Algebra: Introductory and Intermediate

INSTRUCT ANNOTATED EDITION

2nd EDITION

Algebra: Introductory and Intermediate

INSTRUCTOR'S ANNOTATED EDITION

Richard N. Aufmann
Palomar College, California

Vernon C. Barker
Palomar College, California

Joanne S. Lockwood
Plymouth State College, New Hampshire

HOUGHTON MIFFLIN COMPANY

Boston   New York

Senior Sponsoring Editor: *Maureen O'Connor*
Senior Associate Editor: *Dawn M. Nuttall*
Editorial Assistant: *Amanda Bafaro*
Project Editor: *Tamela Ambush*
Editorial Assistant: *Ryan Jones*
Senior Production/Design Coordinator: *Carol Merrigan*
Senior Manufacturing Coordinator: *Sally Culler*
Marketing Manager: *Ros Kane*

Cover design: Diana Coe/Ko Design

Cover image: Andre Baranowski. Graphistock, Inc.

Photo credits:

Chapter 1: Peter Beck/The Stock Market; *Chapter 2:* Elena Rooraid/PhotoEdit; *Chapter 3:* Doug Armand/TSI; *Chapter 4:* Jeff Zaruba/The Stock Market; *Chapter 5:* Bruce Ayers/TSI; *Chapter 6:* Brownie Harris/The Stock Market; *Chapter 7:* Carol Lundeen; *Chapter 8:* Michael Newman/PhotoEdit; *Chapter 9:* David Frazier/Photo Researchers, Inc.; *Chapter 10:* Bruce Hands/TSI; *Chapter 11:* Michael Rosenfeld/TSI; *Chapter 12:* Lee Snyder/Photo Researchers (#7T0321).

Printed in the U.S.A.

Library of Congress Catalog Card Number: 99-72031

ISBN
Text: 0-395-97603-0
Instructor's Annotated Edition: 0-395-97604-9

123456789-WC-03-02-01-00-99

Contents

6   Polynomials   319

7   Factoring   369

8   Rational Expressions   421

11 Functions and Relations   581

12 Exponential and Logarithmic Functions   641

Preface

The second edition of *Algebra: Introductory and Intermediate* examines the fundamental ideas of algebra. Recognizing that the basic principles of geometry are a necessary part of mathematics, we have also included a separate chapter on geometry (Chapter 3) and have integrated geometry topics, where appropriate, throughout the text. The text has been designed not only to meet the needs of the traditional college student but also to serve the needs of returning students whose mathematical proficiency may have declined during years away from formal education.

In this new edition of *Algebra: Introductory and Intermediate*, we have continued to integrate some of the approaches suggested by AMATYC. Each chapter begins with a mathematical vignette in which there may be a historical note, an application, or a curiosity related to mathematics. At the end of each section there are "Applying the Concepts" exercises that include writing, synthesis, critical thinking, and challenge problems. At the end of each chapter there is a "Focus on Problem Solving" that introduces students to various problem-solving strategies. This is followed by "Projects and Group Activities" that can be used for cooperative learning activities.

INSTRUCTIONAL FEATURES

Interactive Approach

Algebra: Introductory and Intermediate uses an interactive style that provides a student with an opportunity to try a skill as it is presented. Each section is divided into objectives, and every objective contains one or more sets of matched-pair examples. The first example in each set is worked out; the second example, called "You Try It," is for the student to work. By solving this problem, the student practices concepts as they are presented in the text. There are complete worked-out solutions to these examples in an appendix at the end of the book. By comparing their solution to the solution in the appendix, students are able to obtain immediate feedback on and reinforcement of the concept.

Emphasis on Problem-Solving Strategies

Algebra: Introductory and Intermediate features a carefully developed approach to problem solving that emphasizes developing strategies to solve problems. Students are encouraged to develop their own strategies, to draw diagrams, and to write strategies as part of their solution to a problem. In each case, model strategies are presented as guides for students to follow as they attempt the "You Try It" problem. Having students provide strategies is a natural way to incorporate writing into the math curriculum.

Emphasis on Applications

The traditional approach to teaching algebra covers only the straightforward manipulation of numbers and variables and thereby fails to teach students the practical value of algebra. By contrast, *Algebra: Introductory and Intermediate* contains an extensive collection of contemporary application problems. Wherever appropriate, the last objective of a section presents applications that require the student to use the skills covered in that section to solve practical problems. This carefully integrated applied approach generates student awareness of the value of algebra as a real-life tool.

Completely Integrated Learning System Organized by Objectives

Each chapter begins with a list of the learning objectives included within that chapter. Each of the objectives is then restated in the chapter to remind the student of the current topic of discussion. The same objectives that organize the text are also used as the structure for exercises, testing programs, and the HM³ Tutorial. For each objective in the text, there is a corresponding computer tutorial and a corresponding set of test questions.

AN INTERACTIVE APPROACH

Instructors have long realized the need for a text that requires students to use a skill as it is being taught. *Algebra: Introductory and Intermediate* uses an interactive technique that meets this need. Every objective, including the one shown below, contains at least one pair of examples. One of the examples is worked. The second example in the pair (You Try It) is not worked so that students may "interact" with the text by solving it. To provide immediate feedback, a complete solution to this example is provided in the Answer Section at the end of the book. The benefit of this interactive style is that students can check that a new skill has been learned before attempting a homework assignment.

An explanatory passage begins each objective.

Paired examples follow the explanatory passage.

The interactive key is the You Try It in each pair. It has not been worked, so that the student may practice the skill, referring to the worked example at the left if necessary.

Reference to the Solutions Section allows the student to check full solutions immediately.

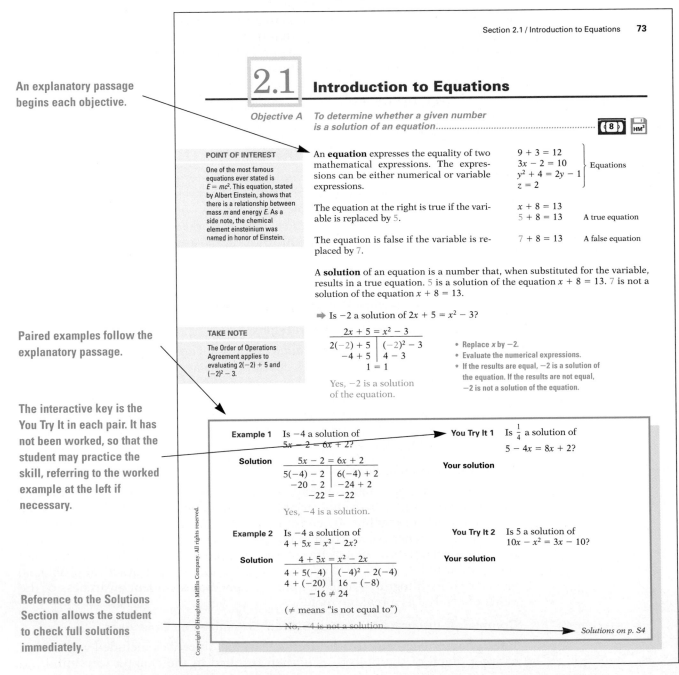

2.1 Introduction to Equations

Objective A   *To determine whether a given number is a solution of an equation* .... (8) HM³

POINT OF INTEREST

One of the most famous equations ever stated is $E = mc^2$. This equation, stated by Albert Einstein, shows that there is a relationship between mass m and energy E. As a side note, the chemical element einsteinium was named in honor of Einstein.

An **equation** expresses the equality of two mathematical expressions. The expressions can be either numerical or variable expressions.

$$\left.\begin{array}{l} 9 + 3 = 12 \\ 3x - 2 = 10 \\ y^2 + 4 = 2y - 1 \\ z = 2 \end{array}\right\} \text{Equations}$$

The equation at the right is true if the variable is replaced by 5.

$x + 8 = 13$
$5 + 8 = 13$ A true equation

The equation is false if the variable is replaced by 7.

$7 + 8 = 13$ A false equation

A **solution** of an equation is a number that, when substituted for the variable, results in a true equation. 5 is a solution of the equation $x + 8 = 13$. 7 is not a solution of the equation $x + 8 = 13$.

➡ Is -2 a solution of $2x + 5 = x^2 - 3$?

TAKE NOTE

The Order of Operations Agreement applies to evaluating $2(-2) + 5$ and $(-2)^2 - 3$.

$$\begin{array}{c|c} 2x + 5 = x^2 - 3 \\ \hline 2(-2) + 5 & (-2)^2 - 3 \\ -4 + 5 & 4 - 3 \\ 1 = 1 \end{array}$$

• Replace x by -2.
• Evaluate the numerical expressions.
• If the results are equal, -2 is a solution of the equation. If the results are not equal, -2 is not a solution of the equation.

Yes, -2 is a solution of the equation.

Example 1   Is -4 a solution of $5x - 2 = 6x + 2$?

Solution
$$\begin{array}{c|c} 5x - 2 = 6x + 2 \\ \hline 5(-4) - 2 & 6(-4) + 2 \\ -20 - 2 & -24 + 2 \\ -22 = -22 \end{array}$$

Yes, -4 is a solution.

You Try It 1   Is $\frac{1}{4}$ a solution of $5 - 4x = 8x + 2$?

Your solution

Example 2   Is -4 a solution of $4 + 5x = x^2 - 2x$?

Solution
$$\begin{array}{c|c} 4 + 5x = x^2 - 2x \\ \hline 4 + 5(-4) & (-4)^2 - 2(-4) \\ 4 + (-20) & 16 - (-8) \\ -16 \neq 24 \end{array}$$

($\neq$ means "is not equal to")

No, -4 is not a solution.

You Try It 2   Is 5 a solution of $10x - x^2 = 3x - 10$?

Your solution

Solutions on p. S4

AN EMPHASIS ON APPLICATIONS

The traditional teaching approach neglects the difficulties that students have in making the transition from arithmetic to algebra. One of the most troublesome and uncomfortable transitions for the student is from concrete arithmetic to symbolic algebra. *Algebra: Introductory and Intermediate* recognizes the formidable task the student faces by introducing variables in a very natural way—through applications of mathematics. A secondary benefit of this approach is that the student becomes aware of the value of algebra as a real-life tool.

The solution of an application problem in *Algebra: Introductory and Intermediate* is always accompanied by two parts: **Strategy** and **Solution**. The strategy is a written description of the steps that are necessary to solve the problem; the solution is the implementation of the strategy. This format provides students with a structure for problem solving. It also encourages students to write strategies for solving problems, which, in turn, fosters organizing problem-solving strategies in a logical way.

A strategy, which the student may use in solving an application problem, is stated.

The strategy is used in the solution of the worked example.

Students are encouraged to write a strategy for the application problem they solve.

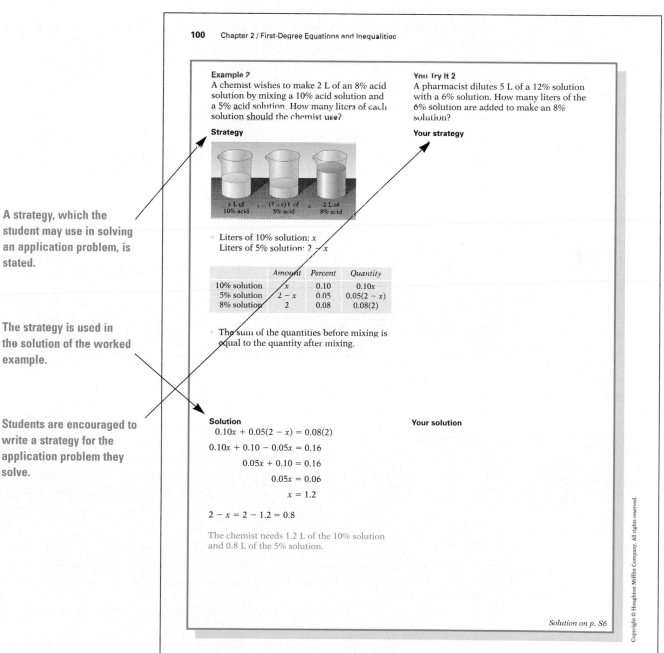

100   Chapter 2 / First-Degree Equations and Inequalities

Example 2
A chemist wishes to make 2 L of an 8% acid solution by mixing a 10% acid solution and a 5% acid solution. How many liters of each solution should the chemist use?

Strategy

x L of 10% acid $(2 - x)$ L of 5% acid   2 L of 8% acid

- Liters of 10% solution: x
  Liters of 5% solution: $2 - x$

	Amount	Percent	Quantity
10% solution	x	0.10	$0.10x$
5% solution	$2 - x$	0.05	$0.05(2 - x)$
8% solution	2	0.08	$0.08(2)$

- The sum of the quantities before mixing is equal to the quantity after mixing.

Solution
$$0.10x + 0.05(2 - x) = 0.08(2)$$
$$0.10x + 0.10 - 0.05x = 0.16$$
$$0.05x + 0.10 = 0.16$$
$$0.05x = 0.06$$
$$x = 1.2$$

$$2 - x = 2 - 1.2 = 0.8$$

The chemist needs 1.2 L of the 10% solution and 0.8 L of the 5% solution.

You Try It 2
A pharmacist dilutes 5 L of a 12% solution with a 6% solution. How many liters of the 6% solution are added to make an 8% solution?

Your strategy

Your solution

Solution on p. S6

OBJECTIVE-SPECIFIC APPROACH

Many mathematics texts are not organized in a manner that facilitates management of learning. Typically, students are left to wander through a maze of apparently unrelated lessons, exercise sets, and tests. *Algebra: Introductory and Intermediate* solves this problem by organizing all lessons, exercise sets, computer tutorials, and tests around a carefully constructed hierarchy of objectives. The advantage of this objective-by-objective organization is that it enables the student who is uncertain at any step in the learning process to refer easily to the original presentation and review that material.

The Objective-Specific Approach also gives the instructor greater control over the management of student progress. The Computerized Test Generator and the printed Test Bank are organized by the same objectives as the text. These references are provided with the answers to the test items, thereby allowing the instructor to quickly determine those objectives on which a student may need additional instruction.

The HM³ Tutorial is also organized around the objectives of the text. As a result, supplemental instruction is available for any objectives that are troublesome for a student.

An objective statement names the topic of each lesson.

2.2 General Equations

Objective A   *To solve an equation of the form $ax + b = c$* .... ⟨8⟩ HM³

The exercise sets correspond to the objectives in the text.

2.2 Exercises

Objective A

Solve and check.

1. $3x + 1 = 10$ **2.** $4y + 3 = 11$ **3.** $2a - 5 = 7$ **4.** $5m - 6 = 9$

5. $5 = 4x + 9$ **6.** $2 = 5b + 12$ **7.** $2x - 5 = -11$ **8.** $3n - 7 = -19$

The answers to the odd-numbered exercises are provided in the Answer Section.

SECTION 2.1

1. yes   **3.** no   **5.** no   **7.** yes   **9.** yes   **11.** yes   **13.** no   **15.** yes   **17.** yes   **19.** yes   **21.** no
23. 6   **25.** 16   **27.** 7   **29.** −2   **31.** 1   **33.** 0   **35.** 3   **37.** −10   **39.** −3   **41.** −14   **43.** 2

The answers to the Chapter Review Exercises, the Chapter Test, and the Cumulative Review Exercises show the objective to study if the student incorrectly answers the exercise.

CHAPTER REVIEW

1. no   [2.1A]   **2.** 21   [2.1B]   **3.** 20   [2.1C]   **4.** −3   [2.2A]   **5.** $-\frac{6}{7}$ [2.2A]   **6.** $\frac{1}{3}$ [2.2B]   **7.** 4   [2.2B]
8. −2   [2.2C]   **9.** 10   [2.2C]   **10.** $\left\{x \middle| x > \frac{5}{3}\right\}$ [2.4A]   **11.** $\{x | x > -1\}$ [2.4A]   **12.** $\left\{x \middle| -3 < x < \frac{4}{3}\right\}$ [2.4B]

CHAPTER TEST

1. −5   [2.2B]   **2.** −5   [2.1B]   **3.** −3   [2.2A]   **4.** 2   [2.2C]   **5.** no   [2.1A]   **6.** 5   [2.2A]   **7.** 0.04   [2.1D]
8. $-\frac{1}{3}$ [2.2C]   **9.** 2   [2.2B]   **10.** −12   [2.1C]   **11.** $\{x | x \le -3\}$ [2.4A]   **12.** $\{x | x > -1\}$ [2.4A]

CUMULATIVE REVIEW

1. 6   [1.1C]   **2.** −48   [1.1D]   **3.** $-\frac{19}{48}$ [1.2C]   **4.** 54   [1.2E]   **5.** $\frac{49}{40}$ [1.3A]   **6.** 6   [1.4A]   **7.** −17x   [1.4B]
8. −5a − 4b   [1.4B]   **9.** 2x   [1.4C]   **10.** 36y   [1.4C]   **11.** $2x^2 + 6x - 4$ [1.4D]   **12.** −4x + 14   [1.4D]

ADDITIONAL LEARNING AIDS

Chapter Opener

The Chapter Opener relates a historical, contemporary, or interesting note about mathematics or its application.

Focus on Problem Solving

At the end of each chapter there is a Focus on Problem Solving, the purpose of which is to introduce the student to various successful problem-solving strategies. Each Focus consists of a problem and an appropriate strategy to solve the problem. Strategies such as guessing, trying to solve a simpler but similar problem, drawing a diagram, and looking for patterns are some of the techniques that are demonstrated.

Projects and Group Activities

The Projects and Group Activities feature can be used as extra credit or cooperative learning activities. The projects cover various aspects of mathematics including the use of calculators, extended applications, additional problem-solving strategies, and other topics related to mathematics.

Chapter Summaries

At the end of each chapter there is a Chapter Summary that includes Key Words and Essential Rules that were covered in the chapter. These chapter summaries provide a single point of reference as the student prepares for a test.

Study Skills

The To the Student Preface provides suggestions for using this text and approaches to creating good study habits.

HM³ Tutorial

This state-of-the-art tutorial software is a networkable, interactive, algorithmically driven software package that supports *every* objective in the text. Written by the authors, the HM³ Tutorial and the text are in the same voice. Features include full-color graphics, a glossary, extensive hints, animated examples, and a comprehensive classroom management system.

The algorithmic feature essentially provides an infinite number of practice problems for students to attempt. The algorithms have been carefully crafted to present a variety of problems from easy to difficult. Helpful hints and a complete worked-out solution are available for every problem. When a student completes a problem, the student may choose to work another similar problem or move on to a different type of problem. A quiz feature is now also part of the package.

The interactive feature asks students to respond to questions about the topic in the current lesson. In this way, students can assess their understanding of concepts as they are presented. These interactive questions are also algorithmically driven and offer hints as well as full solutions.

The user-friendly classroom management system allows instructors to create a syllabus, post notes to individual students or a class, enter their own assessment items (homework, class participation, test results, etc.), and specify the mastery level. There are a variety of printable reports offered that can be called up by student, by class, by objective, etc. Instructors can use such reports to tell at a glance which students are not achieving the specified mastery level.

Glossary

A Glossary at the end of the book includes definitions of terms used in the text.

Margin Notes

There are three types of margin notes in the student text. *Point of Interest* notes feature interesting sidelights of the topic being discussed. The *Take Note* feature warns students that a procedure may be particularly involved or reminds students that there are certain checks of their work that should be performed. *Calculator Notes* provide suggestions for using a calculator in certain situations. In addition, there are *Instructor Notes,* which are printed only in the Instructor's Annotated Edition. These notes provide suggestions for presenting the material or related material that can be used in class.

Index of Applications

The Index of Applications illustrates the power and scope of mathematics and its application. This may help some students see the benefits of mathematics as a tool that is used in everyday experiences.

EXERCISES

End-of-Section Exercises

Algebra: Introductory and Intermediate contains more than 6000 exercises. At the end of each section there are exercise sets that are keyed to the corresponding learning objectives. The exercises are carefully developed to ensure that students can apply the concepts in the section to a variety of problem situations. Data analysis exercises are identified by ⬤. Calculator exercises are identified by ▦ .

Applying the Concepts Exercises

The End-of-Section Exercises are followed by Applying the Concepts Exercises. These sections contain a variety of exercise types, including:

* challenge problems
* problems that require the student to determine if a statement is always true, sometimes true, or never true
* problems that ask students to determine incorrect procedures

Writing Exercises

Within the "Applying the Concepts Exercises," there are Writing Exercises denoted by ✎ . These exercises ask students to write about a topic in the section or to research and report on a related topic.

Chapter Review Exercises

Review Exercises are found at the end of each chapter. These exercises are selected to help the student integrate all of the topics presented in the chapter. The answers to all Chapter Review Exercises are given in the answer section at the end of the book. Along with the answer, there is a reference to the objective that pertains to each exercise.

Chapter Test Exercises

The Chapter Test Exercises are designed to simulate a possible test of the material in the chapter. The answers to all Chapter Test Exercises are given in the answer section at the end of the book. Along with the answer, there is a reference to the objective that pertains to each exercise.

Cumulative Review Exercises

Cumulative Review Exercises, which appear at the end of each chapter (beginning with Chapter 2), help students maintain skills learned in previous chapters. The answers to all Cumulative Review Exercises are given in the answer section. Along with the answer, there is a reference to the objective that pertains to each exercise.

NEW TO THIS EDITION

In response to suggestions by users, we now offer an Instructor's Annotated Edition for *Algebra: Introductory and Intermediate*. It is an exact replica of the full-color student text except that it also offers answers to all the exercises as well as helpful Instructor Notes in the margin.

A Chapter Test has been added for each chapter in the text.

A new Calculator Note margin feature has been added.

We have more than doubled the number of projects found at the end of the chapters. In addition, those projects involving calculators and Internet sites have been easily identified with the appropriate icon. Graph interpretation exercises have also been added to the projects.

Career notes and photos have been added to the chapter openers to illustrate to students the diverse ways in which mathematics is used in the workplace.

New and colorful icons have been added for the Writing, Data, Calculator, and Internet exercises.

All the real sourced data exercises and examples have been updated, and many new data problems have been added.

SUPPLEMENTS FOR THE INSTRUCTOR

Instructor's Annotated Edition

The Instructor's Annotated Edition is an exact replica of the student text except that answers to all exercises are given in the text. Also, there are Instructor Notes in the margin that offer suggestions for presenting the material in that objective.

Instructor's Resource Manual with Solutions Manual

The Instructor's Resource Manual includes suggestions for course sequencing and outlines for the answers to the writing exercises. The Solutions Manual contains worked-out solutions for all end-of-section exercises, Applying the Concepts exercises, Chapter Review Exercises, Chapter Tests, and Cumulative Review Exercises as well as appropriate Focus on Problem Solving and Projects and Group Activities.

Computerized Test Generator

The Computerized Test Generator is the first of three testing materials. The database contains more than 2000 test items. These questions are unique to the Test Generator. The Test Generator is designed to provide an unlimited number of tests for each chapter, cumulative chapter tests, and a final exam. It is available for Microsoft Windows® and the Macintosh. Both versions provide **algorithms, on-line testing,** and **gradebook** functions.

Printed Test Bank with Chapter Tests

The Printed Test Bank, the second component of the testing material, is a printout of all items in the Computerized Test Generator. Instructors who do not have access to a computer can use the test bank to select items to include on a test being prepared by hand. Chapter tests contain the printed testing program, which is the third source of testing material. Four printed tests, two free response and two multiple choice, are provided for each chapter. In addition, there are cumulative tests after Chapters 4, 8, and 12, and a final exam.

SUPPLEMENTS FOR THE STUDENT

Student Solutions Manual

The Student Solutions Manual contains the complete solution to all odd-numbered exercises in the text.

HM³ Tutorial

The content of this new, interactive, state-of-the-art tutorial software was written by the authors and is in the same voice as the text. The HM³ Tutorial supports every objective in the text. Problems are algorithmically generated, lessons provide animated examples, lessons and problems are presented in a colorful, lively manner, and an integrated classroom management system tracks and reports student performance. Features include:

- assessment
- free-response problems
- ability to repeat same problem type
- printing capability
- glossary
- resizable screen

- pedagogical animations
- interactivity within lessons
- algorithms
- extensive classroom management with
  —syllabus customization
  —variety of reports

The HM³ Tutorial can be used in several ways: (1) to cover material the student missed because of an absence; (2) to reinforce instruction on a concept that the student has not yet mastered; (3) to review material in preparation for exams; (4) for self-instruction.

The networkable HM³ Tutorial is available on CD-ROM for Windows. There is also an alternate version offered for the Macintosh, available only on floppy disk. The HM³ Tutorial is free to any school upon adoption of this text; however, students can purchase a non-networkable copy of the HM³ Tutorial for home use.

Within each section of the book, a computer icon HM³ appears next to each objective. The icon serves as a reminder that there is an HM³ Tutorial lesson corresponding to that objective.

Videotapes

Within each section of the text, a videotape icon appears next to an objective for which there is a corresponding video. The icon contains the reference number of the appropriate video. Each video topic is related to an application, and the necessary mathematics to solve that problem are then presented.

ACKNOWLEDGMENTS

The authors would like to thank the people who have reviewed this manuscript and provided many valuable suggestions:

Thomas J. Blackburn, *Northeastern Illinois University;* **James Brasel,** *Philips Community College, AR;* **Dr. Kay Dundas,** *Hutchinson Community College, KS;* **Larry Friesen,** *Butler County Community College, KS;* **Ron Harris,** *Bowling Green State University, OH;* **Edith Haight Hays,** *Texas Woman's University;* **Cheryl Keeton,** *College of the Albemarle, NC;* **Georgia K. Mederer; Carol Metz,** *Westchester Community College, NY;* **Linda J. Murphy,** *Northern Essex Community College, MA;* **John Odell,** *Richland Community College, IL;* **Thomas M. O'Keefe,** *Bucks County Community College, PA;* **Mark Serebransky,** *Camden County College, NJ*

To the Student

Take an active role in the learning process.

Many students feel that they will never understand math, while others appear to do very well with little effort. Oftentimes what makes the difference is that successful students take an active role in the learning process.

Do the homework.

Attend class regularly.

Participate in class.

Learning mathematics requires your *active* participation. Although doing homework is one way you can actively participate, it is not the only way. First, you must attend class regularly and become an active participant. Second, you must become actively involved with the textbook.

Algebra: Introductory and Intermediate was written and designed with you in mind as a participant. Here are some suggestions on how to use the features of this textbook.

Use the features of the text.

   Read the objective statement.

   Read the objective material.

   Study the in-text examples.

There are 12 chapters in this text. Each chapter is divided into sections, and each section is subdivided into learning objectives. Each learning objective is labeled with a letter from A to G.

First, read each objective statement carefully so you will understand the learning goal that is being presented. Next, read the objective material carefully, being sure to note each bold word. These words indicate important concepts that you should familiarize yourself with. Study carefully each in-text example (denoted by an orange arrow), noting the techniques and strategies used to solve the example.

Use the boxed examples.

1. **Study the example on the left.**

2. **Solve the You Try It example.**

3. **Check your work against the solution in the back of the book.**

You will then come to the key learning feature of this text, the *boxed examples*. These examples have been designed to assist you in a very specific way. Notice that in each example box, the example on the left is completely worked out and the "You Try It" example on the right is not. *You* are expected to work the right-hand example (in the space provided) in order to immediately test your understanding of the material you have just studied.

You should study the worked-out example carefully by working through each step presented. This allows you to focus on each step and reinforces the technique for solving that type of problem. You can then use the worked-out example as a model for solving similar problems.

Next, try to solve the "You Try It" example using the problem-solving techniques that you have just studied. When you have completed your solution, check your work by turning to the page in the Appendix where the complete solution can be found. The page number on which the solution appears is printed at the bottom of the example box in the right-hand corner. By checking your solution, you will know immediately whether or not you fully understand the skill you just studied.

Do the exercises.

Check your answers to the odd-numbered exercises.

When you have completed studying an objective, do the exercises in the exercise set that correspond with that objective. The exercises are labeled with the same letter as the objective. Algebra is a subject that needs to be learned in small sections and practiced continually in order to be mastered. Doing all of the exercises in each exercise set will help you to master the problem-solving techniques necessary for success. As you work through the exercises for an objective, check your answers to the odd-numbered exercises with those in the back of the book.

Read the Chapter Summary.

Do the Chapter Review exercises.

After completing a chapter, read the Chapter Summary. This summary highlights the important topics covered in the chapter. Following the Chapter Summary are a Chapter Review, a Chapter Test, and a Cumulative Review (beginning with Chapter 2). Doing the review exercises is an important way of testing your understanding of the chapter. The answer to each review exercise is given in an

Check your answers.

Restudy objectives you missed.

Appendix at the back of the book. Each answer is followed by a reference that tells which objective that exercise was taken from. For example, (4.2B) means Section 4.2, Objective B. After checking your answers, restudy any objective that you missed. It may be very helpful to retry some of the exercises for that objective to reinforce your problem-solving techniques.

Do the Chapter Test.

The Chapter Test should be used to prepare for an exam. We suggest that you try the Chapter Test a few days before your actual exam. Take the test in a quiet place and try to complete the test in the same amount of time you will be allowed for your exam. When taking the Chapter Test, practice the strategies of successful test takers: 1) scan the entire test to get a feel for the questions; 2) read the directions carefully; 3) work the problems that are easiest for you first; and, perhaps most importantly, 4) try to stay calm.

Check your answers.

Restudy objectives you missed.

When you have completed the Chapter Test, check your answers. If you missed a question, review the material in that objective and rework some of the exercises from that objective. This will strengthen your ability to perform the skills in that objective.

The Cumulative Review allows you to refresh the skills you have learned in previous chapters. This is very important in mathematics. By consistently reviewing previous material, you will retain the skills already learned as you build new ones.

Remember, to be successful: attend class regularly; read the textbook carefully; actively participate in class; work with your textbook using the "You Try It" examples for immediate feedback and reinforcement of each skill; do all of the homework assignments; review constantly; and work carefully.

Index of Applications

1

Real Numbers and Variable Expressions

County agricultural agents work with farmers to help them produce better crops. Many agents are specialists in soils. They teach farmers about the physical and chemical characteristics of the soil, helping them to make the most productive use of their land. Agricultural agents must have a good understanding of percents in order to analyze the composition of nutrients in farmland. Their goal is to assist farmers in improving the quality and quantity of crop yields and in controlling diseases and pests.

Objectives

Section 1.1
To use inequality symbols with integers
To find the additive inverse and absolute value of a number
To add or subtract integers
To multiply or divide integers
To solve application problems

Section 1.2
To write a rational number as a decimal
To convert among percents, fractions, and decimals
To add or subtract rational numbers
To multiply or divide rational numbers
To evaluate exponential expressions
To simplify numerical radical expressions
To solve application problems

Section 1.3
To use the Order of Operations Agreement to simplify expressions

Section 1.4
To evaluate a variable expression
To simplify a variable expression using the Properties of Addition
To simplify a variable expression using the Properties of Multiplication
To simplify a variable expression using the Distributive Property
To translate a verbal expression into a variable expression

Section 1.5
To write a set using the roster method
To write a set using set-builder notation
To graph an inequality on the number line

History of Variables

Prior to the 16th century, unknown quantities were represented by words. In Latin, the language in which most scholarly works were written, the word *res*, meaning "thing," was used. In Germany the word *zahl*, meaning "number," was used. In Italy the word *cosa*, also meaning "thing," was used.

Then in 1637, René Descartes, a French mathematician, began using the letters x, y, and z to represent variables. It is interesting to note, upon examining Descartes's work, that toward the end of the book the letters y and z were no longer used and x became the choice for a variable.

One explanation of why the letters y and z appeared less frequently has to do with the nature of printing presses during Descartes's time. A printer had a large tray that contained all the letters of the alphabet. There were many copies of each letter, especially those letters that are used frequently. For example, there were more e's than q's. Because the letters y and z do not occur frequently in French, a printer would have few of these letters on hand. Consequently, when Descartes started using these letters as variables the printer's supply was quickly depleted and x's had to be used instead.

Today, x is used by most nations as the standard letter for a single unknown. In fact, x rays were so named because the scientists who discovered them did not know what they were and thus labeled them the "unknown rays" or x rays.

1.1   Integers

Objective A   *To use inequality symbols with integers* ....

It seems to be a human characteristic to put similar items in the same place. For instance, a biologist places similar animals in groups called *phyla,* and a geologist divides the history of the earth into *eras.*

Mathematicians likewise place objects with similar properties in *sets* and use braces to surround the objects in the set. The numbers that we use to count objects, such as the number of people at a baseball game or the number of horses on a ranch, have similar characteristics. These numbers are the *natural numbers.*

Natural numbers = {1, 2, 3, 4, 5, 6, 7, 8, 9, 10, 11, ...}

The natural numbers alone do not provide all the numbers that are useful in applications. For instance, a meteorologist needs numbers below zero and above zero.

Integers = {..., −5, −4, −3, −2, −1, 0, 1, 2, 3, 4, 5, ...}

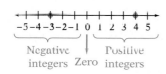

Each integer can be shown on a **number line**. The **graph** of an integer is shown by placing a heavy dot on the number line directly above the number. The graph of −3 and that of 4 are shown on the number line at the left.

The integers to the left of zero are **negative integers**. The integers to the right of zero are **positive integers**. Zero is neither a positive nor a negative integer.

Consider the sentences below.

The quarterback threw the football and the receiver caught *it.*
An accountant purchased a calculator and placed *it* in a briefcase.

In the first sentence, *it* means football; in the second sentence, *it* means calculator. In language, the word *it* can stand for many different objects. Similarly, in mathematics, a letter of the alphabet can be used to stand for a number. Such a letter is called a **variable**. Variables are used in the next definition.

Definition of Inequality Symbols

If *a* and *b* are two numbers and *a* is to the left of *b* on the number line, then *a* is **less than** *b*. This is written $a < b$.

If *a* and *b* are two numbers and *a* is to the right of *b* on the number line, then *a* is **greater than** *b*. This is written $a > b$.

There are also inequality symbols for **less than or equal to** ($\leq$) and **greater than or equal to** ($\geq$). For instance,

$6 \leq 6$ because $6 = 6$. $7 \leq 15$ because $7 < 15$.

It is convenient to use a variable to represent, or stand for, any one of the elements of a set. For instance, the statement "*x* is an *element of* the set {0, 2, 4, 6}" means that *x* can be replaced by 0, 2, 4, or 6. The symbol for "is an element of" is $\in$; the symbol for "is not an element of" is $\notin$. For example,

$2 \in \{0, 2, 4, 6\}$ $6 \in \{0, 2, 4, 6\}$ $7 \notin \{0, 2, 4, 6\}$

Example 1

Let $x \in \{-6, -2, 0\}$. For which values of x is the inequality $x \le -2$ a true statement?

Solution

Replace x by each element of the set and determine whether the inequality is true.

$$x \le -2$$
$$-6 \le -2 \quad \text{True.} \quad -6 < -2$$
$$-2 \le -2 \quad \text{True.} \quad -2 = -2$$
$$0 \le -2 \quad \text{False.}$$

The inequality is true for -6 and -2.

You Try It 1

Let $y \in \{-5, -1, 5\}$. For which values of y is the inequality $y > -1$ a true statement?

Your solution

5

Solution on p. S1

Objective B   To find the additive inverse and absolute value of a number .....

$-5-4-3-2-1\ 0\ 1\ 2\ 3\ 4\ 5$

On the number line, the numbers 5 and -5 are the same distance from zero but on opposite sides of zero. The numbers 5 and -5 are called **opposites** or **additive inverses** of each other. (See the number line at the left.)

TAKE NOTE

The distance from 0 to 5 is 5; $|5| = 5$. The distance from 0 to -5 is 5; $|-5| = 5$.

The opposite (or additive inverse) of 5 is -5. The opposite of -5 is 5. The symbol for opposite is $-$.

$-(5)$ means the opposite of *positive* 5. $-(5) = -5$
$-(-5)$ means the opposite of *negative* 5. $-(-5) = 5$

The **absolute value** of a number is its distance from zero on the number line. The symbol for absolute value is two vertical bars, $|\ |$.

POINT OF INTEREST

The definition of absolute value that we have given in the box is written in what is called "rhetorical style." That is, it is written without the use of variables. This is how *all* mathematics was written prior to the Renaissance. During that period, from the 14th to the 16th century, the idea of expressing a variable symbolically was developed.

> **Absolute Value**
>
> The absolute value of a positive number is the number itself. The absolute value of zero is zero. The absolute value of a negative number is the opposite of the negative number.

$|9| = 9$

$|-7| = 7$

➡ Evaluate: $-|-12|$

$$-|-12| = -12$$

• The absolute value sign does not affect the negative sign in front of the absolute value sign.

Example 2

Let $a \in \{-12, 0, 4\}$. Find the additive inverse of a and the absolute value of a for each element of the set.

Solution

Replace a by each element of the set.

$$\begin{array}{ll} -a & |a| \\ -(-12) = 12 & |-12| = 12 \\ -(0) = 0 & |0| = 0 \\ -(4) = -4 & |4| = 4 \end{array}$$

You Try It 2

Let $z \in \{-11, 0, 8\}$. Find the additive inverse of z and the absolute value of z for each element of the set.

Your solution

11; 11
0; 0
-8; 8

Solution on p. S1

Objective C   *To add or subtract integers* ....

A number can be represented anywhere along the number line by an arrow. A positive number is represented by an arrow pointing to the right, and a negative number is represented by an arrow pointing to the left. The size of the number is represented by the length of the arrow.

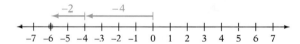

Addition of integers can be shown on the number line. To add integers, start at zero and draw an arrow representing the first number. At the tip of the first arrow, draw a second arrow representing the second number. The sum is below the tip of the second arrow.

$4 + 2 = 6$

$-4 + (-2) = -6$

$-4 + 2 = -2$

$4 + (-2) = 2$

The pattern for the addition of integers shown on the number line can be summarized in the following rule.

> **Addition of Integers**
>
> - *Numbers with the same sign*
>   To add two numbers with the same sign, add the absolute values of the numbers. Then attach the sign of the addends.
>
> - *Numbers with different signs*
>   To add two numbers with different signs, find the absolute value of each number. Then subtract the smaller of these numbers from the larger one. Attach the sign of the number with the larger absolute value.

➡ Add: $(-9) + 8$

$|-9| = 9 \quad |8| = 8$ • The signs are different. Find the absolute value of each number.

$9 - 8 = 1$ • Subtract the smaller number from the larger.

$(-9) + 8 = -1$ • Attach the sign of the number with the larger absolute value. Because $|-9| > |8|$, use the sign of -9.

➡ Add: $(-23) + 47 + (-18) + 5$

To add more than two numbers, add the first two numbers. Then add the sum to the third number. Continue until all the numbers are added.

$$\begin{aligned}(-23) + 47 + (-18) + 5 &= 24 + (-18) + 5 \\ &= 6 + 5 \\ &= 11\end{aligned}$$

Look at the two expressions below and note that each expression equals the same number.

$$8 - 3 = 5 \qquad \text{8 minus 3 is 5.}$$
$$8 + (-3) = 5 \qquad \text{8 plus the opposite of 3 is 5.}$$

This example suggests that to subtract two numbers, we add the opposite of the second number to the first number.

first number	$-$	second number	$=$	first number	$+$	the opposite of the second number	
40	$-$	60	$=$	40	$+$	(-60)	$= -20$
-40	$-$	60	$=$	-40	$+$	(-60)	$= -100$
-40	$-$	(-60)	$=$	-40	$+$	60	$= 20$
40	$-$	(-60)	$=$	40	$+$	60	$= 100$

➡ Subtract: $-21 - (-40)$

Change this sign to plus.

$$-21 - (-40) = -21 + 40 = 19$$

Change -40 to the opposite of -40.

• Rewrite each subtraction as addition of the opposite. Then add.

➡ Subtract: $15 - 51$

Change this sign to plus.

$$15 - 51 = 15 + (-51) = -36$$

Change 51 to the opposite of 51.

• Rewrite each subtraction as addition of the opposite. Then add.

➡ Subtract: $-12 - (-21) - 15$

$$\begin{aligned}-12 - (-21) - 15 &= -12 + 21 + (-15) \\ &= 9 + (-15) \\ &= -6\end{aligned}$$

• Rewrite each subtraction as addition of the opposite. Then add.

Example 3 Add: $(-52) + (-39)$

Solution The signs are the same. Add the absolute values of the numbers:
$52 + 39 = 91$

Attach the sign of the addends:
$(-52) + (-39) = -91$

You Try It 3 Add: $100 + (-43)$

Your solution 57

Example 4 Add:
$37 + (-52) + (-21) + (-7)$

Solution $37 + (-52) + (-21) + (-7)$
$= -15 + (-21) + (-7)$
$= -36 + (-7)$
$= -43$

You Try It 4 Add:
$(-51) + 42 + 17 + (-102)$

Your solution -94

Example 5 Subtract: $-11 - 15$

Solution $-11 - 15 = -11 + (-15)$
$= 26$

You Try It 5 Subtract: $19 - (-32)$

Your solution 51

Example 6 Subtract:
$-14 - 18 - (-21) - 4$

Solution $-14 - 18 - (-21) - 4$
$= -14 + (-18) + 21 + (-4)$
$= -32 + 21 + (-4)$
$= -11 + (-4)$
$= -15$

You Try It 6 Subtract:
$-9 - (-12) - 17 - 4$

Your solution 18

Solutions on p. S1

Objective D   To multiply or divide integers...

Multiplication is the repeated addition of the same number. The product 3×5 is shown on the number line below.

5   5   5

0 1 2 3 4 5 6 7 8 9 10 11 12 13 14 15

5 is added 3 times.

$3 \times 5 = 5 + 5 + 5 = 15$

To indicate multiplication, several different symbols are used.

$$3 \times 5 = 15 \qquad 3 \cdot 5 = 15 \qquad (3)(5) = 15 \qquad 3(5) = 15 \qquad (3)5 = 15$$

POINT OF INTEREST

The cross $\times$ was first used as a symbol for multiplication in 1631 in a book titled *The Key to Mathematics.* Also in that year, another book, *Practice of the Analytical Art,* advocated the use of a dot to indicate multiplication.

Note that when parentheses are used and there is no arithmetic operation symbol, the operation is multiplication. Each number in a product is called a **factor**. For instance, 3 and 5 are factors of the product $3 \cdot 5 = 15$.

Now consider the product of a positive and a negative number.

$$\overbrace{-5 \text{ is added 3 times.}}$$

$$3(-5) = (-5) + (-5) + (-5) = -15 \qquad \bullet \text{ Multiplication is repeated addition.}$$

This suggests that the product of a positive number and a negative number is negative. Here are a few more examples.

$$4(-7) = -28 \qquad (-6)5 = -30 \qquad (-5) \cdot 7 = -35$$

To find the product of two negative numbers, look at the pattern at the right. As -5 multiplies a sequence of decreasing integers, the products increase by 5.

The pattern can be continued by requiring that the product of two negative numbers be positive.

These numbers decrease by 1. ⟶   These numbers increase by 5.

$$-5(3) = -15$$
$$-5(2) = -10$$
$$-5(1) = -5$$
$$-5(0) = 0$$
$$-5(-1) = 5$$
$$-5(-2) = 10$$
$$-5(-3) = 15$$

Multiplication of Integers

- *Numbers with the same sign*
  To multiply two numbers with the same sign, multiply the absolute values of the numbers. The product is positive.

- *Numbers with different signs*
  To multiply two numbers with different signs, multiply the absolute values of the numbers. The product is negative.

➡ Multiply: $-2(5)(-7)(-4)$

$$-2(5)(-7)(-4) = -10(-7)(-4)$$
$$= 70(-4) = -280$$

• To multiply more than two numbers, multiply the first two. Then multiply the product by the third number. Continue until all the numbers are multiplied.

For every division problem there is a related multiplication problem.

$$\frac{8}{2} = 4 \qquad \text{because} \qquad 4 \cdot 2 = 8$$

Division   Related multiplication

This fact and the rules for multiplying integers can be used to illustrate the rules for dividing integers.

Note in the following examples that the quotient of two numbers with the same sign is positive.

$$\frac{12}{3} = 4 \text{ because } 4 \cdot 3 = 12 \qquad \frac{-12}{-3} = 4 \text{ because } 4 \cdot (-3) = -12$$

The next two examples illustrate that the quotient of two numbers with different signs is negative.

$$\frac{12}{-3} = -4 \text{ because } (-4)(-3) = 12 \qquad \frac{-12}{3} = -4 \text{ because } (-4) \cdot 3 = -12$$

> **Division of Integers**
>
> - *Numbers with the same sign*
>   To divide two numbers with the same sign, divide the absolute values of the numbers. The quotient is positive.
>
> - *Numbers with different signs*
>   To divide two numbers with different signs, divide the absolute values of the numbers. The quotient is negative.

➡ Simplify: $-\dfrac{-56}{7}$

$$-\frac{-56}{7} = -\left(\frac{-56}{7}\right) = -(-8) = 8$$

Note that $\dfrac{-12}{3} = -4$, $\dfrac{12}{-3} = -4$, and $-\dfrac{12}{3} = -4$. This suggests the following rule.

> If a and b are integers, and $b \neq 0$, then $\dfrac{-a}{b} = \dfrac{a}{-1} = -\dfrac{a}{b}$.

PROPERTIES OF ZERO AND ONE IN DIVISION

- Zero divided by any number other than zero is zero.

$$\frac{0}{a} = 0 \qquad \text{because} \qquad 0 \cdot a = 0 \qquad\qquad \text{For example, } \frac{0}{7} = 0 \text{ because } 0 \cdot 7 = 0.$$

- Division by zero is not defined.

To understand that division by zero is not permitted, suppose that $\dfrac{4}{0}$ were equal to n, where n is some number. Because each division problem has a related multiplication problem, $\dfrac{4}{0} = n$ means $n \cdot 0 = 4$. But $n \cdot 0 = 4$ is impossible because any number times 0 is 0. Therefore, division by 0 is not defined.

- Any number other than zero divided by itself is 1.

$$\frac{a}{a} = 1, \ a \neq 0 \qquad\qquad\qquad \text{For example, } \frac{-8}{-8} = 1.$$

- Any number divided by one is the number.

$$\frac{a}{1} = a \qquad\qquad\qquad \text{For example, } \frac{9}{1} = 9.$$

Example 7	Multiply: $(-3)4(-5)$	**You Try It 7**	Multiply: $8(-9)10$
Solution	$(-3)4(-5) = (-12)(-5) = 60$	**Your solution**	-720

Solution on p. S1

Example 8   Multiply: $12(-4)(-3)(-5)$

Solution $12(-4)(-3)(-5)$
$= (-48)(-3)(-5)$
$= 144(-5) = -720$

You Try It 8   Multiply: $(-2)3(-8)7$

Your solution   336

Example 9   Divide: $(-120) \div (-8)$

Solution $(-120) \div (-8) = 15$

You Try It 9   Divide: $(-135) \div (-9)$

Your solution   15

Example 10   Divide: $\dfrac{95}{-5}$

Solution $\dfrac{95}{-5} = -19$

You Try It 10   Divide: $\dfrac{-72}{4}$

Your solution -18

Example 11   Divide: $-\dfrac{-81}{3}$

Solution $-\dfrac{-81}{3} = -(-27) = 27$

You Try It 11   Divide: $-\dfrac{36}{-12}$

Your solution   3

Solutions on p. S1

Objective E   To solve application problems...

To solve an application problem, first read the problem carefully. The Strategy involves identifying the quantity to be found and planning the steps that are necessary to find that quantity. The Solution involves performing each operation stated in the Strategy and writing the answer.

Example 12
The average temperature on Mercury's sunlit side is 950°F. The average temperature on Mercury's dark side is −346°F. Find the difference between these two average temperatures.

You Try It 12
The daily low temperatures (in degrees Celsius) during one week were recorded as follows: −6°, −7°, 0°, −5°, −8°, −1°, −1°. Find the average daily low temperature.

Strategy
To find the difference, subtract the average temperature on the dark side (−346) from the average temperature on the sunlit side (950).

Your strategy

Solution
$950 - (-346) = 950 + 346$
$= 1296$
The difference between these average temperatures is 1296°F.

Your solution
−4°C

Solution on p. S1

1.1 Exercises

TAKE NOTE

"To the Student" on page xxi discusses the exercise sets in this textbook.

Objective A

Place the correct symbol, < or >, between the two numbers.

1. $8 > -6$ **2.** $-14 < 16$ **3.** $-12 < 1$ **4.** $35 > 28$ **5.** $42 > 19$

6. $-42 < 27$ **7.** $0 > -31$ **8.** $-17 < 0$ **9.** $53 > -46$ **10.** $-27 > -39$

Answer true or false.

11. $-13 > 0$
false

12. $-20 > 3$
false

13. $12 > -31$
true

14. $9 > 7$
true

15. $-5 > -2$
false

16. $-44 > -21$
false

17. $-4 > -120$
true

18. $0 > -8$
true

19. $-1 > 0$
false

20. $-10 > 88$
true

21. Let $x \in \{-23, -18, -8, 0\}$. For which values of x is the inequality $x < -8$ a true statement?
$-23, -18$

22. Let $w \in \{-33, -24, -10, 0\}$. For which values of w is the inequality $w < -10$ a true statement?
$-33, -24$

23. Let $a \in \{-33, -15, 21, 37\}$. For which values of a is the inequality $a > -10$ a true statement?
$21, 37$

24. Let $v \in \{-27, -14, 14, 27\}$. For which values of v is the inequality $v > -15$ a true statement?
$-14, 14, 27$

25. Let $n \in \{-23, -1, 0, 4, 29\}$. For which values of n is the inequality $-6 > n$ a true statement?
-23

26. Let $m \in \{-33, -11, 0, 12, 45\}$. For which values of m is the inequality $-15 > m$ a true statement?
-33

Objective B

Find the additive inverse.

27. 4
-4

28. 8
-8

29. -9
9

30. -12
12

31. -28
28

32. -36
36

Evaluate.

33. $-(-14)$
14

34. $-(-40)$
40

35. $-(77)$
-77

36. $-(39)$
-39

37. $-(0)$
0

38. $-(-13)$
13

39. $|-74|$
74

40. $|-96|$
96

41. $-|-82|$
-82

42. $-|-53|$
-53

43. $-|81|$
-81

44. $-|38|$
-38

Place the correct symbol, < or >, between the values of the two numbers.

45. $|-83| > |58|$ **46.** $|22| > |-19|$ **47.** $|43| < |-52|$ **48.** $|-71| < |-92|$

49. $|-68| > |-42|$ **50.** $|12| < |-31|$ **51.** $|-45| < |-61|$ **52.** $|-28| < |43|$

53. Let $p \in \{-19, 0, 28\}$. Evaluate $-p$ for each element of the set.
19, 0, −28

54. Let $q \in \{-34, 0, 31\}$. Evaluate $-q$ for each element of the set.
34, 0, −31

55. Let $x \in \{-45, 0, 17\}$. Evaluate $-|x|$ for each element of the set.
−45, 0, −17

56. Let $y \in \{-91, 0, 48\}$. Evaluate $-|y|$ for each element of the set.
−91, 0, −48

Objective C

Add or subtract.

57. $-3 + (-8)$
−11

58. $-6 + (-9)$
−15

59. $-8 + 3$
−5

60. $-9 + 2$
−7

61. $-3 + (-80)$
−83

62. $-12 + (-1)$
−13

63. $-23 + (-23)$
−46

64. $-12 + (-12)$
−24

65. $16 + (-16)$
0

66. $-17 + 17$
0

67. $48 + (-53)$
−5

68. $19 + (-41)$
−22

69. $-17 + (-3) + 29$
9

70. $13 + 62 + (-38)$
37

71. $-3 + (-8) + 12$
1

72. $-27 + (-42) + (-18)$
−87

73. $16 - 8$
8

74. $12 - 3$
9

75. $7 - 14$
−7

76. $6 - 9$
−3

77. $-7 - 2$
−9

78. $-9 - 4$
−13

79. $7 - (-2)$
9

80. $3 - (-4)$
7

81. $-6 - (-3)$
−3

82. $-4 - (-2)$
−2

83. $6 - (-12)$
18

84. $-12 - 16$
−28

85. $13 + (-22) + 4 + (-5)$
−10

86. $-14 + (-3) + 7 + (-21)$
−31

87. $-22 + 20 + 2 + (-18)$
−18

88. $-6 + (-8) + 14 + (-4)$
−4

89. $-16 + (-17) + (-18) + 10$
-41

90. $-25 + (-31) + 24 + 19$
-13

91. $26 + (-15) + (-11) + (-12)$
-12

92. $-32 + 40 + (-8) + (-19)$
-19

93. $-17 + (-18) + 45 + (-10)$
0

94. $23 + (-15) + 9 + (-15)$
2

95. $46 + (-17) + (-13) + (-50)$
-34

96. $-37 + (-17) + (-12) + (-15)$
-81

97. $-14 + (\ \ 15) + (-11) + 40$
0

98. $28 + (-19) + (-8) + (-1)$
0

99. $-4 - 3 - 2$
-9

100. $4 - 5 - 12$
-13

101. $12 - (-7) - 8$
11

102. $-12 - (-3) - (-15)$
6

103. $-19 - (-19) - 18$
-18

104. $-8 - (-8) - 14$
-14

105. $-17 - (-8) - (-9)$
0

106. $7 - 8 - (-1)$
0

107. $-30 - (-65) - 29 - 4$
2

108. $42 - (-82) - 65 - 7$
52

109. $-16 - 47 - 63 - 12$
-138

110. $42 - (-30) - 65 - (-11)$
18

111. $-47 - (-67) - 13 - 15$
-8

112. $-18 - 49 - (-84) - 27$
-10

113. $-19 - 17 - (-36) - 12$
-12

114. $48 - 19 - 29 - 51$
-51

115. $21 - (-14) - 43 - 12$
-20

116. $17 - (-17) - 14 - 21$
-1

Objective D

Multiply or divide.

117. (14)3   **118.** (17)6   **119.** $-7 \cdot 4$ **120.** $-8 \cdot 7$ **121.** $(-12)(-5)$ **122.** $(-13)(-9)$
   42   102 -28 -56 60   117

123. $-11(23)$ **124.** $-8(21)$ **125.** $(-17)14$ **126.** $(-15)12$ **127.** $6(-19)$ **128.** $17(-13)$
   -253 -168 -238 -180 -114 -221

129. $12 \div (-6)$ **130.** $18 \div (-3)$ **131.** $(-72) \div (-9)$ **132.** $(-64) \div (-8)$ **133.** $-42 \div 6$
   -2 -6 8   8 -7

134. $(-56) \div 8$ **135.** $(-144) \div 12$ **136.** $(-93) \div (-3)$ **137.** $48 \div (-8)$ **138.** $57 \div (-3)$
   -7 -12 31 -6 -19

139. $\dfrac{-49}{7}$ **140.** $\dfrac{-45}{5}$ **141.** $\dfrac{-44}{-4}$ **142.** $\dfrac{-36}{-9}$ **143.** $\dfrac{98}{-7}$
   -7 -9 11   4 -14

144. $\dfrac{85}{-5}$ **145.** $-\dfrac{-120}{8}$ **146.** $-\dfrac{-72}{4}$ **147.** $-\dfrac{-80}{-5}$ **148.** $-\dfrac{-114}{-6}$
   -17 15   18 -16 -19

149. $0 \div (-9)$ **150.** $0 \div (-14)$ **151.** $\dfrac{-261}{9}$ **152.** $\dfrac{-128}{4}$ **153.** $9 \div 0$
   0   0 -29 -32 undefined

154. $(-21) \div 0$ **155.** $\dfrac{132}{-12}$ **156.** $\dfrac{250}{-25}$ **157.** $\dfrac{0}{0}$ **158.** $\dfrac{-58}{0}$
   undefined -11 -10 undefined   undefined

159. $7(5)(-3)$ **160.** $(-3)(-2)8$ **161.** $9(-7)(-4)$ **162.** $(-2)(6)(-4)$
   -105 48   252   48

163. $16(-3)5$ **164.** $20(-4)3$ **165.** $-4(-3)8$ **166.** $-5(-9)6$
   -240 -240 96   270

167. $-3(-8)(-9)$ **168.** $-7(-6)(-5)$ **169.** $(-9)7(5)$ **170.** $(-8)7(10)$
   -216 -210 -315 -560

171. $7(-2)(5)(-6)$ **172.** $(-3)7(-2)8$ **173.** $-9(-4)-8)(-10)$ **174.** $-11(-3)(-5)(-2)$
   420   336   2880   330

175. $7(9)(-11)4$ **176.** $-12(-4)7(-2)$ **177.** $(-14)9(-11)0$ **178.** $(-13)(15)(-19)0$
   -2772 -672 0   0

Objective E   *Application Problems*

The elevation, or height, of places on the earth is measured in relation to sea level, or the average level of the ocean's surface. The table below shows height above sea level as a positive number and depth below sea level as a negative number. Use the table for Exercises 179 to 181.

Continent	Highest Elevation (in meters)		Lowest Elevation (in meters)	
Africa	Mt. Kilimanjaro	5895	Qattara Depression	−133
Asia	Mt. Everest	8848	Dead Sea	−400
Europe	Mt. Elbrus	5634	Caspian Sea	−28
America	Mt. Aconcagua	6960	Death Valley	−86

179. Find the difference in elevation between Mt. Aconcagua and Death Valley.

7046 m

180. What is the difference in elevation between Mt. Kilimanjaro and the Qattara Depression?

6028 m

181. For which continent shown is the difference between the highest and lowest elevations greatest?

Asia

The table at the right shows the boiling point and the melting point in degrees Celsius of three chemical elements. Use this table for Exercises 182 and 183.

Chemical Element	Boiling Point	Melting Point
Carbon	4827	−355
Radon	−62	−71
Xenon	−107	−112

182. Find the difference between the boiling point and the melting point of carbon.

5182°C

183. Find the difference between the boiling point and the melting point of xenon.

5°C

184. To discourage random guessing on a multiple-choice exam, a professor assigns 5 points for a correct answer, −2 points for an incorrect answer, and 0 points for leaving the question blank. What is the score for a student who had 20 correct answers, had 13 incorrect answers, and left 7 questions blank?

74

185. To discourage random guessing on a multiple-choice exam, a professor assigns 7 points for a correct answer, −3 points for an incorrect answer, and −1 point for leaving the question blank. What is the score for a student who had 17 correct answers, had 8 incorrect answers, and left 2 questions blank?

93

The bar graph at the right shows the net income or loss for US Airways for the years 1992 to 1997. Use this graph for Exercises 186 to 188.

186. What was the total net income or loss for the years shown in the graph?
−$900 million

187. What was the difference between the net income or loss in 1993 and 1994?
$292 million

188. What was the difference between the net income or loss in 1995 and 1994?
$804 million

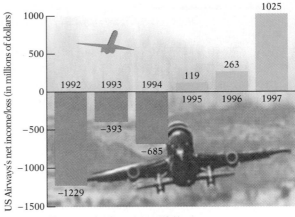

Sources: Transportation Department, US Airways

A meteorologist may report a wind-chill temperature. This is the equivalent temperature, including the effects of wind and temperature, that a person would feel in calm air conditions. The table below gives the wind-chill temperature for various wind speeds and temperatures. For instance, when the temperature is 5°F and the wind is blowing at 15 mph, the wind-chill temperature is −25°F. Use this table for Exercises 189 and 190.

Wind Speed (mph)						*Thermometer Reading (degrees Fahrenheit)*											
	35	**30**	**25**	**20**	**15**	**10**	**5**	**0**	**−5**	**−10**	**−15**	**−20**	**−25**	**−30**	**−35**	**−40**	**−45**
5	33	27	21	19	12	7	0	−5	−10	−15	−21	−26	−31	−36	−42	−47	−52
10	22	16	10	3	−3	−9	−15	−22	−27	−34	−40	−46	−52	−58	−64	−71	−77
15	16	9	2	−5	−11	−18	−25	−31	−38	−45	−51	−58	−65	−72	−78	−85	−92
20	12	4	−3	−10	−17	−24	−31	−39	−46	−53	−60	−67	−74	−81	−88	−95	−103
25	8	1	−7	−15	−22	−29	−36	−44	−51	−59	−66	−74	−81	−88	−96	−103	−110
30	6	−2	−10	−18	−25	−33	−41	−49	−56	−64	−71	−79	−86	−93	−101	−109	−116
35	4	−4	−12	−20	−27	−35	−43	−52	−58	−67	−74	−82	−89	−97	−105	−113	−120
40	3	−5	−13	−21	−29	−37	−45	−53	−60	−69	−76	−84	−92	−100	−107	−115	−123
45	2	−6	−14	−22	−30	−38	−46	−54	−62	−70	−78	−85	−93	−102	−109	−117	−125

Title row: *Wind-Chill Factors*

189. When the thermometer reading is −5°F, what is the difference between the wind-chill factor when the wind is blowing 10 mph and when the wind is blowing 30 mph?
29°F

190. When the thermometer reading is −20°F, what is the difference between the wind-chill factor when the wind is blowing 15 mph and when the wind is blowing 25 mph?
16°F

APPLYING THE CONCEPTS

191. If $-4x$ equals a positive integer, is x a positive or a negative integer? Explain your answer.
x is negative.

192. Is the difference between two integers always smaller than either of the integers? If not, give an example for which the difference between two integers is greater than either integer.
No. For example, $10 - (-8) = 18$.

1.2 Rational and Irrational Numbers

Objective A   **To write a rational number as a decimal**..

A *rational number* is the quotient of two integers. A rational number written in this way is commonly called a fraction. Here are some examples of rational numbers.

$$\frac{3}{4}, \quad \frac{-4}{9}, \quad \frac{15}{-4}, \quad \frac{8}{1}, \quad -\frac{5}{6}$$

> **Rational Numbers**
>
> A **rational number** is a number that can be written in the form $\frac{a}{b}$, where a and b are integers and $b \neq 0$.

Because an integer can be written as the quotient of the integer and 1, every integer is a rational number. For instance,

$$\frac{6}{1} = 6 \qquad \frac{-8}{1} = -8$$

A number written in **decimal notation** is also a rational number.

three-tenths $0.3 = \dfrac{3}{10}$ forty-three thousandths $0.043 = \dfrac{43}{1000}$

A rational number written as a fraction can be written in decimal notation.

Write $\dfrac{5}{8}$ as a decimal.

The fraction bar can be read "÷".

$$\frac{5}{8} = 5 \div 8$$

$$
\begin{array}{r}
0.625 \\
8\overline{)5.000} \\
-4\ 8 \\
\hline
20 \\
-16 \\
\hline
40 \\
-40 \\
\hline
0
\end{array}
$$
← This is called a **terminating decimal.**

← The remainder is zero.

$$\frac{5}{8} = 0.625$$

Write $\dfrac{4}{11}$ as a decimal.

$$
\begin{array}{r}
0.3636\ldots \\
11\overline{)4.0000} \\
-3\ 3 \\
\hline
70 \\
-66 \\
\hline
40 \\
-33 \\
\hline
70 \\
-66 \\
\hline
4
\end{array}
$$
← This is called a **repeating decimal.**

← The remainder is never zero.

$$\frac{4}{11} = 0.\overline{36}$$
← The bar over the digits 3 and 6 is used to show that these digits repeat.

Example 1 Write $\frac{8}{11}$ as a decimal. Place a bar over the repeating digits of the decimal.

Solution $\frac{8}{11} = 8 \div 11 = 0.7272\ldots = 0.\overline{72}$

You Try It 1 Write $\frac{4}{9}$ as a decimal. Place a bar over the repeating digits of the decimal.

Your solution $0.\overline{4}$

Solution on p. S1

Objective B **To convert among percents, fractions, and decimals** ......

Percent means "parts of 100." Thus 27% means 27 parts of 100.

In applied problems involving percent, it may be necessary to rewrite a percent as a fraction or decimal or to rewrite a fraction or decimal as a percent.

To write a percent as a fraction, remove the percent sign and multiply by $\frac{1}{100}$.

➡ Write 27% as a fraction.

$$27\% = 27\left(\frac{1}{100}\right) = \frac{27}{100}$$ • Remove the percent sign and multiply by $\frac{1}{100}$.

To write a percent as a decimal, remove the percent sign and multiply by 0.01.

$$33\% \quad = \quad 33(0.01) \quad = \quad 0.33$$

| Move the decimal point two places to the left. Then remove the percent sign. |

A fraction or decimal can be written as a percent by multiplying by 100%.

$$\frac{5}{8} = \frac{5}{8}(100\%) = \frac{500}{8}\% = 62.5\%, \text{ or } 62\frac{1}{2}\%$$

$$0.82 \quad = \quad 0.82(100\%) \quad = \quad 82\%$$

| Move the decimal point two places to the right. Then write the percent sign. |

Example 2
Write 130% as a fraction and as a decimal.

Solution

$$130\% = 130\left(\frac{1}{100}\right) = \frac{130}{100} = \frac{13}{10}$$

$$130\% = 130(0.01) = 1.30$$

You Try It 2
Write 125% as a fraction and as a decimal.

Your solution

$\frac{5}{4}$; 1.25

Solution on p. S1

Example 3	Write $\frac{5}{6}$ as a percent.	**You Try It 3**	Write $\frac{1}{3}$ as a percent.
Solution	$\frac{5}{6} = \frac{5}{6}(100\%) = \frac{500}{6}\% = 83\frac{1}{3}\%$	**Your solution**	$33\frac{1}{3}\%$
Example 4	Write 0.092 as a percent.	**You Try It 4**	Write 0.043 as a percent.
Solution	$0.092 = 0.092(100\%) = 9.2\%$	**Your solution**	4.3%

Solutions on p. S2

Objective C   To add or subtract rational numbers ....

Fractions with the same denominator are added by adding the numerators and placing the sum over the common denominator.

> **Addition of Fractions**
>
> To add two fractions with the same denominator, add the numerators and place the sum over the common denominator.
>
> $$\frac{a}{c} + \frac{b}{c} = \frac{a+b}{c}$$

To add fractions with different denominators, first rewrite the fractions as equivalent fractions with a common denominator. Then add the fractions.

The least common denominator is the **least common multiple** (LCM) of the denominators. This is the smallest number that is a multiple of each of the denominators.

TAKE NOTE

You can find the LCM by multiplying the denominators and then dividing by the *common factor* of the two denominators. In the case of 6 and 10, 6 · 10 = 60. Now divide by 2, the common factor of 6 and 10.

60 ÷ 2 = 30.

➡ Add: $-\frac{5}{6} + \frac{3}{10}$

The LCM of 6 and 10 is 30. Rewrite the fractions as equivalent fractions with the denominator 30. Then add the fractions.

$$-\frac{5}{6} + \frac{3}{10} = -\frac{5}{6} \cdot \frac{5}{5} + \frac{3}{10} \cdot \frac{3}{3} = -\frac{25}{30} + \frac{9}{30} = \frac{-25 + 9}{30} = \frac{-16}{30} = -\frac{8}{15}$$

To subtract fractions with the same denominator, subtract the numerators and place the difference over the common denominator.

TAKE NOTE

The least common multiple of the denominators is frequently called the **least common denominator** (LCD).

➡ Subtract: $-\frac{4}{9} - \left(-\frac{7}{12}\right)$

The LCM of 9 and 12 is 36. Rewrite the fractions as equivalent fractions with the denominator 36. Then subtract the fractions.

$$-\frac{4}{9} - \left(-\frac{7}{12}\right) = -\frac{16}{36} - \left(-\frac{21}{36}\right) = \frac{-16 - (-21)}{36} = \frac{-16 + 21}{36} = \frac{5}{36}$$

INSTRUCTOR NOTE
One of the pedagogical features of this text is paired examples like those in the box below. The example in the left-hand column is worked completely. After studying that example, the student should attempt the corresponding You Try It. A *complete solution* of that example can be found at the back of the book so that the student can compare the *answer* and the *procedure*.

To add or subtract decimals, write the numbers so that the decimal points are in a vertical line. Then proceed as in the addition or subtraction of integers. Write the decimal point in the answer directly below the decimal points in the problem.

➡ Add: $-114.039 + 84.76$

$|-114.039| = 114.039$

$|84.76| = 84.76$

- The signs are different. Find the absolute value of each number.

$$\begin{array}{r} 114.039 \\ -\ \ 84.76 \\ \hline 29.279 \end{array}$$

- Subtract the smaller of these numbers from the larger.

$-114.039 + 84.76 = -29.279$

- Attach the sign of the number with the larger absolute value. Because $|-114.039| > |84.76|$, use the sign of -114.039.

Example 5   Simplify: $-\dfrac{3}{4} + \dfrac{1}{6} - \dfrac{5}{8}$

Solution   The LCM of 4, 6, and 8 is 24.

$$-\frac{3}{4} + \frac{1}{6} - \frac{5}{8} = -\frac{18}{24} + \frac{4}{24} - \frac{15}{24}$$

$$= \frac{-18 + 4 - 15}{24}$$

$$= \frac{-29}{24} = -\frac{29}{24}$$

You Try It 5   Simplify: $-\dfrac{7}{8} - \dfrac{5}{6} + \dfrac{3}{4}$

Your solution $-\dfrac{23}{24}$

Example 6   Subtract: $42.987 - 98.61$

Solution $42.987 - 98.61$

$= 42.987 + (-98.61)$

$= -55.623$

You Try It 6   Subtract: $16.127 - 67.91$

Your solution -51.783

Solutions on p. S2

Objective D   **To multiply or divide rational numbers** ....

The product of two fractions is the product of the numerators divided by the product of the denominators.

$$\frac{a}{b} \cdot \frac{c}{d} = \frac{ac}{bd}$$

➡ Multiply: $\dfrac{3}{8} \cdot \dfrac{12}{17}$

$$\frac{3}{8} \cdot \frac{12}{17} = \frac{3 \cdot 12}{8 \cdot 17}$$

- Multiply the numerators. Multiply the denominators.

$$= \frac{3 \cdot \overset{1}{\cancel{2}} \cdot \overset{1}{\cancel{2}} \cdot 3}{2 \cdot \underset{1}{\cancel{2}} \cdot \underset{1}{\cancel{2}} \cdot 17}$$

- Write the prime factorization of each factor. Divide by the common factors.

$$= \frac{9}{34}$$

- Multiply the factors in the numerator and in the denominator.

TAKE NOTE

To invert the divisor means to write its reciprocal. The reciprocal of $\frac{18}{25}$ is $\frac{25}{18}$.

To divide fractions, invert the divisor. Then multiply the fractions.

➡ Divide: $\frac{3}{10} \div \left(-\frac{18}{25}\right)$

The signs are different. The quotient is negative.

$$\frac{3}{10} \div \left(-\frac{18}{25}\right) = -\left(\frac{3}{10} \div \frac{18}{25}\right) = -\left(\frac{3}{10} \cdot \frac{25}{18}\right) = -\left(\frac{3 \cdot 25}{10 \cdot 18}\right)$$

$$= -\left(\frac{\overset{1}{\cancel{3}} \cdot \overset{1}{\cancel{5}} \cdot 5}{2 \cdot \underset{1}{\cancel{5}} \cdot 2 \cdot \underset{1}{\cancel{3}} \cdot 3}\right) = -\frac{5}{12}$$

INSTRUCTOR NOTE

Simon Stevin (1548–1620), a Dutch mathematician, wrote *De Thiende (The Art of the Tenth),* in which he showed a systematic method of computing with decimals.

To multiply decimals, multiply as with integers. Write the decimal point in the product so that the number of decimal places in the product equals the sum of the decimal places in the factors.

➡ Multiply: $-6.89(0.00035)$

$$
\begin{array}{r}
6.89 \\
\times\ 0.00035 \\
\hline
3445 \\
2067 \\
\hline
0.0024115
\end{array}
$$

2 decimal places
5 decimal places   • **Multiply the absolute values.**

7 decimal places

$-6.89(0.00035) = -0.0024115$ • **The signs are different. The product is negative.**

To divide decimals, move the decimal point in the divisor to the right to make it a whole number. Move the decimal point in the dividend the same number of places to the right. Place the decimal point in the quotient directly over the decimal point in the dividend. Then divide as with whole numbers.

TAKE NOTE

The symbol ≈ is used to indicate that the quotient is an approximate value that has been rounded off.

➡ Divide: $1.32 \div 0.27$. Round to the nearest tenth.

$$
\begin{array}{r}
4.88 \approx 4.9 \\
0.27.\overline{)1.32.00} \\
-1\ 08 \\
\hline
240 \\
-216 \\
\hline
240 \\
-216 \\
\hline
24
\end{array}
$$

• **Move the decimal point 2 places to the right in the divisor and then in the dividend. Place the decimal point in the quotient.**

Example 7   Divide: $-\frac{5}{8} \div \left(-\frac{5}{40}\right)$

Solution   The quotient is positive.

$$-\frac{5}{8} \div \left(-\frac{5}{40}\right) = \frac{5}{8} \div \frac{5}{40} = \frac{5}{8} \cdot \frac{40}{5} = \frac{5 \cdot 40}{8 \cdot 5}$$

$$= \frac{\overset{1}{\cancel{5}} \cdot \overset{1}{\cancel{2}} \cdot \overset{1}{\cancel{2}} \cdot \overset{1}{\cancel{2}} \cdot 5}{2 \cdot 2 \cdot 2 \cdot \underset{1}{\cancel{5}}} = \frac{5}{1} = 5$$

You Try It 7   Divide: $-\frac{3}{8} \div \left(-\frac{5}{12}\right)$

Your solution $\frac{9}{10}$

Solution on p. S2

Example 8   Multiply: $-4.29(8.2)$

Solution   The product is negative.

$$\begin{array}{r} 4.29 \\ \times\ 8.2 \\ \hline 858 \\ 3432 \\ \hline 35.178 \end{array}$$

$$-4.29(8.2) = -35.178$$

You Try It 8   Multiply: $-5.44(3.8)$

Your solution -20.672

Solution on p. S2

Objective E   **To evaluate exponential expressions**..

Repeated multiplication of the same factor can be written using an exponent.

$$2 \cdot 2 \cdot 2 \cdot 2 \cdot 2 = 2^5 \quad \overset{\textbf{exponent}}{\underset{\textbf{base}}{\uparrow}}$$

$$a \cdot a \cdot a \cdot a = a^4 \quad \overset{\textbf{exponent}}{\underset{\textbf{base}}{\uparrow}}$$

The **exponent** indicates how many times the factor, called the **base**, occurs in the multiplication. The multiplication $2 \cdot 2 \cdot 2 \cdot 2 \cdot 2$ is in **factored form**. The exponential expression 2^5 is in **exponential form**.

2^1 is read "the first power of 2" or just 2. Usually the exponent 1 is not written.

2^2 is read "the second power of 2" or "2 squared."

2^3 is read "the third power of 2" or "2 cubed."

2^4 is read "the fourth power of 2."

a^4 is read "the fourth power of a."

There is a geometric interpretation of the first three natural-number powers.

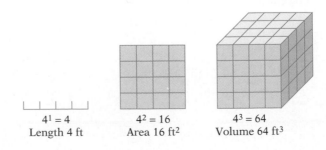

$4^1 = 4$
Length 4 ft

$4^2 = 16$
Area 16 ft^2

$4^3 = 64$
Volume 64 ft^3

To evaluate an exponential expression, write each factor as many times as indicated by the exponent. Then multiply.

➡ Evaluate $(-2)^4$.

$$(-2)^4 = (-2)(-2)(-2)(-2)$$ • Write (-2) as a factor 4 times.
$$= 16$$ • Multiply.

➡ Evaluate -2^4.

$$-2^4 = -(2 \cdot 2 \cdot 2 \cdot 2)$$ • Write 2 as a factor 4 times.
$$= -16$$ • Multiply.

From these last two examples, note the difference between $(-2)^4$ and -2^4.

$$(-2)^4 = 16$$
$$-2^4 = -(2^4) = -16$$

Example 9   Evaluate -5^3.

Solution $-5^3 = -(5 \cdot 5 \cdot 5) = -125$

You Try It 9   Evaluate -6^3.

Your solution -216

Example 10   Evaluate $(-4)^4$.

Solution $(-4)^4 = (-4)(-4)(-4)(-4)$
$$= 256$$

You Try It 10   Evaluate $(-3)^4$.

Your solution   81

Example 11   Evaluate $(-3)^2 \cdot 2^3$.

Solution $(-3)^2 \cdot 2^3 = (-3)(-3) \cdot (2)(2)(2)$
$$= 9 \cdot 8 = 72$$

You Try It 11   Evaluate $(3^3)(-2)^3$.

Your solution -216

Example 12   Evaluate $\left(-\dfrac{2}{3}\right)^3$.

Solution $\left(-\dfrac{2}{3}\right)^3 = \left(-\dfrac{2}{3}\right)\left(-\dfrac{2}{3}\right)\left(-\dfrac{2}{3}\right)$
$$= -\dfrac{2 \cdot 2 \cdot 2}{3 \cdot 3 \cdot 3} = -\dfrac{8}{27}$$

You Try It 12   Evaluate $\left(-\dfrac{2}{5}\right)^2$.

Your solution $\dfrac{4}{25}$

Example 13   Evaluate $-4(0.7)^2$.

Solution $-4(0.7)^2 = -4(0.7)(0.7)$
$$= -2.8(0.7) = -1.96$$

You Try It 13   Evaluate $-3(0.3)^3$.

Your solution -0.081

Solutions on p. S2

Objective F   *To simplify numerical radical expressions* ....

A **square root** of a positive number x is a number whose square is x.

A square root of 16 is 4 because $4^2 = 16$.
A square root of 16 is -4 because $(-4)^2 = 16$.

POINT OF INTEREST

The radical sign was first used in 1525 but was written as √. Some historians suggest that the radical sign also developed into the symbols for "less than" and "greater than." Because typesetters of that time did not want to make additional symbols, the radical sign was rotated to the position ⟍ and used as a "greater than" symbol and rotated to ⟋ and used for the "less than" symbol. Other evidence, however, suggests that the "less than" and "greater than" symbols were developed independently of the radical sign.

Every positive number has two square roots, one a positive and one a negative number. The symbol "$\sqrt{}$," called a **radical sign**, is used to indicate the positive or **principal square root** of a number. For example, $\sqrt{16} = 4$ and $\sqrt{25} = 5$. The number under the radical sign is called the **radicand**.

When the negative square root of a number is to be found, a negative sign is placed in front of the radical. For example, $-\sqrt{16} = -4$ and $-\sqrt{25} = -5$.

The square of an integer is a **perfect square**. 49, 81, and 144 are examples of perfect squares.

$$7^2 = 49$$
$$9^2 = 81$$
$$12^2 = 144$$

An integer that is a perfect square can be written as the product of prime factors, each of which has an even exponent when expressed in exponential form.

$$49 = 7 \cdot 7 = 7^2$$
$$81 = 3 \cdot 3 \cdot 3 \cdot 3 = 3^4$$
$$144 = 2 \cdot 2 \cdot 2 \cdot 2 \cdot 3 \cdot 3 = 2^4 3^2$$

➡ Simplify $\sqrt{625}$.

TAKE NOTE

To find the square root of a perfect square written in exponential form, remove the radical sign and multiply the exponent by $\frac{1}{2}$.

$$\sqrt{625} = \sqrt{5^4}$$

   • Write the prime factorization of the radicand in exponential form.

$$= 5^2$$

   • Remove the radical sign and multiply the exponent by $\frac{1}{2}$.

$$= 25$$

   • Simplify.

If a number is not a perfect square, its square root can only be approximated. For example, 2 and 7 are not perfect squares. The square roots of these numbers are **irrational numbers**. Their decimal representations never terminate or repeat.

$$\sqrt{2} \approx 1.4142135\ldots \qquad \sqrt{7} \approx 2.6457513\ldots$$

Recall that rational numbers are fractions such as $-\frac{6}{7}$ or $-\frac{10}{3}$, where the numerator and denominator are integers. Rational numbers are also represented by repeating decimals, such as $0.25767676\ldots$, and by terminating decimals, such as 1.73. An irrational number is neither a repeating nor a terminating decimal. For instance, $2.45445444544445\ldots$ is an irrational number.

> **Real Numbers**
>
> The rational numbers and the irrational numbers taken together are called the **real numbers**.

A radical expression is in simplest form when the radicand contains no factor greater than 1 that is a perfect square. The Product Property of Square Roots is used to simplify radical expressions.

The Product Property of Square Roots

If a and b are positive real numbers, then $\sqrt{ab} = \sqrt{a} \cdot \sqrt{b}$.

➡ Simplify: $\sqrt{360}$

$\sqrt{360} = \sqrt{2^3 \cdot 3^2 \cdot 5}$

- Write the prime factorization of the radicand.

$\qquad = \sqrt{(2^2 \cdot 3^2)(2 \cdot 5)}$

- Write the radicand as a product of a perfect square and factors that do not contain perfect-square factors.

$\qquad = \sqrt{2^2 \cdot 3^2}\,\sqrt{2 \cdot 5}$

- Use the Product Property of Square Roots.

$\qquad = 2 \cdot 3\sqrt{10}$

- Take the square root of the perfect squares.

$\qquad = 6\sqrt{10}$

From the last example, note than $\sqrt{360} = 6\sqrt{10}$. The two expressions are different representations of the same number. Using a calculator, we find that $\sqrt{360} \approx 18.973666$ and $6\sqrt{10} \approx 6(3.1622777) = 18.973666$.

➡ Simplify: $\sqrt{-16}$

Because the square of any real number is positive, there is no real number whose square is -16. $\sqrt{-16}$ is not a real number.

Example 14 Simplify: $3\sqrt{90}$

Solution $3\sqrt{90} = 3\sqrt{2 \cdot 3^2 \cdot 5}$
$\qquad\qquad = 3\sqrt{3^2(2 \cdot 5)}$
$\qquad\qquad = 3\sqrt{3^2}\,\sqrt{2 \cdot 5}$
$\qquad\qquad = 3 \cdot 3\sqrt{10} = 9\sqrt{10}$

You Try It 14 Simplify: $-5\sqrt{32}$

Your solution $-20\sqrt{2}$

Example 15 Simplify: $\sqrt{252}$

Solution $\sqrt{252} = \sqrt{2^2 \cdot 3^2 \cdot 7}$
$\qquad\qquad = \sqrt{2^2 \cdot 3^2}\,\sqrt{7}$
$\qquad\qquad = 2 \cdot 3\sqrt{7}$
$\qquad\qquad = 6\sqrt{7}$

You Try It 15 Simplify: $\sqrt{216}$

Your solution $6\sqrt{6}$

Solutions on p. S2

Objective G *To solve application problems*...

One of the applications of percent is to express a portion of a total as a percent. For instance, a recent survey of 450 mall shoppers found that 270 preferred the mall closest to their home even though it did not have as much store variety as a mall farther from home. The percent of shoppers who preferred the mall closest to home can be found by converting a fraction to a percent.

$$\frac{\text{Portion preferring mall closest to home}}{\text{Total number surveyed}} = \frac{270}{450}$$

$$= 0.60 = 60\%$$

According to the Congressional Budget Office, the U.S. federal budget deficit in 1996 was $107.3 billion. The number 107.3 billion means

$$107.3 \times \underbrace{1,000,000,000}_{\text{1 billion}} = 107,300,000,000$$

Numbers such as 107.3 billion are used in many instances because they are easy to read and offer an approximation to the actual number. Such numbers are used in Example 16 and You Try It 16.

Example 16

The actual and projected spending for software, equipment, and services for intranets is shown in the bar graph below. Find the difference between expenditures in 2000 and in 1998.

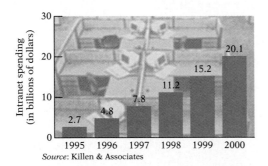

Source: Killen & Associates

Strategy
To find the difference, subtract the expenditures in 1998 ($11.2 billion) from those in 2000 ($20.1 billion).

Solution
$20.1 - 11.2 = 8.9$

The difference is $8.9 billion.

You Try It 16

The circle graph below shows the breakdown of the population of the United States by generation. What percent of the population of the United States is in the baby-boomer generation? Round to the nearest percent.

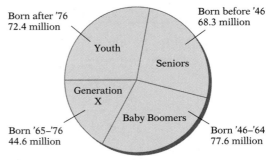

Source: Data from U.S. Census Bureau

Your strategy

Your solution
30%

Solution on p. S2

1.2 Exercises

· ·

Objective A

Write as a decimal. Place a bar over the repeating digits of a repeating decimal.

1. $\dfrac{1}{8}$

0.125

2. $\dfrac{7}{8}$

0.875

3. $\dfrac{2}{9}$

$0.\overline{2}$

4. $\dfrac{8}{9}$

$0.\overline{8}$

5. $\dfrac{1}{6}$

$0.1\overline{6}$

6. $\dfrac{5}{6}$

$0.8\overline{3}$

7. $\dfrac{9}{16}$

0.5625

8. $\dfrac{15}{16}$

0.9375

9. $\dfrac{7}{12}$

$0.583\overline{3}$

10. $\dfrac{11}{12}$

$0.91\overline{6}$

11. $\dfrac{6}{25}$

0.24

12. $\dfrac{14}{25}$

0.56

13. $\dfrac{9}{40}$

0.225

14. $\dfrac{21}{40}$

0.525

15. $\dfrac{5}{11}$

$0.\overline{45}$

Objective B

Write as a fraction and as a decimal.

16. 75%

$\dfrac{3}{4}$, 0.75

17. 40%

$\dfrac{2}{5}$, 0.40

18. 64%

$\dfrac{16}{25}$, 0.64

19. 88%

$\dfrac{22}{25}$, 0.88

20. 125%

$\dfrac{5}{4}$, 1.25

21. 160%

$\dfrac{8}{5}$, 1.6

22. 19%

$\dfrac{19}{100}$, 0.19

23. 87%

$\dfrac{87}{100}$, 0.87

24. 5%

$\dfrac{1}{20}$, 0.05

25. 450%

$\dfrac{9}{2}$, 4.50

Write as a fraction.

26. $11\dfrac{1}{9}\%$

$\dfrac{1}{9}$

27. $4\dfrac{2}{7}\%$

$\dfrac{3}{70}$

28. $12\dfrac{1}{2}\%$

$\dfrac{1}{8}$

29. $37\dfrac{1}{2}\%$

$\dfrac{3}{8}$

30. $66\dfrac{2}{3}\%$

$\dfrac{2}{3}$

31. $\dfrac{1}{4}\%$

$\dfrac{1}{400}$

32. $\dfrac{1}{2}\%$

$\dfrac{1}{200}$

33. $6\dfrac{1}{4}\%$

$\dfrac{1}{16}$

34. $83\dfrac{1}{3}\%$

$\dfrac{5}{6}$

35. $5\dfrac{3}{4}\%$

$\dfrac{23}{400}$

Write as a decimal.

36. 7.3%

0.073

37. 9.1%

0.091

38. 15.8%

0.158

39. 16.7%

0.167

40. 0.3%

0.003

41. 0.9%

0.009

42. 9.9%

0.099

43. 9.15%

0.0915

44. 121.2%

1.212

45. 18.23%

0.1823

Write as a percent.

46. 0.15
15%

47. 0.37
37%

48. 0.05
5%

49. 0.02
2%

50. 0.175
17.5%

51. 0.125
12.5%

52. 1.15
115%

53. 1.36
136%

54. 0.008
0.8%

55. 0.004
0.4%

56. $\dfrac{27}{50}$
54%

57. $\dfrac{83}{100}$
83%

58. $\dfrac{1}{3}$
$33\dfrac{1}{3}\%$

59. $\dfrac{3}{8}$
$37\dfrac{1}{2}\%$

60. $\dfrac{5}{11}$
$45\dfrac{5}{11}\%$

61. $\dfrac{4}{9}$
$44\dfrac{4}{9}\%$

62. $\dfrac{7}{8}$
$87\dfrac{1}{2}\%$

63. $\dfrac{9}{20}$
45%

64. $1\dfrac{2}{3}$
$166\dfrac{2}{3}\%$

65. $2\dfrac{1}{2}$
250%

Objective C

Add or subtract.

66. $\dfrac{1}{2}+\dfrac{3}{8}$
$\dfrac{7}{8}$

67. $\dfrac{5}{8}-\dfrac{5}{6}$
$-\dfrac{5}{24}$

68. $\dfrac{1}{9}-\dfrac{5}{27}$
$-\dfrac{2}{27}$

69. $-\dfrac{5}{12}-\dfrac{3}{8}$
$-\dfrac{19}{24}$

70. $-\dfrac{5}{6}-\dfrac{5}{9}$
$-\dfrac{25}{18}$

71. $-\dfrac{6}{13}+\dfrac{17}{26}$
$\dfrac{5}{26}$

72. $-\dfrac{7}{12}+\dfrac{5}{8}$
$\dfrac{1}{24}$

73. $\dfrac{5}{8}-\left(-\dfrac{3}{4}\right)$
$\dfrac{11}{8}$

74. $\dfrac{3}{5}-\dfrac{11}{12}$
$-\dfrac{19}{60}$

75. $\dfrac{11}{12}-\dfrac{5}{6}$
$\dfrac{1}{12}$

76. $-\dfrac{2}{3}-\left(-\dfrac{11}{18}\right)$
$-\dfrac{1}{18}$

77. $-\dfrac{5}{8}-\left(-\dfrac{11}{12}\right)$
$\dfrac{7}{24}$

78. $\dfrac{1}{3}+\dfrac{5}{6}-\dfrac{2}{9}$
$\dfrac{17}{18}$

79. $\dfrac{1}{2}-\dfrac{2}{3}+\dfrac{1}{6}$
0

80. $-\dfrac{5}{16}+\dfrac{3}{4}-\dfrac{7}{8}$
$-\dfrac{7}{16}$

81. $\dfrac{1}{2}-\dfrac{3}{8}-\left(-\dfrac{1}{4}\right)$
$\dfrac{3}{8}$

82. $\dfrac{3}{4}-\left(-\dfrac{7}{12}\right)-\dfrac{7}{8}$
$\dfrac{11}{24}$

83. $\dfrac{1}{3}-\dfrac{1}{4}-\dfrac{1}{5}$
$-\dfrac{7}{60}$

84. $\dfrac{2}{3}-\dfrac{1}{2}+\dfrac{5}{6}$
1

85. $\dfrac{5}{16}+\dfrac{1}{8}-\dfrac{1}{2}$
$-\dfrac{1}{16}$

86. $7.56 + 0.462$
8.022

87. $1.09 + 6.2$
7.29

88. $-32.1 - 6.7$
−38.8

89. $5.13 - 8.179$
−3.049

90. $-13.092 + 6.9$
−6.192

91. $2.54 - 3.6$
−1.06

92. $5.43 + 7.925$
13.355

93. $-16.92 - 6.925$
−23.845

94. $-3.87 + 8.546$
4.676

95. $6.9027 - 17.692$
−10.7893

96. $2.09 - 6.72 - 5.4$
−10.03

97. $-18.39 + 4.9 - 23.7$
−37.19

98. $19 - (-3.72) - 82.75$
−60.03

99. $-3.07 - (-2.97) - 17.4$
−17.5

100. $16.4 - (-3.09) - 7.93$
11.56

101. $-3.09 - 4.6 - (-27.3)$
19.61

102. $2.66 - (-4.66) - 8.2$
−0.88

Objective D

Multiply or divide.

103. $\dfrac{1}{2}\left(-\dfrac{3}{4}\right)$
$-\dfrac{3}{8}$

104. $-\dfrac{2}{9}\left(-\dfrac{3}{14}\right)$
$\dfrac{1}{21}$

105. $\left(-\dfrac{3}{8}\right)\left(-\dfrac{4}{15}\right)$
$\dfrac{1}{10}$

106. $\left(-\dfrac{3}{4}\right)\left(-\dfrac{8}{27}\right)$
$\dfrac{2}{9}$

107. $-\dfrac{1}{2}\left(\dfrac{8}{9}\right)$
$-\dfrac{4}{9}$

108. $\dfrac{5}{12}\left(-\dfrac{8}{15}\right)$
$-\dfrac{2}{9}$

109. $\dfrac{5}{8}\left(-\dfrac{7}{12}\right)\dfrac{16}{25}$
$-\dfrac{7}{30}$

110. $\left(\dfrac{5}{12}\right)\left(-\dfrac{8}{15}\right)\left(-\dfrac{1}{3}\right)$
$\dfrac{2}{27}$

111. $\dfrac{1}{2}\left(-\dfrac{3}{4}\right)\left(-\dfrac{5}{8}\right)$
$\dfrac{15}{64}$

112. $\dfrac{3}{8} \div \dfrac{1}{4}$
$\dfrac{3}{2}$

113. $\dfrac{5}{6} \div \left(-\dfrac{3}{4}\right)$
$-\dfrac{10}{9}$

114. $-\dfrac{5}{12} \div \dfrac{15}{32}$
$-\dfrac{8}{9}$

115. $-\dfrac{7}{8} \div \dfrac{4}{21}$
$-\dfrac{147}{32}$

116. $\dfrac{7}{10} \div \dfrac{2}{5}$
$\dfrac{7}{4}$

117. $-\dfrac{15}{64} \div \left(-\dfrac{3}{40}\right)$
$\dfrac{25}{8}$

118. $\dfrac{1}{8} \div \left(-\dfrac{5}{12}\right)$
$-\dfrac{3}{10}$

119. $-\dfrac{4}{9} \div \left(-\dfrac{2}{3}\right)$
$\dfrac{2}{3}$

120. $-\dfrac{6}{11} \div \dfrac{4}{9}$
$-\dfrac{27}{22}$

121. 1.2(3.47)
4.164

122. (−0.8)6.2
−4.96

123. (−1.89)(−2.3)
4.347

124. (6.9)(−4.2)
−28.98

125. 1.06(−3.8)
−4.028

126. −2.7(−3.5)
9.45

127. 1.2(−0.5)(3.7)
−2.22

128. −2.4(6.1)(0.9)
−13.176

129. 2.3(−0.6)(0.8)
−1.104

130. −1.2(−0.55)(1.9)
1.254

131. 0.44(−2.3)(−0.5)
0.506

132. −3.4(−22.1)(−0.5)
−37.57

133. 1.8(0.33)(−0.4)
−0.2376

134. 4.5(−0.22)(−0.8)
0.792

135. −24.7 ÷ 0.09
−274.$\overline{4}$

Divide. Round to the nearest hundredth.

136. −1.27 ÷ (−1.7)
0.75

137. 9.07 ÷ (−3.5)
−2.59

138. 0.0976 ÷ 0.042
2.32

139. −6.904 ÷ 1.35
−5.11

140. −7.894 ÷ (−2.06)
3.83

141. −354.2086 ÷ 0.1719
−2060.55

**Objective E**

Evaluate.

142. 6^2
36

143. 7^4
2401

144. -7^2
−49

145. -4^3
−64

146. $(-3)^2$
9

147. $(-2)^3$
−8

148. $(-3)^4$
81

149. $(-5)^3$
−125

150. $\left(\dfrac{1}{2}\right)^2$
$\dfrac{1}{4}$

151. $\left(-\dfrac{3}{4}\right)^3$
$-\dfrac{27}{64}$

152. $(0.3)^2$
0.09

153. $(1.5)^3$
3.375

154. $\left(\dfrac{2}{3}\right)^2 \cdot 3^3$
12

155. $\left(-\dfrac{1}{2}\right)^3 \cdot 8$
−1

156. $(0.3)^3 \cdot 2^3$
0.216

157. $(0.5)^2 \cdot 3^3$
6.75

158. $(-3) \cdot 2^2$
−12

159. $(-5) \cdot 3^4$
−405

160. $(-2) \cdot (-2)^3$
16

161. $(-2) \cdot (-2)^2$
−8

162. $2^3 \cdot 3^3 \cdot (-4)$
−864

163. $(-3)^3 \cdot 5^2 \cdot 10$
−6750

164. $(-7) \cdot 4^2 \cdot 3^2$
−1008

165. $(-2) \cdot 2^3 \cdot (-3)^2$
−144

166. $\left(\dfrac{2}{3}\right)^2 \cdot \dfrac{1}{4} \cdot 3^3$
3

167. $\left(\dfrac{3}{4}\right)^2 \cdot (-4) \cdot 2^3$
−18

168. $8^2 \cdot (-3)^5 \cdot 5$
−77,760

Objective F

Simplify.

169. $\sqrt{16}$ **170.** $\sqrt{64}$ **171.** $\sqrt{49}$ **172.** $\sqrt{144}$ **173.** $\sqrt{32}$ **174.** $\sqrt{50}$
4   8   7   12 $4\sqrt{2}$ $5\sqrt{2}$

175. $\sqrt{8}$ **176.** $\sqrt{12}$ **177.** $6\sqrt{18}$ **178.** $-3\sqrt{48}$ **179.** $5\sqrt{40}$ **180.** $2\sqrt{28}$
$2\sqrt{2}$ $2\sqrt{3}$ $18\sqrt{2}$ $-12\sqrt{3}$ $10\sqrt{10}$ $4\sqrt{7}$

181. $\sqrt{15}$ **182.** $\sqrt{21}$ **183.** $\sqrt{29}$ **184.** $\sqrt{13}$ **185.** $-9\sqrt{72}$ **186.** $11\sqrt{80}$
$\sqrt{15}$ $\sqrt{21}$ $\sqrt{29}$ $\sqrt{13}$ $-54\sqrt{2}$ $44\sqrt{5}$

187. $\sqrt{45}$ **188.** $\sqrt{225}$ **189.** $\sqrt{0}$ **190.** $\sqrt{210}$ **191.** $6\sqrt{128}$ **192.** $9\sqrt{288}$
$3\sqrt{5}$ 15   0 $\sqrt{210}$ $48\sqrt{2}$ $108\sqrt{2}$

Find the decimal approximation rounded to the nearest thousandth.

193. $\sqrt{240}$ **194.** $\sqrt{300}$ **195.** $\sqrt{288}$ **196.** $\sqrt{600}$ **197.** $\sqrt{256}$ **198.** $\sqrt{324}$
15.492   17.321   16.971   24.495   16   18

199. $\sqrt{275}$ **200.** $\sqrt{450}$ **201.** $\sqrt{245}$ **202.** $\sqrt{525}$ **203.** $\sqrt{352}$ **204.** $\sqrt{363}$
16.583   21.213   15.652   22.913   18.762   19.053

Objective G   *Application Problems*

205. Movies made in the United States that are not blockbusters in this country may make considerable money abroad. At the right is a table showing five films and their box-office grosses, in millions of dollars, at home and in foreign countries.
  a. What percent of *Waterworld*'s total gross was from foreign countries? Round to the nearest percent.   47%
  b. What percent of *Judge Dredd*'s total gross here and abroad was its U.S. box-office gross? Round to the nearest percent.   44%
  c. Which of the films listed grossed more than half their box-office income in foreign countries?   *Judge Dredd, Spy Hard*

Box-Office Grosses (in millions of dollars)

Film	U. S.	Foreign
Judge Dredd	34.7	44.1
Spy Hard	26.6	30.6
Waterworld	88.2	78.2
The Juror	22.7	17.6
Highlander III	13.8	9.1

Source: Time Magazine, July 7, 1997

206. According to the Federal Highway Administration, the average car is driven approximately 10,300 mi per year and uses approximately 495 gal of gas. Assuming that the average cost of gasoline is $1.097 per gallon, which includes $.443 for all taxes, and that there are 1.53 million cars on the road, determine how much total tax is paid for gasoline in one year. (You may not need all the data given in this problem.)
$335,506,050

207. When a U.S. company does business with another country, it is necessary to convert U.S. currency into the currency of the other country. These *exchange rates* are determined by various factors. The exchange rates for some currencies during one day in July 1998 are shown in the table at the right.

Foreign Currency per U.S. Dollar	
Canadian dollar	1.505
French franc	5.987
British pound	0.6038

  a. If you sold goods worth 1.2 million U.S. dollars to France, how many French francs would you receive?   7.1844 million French francs

  b. How many U.S. dollars, to the nearest cent, are equivalent to 1 British pound? $1.66

208. The circle graph at the right shows the sources of donations to social causes. What percent of the total is contributed by corporations? Round to the nearest percent.   5%

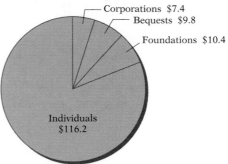

Giving, by Source (in billions of dollars)
Corporations $7.4
Bequests $9.8
Foundations $10.4
Individuals $116.2

Source: *Giving USA*, 1996, AAFRC Trust for Philanthropy

209. The table below shows the first-quarter profits and losses for 1997 for three companies in the toy industry. Profits are shown as positive numbers; losses are shown as negative numbers. One-quarter of a year is three months.

  a. If earnings were to continue throughout the year at the same level, what would the annual earnings or losses be for Mattel, Inc.?
  −$818.496 million

  b. For the quarter shown, what was the average monthly profit or loss for Acclaim Entertainment?   −$5.614 million

Toy Company	First Quarter 1997 Profits
Acclaim Entertainment	−16.842 million
Hasbro, Inc.	25.694 million
Mattel, Inc.	−204.624 million

Source: *The Wall Street Journal*, May 5, 1997

APPLYING THE CONCEPTS

210. Use a calculator to determine the decimal representations of $\frac{17}{99}$, $\frac{45}{99}$, and $\frac{73}{99}$. Make a conjecture as to the decimal representation of $\frac{83}{99}$. Does your conjecture work for $\frac{33}{99}$? What about $\frac{1}{99}$?

211. List the whole numbers between $\sqrt{8}$ and $\sqrt{90}$.
  3, 4, 5, 6, 7, 8, 9

212. Describe in your own words how to simplify a radical expression.

213. Explain why $2\sqrt{2}$ is in simplest form and $\sqrt{8}$ is not in simplest form.

1.3   The Order of Operations Agreement

Objective A   *To use the Order of Operations Agreement to simplify expressions* ....

Let's evaluate $2 + 3 \cdot 5$.

There are two arithmetic operations, addition and multiplication, in this expression. The operations could be performed in different orders.

Multiply first.	$2 + \underbrace{3 \cdot 5}$	Add first.	$\underbrace{2 + 3} \cdot 5$
Then add.	$\underbrace{2 + 15}$	Then multiply.	$\underbrace{5 \cdot 5}$
	17		25

In order to prevent there being more than one answer for a numerical expression, an Order of Operations Agreement has been established.

THE ORDER OF OPERATIONS AGREEMENT

> **Step 1** Perform operations inside grouping symbols. Grouping symbols include parentheses ( ), brackets [ ], braces { }, absolute value symbols | |, and the fraction bar.
> **Step 2** Simplify exponential expressions.
> **Step 3** Do multiplication and division as they occur from left to right.
> **Step 4** Do addition and subtraction as they occur from left to right.

➡ Evaluate $12 - 24(8 - 5) \div 2^2$.

$$12 - 24(8 - 5) \div 2^2 = 12 - 24(3) \div 2^2$$
  • Perform operations inside grouping symbols.

$$= 12 - 24(3) \div 4$$
  • Simplify exponential expressions.

$$= 12 - 72 \div 4$$
  • Do multiplication and division as they occur from left to right.

$$= 12 - 18$$

$$= -6$$
  • Do addition and subtraction as they occur from left to right.

One or more of the above steps may not be needed to evaluate an expression. In that case, proceed to the next step in the Order of Operations Agreement.

When an expression has grouping symbols inside grouping symbols, perform the operations inside the inner grouping symbols first.

➡ Evaluate $6 \div [4 - (6 - 8)] + 2^2$.

$$6 \div [4 - (6 - 8)] + 2^2 = 6 \div [4 - (-2)] + 2^2$$

- Perform operations inside grouping symbols.

$$= 6 \div 6 + 2^2$$

$$= 6 \div 6 + 4$$

- Simplify exponential expressions.

$$= 1 + 4$$

- Do multiplication and division as they occur from left to right.

$$= 5$$

- Do addition and subtraction as they occur from left to right.

Example 1
Evaluate $4 - 3[4 - 2(6 - 3)] \div 2$.

Solution
$4 - 3[4 - 2(6 - 3)] \div 2$
$= 4 - 3[4 - 2 \cdot 3] \div 2$
$= 4 - 3[4 - 6] \div 2$
$= 4 - 3[-2] \div 2$
$= 4 + 6 \div 2$
$= 4 + 3$
$= 7$

You Try It 1
Evaluate $18 - 5[8 - 2(2 - 5)] \div 10$.

Your solution
11

Example 2
Evaluate $27 \div (5 - 2)^2 + (-3)^2 \cdot 4$.

Solution
$27 \div (5 - 2)^2 + (-3)^2 \cdot 4$
$= 27 \div 3^2 + (-3)^2 \cdot 4$
$= 27 \div 9 + 9 \cdot 4$
$= 3 + 9 \cdot 4$
$= 3 + 36$
$= 39$

You Try It 2
Evaluate $36 \div (8 - 5)^2 - (-3)^2 \cdot 2$.

Your solution
-14

Example 3
Evaluate $(1.75 - 1.3)^2 \div 0.025 + 6.1$.

Solution
$(1.75 - 1.3)^2 \div 0.025 + 6.1$
$= (0.45)^2 \div 0.025 + 6.1$
$= 0.2025 \div 0.025 + 6.1$
$= 8.1 + 6.1$
$= 14.2$

You Try It 3
Evaluate $(6.97 - 4.72)^2 \cdot 4.5 \div 0.05$.

Your solution
455.625

Solutions on p. S3

1.3 Exercises

· ·

Objective A

Evaluate by using the Order of Operations Agreement.

1. $4 - 8 \div 2$
0

2. $2^2 \cdot 3 - 3$
9

3. $2(3 - 4) - (-3)^2$
−11

4. $16 - 32 \div 2^3$
12

5. $24 - 18 \div 3 + 2$
20

6. $8 - (-3)^2 - (-2)$
1

7. $8 - 2(3)^2$
−10

8. $16 - 16 \cdot 2 \div 4$
8

9. $12 + 16 \div 4 \cdot 2$
20

10. $16 - 2 \cdot 4^2$
−16

11. $27 - 18 \div (-3^2)$
29

12. $4 + 12 \div 3 \cdot 2$
12

13. $16 + 15 \div (-5) - 2$
11

14. $14 - 2^2 - (4 - 7)$
13

15. $14 - 2^2 - |4 - 7|$
7

16. $10 - |5 - 8| + 2^3$
15

17. $3 - 2[8 - (3 - 2)]$
−11

18. $-2^2 + 4[16 \div (3 - 5)]$
−36

19. $6 + \dfrac{16 - 4}{2^2 + 2} - 2$
6

20. $24 \div \dfrac{3^2}{8 - 5} - (-5)$
13

21. $18 \div |9 - 2^3| + (-3)$
15

22. $96 \div 2[12 + (6 - 2)] - 3^2$
759

23. $4[16 - (7 - 1)] \div 10$
4

24. $18 \div 2 - 4^2 - (-3)^2$
−16

25. $20 \div (10 - 2^3) + (-5)$
5

26. $16 - 3(8 - 3)^2 \div 5$
1

27. $4(-8) \div [2(7 - 3)^2]$
−1

28. $\dfrac{(-10) + (-2)}{6^2 - 30} \div |2 - 4|$
−1

29. $16 - 4 \cdot \dfrac{3^3 - 7}{2^3 + 2} - (-2)^2$
4

30. $(0.2)^2 \cdot (-0.5) + 1.72$
1.70

31. $0.3(1.7 - 4.8) + (1.2)^2$
0.51

32. $(1.8)^2 - 2.52 \div 1.8$
1.84

33. $(1.65 - 1.05)^2 \div 0.4 + 0.8$
1.7

34. $\dfrac{3}{8} \div \left(\dfrac{5}{6} + \dfrac{2}{3}\right)$

$\dfrac{1}{4}$

35. $\left(\dfrac{5}{12} - \dfrac{9}{16}\right)\dfrac{3}{7}$

$-\dfrac{1}{16}$

36. $\left(\dfrac{3}{4}\right)^2 - \left(\dfrac{1}{2}\right)^3 \div \dfrac{3}{5}$

$\dfrac{17}{48}$

APPLYING THE CONCEPTS

37. Find two fractions between $\dfrac{2}{3}$ and $\dfrac{3}{4}$. (There is more than one answer to this question.)

Answers will vary. For example, $\dfrac{17}{24}$ and $\dfrac{33}{48}$.

38. A magic square is one in which the numbers in every row, column, and diagonal sum to the same number. Complete the magic square at the right.

$\dfrac{2}{3}$	$-\dfrac{1}{6}$	0
$-\dfrac{1}{2}$	$\dfrac{1}{6}$	$\dfrac{5}{6}$
$\dfrac{1}{3}$	$\dfrac{1}{2}$	$-\dfrac{1}{3}$

39. For each part below, find a rational number r that satisfies the condition.
a. $r^2 < r$ **b.** $r^2 = r$ **c.** $r^2 > r$

Answers will vary. For example, a. $\dfrac{1}{2}$, b. 1, c. 2

40. In a survey of consumers, approximately 43% said they would be willing to pay between \$1000 and \$2000 more for a new car if the car had an EPA rating of 80 mpg. If your car now gets 28 mpg and you drive approximately 10,000 mi per year, in how many months would your savings on gasoline pay for the increased cost of such a car? Assume the average cost for gasoline is \$1.06 per gallon.

48.8 to 97.5 months

41. Find three different natural numbers a, b, and c such that $\dfrac{1}{a} + \dfrac{1}{b} + \dfrac{1}{c}$ is a natural number.

$a = 2$, $b = 3$, $c = 6$

42. The following was offered as the simplification of $6 + 2(4 - 9)$.

$$6 + 2(4 - 9) = 6 + 2(-5)$$
$$= 8(-5)$$
$$= -40$$

Is this a correct simplification? Explain your answer.

43. The following was offered as the simplification of $2 \cdot 3^3$.

$$2 \cdot 3^3 = 6^3 = 216$$

Is this is a correct simplification? Explain your answer.

44. If a and b are rational numbers and $a < b$, is it always possible to find a rational number c such that $a < c < b$? If not, explain why. If so, show how to find one.

1.4 Variable Expressions

Objective A   *To evaluate a variable expression* ....

Often we discuss a quantity without knowing its exact value—for example, the price of gold next month, the cost of a new automobile next year, or the tuition cost for next semester. Recall that a letter of the alphabet can be used to stand for a quantity that is unknown or that can change, or *vary*. Such a letter is called a variable. An expression that contains one or more variables is called a **variable expression**.

A variable expression is shown at the right. The expression can be re-written by writing subtraction as the addition of the opposite.

$$3x^2 - 5y + 2xy - x - 7$$

$$3x^2 + (-5y) + 2xy + (-x) + (-7)$$

Note that the expression has 5 addends. The **terms** of a variable expression are the addends of the expression. The expression has 5 terms.

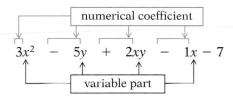

The terms $3x^2$, $-5y$, $2xy$, and $-x$ are **variable terms.**

The term -7 is a **constant term**, or simply a **constant.**

Each variable term is composed of a **numerical coefficient** and a **variable part** (the variable or variables and their exponents).

$$3x^2 - 5y + 2xy - 1x - 7$$

When the numerical coefficient is 1 or -1, the 1 is usually not written ($x = 1x$ and $-x = -1x$).

Replacing each variable by its value and then simplifying the resulting numerical expression is called **evaluating the variable expression**.

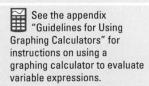

➡ Evaluate $ab - b^2$ when $a = 2$ and $b = -3$.

$ab - b^2$

$2(-3) - (-3)^2$ • Replace each variable in the expression by its value.

$= 2(-3) - 9$ • Use the Order of Operations Agreement to simplify the resulting numerical expression.

$= -6 - 9$

$= -15$

Example 1   Evaluate $\dfrac{a^2 - b^2}{a - b}$ when $a = 3$ and $b = -4$.

Solution $\dfrac{a^2 - b^2}{a - b}$

$\dfrac{3^2 - (-4)^2}{3 - (-4)} = \dfrac{9 - 16}{3 - (-4)}$

$= \dfrac{-7}{7} = -1$

You Try It 1   Evaluate $\dfrac{a^2 + b^2}{a + b}$ when $a = 5$ and $b = -3$.

Your solution   17

Example 2   Evaluate $x^2 - 3(x - y) - z^2$ when $x = 2$, $y = -1$, and $z = 3$.

Solution $x^2 - 3(x - y) - z^2$

$2^2 - 3[2 - (-1)] - 3^2$
$= 2^2 - 3(3) - 3^2$
$= 4 - 3(3) - 9$
$= 4 - 9 - 9$
$= -5 - 9$
$= -14$

You Try It 2   Evaluate $x^3 - 2(x + y) + z^2$ when $x = 2$, $y = -4$, and $z = -3$.

Your solution   21

Solutions on p. S3

Objective B   **To simplify a variable expression using the Properties of Addition** .... 🎞 6 HM³

Like terms of a variable expression are terms with the same variable part. (Because $x^2 = x \cdot x$, x^2 and x are not like terms.)

Constant terms are like terms. 4 and 9 are like terms.

To simplify a variable expression, use the Distributive Property to combine like terms by adding the numerical coefficients. The variable part remains unchanged.

> **Distributive Property**
>
> If a, b, and c are real numbers, then $a(b + c) = ab + ac$.

The Distributive Property can also be written as $ba + ca = (b + c)a$. This form is used to simplify a variable expression.

➡ Simplify: $2x + 3x$

Use the Distributive Property to add the numerical coefficients of the like variable terms. This is called **combining like terms**.

$$2x + 3x = (2 + 3)x$$ • Use the Distributive Property.
$$= 5x$$

➡ Simplify: $5y - 11y$

$$5y - 11y = \boxed{(5 - 11)y}$$ • Use the Distributive Property. This step is usually done mentally.
$$= -6y$$

➡ Simplify: $5 + 7p$

The terms 5 and $7p$ are not like terms.

The expression $5 + 7p$ is in simplest form.

In simplifying variable expressions, the following Properties of Addition are used.

The Associative Property of Addition

If a, b, and c are real numbers, then $(a + b) + c = a + (b + c)$.

When three or more like terms are added, the terms can be grouped (with parentheses, for example) in any order. The sum is the same. For example,

$$(3x + 5x) + 9x = 3x + (5x + 9x)$$
$$8x + 9x = 3x + 14x$$
$$17x = 17x$$

The Commutative Property of Addition

If a and b are real numbers, then $a + b = b + a$.

When two like terms are added, the terms can be added in either order. The sum is the same. For example,

$$2x + (-4x) = -4x + 2x$$
$$-2x = -2x$$

The Addition Property of Zero

If a is a real number, then $a + 0 = 0 + a = a$.

The sum of a term and zero is the term. For example,

$$5x + 0 = 0 + 5x = 5x$$

> **The Inverse Property of Addition**
>
> If a is a real number, then $a + (-a) = (-a) + a = 0$.

The sum of a term and its opposite is zero. The opposite of a number is called its **additive inverse**.

$$7x + (-7x) = -7x + 7x = 0$$

➡ Simplify: $8x + 4y - 8x + y$

Use the Commutative and Associative Properties of Addition to rearrange and group like terms. Then combine like terms.

$8x + 4y - 8x + y = \underline{(8x - 8x) + (4y + y)}$ • This step is usually done mentally.

$\qquad\qquad\qquad\quad = 0 + 5y$

$\qquad\qquad\qquad\quad = 5y$

➡ Simplify: $4x^2 + 5x - 6x^2 - 2x + 1$

Use the Commutative and Associative Properties of Addition to rearrange and group like terms. Then combine like terms.

$4x^2 + 5x - 6x^2 - 2x + 1 = (4x^2 - 6x^2) + (5x - 2x) + 1$

$\qquad\qquad\qquad\qquad\qquad\quad = -2x^2 + 3x + 1$

Example 3	Simplify: $3x + 4y - 10x + 7y$	**You Try It 3**	Simplify: $3a - 2b - 5a + 6b$
Solution	$3x + 4y - 10x + 7y = -7x + 11y$	**Your solution**	$-2a + 4b$
Example 4	Simplify: $x^2 - 7 + 4x^2 - 16$	**You Try It 4**	Simplify: $-3y^2 + 7 + 8y^2 - 14$
Solution	$x^2 - 7 + 4x^2 - 16 = 5x^2 - 23$	**Your solution**	$5y^2 - 7$

Solutions on p. S3

Objective C   ***To simplify a variable expression using the Properties of Multiplication*** ....

In simplifying variable expressions, the following Properties of Multiplication are used.

> **The Associative Property of Multiplication**
>
> If a, b, and c are real numbers, then $(a \cdot b) \cdot c = a \cdot (b \cdot c)$.

When three or more factors are multiplied, the factors can be grouped in any order. The product is the same. For example,

$$2(3x) = (2 \cdot 3)x = 6x$$

> **The Commutative Property of Multiplication**
>
> If a and b are real numbers, then $a \cdot b = b \cdot a$.

Two factors can be multiplied in either order. The product is the same. For example,

$$(2x) \cdot 3 = 3 \cdot (2x) = 6x$$

> **The Multiplication Property of One**
>
> If a is a real number, then $a \cdot 1 = 1 \cdot a = a$.

The product of a term and one is the term. For example,

$$(8x)(1) = (1)(8x) = 8x$$

> **The Inverse Property of Multiplication**
>
> If a is a real number, and a is not equal to zero, then
>
> $$a \cdot \frac{1}{a} = \frac{1}{a} \cdot a = 1.$$

$\frac{1}{a}$ is called the **reciprocal** of a. $\frac{1}{a}$ is also called the **multiplicative inverse** of a.

The product of a number and its reciprocal is one. For example,

$$7 \cdot \frac{1}{7} = \frac{1}{7} \cdot 7 = 1$$

The multiplication properties just discussed are used to simplify variable expressions.

➡ Simplify: $2(-x)$

$$\begin{aligned}
2(-x) &= 2(-1 \cdot x) \\
&= [2(-1)]x \\
&= -2x
\end{aligned}$$

- Use the Associative Property of Multiplication to group factors.

INSTRUCTOR NOTE

Simplifying expressions such as these prepares the student for solving equations.

➡ Simplify: $\frac{3}{2}\left(\frac{2x}{3}\right)$

Use the Associative Property of Multiplication to group factors.

$$\begin{aligned}
\frac{3}{2}\left(\frac{2x}{3}\right) &= \frac{3}{2}\left(\frac{2}{3}x\right) \\
&= \left(\frac{3}{2} \cdot \frac{2}{3}\right)x \\
&= 1 \cdot x \\
&= x
\end{aligned}$$

- Note that $\frac{2x}{3} = \frac{2}{3}x$.

- The steps in the dashed box are usually done mentally.

➡ Simplify: $(16x)2$

Use the Commutative and Associative Properties of Multiplication to re-arrange and group factors.

$$(16x)2 = \boxed{\begin{aligned} 2(16x) \\ (2 \cdot 16)x \end{aligned}}$$
$$= 32x$$

• The steps in the dashed box are usually done mentally.

Example 5	Simplify: $-2(3x^2)$	**You Try It 5**	Simplify: $-5(4y^2)$
Solution	$-2(3x^2) = -6x^2$	**Your solution**	$-20y^2$
Example 6	Simplify: $-5(-10x)$	**You Try It 6**	Simplify: $-7(-2a)$
Solution	$-5(-10x) = 50x$	**Your solution**	$14a$
Example 7	Simplify: $(6x)(-4)$	**You Try It 7**	Simplify: $(-5x)(-2)$
Solution	$(6x)(-4) = -24x$	**Your solution**	$10x$

Solutions on p. S3

Objective D *To simplify a variable expression using the Distributive Property* ....

Recall that the Distributive Property states that if *a*, *b*, and *c* are real numbers, then

$$a(b + c) = ab + ac$$

The Distributive Property is used to remove parentheses from a variable expression.

➡ Simplify: $3(2x + 7)$

$$3(2x + 7) = \boxed{3(2x) + 3(7)}$$
$$= 6x + 21$$

• Use the Distributive Property. Do this step mentally.

➡ Simplify: $-5(4x + 6)$

$$-5(4x + 6) = \boxed{-5(4x) + (-5) \cdot 6}$$
$$= -20x - 30$$

• Use the Distributive Property. Do this step mentally.

➡ Simplify: $-(2x - 4)$

$$-(2x - 4) = \boxed{\begin{array}{l} -1(2x - 4) \\ -1(2x) - (-1)(4) \end{array}}$$

$$= -2x + 4$$

• Use the Distributive Property.
  Do these steps mentally.

Note: When a negative sign immediately precedes the parentheses, the sign of each term inside the parentheses is changed.

➡ Simplify: $-\dfrac{1}{2}(8x - 12y)$

$$-\frac{1}{2}(8x - 12y) = \boxed{-\frac{1}{2}(8x) - \left(-\frac{1}{2}\right)(12y)}$$

$$= -4x + 6y$$

• Use the Distributive Property.
  Do this step mentally.

➡ Simplify: $4(x - y) - 2(-3x + 6y)$

$$4(x - y) - 2(-3x + 6y) = 4x - 4y + 6x - 12y$$

• Use the Distributive
  Property twice.

$$= 10x - 16y$$

• Combine like terms.

An extension of the Distributive Property is used when an expression inside parentheses contains more than two terms.

➡ Simplify: $3(4x - 2y - z)$

$$3(4x - 2y - z) = \boxed{3(4x) - 3(2y) - 3(z)}$$

$$= 12x - 6y - 3z$$

• Use the Distributive Property.
  Do this step mentally.

Example 8   Simplify: $-3(-5a + 7b)$

Solution $-3(-5a + 7b) = 15a - 21b$

You Try It 8   Simplify: $-8(-2a + 7b)$

Your solution $16a - 56b$

Example 9   Simplify: $(2x - 6)2$

Solution $(2x - 6)2 = 4x - 12$

You Try It 9   Simplify: $(3a - 1)5$

Your solution $15a - 5$

Solutions on p. S3

Example 10   Simplify: $3(x^2 - x - 5)$

   Solution $3(x^2 - x - 5) = 3x^2 - 3x - 15$

You Try It 10   Simplify: $2(x^2 - x + 7)$

   Your solution $2x^2 - 2x + 14$

Example 11   Simplify: $2x - 3(2x - 7y)$

   Solution $2x - 3(2x - 7y) = 2x - 6x + 21y$
$$= -4x + 21y$$

You Try It 11   Simplify: $3y - 2(y - 7x)$

   Your solution $14x + y$

Example 12   Simplify:
$7(x - 2y) - (-x - 2y)$

   Solution $7(x - 2y) - (-x - 2y)$
$$= 7x - 14y + x + 2y$$
$$= 8x - 12y$$

You Try It 12   Simplify:
$-2(x - 2y) - (-x + 3y)$

   Your solution $-x + y$

Example 13   Simplify:
$2x - 3[2x - 3(x + 7)]$

   Solution $2x - 3[2x - 3(x + 7)]$
$$= 2x - 3[2x - 3x - 21]$$
$$= 2x - 3[-x - 21]$$
$$= 2x + 3x + 63$$
$$= 5x + 63$$

You Try It 13   Simplify:
$3y - 2[x - 4(2 - 3y)]$

   Your solution $-2x - 21y + 16$

Solutions on p. S3

Objective E   *To translate a verbal expression into a variable expression*........

One of the major skills required in applied mathematics is the ability to translate a verbal expression into a variable expression. This requires recognizing the verbal phrases that translate into mathematical operations. A partial list of the verbal phrases used to indicate the different mathematical operations follows.

Addition	added to	6 added to y	$y + 6$
	more than	8 more than x	$x + 8$
	the sum of	the sum of x and z	$x + z$
	increased by	t increased by 9	$t + 9$
	the total of	the total of 5 and y	$5 + y$

Subtraction	minus	x minus 2	$x - 2$
	less than	7 less than t	$t - 7$
	decreased by	m decreased by 3	$m - 3$
	the difference between	the difference between y and 4	$y - 4$

Multiplication	times	10 times t	$10t$
	of	one-half of x	$\dfrac{1}{2}x$
	the product of	the product of y and z	yz
	multiplied by	y multiplied by 11	$11y$
	twice	twice d	$2d$

Division	divided by	x divided by 12	$\dfrac{x}{12}$
	the quotient of	the quotient of y and z	$\dfrac{y}{z}$
	the ratio of	the ratio of t to 9	$\dfrac{t}{9}$

| **Power** | the square of | the square of x | x^2 |
| | the cube of | the cube of a | a^3 |

➡ Translate "14 less than the cube of x" into a variable expression.

14 *less than* the *cube* of x · Identify the words that indicate the mathematical operations.

$x^3 - 14$ · Use the identified operations to write the variable expression.

In most applications that involve translating phrases into variable expressions, the variable to be used is not given. To translate these phrases, a variable must be assigned to an unknown quantity before the variable expression can be written.

➡ Translate "the sum of two consecutive integers" into a variable expression. Then simplify.

the first integer: n · Assign a variable to one of the unknown quantities.

the next consecutive integer: $n + 1$ · Use the assigned variable to write an expression for any other unknown quantity.

$n + (n + 1)$ · Use the assigned variable to write the variable expression.

$(n + n) + 1$ · Simplify the variable expression.

$2n + 1$

Many of the applications of mathematics require that you identify an unknown quantity, assign a variable to that quantity, and then attempt to express another unknown quantity in terms of the variable.

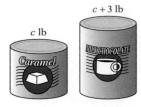

➡ A confectioner makes a mixture of candy that contains 3 lb more of milk chocolate than of caramel. Express the amount of milk chocolate in the mixture in terms of the amount of caramel in the mixture.

Amount of caramel
in the mixture: c

• Assign a variable to the amount
of caramel in the mixture.

Amount of milk chocolate
in the mixture: $c + 3$

• Express the amount of milk chocolate
in the mixture in terms of c.

Example 14
Translate "four times the sum of half of a number and fourteen" into a variable expression. Then simplify.

Solution
the unknown number: n

half of the number: $\frac{1}{2}n$

the sum of half of the number and

fourteen: $\frac{1}{2}n + 14$

$4\left(\frac{1}{2}n + 14\right)$

$2n + 56$

You Try It 14
Translate "five times the difference between a number and sixty" into a variable expression. Then simplify.

Your solution
$5(x - 60); 5x - 300$

Example 15
The length of a swimming pool is 4 ft less than two times the width. Express the length of the pool in terms of the width.

Solution
the width of the pool: w
the length is 4 ft less than two times the width: $2w - 4$

You Try It 15
The speed of a new printer is twice the speed of an older model. Express the speed of the new model in terms of the speed of the older model.

Your solution
the speed of the older model: s
the speed of the new model: $2s$

Example 16
A banker divided $5000 between two accounts, one paying 10% annual interest and the second paying 8% annual interest. Express the amount invested in the 10% account in terms of the amount invested in the 8% account.

Solution
the amount invested at 8%: x
the amount invested at 10%: $5000 - x$

You Try It 16
A guitar string 6 ft long was cut into two pieces. Express the length of the shorter piece in terms of the length of the longer piece.

Your solution
the length of the longer piece: L
the length of the shorter piece: $6 - L$

Solutions on p. S4

1.4 Exercises

Objective A

Evaluate the variable expression when $a = 2$, $b = 3$, and $c = -4$.

1. $6b \div (-a)$
-9

2. $bc \div (2a)$
-3

3. $b^2 - 4ac$
41

4. $a^2 - b^2$
-5

5. $b^2 - c^2$
-7

6. $(a + b)^2$
25

7. $a^2 + b^2$
13

8. $2a - (c + a)^2$
0

9. $(b - a)^2 + 4c$
-15

10. $b^2 - \dfrac{ac}{8}$
10

11. $\dfrac{5ab}{6} - 3cb$
41

12. $(b - 2a)^2 + bc$
-11

Evaluate the variable expression when $a = -2$, $b = 4$, $c = -1$, and $d = 3$.

13. $\dfrac{b + c}{d}$
1

14. $\dfrac{d - b}{c}$
1

15. $\dfrac{2d + b}{-a}$
5

16. $\dfrac{b + 2d}{b}$
$\dfrac{5}{2}$

17. $\dfrac{b - d}{c - a}$
1

18. $\dfrac{2c - d}{ad}$
$-\dfrac{5}{6}$

19. $(b + d)^2 - 4a$
57

20. $(d - a)^2 - 3c$
28

21. $(d - a)^2 \div 5$
5

22. $3(b - a) - bc$
22

23. $\dfrac{b - 2a}{bc^2 - d}$
8

24. $\dfrac{b^2 - a}{ad + 3c}$
-2

25. $\dfrac{1}{3} d^2 - \dfrac{3}{8} b^2$
-3

26. $\dfrac{5}{8} a^4 - c^2$
9

27. $\dfrac{-4bc}{2a - b}$
-2

28. $-\dfrac{3}{4} b + \dfrac{1}{2} (ac + bd)$
4

29. $-\dfrac{2}{3} d - \dfrac{1}{5} (bd - ac)$
-4

30. $(b - a)^2 - (d - c)^2$
20

31. $(b + c)^2 + (a + d)^2$
10

32. $4ac + (2a)^2$
24

33. $3dc - (4c)^2$
-25

Objective B

Simplify.

34. $6x + 8x$
$14x$

35. $12x + 13x$
$25x$

36. $9a - 4a$
$5a$

37. $12a - 3a$
$9a$

38. $4y + (-10y)$
$-6y$

39. $8y + (-6y)$
$2y$

40. $-3b - 7$
$-3b - 7$

41. $-12y - 3$
$-12y - 3$

42. $-12a + 17a$
$5a$

43. $-3a + 12a$
$9a$

44. $5ab - 7ab$
$-2ab$

45. $9ab - 3ab$
$6ab$

46. $-12xy + 17xy$
$5xy$

47. $-15xy + 3xy$
$-12xy$

48. $-3ab + 3ab$
0

49. $-7ab + 7ab$
0

50. $-\dfrac{1}{2}x - \dfrac{1}{3}x$
$-\dfrac{5}{6}x$

51. $-\dfrac{2}{5}y + \dfrac{3}{10}y$
$-\dfrac{1}{10}y$

52. $\dfrac{3}{8}x^2 - \dfrac{5}{12}x^2$
$-\dfrac{1}{24}x^2$

53. $\dfrac{2}{3}y^2 - \dfrac{4}{9}y^2$
$\dfrac{2}{9}y^2$

54. $3x + 5x + 3x$
$11x$

55. $8x + 5x + 7x$
$20x$

56. $5a - 3a + 5a$
$7a$

57. $10a - 17a + 3a$
$-4a$

58. $-5x^2 - 12x^2 + 3x^2$
$-14x^2$

59. $-y^2 - 8y^2 + 7y^2$
$-2y^2$

60. $7x + (-8x) + 3y$
$-x + 3y$

61. $8y + (-10x) + 8x$
$-2x + 8y$

62. $7x - 3y + 10x$
$17x - 3y$

63. $8y + 8x - 8y$
$8x$

64. $3a + (-7b) - 5a + b$
$-2a - 6b$

65. $-5b + 7a - 7b + 12a$
$19a - 12b$

66. $3x + (-8y) - 10x + 4x$
$-3x - 8y$

67. $3y + (-12x) - 7y + 2y$
$-12x - 2y$

68. $x^2 - 7x + (-5x^2) + 5x$
$-4x^2 - 2x$

69. $3x^2 + 5x - 10x^2 - 10x$
$-7x^2 - 5x$

Objective C

Simplify.

70. $4(3x)$
$12x$

71. $12(5x)$
$60x$

72. $-3(7a)$
$-21a$

73. $-2(5a)$
$-10a$

74. $-2(-3y)$
$6y$

75. $-5(-6y)$
$30y$

76. $(4x)2$
$8x$

77. $(6x)12$
$72x$

78. $(3a)(-2)$
$-6a$

79. $(7a)(-4)$
$-28a$

80. $(-3b)(-4)$
$12b$

81. $(-12b)(-9)$
$108b$

82. $-5(3x^2)$
$-15x^2$

83. $-8(7x^2)$
$-56x^2$

84. $\frac{1}{3}(3x^2)$
x^2

85. $\frac{1}{6}(6x^2)$
x^2

86. $\frac{1}{5}(5a)$
a

87. $\frac{1}{8}(8x)$
x

88. $-\frac{1}{2}(-2x)$
x

89. $-\frac{1}{4}(-4a)$
a

90. $-\frac{1}{7}(-7n)$
n

91. $-\frac{1}{9}(-9b)$
b

92. $(3x)\left(\frac{1}{3}\right)$
x

93. $(12x)\left(\frac{1}{12}\right)$
x

94. $(-6y)\left(-\frac{1}{6}\right)$
y

95. $(-10n)\left(-\frac{1}{10}\right)$
n

96. $\frac{1}{3}(9x)$
$3x$

97. $\frac{1}{7}(14x)$
$2x$

98. $-\frac{1}{5}(10x)$
$-2x$

99. $\frac{1}{8}(16x)$
$-2x$

100. $-\frac{2}{3}(12a^2)$
$-8a^2$

101. $-\frac{5}{8}(24a^2)$
$-15a^2$

102. $-\frac{1}{2}(-16y)$
$8y$

103. $-\frac{3}{4}(-8y)$
$6y$

104. $(16y)\left(\frac{1}{4}\right)$
$4y$

105. $(33y)\left(\frac{1}{11}\right)$
$3y$

106. $(-6x)\left(\frac{1}{3}\right)$
$-2x$

107. $(-10x)\left(\frac{1}{5}\right)$
$-2x$

108. $(-8a)\left(-\frac{3}{4}\right)$
$6a$

109. $(21y)\left(-\frac{3}{7}\right)$
$-9y$

Objective D

Simplify.

110. $-(x+2)$
$-x-2$

111. $-(x+7)$
$-x-7$

112. $2(4x-3)$
$8x-6$

113. $5(2x-7)$
$10x-35$

114. $-2(a+7)$
$-2a-14$

115. $-5(a+16)$
$-5a-80$

116. $-3(2y-8)$
$-6y+24$

117. $-5(3y-7)$
$-15y+35$

118. $(5 - 3b)7$

$35 - 21b$

119. $(10 - 7b)2$

$20 - 14b$

120. $\frac{1}{3}(6 - 15y)$

$2 - 5y$

121. $\frac{1}{2}(-8x + 4y)$

$-4x + 2y$

122. $3(5x^2 + 2x)$

$15x^2 + 6x$

123. $6(3x^2 + 2x)$

$18x^2 + 12x$

124. $-2(-y + 9)$

$2y - 18$

125. $-5(-2x + 7)$

$10x - 35$

126. $(-3x - 6)5$

$-15x - 30$

127. $(-2x + 7)7$

$-14x + 49$

128. $2(-3x^2 - 14)$

$-6x^2 - 28$

129. $5(-6x^2 - 3)$

$-30x^2 - 15$

130. $-3(2y^2 - 7)$

$-6y^2 + 21$

131. $-8(3y^2 - 12)$

$-24y^2 + 96$

132. $3(x^2 - y^2)$

$3x^2 - 3y^2$

133. $5(x^2 + y^2)$

$5x^2 + 5y^2$

134. $-\frac{2}{3}(6x - 18y)$

$-4x + 12y$

135. $-\frac{1}{2}(x - 4y)$

$-\frac{1}{2}x + 2y$

136. $-(6a^2 - 7b^2)$

$-6a^2 + 7b^2$

137. $3(x^2 + 2x - 6)$

$3x^2 + 6x - 18$

138. $4(x^2 - 3x + 5)$

$4x^2 - 12x + 20$

139. $-2(y^2 - 2y + 4)$

$-2y^2 + 4y - 8$

140. $\frac{1}{2}(2x - 6y + 8)$

$x - 3y + 4$

141. $-\frac{1}{3}(6x - 9y + 1)$

$-2x + 3y - \frac{1}{3}$

142. $4(-3a^2 - 5a + 7)$

$-12a^2 - 20a + 28$

143. $-5(-2x^2 - 3x + 7)$

$10x^2 + 15x - 35$

144. $-3(-4x^2 + 3x - 4)$

$12x^2 - 9x + 12$

145. $3(2x^2 + xy - 3y^2)$

$6x^2 + 3xy - 9y^2$

146. $5(2x^2 - 4xy - y^2$

$10x^2 - 20xy - 5y^2$

147. $-(3a^2 + 5a - 4)$

$-3a^2 - 5a + 4$

148. $-(8b^2 - 6b + 9)$

$-8b^2 + 6b - 9$

149. $4x - 2(3x + 8)$

$-2x - 16$

150. $6a - (5a + 7)$

$a - 7$

151. $9 - 3(4y + 6)$

$-12y - 9$

152. $10 - (11x - 3)$

$-11x + 13$

153. $5n - (7 - 2n)$

$7n - 7$

154. $8 - (12 + 4y)$

$-4y - 4$

155. $3(x + 2) - 5(x - 7)$

$-2x + 41$

156. $2(x - 4) - 4(x + 2)$

$-2x - 16$

157. $12(y - 2) + 3(7 - 3y)$

$3y - 3$

158. $6(2y - 7) - (3 - 2y)$

$14y - 45$

159. $3(a - b) - (a + b)$

$2a - 4b$

160. $2(a + 2b) - (a - 3b)$

$a + 7b$

161. $4[x - 2(x - 3)]$

$-4x + 24$

162. $2[x + 2(x + 7)]$

$6x + 28$

163. $-2[3x + 2(4 - x)]$

$-2x - 16$

164. $-5[2x + 3(5 - x)]$

$5x - 75$

165. $-3[2x - (x + 7)]$

$-3x + 21$

166. $-2[3x - (5x - 2)]$

$4x - 4$

167. $2x - 3[x - (4 - x)]$

$-4x + 12$

168. $-7x + 3[x - (3 - 2x)]$

$2x - 9$

169. $-5x - 2[2x - 4(x + 7)] - 6$

$-x + 50$

Objective E

Translate into a variable expression. Then simplify.

170. twelve minus a number

$12 - x$

171. a number divided by eighteen

$\dfrac{x}{18}$

172. two-thirds of a number

$\dfrac{2}{3}x$

173. twenty more than a number

$x + 20$

174. the quotient of twice a number and nine

$\dfrac{2x}{9}$

175. ten times the difference between a number and fifty

$10(x - 50); 10x - 500$

176. eight less than the product of eleven and a number

$11x - 8$

177. the sum of five-eighths of a number and six

$\dfrac{5}{8}x + 6$

178. nine less than the total of a number and two

$(x + 2) - 9; x - 7$

179. the difference between a number and three more than the number

$x - (x + 3); -3$

180. the quotient of seven and the total of five and a number

$$\dfrac{7}{5 + x}$$

181. four times the sum of a number and nineteen

$4(x + 19); 4x + 76$

182. five increased by one-half of the sum of a number and three

$5 + \dfrac{1}{2}(x + 3); \dfrac{1}{2}x + \dfrac{13}{2}$

183. the quotient of fifteen and the sum of a number and twelve

$$\dfrac{15}{x + 12}$$

184. a number added to the difference between twice the number and four

$(2x - 4) + x; 3x - 4$

185. the product of two-thirds and the sum of a number and seven

$\dfrac{2}{3}(x + 7); \dfrac{2}{3}x + \dfrac{14}{3}$

186. the product of five less than a number and seven

$(x - 5)7; 7x - 35$

187. the difference between forty and the quotient of a number and twenty

$40 - \dfrac{x}{20}$

188. the quotient of five more than twice a number and the number

$$\dfrac{2x + 5}{x}$$

189. the sum of the square of a number and twice the number

$x^2 + 2x$

190. a number decreased by the difference between three times the number and eight

$x - (3x - 8); -2x + 8$

191. the sum of eight more than a number and one-third of the number

$(x + 8) + \dfrac{1}{3}x; \dfrac{4}{3}x + 8$

192. a number added to the product of three and the number

$3x + x; 4x$

193. a number increased by the total of the number and nine

$x + (x + 9); 2x + 9$

194. five more than the sum of a number and six

$(x + 6) + 5; x + 11$

195. a number decreased by the difference between eight and the number

$x - (8 - x); 2x - 8$

196. a number minus the sum of the number and ten

$x - (x + 10); -10$

197. the difference between one-third of a number and five-eighths of the number

$\dfrac{1}{3}x - \dfrac{5}{8}x; -\dfrac{7}{24}$

198. the sum of one-sixth of a number and four-ninths of the number

$\dfrac{1}{6}x + \dfrac{4}{9}x; \dfrac{11}{18}x$

199. two more than the total of a number and five

$(x + 5) + 2; x + 7$

200. the sum of a number divided by three and the number

$\dfrac{x}{3} + x; \dfrac{4x}{3}$

201. twice the sum of six times a number and seven

$2(6x + 7); 12x + 14$

202. In a recent year, the average sale price of a home in Vail, Colorado, was $143,600 more than the average sale price of a home in Carmel, California. Express the average sale price of a home in Vail in terms of the average sale price of a home in Carmel.

$P + 143{,}600$

203. According to *USA Today*, in Norway, annual spending per person for books is $40 more than it is in the United States. Express the annual spending per person for books in Norway in terms of the annual spending per person for books in the United States.

$B + 40$

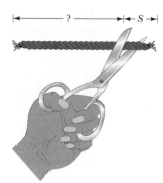

204. A rope 12 ft long was cut into two pieces of different lengths. Use one variable to express the lengths of the two pieces.

$S, 12 - S$

205. Twenty gallons of crude oil were poured into two containers of different sizes. Use one variable to express the amount of oil poured into each container.

$g, 20 - g$

206. Two cars start at the same place and travel at different rates in opposite directions. Two hours later the cars are 200 mi apart. Express the distance traveled by the faster car in terms of distance traveled by the slower car.

$200 - x$

207. According to the *Wall Street Journal*, in a recent year, the retail sales in Boston were one-half the retail sales in Los Angeles. Express the retail sales in Boston in terms of the retail sales in Los Angeles.

$\frac{1}{2}L$

208. According to the IRS, it should take about one-fourth the time to prepare Schedule A than it takes to prepare Form 1040. Express the time it should take to prepare Schedule A in terms of the time it should take to prepare Form 1040.

$\frac{1}{4}t$

209. The diameter of a basketball is approximately 4 times the diameter of a baseball. Express the diameter of a basketball in terms of the diameter of a baseball.

$4d$

210. The world population in the year 2050 is expected to be twice the world population in 1990. Express the world population in 2050 in terms of the world population in 1990.

$2p$

APPLYING THE CONCEPTS

211. Does every number have an additive inverse? If not, which real numbers do not have an additive inverse?
yes

212. Does every number have a multiplicative inverse? If not, which real numbers do not have a multipicative inverse?
No. 0 does not have a multiplicative inverse.

213. The chemical formula for glucose (sugar) is $C_6H_{12}O_6$. This formula means that there are twelve hydrogen atoms, six carbon atoms, and six oxygen atoms in each molecule of glucose. If x represents the number of atoms of oxygen in a pound of sugar, express the number of hydrogen atoms in the pound of sugar.
$2x$

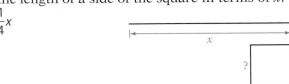

214. Determine whether the statement is true or false. If the statement is false, give an example that illustrates that it is false.
  a. Division is a commutative operation. false
  b. Division is an associative operation. false
  c. Subtraction is an associative operation. false
  d. Subtraction is a commutative operation. false
  e. Addition is a commutative operation. true

215. A wire whose length is given as x inches is bent into a square. Express the length of a side of the square in terms of x.
$\frac{1}{4}x$

216. For each of the following, determine the first natural number x, greater than 2, for which the second expression is larger than the first.

  a. $x^3, 3x$ 4   **b.** $x^4, 4x$ 5   **c.** $x^5, 5x$ 6   **d.** $x^6, 6x$ 7

On the basis of your answers, make a conjecture that appears to be true about the expressions x^n and n^x, where $n = 3, 4, 5, 6, 7, \ldots$ and x is a natural number greater than 2.
$n^x > x^n$ if $x \geq n + 1$

217. A block-and-tackle system is designed so that pulling five feet on one end of a rope will move a weight on the other end a distance of three feet. If x represents the distance the rope is pulled, express the distance the weight moves in terms of x. $\frac{3}{5}x$

218. Give examples of two operations that occur in everyday experience that are not commutative (for example, putting on socks and then shoes).

219. Choose any number a. Evaluate the expressions $6a^2 + 2a - 10$ and $2a(3a - 4) + 10(a - 1)$. Now choose a different number and evaluate the expressions again. Repeat this two more times with different numbers. What conclusions might you draw from your evaluations?

1.5 Sets

Objective A   *To write a set using the roster method* ....

A **set** is a collection of objects, which are called the **elements** of the set. The **roster method** of writing a set encloses a list of the elements in braces.

The set of the last three letters of the alphabet is written $\{x, y, z\}$.

The set of the positive integers less than 5 is written $\{1, 2, 3, 4\}$.

⟹ Use the roster method to write the set of integers between 0 and 10.

$A = \{1, 2, 3, 4, 5, 6, 7, 8, 9\}$

A set can be designated by a capital letter.
Note that 0 and 10 are not elements of set A.

⟹ Use the roster method to write the set of natural numbers.

$A = \{1, 2, 3, 4, \ldots\}$ • The three dots mean that the pattern of numbers continues without end.

INSTRUCTOR NOTE
Students want to write the empty set as $\{\varnothing\}$. It is very difficult to convince them that this is incorrect. Students, in general, have a difficult time with the idea that a set can be an element of another set.

The **empty set**, or **null set**, is the set that contains no elements. The symbol $\varnothing$ or $\{\ \}$ is used to represent the empty set.

The set of people who have run a two-minute mile is the empty set.

The **union** of two sets, written $A \cup B$, is the set that contains the elements of A and the elements of B.

⟹ Find $A \cup B$, given $A = \{1, 2, 3, 4\}$ and $B = \{3, 4, 5, 6\}$.

$A \cup B = \{1, 2, 3, 4, 5, 6\}$ • The union of A and B contains all the elements of A and all the elements of B. Any elements that are in both A and B are listed only once.

The **intersection** of two sets, written $A \cap B$, is the set that contains the elements that are common to both A and B.

⟹ Find $A \cap B$, given $A = \{1, 2, 3, 4\}$ and $B = \{3, 4, 5, 6\}$.

$A \cap B = \{3, 4\}$ • The intersection of A and B contains the elements common to A and B.

Example 1
Use the roster method to write the set of the odd positive integers less than 12.

Solution
$A = \{1, 3, 5, 7, 9, 11\}$

You Try It 1
Use the roster method to write the set of the odd negative integers greater than -10.

Your solution
$A = \{-9, -7, -5, -3, -1\}$

Solution on p. S4

Example 2
Use the roster method to write the set of the even positive integers.

Solution
$A = \{2, 4, 6, \ldots\}$

You Try It 2
Use the roster method to write the set of the odd positive integers.

Your solution
$A = \{1, 3, 5, \ldots\}$

Example 3
Find $D \cup E$, given $D = \{6, 8, 10, 12\}$ and $E = \{-8, -6, 10, 12\}$.

Solution
$D \cup E = \{-8, -6, 6, 8, 10, 12\}$

You Try It 3
Find $A \cup B$, given $A = \{-2, -1, 0, 1, 2\}$ and $B = \{0, 1, 2, 3, 4\}$.

Your solution
$A \cup B = \{-2, -1, 0, 1, 2, 3, 4\}$

Example 4
Find $A \cap B$, given $A = \{5, 6, 9, 11\}$ and $B = \{5, 9, 13, 15\}$.

Solution
$A \cap B = \{5, 9\}$

You Try It 4
Find $C \cap D$, given $C = \{10, 12, 14, 16\}$ and $D = \{10, 16, 20, 26\}$.

Your solution
$C \cap D = \{10, 16\}$

Example 5
Find $A \cap B$ given $A = \{1, 2, 3, 4\}$ and $B = \{8, 9, 10, 11\}$.

Solution
$A \cap B = \varnothing$

You Try It 5
Find $A \cap B$, given $A = \{-5, -4, -3, -2\}$ and $B = \{2, 3, 4, 5\}$.

Your solution
$A \cap B = \varnothing$

Solutions on p. S4

Objective B   ***To write a set using set-builder notation*** ....

POINT OF INTEREST

The symbol $\in$ was first used in the book *Arithmeticae Principia,* published in 1889. It was the first letter of the Greek word εστι, which means "is." The symbols for union and intersection were also introduced at that time.

Another method of representing sets is called **set-builder notation.** Using set-builder notation, the set of all positive integers less than 10 is as follows:

$\{x \mid x < 10, x \in \text{positive integers}\}$, which is read "the set of all x such that x is less than 10 and x is an element of the positive integers."

➡ Use set-builder notation to write the set of real numbers greater than 4.

$\{x \mid x > 4, x \in \text{real numbers}\}$

• "$x \in$ real numbers" is read "x is an element of the real numbers."

Example 6
Use set-builder notation to write the set of negative integers greater than -100.

Solution
$\{x|x > -100, x \in \text{negative integers}\}$

You Try It 6
Use set-builder notation to write the set of positive even integers less than 59.

Your solution
$\{x|x < 59, x \in \text{positive even integers}\}$

Example 7
Use set-builder notation to write the set of real numbers less than 60.

Solution
$\{x|x < 60, x \in \text{real numbers}\}$

You Try It 7
Use set-builder notation to write the set of real numbers greater than -3.

Your solution
$\{x|x > -3, x \in \text{real numbers}\}$

Solutions on p. S4

Objective C   *To graph an inequality on the number line* ....

An expression that contains the symbol $>$, $<$, $\geq$, or $\leq$ is called an **inequality**. An inequality expresses the relative order of two mathematical expressions. The expressions can be either numerical or variable.

$$\left.\begin{array}{l} 4 > 2 \\ 3x \leq 7 \\ x^2 - 2x > y + 4 \end{array}\right\} \text{Inequalities}$$

An inequality can be graphed on the number line.

➡ Graph: $x > 1$

The graph is the real numbers greater than 1. The parenthesis at 1 indicates that 1 is not included in the graph.

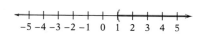

➡ Graph: $x \geq 1$

The bracket at 1 indicates that 1 is included in the graph.

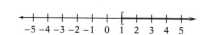

➡ Graph: $-1 > x$

$-1 > x$ is equivalent to $x < -1$. The numbers less than -1 are to the left of -1 on the number line.

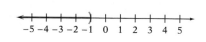

The union of two sets is the set that contains all the elements of each set.

➡ Graph: $\{x|x > 4\} \cup \{x|x < 1\}$

The graph is the numbers greater than 4 and the numbers less than 1.

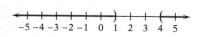

The intersection of two sets is the set that contains the elements common to both sets.

➡ Graph: $\{x|x > -1\} \cap \{x|x < 2\}$

The graphs of $\{x|x > -1\}$ and $\{x|x < 2\}$ are shown at the right.

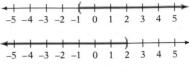

The graph of $\{x|x > -1\} \cap \{x|x < 2\}$ is the numbers between -1 and 2.

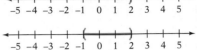

Example 8
Graph: $x < 5$

Solution
The graph is the numbers less than 5.

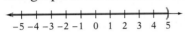

You Try It 8
Graph: $-2 <$ ♪

Your solution

Example 9
Graph: $\{x|x > 3\} \cup \{x|x < 1\}$

Solution
The graph is the numbers greater than 3 and the numbers less than 1.

You Try It 9
Graph: $\{x|x > -1\} \cup \{x|x < -3\}$

Your solution

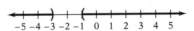

Example 10
Graph: $\{x|x > -2\} \cap \{x|x < 1\}$

Solution
The graph is the numbers between -2 and 1.

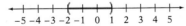

You Try It 10
Graph: $\{x|x \leq 4\} \cap \{x|x \geq -4\}$

Your solution

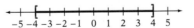

Example 11
Graph: $\{x|x \leq 5\} \cup \{x|x \geq -3\}$

Solution
The graph is the real numbers.

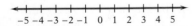

You Try It 11
Graph: $\{x|x < 2\} \cup \{x|x \geq -2\}$

Your solution

Solutions on p. S4

1.5 Exercises

· ·

Objective A

Use the roster method to write the set.

1. the integers between 15 and 22
$A = \{16, 17, 18, 19, 20, 21\}$

2. the integers between −10 and −4
$A = \{-9, -8, -7, -6, -5\}$

3. the odd integers between 8 and 18
$A = \{9, 11, 13, 15, 17\}$

4. the even integers between −11 and −1
$A = \{-10, -8, -6, -4, -2\}$

5. the letters of the alphabet between a and d
$A = \{b, c\}$

6. the letters of the alphabet between p and v
$A = \{q, r, s, t, u\}$

Find $A \cup B$.

7. $A = \{3, 4, 5\}$ $B = \{4, 5, 6\}$
$A \cup B = \{3, 4, 5, 6\}$

8. $A = \{-3, -2, -1\}$ $B = \{-2, -1, 0\}$
$A \cup B = \{-3, -2, -1, 0\}$

9. $A = \{-10, -9, -8\}$ $B = \{8, 9, 10\}$
$A \cup B = \{-10, -9, -8, 8, 9, 10\}$

10. $A = \{a, b, c\}$ $B = \{x, y, z\}$
$A \cup B = \{a, b, c, x, y, z\}$

11. $A = \{a, b, d, e\}$ $B = \{c, d, e, f\}$
$A \cup B = \{a, b, c, d, e, f\}$

12. $A = \{m, n, p. q\}$ $B = \{m, n, o\}$
$A \cup B \{m, n, o, p, q\}$

13. $A = \{1, 3, 7, 9\}$ $B = \{7, 9, 11, 13\}$
$A \cup B = \{1, 3, 7, 9, 11, 13\}$

14. $A = \{-3, -2, -1\}$ $B = \{-1, 1, 2\}$
$A \cup B = \{-3, -2, -1, 1, 2\}$

Find $A \cap B$.

15. $A = \{3, 4, 5\}$ $B = \{4, 5, 6\}$
$A \cap B = \{4, 5\}$

16. $A = \{-4, -3, -2\}$ $B = \{-6, -5, -4\}$
$A \cap B = \{-4\}$

17. $A = \{-4, -3, -2\}$ $B = \{2, 3, 4\}$
$A \cap B = \varnothing$

18. $A = \{1, 2, 3, 4\}$ $B = \{1, 2, 3, 4\}$
$A \cap B = \{1, 2, 3, 4\}$

19. $A = \{a, b, c, d, e\}$ $B = \{c, d, e, f, g\}$
$A \cap B = \{c, d, e\}$

20. $A = \{m, n, o, p\}$ $B = \{k, l, m, n\}$
$A \cap B = \{m, n\}$

Objective B

Use set-builder notation to write the set.

21. the negative integers greater than −5
$\{x \mid x > -5, x \in \text{negative integers}\}$

22. the positive integers less than 5
$\{x \mid x < 5, x \in \text{positive integers}\}$

23. the integers greater than 30
$\{x \mid x > 30, x \in \text{integers}\}$

24. the integers less than −70
$\{x \mid x < -70, x \in \text{integers}\}$

25. the even integers greater than 5
$\{x \mid x > 5, x \in \text{even integers}\}$

26. the odd integers less than −2
$\{x \mid x < -2, x \in \text{odd integers}\}$

27. the real numbers greater than 8
$\{x \mid x > 8, x \in \text{real numbers}\}$

28. the real numbers less than 57
$\{x \mid x < 57, x \in \text{real numbers}\}$

Objective C

Graph.

29. $x > 2$

$$\text{—} \mid \text{—} \mid \text{—} \mid \text{—} \mid \text{—} \mid \text{—} \mid \text{—} (\text{—} \mid \text{—} \mid \text{—}$$
$$-5\ -4\ -3\ -2\ -1\ \ 0\ \ 1\ \ 2\ \ 3\ \ 4\ \ 5$$

30. $x \geq -1$

$$-5\ -4\ -3\ -2\ -1\ \ 0\ \ 1\ \ 2\ \ 3\ \ 4\ \ 5$$

31. $0 \geq x$

$$-5\ -4\ -3\ -2\ -1\ \ 0\ \ 1\ \ 2\ \ 3\ \ 4\ \ 5$$

32. $4 > x$

$$-5\ -4\ -3\ -2\ -1\ \ 0\ \ 1\ \ 2\ \ 3\ \ 4\ \ 5$$

33. $\{x | x > -2\} \cup \{x | x < -4\}$

$$-5\ -4\ -3\ -2\ -1\ \ 0\ \ 1\ \ 2\ \ 3\ \ 4\ \ 5$$

34. $\{x | x > 4\} \cup \{x | x < -2\}$

$$-5\ -4\ -3\ -2\ -1\ \ 0\ \ 1\ \ 2\ \ 3\ \ 4\ \ 5$$

35. $\{x | x > -2\} \cap \{x < 4\}$

$$-5\ -4\ -3\ -2\ -1\ \ 0\ \ 1\ \ 2\ \ 3\ \ 4\ \ 5$$

36. $\{x | x > -3\} \cap \{x | x < 3\}$

$$-5\ -4\ -3\ -2\ -1\ \ 0\ \ 1\ \ 2\ \ 3\ \ 4\ \ 5$$

37. $\{x | x \geq -2\} \cup \{x | x < 4\}$

$$-5\ -4\ -3\ -2\ -1\ \ 0\ \ 1\ \ 2\ \ 3\ \ 4\ \ 5$$

38. $\{x | x > 0\} \cup \{x | x \leq 4\}$

$$-5\ -4\ -3\ -2\ -1\ \ 0\ \ 1\ \ 2\ \ 3\ \ 4\ \ 5$$

APPLYING THE CONCEPTS

39. Explain how to find the union of two sets.

40. Explain how to find the intersection of two sets.

41. Determine whether the statement is always true, sometimes true, or never true.
 a. Given that $a > 0$ and $b < 0$, then $ab > 0$.   never true
 b. Given that $a < 0$, then $a^2 > 0$.   always true
 c. Given that $a > 0$ and $b < 0$, then $a^2 > b$.   always true

42. By trying various sets, make a conjecture as to whether the union of two sets is
 a. a commutative operation   yes
 b. an associative operation   yes

43. By trying various sets, make a conjecture as to whether the intersection of two sets is
 a. a commutative operation   yes
 b. an associative operation   yes

Focus on Problem Solving

Inductive Reasoning

INSTRUCTOR NOTE

The feature entitled "Focus on Problem Solving" appears at the end of every chapter of the text. It provides optional material that can be used to enhance your students' problem-solving skills.

Suppose you take 9 credit hours each semester. The total number of credit hours you have taken at the end of each semester can be described in a list of numbers.

$$9, 18, 27, 36, 45, 54, 63, \ldots$$

The list of numbers that indicates the total credit hours is an ordered list of numbers, called a **sequence.** Each number in a sequence is called a **term** of the sequence. The list is ordered because the position of a number in the list indicates the semester in which that number of credit hours has been taken. For example, the 7th term of the sequence is 63, and a total of 63 credit hours have been taken after the 7th semester.

Assuming the pattern is continued, find the next three numbers in the pattern

$$-6, -10, -14, -18, \ldots$$

This list of numbers is a sequence. The first step in solving this problem is to observe the pattern in the list of numbers. In this case, each number in the list is 4 less than the previous number. The next three numbers are $-22, -26, -30$.

This process of discovering the pattern in a list of numbers is inductive reasoning. **Inductive reasoning** involves making generalizations from specific examples; in other words, we reach a conclusion by making observations about particular facts or cases.

Try the following exercises. Each exercise requires inductive reasoning.

Name the next two terms in the sequence.

1. 1, 3, 5, 7, 1, 3, 5, 7, 1, . . .

2. 1, 4, 2, 5, 3, 6, 4, . . .

3. 1, 2, 4, 7, 11, 16, . . .

4. A, B, C, G, H, I, M, . . .

Draw the next shape in the sequence.

5.

6. |• ||• ||•• |||•• |||•••

Solve.

7. Convert $\frac{1}{11}$, $\frac{2}{11}$, $\frac{3}{11}$, $\frac{4}{11}$, and $\frac{5}{11}$ to decimals. Then use the pattern you observe to convert $\frac{6}{11}$, $\frac{7}{11}$, and $\frac{9}{11}$ to decimals.

8. Convert $\frac{1}{33}$, $\frac{2}{33}$, $\frac{4}{33}$, $\frac{5}{33}$, and $\frac{7}{33}$ to decimals. Then use the pattern you observe to convert $\frac{8}{33}$, $\frac{13}{33}$, and $\frac{19}{33}$ to decimals.

Projects and Group Activities

Calculators

INSTRUCTOR NOTE
"Projects and Group Activities" appear at the end of each chapter in this text. The feature can be used for individual assignments, such as extra credit, or for cooperative learning exercises, such as small-group projects, or for class discussions.

Does your calculator use the Order of Operations Agreement? To find out, try this problem:

$$2 + 4 \cdot 7$$

If your answer is 30, then the calculator uses the Order of Operations Agreement. If your answer is 42, it does not use that agreement.

Even if your calculator does not use the order of Operations Agreement, you can still correctly evaluate numerical expressions. The parentheses keys, ⬚ and ⬚, are used for this purpose.

Remember that $2 + 4 \cdot 7$ means $2 + (4 \cdot 7)$ because the multiplication must be completed before the addition. To evaluate this expression, enter the following:

Enter: 2   ⊞   ⬚(4   ⊠   7   ⬚)   ⊟

Display: 2   2   ⬚(4   4   7   28   30

When using your calculator to evaluate numerical expressions, insert parentheses around multiplications or divisions. This has the effect of forcing the calculator to do the operations in the order you want rather than in the order the calculator wants.

Evaluate.

1. $3 \cdot (15 - 2 \cdot 3) - 36 \div 3$ **2.** $4 \cdot 2^2 - (12 + 24 \div 6) - 5$

3. $16 \div 4 \cdot 3 + (3 \cdot 4 - 5) + 2$ **4.** $15 \cdot 3 \div 9 + (2 \cdot 6 - 3) + 4$

Using your calculator to simplify numerical expressions sometimes requires use of the ⬚+/− key or, on some calculators, the negative key, which is frequently shown as ⬚(−). These keys change the sign of the number currently in the display. To enter −4:

- For those calculators with ⬚+/−, press 4 and then ⬚+/−.
- For those calculators with ⬚(−), press ⬚(−) and then 4.

Here are the keystrokes for evaluating the expression $3(-4) - (-5)$.

Calculators with ⬚+/− key: 3 ⊠ 4 ⬚+/− − 5 ⬚+/− ⊟

Calculators with ⬚(−) key: 3 ⊠ ⬚(−) 4 ⊟ ⬚(−) 5 ⊟

This example illustrates that calculators make a distinction between negative and minus. To perform the operation $3 - (-3)$, you cannot enter 3 ⊟ ⊟ 3. This would result in 0, which is not the correct answer. You must enter

3 ⊟ 3 ⬚+/− ⊟   or   3 ⊟ ⬚(−) 3 ⊟

Use a calculator to evaluate each of the following exercises.

5. $-16 \div 2$ **6.** $3(-8)$ **7.** $47 - (-9)$

8. $-50 - (-14)$ **9.** $4 - (-3)^2$ **10.** $-8 + (-6)^2 - 7$

Moving Averages

Stock	Div	PE	Sales 100s	High	Low	Close	Chg.
			A				
AAR	.48	23	2495	13¼	11⅞	12¼	−⅞
ACMin	.96		814	11⅛	11	11	−⅛
ACM Op	.80a		324	9¾	9⅜	9⅝	+¼
ACM Sc	.96a		1104	11⅜	11¼	11⅜	
ACMSp	.80a		497	9½	9⅜	9½	
ACM MI	1.08a		678	10¾	10⅝	10¾	+⅛
ACMMM	.78		156	9¼	9⅛	9⅛	
ADT wt			742	1⅝	1⅜	1½	
ADT			4357	9½	9	9⅛	
AFLAC	.44	16	1355	35½	34¾	34⅞	−½
AL Lab	.18	168	911	23½	22¼	23½	+1⅜

In many courses, your course grade depends on the *average* of all your test scores. You compute the average by calculating the sum of all your test scores and then dividing that result by the number of tests. Statisticians call this average an **arithmetic mean.** Besides its application to finding the average of your test scores, the arithmetic mean is used in many other situations.

Stock market analysts calculate the **moving average** of a stock. This is the arithmetic mean of the changes in the value of a stock for a given number of days. To illustrate the procedure, we will calculate the 5-day moving average of a stock. In actual practice, a stock market analyst may use 15 days, 30 days, or some other number.

The table below shows the amount of increase or decrease, in cents, in the closing price of a stock for a 10-day period.

Day 1	Day 2	Day 3	Day 4	Day 5	Day 6	Day 7	Day 8	Day 9	Day 10
+50	−175	+225	0	−275	−75	−50	+50	−475	−50

To calculate the 5-day moving average of this stock, determine the average of the stock for days 1 through 5, days 2 through 6, days 3 through 7, and so on.

Days 1–5	Days 2–6	Days 3–7	Days 4–8	Days 5–9	Days 6–10
+50	−175	+225	0	−275	−75
−175	+225	0	−275	−75	−50
+225	0	−275	−75	−50	+50
0	−275	−75	−50	+50	−475
−275	−75	−50	+50	−475	−50
Sum = −175	Sum = −300	Sum = −175	Sum = −350	Sum = −825	Sum = −600
$Av = \dfrac{-175}{5} = -35$	$Av = \dfrac{-300}{5} = -60$	$Av = \dfrac{-175}{5} = -35$	$Av = \dfrac{-350}{5} = -70$	$Av = \dfrac{-825}{5} = -165$	$Av = \dfrac{-600}{5} = -120$

The 5-day moving average is the list of means: $-35, -60, -35, -70, -165$, and -120. If the numbers in the list tend to increase, the price of the stock is showing an upward trend; if they decrease, the price of the stock is showing a downward trend. For the stock shown above, the price of the stock is showing a downward trend. These trends help an analyst determine whether to recommend a stock. (You can also look up stock prices on the internet by using a search engine and typing in "stocks.")

11. The value of a share of McDonald's stock on June 12, 1998, was $64.25. The table below shows the amount of increase or decrease, to the nearest 10 cents, from the June 12 closing price of the stock for a 10-day period. Calculate the 5-day moving average for this stock.

Day 1	Day 2	Day 3	Day 4	Day 5	Day 6	Day 7	Day 8	Day 9	Day 10
+40	−90	+40	+130	+240	+20	−10	−50	+10	+40

12. The value of a share of Disney stock on June 12, 1998, was $116.1875. The table below shows the amount of increase or decrease, to the nearest 10 cents, from the June 12 closing price of the stock for a 10-day period. Calculate the 5-day moving average for this stock.

Day 1	Day 2	Day 3	Day 4	Day 5	Day 6	Day 7	Day 8	Day 9	Day 10
−110	−290	+70	+140	−230	−440	+120	+100	+290	−20

13. Calculate the 5-day moving average for at least three different stocks. Discuss and compare the results for the different stocks. For this project, you will need to use stock tables, which are printed in the business section of major newspapers. Your college library should have copies of these publications. In a stock table, the column headed "Chg" provides the change in the price of a share of the stock; that is, it gives the difference between the closing price for the day shown and the closing price for the previous day. The symbol + indicates that the change was an increase in price; the symbol − indicates that the change was a decrease in price.

www.fedstats.gov

Information regarding the history of the federal budget can be found on the World Wide Web. Go to the web site www.fedstats.gov. Click on "Fast Facts" and then on "Frequently Requested Tables." In the list of tables printed to the screen, find the table entitled "Federal Budget—Summary." Click on it. When the federal budget table appears on the screen, look for the column that lists each year's surplus or deficit. You will see that a negative sign (−) is used to show a deficit. Note that it states near the top of the screen that the figures in the table are in millions of dollars.

14. During which years shown in the table was there a surplus?

15. During which year was the deficit the greatest?

16. Find the difference between the surplus or deficit this year and the surplus or deficit five years ago.

17. What is the difference between the surplus or deficit this year and the surplus or deficit a decade ago?

18. Determine what two numbers in the table are being subtracted in each row in order to arrive at the number in the surplus or deficit column.

19. Describe the trend of the federal deficit over the last ten years.

Chapter Summary

Key Words

A *set* is a collection of objects. The objects in the set are called the *elements* of the set. The *roster method* of writing sets encloses a list of the elements in braces.

The set of *natural numbers* is $\{1, 2, 3, 4, 5, 6, 7, \ldots\}$. The set of *integers* is $\{\ldots, -4, -3, -2, -1, 0, 1, 2, 3, 4, \ldots\}$.

The *empty set* or *null set*, written $\varnothing$ or $\{\ \}$, is the set that contains no elements.

A number a *is less than* another number b, written $a < b$, if a is to the left of b on the number line. A number a *is greater than* another number b, written $a > b$, if a is to the right of b on the number line. The symbol $\leq$ means *is less than or equal to.* The symbol $\geq$ means *is greater than or equal to.* An expression that contains the symbol $>$, $<$, $\geq$, or $\leq$ is an *inequality.*

Two numbers that are the same distance from zero on the number line but on opposite sides of zero are *opposite numbers,* or *opposites.* The *additive inverse* of a number is the opposite of the number.

The *multiplicative inverse* of a number is the reciprocal of the number.

The *absolute value* of a number is its distance from zero on the number line.

A *rational number* is a number that can be written in the form $\frac{a}{b}$, where a and b are integers and $b \neq 0$. An *irrational number* is a number that has a decimal representation that never terminates or repeats. The rational numbers and the irrational numbers taken together are called the *real numbers*.

Percent means "parts of 100."

An expression of the form a^n is in *exponential form*, where a is the base and n is the exponent.

A *square root* of a positive number x is a number whose square is x. The *principal square root* of a number is the positive square root. The symbol $\sqrt{\ }$ is called a *radical sign* and is used to indicate the principal square root of a number. The *radicand* is the number under the radical sign.

The square of an integer is a *perfect square*. If a number is not a perfect square, its square root can only be approximated.

A *variable* is a letter that is used to stand for a quantity that is unknown or that varies. A *variable expression* is an expression that contains one or more variables.

The *terms* of a variable expression are the addends of the expression. A *variable term* is composed of a numerical coefficient and a variable part. *Like terms* of a variable expression are terms with the same variable part.

The *union* of two sets, written $A \cup B$, is the set that contains all the elements of A and all the elements of B. (Any elements that are in both set A and set B are listed only once.) The *intersection* of two sets, written $A \cap B$, is the set that contains the elements that are common to both A and B.

Essential Rules

To add two numbers with the same sign, add the absolute values of the numbers. Then attach the sign of the addends.

To add two numbers with different signs, find the absolute value of each number. Subtract the smaller of these from the larger. Attach the sign of the addend with the larger absolute value.

To subtract two numbers, add the opposite of the second number to the first number.

To multiply two numbers with the same sign, multiply the absolute values of the factors. The product is positive.

To multiply two numbers with different signs, multiply the absolute values of the factors. The product is negative.

To divide two numbers with the same sign, divide the absolute values of the numbers. The quotient is positive.

To divide two numbers with different signs, divide the absolute values of the numbers. The quotient is negative.

To convert a percent to a decimal, remove the percent sign and multiply by 0.01.

To convert a percent to a fraction, remove the percent sign and multiply by $\frac{1}{100}$.

To convert a decimal or a fraction to a percent, multiply by 100%.

Product Property of Square Roots	$\sqrt{ab} = \sqrt{a} \cdot \sqrt{b}$
Addition Property of Zero	$a + 0 = a$ or $0 + a = a$
Commutative Property of Addition	$a + b = b + a$
Associative Property of Addition	$(a + b) + c = a + (b + c)$
Inverse Property of Addition	$a + (-a) = 0$ or $-a + a = 0$
Multiplication Property of Zero	$a \cdot 0 = 0$ or $0 \cdot a = 0$
Multiplication Property of One	$a \cdot 1 = a$ or $1 \cdot a = a$
Commutative Property of Multiplication	$a \cdot b = b \cdot a$
Associative Property of Multiplication	$(a \cdot b) \cdot c = a \cdot (b \cdot c)$
Inverse Property of Multiplication	$a \cdot \frac{1}{a} = \frac{1}{a} \cdot a = 1, a \neq 0$
Division Properties of Zero and One	If $a \neq 0$, $0 \div a = 0$. If $a \neq 0$, $a \div a = 1$. $a \div 1 = a$ $a \div 0$ is undefined.
Distributive Property	$a(b + c) = ab + ac$

The Order of Operations Agreement

Step 1 Perform operations inside grouping symbols. The grouping symbols include parentheses, brackets, braces, absolute value symbols, and the fraction bar.

Step 2 Simplify exponential expressions.

Step 3 Do multiplication and division as they occur from left to right.

Step 4 Do addition and subtraction as they occur from left to right.

Chapter Review

1. Let $x \in \{-4, 0, 11\}$. For what values of x is the inequality $x < 1$ a true statement?

$-4, 0$ [1.1A]

2. Find the additive inverse of -4.

4 [1.1B]

3. Evaluate $-|-5|$.

-5 [1.1B]

4. Add: $-3 + (-12) + 6 + (-4)$

-13 [1.1C]

5. Subtract: $16 - (-3) - 18$

1 [1.1C]

6. Multiply: $(-6)(7)$

-42 [1.1D]

7. Divide: $-100 \div 5$

-20 [1.1D]

8. Write $\frac{7}{25}$ as a decimal.

0.28 [1.2A]

9. Write 6.2% as a decimal.

0.062 [1.2B]

10. Write $\frac{5}{8}$ as a percent.

62.5% [1.2B]

11. Simplify: $\frac{1}{3} - \frac{1}{6} + \frac{5}{12}$

$\frac{7}{12}$ [1.2C]

12. Subtract: $5.17 - 6.238$

-1.068 [1.2C]

13. Divide: $-\frac{18}{35} \div \frac{17}{28}$

$-\frac{72}{85}$ [1.2D]

14. Multiply: $4.32(-1.07)$

-4.6224 [1.2D]

15. Evaluate $\left(-\frac{2}{3}\right)^4$.

$\frac{16}{81}$ [1.2E]

16. Simplify: $2\sqrt{36}$

12 [1.2F]

17. Simplify: $-3\sqrt{120}$

$-6\sqrt{30}$ [1.2F]

18. Evaluate $-3^2 + 4[18 + (12 - 20)]$.

31 [1.3A]

19. Evaluate $(b - a)^2 + c$ when $a = -2$, $b = 3$, and $c = 4$.

29 [1.4A]

20. Simplify: $6a - 4b + 2a$

$8a - 4b$ [1.4B]

21. Simplify: $-3(-12y)$

$36y$ [1.4C]

22. Simplify: $5(2x - 7)$

$10x - 35$ [1.4D]

23. Simplify: $-4(2x - 9) + 5(3x + 2)$

$7x + 46$ [1.4D]

24. Simplify: $5[2 - 3(6x - 1)]$

$-90x + 25$ [1.4D]

25. Use the roster method to write the set of odd positive integers less than 8.

$\{1, 3, 5, 7\}$ [1.5A]

26. Find $A \cap B$, given $A = \{1, 5, 9, 13\}$ and $B = \{1, 3, 5, 7, 9\}$.

$A \cap B = \{1, 5, 9\}$ [1.5A]

27. Graph: $x > 3$

$$\overset{-5\ -4\ -3\ -2\ -1\ \ 0\ \ 1\ \ 2\ \ 3\ \ 4\ \ 5}{\longleftrightarrow}$$ [1.5C]

28. Graph $\{x | x \leq 3\} \cup \{x | x < -2\}$.

$$\overset{-5\ -4\ -3\ -2\ -1\ \ 0\ \ 1\ \ 2\ \ 3\ \ 4\ \ 5}{\longleftrightarrow}$$ [1.5C]

29. To discourage random guessing on a multiple-choice exam, a professor assigns 6 points for a correct answer, -4 points for an incorrect answer, and -2 points for leaving a question blank. What is the score for a student who had 21 correct answers, had 5 incorrect answers, and left 4 questions blank?

98 [1.1E]

30. The exchange rates on July 19, 1998 for some currencies are shown at the right. If you are in Sweden and purchase a car for 84,000 krona, what is the value of the purchase in U.S. dollars?

$10,632.91 [1.2G]

Foreign Currency per U.S. Dollar	
Hong Kong dollar	7.75
Swedish krona	7.90
Japanese yen	142.7

31. Translate "the difference between twice a number and one-half of the number" into a variable expression. Then simplify.

$2x - \frac{1}{2}x; \frac{3}{2}x$ [1.4E]

32. A baseball card collection contains five times as many National League players' cards as American League players' cards. Express the number of National League players' cards in terms of the number of American League players' cards.

number of American League players' cards: A
number of National League players' cards: $5A$ [1.4E]

33. A club treasurer has some five-dollar bills and some ten-dollar bills. The treasurer has a total of 35 bills. Express the number of five-dollar bills in terms of the number of ten-dollar bills.

number of ten-dollar bills: T
number of five-dollar bills: $35 - T$ [1.4E]

Chapter Test

1. Place the correct symbol, $<$ or $>$, between the two numbers.

   $-2 > -40$ [1.1A]

2. Find the opposite of -4.

   4   [1.1B]

3. Evaluate $-|-4|$.

   -4 [1.1B]

4. Subtract: $16 - 30$

   -14 [1.1C]

5. Add: $-22 + 14 + (-8)$

   -16 [1.1C]

6. Subtract: $16 - (-30) - 42$

   4   [1.1C]

7. Divide: $-561 \div (-33)$

   17   [1.1D]

8. Write $\frac{7}{9}$ as a decimal. Place a bar over the repeating digit of the decimal.

   $0.\overline{7}$ [1.2A]

9. Write 45% as a fraction and as a decimal.

   $\frac{9}{20}$, 0.45   [1.2B]

10. Add: $-\frac{2}{5} + \frac{7}{15}$

    $\frac{1}{15}$ [1.2C]

11. Multiply: $6.02(-0.89)$

    -5.3578 [1.2D]

12. Divide: $\frac{5}{12} \div \left(-\frac{5}{6}\right)$

    $-\frac{1}{2}$ [1.2D]

13. Evaluate $\frac{3}{4} \cdot (4)^2$

    12   [1.2E]

14. Simplify: $-2\sqrt{45}$

    $-6\sqrt{5}$ [1.2F]

15. Evaluate $16 \div 2[8 - 3(4 - 2)] + 1$.

    17   [1.3A]

16. Evaluate $b^2 - 3ab$ when $a = 3$ and $b = -2$.

    22   [1.4A]

17. Simplify: $3x - 5x + 7x$

    $5x$ [1.4B]

18. Simplify: $\frac{1}{5}(10x)$

    $2x$ [1.4C]

19. Simplify: $-3(2x^2 - 7y^2)$

$-6x^2 + 21y^2$ [1.4D]

20. Simplify: $2x - 3(x - 2)$

$-x + 6$ [1.4D]

21. Simplify: $2x + 3[4 - (3x - 7)]$

$-7x + 33$ [1.4D]

22. Use the roster method to write the set of integers between -3 and 4.

$\{-2, -1, 0, 1, 2, 3\}$ [1.5A]

23. Use set-builder notation to write the set of real numbers less than -3.

$\{x \,|\, x < -3\}$ [1.5B]

24. Find $A \cup B$ given $A = \{1, 3, 5, 7\}$ and $B = \{2, 4, 6, 8\}$.

$A \cup B = \{1, 2, 3, 4, 5, 6, 7, 8\}$ [1.5A]

25. Graph $x < 1$.

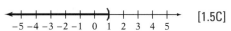
[1.5C]

26. Graph $\{x \,|\, x \le -3\} \cup \{x \,|\, x > 0\}$.

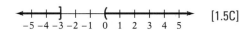
[1.5C]

27. Translate "ten times the difference between a number and 3" into a variable expression. Then simplify.

$10(x - 3); 10x - 30$ [1.4E]

28. The speed of a pitcher's fastball is twice the speed of the catcher's return throw. Express the speed of the fastball in terms of the speed of the return throw.

speed of return: s; speed of fastball: $2s$ [1.4E]

29. The table below shows the first-quarter profits and losses for 1997 for five companies in the paper industry. Profits are shown as positive numbers; losses are shown as negative numbers. One-quarter of a year is three months.
   a. If earnings were to continue throughout the year at the same level, what would be the annual earnings or losses for Bowater, Inc.?
   b. For the quarter shown, what was the average monthly profit or loss for Boise Cascade?

Paper Company	First Quarter 1997 Profits
Boise Cascade	-15,210,000
Bowater, Inc.	-3,140,000
Champion International	-37,083,000
Consolidated Paper	28,056,000
International Paper Company	34,000,000

Source: *The Wall Street Journal*, May 5, 1997

a. −$12,560,000   b. −$5,070,000   [1.1E]

30. At the end of the trading day on July 30, the price of one share of Nike stock was $\$62\frac{3}{4}$. The change in the price of a share on July 31 was $-\frac{1}{8}$. What was the price of one share of Nike stock at the end of the trading day on July 31?

$\$62\frac{5}{8}$ [1.2G]

2

First-Degree Equations and Inequalities

It is the job of construction electricians to install heating, lighting, air conditioning, controls, communications, and other types of electrical equipment. Electricians follow specifications such as blueprints to connect equipment to power sources and circuit breakers. In their work, they must apply various algebraic and scientific formulas. One equation in Ohm's Law is $IR = V$, where I is current, R is resistance, and V is voltage. For example, if $I = 10$ amperes and $R = 12$ ohms, then $V = 120$ volts.

Objectives

Section 2.1
To determine whether a given number is a solution of an equation
To solve an equation of the form $x + a = b$
To solve an equation of the form $ax = b$
To solve application problems using the basic percent equation

Section 2.2
To solve an equation of the form $ax + b = c$
To solve an equation of the form $ax + b = cx + d$
To solve an equation containing parentheses
To translate a sentence into an equation and solve

Section 2.3
To solve value mixture problems
To solve percent mixture problems
To solve investment problems
To solve uniform motion problems

Section 2.4
To solve an inequality in one variable
To solve a compound inequality
To solve application problems

Section 2.5
To solve an absolute value equation
To solve an absolute value inequality
To solve application problems

Mersenne Primes

A **prime number** is a natural number greater than 1 whose only natural-number factors are itself and 1. The number 7 is a prime number because the only natural-number factors of 7 are 7 and 1.

A prime number that can be written in the form $2^n - 1$, where n is also prime, is called a **Mersenne prime**. The table below shows some Mersenne primes.

$$3 = 2^2 - 1$$
$$7 = 2^3 - 1$$
$$31 = 2^5 - 1$$
$$127 = 2^7 - 1$$

Not every prime number is a Mersenne prime. For example, 5 is a prime number but not a Mersenne prime. Also, not all numbers in the form $2^n - 1$, where n is prime, yield a prime number. For example, $2^{11} - 1 = 2047$ is not a prime number.

The search for Mersenne primes has been quite extensive, especially since the advent of the computer. One reason for the extensive research into large prime numbers (not only Mersenne primes) has to do with cryptology.

Cryptology is the study of making or breaking secret codes. One method for making a code that is difficult to break is called public key cryptology. For this method to work, it is necessary to use very large prime numbers. To keep anyone from breaking the code, each prime should have at least 200 digits.

Today the largest known Mersenne prime is $2^{216091} - 1$. This number has 65,050 digits in its representation.

Another Mersenne prime got special recognition in a postage-meter stamp! It is the number $2^{11213} - 1$. This number has 3276 digits in its representation.

2.1 Introduction to Equations

Objective A *To determine whether a given number is a solution of an equation* ....

An **equation** expresses the equality of two mathematical expressions. The expressions can be either numerical or variable expressions.

$$\left.\begin{array}{l} 9 + 3 = 12 \\ 3x - 2 = 10 \\ y^2 + 4 = 2y - 1 \\ z = 2 \end{array}\right\} \text{Equations}$$

The equation at the right is true if the variable is replaced by 5.

$x + 8 = 13$
$5 + 8 = 13$ A true equation

The equation is false if the variable is replaced by 7.

$7 + 8 = 13$ A false equation

A **solution** of an equation is a number that, when substituted for the variable, results in a true equation. 5 is a solution of the equation $x + 8 = 13$. 7 is not a solution of the equation $x + 8 = 13$.

➡ Is -2 a solution of $2x + 5 = x^2 - 3$?

$$\begin{array}{c|c} \multicolumn{2}{c}{2x + 5 = x^2 - 3} \\ \hline 2(-2) + 5 & (-2)^2 - 3 \\ -4 + 5 & 4 - 3 \\ \multicolumn{2}{c}{1 = 1} \end{array}$$

• Replace x by -2.
• Evaluate the numerical expressions.
• If the results are equal, -2 is a solution of the equation. If the results are not equal, -2 is not a solution of the equation.

Yes, -2 is a solution of the equation.

Example 1 Is -4 a solution of $5x - 2 = 6x + 2$?

Solution
$$\begin{array}{c|c} \multicolumn{2}{c}{5x - 2 = 6x + 2} \\ \hline 5(-4) - 2 & 6(-4) + 2 \\ -20 - 2 & -24 + 2 \\ \multicolumn{2}{c}{-22 = -22} \end{array}$$

Yes, -4 is a solution.

You Try It 1 Is $\dfrac{1}{4}$ a solution of $5 - 4x = 8x + 2$?

Your solution yes

Example 2 Is -4 a solution of $4 + 5x = x^2 - 2x$?

Solution
$$\begin{array}{c|c} \multicolumn{2}{c}{4 + 5x = x^2 - 2x} \\ \hline 4 + 5(-4) & (-4)^2 - 2(-4) \\ 4 + (-20) & 16 - (-8) \\ \multicolumn{2}{c}{-16 \neq 24} \end{array}$$

($\neq$ means "is not equal to")

No, -4 is not a solution.

You Try It 2 Is 5 a solution of $10x - x^2 = 3x - 10$?

Your solution no

Solutions on p. S4

Objective B   **To solve an equation of the form x + a = b** ....

To **solve an equation** means to find a solution of the equation. The simplest equation to solve is an equation of the form *variable* = *constant*, because the constant is the solution.

The solution of the equation $x = 5$ is 5 because $5 = 5$ is a true equation.

The solution of the equation at the right is 7 because $7 + 2 = 9$ is a true equation.

$$x + 2 = 9 \qquad 7 + 2 = 9$$

Note that if 4 is added to each side of the equation $x + 2 = 9$, the solution is still 7.

$$x + 2 = 9$$
$$x + 2 + 4 = 9 + 4$$
$$x + 6 = 13 \qquad 7 + 6 = 13$$

If -5 is added to each side of the equation $x + 2 = 9$, the solution is still 7.

$$x + 2 = 9$$
$$x + 2 + (-5) = 9 + (-5)$$
$$x - 3 = 4 \qquad 7 - 3 = 4$$

Equations that have the same solution are **equivalent equations**. The equations $x + 2 = 9$, $x + 6 = 13$, and $x - 3 = 4$ are equivalent equations; each equation has 7 as its solution. These examples suggest that adding the same number to each side of an equation produces equivalent equations. This is called the *Addition Property of Equations*.

Addition Property of Equations

The same number can be added to each side of an equation without changing its solution. In symbols, the equation $a = b$ has the same solution as the equation $a + c = b + c$.

In solving an equation, the goal is to rewrite the given equation in the form *variable* = *constant*. The Addition Property of Equations is used to remove a *term* from one side of the equation by adding the opposite of that term to each side of the equation.

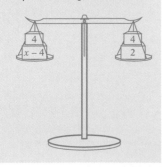

➡ Solve: $x - 4 = 2$

$$x - 4 = 2$$ • The goal is to rewrite the equation as *variable* = *constant*.
$$x - 4 + 4 = 2 + 4$$ • Add 4 to each side of the equation.
$$x + 0 = 6$$ • Simplify.
$$x = 6$$ • The equation is in the form *variable* = *constant*.

Check: $x - 4 = 2$
$$6 - 4 \,|\, 2$$
$$2 = 2 \qquad \text{A true equation}$$

The solution is 6.

Because subtraction is defined in terms of addition, the Addition Property of Equations also makes it possible to subtract the same number from each side of an equation without changing the solution of the equation.

➡ Solve: $y + \frac{3}{4} = \frac{1}{2}$

$$y + \frac{3}{4} = \frac{1}{2}$$

- The goal is to rewrite the equation in the form *variable = constant*.

$$y + \frac{3}{4} - \frac{3}{4} = \frac{1}{2} - \frac{3}{4}$$

- Subtract $\frac{3}{4}$ from each side of the equation.

$$y + 0 = \frac{2}{4} - \frac{3}{4}$$

- Simplify.

$$y = -\frac{1}{4}$$

- The equation is in the form *variable = constant*.

The solution is $-\frac{1}{4}$. You should check this solution.

Example 3 Solve: $x + \frac{3}{4} = \frac{1}{3}$

Solution

$$x + \frac{3}{4} = \frac{1}{3}$$

$$x + \frac{3}{4} - \frac{3}{4} = \frac{1}{3} - \frac{3}{4}$$

$$x + 0 = \frac{4}{12} - \frac{9}{12}$$

$$x = -\frac{5}{12}$$

The solution is $-\frac{5}{12}$.

You Try It 3 Solve: $\frac{5}{6} = y - \frac{3}{8}$

Your solution $\frac{29}{24}$

Solution on p. S4

Objective C **To solve an equation of the form $ax = b$** ....

The solution of the equation at the right is 3 because $2 \cdot 3 = 6$ is a true equation.

$$2x = 6 \qquad 2 \cdot 3 = 6$$

Note that if each side of $2x = 6$ is multiplied by 5, the solution is still 3.

$$2x = 6$$
$$5(2x) = 5 \cdot 6$$
$$10x = 30 \qquad 10 \cdot 3 = 30$$

If each side of $2x = 6$ is multiplied by -4, the solution is still 3.

$$2x = 6$$
$$(-4)(2x) = (-4) \cdot 6$$
$$-8x = -24 \qquad -8 \cdot 3 = -24$$

INSTRUCTOR NOTE

The requirement that each side be multiplied by a *nonzero* number is important. Students will solve some equations by multiplying each side by a variable expression whose value may be zero. This can yield extraneous solutions.

The equations $2x = 6$, $10x = 30$, and $-8x = -24$ are equivalent equations; each equation has 3 as its solution. These examples suggest that multiplying each side of an equation by the same number produces equivalent equations.

Multiplication Property of Equations

Each side of an equation can be multiplied by the same *nonzero* number without changing the solution of the equation. In symbols, if $c \neq 0$, then the equation $a = b$ has the same solutions as the equation $ac = bc$.

INSTRUCTOR NOTE

Solving equations such as $ax = b$ has appeared in algebra texts for a long time. The problem below is an adaptation from Fibonacci's text *Liber Abaci,* which dates from 1202.

   A merchant purchased 7 eggs for 1 denarius and sold them at a rate of 5 eggs for 1 denarius. The merchant's profit was 18 denarii. How much did the merchant invest?

   The resulting equation is

$$\frac{7}{5}x - x = 18$$

Solving this equation can serve as a classroom exercise. The solution is 45 denarii.

TAKE NOTE

Remember to check the solution.

Check: $6x = 14$

$$6\left(\frac{7}{3}\right) \Big|\ 14$$

$$14 = 14$$

The Multiplication Property of Equations is used to remove a coefficient by multiplying each side of the equation by the reciprocal of the coefficient.

➡ Solve: $\frac{3}{4}z = 9$

$\dfrac{3}{4}z = 9$	• The goal is to rewrite the equation in the form *variable* = *constant*.
$\dfrac{4}{3} \cdot \dfrac{3}{4}z = \dfrac{4}{3} \cdot 9$	• Multiply each side of the equation by $\dfrac{4}{3}$.
$1 \cdot z = 12$	• Simplify.
$z = 12$	• The equation is in the form *variable* = *constant*.

The solution is 12. **You should check this solution.**

Because division is defined in terms of multiplication, each side of an equation can be divided by the same nonzero number without changing the solution of the equation.

➡ Solve: $6x = 14$

$6x = 14$	• The goal is to rewrite the equation in the form *variable* = *constant*.
$\dfrac{6x}{6} = \dfrac{14}{6}$	• Divide each side of the equation by 6.
$x = \dfrac{7}{3}$	• Simplify. The equation is in the form *variable* = *constant*.

The solution is $\frac{7}{3}$.

When using the Multiplication Property of Equations, multiply each side of the equation by the reciprocal of the coefficient when the coefficient is a fraction. Divide each side of the equation by the coefficient when the coefficient is an integer or decimal.

Example 4   Solve: $\dfrac{3x}{4} = -9$

Solution
$$\frac{3x}{4} = -9$$
$$\frac{4}{3} \cdot \frac{3}{4}x = \frac{4}{3}(-9) \quad \bullet \left[\frac{3x}{4} = \frac{3}{4}x\right]$$
$$x = -12$$

The solution is -12.

You Try It 4   Solve: $-\dfrac{2x}{5} = 6$

Your solution -15

Example 5   Solve: $5x - 9x = 12$

Solution
$$5x - 9x = 12$$
$$-4x = 12 \quad \bullet \text{ Combine like terms.}$$
$$\frac{-4x}{-4} = \frac{12}{-4}$$
$$x = -3$$

The solution is -3.

You Try It 5   Solve: $4x - 8x = 16$

Your solution -4

Solutions on pp. S4–S5

Objective D   ***To solve application problems using***
the basic percent equation..

An equation that is used frequently in mathematics applications is the basic percent equation.

> **Basic Percent Equation**
>
> Percent · Base = Amount
>
> $P \quad \cdot \quad B \ = \quad A$

In many application problems involving percent, the base follows the word "of."

➡ 20% of what number is 30?

$$P \cdot B = A$$
$$0.20B = 30$$
$$\frac{0.20B}{0.20} = \frac{30}{0.20}$$
$$B = 150$$

- Use the basic percent equation.
- $P = 20\% = 0.20$, $A = 30$, and B is unknown.
- Solve for B.

The number is 150.

➡ 70 is what percent of 80?

$$P \cdot B = A$$
$$P(80) = 70$$
$$\frac{P(80)}{80} = \frac{70}{80}$$
$$P = 0.875$$
$$P = 87.5\%$$

- Use the basic percent equation.
- $B = 80$, $A = 70$, and P is unknown.
- Solve for P.
- The question asked for a percent. Convert the decimal to a percent.

70 is 87.5% of 80.

➡ According to the Travel Industry Association of America, a typical traveler's total vacation bill is $1442. Of that amount, $735 is paid in cash. To the nearest percent, what percent of a typical traveler's vacation bill is paid in cash?

Strategy   To determine the percent, use the basic percent equation.
$B = 1442$, $A = 735$, and P is unknown.

Solution
$$P \cdot B = A$$
$$P(1442) = 735$$
$$\frac{P(1442)}{1442} = \frac{735}{1442}$$
$$P \approx 0.51 = 51\%$$

A typical traveler pays 51% of the vacation bill in cash.

In most cases, you should write the percent as a decimal before solving the basic percent equation. However, some percents are more easily written as a fraction. For example,

$$33\frac{1}{3}\% = \frac{1}{3} \qquad\qquad 66\frac{2}{3}\% = \frac{2}{3} \qquad\qquad 16\frac{2}{3}\% = \frac{1}{6} \qquad\qquad 83\frac{1}{3}\% = \frac{5}{6}$$

Example 6

12 is $33\frac{1}{3}\%$ of what number?

Solution

$$P \cdot B = A$$

$$\frac{1}{3}B = 12 \qquad \bullet\ \mathbf{33\frac{1}{3}\% = \frac{1}{3}}$$

$$3 \cdot \frac{1}{3}B = 3 \cdot 12$$

$$B = 36$$

12 is $33\frac{1}{3}\%$ of 36.

You Try It 6

18 is $16\frac{2}{3}\%$ of what number?

Your solution

108

Example 7

In a recent year, 238 U.S. airports collected \$1.1 billion in passenger taxes. Of this amount, \$88 million was spent on noise reduction. What percent of the passenger taxes collected was spent on noise reduction?

Strategy

To find the percent, solve the basic percent equation using $B = 1.1$ billion $= 1100$ million and $A = 88$ million. The percent is unknown.

Solution

$$P \cdot B = A$$

$$P(1100) = 88$$

$$\frac{P(1100)}{1100} = \frac{88}{1100}$$

$$P = 0.08$$

8% of the passenger taxes collected was spent on noise reduction.

You Try It 7

The federal government ran a deficit of \$23.1 billion in March of 1997. The deficit in March of 1996 was \$47.1 billion. What percent of the March 1996 deficit was the March 1997 deficit? Round to the nearest tenth of a percent.

Your strategy

Your solution

49.0%

Solutions on p. S5

2.1 Exercises

· ·

Objective A

1. Is 4 a solution of
$2x = 8$?
yes

2. Is 3 a solution of
$y + 4 = 7$?
yes

3. Is -1 a solution of
$2b - 1 = 3$?
no

4. Is -2 a solution of
$3a - 4 = 10$?
no

5. Is 1 a solution of
$4 - 2m = 3$?
no

6. Is 2 a solution of
$7 - 3n = 2$?
no

7. Is 5 a solution of
$2x + 5 = 3x$?
yes

8. Is 4 a solution of
$3y - 4 = 2y$?
yes

9. Is 0 a solution of
$4a + 5 = 3a + 5$?
yes

10. Is 3 a solution of
$z^2 + 1 = 4 + 3z$?
no

11. Is 2 a solution of
$2x^2 - 1 = 4x - 1$?
yes

12. Is -1 a solution of
$y^2 - 1 = 4y + 3$?
no

13. Is -2 a solution of
$m^2 - 4 = m + 3$?
no

14. Is 5 a solution of
$x^2 + 2x + 1 = (x + 1)^2$?
yes

15. Is -6 a solution of
$(n - 2)^2 = n^2 - 4n + 4$?
yes

16. Is 4 a solution of
$x(x + 1) = x^2 + 5$?
no

17. Is 3 a solution of
$2a(a - 1) = 3a + 3$?
yes

18. Is $-\dfrac{1}{4}$ a solution of
$8t + 1 = -1$?
yes

19. Is $\dfrac{1}{2}$ a solution of
$4y + 1 = 3$?
yes

20. Is $\dfrac{2}{5}$ a solution of
$5m + 1 = 10m - 3$?
no

21. Is $\dfrac{3}{4}$ a solution of
$8x - 1 = 12x + 3$?
no

Objective B

Solve and check.

22. $x + 5 = 7$
2

23. $y + 3 = 9$
6

24. $b - 4 = 11$
15

25. $z - 6 = 10$
16

26. $2 + a = 8$
6

27. $5 + x = 12$
7

28. $m + 9 = 3$
-6

29. $t + 12 = 10$
-2

30. $n - 5 = -2$
3

31. $x - 6 = -5$
1

32. $b + 7 = 7$
0

33. $y - 5 = -5$
0

34. $a - 3 = -5$
-2

35. $x - 6 = -3$
3

36. $z + 9 = 2$
-7

37. $n + 11 = 1$
-10

38. $10 + m = 3$
-7

39. $8 + x = 5$
-3

40. $9 + x = -3$
-12

41. $10 + y = -4$
-14

42. $b - 5 = -3$
2

43. $t - 6 = -4$
2

44. $4 + x = 10$
6

45. $9 + a = 20$
11

46. $2 = x + 7$
-5

47. $-8 = n + 1$
-9

48. $4 = m - 11$
15

49. $-6 = y - 5$
-1

50. $12 = 3 + w$
9

51. $-9 = 5 + x$
-14

52. $4 = -10 + b$
14

53. $-7 = -2 + x$
-5

54. $13 = -6 + a$
19

55. $m + \dfrac{2}{3} = -\dfrac{1}{3}$
-1

56. $c + \dfrac{3}{4} = -\dfrac{1}{4}$
-1

57. $x - \dfrac{1}{2} = \dfrac{1}{2}$
1

58. $x - \dfrac{2}{5} = \dfrac{3}{5}$
1

59. $\dfrac{5}{8} + y = \dfrac{1}{8}$
$-\dfrac{1}{2}$

60. $\dfrac{4}{9} + a = -\dfrac{2}{9}$
$-\dfrac{2}{3}$

61. $m + \dfrac{1}{2} = -\dfrac{1}{4}$
$-\dfrac{3}{4}$

62. $b + \dfrac{1}{6} = -\dfrac{1}{3}$
$-\dfrac{1}{2}$

63. $x + \dfrac{2}{3} = \dfrac{3}{4}$
$\dfrac{1}{12}$

64. $n + \dfrac{2}{5} = \dfrac{2}{3}$
$\dfrac{4}{15}$

65. $-\dfrac{5}{6} = x - \dfrac{1}{4}$
$-\dfrac{7}{12}$

66. $-\dfrac{1}{4} = c - \dfrac{2}{3}$
$\dfrac{5}{12}$

67. $d + 1.3619 = 2.0148$
0.6529

68. $w + 2.932 = 4.801$
1.869

69. $-0.813 + x = -1.096$
-0.283

70. $-1.926 + t = -1.042$
0.884

71. $6.149 = -3.108 + z$
9.257

72. $5.237 = -2.014 + x$
7.251

Objective C

Solve and check.

73. $5x = -15$
-3

74. $4y = -28$
-7

75. $3b = 0$
0

76. $2a = 0$
0

77. $-3x = 6$
-2

78. $-5m = 20$
-4

79. $-3x = -27$
9

80. $-\dfrac{1}{6}n = -30$
180

81. $20 = \dfrac{1}{4}c$
80

82. $18 = 2t$
9

83. $-32 = 8w$
-4

84. $-56 = 7x$
-8

85. $0 = -5x$
0

86. $0 = -8a$
0

87. $-32 = -4y$
8

88. $-54 = 6c$
-9

89. $49 = -7t$
-7

90. $\dfrac{x}{3} = 2$
6

91. $\dfrac{x}{4} = 3$
12

92. $-\dfrac{y}{2} = 5$
-10

93. $-\dfrac{b}{3} = 6$
-18

94. $\dfrac{3}{4}y = 9$
12

95. $\dfrac{2}{5}x = 6$
15

96. $-\dfrac{2}{3}d = 8$
-12

97. $-\dfrac{3}{5}m = 12$
-20

98. $\dfrac{2n}{3} = 0$
0

99. $\dfrac{5x}{6} = 0$
0

100. $\dfrac{-3z}{8} = 9$
-24

101. $\dfrac{-4x}{5} = -12$
15

102. $-6 = -\dfrac{2}{3}y$
9

103. $-15 = -\dfrac{1}{5}x$
75

104. $\dfrac{2}{5}a = 3$
$\dfrac{15}{2}$

105. $\dfrac{3x}{4} = 2$
$\dfrac{8}{3}$

106. $\dfrac{3}{4}c = \dfrac{3}{5}$
$\dfrac{4}{5}$

107. $\dfrac{2}{9} = \dfrac{2}{3}y$
$\dfrac{1}{3}$

108. $-\dfrac{6}{7} = -\dfrac{3}{4}b$
$\dfrac{8}{7}$

109. $\dfrac{1}{5}x = -\dfrac{1}{10}$
$-\dfrac{1}{2}$

110. $-\dfrac{2}{3}y = -\dfrac{8}{9}$
$\dfrac{4}{3}$

111. $-1 = \dfrac{2n}{3}$
$-\dfrac{3}{2}$

112. $-\dfrac{3}{4} = \dfrac{a}{8}$
-6

113. $-\dfrac{2}{5}m = -\dfrac{6}{7}$

$\dfrac{15}{7}$

114. $5x + 2x = 14$

2

115. $3n + 2n = 20$

4

116. $7d - 4d = 9$

3

117. $10y - 3y = 21$

3

118. $2x - 5x = 9$

−3

119. $\dfrac{x}{1.46} = 3.25$

4.745

120. $\dfrac{z}{2.95} = -7.88$

−23.246

121. $3.47a = 7.1482$

2.06

122. $2.31m = 2.4255$

1.05

123. $-3.7x = 7.881$

−2.13

124. $\dfrac{n}{2.65} = 9.08$

24.062

Objective D

125. What is 35% of 80?
28

126. What percent of 8 is 0.5?
6.25%

127. Find 1.2% of 60.
0.72

128. 8 is what percent of 5?
160%

129. 125% of what is 80?
64

130. What percent of 20 is 30?
150%

131. 12 is what percent of 50?
24%

132. What percent of 125 is 50?
40%

133. Find 18% of 40.
7.2

134. What is 25% of 60?
15

135. 12% of what is 48?
400

136. 45% of what is 9?
20

137. What is $33\dfrac{1}{3}$% of 27?
9

138. Find $16\dfrac{2}{3}$% of 30.
5

139. What percent of 12 is 3?
25%

140. 10 is what percent of 15?
$66\dfrac{1}{2}$%

141. 60% of what is 3?
5

142. 75% of what is 6?
8

143. 12 is what percent of 6?
200%

144. 20 is what percent of 16?
125%

145. $5\dfrac{1}{4}$% of what is 21?
400

146. $37\frac{1}{2}$% of what is 15?

40

147. Find 15.4% of 50.

7.7

148. What is 18.5% of 46?

8.51

149. 1 is 0.5% of what?

200

150. 3 is 1.5% of what?

200

151. $\frac{3}{4}$% of what is 3?

400

152. $\frac{1}{2}$% of what is 3?

600

153. Find 125% of 16.

20

154. What is 250% of 12?

30

155. 16.43 is what percent of 20.45? Round to the nearest hundredth of a percent.
80.34%

156. Find 18.37% of 625.43. Round to the nearest hundredth.
114.89

157. A university consists of three colleges: business, engineering, and fine arts. There are 2900 students in the business college, 1500 students in the engineering college, and 1000 students in the fine arts college. What percent of the total number of students in the university are in the fine arts college? Round to the nearest percent.
19%

158. Approximately 21% of air is oxygen. Using this estimate, determine how many liters of oxygen there are in a room containing 21,600 L of air.
4536 L

Corporate Sponsorships
(in millions of dollars)

Sports
$3,900

Fine Arts
$360

Charity
$540

Other
$1,200

Source: IEG Sponsorship Report

159. The circle graph at the right represents corporate spending in 1997 of $6 billion to sponsor events. What percent of the amount spent by companies was spent on sports?
65%

160. In 1950, 12% of mothers with children under age 6 worked outside the home. By 1995, that percent had increased to 64%. How many more mothers with children under age 6 worked outside the home in 1995 than in 1950?
insufficient information

161. The Energy Information Administration reports that if every U.S. household switched 4 h of lighting per day from incandescent bulbs to compact fluorescent bulbs, we would save 31.7 billion kilowatt-hours (kWh) a year, or 33% of the total electricity used for home lighting. What is the total electricity used for home lighting in this country? Round to the nearest tenth of a billion.
96.1 billion kWh

162. To override a presidential veto, at least $66\frac{2}{3}\%$ of the Senate must vote to override the veto. There are 100 senators in the Senate. What is the minimum number of votes needed to override a veto?   67 votes

163. According to *Time* (March 1997), in 1996 The Coca-Cola Company declared its intention to repurchase 206 million shares of the company, or 8.3% of the company's outstanding common stock. How many shares of The Coca-Cola Company common stock were outstanding at the time of this announcement? Round to the nearest million.
2,482 million shares

164. A Holstein cow in Wisconsin recently set a milk production record. She averaged 174 lb of milk per day for 365 days. What percent of the average daily milk production in 1996 was the production by this Wisconsin Holstein? See the graph at the right. Round to the nearest percent.   385%

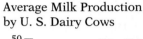

Average Milk Production
by U. S. Dairy Cows

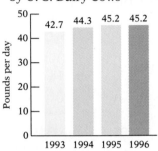

Source: Department of Agriculture

165. According to *Working Woman* (July–August 1997), in 1996, total consumer spending in the United States was $4.69 trillion. Of that amount, 1.58% was spent on new cars. In 1986, total consumer spending in the United States was $3.72 trillion, of which 3.09% was spent on new cars.
 a. During which year was more money spent on new cars?
 b. How much more? Round to the nearest billion.
  a. 1986   b. $41 billion

APPLYING THE CONCEPTS

166. Solve the equation $ax = b$ for x. Is the solution you have written valid for all real numbers a and b?
$x = \dfrac{b}{a}, a \neq 0$

167. **a.** Make up an equation of the form $x + a = b$ that has 2 as a solution.
 b. Make up an equation of the form $ax = b$ that has -1 as a solution.
 a. Answers will vary.   b. Answers will vary.

168. Solve.   **a.** $\dfrac{\frac{3}{1}}{x} = 5$ $\frac{5}{3}$ **b.** $\dfrac{\frac{2}{1}}{y} = -2$ -1 **c.** $\dfrac{3x + 2x}{3} = 2$ $\frac{6}{5}$

169. Write out the steps for solving the equation $\frac{1}{2}x = -3$. Identify each Property of Real Numbers or Property of Equations as you use it.

170. In your own words, state the Addition Property and the Multiplication Property of Equations.

171. If a quantity increases by 100%, how many times its original value is the new value?   2 times

2.2   **General Equations**

Objective A   **To solve an equation of the form *ax* + *b* = *c*** ....

In solving an equation of the form $ax + b = c$, the goal is to rewrite the equation in the form *variable = constant*. This requires the application of both the Addition and the Multiplication Properties of Equations.

➡ Solve: $\frac{3}{4}x - 2 = -11$

The goal is to write the equation in the form *variable = constant*.

$$\frac{3}{4}x - 2 = -11$$

$$\frac{3}{4}x - 2 + 2 = -11 + 2$$ • Add 2 to each side of the equation.

$$\frac{3}{4}x = -9$$ • Simplify.

$$\frac{4}{3} \cdot \frac{3}{4}x = \frac{4}{3}(-9)$$ • Multiply each side of the equation by $\frac{4}{3}$.

$$x = -12$$ • The equation is of the form *variable = constant*.

Check: • Check the solution.

$$\frac{3}{4}x - 2 = -11$$

$$\frac{3}{4}(-12) - 2 \mid -11$$

$$-9 - 2 \mid -11$$

$$-11 = -11$$ • A true equation

The solution is -12.

Example 1   Solve: $3x - 7 = -5$

Solution
$$3x - 7 = -5$$
$$3x - 7 + 7 = -5 + 7$$
$$3x = 2$$
$$\frac{3x}{3} = \frac{2}{3}$$
$$x = \frac{2}{3}$$

The solution is $\frac{2}{3}$.

You Try It 1   Solve: $5x + 7 = 10$

Your solution $\frac{3}{5}$

Solution on p. S5

Example 2

Solve: $5 = 9 - 2x$

Solution

$$5 = 9 - 2x$$
$$5 - 9 = 9 - 9 - 2x$$
$$-4 = -2x$$
$$\frac{-4}{-2} = \frac{-2x}{-2}$$
$$2 = x$$

The solution is 2.

You Try It 2

Solve: $2 = 11 + 3x$

Your solution

-3

Example 3

Solve: $2x + 4 - 5x = 10$

Solution

$$2x + 4 - 5x = 10$$
$$-3x + 4 = 10 \qquad \bullet \text{ Combine like terms.}$$
$$-3x + 4 - 4 = 10 - 4$$
$$-3x = 6$$
$$\frac{-3x}{-3} = \frac{6}{-3}$$
$$x = -2$$

The solution is -2.

You Try It 3

Solve: $x - 5 + 4x = 25$

Your solution

6

Solutions on p. S5

Objective B   *To solve an equation of the form* ***ax + b = cx + d*** ....

In solving an equation of the form $ax + b = cx + d$, the goal is to rewrite the equation in the form *variable = constant*. Begin by rewriting the equation so that there is only one variable term in the equation. Then rewrite the equation so that there is only one constant term.

➡ Solve: $2x + 3 = 5x - 9$

$$2x + 3 = 5x - 9$$

$$2x - 5x + 3 = 5x - 5x - 9 \qquad \bullet \text{ Subtract } 5x \text{ from each side of the equation.}$$

$$-3x + 3 = -9 \qquad \bullet \text{ Simplify.}$$

$$-3x + 3 - 3 = -9 - 3 \qquad \bullet \text{ Subtract 3 from each side of the equation.}$$

$$-3x = -12 \qquad \bullet \text{ Simplify.}$$

$$\frac{-3x}{-3} = \frac{-12}{-3} \qquad \bullet \text{ Divide each side of the equation by } -3.$$

$$x = 4 \qquad \bullet \text{ The equation is in the form } \textit{variable = constant.}$$

The solution is 4. You should verify this by checking this solution.

Example 4

Solve: $4x - 5 = 8x - 7$

Solution

$$4x - 5 = 8x - 7$$

$$4x - 8x - 5 = 8x - 8x - 7$$

$$-4x - 5 = -7$$

$$-4x - 5 + 5 = -7 + 5$$

$$-4x = -2$$

$$\frac{-4x}{-4} = \frac{-2}{-4}$$

$$x = \frac{1}{2}$$

The solution is $\frac{1}{2}$.

You Try It 4

Solve: $5x + 4 = 6 + 10x$

Your solution

$-\dfrac{2}{5}$

Example 5

Solve: $3x + 4 - 5x = 2 - 4x$

Solution

$$3x + 4 - 5x = 2 - 4x$$

$$-2x + 4 = 2 - 4x$$

$$-2x + 4x + 4 = 2 - 4x + 4x$$

$$2x + 4 = 2$$

$$2x + 4 - 4 = 2 - 4$$

$$2x = -2$$

$$\frac{2x}{2} = \frac{-2}{2}$$

$$x = -1$$

The solution is -1.

You Try It 5

Solve: $5x - 10 - 3x = 6 - 4x$

Your solution

$\dfrac{8}{3}$

Solutions on p. S5

Objective C *To solve an equation containing parentheses* ....

When an equation contains parentheses, one of the steps in solving the equation requires the use of the Distributive Property. The Distributive Property is used to remove parentheses from a variable expression.

INSTRUCTOR NOTE
Remind students that the goal
is still *variable = constant.*

➡ Solve: $4 + 5(2x - 3) = 3(4x - 1)$

$$4 + 5(2x - 3) = 3(4x - 1)$$

$$4 + 10x - 15 = 12x - 3$$ • Use the Distributive Property. Then simplify.

$$10x - 11 = 12x - 3$$

$$10x - 12x - 11 = 12x - 12x - 3$$ • Subtract **12x** from each side of the equation.

$$-2x - 11 = -3$$ • Simplify.

$$-2x - 11 + 11 = -3 + 11$$ • Add 11 to each side of the equation.

$$-2x = 8$$ • Simplify.

$$\frac{-2x}{-2} = \frac{8}{-2}$$ • Divide each side of the equation by −2.

$$x = -4$$ • The equation is in the form *variable = constant.*

The solution is -4. You should verify this by checking this solution.

Example 6
Solve: $3x - 4(2 - x) = 3(x - 2) - 4$

Solution
$$3x - 4(2 - x) = 3(x - 2) - 4$$
$$3x - 8 + 4x = 3x - 6 - 4$$
$$7x - 8 = 3x - 10$$
$$7x - 3x - 8 = 3x - 3x - 10$$
$$4x - 8 = -10$$
$$4x - 8 + 8 = -10 + 8$$
$$4x = -2$$
$$\frac{4x}{4} = \frac{-2}{4}$$
$$x = -\frac{1}{2}$$

The solution is $-\frac{1}{2}$.

You Try It 6
Solve: $5x - 4(3 - 2x) = 2(3x - 2) + 6$

Your solution
2

Solution on p. S5

Example 7

Solve: $3[2 - 4(2x - 1)] = 4x - 10$

Solution

$$3[2 - 4(2x - 1)] = 4x - 10$$
$$3[2 - 8x + 4] = 4x - 10$$
$$3[6 - 8x] = 4x - 10$$
$$18 - 24x = 4x - 10$$
$$18 - 24x - 4x = 4x - 4x - 10$$
$$18 - 28x = -10$$
$$18 - 18 - 28x = -10 - 18$$
$$-28x = -28$$
$$\frac{-28x}{-28} = \frac{-28}{-28}$$
$$x = 1$$

The solution is 1.

You Try It 7

Solve: $-2[3x - 5(2x - 3)] = 3x - 8$

Your solution

2

Solution on p. S5

Objective D   *To translate a sentence into an equation and solve* ....

An equation states that two mathematical expressions are equal. Therefore, to translate a sentence into an equation requires recognition of the words or phrases that mean "equals." Some of these words and phrases are listed below.

> *equals*   *is*   *totals*   *is the same as*

➡ Translate "five less than four times a number is four more than the number" into an equation and solve.

the unknown number: n

• Assign a variable to the unknown number.

five less than four times a number	is	four more than the number

• Find two verbal expressions for the same value.

$$4n - 5 = n + 4$$
$$4n - n - 5 = n - n + 4$$
$$3n - 5 = 4$$
$$3n - 5 + 5 = 4 + 5$$
$$3n = 9$$
$$\frac{3n}{3} = \frac{9}{3}$$
$$n = 3$$

The number is 3.

• Write an equation.

• Solve the equation.

• *Check:*

5 less than 4 times 3	4 more than 3
$4 \cdot 3 - 5$	$3 + 4$
$12 - 5$	7

$$7 = 7$$

Many of the applications of mathematics require that you identify an unknown quantity, assign a variable to that quantity, and then attempt to express another unknown quantity in terms of that variable.

Suppose we know that the sum of two numbers is 10 and that one of the two numbers is 4. We can find the other number by subtracting 4 from 10.

one number: 4
other number: $10 - 4 = 6$
The two numbers are 4 and 6.

Now suppose we know that the sum of two numbers is 10, we don't know either number, and we want to express *both* numbers in terms of the *same* variable. Let one number be x. Again, we can find the other number by subtracting x from 10.

one number: x
other number: $10 - x$
The two numbers are x and $10 - x$.

Note that the sum of x and $10 - x$ is 10.

$x + (10 - x) = x + 10 - x = 10$

Example 8

The sum of two numbers is 9. Eight times the smaller number is five less than three times the larger number. Find the numbers.

Solution

the smaller number: p
the larger number: $9 - p$

eight times the smaller number	is	five less than three times the larger number

$$8p = 3(9 - p) - 5$$
$$8p = 27 - 3p - 5$$
$$8p = 22 - 3p$$
$$8p + 3p = 22 - 3p + 3p$$
$$11p = 22$$
$$\frac{11p}{11} = \frac{22}{11}$$
$$p = 2$$

$9 - p = 9 - 2 = 7$

These numbers check as solutions.

The smaller number is 2.
The larger number is 7.

You Try It 8

The sum of two numbers is 14. One more than three times the smaller number equals the sum of the larger number and three. Find the two numbers.

Your solution

4 and 10

Solution on p. S6

2.2 Exercises

- -

Objective A

Solve and check.

1. $3x + 1 = 10$
3

2. $4y + 3 = 11$
2

3. $2a - 5 = 7$
6

4. $5m - 6 = 9$
3

5. $5 = 4x + 9$
-1

6. $2 = 5b + 12$
-2

7. $2x - 5 = -11$
-3

8. $3n - 7 = -19$
-4

9. $4 - 3w = -2$
2

10. $5 - 6x = -13$
3

11. $8 - 3t = 2$
2

12. $12 - 5x = 7$
1

13. $4a - 20 = 0$
5

14. $3y - 9 = 0$
3

15. $6 + 2b = 0$
-3

16. $10 + 5m = 0$
-2

17. $-2x + 5 = -7$
6

18. $-5d + 3 = -12$
3

19. $-12x + 30 = -6$
3

20. $-13 - -11y + 9$
2

21. $2 = 7 - 5a$
1

22. $3 = 11 - 4n$
2

23. $-35 = -6b + 1$
6

24. $-8x + 3 = -29$
4

25. $-3m - 21 = 0$
-7

26. $-5x - 30 = 0$
-6

27. $-4y + 15 = 15$
0

28. $-3x + 19 = 19$
0

29. $9 - 4x = 6$
$\dfrac{3}{4}$

30. $3t - 2 = 0$
$\dfrac{2}{3}$

31. $9x - 4 = 0$
$\dfrac{4}{9}$

32. $7 - 8z = 0$
$\dfrac{7}{8}$

33. $1 - 3x = 0$
$\dfrac{1}{3}$

34. $9d + 10 = 7$
$-\dfrac{1}{3}$

35. $12w + 11 = 5$
$-\dfrac{1}{2}$

36. $6y - 5 = -7$
$-\dfrac{1}{3}$

37. $8b - 3 = -9$
$-\dfrac{3}{4}$

38. $5 - 6m = 2$
$\dfrac{1}{2}$

39. $7 - 9a = 4$
$\dfrac{1}{3}$

40. $9 = -12c + 5$
$-\dfrac{1}{3}$

41. $10 = -18x + 7$

$-\dfrac{1}{6}$

42. $2y + \dfrac{1}{3} = \dfrac{7}{3}$

1

43. $4a + \dfrac{3}{4} = \dfrac{19}{4}$

1

44. $2n - \dfrac{3}{4} = \dfrac{13}{4}$

2

45. $3x - \dfrac{5}{6} = \dfrac{13}{6}$

1

46. $5y + \dfrac{3}{7} = \dfrac{3}{7}$

0

47. $9x + \dfrac{4}{5} = \dfrac{4}{5}$

0

48. $8 = 7d - 1$

$\dfrac{9}{7}$

49. $8 = 10x - 5$

$\dfrac{13}{10}$

50. $4 = 7 - 2w$

$\dfrac{3}{2}$

51. $7 = 9 - 5a$

$\dfrac{2}{5}$

52. $8t + 13 = 3$

$-\dfrac{5}{4}$

53. $12x + 19 = 3$

$-\dfrac{4}{3}$

54. $-6y + 5 = 13$

$-\dfrac{4}{3}$

55. $-4x + 3 = 9$

$-\dfrac{3}{2}$

56. $\dfrac{1}{2}a - 3 = 1$

8

57. $\dfrac{1}{3}m - 1 = 5$

18

58. $\dfrac{2}{5}y + 4 = 6$

5

59. $\dfrac{3}{4}n + 7 = 13$

8

60. $-\dfrac{2}{3}x + 1 = 7$

-9

61. $-\dfrac{3}{8}b + 4 = 10$

-16

62. $\dfrac{x}{4} - 6 = 1$

28

63. $\dfrac{y}{5} - 2 = 3$

25

64. $\dfrac{2x}{3} - 1 = 5$

9

65. $\dfrac{3c}{7} - 1 = 8$

21

66. $4 - \dfrac{3}{4}z = -2$

8

67. $3 - \dfrac{4}{5}w = -9$

15

68. $5 + \dfrac{2}{3}y = 3$

-3

69. $17 + \dfrac{5}{8}x = 7$

-16

70. $17 = 7 - \dfrac{5}{6}t$

-12

71. $9 = 3 - \dfrac{2x}{7}$

-21

72. $3 = \dfrac{3a}{4} + 1$

$\dfrac{8}{3}$

73. $7 = \dfrac{2x}{5} + 4$

$\dfrac{15}{2}$

74. $5 - \dfrac{4c}{7} = 8$

$-\dfrac{21}{4}$

75. $7 - \dfrac{5}{9}y = 9$

$-\dfrac{18}{5}$

76. $6a + 3 + 2a = 11$

1

77. $5y + 9 + 2y = 23$

2

78. $7x - 4 - 2x = 6$

2

79. $11z - 3 - 7z = 9$

3

80. $2x - 6x + 1 = 9$

-2

81. $b - 8b + 1 = -6$

1

82. $3 = 7x + 9 - 4x$

-2

83. $-1 = 5m + 7 - m$

-2

84. $8 = 4n - 6 + 3n$

2

Objective B

Solve and check.

85. $8x + 5 = 4x + 13$
2

86. $6y + 2 = y + 17$
3

87. $5x - 4 = 2x + 5$
3

88. $13b - 1 = 4b - 19$
−2

89. $15x - 2 = 4x - 13$
−1

90. $7a - 5 = 2a - 20$
−3

91. $3x + 1 = 11 - 2x$
2

92. $n - 2 = 6 - 3n$
2

93. $2x - 3 = -11 - 2x$
−2

94. $4y - 2 = -16 - 3y$
−2

95. $2b + 3 = 5b + 12$
−3

96. $m + 4 = 3m + 8$
−2

97. $4y - 8 = y - 8$
0

98. $5a + 7 = 2a + 7$
0

99. $6 - 5x = 8 - 3x$
−1

100. $10 - 4n = 16 - n$
−2

101. $5 + 7x = 11 + 9x$
−3

102. $3 - 2y = 15 + 4y$
−2

103. $2x - 4 = 6x$
−1

104. $2b - 10 = 7b$
−2

105. $8m - 3m + 20$
4

106. $9y = 5y + 16$
4

107. $8b + 5 = 5b + 7$
$\dfrac{2}{3}$

108. $6y - 1 = 2y + 2$
$\dfrac{3}{4}$

109. $7x - 8 = x - 3$
$\dfrac{5}{6}$

110. $2y - 7 = -1 - 2y$
$\dfrac{3}{2}$

111. $2m - 1 = -6m + 5$
$\dfrac{3}{4}$

Objective C

Solve and check.

112. $5x + 2(x + 1) = 23$
3

113. $6y + 2(2y + 3) = 16$
1

114. $9n - 3(2n - 1) = 15$
4

115. $12x - 2(4x - 6) = 28$
4

116. $7a - (3a - 4) = 12$
2

117. $9m - 4(2m - 3) = 11$
−1

118. $5(3 - 2y) + 4y = 3$
2

119. $4(1 - 3x) + 7x = 9$
−1

120. $5y - 3 = 7 + 4(y - 2)$
2

121. $5 + 2(3b + 1) = 3b + 5$
$-\dfrac{2}{3}$

122. $6 - 4(3a - 2) = 2(a + 5)$
$\dfrac{2}{7}$

123. $7 - 3(2a - 5) = 3a + 10$
$\dfrac{4}{3}$

124. $2a - 5 = 4(3a + 1) - 2$
$-\dfrac{7}{10}$

125. $5 - (9 - 6x) = 2x - 2$
$\dfrac{1}{2}$

126. $7 - (5 - 8x) = 4x + 3$
$\dfrac{1}{4}$

127. $3[2 - 4(y - 1)] = 3(2y + 8)$
$-\dfrac{1}{3}$

128. $5[2 - (2x - 4)] = 2(5 - 3x)$
5

129. $3a + 2[2 + 3(a - 1)] = 2(3a + 4)$
$\dfrac{10}{3}$

130. $5 + 3[1 + 2(2x - 3)] = 6(x + 5)$
$\dfrac{20}{3}$

131. $-2[4 - (3b + 2)] = 5 - 2(3b + 6)$
$-\dfrac{1}{4}$

132. $-4[x - 2(2x - 3)] + 1 = 2x - 3$
2

Objective D

Translate into an equation and solve.

133. The sum of a number and twelve is twenty. Find the number.
$x + 12 = 20$; 8

134. The difference between nine and a number is seven. Find the number.
$9 - x = 7$; 2

135. Three-fifths of a number is negative thirty. Find the number.
$\dfrac{3}{5}x = -30$; −50

136. The quotient of a number and six is twelve. Find the number.
$\dfrac{x}{6} = 12$; 72

137. Four more than three times a number is thirteen. Find the number.
$3x + 4 = 13$; 3

138. The sum of twice a number and five is fifteen. Find the number.
$2x + 5 = 15$; 5

139. The difference between nine times a number and six is twelve. Find the number.
$9x - 6 = 12$; 2

140. Six less than four times a number is twenty-two. Find the number.
$4x - 6 = 22; 7$

141. The sum of a number and twice the number is nine. Find the number.
$x + 2x = 9; 3$

142. Eleven more than negative four times a number is three. Find the number.
$-4x + 11 = 3; 2$

143. Seventeen less than the product of five and a number is two. Find the number.
$5x - 17 = 2; \dfrac{19}{5}$

144. Eight less than the product of eleven and a number is negative nineteen. Find the number.
$11x - 8 = -19; -1$

145. Seven more than the product of six and a number is eight less than the product of three and the number. Find the number.
$6x + 7 = 3x - 8; -5$

146. Fifteen less than the product of four and a number is the difference between six times the number and eleven. Find the number.
$4x - 15 = 6x - 11; -2$

147. Thirty equals nine less than the product of seven and a number. Find the number.
$30 = 7x - 9; \dfrac{39}{7}$

148. Twenty-three equals the difference between eight and the product of five and a number. Find the number.
$23 - 8 - 5x; -3$

149. The sum of two numbers is twenty-one. Twice the smaller number is three more than the larger number. Find the two numbers.
$2x = (21 - x) + 3; 8, 13$

150. The sum of two numbers is thirty. Three times the smaller number is twice the larger number. Find the two numbers.
$3x = 2(30 - x); 12, 18$

151. The sum of two numbers is twenty-three. The larger number is five more than twice the smaller number. Find the two numbers.
$23 - x = 2x + 5; 6, 17$

152. The sum of two numbers is twenty-five. The larger number is ten less than four times the smaller number. Find the two numbers.
$25 - x = 4x - 10; 7, 18$

APPLYING THE CONCEPTS

153. If $2x - 3 = 7$, evaluate $3x + 4$.
19

154. If $3x + 5 = -4$, evaluate $2x - 5$.
-11

155. If $5x = 3x - 8$, evaluate $4x + 2$.
-14

156. If $7x + 3 = 5x - 7$, evaluate $3x - 2$.
-17

157. Solve: $x \div 28 = 1481$ remainder 25
41,493

158. If $3 + 2(4a - 3) = 5$ and $4 - 3(2 - 3b) = 11$, which is larger, a or b?
b

159. Does the sentence "Solve $2x - 3(4x + 1)$" make sense? Why or why not?

Solve. If the equation has no solution, write "No solution."

160. $3(2x - 1) - (6x - 4) = -9$
no solution

161. $7(3x + 6) - 4(3 + 5x) = 13 + x$
no solution

162. $\frac{1}{5}(25 - 10a) + 4 = \frac{1}{3}(12a - 15) + 14$
0

163. $5[m + 2(3 - m)] = 3[2(4 - m) - 5]$
-21

164. Solve the equation $x + a = b$ for x. Is the solution you have written valid for all real numbers a and b?
$x = b - a$. Yes.

165. Explain in your own words the steps you would take to solve the equation $\frac{2}{3}x - 4 = 10$. State the Property of Real Numbers or the Property of Equations that is used at each step.

166. The equation $x = x + 1$ has no solution, whereas the solution of the equation $2x + 3 = 3$ is zero. Is there a difference between no solution and a solution of zero? Explain your answer.

167. Explain the difference between the word *equation* and the word *expression*.

168. The following problem does not contain enough information for us to find only one solution. Supply some additional information so that the problem has exactly one solution. Then write and solve an equation.
"The sum of two numbers is 15. Find the numbers."

2.3 Mixture, Investment, and Motion Problems

Objective A *To solve value mixture problems* ....

TAKE NOTE

The equation $AC = V$ is used to find the value of an ingredient. For example, the value of 4 lb of cashews costing $6 per pound is
$$AC = V$$
$$4 \cdot 6 = V$$
$$\$24 = V$$

A value mixture problem involves combining two ingredients that have different prices into a single blend. For example, a coffee merchant may blend two types of coffee into a single blend, or a candy manufacturer may combine two types of candy to sell as a "variety pack."

The solution of a value mixture problem is based on the equation $V = AC$, where V is the value of an ingredient, A is the amount of the ingredient, and C is the cost per unit of the ingredient.

➡ A coffee merchant wants to make 6 lb of a blend of coffee costing $5 per pound. The blend is made using a $6-per-pound grade of coffee and a $3-per-pound grade. How many pounds of each of these grades should be used?

> **Strategy for Solving a Value Mixture Problem**
>
> 1. For each ingredient in the mixture, write a numerical or variable expression for the amount of the ingredient used, the unit cost of the ingredient, and the value of the amount used. For the blend, write a numerical or variable expression for the amount, the unit cost of the blend, and the value of the amount. The results can be recorded in a table.

Amount of $6 coffee: x • The sum of the amounts is 6 lb.
Amount of $3 coffee: $6 - x$

TAKE NOTE

Use the information given in the problem to fill in the "Amount" and "Unit Cost" columns of the table. Fill in the "Value" column by multiplying the two expressions you wrote in each row. Use the expressions in the last column to write the equation.

	Amount, A	·	*Unit Cost, C*	=	*Value, V*
$6 grade	x	·	6	=	$6x$
$3 grade	$6 - x$	·	3	=	$3(6 - x)$
$5 blend	6	·	5	=	$5(6)$

> 2. Determine how the values of the individual ingredients are related. Use the fact that the sum of the values of these ingredients is equal to the value of the blend.

$$6x + 3(6 - x) = 5(6)$$ • The sum of the values of the $6 grade
$$6x + 18 - 3x = 30$$ and the $3 grade is equal to the value of
$$3x + 18 = 30$$ the $5 blend.
$$3x = 12$$
$$x = 4$$

$$6 - x = 6 - 4 = 2$$ • Find the amount of $3 coffee.

The merchant must use 4 lb of the $6 coffee and 2 lb of the $3 coffee.

Example 1

How many ounces of a silver alloy that costs $4 an ounce must be mixed with 10 oz of an alloy that costs $6 an ounce to make a mixture that costs $4.32 an ounce?

You Try It 1

A gardener has 20 lb of a lawn fertilizer that costs $.80 per pound. How many pounds of a fertilizer that costs $.55 per pound should be mixed with this 20 lb of lawn fertilizer to produce a mixture that costs $.75 per pound?

Strategy

- Ounces of $4 alloy: x

	Amount	*Cost*	*Value*
$4 alloy	x	4	$4x$
$6 alloy	10	6	6(10)
$4.32 mixture	$10 + x$	4.32	$4.32(10 + x)$

- The sum of the values before mixing equals the value after mixing.

Your strategy

Solution

$$4x + 6(10) = 4.32(10 + x)$$

$$4x + 60 = 43.2 + 4.32x$$

$$-0.32x + 60 = 43.2$$

$$-0.32x = -16.8$$

$$x = 52.5$$

52.5 oz of the $4 silver alloy must be used.

Your solution

5 lb

Solution on p. S6

Objective B **To solve percent mixture problems** ....

The amount of a substance in a solution can be given as a percent of the total solution. For example, a 5% saltwater solution means that 5% of the total solution is salt. The remaining 95% is water.

The solution of a percent mixture problem is based on the equation $Q = Ar$, where Q is the quantity of a substance in the solution, r is the percent of concentration, and A is the amount of solution.

➡ A 500-milliliter bottle contains a 4% solution of hydrogen peroxide. Find the amount of hydrogen peroxide in the solution.

$$Q = Ar$$
$$Q = 500(0.04)$$
$$Q = 20$$

• Given: $A = 500$; $r = 4\% = 0.04$

The bottle contains 20 ml of hydrogen peroxide.

➡ How many gallons of a 20% salt solution must be mixed with 6 gal of a 30% salt solution to make a 22% salt solution?

> **Strategy for Solving a Percent Mixture Problem**
>
> 1. For each solution, use the equation $Ar = Q$. Write a numerical or variable expression for the amount of solution, the percent of concentration, and the quantity of the substance in the solution. The results can be recorded in a table.

The unknown quantity of 20% solution: x

	Amount of Solution, A	·	Percent of Concentration, r	=	Quantity of Substance, Q
20% solution	x	·	0.20	=	$0.20x$
30% solution	6	·	0.30	=	$0.30(6)$
22% solution	$x + 6$	·	0.22	=	$0.22(x + 6)$

> 2. Determine how the quantities of the substance in the individual solutions are related. Use the fact that the sum of the quantities of the substances being mixed is equal to the quantity of the substance after mixing.

$$0.20x + 0.30(6) = 0.22(x + 6)$$
$$0.20x + 1.80 = 0.22x + 1.32$$
$$-0.02x + 1.80 = 1.32$$
$$-0.02x = -0.48$$
$$x = 24$$

• The sum of the quantities of the substance in the 20% solution and the 30% solution is equal to the quantity of the substance in the 22% solution.

24 gal of the 20% solution are required.

Example 2

A chemist wishes to make 2 L of an 8% acid solution by mixing a 10% acid solution and a 5% acid solution. How many liters of each solution should the chemist use?

Strategy

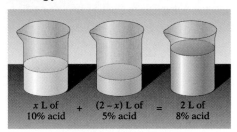

x L of 10% acid + $(2 - x)$ L of 5% acid = 2 L of 8% acid

- Liters of 10% solution: x
  Liters of 5% solution: $2 - x$

	Amount	Percent	Quantity
10% solution	x	0.10	$0.10x$
5% solution	$2 - x$	0.05	$0.05(2 - x)$
8% solution	2	0.08	$0.08(2)$

- The sum of the quantities before mixing is equal to the quantity after mixing.

Solution

$$0.10x + 0.05(2 - x) = 0.08(2)$$

$$0.10x + 0.10 - 0.05x = 0.16$$

$$0.05x + 0.10 = 0.16$$

$$0.05x = 0.06$$

$$x = 1.2$$

$$2 - x = 2 - 1.2 = 0.8$$

The chemist needs 1.2 L of the 10% solution and 0.8 L of the 5% solution.

You Try It 2

A pharmacist dilutes 5 L of a 12% solution with a 6% solution. How many liters of the 6% solution are added to make an 8% solution?

Your strategy

Your solution

10 L

Solution on p. S6

Objective C **To solve investment problems** .... 10 HM³

The annual simple interest that an investment earns is given by the equation $I = Pr$, where I is the simple interest, P is the principal, or the amount invested, and r is the simple interest rate.

➡ The annual interest rate on a $2500 investment is 8%. Find the annual simple interest earned on the investment.

$I = Pr$ • Given: $P = \$2500$; $r = 8\% = 0.08$
$I = 2500(0.08)$
$I = 200$

The annual simple interest is $200.

➡ An investor has a total of $10,000 deposited in two simple interest accounts. On one account, the annual simple interest rate is 6%. On the second account, the annual simple interest rate is 10%. How much is invested in the 6% account if the total annual interest earned is $900?

> **Strategy for Solving a Problem Involving Money Deposited in Two Simple Interest Accounts**
>
> 1. For each amount invested, use the equation $Pr = I$. Write a numerical or variable expression for the principal, the interest rate, and the interest earned. The results can be recorded in a table.

Amount invested at 6%: x • The sum of the amounts
Amount invested at 10%: $\$10,000 - x$ invested is $10,000.

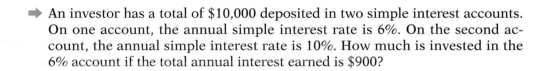

	Principal, P	·	Interest Rate, r	=	Interest Earned, I
Amount at 6%	x	·	0.06	=	$0.06x$
Amount at 10%	$10,000 - x$	·	0.10	=	$0.10(10,000 - x)$

> 2. Determine how the amounts of interest earned on the individual amounts are related. For example, the total interest earned by both accounts may be known, or it may be known that the interest earned on one account is equal to the interest earned on the other account.

$0.06x + 0.10(10,000 - x) = 900$ • The sum of the interest earned on the
$0.06x + 1000 - 0.10x = 900$ two accounts is $900.
$-0.04x + 1000 = 900$
$-0.04x = -100$
$x = 2500$

The amount invested at 6% is $2500.

Example 3

An investment counselor invested 75% of a client's money in a 9% annual simple interest money market fund. The remainder was invested in 7% annual simple interest government securities. Find the amount invested in each if the total annual interest earned is $3825.

You Try It 3

An investment of $5000 is made at an annual simple interest rate of 8%. How much additional money must be invested at 11% so that the total interest earned will be 9% of the total investment?

Strategy

• Amount invested: x
 Amount invested at 7%: $0.25x$
 Amount invested at 9%: $0.75x$

	Principal	Rate	Interest
Amount at 7%	$0.25x$	0.07	$0.0175x$
Amount at 9%	$0.75x$	0.09	$0.0675x$

• The sum of the interest earned by the two investments equals the total annual interest earned ($3825).

Your strategy

Solution

$0.0175x + 0.0675x = 3825$

$\qquad\qquad 0.085x = 3825$

$\qquad\qquad\qquad x = 45{,}000$

$0.25x = 0.25(45{,}000) = 11{,}250$

$0.75x = 0.75(45{,}000) = 33{,}750$

The amount invested at 7% is $11,250.
The amount invested at 9% is $33,750.

Your solution

$2500

Solution on p. S6

Objective D   *To solve uniform motion problems*..

A train that travels constantly in a straight line at 50 mph is in *uniform motion*. **Uniform motion** means that the speed or direction of an object does not change.

The solution of a uniform motion problem is based on the equation $d = rt$, where d is the distance traveled, r is the rate of travel, and t is the time traveled.

A train traveled at a speed of 55 mph for 3 h. The distance traveled by the train can be found by the equation $d = rt$.

$$d = rt$$
$$d = (55)(3)$$
$$d = 165$$

The distance traveled is 165 mi.

➡ A car leaves a town traveling at 40 mph. Two hours later, a second car leaves the same town, on the same road, traveling at 60 mph. In how many hours will the second car pass the first car?

> **Strategy for Solving a Uniform Motion Problem**
>
> 1. For each object, use the equation $d = rt$. Write a numerical or variable expression for the distance, rate, and time. The results can be recorded in a table.

The first car traveled 2 h longer than the second car.

First car $d = 40(t + 2)$

Unknown time for the second car: t
Time for the first car: $t + 2$

Second car $d = 60t$

	Rate, r	·	Time, t	=	Distance, d
First car	40	·	$t + 2$	=	$40(t + 2)$
Second car	60	·	t	=	$60t$

> 2. Determine how the distances traveled by the individual objects are related. For example, the total distance traveled by both objects may be known, or it may be known that the two objects traveled the same distance.

The two cars travel the same distance.

$$40(t + 2) = 60t$$
$$40t + 80 = 60t$$
$$80 = 20t$$
$$4 = t$$

The second car will pass the first car in 4 h.

Example 4

Two cars, one traveling 10 mph faster than the other, start at the same time from the same point and travel in opposite directions. In 3 h they are 300 mi apart. Find the rate of each car.

Strategy

* Rate of 1st car: r
* Rate of 2nd car: $r + 10$

	Rate	Time	Distance
1st car	r	3	$3r$
2nd car	$r + 10$	3	$3(r + 10)$

* The total distance traveled by the two cars is 300 mi.

Solution

$$3r + 3(r + 10) = 300$$
$$3r + 3r + 30 = 300$$
$$6r + 30 = 300$$
$$6r = 270$$
$$r = 45$$

$$r + 10 = 45 + 10 = 55$$

The first car is traveling 45 mph.
The second car is traveling 55 mph.

Example 5

How far can the members of a bicycling club ride out into the country at a speed of 12 mph and return over the same road at 8 mph if they travel a total of 10 h?

Strategy

* Time spent riding out: t
  Time spent riding back: $10 - t$

	Rate	Time	Distance
Out	12	t	$12t$
Back	8	$10 - t$	$8(10 - t)$

* The distance out equals the distance back.

Solution

$$12t = 8(10 - t)$$
$$12t = 80 - 8t$$
$$20t = 80$$
$$t = 4 \quad \text{(The time is 4 h.)}$$

The distance out $= 12t = 12(4) = 48$ mi.
The club can ride 48 mi into the country.

You Try It 4

Two trains, one traveling at twice the speed of the other, start at the same time on parallel tracks from stations that are 288 mi apart and travel toward each other. In 3 h, the trains pass each other. Find the rate of each train.

Your strategy

Your solution
32 mph; 64 mph

You Try It 5

A pilot flew out to a parcel of land and back in 5 h. The rate out was 150 mph, and the rate returning was 100 mph. How far away was the parcel of land?

Your strategy

Your solution
300 mi

Solutions on pp. S6–S7

2.3 Exercises

Objective A   Application Problems

1. An herbalist has 30 oz of herbs costing $2 per ounce. How many ounces of herbs costing $1 per ounce should be mixed with the 30 oz to produce a mixture costing $1.60 per ounce?
20 oz

2. The manager of a farmer's market has 500 lb of grain that costs $1.20 per pound. How many pounds of meal costing $.80 per pound should be mixed with the 500 lb of grain to produce a mixture that costs $1.05 per pound?
300 lb

3. Find the cost per pound of a meatloaf mixture made from 3 lb of ground beef costing $1.99 per pound and 1 lb of ground turkey costing $1.39 per pound.
$1.84

4. Find the cost per ounce of a sunscreen made from 100 oz of a lotion that costs $2.50 per ounce and 50 oz of a lotion that costs $4.00 per ounce.
$3

5. A snack food is made by mixing 5 lb of popcorn that costs $.80 per pound with caramel that costs $2.40 per pound. How much caramel is needed to make a mixture that costs $1.40 per pound?
3 lb

6. A wild birdseed mix is made by combining 100 lb of millet seed costing $.60 per pound with sunflower seeds costing $1.10 per pound. How many pounds of sunflower seeds are needed to make a mixture that costs $.70 per pound?
25 lb

7. Ten cups of a restaurant's house Italian dressing is made by blending olive oil costing $1.50 per cup with vinegar that costs $.25 per cup. How many cups of each are used if the cost of the blend is $.50 per cup?
olive oil: 2 c; vinegar: 8 c

8. A high-protein diet supplement that costs $6.75 per pound is mixed with a vitamin supplement that costs $3.25 per pound. How many pounds of each should be used to make 5 lb of a mixture that costs $4.65 per pound?
diet supplement: 2 lb; vitamin supplement: 3 lb

9. Find the cost per ounce of a mixture of 200 oz of a cologne that costs $5.50 per ounce and 500 oz of a cologne that costs $2.00 per ounce.
$3.00

10. Find the cost per pound of a trail mix made from 40 lb of raisins that cost $4.40 per pound and 100 lb of granola that costs $2.30 per pound.
$2.90

11. Twenty ounces of a platinum alloy that costs $220 per ounce are mixed with an alloy that costs $400 per ounce. How many ounces of the $400 alloy should be used to make an alloy that costs $300 per ounce?
16 oz

12. How many liters of a blue dye that costs $1.60 per liter must be mixed with 18 L of anil that costs $2.50 per liter to make a mixture that costs $1.90 per liter?
36 L

13. The manager of a specialty food store combined almonds that cost $4.50 per pound with walnuts that cost $2.50 per pound. How many pounds of each were used to make a 100-pound mixture that costs $3.24 per pound?
almonds: 37 lb; walnuts: 63 lb

14. A goldsmith combined an alloy that cost $4.30 per ounce with an alloy that cost $1.80 per ounce. How many ounces of each were used to make a mixture of 200 oz costing $2.50 per ounce?
$4.30 alloy: 56 oz; $1.80 alloy: 144 oz

15. Adult tickets for a play cost $6.00 and children's tickets cost $2.50. For one performance, 370 tickets were sold. Receipts for the performance were $1723. Find the number of adult tickets sold.
228 adult tickets

16. Tickets for a piano concert sold for $4.50 for each adult. Student tickets sold for $2.00 each. The total receipts for 1720 tickets were $5980. Find the number of adult tickets sold.
1016 adult tickets

17. Find the cost per pound of sugar-coated breakfast cereal made from 40 lb of sugar that costs $1.00 per pound and 120 lb of corn flakes that cost $.60 per pound.
$.70

18. Find the cost per pound of a coffee mixture made from 8 lb of coffee that costs $9.20 per pound and 12 lb of coffee that costs $5.50 per pound.
$6.98

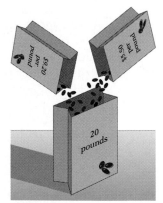

Objective B   *Application Problems*

19. Forty ounces of a 30% gold alloy are mixed with 60 oz of a 20% gold alloy. Find the percent concentration of the resulting gold alloy.
24%

20. One hundred ounces of juice that is 50% tomato juice are added to 200 oz of a vegetable juice that is 25% tomato juice. What is the percent concentration of tomato juice in the resulting mixture?
$33\frac{1}{3}$%

21. How many gallons of a 15% acid solution must be mixed with 5 gal of a 20% acid solution to make a 16% acid solution?
20 gal

22. How many pounds of a chicken feed that is 50% corn must be mixed with 400 lb of a feed that is 80% corn to make a chicken feed that is 75% corn?
80 lb

23. A rug is made by weaving 20 lb of yarn that is 50% wool with a yarn that is 25% wool. How many pounds of the yarn that is 25% wool are used if the finished rug is 35% wool?
30 lb

24. Five gallons of a dark green latex paint that is 20% yellow paint are combined with a lighter green latex paint that is 40% yellow paint. How many gallons of the lighter green paint must be used to create a green paint that is 25% yellow paint?
$1\frac{2}{3}$ % gal

25. How many gallons of a plant food that is 9% nitrogen must be combined with another plant food that is 25% nitrogen to make 10 gal of a solution that is 15% nitrogen?
6.25 gal

26. A chemist wants to make 50 ml of a 16% acid solution by mixing a 13% acid solution and an 18% acid solution. How many milliliters of each solution should the chemist use?
13% solution: 20 ml; 18% solution: 30 ml

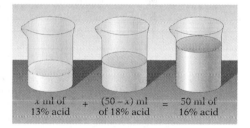

x ml of 13% acid + $(50 - x)$ ml of 18% acid = 50 ml of 16% acid

27. Five grams of sugar are added to a 45-gram serving of a breakfast cereal that is 10% sugar. What is the percent concentration of sugar in the resulting mixture?
19%

28. A goldsmith mixes 8 oz of a 30% gold alloy with 12 oz of a 25% gold alloy. What is the percent concentration of the resulting alloy?
27%

29. How many pounds of coffee that is 40% java beans must be mixed with 80 lb of coffee that is 30% java beans to make a coffee blend that is 32% java beans?
20 lb

30. The manager of a garden shop mixes grass seed that is 60% rye grass with 70 lb of grass seed that is 80% rye grass to make a mixture that is 74% rye grass. How much of the 60% rye grass is used?
30 lb

31. A hair dye is made by blending a 7% hydrogen peroxide solution and a 4% hydrogen peroxide solution. How many milliliters of each are used to make a 300-milliliter solution that is 5% hydrogen peroxide?
7% solution: 100 ml; 4% solution: 200 ml

32. A tea that is 20% jasmine is blended with a tea that is 15% jasmine. How many pounds of each tea are used to make 5 lb of tea that is 18% jasmine?
20% jasmine: 3 lb; 15% jasmine: 2 lb

33. How many ounces of pure chocolate must be added to 150 oz of chocolate topping that is 50% chocolate to make a topping that is 75% chocolate?
150 oz

34. How many ounces of pure bran flakes must be added to 50 oz of cereal that is 40% bran flakes to produce a mixture that is 50% bran flakes?
10 oz

35. Thirty ounces of pure silver are added to 50 oz of a silver alloy that is 20% silver. What is the percent concentration of the resulting alloy?
50%

36. A clothing manufacturer has some pure silk thread and some thread that is 85% silk. How many kilograms of each must be woven together to make 75 kg of cloth that is 96% silk?
pure silk: 55 kg; 85% silk: 20 kg

Objective C   *Application Problems*

37. An investment of $3000 is made at an annual simple interest rate of 5%. How much additional money must be invested at an annual simple interest rate of 9% so that the total annual interest earned is 7.5% of the total investment?
$5000

38. A total of $6000 is invested into two simple interest accounts. The annual simple interest rate on one account is 9%; on the second account, the annual simple interest rate is 6%. How much should be invested in each account so that both accounts earn the same amount of annual interest?
$2400 @ 9%; $3600 @ 6%

39. An engineer invested a portion of $15,000 in a 7% annual simple interest account and the remainder in a 6.5% annual simple interest government bond. The amount of interest earned for one year was $1020. How much was invested in each account?
$9000 @ 7%; $6000 @ 6.5%

40. An investment club invested part of $20,000 in preferred stock that pays 8% annual simple interest and the remainder in a municipal bond that pays 7% annual simple interest. The amount of interest earned each year is $1520. How much was invested in each account?
$12,000 @ 8%; $8000 @ 7%

41. A grocery checker deposited an amount of money into a high-yield mutual fund that returns a 9% annual simple interest rate. A second deposit, $2500 more than the first, was placed in a certificate of deposit that returns a 5% annual simple interest rate. The total interest earned on both investments for one year was $475. How much money was deposited in the mutual fund?
$2500

42. A deposit was made into a 7% annual simple interest account. Another deposit, $1500 less than the first deposit, was placed in a 9% annual simple interest certificate of deposit. The total interest earned on both accounts for one year was $505. How much money was deposited in the certificate of deposit?
$2500

43. A corporation gave a university $300,000 to support product safety research. The university deposited some of the money in a 10% simple interest account and the remainder in an 8.5% simple interest account. How much was deposited in each account if the annual interest earned is $28,500?
$200,000 @ 10%; $100,000 @ 8.5%

44. A financial consultant advises a client to invest part of $30,000 in municipal bonds that earn 6.5% annual simple interest and the remainder of the money in 8.5% corporate bonds. How much should be invested in each type of bond so that the total annual interest earned each year is $2190?
$18,000 @ 6.5%; $12,000 @ 8.5%

45. To provide for retirement income, an auto mechanic purchases a $5000 bond that earns 7.5% annual simple interest. How much money must be invested in additional bonds that have an interest rate of 8% so that the total annual interest earned from the two investments is $615?
$3000

46. The portfolio manager for an investment group invested $40,000 in a certificate of deposit that earns 7.25% annual simple interest. How much money must be invested in additional certificates that have an interest rate of 8.5% so that the total annual interest earned from the two investments is $5025?
$25,000

47. A charity deposited a total of $54,000 into two simple interest accounts. The annual simple interest rate on one account is 8%. The annual simple interest rate on the second account is 12%. How much was invested in each account if the total interest earned is 9% of the total investment?
$40,500 @ 8%; $13,500 @ 12%

48. A college sports foundation deposited a total of $24,000 into two simple interest accounts. The annual simple interest rate on one account is 7%. The annual simple interest rate on the second account is 11%. How much was invested in each account if the total annual interest earned is 10% of the total investment?
$6000 @ 7%; $18,000 @ 11%

49. An investment banker invested 55% of the bank's available cash in an account that earns 8.25% annual simple interest. The remainder of the cash was placed in an account that earns 10% annual simple interest. The interest earned in one year was $58,743.75. Find the total amount invested.
$650,000

50. A financial planner invested 40% of a client's cash account in preferred stock that earns 9% annual simple interest. The remainder of the client's cash was placed in treasury bonds that earn 7% annual interest. The total annual interest earned from the two investments was $2496. What was the total amount invested?
$32,000

51. The manager of a mutual fund placed 30% of the fund's available cash in a 6% simple interest account, 25% in 8% corporate bonds, and the remainder in a money market fund that earns 7.5% annual simple interest. The total annual interest from the investments was $35,875. What was the total amount invested?
$500,000

52. The manager of a trust decided to invest 30% of a client's cash in government bonds that earn 6.5% annual simple interest. Another 30% was placed in utility stocks that earn 7% annual simple interest. The remainder of the cash was placed in an account earning 8% annual simple interest. The total annual interest earned from the investments was $5437.50. What was the total amount invested?
$75,000

Objective D   *Application Problems*

53. Two small planes start from the same point and fly in opposite directions. The first plane is flying 25 mph slower than the second plane. In 2 h, the planes are 470 mi apart. Find the rate of each plane.
105 mph, 130 mph

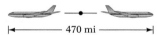
470 mi

54. Two cyclists start from the same point and ride in opposite directions. One cyclist rides twice as fast as the other. In 3 h, they are 81 mi apart. Find the rate of each cyclist.
9 mph, 18 mph

55. Two planes leave an airport at 8 A.M., one flying north at 480 km/h and the other flying south at 520 km/h. At what time will they be 3000 km apart?
11 A.M.

56. A long-distance runner started on a course running at an average speed of 6 mph. One-half hour later, a second runner began the same course at an average speed of 7 mph. How long after the second runner started will the second runner overtake the first runner?
3 h

TAKE NOTE

Any time an inequality is multiplied or divided by a negative number, the inequality symbol must be reversed. Compare the next two examples.

$2x < -4$ Divide each side
$\dfrac{2x}{2} < \dfrac{-4}{2}$ by *positive* 2. Inequality *is not* reversed.
$x < -2$

$-2x < 4$ Divide each
$\dfrac{-2x}{-2} > \dfrac{4}{-2}$ side by *negative* 2. Inequality *is* reversed.
$x > -2$

➡ Solve: $3x + 2 < -4$

$3x + 2 < -4$

$3x < -6$ • Subtract 2 from each side of the inequality.

$\dfrac{3x}{3} < \dfrac{-6}{3}$ • Divide each side of the inequality by the coefficient 3.

$x < -2$

The solution set is $\{x \mid x < -2\}$.

➡ Solve: $2x - 9 > 4x + 5$

$2x - 9 > 4x + 5$

$-2x - 9 > 5$ • Subtract 4x from each side of the inequality.

$-2x > 14$ • Add 9 to each side of the inequality.

$\dfrac{-2x}{-2} < \dfrac{14}{-2}$ • Divide each side of the inequality by the coefficient −2. Reverse the inequality symbol.

$x < -7$

The solution set is $\{x \mid x < -7\}$.

TAKE NOTE

Solving these inequalities is similar to solving the equations solved in Section 2 *except* that when you multiply or divide the inequality by a negative number, you must reverse the inequality symbol.

➡ Solve: $5(x - 2) \geq 9x - 3(2x - 4)$

$5(x - 2) \geq 9x - 3(2x - 4)$

$5x - 10 \geq 9x - 6x + 12$ • Use the Distributive Property to remove parentheses.

$5x - 10 \geq 3x + 12$ • Combine like terms.

$2x - 10 \geq 12$ • Subtract 3x from each side of the inequality.

$2x \geq 22$ • Add 10 to each side of the inequality.

$\dfrac{2x}{2} \geq \dfrac{22}{2}$ • Divide each side of the inequality by the coefficient 2.

$x \geq 11$

The solution set is $\{x \mid x \geq 11\}$.

Example 1

Solve: $x + 3 > 4x + 6$

Solution

$x + 3 > 4x + 6$

$-3x + 3 > 6$ • Subtract 4x from each side.

$-3x > 3$ • Subtract 3 from each side.

$\dfrac{-3x}{-3} < \dfrac{3}{-3}$ • Divide each side by −3.

$x < -1$

The solution set is $\{x \mid x < -1\}$.

You Try It 1

Solve: $2x - 1 < 6x + 7$

Your solution

$\{x \mid x > -2\}$

Solution on p. S7

Example 2 Solve:
$$3x - 5 \le 3 - 2(3x + 1)$$

Solution
$$3x - 5 \le 3 - 2(3x + 1)$$
$$3x - 5 \le 3 - 6x - 2$$
$$3x - 5 \le 1 - 6x$$
$$9x - 5 \le 1$$
$$9x \le 6$$
$$\frac{9x}{9} \le \frac{6}{9}$$
$$x \le \frac{2}{3}$$
$$\left\{ x \mid x \le \frac{2}{3} \right\}$$

You Try It 2 Solve:
$$5x - 2 \le 4 - 3(x - 2)$$

Your solution
$$\left\{ x \mid x \le \frac{3}{2} \right\}$$

Solution on p. S7

Objective B **To solve a compound inequality** ....

INSTRUCTOR NOTE

The compound inequalities in this section prepare the student to solve absolute value inequalities, which are given in the next section.

A **compound inequality** is formed by joining two inequalities with a connective word such as *and* or *or*. The inequalities at the right are compound inequalities.

$$2x < 4 \text{ and } 3x - 2 > -8$$

$$2x + 3 > 5 \text{ or } x + 2 < 5$$

The solution set of a compound inequality with the connective word *and* is the set of all elements that appear in the solution sets of both inequalities. Therefore, it is the intersection of the solution sets of the two inequalities.

➡ Solve: $2x < 6$ and $3x + 2 > -4$

$$
\begin{array}{lll}
2x < 6 & \text{and} & 3x + 2 > -4 \\
x < 3 & & 3x > -6 \\
\{x \mid x < 3\} & & x > -2 \\
& & \{x \mid x > -2\}
\end{array}
$$
• Solve each inequality.

TAKE NOTE

The intersection
$\{x \mid x < 3\} \cap \{x \mid x > -2\}$
can be written
$\{x \mid x > -2 \text{ and } x < 3\}$.
However, it is more commonly written $\{x \mid -2 < x < 3\}$. This is read "the set of all x such that x is greater than -2 *and* less than 3."

The solution of a compound inequality with *and* is the intersection of the solution sets of the two inequalities.

$$\{x \mid x < 3\} \cap \{x \mid x > -2\} = \{x \mid -2 < x < 3\}$$

➡ Solve: $-3 < 2x + 1 < 5$

This inequality is equivalent to the compound inequality shown at the right.

$$-3 < 2x + 1 \text{ and } 2x + 1 < 5$$

$$
\begin{array}{lll}
-3 < 2x + 1 & \text{and} & 2x + 1 < 5 \\
-4 < 2x & & 2x < 4 \\
-2 < x & & x < 2 \\
\{x \mid x > -2\} & & \{x \mid x < 2\}
\end{array}
$$
• Solve each inequality.

$$\{x \mid x > -2\} \cap \{x \mid x < 2\} = \{x \mid -2 < x < 2\}$$

There is an alternative method for solving the inequality in the last example.

➡ Solve: $-3 < 2x + 1 < 5$

$$-3 < 2x + 1 < 5$$

$$-3 - 1 < 2x + 1 - 1 < 5 - 1$$ • **Subtract 1 from each of the three parts of the inequality.**

$$-4 < 2x < 4$$

$$\frac{-4}{2} < \frac{2x}{2} < \frac{4}{2}$$ • **Divide each of the three parts of the inequality by the coefficient 2.**

$$-2 < x < 2$$

The solution set is $\{x | -2 < x < 2\}$.

The solution set of a compound inequality with the connective word *or* is the union of the solution sets of the two inequalities.

➡ Solve: $2x + 3 > 7$ or $4x - 1 < 3$

$$2x + 3 > 7 \quad \text{or} \quad 4x - 1 < 3$$

$$2x > 4 \qquad\qquad 4x < 4$$ • **Solve each inequality.**

$$x > 2 \qquad\qquad x < 1$$

$$\{x | x > 2\} \qquad \{x | x < 1\}$$

$$\{x | x > 2\} \cup \{x | x < 1\} = \{x | x > 2 \text{ or } x < 1\}$$ • **Find the union of the solution sets.**

Example 3

Solve: $1 < 3x - 5 < 4$

Solution

$$1 < 3x - 5 < 4$$

$$1 + 5 < 3x - 5 + 5 < 4 + 5$$

$$6 < 3x < 9$$

$$\frac{6}{3} < \frac{3x}{3} < \frac{9}{3}$$

$$2 < x < 3$$

$$\{x | 2 < x < 3\}$$

You Try It 3

Solve: $-2 \le 5x + 3 \le 13$

Your solution

$\{x | -1 \le x \le 2\}$

Example 4

Solve: $11 - 2x > -3$ and $7 - 3x < 4$

Solution

$$11 - 2x > -3 \quad \text{and} \quad 7 - 3x < 4$$

$$-2x > -14 \qquad\qquad -3x < -3$$

$$x < 7 \qquad\qquad\qquad x > 1$$

$$\{x | x < 7\} \qquad\qquad \{x | x > 1\}$$

$$\{x | x < 7\} \cap \{x | x > 1\} = \{x | 1 < x < 7\}$$

You Try It 4

Solve: $2 - 3x > 11$ or $5 + 2x > 7$

Your solution

$\{x | x < -3 \text{ or } x > 1\}$

Solutions on p. S7

Objective C   To solve application problems..

Example 5

A rectangle is 10 ft wide and $(2x + 4)$ ft long. Express as an integer the maximum length of the rectangle when the area is less than 200 ft². (The area of a rectangle is equal to its length times its width.)

Strategy

(2x + 4) ft

10 ft

To find the maximum length:

• Replace the variables in the area formula by the given values and solve for x.

• Replace the variable in the expression $2x + 4$ with the value found for x.

Solution

Length times width	is less than	200 ft²

$$(2x + 4)10 < 200$$
$$20x + 40 < 200$$
$$20x + 40 - 40 < 200 - 40$$
$$20x < 160$$
$$\frac{20x}{20} < \frac{160}{20}$$
$$x < 8$$

The length is $(2x + 4)$ ft. Because $x < 8$, $2x + 4 < 2(8) + 4 = 20$. Therefore, the length is less than 20 ft.

The maximum length is 19 ft.

You Try It 5

Company A rents cars for $8 a day and 10¢ for every mile driven. Company B rents cars for $10 a day and 8¢ per mile driven. You want to rent a car for one week. What is the maximum number of miles you can drive a Company A car if it is to cost you less than a Company B car?

Your strategy

Your solution
699 mi

Solution on p. S7

2.4 Exercises

· ·

Objective A

Solve.

1. $x - 3 < 2$
$\{x \mid x < 5\}$

2. $x + 4 \geq 2$
$\{x \mid x \geq -2\}$

3. $4x \leq 8$
$\{x \mid x \leq 2\}$

4. $6x > 12$
$\{x \mid x > 2\}$

5. $-2x > 8$
$\{x \mid x < -4\}$

6. $-3x \leq -9$
$\{x \mid x \geq 3\}$

7. $3x - 1 > 2x + 2$
$\{x \mid x > 3\}$

8. $5x + 2 \geq 4x - 1$
$\{x \mid x \geq -3\}$

9. $2x - 1 > 7$
$\{x \mid x > 4\}$

10. $3x + 2 < 8$
$\{x \mid x < 2\}$

11. $5x - 2 \leq 8$
$\{x \mid x \leq 2\}$

12. $4x + 3 \leq -1$
$\{x \mid x \leq -1\}$

13. $6x + 3 > 4x - 1$
$\{x \mid x > -2\}$

14. $7x + 4 < 2x - 6$
$\{x \mid x < -2\}$

15. $8x + 1 \geq 2x + 13$
$\{x \mid x \geq 2\}$

16. $5x - 4 < 2x + 5$
$\{x \mid x < 3\}$

17. $4 - 3x < 10$
$\{x \mid x > -2\}$

18. $2 - 5x > 7$
$\{x \mid x < -1\}$

19. $7 - 2x \geq 1$
$\{x \mid x \leq 3\}$

20. $3 - 5x \leq 18$
$\{x \mid x \geq -3\}$

21. $-3 - 4x > -11$
$\{x \mid x < 2\}$

22. $-2 - x < 7$
$\{x \mid x > -9\}$

23. $4x - 2 < x - 11$
$\{x \mid x < -3\}$

24. $6x + 5 \leq x - 10$
$\{x \mid x \leq -3\}$

25. $x + 7 \geq 4x - 8$
$\{x \mid x \leq 5\}$

26. $3x + 1 \leq 7x - 15$
$\{x \mid x \geq 4\}$

27. $3x + 2 \leq 7x + 4$
$\left\{ x \mid x \geq -\dfrac{1}{2} \right\}$

28. $3x - 5 \geq -2x + 5$
$\{x \mid x \geq 2\}$

29. $\dfrac{3}{5}x - 2 < \dfrac{3}{10} - x$
$\left\{ x \mid x < \dfrac{23}{16} \right\}$

30. $\dfrac{5}{6}x - \dfrac{1}{6} < x - 4$
$\{x \mid x > 23\}$

31. $\dfrac{2}{3}x - \dfrac{3}{2} < \dfrac{7}{6} - \dfrac{1}{3}x$

$\left\{ x \mid x < \dfrac{8}{3} \right\}$

32. $\dfrac{7}{12}x - \dfrac{3}{2} < \dfrac{2}{3}x + \dfrac{5}{6}$

$\{ x \mid x > -28 \}$

33. $\dfrac{1}{2}x - \dfrac{3}{4} < \dfrac{7}{4}x - 2$

$\{ x \mid x > 1 \}$

34. $6 - 2(x - 4) \le 2x + 10$

$\{ x \mid x \ge 1 \}$

35. $4(2x - 1) > 3x - 2(3x - 5)$

$\left\{ x \mid x > \dfrac{14}{11} \right\}$

36. $2(1 - 3x) - 4 > 10 + 3(1 - x)$

$\{ x \mid x < -5 \}$

37. $2 - 5(x + 1) \ge 3(x - 1) - 8$

$\{ x \mid x \le 1 \}$

38. $7 + 2(4 - x) < 9 - 3(6 + x)$

$\{ x \mid x < -24 \}$

39. $3(4x + 3) \le 7 - 4(x - 2)$

$\left\{ x \mid x \le \dfrac{3}{8} \right\}$

40. $2 - 2(7 - 2x) < 3(3 - x)$

$\{ x \mid x < 3 \}$

41. $3 + 2(x + 5) \ge x + 5(x + 1) + 1$

$\left\{ x \mid x \le \dfrac{7}{4} \right\}$

42. $10 - 13(2 - x) < 5(3x - 2)$

$\{ x \mid x > -3 \}$

43. $3 - 4(x + 2) \le 6 + 4(2x + 1)$

$\left\{ x \mid x \ge -\dfrac{5}{4} \right\}$

44. $3x - 2(3x - 5) \le 2 - 5(x - 4)$
$\{ x \mid x \le 6 \}$

45. $12 - 2(3x - 2) \ge 5x - 2(5 - x)$
$\{ x \mid x \le 2 \}$

Objective B

Solve.

46. $3x < 6$ and $x + 2 > 1$
$\{ x \mid -1 < x < 2 \}$

47. $x - 3 \le 1$ and $2x \ge -4$
$\{ x \mid -2 \le x \le 4 \}$

48. $x + 2 \ge 5$ or $3x \le 3$
$\{ x \mid x \ge 3 \text{ or } x \le 1 \}$

49. $2x < 6$ or $x - 4 > 1$
$\{ x \mid x < 3 \text{ or } x > 5 \}$

50. $-2x > -8$ and $-3x < 6$

$\{ x \mid -2 < x < 4 \}$

51. $\dfrac{1}{2}x > -2$ and $5x < 10$

$\{ x \mid -4 < x < 2 \}$

52. $\frac{1}{3}x < -1$ or $2x > 0$
$\{x \mid x < -3 \text{ or } x > 0\}$

53. $\frac{2}{3}x > 4$ or $2x < -8$
$\{x \mid x > 6 \text{ or } x < -4\}$

54. $x + 4 \geq 5$ and $2x \geq 6$
$\{x \mid x \geq 3\}$

55. $3x < -9$ and $x - 2 < 2$
$\{x \mid x < -3\}$

56. $-5x > 10$ and $x + 1 > 6$
$\varnothing$

57. $7x < 14$ and $1 - x < 4$
$\{x \mid -3 < x < 2\}$

58. $2x - 3 > 1$ and $3x - 1 < 2$
$\varnothing$

59. $4x + 1 < 5$ and $4x + 7 > -1$
$\{x \mid -2 < x < 1\}$

60. $3x + 7 < 10$ or $2x - 1 > 5$
$\{x \mid x < 1 \text{ or } x > 3\}$

61. $6x - 2 < -14$ or $5x + 1 > 11$
$\{x \mid x < -2 \text{ or } x > 2\}$

62. $-5 < 3x + 4 < 16$
$\{x \mid -3 < x < 4\}$

63. $5 < 4x - 3 < 21$
$\{x \mid 2 < x < 6\}$

64. $0 < 2x - 6 < 4$
$\{x \mid 3 < x < 5\}$

65. $-2 < 3x + 7 < 1$
$\{x \mid -3 < x < -2\}$

66. $4x - 1 > 11$ or $4x - 1 \leq -11$
$\left\{x \mid x > 3 \text{ or } x \leq -\frac{5}{2}\right\}$

67. $3x - 5 > 10$ or $3x - 5 < -10$
$\left\{x \mid x > 5 \text{ or } x < -\frac{5}{3}\right\}$

68. $2x - 3 \geq 5$ and $3x - 1 > 11$
$\{x \mid x > 4\}$

69. $6x - 2 < 5$ or $7x - 5 < 16$
$\{x \mid x < 3\}$

70. $9x - 2 < 7$ and $3x - 5 > 10$
$\varnothing$

71. $8x + 2 \leq -14$ and $4x - 2 > 10$
$\varnothing$

72. $3x - 11 < 4$ or $4x + 9 \geq 1$
The set of real numbers

73. $5x + 12 \geq 2$ or $7x - 1 \leq 13$
The set of real numbers

74. $-6 \le 5x + 14 \le 24$

$\{x \mid -4 \le x \le 2\}$

75. $3 \le 7x - 14 \le 31$

$\left\{ x \mid \dfrac{17}{7} \le x \le \dfrac{45}{7} \right\}$

76. $3 - 2x > 7$ and $5x + 2 > -18$

$\{x \mid -4 < x < -2\}$

77. $1 - 3x < 16$ and $1 - 3x > -16$

$\left\{ x \mid -5 < x < \dfrac{17}{3} \right\}$

78. $5 - 4x > 21$ or $7x - 2 > 19$

$\{x \mid x < -4 \text{ or } x > 3\}$

79. $6x + 5 < -1$ or $1 - 2x < 7$

the set of real numbers

80. $3 - 7x \le 31$ and $5 - 4x > 1$

$\{x \mid -4 \le x < 1\}$

81. $9 - x \ge 7$ and $9 - 2x < 3$

$\varnothing$

Objective C   *Application Problems*

82. Five times the difference between a number and two is greater than the quotient of two times the number and three. Find the smallest integer that will satisfy the inequality.

3

83. Two times the difference between a number and eight is less than or equal to five times the sum of the number and four. Find the smallest number that will satisfy the inequality.

-12

84. The length of a rectangle is 2 ft more than four times the width. Express as an integer the maximum width of the rectangle when the perimeter is less than 34 ft.

2 ft

85. The length of a rectangle is 5 cm less than twice the width. Express as an integer the maximum width of the rectangle when the perimeter is less than 60 cm.

11 cm

86. In 1997, the computer service America Online offered its customers a rate of $19.95 per month for unlimited use or $4.95 per month with 3 free hours plus $2.50 for each hour thereafter. How many hours can you use this service per month if the second plan is to cost you less than the first?

less than 9 h

87. TopPage advertises local paging service for $6.95 per month for up to 400 pages and $.10 per page thereafter. A competitor advertises service for $3.95 per month for up to 400 pages and $.15 per page thereafter. For what number of pages per month is the TopPage plan less expensive?
more than 460 pages

88. Suppose PayRite Rental Cars rents compact cars for $32 per day with unlimited mileage and Otto Rentals offers compact cars for $19.99 per day but charges $.19 for each mile beyond 100 mi driven per day. You want to rent a car for one week. How many miles can you drive during the week if Otto Rentals is to be less expensive than PayRite?
less than 1143 mi

89. During a weekday, to call a city 40 mi away from a certain pay phone costs $.70 for the first 3 min and $.15 for each additional minute. If you use a calling card, there is a $.35 fee and then the rates are $.196 for the first minute and $.126 for each additional minute. How long must a call be for it to be cheaper to pay with coins rather than a calling card?
7 min or less

90. The temperature range for a week was between 14°F and 77°F. Find the temperature range in Celsius degrees. $F = \frac{9}{5}C + 32$

$-10° < C < 25°$

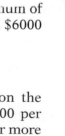

91. The temperature range for a week in a mountain town was between 0°C and 30°C. Find the temperature range in Fahrenheit degrees.
$C = \frac{5(F - 32)}{9}$
$32° < F < 86°$

92. You are a sales account executive earning $1200 per month plus 6% commission on the amount of sales. Your goal is to earn a minimum of $6000 per month. What amount of sales will enable you to earn $6000 or more per month?
$80,000 or more

93. George Stoia earns $1000 per month plus 5% commission on the amount of sales. George's goal is to earn a minimum of $3200 per month. What amount of sales will enable George to earn $3200 or more per month?
$44,000 or more

94. Heritage National Bank offers two different checking accounts. The first charges $3 per month and $.50 per check after the first 10 checks. The second account charges $8 per month with unlimited check writing. How many checks can be written per month if the first account is to be less expensive than the second account?
less than 20 checks

95. Glendale Federal Bank offers a checking account to small businesses. The charge is $8 per month plus $.12 per check after the first 100 checks. A competitor is offering an account for $5 per month plus $.15 per check after the first 100 checks. If a business chooses the first account, how many checks does the business write monthly if it is assumed that the first account will cost less than the competitor's account?
more than 200 checks

96. An average score of 90 or above in a history class receives an A grade. You have grades of 95, 89, and 81 on three exams. Find the range of scores on the fourth exam that will give you an A grade for the course.
$95 \leq N \leq 100$

97. An average of 70 to 79 in a mathematics class receives a C grade. A student has grades of 56, 91, 83, and 62 on four tests. Find the range of scores on the fifth test that will give the student a C for the course.
$58 \leq N \leq 100$

98. Grade A hamburger cannot contain more than 20% fat. How much fat can a butcher mix with 300 lb of lean meat to meet the 20% requirement?
maximum amount: 75 lb

99. A shuttle service taking skiers to a ski area charges $8 per person each way. Four skiers are debating whether to take the shuttle bus or rent a car for $45 plus $.25 per mile. The skiers will share the cost of the car, and they want the least expensive method of transportation. How far away is the ski area if they choose the shuttle service?
more than 38 mi away

APPLYING THE CONCEPTS

100. Determine whether the statement is always true, sometimes true, or never true, given that a, b, and c are real numbers.
a. If $a > b$, then $-a > -b$.   never true
b. If $a < b$, then $ac < bc$.   sometimes true
c. If $a > b$, then $a + c > b + c$.   always true
d. If $a \neq 0$, $b \neq 0$, and $a > b$, then $\frac{1}{a} > \frac{1}{b}$.   sometimes true

101. Use the roster method to list the set of positive integers that are solutions of the inequality $7 - 2b \leq 15 - 5b$.
$\{1, 2\}$

102. Determine the solution set of $2 - 3(x + 4) < 5 - 3x$.
$\{x \mid x \in \text{real numbers}\}$

103. Determine the solution set of $3x + 2(x - 1) > 5(x + 1)$.
$\varnothing$

104. In your own words, state the Multiplication Property of Inequalities.

2.5 Absolute Value Equations and Inequalities

Objective A   *To solve an absolute value equation* ....

The **absolute value** of a number is its distance from zero on the number line. Distance is always a positive number or zero. Therefore, the absolute value of a number is always a positive number or zero.

The distance from 0 to 3 or from 0 to -3 is 3 units.

$|3| = 3 \qquad |-3| = 3$

An equation that contains an absolute value symbol is called an **absolute value equation**. The solution of an absolute value equation is based on the following property:

If $a \geq 0$ and $|x| = a$, then $x = a$ or $x = -a$.

For instance, given $|x| = 3$, then $x = 3$ or $x = -3$, because $|3| = 3$ and $|-3| = 3$.

➡ Solve: $|x + 2| = 8$

$$|x + 2| = 8$$
$$x + 2 = 8 \qquad x + 2 = -8$$
$$x = 6 \qquad x = -10$$

- Remove the absolute value sign and rewrite as two equations.
- Solve each equation.

Check:

$|x + 2| = 8$		$|x + 2| = 8$	
$|6 + 2|$	8	$|-10 + 2|$	8
$|8|$	8	$|-8|$	8
$8 = 8$		$8 = 8$	

The solutions are 6 and -10.

➡ Solve: $|5 - 3x| - 8 = -4$

$$|5 - 3x| - 8 = -4$$
$$|5 - 3x| = 4$$
$$5 - 3x = 4 \qquad 5 - 3x = -4$$
$$-3x = -1 \qquad -3x = -9$$
$$x = \frac{1}{3} \qquad x = 3$$

- Solve for the absolute value.
- Remove the absolute value sign and rewrite as two equations.
- Solve each equation.

Check:

$|5 - 3x| - 8 = -4$		$|5 - 3x| - 8 = -4$	
$\left|5 - 3\left(\frac{1}{3}\right)\right| - 8$	-4	$|5 - 3(3)| - 8$	-4
$|5 - 1| - 8$	-4	$|5 - 9| - 8$	-4
$4 - 8$	-4	$4 - 8$	-4
$-4 = -4$		$-4 = -4$	

The solutions are $\frac{1}{3}$ and 3.

Example 1
Solve: $|2 - x| = 12$

Solution
$$|2 - x| = 12$$

$2 - x = 12$	$2 - x = -12$
$-x = 10$	$-x = -14$
$x = -10$	$x = 14$

The solutions are -10 and 14.

You Try It 1
Solve: $|2x - 3| = 5$

Your solution
$4, -1$

Example 2
Solve: $3 - |2x - 4| = -5$

Solution
$$3 - |2x - 4| = -5$$
$$-|2x - 4| = -8$$
$$|2x - 4| = 8$$

$2x - 4 = 8$	$2x - 4 = -8$
$2x = 12$	$2x = -4$
$x = 6$	$x = -2$

The solutions are 6 and -2.

You Try It 2
Solve: $5 - |3x + 5| = 3$

Your solution
$-1, -\dfrac{7}{3}$

Solutions on p. S7

Objective B   To solve an absolute value inequality ....

Recall that absolute value represents the distance between two points. For example, the solutions of the absolute value equation $|x - 1| = 3$ are the numbers whose distance from 1 is 3. Therefore, the solutions are -2 and 4.

The solutions of the absolute value inequality $|x - 1| < 3$ are the numbers whose distance from 1 is less than 3. Therefore, the solutions are the numbers greater than -2 and less than 4. The solution set is $\{x \mid -2 < x < 4\}$.

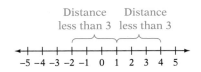

To solve an absolute value inequality of the form $|ax + b| < c$, solve the equivalent compound inequality $-c < ax + b < c$.

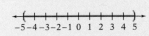
➡ Solve: $|3x - 1| < 5$

$$|3x - 1| < 5$$
$$-5 < 3x - 1 < 5$$ • Solve the equivalent compound inequality.
$$-5 + 1 < 3x - 1 + 1 < 5 + 1$$
$$-4 < 3x < 6$$
$$\frac{-4}{3} < \frac{3x}{3} < \frac{6}{3}$$
$$-\frac{4}{3} < x < 2$$
$$\left\{ x \mid -\frac{4}{3} < x < 2 \right\}$$

The solutions of the absolute value inequality $|x + 1| > 2$ are the numbers whose distance from -1 is greater than 2. Therefore, the solutions are the numbers that are less than -3 or greater than 1. The solution set of $|x + 1| > 2$ is $\{x \mid x < -3 \text{ or } x > 1\}$.

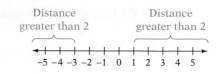

Distance greater than 2   Distance greater than 2

TAKE NOTE

Because the absolute value of $3 - 2x$ is greater than 1, the number $3 - 2x$ is more than 1 unit from 0 on the number line.

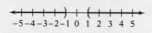

Therefore, $3 - 2x$ is less than -1 or greater than 1.

To solve an absolute value inequality of the form $|ax + b| > c$, solve the equivalent compound inequality $ax + b < -c$ or $ax + b > c$.

➡ Solve: $|3 - 2x| > 1$

$$3 - 2x < -1 \quad \text{or} \quad 3 - 2x > 1$$
$$-2x < -4 \qquad\qquad -2x > -2$$
$$x > 2 \qquad\qquad\quad x < 1$$
$$\{x \mid x > 2\} \qquad\quad \{x \mid x < 1\}$$

- Solve each inequality.

$$\{x \mid x > 2\} \cup \{x \mid x < 1\}$$
$$= \{x \mid x > 2 \text{ or } x < 1\}$$

- Find the union of the solution sets of the two inequalities.

Example 3 Solve: $|4x - 3| < 5$

Solution Solve the equivalent compound inequality.

$$-5 < 4x - 3 < 5$$
$$-5 + 3 < 4x - 3 + 3 < 5 + 3$$
$$-2 < 4x < 8$$
$$\frac{-2}{4} < \frac{4x}{4} < \frac{8}{4}$$
$$-\frac{1}{2} < x < 2$$
$$\left\{ x \mid -\frac{1}{2} < x < 2 \right\}$$

You Try It 3 Solve: $|3x + 2| < 8$

Your solution
$$\left\{ x \mid -\frac{10}{3} < x < 2 \right\}$$

Example 4 Solve: $|2x - 1| > 7$

Solution Solve the equivalent compound inequality.

$$2x - 1 < -7 \quad \text{or} \quad 2x - 1 > 7$$
$$2x < -6 \qquad\qquad 2x > 8$$
$$x < -3 \qquad\qquad x > 4$$
$$\{x \mid x < -3\} \qquad \{x \mid x > 4\}$$
$$\{x \mid x < -3\} \cup \{x \mid x > 4\}$$
$$= \{x \mid x < -3 \text{ or } x > 4\}$$

You Try It 4 Solve: $|5x + 3| > 8$

Your solution
$$\left\{ x \mid x < -\frac{11}{5} \text{ or } x > 1 \right\}$$

Solutions on pp. S7–S8

Objective C   *To solve application problems* ....

The **tolerance** of a component, or part, is the acceptable amount by which the component may vary from a given measurement. For example, the diameter of a piston may vary from the given measurement of 9 cm by 0.001 cm. This is written 9 cm ± 0.001 cm and is read "9 centimeters plus or minus 0.001 centimeter." The maximum diameter, or **upper limit**, of the piston is 9 cm + 0.001 cm = 9.001 cm. The minimum diameter, or **lower limit**, is 9 cm − 0.001 cm = 8.999 cm.

The lower and upper limits of the diameter of the piston could also be found by solving the absolute value inequality $|d - 9| \le 0.001$, where d is the diameter of the piston.

$$|d - 9| \le 0.001$$

$$-0.001 \le d - 9 \le 0.001$$

$$-0.001 + 9 \le d - 9 + 9 \le 0.001 + 9$$

$$8.999 \le d \le 9.001$$

The lower and upper limits of the diameter of the piston are 8.999 cm and 9.001 cm.

Example 5

A doctor has prescribed 2 cc of medication for a patient. The tolerance is 0.03 cc. (In the medical field, cubic centimeter is usually abbreviated cc.) Find the lower and upper limits of the amount of medication to be given.

Strategy

Let p represent the prescribed amount of medication, T the tolerance, and m the given amount of medication. Solve the absolute value inequality $|m - p| \le T$ for m.

Solution

$|m - p| \le T$
$|m - 2| \le 0.03$

$$-0.03 \le m - 2 \le 0.03$$
$$-0.03 + 2 \le m - 2 + 2 \le 0.03 + 2$$
$$1.97 \le m \le 2.03$$

The lower and upper limits of the amount of medication to be given are 1.97 cc and 2.03 cc.

You Try It 5

A machinist must make a bushing that has a diameter of 2.55 in. The tolerance of the bushing is 0.003 in. Find the lower and upper limits of the diameter of the bushing.

Your strategy

Your solution
2.547 in., 2.553 in.

Solution on p. S8

2.5 Exercises

Objective A

Solve.

1. $|x| = 7$
7, −7

2. $|a| = 2$
2, −2

3. $|b| = 4$
4, −4

4. $|c| = 12$
12, −12

5. $|-y| = 6$
6, −6

6. $|-t| = 3$
3, −3

7. $|-a| = 7$
7, −7

8. $|-x| = 3$
3, −3

9. $|x| = -4$
no solution

10. $|y| = -3$
no solution

11. $|-t| = -3$
no solution

12. $|-y| = -2$
no solution

13. $|x + 2| = 3$
1, −5

14. $|x + 5| = 2$
−3, −7

15. $|y - 5| = 3$
8, 2

16. $|y - 8| = 4$
12, 4

17. $|a - 2| = 0$
2

18. $|a + 7| = 0$
7

19. $|x - 2| = -4$
no solution

20. $|x + 8| = -2$
no solution

21. $|3 - 4x| = 9$
$-\dfrac{3}{2}, 3$

22. $|2 - 5x| = 3$
$-\dfrac{1}{5}, 1$

23. $|2x - 3| = 0$
$\dfrac{3}{2}$

24. $|5x + 5| = 0$
−1

25. $|3x - 2| = -4$
no solution

26. $|2x + 5| = -2$
no solution

27. $|x - 2| - 2 = 3$
7, −3

28. $|x - 9| - 3 = 2$
14, 4

29. $|3a + 2| - 4 = 4$
$2, -\dfrac{10}{3}$

30. $|2a + 9| + 4 = 5$
−4, −5

31. $|2 - y| + 3 = 4$
1, 3

32. $|8 - y| - 3 = 1$
4, 12

33. $|2x - 3| + 3 = 3$
$\dfrac{3}{2}$

34. $|4x - 7| - 5 = -5$
$\dfrac{7}{4}$

35. $|2x - 3| + 4 = -4$
no solution

36. $|3x - 2| + 1 = -1$
no solution

37. $|6x - 5| - 2 = 4$

$\dfrac{11}{6}, -\dfrac{1}{6}$

38. $|4b + 3| - 2 = 7$

$\dfrac{3}{2}, -3$

39. $|3t + 2| + 3 = 4$

$-\dfrac{1}{3}, -1$

40. $|5x - 2| + 5 = 7$

$\dfrac{4}{5}, 0$

41. $3 - |x - 4| = 5$

no solution

42. $2 - |x - 5| = 4$

no solution

43. $8 - |2x - 3| = 5$

$3, 0$

44. $8 - |3x + 2| = 3$

$1, -\dfrac{7}{3}$

45. $|2 - 3x| + 7 = 2$

no solution

46. $|1 - 5a| + 2 = 3$

$0, \dfrac{2}{5}$

47. $|8 - 3x| - 3 = 2$

$1, \dfrac{13}{3}$

48. $|6 - 5b| - 4 = 3$

$-\dfrac{1}{5}, \dfrac{13}{5}$

49. $|2x - 8| + 12 = 2$

no solution

50. $|3x - 4| + 8 = 3$

no solution

51. $2 + |3x - 4| = 5$

$\dfrac{7}{3}, \dfrac{1}{3}$

52. $5 + |2x + 1| = 8$

$1, -2$

53. $5 - |2x + 1| = 5$

$-\dfrac{1}{2}$

54. $3 - |5x + 3| = 3$

$-\dfrac{3}{5}$

55. $6 - |2x + 4| = 3$

$-\dfrac{1}{2}, -\dfrac{7}{2}$

56. $8 - |3x - 2| = 5$

$\dfrac{5}{3}, -\dfrac{1}{3}$

57. $8 - |1 - 3x| = -1$

$-\dfrac{8}{3}, \dfrac{10}{3}$

58. $3 - |3 - 5x| = -2$

$-\dfrac{2}{5}, \dfrac{8}{5}$

59. $5 + |2 - x| = 3$

no solution

60. $6 + |3 - 2x| = 2$

no solution

Objective B

Solve.

61. $|x| > 3$

$\{x | x > 3 \text{ or } x < -3\}$

62. $|x| < 5$

$\{x | -5 < x < 5\}$

63. $|x + 1| > 2$

$\{x | x > 1 \text{ or } x < -3\}$

64. $|x - 2| > 1$

$\{x | x > 3 \text{ or } x < 1\}$

65. $|x - 5| \leq 1$

$\{x | 4 \leq x \leq 6\}$

66. $|x - 4| \leq 3$

$\{x | 1 \leq x \leq 7\}$

67. $|2 - x| \geq 3$

$\{x | x \geq 5 \text{ or } x \leq -1\}$

68. $|3 - x| \geq 2$

$\{x | x \leq 1 \text{ or } x \geq 5\}$

69. $|2x + 1| < 5$

$\{x | -3 < x < 2\}$

70. $|3x - 2| < 4$

$\left\{ x \middle| -\dfrac{2}{3} < x < 2 \right\}$

71. $|5x + 2| > 12$

$\left\{ x \middle| x > 2 \text{ or } x < -\dfrac{14}{5} \right\}$

72. $|7x - 1| > 13$

$\left\{ x \middle| x > 2 \text{ or } x < -\dfrac{12}{7} \right\}$

73. $|4x - 3| \leq -2$

$\varnothing$

74. $|5x + 1| \leq -4$

$\varnothing$

75. $|2x + 7| > -5$

the set of real numbers

76. $|3x - 1| > -4$

the set of real numbers

77. $|4 - 3x| \geq 5$

$\left\{ x \middle| x \leq -\dfrac{1}{3} \text{ or } x \geq 3 \right\}$

78. $|7 - 2x| > 9$

$\{ x | x < -1 \text{ or } x > 8 \}$

79. $|5 - 4x| \leq 13$

$\left\{ x \middle| -2 \leq x \leq \dfrac{9}{2} \right\}$

80. $|3 - 7x| < 17$

$\left\{ x \middle| -2 < x < \dfrac{20}{7} \right\}$

81. $|6 - 3x| \leq 0$

$\{ x | x = 2 \}$

82. $|10 - 5x| \geq 0$

the set of real numbers

83. $|2 - 9x| > 20$

$\left\{ x \middle| x < -2 \text{ or } x > \dfrac{22}{9} \right\}$

84. $|5x - 1| < 16$

$\left\{ x \middle| -3 < x < \dfrac{17}{5} \right\}$

85. $|2x - 3| + 2 < 8$

$\left\{ x \middle| -\dfrac{3}{2} < x < \dfrac{9}{2} \right\}$

86. $|3x - 5| + 1 < 7$

$\left\{ x \middle| -\dfrac{1}{3} < x < \dfrac{11}{3} \right\}$

87. $|2 - 5x| - 4 > -2$

$\left\{ x \middle| x < 0 \text{ or } x > \dfrac{4}{5} \right\}$

88. $|4 - 2x| - 9 > -3$

$\{ x | x < -1 \text{ or } x > 5 \}$

89. $8 - |2x - 5| < 3$

$\{ x | x > 5 \text{ or } x < 0 \}$

90. $12 - |3x - 4| > 7$

$\left\{ x \middle| -\dfrac{1}{3} < x < 3 \right\}$

Objective C   *Application Problems*

91. The diameter of a bushing is 1.75 in. The bushing has a tolerance of 0.008 in. Find the lower and upper limits of the diameter of the bushing.
1.742 in.; 1.758 in.

92. A machinist must make a bushing that has a tolerance of 0.004 in. The diameter of the bushing is 3.48 in. Find the lower and upper limits of the diameter of the bushing.
3.476 in.; 3.484 in.

93. An electric motor is designed to run on 220 volts plus or minus 25 volts. Find the lower and upper limits of voltage on which the motor will run.
195 volts; 245 volts

94. A power strip is utilized on a computer to prevent the loss of programming by electrical surges. The power strip is designed to allow 110 volts plus or minus 16.5 volts. Find the lower and upper limits of voltage to the computer.

93.5 volts; 126.5 volts

95. A piston rod for an automobile is $9\frac{5}{8}$ in. long with a tolerance of $\frac{1}{32}$ in. Find the lower and upper limits of the length of the piston rod.

$9\frac{19}{32}$ in.; $9\frac{21}{32}$ in.

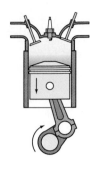

96. A piston rod for an automobile is $9\frac{3}{8}$ in. long with a tolerance of $\frac{1}{64}$ in. Find the lower and upper limits of the length of the piston rod.

$9\frac{23}{64}$ in.; $9\frac{25}{64}$ in.

The tolerance of the resistors used in electronics is given as a percent. Use your calculator for the following exercises.

97. Find the lower and upper limits of a 29,000-ohm resistor with a 2% tolerance.

28,420 ohms; 29,580 ohms

98. Find the lower and upper limits of a 15,000-ohm resistor with a 10% tolerance.

13,500 ohms; 16,500 ohms

99. Find the lower and upper limits of a 25,000-ohm resistor with a 5% tolerance.

23,750 ohms; 26,250 ohms

100. Find the lower and upper limits of a 56-ohm resistor with a 5% tolerance.

53.2 ohms; 58.8 ohms

APPLYING THE CONCEPTS

101. For what values of the variable is the equation true? Write the solution set in set-builder notation.
   a. $|x + 3| = x + 3$ **b.** $|a - 4| = 4 - a$
   a. $\{x \mid x \geq -3\}$ **b.** $\{a \mid a \leq 4\}$

102. Write an absolute value inequality to represent all real numbers within 5 units of 2.
   $|x - 2| < 5$

103. Replace the question mark with $\leq$, $\geq$, or $=$.
   a. $|x + y| \; ? \; |x| + |y|$ $\leq$ **b.** $|x - y| \; ? \; |x| - |y|$ $\geq$

   c. $||x| - |y|| \; ? \; |x| - |y|$ $\geq$ **d.** $\left|\frac{x}{y}\right| \; ? \; \frac{|x|}{|y|}, y \neq 0$ $=$

   e. $|xy| \; ? \; |x||y|$ $=$

Focus on Problem Solving

From Concrete to Abstract

In your study of algebra, you will find that the problems are less concrete than those you studied in arithmetic. Problems that are concrete provide information pertaining to a specific instance. Algebra is more abstract. Abstract problems are theoretical; they are stated without reference to a specific instance. Let's look at an example of an abstract problem.

How many minutes are in h hours?

A strategy that can be used to solve this problem is to solve the same problem after substituting a number for the variable.

How many minutes are in 5 hours?

You know that there are 60 minutes in 1 hour. To find the number of minutes in 5 hours, multiply 5 by 60.

$$60 \cdot 5 = 300 \qquad \text{There are 300 minutes in 5 hours.}$$

Use the same procedure to find the number of minutes in h hours: multiply h by 60.

$$60 \cdot h = 60h \qquad \text{There are } 60h \text{ minutes in } h \text{ hours.}$$

This problem might be taken a step further:

If you walk one mile in x minutes, how far can you walk in h hours?

Consider the same problem using numbers in place of the variables.

If you walk one mile in 20 minutes, how far can you walk in 3 hours?

To solve this problem, you need to calculate the number of minutes in 3 hours (multiply 3 by 60), and divide the result by the number of minutes it takes to walk one mile (20 minutes).

$$\frac{60 \cdot 3}{20} = \frac{180}{20} = 9 \qquad \text{If you walk one mile in 20 minutes, you can walk 9 miles in 3 hours.}$$

Use the same procedure to solve the related abstract problem. Calculate the number of minutes in h hours (multiply h by 60), and divide the result by the number of minutes it takes to walk one mile (x minutes).

$$\frac{60 \cdot h}{x} = \frac{60h}{x} \qquad \text{If you walk one mile in } x \text{ minutes, you can walk } \frac{60h}{x} \text{ miles in } h \text{ hours.}$$

At the heart of the study of algebra is the use of variables. It is the variables in the problems above that make them abstract. But it is variables that allow us to generalize situations and state rules about mathematics.

Try each of the following problems.

1. How many hours are in d days?
2. You earn d dollars an hour. What are your wages for working h hours?

3. If p is the price of one share of stock, how many shares can you purchase with d dollars?

4. A company pays a television station d dollars to air a commercial lasting s seconds. What is the cost per second?

5. After every v videotape rentals, you are entitled to one free rental. You have rented t tapes, where $t < v$. How many more do you need to rent before you are entitled to a free rental?

6. Your car gets g miles per gallon. How many gallons of gasoline does your car consume traveling t miles?

7. If you drink j ounces of juice each day, how many days will q quarts of the juice last?

8. A TV station has m minutes of commercials each hour. How many ads lasting s seconds each can be sold for each hour of programming?

9. A factory worker can assemble p products in m minutes. How many products can the factory worker assemble in h hours?

10. If one candy bar costs n nickels, how many candy bars can be purchased with q quarters?

| Projects and Group Activities

Prime and Composite Numbers

A **prime number** is a natural number greater than 1 whose only natural-number factors are itself and 1. The number 11 is a prime number because the only natural-number factors of 11 are 11 and 1.

Eratosthenes, a Greek philosopher and astronomer who lived from 270 to 190 B.C., devised a method of identifying prime numbers. It is called the **Sieve of Eratosthenes**. The procedure is illustrated below.

1̸	②	③	4̸	⑤	6̸	⑦	8̸	9̸	1̸0̸
⑪	1̸2̸	⑬	1̸4̸	1̸5̸	1̸6̸	⑰	1̸8̸	⑲	2̸0̸
2̸1̸	2̸2̸	㉓	2̸4̸	2̸5̸	2̸6̸	2̸7̸	2̸8̸	㉙	3̸0̸
㉛	3̸2̸	3̸3̸	3̸4̸	3̸5̸	3̸6̸	㊲	3̸8̸	3̸9̸	4̸0̸
㊶	4̸2̸	㊸	4̸4̸	4̸5̸	4̸6̸	㊼	4̸8̸	4̸9̸	5̸0̸
5̸1̸	5̸2̸	㊿	5̸4̸	5̸5̸	5̸6̸	5̸7̸	5̸8̸	㊾	6̸0̸
㊿	6̸2̸	6̸3̸	6̸4̸	6̸5̸	6̸6̸	㊿	6̸8̸	6̸9̸	7̸0̸
㊼	7̸2̸	㊼	7̸4̸	7̸5̸	7̸6̸	7̸7̸	7̸8̸	㊿	8̸0̸
8̸1̸	8̸2̸	㊿	8̸4̸	8̸5̸	8̸6̸	8̸7̸	8̸8̸	㊿	9̸0̸
9̸1̸	9̸2̸	9̸3̸	9̸4̸	9̸5̸	9̸6̸	㊾	9̸8̸	9̸9̸	1̸0̸0̸

List all the natural numbers from 1 to 100. Cross out the number 1, because it is not a prime number. The number 2 is prime; circle it. Cross out all the other multiples of 2 (4, 6, 8, ...), because they are not prime. The number 3 is prime; circle it. Cross out all the other multiples of 3 (6, 9, 12, ...) that are not already crossed out. The number 4, the next consecutive number in the list, has already been crossed out. The number 5 is prime; circle it. Cross out all the other multiples of 5 that are not already crossed out. Continue in this manner until all the prime numbers less than 100 are circled.

A **composite number** is a natural number greater than 1 that has a natural-number factor other than itself and 1. The number 21 is a composite number because it has factors of 3 and 7. All the numbers crossed out in the preceding table, except the number 1, are composite numbers.

1. Use the Sieve of Eratosthenes to find the prime numbers between 100 and 200.

2. How many prime numbers are even numbers?

3. Find the "twin primes" between 1 and 200. Twin primes are two prime numbers whose difference is 2. For instance, 3 and 5 are twin primes; 5 and 7 are also twin primes.

4. **a.** List two prime numbers that are consecutive natural numbers.
   b. Can there be any other pairs of prime numbers that are consecutive natural numbers?

5. Some primes are the sum of a square and 1. For example, $5 = 2^2 + 1$. Find another prime p such that $p = n^2 + 1$, where n is a natural number.

6. Find a prime number p such that $p = n^2 - 1$, where n is a natural number.

7. **a.** 4! (which is read "4 factorial") is equal to $4 \cdot 3 \cdot 2 \cdot 1$. Show that $4! + 2$, $4! + 3$, and $4! + 4$ are all composite numbers.
   b. 5! (which is read "5 factorial") is equal to $5 \cdot 4 \cdot 3 \cdot 2 \cdot 1$. Will $5! + 2$, $5! + 3$, $5! + 4$, and $5! + 5$ generate four consecutive composite numbers?
   c. Use the notation 6! to represent a list of five consecutive composite numbers.

Investigation into Operations with Even and Odd Integers

Complete each statement with the word *even* or *odd*.

1. If k is an odd integer, then $k + 1$ is an _____ integer.

2. If k is an odd integer, then $k - 2$ is an _____ integer.

3. If n is an integer, then $2n$ is an _____ integer.

4. If m and n are even integers, then $m - n$ is an _____ integer.

5. If m and n are even integers, then mn is an _____ integer.

6. If m and n are odd integers, then $m + n$ is an _____ integer.

7. If m and n are odd integers, then $m - n$ is an _____ integer.

8. If m and n are odd integers, then mn is an _____ integer.

9. If m is an even integer and n is an odd integer, then $m - n$ is an _____ integer.

10. If m is an even integer and n is an odd integer, than $m + n$ is an _____ integer.

Chapter Summary

Key Words An *equation* expresses the equality of two mathematical expressions. A *solution* of an equation is a number that, when substituted for the variable, results in a true equation. To *solve* an equation means to find a solution of the equation.

An *inequality* is an expression that contains the symbol $>$, $<$, $\geq$, or $\leq$. The *solution set of an inequality* is a set of numbers, each element of which, when substituted for the variable, results in a true inequality.

A *compound inequality* is formed by joining two inequalities with a connective word such as *and* or *or*.

The *absolute value* of a number is its distance from zero on the number line. An equation that contains an absolute value symbol is an *absolute value equation*.

Essential Rules

Addition Property of Equations If $a = b$, then $a + c = b + c$.

Multiplication Property of Equations If $a = b$ and $c \neq 0$, then $ac = bc$.

Addition Property of Inequalities If $a > b$, then $a + c > b + c$.
If $a < b$, then $a + c < b + c$.

Multiplication Property of Inequalities **Rule 1**
If $a > b$ and $c > 0$, then $ac > bc$.
If $a < b$ and $c > 0$, then $ac < bc$.
Rule 2
If $a > b$ and $c < 0$, then $ac < bc$.
If $a < b$ and $c < 0$, then $ac > bc$.

Basic Percent Equation Percent $\cdot$ base = amount
$$P \cdot B = A$$

Value Mixture Equation Amount $\cdot$ unit cost = value
$$A \cdot C = V$$

Percent Mixture Equation Amount of solution $\cdot$ percent of concentration $=$ quantity of substance
$$A \cdot r = Q$$

Annual Simple Interest Equation Principal $\cdot$ interest rate $=$ interest earned
$$P \cdot r = I$$

Uniform Motion Equation Rate $\cdot$ time = distance
$$r \cdot t = d$$

To solve an absolute value inequality of the form $|ax + b| < c$, solve the equivalent compound inequality $-c < ax + b < c$.

To solve an absolute value inequality of the form $|ax + b| > c$, solve the equivalent compound inequality $ax + b < -c$ or $ax + b > c$.

Chapter Review

1. Is 3 a solution of $5x - 2 = 4x + 5$?
no   [2.1A]

2. Solve: $x + 3 = 24$
21   [2.1B]

3. Solve: $\dfrac{3}{5}a = 12$
20   [2.1C]

4. Solve: $-4x - 2 = 10$
-3 [2.2A]

5. Solve: $14x + 7x + 8 = -10$
$-\dfrac{6}{7}$ [2.2A]

6. Solve: $12y - 1 = 3y + 2$
$\dfrac{1}{3}$ [2.2B]

7. Solve: $-6x + 16 = -2x$
4   [2.2B]

8. Solve: $6x + 3(2x - 1) = -27$
-2 [2.2C]

9. Solve: $x + 5(3x - 20) = 10(x - 4)$
10   [2.2C]

10. Solve: $3x - 7 > -2$
$\left\{ x \mid x > \dfrac{5}{3} \right\}$ [2.4A]

11. Solve: $4 - 3(x + 2) < 2(2x + 3) - 1$
$\{x \mid x > -1\}$ [2.4A]

12. Solve: $3x < 4$ and $x + 2 > -1$
$\left\{ x \mid -3 < x < \dfrac{4}{3} \right\}$ [2.4B]

13. Solve: $3x - 2 > x - 4$ or $7x - 5 < 3x + 3$
$\{x \mid x \in$ real numbers$\}$ [2.4B]

14. Solve: $|3 - 5x| = 12$
$-\dfrac{9}{5}, 3$ [2.5A]

15. Solve: $|x - 4| - 8 = -3$
$9, -1$ [2.5A]

16. Solve: $|2x - 5| < 3$
$\{x \mid 1 < x < 4\}$ [2.5B]

17. Solve: $|4x - 5| \geq 3$
$\left\{ x \mid x \geq 2 \text{ or } x \leq \dfrac{2}{3} \right\}$ [2.5B]

18. 30 is what percent of 12?
250%   [2.1D]

19. $\dfrac{1}{2}\%$ of what is 8?

1600   [2.1D]

20. Translate "four less than the product of five and a number is sixteen" into an equation and solve.

$5x - 4 = 16$; $x = 4$ [2.2D]

21. The sum of two numbers is twenty-one. Three times the smaller number is two less than twice the larger number. Translate into an equation. Then find the two numbers.

$3x = 2(21 - x) - 2$; 8, 13   [2.2D]

22. An airline knowingly overbooks certain flights by selling 18% more tickets than there are available seats. How many tickets would this airline sell for an airplane that has 150 seats?   177 tickets   [2.1D]

23. An auto manufacturer offers a rebate of $1000 on each car sold by a dealership. A customer bought a car from the dealership for $16,500. What percent of the cost is the $1000 rebate? Round to the nearest tenth of a percent.   6.1%   [2.1D]

24. A health food store combined cranberry juice that costs $1.79 per quart with apple juice that costs $1.19 per quart. How many quarts of each were used to make 10 qt of a cranapple juice mixture that costs $1.61 per quart?
7 qt of cranberry juice; 3 qt of apple juice   [2.3A]

25. Find the cost per ounce of a sun screen made from 100 oz of a lotion that costs $2.50 per ounce and 50 oz of a lotion that costs $4.00 per ounce. $3   [2.3A]

26. A dairy mixed 5 gal of cream that is 30% butterfat with 8 gal of milk that is 4% butterfat. What is the percent concentration of butterfat in the resulting mixture?   14%   [2.3B]

27. An alloy containing 30% tin is mixed with an alloy containing 70% tin. How many pounds of each were used to make 500 lb of an alloy containing 40% tin?   375 lb of the 30% tin alloy; 125 lb of the 70% tin alloy   [2.3B]

28. An investment banker invested 45% of the bank's available cash in an account earning 8.5% annual simple interest. The remainder of the cash was placed in an account earning 10% annual simple interest. The interest earned in one year was $41,962.50. What was the total amount invested?
$450,000   [2.3C]

29. A club treasurer deposited $2400 into two simple interest accounts. On one account the annual simple interest rate was 6.75%. The annual simple interest rate on the other account was 9.45%. How much was deposited in each account if both accounts earned the same amount of interest?
$1400 @ 6.75%; $1000 @ 9.45%   [2.3C]

30. A jet plane traveling at 600 mph overtakes a propeller-driven plane that had a 2-hour headstart. The propeller-driven plane is traveling at 200 mph. How far from the starting point does the jet overtake the propeller-driven plane?
600 mi   [2.3D]

31. A bus traveled on a straight road for 2 h at an average speed that was 20 mph faster than it traveled on a winding road. The time spent on the winding road was 3 h. Find the average speed on the winding road if the total trip was 200 mi.   32 mph   [2.3D]

32. An average score of 80 to 90 in a psychology class receives a B grade. A student has grades of 92, 66, 72, and 88 on four tests. Find the range of scores on the fifth test that will earn the student a B for the course.
$82 \le x \le 100$ [2.4C]

33. A doctor has prescribed 2 cc of medication for a patient. The tolerance is 0.25 cc. Find the lower and upper limits of the amount of medication to be given.   1.75 cc and 2.25 cc   [2.5C]

Chapter Test

1. Solve: $3x - 2 = 5x + 8$

-5 [2.2B]

2. Solve: $x - 3 - -8$

-5 [2.1B]

3. Solve: $3x - 5 = -14$

-3 [2.2A]

4. Solve: $4 - 2(3 - 2x) = 2(5 - x)$

2 [2.2C]

5. Is -2 a solution of $x^2 - 3x = 2x - 6$?

no   [2.1A]

6. Solve: $7 - 4x = -13$

5 [2.2A]

7. What is 0.5% of 8?

0.04   [2.1D]

8. Solve: $5x - 2(4x - 3) = 6x + 9$

$-\dfrac{1}{3}$ [2.2C]

9. Solve: $5x + 3 - 7x = 2x - 5$

2 [2.2B]

10. Solve: $\dfrac{3}{4}x = -9$

-12 [2.1C]

11. Solve: $3x - 2 \geq 6x + 7$

$\{x \mid x \leq -3\}$ [2.4A]

12. Solve: $4 - 3(x + 2) < 2(2x + 3) - 1$

$\{x \mid x > -1\}$ [2.4A]

13. Solve: $4x - 1 > 5$ or $2 - 3x < 8$

$\{x \mid x > -2\}$ [2.4B]

14. Solve: $4 - 3x \geq 7$ and $2x + 3 \geq 7$

$\varnothing$ [2.4B]

15. Solve: $|3 - 5x| = 12$

$3, -\dfrac{9}{5}$ [2.5A]

16. Solve: $2 - |2x - 5| = -7$

$7, -2$ [2.5A]

17. Solve: $|3x - 5| \leq 4$

$\left\{x \mid \dfrac{1}{3} \leq x \leq 3\right\}$ [2.5B]

18. Solve: $|4x - 3| > 5$

$\left\{x \mid x > 2 \text{ or } x < -\dfrac{1}{2}\right\}$ [2.5B]

19. The sum of two integers is fifteen. Eight times the smaller integer is one less than three times the larger integer. Find the integers.

4, 11   [2.2D]

20. A butcher combines 100 lb of hamburger that costs $1.60 per pound with 60 lb of hamburger that costs $3.20 per pound. Find the cost of the hamburger mixture.

$2.20 per pound   [2.3A]

21. How many gallons of water must be mixed with 5 gal of a 20% salt solution to make a 16% salt solution?

1.25 gal   [2.3B]

22. A trust administrator divided $20,000 between two accounts. One account earns an annual simple interest rate of 3%, and the second account earns an annual simple interest rate of 7%. The total annual income from the two accounts is $1200. How much is invested in each account?

$5000 @ 3%; $15,000 @ 7%   [2.3C]

23. A cross-country skier leaves a camp to explore a wilderness area. Two hours later a friend leaves the camp in a snowmobile, traveling 4 mph faster than the skier, and meets the skier 1 h later. Find the rate of the snowmobile.

6 mph   [2.3D]

24. Gambelli Agency rents cars for $12 a day and 10¢ for every mile driven. McDougal Rental rents cars for $24 a day with unlimited mileage. How many miles a day can you drive a Gambelli Agency car if it is to cost you less than a McDougal Rental car?

less than 120 mi   [2.4C]

25. A machinist must make a bushing that has a tolerance of 0.002 in. The diameter of the bushing is 2.65 in. Find the lower and upper limits of the diameter of the bushing.

2.648 in.; 2.652 in.   [2.5C]

Cumulative Review

1. Subtract: $-6 - (-20) - 8$

6   [1.1C]

2. Multiply: $(-2)(-6)(-4)$

-48 [1.1D]

3. Subtract: $-\dfrac{5}{6} - \left(-\dfrac{7}{16}\right)$

$-\dfrac{19}{48}$ [1.2C]

4. Simplify: $-4^2 \cdot \left(-\dfrac{3}{2}\right)^3$

54   [1.2E]

5. Simplify: $\dfrac{5}{8} - \left(\dfrac{1}{2}\right)^2 \div \left(\dfrac{1}{3} - \dfrac{3}{4}\right)$

$\dfrac{49}{40}$ [1.3A]

6. Evaluate $3(a - c) - 2ab$ when $a = 2$, $b = 3$, and $c = -4$.

6   [1.4A]

7. Simplify: $3x - 8x + (-12x)$

$-17x$ [1.4B]

8. Simplify: $2a - (-b) - 7a - 5b$

$-5a - 4b$ [1.4B]

9. Simplify: $(16x)\left(\dfrac{1}{8}\right)$

$2x$ [1.4C]

10. Simplify: $-4(-9y)$

$36y$ [1.4C]

11. Simplify: $-2(-x^2 - 3x + 2)$

$2x^2 + 6x - 4$ [1.4D]

12. Simplify: $-2(x - 3) + 2(4 - x)$

$-4x + 14$ [1.4D]

13. Simplify: $-3[2x - 4(x - 3)] + 2$

$6x - 34$ [1.4D]

14. Find $A \cap B$ given $A = \{-4, -2, 0, 2\}$ and $B = \{-4, 0, 4, 8\}$.

$A \cap B = \{-4, 0\}$ [1.5B]

15. Graph: $\{x \mid x < 3\} \cap \{x \mid x > -2\}$

[1.5C]

16. Is -3 a solution of $x^2 + 6x + 9 = x + 3$?

yes   [2.1A]

17. Solve: $\dfrac{3}{5}x = -15$

-25 [2.1C]

18. Solve: $7x - 8 = -29$

-3 [2.2A]

19. Solve: $13 - 9x = -14$

    3   [2.2A]

20. Solve: $5x - 8 = 12x + 13$

    −3   [2.2B]

21. Solve: $11 - 4x = 2x + 8$

    $\dfrac{1}{2}$ [2.2B]

22. Solve: $8x - 3(4x - 5) = -2x - 11$

    13   [2.2C]

23. Solve: $3 - 2(2x - 1) \geq 3(2x - 2) + 1$

    $\{x \,|\, x \leq 1\}$ [2.4A]

24. Solve: $3x + 2 \leq 5$ and $x + 5 \geq 1$

    $\{x \,|\, -4 \leq x \leq 1\}$ [2.4B]

25. Solve: $|3 - 2x| = 5$

    −1, 4   [2.5A]

26. Solve: $|3x - 1| > 5$

    $\left\{x \,\middle|\, x > 2 \text{ or } x < -\dfrac{4}{3}\right\}$ [2.5B]

27. Write 55% as a fraction.

    $\dfrac{11}{20}$ [1.2B]

28. Write 1.03 as a percent.

    103%   [1.2B]

29. 25% of what number is 30?

    120   [2.1D]

30. Translate "the sum of six times a number and thirteen is five less than the product of three and the number" into an equation and solve.

    $6x + 13 = 3x - 5$; −6   [2.2D]

31. How many pounds of an oat flour that costs $.80 per pound must be mixed with 40 lb of a wheat flour that costs $.50 per pound to make a blend that costs $.60 per pound?

    20 lb   [2.3A]

32. How many grams of pure gold must be added to 100 g of a 20% gold alloy to make an alloy that is 36% gold?

    25 g   [2.3B]

33. A sprinter ran to the end of a track at an average rate of 8 m/s and then jogged back to the starting point at an average rate of 3 m/s. The sprinter took 55 s to run to the end of the track and jog back. Find the length of the track.

    120 m   [2.3D]

CHAPTER

3 Geometry

Architects use geometric objects to design skyscrapers, homes, and shopping malls. By understanding the properties of these geometric objects, an architect can combine various geometric figures to create structures that are functional and attractive. For example, the architect I. M. Pei used a series of glass pyramids to create a new entrance to the Louvre in Paris, France.

Objectives

Section 3.1
To solve problems involving lines and angles
To solve problems involving angles formed by
   intersecting lines
To solve problems involving the angles of a triangle

Section 3.2
To solve problems involving the perimeter of
   geometric figures
To solve problems involving the area of
   geometric figures

Section 3.3
To solve problems involving the volume of a solid
To solve problems involving the surface area of a solid

Mobius Strips and Klein Bottles

Some geometric shapes have very unusual characteristics. Among these figures are Mobius strips and Klein bottles.

A Mobius strip is formed by taking a long strip of paper and twisting it one-half turn. The resulting figure is called a "one-sided" surface. It is one-sided in the sense that if you tried to paint the strip in one continuous motion beginning at one spot, the entire surface would be painted the same color, unlike a strip that has not been twisted.

Another remarkable result of its being one-sided can be demonstrated by making a Mobius strip and sealing the junction with tape. Now cut the strip by cutting along the center of the strip. Try this; you will be amazed at the result.

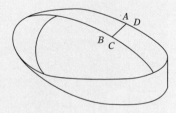

A second interesting surface is called a Klein bottle, which is a one-sided surface with no edges and no "inside" or "outside." A Klein bottle is formed by pulling the small open end of a tapering tube through the side of the tube and joining the ends of the small open end to the ends of the larger open end.

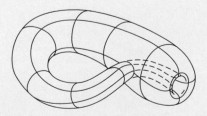

3.1 Introduction to Geometry

Objective A   *To solve problems involving lines and angles* ....

The word *geometry* comes from the Greek words for "earth" and "measure." The original purpose of geometry was to measure land. Today geometry is used in many fields, such as physics, medicine, and geology, and is applied in such areas as mechanical drawing and astronomy. Geometric forms are also used in art and design.

Three basic concepts of geometry are the point, line, and plane. A **point** is symbolized by drawing a dot. A **line** is determined by two distinct points and extends indefinitely in both directions, as the arrows on the line shown at the right indicate. This line contains points *A* and *B* and is represented by $\overleftrightarrow{AB}$. A line can also be represented by a single letter, such as ℓ.

A **ray** starts at a point and extends indefinitely in *one* direction. The point at which a ray starts is called the **endpoint** of the ray. The ray shown at the right is denoted by $\overrightarrow{AB}$. Point *A* is the endpoint of the ray.

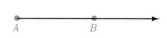

A **line segment** is part of a line and has two endpoints. The line segment shown at the right is denoted by $\overline{AB}$.

The distance between the endpoints of $\overline{AC}$ is denoted by *AC*. If *B* is a point on $\overline{AC}$, then *AC* (the distance from *A* to *C*) is the sum of *AB* (the distance from *A* to *B*) and *BC* (the distance from *B* to *C*).

$$AC = AB + BC$$

➡ Given *AB* = 22 cm and *AC* = 31 cm, find *BC*.

$AC = AB + BC$ • Write an equation for the distances between points on the line segment.

$31 = 22 + BC$ • Substitute the given distances for **AB** and **AC** into the equation.

$9 = BC$ • Solve for **BC**.

$BC = 9$ cm

In this section we will be discussing figures that lie in a plane. A **plane** is a flat surface and can be pictured as a table top or blackboard that extends in all directions. Figures that lie in a plane are called **plane figures**.

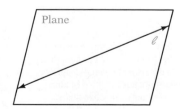

Lines in a plane can be intersecting or parallel. **Intersecting lines** cross at a point in the plane. **Parallel lines** never meet. The distance between them is always the same.

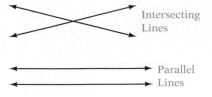

The symbol ∥ means "is parallel to." In the figure at the right, $j \parallel k$ and $\overline{AB} \parallel \overline{CD}$. Note that j contains $\overline{AB}$ and k contains $\overline{CD}$. Parallel lines contain parallel line segments.

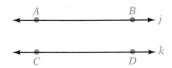

An **angle** is formed by two rays with the same endpoint. The **vertex** of the angle is the point at which the two rays meet. The rays are called the **sides** of the angle.

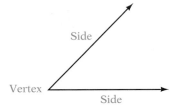

If A and C are points on rays r_1 and r_2, and B is the vertex, then the angle is called $\angle B$ or $\angle ABC$, where $\angle$ is the symbol for angle. Note that either the angle is named by the vertex, or the vertex is the second point listed when the angle is named by giving three points. $\angle ABC$ could also be called $\angle CBA$.

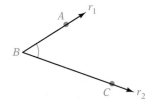

An angle can also be named by a variable written between the rays close to the vertex. In the figure at the right, $\angle x = \angle QRS$ and $\angle y = \angle SRT$. Note that in this figure, more than two rays meet at R. In this case, the vertex cannot be used to name an angle.

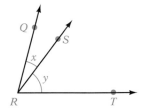

POINT OF INTEREST

The first woman mathematician for whom documented evidence exists is Hypatia (370–415). She lived in Alexandria, Egypt, and lectured at the Museum, the forerunner of our modern university. She made important contributions in mathematics, astronomy, and philosophy.

An angle is measured in **degrees**. The symbol for degrees is a small raised circle, °. Probably because early Babylonians believed that Earth revolves around the sun in approximately 360 days, the angle formed by a circle has a measure of 360° (360 degrees).

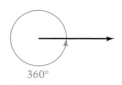

A **protractor** is used to measure an angle. Place the center of the protractor at the vertex of the angle with the edge of the protractor along a side of the angle. The angle shown in the figure below measure 58°.

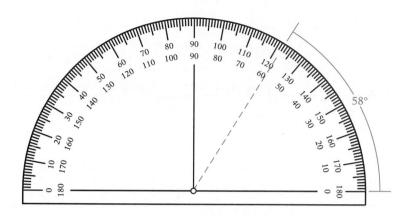

TAKE NOTE

The corner of a page of this book is a good example of a 90° angle.

A 90° angle is called a **right angle**. The symbol ∟ represents a right angle.

90°

Perpendicular lines are intersecting lines that form right angles.

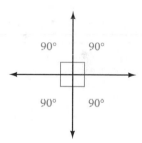

90° | 90°
90° | 90°

The symbol ⊥ means "is perpendicular to." In the figure at the right, $p \perp q$ and $\overline{AB} \perp \overline{CD}$. Note that line p contains $\overline{AB}$ and line q contains $\overline{CD}$. Perpendicular lines contain perpendicular line segments.

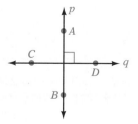

Complementary angles are two angles whose measures have the sum 90°.

$$\angle A + \angle B = 70° + 20° = 90°$$

$\angle A$ and $\angle B$ are complementary angles.

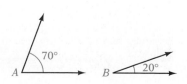

A 180° angle is called a **straight angle**.

$\angle AOB$ is a straight angle.

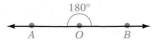

Supplementary angles are two angles whose measures have the sum $180°$.

$$\angle A + \angle B = 130° + 50° = 180°$$

$\angle A$ and $\angle B$ are supplementary angles.

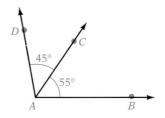

An **acute angle** is an angle whose measure is between 0° and 90°. $\angle B$ above is an acute angle. An **obtuse angle** is an angle whose measure is between 90° and 180°. $\angle A$ above is an obtuse angle.

Two angles that share a common side are **adjacent angles**. In the figure at the right, $\angle DAC$ and $\angle CAB$ are adjacent angles. $\angle DAC = 45°$ and $\angle CAB = 55°$.

$$\angle DAB = \angle DAC + \angle CAB$$
$$= 45° + 55° = 100°$$

➡ In the figure at the right, $\angle EDG = 80°$. $\angle FDG$ is three times the measure of $\angle EDF$. Find the measure of $\angle EDF$.

Let x = the measure of $\angle EDG$. Then $3x$ = the measure of $\angle FDG$. Write an equation and solve for x, the measure of $\angle EDF$.

$$\angle EDF + \angle FDG = \angle EDG$$
$$x + 3x = 80$$
$$4x = 80$$
$$x = 20$$

$\angle EDF = 20°$

Example 1
Given $MN = 15$ mm, $NO = 18$ mm, and $MP = 48$ mm, find OP.

Solution
$$MN + NO + OP = MP$$
$$15 + 18 + OP = 48$$
$$33 + OP = 48$$
$$OP = 15$$
$OP = 15$ mm

You Try It 1
Given $QR = 24$ cm, $ST = 17$ cm, and $QT = 62$ cm, find RS.

Your solution
21 cm

Solution on p. S8

Example 2
Given $XY = 9$ m and YZ is twice XY, find XZ.

Solution
$XZ = XY + YZ$
$XZ = XY + 2(XY)$
$XZ = 9 + 2(9)$
$XZ = 9 + 18$
$XZ = 27$

$XZ = 27$ m

You Try It 2
Given $BC = 16$ ft and $AB = \frac{1}{4}(BC)$, find AC.

Your solution
20 ft

Example 3
Find the complement of a 38° angle.

Strategy
Complementary angles are two angles whose sum is 90°. To find the complement, let x represent the complement of a 38° angle. Write an equation and solve for x.

Solution
$x + 38° = 90°$
$\quad\ x = 52°$

The complement of a 38° angle is a 52° angle.

You Try It 3
Find the supplement of a 129° angle.

Your strategy

Your solution
51°

Example 4
Find the measure of $\angle x$.

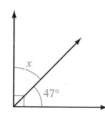

Strategy
To find the measure of $\angle x$, write an equation using the fact that the sum of the measure of $\angle x$ and 47° is 90°. Solve for $\angle x$.

Solution
$\angle x + 47° = 90°$
$\quad\ \angle x = 43°$

The measure of $\angle x$ is 43°.

You Try It 4
Find the measure of $\angle a$.

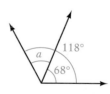

Your strategy

Your solution
50°

Solutions on p. S8

Objective B **To solve problems involving angles formed by intersecting lines** ....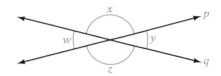

Four angles are formed by the intersection of two lines. If the two lines are perpendicular, each of the four angles is a right angle. If the two lines are not perpendicular, then two of the angles formed are acute angles and two of the angles are obtuse angles. The two acute angles are always opposite each other, and the two obtuse angles are always opposite each other.

In the figure at the right, $\angle w$ and $\angle y$ are acute angles. $\angle x$ and $\angle z$ are obtuse angles.

Two angles that are on opposite sides of the intersection of two lines are called **vertical angles**. Vertical angles have the same measure. $\angle w$ and $\angle y$ are vertical angles. $\angle x$ and $\angle z$ are vertical angles.

Vertical angles have the same measure.

$$\angle w = \angle y$$
$$\angle x = \angle z$$

Two angles that share a common side are called **adjacent angles**. For the figure shown above, $\angle x$ and $\angle y$ are adjacent angles, as are $\angle y$ and $\angle z$, $\angle z$ and $\angle w$, and $\angle w$ and $\angle x$. Adjacent angles of intersecting lines are supplementary angles.

Adjacent angles of intersecting lines are supplementary angles.

$$\angle x + \angle y = 180°$$
$$\angle y + \angle z = 180°$$
$$\angle z + \angle w = 180°$$
$$\angle w + \angle x = 180°$$

➡ Given that $\angle c = 65°$, find the measures of angles a, b, and d.

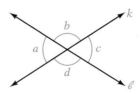

$\angle a = 65°$

• $\angle a = \angle c$ because $\angle a$ and $\angle c$ are vertical angles.

$\angle b + \angle c = 180°$
$\angle b + 65° = 180°$
$\angle b = 115°$

• $\angle b$ is supplementary to $\angle c$ because $\angle b$ and $\angle c$ are adjacent angles of intersecting lines.

$\angle d = 115°$

• $\angle d = \angle b$ because $\angle d$ and $\angle b$ are vertical angles.

A line that intersects two other lines at different points is called a **transversal**.

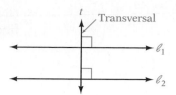

If the lines cut by a transversal t are parallel lines and the transversal is perpendicular to the parallel lines, all eight angles formed are right angles.

If the lines cut by a transversal t are parallel lines and the transversal is not perpendicular to the parallel lines, all four acute angles have the same measure and all four obtuse angles have the same measure. For the figure at the right,

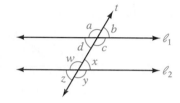

$$\angle b = \angle d = \angle x = \angle z$$
$$\angle a = \angle c = \angle w = \angle y$$

Alternate interior angles are two angles that are on opposite sides of the transversal and lie between the parallel lines. In the figure above, $\angle c$ and $\angle w$ are alternate interior angles; $\angle d$ and $\angle x$ are alternate interior angles. Alternate interior angles have the same measure.

Alternate interior angles have the same measure.

$$\angle c = \angle w$$
$$\angle d = \angle x$$

Alternate exterior angles are two angles that are on opposite sides of the transversal and lie outside the parallel lines. In the figure above, $\angle a$ and $\angle y$ are alternate exterior angles; $\angle b$ and $\angle z$ are alternate exterior angles. Alternate exterior angles have the same measure.

Alternate exterior angles have the same measure.

$$\angle a = \angle y$$
$$\angle b = \angle z$$

Corresponding angles are two angles that are on the same side of the transversal and are both acute angles or are both obtuse angles. For the figure above, the following pairs of angles are corresponding angles: $\angle a$ and $\angle w$, $\angle d$ and $\angle z$, $\angle b$ and $\angle x$, and $\angle c$ and $\angle y$. Corresponding angles have the same measure.

Corresponding angles have the same measure.

$$\angle a = \angle w$$
$$\angle d = \angle z$$
$$\angle b = \angle x$$
$$\angle c = \angle y$$

➡ Given that $\ell_1 \parallel \ell_2$ and $\angle c = 58°$, find the measures of $\angle f$, $\angle h$, and $\angle g$.

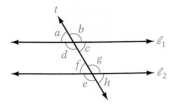

$\angle f = \angle c = 58°$ • $\angle c$ and $\angle f$ are alternate interior angles.

$\angle h = \angle c = 58°$ • $\angle c$ and $\angle h$ are corresponding angles.

$\angle g + \angle h = 180°$ • $\angle g$ is supplementary to $\angle h$.

$\angle g + 58° = 180°$

$\angle g = 122°$

Example 5

Find x.

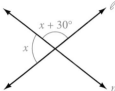

Strategy

The angles labeled are adjacent angles of intersecting lines and are, therefore, supplementary angles. To find x, write an equation and solve for x.

Solution

$x + (x + 30°) = 180°$

$2x + 30° = 180°$

$2x = 150°$

$x = 75°$

You Try It 5

Find x.

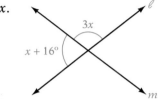

Your strategy

Your solution

41°

Example 6

Given $\ell_1 \parallel \ell_2$, find x.

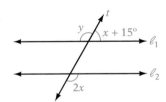

Strategy

$2x = y$ because alternate exterior angles have the same measure.

$(x + 15°) + y = 180°$ because adjacent angles of intersecting lines are supplementary angles. Substitute $2x$ for y and solve for x.

Solution

$(x + 15°) + 2x = 180°$

$3x + 15° = 180°$

$3x = 165°$

$x = 55°$

You Try It 6

Given $\ell_1 \parallel \ell_2$, find x.

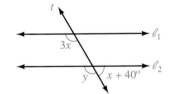

Your strategy

Your solution

35°

Solutions on p. S8

Objective C   *To solve problems involving the angles of a triangle*................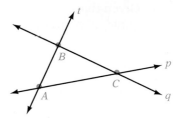

If the lines cut by a transversal are not parallel lines, the three lines will intersect at
three points. In the figure at the right, the
transversal t intersects lines p and q. The
three lines intersect at points A, B, and C.
These three points define three line seg-
ments: $\overline{AB}$, $\overline{BC}$, and $\overline{AC}$. The plane figure
formed by these three line segments is
called a **triangle**.

Each of the three points of intersection is
the vertex of four angles. The angles within
the region enclosed by the triangle are
called **interior angles**. In the figure at the
right, angles a, b, and c are interior angles.
The sum of the measures of the interior
angles of a triangle is $180°$.

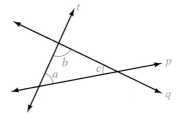

$$\angle a + \angle b + \angle c = 180°$$

**The Sum of the Measures of the
Interior Angles of a Triangle**

The sum of the measures of the interior
angles of a triangle is 180°.

An angle adjacent to an interior angle is an
exterior angle. In the figure at the right,
angles m and n are exterior angles for angle
a. The sum of the measures of an interior
and an exterior angle is $180°$.

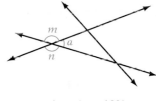

$$\angle a + \angle m = 180°$$
$$\angle a + \angle n = 180°$$

➡ Given the $\angle c = 40°$ and $\angle d = 100°$,
find the measure of $\angle e$.

$\angle d$ and $\angle b$ are supplementary angles.

$$\angle d + \angle b = 180°$$
$$100° + \angle b = 180°$$
$$\angle b = 80°$$

The sum of the interior angles is 180°.

$$\angle c + \angle b + \angle a = 180°$$
$$40° + 80° + \angle a = 180°$$
$$120° + \angle a = 180°$$
$$\angle a = 60°$$

$\angle a$ and $\angle e$ are vertical angles.

$$\angle e = \angle a = 60°$$

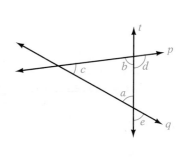

Example 7

Given that $\angle y = 55°$, find the measures of angles a, b, and d.

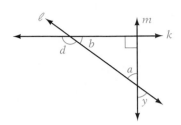

Strategy

• To find the measure of angle a, use the fact that $\angle a$ and $\angle y$ are vertical angles.
• To find the measure of angle b, use the fact that the sum of the measures of the interior angles of a triangle is 180°.
• To find the measure of angle d, use the fact that the sum of an interior and an exterior angle is 180°.

Solution

$\angle a = \angle y = 55°$

$\angle a + \angle b + 90° = 180°$
$55° + \angle b + 90° = 180°$
$\angle b + 145° = 180°$
$\angle b = 35°$

$\angle d + \angle b = 180°$
$\angle d + 35° = 180°$
$\angle d = 145°$

Example 8

Two angles of a triangle measure 53° and 78°. Find the measure of the third angle.

Strategy

To find the measure of the third angle, use the fact that the sum of the measures of the interior angles of a triangle is 180°. Write an equation using x to represent the measure of the third angle. Solve the equation for x.

Solution

$x + 53° + 78° = 180°$
$x + 131° = 180°$
$x = 49°$

The measure of the third angle is 49°.

You Try It 7

Given that $\angle a = 45°$ and $\angle x = 100°$, find the measures of angles b, c, and y.

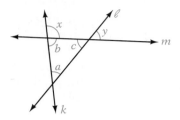

Your strategy

Your solution

$\angle b = 80°$,
$\angle y = \angle c = 55°$

You Try It 8

One angle in a triangle is a right angle, and one angle measures 34°. Find the measure of the third angle.

Your strategy

Your solution

56°

Solutions on pp. S8–S9

3.1 Exercises

· ·

Objective A

Use a protractor to measure the angle. State whether the angle is acute, obtuse, or right.

1.
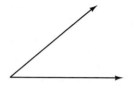
40°; acute

2.
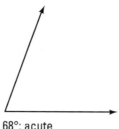
68°; acute

3.
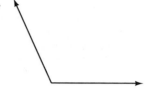
115°; obtuse

4.
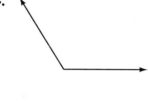
122°; obtuse

5.
90°; right

6.
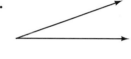
20°; acute

Solve.

7. Find the complement of a 62° angle.   28°

8. Find the complement of a 31° angle.   59°

9. Find the supplement of a 162° angle.   18°

10. Find the supplement of a 72° angle.   108°

11. Given $AB = 12$ cm, $CD = 9$ cm, and $AD = 35$ cm, find the length of BC.   14 cm

12. Given $AB = 21$ mm, $BC = 14$ mm, and $AD = 54$ mm, find the length of CD.   19 mm

13. Given $QR = 7$ ft and RS is three times the length of QR, find the length of QS.   28 ft

14. Given $QR = 15$ in. and RS is twice the length of QR, find the length of QS.   45 in.

15. Given $EF = 20$ m and FG is $\frac{1}{2}$ the length of EF, find the length of EG.   30 m

16. Given $EF = 18$ cm and FG is $\frac{1}{3}$ the length of EF, find the length of EG.
24 cm

17. Given $\angle LOM = 53°$ and $\angle LON = 139°$, find the measure of $\angle MON$.
86°

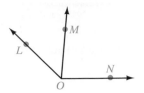

18. Given $\angle MON = 38°$ and $\angle LON = 85°$, find the measure of $\angle LOM$.
47°

Find the measure of $\angle x$.

19.

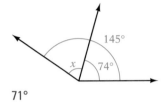

71°

20.

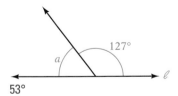

63°

Given that $\angle LON$ is a right angle, find the measure of $\angle x$.

21.

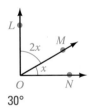

30°

22.

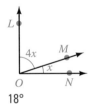

18°

23.

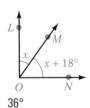

36°

24.

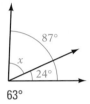

33°

Find the measure of $\angle a$.

25.

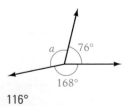

127°

26.

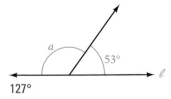

53°

27.

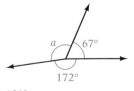

116°

28.

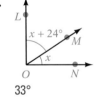

121°

Find x.

29.

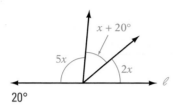

20°

30.

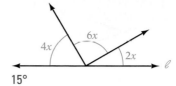

15°

31.

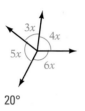

20°

32.

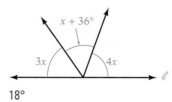

18°

33.

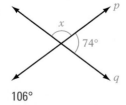

20°

34.

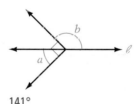

45°

Solve.

35.   Given $\angle a = 51°$, find the measure of $\angle b$.

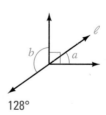

141°

36.   Given $\angle a = 38°$, find the measure of $\angle b$.

128°

─────────────
Objective B

Find the measure of $\angle x$.

37.

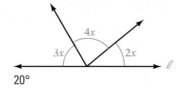

106°

38.

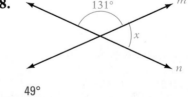

49°

Find x.

39.

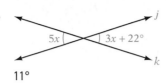

11°

40.

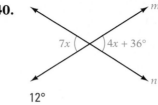

12°

Given that $\ell_1 \parallel \ell_2$, find the measures of angles a and b.

41.

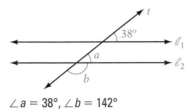

$\angle a = 38°$, $\angle b = 142°$

42.

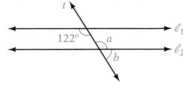

$\angle a = 122°$, $\angle b = 58°$

43.

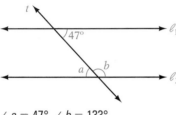

$\angle a = 47°$, $\angle b = 133°$

44.

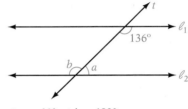

$\angle a = 44°$, $\angle b = 136°$

Given that $\ell_1 \parallel \ell_2$, find x.

45.

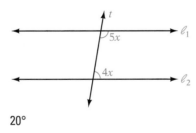

20°

46.

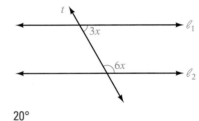

20°

47.

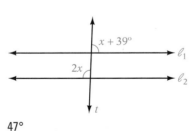

47°

48.

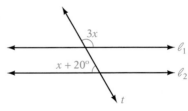

40°

Objective C

Solve.

49. Given that $\angle a = 95°$ and $\angle b = 70°$, find the measures of angles x and y.
$\angle x = 155°$, $\angle y = 70°$

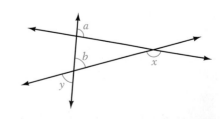

50. Given that $\angle a = 35°$ and $\angle b = 55°$, find the measures of angles x and y.
   $\angle x = 160°$,
   $\angle y = 145°$

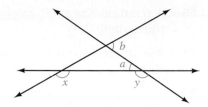

51. Given that $\angle y = 45°$, find the measures of angles a and b.
   $\angle a = 45°$,
   $\angle b = 135°$

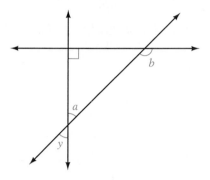

52. Given that $\angle y = 130°$, find the measures of angles a and b.
   $\angle a = 40°$,
   $\angle b = 140°$

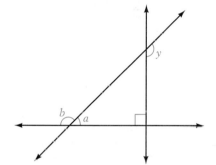

53. Given that $\overline{AO} \perp \overline{OB}$, express in terms of x the number of degrees in $\angle BOC$.
   $90° - x$

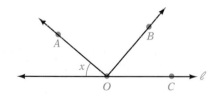

54. Given that $\overline{AO} \perp \overline{OB}$, express in terms of x the number of degrees in $\angle AOC$.
   $75° - x$

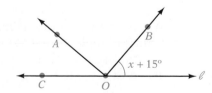

55. One angle in a triangle is a right angle, and one angle is equal to 30°. What is the measure of the third angle?
   $60°$

56. A triangle has a 45° angle and a right angle. Find the measure of the third angle.   45°

57. Two angles of a triangle measure 42° and 103°. Find the measure of the third angle.   35°

58. Two angles of a triangle measure 62° and 45°. Find the measure of the third angle.   73°

59. A triangle has a 13° angle and a 65° angle. What is the measure of the third angle?   102°

60. A triangle has a 105° angle and a 32° angle. What is the measure of the third angle?   43°

APPLYING THE CONCEPTS

61. **a.** What is the smallest possible whole number of degrees in an angle of a triangle?   1°
   b. What is the largest possible whole number of degrees in an angle of a triangle?   179°

62. Cut out a triangle and then tear off two of the angles, as shown at the right. Position the pieces you tore off so that angle a is adjacent to angle b and angle c is adjacent to angle b (on the other side). Describe what you observe. What does this demonstrate?   See the *Solutions Manual.*

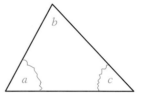

63. Construct a triangle with the given angle measures.
   a. 45°, 45°, and 90°
   b. 30°, 60°, and 90°
   c. 40°, 40°, and 100°

64. Determine whether the statement is always true, sometimes true, or never true.
   a. Two lines that are parallel to a third line are parallel to each other.   always true
   b. A triangle contains two acute angles.   always true
   c. Vertical angles are complementary angles.   sometimes true

65. For the figure at the right, find the sum of the measures of angles x, y, and z.   360°

66. For the figure at the right, explain why $\angle a + \angle b = \angle x$. Write a rule that describes the relationship between an exterior angle of a triangle and the opposite interior angles. Use the rule to write an equation involving angles a, c, and z.

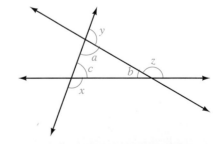

67. If $\overline{AB}$ and $\overline{CD}$ intersect at point O, and $\angle AOC = \angle BOC$, explain why $\overline{AB} \perp \overline{CD}$.

68. Do some research on the principle of reflection. Explain how this principle applies to the operation of a periscope and to the game of billiards.

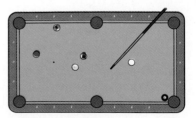

3.2 Plane Geometric Figures

Objective A *To solve problems involving the perimeter of geometric figures* ....

A **polygon** is a closed figure determined by three or more line segments that lie in a plane. The line segments that form the polygon are called its **sides**. The figures below are examples of polygons.

 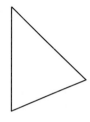 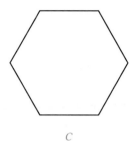 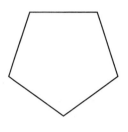 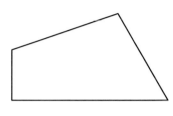

A   B   C   D   E

A **regular polygon** is one in which each side has the same length and each angle has the same measure. The polygons in Figures *A*, *C*, and *D* above are regular polygons.

The name of a polygon is based on the number of its sides. The table below lists the names of polygons that have from 3 to 10 sides.

Number of Sides	Name of the Polygon
3	Triangle
4	Quadrilateral
5	Pentagon
6	Hexagon
7	Heptagon
8	Octagon
9	Nonagon
10	Decagon

Triangles and quadrilaterals are two of the most common types of polygons. Triangles are distinguished by the number of equal sides and also by the measures of their angles.

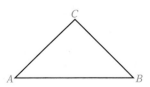 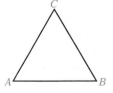 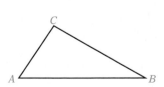

An **isosceles triangle** has two sides of equal length. The angles opposite the equal sides are of equal measure.
$AC = BC$
$\angle A = \angle B$

The three sides of an **equilateral triangle** are of equal length. The three angles are of equal measure.
$AB = BC = AC$
$\angle A = \angle B = \angle C$

A **scalene triangle** has no two sides of equal length. No two angles are of equal measure.

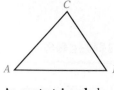

An **acute triangle** has three acute angles.

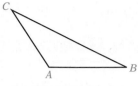

An **obtuse triangle** has one obtuse angle.

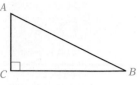

A **right triangle** has a right angle.

Quadrilaterals are also distinguished by their sides and angles, as shown below. Note that a rectangle, a square, and a rhombus are different forms of a parallelogram.

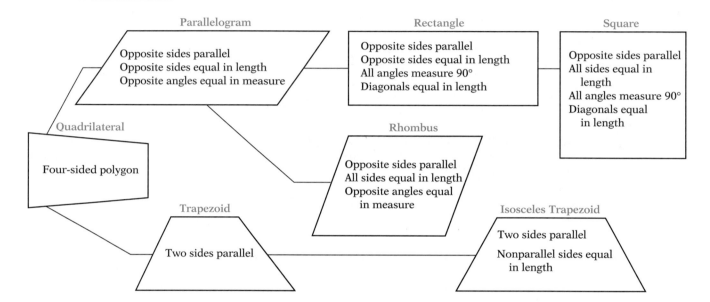

The **perimeter** of a plane geometric figure is a measure of the distance around the figure. Perimeter is used in buying fencing for a lawn or determining how much baseboard is needed for a room.

The perimeter of a triangle is the sum of the length of the three sides.

Perimeter of a Triangle

Let a, b, and c be the lengths of the sides of a triangle. The perimeter, P, of the triangle is given by $P = a + b + c$.

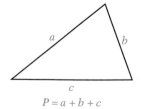

$P = a + b + c$

➡ Find the perimeter of the triangle shown at the right.

$P = 5 + 7 + 10 = 22$

The perimeter is 22 ft.

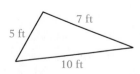

The perimeter of a quadrilateral is the sum of the lengths of its four sides.

A rectangle is a quadrilateral with opposite sides of equal length. Usually the length, L, of a rectangle refers to the length of one of the longer sides of the rectangle, and the width, W, refers to the length of one of the shorter sides. The perimeter can then be represented $P = L + W + L + W$.

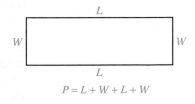

$$P = L + W + L + W$$

The formula for the perimeter of a rectangle is derived by combining like terms.

$$P = 2L + 2W$$

Perimeter of a Rectangle

Let L represent the length and W the width of a rectangle. The perimeter, P, of the rectangle is given by $P = 2L + 2W$.

➡ Find the perimeter of the rectangle shown at the right.

$P = 2L + 2W$

$P = 2(5) + 2(2)$ • **The length is 5 m. Substitute 5 for L.**
                              The width is 2 m. Substitute 2 for W.

$P = 10 + 4$ • **Solve for P.**

$P = 14$

The perimeter is 14 m.

A square is a rectangle in which each side has the same length. Let s represent the length of each side of a square. Then the perimeter of a square can be represented $P = s + s + s + s$.

The formula for the perimeter of a square is derived by combining like terms.

$$P = s + s + s + s$$

$$P = 4s$$

Perimeter of a Square

Let s represent the length of a side of a square. The perimeter, P, of the square is given by $P = 4s$.

➡ Find the perimeter of the square shown at the right.

$P = 4s = 4(8) = 32$

The perimeter is 32 in.

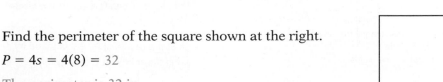

A **circle** is a plane figure in which all points are the same distance from point O, which is called the **center** of the circle.

The **diameter** of a circle is a line segment across the circle through point O. AB is a diameter of the circle at the right. The variable d is used to designate the diameter of a circle.

The **radius** of a circle is a line segment from the center of the circle to a point on the circle. OC is a radius of the circle at the right. The variable r is used to designate a radius of a circle.

The length of the diameter is twice the length of the radius.

$$d = 2r \text{ or } r = \frac{1}{2}d$$

The distance around a circle is called the **circumference**. The circumference, C, of a circle is equal to the product of π (pi) and the diameter.

$$C = \pi d$$

Because $d = 2r$, the formula for the circumference can be written in terms of r.

$$C = 2\pi r$$

The Circumference of a Circle

The circumference, C, of a circle with diameter d and radius r is given by $C = \pi d$ or $C = 2\pi r$.

The formula for circumference uses the number π, which is an irrational number. The value of π can be approximated by a fraction or by a decimal.

$$\pi \approx \frac{22}{7} \text{ or } \pi \approx 3.14$$

The π key on a scientific calculator gives a closer approximation of π than 3.14. Use a scientific calculator to find approximate values in calculations involving π.

⇒ Find the circumference of a circle with a diameter of 6 in.

$C = \pi d$ • The diameter of the circle is given.

$C = \pi(6)$ Use the circumference formula that involves the diameter. $d = 6$.

$C = 6\pi$ • The exact circumference of the circle is 6π in.

$C \approx 18.85$ • An approximate measure is found by using the π key on a calculator.

The circumference is approximately 18.85 in.

Example 1

A carpenter is designing a square patio with a perimeter of 44 ft. What is the length of each side?

Strategy

To find the length of each side, use the formula for the perimeter of a square. Substitute 44 for P and solve for s.

Solution

$P = 4s$
$44 = 4s$
$11 = s$

The length of each side of the patio is 11 ft.

Example 2

The dimensions of a triangular sail are 18 ft, 11 ft, and 15 ft. What is the perimeter of the sail?

Strategy

To find the perimeter, use the formula for the perimeter of a triangle. Substitute 18 for a, 11 for b, and 15 for c. Solve for P.

Solution

$P = a + b + c$
$P = 18 + 11 + 15$
$P = 44$

The perimeter of the sail is 44 ft.

Example 3

Find the circumference of a circle with a radius of 15 cm. Round to the nearest hundredth.

Strategy

To find the circumference, use the circumference formula that involves the radius. An approximation is asked for; use the π key on a calculator. $r = 15$.

Solution

$C = 2\pi r = 2\pi(15) = 30\pi \approx 94.25$

The circumference is 94.25 cm.

You Try It 1

The infield for a softball field is a square with each side of length 60 ft. Find the perimeter of the infield.

Your strategy

Your solution

240 ft

You Try It 2

What is the perimeter of a standard piece of typing paper that measures $8\frac{1}{2}$ in. by 11 in.?

Your strategy

Your solution

39 in.

You Try It 3

Find the circumference of a circle with a diameter of 9 in. Give the exact measure.

Your strategy

Your solution

9π in.

Solutions on p. S9

Objective B **To solve problems involving the area of geometric figures** ....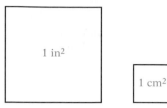

Area is the amount of surface in a region. Area can be used to describe the size of a rug, a parking lot, a farm, or a national park. Area is measured in square units.

A square that measures 1 in. on each side has an area of 1 square inch, written 1 in^2.

A square that measures 1 cm on each side has an area of 1 square centimeter, written 1 cm^2.

1 in^2

1 cm^2

Larger areas can be measured in square feet (ft^2), square meters (m^2), square miles (mi^2), acres (43,560 ft^2), or any other square unit.

The area of a geometric figure is the number of squares that are necessary to cover the figure. In the figures below, two rectangles have been drawn and covered with squares. In the figure on the left, 12 squares, each of area 1 cm^2, were used to cover the rectangle. The area of the rectangle is 12 cm^2. In the figure on the right, 6 squares, each of area 1 in^2, were used to cover the rectangle. The area of the rectangle is 6 in^2.

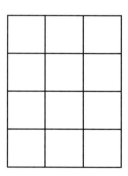

The area of the rectangle is 12 cm^2.

The area of the rectangle is 6 in^2.

Note from the above figures that the area of a rectangle can be found by multiplying the length of the rectangle by its width.

Area of a Rectangle

Let *L* represent the length and *W* the width of a rectangle. The area, *A*, of the rectangle is given by *A* = *LW*.

➡ Find the area of the rectangle shown at the right.

$$A = LW = 11(7) = 77$$

The area is 77 m^2.

7 m

11 m

A square is a rectangle in which all sides are the same length. Therefore, both the length and the width of a square can be represented by s, and $A = LW = s \cdot s = s^2$.

Area of a Square

Let s represent the length of a side of a square. The area, A, of the square is given by $A = s^2$.

$A = s \cdot s = s^2$

➡ Find the area of the square shown at the right.

$A = s^2 = 9^2 = 81$

The area is 81 mi².

9 mi

Figure $ABCD$ is a parallelogram. BC is the **base**, b, of the parallelogram. AE, perpendicular to the base, is the **height**, h, of the parallelogram.

Any side of a parallelogram can be designated as the base. The corresponding height is found by drawing a line segment perpendicular to the base from the opposite side.

A rectangle can be formed from a parallelogram by cutting a right triangle from one end of the parallelogram and attaching it to the other end. The area of the resulting rectangle will equal the area of the original parallelogram.

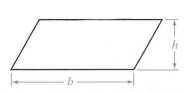

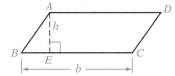

Area of a Parallelogram

Let b represent the length of the base and h the height of a parallelogram. The area, A, of the parallelogram is given by $A = bh$.

➡ Find the area of the parallelogram shown at the right.

$A = bh = 12 \cdot 6 = 72$

The area is 72 m².

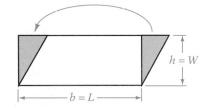

6 m

12 m

Figure ABC is a triangle. AB is the **base**, b, of the triangle. CD, perpendicular to the base, is the **height**, h, of the triangle.

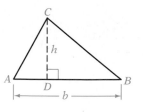

Any side of a triangle can be designated as the base. The corresponding height is found by drawing a line segment perpendicular to the base from the vertex opposite the base.

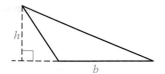

Consider the triangle with base b and height h shown at the right. By extending a line from C parallel to the base AB and equal in length to the base, and extending a line from B parallel to AC and equal in length to AC, a parallelogram is formed. The area of the parallelogram is bh and is twice the area of the triangle. Therefore, the area of the triangle is one-half the area of the parallelogram, or $\frac{1}{2}bh$.

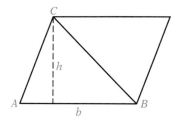

Area of a Triangle

Let b represent the length of the base and h the height of a triangle. The area, A, of the triangle is given by $A = \frac{1}{2}bh$.

➡ Find the area of a triangle with a base of 18 cm and a height of 6 cm.

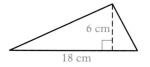

$$A = \frac{1}{2}bh = \frac{1}{2} \cdot 18 \cdot 6 = 54$$

The area is 54 cm².

Figure $ABCD$ is a trapezoid. AB is one **base**, b_1, of the trapezoid, and CD is the other base, b_2. AE, perpendicular to the two bases, is the **height**, h.

In the trapezoid at the right, the line segment BD divides the trapezoid into two triangles, ABD and BCD. In triangle ABD, b_1 is the base and h is the height. In triangle BCD, b_2 is the base and h is the height. The area of the trapezoid is the sum of the areas of the two triangles.

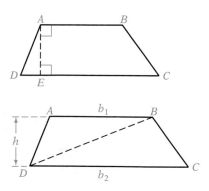

Area of trapezoid $ABCD$ = area of triangle ABD + area of triangle BCD

$$= \frac{1}{2}b_1 h + \frac{1}{2}b_2 h = \frac{1}{2}h(b_1 + b_2)$$

> **Area of a Trapezoid**
>
> Let b_1 and b_2 represent the lengths of the bases and h the height of a trapezoid. The area, A, of the trapezoid is given by
>
> $$A = \frac{1}{2}h(b_1 + b_2).$$

➡ Find the area of a trapezoid that has bases measuring 15 in. and 5 in. and a height of 8 in.

$$A = \frac{1}{2}h(b_1 + b_2)$$

$$= \frac{1}{2} \cdot 8(15 + 5) = 4(20) = 80$$

The area is 80 in².

The area of a circle is equal to the product of π and the square of the radius.

$A = \pi r^2$

POINT OF INTEREST

Ancient Egyptians gave the formula for the area of a circle as $\left(\frac{8}{9}d\right)^2$. Does this formula give an area that is less than or greater than the correct formula?

> **Area of a Circle**
>
> The area, A, of a circle with radius r is given by $A = \pi r^2$.

CALCULATOR NOTE

To approximate 36π on your calculator, enter $36 \boxed{\times} \boxed{\pi} \boxed{=}$.

➡ Find the area of a circle that has a radius of 67 cm.

$A = \pi r^2$ • Use the formula for the area of a
$A = \pi(6)^2$ circle. $r = 6$
$A = \pi(36)$

$A = 36\pi$ • The exact area of the circle is 36π cm².

$A \approx 113.10$ • An approximate measure is found
                       by using the π key on a calculator.

The approximate area of the circle is 113.10 cm².

For your reference, all of the formulas for the perimeters and areas of the geometric figures presented in this section are listed in the Chapter Summary located at the end of this chapter.

Example 4

The Parks and Recreation Department of a city plans to plant grass seed in a playground that has the shape of a trapezoid, as shown below. Each bag of grass seed will seed 1500 ft². How many bags of grass seed should the department purchase?

Strategy

To find the number of bags to be purchased:
- Use the formula for the area of a trapezoid to find the area of the playground.
- Divide the area of the playground by the area one bag will seed (1500).

Solution

$$A = \frac{1}{2} h(b_1 + b_2)$$

$$A = \frac{1}{2} \cdot 64(80 + 115)$$

$A = 6240$ • The area of the playground is 6240 ft².

$6240 \div 1500 = 4.16$

Because a portion of a fifth bag is needed, 5 bags of grass seed should be purchased.

You Try It 4

An interior designer decides to wallpaper two walls of a room. Each roll of wallpaper will cover 30 ft². Each wall measures 8 ft by 12 ft. How many rolls of wallpaper should be purchased?

Your strategy

Your solution

7 rolls

Example 5

Find the area of a circle with a diameter of 5 ft. Give the exact measure.

Strategy

To find the area:
- Find the radius of the circle.
- Use the formula for the area of a circle. Leave the answer in terms of π.

Solution

$$r = \frac{1}{2}d = \frac{1}{2}(5) = 2.5$$

$$A = \pi r^2 = \pi(2.5)^2 = \pi(6.25) = 6.25\pi$$

The area of the circle is 6.25π ft².

You Try It 5

Find the area of a circle with a radius of 11 cm. Round to the nearest hundredth.

Your strategy

Your solution

380.13 cm²

Solutions on p. S9

3.2 Exercises

. . . .

Objective A

Name each polygon.

1.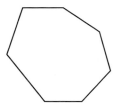

hexagon

2.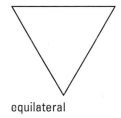

heptagon

3.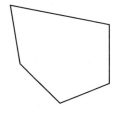

pentagon

4.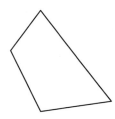

quadrilateral

Classify the triangle as isosceles, equilateral, or scalene.

5.

scalene

6.

isosceles

7.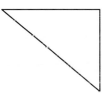

equilateral

8.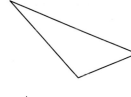

scalene

Classify the triangle as acute, obtuse, or right.

9.

obtuse

10.

right

11.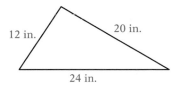

acute

12.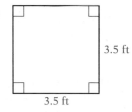

obtuse

Find the perimeter of the figure.

13.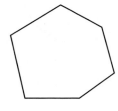

12 in.   20 in.   24 in.

56 in.

14.

7 cm   11 cm

36 cm

15.

3.5 ft   3.5 ft

14 ft

16.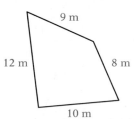

9 m   12 m   8 m   10 m

39 m

17.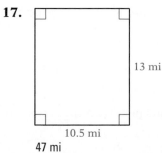

13 mi   10.5 mi

47 mi

18.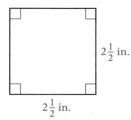

$2\frac{1}{2}$ in. $2\frac{1}{2}$ in.

10 in.

Find the circumference of the figure. Give both the exact value and an approximation to the nearest hundredth.

19.

4 cm

8π cm; 25.13 cm

20.

12 m

24π m; 75.40 m

21.

5.5 mi

11π mi; 34.56 mi

22.

18 in.

18π in.; 56.55 in.

23.

17 ft

17π ft; 53.41 ft

24.

6.6 km

6.6π km; 20.73 km

Solve.

25. The lengths of the three sides of a triangle are 3.8 cm, 5.2 cm, and 8.4 cm. Find the perimeter of the triangle.   17.4 cm

26. The lengths of the three sides of a triangle are 7.5 m, 6.1 m, and 4.9 m. Find the perimeter of the triangle.   18.5 m

27. The length of each of two sides of an isosceles triangle is $2\frac{1}{2}$ cm. The third side measures 3 cm. Find the perimeter of the triangle.   8 cm

28. The length of each side of an equilateral triangle is $4\frac{1}{2}$ in. Find the perimeter of the triangle. $13\frac{1}{2}$ in.

29. A rectangle has a length of 8.5 m and a width of 3.5 m. Find the perimeter of the rectangle.   24 m

30. Find the perimeter of a rectangle that has a length of $5\frac{1}{2}$ ft and a width of 4 ft.   19 ft

31. The length of each side of a square is 12.2 cm. Find the perimeter of the square.   48.8 cm

32. Find the perimeter of a square that measures 0.5 m on each side.   2 m

33. Find the perimeter of a regular pentagon that measures 3.5 in. on each side.   17.5 in.

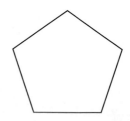

34. What is the perimeter of a regular hexagon that measures 8.5 cm on each side?   51 cm

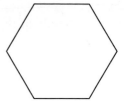

35. The radius of a circle is 4.2 cm. Find the length of a diameter of the circle.   8.4 cm

36. The diameter of a circle is 0.56 m. Find the length of a radius of the circle.   0.28 m

37. Find the circumference of a circle that has a diameter of 1.5 in. Give the exact value.   1.5π in.

38. The diameter of a circle is 4.2 ft. Find the circumference of the circle. Round to the nearest hundredth.   13.19 ft

39. The radius of a circle is 36 cm. Find the circumference of the circle. Round to the nearest hundredth.   226.19 cm

40. Find the circumference of a circle that has a radius of 2.5 m. Give the exact value.   5π m

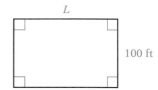

41. How many feet of fencing should be purchased for a rectangular garden that is 18 ft long and 12 ft wide?   60 ft

42. How many meters of binding are required to bind the edge of a rectangular quilt that measures 3.5 m by 8.5 m?   24 m

43. Wall-to-wall carpeting is installed in a room that is 12 ft long and 10 ft wide. The edges of the carpet are nailed to the floor. Along how many feet must the carpet be nailed down?   44 ft

44. The length of a rectangular park is 55 yd. The width is 47 yd. How many yards of fencing are needed to surround the park?   204 yd

45. The perimeter of a rectangular playground is 440 ft. If the width is 100 ft, what is the length of the playground?   120 ft

46. A rectangular vegetable garden has a perimeter of 64 ft. The length of the garden is 20 ft. What is the width of the garden?   12 ft

47. Each of two sides of a triangular banner measures 18 in. If the perimeter of the banner is 46 in., what is the length of the third side of the banner?   10 in.

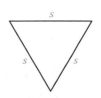

48. The perimeter of an equilateral triangle is 13.2 cm. What is the length of each side of the triangle?   4.4 cm

49. The perimeter of a square picture frame is 48 in. Find the length of each side of the frame.   12 in.

50. A square rug has a perimeter of 32 ft. Find the length of each edge of the rug.   8 ft

51. The circumference of a circle is 8 cm. Find the length of a diameter of the circle. Round to the nearest hundredth.   2.55 cm

52. The circumference of a circle is 15 in. Find the length of a radius of the circle. Round to the nearest hundredth.   2.39 in.

53. Find the length of molding needed to put around a circular table that is 4.2 ft in diameter. Round to the nearest hundredth.   13.19 ft

54. How much binding is needed to bind the edge of a circular rug that is 3 m in diameter? Round to the nearest hundredth.   9.42 m

55. A bicycle tire has a diameter of 24 in. How many feet does the bicycle travel when the wheel makes eight revolutions? Round to the nearest hundredth.   50.27 ft

56. A tricycle tire has a diameter of 12 in. How many feet does the tricycle travel when the wheel makes twelve revolutions? Round to the nearest hundredth.   37.70 ft

57. The distance from the surface of Earth to its center is 6356 km. What is the circumference of Earth? Round to the nearest hundredth.
39,935.93 km

58. Bias binding is to be sewed around the edge of a rectangular tablecloth measuring 72 in. by 45 in. If the bias binding comes in packages containing 15 ft of binding, how many packages of bias binding are needed for the tablecloth?   2 packages

Objective B

Find the area of the figure.

59.
5 ft
12 ft
60 ft²

60.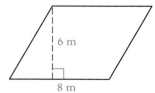
6 m
8 m
48 m²

61.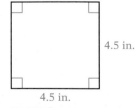
4.5 in.
4.5 in.
20.25 in²

62.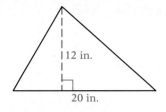

120 in²

63.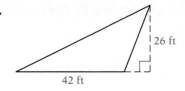

546 ft²

64.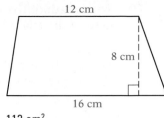

112 cm²

Find the area of the figure. Give both the exact value and an approximation to the nearest hundredth.

65.

16π cm²; 50.27 cm²

66.

144π m²; 452.39 m²

67.

30.25π mi²; 95.03 mi²

68.

81π in²; 254.47 in²

69.

72.25π ft²; 226.98 ft²

70.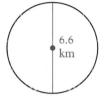

10.89π km²; 34.21 km²

Solve.

71. The length of a side of a square is 12.5 cm. Find the area of the square.
156.25 cm²

72. Each side of a square measures $3\frac{1}{2}$ in. Find the area of the square.

12.25 in²

73. The length of a rectangle is 38 in., and the width is 15 in. Find the area of the rectangle.
570 in²

74. Find the area of a rectangle that has a length of 6.5 m and a width of 3.8 m.
24.7 m²

75. The length of the base of a parallelogram is 16 in., and the height is 12 in. Find the area of the parallelogram.
192 in²

76. The height of a parallelogram is 3.4 m, and the length of the base is 5.2 m. Find the area of the parallelogram.
17.68 m²

77. The length of the base of a triangle is 6 ft. The height is 4.5 ft. Find the area of the triangle.   13.5 ft²

78. The height of a triangle is 4.2 cm. The length of the base is 5 cm. Find the area of the triangle.   10.5 cm²

79. The length of one base of a trapezoid is 35 cm, and the length of the other base is 20 cm. If the height is 12 cm, what is the area of the trapezoid?   330 cm²

80. The height of a trapezoid is 5 in. The bases measure 16 in. and 18 in. Find the area of the trapezoid.   85 in²

81. The radius of a circle is 5 in. Find the area of the circle. Give the exact value. 25π in²

82. Find the area of a circle with a radius of 14 m. Round to the nearest hundredth.   615.75 m²

83. Find the area of a circle that has a diameter of 3.4 ft. Round to the nearest hundredth.   9.08 ft²

84. The diameter of a circle is 6.5 m. Find the area of the circle. Give the exact value. 10.5625π m²

85. The dome of the Hale telescope at Mount Palomar, California, has a diameter of 200 in. Find the area across the dome. Give the exact value. $10{,}000\pi$ in²

86. An irrigation system waters a circular field that has a 50-foot radius. Find the area watered by the irrigation system. Give the exact value. 2500π ft²

87. Find the area of a rectangular flower garden that measures 14 ft by 9 ft.   126 ft²

88. What is the area of a square patio that measures 8.5 m on each side?   72.25 m²

89. Artificial turf is being used to cover a playing field. If the field is rectangular with a length of 100 yd and a width of 75 yd, how much artificial turf must be purchased to cover the field?   7500 yd²

90. A fabric wall hanging is to fill a space that measures 5 m by 3.5 m. Allowing for 0.1 m of the fabric to be folded back along each edge, how much fabric must be purchased for the wall hanging?   19.24 m²

91. The area of a rectangle is 300 in². If the length of the rectangle is 30 in., what is the width?   10 in.

30 in.

W

92. The width of the rectangle is 12 ft. If the area is 312 ft², what is the length of the rectangle?   26 ft

93. The height of a triangle is 5 m. The area of the triangle is 50 m². Find the length of the base of the triangle.   20 m

94. The area of a parallelogram is 42 m². If the height of the parallelogram is 7 m, what is the length of the base?   6 m

95. You plan to stain the wooden deck attached to your house. The deck measures 10 ft by 8 ft. If a quart of stain will cover 50 ft², how many quarts of stain should you buy?   2 qt

96. You want to tile your kitchen floor. The floor measures 12 ft by 9 ft. How many tiles, each a square with side $1\frac{1}{2}$ ft, should you purchase for the job?   48 tiles

97. You are wallpapering two walls of a child's room, one measuring 9 ft by 8 ft and the other measuring 11 ft by 8 ft. The wallpaper costs $18.50 per roll, and each roll of the wallpaper will cover 40 ft². What will it cost to wallpaper the two walls? $74

98. An urban renewal project involves reseeding a park that is in the shape of a square 60 ft on each side. Each bag of grass seed costs $5.75 and will seed 1200 ft². How much money should be budgeted for buying grass seed for the park? $17.25

99. A circle has a radius of 8 in. Find the increase in area when the radius is increased by 2 in. Round to the nearest hundredth.   113.10 in²

100. A circle has a radius of 6 cm. Find the increase in area when the radius is doubled. Round to the nearest hundredth.   339.29 cm²

101. You want to install wall-to-wall carpeting in your living room, which measures 15 ft by 24 ft. If the cost of the carpet you would like to purchase is $15.95 per square yard, what will be the cost of the carpeting for your living room? (*Hint:* 9 ft² = 1 yd²) $638

102. You want to paint the walls of your bedroom. Two walls measure 15 ft by 9 ft, and the other two walls measure 12 ft by 9 ft. The paint you wish to purchase costs $12.98 per gallon, and each gallon will cover 400 ft² of wall. Find the total amount you will spend on paint. $25.96

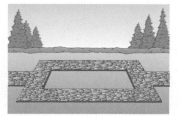

103. A walkway 2 m wide surrounds a rectangular plot of grass. The plot is 30 m long and 20 m wide. What is the area of the walkway?   216 m²

104. Pleated draperies for a window must be twice as wide as the width of the window. Draperies are being made for four windows, each 2 ft wide and 4 ft high. Because the drapes will fall slightly below the window sill, and because extra fabric will be needed for hemming the drapes, 1 ft must be added to the height of the window. How much material must be purchased to make the drapes?   80 ft²

APPLYING THE CONCEPTS

105. Find the ratio of the areas of two squares if the ratio of the lengths of their sides is 2 : 3.   4 : 9

106. If both the length and the width of a rectangle are doubled, how many times larger is the area of the resulting rectangle?   4 times

107. A **hexagram** is a six-pointed star, formed by extending each of the sides of a regular hexagon into an equilateral triangle. A hexagram is shown at the right. Use a pencil, paper, protractor, and ruler to create a hexagram.

108. If the formula $C = \pi d$ is solved for π, the resulting equation is $\pi = \dfrac{C}{d}$. Therefore, π is the ratio of the circumference of a circle to the length of its diameter. Use several circular objects, such as coins, plates, tin cans, and wheels, to show that the ratio of the circumference of each object to its diameter is approximately equal to 3.14.

109. Derive a formula for the area of a circle in terms of the diameter of the circle. $A = \dfrac{\pi d^2}{4}$

110. Determine whether the statement is always true, sometimes true, or never true.
    a. If two triangles have the same perimeter, then they have the same area.   sometimes true
    b. If two rectangles have the same area, then they have the same perimeter.   sometimes true
    c. If two squares have the same area, then the sides of the squares have the same length.   always true
    d. An equilateral triangle is also an isosceles triangle.   always true
    e. All the radii (plural of radius) of a circle are equal.   always true
    f. All the diameters of a circle are equal.   always true

111. Suppose a circle is cut into 16 equal pieces, which are then arranged as shown at the right. The figure formed resembles a parallelogram. What variable expression could describe the base of the parallelogram? What variable could describe its height? Explain how the formula for the area of a circle is derived from this approach.

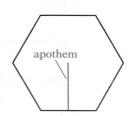

apothem

112. The **apothem** of a regular polygon is the distance from the center of the polygon to a side. Explain how to derive a formula for the area of a regular polygon using the apothem. (*Hint:* Use the formula for the area of a triangle.)

3.3 Solids

Objective A   *To solve problems involving the volume of a solid* ....

Geometric solids are figures in space. Five common geometric solids are the rectangular solid, the sphere, the cylinder, the cone, and the pyramid.

A **rectangular solid** is one in which all six sides, called **faces**, are rectangles. The variable *L* is used to represent the length of a rectangular solid, *W* its width, and *H* its height.

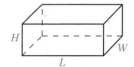

A **sphere** is a solid in which all points are the same distance from point *O*, which is called the **center** of the sphere. The **diameter**, *d*, of a sphere is a line across the sphere going through point *O*. The **radius**, *r*, is a line from the center to a point on the sphere. *AB* is a diameter and *OC* is a radius of the sphere shown at the right.

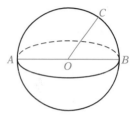

$$d = 2r \text{ or } r = \frac{1}{2}d$$

The most common cylinder, called a **right circular cylinder**, is one in which the bases are circles and are perpendicular to the height of the cylinder. The variable *r* is used to represent the radius of a base of a cylinder, and *h* represents the height. In this text, only right circular cylinders are discussed.

A **right circular cone** is obtained when one base of a right circular cylinder is shrunk to a point, called a **vertex**, *V*. The variable *r* is used to represent the radius of the base of the cone, and *h* represents the height. The variable ℓ is used to represent the **slant height**, which is the distance from a point on the circumference of the base to the vertex. In this text, only right circular cones are discussed.

The base of a **regular pyramid** is a regular polygon, and the sides are isosceles triangles. The height, *h*, is the distance from the vertex, *V*, to the base and is perpendicular to the base. The variable ℓ is used to represent the **slant height**, which is the height of one of the isosceles triangles on the face of the pyramid. The regular square pyramid at the right has a square base. This is the only type of pyramid discussed in this text.

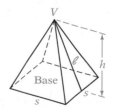

A **cube** is a special type of rectangular solid. Each of the six faces of a cube is a square. The variable s is used to represent the length of one side of a cube.

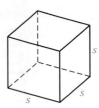

Volume is a measure of the amount of space inside a figure in space. Volume can be used to describe the amount of heating gas used for cooking, the amount of concrete delivered for the foundation of a house, or the amount of water in storage for a city's water supply.

A cube that is 1 ft on each side has a volume of 1 cubic foot, which is written 1 ft³. A cube that measures 1 cm on each side has a volume of 1 cubic centimeter, which is written 1 cm³.

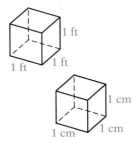

The volume of a solid is the number of cubes that are necessary to exactly fill the solid. The volume of the rectangular solid at the right is 24 cm³ because it will hold exactly 24 cubes, each 1 cm on a side. Note that the volume can be found by multiplying the length times the width times the height.

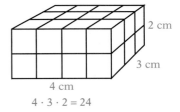

$4 \cdot 3 \cdot 2 = 24$

The formulas for the volumes of the geometric solids described above are given below.

Volumes of Geometric Solids

The volume, V, of a **rectangular solid** with length L, width W, and height H is given by $V = LWH$.

The volume, V, of a **cube** with side s is given by $V = s^3$.

The volume, V, of a **sphere** with radius r is given by $V = \frac{4}{3}\pi r^3$.

The volume, V, of a **right circular cylinder** is given by $V = \pi r^2 h$, where r is the radius of the base and h is the height.

The volume, V, of a **right circular cone** is given by $V = \frac{1}{3}\pi r^2 h$, where r is the radius of the circular base and h is the height.

The volume, V, of a **regular square pyramid** is given by $V = \frac{1}{3}s^2 h$, where s is the length of a side of the base and h is the height.

➡ Find the volume of a sphere with a diameter of 6 in.

$r = \dfrac{1}{2}d = \dfrac{1}{2}(6) = 3$ • First find the radius of the sphere.

$V = \dfrac{4}{3}\pi r^3$ • Use the formula for the volume of a sphere.

$V = \dfrac{4}{3}\pi(3)^3$

$V = \dfrac{4}{3}\pi(27)$

$V = 36\pi$ • The exact volume of the sphere is 36π in^3.

$V \approx 113.10$ • An approximate measure can be found by using the π key on a calculator.

The approximate volume is 113.10 in^3.

CALCULATOR NOTE

To approximate 36π on your calculator, enter $36\;\boxed{\times}\;\boxed{\pi}\;\boxed{=}$.

Example 1
The length of a rectangular solid is 5 m, the width is 3.2 m, and the height is 4 m. Find the volume of the solid.

Strategy
To find the volume, use the formula for the volume of a rectangular solid. $L = 5$, $W = 3.2$, $H = 4$.

Solution
$V = LWH = 5(3.2)(4) = 64$

The volume of the rectangular solid is 64 m^3.

You Try It 1
Find the volume of a cube that measures 2.5 m on a side.

Your strategy

Your solution
15.625 m^3

Example 2
The radius of the base of a cone is 8 cm. The height is 12 cm. Find the volume of the cone. Round to the nearest hundredth.

Strategy
To find the volume, use the formula for the volume of a cone. An approximation is asked for; use the π key on a calculator. $r = 8$, $h = 12$.

Solution

$V = \dfrac{1}{3}\pi r^2 h$

$V = \dfrac{1}{3}\pi(8)^2(12) = \dfrac{1}{3}\pi(64)(12) = 256\pi$

≈ 804.25

The volume is approximately 804.25 cm^3.

Your Try It 2
The diameter of the base of a cylinder is 8 ft. The height of the cylinder is 22 ft. Find the exact volume of the cylinder.

Your strategy

Your solution
352π ft^3

Solutions on pp. S9–S10

Objective B   **To solve problems involving the surface area of a solid**..........................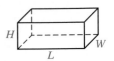

The surface area of a solid is the total area on the surface of the solid.

When a rectangular solid is cut open and flattened out, each face is a rectangle. The surface area, *SA*, of the rectangular solid is the sum of the areas of the six rectangles:

$$SA = LW + LH + WH + LW + WH + LH$$

which simplifies to

$$SA = 2LW + 2LH + 2WH$$

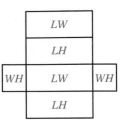

The surface area of a cube is the sum of the areas of the six faces of the cube. The area of each face is s^2. Therefore, the surface area, *SA*, of a cube is given by the formula $SA = 6s^2$.

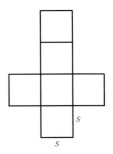

When a cylinder is cut open and flattened out, the top and bottom of the cylinder are circles. The side of the cylinder flattens out to a rectangle. The length of the rectangle is the circumference of the base, which is $2\pi r$; the width is *h*, the height of the cylinder. Therefore, the area of the rectangle is $2\pi rh$. The surface area, *SA*, of the cylinder is

$$SA = \pi r^2 + 2\pi rh + \pi r^2$$

which simplifies to

$$SA = 2\pi r^2 + 2\pi rh$$

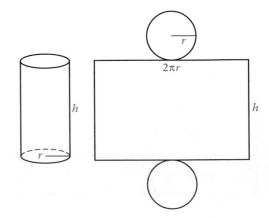

The surface area of a pyramid is the area of the base plus the area of the four isosceles triangles. A side of the square base is s; therefore, the area of the base is s^2. The slant height, ℓ, is the height of each triangle, and s is the base of each triangle. The surface area, SA, of a pyramid is

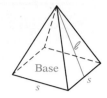

$$SA = s^2 + 4\left(\frac{1}{2}s\ell\right)$$

which simplifies to

$$SA = s^2 + 2s\ell$$

Formulas for the surface areas of geometric solids are given below.

Surface Areas of Geometric Solids

The surface area, SA, of a **rectangular solid** with length L, width W, and height H is given by $SA = 2LW + 2LH + 2WH$.

The surface area, SA, of a **cube** with side s is given by $SA = 6s^2$.

The surface area, SA, of a **sphere** with radius r is given by $SA = 4\pi r^2$.

The surface area, SA, of a **right circular cylinder** is given by $SA = 2\pi r^2 + 2\pi rh$, where r is the radius of the base and h is the height.

The surface area, SA, of a **right circular cone** is given by $SA = \pi r^2 + \pi r\ell$, where r is the radius of the circular base and ℓ is the slant height.

The surface area, SA, of a **regular pyramid** is given by $SA = s^2 + 2s\ell$, where s is the length of a side of the base and ℓ is the slant height.

➡ Find the surface area of a sphere with a diameter of 18 cm.

$r = \dfrac{1}{2}d = \dfrac{1}{2}(18) = 9$ • **First find the radius of the sphere.**

$SA = 4\pi r^2$ • **Use the formula for the surface**

$SA = 4\pi(9)^2$ **area of a sphere.**

$SA = 4\pi(81)$

$SA \approx 324\pi$ • **The exact surface area of the sphere is 324 π cm².**

$SA \approx 1017.88$ • **An approximate measure can be found by using the π key on a calculator.**

The approximate surface area is 1017.88 cm².

Example 3

The diameter of the base of a cone is 5 m, and the slant height is 4 m. Find the surface area of the cone. Give the exact measure.

Strategy

To find the surface area of the cone:
- Find the radius of the base of the cone.
- Use the formula for the surface area of a cone. Leave the answer in terms of π.

Solution

$$r = \frac{1}{2}d = \frac{1}{2}(5) = 2.5$$

$$SA = \pi r^2 + \pi r\ell$$
$$SA = \pi(2.5)^2 + \pi(2.5)(4)$$
$$SA = \pi(6.25) + \pi(2.5)(4)$$
$$SA = 6.25\pi + 10\pi$$
$$SA = 16.25\pi$$

The surface area of the cone is 16.25π m².

You Try It 3

The diameter of the base of a cylinder is 6 ft, and the height is 8 ft. Find the surface area of the cylinder. Round to the nearest hundredth.

Your strategy

Your solution
207.35 ft²

Example 4

Find the area of a label used to cover a soup can that has a radius of 4 cm and a height of 12 cm. Round to the nearest hundredth.

Strategy

To find the area of the label, use the fact that the surface area of the sides of a cylinder is given by $2\pi rh$. An approximation is asked for; use the π key on a calculator. $r = 4$, $h = 12$.

Solution

Area of the label = $2\pi rh$
Area of the label = $2\pi(4)(12) = 96\pi$
$$\approx 301.59$$

The area is approximately 301.59 cm².

You Try It 4

Which has a larger surface area, a cube with a side measuring 10 cm or a sphere with a diameter measuring 8 cm?

Your strategy

Your solution
the cube

Solutions on p. S10

3.3 Exercises

Objective A

Find the volume of the figure. For calculations involving π, give both the exact value and an approximation to the nearest hundredth.

1.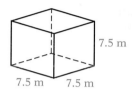

840 in³

2.

168π ft³; 527.79 ft³

3.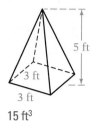

15 ft³

4.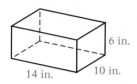

421.88 m³

5.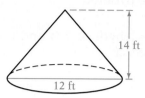

4.5π cm³; 14.14 cm³

6.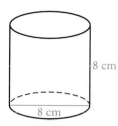

128π cm³; 402.12 cm³

Solve.

7. A rectangular solid has a length of 6.8 m, a width of 2.5 m, and a height of 2 m. Find the volume of the solid.   34 m³

8. Find the volume of a rectangular solid that has a length of 4.5 ft, a width of 3 ft, and a height of 1.5 ft.   20.25 ft³

9. Find the volume of a cube whose side measures 3.5 in.   42.875 in³

10. The length of a side of a cube is 7 cm. Find the volume of the cube. 343 cm³

11. The diameter of a sphere is 6 ft. Find the volume of the sphere. Give the exact measure.   36π ft³

12. Find the volume of a sphere that has a radius of 1.2 m. Round to the nearest tenth.   7.2 m³

13. The diameter of the base of a cylinder is 24 cm. The height of the cylinder is 18 cm. Find the volume of the cylinder. Round to the nearest hundredth.   8143.01 cm³

14. The height of a cylinder is 7.2 m. The radius of the base is 4 m. Find the volume of the cylinder. Give the exact measure.   115.2π m³

15. The radius of the base of a cone is 5 in. The height of the cone is 9 in. Find the volume of the cone. Give the exact measure.   75π in³

16. The height of a cone is 15 cm. The diameter of the cone is 10 cm. Find the volume of the cone. Round to the nearest hundredth.   392.70 cm³

17. The length of a side of the base of a pyramid is 6 in., and the height is 10 in. Find the volume of the pyramid.   120 in³

18. The height of a pyramid is 8 m, and the length of a side of the base is 9 m. What is the volume of the pyramid?   216 m³

19. The volume of a freezer with a length of 7 ft and a height of 3 ft is 52.5 ft³. Find the width of the freezer.   2.5 ft

20. The length of an aquarium is 18 in., and the width is 12 in. If the volume of the aquarium is 1836 in³, what is the height of the aquarium?
     8.5 in.

21. The volume of a cylinder with a height of 10 in. is 502.4 in³. Find the radius of the base of the cylinder. Round to the nearest hundredth.
     4.00 in.

22. The diameter of the base of a cylinder is 14 cm. If the volume of the cylinder is 2310 cm³, find the height of the cylinder. Round to the nearest hundredth.   15.01 cm

23. A rectangular solid has a square base and a height of 5 in. If the volume of the solid is 125 in³, find the length and the width.
     length: 5 in.; width: 5 in.

24. The volume of a rectangular solid is 864 m³. The rectangular solid has a square base and a height of 6 m. Find the dimensions of the solid.
     length: 12 m; width: 12 m

25. An oil storage tank, which is in the shape of a cylinder, is 4 m high and has a diameter of 6 m. The oil tank is two-thirds full. Find the number of cubic meters of oil in the tank. Round to the nearest hundredth.   75.40 m³

26. A silo, which is in the shape of a cylinder, is 16 ft in diameter and has a height of 30 ft. The silo is three-fourths full. Find the volume of the portion of the silo that is not being used for storage. Round to the nearest hundredth.   1507.96 ft³

Objective B

Find the surface area of the figure.

27.

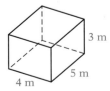

3 m
4 m
5 m

94 m²

28.

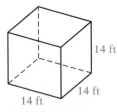

14 ft
14 ft
14 ft

1176 ft²

29.

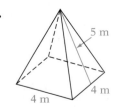

5 m
4 m
4 m

56 m²

Find the surface area of the figure. Give both the exact value and an approximation to the nearest hundredth.

30.

4π cm²; 12.57 cm²

31.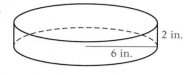

96π in²; 301.59 in²

32.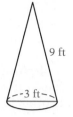

15.75π ft²; 49.48 ft²

Solve.

33. The height of a rectangular solid is 5 ft. The length is 8 ft, and the width is 4 ft. Find the surface area of the solid.   184 ft²

34. The width of a rectangular solid is 32 cm. The length is 60 cm, and the height is 14 cm. What is the surface area of the solid?   6416 cm²

35. The side of a cube measures 3.4 m. Find the surface area of the cube. 69.36 m²

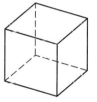

36. Find the surface area of a cube that has a side measuring 1.5 in. 13.5 in²

37. Find the surface area of a sphere with a diameter of 15 cm. Give the exact value.   225π cm²

38. The radius of a sphere is 2 in. Find the surface area of the sphere. Round to the nearest hundredth.   50.27 in²

39. The radius of the base of a cylinder is 4 in. The height of the cylinder is 12 in. Find the surface area of the cylinder. Round to the nearest hundredth.   402.12 in²

40. The diameter of the base of a cylinder is 1.8 m. The height of the cylinder is 0.7 m. Find the surface area of the cylinder. Give the exact value.   2.88π m²

41. The slant height of a cone is 2.5 ft. The radius of the base is 1.5 ft. Find the surface area of the cone. Give the exact value.   6π ft²

42. The diameter of the base of a cone is 21 in. The slant height is 16 in. What is the surface area of the cone? Round to the nearest hundredth. 874.15 in²

43. The length of a side of the base of a pyramid is 9 in., and the slant height is 12 in. Find the surface area of the pyramid.   297 in²

44. The slant height of a pyramid is 18 m, and the length of a side of the base is 16 m. What is the surface area of the pyramid?   832 m²

45. The surface area of a rectangular solid is 108 cm². The height of the solid is 4 cm, and the length is 6 cm. Find the width of the rectangular solid.   3 cm

46. The length of a rectangular solid is 12 ft. The width is 3 ft. If the surface area is 162 ft², find the height of the rectangular solid.   3 ft

47. A can of paint will cover 300 ft². How many cans of paint should be purchased in order to paint a cylinder that has a height of 30 ft and a radius of 12 ft?   11 cans

48. A hot air balloon is in the shape of a sphere. Approximately how much fabric was used to construct the balloon if its diameter is 32 ft? Round to the nearest whole number.   3217 ft²

49. How much glass is needed to make a fish tank that is 12 in. long, 8 in. wide, and 9 in. high? The fish tank is open at the top.   456 in²

50. Find the area of a label used to cover a can of juice that has a diameter of 16.5 cm and a height of 17 cm. Round to the nearest hundredth.
881.22 cm²

51. The length of a side of the base of a pyramid is 5 cm, and the slant height is 8 cm. How much larger is the surface area of this pyramid than the surface area of a cone with a diameter of 5 cm and a slant height of 8 cm? Round to the nearest hundredth.   22.53 cm²

APPLYING THE CONCEPTS

52. Half of a sphere is called a **hemisphere**. Derive formulas for the volume and surface area of a hemisphere.   See the *Solutions Manual.*

53. Determine whether the statement is always true, sometimes true, or never true.
   a. The slant height of a regular pyramid is longer than the height.   always true
   b. The slant height of a cone is shorter than the height.   never true
   c. The four triangular faces of a regular pyramid are equilateral triangles.   sometimes true

54. **a.** What is the effect on the surface area of a rectangular solid when the width and height are doubled?   doubled plus 4*WH*
   b. What is the effect on the volume of a rectangular solid when both the length and the width are doubled?   quadrupled
   c. What is the effect on the volume of a cube when the length of each side of the cube is doubled?   8 times as large
   d. What is the effect on the surface area of a cylinder when the radius and height are doubled?   4 times as large

55. Explain how you could cut through a cube so that the face of the resulting solid is
   a. a square
   b. an equilateral triangle
   c. a trapezoid
   d. a hexagon

Focus on Problem Solving

Trial and Error

Some problems in mathematics are solved by using **trial and error**. The trial-and-error method of arriving at a solution to a problem involves repeated tests or experiments until a satisfactory conclusion is reached.

Many of the Applying the Concepts exercises in this text require a trial and error method of solution. For example, an exercise in Section 3 of this chapter reads:

Explain how you could cut through a cube so that the face of the resulting solid is **(a)** a square, **(b)** an equilateral triangle, **(c)** a trapezoid, **(d)** a hexagon.

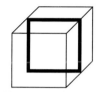

There is no formula to apply to this problem; there is no computation to perform. This problem requires picturing a cube and the results after cutting through it at different places on its surface and at different angles. For part (a), cutting perpendicular to the top and bottom of the cube and parallel to two of its sides will result in a square. The other shapes may prove more difficult.

When solving problems of this type, keep an open mind. Sometimes when using the trial-and-error method, we are hampered by narrowness of vision; we cannot expand our thinking to include other possibilities. Then when we see someone else's solution, it appears so obvious to us! For example, for the Applying the Concepts question above, it is necessary to conceive of cutting through the cube at places other than the top surface; we need to be open to the idea of beginning the cut at one of the corner points of the cube.

A topic of the Projects and Group Activities in this chapter is symmetry. Here again, trial and error is used to determine the lines of symmetry inherent in an object. For example, in determining lines of symmetry for a square, begin by drawing a square. The horizontal line of symmetry and the vertical line of symmetry may be immediately obvious to you.

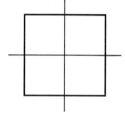

But there are two others. Do you see that a line drawn through opposite corners of the square is also a line of symmetry?

Many of the questions in this text that require an answer of "always true, sometimes true, or never true" are best solved by the trial-and-error method. For example, consider the statement presented in Section 2 of this chapter.

If two rectangles have the same area, then they have the same perimeter.

Try some numbers. Each of two rectangles, one measuring 6 units by 2 units and another measuring 4 units by 3 units, has an area of 12 square units, but the perimeter of the first is 16 units and the perimeter of the second is 14 units. So the answer "always true" has been eliminated. We still need to determine whether there is a case when it is true. After experimenting with a lot of numbers, you may come to realize that we are trying to determine if it is possible for two different pairs of factors of a number to have the same sum. Is it?

Don't be afraid to make many experiments, and remember that *errors*, or tests that "don't work," are a part of the trial-and-*error* process.

Projects and Group Activities

Investigating Perimeter

The perimeter of the square at the right is 4 units.

If two squares are joined along one of the sides, the perimeter is 6 units. Note that it does not matter which sides are joined; the perimeter is still 6 units.

If three squares are joined, the perimeter of the resulting figure is 8 units for each possible placement of the squares.

Four squares can be joined in five different ways as shown. There are two possible perimeters, 10 units for A, B, C, and D, and 8 for E.

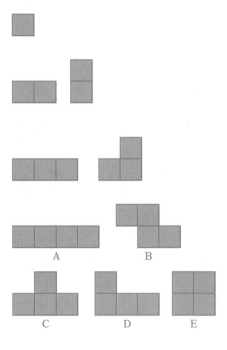

1. If five squares are joined, what is the maximum perimeter possible?

2. If five squares are joined, what is the minimum perimeter possible?

3. If six squares are joined, what is the maximum perimeter possible?

4. If six squares are joined, what is the minimum perimeter possible?

Symmetry   Look at the letter A printed at the left. If the letter were folded along line ℓ, the two sides of the letter would match exactly. This letter has **symmetry** with respect to line ℓ. Line ℓ is called the **axis of symmetry**.

Now consider the letter H printed below at the left. Both lines ℓ_1 and ℓ_2 are axes of symmetry for this letter; the letter could be folded along either line and the two sides would match exactly.

1. Does the letter A have more than one axis of symmetry?

2. Find axes of symmetry for other capital letters of the alphabet.

3. Which lowercase letters have one axis of symmetry?

4. Do any of the lowercase letters have more than one axis of symmetry?

5. Find the number of axes of symmetry for each of the plane geometric figures presented in this chapter.

6. There are other types of symmetry. Look up the meaning of point symmetry and rotational symmetry. Which plane geometric figures provide examples of these types of symmetry?

7. Find examples of symmetry in nature, art, and architecture.

Chapter Summary

Key Words   A *line* is determined by two distinct points and extends indefinitely in both directions. A *line segment* is part of a line that has two endpoints. *Parallel lines* never meet; the distance between them is always the same. *Perpendicular lines* are intersecting lines that form right angles.

A *ray* starts at a point and extends indefinitely in one direction. The point at which a ray starts is the *endpoint* of the ray. An *angle* is formed by two rays with the same endpoint. The *vertex* of an angle is the point at which the two rays meet. An angle is measured in *degrees*. A 90° angle is a *right angle*. A 180° angle is a *straight angle*. An *acute angle* is an angle whose measure is between 0° and 90°. An *obtuse angle* is an angle whose measure is between 90° and 180°. *Complementary angles* are two angles whose measures have the sum 90°. *Supplementary angles* are two angles whose measures have the sum 180°.

Two angles that are on opposite sides of the intersection of two lines are *vertical angles;* vertical angles have the same measure. Two angles that share a common side are *adjacent angles;* adjacent angles of intersecting lines are supplementary angles.

A line that intersects two other lines at two different points is a *transversal*. If the lines cut by a transversal are parallel lines, equal angles are formed: *alternate interior angles, alternate exterior angles,* and *corresponding angles*.

A *polygon* is a closed figure determined by three or more line segments. The line segments that form the polygon are its *sides*. A *regular polygon* is one in which each side has the same length and each angle has the same measure. Polygons are classified by the number of sides.

A *triangle* is a plane figure formed by three line segments. An *isosceles triangle* has two sides of equal length. The three sides of an *equilateral triangle* are of equal length. A *scalene triangle* has no two sides of equal length. An *acute triangle* has three acute angles. An *obtuse triangle* has one obtuse angle. A *right triangle* has a right angle.

A *quadrilateral* is a four-sided polygon. A parallelogram, a rectangle, a square, a rhombus, and a trapezoid are all quadrilaterals.

A *circle* is a plane figure in which all points are the same distance from the center of the circle. A *diameter* of a circle is a line segment across the circle through the center. A *radius* of a circle is a line segment from the center of the circle to a point on the circle.

The *perimeter* of a plane geometric figure is a measure of the distance around the figure. The distance around a circle is called the *circumference*. *Area* is the amount of surface in a region. *Volume* is a measure of the amount of space inside a figure in space. The *surface area* of a solid is the total area on the surface of the solid.

Essential Rules

Triangles

Sum of the measures of the interior angles = 180°

Sum of an interior and corresponding exterior angle = 180°

Perimeter

Triangle:	$P = a + b + c$
Rectangle:	$P = 2L + 2W$
Square:	$P = 4s$
Circle:	$C = \pi d$ or $C = 2\pi r$

Area

Triangle:	$A = \dfrac{1}{2}bh$
Rectangle:	$A = LW$
Square:	$A = s^2$
Circle:	$A = \pi r^2$
Parallelogram:	$A = bh$
Trapezoid:	$A = \dfrac{1}{2}h(b_1 + b_2)$

Volume

Rectangular solid:	$V = LWH$
Cube:	$V = s^3$
Sphere:	$V = \dfrac{4}{3}\pi r^3$
Right circular cylinder:	$V = \pi r^2 h$
Right circular cone:	$V = \dfrac{1}{3}\pi r^2 h$
Regular pyramid:	$V = \dfrac{1}{3}s^2 h$

Surface Area

Rectangular solid:	$SA = 2LW + 2LH + 2WH$
Cube:	$SA = 6s^2$
Sphere:	$SA = 4\pi r^2$
Right circular cylinder:	$SA = 2\pi r^2 + 2\pi rh$
Right circular cone:	$SA = \pi r^2 + \pi r\ell$
Regular pyramid:	$SA = s^2 + 2s\ell$

Chapter Review

1. Given that $\angle a = 74°$ and $\angle b = 52°$, find the measures of angles x and y.

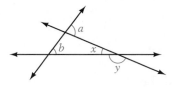

$\angle x = 22°$; $\angle y = 158°$ [3.1C]

2. Find the measure of $\angle x$.

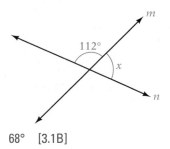

68°   [3.1B]

3. Given that $BC = 11$ cm and AB is three times the length of BC, find the length of AC.

44 cm   [3.1A]

4. Find x.

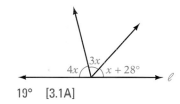

19°   [3.1A]

5. Find the volume of the figure.

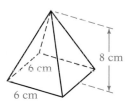

96 cm³   [3.3A]

6. Given that $\ell_1 \parallel \ell_2$, find the measures of angles a and b.

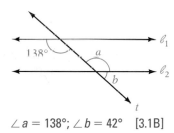

$\angle a = 138°$; $\angle b = 42°$ [3.1B]

7. Find the surface area of the figure.

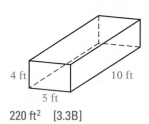

220 ft²   [3.3B]

8. Find the supplement of a 32° angle.
148°   [3.1A]

9. Determine the area of a rectangle with a length of 12 cm and a width of 6.5 cm.
78 cm²   [3.2B]

10. Determine the area of a triangle whose base is 9 m and whose height is 14 m.
63 m²   [3.2B]

11. Find the volume of a rectangular solid with a length of 6.5 ft, a width of 2 ft, and a height of 3 ft.
39 ft³ [3.3A]

12. Two angles of a triangle measure 37° and 48°. Find the measure of the third angle.
95° [3.1C]

13. The height of a triangle is 7 cm. The area of the triangle is 28 cm². Find the length of the base of the triangle.
8 cm [3.2B]

14. Find the volume of a sphere that has a diameter of 12 mm. Find the exact value.
288π mm³ [3.3A]

15. Determine the exact volume of a right circular cone whose radius is 7 cm and whose height is 16 cm.
$\frac{784\pi}{3}$ cm³ [3.3A]

16. The perimeter of a square picture frame is 86 cm. Find the length of each side of the frame.
21.5 cm [3.2A]

17. A can of paint will cover 200 ft². How many cans of paint should be purchased in order to paint a cylinder that has a height of 15 ft and a radius of 6 ft?
4 cans [3.3B]

18. The length of a rectangular park is 56 yd. The width is 48 yd. How many yards of fencing are needed to surround the park?
208 yd [3.2A]

19. What is the area of a square patio that measures 9.5 m on each side?
90.25 m² [3.2B]

20. A walkway 2 m wide surrounds a rectangular plot of grass. The plot is 40 m long and 25 m wide. What is the area of the walkway?
276 m² [3.2B]

Chapter Test

1. The diameter of a sphere is 1.5 m. Find the radius of the sphere.

0.75 m   [3.2A]

2. Find the circumference of a circle with a radius of 5 cm. Use 3.14 for π.

31.4 cm   [3.2A]

3. Find the perimeter of the rectangle in the figure below.

26 ft   [3.2A]

4. Given $AB = 15$, $CD = 6$, and $AD = 24$, find the length of BC.

3   [3.1A]

5. Find the volume of a sphere with a diameter of 8 ft. Use 3.14 for π. Round to the nearest tenth.

267.9 ft³   [3.3A]

6. Find the area of the circle shown below. Use 3.14 for π.

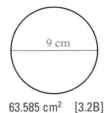

63.585 cm²   [3.2B]

7. Given that $\ell_1 \parallel \ell_2$, find the measures of angles a and b.

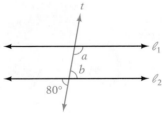

$a = 100°$, $b = 80°$ [3.1B]

8. Find the supplement of a 105° angle.

75°   [3.1A]

9. Given that $\ell_1 \parallel \ell_2$, find the measures of angles a and b.

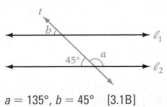

$a = 135°$, $b = 45°$ [3.1B]

10. Find the area of the rectangle shown below.

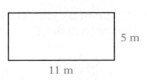

55 m²   [3.2B]

11. Find the volume of a cylinder with a height of 6 m and a radius of 3 m. Use 3.14 for π.
169.56 m³ [3.3A]

12. Find the perimeter of a rectangle that has a length of 2 m and a width of 1.4 m.
6.8 m [3.2A]

13. Find the complement of a 32° angle.
58° [3.1A]

14. Find the surface area of the figure. Round to the nearest hundredth.

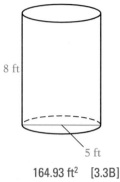

8 ft

5 ft

164.93 ft² [3.3B]

15. How much more pizza is contained in a pizza with radius 10 in. than in one with radius 8 in.? Use 3.14 for π.
113.04 in² [3.2B]

16. A right triangle has a 32° angle. Find the measures of the other two angles.
58° and 90° [3.1C]

17. A bicycle tire has a diameter of 28 in. How many feet does the bicycle travel if the wheel makes 10 revolutions? Use 3.14 for π. Round to the nearest tenth of a foot.
73.3 ft [3.2A]

28 in.

18. New carpet is installed in a room measuring 18 ft by 14 ft. Find the area of the room in square yards. (9 ft² = 1 yd²)
28 yd² [3.2B]

19. A silo, which is in the shape of a cylinder, is 9 ft in diameter and has a height of 18 ft. Find the volume of the silo. Use 3.14 for π.
1144.53 ft³ [3.3A]

20. Find the area of a right triangle with a base of 8 m and a height of 2.75 m.
11 m² [3.2B]

Cumulative Review

1. Let $x \in \{-3, 0, 1\}$. For what values of x is the inequality $x \le 1$ a true statement?
   $-3, 0, 1$ [1.1A]

2. Write 8.9% as a decimal.
   0.089   [1.2B]

3. Write $\frac{7}{20}$ as a percent.
   35%   [1.2B]

4. Divide: $-\frac{4}{9} \div \frac{2}{3}$
   $-\frac{2}{3}$ [1.2D]

5. Multiply: 5.7 (−4.3)
   −24.51   [1.2D]

6. Simplify: $-\sqrt{125}$
   $-5\sqrt{5}$ [1.2F]

7. Evaluate $5 - 3[10 + (5 - 6)^2]$.
   −28   [1.3A]

8. Evaluate $a(b - c)^3$ when $a = -1$, $b = -2$, and $c = -4$.
   −8   [1.4A]

9. Simplify: $5m + 3n - 8m$
   $-3m + 3n$ [1.4B]

10. Simplify: $-7(-3y)$
    21y   [1.4C]

11. Simplify: $4(3x + 2) - (5x - 1)$
    7x + 9   [1.4D]

12. Use the roster method to write the set of negative integers greater than or equal to −2.
    $\{-2, -1\}$ [1.5A]

13. Find $C \cup D$, given $C = \{0, 10, 20, 30\}$ and $D = \{-10, 0, 10\}$.
    $C \cup D = \{-10, 0, 10, 20, 30\}$ [1.5A]]

14. Graph: $x \le 1$

    [1.5C]

15. Solve: $4x + 2 = 6x - 8$
    5   [2.2B]

16. Solve: $3(2x + 5) = 18$
    $\frac{1}{2}$ [2.2C]

17. Solve: $4y - 3 \ge 6y + 5$
    $\{y \mid y \le -4\}$ [2.4A]

18. Solve: $8 - 4(3x + 5) \le 6(x - 8)$
    $\{x \mid x \ge 2\}$ [2.4A]

19. Solve: $2x - 3 > 5$ or $x + 4 < 1$
$\{x \mid x < -3 \text{ or } x > 4\}$ [2.4B]

20. Solve: $-3 \leq 2x - 7 \leq 5$
$\{x \mid 2 \leq x \leq 6\}$ [2.4B]

21. Solve: $|3x - 1| = 2$
$1, -\dfrac{1}{3}$ [2.5A]

22. Solve: $|x - 8| \leq 2$
$\{x \mid 6 \leq x \leq 10\}$ [2.5B]

23. Find the measure of $\angle x$.
131°   [3.1B]

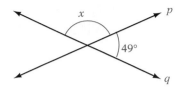

24. Translate "the difference between four times a number and ten is two" into an equation and solve.
$4x - 10 = 2$; $x = 3$ [2.2D]

25. Two angles of a triangle measure 37° and 21°. Find the measure of the third angle of the triangle.
122°   [3.1C]

26. An engineering consultant invested $14,000 in a 5.5% annual simple interest account. How much additional money is deposited in an account that pays 9.5% annual simple interest if the total interest earned on both accounts is $1245?
$5000   [2.3C]

27. Two sides of an isosceles triangle measure 7.5 m. The perimeter of the triangle is 19.5 m. Find the measure of the third side of the triangle.
4.5 m   [3.2A]

28. Of the 375 students in a high school graduating class, 300 students went on to college. What percent of the students in the class went on to college?
80%   [2.1D]

29. Find the exact area of a circle that has a diameter of 9 cm.
20.25π cm^2 [3.2B]

30. The volume of a box is 144 ft³. The length of the box is 12 ft, and the width is 4 ft. Find the height of the box.
3 ft   [3.3A]

4

Linear Equations and Inequalities in Two Variables

Broadcast technicians operate the electronic equipment used to record and transmit radio and television programs, and they help prepare movie soundtracks for production studios. They work with television cameras, microphones, tape recorders, light and sound effects, transmitters, antennas, and other equipment. These technicians must be able to read and interpret graphs such as those discussed in this chapter.

Objectives

Section 4.1
To graph points in a rectangular coordinate system
To determine ordered-pair solutions of an equation in two variables
To determine whether a set of ordered pairs is a function
To evaluate a function written in functional notation

Section 4.2
To graph an equation of the form $y = mx + b$
To graph an equation of the form $Ax + By = C$
To solve application problems

Section 4.3
To find the slope of a straight line
To graph a line using the slope and the y-intercept

Section 4.4
To find the equation of a line given a point and the slope
To find the equation of a line given two points
To solve application problems

Section 4.5
To find parallel and perpendicular lines

Section 4.6
To graph an inequality in two variables

Magic Squares

A magic square is a square array of distinct integers arranged in such a way that the numbers along any row, column, or main diagonal have the same sum. An example of a magic square is shown at the right.

8	3	4
1	5	9
6	7	2

The oldest known example of a magic square comes from China. Estimates are that this magic square is over 4000 years old. It is shown at the left.

There is a simple way to produce a magic square with an odd number of cells. Start by writing a 1 in the top middle cell. The rule then is to proceed diagonally upward to the right with the successive integers. See Figure A.

When the rule takes you outside the square, write the number by shifting either across the square from right to left or down the square from top to bottom, as the case may be. For example, in Figure B the second number (2) is outside the square above a column. Because the 2 is above a column, it should be shifted down to the bottom cell in that column. In Figure C, the 3 is outside the square to the right of a column and should therefore be shifted all the way to the left.

If the rule takes you to a square that is already filled (as shown in Figure C), then write the number in the cell directly below the last number written (see Figure D). Continue until the entire square is filled.

It is possible to begin a magic square with any integer and proceed by using the above rule and consecutive integers.

For an odd magic square beginning with 1, the sum of a row, column, or diagonal is $\dfrac{n(n^2 + 1)}{2}$, where n is the number of rows.

Figure A

Figure B

Figure C

Figure D

Figure E

Figure F

Figure G

Figure H

奇異方格

4.1 The Rectangular Coordinate System

Objective A   *To graph points in a rectangular coordinate system*..................

Before the 15th century, geometry and algebra were considered separate branches of mathematics. That all changed when René Descartes, a French mathematician who lived from 1596 to 1650, developed **analytic geometry**. In this geometry, a *coordinate system* is used to study relationships between variables.

A **rectangular coordinate system** is formed by two number lines, one horizontal and one vertical, that intersect at the zero point of each line. The point of intersection is called the **origin**. The two lines are called **coordinate axes**, or simply **axes**. Generally, the horizontal axis is labeled the *x*-axis and the vertical axis is labeled the *y*-axis.

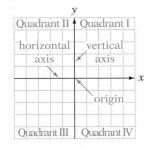

The axes determine a **plane**, which can be thought of as a large, flat sheet of paper. The two axes divide the plane into four regions called **quadrants**, which are numbered counterclockwise from I to IV starting from the upper right.

Each point in the plane can be identified by a pair of numbers called an **ordered pair**. The first number of the ordered pair measures a horizontal distance and is called the **abscissa**, or **x-coordinate**. The second number of the pair measures a vertical distance and is called the **ordinate**, or **y-coordinate**. The ordered pair (x, y) associated with a point is also called the **coordinates** of the point.

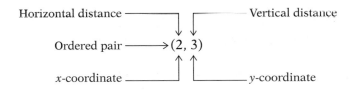

To **graph** or **plot** a point in the plane, place a dot at the location given by the ordered pair. The **graph of an ordered pair** is the dot drawn at the coordinates of the point in the plane. The points whose coordinates are (3, 4) and (−2.5, −3) are graphed in the figures below.

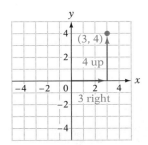

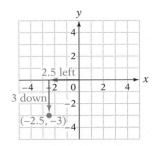

The points whose coordinates are $(3, -1)$ and $(-1, 3)$ are graphed at the right. Note that the graphed points are in different locations. *The order of the coordinates of an ordered pair is important.*

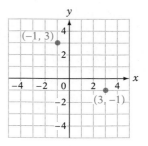

INSTRUCTOR NOTE

It may help students to think of an ordered pair as the address (location) of a point in the plane.

Each point in the plane is associated with an ordered pair, and each ordered pair is associated with a point in the plane. Although only the labels for integers are given on a coordinate grid, the graph of any ordered pair can be approximated. For example, the points whose coordinates are $(-2.3, 4.1)$ and $(\pi, 1)$ are shown on the graph at the right.

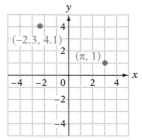

Example 1   Graph the ordered pairs $(-2, -3)$, $(3, -2)$, $(0, -2)$, and $(3, 0)$.

Solution

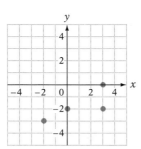

You Try It 1   Graph the ordered pairs $(-4, 1)$, $(3, -3)$, $(0, 4)$, and $(-3, 0)$.

Your solution

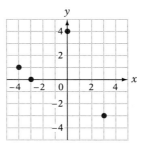

Example 2   Give the coordinates of the points labeled A and B. Give the abscissa of point C and the ordinate of point D.

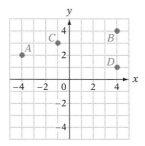

You Try It 2   Give the coordinates of the points labeled A and B. Give the abscissa of point D and the ordinate of point C.

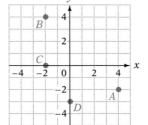

Solution   The coordinates of A are $(-4, 2)$.
The coordinates of B are $(4, 4)$.
The abscissa of C is -1.
The ordinate of D is 1.

Your solution $A(4, -2)$, $B(-2, 4)$. The abscissa of D is 0. The ordinate of C is 0.

Solutions on p. S10

Objective B **To determine ordered-pair solutions of an equation in two variables**..

A coordinate system is used to study the relationship between two variables. Frequently this relationship is given by an equation. Examples of equations in two variables include

$$y = 2x - 3 \qquad 3x + 2y = 6 \qquad x^2 - y = 0$$

A **solution of an equation in two variables** is an ordered pair (x, y) whose coordinates make the equation a true statement.

➡ Is the ordered pair $(-3, 7)$ a solution of the equation $y = -2x + 1$?

$$\begin{array}{c|c} y = -2x + 1 \\ \hline 7 & -2(-3) + 1 \\ 7 & 6 + 1 \\ 7 = 7 \end{array}$$

• Replace x by -3 and y by 7.
• Simplify.
• Compare the results. If the resulting equation is a true statement, the ordered pair is a solution of the equation. If it is not a true statement, the ordered pair is not a solution of the equation.

Yes, the ordered pair $(-3, 7)$ is a solution of the equation.

Besides $(-3, 7)$, there are many other ordered-pair solutions of $y = -2x + 1$. For example, $(0, 1)$, $\left(-\dfrac{3}{2}, 4\right)$, and $(4, -7)$ are also solutions. In general, an equation in two variables has an infinite number of solutions. By choosing any value of x and substituting that value into the equation, we can calculate a corresponding value of y.

➡ Find the ordered-pair solution of $y = \dfrac{2}{3}x - 3$ that corresponds to $x = 6$.

$$y = \dfrac{2}{3}x - 3$$
$$\quad = \dfrac{2}{3}(6) - 3 \qquad \text{• Replace } x \text{ by 6.}$$
$$\quad = 4 - 3 \qquad\qquad \text{• Solve for } y.$$
$$\quad = 1$$

The ordered-pair solution is $(6, 1)$.

The solution of an equation in two variables can be graphed in an xy-coordinate system.

➡ Graph the ordered-pair solutions of $y = -2x + 1$ when $x = -2, -1, 0, 1,$ and 2.

Use the values of x to determine ordered-pair solutions of the equation. It is convenient to record these in a table.

x	$y = -2x + 1$	y	(x, y)
-2	$-2(-2) + 1$	5	$(-2, 5)$
-1	$-2(-1) + 1$	3	$(-1, 3)$
0	$-2(0) + 1$	1	$(0, 1)$
1	$-2(1) + 1$	-1	$(1, -1)$
2	$-2(2) + 1$	-3	$(2, -3)$

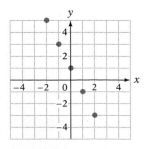

Example 3

Is $(3, -2)$ a solution of $3x - 4y = 15$?

Solution

$$3x - 4y = 15$$

$3(3) - 4(-2)$	15
$9 + 8$	15
$17 \neq 15$	

• Replace x by 3 and y by -2.

No, $(3, -2)$ is not a solution of $3x - 4y = 15$.

You Try It 3

Is $(-2, 4)$ a solution of $x - 3y = -14$?

Your solution

yes

Example 4

Find the ordered-pair solution of $y = \dfrac{x}{x - 2}$ corresponding to $x = 4$.

Solution

Replace x by 4 and solve for y.

$$y = \frac{x}{x - 2} = \frac{4}{4 - 2} = \frac{4}{2} = 2$$

The ordered-pair solution is $(4, 2)$.

You Try It 4

Find the ordered-pair solution of $y = \dfrac{3x}{x + 1}$ corresponding to $x = -2$.

Your solution

$(-2, 6)$

Example 5

Graph the ordered-pair solutions of $y = \dfrac{2}{3}x - 2$ when $x = -3, 0, 3, 6$.

Solution

Replace x in $y = \dfrac{2}{3}x - 2$ by $-3, 0, 3$, and 6. For each value of x, determine the value of y.

x	$y = \dfrac{2}{3}x - 2$	y	(x, y)
-3	$\dfrac{2}{3}(-3) - 2$	-4	$(-3, -4)$
0	$\dfrac{2}{3}(0) - 2$	-2	$(0, -2)$
3	$\dfrac{2}{3}(3) - 2$	0	$(3, 0)$
6	$\dfrac{2}{3}(6) - 2$	2	$(6, 2)$

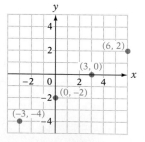

You Try It 5

Graph the ordered-pair solutions of $y = -\dfrac{1}{2}x + 2$ when $x = -4, -2, 0, 2$.

Your solution

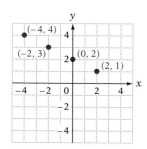

Solutions on pp. S10–S11

Objective C   *To determine whether a set of ordered pairs is a function..........*

Discovering a relationship between two variables is an important task in the application of mathematics. Here are some examples.

• Botanists study the relationship between the number of bushels of wheat yielded per acre and the amount of watering per acre.
• Environmental scientists study the relationship between the incidence of skin cancer and the amount of ozone in the atmosphere.
• Business analysts study the relationship between the price of a product and the number of products that are sold at that price.

Each of these relationships can be described by a set of ordered pairs.

Definition of a Relation

A **relation** is any set of ordered pairs.

The following table shows the number of hours that each of 9 students spent studying for a midterm exam and the grade that each of these 9 students received.

Hours	3	3.5	2.75	2	4	4.5	3	2.5	5
Grade	78	75	70	65	85	85	80	75	90

This information can be written as the relation

{(3, 78), (3.5, 75), (2.75, 70), (2, 65), (4, 85), (4.5, 85), (3, 80), (2.5, 75), (5, 90)}

where the first coordinate of each ordered pair is the hours spent studying and the second coordinate is the score on the midterm.

The **domain** of a relation is the set of first coordinates of the ordered pairs; the **range** is the set of second coordinates. For the relation above,

Domain = {2, 2.5, 2.75, 3, 3.5, 4, 4.5, 5}   Range = {65, 70, 75, 78, 80, 85, 90}

The **graph of a relation** is the graph of the ordered pairs that belong to the relation. The graph of the relation given above is shown at the right. The horizontal axis represents the hours spent studying (the domain); the vertical axis represents the test score (the range). The axes could be labeled H for hours studied and S for test score.

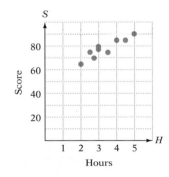

INSTRUCTOR NOTE

An extra-credit problem for interested students is to define three situations that are functions and three that are relations but not functions. Here's an example of a relation: The ordered pairs whose first coordinate is the runs scored by a baseball team and whose second coordinate is W for win or L for loss.

A *function* is a special type of relation for which no two ordered pairs have the same first coordinate.

Definition of a Function

A **function** is a relation in which no two ordered pairs that have the same first coordinate have different second coordinates.

The table at the right is the grading scale for a 100-point test. This table defines a relationship between the *score* on the test and a *letter grade*. Some of the ordered pairs of this function are (78, C), (97, A), (84, B), and (82, B).

Score	Grade
90–100	A
80–89	B
70–79	C
60–69	D
0–59	F

The grading-scale table defines a function, because no two ordered pairs can have the *same* first coordinate and *different* second coordinates. For instance, it is not possible to have the ordered pairs (72, C) and (72, B)—the same first coordinate (test score) but a different second coordinate (test grade). The domain of this function is {0, 1, 2, . . . , 99, 100}. The range is {A, B, C, D, F}.

The example of hours spent studying and test score given earlier is *not* a function, because (3, 78) and (3, 80) are ordered pairs of the relation that have the *same* first coordinate but *different* second coordinates.

Consider, again, the grading-scale example. Note that (84, B) and (82, B) are ordered pairs of the function. Ordered pairs of a function may have the same *second* coordinates, but not the same first coordinates.

Although relations and functions can be given by tables, they are frequently given by an equation in two variables.

The equation $y = 2x$ expresses the relationship between a number, x, and twice the number, y. For instance, if $x = 3$, then $y = 6$, which is twice 3. To indicate exactly which ordered pairs are determined by the equation, the domain (values of x) is specified. If $x \in \{-2, -1, 0, 1, 2\}$, then the ordered pairs determined by the equation are $\{(-2, -4), (-1, -2), (0, 0), (1, 2), (2, 4)\}$. This relation is a function because no two ordered pairs have the same first coordinate.

INSTRUCTOR NOTE

The concept of a function was beginning to form with the work of Fermat and Descartes. However, it was Euler who gave us the word and its first definition: "A function of a variable quantity is an analytic expression composed in any way whatsoever of the variable quantity and numbers or constant quantities."
   This sense of function in Euler's definition is that of "*y* is a function of *x*," but it does not encompass the more general notion of a function as a certain set of ordered pairs.

The graph of the function $y = 2x$ with domain $\{-2, -1, 0, 1, 2\}$ is shown at the right. The horizontal axis (domain) is labeled x; the vertical axis (range) is labeled y.

The domain $\{-2, -1, 0, 1, 2\}$ was chosen arbitrarily. Other domains could have been selected. The type of application usually influences the choice of the domain.

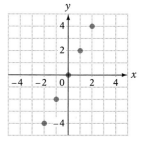

For the equation $y = 2x$, we say that "y is a function of x" because the set of ordered pairs is a function.

Not all equations, however, define a function. For instance, the equation $|y| = x + 2$ does not define y as a function of x. The ordered pairs (2, 4) and (2, −4) both satisfy the equation. Thus there are two ordered pairs with the same first coordinate but different second coordinates.

Objective C

35. The speeds of a car in miles per hour and the distance needed to stop at those speeds are recorded in the table at the right. Write a relation in which the first co-ordinate is the speed in miles per hour and the second coordinate is the distance needed to stop. Is the relation a function?

{(55, 273),(65, 355), (75, 447), (85, 549)}; yes

Speed (in miles per hour)	Distance Needed to Stop (in feet)
55	273
65	355
75	447
85	549

Source: AAA Foundation for Traffic Safety

36. The number of runs scored by the American League and by the National League in each of the Major League Baseball All-Star Games from 1990 to 1997 are recorded in the table at the right. Write a relation in which the first coordinate is the number of runs scored by the American League and the second coordinate is the number of runs scored by the National League. Is the relation a function?

{(0, 2), (4, 2), (13, 6), (9, 3), (7, 8), (2, 3), (0, 6), (3, 1)}; yes

Year	American League	National League
1990	0	2
1991	4	2
1992	13	6
1993	9	3
1994	7	8
1995	2	3
1996	0	6
1997	3	1

37. The number of sunny days in a year in five different cities and the average cost of a four-bedroom house (in thousands of dollars) in those cities is given in the table to the right. Write a relation in which the first component is the number of sunny days annually and the second component is the cost of a house. Is the relation a function?

{(197, 125), (205, 122), (257, 490), (226, 108), (205, 150)}; no

City	Sunny Days Annually	4-Bedroom House Cost
Nashua, NH	197	125
Portsmouth, NH	205	122
San Jose, CA	257	498
Jacksonville, FL	226	108
Manchester, NH	205	150

Source: Money Magazine, July, 1997

38. The budgets (in millions of dollars) for several movies and the gross ticket sales (in millions of dollars) are recorded in the table to the right. Write a relation in which the first component is the budget and the second component is the gross sales. Is the relation a function?

{(30, 93), (62, 172), (30, 15), (50, 200), (100, 184)}; no

Movie	Budget	Gross Sales
Seven	30	93
Apollo 13	62	172
Nixon	30	15
Toy Story	50	200
Batman Forever	100	184

39. Does $y = -2x - 3$, where $x \in \{-2, -1, 0, 3\}$, define y as a function of x?

yes

40. Does $y = 2x + 3$, where $x \in \{-2, -1, 1, 4\}$, define y as a function of x?

yes

41. Does $|y| = x - 1$, where $x \in \{1, 2, 3, 4\}$, define y as a function of x?

no

42. Does $|y| = x + 2$, where $x \in \{-2, -1, 0, 3\}$, define y as a function of x?

no

43. Does $y = x^2$, where $x \in \{-2, -1, 0, 1, 2\}$, define y as a function of x?

yes

44. Does $y = x^2 - 1$, where $x \in \{-2, -1, 0, 1, 2\}$, define y as a function of x?

yes

Objective D

45. Given $f(x) = 3x - 4$, find $f(4)$.
8

46. Given $f(x) = 5x + 1$, find $f(2)$.
11

47. Given $f(x) = x^2$, find $f(3)$.
9

48. Given $f(x) = x^2 - 1$, find $f(1)$.
0

49. Given $G(x) = x^2 + x$, find $G(-2)$.
2

50. Given $H(x) = x^2 - x$, find $H(-2)$.
6

51. Given $s(t) = \dfrac{3}{t - 1}$, find $s(-2)$.

-1

52. Given $P(x) = \dfrac{4}{2x + 1}$, find $P(-2)$.

$-\dfrac{4}{3}$

53. Given $h(x) = 3x^2 - 2x + 1$, find $h(3)$.
22

54. Given $Q(r) = 4r^2 - r - 3$, find $Q(2)$.
11

55. Given $f(x) = \dfrac{x}{x + 5}$, find $f(-3)$.

$-\dfrac{3}{2}$

56. Given $v(t) = \dfrac{2t}{2t + 1}$, find $v(3)$.

$\dfrac{6}{7}$

57. Given $g(x) = x^3 - x^2 + 2x - 7$, find $g(0)$.
-7

58. Given $F(z) = \dfrac{z}{z^2 + 1}$, find $F(0)$.
0

APPLYING THE CONCEPTS

59. Suppose you are helping a student who is having trouble graphing ordered pairs. The work of the student is at the right. What can you say to this student to correct the error that is being made?

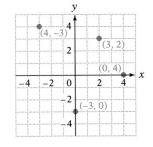

60. Write a few sentences that describe the similiarities and differences between relations and functions.

61. The graph of $y^2 = x$, where $x \in \{0, 1, 4, 9\}$, is shown at the right. Is this the graph of a function? Explain your answer.

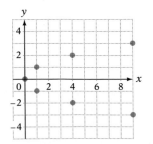

62. Is it possible to evaluate $f(x) = \dfrac{5}{x - 1}$ when $x = 1$? If so, what is $f(1)$? If not, explain why not.

4.2 Linear Equations in Two Variables

Objective A   *To graph an equation of the form y = mx + b* ....

The **graph of an equation in two variables** is a graph of the ordered-pair solutions of the equation.

Consider $y = 2x + 1$. Choosing $x = -2$, -1, 0, 1, and 2 and determining the corresponding values of y produces some of the ordered pairs of the equation. These are recorded in the table at the right. See the graph of the ordered pairs in Figure 1.

x	$y = 2x + 1$	y	(x, y)
-2	$2(-2) + 1$	-3	$(-2, -3)$
-1	$2(-1) + 1$	-1	$(-1, -1)$
0	$2(0) + 1$	1	$(0, 1)$
1	$2(1) + 1$	3	$(1, 3)$
2	$2(2) + 1$	5	$(2, 5)$

Choosing values of x that are not integers produces more ordered pairs to graph, such as $\left(-\frac{5}{2}, -4\right)$ and $\left(\frac{3}{2}, 4\right)$, as shown in Figure 2. Choosing still other values of x would result in more and more ordered pairs being graphed. The result would be so many dots that the graph would appear as the straight line shown in Figure 3, which is the graph of $y = 2x + 1$.

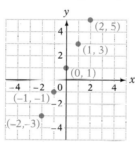

Figure 1

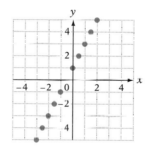

Figure 2

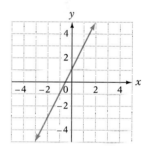

Figure 3

Equations in two variables have characteristic graphs. The equation $y = 2x + 1$ is an example of a *linear equation,* or *linear function,* because its graph is a straight line. It is also called a *first-degree equation* in two variables because the exponent on each variable is the first power.

> **Linear Equation in Two Variables**
>
> Any equation of the form $y = mx + b$, where m is the coefficient of x and b is a constant, is a **linear equation in two variables or a first-degree equation in two variables.** The graph of a linear equation in two variables is a straight line.

Examples of linear equations are shown at the right. These equations represent linear functions because there is only one possible y for each x. Note that for $y = 3 - 2x$, m is the coefficient of x and b is the constant.

$y = 2x + 1$ $(m = 2, b = 1)$

$y = x - 4$ $(m = 1, b = -4)$

$y = -\dfrac{3}{4}x$ $\left(m = -\dfrac{3}{4}, b = 0\right)$

$y = 3 - 2x$ $(m = -2, b = 3)$

The equation $y = x^2 + 4x + 3$ is not a linear equation in two variables because there is a term with a variable squared. The equation $y = \dfrac{3}{x - 4}$ is not a linear equation because a variable occurs in the denominator of a fraction.

To graph a linear equation, find ordered-pair solutions of the equation. Do this by choosing any value of x and finding the corresponding value of y. Repeat this procedure, choosing different values for x, until you have found the number of solutions desired.

Because the graph of a linear equation in two variables is a straight line, and a straight line is determined by two points, it is necessary to find only two solutions. However, it is recommended that at least three points be used to ensure accuracy.

➡ Graph $y = 2x + 1$.

Choose any values of x, and then find corresponding values of y. The numbers 0, 2, and -1 were chosen arbitrarily for x. It is convenient to record these solutions in a table.

Graph the ordered-pair solutions $(0,\ 1)$, $(2, 5)$, and $(-1, -1)$. Draw a line through the ordered-pair solutions.

x	$y = 2x + 1$	y
0	$2(0) + 1$	1
2	$2(2) + 1$	5
-1	$2(-1) + 1$	-1

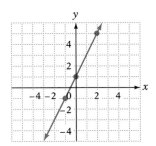

Remember that a graph is a drawing of the ordered-pair solutions of the equation. Therefore, every point on the graph is a solution of the equation, and every solution of the equation is a point on the graph.

The graph at the right is the graph of $y = x + 2$. Note that $(-4, -2)$ and $(1, 3)$ are points on the graph and that these points are solutions of $y = x + 2$. The point whose coordinates are $(4, 1)$ is not a point on the graph and is not a solution of the equation.

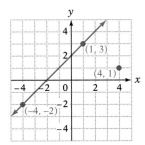

When m is a fraction in the equation $y = mx + b$, choose values of x that will simplify the evaluation.

➡ Graph $y = \frac{1}{3}x - 1$.

m is a fraction. $\left(m = \frac{1}{3} \right)$

Choose values of x that are multiples of the denominator. The numbers 0, 3, and -3 are used here.

x	y
0	-1
3	0
-3	-2

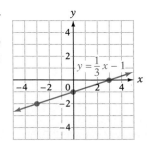

Example 1   Graph $y = 3x - 2$.

Solution

x	y
0	-2
-1	-5
2	4

You Try It 1   Graph $y = 3x + 1$.

Your solution

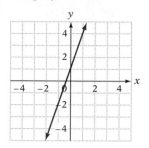

Example 2   Graph $y = 2x$.

Solution

x	y
0	0
2	4
-2	-4

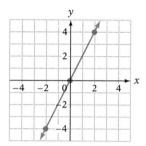

You Try It 2   Graph $y = -2x$.

Your solution

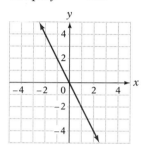

Example 3   Graph $y = \frac{1}{2}x - 1$.

Solution

x	y
0	-1
2	0
-2	-2

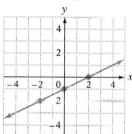

You Try It 3   Graph $y = \frac{1}{3}x - 3$.

Your solution

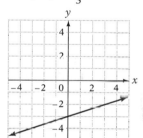

Solutions on p. S11

Objective B   **To graph an equation of the form Ax + By = C** ....

An equation in the form $Ax + By = C$ is also a linear equation. Examples of these equations are shown below.

$$2x + 3y = 6 \qquad (A = 2, B = 3, \quad C = 6)$$
$$x - 2y = -4 \qquad (A = 1, B = -2, C = -4)$$
$$2x + y = 0 \qquad (A = 2, B = 1, \quad C = 0)$$
$$4x - 5y = 2 \qquad (A = 4, B = -5, C = 2)$$

One method of graphing an equation of the form $Ax + By = C$ involves first solving the equation for y and then following the same procedure used for graphing an equation of the form $y = mx + b$. To solve the equation for y means to rewrite the equation so that y is alone on one side of the equation and the term containing x and the constant are on the other side of the equation. The Addition and Multiplication Properties of Equations are used to rewrite an equation of the form $Ax + By = C$ in the form $y = mx + b$.

➡ Solve the equation $3x + 2y = 4$ for y.

$$3x + 2y = 4$$
- The equation is in the form $Ax + By = C$.

$$3x - 3x + 2y = -3x + 4$$
- Use the Addition Property of Equations to subtract the term $3x$ from each side of the equation.

$$2y = -3x + 4$$
- Simplify. Note that on the right side of the equation, the term containing x is first, followed by the constant.

$$\frac{1}{2} \cdot 2y = \frac{1}{2}(-3x + 4)$$
- Use the Multiplication Property of Equations to multiply each side of the equation by the reciprocal of the coefficient of y. (The coefficient of y is 2; the reciprocal of 2 is $\frac{1}{2}$.)

$$y = \frac{1}{2}(-3x) + \frac{1}{2}(4)$$
- Simplify. Use the Distributive Property on the right side of the equation.

$$y = -\frac{3}{2}x + 2$$
- The equation is now in the form $y = mx + b$, with $m = -\frac{3}{2}$ and $b = 2$.

In solving the equation $3x + 2y = 4$ for y, where we multiplied both sides of the equation by $\frac{1}{2}$, we could have divided both sides of the equation by 2, as shown at the right. In simplifying the right side after dividing both sides by 2, be sure to divide *each term* by 2.

$$2y = -3x + 4$$
$$\frac{2y}{2} = \frac{-3x + 4}{2}$$
$$y = \frac{-3x}{2} + \frac{4}{2}$$
$$y = -\frac{3}{2}x + 2$$

➡ Graph $3x + 4y = 12$.

$$3x + 4y = 12$$
- Solve the equation for y.

$$4y = -3x + 12$$
- Subtract $3x$ from each side of the equation.

$$y = -\frac{3}{4}x + 3$$
- Divide each side of the equation by 4.

x	y
0	3
4	0
-4	6

- Find three ordered-pair solutions of the equation.

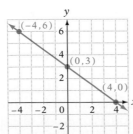

- Graph the ordered pairs and then draw a line through the points.

The graph of the equation $2x + 3y = 6$ is shown at the right. The graph crosses the x-axis at the point $(3, 0)$. This point is called the **x-intercept**. The graph also crosses the y-axis at the point $(0, 2)$. This point is called the **y-intercept**.

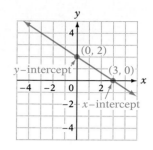

We can find the x-intercept and the y-intercept of the graph of the equation $2x + 3y = 6$ algebraically.

To find the x-intercept, let $y = 0$.
(Any point on the x-axis has y-coordinate 0.)

$$2x + 3y = 6$$
$$2x + 3(0) = 6$$
$$2x = 6$$
$$x = 3$$

The x-intercept is $(3, 0)$.

To find the y-intercept, let $x = 0$.
(Any point on the y-axis has x-coordinate 0.)

$$2x + 3y = 6$$
$$2(0) + 3y = 6$$
$$3y = 6$$
$$y = 2$$

The y-intercept is $(0, 2)$.

Another method of graphing an equation of the form $Ax + By = C$ is to find the x- and y-intercepts, plot both intercepts, and then draw a line through the two points. This method of graphing the equation $3x + 4y = 12$ is shown below. Note that this is the same equation graphed at the bottom of the previous page.

➡ Graph $3x + 4y = 12$ by using the x- and y-intercepts.

x-intercept: $3x + 4y = 12$
$\qquad\qquad 3x + 4(0) = 12$
$\qquad\qquad\qquad 3x = 12$
$\qquad\qquad\qquad\quad x = 4$

- To find the x-intercept, let $y = 0$.

- The x-intercept is $(4, 0)$.

y-intercept: $3x + 4y = 12$
$\qquad\qquad 3(0) + 4y = 12$
$\qquad\qquad\qquad 4y = 12$
$\qquad\qquad\qquad\ y = 3$

- To find the y-intercept, let $x = 0$.

- The y-intercept is $(0, 3)$.

- Graph the ordered pairs $(4, 0)$, and $(0, 3)$. Draw a straight line through the points.

The graph of a linear equation with one of the variables missing is either a horizontal or a vertical line.

The equation $y = 2$ could be written $0x + y = 2$. Because $0x = 0$ for any value of x, the value of y is always 2, no matter what value of x is chosen. For instance, replace x by -4, -1, 0, or 3. In each case, $y = 2$.

$$0x + y = 2$$
$$0(-4) + y = 2 \qquad (-4, 2) \text{ is a solution.}$$
$$0(-1) + y = 2 \qquad (-1, 2) \text{ is a solution.}$$
$$0(0) + y = 2 \qquad (0, 2) \text{ is a solution.}$$
$$0(3) + y = 2 \qquad (3, 2) \text{ is a solution.}$$

The solutions are plotted in the graph to the right, and a line is drawn through the plotted points. Note that the line is horizontal.

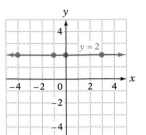

INSTRUCTOR NOTE

As an oral exercise, ask students for the equation of the x-axis.

> **Graph of a Horizontal Line**
>
> The graph of $y = b$ is a horizontal line passing through $(0, b)$.

The equation $x = -2$ could be written $x + 0y = -2$. Because $0y = 0$ for any value of y, the value of x is always -2, no matter what value of y is chosen. For instance, replace y by -2, 0, 2, or 3. In each case, $x = -2$.

$$x + 0y = -2$$
$$x + 0(-2) = -2 \qquad (-2, -2) \text{ is a solution.}$$
$$x + 0(0) = -2 \qquad (-2, 0) \text{ is a solution.}$$
$$x + 0(2) = -2 \qquad (-2, 2) \text{ is a solution.}$$
$$x + 0(3) = -2 \qquad (-2, 3) \text{ is a solution.}$$

The solutions are plotted in the graph at the right, and a line is drawn through the plotted points. Note that the line is vertical.

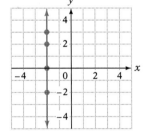

INSTRUCTOR NOTE

As an oral exercise, ask students for the equation of the y-axis.

> **Graph of a Vertical Line**
>
> The graph of $x = a$ is a vertical line passing through $(a, 0)$.

⟹ Graph $x = -3$ and $y = 2$ on the same coordinate grid.

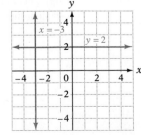

• The graph of $x = -3$ is a vertical line passing through $(-3, 0)$.

• The graph of $y = 2$ is a horizontal line passing through $(0, 2)$.

Example 4

Solve the equation $2x - 5y = 10$ for y.
Then graph the equation.

Solution

$2x - 5y = 10$

$\quad -5y = -2x + 10$

$\qquad y = \dfrac{2}{5}x - 2$

x	y
0	-2
5	0
-5	-4

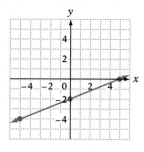

You Try It 4

Solve the equation $5x - 2y = 10$ for y.
Then graph the equation.

Your solution

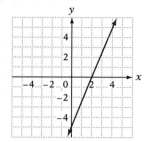

Example 5

Find the x- and y-intercepts of
$x - 2y = 4$. Graph the line.

Solution

x-intercept:

$\quad x - 2y = 4$

$x - 2(0) = 4$

$\qquad\quad x = 4$

$(4, 0)$

y-intercept:

$\quad x - 2y = 4$

$\quad 0 - 2y = 4$

$\quad\;\; -2y = 4$

$\qquad\;\; y = -2$

$(0, -2)$

You Try It 5

Find the x- and y-intercepts of
$x - 4y = -4$. Graph the line.

Your solution

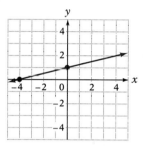

Example 6

Graph $y = -2$.

Solution

The graph of an equation of the form
$y = b$ is a horizontal line passing
through the point $(0, b)$.

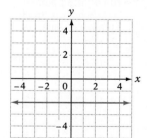

You Try It 6

Graph $x = -4$.

Your solution

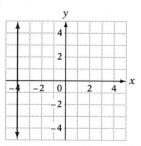

Solutions on p. S11

Objective C *To solve application problems* ....

INSTRUCTOR NOTE
Part b of the example problem at the right asks the student to write a sentence that explains the meaning of the answer. These questions require the student to do more than just manipulate. They require an understanding of the final result in the context of the application.

There are a variety of applications of linear functions.

➡ Solve: An installer of marble kitchen countertops charges $250 plus $180 per foot of countertop. The equation that describes the total cost, C, to have x feet of countertop installed is $C = 180x + 250$.

a. Graph this equation for $0 \leq x \leq 25$. (*Note:* In many applications, the domain of the variable is given so that the equation makes sense. For instance, it would not be sensible to have values of x that are less than 0. This would mean negative countertop! The choice of 25 is somewhat arbitrary, but most kitchens have less than 25 ft of counter space.)

b. The point whose coordinates are (8, 1690) is on the graph. Write a sentence that describes this ordered pair.

Solution

a.

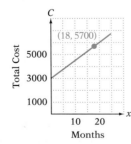

• Choosing $x = 0$, 5, and 10, you find that the corresponding ordered pairs are (0, 250), (5, 1150), and (10, 2050). Plot these points and draw a line through them.

b. The point whose coordinates are (8, 1690) means that 8 ft of countertop costs $1690 to install.

Example 7
A local car dealer is advertising a 2-year lease for a new Honda Civic. The upfront cost is $3000 with a monthly lease payment of $150. The total cost, C, after x months of the lease is given by $C = 150x + 3000$. Graph this equation for $0 \leq x \leq 24$. The point whose coordinates are (18, 5700) is on the graph. Write a sentence that describes this ordered pair.

Solution

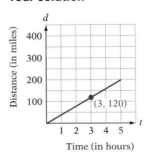

The ordered pair (18, 5700) means that the total cost of the lease payments for 18 months is $5700.

You Try It 7
A car is traveling at a uniform speed of 40 mph. The distance, d, that the car travels in t hours is given by $d = 40t$. Graph this equation for $0 \leq t \leq 5$. The point whose coordinates are (3, 120) is on the graph. Write a sentence that describes this ordered pair.

Your solution

The ordered pair (3, 120) means that in 3 h the car will travel 120 mi.

Solution on p. S11

4.2 Exercises

Objective A

Graph.

1. $y = 2x - 3$

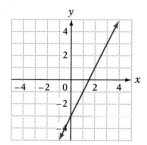

2. $y = -2x + 2$

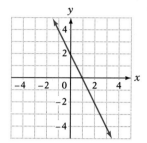

3. $y = \dfrac{1}{3}x$

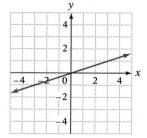

4. $y = -3x$

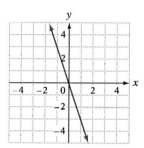

5. $y = \dfrac{2}{3}x - 1$

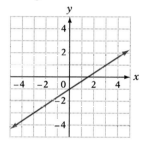

6. $y = \dfrac{3}{4}x + 2$

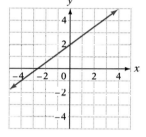

7. $y = -\dfrac{1}{4}x + 2$

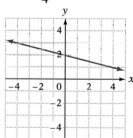

8. $y = -\dfrac{1}{3}x + 1$

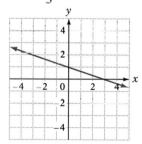

9. $y = -\dfrac{2}{5}x + 1$

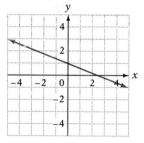

10. $y = -\dfrac{1}{2}x + 3$

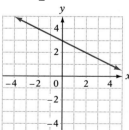

11. $y = 2x - 4$

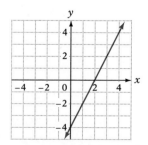

12. $y = 3x - 4$

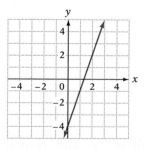

13. $y = x - 3$

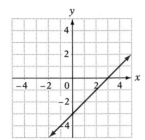

14. $y = x + 2$

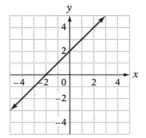

15. $y = -x + 2$

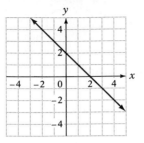

16. $y = -x - 1$

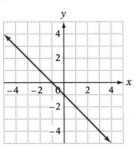

17. $y = -\dfrac{2}{3}x + 1$

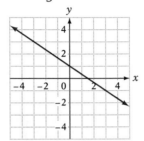

18. $y = 5x - 4$

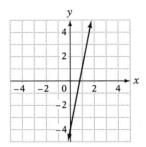

Objective B

Find the *x*- and *y*-intercepts.

19. $x - y = 3$
(3, 0), (0, −3)

20. $3x + 4y = 12$
(4, 0), (0, 3)

21. $x - 5y = 10$
(10, 0), (0, −2)

22. $3x + 2y = 12$
(4, 0), (0, 6)

23. $2x - 3y = 0$
(0, 0), (0, 0)

24. $3x + 4y = 0$
(0, 0), (0, 0)

Graph.

25. $3x + y = 3$

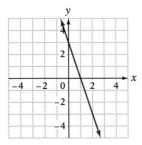

26. $2x + y = 4$

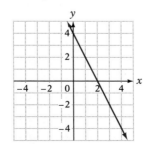

27. $2x + 3y = 6$

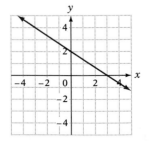

28. $3x + 2y = 4$

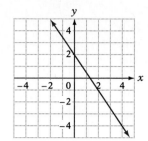

29. $x - 2y = 4$

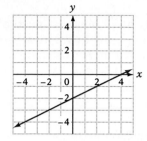

30. $x - 3y = 6$

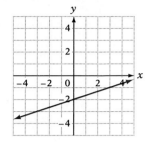

31. $2x - 3y = 6$

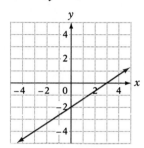

32. $3x - 2y = 8$

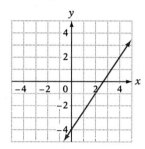

33. $2x + 5y = 10$

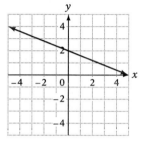

34. $3x + 4y = 12$

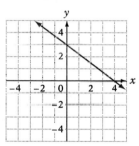

35. $x = 3$

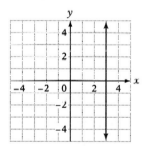

36. $y = -4$

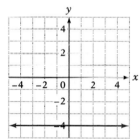

37. $x + 4y = 4$

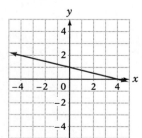

38. $4x - 3y = 12$

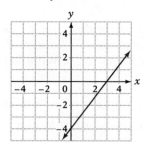

39. $y = 4$

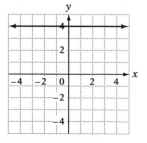

Objective C   *Application Problems*

40. A rescue helicopter is rushing at a constant speed of 150 mph to reach several people stranded in the ocean 11 mi away after their boat sank. The rescuers can determine how far they are from the victims using the equation $D = 11 - 2.5t$, where D is the distance in miles and t is the time elapsed in minutes. Graph this equation for $0 \le t \le 4$. The point $(3, 3.5)$ is on the graph. Write a sentence that describes the meaning of this ordered pair.
After flying for 3 min, the helicopter is 3.5 mi away from the victims.

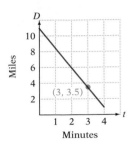

41. A custom-illustrated sign or banner can be commissioned for a cost of $25 for the material and $10.50 per square foot for the artwork. The equation that represents this cost is given by $y = 10.50x + 25$, where y is the cost and x is the number of square feet in the sign. Graph this equation for $0 \le x \le 20$. The point $(15, 182.5)$ is on the graph. Write a sentence that describes the meaning of this ordered pair.
It costs $182.50 for a custom sign 15 ft² in area.

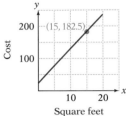

42. According to some veterinarians, the age, x, of a dog can be translated to "human years" by using the equation $H = 4x + 16$, where H is the human equivalent age for the dog. Graph this equation for $2 \le x \le 21$. The point whose coordinates are $(6, 40)$ is on this graph. Write a sentence that explains the meaning of this ordered pair.
A dog 6 years old is equivalent in age to a human 40 years old.

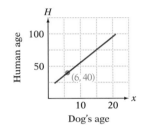

43. One projection for the total value, V, of stocks that will be bought and sold over the Internet for the years 1997 through 2002 is given by the equation $V = 380x + 300$, where $0 \le x \le 5$ and 0 corresponds to the year 1997. Graph the equation. The point whose coordinates are $(3, 1440)$ is on the graph. Write a sentence that describes the meaning of this ordered pair.
In the year 2000, it is projected that $1440 million ($1.44 billion) in stocks will be traded over the Internet.

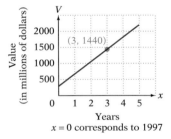

APPLYING THE CONCEPTS

44. Graph $y = 2x - 2$, $y = 2x$, and $y = 2x + 3$ in the first coordinate system at the right. What observation can you make about the graphs?
They are parallel.

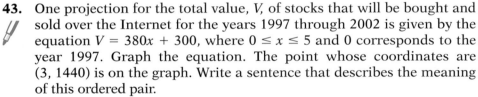

45. For the equation $y = 3x + 2$, when the value of x changes from 1 to 2, does the value of y increase or decrease? What is the change in y? Suppose that the value of x changes from 13 to 14. What is the change in y?
increases; 3; 3

46. For the equation $y = -2x + 1$, when the value of x changes from 1 to 2, does the value of y increase or decrease? What is the change in y? Suppose the value of x changes from 13 to 14. What is the change in y?
decreases; -2; -2

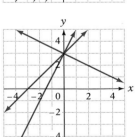

47. Graph $y = x + 3$, $y = 2x + 3$, and $y = -\frac{1}{2}x + 3$ in the second coordinate system at the right. What observation can you make about the graphs?
They pass through the same point on the y-axis.

4.3 Slopes of Straight Lines

Objective A   *To find the slope of a straight line*....................................

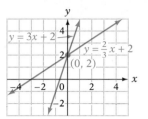

The graphs of $y = 3x + 2$ and $y = \frac{2}{3}x + 2$ are shown at the left. Each graph crosses the y-axis at the point (0, 2), but the graphs have different slants. The **slope** of a line is a measure of the slant of the line. The symbol for slope is m.

The slope of a line containing two points is the ratio of the change in the y values between the two points to the change in the x values. The line containing the points whose coordinates are $(-1, -3)$ and $(5, 2)$ is shown below.

The change in the y values is the difference between the y-coordinates of the two points.

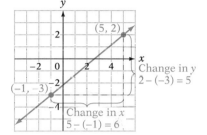

$$\text{Change in } y = 2 - (-3) = 5$$

The change in the x values is the difference between the x-coordinates of the two points.

$$\text{Change in } x = 5 - (-1) = 6$$

The slope of the line between the two points is the ratio of the change in y to the change in x.

$$\text{Slope} = m = \frac{\text{change in } y}{\text{change in } x} = \frac{5}{6} \qquad\qquad m = \frac{2 - (-3)}{5 - (-1)} = \frac{5}{6}$$

In general, if $P_1(x_1, y_1)$ and $P_2(x_2, y_2)$ are two points on a line, then

$$\text{Change in } y = y_2 - y_1 \qquad\qquad \text{Change in } x = x_2 - x_1$$

Using these ideas, we can state a formula for slope.

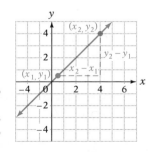

> **Slope Formula**
>
> The slope of the line containing the two points $P_1(x_1, y_1)$ and $P_2(x_2, y_2)$ is given by
>
> $$m = \frac{y_2 - y_1}{x_2 - x_1}, \ x_1 \neq x_2$$

Frequently, the Greek letter Δ is used to designate the change in a variable. Using this notation, we can write the equations for the change in y and the change in x as follows:

$$\text{Change in } y = \Delta y = y_2 - y_1 \qquad\qquad \text{Change in } x = \Delta x = x_2 - x_1$$

With this notation, the slope formula is written $m = \frac{\Delta y}{\Delta x}$.

➡ Find the slope of the line containing the points whose coordinates are $(-2, 0)$ and $(4, 5)$.

Let $P_1 = (-2, 0)$ and $P_2 = (4, 5)$. (It does not matter which point is named P_1 or P_2; the slope will be the same.)

$$m = \frac{y_2 - y_1}{x_2 - x_1} = \frac{5 - 0}{4 - (-2)} = \frac{5}{6}$$

A line that slants upward to the right always has a **positive slope**.

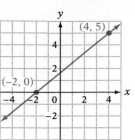

Positive slope

➡ Find the slope of the line containing the points whose coordinates are $(-3, 4)$ and $(4, 2)$.

Let $P_1 = (-3, 4)$ and $P_2 = (4, 2)$.

$$m = \frac{y_2 - y_1}{x_2 - x_1} = \frac{2 - 4}{4 - (-3)} = \frac{-2}{7} = -\frac{2}{7}$$

A line that slants downward to the right always has a **negative slope**.

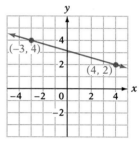

Negative slope

➡ Find the slope of the line containing the points whose coordinates are $(-2, 2)$ and $(4, 2)$.

Let $P_1 = (-2, 2)$ and $P_2 = (4, 2)$.

$$m = \frac{y_2 - y_1}{x_2 - x_1} = \frac{2 - 2}{4 - (-2)} = \frac{0}{6} = 0$$

A horizontal line has **zero slope**.

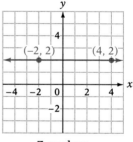

Zero slope

➡ Find the slope of the line containing the points whose coordinates are $(1, -2)$ and $(1, 3)$.

Let $P_1 = (1, -2)$ and $P_2 = (1, 3)$.

$$m = \frac{y_2 - y_1}{x_2 - x_1} = \frac{3 - (-2)}{1 - 1} = \frac{5}{0} \quad \text{Not a real number}$$

The slope of a vertical line is **undefined**.

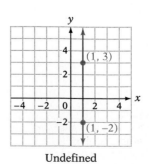

Undefined

There are many applications of the concept of slope. Here are two possibilities.

In 1988, when Florence Griffith-Joyner set the world record for the 100-meter dash, her average rate of speed was approximately 9.5 m/s. The graph at the right shows the distance she ran during her record-setting run. From the graph, note that after 4 s she had traveled 38 m and that after 6 s she had traveled 57 m. The slope of the line between these two points is

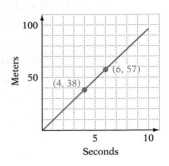

$$m = \frac{57 - 38}{6 - 4} = \frac{19}{2} = 9.5$$

Note that the slope of the line is the same as the rate she was running, 9.5 m/s. The average speed of an object is related to slope.

Here is another example, this one related to the world of finance.

The number of banks in the United States has been decreasing as a consequence of bank mergers. The graph at the right shows the number of banks in the United States from 1990 to 1997. The numbers have been rounded to the nearest hundred.

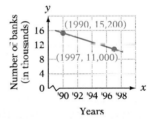

According to the graph, the number of banks in 1990 was 15,200, and the number of banks in 1997 was 11,000. The slope of the line between the two points is

$$m = \frac{11,000 - 15,200}{1997 - 1990} = \frac{-4200}{7} = -600$$

INSTRUCTOR NOTE

Just as the phrase *the sum of* means to add, any expression that contains the word *per* translates mathematically as slope. Have students suggest some everyday situations that involve slope. Some examples might include miles per gallon or feet per second.

Note that if we interpret negative slope as decreasing, then the slope of the line is the same as the rate at which the number of banks decreased from 1990 to 1997, 600 per year.

In general, any quantity that is expressed by using the word *per* is represented mathematically as slope. In the first example, slope was 9.5 meters *per* second; in the second example, slope was −600 *per* year.

Example 1

Find the slope of the line containing the points $(2, -5)$ and $(-4, 2)$.

Solution

Let $P_1 = (2, -5)$ and $P_2 = (-4, 2)$.

$$m = \frac{y_2 - y_1}{x_2 - x_1} = \frac{2 - (-5)}{-4 - 2} = \frac{7}{-6}$$

The slope is $-\frac{7}{6}$.

You Try It 1

Find the slope of the line containing the points $(4, -3)$ and $(2, 7)$.

Your solution

-5

Example 2

Find the slope of the line containing the points $(-3, 4)$ and $(5, 4)$.

Solution

Let $P_1 = (-3, 4)$ and $P_2 = (5, 4)$.

$$m = \frac{y_2 - y_1}{x_2 - x_1} = \frac{4 - 4}{5 - (-3)} = \frac{0}{8} = 0$$

The slope of the line is zero.

You Try It 2

Find the slope of the line containing the points $(6, -1)$ and $(6, 7)$.

Your solution

The slope of the line is undefined.

Example 3

The graph below shows the height of a plane above an airport during its 30-minute descent from cruising altitude to landing. Find the slope of the line. Write a sentence that explains the meaning of the slope.

Solution

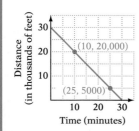

$$m = \frac{5000 - 20,000}{25 - 10} = \frac{-15,000}{15}$$

$$= -1000$$

A slope of -1000 means that the height of the plane is *decreasing* at the rate of 1000 ft/min.

You Try It 3

The graph below shows the approximate decline in the value of a used car over a five-year period. Find the slope of the line. Write a sentence that states the meaning of the slope.

Your solution

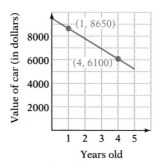

$m = -850$

A slope of -850 means that the value of the car is decreasing at a rate of $850 per year.

Solutions on pp. S11–S12

Objective B **To graph a line using the slope and the *y*-intercept** ....

Recall that we can find the *y*-intercept of a linear equation by letting $x = 0$.

➡ Find the *y*-intercept of $y = 3x + 4$.

$y = 3x + 4 = 3(0) + 4 = 4$ • Let $x = 0$.

The *y*-intercept is $(0, 4)$.

For any equation of the form $y = mx + b$, the *y*-intercept is $(0, b)$.

The graph of the equation $y = \frac{2}{3}x + 1$ is shown at the right. The points $(-3, -1)$ and $(3, 3)$ are on the graph. The slope of the line between the two points is

$$m = \frac{3 - (-1)}{3 - (-3)} = \frac{4}{6} = \frac{2}{3}$$

Observe that the slope of the line is the coefficient of *x* in the equation $y = \frac{2}{3}x + 1$.

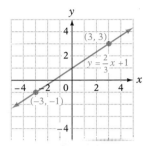

Slope–Intercept Form of a Straight Line

An equation of the form $y = mx + b$ is called the **slope–intercept** form of a straight line. The slope of the line is *m*, the coefficient of *x*. The *y*-intercept is $(0, b)$, where *b* is the constant term of the equation.

The following equations are written in slope–intercept form.

$y = 2x - 3$ Slope $= 2$, *y*-intercept $= (0, -3)$

$y = -x + 2$ Slope $= -1\ (-x = -1x)$, *y*-intercept $= (0, 2)$

$y = \frac{1}{2}x$ Slope $= \frac{1}{2}$, *y*-intercept $= (0, 0)$

When the equation of a straight line is in the form $y = mx + b$, the graph can be drawn by using the slope and the *y*-intercept. First locate the *y*-intercept. Use the slope to find a second point on the line. Then draw a line through the two points.

➡ Graph $y = \frac{5}{3}x - 4$ by using the slope and *y*-intercept.

The slope is the coefficient of *x*:

$$m = \frac{5}{3} = \frac{\text{change in } y}{\text{change in } x}$$

The *y*-intercept is $(0, -4)$.

Beginning at the *y*-intercept $(0, -4)$, move right 3 units (change in *x*) and then up 5 units (change in *y*).

The point whose coordinates are $(3, 1)$ is a second point on the graph. Draw a line through the points $(0, -4)$ and $(3, 1)$.

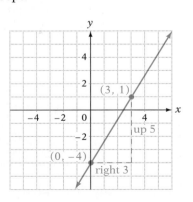

TAKE NOTE

When graphing a line by using its slope and *y*-intercept, *always* start at the *y*-intercept.

➡ Graph $y = 2x - 3$.

y-intercept $= (0, b) = (0, -3)$

$m = 2 = \dfrac{2}{1} = \dfrac{\text{change in } y}{\text{change in } x}$

Beginning at the y-intercept, move right 1 unit (change in x) and then up 2 units (change in y).

$(1, -1)$ is a second point on the graph.

Draw a line through the two points $(0, -3)$ and $(1, -1)$.

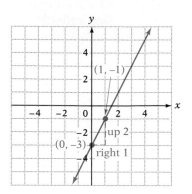

Example 4 Graph $y = -\dfrac{2}{3}x + 1$ by using the slope and y-intercept.

Solution y-intercept $= (0, b) = (0, 1)$

$m = -\dfrac{2}{3} = \dfrac{-2}{3}$

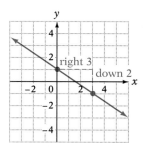

You Try It 4 Graph $y = -\dfrac{1}{4}x - 1$ by using the slope and y-intercept.

Your solution

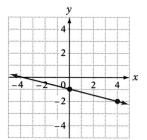

Example 5 Graph $2x - 3y = 6$ by using the slope and y-intercept.

Solution Solve the equation for y.

$2x - 3y = 6$

$-3y = -2x + 6$

$y = \dfrac{2}{3}x - 2$

y-intercept $= (0, -2)$; $m = \dfrac{2}{3}$

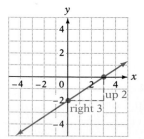

You Try It 5 Graph $x - 2y = 4$ by using the slope and y-intercept.

Your solution

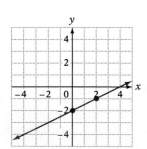

Solutions on p. S12

4.3 Exercises

· ·

Objective A

Find the slope of the line containing the points.

1. $P_1(1, 3), P_2(3, 1)$
−1

2. $P_1(2, 3), P_2(5, 1)$
$-\dfrac{2}{3}$

3. $P_1(-1, 4), P_2(2, 5)$
$\dfrac{1}{3}$

4. $P_1(3, -2), P_2(1, 4)$
−3

5. $P_1(-1, 3), P_2(-4, 5)$
$-\dfrac{2}{3}$

6. $P_1(-1, -2), P_2(-3, 2)$
−2

7. $P_1(0, 3), P_2(4, 0)$
$-\dfrac{3}{4}$

8. $P_1(-2, 0), P_2(0, 3)$
$\dfrac{3}{2}$

9. $P_1(2, 4), P_2(2, -2)$
undefined

10. $P_1(4, 1), P_2(4, -3)$
undefined

11. $P_1(2, 5), P_2(-3, -2)$
$\dfrac{7}{5}$

12. $P_1(4, 1), P_2(-1, -2)$
$\dfrac{3}{5}$

13. $P_1(2, 3), P_2(-1, 3)$
zero slope

14. $P_1(3, 4), P_2(0, 4)$
zero slope

15. $P_1(0, 4), P_2(-2, 5)$
$-\dfrac{1}{2}$

16. $P_1(-2, 3), P_2(-2, 5)$
undefined

17. $P_1(-3, -1), P_2(-3, 4)$
undefined

18. $P_1(-2, -5), P_2(-4, -1)$
−2

19. One measure of the affordability of a home for a given population is the percent of the population that has the necessary income to purchase a median-priced new home ($136,000 in 1996). The graph at the right shows the decrease in the percent of the population that can afford a new home. Find the slope of the line and write a sentence that states its meaning.

$m = -0.4$. The percent of the population that can afford a median-priced new home has decreased by 0.4% per year.

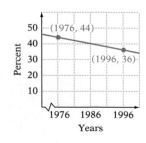

20. The graph at the right shows the cost, in dollars, to make a transatlantic telephone call. Find the slope of the line. Write a sentence that states the meaning of the slope.
$m = 0.8$. After being connected, each minute of a transatlantic phone call costs $.80.

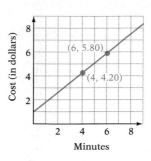

21. a. The pressure, in pounds per square inch, on a diver is shown in the graph at the right. Find the slope of the line. Write a sentence that explains the meaning of the slope.
$m = 0.5$. For each additional foot a diver descends below the surface of the water, the pressure on the diver increases by 0.5 pound per square inch.

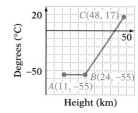

b. What does the *y*-intercept represent?
The *y*-intercept represents the pressure on a person at sea level.

22. The stratosphere extends from approximately 11 km to 50 km above Earth. The graph at the right shows how the temperature in degrees Celsius changes in the stratosphere. Explain the meaning of the horizontal line segment from *A* to *B*. Find the slope of the line from *B* to *C* and explain its meaning.
The temperature remains constant from *A* to *B*. $m = 3$. The temperature is increasing at 3°C per kilometer.

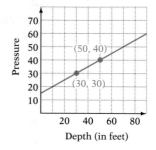

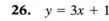

Objective B

23. Explain why $y = mx + b$ is called the slope–intercept form of the equation of a straight line.

24. Do all straight lines have a *y*-intercept? If not, give an example of one that does not.   No. For instance, the graph of $x = 3$.

25. If two lines have the same slope and the same *y*-intercept, must the graphs of the lines be the same? If not, give an example.   yes

Graph by using the slope and *y*-intercept.

26. $y = 3x + 1$

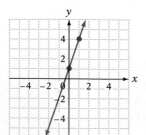

27. $y = -2x - 1$

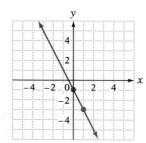

28. $y = \dfrac{2}{5}x - 2$

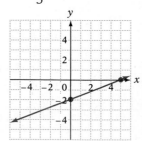

29. $y = \dfrac{3}{4}x + 1$

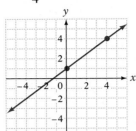

30. $2x + y = 3$

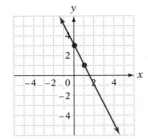

31. $3x - y = 1$

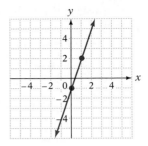

32. $x - 2y = 4$

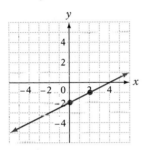

33. $x + 3y = 6$

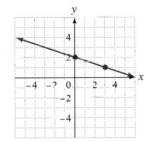

34. $y = \dfrac{2}{3}x$

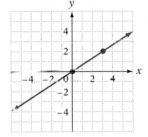

35. $y = \dfrac{1}{2}x$

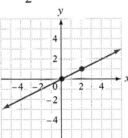

36. $y = -x + 1$

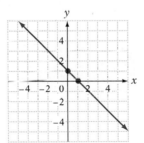

37. $y = -x - 3$

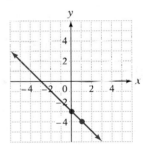

38. $3x - 4y = 12$

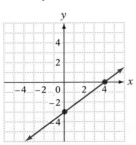

39. $5x - 2y = 10$

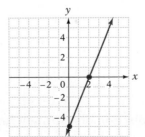

40. $y = -4x + 2$

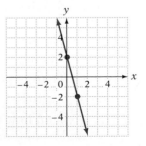

APPLYING THE CONCEPTS

Complete the following sentences.

41. If a line has a slope of 2, then the value of y <u>increases/decreases</u> by
_____ as the value of x increases by 1.
increases by 2

42. If a line has a slope of -3, then the value of y <u>increases/decreases</u> by
_____ as the value of x increases by 1.
decreases by 3

43. If a line has a slope of -2, the the value of y <u>increases/decreases</u> by
_____ as the value of x decreases by 1.
increases by 2

44. If a line has a slope of 3, then the value of y <u>increases/decreases</u> by
_____ as the value of x decreases by 1.
decreases by 3

45. Draw the graphs of   **a.** $\frac{x}{3} + \frac{y}{4} = 1$ **b.** $\frac{x}{2} - \frac{y}{3} = 1$ **c.** $-\frac{x}{4} + \frac{y}{2} = 1$.

What observations can you make about the x- and y-intercepts of these
graphs and the coefficients of x and y?

d. Use this observation to draw the graph of $\frac{x}{4} - \frac{y}{3} = 1$.

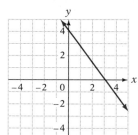 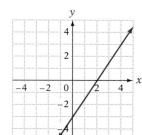 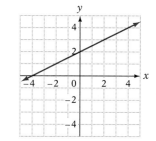 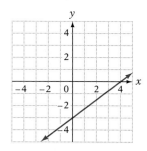

The reciprocals of the coefficients of x and y are the x- and y-intercepts of the graphs
of the lines.

46. What does the highway sign at the right have to do with slope?
$6\% = 0.06 = \frac{6}{100}$. A 6% grade means that the average slope of the road is $\frac{6}{100}$.

Grade
6%

Determine the value of k such that the points whose coordinates are given
below lie on the same line.

47. $(3, 2), (4, 6), (5, k)$ 10

48. $(-2, 3), (1, 0), (k, 2)$ -1

49. $(k, 1), (0, -1), (2, -2)$ -4

50. $(4, -1), (3, -4), (k, k)$ $\frac{13}{2}$

51. Explain how to graph the equation of a straight line by using its slope
and a point on the line.

4.4   Equations of Straight Lines

Objective A   ***To find the equation of a line given a point and the slope...........***

In earlier sections, the equation of a line was given and you were asked to determine some properties of the line, such as its intercepts and slope. Here, the process is reversed: Given properties of a line, determine its equation.

If the slope and y-intercept of a line are known, the equation of the line can be determined by using the slope–intercept form of a straight line.

➡ Find the equation of the line with slope $-\frac{1}{2}$ and y-intercept $(0, 3)$.

$$y = mx + b$$ • **Use the slope–intercept formula.**

$$y = -\frac{1}{2}x + 3$$ • $m = -\frac{1}{2}$; $(0, b) = (0, 3)$, so $b = 3$.

The equation of the line is $y = -\frac{1}{2}x + 3$.

When the slope and the coordinates of a point other than the y-intercept are known, the equation of the line can be found by using the formula for slope.

Suppose a line passes through the point $(3, 1)$ and has a slope of $\frac{2}{3}$. The equation of the line with these properties is determined by letting (x, y) be the coordinates of an unknown point on the line. Because the slope of the line is known, use the slope formula to write an equation. Then solve for y.

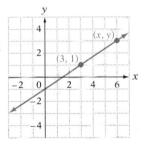

$$\frac{y - 1}{x - 3} = \frac{2}{3}$$ • $\frac{y_2 - y_1}{x_2 - x_1} = m$; $m = \frac{2}{3}$; $(x_2, y_2) = (x, y)$; $(x_1, y_1) = (3, 1)$

$$\frac{y - 1}{x - 3}(x - 3) = \frac{2}{3}(x - 3)$$ • **Multiply each side by $(x - 3)$.**

$$y - 1 = \frac{2}{3}x - 2$$ • **Simplify.**

$$y = \frac{2}{3}x - 1$$ • **Solve for y.**

The equation of the line is $y = \frac{2}{3}x - 1$.

The same procedure that was used above is used to derive the *point–slope formula*. We use this formula to determine the equation of a line when we are given the coordinates of a point on the line and the slope of the line.

Let (x_1, y_1) be the given coordinates of a point on a line, m the given slope of the line, and (x, y) the coordinates of an unknown point on the line. Then

$$\frac{y - y_1}{x - x_1} = m$$ • **Formula for slope.**

$$\frac{y - y_1}{x - x_1}(x - x_1) = m(x - x_1)$$ • **Multiply each side by $x - x_1$.**

$$y - y_1 = m(x - x_1)$$ • **Simplify.**

> **Point–Slope Formula**
>
> If (x_1, y_1) is a point on a line with slope m, then $y - y_1 = m(x - x_1)$.

INSTRUCTOR NOTE
A model of the point–slope formula with open parentheses may help some students substitute correctly.
$$y - y_1 = m[x - x_1]$$
$$\downarrow \quad \downarrow \quad \downarrow$$
$$y - (\ ) = (\ )[x - (\ )]$$

⇒ Find the equation of the line that passes through point (2, 3) and has slope -2.

$y - y_1 = m(x - x_1)$ • Use the point–slope formula.

$y - 3 = -2(x - 2)$ • $m = -2$; $(x_1, y_1) = (2, 3)$

$y - 3 = -2x + 4$ • Slope for y.

$y = -2x + 7$

The equation of the line is $y = -2x + 7$.

Example 1

Find the equation of the line whose slope is $-\dfrac{2}{3}$ and whose y-intercept is $(0, -1)$.

Solution

Because the slope and y-intercept are known, use the slope–intercept form of a straight line, $y = mx + b$.

$y = -\dfrac{2}{3}x - 1$ • $m = -\dfrac{2}{3}$; $b = -1$

Example 2

Use the point–slope formula to find the equation of the line that passes through the point $(-2, -1)$ and has slope $\dfrac{3}{2}$.

Solution

$y - y_1 = m(x - x_1)$

$y - (-1) = \dfrac{3}{2}[x - (-2)]$ • $m = \dfrac{3}{2}$;

$y + 1 = \dfrac{3}{2}(x + 2)$ $(x_1, y_1) = (-2, -1)$

$y + 1 = \dfrac{3}{2}x + 3$

$y = \dfrac{3}{2}x + 2$

The equation of the line is $y = \dfrac{3}{2}x + 2$.

You Try It 1

Find the equation of the line whose slope is $\dfrac{5}{3}$ and whose y-intercept is $(0, 2)$.

Your solution

$y = \dfrac{5}{3}x + 2$

You Try It 2

Use the point–slope formula to find the equation of the line that passes through the point $(4, -2)$ and has slope $\dfrac{3}{4}$.

Your solution

$y = \dfrac{3}{4}x - 5$

Solutions on p. S12

Objective B **To find the equation of a line given two points**............................

The point–slope formula is used to find the equation of a line when a point on the line and the slope of the line are known. But this formula can also be used to find the equation of a line given two points on the line. In this case,

1. Use the slope formula to determine the slope of the line between the points.

2. Use the point–slope formula, the slope you just calculated, and one of the given points to find the equation of the line.

➡ Find the equation of the line that passes through the points whose coordinates are $(-3, -1)$ and $(3, 3)$.

Use the slope formula to determine the slope of the line between the points.

$$m = \frac{y_2 - y_1}{x_2 - x_1} = \frac{3 - (-1)}{3 - (-3)} = \frac{4}{6} = \frac{2}{3} \qquad \bullet \; (x_1, y_1) = (-3, -1); (x_2, y_2) = (3, 3)$$

Use the point–slope formula, the slope you just calculated, and one of the given points to find the equation of the line.

INSTRUCTOR NOTE

Show students that it does not matter which ordered pair is selected to use in the point–slope formula.

$$y - y_1 = m(x - x_1) \qquad \bullet \; \text{Point–slope formula}$$

$$y - (-1) = \frac{2}{3}[x - (-3)] \qquad \bullet \; m = \frac{2}{3}; (x_1, y_1) = (-3, -1)$$

$$y + 1 = \frac{2}{3}(x + 3)$$

$$y + 1 = \frac{2}{3}x + 2$$

$$y = \frac{2}{3}x + 1$$

TAKE NOTE

You can verify that the equation $y = \frac{2}{3}x + 1$ passes through the points $(-3, -1)$ and $(3, 3)$ by substituting the coordinates of these points into the equation.

$$
\begin{array}{c|c}
y = \frac{2}{3}x + 1 \\
\hline
-1 & \frac{2}{3}(-3) + 1 \\
-1 & -2 + 1 \\
-1 = -1
\end{array}
\qquad \bullet \; (x, y) = (-3, -1)
$$

$$
\begin{array}{c|c}
y = \frac{2}{3}x + 1 \\
\hline
3 & \frac{2}{3}(3) + 1 \\
3 & 2 + 1 \\
3 = 3
\end{array}
\qquad \bullet \; (x, y) = (3, 3)
$$

The equation of the line that passes through the two points is $y = \frac{2}{3}x + 1$.

Example 3

Find the equation of the line that passes through the points $(-4, 0)$ and $(2, -3)$.

Solution

Find the slope of the line between the two points.

$$m = \frac{y_2 - y_1}{x_2 - x_1} = \frac{-3 - 0}{2 - (-4)} = \frac{-3}{6} = -\frac{1}{2}$$

Use the point–slope formula.

$$y - y_1 = m(x - x_1)$$

$$y - 0 = -\frac{1}{2}[x - (-4)] \qquad \bullet \; \text{Point–slope formula}$$

$$\qquad \bullet \; m = -\frac{1}{2}; (x_1, y_1) = (4, 0)$$

$$y = -\frac{1}{2}(x + 4)$$

$$y = -\frac{1}{2}x - 2$$

The equation of the line is $y = -\frac{1}{2}x - 2$.

You Try It 3

Find the equation of the line that passes through the points $(-6, -1)$ and $(3, 1)$.

Your solution

$$y = \frac{2}{9}x + \frac{1}{3}$$

Solution on p. S12

Objective C **To solve application problems**...

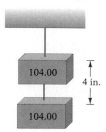

A **linear model** is a first-degree equation that is used to describe a relationship between quantities. In many cases, a linear model is used to approximate collected data. The data are graphed as points in a coordinate system, and then a line is drawn that approximates the data. The graph of the points is called a **scatter diagram**; the line is called a **line of best fit**.

Consider an experiment to determine the weight required to stretch a spring a certain distance. Data from such an experiment are shown in the table below.

Distance (in inches)	2.5	4	2	3.5	1	4.5
Weight (in pounds)	63	104	47	85	27	115

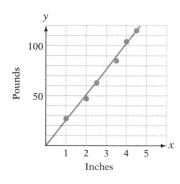

The accompanying graph shows the scatter diagram, which is the plotted points, and the line of best fit, which is the line that approximately goes through the plotted points. The equation of the line of best fit is $y = 25.7x - 1.3$, where x is the number of inches the spring is stretched and y is the weight in pounds.

The table below shows the values that the model would predict to the nearest tenth. Good linear models should predict values that are close to the actual values. A more thorough analysis of lines of best fit is undertaken in statistics courses.

Distance, x	2.5	4	2	3.5	1	4.5
Weight predicted using $y = 25.7x - 1.3$	63.0	101.5	50.1	88.7	24.4	114.4

Example 4

The data in the table below show the size of a house in square feet and the cost to build the house. The line of best fit is $y = 70.3x + 41,100$, where x is the number of square feet and y is the cost of the house.

Square feet	1250	1400	1348	2675	2900
Cost	128,000	140,000	136,100	233,450	241,500

Graph the data and the line of best fit in the coordinate system below. Write a sentence that describes the meaning of the slope of the line of best fit.

Solution

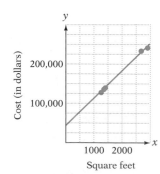

The slope of the line means that the cost to build the house increases $70.30 for each additional square foot in the size of the house.

You Try It 4

The data in the table below show a reading test grade and the final exam grade in a history class. The line of best fit is $y = 8.3x - 7.8$, where x is the reading test score and y is the history test score.

Reading	8.5	9.4	10.0	11.4	12.0
History	64	68	76	87	92

Graph the data and the line of best fit in the coordinate system below. Write a sentence that describes the meaning of the slope of the line of best fit.

Your solution

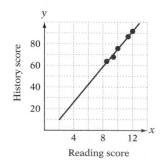

The slope of the line means that the grade on the history test increases 8.3 points for each 1-point increase in the grade on the reading test.

Solution on p. S12

4.4 Exercises

· ·

Objective A

1. Find the equation of the line that contains the point (0, 2) and has slope 2.
   $y = 2x + 2$

2. Find the equation of the line that contains the point (0, −1) and has slope −2.
   $y = -2x - 1$

3. Find the equation of the line that contains the point (−1, 2) and has slope −3.
   $y = -3x - 1$

4. Find the equation of the line that contains the point (2, −3) and has slope 3.
   $y = 3x \quad 9$

5. Find the equation of the line that contains the point (3, 1) and has slope $\frac{1}{3}$.
   $y = \frac{1}{3}x$

6. Find the equation of the line that contains the point (−2, 3) and has slope $\frac{1}{2}$.
   $y = \frac{1}{2}x + 4$

7. Find the equation of the line that contains the point (4, −2) and has slope $\frac{3}{4}$.
   $y = \frac{3}{4}x - 5$

8. Find the equation of the line that contains the point (2, 3) and has slope $-\frac{1}{2}$.
   $y = -\frac{1}{2}x + 4$

9. Find the equation of the line that contains the point (5, −3) and has slope $-\frac{3}{5}$.
   $y = -\frac{3}{5}x$

10. Find the equation of the line that contains the point (5, −1) and has slope $\frac{1}{5}$.
    $y = \frac{1}{5}x - 2$

11. Find the equation of the line that contains the point (2, 3) and has slope $\frac{1}{4}$.
    $y = \frac{1}{4}x + \frac{5}{2}$

12. Find the equation of the line that contains the point (−1, 2) and has slope $-\frac{1}{2}$.
    $y = -\frac{1}{2}x + \frac{3}{2}$

Objective B

13. Find the equation of the line that passes through the points $(1, -1)$ and $(-2, -7)$.
$y = 2x - 3$

14. Find the equation of the line that passes through the points $(2, 3)$ and $(3, 2)$.
$y = -x + 5$

15. Find the equation of the line that passes through the points $(-2, 1)$ and $(1, -5)$.
$y = -2x - 3$

16. Find the equation of the line that passes through the points $(-1, -3)$ and $(2, -12)$.
$y = -3x - 6$

17. Find the equation of the line that passes through the points $(0, 0)$ and $(-3, -2)$.
$y = \dfrac{2}{3}x$

18. Find the equation of the line that passes through the points $(0, 0)$ and $(-5, 1)$.
$y = -\dfrac{1}{5}x$

19. Find the equation of the line that passes through the points $(2, 3)$ and $(-4, 0)$.
$y = \dfrac{1}{2}x + 2$

20. Find the equation of the line that passes through the points $(3, -1)$ and $(0, -3)$.
$y = \dfrac{2}{3}x - 3$

21. Find the equation of the line that passes through the points $(-4, 1)$ and $(4, -5)$.
$y = -\dfrac{3}{4}x - 2$

22. Find the equation of the line that passes through the points $(-5, 0)$ and $(10, -3)$.
$y = -\dfrac{1}{5}x - 1$

23. Find the equation of the line that passes through the points $(-2, 1)$ and $(2, 4)$.
$y = \dfrac{3}{4}x + \dfrac{5}{2}$

24. Find the equation of the line that passes through the points $(3, -2)$ and $(-3, -3)$.
$y = \dfrac{1}{6}x - \dfrac{5}{2}$

Objective C   *Application Problems*

25. The data in the table below are estimates that a study projected for the number of hours, on average, a person will spend watching "basic cable" television channels each year. The line of best fit is $y = 12.9x + 332$, where x is the year (with $x = 0$ corresponding to 1990) and y is the number of hours per person.

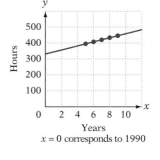

Year, x	5	6	7	8	9
Hours per Person, y	398	408	420	435	449

Graph the data and the line of best fit in the coordinate system at the right. Write a sentence that describes the meaning of the slope of the line of best fit.
The number of hours of "basic cable" watched per person increases by 12.9 h per year.

26. The data in the table below show the projected median annual income for a four-person family during different years. The line of best fit is $y = 1460x + 47,016$, where x is the year (with $x = 0$ corresponding to 1994) and y is the annual income.

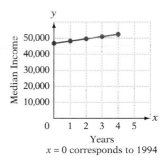

Year, x	0	1	2	3	4
Annual Income, y	47,012	48,452	49,987	51,406	52,843

Graph the data and the line of best fit in the coordinate system at the right. Write a sentence that describes the meaning of the slope of the line of best fit.
The median annual income is increasing by $1460 per year.

27. The data in the table below show the number of visitors (in millions) to U.S. national parks during different years. The line of best fit is $y = -2.1x + 275$, where x is the year (with $x = 0$ corresponding to 1992) and y is the number of visitors in millions.

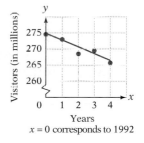

Year, x	0	1	2	3	4
Visitors (in millions), y	274.7	273.1	268.6	269.6	265.8

Graph the data and the line of best fit in the coordinate system at the right. Write a sentence that describes the meaning of the slope of the line of best fit.
The number of visitors is decreasing by 2.1 million per year.

28. The data in the table below show the average lifetime for women in the United States during different years. The line of best fit is $y = 0.2x + 73$, where x is the year (with $x = 0$ corresponding to 1960) and y is the length of the lifetime in years.

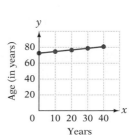

Year, x	0	10	20	30	40
Life Expectancy (in years), y	73.1	74.7	77.4	78.8	81.2

Graph the data and the line of best fit in the coordinate system at the right. Write a sentence that describes the meaning of the slope of the line of best fit.
The life expectancy of a woman is increasing by 0.2 year each year.

APPLYING THE CONCEPTS

In Exercises 29 to 32, the first two given points are on a line. Determine whether the third point is on the line.

29. $(-3, 2), (4, 1); (-1, 0)$
no

30. $(2, -2), (3, 4); (-1, 5)$
no

31. $(-3, -5), (1, 3); (4, 9)$
yes

32. $(-3, 7), (0, -2); (1, -5)$
yes

33. If $(-2, 4)$ are the coordinates of a point on the line whose equation is $y = mx + 1$, what is the slope of the line?
$-\dfrac{3}{2}$

34. If $(3, 1)$ are the coordinates of a point on the line whose equation is $y = mx - 3$, what is the slope of the line?
$\dfrac{4}{3}$

35. If $(0, -3), (6, -7),$ and $(3, n)$ are coordinates of points on the same line, determine n.
-5

36. If $(-4, 11), (2, -4),$ and $(6, n)$ are coordinates of points on the same line, determine n.
-14

The formula $y - y_1 = \dfrac{y_2 - y_1}{x_2 - x_1}(x - x_1)$, where $x_1 \neq x_2$, is called the **two-point formula** for a straight line. This formula can be used to find the equation of a line given two points. Use this formula for Exercises 37 and 38.

37. Find the equation of the line passing through $(-2, 3)$ and $(4, -1)$.
$y = -\dfrac{2}{3}x + \dfrac{5}{3}$

38. Find the equation of the line passing through $(3, -1)$ and $(4, -3)$.
$y = -2x + 5$

39. Explain why the condition $x_1 \neq x_2$ is placed on the two-point formula given above.

40. Explain how the two-point formula given above can be derived from the point–slope formula.

4.5 Parallel and Perpendicular Lines

Objective A   *To find parallel and perpendicular lines* ....

Two lines that have the same slope do not intersect and are called **parallel lines**.

The slope of each of the lines at the right is $\frac{2}{3}$.

The lines are parallel.

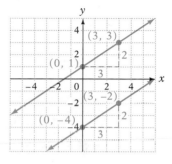

INSTRUCTOR NOTE

When students are attempting to find the equations of parallel or perpendicular lines, it may help to use the model given in the last section.

$$y - y_1 = m(x - x_1)$$
$$\downarrow \quad \downarrow \qquad \downarrow$$
$$y - (\ ) = (\ )[x - (\ )]$$

If the lines are parallel, m has the same value as the slope of the line to which it is parallel.

If the lines are perpendicular, m is the negative reciprocal of the slope of the line to which it is perpendicular.

> **Slopes of Parallel Lines**
>
> Two nonvertical lines with slopes of m_1 and m_2 are parallel if and only if $m_1 = m_2$. Any two vertical lines are parallel.

➡ Is the line containing the points $(-2, 1)$ and $(-5, -1)$ parallel to the line that contains the points $(1, 0)$ and $(4, 2)$?

$$m_1 = \frac{-1 - 1}{-5 - (-2)} = \frac{-2}{-3} = \frac{2}{3}$$

• Find the slope of the line through $(-2, 1)$ and $(-5, -1)$.

$$m_2 = \frac{2 - 0}{4 - 1} = \frac{2}{3}$$

• Find the slope of the line through $(1, 0)$ and $(4, 2)$.

Because $m_1 = m_2$, the lines are parallel.

➡ Find the equation of the line that contains the point $(2, 3)$ and is parallel to the line $y = \frac{1}{2}x - 4$.

The slope of the given line is $\frac{1}{2}$. Because parallel lines have the same slope, the slope of the unknown line is also $\frac{1}{2}$.

$$y - y_1 = m(x - x_1)$$

• Use the point–slope formula.

$$y - 3 = \frac{1}{2}(x - 2)$$

• $m = \frac{1}{2}$, $(x_1, y_1) = (2, 3)$

$$y - 3 = \frac{1}{2}x - 1$$

• Simplify.

$$y = \frac{1}{2}x + 2$$

• Write the equation in the form $y = mx + b$.

The equation of the line is $y = \frac{1}{2}x + 2$.

⇒ Find the equation of the line that contains the point $(-1, 4)$ and is parallel to the line $2x - 3y = 5$.

Because the lines are parallel, the slope of the unknown line is the same as the slope of the given line. Solve $2x - 3y = 5$ for y and determine its slope.

$$2x - 3y = 5$$
$$-3y = -2x + 5$$
$$y = \frac{2}{3}x - \frac{5}{3}$$

The slope of the given line is $\frac{2}{3}$. Because the lines are parallel, this is the slope of the unknown line. Use the point–slope formula to determine the equation.

$y - y_1 = m(x - x_1)$ • Use the point–slope formula.

$y - 4 = \frac{2}{3}[x - (-1)]$ • $m = \frac{2}{3}$, $(x_1, y_1) = (-1, 4)$

$y - 4 = \frac{2}{3}x + \frac{2}{3}$ • Simplify.

$y = \frac{2}{3}x + \frac{14}{3}$ • Write the equation in the form $y = mx + b$.

The equation of the line is $y = \frac{2}{3}x + \frac{14}{3}$.

Two lines that intersect at right angles are **perpendicular lines**.

Any horizontal line is perpendicular to any vertical line. For example, $x = 3$ is perpendicular to $y = -2$.

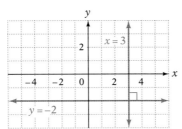

tangent line

Force

Slopes of Perpendicular Lines

If m_1 and m_2 are the slopes of two lines, neither of which is vertical, then the lines are perpendicular if and only if $m_1 \cdot m_2 = -1$.

A vertical line is perpendicular to a horizontal line.

Solving $m_1 \cdot m_2 = -1$ for m_1 gives $m_1 = -\frac{1}{m_2}$. This last equation states that the slopes of perpendicular lines are *negative reciprocals* of each other.

⇒ Is the line that contains the points $(4, 2)$ and $(-2, 5)$ perpendicular to the line that contains the points $(-4, 3)$ and $(-3, 5)$?

$m_1 = \dfrac{5 - 2}{-2 - 4} = \dfrac{3}{-6} = -\dfrac{1}{2}$ • Find the slope of the line through $(4, 2)$ and $(-2, 5)$.

$m_2 = \dfrac{5 - 3}{-3 - (-4)} = \dfrac{2}{1} = 2$ • Find the slope of the line through $(-4, 3)$ and $(-3, 5)$.

$m_1 \cdot m_2 = -\dfrac{1}{2}(2) = -1$ • Find the product of the two slopes.

Because $m_1 \cdot m_2 = -1$, the lines are perpendicular.

➡ Are the graphs of the equations $3x + 4y = 8$ and $8x + 6y = 5$ perpendicular?

To determine whether the lines are perpendicular, solve each equation for y and find the slope of each line. Then use the equation $m_1 \cdot m_2 = -1$.

$$3x + 4y = 8 \qquad\qquad\qquad 8x + 6y = 5$$
$$4y = -3x + 8 \qquad\qquad\quad 6y = -8x + 5$$
$$y = -\frac{3}{4}x + 2 \quad m_1 = -\frac{3}{4} \qquad y = -\frac{4}{3}x + \frac{5}{6} \quad m_2 = -\frac{4}{3}$$

$$m_1 \cdot m_2 = \left(-\frac{3}{4}\right)\left(-\frac{4}{3}\right) = 1$$

Because $m_1 \cdot m_2 = 1 \neq -1$, the lines are not perpendicular.

➡ Find the equation of the line that contains the point $(-2, 1)$ and is perpendicular to the line $y = -\frac{2}{3}x + 2$.

The slope of the given line is $-\frac{2}{3}$. The slope of the line perpendicular to the given line is the negative reciprocal of $-\frac{2}{3}$, which is $\frac{3}{2}$.

$$y - y_1 = m(x - x_1)$$ • Use the point–slope formula.

$$y - 1 = \frac{3}{2}[x - (-2)]$$ • $m = \frac{3}{2}, (x_1, y_1) = (-2, 1)$

$$y - 1 = \frac{3}{2}x + 3$$ • Write in the form $y = mx + b$.

$$y = \frac{3}{2}x + 4$$

The equation of the perpendicular line is $y = \frac{3}{2}x + 4$.

➡ Find the equation of the line that contains the point $(3, -4)$ and is perpendicular to the line $2x - y = -3$.

$$2x - y = -3$$ • Find the slope of the given line.
$$-y = -2x - 3$$
$$y = 2x + 3$$ • The slope is 2. The slope of the line perpendicular to this line is $-\frac{1}{2}$.

$$y - y_1 = m(x - x_1)$$ • Use the point–slope formula.

$$y - (-4) = -\frac{1}{2}(x - 3)$$ • $m = -\frac{1}{2}, (x_1, y_1) = (3, -4)$

$$y + 4 = -\frac{1}{2}x + \frac{3}{2}$$ • Write in the form $y = mx + b$.

$$y = -\frac{1}{2}x - \frac{5}{2}$$

The equation of the perpendicular line is $y = -\frac{1}{2}x - \frac{5}{2}$.

Example 1

Is the line that contains the points $(-4, 2)$ and $(1, 6)$ parallel to the line that contains the points $(2, -4)$ and $(7, 0)$?

Solution

$$m_1 = \frac{6 - 2}{1 - (-4)} = \frac{4}{5}$$

$$m_2 = \frac{0 - (-4)}{7 - 2} = \frac{4}{5}$$

$$m_1 = m_2 = \frac{4}{5}$$

The lines are parallel.

You Try It 1

Is the line that contains the points $(-2, -3)$ and $(7, 1)$ perpendicular to the line that contains the points $(4, 1)$ and $(6, -5)$?

Your solution

no

Example 2

Are the lines $4x - y = -2$ and $x + 4y = -12$ perpendicular?

Solution

$4x - y = -2$
$\quad -y = -4x - 2$
$\quad\quad y = 4x + 2$ • $m_1 = 4$

$x + 4y = -12$
$\quad 4y = -x - 12$
$\quad\quad y = -\frac{1}{4}x - 3$ • $m_2 = -\frac{1}{4}$

$$m_1 \cdot m_2 = 4\left(-\frac{1}{4}\right) = -1$$

The lines are perpendicular.

You Try It 2

Are the lines $5x + 2y = 2$ and $5x + 2y = -6$ parallel?

Your solution

yes

Example 3

Find the equation of the line that contains the point $(3, -1)$ and is parallel to the line $y = \frac{3}{2}x - 2$.

Solution

$$y - y_1 = m(x - x_1)$$

$$y - (-1) = \frac{3}{2}(x - 3) \quad • \ m = \frac{3}{2}$$

$$y + 1 = \frac{3}{2}x - \frac{9}{2}$$

$$y = \frac{3}{2}x - \frac{11}{2}$$

The equation of the line is $y = \frac{3}{2}x - \frac{11}{2}$.

You Try It 3

Find the equation of the line that contains the point $(-2, 2)$ and is perpendicular to the line $y = \frac{1}{4}x - 3$.

Your solution

$y = -4x - 6$

Solutions on pp. S12–S13

4.5 Exercises

· ·

Objective A

1. Is the line $x = -2$ perpendicular to the line $y = 3$?

   yes

2. Is the line $y = \frac{1}{2}$ perpendicular to the line $y = -4$?

   no

3. Is the line $x = -3$ parallel to the line $y = \frac{1}{3}$?

   no

4. Is the line $x = 4$ parallel to the line $x = -4$?

   yes

5. Is the line $y = \frac{2}{3}x - 4$ parallel to the line $y = -\frac{3}{2}x - 4$?

   no

6. Is the line $y = -2x + \frac{2}{3}$ parallel to the line $y = -2x + 3$?

   yes

7. Is the line $y = \frac{4}{3}x - 2$ perpendicular to the line $y = -\frac{3}{4}x + 2$?

   yes

8. Is the line $y = \frac{1}{2}x + \frac{3}{2}$ perpendicular to the line $y = -\frac{1}{2}x + \frac{3}{2}$?

   no

9. Are the lines $2x + 3y = 2$ and $2x + 3y = -4$ parallel?

   yes

10. Are the lines $2x - 4y = 3$ and $2x + 4y = -3$ parallel?

    no

11. Are the lines $x - 4y = 2$ and $4x + y = 8$ perpendicular?

    yes

12. Are the lines $4x - 3y = 2$ and $4x + 3y = -7$ perpendicular?

    no

13. Is the line that contains the points $(3, 2)$ and $(1, 6)$ parallel to the line that contains the points $(-1, 3)$ and $(-1, -1)$?

    no

14. Is the line that contains the points $(4, -3)$ and $(2, 5)$ parallel to the line that contains the points $(-2, -3)$ and $(-4, 1)$?

    no

15. Is the line that contains the points $(-3, 2)$ and $(4, -1)$ perpendicular to the line that contains the points $(1, 3)$ and $(-2, -4)$?

    yes

16. Is the line that contains the points $(-1, 2)$ and $(3, 4)$ perpendicular to the line that contains the points $(-1, 3)$ and $(-4, 1)$?

    no

17. Is the line that contains the points $(-5, 0)$ and $(0, 2)$ parallel to the line that contains the points $(5, 1)$ and $(0, -1)$?

    yes

18. Is the line that contains the points $(3, 5)$ and $(-3, 3)$ perpendicular to the line that contains the points $(2, -5)$ and $(-4, 4)$?

    no

19. Find the equation of the line containing the point $(-2, -4)$ and parallel to the line $2x - 3y = 2$.

$y = \dfrac{2}{3}x - \dfrac{8}{3}$

20. Find the equation of the line containing the point $(3, 2)$ and parallel to the line $3x + y = -3$.

$y = -3x + 11$

21. Find the equation of the line containing the point $(4, 1)$ and perpendicular to the line $y = -3x + 4$.

$y = \dfrac{1}{3}x - \dfrac{1}{3}$

22. Find the equation of the line containing the point $(2, -5)$ and perpendicular to the line $y = \dfrac{5}{2}x - 4$.

$y = -\dfrac{2}{5}x - \dfrac{21}{5}$

23. Find the equation of the line containing the point $(-1, -3)$ and perpendicular to the line $3x - 5y = 2$.

$y = -\dfrac{5}{3}x - \dfrac{14}{3}$

24. Find the equation of the line containing the point $(-1, 3)$ and perpendicular to the line $2x + 4y = -1$.

$y = 2x + 5$

APPLYING THE CONCEPTS

25. Explain how to determine whether the graphs of two lines are parallel.

26. Explain how to determine whether the graphs of two lines are perpendicular.

27. If the graphs of $A_1x + B_1y = C_1$ and $A_2x + B_2y = C_2$ are perpendicular, express $\dfrac{A_1}{B_1}$ in terms of A_2 and B_2. $\dfrac{A_1}{B_1} = -\dfrac{B_2}{A_2}$

28. If the graphs of $A_1x + B_1y = C_1$ and $A_2x + B_2y = C_2$ are parallel, express $\dfrac{A_1}{B_1}$ in terms of A_2 and B_2. $\dfrac{A_1}{B_1} = \dfrac{A_2}{B_2}$

29. The graphs of $y = -\dfrac{1}{2}x + 2$ and $y = \dfrac{2}{3}x - 5$ intersect at the point whose coordinates are $(6, -1)$. Find the equation of a line whose graph intersects the graphs of the given lines to form a right triangle. (*Hint:* There is more than one answer to this question.)

Any equation of the form $y = 2x + b$ where $b \neq -13$ or of the form $y = -\dfrac{3}{2}x + c$ where $c \neq 8$.

30. A theorem from geometry states that a line passing through the center of a circle and through a point P on the circle is perpendicular to the tangent line at P. (See the figure at the right.) If the coordinates of P are $(5, 4)$ and the coordinates of C are $(3, 2)$, what is the equation of the tangent line?

$y = -x + 9$

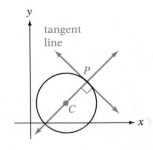

31. Find the x- and y-intercepts of the tangent line in Exercise 30.

x-intercept: $(9, 0)$; y-intercept: $(0, 9)$

4.6 Graphing Linear Inequalities

Objective A   ***To graph an inequality in two variables***.....................................

The graph of the linear equation $y = x - 2$ separates a plane into three sets:

the set of points on the line
the set of points above the line
the set of points below the line

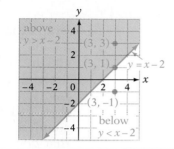

The point (3, 1) is a solution of $y = x - 2$.

$$\begin{array}{c|c} y = x - 2 \\ \hline 1 & 3 - 2 \\ \\ 1 = 1 \end{array}$$

The point (3, 3) is a solution of $y > x$ 2.

$$\begin{array}{c|c} y > x - 2 \\ \hline 3 & 3 - 2 \\ \\ 3 > 1 \end{array}$$

Any point above the line is a solution of $y > x - 2$.

The point (3, −1) is a solution of $y < x - 2$.

$$\begin{array}{c|c} y < x - 2 \\ \hline -1 & 3 - 2 \\ \\ -1 < 1 \end{array}$$

Any point below the line is a solution of $y < x - 2$.

The solution set of $y = x - 2$ is all points on the line. The solution set of $y > x - 2$ is all points above the line. The solution set of $y < x - 2$ is all points below the line. The solution set of an inequality in two variables is a **half-plane**.

The following illustrates the procedure for graphing a linear inequality.

➡ Graph the solution set of $2x + 3y \leq 6$.

Solve the inequality for y.

$$\begin{aligned} 2x + 3y &\leq 6 \\ 2x - 2x + 3y &\leq -2x + 6 \\ 3y &\leq -2x + 6 \\ \frac{3y}{3} &\leq \frac{-2x + 6}{3} \\ y &\leq -\frac{2}{3}x + 2 \end{aligned}$$

• Subtract 2x from each side.
• Simplify.

• Divide each side by 3.

• Simplify.

Change the inequality to an equality and graph $y = -\frac{2}{3}x + 2$. If the inequality is $\geq$ or $\leq$, the line is in the solution set and is shown by a **solid line**. If the inequality is $>$ or $<$, the line is not a part of the solution set and is shown by a **dotted line**.

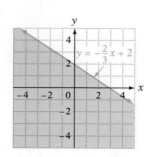

If the inequality is $>$ or $\geq$, shade the **upper half-plane**. If the inequality is $<$ or $\leq$, shade the **lower half-plane**.

The inequality $2x + 3y \leq 6$ can also be graphed as shown below.

$$2x + 3y = 6$$ • **Change the inequality to an equality.**

$$2x + 3(0) = 6$$ • **Find the x- and y-intercepts of the equation.**
$$2x = 6$$
$$x = 3$$ • **The x-intercept is (3, 0).**

$$2(0) + 3y = 6$$
$$3y = 6$$
$$y = 2$$ • **The y-intercept is (0, 2).**

Graph the ordered pairs $(3, 0)$ and $(0, 2)$. Draw a solid line through the points because the inequality is $\leq$. The point $(0, 0)$ can be used to determine which region to shade. If $(0, 0)$ is a solution of the inequality, then shade the region that includes the point $(0, 0)$. If $(0, 0)$ is not a solution of the inequality, then shade the region that does not include the point $(0, 0)$. For this example, $(0, 0)$ is a solution of the inequality. The region that contains the point $(0, 0)$ is shaded.

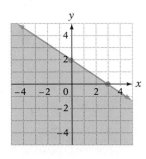

$$2x + 3y \leq 6$$
$$2(0) + 3(0) \leq 6$$
$$0 \leq 6 \quad \text{True}$$

TAKE NOTE

Any ordered pair is of the form (x, y). For the point $(0, 0)$, substitute 0 for x and 0 for y in the inequality.

If the line passes through point $(0, 0)$, another point must be used to determine which region to shade. For example, use the point $(1, 0)$.

It is important to note that every point in the shaded region is a solution of the inequality and that every solution of the inequality is a point in the shaded region. No point outside the shaded region is a solution of the inequality.

Example 1
Graph the solution set of $3x + y > -2$.

Solution
$$3x + y > -2$$
$$3x - 3x + y > -3x - 2$$
$$y > -3x - 2$$

Graph $y = -3x - 2$ as a dashed line.
Shade the upper half-plane.

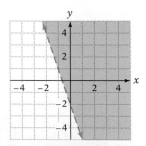

You Try It 1
Graph the solution set of $x - 3y < 2$.

Your solution

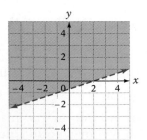

Solution on p. S13

4.6 Exercises

· ·

Objective A

Graph the solution set.

1. $y > -x + 4$

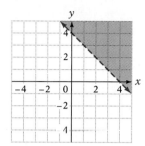

2. $y < x + 3$

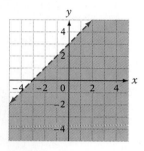

3. $y > 2x + 3$

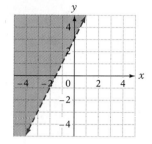

4. $y \geq -2x + 4$

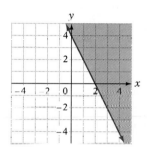

5. $y > \dfrac{3}{2}x - 4$

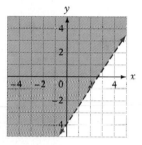

6. $y > -\dfrac{5}{4}x + 1$

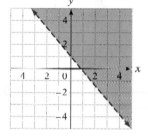

7. $y \leq -\dfrac{3}{4}x - 1$

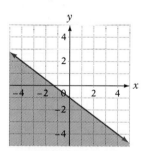

8. $y \leq -\dfrac{5}{2}x - 4$

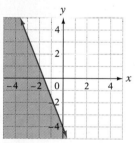

9. $y \leq -2$

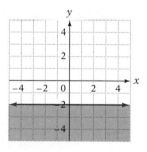

10. $y > 3$

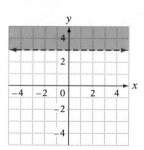

11. $y < \dfrac{4}{5}x + 3$

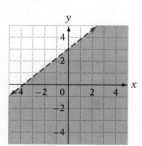

12. $y \leq -\dfrac{6}{5}x - 2$

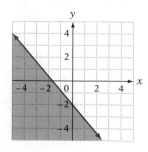

13. $3x - y < 9$

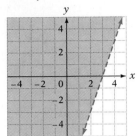

14. $3x + y \geq 6$

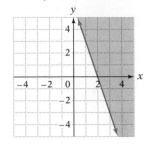

15. $2x + 2y \leq -4$

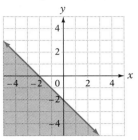

16. $-4x + 3y < -12$

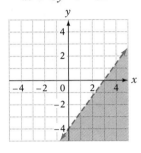

17. $-2x + 3y \leq 6$

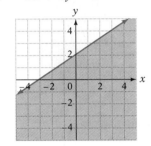

18. $3x - 4y > 12$

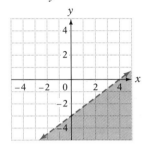

APPLYING THE CONCEPTS

Graph the solution set.

19. $\dfrac{x}{4} + \dfrac{y}{2} > 1$

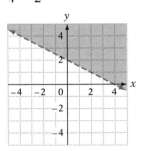

20. $2x - 3(y + 1) > y - (4 - x)$

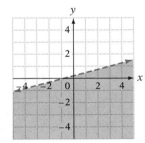

Write the inequality given its graph.

21.

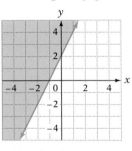

$y \geq 2x + 2$

22.

$y \leq -\dfrac{2}{3}x + 2$

23. Are there any points whose coordinates satisfy both $y \leq x + 3$ and $y \geq -\dfrac{1}{2}x + 1$? If so, give the coordinates of three such points. If not, explain why not.

24. Are there any points whose coordinates satisfy both $y \leq x - 1$ and $y \geq x + 2$? If so, give the coordinates of three such points. If not, explain why not.

Focus on Problem Solving

Counterexamples
Some of the exercises in this text ask you to determine whether a statement is true or false. For instance, the statement "every real number has a reciprocal" is false because 0 is a real number and 0 does not have a reciprocal.

Finding an example, such as 0 has no reciprocal, to show that a statement is not always true is called "finding a counterexample." A counterexample is an example that shows that a statement is not always true.

Consider the statement "the product of two numbers is greater than either factor." A counterexample to this statement is the factors $\frac{2}{3}$ and $\frac{3}{4}$. The product of these numbers is $\frac{1}{2}$, and $\frac{1}{2}$ is smaller than either $\frac{2}{3}$ or $\frac{3}{4}$. There are many other counterexamples to the given statement.

Here are some counterexamples to the statement "the square of a number is always larger than the number."

$$\left(\frac{1}{2}\right)^2 = \frac{1}{4} \quad \text{but} \quad \frac{1}{4} < \frac{1}{2} \qquad\qquad 1^2 = 1 \quad \text{but} \quad 1 = 1$$

For each of the next five statements, find at least one counterexample to show that the statement, or conjecture, is false.

1. The product of two integers is always a positive number.
2. The sum of two prime numbers is never a prime number.
3. For all real numbers, $|x + y| = |x| + |y|$.
4. If x and y are nonzero real numbers and $x > y$, then $x^2 > y^2$.
5. The quotient of any two nonzero real numbers is less than either one of the numbers.

When a problem is posed, it may not be known whether the statement is true or false. For instance, Christian Goldbach (1690–1764) stated that every even integer greater than 2 can be written as the sum of two prime numbers. No one has been able to find a counterexample to this statement, but neither has anyone been able to prove that it is always true.

In the next five exercises, answer true if the statement is always true. If there is an instance when the statement is false, give a counterexample.

6. The reciprocal of a positive number is always smaller than the number.
7. If $x < 0$, then $|x| = -x$.
8. For any two real numbers x and y, $x + y > x - y$.
9. For any positive integer n, $n^2 + n + 17$ is a prime number.
10. The list of numbers 1, 11, 111, 1111, 11111, . . . contains infinitely many composite numbers. (*Hint:* A number is divisible by 3 if the sum of the digits of the number is divisible by 3.)

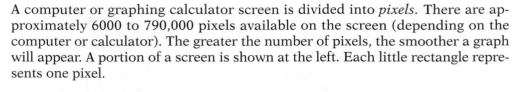

Projects and Group Activities

Graphing Linear Equations with a Graphing Utility

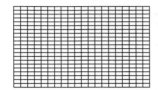

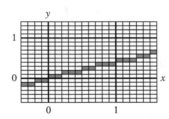

A computer or graphing calculator screen is divided into *pixels*. There are approximately 6000 to 790,000 pixels available on the screen (depending on the computer or calculator). The greater the number of pixels, the smoother a graph will appear. A portion of a screen is shown at the left. Each little rectangle represents one pixel.

The graphing utilities that are used by computers or calculators to graph an equation do basically what we have shown in the text: They choose values of x and, for each, calculate the corresponding value of y. The pixel corresponding to the ordered pair is then turned on. The graph is jagged because pixels are much larger than the dots we draw on paper.

The graph of $y = 0.45x$ is shown at the left as the calculator drew it (jagged). The x- and y-axes have been chosen so that each pixel represents $\frac{1}{10}$ of a unit. Consider the region of the graph where $x = 1$, 1.1, and 1.2.

The corresponding values of y are 0.45, 0.495, and 0.54. Because the y-axis is in tenths, the numbers 0.45, 0.495, and 0.54 are rounded to the nearest tenth before plotting. Rounding 0.45, 0.495, and 0.54 to the nearest tenth results in 0.5 for each number. Thus the ordered pairs (1, 0.45), (1.1, 0.495), and (1.2, 0.54) are graphed as (1, 0.5), (1.1, 0.5), and (1.2, 0.5). These points appear as three illuminated horizontal pixels. The graph of the line appears horizontal. However, if you use the TRACE feature of the calculator (see the appendix), the actual y-coordinate for each value of x is displayed.

TAKE NOTE

Xmin and Xmax are the smallest and largest values of x that will be shown on the screen. Ymin and Ymax are the smallest and largest values of y that will be shown on the screen.

Here are the keystrokes to graph $y = \frac{2}{3}x + 1$. First the equation is entered. Then the domain (Xmin to Xmax) and the range (Ymin to Ymax) are entered. This is called the **viewing window**. By changing the keystrokes 2 ⬚X, T, θ, n⬚ ⬚÷⬚ 3 ⬚+⬚ 1 (use ⬚X/θ/T/n⬚ for the Sharp EL-9600 or use ⬚X,θ,T⬚ for the Casio CFX-9850), you can graph different equations.

TI-83	*SHARP EL-9600*	*CASIO CFX-9850*
⬚Y =⬚ ⬚CLEAR⬚ 2 ⬚X, T, θ, n⬚ ⬚÷⬚ 3	⬚Y =⬚ ⬚CL⬚ 2 ⬚X/θ/T/n⬚ ⬚÷⬚ 3 ⬚+⬚ 1	⬚MENU⬚ 5 ⬚F2⬚ ⬚F1⬚ 2 ⬚X,θ,T⬚
⬚+⬚ 1 ⬚WINDOW⬚ ⬚(−)⬚ 10	⬚WINDOW⬚ ⬚(−)⬚ 10 ⬚ENTER⬚ 10	⬚÷⬚ 3 ⬚+⬚ ⬚EXE⬚ ⬚SHIFT⬚ F3
⬚ENTER⬚ 10 ⬚ENTER⬚ 1 ⬚ENTER⬚	⬚ENTER⬚ 1 ⬚ENTER⬚ ⬚(−)⬚ 10	⬚(−)⬚ 10 ⬚EXE⬚ 10 ⬚EXE⬚ 1 ⬚EXE⬚
⬚(−)⬚ 10 ⬚ENTER⬚ 10 ⬚ENTER⬚ 1	⬚ENTER⬚ 10 ⬚ENTER⬚ 1 ⬚ENTER⬚	⬚(−)⬚ 10 ⬚EXE⬚ 10 ⬚EXE⬚ 1 ⬚EXE⬚
⬚ENTER⬚ ⬚GRAPH⬚	⬚GRAPH⬚	⬚EXIT⬚ ⬚F6⬚

1. $y = 2x + 1$ — For $2x$, you may enter $2 \times x$ or just $2x$. The times sign $\times$ is not necessary on many graphing calculators.

2. $y = -\frac{1}{2}x - 2$ — Use the ⬚(−)⬚ key to enter a negative sign.

3. $3x + 2y = 6$ — Solve for y. Then enter the equation.

4. $4x + 3y = 75$ — You must adjust the viewing window. *Suggestion:* Xmin = −25, Xmax = 25, Xscl = 5, Ymin = −35, Ymax = 35, Yscl = 5. See the appendix for assistance.

Graphs of Motion A graph can be useful in analyzing the motion of a body. For example, consider an airplane in uniform motion traveling at 100 m/s. The table at the right shows the distance, in meters, traveled by the plane at the end of each of five one-second intervals.

Time (in seconds)	Distance (in meters)
0	0
1	100
2	200
3	300
4	400
5	500

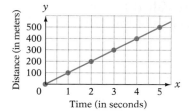

These data can be graphed on a rectangular coordinate system and a straight line drawn through the points plotted. The travel time is shown along the horizontal axis, and the distance traveled by the plane is shown along the vertical axis. (Note that the units along the two axes are not the same length.)

To write the equation for the line just graphed, use the coordinates of any two points on the line to find the slope. The y-intercept is (0, 0).

Let $(x_1, y_1) = (1, 100)$ and $(x_2, y_2) = (2, 200)$.

$$m = \frac{y_2 - y_1}{x_2 - x_1} = \frac{200 - 100}{2 - 1} = 100$$

$$y = mx + b$$
$$y = 100x + 0$$
$$y = 100x$$

Note that the slope of the line, 100, is equal to the speed, 100 m/s. *The slope of a distance-time graph represents the speed of the object.*

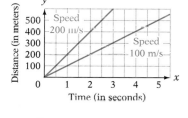

The distance-time graphs for two planes are shown at the left. One plane is traveling at 100 m/s, and the other is traveling at 200 m/s. The slope of the line representing the faster plane is greater than the slope of the line representing the slower plane.

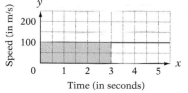

In the speed-time graph at the left, the time a plane has been flying at 100 m/s is shown along the horizontal axis and its speed is shown along the vertical axis. Because the speed is constant, the graph is a horizontal line.

The area between the horizontal line graphed and the horizontal axis is equal to the distance traveled by the plane up to that time. For example, the area of the shaded region on the graph is

$$\text{Length} \cdot \text{width} = (3 \text{ s})(100 \text{ m/s}) = 300 \text{ m}$$

The distance traveled by the plane in 3 s is equal to 300 m.

1. A car in uniform motion is traveling at 20 m/s.
   a. Prepare a distance-time graph for the car for 0 s to 5 s.
   b. Find the slope of the line.
   c. Find the equation of the line.
   d. Prepare a speed-time graph for the car for 0 s to 5 s.
   e. Find the distance traveled by the car after 3 s.

2. One car in uniform motion is traveling at 10 m/s. A second car in uniform motion is traveling at 15 m/s.
   a. Prepare one distance-time graph for both cars for 0 s to 5 s.
   b. Find the slope of each line.
   c. Find the equation of each line graphed.
   d. Assuming that the cars started at the same point at 0 s, find the distance between the cars at the end of 5 s.

3. a. In a distance-time graph, is it possible for the graph to be a horizontal line?
   b. What does a horizontal line reveal about the motion of the object during that time period?

Chapter Summary

Key Words   A *rectangular coordinate system* is formed by two number lines, one horizontal and one vertical, that intersect at the zero point of each line. A rectangular coordinate system divides the plane into four regions called *quadrants*. The number lines that make up a rectangular coordinate system are called the *coordinate axes*, or simply the *axes*. The *origin* is the point of intersection of the two coordinate axes.

Every point in the plane can be identified by an ordered pair (x, y). The first number in an ordered pair is called the *abscissa* or *x*-coordinate. The second number is called the *ordinate* or *y*-coordinate. The *coordinates* of a point are the numbers in the ordered pair associated with the point.

A *relation* is any set of ordered pairs. The *domain* of a relation is the set of first coordinates of the ordered pairs. The *range* is the set of second coordinates of the ordered pairs. A *function* is a relation in which no two ordered pairs have the same first coordinate and different second coordinates. A function designated by $f(x)$ is written in *functional notation*. The *value* of the function at x is $f(x)$.

An equation of the form $y = mx + b$, where m is the coefficient of x and b is a constant, is a *linear equation in two variables*. m is the slope of the line, and $(0, b)$ is the *y*-intercept. An equation of the form $Ax + By = C$ is also a linear equation in two variables. A *solution* of a linear equation in two variables is an ordered pair (x, y) that makes the equation a true statement. The *graph of a linear equation* is a straight line.

The point at which a graph crosses the *x*-axis is called the *x-intercept*. The point at which a graph crosses the *y*-axis is called the *y-intercept*.

The *slope* of a line is a measure of the slant of the line. The symbol for slope is m. A line that slants upward to the right has a *positive slope*. A line that slants downward to the right has a *negative slope*. A horizontal line has *zero slope*. The slope of a vertical line is *undefined*.

Two lines that have the same slope do not intersect and are *parallel lines*. Two lines that intersect at right angles are *perpendicular lines*.

An inequality of the form $y > mx + b$ or $Ax + By > C$ is a *linear inequality in two variables*. The symbol $>$ here could be replaced by $\geq$, $<$, or $\leq$. The solution set of an inequality in two variables is a *half-plane*.

Essential Rules   **To find the *x*-intercept,** let $y = 0$
To find the *y*-intercept, let $x = 0$.

Slope of a Linear Equation	Slope $= m = \dfrac{y_2 - y_1}{x_2 - x_1}, x_1 \neq x_2$
Slope–Intercept Form of a Straight Line	$y = mx + b$
Point–Slope Formula	$y - y_1 = m(x - x_1)$
Slopes of Parallel Lines	$m_1 = m_2$
Slopes of Perpendicular Lines	$m_1 \cdot m_2 = -1$

Chapter Review

1. **a.** Graph the ordered pairs $(-2, 4)$ and $(3, -2)$.
  b. Name the abscissa of point A. -2
  c. Name the ordinate of point B. -4

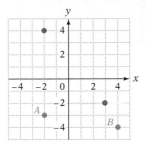

[4.1A]

2. Graph the ordered-pair solutions of $y = -\frac{1}{2}x - 2$ when $x = -4, -2, 0,$ and 2.

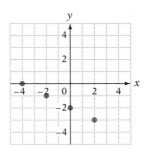

[4.1B]

3. Does $y = -x + 3$, where $x \in \{-2, 0, 3, 5\}$, define y as a function of x?
yes [4.1C]

4. Given $f(x) = x^2 - 2$, find $f(-1)$.
-1 [4.1D]

5. Graph $x = -3$.

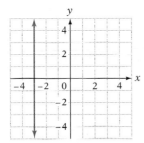

[4.2B]

6. Graph the line that has slope $-\frac{2}{3}$ and y-intercept $(0, 2)$.

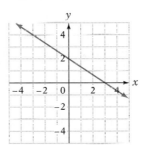

[4.3B]

7. Graph $y = -2x - 1$.

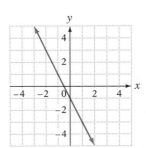

[4.2A]

8. Graph $y = \frac{1}{4}x + 3$.

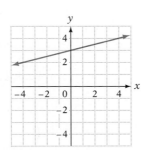

[4.2A]

9. Find the slope of the line containing the points $(-2, -3)$ and $(4, -3)$.
0 [4.3A]

10. Find the slope of the line containing the points $(9, 8)$ and $(-2, 1)$.
$\frac{7}{11}$ [4.3A]

11. Find the x- and y-intercepts of $3x - 2y = 24$.
$(8, 0), (0, -12)$ [4.2B]

12. Graph $3x - 2y = -6$.

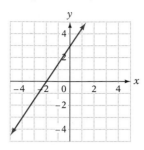

[4.2B]

13. Graph the solution set of $3x - 4y > 8$.

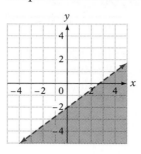

[4.6A]

14. Determine the equation of the line that passes through the points $(-1, 3)$ and $(2, -5)$.

$y = -\dfrac{8}{3}x + \dfrac{1}{3}$ [4.4B]

15. Determine the equation of the line that passes through the point $(6, 1)$ and has slope $-\dfrac{5}{2}$.

$y = -\dfrac{5}{2}x + 16$ [4.4A]

16. Find the equation of the line that contains the ordered pair $(-2, -4)$ and is parallel to the graph of $4x - 2y = 7$.

$y = 2x$ [4.5A]

17. Find the equation of the line that contains the point $(-2, -3)$ and is perpendicular to the line $y = -\dfrac{1}{2}x - 3$.

$y = 2x + 1$ [4.5A]

18. The height and weight of 8 seventh-grade students are shown in the following table. Write a relation in which the first coordinate is height, in inches, and the second coordinate is weight, in pounds. Is the relation a function?

Height	55	57	53	57	60	61	58	54
Weight	95	101	94	98	100	105	97	95

{(55, 95), (57, 101), (53, 94), (57, 98), (60, 100), (61, 105), (58, 97), (54, 95)}; no   [4.1C]

19. An on-line research service charges a monthly access fee of $75 plus $.45 per minute to use the service. An equation that represents the monthly cost to use this service is $C = 0.45x + 75$, where C is the monthly cost and x is the number of minutes. Graph this equation for $0 \le x \le 100$. The point $(50, 97.5)$ is on the graph. Write a sentence that describes the meaning of this ordered pair.
The cost of 50 min of access time for one month is $97.50.   [4.2C]

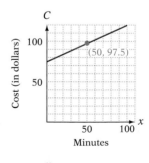

20. The data in the table below show the amount spent on health care in the United States. The line of best fit for these data is $y = 3.85x + 15.78$, where $x = 0$ corresponds to the year 1990. Graph the data and the line of best fit in the coordinate system at the right. How much is the amount spent on health care increasing each year?

Year	1990	1992	1994	1996	1998
Amount spent (billions)	14.9	22.7	30.9	36.0	42.1*

*Projected
The amount spent on health care increased $3.85 billion per year.   [4.4C]

Chapter Test

1. Find the ordered-pair solution of $2x - 3y = 15$ corresponding to $x = 3$.

$(3, -3)$ [4.1B]

2. Given $f(t) = t^2 + t$, find $f(2)$.

6   [4.1D]

3. The distance a house is from a fire station and the amount of damage that the house sustained in a fire are given in the following table. Write a relation in which the first coordinate of the ordered pair is the distance in miles from the fire station and the second coordinate is the amount of damage in thousands of dollars. Is the relation a function?

Distance	3.5	4.0	5.2	5.0	4.0	6.3	5.4
Damage	25	30	45	38	42	12	34

{(3.5, 25), (4.0, 30), (5.2, 45), (5.0, 38), (4.0, 42), (6.3, 12), (5.4, 34)}; no   [4.1C]

4. Graph the ordered-pair solutions of $y = -\frac{3}{2}x + 1$ when $x = -2, 0,$ and 4.

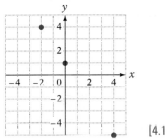

[4.1B]

5. Graph $y = -\frac{3}{4}x + 3$.

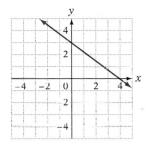

[4.2A]

6. Graph $3x - 2y = 6$.

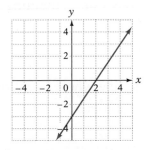

[4.2B]

7. Graph the line that has slope $-\frac{2}{3}$ and y-intercept $(0, 4)$.

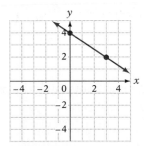

[4.3B]

8. Graph the solution set of $y \geq 2x - 3$.

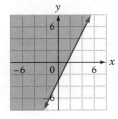

[4.6A]

9. Graph the solution set of $3x - 2y \leq 6$.

[4.6A]

10. The equation for the speed of a ball that is thrown straight up with an initial speed of 128 ft/s is $v = 128 - 32t$, where v is the speed of the ball after t seconds. Graph this equation for $0 \leq t \leq 4$. The point whose coordinates are (1, 96) is on the graph in Figure 1. Write a sentence that describes this ordered pair.

After 1 s, the ball is traveling 96 ft/s.   [4.2C]

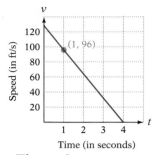

Figure 1

11. The graph in Figure 2 shows the increase in the cost of tuition for a college for the years 1993 through 1998 (with 1993 as 0). Find the slope of the line. Write a sentence that states the meaning of the slope.

$m = 1500$. The tuition increased by $1500 per year.   [4.4C]

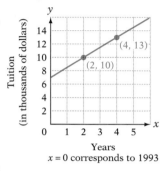

Figure 2

12. The data in the following table show the number of mutual fund companies for selected years between 1983 and 1993. The line of best fit is $y = 330x + 1016$, where x is the year (with 1983 as 0) and y is the number of mutual fund companies.

Year, x	0 (1983)	3 (1986)	5 (1988)	8 (1991)	10 (1993)
No. of companies, y	1020	2000	2670	3660	4320

Graph the data and the line of best fit in the coordinate system in Figure 3. Write a sentence that describes the meaning of the slope of the line of best fit.

The number of mutual fund companies increased by 330 each year.   [4.4C]

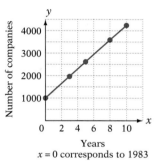

Figure 3

13. Find the x- and y-intercepts for $6x - 4y = 12$.

(2, 0), (0, −3)   [4.2B]

14. Find the slope of the line containing the points (2, −3) and (4, 1).

2   [4.3A]

15. Find the slope of the line containing the points (−5, 2) and (−5, 7).

undefined   [4.3A]

16. Find the slope of the line whose equation is $2x + 3y = 6$.

$-\dfrac{2}{3}$ [4.2B]

17. Find the equation of the line that contains the point (−3, 1) and has slope $\dfrac{2}{3}$.

$y = \dfrac{2}{3}x + 3$ [4.4A]

18. Find the equation of the line that passes through the points (−2, 0) and 5, −2).

$y = -\dfrac{2}{7}x - \dfrac{4}{7}$ [4.4B]

19. Find the equation of the line that contains the ordered pair (3, −2) and is parallel to the graph of $y = -3x + 4$.

$y = -3x + 7$ [4.5A]

20. Find the equation of the line that contains the ordered pair (2, 5) and is perpendicular to the graph of the line $y = -\dfrac{2}{3}x + 6$.

$y = \dfrac{3}{2}x + 2$ [4.5A]

Cumulative Review

1. Let $x \in \{-5, -3, -1\}$. For what values of x is the inequality $x \leq -3$ a true statement?
$-5, -3$ [1.1A]

2. Write $\frac{17}{20}$ as a decimal.
0.85 [1.2B]

3. Simplify: $3\sqrt{45}$
$9\sqrt{5}$ [1.2F]

4. Simplify: $12 - 18 \div 3(-2)^2$
-12 [1.3A]

5. Evaluate $\frac{a-b}{a^2-c}$ when $a = -2$, $b = 3$, and $c = -4$.
$-\dfrac{5}{8}$ [1.4A]

6. Simplify: $3d - 9 - 7d$
$-4d - 9$ [1.4B]

7. Simplify: $4(-8z)$
$-32z$ [1.4C]

8. Simplify: $2(x + y) - 5(3x - y)$
$-13x + 7y$ [1.4D]

9. Graph: $\{x \mid x < -2\} \cup \{x \mid x > 0\}$

[1.5C]

10. Solve: $2x - \dfrac{2}{3} = \dfrac{7}{3}$
$\dfrac{3}{2}$ [2.2A]

11. Solve: $3x - 2(10x - 6) = x - 6$
1 [2.2C]

12. Solve: $4x - 3 < 9x + 2$
$\{x \mid x > -1\}$ [2.4A]

13. Solve: $3x - 1 < 4$ and $x - 2 > 2$
The solution set is $\varnothing$.   [2.4B]

14. Solve: $|3x - 5| < 5$
$\left\{x \mid 0 < x < \dfrac{10}{3}\right\}$ [2.5B]

15. Given $f(t) = t^2 + t$, find $f(2)$.
6 [4.1D]

16. Find the slope of the line containing the points $(2, -3)$ and $(4, 1)$.
2 [4.3A]

17. Graph $y = 3x + 1$.

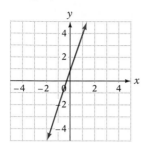

[4.2A]

18. Graph $x = -3$.

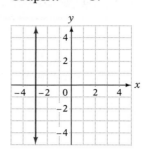

[4.2B]

19. Graph the line that has slope $\frac{1}{2}$ and y-intercept $(0, -1)$.

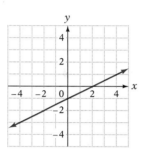

[4.3B]

20. Graph the solution set of $3x - 2y \geq 6$.

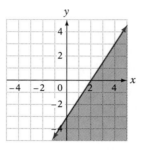

[4.6A]

21. Find the equation of the line that passes through the points $(6, -4)$ and $(-3, -1)$.

$y = -\frac{1}{3}x - 2$ [4.4B]

22. Find the equation of the line that contains the point $(2, 4)$ and is parallel to the line $y = -\frac{3}{2}x + 2$.

$y = -\frac{3}{2}x + 7$ [4.5A]

23. Two planes are 1800 mi apart and traveling toward each other. The first plane is traveling at twice the speed of the second plane. The planes meet in 3 h. Find the speed of each plane.

first plane: 400 mph; second plane: 200 mph [2.3D]

24. A grocer combines coffee that costs $8 per pound with coffee that costs $3 per pound. How many pounds of each should be used to make 80 lb of a blend that costs $5 per pound?

48 lb of $3 coffee; 32 lb of $8 coffee [2.3A]

25. The graph at the right shows the relationship between the cost of a rental house and the depreciation allowed for income tax purposes. Find the slope of the line between the two points on the graph. Write a sentence that states the meaning of the slope.

$m = -\dfrac{10,000}{3}$. The value of the house decreases by $3333.33 each year. [4.3A]

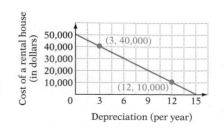

5

Systems of Linear Equations and Inequalities

A budget analyst provides advice and technical assistance in the preparation of annual budgets. Managers and department heads submit proposed operating and financial plans to the budget analyst for review. These plans outline proposed program increases or new products, estimated costs and expenses, and capital expenditures needed to finance these programs. Analyzing the different needs of each department or division requires solving large systems of equations.

Objectives

Section 5.1
To solve a system of linear equations by graphing

Section 5.2
To solve a system of linear equations by the substitution method

Section 5.3
To solve a system of two linear equations in two variables by the addition method
To solve a system of three linear equations in three variables by the addition method

Section 5.4
To evaluate a determinant
To solve a system of equations by using Cramer's Rule

Section 5.5
To solve rate-of-wind or rate-of-current problems
To solve application problems using two variables

Section 5.6
To graph the solution set of a system of linear inequalities

Input–Output Analysis

The economies of the industrial nations are very complex; they comprise hundreds of different industries, and each industry supplies other industries with goods and services needed in the production process. For example, the steel industry requires coal to produce steel, and the coal industry requires steel (in the form of machinery) to mine and transport coal.

Wassily Leontief, a Russian-born economist, developed a method of describing mathematically the interactions of an economic system. His technique was to examine various sectors of an economy (the steel industry, oil, farms, autos, and so on) and determine how each sector interacted with the others. More than five hundred sectors of the economy were studied.

The interactions of every sector with the others were expressed as a series of equations. This series of equations is called a *system of equations*. Using a computer, economists searched for a solution to the system of equations that would determine the output levels various sectors would have to meet to satisfy the requests from other sectors. The method is called input–output analysis.

Input–output analysis has many applications. For example, it is used today to predict the production needs of large corporations and to determine the effect of price changes on the economy. In recognition of the importance of his ideas, Leontief was awarded the Nobel Prize in Economics in 1973.

This chapter begins the study of systems of equations.

5.1 Solving Systems of Linear Equations by Graphing

Objective A *To solve a system of linear equations by graphing* ....

INSTRUCTOR NOTE
The idea of a system of equations is fairly difficult for students. You might try to motivate the discussion by first asking, "Find two numbers whose sum is 20." It will not take students too long to realize that there are infinitely many solutions to this question. By guiding your students a little further, you can show that the solution set is the set of points whose coordinates satisfy $x + y = 20$.

Now ask, "Find two numbers whose difference is 4." This will provide another line.

Finally, ask, "Find two numbers whose sum is 20 and whose difference is 4." You might have students guess and check until they find the solution and then show them that the solution is the coordinates of the point of intersection of the two lines.

You can extend this number problem to illustrate inconsistent and dependent systems of equations:

"Find two numbers whose sum is 5 and whose sum is 8." This is obviously not possible, and the graphs of the lines are parallel.

"Find two numbers whose sum is 10 such that the larger number is the difference between 10 and the smaller number." This is always true, and the graphs are the same line.

A **system of equations** is two or more equations considered together. The system at the right is a system of two linear equations in two variables. The graphs of the equations are straight lines.

$$3x + 4y = 7$$
$$2x - 3y = 6$$

A **solution of a system of equations in two variables** is an ordered pair that is a solution of each equation of the system.

➡ Is $(3, -2)$ a solution of the system $2x - 3y = 12$
$5x + 2y = 11$?

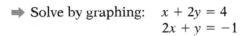

$2x - 3y = 12$	
$2(3) - 3(-2)$	12
$6 - (-6)$	
	$12 = 12$ True

$5x + 2y = 11$	
$5(3) + 2(-2)$	11
$15 + (-4)$	
	$11 = 11$ True

• **Replace x by 3 and y by -2.**

Yes, because $(3, -2)$ is a solution of each equation, it is a solution of the system of equations.

A solution of a system of linear equations can be found by graphing the lines of the system on the same coordinate axes. The point of intersection of the lines is the ordered pair that lies on both lines. It is the solution of the system of equations.

➡ Solve by graphing: $x + 2y = 4$
$2x + y = -1$

Graph each line.

Find the point of intersection.

The ordered pair $(-2, 3)$ lies on each line.

The solution is $(-2, 3)$.

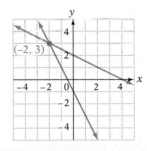

When the graphs of a system of equations intersect at only one point, the system of equations is called an **independent system of equations**.

➡ Solve by graphing: $2x + 3y = 6$
$4x + 6y = -12$

Graph each line.

The lines are parallel and therefore do not intersect. The system of equations has no solution.

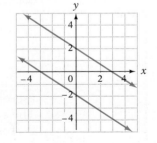

When a system of equations has no solution, it is called an **inconsistent system of equations**.

➡ Solve by graphing: $x - 2y = 4$
                             $2x - 4y = 8$

Graph each line.

The two equations represent the same line. This is a **dependent system of equations**. When a system of two equations is dependent, solve (if necessary) one of the equations of the system for y. The solutions of the dependent system are $(x, mx + b)$, where $y = mx + b$. For this system,

$$x - 2y = 4$$
$$-2y = -x + 4$$
$$y = \frac{1}{2}x - 2$$

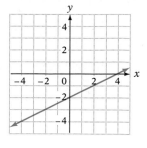

The solutions are the ordered pairs $\left(x, \frac{1}{2}x - 2\right)$.

TAKE NOTE

Keep in mind the ways in which independent, dependent, and inconsistent systems of equations differ. You should be able to express your understanding of these terms by using graphs.

Example 1   Solve by graphing:
                 $2x - y = 3$
                 $3x + y = 2$

Solution

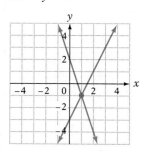

The solution is $(1, -1)$.

You Try It 1   Solve by graphing:
                 $x + y = 1$
                 $2x + y = 0$

Your solution

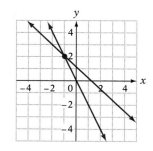

$(-1, 2)$

Example 2   Solve by graphing:
                 $2x + 3y = 6$
                 $y = -\frac{2}{3}x + 1$

Solution

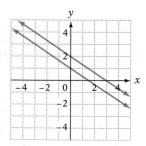

The lines are parallel and therefore do not intersect. The system of equations has no solution. It is inconsistent.

You Try It 2   Solve by graphing:
                 $3x - 4y = 12$
                 $y = \frac{3}{4}x - 3$

Your solution

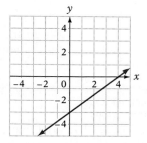

The system of equations is dependent. The solutions are the ordered pairs $\left(x, \frac{3}{4}x - 3\right)$.

Solutions on p. S13

5.1 Exercises

. . . .

Objective A

1. Is (2, 3) a solution of the system
$$3x + 4y = 18$$
$$2x - y = 1?$$
yes

2. Is (2, −1) a solution of the system
$$x - 2y = 4$$
$$2x + y = 3?$$
yes

3. Is (1, −2) a solution of the system
$$3x - y = 5$$
$$2x + 5y = -8?$$
yes

4. Is (−1, −1) a solution of the system
$$x - 4y = 3$$
$$3x + y = 2?$$
no

5. Is (4, 3) a solution of the system
$$5x - 2y = 14$$
$$x + y = 8?$$
no

6. Is (2, 5) a solution of the system
$$3x + 2y = 16$$
$$2x - 3y = 4?$$
no

7. Is (−1, 3) a solution of the system
$$4x - y = -5$$
$$2x + 5y = 13?$$
no

8. Is (4, −1) a solution of the system
$$x - 4y = 9$$
$$2x - 3y = 11?$$
no

9. Is (0, 0) a solution of the system
$$4x + 3y = 0$$
$$2x - y = 1?$$
no

10. Is (2, 0) a solution of the system
$$3x - y = 6$$
$$x + 3y = 2?$$
yes

11. Is (2, −3) a solution of the system
$$y = 2x - 7$$
$$3x - y = 9?$$
yes

12. Is (−1, −2) a solution of the system
$$3x - 4y = 5$$
$$y = x - 1?$$
yes

13. Is (5, 2) a solution of the system
$$y = 2x - 8$$
$$y = 3x - 13?$$
yes

14. Is (−4, 3) a solution of the system
$$y = 2x + 11$$
$$y = 5x - 19?$$
no

15. Is (−2, −3) a solution of the system
$$3x - 4y = 6$$
$$2x - 7y = 17?$$
yes

16. Is (0, 0) a solution of the system
$$y = 2x$$
$$3x + 5y = 0?$$
yes

17. Is (0, −3) a solution of the system
$$4x - 3y = 9$$
$$2x + 5y = 15?$$
no

18. Is (4, 0) a solution of the system
$$2x + 3y = 8$$
$$x - 5y = 4?$$
yes

19. How is a solution of a system of equations in two variables represented?

20. For a system of two linear equations in two variables, explain, in geometric terms, each of the following: dependent system of equations, inconsistent system of equations, independent system of equations.

Solve by graphing.

21. $x + y = 2$
$x - y = 4$

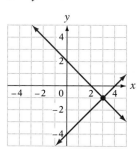

$(3, -1)$

22. $x + y = 1$
$3x - y = -5$

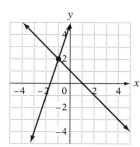

$(-1, 2)$

23. $x - y = -2$
$x + 2y = 10$

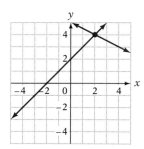

$(2, 4)$

24. $2x - y = 5$
$3x + y = 5$

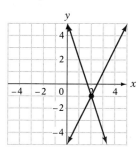

$(2, -1)$

25. $3x - 2y = 6$
$y = 3$

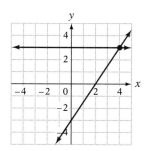

$(4, 3)$

26. $x = 4$
$3x - 2y = 4$

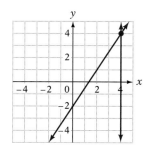

$(4, 4)$

27. $x = 4$
$y = -1$

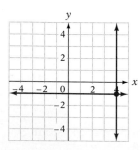

$(4, -1)$

28. $x + 2 = 0$
$y - 1 = 0$

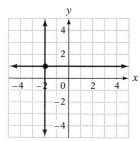

$(-2, 1)$

29. $2x + y = 3$
$x - 2 = 0$

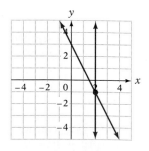

$(2, -1)$

30. $x - 3y = 6$
$y + 3 = 0$

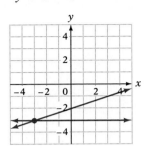

$(-3, -3)$

31. $x - y = 6$
$x + y = 2$

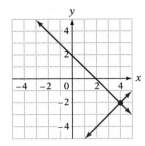

$(4, -2)$

32. $2x + y = 2$
$-x + y = 5$

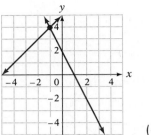

$(-1, 4)$

33. $y = x - 5$
$2x + y = 4$

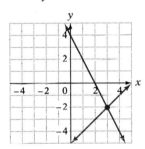

$(3, -2)$

34. $2x - 5y = 4$
$y = x + 1$

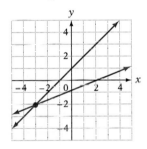

$(-3, -2)$

35. $y = \dfrac{1}{2}x - 2$
$x - 2y = 8$

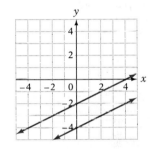

no
solution

36. $2x + 3y = 6$
$y = -\dfrac{2}{3}x + 1$

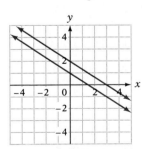

no
solution

37. $2x - 5y = 10$
$y = \dfrac{2}{5}x - 2$

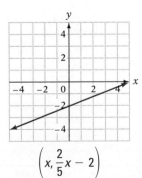

$\left(x, \dfrac{2}{5}x - 2\right)$

38. $3x - 2y = 6$
$y = \dfrac{3}{2}x - 3$

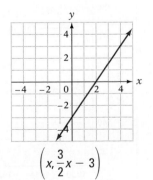

$\left(x, \dfrac{3}{2}x - 3\right)$

39. $3x - 4y = 12$
$5x + 4y = -12$

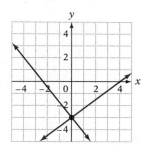

$(0, -3)$

40. $2x - 3y = 6$
$2x - 5y = 10$

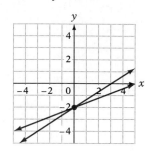

$(0, -2)$

41. $2x - 3y = 2$
$5x + 4y = 5$

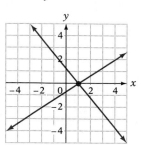

$(1, 0)$

APPLYING THE CONCEPTS

42. Determine whether the statement is always true, sometimes true, or never true.
  a. A solution of a system of two equations in two variables is a point in the plane.   sometimes true
  b. Two parallel lines have the same slope.   always true
  c. Two different lines with the same y-intercept are parallel.   never true
  d. Two different lines with the same slope are parallel.   always true

Use a graphing calculator to solve each of the following systems of equations. Round answers to the nearest hundredth. See the Projects and Group Activities at the end of this chapter for assistance.

43. $y = -\dfrac{1}{2}x + 2$
$y = 2x - 1$
$(1.20, 1.40)$

44. $y = 1.2x + 2$
$y = -1.3x - 3$
$(-2, -0.4)$

45. $y = \sqrt{2}x - 1$
$y = -\sqrt{3}x + 1$
$(0.64, -0.10)$

46. $y = \pi x - \dfrac{2}{3}$
$y = -x + \dfrac{\pi}{2}$
$(0.54, 1.03)$

47. Write three different systems of equations: (a) one that has $(-3, 5)$ as its only solution, (b) one for which there is no solution, and (c) one that is a dependent system of equations.   Answers will vary.

48. The graph below shows the life expectancy at birth for males and females. Write an essay describing your interpretation of the data presented. Be sure to include in your discussion an interpretation of the point at which the two lines intersect.

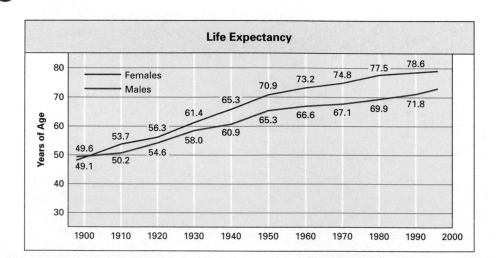

5.2 Solving Systems of Linear Equations by the Substitution Method

Objective A *To solve a system of linear equations by the substitution method* ....

A graphical solution of a system of equations is based on approximating the coordinates of a point of intersection. An algebraic method called the **substitution method** can be used to find an exact solution of a system of equations.

➡ Solve by the substitution method: (1) $2x + 5y = -11$
                                        (2) $y = 3x - 9$

Equation (2) states that $y = 3x - 9$. Substitute $3x - 9$ for y in Equation (1).

$2x + 5y = -11$ • This is Equation (1).
$2x + 5(3x - 9) = -11$ • From Equation (2), substitute $3x - 9$ for y.
$2x + 15x - 45 = -11$ • Solve for x.
$17x - 45 = -11$
$17x = 34$
$x = 2$

Now substitute the value of x into Equation (2) and solve for y.

$y = 3x - 9$ • This is Equation (2).
$y = 3(2) - 9$ • Substitute 2 for x.
$y = 6 - 9 = -3$

The solution is the ordered pair $(2, -3)$.

The graph of the equations in this system of equations is shown at the right. Note that the lines intersect at the point whose coordinates are $(2, -3)$, which is the algebraic solution we determined by the substitution method.

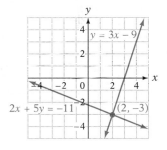

To solve a system of equations by the substitution method, sometimes we must solve one of the equations in the system of equations for one of its variables. For instance, the first step in solving the system of equations

(1) $x + 2y = -3$
(2) $2x - 3y = 5$

is to solve an equation of the system for one of its variables. Either equation can be used.

Solving Equation (1) for x: Solving Equation (2) for x:

$x + 2y = -3$ $2x - 3y = 5$
$x = -2y - 3$ $2x = 3y + 5$
                                            $x = \dfrac{3y + 5}{2}$

Because solving Equation (1) for x does not result in fractions, it is the easier of the two equations to use.

Here is the solution of the system of equations given on the previous page.

➡ Solve by the substitution method: (1) $x + 2y = -3$
(2) $2x - 3y = 5$

To use the substitution method, we must solve an equation for one of its variables. Equation (1) is used here because solving it for x does not result in fractions.

$$x + 2y = -3$$

(3) $\qquad x = -2y - 3$ • Solve for x. This is Equation (3).

Now substitute $-2y - 3$ for x in Equation (2) and solve for y.

$$2x - 3y = 5 \qquad \text{• This is Equation (2).}$$
$$2(-2y - 3) - 3y = 5 \qquad \text{• From Equation (3), substitute } -2y - 3 \text{ for } x.$$
$$-4y - 6 - 3y = 5 \qquad \text{• Solve for } y.$$
$$-7y - 6 = 5$$
$$-7y = 11$$
$$y = -\frac{11}{7}$$

INSTRUCTOR NOTE

It may benefit some students to see a demonstration that the same value of x is determined by substituting the value of y into any one of the equations of the system of equations.

Substitute the value of y into Equation (3) and solve for x.

$$x = -2y - 3 \qquad \text{• This is Equation (3).}$$
$$= -2\left(-\frac{11}{7}\right) - 3 \qquad \text{• Substitute } -\frac{11}{7} \text{ for } y.$$
$$= \frac{22}{7} - 3 = \frac{22}{7} - \frac{21}{7} = \frac{1}{7}$$

The solution is $\left(\frac{1}{7}, -\frac{11}{7}\right)$.

The graph of the system of equations given above is shown at the right. It would be difficult to determine the exact solution of this system of equations from the graphs of the equations.

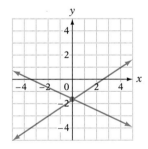

➡ Solve by the substitution method: (1) $y = 3x - 1$
(2) $y = -2x - 6$

$$y = -2x - 6$$
$$3x - 1 = -2x - 6 \qquad \text{• Substitute } 3x - 1 \text{ for } y \text{ in Equation (2).}$$
$$5x = -5 \qquad \text{• Solve for } x.$$
$$x = -1$$

TAKE NOTE

You can *always* check the solution to an independent system of equations. Use the skill you developed in Objective 5.1A to check that the ordered pair is a solution to each equation in the system.

Substitute this value of x into Equation (1) or Equation (2) and solve for y. Equation (1) is used here.

$$y = 3x - 1$$
$$y = 3(-1) - 1 = -4$$

The solution is $(-1, -4)$.

The substitution method can be used on inconsistent and dependent systems of equations.

➡ Solve by the substitution method: (1) $2x + 3y = 3$

(2) $y = -\dfrac{2}{3}x + 3$

$2x + 3y = 3$ • This is Equation (1).

$2x + 3\left(-\dfrac{2}{3}x + 3\right) = 3$ • From Equation (2), replace y with $-\dfrac{2}{3}x + 3$.

$2x - 2x + 9 = 3$ • Solve for x.

$9 = 3$ • This is not a true equation.

Because $9 = 3$ is not a true equation, the system of equations has no solution.

Solving Equation (1) above for y, we have $y = -\dfrac{2}{3}x + 1$. Comparing this with Equation (2) reveals that the slopes are equal and the y-intercepts are different. The graphs of the equations that make up this system of equations are parallel and thus never intersect. Because the graphs do not intersect, there are no solutions of the system of equations. The system of equations is inconsistent.

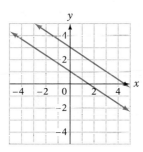

➡ Solve by the substitution method: (1) $x = 2y + 3$
(2) $4x - 8y = 12$

$4x - 8y = 12$ • This is Equation (2).

$4(2y + 3) - 8y = 12$ • From Equation (1), replace x by $2y + 3$.

$8y + 12 - 8y = 12$ • Solve for y.

$12 = 12$ • This is a true equation.

The true equation $12 = 12$ indicates that any ordered pair (x, y) that satisfies one equation of the system satisfies the other equation. Therefore, the system of equations has an infinite number of solutions.

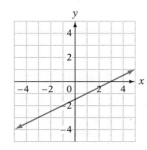

INSTRUCTOR NOTE
Some students will wonder which equation of a system to use to represent the solutions of a dependent system of equations. To them it seems that the two equations of the system are different. If they write the equations in slope–intercept form as we have shown, they may better understand that either equation can be used.

If we write Equation (1) and Equation (2) in slope–intercept form, we have

$$x = 2y + 3 \qquad\qquad 4x - 8y = 12$$

$$y = \dfrac{1}{2}x - \dfrac{3}{2} \qquad\qquad y = \dfrac{1}{2}x - \dfrac{3}{2}$$

The slope–intercept forms of the equations are the same, and therefore the graphs are the same. If we graph these two equations, we essentially graph one over the other. Accordingly, the graphs intersect at an infinite number of points. The solutions are the ordered pairs $\left(x, \dfrac{1}{2}x - \dfrac{3}{2}\right)$.

Example 1   Solve by substitution:
(1) $3x + 4y = -2$
(2) $-x + 2y = 4$

Solution   Solve Equation (2) for x.
$$-x + 2y = 4$$
$$-x = -2y + 4$$
$$x = 2y - 4$$

Substitute in Equation (1).
(1) $3x + 4y = -2$
$$3(2y - 4) + 4y = -2$$
$$6y - 12 + 4y = -2$$
$$10y - 12 = -2$$
$$10y = 10$$
$$y = 1$$

Substitute in Equation (2).
(2) $-x + 2y = 4$
$$-x + 2(1) = 4$$
$$-x + 2 = 4$$
$$-x = 2$$
$$x = -2$$

The solution is $(-2, 1)$.

You Try It 1   Solve by substitution:
$$7x - y = 4$$
$$3x + 2y = 9$$

Your solution $(1, 3)$

Example 2   Solve by substitution:
$$4x + 2y = 5$$
$$y = -2x + 1$$

Solution $4x + 2y = 5$
$$4x + 2(-2x + 1) = 5$$
$$4x - 4x + 2 = 5$$
$$2 = 5$$

This is not a true equation. The system of equations is inconsistent and therefore does not have a solution.

You Try It 2   Solve by substitution:
$$3x - y = 4$$
$$y = 3x + 2$$

Your solution   The system of equations is inconsistent and therefore does not have a solution.

Example 3   Solve by substitution:
$$y = 3x - 2$$
$$6x - 2y = 4$$

Solution $6x - 2y = 4$
$$6x - 2(3x - 2) = 4$$
$$6x - 6x + 4 = 4$$
$$4 = 4$$

This is a true equation. The system of equations is dependent. The solutions are the ordered pairs $(x, 3x - 2)$.

You Try It 3   Solve by substitution:
$$y = -2x + 1$$
$$6x + 3y = 3$$

Your solution   The system of equations is dependent. The solutions are the ordered pairs $(x, -2x + 1)$.

Solutions on p. S13

5.2 Exercises

Objective A

Solve by substitution.

1. $2x + 3y = 7$
$\quad x = 2$
(2, 1)

2. $\quad y = 3$
$3x - 2y = 6$
(4, 3)

3. $\quad y = x - 3$
$x + y = 5$
(4, 1)

4. $\quad y = x + 2$
$x + y = 6$
(2, 4)

5. $\quad x = y - 2$
$x + 3y = 2$
(−1, 1)

6. $\quad x = y + 1$
$x + 2y = 7$
(3, 2)

7. $\quad y = 4 - 3x$
$3x + y = 5$
inconsistent

8. $\quad y = 2 - 3x$
$6x + 2y = 7$
inconsistent

9. $\quad x = 3y + 3$
$2x - 6y = 12$
inconsistent

10. $\quad x = 2 - y$
$3x + 3y = 6$
$(x, 2-x)$

11. $3x + 5y = -6$
$\quad x = 5y + 3$
$\left(-\dfrac{3}{4}, -\dfrac{3}{4}\right)$

12. $\quad y = 2x + 3$
$4x - 3y = 1$
(−5, −7)

13. $3x + y = 4$
$4x - 3y = 1$
(1, 1)

14. $x - 4y = 9$
$2x - 3y = 11$
$\left(\dfrac{17}{5}, -\dfrac{7}{5}\right)$

15. $3x - y = 6$
$x + 3y = 2$
(2, 0)

16. $4x - y = -5$
$2x + 5y = 13$
$\left(-\dfrac{6}{11}, \dfrac{31}{11}\right)$

17. $3x - y = 5$
$2x + 5y = -8$
(1, −2)

18. $3x + 4y = 18$
$2x - y = 1$
(2, 3)

19. $4x + 3y = 0$
$2x - y = 0$
(0, 0)

20. $5x + 2y = 0$
$x - 3y = 0$
(0, 0)

21. $2x - y = 2$
$6x - 3y = 6$
$(x, 2x - 2)$

22. $3x + y = 4$
        $9x + 3y = 12$
        $(x, -3x + 4)$

23. $x = 3y + 2$
       $y = 2x + 6$
       $(-4, -2)$

24. $x = 4 - 2y$
       $y = 2x - 13$
       $(6, -1)$

25. $y = 2x + 11$
       $y = 5x - 19$
       $(10, 31)$

26. $y = 2x - 8$
       $y = 3x - 13$
       $(5, 2)$

27. $y = -4x + 2$
       $y = -3x - 1$
       $(3, -10)$

28. $x = 3y + 7$
       $x = 2y - 1$
       $(-17, -8)$

29. $x = 4y - 2$
       $x = 6y + 8$
       $(-22, -5)$

30. $x = 3 - 2y$
       $x = 5y - 10$
       $\left(-\dfrac{5}{7}, \dfrac{13}{7}\right)$

APPLYING THE CONCEPTS

For what value of k does the system of equations have no solution?

31. $2x - 3y = 7$
       $kx - 3y = 4$
       2

32. $8x - 4y = 1$
       $2x - ky = 3$
       1

33. $x = 4y + 4$
       $kx - 8y = 4$
       2

34. The following was offered as a solution to the system of equations

    (1) $y = \dfrac{1}{2}x + 2$

    (2) $2x + 5y = 10$

$$2x + 5y = 10 \qquad \bullet \text{ This is Equation (2).}$$
$$2x + 5\left(\frac{1}{2}x + 2\right) = 10 \qquad \bullet \text{ Substitute } \tfrac{1}{2}x + 2 \text{ for } y.$$
$$2x + \frac{5}{2}x + 10 = 10 \qquad \bullet \text{ Solve for } x.$$
$$\frac{9}{2}x = 0$$
$$x = 0$$

At this point the student stated that because $x = 0$, the system of equations has no solution. If this assertion is correct, is the system of equations independent, dependent, or inconsistent? If the assertion is not correct, what is the correct solution?
The assertion is false. The solution is (0, 2).

35. Describe in your own words the process of solving a system of equations by the substitution method.

36. When you solve a system of equations by the substitution method, how do you determine whether the system of equations is dependent?

37. When you solve a system of equations by the substitution method, how do you determine whether the system of equations is inconsistent?

5.3 Solving Systems of Linear Equations by the Addition Method

Objective A   *To solve a system of two linear equations in two variables by the addition method* ....

The **addition method** is an alternative method for solving a system of equations. This method is based on the Addition Property of Equations. Use the addition method when it is not convenient to solve one equation for one variable in terms of the other variable.

Note, for the system of equations at the right, the effect of adding Equation (2) to Equation (1). Because $-3y$ and $3y$ are additive inverses, adding the equations results in an equation with only one variable.

$$(1) \quad 5x - 3y = 14$$
$$(2) \quad 2x + 3y = -7$$
$$ \quad 7x + 0y = 7$$
$$ \quad 7x = 7$$

The solution of the resulting equation is the first component of the ordered-pair solution of the system.

$$7x = 7$$
$$x = 1$$

The second component is found by substituting the value of x into Equation (1) or (2) and then solving for y. Equation (1) is used here.

$$(1) \quad 5x - 3y = 14$$
$$5(1) - 3y = 14$$
$$5 - 3y = 14$$
$$-3y = 9$$
$$y = -3$$

The solution is $(1, -3)$.

Sometimes each equation of the system of equations must be multiplied by a constant so that the coefficients of one of the variables are opposites.

➡ Solve by the addition method:
$$(1) \quad 3x + 4y = 2$$
$$(2) \quad 2x + 5y = -1$$

To eliminate x, multiply Equation (1) by 2 and Equation (2) by -3. Note at the right how the constants are chosen.

$$2(3x + 4y) = 2 \cdot 2$$
$$\cancel{}$$
$$-3(2x + 5y) = -3(-1)$$

• The negative is used so that the coefficients will be opposites.

$$6x + 8y = 4$$
$$\underline{-6x - 15y = 3}$$
$$-7y = 7$$
$$y = -1$$

• 2 times Equation (1)
• −3 times Equation (2)
• Add the equations.
• Solve for *y*.

Substitute the value of y into Equation (1) or Equation (2) and solve for x. Equation (1) will be used here.

$$(1) \quad 3x + 4y = 2$$
$$3x + 4(-1) = 2$$
$$3x - 4 = 2$$
$$3x = 6$$
$$x = 2$$

• Substitute −1 for *y*.
• Solve for *x*.

The solution is $(2, -1)$.

➡ Solve by the addition method: (1) $\frac{2}{3}x + \frac{1}{2}y = 4$

(2) $\frac{1}{4}x - \frac{3}{8}y = -\frac{3}{4}$

Clear fractions. Multiply each equation by the LCM of the denominators.

$$6\left(\frac{2}{3}x + \frac{1}{2}y\right) = 6(4)$$
$$8\left(\frac{1}{4}x - \frac{3}{8}y\right) = 8\left(-\frac{3}{4}\right)$$

$$4x + 3y = 24$$
$$2x - 3y = -6$$

$$6x = 18 \qquad \bullet \text{ Eliminate } y. \text{ Add the equations.}$$
$$x = 3 \qquad \bullet \text{ Solve for } x.$$

Substitute the value of x into Equation (1) and solve for y.

$$\frac{2}{3}x + \frac{1}{2}y = 4 \qquad \bullet \text{ This is Equation (1).}$$

$$\frac{2}{3}(3) + \frac{1}{2}y = 4 \qquad \bullet \ x = 3$$

$$2 + \frac{1}{2}y = 4$$

$$\frac{1}{2}y = 2$$

$$y = 4$$

The solution is (3, 4).

➡ Solve by the addition method: (1) $2x - y = 3$
(2) $4x - 2y = 6$

Eliminate y. Multiply Equation (1) by -2.

(1) $-2(2x - y) = -2(3)$ $\bullet$ Multiply both sides of Equation (1) by -2.
(3) $-4x + 2y = -6$ $\bullet$ This is Equation (3).

Add Equation (3) to Equation (2).

(2) $4x - 2y = 6$
(3) $\underline{-4x + 2y = -6}$
              $0 = 0$ $\bullet$ This is a true equation.

The equation $0 = 0$ indicates that the system of equations is dependent. This means that the graphs of the two lines are the same. Therefore, the solutions of the system of equations are the ordered-pair solutions of the equation of the line. Solve Equation (1) for y.

$$2x - y = 3$$
$$-y = -2x + 3$$
$$y = 2x - 3$$

The ordered-pair solutions are $(x, 2x - 3)$.

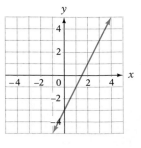

Example 1   Solve by the addition method:
(1) $3x - 2y = 2x + 5$
(2) $2x + 3y = -4$

Solution   Write Equation (1) in the form
$Ax + By = C$.

$$3x - 2y = 2x + 5$$
$$x - 2y = 5$$

Solve the system:

$$x - 2y = 5$$
$$2x + 3y = -4$$

Eliminate x.

$$-2(x - 2y) = -2(5)$$
$$2x + 3y = -4$$

$$-2x + 4y = -10$$
$$2x + 3y = -4$$

Add the equations.

$$7y = -14$$
$$y = -2$$

Replace y in Equation (2).

$$2x + 3y = -4$$
$$2x + 3(-2) = -4$$
$$2x - 6 = -4$$
$$2x = 2$$
$$x = 1$$

The solution is $(1, -2)$.

You Try It 1   Solve by the addition method:
$2x + 5y = 6$
$3x - 2y = 6x + 2$

Your solution $(-2, 2)$

Example 2   Solve by the addition method:
(1) $4x - 8y = 36$
(2) $3x - 6y = 27$

Solution   Eliminate x.

$$3(4x - 8y) = 3(36)$$
$$-4(3x - 6y) = -4(27)$$

$$12x - 24y = 108$$
$$-12x + 24y = -108$$

Add the equations.

$$0 = 0$$

The system of equations is
dependent. The solutions are
the ordered pairs
$\left(x, \frac{1}{2}x - \frac{9}{2}\right)$.

You Try It 2   Solve by the addition method:
$2x + y = 5$
$4x + 2y = 6$

Your solution   The system of equations is
inconsistent and therefore has no
solution.

Solutions on p. S14

Objective B   *To solve a system of three linear equations in three variables by the addition method* ....

An equation of the form $Ax + By + Cz = D$, where A, B, and C are coefficients and D is a constant, is a **linear equation in three variables.** Examples of these equations are shown at the right. The graph of a linear equation in three variables is a plane.

$$2x + 4y - 3z = 7$$

$$x - 6y + z = -3$$

Graphing an equation in three variables requires a third coordinate axis perpendicular to the *xy*-plane. The third axis is commonly called the *z*-axis. The result is a three-dimensional coordinate system called the *xyz*-coordinate system. To help visualize a three-dimensional coordinate system, think of a corner of a room: the floor is the *xy*-plane, one wall is the *yz*-plane, and the other wall is the *xz*-plane. A three-dimensional coordinate system is shown at the right.

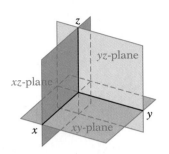

The graph of a point in an *xyz*-coordinate system is an ordered triple (x, y, z). Graphing an ordered triple requires three moves, the first along the *x*-axis, the second parallel to the *y*-axis, and the third parallel to the *z*-axis. The graphs of the points $(-4, 2, 3)$ and $(3, 4, -2)$ are shown at the right.

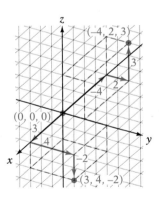

The graph of a linear equation in three variables is a plane. That is, if all the solutions of a linear equation in three variables were plotted in an *xyz*-coordinate system, the graph would look like a large piece of paper extending infinitely. The graph of $x + y + z = 3$ is shown at the right.

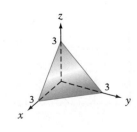

There are different ways in which three planes can be oriented in an *xyz*-coordinate system. The systems of equations represented by the planes below are inconsistent.

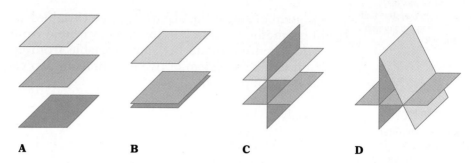

Graphs of Inconsistent Systems of Equations

For a system of three equations in three variables to have a solution, the graphs of the planes must intersect at a single point, they must intersect along a common line, or all equations must have a graph that is the same plane. These situations are shown in the figures below.

The three planes shown in Figure E intersect at a point. A system of equations represented by planes that intersect at a point is independent.

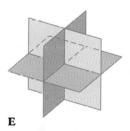

An Independent System of Equations

The planes shown in Figures F and G intersect along a common line. The system of equations represented by the planes in Figure H has a graph that is the same plane. The systems of equations represented by these three graphs are dependent.

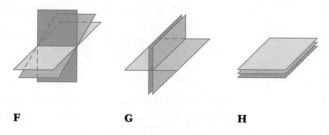

Dependent Systems of Equations

Just as a solution of an equation in two variables is an ordered pair (x, y), a **solution of an equation in three variables** is an ordered triple (x, y, z). For example, $(2, 1, -3)$ is a solution of the equation $2x - y - 2z = 9$. The ordered triple $(1, 3, 2)$ is not a solution.

POINT OF INTEREST

In the early 1980s, Stephen Hoppe became interested in winning Monopoly strategies. Finding these strategies required solving a system that contained 123 equations with 123 variables!

A **system of linear equations in three variables** is shown at the right. A **solution of a system of equations in three variables** is an ordered triple that is a solution of each equation of the system.

$$x - 2y + z = 6$$
$$3x + y - 2z = 2$$
$$2x - 3y + 5z = 1$$

A system of linear equations in three variables can be solved by using the addition method. First, eliminate one variable from any two of the given equations. Then eliminate the same variable from any other two equations. The result will be a system of two equations in two variables. Solve this system by the addition method.

INSTRUCTOR NOTE

Show students that the goal of solving a system of three equations in three variables is to replace it with an equivalent system of two equations in two variables that can be solved by using the techniques of the previous objective.

➡ Solve: (1) $x + 4y - z = 10$
(2) $3x + 2y + z = 4$
(3) $2x - 3y + 2z = -7$

Eliminate z from Equations (1) and (2) by adding the two equations.

$$x + 4y - z = 10$$
$$3x + 2y + z = 4$$
(4) $4x + 6y = 14$ • Add the equations. This is Equation (4).

Eliminate z from Equations (1) and (3). Multiply Equation (1) by 2 and add to Equation (3).

$$2x + 8y - 2z = 20$$ • 2 times Equation (1)
$$2x - 3y + 2z = -7$$ • This is Equation (3).
(5) $4x + 5y = 13$ • Add the equations. This is Equation (5).

Using Equations (4) and (5), solve the system of two equations in two variables.

(4) $4x + 6y = 14$
(5) $4x + 5y = 13$

Eliminate x. Multiply Equation (5) by -1 and add to Equation (4).

$$4x + 6y = 14$$ • This is Equation (4).
$$-4x - 5y = -13$$ • -1 times Equation (5)
$$y = 1$$ • Add the equations.

Substitute the value of y into Equation (4) or Equation (5) and solve for x. Equation (4) is used here.

$$4x + 6y = 14$$ • This is Equation (4).
$$4x + 6(1) = 14$$ • $y = 1$
$$4x + 6 = 14$$ • Solve for x.
$$4x = 8$$
$$x = 2$$

Substitute the value of y and the value of x into one of the equations in the original system. Equation (2) is used here.

$$3x + 2y + z = 4$$
$$3(2) + 2(1) + z = 4$$ • $x = 2, y = 1$
$$6 + 2 + z = 4$$
$$8 + z = 4$$
$$z = -4$$

The solution is $(2, 1, -4)$.

➡ Solve:
(1) $\quad 2x - 3y - z = 1$
(2) $\quad x + 4y + 3z = 2$
(3) $\quad 4x - 6y - 2z = 5$

Eliminate x from Equations (1) and (2).

$$2x - 3y - z = 1$$
$$-2x - 8y - 6z = -4$$
$$\overline{\quad -11y - 7z = -3}$$

- This is Equation (1).
- -2 times Equation (2)
- Add the equations.

Eliminate x from Equations (1) and (3).

$$-4x + 6y + 2z = -2$$
$$4x - 6y - 2z = 5$$
$$\overline{\qquad\qquad 0 = 3}$$

- -2 times Equation (1)
- This is Equation (3).
- Add the equations.

The equation $0 = 3$ is not a true equation. The system of equations is inconsistent and therefore has no solution.

➡ Solve:
(1) $\quad 3x - z = -1$
(2) $\quad 2y - 3z = 10$
(3) $\quad x + 3y - z = 7$

Eliminate x from Equations (1) and (3). Multiply Equation (3) by -3 and add to Equation (1).

$$3x - z = -1$$
$$-3x - 9y + 3z = -21$$
(4) $\quad \overline{\quad -9y + 2z = -22}$

- This is Equation (1).
- -3 times Equation (3)
- Add the equations.

Use Equations (2) and (4) to form a system of equations in two variables.

(2) $\quad 2y - 3z = 10$
(4) $\quad -9y + 2z = -22$

Eliminate z. Multiply Equation (2) by 2 and Equation (4) by 3.

$$4y - 6z = 20$$
$$-27y + 6z = -66$$
$$\overline{\quad -23y = -46}$$
$$y = 2$$

- 2 times Equation (2)
- 3 times Equation (4)
- Add the equations.
- Solve for y.

Substitute the value of y into Equation (2) or Equation (4) and solve for z. Equation (2) is used here.

(2)
$$2y - 3z = 10$$
$$2(2) - 3z = 10$$
$$4 - 3z = 10$$
$$-3z = 6$$
$$z = -2$$

- This is Equation (2).
- $y = 2$
- Solve for z.

Substitute the value of z into Equation (1) and solve for x.

(1)
$$3x - z = -1$$
$$3x - (-2) = -1$$
$$3x + 2 = -1$$
$$3x = -3$$
$$x = -1$$

- This is Equation (1).
- $z = -2$
- Solve for x.

The solution is $(-1, 2, -2)$.

Example 3   Solve: (1) $\quad 3x - y + 2z = 1$
            (2) $\quad 2x + 3y + 3z = 4$
            (3) $\quad\;\; x + y - 4z = -9$

You Try It 3   Solve: $\quad x - y + z = 6$
            $\quad 2x + 3y - z = 1$
            $\quad x + 2y + 2z = 5$

Solution   Eliminate y. Add
            Equations (1) and (3).

$$3x - y + 2z = 1$$
$$\underline{x + y - 4z = -9}$$
$$4x \quad\;\; - 2z = -8$$

Multiply each side of the
equation by $\frac{1}{2}$.

(4) $\quad 2x - z = -4$

Multiply Equation (1) by 3
and add to Equation (2).

$$9x - 3y + 6z = 3$$
$$\underline{2x + 3y + 3z = 4}$$
(5) $\quad\;\; 11x \quad\;\; + 9z = 7$

Solve the system of two
equations.

(4) $\qquad 2x - z = -4$
(5) $\qquad 11x + 9z = 7$

Multiply Equation (4) by 9
and add to Equation (5).

$$18x - 9z = -36$$
$$\underline{11x + 9z = 7}$$
$$29x \qquad = -29$$
$$x = -1$$

Replace x by -1 in Equation
(4).

$$2x - z = -4$$
$$2(-1) - z = -4$$
$$-2 - z = -4$$
$$-z = -2$$
$$z = 2$$

Replace x by -1 and z by 2 in
Equation (3).

$$x + y - 4z = -9$$
$$-1 + y - 4(2) = -9$$
$$-9 + y = -9$$
$$y = 0$$

The solution is $(-1, 0, 2)$.

Your solution $(3, -1, 2)$

Solution on p. S14

5.3 Exercises

Objective A

Solve by the addition method.

1. $x - y = 5$
$x + y = 7$
$(6, 1)$

2. $x + y = 1$
$2x - y = 5$
$(2, -1)$

3. $3x + y = 4$
$x + y = 2$
$(1, 1)$

4. $x - 3y = 4$
$x + 5y = -4$
$(1, -1)$

5. $3x + y = 7$
$x + 2y = 4$
$(2, 1)$

6. $x - 2y = 7$
$3x - 2y = 9$
$(1, -3)$

7. $2x + 3y = -1$
$x + 5y = 3$
$(-2, 1)$

8. $x + 5y = 7$
$2x + 7y = 8$
$(-3, 2)$

9. $3x - y = 4$
$6x - 2y = 8$
$(x, 3x - 4)$

10. $x - 2y = -3$
$-2x + 4y = 6$
$\left(x, \dfrac{1}{2}x + \dfrac{3}{2}\right)$

11. $2x + 5y = 9$
$4x - 7y = -16$
$\left(-\dfrac{1}{2}, 2\right)$

12. $8x - 3y = 21$
$4x + 5y = -9$
$\left(\dfrac{3}{2}, -3\right)$

13. $4x - 6y = 5$
$2x - 3y = 7$
inconsistent

14. $3x + 6y = 7$
$2x + 4y = 5$
inconsistent

15. $3x - 5y = 7$
$x - 2y = 3$
$(-1, -2)$

16. $3x + 4y = 25$
$2x + y = 10$
$(3, 4)$

17. $x + 3y = 7$
$-2x + 3y = 22$
$(-5, 4)$

18. $2x - 3y = 14$
$5x - 6y = 32$
$(4, -2)$

19. $3x + 2y = 16$
$2x - 3y = -11$
$(2, 5)$

20. $2x - 5y = 13$
$5x + 3y = 17$
$(4, -1)$

21. $4x + 4y = 5$
$2x - 8y = -5$
$\left(\dfrac{1}{2}, \dfrac{3}{4}\right)$

22. $3x + 7y = 16$
$4x - 3y = 9$
$(3, 1)$

23. $5x + 4y = 0$
$3x + 7y = 0$
$(0, 0)$

24. $3x - 4y = 0$
$4x - 7y = 0$
$(0, 0)$

25. $5x + 2y = 1$
$2x + 3y = 7$
$(-1, 3)$

26. $3x + 5y = 16$
$5x - 7y = -4$
$(2, 2)$

27. $3x - 6y = 6$
$9x - 3y = 8$
$\left(\dfrac{2}{3}, -\dfrac{2}{3} \right)$

28. $\dfrac{2}{3}x - \dfrac{1}{2}y = 3$
$\dfrac{1}{3}x - \dfrac{1}{4}y = \dfrac{3}{2}$
$\left(x, \dfrac{4}{3}x - 6 \right)$

29. $\dfrac{3}{4}x + \dfrac{1}{3}y = -\dfrac{1}{2}$
$\dfrac{1}{2}x - \dfrac{5}{6}y = -\dfrac{7}{2}$
$(-2, 3)$

30. $\dfrac{2}{5}x - \dfrac{1}{3}y = 1$
$\dfrac{3}{5}x + \dfrac{2}{3}y = 5$
$(5, 3)$

31. $\dfrac{5x}{6} + \dfrac{y}{3} = \dfrac{4}{3}$
$\dfrac{2x}{3} - \dfrac{y}{2} = \dfrac{11}{6}$
$(2, -1)$

32. $\dfrac{3x}{4} + \dfrac{2y}{5} = -\dfrac{3}{20}$
$\dfrac{3x}{2} - \dfrac{y}{4} = \dfrac{3}{4}$
$\left(\dfrac{1}{3}, -1 \right)$

33. $\dfrac{2x}{5} - \dfrac{y}{2} = \dfrac{13}{2}$
$\dfrac{3x}{4} - \dfrac{y}{5} = \dfrac{17}{2}$
$(10, -5)$

34. $\dfrac{x}{2} + \dfrac{y}{3} = \dfrac{5}{12}$
$\dfrac{x}{2} - \dfrac{y}{3} = \dfrac{1}{12}$
$\left(\dfrac{1}{2}, \dfrac{1}{2} \right)$

35. $\dfrac{3x}{2} - \dfrac{y}{4} = -\dfrac{11}{12}$
$\dfrac{x}{3} - y = -\dfrac{5}{6}$
$\left(-\dfrac{1}{2}, \dfrac{2}{3} \right)$

36. $\dfrac{3x}{4} - \dfrac{2y}{3} = 0$
$\dfrac{5x}{4} - \dfrac{y}{3} = \dfrac{7}{12}$
$\left(\dfrac{2}{3}, \dfrac{3}{4} \right)$

37. $4x - 5y = 3y + 4$
$2x + 3y = 2x + 1$
$\left(\dfrac{5}{3}, \dfrac{1}{3} \right)$

38. $5x - 2y = 8x - 1$
$2x + 7y = 4y + 9$
$(-3, 5)$

39. $2x + 5y = 5x + 1$
$3x - 2y = 3y + 3$
inconsistent

40. $4x - 8y = 5$
$8x + 2y = 1$
$\left(\dfrac{1}{4}, -\dfrac{1}{2} \right)$

41. $5x + 2y = 2x + 1$
$2x - 3y = 3x + 2$
$(1, -1)$

42. $3x + 3y = y + 1$
$x + 3y = 9 - x$
$(-3, 5)$

Objective B

Solve by the addition method.

43. $x + 2y - z = 1$
$2x - y + z = 6$
$x + 3y - z = 2$
$(2, 1, 3)$

44. $x + 3y + z = 6$
$3x + y - z = -2$
$2x + 2y - z = 1$
$(-1, 2, 1)$

45. $2x - y + 2z = 7$
$x + y + z = 2$
$3x - y + z = 6$
$(1, -1, 2)$

46. $x - 2y + z = 6$
$x + 3y + z = 16$
$3x - y - z = 12$
$(6, 2, 4)$

47. $3x + y = 5$
$3y - z = 2$
$x + z = 5$
$(1, 2, 4)$

48. $2y + z = 7$
$2x - z = 3$
$x - y = 3$
$(4, 1, 5)$

49. $x - y + z = 1$
$2x + 3y - z = 3$
$-x + 2y - 4z = 4$
$(2, -1, -2)$

50. $2x + y - 3z = 7$
$x - 2y + 3z = 1$
$3x + 4y - 3z = 13$
$(3, 1, 0)$

51. $2x + 3z = 5$
$3y + 2z = 3$
$3x + 4y = -10$
$(-2, -1, 3)$

52. $3x + 4z = 5$
$2y + 3z = 2$
$2x - 5y = 8$
$(-1, -2, 2)$

53. $2x + 4y - 2z = 3$
$x + 3y + 4z = 1$
$x + 2y - z = 4$
inconsistent

54. $x - 3y + 2z = 1$
$x - 2y + 3z = 5$
$2x - 6y + 4z = 3$
inconsistent

55. $2x + y - z = 5$
$x + 3y + z = 14$
$3x - y + 2z = 1$
$(1, 4, 1)$

56. $3x - y - 2z = 11$
$2x + y - 2z = 11$
$x + 3y - z = 8$
$(2, 1, -3)$

57. $3x + y - 2z = 2$
$x + 2y + 3z = 13$
$2x - 2y + 5z = 6$
$(1, 3, 2)$

58. $4x + 5y + z = 6$
$2x - y + 2z = 11$
$x + 2y + 2z = 6$
$(2, -1, 3)$

59. $2x - y + z = 6$
$3x + 2y + z = 4$
$x - 2y + 3z = 12$
$(1, -1, 3)$

60. $3x + 2y - 3z = 8$
$2x + 3y + 2z = 10$
$x + y - z = 2$
$(6, -2, 2)$

61. $3x - 2y + 3z = -4$
$2x + y - 3z = 2$
$3x + 4y + 5z = 8$
$(0, 2, 0)$

62. $3x - 3y + 4z = 6$
$4x - 5y + 2z = 10$
$x - 2y + 3z = 4$
$(0, -2, 0)$

63. $3x - y + 2z = 2$
$4x + 2y - 7z = 0$
$2x + 3y - 5z = 7$
$(1, 5, 2)$

64. $2x + 2y + 3z = 13$
$-3x + 4y - z = 5$
$5x - 3y + z = 2$
$(2, 3, 1)$

65. $2x - 3y + 7z = 0$
$x + 4y - 4z = -2$
$3x + 2y + 5z = 1$
$(-2, 1, 1)$

66. $5x + 3y - z = 5$
$3x - 2y + 4z = 13$
$4x + 3y + 5z = 22$
$(1, 1, 3)$

APPLYING THE CONCEPTS

67. The point of intersection of the graphs of the equations $Ax + 2y = 2$ and $2x + By = 10$ is $(2, -2)$. Find A and B.
$A = 3, B = -3$

68. The point of intersection of the graphs of the equations $Ax - 4y = 9$ and $4x + By = -1$ is $(-1, -3)$. Find A and B.
$A = 3, B = -1$

69. For what value of k is the system of equations dependent?

   a. $2x + 3y = 7$
   $4x + 6y = k$ 14

   b. $y = \frac{2}{3}x - 3$
   $y = kx - 3$ $\frac{2}{3}$

   c. $x = ky - 1$
   $y = 2x + 2$ $\frac{1}{2}$

70. For what values of k is the system of equations independent?

   a. $x + y = 7$
   $kx + y = 3$ $k \neq 1$

   b. $x + 2y = 4$
   $kx + 3y = 2$ $k \neq \frac{3}{2}$

   c. $2x + ky = 1$
   $x + 2y = 2$ $k \neq 4$

71. Given that the graphs of the equations $2x - y = 6$, $3x - 4y = 4$, and $Ax - 2y = 0$ all intersect at the same point, find A.
1

72. Given that the graphs of the equations $3x - 2y = -2$, $2x - y = 0$, and $Ax + y = 8$ all intersect at the same point, find A.
2

73. Describe in your own words the process of solving a system of two linear equations in two variables by the addition method.

74. Explain, graphically, the following situations when they are related to a system of three linear equations in three variables.
   a. The system of equations has no solution.
   b. The system of equations has exactly one solution.
   c. The system of equations has infinitely many solutions.

5.4 Solving Systems of Equations by Using Determinants

Objective A   To evaluate a determinant ....

A **matrix** is a rectangular array of numbers. Each number in the matrix is called an **element** of the matrix. The matrix at the right, with three rows and four columns, is called a 3×4 (read "3 by 4") matrix.

$$A = \begin{pmatrix} 1 & -3 & 2 & 4 \\ 0 & 4 & -3 & 2 \\ 6 & -5 & 4 & -1 \end{pmatrix}$$

A matrix of m rows and n columns is said to be of **order $m \times n$.** The matrix above has order 3×4. The notation a_{ij} refers to the element of a matrix in the ith row and the jth column. For matrix A, $a_{23} = -3$, $a_{31} = 6$, and $a_{13} = 2$.

A **square matrix** is one that has the same number of rows as columns. A 2×2 matrix and a 3×3 matrix are shown at the right.

$$\begin{pmatrix} -1 & 3 \\ 5 & 2 \end{pmatrix} \quad \begin{pmatrix} 4 & 0 & 1 \\ 5 & -3 & 7 \\ 2 & 1 & 4 \end{pmatrix}$$

Associated with every square matrix is a number called its **determinant**.

TAKE NOTE

Note that vertical bars are used to represent the determinant and that parentheses are used to represent the matrix.

Determinant of a 2 × 2 Matrix

The **determinant** of a 2×2 matrix $\begin{pmatrix} a_{11} & a_{12} \\ a_{21} & a_{22} \end{pmatrix}$ is written $\begin{vmatrix} a_{11} & a_{12} \\ a_{21} & a_{22} \end{vmatrix}$.

The value of this determinant is given by the formula

$$\begin{vmatrix} a_{11} & a_{12} \\ a_{21} & a_{22} \end{vmatrix} = a_{11}a_{22} - a_{12}a_{21}$$

⟹ Find the value of the determinant $\begin{vmatrix} 3 & 4 \\ -1 & 2 \end{vmatrix}$.

$$\begin{vmatrix} 3 & 4 \\ -1 & 2 \end{vmatrix} = 3 \cdot 2 - 4(-1) = 6 - (-4) = 10$$

The value of the determinant is 10.

For a square matrix whose order is 3×3 or greater, the value of the determinant of that matrix is found by using 2×2 determinants.

The **minor of an element** in a 3×3 determinant is the 2×2 determinant that is obtained by eliminating the row and column that contain that element.

⟹ Find the minor of -3 for the determinant $\begin{vmatrix} 2 & -3 & 4 \\ 0 & 4 & 8 \\ -1 & 3 & 6 \end{vmatrix}$.

The minor of -3 is the 2×2 determinant created by eliminating the row and column that contain -3.

Eliminate the row and column as shown: $\begin{vmatrix} 2 & -3 & 4 \\ 0 & 4 & 8 \\ -1 & 3 & 6 \end{vmatrix}$

The minor of -3 is $\begin{vmatrix} 0 & 8 \\ -1 & 6 \end{vmatrix}$.

Copyright © Houghton Mifflin Company. All rights reserved.

TAKE NOTE

The only difference between the cofactor and the minor is one of sign. The definition at the right can be stated symbolically as follows: If C_{ij} is the cofactor and M_{ij} is the minor of the matrix element a_{ij}, then $C_{ij} = (-1)^{i+j}M_{ij}$. If $i + j$ is an even number, then $(-1)^{i+j} = 1$ and $C_{ij} = M_{ij}$. If $i + j$ is an odd number, then $(-1)^{i+j} = -1$ and $C_{ij} = -M_{ij}$.

Cofactor of an Element of a Matrix

The **cofactor** of an element of a matrix is $(-1)^{i+j}$ times the minor of that element, where i is the row number of the element and j is the column number of the element.

➡ For the determinant $\begin{vmatrix} 3 & -2 & 1 \\ 2 & -5 & -4 \\ 0 & 3 & 1 \end{vmatrix}$, find the cofactor of -2 and of -5.

Because -2 is in the first row and the second column, $i = 1$ and $j = 2$. Thus $(-1)^{i+j} = (-1)^{1+2} = (-1)^3 = -1$. The cofactor of -2 is $(-1)\begin{vmatrix} 2 & -4 \\ 0 & 1 \end{vmatrix}$.

Because -5 is in the second row and the second column, $i = 2$ and $j = 2$. Thus $(-1)^{i+j} = (-1)^{2+2} = (-1)^4 = 1$. The cofactor of -5 is $1 \cdot \begin{vmatrix} 3 & 1 \\ 0 & 1 \end{vmatrix}$.

Note from this example that the cofactor of an element is -1 times the minor of that element or 1 times the minor of that element, depending on whether the sum $i + j$ is an odd or even integer.

The value of a 3×3 or larger determinant can be found by **expanding by cofactors** of *any* row or any column. The result of expanding by cofactors using the first row of a 3×3 matrix is shown below.

$$\begin{vmatrix} a_{11} & a_{12} & a_{13} \\ a_{21} & a_{22} & a_{23} \\ a_{31} & a_{32} & a_{33} \end{vmatrix} = a_{11}(-1)^{1+1}\begin{vmatrix} a_{22} & a_{23} \\ a_{32} & a_{33} \end{vmatrix} + a_{12}(-1)^{1+2}\begin{vmatrix} a_{21} & a_{23} \\ a_{31} & a_{33} \end{vmatrix} + a_{13}(-1)^{1+3}\begin{vmatrix} a_{21} & a_{22} \\ a_{31} & a_{32} \end{vmatrix}$$

$$= a_{11}\begin{vmatrix} a_{22} & a_{23} \\ a_{32} & a_{33} \end{vmatrix} - a_{12}\begin{vmatrix} a_{21} & a_{23} \\ a_{31} & a_{33} \end{vmatrix} + a_{13}\begin{vmatrix} a_{21} & a_{22} \\ a_{31} & a_{32} \end{vmatrix}$$

INSTRUCTOR NOTE

Emphasize to students that expanding by cofactors does not depend on the row or column that is selected. Students should choose the row or column with the most zeros; that will reduce the amount of computation.

INSTRUCTOR NOTE

Another method for expanding a 3×3 determinant is to reproduce the first two columns, find the sum of the products along the downward arrows, and subtract the sum of the products along the upward arrows. This is shown below.

$[-2 + (-8) + 0] - [-1 + 0 + (-6)] = -3$

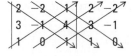

If you show students this method, mention that it works only for 3×3 determinants.

➡ Find the value of the determinant $\begin{vmatrix} 2 & -3 & 2 \\ 1 & 3 & -1 \\ 0 & -2 & 2 \end{vmatrix}$.

Expand by cofactors of the first row.

$$\begin{vmatrix} 2 & -3 & 2 \\ 1 & 3 & -1 \\ 0 & -2 & 2 \end{vmatrix} = 2\begin{vmatrix} 3 & -1 \\ -2 & 2 \end{vmatrix} - (-3)\begin{vmatrix} 1 & -1 \\ 0 & 2 \end{vmatrix} + 2\begin{vmatrix} 1 & 3 \\ 0 & -2 \end{vmatrix}$$

$$= 2(6 - 2) - (-3)(2 - 0) + 2(-2 - 0)$$

$$= 2(4) - (-3)(2) + 2(-2) = 8 - (-6) + (-4) = 10$$

To illustrate a statement made earlier, the value of this determinant will now be found by expanding by cofactors using the second column.

$$\begin{vmatrix} 2 & -3 & 2 \\ 1 & 3 & -1 \\ 0 & -2 & 2 \end{vmatrix} = -3(-1)^{1+2}\begin{vmatrix} 1 & -1 \\ 0 & 2 \end{vmatrix} + 3(-1)^{2+2}\begin{vmatrix} 2 & 2 \\ 0 & 2 \end{vmatrix} + (-2)(-1)^{3+2}\begin{vmatrix} 2 & 2 \\ 1 & -1 \end{vmatrix}$$

$$= -3(-1)\begin{vmatrix} 1 & -1 \\ 0 & 2 \end{vmatrix} + 3(1)\begin{vmatrix} 2 & 2 \\ 0 & 2 \end{vmatrix} + (-2)(-1)\begin{vmatrix} 2 & 2 \\ 1 & -1 \end{vmatrix}$$

$$= 3(2 - 0) + 3(4 - 0) + 2(-2 - 2)$$

$$= 3(2) + 3(4) + 2(-4) = 6 + 12 + (-8) = 10$$

Note that the value of the determinant is the same whether the first row or the second column is used to expand by cofactors. *Any row or column* can be used to evaluate a determinant by expanding by cofactors.

Example 1

Find the value of $\begin{vmatrix} 3 & -2 \\ 6 & -4 \end{vmatrix}$.

Solution

$\begin{vmatrix} 3 & -2 \\ 6 & -4 \end{vmatrix} = 3(-4) - (-2)(6) = -12 + 12 = 0$

The value of the determinant is 0.

You Try It 1

Find the value of $\begin{vmatrix} -1 & -4 \\ 3 & -5 \end{vmatrix}$.

Your solution

17

Example 2

Find the value of $\begin{vmatrix} -2 & 3 & 1 \\ 4 & -2 & 0 \\ 1 & -2 & 3 \end{vmatrix}$.

Solution

Expand by cofactors of the first row.

$\begin{vmatrix} -2 & 3 & 1 \\ 4 & -2 & 0 \\ 1 & -2 & 3 \end{vmatrix}$

$= -2 \begin{vmatrix} -2 & 0 \\ -2 & 3 \end{vmatrix} - 3 \begin{vmatrix} 4 & 0 \\ 1 & 3 \end{vmatrix} + 1 \begin{vmatrix} 4 & -2 \\ 1 & -2 \end{vmatrix}$

$= -2(-6 - 0) - 3(12 - 0) + 1(-8 + 2)$

$= -2(-6) - 3(12) + 1(-6)$

$= 12 - 36 - 6$

$= -30$

The value of the determinant is -30.

You Try It 2

Find the value of $\begin{vmatrix} 1 & 4 & -2 \\ 3 & 1 & 1 \\ 0 & -2 & 2 \end{vmatrix}$.

Your solution

-8

Example 3

Find the value of $\begin{vmatrix} 0 & -2 & 1 \\ 1 & 4 & 1 \\ 2 & -3 & 4 \end{vmatrix}$.

Solution

$\begin{vmatrix} 0 & -2 & 1 \\ 1 & 4 & 1 \\ 2 & -3 & 4 \end{vmatrix}$

$= 0 \begin{vmatrix} 4 & 1 \\ -3 & 4 \end{vmatrix} - (-2) \begin{vmatrix} 1 & 1 \\ 2 & 4 \end{vmatrix} + 1 \begin{vmatrix} 1 & 4 \\ 2 & -3 \end{vmatrix}$

$= 0 - (-2)(4 - 2) + 1(-3 - 8)$

$= 2(2) + 1(-11)$

$= 4 - 11$

$= -7$

The value of the determinant is -7.

You Try It 3

Find the value of $\begin{vmatrix} 3 & -2 & 0 \\ 1 & 4 & 2 \\ -2 & 1 & 3 \end{vmatrix}$.

Your solution

44

Solutions on pp. S14–S15

Objective B **To solve a system of equations by using Cramer's Rule**..........................

The connection between determinants and systems of equations can be understood by solving a general system of linear equations.

Solve: (1) $a_1 x + b_1 y = c_1$
$\quad\quad$ (2) $a_2 x + b_2 y = c_2$

Eliminate y. Multiply Equation (1) by b_2 and Equation (2) by $-b_1$.

$a_1 b_2 x + b_1 b_2 y = c_1 b_2$ $\quad\quad$ • b_2 times Equation (1).
$-a_2 b_1 x - b_1 b_2 y = -c_2 b_1$ $\quad\quad$ • $-b_1$ times Equation (2).

Add the equations.

$a_1 b_2 x - a_2 b_1 x = c_1 b_2 - c_2 b_1$
$(a_1 b_2 - a_2 b_1)x = c_1 b_2 - c_2 b_1$ $\quad\quad$ • Solve for x, assuming $a_1 b_2 - a_2 b_1 \neq 0$.

$$x = \frac{c_1 b_2 - c_2 b_1}{a_1 b_2 - a_2 b_1}$$

The denominator $a_1 b_2 - a_2 b_1$ is the determinant of the coefficients of x and y. This is called the **coefficient determinant**.

$$a_1 b_2 - a_2 b_1 = \begin{vmatrix} a_1 & b_1 \\ a_2 & b_2 \end{vmatrix}$$

coefficients of x ————
coefficients of y ————

The numerator $c_1 b_2 - c_2 b_1$ is the determinant obtained by replacing the first column in the coefficient determinant by the constants c_1 and c_2. This is called a **numerator determinant**.

$$c_1 b_2 - c_2 b_1 = \begin{vmatrix} c_1 & b_1 \\ c_2 & b_2 \end{vmatrix}$$

constants of ————
the equations

Following a similar procedure and eliminating x, it is possible also to express the y-component of the solution in determinant form. These results are summarized in Cramer's Rule.

Cramer's Rule

The solution of the system of equations $\begin{aligned} a_1 x + b_1 y &= c_1 \\ a_2 x + b_2 y &= c_2 \end{aligned}$ is given by

$x = \dfrac{D_x}{D}$ and $y = \dfrac{D_y}{D}$, where $D = \begin{vmatrix} a_1 & b_1 \\ a_2 & b_2 \end{vmatrix}$, $D_x = \begin{vmatrix} c_1 & b_1 \\ c_2 & b_2 \end{vmatrix}$,

$D_y = \begin{vmatrix} a_1 & c_1 \\ a_2 & c_2 \end{vmatrix}$, and $D \neq 0$.

➡ Solve by using Cramer's Rule: $3x - 2y = 1$
$\quad\quad\quad\quad\quad\quad\quad\quad\quad\quad\quad 2x + 5y = 3$

$$D = \begin{vmatrix} 3 & -2 \\ 2 & 5 \end{vmatrix} = 19$$ $\quad\quad$ • Find the value of the coefficient determinant.

$$D_x = \begin{vmatrix} 1 & -2 \\ 3 & 5 \end{vmatrix} = 11, \; D_y = \begin{vmatrix} 3 & 1 \\ 2 & 3 \end{vmatrix} = 7$$ $\quad\quad$ • Find the value of each of the numerator determinants.

$$x = \frac{D_x}{D} = \frac{11}{19}, \; y = \frac{D_y}{D} = \frac{7}{19}$$ $\quad\quad$ • Use Cramer's Rule to write the solution.

The solution is $\left(\dfrac{11}{19}, \dfrac{7}{19} \right)$.

A procedure similar to that followed for a system of two equations in two variables can be used to extend Cramer's Rule to a system of three equations in three variables.

Cramer's Rule for a System of Three Equations in Three Variables

$$a_1x + b_1y + c_1z = d_1$$

The solution of the system of equations $a_2x + b_2y + c_2z = d_2$

$$a_3x + b_3y + c_3z = d_3$$

is given by $x = \dfrac{D_x}{D}$, $y = \dfrac{D_y}{D}$, and $z = \dfrac{D_z}{D}$, where

$$D = \begin{vmatrix} a_1 & b_1 & c_1 \\ a_2 & b_2 & c_2 \\ a_3 & b_3 & c_3 \end{vmatrix}, D_x = \begin{vmatrix} d_1 & b_1 & c_1 \\ d_2 & b_2 & c_2 \\ d_3 & b_3 & c_3 \end{vmatrix}, D_y = \begin{vmatrix} a_1 & d_1 & c_1 \\ a_2 & d_2 & c_2 \\ a_3 & d_3 & c_3 \end{vmatrix}, D_z = \begin{vmatrix} a_1 & b_1 & d_1 \\ a_2 & b_2 & d_2 \\ a_3 & b_3 & d_3 \end{vmatrix}, \text{ and } D \neq 0.$$

➡️ Solve by using Cramer's Rule: $2x - y + z = 1$
$$x + 3y - 2z = -2$$
$$3x + y + 3z = 4$$

Find the value of the coefficient determinant.

$$D = \begin{vmatrix} 2 & -1 & 1 \\ 1 & 3 & -2 \\ 3 & 1 & 3 \end{vmatrix} = 2\begin{vmatrix} 3 & -2 \\ 1 & 3 \end{vmatrix} - (-1)\begin{vmatrix} 1 & -2 \\ 3 & 3 \end{vmatrix} + 1\begin{vmatrix} 1 & 3 \\ 3 & 1 \end{vmatrix}$$

$$= 2(11) + 1(9) + 1(-8)$$

$$= 23$$

Find the value of each of the numerator determinants.

$$D_x = \begin{vmatrix} 1 & -1 & 1 \\ -2 & 3 & -2 \\ 4 & 1 & 3 \end{vmatrix} = 1\begin{vmatrix} 3 & -2 \\ 1 & 3 \end{vmatrix} - (-1)\begin{vmatrix} -2 & -2 \\ 4 & 3 \end{vmatrix} + 1\begin{vmatrix} -2 & 3 \\ 4 & 1 \end{vmatrix}$$

$$= 1(11) + 1(2) + 1(-14)$$

$$= -1$$

$$D_y = \begin{vmatrix} 2 & 1 & 1 \\ 1 & -2 & -2 \\ 3 & 4 & 3 \end{vmatrix} = 2\begin{vmatrix} -2 & -2 \\ 4 & 3 \end{vmatrix} - 1\begin{vmatrix} 1 & -2 \\ 3 & 3 \end{vmatrix} + 1\begin{vmatrix} 1 & -2 \\ 3 & 4 \end{vmatrix}$$

$$= 2(2) - 1(9) + 1(10)$$

$$= 5$$

$$D_z = \begin{vmatrix} 2 & -1 & 1 \\ 1 & 3 & -2 \\ 3 & 1 & 4 \end{vmatrix} = 2\begin{vmatrix} 3 & -2 \\ 1 & 4 \end{vmatrix} - (-1)\begin{vmatrix} 1 & -2 \\ 3 & 4 \end{vmatrix} + 1\begin{vmatrix} 1 & 3 \\ 3 & 1 \end{vmatrix}$$

$$= 2(14) + 1(10) + 1(-8)$$

$$= 30$$

Use Cramer's Rule to write the solution.

$$x = \frac{D_x}{D} = \frac{-1}{23}, \qquad y = \frac{D_y}{D} = \frac{5}{23}, \qquad z = \frac{D_z}{D} = \frac{30}{23}$$

The solution is $\left(-\dfrac{1}{23}, \dfrac{5}{23}, \dfrac{30}{23}\right)$.

Example 4
Solve by using Cramer's Rule:
$6x - 9y = 5$
$4x - 6y = 4$

Solution

$D = \begin{vmatrix} 6 & -9 \\ 4 & -6 \end{vmatrix} = -36 + 36 = 0$

Because $D = 0$, $\dfrac{D_x}{D}$ is undefined.

Therefore, the system is dependent or inconsistent.

It is not possible to solve this system by using Cramer's Rule.

You Try It 4
Solve by using Cramer's Rule:
$3x - y = 4$
$6x - 2y = 5$

Your solution
It is not possible to solve this system by using Cramer's Rule.

Example 5
Solve by using Cramer's Rule:
$3x - y + z = 5$
$x + 2y - 2z = -3$
$2x + 3y + z = 4$

Solution

$D = \begin{vmatrix} 3 & -1 & 1 \\ 1 & 2 & -2 \\ 2 & 3 & 1 \end{vmatrix} = 28$

$D_x = \begin{vmatrix} 5 & -1 & 1 \\ -3 & 2 & -2 \\ 4 & 3 & 1 \end{vmatrix} = 28$

$D_y = \begin{vmatrix} 3 & 5 & 1 \\ 1 & -3 & -2 \\ 2 & 4 & 1 \end{vmatrix} = 0$

$D_z = \begin{vmatrix} 3 & -1 & 5 \\ 1 & 2 & -3 \\ 2 & 3 & 4 \end{vmatrix} = 56$

$x = \dfrac{D_x}{D} = \dfrac{28}{28} = 1, \quad y = \dfrac{D_y}{D} = \dfrac{0}{28} = 0,$

$z = \dfrac{D_z}{D} = \dfrac{56}{28} = 2$

The solution is (1, 0, 2).

You Try It 5
Solve by using Cramer's Rule:
$2x - y + z = -1$
$3x + 2y - z = 3$
$x + 3y + z = -2$

Your solution
$\left(\dfrac{3}{7}, -\dfrac{1}{7}, -2\right)$

Solutions on p. S15

5.4 Exercises
. . . .

Objective A

Evaluate the determinant.

1. $\begin{vmatrix} 2 & -1 \\ 3 & 4 \end{vmatrix}$

11

2. $\begin{vmatrix} 5 & 1 \\ -1 & 2 \end{vmatrix}$

11

3. $\begin{vmatrix} 6 & -2 \\ -3 & 4 \end{vmatrix}$

18

4. $\begin{vmatrix} -3 & 5 \\ 1 & 7 \end{vmatrix}$

-26

5. $\begin{vmatrix} 3 & 6 \\ 2 & 4 \end{vmatrix}$

0

6. $\begin{vmatrix} 5 & -10 \\ 1 & -2 \end{vmatrix}$

0

7. $\begin{vmatrix} 1 & -1 & 2 \\ 3 & 2 & 1 \\ 1 & 0 & 4 \end{vmatrix}$

15

8. $\begin{vmatrix} 4 & 1 & 3 \\ 2 & -2 & 1 \\ 3 & 1 & 2 \end{vmatrix}$

3

9. $\begin{vmatrix} 3 & -1 & 2 \\ 0 & 1 & 2 \\ 3 & 2 & -2 \end{vmatrix}$

-30

10. $\begin{vmatrix} 4 & 5 & -2 \\ 3 & -1 & 5 \\ 2 & 1 & 4 \end{vmatrix}$

-56

11. $\begin{vmatrix} 4 & 2 & 6 \\ -2 & 1 & 1 \\ 2 & 1 & 3 \end{vmatrix}$

0

12. $\begin{vmatrix} 3 & 6 & -3 \\ 4 & -1 & 6 \\ -1 & -2 & 3 \end{vmatrix}$

-54

Objective B

Solve by using Cramer's Rule.

13. $2x - 5y = 26$
$5x + 3y = 3$
$(3, -4)$

14. $3x + 7y = 15$
$2x + 5y = 11$
$(-2, 3)$

15. $x - 4y = 8$
$3x + 7y = 5$
$(4, -1)$

16. $5x + 2y = -5$
$3x + 4y = 11$
$(-3, 5)$

17. $2x + 3y = 4$
$6x - 12y = -5$
$\left(\dfrac{11}{14}, \dfrac{17}{21}\right)$

18. $5x + 4y = 3$
$15x - 8y = -21$
$\left(-\dfrac{3}{5}, \dfrac{3}{2}\right)$

19. $2x + 5y = 6$
$6x - 2y = 1$
$\left(\dfrac{1}{2}, 1\right)$

20. $7x + 3y = 4$
$5x - 4y = 9$
$(1, -1)$

21. $-2x + 3y = 7$
$4x - 6y = 9$

not independent

22. $9x + 6y = 7$
$3x + 2y = 4$

not independent

23. $2x - 5y = -2$
$3x - 7y = -3$
$(-1, 0)$

24. $8x + 7y = -3$
$2x + 2y = 5$
$\left(-\dfrac{41}{2}, 23\right)$

25. $2x - y + 3z = 9$
$x + 4y + 4z = 5$
$3x + 2y + 2z = 5$

$(1, -1, 2)$

26. $3x - 2y + z = 2$
$2x + 3y + 2z = -6$
$3x - y + z = 0$

$(-1, -2, 1)$

27. $3x - y + z = 11$
$x + 4y - 2z = -12$
$2x + 2y - z = -3$

$(2, -2, 3)$

28. $x + 2y + 3z = 8$
$2x - 3y + z = 5$
$3x - 4y + 2z = 9$

$(-3, -2, 5)$

29. $4x - 2y + 6z = 1$
$3x + 4y + 2z = 1$
$2x - y + 3z = 2$

not independent

30. $x - 3y + 2z = 1$
$2x + y - 2z = 3$
$3x - 9y + 6z = -3$

not independent

31. $5x - 4y + 2z = 4$
$3x - 5y + 3z = -4$
$3x + y - 5z = 12$

$\left(\dfrac{68}{25}, \dfrac{56}{25}, -\dfrac{8}{25} \right)$

32. $2x + 4y + z = 7$
$x + 3y - z = 1$
$3x + 2y - 2z = 5$

$\left(\dfrac{53}{19}, -\dfrac{1}{19}, \dfrac{31}{19} \right)$

33. $3x - 2y + 2z = 5$
$6x + 3y - 4z = -1$
$3x - y + 2z = 4$

$\left(\dfrac{2}{3}, -1, \dfrac{1}{2} \right)$

APPLYING THE CONCEPTS

34. Determine whether the following statements are always true, sometimes true, or never true.
a. The determinant of a matrix is a positive number.   sometimes true
b. A determinant can be evaluated by expanding about any row or column of the matrix.   always true
c. Cramer's Rule can be used to solve a system of linear equations in three variables.   sometimes true

Complete.

35. If all the elements in one row or one column of a 2×2 matrix are zeros, the value of the determinant of the matrix is _____.   0

36. If all the elements in one row or one column of a 3×3 matrix are zeros, the value of the determinant of the matrix is _____.   0

37. **a.** The value of the determinant $\begin{vmatrix} x & x & a \\ y & y & b \\ z & z & c \end{vmatrix}$ is _____.   0

b. If two columns of a 3×3 matrix contain identical elements, the value of the determinant is _____.   0

5.5 Application Problems in Two Variables

Objective A   *To solve rate-of-wind or rate-of-current problems* ....

Motion problems that involve an object moving with or against a wind or current normally require two variables to solve.

➡ A motorboat traveling with the current can go 24 mi in 2 h. Against the current, it takes 3 h to go the same distance. Find the rate of the motorboat in calm water and the rate of the current.

> **Strategy for Solving Rate-of-Wind or Rate-of-Current Problems**
>
> 1. Choose one variable to represent the rate of the object in calm conditions and a second variable to represent the rate of the wind or current. Using these variables, express the rate of the object with and against the wind or current. Use the equation $rt = d$ to write expressions for the distance traveled by the object. The results can be recorded in a table.

Rate of the boat in calm water: x
Rate of the current: y

	Rate	·	*Time*	=	*Distance*
With the current	$x + y$	·	2	=	$2(x + y)$
Against the current	$x - y$	·	3	=	$3(x - y)$

> 2. Determine how the expressions for distance are related.

The distance traveled with the current is 24 mi: $2(x + y) = 24$
The distance traveled against the current is 24 mi: $3(x - y) = 24$

$2(x + y) = 24$ • Solve this system of equations.
$3(x - y) = 24$

$x + y = 12$ • Divide each side of the first equation by 2.
$x - y = 8$ • Divide each side of the second equation by 3.

$2x = 20$ • Add the equations.
$x = 10$ • Solve the equation for *x*.

$x + y = 12$
$10 + y = 12$ • Replace *x* by 10 in the equation $x + y = 12$
$y = 2$ and solve for *y*.

The rate of the boat in calm water is 10 mph.
The rate of the current is 2 mph.

Example 1

Flying with the wind, a plane flew 1000 mi in 5 h. Flying against the wind, the plane could fly only 500 mi in the same amount of time. Find the rate of the plane in calm air and the rate of the wind.

Strategy

● Rate of the plane in still air: p
  Rate of the wind: w

	Rate	Time	Distance
With wind	$p + w$	5	$5(p + w)$
Against wind	$p - w$	5	$5(p - w)$

● The distance traveled with the wind is 1000 mi.
  The distance traveled against the wind is 500 mi.

Solution

$5(p + w) = 1000$
$5(p - w) = 500$

$p + w = 200$ ● **Divide each side of**
$p - w = 100$ **each equation by 5.**

$2p = 300$
$p = 150$

$p + w = 200$
$150 + w = 200$
$w = 50$

The rate of the plane in calm air is 150 mph. The rate of the wind is 50 mph.

You Try It 1

A rowing team rowing with the current traveled 18 mi in 2 h. Against the current, the team rowed 10 mi in 2 h. Find the rate of the rowing team in calm water and the rate of the current.

Your strategy

Your solution
rate of the rowing team in calm water:
7 mph;
rate of the current: 2 mph

Solution on p. S15

Objective B   **To solve application problems using two variables** ....

The application problems in this section are varieties of problems solved earlier in the text. Each of the strategies for the problems in this section will result in a system of equations.

➡ A store owner purchased twenty 60-watt light bulbs and 30 fluorescent bulbs for a total cost of $40. A second purchase, at the same prices, included thirty 60-watt light bulbs and 10 fluorescent bulbs for a total cost of $25. Find the cost of a 60-watt bulb and that of a fluorescent bulb.

POINT OF INTEREST

The Babylonians had a method for solving a system of equations. Here is an adaptation of a problem from an ancient (around 1500 B.C.) Babylonian text. "There are two silver blocks. The sum of $\frac{1}{7}$ of the first block and $\frac{1}{11}$ of the second block is one sheqel (a weight). The first block diminished by $\frac{1}{7}$ of its weight equals the second diminished by $\frac{1}{11}$ of its weight. What are the weights of the two blocks?"

Strategy for Solving an Application Problem in Two Variables

1. Choose one variable to represent one of the unknown quantities and a second variable to represent the other unknown quantity. Write numerical or variable expressions for all the remaining quantities. These results can be recorded in tables.

Cost of a 60-watt bulb: b
Cost of a fluorescent bulb: f

First purchase

	Amount	·	Unit Cost	=	Value
60-watt	20	·	b	=	$20b$
Fluorescent	30	·	f	=	$30f$

Second purchase

	Amount	·	Unit Cost	=	Value
60-watt	30	·	b	=	$30b$
Fluorescent	10	·	f	=	$10f$

---

2. Determine a system of equations. The strategies presented in Chapter 2 can be used to determine the relationships between the expressions in the tables.

The total of the first purchase was \$40: $20b + 30f = 40$
The total of the second purchase was \$25: $30b + 10f = 25$

Solve the system of equations: (1) $20b + 30f = 40$
$\qquad\qquad\qquad\qquad\qquad\quad$ (2) $30b + 10f = 25$

$$\begin{aligned} 60b + 90f &= 120 \\ -60b - 20f &= -50 \\ 70f &= 70 \\ f &= 1 \end{aligned}$$

• 3 times Equation (1)
• −2 times Equation (2)

Replace f by 1 in Equation (1). Solve for b.

$$\begin{aligned} 20b + 30f &= 40 \\ 20b + 30(1) &= 40 \\ 20b + 30 &= 40 \\ 20b &= 10 \\ b &= 0.5 \end{aligned}$$

The cost of a 60-watt bulb was \$.50.
The cost of a fluorescent bulb was \$1.00.

Example 2

A total of 260 tickets were sold for a softball game. Adult tickets sold for $6 each, and children's tickets sold for $2 each. If the total receipts were $1220, how many adult tickets and how many children's tickets were sold?

Strategy

- Number of adult tickets sold: A
  Number of children's tickets sold: C

Ticket	Price	Number Sold	Total Receipts
Adult	6	A	$6A$
Children	2	C	$2C$

- The total number of tickets sold was 260.
  The total receipts were $1220.

Solution

$$A + C = 260$$
$$6A + 2C = 1220$$

$$-2A - 2C = -520$$
$$6A + 2C = 1220$$
$$4A = 700$$
$$A = 175$$

$$A + C = 260$$
$$175 + C = 260$$
$$C = 85$$

There were 175 adult tickets sold.
There were 85 children's tickets sold.

You Try It 2

An investment adviser invested $15,000 in two accounts. One investment earned 8% annual simple interest. The other investment earned 7% annual simple interest. The total interest in one year was $1170. How much was invested in each account?

Your strategy

Your solution

$12,000 @ 8%;
$3000 @ 7%

Solution on p. S15

5.5 Exercises

· ·

Objective A   *Application Problems*

1. A motorboat traveling with the current went 36 mi in 2 h. Against the current, it took 3 h to travel the same distance. Find the rate of the boat in calm water and the rate of the current.
   rate of the motorboat in calm water: 15 mph;
   rate of the current: 3 mph

2. A cabin cruiser traveling with the current went 45 mi in 3 h. Against the current, it took 5 h to travel the same distance. Find the rate of the cabin cruiser in calm water and the rate of the current.
   rate of the cabin cruiser in calm water: 12 mph;
   rate of the current: 3 mph

3. A jet plane flying with the wind went 2200 mi in 4 h. Against the wind, the plane could fly only 1820 mi in the same amount of time. Find the rate of the plane in calm air and the rate of the wind.
   rate of the plane in calm air: 502.5 mph;
   rate of the wind: 47.5 mph

4. Flying with the wind, a small plane flew 300 mi in 2 h. Against the wind, the plane could fly only 270 mi in the same amount of time. Find the rate of the plane in calm air and the rate of the wind.
   rate of the plane in calm air: 142.5 mph;
   rate of the wind: 7.5 mph

5. A rowing team rowing with the current traveled 20 km in 2 h. Rowing against the current, the team rowed 12 km in the same amount of time. Find the rate of the rowing team in calm water and the rate of the current.
   rate of the team in calm water: 8 km/h;
   rate of the current: 2 km/h

6. A motorboat traveling with the current went 72 km in 3 h. Against the current, the boat could go only 48 km in the same amount of time. Find the rate of the boat in calm water and the rate of the current.
   rate of the boat in calm water: 20 km/h;
   rate of the current: 4 km/h

7. A turbo-prop plane flying with the wind flew 800 mi in 4 h. Flying against the wind, the plane required 5 h to travel the same distance. Find the rate of the wind and the rate of the plane in calm air.
   rate of the plane in calm air: 180 mph;
   rate of the wind: 20 mph

8. Flying with the wind, a pilot flew 600 mi between two cities in 4 h. The return trip against the wind took 5 h. Find the rate of the plane in calm air and the rate of the wind.
   rate of the plane in calm air: 135 mph;
   rate of the wind: 15 mph

9. A plane flying with a tailwind flew 600 mi in 5 h. Against the wind, the plane required 6 h to fly the same distance. Find the rate of the plane in calm air and the rate of the wind.
   rate of the plane in calm air: 110 mph;
   rate of the wind: 10 mph

10. Flying with the wind, a plane flew 720 mi in 3 h. Against the wind, the plane required 4 h to fly the same distance. Find the rate of the plane in calm air and the rate of the wind.
    rate of the plane in calm air: 210 mph;
    rate of the wind: 30 mph

11. A motorboat traveling with the current went 48 mi in 3 h. Against the current, it took 4.8 h to travel the same distance. Find the rate of the boat in calm water and the rate of the current.
    rate of the boat in calm water: 13 mph;
    rate of the current: 3 mph

12. A plane traveling with the wind flew 3625 mi in 6.25 h. Against the wind, the plane required 7.25 h to fly the same distance. Find the rate of the plane in calm air and the rate of the wind.
    rate of the plane in calm air: 540 mph;
    rate of the wind: 40 mph

13. A cabin cruiser traveling with the current went 45 mi in 2.5 h. Against the current, the boat could go only 30 mi in the same amount of time. Find the rate of the cabin cruiser and the rate of the current.
    rate of the cruiser in calm water: 15 mph;
    rate of the current: 3 mph

14. Flying with the wind, a plane flew 450 mi in 3 h. Against the wind, the plane could fly only 270 mi in the same amount of time. Find the rate of the plane in calm air and the rate of the wind.
    rate of the plane in calm air: 120 mph;
    rate of the wind: 30 mph

Objective B   *Application Problems*

15. A merchant mixed 10 lb of a cinnamon tea with 5 lb of spice tea. The 15-pound mixture cost $40. A second mixture included 12 lb of the cinnamon tea and 8 lb of the spice tea. The 20-pound mixture cost $54. Find the cost per pound of the cinnamon tea and the spice tea.
    cinnamon tea: $2.50/lb;
    spice tea: $3.00/lb

16. A carpenter purchased 60 ft of redwood and 80 ft of pine for a total cost of $27. A second purchase, at the same prices, included 100 ft of redwood and 60 ft of pine for a total of $34. Find the cost per foot of redwood and the cost per foot of pine.
    pine: $.15 per foot;
    redwood: $.25 per foot

17. A contractor buys 16 yd of nylon carpet and 20 yd of wool carpet for $920. A second purchase, at the same prices, includes 18 yd of nylon carpet and 25 yd of wool carpet for $1100. Find the cost per yard of the wool carpet.
$26/yd

18. During one month, a homeowner used 500 units of electricity and 100 units of gas, for a total cost of $88. The next month, 400 units of electricity and 150 units of gas were used, for a total cost of $76. Find the cost per unit of gas.
$.08

19. A company manufactures both 10-speed and standard model bicycles. The cost of materials for a 10-speed bicycle is $35, and the cost of materials for a standard bicycle is $25. The cost of labor to manufacture a 10-speed bicycle is $40, and the cost of labor to manufacture a standard bicycle is $20. During a week when the company has budgeted $1250 for materials and $1300 for labor, how many 10-speed bicycles does the company plan to manufacture?
25 10-speed bicycles

20. A company manufactures both color and black-and-white television sets. The cost of materials for a black-and-white TV is $20, and the cost of materials for a color TV is $80. The cost of labor to manufacture a black-and-white TV is $30, and the cost of labor to manufacture a color TV is $50. During a week when the company has budgeted $4200 for materials and $2800 for labor, how many color TVs does the company plan to manufacture?
50 color TVs

21. A chemist has two alloys, one of which is 10% gold and 15% lead and the other of which is 30% gold and 40% lead. How many grams of each of the two alloys should be used to make an alloy that contains 60 g of gold and 88 g of lead?
480 g of the first alloy; 40 g of the second alloy

22. A pharmacist has two vitamin-supplement powders. The first powder is 20% vitamin B_1 and 10% vitamin B_2. The second is 15% vitamin B_1 and 20% vitamin B_2. How many milligrams of each of the two powders should the pharmacist use to make a mixture that contains 130 mg of vitamin B_1 and 80 mg of vitamin B_2?
560 mg of the first powder; 120 mg of the second powder

23. Two angles are complementary. The larger angle is 9° more than eight times the measure of the smaller angle. Find the measure of the two angles. (Complementary angles are two angles whose sum is 90°.)
9°, 81°

24. Two angles are supplementary. The larger angle is 40° more than three times the measure of the smaller angle. Find the measure of the two angles. (Supplementary angles are two angles whose sum is 180°.)
35°, 145°

25. The total receipts from 245 tickets sold to a play were $1045. Adult tickets sold for $5 each, and student tickets sold for $3 each. Find the number of adult tickets and the number of student tickets sold.
155 adult tickets; 90 student tickets

26. The income from a theater production was $4150. The price of a student ticket was $6, and the price of a nonstudent ticket was $10. Find the number of student tickets and the number of nonstudent tickets sold.
290 student tickets; 241 nonstudent tickets

27. You have a total of $5000 invested in two simple interest accounts. On one account, the annual simple interest rate is 6%. On the second account, the annual simple interest rate is 8%. The total annual interest earned in one year is $370. How much is invested in each account?
$1500 @ 6%; $3500 @ 8%

28. Two investments earn total annual interest of $970. One investment is in a 7.5% annual simple interest account. The other investment is in a 9.5% annual simple interest account. The total in the two investments is $12,000. How much is invested in each account?
$8500 @ 7.5%; $3500 @ 9.5%

APPLYING THE CONCEPTS

29. The sum of the digits of a two-digit number equals $\frac{1}{7}$ of the number. If the digits of the number are reversed, the new number is equal to 36 less than the original number. Find the original number.
84

30. The sum of the digits of a two-digit number equals $\frac{1}{5}$ of the number. If the digits of the number are reversed, the new number is equal to 9 more than the original number. Find the original number.
45

31. A coin bank contains only nickels and dimes. The total value of the coins in the bank is $2.50. If the nickels were dimes and the dimes were nickels, the total value of the coins would be $3.50. Find the number of nickels in the bank.
30 nickels

32. The total value of the quarters and dimes in a coin bank is $5.75. If the quarters were dimes and the dimes were quarters, the total value of the coins would be $6.50. Find the number of quarters in the bank.
15 quarters

5.6 Solving Systems of Linear Inequalities

Objective A   *To graph the solution set of a system of linear inequalities* ....

Two or more inequalities considered together are called a **system of inequalities**. The **solution set of a system of inequalities** is the intersection of the solution sets of the individual inequalities. To graph the solution set of a system of inequalities, first graph the solution set of each inequality. The solution set of the system of inequalities is the region of the plane represented by the intersection of the two shaded areas.

➡ Graph the solution set: $2x - y \le 3$
$$3x + 2y > 8$$

Solve each inequality for y.

$$2x - y \le 3 \qquad\qquad 3x + 2y > 8$$
$$-y \le -2x + 3 \qquad\qquad 2y > -3x + 8$$
$$y \ge 2x - 3 \qquad\qquad y > -\frac{3}{2}x + 4$$

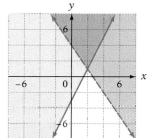

Graph $y = 2x - 3$ as a solid line. Because the inequality is $\ge$, shade above the line.

Graph $y = -\frac{3}{2}x + 4$ as a dotted line. Because the inequality is $>$, shade above the line.

The solution set of the system is the region of the plane represented by the intersection of the solution sets of the individual inequalities.

➡ Graph the solution set: $-x + 2y \ge 4$
$$x - 2y \ge 6$$

Solve each inequality for y.

$$-x + 2y \ge 4 \qquad\qquad x - 2y \ge 6$$
$$2y \ge x + 4 \qquad\qquad -2y \ge -x + 6$$
$$y \ge \frac{1}{2}x + 2 \qquad\qquad y \le \frac{1}{2}x - 3$$

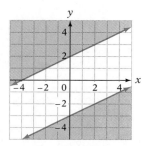

Shade above the solid line $y = \frac{1}{2}x + 2$.

Shade below the solid line $y = \frac{1}{2}x - 3$.

Because the solution sets of the two inequalities do not intersect, the solution of the system is the empty set.

Example 1

Graph the solution set: $y \geq x - 1$
$$y < -2x$$

Solution

Shade above the solid line $y = x - 1$.
Shade below the dotted line $y = -2x$.

The solution of the system is the intersection of the solution sets of the individual inequalities.

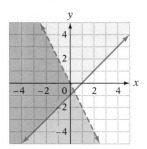

You Try It 1

Graph the solution set: $y \geq 2x - 3$
$$y > -3x$$

Your solution

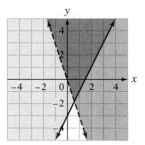

Example 2

Graph the solution set: $2x + 3y > 9$
$$y < -\frac{2}{3}x + 1$$

Solution

$2x + 3y > 9$
$$3y > -2x + 9$$
$$y > -\frac{2}{3}x + 3$$

Graph above the dotted line $y = -\frac{2}{3}x + 3$.

Graph below the dotted line $y = -\frac{2}{3}x + 1$.

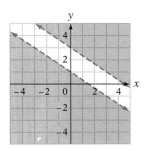

The intersection of the system is the empty set, because the solution sets of the two inequalities do not intersect.

You Try It 2

Graph the solution set: $3x + 4y > 12$
$$y < \frac{3}{4}x - 1$$

Your solution

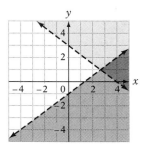

Solutions on p. S16

5.6 Exercises

· ·

Objective A

Graph the solution set.

1. $x - y \geq 3$
$\quad x + y \leq 5$

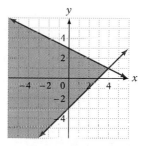

2. $2x - y < 4$
$\quad x + y < 5$

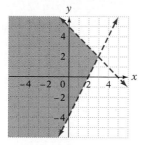

3. $3x - y < 3$
$\quad 2x + y \geq 2$

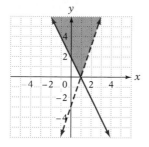

4. $x + 2y \leq 6$
$\quad x - y \leq 3$

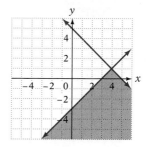

5. $\quad 2x + y \geq -2$
$\quad 6x + 3y \leq 6$

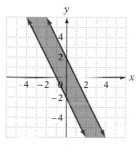

6. $\quad x + y \geq 5$
$\quad 3x + 3y < 6$

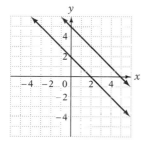

7. $3x - 2y < 6$
$\quad\quad y \leq 3$

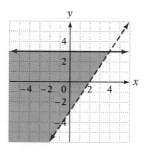

8. $\quad\quad x \leq 2$
$\quad 3x + 2y > 4$

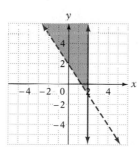

9. $\quad\quad y > 2x - 6$
$\quad x + y < 0$

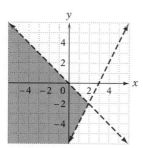

10. $x < 3$
$\quad\; y < -2$

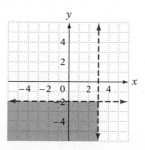

11. $x + 1 \geq 0$
$\quad\; y - 3 \leq 0$

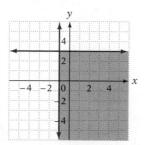

12. $5x - 2y \geq 10$
$\quad 3x + 2y \geq 6$

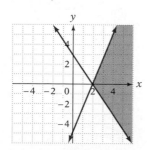

13. $2x + y \geq 4$
$3x - 2y < 6$

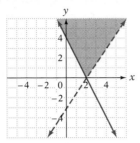

14. $3x - 4y < 12$
$x + 2y < 6$

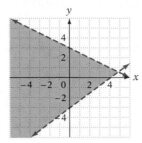

15. $x - 2y \leq 6$
$2x + 3y \leq 6$

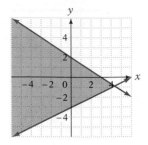

16. $x - 3y > 6$
$2x + y > 5$

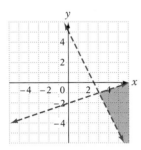

17. $x - 2y \leq 4$
$3x + 2y \leq 8$
$x > -1$

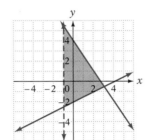

18. $3x - 2y < 0$
$5x + 3y > 9$
$y < 4$

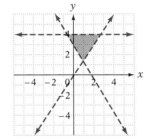

APPLYING THE CONCEPTS

Graph the solution set.

19. $2x + 3y \leq 15$
$3x - y \leq 6$
$y \geq 0$

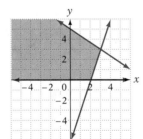

20. $x + y \leq 6$
$x - y \leq 2$
$x \geq 0$

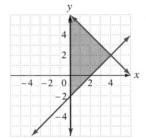

21. $x - y \leq 5$
$2x - y \geq 6$
$y \geq 0$

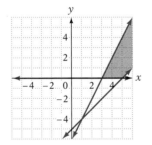

22. $x - 3y \leq 6$
$5x - 2y \geq 4$
$y \geq 0$

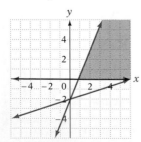

23. $2x - y \leq 4$
$3x + y < 1$
$y \leq 0$

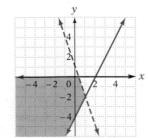

24. $x - y \leq 4$
$2x + 3y > 6$
$x \geq 0$

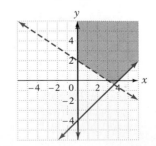

Focus on Problem Solving

Solve an Easier Problem

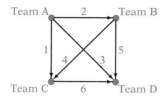

Team A   2   Team B
1   4   3   5
Team C   6   Team D

Suppose you are in charge of your softball league, which consists of 15 teams. You must devise a schedule in which each team plays every other team once. How many games must be scheduled?

To solve this problem, we will attempt an easier problem first. Suppose that your league contains only a small number of teams. For instance, if there were only 1 team, you would schedule 0 games. If there were 2 teams, you would schedule 1 game. If there were 3 teams, you would schedule 3 games. The diagram at the left shows that 6 games must be scheduled when there are 4 teams in the league.

Here is a table of our results so far. (Remember that making a table is another strategy to be used in problem solving.)

Number of Teams	Number of Games	Possible Pattern
1	0	0
2	1	1
3	3	1 + 2
4	6	1 + 2 + 3

1. Draw a diagram with 5 dots to represent the teams. Draw lines from each dot to a second dot, and determine the number of games required.

2. What is the apparent pattern for the number of games required?

3. Assuming that the pattern continues, how many games must be scheduled for the 15 teams of the original problem?

After solving a problem, good problem solvers ask whether it is possible to solve the problem in a different manner. Here is a possible alternative method of solving the scheduling problem.

Begin with one of the 15 teams (say team A) and ask, "How many games must this team play?" Because there are 14 teams left to play, you must schedule 14 games. Now move to team B. It is already scheduled to play team A, and it does not play itself, so there are 13 teams left for it to play. Consequently, you must schedule 14 + 13 games.

4. Continue this reasoning for the remaining teams and determine the number of games that must be scheduled. Does this answer correspond to the answer you obtained with the first method?

5. Visit www.sports.com to get lists of professional sports teams, divisions, etc. Find the strategy used to create the schedule of your favorite team.

6. Making connections to other problems you have solved is an important step toward becoming an excellent problem solver. How does the answer to the scheduling of teams relate to the triangular numbers discussed in the Focus on Problem Solving in the chapter entitled Linear Equations and Inequalities in Two Variables?

Projects and Group Activities

Using a Graphing Calculator to Solve a System of Equations

A graphing calculator can be used to solve a system of equations. For this procedure to work on most calculators, it is necessary that the point of intersection be on the screen. This means that you may have to experiment with Xmin, Xmax, Ymin, and Ymax values until the graphs intersect on the screen.

To solve a system of equations graphically, solve each equation for y. Then graph the equations of the system. Their point of intersection is the solution.

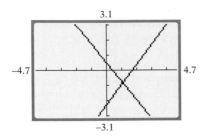

For instance, to solve the system of equations

$$4x - 3y = 7$$
$$5x + 4y = 2$$

first solve each equation for y.

$$4x - 3y = 7 \Rightarrow y = \frac{4}{3}x - \frac{7}{3}$$

$$5x + 4y = 2 \Rightarrow y = -\frac{5}{4}x + \frac{1}{2}$$

The keystrokes to solve this system are given below. We are using a viewing window $[-4.7, 4.7]$ by $[-3.1, 3.1]$.

TI-83	SHARP EL-9600	Casio CFX-9850G
[Y=] [CLEAR] 4 [X, T, θ, n] [÷] 3 [−]	[Y=] [CL] 4 [X/θ/T/n] [÷] 3 [−]	[MENU] 5 [F2] [F1] 4 [X,θ,T] [÷] 3
7 [÷] 3 [ENTER] [CLEAR]	7 [÷] 3 [ENTER] [CL] [(−)]	[−] 7 [÷] 3 [EXE] [F2] [F1]
[(−)] 5 [X, T, θ, n] [÷] 4 [+] 1 [÷]	5 [X/θ/T/n] [÷] 4 [+] 1 [÷] 2	[CLEAR] [(−)] 5 [X,θ,T] [÷] 4
2 [GRAPH]	[GRAPH]	[+] 1 [÷] 2 [EXE] [GRAPH]

Once the calculator has drawn the graphs, use the TRACE feature and move the cursor to the approximate point of intersection. This will give you an approximate solution of the system of equations. The approximate solution is $(1.096774, -0.870968)$. The method by which a more accurate solution can be determined depends on the type of calculator you use. Consult the user's manual under "systems of equations."

Some of the exercises in the first section of this chapter asked you to solve a system of equations by graphing. Try those exercises again, this time using your graphing calculator.

Current models of calculators do not allow you to solve graphically a system of equations in three variables. However, these calculators do have matrix and determinant operations that can be used to solve these systems.

Solving a First-Degree Equation with a Graphing Calculator

A first-degree equation in one variable can be solved graphically by using a graphing calculator. The idea is to rewrite the equation as a system of equations and then solve the system of equations as we illustrated above. For instance, to solve the equation

$$2x + 1 = 5x - 5$$

write the equation as the following system of equations.

$$y = 2x + 1$$
$$y = 5x - 5$$

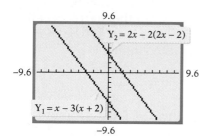

Notice that we have used the left and right sides of the original equation to form the system of equations.

Now graph the equations and find the point of intersection. This is shown at the left using a viewing window of $[-9.6, 9.6]$ by $[-9.6, 9.6]$. The solution of the original equation, $2x + 1 = 5x - 5$, is the x-coordinate of the point of intersection. Thus the solution of the equation is 2.

Recall that not all equations have a solution. Consider the equation

$$x - 3(x + 2) = 2x - 2(2x - 2)$$

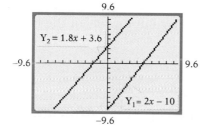

The graphs of the left and right sides of the equation are shown at the left. Note that the lines appear to be parallel and therefore do not intersect. Since the lines do not intersect, there is no solution of the system of equations and thus no solution of the original equation. We algebraically verify this result below.

$$
\begin{aligned}
x - 3(x + 2) &= 2x - 2(2x - 2) \\
x - 3x - 6 &= 2x - 4x + 4 \\
-2x - 6 &= -2x + 4 \\
-6 &= 4
\end{aligned}
$$

• **Use the Distributive Property.**
• **Simplify.**
• **Add 2x to each side of the equation.**

Because $-6 = 4$ is not a true equation, there is no solution.

One last point about the last equation. Note that in the third line of the solution we obtain the expressions $-2x - 6$ and $-2x + 4$. If we were to graph $y = -2x - 6$ and $y = -2x + 4$, the slopes of the lines are equal (both are -2) and therefore the graphs of the lines are parallel.

Before we leave graphical solutions, a few words of caution. Graphs can be deceiving and appear not to intersect when they do, and appear to intersect when they do not. For instance, an attempt to graphically solve

$$2x - 10 = 1.8x + 3.6$$

is shown at the left.

If you use the viewing window $[-9.6, 9.6]$ by $[-9.6, 9.6]$, the graphs will appear to be parallel. However, the graphs of $y = 2x - 10$ and $y = 1.8x + 3.6$ do not have the same slope and therefore must intersect. For this equation, you need a larger viewing window to see the point of intersection.

Solve the following equations by using a graphing calculator.

1. $3x - 1 = 5x + 1$

2. $3x + 2 = 4$

3. $3 + 2(2x - 4) = 5(x - 3)$

4. $2x - 4 = 5x - 3(x + 2) + 2$

5. Find an appropriate viewing window so that you can determine the solution of the equation $2x - 10 = 1.8x + 3.6$ given above.

| Chapter Summary

Key Words   Equations considered together are called a *system of equations*.

A *solution of a system of equations* in two variables is an ordered pair that is a solution of each equation of the system.

When the graphs of a system of equations intersect at only one point, the system is called an *independent system of equations.* When the graphs of a system of equations coincide, the system is called a *dependent system of equations.* When a system of equations has no solution, it is called an *inconsistent system of equations.*

An equation of the form $Ax + By + Cz = D$ is a *linear equation in three variables.* A *solution of a system of equations in three variables* is an ordered triple that is a solution of each equation of the system.

A *matrix* is a rectangular array of numbers. Each number in the matrix is called an *element* of the matrix. A matrix of m rows and n columns is said to be of *order* $m \times n$. A *square matrix* has the same number of rows as columns.

A *determinant* is a number associated with a square matrix.

The *minor of an element* in a 3×3 determinant is the 2×2 determinant obtained by eliminating the row and column that contain that element. The *cofactor* of an element of a matrix is $(-1)^{i+j}$ times the minor of that element, where i is the row number of the element and j is its column number.

The evaluation of the determinant of a 3×3 or larger matrix is accomplished by *expanding by cofactors.*

Inequalities considered together are called a *system of inequalities.* The *solution set of a system of inequalities* is the intersection of the solution sets of the individual inequalities.

Essential Rules   A system of equations can be solved by a graphing method, by the substitution method, or by the addition method.

Cramer's Rule   The solution of the system of equations $\begin{aligned} a_1x + b_1y &= c_1 \\ a_2x + b_2y &= c_2 \end{aligned}$ is

given by $x = \dfrac{D_x}{D}$ and $y = \dfrac{D_y}{D}$, where $D = \begin{vmatrix} a_1 & b_1 \\ a_2 & b_2 \end{vmatrix}$,

$D_x = \begin{vmatrix} c_1 & b_1 \\ c_2 & b_2 \end{vmatrix}$, $D_y = \begin{vmatrix} a_1 & c_1 \\ a_2 & c_2 \end{vmatrix}$, and $D \neq 0$.

The solution of the system of equations

$\begin{aligned} a_1x + b_1y + c_1z &= d_1 \\ a_2x + b_2y + c_2z &= d_2 \\ a_3x + b_3y + c_3z &= d_3 \end{aligned}$ is given by $x = \dfrac{D_x}{D}$, $y = \dfrac{D_y}{D}$, and

$z = \dfrac{D_z}{D}$, where $D = \begin{vmatrix} a_1 & b_1 & c_1 \\ a_2 & b_2 & c_2 \\ a_3 & b_3 & c_3 \end{vmatrix}$, $D_x = \begin{vmatrix} d_1 & b_1 & c_1 \\ d_2 & b_2 & c_2 \\ d_3 & b_3 & c_3 \end{vmatrix}$,

$D_y = \begin{vmatrix} a_1 & d_1 & c_1 \\ a_2 & d_2 & c_2 \\ a_3 & d_3 & c_3 \end{vmatrix}$, $D_z = \begin{vmatrix} a_1 & b_1 & d_1 \\ a_2 & b_2 & d_2 \\ a_3 & b_3 & d_3 \end{vmatrix}$, and $D \neq 0$.

Chapter Review

1. Solve by graphing: $2x - 3y = -6$
$2x - y = 2$

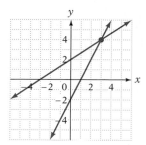

$(3, 4)$　[5.1A]

2. Solve by graphing:　$x - 2y = -5$
$3x + 4y = -15$

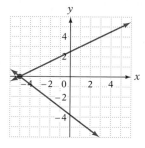

$(-5, 0)$　[5.1A]

3. Graph the solution set:　$2x - y < 3$
$4x + 3y < 11$

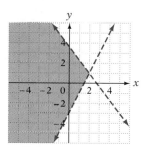

[5.6A]

4. Graph the solution set:　$x + y > 2$
$2x - y < -1$

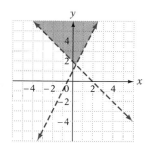

[5.6A]

5. Solve by substitution: $3x + 2y = 4$
$x = 2y - 1$

$\left(\dfrac{3}{4}, \dfrac{7}{8}\right)$　[5.2A]

6. Solve by substitution: $5x + 2y = -23$
$2x + y = -10$

$(-3, -4)$　[5.2A]

7. Solve by substitution: $y = 3x - 7$
$y = -2x + 3$

$(2, -1)$　[5.2A]

8. Solve by the addition method: $3x + 4y = -2$
$2x + 5y = 1$

$(-2, 1)$　[5.3A]

9. Solve by the addition method:
$4x - 6y = 5$
$6x - 9y = 4$

inconsistent　[5.3A]

10. Solve by the addition method:
$3x - y = 2x + y - 1$
$5x + 2y = y + 6$

$(1, 1)$　[5.3A]

11. Solve by the addition method:
$2x + 4y - z = 3$
$x + 2y + z = 5$
$4x + 8y - 2z = 7$

inconsistent　[5.3B]

12. Solve by the addition method:
$x - y - z = 5$
$2x + z = 2$
$3y - 2z = 1$

$(2, -1, -2)$　[5.3B]

13. Evaluate the determinant: $\begin{vmatrix} 3 & -1 \\ -2 & 4 \end{vmatrix}$

    10   [5.4A]

14. Evaluate the determinant: $\begin{vmatrix} 1 & -2 & 3 \\ 3 & 1 & 1 \\ 2 & -1 & -2 \end{vmatrix}$

    -32 [5.4A]

15. Solve by using Cramer's Rule:
    $x - y = 3$
    $2x + y = -4$
    $\left(-\dfrac{1}{3}, -\dfrac{10}{3}\right)$ [5.4B]

16. Solve by using Cramer's Rule:
    $5x + 2y = 9$
    $3x + 5y = -7$
    $\left(\dfrac{59}{19}, -\dfrac{62}{19}\right)$ [5.4B]

17. Solve by using Cramer's Rule:
    $x - y + z = 2$
    $2x - y - z = 1$
    $x + 2y - 3z = -4$
    $\left(\dfrac{1}{5}, -\dfrac{6}{5}, \dfrac{3}{5}\right)$ [5.4B]

18. Solve by using Cramer's Rule:
    $3x + 2y + 2z = 2$
    $x - 2y - z = 1$
    $2x - 3y - 3z = -3$
    $(0, -2, 3)$ [5.4B]

19. A plane flying with the wind went 350 mi in 2 h. The return trip, flying against the wind, took 2.8 h. Find the rate of the plane in calm air and the rate of the wind.
    rate of the plane: 150 mph;
    rate of the wind: 25 mph   [5.5A]

20. A clothing manufacturer purchased 60 yd of cotton and 90 yd of wool for a total cost of $1800. Another purchase, at the same prices, included 80 yd of cotton and 20 yd of wool for a total cost of $1000. Find the cost per yard of the cotton and of the wool.
    cost per yard of cotton: $9;
    cost per yard of wool: $14   [5.5B]

Chapter Test

1. Solve by substitution: $2x - 6y = 15$
$$x = 4y + 8$$

$\left(6, -\frac{1}{2}\right)$ [5.2A]

2. Solve by the addition method: $3x + 2y = 2$
$$x + y = 3$$

$(-4, 7)$ [5.3A]

3. Solve by graphing: $x + y = 3$
$$3x - 2y = -6$$

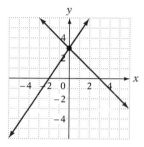

$(0, 3)$ [5.1A]

4. Solve by graphing: $2x - y = 4$
$$y = 2x - 4$$

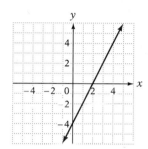

$(x, 2x - 4)$ [5.1A]

5. Solve by substitution: $3x + 12y = 18$
$$x + 4y = 6$$

$\left(x, -\frac{1}{4}x + \frac{3}{2}\right)$ [5.2A]

6. Solve by the addition method: $5x - 15y = 30$
$$x - 3y = 6$$

$\left(x, \frac{1}{3}x - 2\right)$ [5.3A]

7. Solve by the addition method:
$$3x - 4y - 2z = 17$$
$$4x - 3y + 5z = 5$$
$$5x - 5y + 3z = 14$$

$(3, -1, -2)$ [5.3B]

8. Solve by the addition method:
$$3x + y = 13$$
$$2y + 3z = 5$$
$$x + 2z = 11$$

$(5, -2, 3)$ [5.3B]

9. Evaluate the determinant:

$\begin{vmatrix} 6 & 1 \\ 2 & 5 \end{vmatrix}$

28   [5.4A]

10. Evaluate the determinant:

$\begin{vmatrix} 1 & 5 & -2 \\ -2 & 1 & 4 \\ 4 & 3 & -8 \end{vmatrix}$

0   [5.4A]

11. Solve by using Cramer's Rule:
$$2x - y = 7$$
$$3x + 2y = 7$$

(3, −1) [5.4B]

12. Solve by using Cramer's Rule:
$$3x - 4y = 10$$
$$2x + 5y = 15$$

$\left(\dfrac{110}{23}, \dfrac{25}{23}\right)$ [5.4B]

13. Solve by using Cramer's Rule:
$$x + y + z = 0$$
$$x + 2y + 3z = 5$$
$$2x + y + 2z = 3$$

(−1, −3, 4) [5.4B]

14. Solve by using Cramer's Rule:
$$x + 3y + z = 6$$
$$2x + y - z = 12$$
$$x + 2y - z = 13$$

(2, 3, −5) [5.4B]

15. Graph the solution set:
$$x + 3y \leq 6$$
$$2x - y \geq 4$$

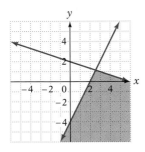

[5.6A]

16. Graph the solution set:
$$2x + 4y \geq 8$$
$$x + y \leq 3$$

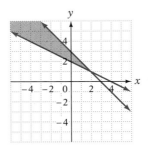

[5.6A]

17. Solve by substitution:
$$3x - 2y = 4$$
$$y = 5x - 9$$

(2, 1) [5.2A]

18. A cabin cruiser traveling with the current went 60 mi in 3 h. Against the current, it took 5 h to travel the same distance. Find the rate of the cabin cruiser in calm water and the rate of the current.
cabin cruiser: 16 mph; current: 4 mph   [5.5A]

19. A pilot flying with the wind flew 600 mi in 3 h. Flying against the wind, the pilot required 4 h to travel the same distance. Find the rate of the plane in calm air and the rate of the wind.
plane: 175 mph; wind: 25 mph   [5.5A]

20. At a movie theater, admission tickets are $5 for children and $8 for adults. The receipts for one Friday evening were $2500. The next day there were three times as many children as the preceding evening and only half the number of adults as the night before, yet the receipts were still $2500. Find the number of children who attended on Friday evening.
100 children   [5.5B]

Cumulative Review

1. Simplify: $-2\sqrt{90}$

    $-6\sqrt{10}$ [1.2F]

2. Solve: $3(x - 5) = 2x + 7$

    22   [2.2C]

3. Simplify: $3[x - 2(5 - 2x) - 4x] + 6$

    $3x - 24$ [1.4D]

4. Evaluate $a + bc \div 2$ when $a = 4$, $b = 8$, and $c = -2$.

    -4 [1.4A]

5. Solve: $2x - 3 < 9$ or $5x - 1 < 4$

    $\{x\,|\,x < 6\}$ [2.4B]

6. Solve: $|x - 2| - 4 < 2$

    $\{x\,|\,-4 < x < 8\}$ [2.5B]

7. Solve: $|2x - 3| > 5$

    $\{x\,|\,x > 4$ or $x < -1\}$ [2.5B]

8. Given $F(x) = x^2 - 3$, find $F(2)$.

    1   [4.1D]

9. Graph the solution set of $\{x\,|\,x \le 2\} \cap \{x\,|\,x > -3\}$.

    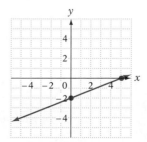   [1.5C]

10. Find the equation of the line that contains the point $(-2, 3)$ and has slope $-\frac{2}{3}$.

    $y = \frac{2}{3}x + \frac{5}{3}$ [4.4A]

11. Find the equation of the line that contains the points $(2, -1)$ and $(3, 4)$.

    $y = 5x - 11$ [4.4B]

12. Find the equation of the line that contains the point $(-1, 2)$ and is perpendicular to the line $2x - 3y = 7$.

    $y = -\frac{3}{2}x + \frac{1}{2}$ [4.5A]

13. Graph $2x - 5y = 10$ by using the slope and y-intercept.

    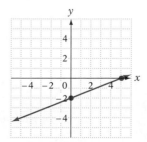

    [4.3B]

14. Graph the solution set of the inequality $3x - 4y \ge 8$.

    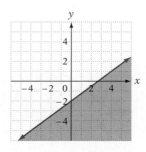

    [4.6A]

15. Solve by graphing:
$5x - 2y = 10$
$3x + 2y = 6$

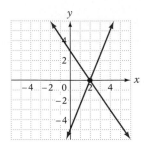

(2, 0)   [5.1A]

16. Solve by substitution:
$3x - 2y = 7$
$\qquad y = 2x - 1$

$(-5, -11)$ [5.2A]

17. Solve by the addition method:
$3x + 2z = 1$
$\quad 2y - z = 1$
$\quad x + 2y = 1$

$(1, 0, -1)$ [5.3B]

18. Evaluate the determinant:
$$\begin{vmatrix} 2 & -5 & 1 \\ 3 & 1 & 2 \\ 6 & -1 & 4 \end{vmatrix}$$

3   [5.4A]

19. Solve by using Cramer's Rule:
$4x - 3y = 17$
$3x - 2y = 12$

$(2, -3)$ [5.4B]

20. Graph the solution set:
$3x - 2y \geq 4$
$\quad x + y < 3$

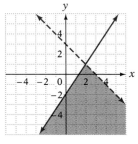

[5.6A]

21. How many milliliters of pure water must be added to 100 ml of a 4% salt solution to make a 2.5% salt solution?
60 ml   [2.3B]

22. Flying with the wind, a small plane required 2 h to fly 150 mi. Against the wind, it took 3 h to fly the same distance. Find the rate of the wind.
12.5 mph   [5.5A]

23. A restaurant manager buys 100 lb of hamburger and 50 lb of steak for a total cost of $490. A second purchase, at the same prices, includes 150 lb of hamburger and 100 lb of steak. The total cost is $860. Find the price of 1 lb of steak.
$5   [5.5B]

24. Find the lower and upper limits of a 12,000-ohm resistor with a 15% tolerance.
10,200 ohms and 13,800 ohms   [2.5C]

25. The graph shows the relationship between the monthly income and the sales of an account executive. Find the slope of the line between the two points shown on the graph. Write a sentence that states the meaning of the slope.
$m = 40$. The slope represents the monthly income (in dollars) per thousand dollars in sales.   [4.3A]

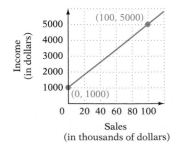

6

Polynomials

It is the job of urban planners to work toward growth and revitalization of urban areas. They must deal not only with such current problems as deterioration and pollution, but also with projections of long-term needs and plans for the future. Making estimations of changes in population, health care requirements, housing needs, and transportation systems requires working with variables.

Objectives

Section 6.1
To multiply monomials
To divide monomials and simplify expressions with negative exponents
To write a number using scientific notation
To solve application problems

Section 6.2
To evaluate polynomial functions
To add or subtract polynomials

Section 6.3
To multiply a polynomial by a monomial
To multiply two polynomials
To multiply two binomials
To multiply binomials that have special products
To solve application problems

Section 6.4
To divide polynomials
To divide polynomials using synthetic division
To evaluate a polynomial using synthetic division

Origins of the Word *Algebra*

The word *algebra* has its origins in an Arabic book written around A.D. 825, *Hisab al-jabr w' almuqa-balah* by al-Khowarizmi. The word *al-jabr*, which literally translated means "reunion," was written as the word *algebra* in Latin translations of al-Khowarizmi's work and became synonymous with equations and the solutions of equations. It is interesting to note that an early meaning of the Spanish word *algebrista* was "bonesetter" or "reuniter of broken bones."

This same al-Khowarizmi also made a second contribution to our language of mathematics. One of the translations of his work into Latin shortened his name to *Algoritmi*. A further modification of this word gives us our present word *algorithm*. An algorithm is a procedure or set of instructions used to solve different types of problems. Computer scientists use algorithms when writing computer programs.

A further historical note: Omar Khayyám, a Persian who probably read al-Khowarizmi's work, is especially noted as a poet and the author of the *Rubáiyat*. However, he was also an excellent mathematician and astronomer and made many contributions to mathematics.

6.1 Exponential Expressions

Objective A   *To multiply monomials*.. (19) HM³

A monomial is a number, a variable, or a product of a number and variables.

The examples at the right are monomials. The **degree of a monomial** is the sum of the exponents of the variables.

x	degree 1 ($x = x^1$)
$3x^2$	degree 2
$4x^2y$	degree 3
$6x^3y^4z^2$	degree 9

In this chapter, the variable n is considered a positive integer when used as an exponent.

x^n degree n

The degree of a nonzero constant term is zero.

6   degree 0

The expression $5\sqrt{x}$ is not a monomial because $\sqrt{x}$ cannot be written as a product of variables. The expression $\dfrac{x}{y}$ is not a monomial because it is a quotient of variables.

The expression x^4 is an exponential expression. The exponent, 4, indicates the number of times the base, x, occurs as a factor.

The product of exponential expressions with the *same* base can be simplified by writing each expression in factored form and writing the result with an exponent.

$$x^3 \cdot x^4 = \overbrace{(x \cdot x \cdot x)}^{3 \text{ factors}} \cdot \overbrace{(x \cdot x \cdot x \cdot x)}^{4 \text{ factors}}$$
$$\underbrace{\qquad\qquad}_{7 \text{ factors}}$$
$$= x^7$$

Note that adding the exponents results in the same product.

$$x^3 \cdot x^4 = x^{3+4} = x^7$$

Rule for Multiplying Exponential Expressions

If m and n are positive integers, then $x^m \cdot x^n = x^{m+n}$.

⇒ Multiply: $(-4x^5y^3)(3xy^2)$

$(-4x^5y^3)(3xy^2) = (-4 \cdot 3)(x^5 \cdot x)(y^3 \cdot y^2)$
- Use the Commutative and Associative Properties of Multiplication to rearrange and group factors.

$= -12(x^{5+1})(y^{3+2})$
- Multiply variables with the same base by adding their exponents. Do these steps mentally.

$= -12x^6y^5$
- Simplify.

The power of a monomial can be simplified by writing the power in factored form and then using the Rule for Multiplying Exponential Expressions.

$$(x^4)^3 = x^4 \cdot x^4 \cdot x^4 \qquad (a^2b^3)^2 = (a^2b^3)(a^2b^3)$$

- Write in factored form.

$$= x^{4+4+4} \qquad\qquad = a^{2+2}b^{3+3}$$

$$= x^{12} \qquad\qquad\quad = a^4b^6$$

- Use the Rule for Multiplying Exponential Expressions.

Note that multiplying each exponent inside the parentheses by the exponent outside the parentheses results in the same product.

$$(x^4)^3 = x^{4 \cdot 3} \qquad\qquad (a^2b^3)^2 = a^{2 \cdot 2}b^{3 \cdot 2}$$

$$= x^{12} \qquad\qquad\qquad = a^4b^6$$

- Multiply each exponent inside the parentheses by the exponent outside the parentheses.

Rule for Simplifying Powers of Exponential Expressions

If m and n are positive integers, then $(x^m)^n = x^{mn}$.

Rule for Simplifying Powers of Products

If m, n, and p are positive integers, then $(x^m y^n)^p = x^{mp} y^{np}$.

➡ Simplify: $(x^4)^5$

Multiply the exponents.

$$(x^4)^5 = x^{4 \cdot 5}$$

- Use the Rule for Simplifying Powers of Exponential Expressions.

$$= x^{20}$$

➡ Simplify: $(2a^3b^4)^3$

Multiply each exponent inside the parentheses by the exponent outside the parentheses.

$$(2a^3b^4)^3 = 2^{1 \cdot 3}a^{3 \cdot 3}b^{4 \cdot 3}$$

- Use the Rule for Simplifying Powers of Products. Note that $2 = 2^1$.

$$= 2^3 a^9 b^{12}$$

$$= 8a^9 b^{12}$$

Example 1

Simplify: $(2xy^2)(-3xy^4)^3$

Solution

$$(2xy^2)(-3xy^4)^3 = (2xy^2)[(-3)^3 x^3 y^{12}]$$

$$= (2xy^2)(-27x^3 y^{12})$$

$$= -54x^4 y^{14}$$

Example 2

Simplify: $(x^{n+2})^5$

Solution

$$(x^{n+2})^5 = x^{5n+10}$$

You Try It 1

Simplify: $(-3a^2b^4)(-2ab^3)^4$

Your solution

$-48a^6 b^{16}$

You Try It 2

Simplify: $(y^{n-3})^2$

Your solution

y^{2n-6}

Solutions on p. S16

Example 3

Simplify: $[(2xy^2)^2]^3$

Solution

$[(2xy^2)^2]^3 = [2^2x^2y^4]^3$
$= 2^6x^6y^{12} = 64x^6y^{12}$

You Try It 3

Simplify: $[(ab^3)^3]^4$

Your solution

$a^{12}b^{36}$

Solution on p. S16

Objective B   **To divide monomials and simplify expressions with negative exponents** ....

The quotient of two exponential expressions with the same base can be simplified by writing each expression in factored form, dividing by the common factors, and then writing the result with an exponent.

$$\frac{x^5}{x^2} = \frac{\overset{1}{\cancel{x}} \cdot \overset{1}{\cancel{x}} \cdot x \cdot x \cdot x}{\underset{1}{\cancel{x}} \cdot \underset{1}{\cancel{x}}} = x^3$$

Note that subtracting the exponents gives the same result.

$$\frac{x^5}{x^2} = x^{5-2} = x^3$$

INSTRUCTOR NOTE

Here we are just verbalizing the rule for division of monomials. The theorem comes after we define negative exponents.

Have students copy this rule onto a piece of paper and then practice a few exercises such as $\frac{a^4}{a^2}$ and $\frac{y^8}{y}$.

It may also help to give $\frac{a^9}{b^5}$

to emphasize that the bases must be the same.

To divide two monomials with the same base, subtract the exponents of the like bases.

➡ Simplify: $\dfrac{z^8}{z^2}$

$$\frac{z^8}{z^2} = \boxed{z^{8-2}}$$
$$= z^6$$

• The bases are the same. Subtract the exponents. This step is often done mentally.

➡ Simplify: $\dfrac{a^5b^9}{a^4b}$

$$\frac{a^5b^9}{a^4b} = \boxed{a^{5-4}b^{9-1}}$$
$$= ab^8$$

• Subtract the exponents of the like bases. This step is often done mentally.

Consider the expression $\dfrac{x^4}{x^4}$, $x \neq 0$. This expression can be simplified, as shown below, by (1) subtracting exponents and (2) dividing by common factors.

TAKE NOTE

A number divided by itself is 1.

Therefore, $\dfrac{8}{8} = 1$, $\dfrac{3^4}{3^4} = 1$, and

for $x \neq 0$, $\dfrac{x^4}{x^4}$.

$$\frac{x^4}{x^4} = x^{4-4} = x^0 \qquad\qquad \frac{x^4}{x^4} = \frac{\overset{1}{\cancel{x}} \cdot \overset{1}{\cancel{x}} \cdot \overset{1}{\cancel{x}} \cdot \overset{1}{\cancel{x}}}{\underset{1}{\cancel{x}} \cdot \underset{1}{\cancel{x}} \cdot \underset{1}{\cancel{x}} \cdot \underset{1}{\cancel{x}}} = 1$$

The equations $\dfrac{x^4}{x^4} = x^0$ and $\dfrac{x^4}{x^4} = 1$ suggest the following definition of x^0.

Definition of Zero as an Exponent

If $x \neq 0$, then $x^0 = 1$. The expression 0^0 is not defined.

➡ Simplify: $(16z^5)^0$, $z \neq 0$

$(16z^5)^0 = 1$ • Any nonzero expression to the zero power is 1.

POINT OF INTEREST

In the 15th century, the expression $12^{2\overline{m}}$ was used to mean $12x^{-2}$. The use of $\overline{m}$ reflects an Italian influence, where m was used for minus and p was used for plus. It was understood that $2\overline{m}$ referred to an unnamed variable. Isaac Newton, in the 17th century, advocated the current use of a negative exponent.

➡ Simplify: $-(7x^4y^3)^0$, $x \neq 0$, $y \neq 0$

$$-(7x^4y^3)^0 = -(1) = -1$$

• The negative outside the parentheses is not affected by the exponent.

Consider the expression $\dfrac{x^4}{x^6}$, $x \neq 0$. This expression can be simplified, as shown below, by (1) subtracting exponents and (2) dividing by common factors.

$$\frac{x^4}{x^6} = x^{4-6} = x^{-2} \qquad \frac{x^4}{x^6} = \frac{\overset{1}{\cancel{x}} \cdot \overset{1}{\cancel{x}} \cdot \overset{1}{\cancel{x}} \cdot \overset{1}{\cancel{x}}}{\underset{1}{\cancel{x}} \cdot \underset{1}{\cancel{x}} \cdot \underset{1}{\cancel{x}} \cdot \underset{1}{\cancel{x}} \cdot x \cdot x} = \frac{1}{x^2}$$

The equations $\dfrac{x^4}{x^6} = x^{-2}$ and $\dfrac{x^4}{x^6} = \dfrac{1}{x^2}$ suggest that $x^{-2} = \dfrac{1}{x^2}$.

Definition of a Negative Exponent

If $x \neq 0$ and n is a positive integer, then

$$x^{-n} = \frac{1}{x^n} \quad \text{and} \quad \frac{1}{x^{-n}} = x^n$$

TAKE NOTE

Note from the example at the right that 2^{-4} is a *positive* number. A negative exponent does not indicate a negative number.

➡ Evaluate: 2^{-4}

$$2^{-4} = \frac{1}{2^4}$$

• Use the Definition of a Negative Exponent.

$$= \frac{1}{16}$$

• Evaluate the expression.

A power of the quotient of two exponential expressions can be simplified by multiplying each exponent in the quotient by the exponent outside the parentheses.

Rule for Simplifying Powers of Quotients

If m, n, and p are integers and $y \neq 0$, then $\left(\dfrac{x^m}{y^n}\right)^p = \dfrac{x^{mp}}{y^{np}}$.

➡ Simplify: $\left(\dfrac{a^2}{b^3}\right)^{-2}$

$$\left(\frac{a^2}{b^3}\right)^{-2} = \frac{a^{2(-2)}}{b^{3(-2)}}$$

• Use the Rule for Simplifying Powers of Quotients.

$$= \frac{a^{-4}}{b^{-6}} = \frac{b^6}{a^4}$$

• Use the Definition of a Negative Exponent.

Simplest Form of an Exponential Expression

An exponential expression is in simplest form when it is written with only positive exponents.

TAKE NOTE

The exponent on n is -5 (*negative* five). The n^{-5} is written in the denominator as n^5. The exponent on 3 is 1 (*positive* one). The 3 remains in the numerator.

➡ Simplify: $3n^{-5}$

$$3n^{-5} = 3 \cdot \frac{1}{n^5} = \frac{3}{n^5}$$

• Use the Definition of Negative Exponents to rewrite the expression with a positive exponent.

➡ Simplify: $\frac{2}{5a^{-4}}$

$$\frac{2}{5a^{-4}} = \frac{2}{5} \cdot \frac{1}{a^{-4}} = \frac{2}{5} \cdot a^4 = \frac{2a^4}{5}$$

• Use the Definition of Negative Exponents to rewrite the expression with a positive exponent.

Now that zero and negative exponents have been defined, a rule for dividing exponential expressions can be stated.

Rule for Dividing Exponential Expressions

If m and n are integers and $x \neq 0$, then $\dfrac{x^m}{x^n} = x^{m-n}$.

➡ Simplify: $\frac{x^4}{x^9}$

$$\frac{x^4}{x^9} = \boxed{x^{4-9}}$$

• Use the Rule for Dividing Exponential Expressions. This step is often done mentally.

$$- x^{-5}$$

• Subtract the exponents.

$$= \frac{1}{x^5}$$

• Use the Definition of Negative Exponents to rewrite the expression with a positive exponent.

The rules for simplifying exponential expressions and powers of exponential expressions are true for all integer exponents. These rules are restated here for your convenience.

Rules of Exponents

If m, n, and p are integers, then

$$x^m \cdot x^n = x^{m+n} \qquad (x^m)^n = x^{mn} \qquad (x^m y^n)^p = x^{mp} y^{np}$$

$$\frac{x^m}{x^n} = x^{m-n}, x \neq 0 \qquad \left(\frac{x^m}{y^n}\right)^p = \frac{x^{mp}}{y^{np}}, y \neq 0 \qquad x^{-n} = \frac{1}{x^n}, x \neq 0$$

$$x^0 = 1, x \neq 0$$

➡ Simplify: $(3ab^{-4})(-2a^{-3}b^7)$

$$(3ab^{-4})(-2a^{-3}b^7) = \boxed{[3 \cdot (-2)](a^{1+(-3)}b^{-4+7})}$$

• When multiplying expressions, add the exponents on like bases. Do this step mentally.

$$= -6a^{-2}b^3$$

$$= -\frac{6b^3}{a^2}$$

➡ Simplify: $\dfrac{4a^{-2}b^5}{6a^5b^2}$

$$\dfrac{4a^{-2}b^5}{6a^5b^2} = \dfrac{\cancel{2}\cdot 2a^{-2}b^5}{\cancel{2}\cdot 3a^5b^2} = \dfrac{2a^{-2}b^5}{3a^5b^2}$$

$$= \dfrac{2a^{-2-5}b^{5-2}}{3}$$

$$= \dfrac{2a^{-7}b^3}{3} = \dfrac{2b^3}{3a^7}$$

- Divide the coefficients by their common factor.
- Use the Rule for Dividing Exponential Expressions.
- Use the Definition of Negative Exponents to rewrite the expression with a positive exponent.

INSTRUCTOR NOTE

There are a few ways to simplify the expression at the right. Students can simplify it by starting as follows:

$$\left(\dfrac{6m^2n^3}{8m^7n^2}\right)^{-3} = \left(\dfrac{8m^7n^2}{6m^2n^3}\right)^{3}$$

➡ Simplify: $\left(\dfrac{6m^2n^3}{8m^7n^2}\right)^{-3}$

$$\left(\dfrac{6m^2n^3}{8m^7n^2}\right)^{-3} = \left(\dfrac{3m^{2-7}n^{3-2}}{4}\right)^{-3}$$

$$= \left(\dfrac{3m^{-5}n}{4}\right)^{-3}$$

$$= \dfrac{3^{-3}m^{15}n^{-3}}{4^{-3}}$$

$$= \dfrac{4^3m^{15}}{3^3n^3} = \dfrac{64m^{15}}{27n^3}$$

- Simplify inside the brackets.
- Subtract the exponents.
- Use the Rule for Simplifying Powers of Quotients.
- Use the Definition of Negative Exponents to rewrite the expression with positive exponents. Then simplify.

Example 4

Simplify: $\dfrac{-28x^6z^{-3}}{42x^{-1}z^4}$

Solution

$$\dfrac{-28x^6z^{-3}}{42x^{-1}z^4} = -\dfrac{14\cdot 2x^{6-(-1)}z^{-3-4}}{14\cdot 3}$$

$$= -\dfrac{2x^7z^{-7}}{3} = -\dfrac{2x^7}{3z^7}$$

Example 5

Simplify: $\dfrac{(3a^{-1}b^4)^{-3}}{(6^{-1}a^{-3}b^{-4})^3}$

Solution

$$\dfrac{(3a^{-1}b^4)^{-3}}{(6^{-1}a^{-3}b^{-4})^3} = \dfrac{3^{-3}a^3b^{-12}}{6^{-3}a^{-9}b^{-12}} = 3^{-3}\cdot 6^3 a^{12}b^0$$

$$= \dfrac{6^3a^{12}}{3^3} = \dfrac{216a^{12}}{27} = 8a^{12}$$

Example 6

Simplify: $\dfrac{x^{4n-2}}{x^{2n-5}}$

Solution

$$\dfrac{x^{4n-2}}{x^{2n-5}} = x^{4n-2-(2n-5)}$$

$$= x^{4n-2-2n+5} = x^{2n+3}$$

You Try It 4

Simplify: $\dfrac{20r^{-2}t^{-5}}{-16r^{-3}s^{-2}}$

Your solution

$$-\dfrac{5rs^2}{4t^5}$$

You Try It 5

Simplify: $\dfrac{(9u^{-6}v^4)^{-1}}{(6u^{-3}v^{-2})^{-2}}$

Your solution

$$\dfrac{4}{v^8}$$

You Try It 6

Simplify: $\dfrac{a^{2n+1}}{a^{n+3}}$

Your solution

$$a^{n-2}$$

Solutions on p. S16

Objective C **To write a number using scientific notation** .... HM³

Integer exponents are used to represent the very large and very small numbers encountered in the fields of science and engineering. For example, the mass of the electron is 0.0000000000000000000000000009 g. Numbers such as this are difficult to read and write, so a more convenient system for writing such numbers has been developed. It is called **scientific notation**.

To express a number in scientific notation, write the number as the product of a number between 1 and 10 and a power of 10. The form for scientific notation is $a \times 10^n$, where $1 \le a < 10$.

For numbers greater than 10, move the decimal point to the right of the first digit. The exponent n is positive and equal to the number of places the decimal point has been moved.

965,000	$= 9.65 \times 10^5$
3,600,000	$= 3.6 \times 10^6$
92,000,000,000	$= 9.2 \times 10^{10}$

For numbers less than 1, move the decimal point to the right of the first nonzero digit. The exponent n is negative. The absolute value of the exponent is equal to the number of places the decimal point has been moved.

0.0002	$= 2 \times 10^{-4}$
0.0000000974	$= 9.74 \times 10^{-8}$
0.000000000086	$= 8.6 \times 10^{-11}$

Converting a number written in scientific notation to decimal notation requires moving the decimal point.

When the exponent is positive, move the decimal point to the right the same number of places as the exponent.

$1.32 \times 10^4 = 13,200$

$1.4 \times 10^8 = 140,000,000$

When the exponent is negative, move the decimal point to the left the same number of places as the absolute value of the exponent.

$1.32 \times 10^{-2} = 0.0132$

$1.4 \times 10^{-4} = 0.00014$

Numerical calculations involving numbers that have more digits than the hand-held calculator is able to handle can be performed using scientific notation.

➡ Simplify: $\dfrac{220,000 \times 0.000000092}{0.0000011}$

$$\frac{220,000 \times 0.000000092}{0.0000011} = \frac{2.2 \times 10^5 \times 9.2 \times 10^{-8}}{1.1 \times 10^{-6}}$$

• Write the numbers in scientific notation.

$$= \frac{(2.2)(9.2) \times 10^{5+(-8)-(-6)}}{1.1}$$

• Simplify.

$$= 18.4 \times 10^3 = 18,400$$

Example 7	Write 0.000041 in scientific notation.	**You Try It 7**	Write 942,000,000 in scientific notation.
Solution	$0.000041 = 4.1 \times 10^{-5}$	**Your solution**	9.42×10^8

Solution on p. S16

Example 8 Write 3.3×10^7 in decimal notation.

Solution $3.3 \times 10^7 = 33{,}000{,}000$

You Try It 8 Write 2.7×10^{-5} in decimal notation.

Your solution 0.000027

Example 9 Simplify:
$$\frac{2{,}400{,}000{,}000 \times 0.0000063}{0.00009 \times 480}$$

Solution
$$\frac{2{,}400{,}000{,}000 \times 0.0000063}{0.00009 \times 480}$$

$$= \frac{2.4 \times 10^9 \times 6.3 \times 10^{-6}}{9 \times 10^{-5} \times 4.8 \times 10^2}$$

$$= \frac{(2.4)(6.3) \times 10^{9+(-6)-(-5)-2}}{(9)(4.8)}$$

$$= 0.35 \times 10^6 = 350{,}000$$

You Try It 9 Simplify:
$$\frac{5{,}600{,}000 \times 0.000000081}{900 \times 0.000000028}$$

Your solution $1.8 \times 10^4 = 18{,}000$

Solutions on p. S16

Objective D   To solve application problems ....

Example 10
How many miles does light travel in one day? The speed of light is 186,000 mi/s. Write the answer in scientific notation.

Strategy
To find the distance traveled:
- Write the speed of light in scientific notation.
- Write the number of seconds in one day in scientific notation.
- Use the equation $d = rt$, where r is the speed of light and t is the number of seconds in one day.

Solution
$r = 186{,}000 = 1.86 \times 10^5$

$t = 24 \cdot 60 \cdot 60 = 86{,}400 = 8.64 \times 10^4$

$d = rt$
$d = (1.86 \times 10^5)(8.64 \times 10^4)$
$\quad = 1.86 \times 8.64 \times 10^9$
$\quad = 16.0704 \times 10^9$
$\quad = 1.60704 \times 10^{10}$

Light travels 1.60704×10^{10} mi in one day.

You Try It 10
A computer can do an arithmetic operation in 1×10^{-7} s. In scientific notation, how many arithmetic operations can the computer perform in 1 min?

Your strategy

Your solution
6×10^8 operations

Solution on p. S16

6.1 Exercises

· ·

Objective A

Simplify.

1. $(ab^3)(a^3b)$
a^4b^4

2. $(-2ab^4)(-3a^2b^4)$
$6a^3b^8$

3. $(9xy^2)(-2x^2y^2)$
$-18x^3y^4$

4. $(x^2y)^2$
x^4y^2

5. $(x^2y^4)^4$
x^8y^{16}

6. $(-2ab^2)^3$
$-8a^3b^6$

7. $(-3x^2y^3)^4$
$81x^8y^{12}$

8. $(2^2a^2b^3)^3$
$64a^6b^9$

9. $(3^3a^5b^3)^2$
$729a^{10}b^6$

10. $(xy)(x^2y)^4$
x^9y^5

11. $(x^2y^2)(xy^3)^3$
x^5y^{11}

12. $[(2x)^4]^2$
$256x^8$

13. $[(3x)^3]^2$
$729x^6$

14. $[(x^2y)^4]^5$
$x^{40}y^{20}$

15. $[(ab)^3]^6$
$a^{18}b^{18}$

16. $[(2ab)^3]^2$
$64a^6b^6$

17. $[(2xy)^3]^4$
$4096x^{12}y^{12}$

18. $[(3x^2y^3)^2]^2$
$81x^8y^{12}$

19. $[(2a^4b^3)^3]^2$
$64a^{24}b^{18}$

20. $y^n \cdot y^{2n}$
y^{3n}

21. $x^n \cdot x^{n+1}$
x^{2n+1}

22. $y^{2n} \cdot y^{4n+1}$
y^{6n+1}

23. $y^{3n} \cdot y^{3n-2}$
y^{6n-2}

24. $(a^n)^{2n}$
a^{2n^2}

25. $(a^{n-3})^{2n}$
a^{2n^2-6n}

26. $(y^{2n-1})^3$
y^{6n-3}

27. $(x^{3n+2})^5$
x^{15n+10}

28. $(b^{2n-1})^n$
b^{2n^2-n}

29. $(2xy)(-3x^2yz)(x^2y^3z^3)$
$-6x^5y^5z^4$

30. $(x^2z^4)(2xyz^4)(-3x^3y^2)$
$-6x^6y^3z^8$

31. $(3b^5)(2ab^2)(-2ab^2c^2)$
$-12a^2b^9c^2$

32. $(-c^3)(-2a^2bc)(3a^2b)$
$6a^4b^2c^4$

33. $(-2x^2y^3z)(3x^2yz^4)$
$-6x^4y^4z^5$

34. $(2a^2b)^3(-3ab^4)^2$
$72a^8b^{11}$

35. $(-3ab^3)^3(-2^2a^2b)^2$
$-432a^7b^{11}$

36. $(4ab)^2(-2ab^2c^3)^3$
$-128a^5b^8c^9$

37. $(-2ab^2)(-3a^4b^5)^3$
$54a^{13}b^{17}$

Objective B

Simplify.

38. 2^{-3}
$\dfrac{1}{8}$

39. $\dfrac{1}{3^{-5}}$
243

40. $\dfrac{1}{x^{-4}}$
x^4

41. $\dfrac{1}{y^{-3}}$
y^3

42. $\dfrac{2x^{-2}}{y^4}$

$\dfrac{2}{x^2y^4}$

43. $\dfrac{a^3}{4b^{-2}}$

$\dfrac{a^3b^2}{4}$

44. $x^{-3}y$

$\dfrac{y}{x^3}$

45. xy^{-4}

$\dfrac{x}{y^4}$

46. $-5x^0$

-5

47. $\dfrac{1}{2x^0}$

$\dfrac{1}{2}$

48. $\dfrac{(2x)^0}{-2^3}$

$-\dfrac{1}{8}$

49. $\dfrac{-3^{-2}}{(2y)^0}$

$-\dfrac{1}{9}$

50. $\dfrac{y^{-7}}{y^{-8}}$

y

51. $\dfrac{y^{-2}}{y^6}$

$\dfrac{1}{y^8}$

52. $(x^2y^{-4})^2$

$\dfrac{x^4}{y^8}$

53. $(x^3y^5)^{-2}$

$\dfrac{1}{x^6y^{10}}$

54. $\dfrac{x^{-2}y^{-11}}{xy^{-2}}$

$\dfrac{1}{x^3y^9}$

55. $\dfrac{x^4y^3}{x^{-1}y^{-2}}$

x^5y^5

56. $\dfrac{a^{-1}b^{-3}}{a^4b^{-5}}$

$\dfrac{b^2}{a^5}$

57. $\dfrac{a^6b^{-4}}{a^{-2}b^5}$

$\dfrac{a^8}{b^9}$

58. $(2a^{-1})^{-2}(2a^{-1})^4$

$\dfrac{4}{a^2}$

59. $(3a)^{-3}(9a^{-1})^{-2}$

$\dfrac{1}{2187a}$

60. $(x^{-2}y)^2(xy)^{-2}$

$\dfrac{1}{x^6}$

61. $(x^{-1}y^2)^{-3}(x^2y^{-4})^{-3}$

$\dfrac{y^6}{x^3}$

62. $\dfrac{50b^{10}}{70b^5}$

$\dfrac{5b^5}{7}$

63. $\dfrac{x^3y^6}{x^6y^2}$

$\dfrac{y^4}{x^3}$

64. $\dfrac{x^{17}y^5}{-x^7y^{10}}$

$-\dfrac{x^{10}}{y^5}$

65. $\dfrac{-6x^2y}{12x^4y}$

$-\dfrac{1}{2x^2}$

66. $\dfrac{2x^2y^4}{(3xy^2)^3}$

$\dfrac{2}{27xy^2}$

67. $\dfrac{-3ab^2}{(9a^2b^4)^3}$

$-\dfrac{1}{243a^5b^{10}}$

68. $\left(\dfrac{-12a^2b^3}{9a^5b^9}\right)^3$

$-\dfrac{64}{27a^9b^{18}}$

69. $\left(\dfrac{12x^3y^2z}{18xy^3z^4}\right)^4$

$\dfrac{16x^8}{81y^4z^{12}}$

70. $\dfrac{(4x^2y)^2}{(2xy^3)^3}$

$\dfrac{2x}{y^7}$

71. $\dfrac{(3a^2b)^3}{(-6ab^3)^2}$

$\dfrac{3a^4}{4b^3}$

72. $\dfrac{(-4x^2y^3)^2}{(2xy^2)^3}$

$2x$

73. $\dfrac{(-3a^2b^3)^2}{(-2ab^4)^3}$

$-\dfrac{9a}{8b^6}$

74. $\dfrac{(-4xy^3)^3}{(-2x^7y)^4}$

$-\dfrac{4y^5}{x^{25}}$

75. $\dfrac{(-8x^2y^2)^4}{(16x^3y^7)^2}$

$\dfrac{16x^2}{y^6}$

76. $\dfrac{a^{5n}}{a^{3n}}$

a^{2n}

77. $\dfrac{b^{6n}}{b^{10n}}$

$\dfrac{1}{b^{4n}}$

78. $\dfrac{-x^{5n}}{x^{2n}}$

$-x^{3n}$

79. $\dfrac{y^{2n}}{-y^{8n}}$

$-\dfrac{1}{y^{6n}}$

80. $\dfrac{x^{2n-1}}{x^{n-3}}$

x^{n+2}

81. $\dfrac{y^{3n+2}}{y^{2n+4}}$

y^{n-2}

82. $\dfrac{a^{3n}b^n}{a^nb^{2n}}$

$\dfrac{a^{2n}}{b^n}$

83. $\dfrac{x^ny^{3n}}{x^ny^{5n}}$

$\dfrac{1}{y^{2n}}$

84. $\dfrac{a^{3n-2}b^{n+1}}{a^{2n+1}b^{2n+2}}$

$\dfrac{a^{n-3}}{b^{n+1}}$

85. $\dfrac{x^{2n-1}y^{n-3}}{x^{n+4}y^{n+3}}$

$\dfrac{x^{n-5}}{y^6}$

86. $\left(\dfrac{4^{-2}xy^{-3}}{x^{-3}y}\right)^3\left(\dfrac{8^{-1}x^{-2}y}{x^4y^{-1}}\right)^{-2}$

$\dfrac{x^{24}}{64y^{16}}$

87. $\left(\dfrac{9ab^{-2}}{8a^{-2}b}\right)^{-2}\left(\dfrac{3a^{-2}b}{2a^2b^{-2}}\right)^3$

$\dfrac{8b^{15}}{3a^{18}}$

88. $\left(\dfrac{2ab^{-1}}{ab}\right)^{-1}\left(\dfrac{3a^{-2}b}{a^2b^2}\right)^{-2}$

$\dfrac{a^8b^4}{18}$

89. $1 + (1 + (1 + 2^{-1})^{-1})^{-1}$

$\dfrac{8}{5}$

90. $2 - (2 - (2 - 2^{-1})^{-1})^{-1}$

$\dfrac{5}{4}$

Objective C

Write in scientific notation.

91. 0.00000467
4.67×10^{-6}

92. 0.00000005
5×10^{-8}

93. 0.00000000017
1.7×10^{-10}

94. 4,300,000
4.3×10^{6}

95. 200,000,000,000
2×10^{11}

96. 9,800,000,000
9.8×10^{9}

Write in decimal notation.

97. 1.23×10^{-7}
0.000000123

98. 6.2×10^{-12}
0.0000000000062

99. 8.2×10^{15}
8,200,000,000,000,000

100. 6.34×10^{5}
634,000

101. 3.9×10^{-2}
0.039

102. 4.35×10^{9}
4,350,000,000

Simplify. Write the answer in decimal notation.

103. $(3 \times 10^{-12})(5 \times 10^{16})$
150,000

104. $(8.9 \times 10^{-5})(3.2 \times 10^{-6})$
0.0000000002848

105. $(0.0000065)(3,200,000,000,000)$
20,800,000

106. $(480,000)(0.0000000096)$
0.004608

107. $\dfrac{9 \times 10^{-3}}{6 \times 10^{5}}$
0.000000015

108. $\dfrac{2.7 \times 10^{4}}{3 \times 10^{-6}}$
9,000,000,000

109. $\dfrac{0.0089}{500,000,000}$
0.0000000000178

110. $\dfrac{4800}{0.00000024}$
20,000,000,000

111. $\dfrac{0.00056}{0.000000000004}$
140,000,000

112. $\dfrac{0.000000346}{0.0000005}$
0.692

113. $\dfrac{(3.3 \times 10^{-11})(2.7 \times 10^{15})}{8.1 \times 10^{-3}}$
11,000,000

114. $\dfrac{(6.9 \times 10^{27})(8.21 \times 10^{-13})}{4.1 \times 10^{15}}$
1.381683

115. $\dfrac{(0.00000004)(84,000)}{(0.0003)(1,400,000)}$
0.000008

116. $\dfrac{(720)(0.0000000039)}{(26,000,000,000)(0.18)}$
0.000000000000006

Objective D   *Application Problems*

Solve. Write the answer in scientific notation.

117. How many kilometers does light travel in one day? The speed of light is 300,000 km/s.
2.592×10^{10} km

118. How many meters does light travel in 8 h? The speed of light is 300,000,000 m/s.
8.64×10^{12} m

119. The rover Sojourner landed on Mars in July of 1997. It took 11 min for the commands from a computer on Earth to travel to the Sojourner, a distance of 119 million miles. How fast did the signals from Earth to Mars travel? Write the answer in scientific notation.
$1.08\overline{1} \times 10^7$ mi/min

120. In early 1997, the gross federal debt was 5.5×10^{12} dollars. How much would each American citizen have to pay in order to pay off the debt? Use 275,000,000 as the number of citizens.
2×10^4 dollars

121. A high-speed centrifuge makes 9×10^7 revolutions each minute. Find the time in seconds for the centrifuge to make one revolution.
$6.\overline{6} \times 10^{-7}$ s

122. How long does it take light to travel to Earth from the sun? The sun is 9.3×10^7 mi from Earth, and light travels 1.86×10^5 mi/s.
5×10^2 s

123. The mass of Earth is 5.9×10^{27} g. The mass of the sun is 2×10^{33} g. How many times heavier is the sun than Earth?
3.38983×10^5 times heavier

124. One astronomical unit (A.U.) is 9.3×10^7 mi. The star Pollux in the constellation Gemini is 1.8228×10^{12} mi from Earth. Find the distance from Pollux to Earth in astronomical units.
1.96×10^4 A.U.

Gemini

125. The weight of 31 million orchid seeds is one ounce. Find the weight of one orchid seed.
3.225806×10^{-8} oz

126. One light year, an astronomical unit of distance, is the distance that light will travel in one year. Light travels 1.86×10^5 mi/s. Find the measure of one light year in miles. Use a 365-day year.
5.865696×10^{12} mi

127. The Coma cluster of galaxies is approximately 2.8×10^8 light years from Earth. Find the distance, in miles, from the Coma cluster to Earth. (See Exercise 126 for the definition of one light year. Use a 365-day year.)
1.6423949×10^{21} mi

APPLYING THE CONCEPTS

128. Which is larger, $(2^3)^3$ or $2^{(3^3)}$?
$2^{(3^3)}$

129. Correct the error in each of the following expressions. Explain which rule or property was used incorrectly.
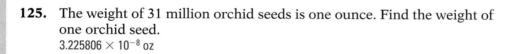
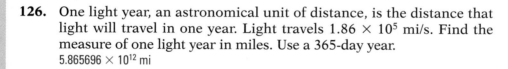
  a. $2x + 3x = 5x^2$ **b.** $a - (b - c) = a - b - c$
  c. $x^0 = 0$ **d.** $(x^4)^5 = x^9$
  e. $x^2 \cdot x^3 = x^6$ **f.** $b^{m+n} = b^m + b^n$

6.2 Introduction to Polynomials

Objective A   *To evaluate polynomial functions* ....

A **polynomial** is a variable expression in which the terms are monomials.

A polynomial of one term is a **monomial**. $5x$

A polynomial of two terms is a **binomial**. $5x^2y + 6x$

A polynomial of three terms is a **trinomial**. $3x^2 + 9xy - 5y$

Polynomials with more than three terms do not have special names.

The **degree of a polynomial** is the greatest of the degrees of any of its terms.

$3x + 2$	degree 1
$3x^2 + 2x - 4$	degree 2
$4x^3y^2 + 6x^4$	degree 5
$3x^{2n} - 5x^n - 2$	degree $2n$

The terms of a polynomial in one variable are usually arranged so that the exponents of the variable decrease from left to right. This is called **descending order**.

$2x^2 - x + 8$

$3y^3 - 3y^2 + y - 12$

For a polynomial in more than one variable, descending order may refer to any one of the variables.

The polynomial at the right is shown first in descending order of the x variable and then in descending order of the y variable.

$2x^2 + 3xy + 5y^2$

$5y^2 + 3xy + 2x^2$

Polynomial functions have many applications in mathematics. The **linear function** given by $f(x) = mx + b$ is an example of a polynomial function. It is a polynomial function of degree one. A second-degree polynomial function, called a **quadratic function**, is given by the equation $f(x) = ax^2 + bx + c$, $a \neq 0$. A third-degree polynomial function is called a **cubic function**. In general, a **polynomial function** is an expression whose terms are monomials.

To evaluate a polynomial function, replace the variable by its value and simplify.

➡ Given $P(x) = x^3 - 3x^2 + 4$, evaluate $P(-3)$.

$$P(x) = x^3 - 3x^2 + 4$$
$$P(-3) = (-3)^3 - 3(-3)^2 + 4 \qquad \bullet \text{ Substitute } -3 \text{ for } x \text{ and simplify.}$$
$$= -27 - 3(9) + 4$$
$$= -27 - 27 + 4$$
$$= -50$$

The **leading coefficient** of a polynomial function is the coefficient of the variable with the largest exponent. The constant term is the term without a variable.

⇒ Find the leading coefficient, the constant term, and the degree of the polynomial function $P(x) = 7x^4 - 3x^2 + 2x - 4$.

The leading coefficient is 7, the constant term is -4, and the degree is 4.

The three equations below do not represent polynomial functions.

$f(x) = 3x^2 + 2x^{-1}$ A polynomial function does not have a variable raised to a negative power.

$g(x) = 2\sqrt{x} - 3$ A polynomial function does not have a variable expression within a radical.

$h(x) = \dfrac{x}{x - 1}$ A polynomial function does not have a variable in the denominator of a fraction.

The graph of a linear function is a straight line and can be found by plotting just two points. The graph of a polynomial function of degree greater than one is a curve. Consequently, many points may have to be found before an accurate graph can be drawn.

Evaluating the quadratic function given by the equation $f(x) = x^2 - x - 6$ when $x = -3, -2, -1, 0, 1, 2, 3$, and 4 gives the points shown in Figure 1 below. For instance, $f(-3) = 6$, so $(-3, 6)$ is graphed; $f(2) = -4$, so $(2, -4)$ is graphed; and $f(4) = 6$, so $(4, 6)$ is graphed. Evaluating the function when x is not an integer, such as $x = -\dfrac{3}{2}$ and $x = \dfrac{5}{2}$, produces more points to graph, as shown in Figure 2. Connecting the points with a smooth curve results in Figure 3, which is the graph of f.

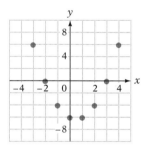

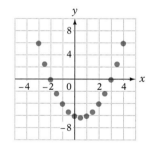

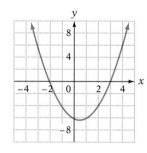

Figure 1   **Figure 2**   **Figure 3**

CALCULATOR NOTE

You can verify the graphs of these polynomial functions by using a graphing calculator. See the Appendix: Guidelines for Using a Graphing Calculator for instructions on graphing functions.

Here is an example of graphing a cubic function, $P(x) = x^3 - 2x^2 - 5x + 6$. Evaluating the function when $x = -2, -1, 0, 1, 2, 3$, and 4 gives the graph in Figure 4 below. Evaluating at some noninteger values gives the graph in Figure 5. Finally, connecting the dots with a smooth curve gives the graph in Figure 6.

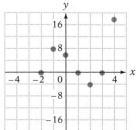

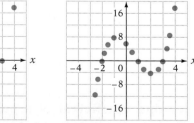

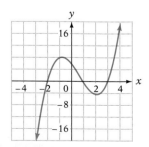

Figure 4   **Figure 5**   **Figure 6**

Example 1

Given $P(x) = x^3 + 3x^2 - 2x + 8$, evaluate $P(-2)$.

Solution

$P(x) = x^3 + 3x^2 - 2x + 8$
$P(-2) = (-2)^3 + 3(-2)^2 - 2(-2) + 8$
$\quad = (-8) + 3(4) + 4 + 8$
$\quad = -8 + 12 + 4 + 8$
$\quad = 16$

You Try It 1

Given $R(x) = -2x^4 - 5x^3 + 2x - 8$, evaluate $R(2)$.

Your solution

-76

Example 2

Find the leading coefficient, the constant term, and the degree of the polynomial.
$P(x) = 5x^6 - 4x^5 - 3x^2 + 7$

Solution

The leading coefficient is 5, the constant term is 7, and the degree is 6.

You Try It 2

Find the leading coefficient, the constant term, and the degree of the polynomial.
$r(x) = -3x^4 + 3x^3 + 3x^2 - 2x - 12$

Your solution

The leading coefficient is -3, the constant term is -12, and the degree is 4.

Example 3

Which of the following is a polynomial function?
a. $P(x) = 3x^{\frac{1}{2}} + 21x^2 - 3$
b. $T(x) = 3\sqrt{x} - 2x^2 - 3x + 2$
c. $R(x) = 14x^3 - \pi x^2 + 3x + 2$

Solution

a. This is not a polynomial function. A polynomial function does not have a variable raised to a fractional power.
b. This is not a polynomial function. A polynomial function does not have a variable expression within a radical.
c. This is a polynomial function.

You Try It 3

Which of the following is a polynomial function?
a. $R(x) = 5x^{14} - 5$
b. $V(x) = -x^{-1} + 2x - 7$
c. $P(x) = 2x^4 - 3\sqrt{x} - 3$

Your solution

a. yes
b. no
c. no

Example 4

Graph $f(x) = x^2 - 2$.

Solution

x	$y = f(x)$
-3	7
-2	2
-1	-1
0	-2
1	-1
2	2
3	7

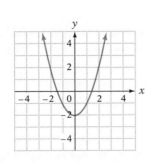

You Try It 4

Graph $f(x) = x^3 + 2$.

Your solution

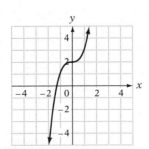

Solutions on p. S17

Example 5

Graph $f(x) = x^3 - 1$.

Solution

x	$y = f(x)$
-2	-9
-1	-2
0	-1
1	0
2	7

You Try It 5

Graph $f(x) = -x^3 + 1$.

Your solution

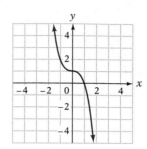

Solution on p. S17

Objective B **To add or subtract polynomials**...

Polynomials can be added by combining like terms. Either a vertical or a horizontal format can be used.

INSTRUCTOR NOTE

It may help to show students that adding polynomials is related to adding whole numbers. Adding the coefficients of like terms is similar to arranging whole numbers to be added in columns with the unit digits aligned.

➡ Add $(3x^3 - 7x + 2) + (7x^2 + 2x - 7)$. Use a horizontal format.

$(3x^3 - 7x + 2) + (7x^2 + 2x - 7)$
$= 3x^3 + 7x^2 + (-7x + 2x) + (2 - 7)$

$= 3x^3 + 7x^2 - 5x - 5$

- Use the Commutative and Associative Properties of Addition to rearrange and group like terms.
- Combine like terms.

➡ Add $(4x^2 + 5x - 3) + (7x^3 - 7x + 1) + (2x - 3x^2 + 4x^3 + 1)$. Use a vertical format.

$$
\begin{array}{r}
4x^2 + 5x - 3 \\
7x^3 \quad\quad - 7x + 1 \\
4x^3 - 3x^2 + 2x + 1 \\
\hline
11x^3 + \ x^2 \quad\quad - 1
\end{array}
$$

- Arrange the terms of each polynomial in descending order with like terms in the same column.
- Add the terms in each column.

TAKE NOTE

The opposite of a polynomial is the polynomial with the sign of every term changed.

The additive inverse of the polynomial $x^2 + 5x - 4$ is $-(x^2 + 5x - 4)$.

To simplify the additive inverse of a polynomial, change the sign of every term inside the parentheses.

$-(x^2 + 5x - 4) = -x^2 - 5x + 4$

To subtract two polynomials, add the additive inverse of the second polynomial to the first.

➡ Subtract $(3x^2 - 7xy + y^2) - (-4x^2 + 7xy - 3y^2)$. Use a horizontal format.

$(3x^2 - 7xy + y^2) - (-4x^2 + 7xy - 3y^2)$
$= (3x^2 - 7xy + y^2) + (4x^2 - 7xy + 3y^2)$
$= 7x^2 - 14xy + 4y^2$

- Rewrite the subtraction as the addition of the additive inverse.
- Combine like terms.

➡ Subtract $(6x^3 - 3x + 7) - (3x^2 - 5x + 12)$. Use a vertical format.

$(6x^3 - 3x + 7) - (3x^2 - 5x + 12)$
$= (6x^3 - 3x + 7) + (-3x^2 + 5x - 12)$

- Rewrite subtraction as the addition of the additive inverse.

$$
\begin{array}{r}
6x^3 \qquad - 3x + \;\;7 \\
-3x^2 + 5x - 12 \\
\hline
6x^3 - 3x^2 + 2x - \;\;5
\end{array}
$$

- Arrange the terms of each polynomial in descending order with like terms in the same column.
- Combine the terms in each column.

Functional notation can be used when adding or subtracting polynomials.

➡ Given $P(x) = 3x^2 - 2x + 4$ and $R(x) = -5x^3 + 4x + 7$, find $P(x) + R(x)$.

$P(x) + R(x) = (3x^2 - 2x + 4) + (-5x^3 + 4x + 7)$
$= -5x^3 + 3x^2 + 2x + 11$

➡ Given $P(x) = -5x^2 + 8x - 4$ and $R(x) = -3x^2 - 5x + 9$, find $P(x) - R(x)$.

$P(x) - R(x) = (-5x^2 + 8x - 4) - (-3x^2 - 5x + 9)$
$= (-5x^2 + 8x - 4) + (3x^2 + 5x - 9)$
$= -2x^2 + 13x - 13$

➡ Given $P(x) = 3x^2 - 5x + 6$ and $R(x) = 2x^2 - 5x - 7$, find $S(x)$, the sum of the two polynomials.

$S(x) = P(x) + R(x) = (3x^2 - 5x + 6) + (2x^2 - 5x - 7)$
$= 5x^2 - 10x - 1$

Note that evaluating $P(x) = 3x^2 - 5x + 6$ and $R(x) = 2x^2 - 5x - 7$ at, for example, $x = 3$, and then adding the values, is the same as evaluating $S(x) = 5x^2 - 10x - 1$ at 3.

$P(3) = 3(3)^2 - 5(3) + 6 = 27 - 15 + 6 = 18$

$R(3) = 2(3)^2 - 5(3) - 7 = 18 - 15 - 7 = -4$

$P(3) + R(3) = 18 + (-4) = 14$

$S(3) = 5(3)^2 - 10(3) - 1 = 45 - 30 - 1 = 14$

Example 6

Add
$(4x^2 - 3xy + 7y^2) + (-3x^2 + 7xy + y^2)$.
Use a vertical format.

Solution

$$\begin{array}{r} 4x^2 - 3xy + 7y^2 \\ -3x^2 + 7xy + y^2 \\ \hline x^2 + 4xy + 8y^2 \end{array}$$

You Try It 6

Add
$(-3x^2 - 4x + 9) + (-5x^2 - 7x + 1)$.
Use a vertical format.

Your solution

$-8x^2 - 11x + 10$

Example 7

Subtract
$(3x^2 - 2x + 4) - (7x^2 + 3x - 12)$.
Use a vertical format.

Solution

Add the additive inverse of $7x^2 + 3x - 12$
to $3x^2 - 2x + 4$.

$$\begin{array}{r} 3x^2 - 2x + 4 \\ -7x^2 - 3x + 12 \\ \hline -4x^2 - 5x + 16 \end{array}$$

You Try It 7

Subtract
$(-5x^2 + 2x - 3) - (6x^2 + 3x - 7)$.
Use a vertical format.

Your solution

$-11x^2 - x + 4$

Example 8

Given $P(x) = -3x^2 + 2x - 6$ and
$R(x) = 4x^3 - 3x + 4$, find
$S(x) = P(x) + R(x)$. Evaluate $S(-2)$.

Solution

$$\begin{aligned} S(x) &= P(x) + R(x) \\ &= (-3x^2 + 2x - 6) + (4x^3 - 3x + 4) \\ &= 4x^3 - 3x^2 - x - 2 \end{aligned}$$

$$\begin{aligned} S(-2) &= 4(-2)^3 - 3(-2)^2 - (-2) - 2 \\ &= 4(-8) - 3(4) - (-2) - 2 \\ &= -32 - 12 + 2 - 2 \\ &= -44 \end{aligned}$$

You Try It 8

Given $P(x) = 4x^3 - 3x^2 + 2$ and
$R(x) = -2x^2 + 2x - 3$, find
$S(x) = P(x) + R(x)$. Evaluate $S(-1)$.

Your solution

$S(x) = 4x^3 - 5x^2 + 2x - 1$
$S(-1) = -12$

Example 9

Given $P(x) = 2x^{2n} - 3x^n + 7$ and
$R(x) = 3x^{2n} + 3x^n + 5$, find
$D(x) = P(x) - R(x)$.

Solution

$$\begin{aligned} D(x) &= P(x) - R(x) \\ &= (2x^{2n} - 3x^n + 7) - (3x^{2n} + 3x^n + 5) \\ &= (2x^{2n} - 3x^n + 7) + (-3x^{2n} - 3x^n - 5) \\ &= -x^{2n} - 6x^n + 2 \end{aligned}$$

You Try It 9

Given $P(x) = 5x^{2n} - 3x^n - 7$ and
$R(x) = -2x^{2n} - 5x^n + 8$, find
$D(x) = P(x) - R(x)$.

Your solution

$7x^{2n} + 2x^n - 15$

Solutions on p. S17

6.2 Exercises

· ·

Objective A

1. Given $P(x) = 3x^2 - 2x - 8$, evaluate $P(3)$.
13

2. Given $P(x) = -3x^2 - 5x + 8$, evaluate $P(-5)$.
-42

3. Given $R(x) = 2x^3 - 3x^2 + 4x - 2$, evaluate $R(2)$.
10

4. Given $R(x) = -x^3 + 2x^2 - 3x + 4$, evaluate $R(-1)$.
10

5. Given $f(x) = x^4 - 2x^2 - 10$, evaluate $f(-1)$.
-11

6. Given $f(x) = x^5 - 2x^3 + 4x$, evaluate $f(2)$.
24

Which of the following define a polynomial function? For those that are polynomial functions, identify **a.** the leading coefficient, **b.** the constant term, and **c.** the degree.

7. $P(x) = -x^2 + 3x + 8$

$-1, 8, 2$

8. $P(x) = 3x^4 - 3x - 7$

$3, -7, 4$

9. $R(x) = \dfrac{x}{x + 1}$

not a polynomial

10. $R(x) = \dfrac{3x^2 - 2x + 1}{x}$

not a polynomial

11. $f(x) = \sqrt{x} - x^2 + 2$

not a polynomial

12. $f(x) = x^2 - \sqrt{x + 2} - 8$

not a polynomial

13. $g(x) = 3x^5 - 2x^2 + \pi$
$3, \pi, 5$

14. $g(x) = -4x^5 - 3x^2 + x - \sqrt{7}$
$-4, -\sqrt{7}, 5$

15. $P(x) = 3x^2 - 5x^3 + 2$
$-5, 2, 3$

16. $P(x) = x^7 - 5x^4 - x^6$

$-1, 0, 6$

17. $R(x) = 14$

$14, 14, 0$

18. $R(x) - \dfrac{1}{x} + 2$

not a polynomial

Graph.

19. $P(x) = x^2 - 1$

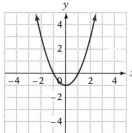

20. $P(x) = 2x^2 + 3$

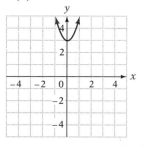

21. $R(x) = x^3 + 2$

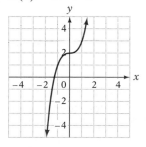

22. $R(x) = x^4 + 1$

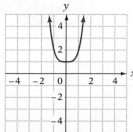

23. $f(x) = x^3 - 2x$

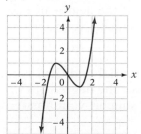

24. $f(x) = x^2 - x - 2$

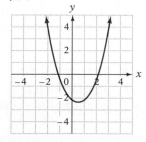

Objective B

Add or subtract. Use a vertical format.

25. $(5x^2 + 2x - 7) + (x^2 - 8x + 12)$
$6x^2 - 6x + 5$

26. $(3x^2 - 2x + 7) + (-3x^2 + 2x - 12)$
-5

27. $(x^2 - 3x + 8) - (2x^2 - 3x + 7)$
$-x^2 + 1$

28. $(2x^2 + 3x - 7) - (5x^2 - 8x - 1)$
$-3x^2 + 11x - 6$

Add or subtract. Use a horizontal format for Exercises 29–32.

29. $(3y^2 - 7y) + (2y^2 - 8y + 2)$
$5y^2 - 15y + 2$

30. $(-2y^2 - 4y - 12) + (5y^2 - 5y)$
$3y^2 - 9y - 12$

31. $(2a^2 - 3a - 7) - (-5a^2 - 2a - 9)$
$7a^2 - a + 2$

32. $(3a^2 - 9a) - (-5a^2 + 7a - 6)$
$8a^2 - 16a + 6$

33. Given $P(x) = x^2 - 3xy + y^2$ and
$R(x) = 2x^2 - 3y^2$, find $P(x) + R(x)$.
$3x^2 - 3xy - 2y^2$

34. Given $P(x) = x^{2n} + 7x^n - 3$ and
$R(x) = -x^{2n} + 2x^n + 8$, find $P(x) + R(x)$.
$9x^n + 5$

35. Given $P(x) = 3x^2 + 2y^2$ and
$R(x) = -5x^2 + 2xy - 3y^2$, find
$P(x) - R(x)$.
$8x^2 - 2xy + 5y^2$

36. Given $P(x) = 2x^{2n} - x^n - 1$ and
$R(x) = 5x^{2n} + 7x^n + 1$, find
$P(x) - R(x)$.
$-3x^{2n} - 8x^n - 2$

37. Given $P(x) = 3x^4 - 3x^3 - x^2$ and
$R(x) = 3x^3 - 7x^2 + 2x$, find
$S(x) = P(x) + R(x)$. Evaluate $S(2)$.
$S(x) = 3x^4 - 8x^2 + 2x$;
$S(2) = 20$

38. Given $P(x) = 3x^4 - 2x + 1$ and
$R(x) = 3x^5 - 5x - 8$, find
$S(x) = P(x) + R(x)$. Evaluate $S(-1)$.
$S(x) = 3x^5 + 3x^4 - 7x - 7$;
$S(-1) = 0$

APPLYING THE CONCEPTS

39. For what value of k is the given equation an identity?
a. $(2x^3 + 3x^2 + kx + 5) - (x^3 + 2x^2 + 3x + 7) = x^3 + x^2 + 5x - 2$
b. $(6x^3 + kx^2 - 2x - 1) - (4x^3 - 3x^2 + 1) = 2x^3 - x^2 - 2x - 2$
a. $k = 8$ b. $k = -4$

40. The deflection D (in inches) of a beam that is uniformly loaded is given by the polynomial function $D(x) = 0.005x^4 - 0.1x^3 + 0.5x^2$, where x is the distance in feet from one end of the beam. See the figure at the right. The maximum deflection occurs when x is the midpoint of the beam. Determine the maximum deflection for the beam in the diagram.
3.125 in.

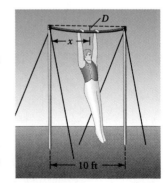

41. If $P(x)$ is a third-degree polynomial and $Q(x)$ is a fourth-degree polynomial, what can be said about the degree of $P(x) + Q(x)$? Give some examples of polynomials that support your answer.

42. If $P(x)$ is a fifth-degree polynomial and $Q(x)$ is a fourth-degree polynomial, what can be said about the degree of $P(x) - Q(x)$? Give some examples of polynomials that support your answer.

6.3 Multiplication of Polynomials

Objective A   To multiply a polynomial by a monomial ....

To multiply a polynomial by a monomial, use the Distributive Property and the Rule for Multiplying Exponential Expressions.

➡ Multiply: $-3a(4a^2 - 5a + 6)$

$$-3a(4a^2 - 5a + 6) = \boxed{-3a(4a^2) - (-3a)(5a) + (-3a)(6)}$$
$$= -12a^3 + 15a^2 - 18a$$

• Use the Distributive Property. This step is frequently done mentally.

Example 1
Multiply: $(5x + 4)(-2x)$

Solution
$(5x + 4)(-2x) = -10x^2 - 8x$

You Try It 1
Multiply: $(-2y + 3)(-4y)$

Your solution
$8y^2 - 12y$

Example 2
Multiply: $2a^2b(4a^2 - 2ab + b^2)$

Solution
$2a^2b(4a^2 - 2ab + b^2)$
$= 8a^4b - 4a^3b^2 + 2a^2b^3$

You Try It 2
Multiply: $-a^2(3a^2 + 2a - 7)$

Your solution
$-3a^4 - 2a^3 + 7a^2$

Solutions on p. S17

Objective B   To multiply two polynomials ....

Multiplication of two polynomials requires the repeated application of the Distributive Property.

$$(y - 2)(y^2 + 3y + 1) = (y - 2)(y^2) + (y - 2)(3y) + (y - 2)(1)$$
$$= y^3 - 2y^2 + 3y^2 - 6y + y - 2$$
$$= y^3 + y^2 - 5y - 2$$

A convenient method of multiplying two polynomials is to use a vertical format similar to that used for multiplication of whole numbers.

$$
\begin{array}{r}
y^2 + 3y + 1 \\
y - 2 \\
\hline
-2y^2 - 6y - 2 \\
y^3 + 3y^2 + y \\
\hline
y^3 + y^2 - 5y - 2
\end{array}
$$

• Multiply $-2(y^2 + 3y + 1)$.
• Multiply $y(y^2 + 3y + 1)$.
• Add the terms in each column.

➡️ Multiply: $(2a^3 + a - 3)(a + 5)$

$$
\begin{array}{r}
2a^3 + a - \;\; 3 \\
a + \;\; 5 \\
\hline
10a^3 \qquad + 5a - 15 \\
2a^4 \qquad + a^2 - 3a \\
\hline
2a^4 + 10a^3 + a^2 + 2a - 15
\end{array}
$$

• Note that spaces are provided in each product so that like terms are in the same column.
• Add the terms in each column.

Example 3
Multiply: $(2b^3 - b + 1)(2b + 3)$

Solution

$$
\begin{array}{r}
2b^3 - b + 1 \\
2b + 3 \\
\hline
6b^3 \qquad - 3b + 3 \\
4b^4 + \qquad - 2b^2 + 2b \\
\hline
4b^4 + 6b^3 - 2b^2 - \;\; b + 3
\end{array}
$$

You Try It 3
Multiply: $(2y^3 + 2y^2 - 3)(3y - 1)$

Your solution
$6y^4 + 4y^3 - 2y^2 - 9y + 3$

Solution on p. S17

Objective C   To multiply two binomials ....

It is frequently necessary to find the product of two binomials. The product can be found using a method called **FOIL**, which is based on the Distributive Property. The letters of FOIL stand for **F**irst, **O**uter, **I**nner, and **L**ast.

➡️ Multiply: $(2x + 3)(x + 5)$

Multiply the **F**irst terms.	$(2x + 3)(x + 5)$	$2x \cdot x = 2x^2$
Multiply the **O**uter terms.	$(2x + 3)(x + 5)$	$2x \cdot 5 = 10x$
Multiply the **I**nner terms.	$(2x + 3)(x + 5)$	$3 \cdot x = 3x$
Multiply the **L**ast terms.	$(2x + 3)(x + 5)$	$3 \cdot 5 = 15$

$$
\begin{array}{ll}
\text{Add the products.} & \quad\quad\quad \text{F} \quad\;\; \text{O} \quad\;\; \text{I} \quad\;\; \text{L} \\
(2x + 3)(x + 5) & = 2x^2 + 10x + 3x + 15 \\
\text{Combine like terms.} & = 2x^2 + 13x + 15
\end{array}
$$

➡️ Multiply: $(4x - 3)(3x - 2)$

$$
\begin{aligned}
(4x - 3)(3x - 2) &= 4x(3x) + 4x(-2) + (-3)(3x) + (-3)(-2) \\
&= 12x^2 - 8x - 9x + 6 \\
&= 12x^2 - 17x + 6
\end{aligned}
$$

• Do this step mentally.

➡️ Multiply: $(3x - 2y)(x + 4y)$

$$
\begin{aligned}
(3x - 2y(x + 4y) &= 3x(x) + 3x(4y) + (-2y)(x) + (-2y)(4y) \\
&= 3x^2 + 12xy - 2xy - 8y^2 \\
&= 3x^2 + 10xy - 8y^2
\end{aligned}
$$

• Do this step mentally.

Example 4

Multiply: $(2a - 1)(3a - 2)$

Solution

$(2a - 1)(3a - 2) = 6a^2 - 4a - 3a + 2$
$= 6a^2 - 7a + 2$

You Try It 4

Multiply: $(4y - 5)(2y - 3)$

Your solution

$8y^2 - 22y + 15$

Example 5

Multiply: $(3x - 2)(4x + 3)$

Solution

$(3x - 2)(4x + 3) = 12x^2 + 9x - 8x - 6$
$= 12x^2 + x - 6$

You Try It 5

Multiply: $(3b + 2)(3b - 5)$

Your solution

$9b^2 - 9b - 10$

Solutions on p. S17

Objective D   ***To multiply binomials that have special products*** ....

Using FOIL, it is possible to find a pattern for the product of the sum and difference of two terms and for the square of a binomial.

The Sum and Difference of Two Terms

$$(a + b)(a - b) = a^2 - ab + ab \quad b^2$$
$$= a^2 - b^2$$

Square of first term ⎯⎯⎯⎯⎯⎯
Square of second term ⎯⎯⎯⎯⎯⎯

The Square of a Binomial

$$(a + b)^2 = (a + b)(a + b) = a^2 + ab + ab + b^2$$
$$= a^2 + 2ab + b^2$$

Square of first term ⎯⎯⎯⎯⎯⎯
Twice the product of the two terms ⎯⎯⎯⎯⎯⎯
Square of the last term ⎯⎯⎯⎯⎯⎯

➡ Multiply: $(2x + 3)(2x - 3)$

$(2x + 3)(2x - 3)$ is the sum and difference of two terms.

$(2x + 3)(2x - 3) = \boxed{(2x)^2 - 3^2}$ • **Do this step mentally.**
$= 4x^2 - 9$

➡ Multiply: $(3x - 2)^2$

$(3x - 2)^2$ is the square of a binomial.

$(3x - 2)^2 = \boxed{(3x)^2 + 2(3x)(-2) + (-2)^2}$ • **Do this step mentally.**
$= 9x^2 - 12x + 4$

Example 6

Multiply: $(4z - 2w)(4z + 2w)$

Solution

$(4z - 2w)(4z + 2w) = 16z^2 - 4w^2$

You Try It 6

Multiply: $(2a + 5c)(2a - 5c)$

Your solution

$4a^2 - 25c^2$

Example 7

Simplify: $(2r - 3s)^2$

Solution

$(2r - 3s)^2 = 4r^2 - 12rs + 9s^2$

You Try It 7

Simplify: $(3x + 2y)^2$

Your solution

$9x^2 + 12xy + 4y^2$

Solutions on p. S17

Objective E   To solve application problems..

Example 8

The length of a rectangle is $(2x + 3)$ ft. The width is $(x - 5)$ ft. Find the area of the rectangle in terms of the variable x.

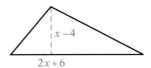

Strategy

To find the area, replace the variables L and W in the equation $A = L \cdot W$ by the given values and solve for A.

Solution

$A = L \cdot W$

$A = (2x + 3)(x - 5)$

$\quad = 2x^2 - 10x + 3x - 15$

$\quad = 2x^2 - 7x - 15$

The area is $(2x^2 - 7x - 15)$ ft².

You Try It 8

The base of a triangle is $(2x + 6)$ ft. The height is $(x - 4)$ ft. Find the area of the triangle in terms of the variable x.

Your strategy

Your solution

$(x^2 - x - 12)$ ft²

Solution on p. S17

6.3 Exercises

· ·

Objective A

Multiply.

1. $x(x - 2)$
$x^2 - 2x$

2. $y(3 - y)$
$-y^2 + 3y$

3. $-x(x + 7)$
$-x^2 - 7x$

4. $-y(7 - y)$
$y^2 - 7y$

5. $3a^2(a - 2)$
$3a^3 - 6a^2$

6. $4b^2(b + 8)$
$4b^3 + 32b^2$

7. $-5x^2(x^2 - x)$
$-5x^4 + 5x^3$

8. $-6y^2(y + 2y^2)$
$-12y^4 - 6y^3$

9. $-x^3(3x^2 - 7)$
$-3x^5 + 7x^3$

10. $-y^4(2y^2 - y^6)$
$y^{10} - 2y^6$

11. $2x(6x^2 - 3x)$
$12x^3 - 6x^2$

12. $3y(4y - y^2)$
$-3y^3 + 12y^2$

13. $(2x - 4)3x$
$6x^2 - 12x$

14. $(3y - 2)y$
$3y^2 - 2y$

15. $(3x + 4)x$
$3x^2 + 4x$

16. $(2x + 1)2x$
$4x^2 + 2x$

17. $-xy(x^2 - y^2)$
$-x^3y + xy^3$

18. $-x^2y(2xy - y^2)$
$-2x^3y^2 + x^2y^3$

19. $x(2x^3 - 3x + 2)$
$2x^4 - 3x^2 + 2x$

20. $y(-3y^2 - 2y + 6)$
$-3y^3 - 2y^2 + 6y$

21. $-a(-2a^2 - 3a - 2)$
$2a^3 + 3a^2 + 2a$

22. $-b(5b^2 + 7b - 35)$
$-5b^3 - 7b^2 + 35b$

23. $x^2(3x^4 - 3x^2 - 2)$
$3x^6 - 3x^4 - 2x^2$

24. $y^3(-4y^3 - 6y + 7)$
$-4y^6 - 6y^4 + 7y^3$

25. $2y^2(-3y^2 - 6y + 7)$
$-6y^4 - 12y^3 + 14y^2$

26. $4x^2(3x^2 - 2x + 6)$
$12x^4 - 8x^3 + 24x^2$

27. $(a^2 + 3a - 4)(-2a)$
$-2a^3 - 6a^2 + 8a$

28. $(b^3 - 2b + 2)(-5b)$
$-5b^4 + 10b^2 - 10b$

29. $-3y^2(-2y^2 + y - 2)$
$6y^4 - 3y^3 + 6y^2$

30. $-5x^2(3x^2 - 3x - 7)$
$-15x^4 + 15x^3 + 35x^2$

31. $xy(x^2 - 3xy + y^2)$
$x^3y - 3x^2y^2 + xy^3$

32. $ab(2a^2 - 4ab - 6b^2)$
$2a^3b - 4a^2b^2 - 6ab^3$

Objective B

Multiply.

33. $(x^2 + 3x + 2)(x + 1)$
$x^3 + 4x^2 + 5x + 2$

34. $(x^2 - 2x + 7)(x - 2)$
$x^3 - 4x^2 + 11x - 14$

35. $(a^2 - 3a + 4)(a - 3)$
$a^3 - 6a^2 + 13a - 12$

36. $(x^2 - 3x + 5)(2x - 3)$
$2x^3 - 9x^2 + 19x - 15$

37. $(-2b^2 - 3b + 4)(b - 5)$
$-2b^3 + 7b^2 + 19b - 20$

38. $(-a^2 + 3a - 2)(2a - 1)$
$-2a^3 + 7a^2 - 7a + 2$

39. $(-2x^2 + 7x - 2)(3x - 5)$
$-6x^3 + 31x^2 - 41x + 10$

40. $(-a^2 - 2a + 3)(2a - 1)$
$-2a^3 - 3a^2 + 8a - 3$

41. $(x^2 + 5)(x - 3)$
$x^3 - 3x^2 + 5x - 15$

42. $(y^2 - 2y)(2y + 5)$
$2y^3 + y^2 - 10y$

43. $(x^3 - 3x + 2)(x - 4)$
$x^4 - 4x^3 - 3x^2 + 14x - 8$

44. $(y^3 + 4y^2 - 8)(2y - 1)$
$2y^4 + 7y^3 - 4y^2 - 16y + 8$

45. $(5y^2 + 8y - 2)(3y - 8)$
$15y^3 - 16y^2 - 70y + 16$

46. $(3y^2 + 3y - 5)(4y - 3)$
$12y^3 + 3y^2 - 29y + 15$

47. $(5a^3 - 5a + 2)(a - 4)$
$5a^4 - 20a^3 - 5a^2 + 22a - 8$

48. $(3b^3 - 5b^2 + 7)(6b - 1)$
$18b^4 - 33b^3 + 5b^2 + 42b - 7$

49. $(y^3 + 2y^2 - 3y + 1)(y + 2)$
$y^4 + 4y^3 + y^2 - 5y + 2$

50. $(2a^3 - 3a^2 + 2a - 1)(2a - 3)$
$4a^4 - 12a^3 + 13a^2 - 8a + 3$

Objective C

Multiply.

51. $(x + 1)(x + 3)$
$x^2 + 4x + 3$

52. $(y + 2)(y + 5)$
$y^2 + 7y + 10$

53. $(a - 3)(a + 4)$
$a^2 + a - 12$

54. $(b - 6)(b + 3)$
$b^2 - 3b - 18$

55. $(y + 3)(y - 8)$
$y^2 - 5y - 24$

56. $(x + 10)(x - 5)$
$x^2 + 5x - 50$

57. $(y - 7)(y - 3)$
$y^2 - 10y + 21$

58. $(a - 8)(a - 9)$
$a^2 - 17a + 72$

59. $(2x + 1)(x + 7)$
$2x^2 + 15x + 7$

60. $(y + 2)(5y + 1)$
$5y^2 + 11y + 2$

61. $(3x - 1)(x + 4)$
$3x^2 + 11x - 4$

62. $(7x - 2)(x + 4)$
$7x^2 + 26x - 8$

63. $(4x - 3)(x - 7)$
$4x^2 - 31x + 21$

64. $(2x - 3)(4x - 7)$
$8x^2 - 26x + 21$

65. $(3y - 8)(y + 2)$
$3y^2 - 2y - 16$

66. $(5y - 9)(y + 5)$
$5y^2 + 16y - 45$

67. $(3x + 7)(3x + 11)$
$9x^2 + 54x + 77$

68. $(5a + 6)(6a + 5)$
$30a^2 + 61a + 30$

69. $(7a - 16)(3a - 5)$
$21a^2 - 83a + 80$

70. $(5a - 12)(3a - 7)$
$15a^2 - 71a + 84$

71. $(3a - 2b)(2a - 7b)$
$6a^2 - 25ab + 14b^2$

72. $(5a - b)(7a - b)$
$35a^2 - 12ab + b^2$

73. $(a - 9b)(2a + 7b)$
$2a^2 - 11ab - 63b^2$

74. $(2a + 5b)(7a - 2b)$
$14a^2 + 31ab - 10b^2$

75. $(10a - 3b)(10a - 7b)$
$100a^2 - 100ab + 21b^2$

76. $(12a - 5b)(3a - 4b)$
$36a^2 - 63ab + 20b^2$

77. $(5x + 12y)(3x + 4y)$
$15x^2 + 56xy + 48y^2$

78. $(11x + 2y)(3x + 7y)$
$33x^2 + 83xy + 14y^2$

79. $(2x - 15y)(7x + 4y)$
$14x^2 - 97xy - 60y^2$

80. $(5x + 2y)(2x - 5y)$
$10x^2 - 21xy - 10y^2$

81. $(8x - 3y)(7x - 5y)$
$56x^2 - 61xy + 15y^2$

82. $(2x - 9y)(8x - 3y)$
$16x^2 - 78xy + 27y^2$

Objective D

Multiply.

83. $(y - 5)(y + 5)$
$y^2 - 25$

84. $(y + 6)(y - 6)$
$y^2 - 36$

85. $(2x + 3)(2x - 3)$
$4x^2 - 9$

86. $(4x - 7)(4x + 7)$
$16x^2 - 49$

87. $(x + 1)^2$
$x^2 + 2x + 1$

88. $(y - 3)^2$
$y^2 - 6y + 9$

89. $(3a - 5)^2$
$9a^2 - 30a + 25$

90. $(6x - 5)^2$
$36x^2 - 60x + 25$

91. $(3x - 7)(3x + 7)$
$9x^2 - 49$

92. $(9x - 2)(9x + 2)$
$81x^2 - 4$

93. $(2a + b)^2$
$4a^2 + 4ab + b^2$

94. $(x + 3y)^2$
$x^2 + 6xy + 9y^2$

95. $(x - 2y)^2$
$x^2 - 4xy + 4y^2$

96. $(2x - 3y)^2$
$4x^2 - 12xy + 9y^2$

97. $(4 - 3y)(4 + 3y)$
$16 - 9y^2$

98. $(4x - 9y)(4x + 9y)$
$16x^2 - 81y^2$

99. $(5x + 2y)^2$
$25x^2 + 20xy + 4y^2$

100. $(2a - 9b)^2$
$4a^2 - 36ab + 81b^2$

Objective E   *Application Problems*

101. The length of a rectangle is $5x$ ft. The width is $(2x - 7)$ ft. Find the area of the rectangle in terms of the variable x.
$(10x^2 - 35x)$ ft²

$5x$
$2x - 7$

102. The width of a rectangle is $(x - 6)$ m. The length is $(2x + 3)$ m. Find the area of the rectangle in terms of the variable x.
$(2x^2 - 9x - 18)$ m²

$2x + 3$
$x - 6$

103. The length of a side of a square is $(2x + 1)$ km. Find the area of the square in terms of the variable x.
$(4x^2 + 4x + 1)$ km^2

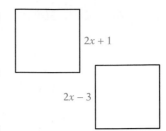

104. The length of a side of a square is $(2x - 3)$ yd. Find the area of the square in terms of the variable x.
$(4x^2 - 12x + 9)$ yd^2

105. The width of a rectangle is $(3x + 1)$ in. The length of the rectangle is twice the width. Find the area of the rectangle in terms of the variable x.
$(18x^2 + 12x + 2)$ in^2

106. The width of a rectangle is $(4x - 3)$ cm. The length of the rectangle is twice the width. Find the area of the rectangle in terms of the variable x.
$(32x^2 - 48x + 18)$ cm^2

107. The base of a triangle is $4x$ m, and the height is $(2x + 5)$ m. Find the area of the triangle in terms of the variable x.
$(4x^2 + 10x)$ m^2

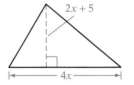

108. The base of a triangle is $(2x + 6)$ in., and the height is $(x - 8)$ in. Find the area of the triangle in terms of the variable x.
$(x^2 - 5x - 24)$ in^2

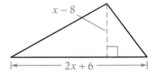

109. An athletic field has dimensions 30 yd by 100 yd. An end zone that is w yd wide borders each end of the field. Express the total area of the field and the end zones in terms of the variable w.
$(3000 + 60w)$ yd^2

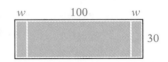

110. A softball diamond has dimensions 45 ft by 45 ft. A base path border x ft wide lies on both the first-base side and the third-base side of the diamond. Express the total area of the softball diamond and the base path in terms of the variable x.
$(2025 + 90x)$ ft^2

APPLYING THE CONCEPTS

Simplify.

111. $(a + b)^2 - (a - b)^2$
$4ab$

112. $(x^2 + x - 3)^2$
$x^4 + 2x^3 - 5x^2 - 6x + 9$

113. $(a + 3)^3$
$a^3 + 9a^2 + 27a + 27$

114. **a.** What polynomial has quotient $3x - 4$ when divided by $4x + 5$?
b. What polynomial has quotient $x^2 + 2x - 1$ when divided by $x + 3$?
a. $12x^2 - x - 20$ b. $x^3 + 5x^2 + 5x - 3$

115. **a.** Add $x^2 + 2x - 3$ to the product of $2x - 5$ and $3x + 1$.
b. Subtract $4x^2 - x - 5$ from the product of $x^2 + x + 3$ and $x - 4$.
a. $7x^2 - 11x - 8$ b. $x^3 - 7x^2 - 7$

6.4 Division of Polynomials

Objective A *To divide polynomials* ....

To divide two polynomials, use a method similar to that used for long division of whole numbers. To check division of polynomials, use

Dividend = (quotient × divisor) + remainder

➡ Divide: $(x^2 + 5x - 7) \div (x + 3)$

Step 1

$$
\begin{array}{r}
x \\
x + 3 \overline{)\, x^2 + 5x - 7} \\
\underline{x^2 + 3x} \quad \downarrow \\
2x - 7
\end{array}
$$

Think: $x\,\overline{)x^2} = \dfrac{x^2}{x} = x$

Multiply: $x(x + 3) = x^2 + 3x$

Subtract: $(x^2 + 5x) - (x^2 + 3x) = 2x$

Bring down the -7.

Step 2

$$
\begin{array}{r}
x + 2 \\
x + 3 \overline{)\, x^2 + 5x - 7} \\
\underline{x^2 + 3x} \\
2x - 7 \\
\underline{2x + 6} \\
-13
\end{array}
$$

Think: $x\,\overline{)2x} = \dfrac{2x}{x} = 2$

Multiply: $2(x + 3) = 2x + 6$

Subtract: $(2x - 7) - (2x + 6) = -13$

The remainder is -13.

Check: (Quotient)(divisor) + remainder

$$= (x + 2)(x + 3) + (-13) = x^2 + 3x + 2x + 6 - 13 = x^2 + 5x - 7$$

$$(x^2 + 5x - 7) \div (x + 3) = x + 2 - \frac{13}{x + 3}$$

➡ Divide: $\dfrac{6 - 6x^2 + 4x^3}{2x + 3}$

INSTRUCTOR NOTE
After you have completed this objective, a possible extra-credit problem might be

$2x - 4 \overline{)\, 3x^3 - 5x^2 - 6x + 8}$.

Arrange the terms in descending order. Note that there is no term of x in $4x^3 - 6x^2 + 6$. Insert a $0x$ for the missing term so that like terms will be in the same columns.

$$
\begin{array}{r}
2x^2 - 6x + 9 \\
2x + 3 \overline{)\, 4x^3 - 6x^2 + 0x + 6} \\
\underline{4x^3 + 6x^2} \\
-12x^2 + 0x \\
\underline{-12x^2 - 18x} \\
18x + 6 \\
\underline{18x + 27} \\
-21
\end{array}
$$

$$\frac{4x^3 - 6x^2 + 6}{2x + 3} = 2x^2 - 6x + 9 - \frac{21}{2x + 3}$$

Example 1

Divide: $\dfrac{12x^2 - 11x + 10}{4x - 5}$

Solution

$$
\begin{array}{r}
3x + 1 \\
4x - 5 \overline{\smash{\big)}\, 12x^2 - 11x + 10} \\
\underline{12x^2 - 15x} \\
4x + 10 \\
\underline{4x - 5} \\
15
\end{array}
$$

$$\frac{12x^2 - 11x + 10}{4x - 5} = 3x + 1 + \frac{15}{4x - 5}$$

You Try It 1

Divide: $\dfrac{15x^2 + 17x - 20}{3x + 4}$

Your solution

$5x - 1 - \dfrac{16}{3x + 4}$

Example 2

Divide: $\dfrac{x^3 + 1}{x + 1}$

Solution

$$
\begin{array}{r}
x^2 - x + 1 \\
x + 1 \overline{\smash{\big)}\, x^3 + 0x^2 + 0x + 1} \\
\underline{x^3 + x^2} \\
- x^2 + 0x \\
\underline{- x^2 - x} \\
x + 1 \\
\underline{x + 1} \\
0
\end{array}
$$

• Insert zeros for the coefficients of the missing terms.

$$\frac{x^3 + 1}{x + 1} = x^2 - x + 1$$

You Try It 2

Divide: $\dfrac{3x^3 + 8x^2 - 6x + 2}{3x - 1}$

Your solution

$x^2 + 3x - 1 + \dfrac{1}{3x - 1}$

Example 3

Divide:
$(2x^4 - 7x^3 + 3x^2 + 4x - 5) \div (x^2 - 2x - 2)$

Solution

$$
\begin{array}{r}
2x^2 - 3x + 1 \\
x^2 - 2x - 2 \overline{\smash{\big)}\, 2x^4 - 7x^3 + 3x^2 + 4x - 5} \\
\underline{2x^4 - 4x^3 - 4x^2} \\
- 3x^3 + 7x^2 + 4x \\
\underline{- 3x^3 + 6x^2 + 6x} \\
x^2 - 2x - 5 \\
\underline{x^2 - 2x - 2} \\
- 3
\end{array}
$$

$(2x^4 - 7x^3 + 3x^2 + 4x - 5) \div (x^2 - 2x - 2)$

$\quad = 2x^2 - 3x + 1 - \dfrac{3}{x^2 - 2x - 2}$

You Try It 3

Divide:
$(3x^4 - 11x^3 + 16x^2 - 16x + 8) \div (x^2 - 3x + 2)$

Your solution

$3x^2 - 2x + 4$

Solutions on p. S18

Objective B   To divide polynomials using synthetic division.. HM³

Synthetic division is a shorter method of dividing a polynomial by a binomial of the form $x - a$.

➡ Divide $(3x^2 - 4x + 6) \div (x - 2)$ by using long division.

$$
\begin{array}{r}
3x + 2 \\
x - 2 \overline{\smash{)}\, 3x^2 - 4x + 6} \\
\underline{3x^2 - 6x} \\
2x + 6 \\
\underline{2x - 4} \\
10
\end{array}
$$

$$(3x^2 - 4x + 6) \div (x - 2) = 3x + 2 + \frac{10}{x - 2}$$

The variables can be omitted because the position of a term indicates the power of the term.

$$
\begin{array}{r}
3 \quad\ \ 2 \\
-2\overline{\smash{)}\, 3 \ \ -4 \quad\ \ 6} \\
\underline{3 \ \ -6} \\
2 \quad\ \ 6 \\
\underline{2 \ \ -4} \\
10
\end{array}
$$

Each number shown in color above is exactly the same as the number above it. Removing the colored numbers condenses the vertical spacing.

$$
\begin{array}{r}
3 \quad\ \ 2 \\
-2\overline{\smash{)}\, 3 \ \ -4 \quad\ \ 6} \\
-6 \ \ -4 \\
\underline{} \\
2 \quad\ 10
\end{array}
$$

The number in color on the top row is the same as the one in the bottom row. Writing the 3 from the top row in the bottom row allows the spacing to be condensed even further.

$$
\begin{array}{c|ccc}
-2 & 3 & -4 & 6 \\
& & -6 & -4 \\
\hline
& 3 & 2 & 10
\end{array}
$$

$\underbrace{\qquad\qquad}_{\substack{\text{Terms of}\\\text{the quotient}}} \quad \underbrace{\qquad}_{\text{Remainder}}$

Because the degree of the dividend $(3x^2 - 4x + 6)$ is 2 and the degree of the divisor $(x - 2)$ is 1, the degree of the quotient is $2 - 1 = 1$. This means that, using the terms of the quotient given above, the quotient is $3x + 2$. The remainder is 10.

In general, the degree of the quotient of two polynomials is the difference between the degree of the dividend and the degree of the divisor.

By replacing the constant term in the divisor by its additive inverse, we may add rather than subtract terms. This is illustrated in the following example.

➡ Divide: $(3x^3 + 6x^2 - x - 2) \div (x + 3)$

The additive inverse of the binomial constant

Coefficients of the polynomial

$$
\begin{array}{c|cccc}
-3 & 3 & 6 & -1 & -2 \\
& \downarrow & & & \\
\hline
& 3 & & &
\end{array}
$$

• Bring down the 3.

$$
\begin{array}{c|cccc}
-3 & 3 & 6 & -1 & -2 \\
& & -9 & & \\
\hline
& 3 & -3 & &
\end{array}
$$

• Multiply $-3(3)$ and add the product to 6.

$$
\begin{array}{c|cccc}
-3 & 3 & 6 & -1 & -2 \\
& & -9 & 9 & \\
\hline
& 3 & -3 & 8 &
\end{array}
$$

• Multiply $-3(-3)$ and add the product to -1.

$$
\begin{array}{c|cccc}
-3 & 3 & 6 & -1 & -2 \\
& & -9 & 9 & -24 \\
\hline
& 3 & -3 & 8 & -26
\end{array}
$$

• Multiply $-3(8)$ and add the product to -2.

$$\underbrace{}_{\substack{\text{Terms of} \\ \text{the quotient}}} \qquad \underbrace{}_{\text{Remainder}}$$

The degree of the dividend is 3 and the degree of the divisor is 1. Therefore, the degree of the quotient is $3 - 1 = 2$.

$$(3x^3 + 6x^2 - x - 2) \div (x + 3) = 3x^2 - 3x + 8 - \frac{26}{x + 3}$$

➡ Divide: $(2x^3 - x + 2) \div (x - 2)$

The additive inverse of the binomial constant

Coefficients of the polynomial

$$
\begin{array}{c|cccc}
2 & 2 & 0 & -1 & 2 \\
& \downarrow & & & \\
\hline
& 2 & & &
\end{array}
$$

• Insert a 0 for the missing term and bring down the 2.

$$
\begin{array}{c|cccc}
2 & 2 & 0 & -1 & 2 \\
& & 4 & & \\
\hline
& 2 & 4 & &
\end{array}
$$

• Multiply $2(2)$ and add the product to 0.

$$
\begin{array}{c|cccc}
2 & 2 & 0 & -1 & 2 \\
& & 4 & 8 & \\
\hline
& 2 & 4 & 7 &
\end{array}
$$

• Multiply $2(4)$ and add the product to -1.

$$
\begin{array}{c|cccc}
2 & 2 & 0 & -1 & 2 \\
& & 4 & 8 & 14 \\
\hline
& 2 & 4 & 7 & 16
\end{array}
$$

• Multiply $2(7)$ and add the product to 2.

$$\underbrace{}_{\substack{\text{Terms of} \\ \text{the quotient}}} \qquad \underbrace{}_{\text{Remainder}}$$

$$(2x^3 - x + 2) \div (x - 2) = 2x^2 + 4x + 7 + \frac{16}{x - 2}$$

Example 4
Divide by using synthetic division:
$(7 - 3x + 5x^2) \div (x - 1)$

Solution
Arrange the coefficients in decreasing powers of x.

$$
\begin{array}{r|rrr}
1 & 5 & -3 & 7 \\
  &   & 5 & 2 \\
\hline
  & 5 & 2 & 9
\end{array}
$$

$(5x^2 - 3x + 7) \div (x - 1) = 5x + 2 + \dfrac{9}{x - 1}$

You Try It 4
Divide by using synthetic division:
$(8x + 6x^2 - 5) \div (x + 2)$

Your solution

$6x - 4 + \dfrac{3}{x + 2}$

Example 5
Divide by using synthetic division:
$(2x^3 + 4x^2 - 3x + 12) \div (x + 4)$

Solution

$$
\begin{array}{r|rrrr}
-4 & 2 & 4 & -3 & 12 \\
   &   & -8 & 16 & -52 \\
\hline
   & 2 & -4 & 13 & -40
\end{array}
$$

$(2x^3 + 4x^2 - 3x + 12) \div (x + 4)$

$= 2x^2 - 4x + 13 - \dfrac{40}{x + 4}$

You Try It 5
Divide by using synthetic division:
$(5x^3 - 12x^2 - 8x + 16) \div (x - 2)$

Your solution

$5x^2 - 2x - 12 - \dfrac{8}{x - 2}$

Example 6
Divide by using synthetic division:
$(3x^4 - 8x^2 + 2x + 1) \div (x + 2)$

Solution
Insert a zero for the missing term.

$$
\begin{array}{r|rrrrr}
-2 & 3 & 0 & -8 & 2 & 1 \\
   &   & -6 & 12 & -8 & 12 \\
\hline
   & 3 & -6 & 4 & -6 & 13
\end{array}
$$

$(3x^4 - 8x^2 + 2x + 1) \div (x + 2)$

$= 3x^3 - 6x^2 + 4x - 6 + \dfrac{13}{x + 2}$

You Try It 6
Divide by using synthetic division:
$(2x^4 - 3x^3 - 8x^2 - 2) \div (x - 3)$

Your solution

$2x^3 + 3x^2 + x + 3 + \dfrac{7}{x - 3}$

Solutions on p. S18

Objective C   **To evaluate a polynomial using synthetic division** ....

A polynomial can be evaluated by using synthetic division. Consider the polynomial $P(x) = 2x^4 - 3x^3 + 4x^2 - 5x + 1$. One way to evaluate the polynomial when $x = 2$ is to replace x by 2 and then simplify the numerical expression.

$$P(x) = 2x^4 - 3x^3 + 4x^2 - 5x + 1$$

$$
\begin{aligned}
P(2) &= 2(2)^4 - 3(2)^3 + 4(2)^2 - 5(2) + 1 \\
&= 2(16) - 3(8) + 4(4) - 5(2) + 1 \\
&= 32 - 24 + 16 - 10 + 1 \\
&= 15
\end{aligned}
$$

Now use synthetic division to divide $(2x^4 - 3x^3 + 4x^2 - 5x + 1) \div (x - 2)$.

$$
\begin{array}{r|rrrr|r}
2 & 2 & -3 & 4 & -5 & 1 \\
  &   & 4 & 2 & 12 & 14 \\
\hline
  & 2 & 1 & 6 & 7 & 15
\end{array}
$$

$$\underbrace{\qquad\qquad\qquad}_{\substack{\text{Terms of} \\ \text{the quotient}}} \qquad \underbrace{\quad}_{\text{Remainder}}$$

Note that the remainder is 15, which is the same value as $P(2)$. This is not a coincidence. The following theorem states that this situation is always true.

Remainder Theorem

If the polynomial $P(x)$ is divided by $x - a$, the remainder is $P(a)$.

➡ Use the Remainder Theorem to evaluate $P(x) = x^4 - 3x^2 + 4x - 5$ when $x = -2$.

The value at which the polynomial is evaluated

$$
\begin{array}{r|rrrrr}
-2 & 1 & 0 & -3 & 4 & -5 \\
   &   & -2 & 4 & -2 & -4 \\
\hline
   & 1 & -2 & 1 & 2 & -9
\end{array}
$$

• A 0 is inserted for the x^3 term.

The remainder

$$P(-2) = -9$$

Example 7

Use the Remainder Theorem to evaluate $P(x) = -x^4 + 3x^3 + 2x^2 - x - 5$ when $x = -2$.

Solution

$$
\begin{array}{r|rrrrr}
-2 & -1 & 3   & 2 & -1 & -5 \\
   &   & 2   & -10 & 16 & -30 \\
\hline
   & -1 & 5   & -8 & 15 & -35
\end{array}
$$

$$P(-2) = -35$$

You Try It 7

Use the Remainder Theorem to evaluate $P(x) = 2x^3 - 5x^2 + 7$ when $x = -3$.

Your solution

-92

Solution on p. S18

6.4 Exercises

. . . .

Objective A

Divide by using long division.

1. $(x^2 + 3x - 40) \div (x - 5)$
$x + 8$

2. $(x^2 - 14x + 24) \div (x - 2)$
$x - 12$

3. $(x^3 - 3x^2 + 2) \div (x - 3)$
$x^2 + \dfrac{2}{x - 3}$

4. $(x^3 + 4x^2 - 8) \div (x + 4)$
$x^2 - \dfrac{8}{x + 4}$

5. $(6x^2 + 13x + 8) \div (2x + 1)$
$3x + 5 + \dfrac{3}{2x + 1}$

6. $(12x^2 + 13x - 14) \div (3x - 2)$
$4x + 7$

7. $(10x^2 + 9x - 5) \div (2x - 1)$
$5x + 7 + \dfrac{2}{2x - 1}$

8. $(18x^2 - 3x + 2) \div (3x + 2)$
$6x - 5 + \dfrac{12}{3x + 2}$

9. $(8x^3 - 9) \div (2x - 3)$
$4x^2 + 6x + 9 + \dfrac{18}{2x - 3}$

10. $(64x^3 + 4) \div (4x + 2)$
$16x^2 - 8x + 4 - \dfrac{4}{4x + 2}$

11. $(6x^4 - 13x^2 - 4) \div (2x^2 - 5)$
$3x^2 + 1 + \dfrac{1}{2x^2 - 5}$

12. $(12x^4 - 11x^2 + 10) \div (3x^2 + 1)$
$4x^2 - 5 + \dfrac{15}{3x^2 + 1}$

13. $\dfrac{-10 - 33x + 3x^3 - 8x^2}{3x + 1}$
$x^2 - 3x - 10$

14. $\dfrac{10 - 49x + 38x^2 - 8x^3}{1 - 4x}$
$2x^2 - 9x + 10$

15. $\dfrac{x^3 - 5x^2 + 7x - 4}{x - 3}$
$x^2 - 2x + 1 - \dfrac{1}{x - 3}$

16. $\dfrac{2x^3 - 3x^2 + 6x + 4}{2x + 1}$
$x^2 - 2x + 4$

17. $\dfrac{16x^2 - 13x^3 + 2x^4 + 20 - 9x}{x - 5}$

$2x^3 - 3x^2 + x - 4$

18. $\dfrac{x - x^2 + 5x^3 + 3x^4 - 2}{x + 2}$

$3x^3 - x^2 + x - 1$

19. $\dfrac{2x^3 + 4x^2 - x + 2}{x^2 + 2x - 1}$

$2x + \dfrac{x + 2}{x^2 + 2x - 1}$

20. $\dfrac{3x^3 - 2x^2 + 5x - 4}{x^2 - x + 3}$

$3x + 1 + \dfrac{-3x - 7}{x^2 - x + 3}$

21. $\dfrac{x^4 + 2x^3 - 3x^2 - 6x + 2}{x^2 - 2x - 1}$

$x^2 + 4x + 6 + \dfrac{10x + 8}{x^2 - 2x - 1}$

22. $\dfrac{x^4 - 3x^3 + 4x^2 - x + 1}{x^2 + x - 3}$

$x^2 - 4x + 11 + \dfrac{-24x + 34}{x^2 + x - 3}$

23. $\dfrac{x^4 + 3x^2 - 4x + 5}{x^2 + 2x + 3}$

$x^2 - 2x + 4 + \dfrac{-6x - 7}{x^2 + 2x + 3}$

24. $\dfrac{x^4 + 2x^3 - x + 2}{x^2 - x - 1}$

$x^2 + 3x + 4 + \dfrac{6x + 6}{x^2 - x - 1}$

Objective B

Divide by using synthetic division.

25. $(2x^2 - 6x - 8) \div (x + 1)$
$2x - 8$

26. $(3x^2 + 19x + 20) \div (x + 5)$
$3x + 4$

27. $(3x^2 - 14x + 16) \div (x - 2)$
$3x - 8$

28. $(4x^2 - 23x + 28) \div (x - 4)$
$4x - 7$

29. $(3x^2 - 4) \div (x - 1)$
$3x + 3 - \dfrac{1}{x - 1}$

30. $(4x^2 - 8) \div (x - 2)$
$4x + 8 + \dfrac{8}{x - 2}$

31. $(2x^3 - x^2 + 6x + 9) \div (x + 1)$
$2x^2 - 3x + 9$

32. $(3x^3 + 10x^2 + 6x - 4) \div (x + 2)$
$3x^2 + 4x - 2$

33. $(18 + x - 4x^3) \div (2 - x)$

$4x^2 + 8x + 15 + \dfrac{12}{x - 2}$

34. $(12 - 3x^2 + x^3) \div (x + 3)$

$x^2 - 6x + 18 - \dfrac{42}{x + 3}$

35. $(2x^3 + 5x^2 - 5x + 20) \div (x + 4)$

$2x^2 - 3x + 7 - \dfrac{8}{x + 4}$

36. $(5x^3 + 3x^2 - 17x + 6) \div (x + 2)$

$5x^2 - 7x - 3 + \dfrac{12}{x + 2}$

37. $\dfrac{5 + 5x - 8x^2 + 4x^3 - 3x^4}{2 - x}$

$3x^3 + 2x^2 + 12x + 19 + \dfrac{33}{x - 2}$

38. $\dfrac{3 - 13x - 5x^2 + 9x^3 - 2x^4}{3 - x}$

$2x^3 - 3x^2 - 4x + 1$

39. $\dfrac{3x^4 + 3x^3 - x^2 + 3x + 2}{x + 1}$

$3x^3 - x + 4 - \dfrac{2}{x + 1}$

40. $\dfrac{4x^4 + 12x^3 - x^2 - x + 2}{x + 3}$

$4x^3 - x + 2 - \dfrac{4}{x + 3}$

41. $\dfrac{2x^4 - x^2 + 2}{x - 3}$

$2x^3 + 6x^2 + 17x + 51 + \dfrac{155}{x - 3}$

42. $\dfrac{x^4 - 3x^3 - 30}{x + 2}$

$x^3 - 5x^2 + 10x - 20 + \dfrac{10}{x + 2}$

Objective C

Use the Remainder Theorem to evaluate the polynomial.

43. $P(x) = 2x^2 - 3x - 1; P(3)$

8

44. $Q(x) = 3x^2 - 5x - 1; Q(2)$

1

45. $R(x) = x^3 - 2x^2 + 3x - 1; R(4)$

43

46. $F(x) = x^3 + 4x^2 - 3x + 2; F(3)$

56

47. $P(z) = 2z^3 - 4z^2 + 3z - 1; P(-2)$

-39

48. $R(t) = 3t^3 + t^2 - 4t + 2; R(-3)$

-58

49. $Z(p) = 2p^3 - p^2 + 3; Z(-3)$
-60

50. $P(y) = 3y^3 + 2y^2 - 5; P(-2)$
-21

51. $Q(x) = x^4 + 3x^3 - 2x^2 + 4x - 9; Q(2)$
31

52. $Y(z) = z^4 - 2z^3 - 3z^2 - z + 7; Y(3)$
4

53. $F(x) = 2x^4 - x^3 + 2x - 5; F(-3)$
178

54. $Q(x) = x^4 - 2x^3 + 4x - 2; Q(-2)$
22

55. $P(x) = x^3 - 3; P(5)$
122

56. $S(t) = 4t^3 + 5; S(-4)$
-251

57. $R(t) = 4t^4 - 3t^2 + 5; R(-3)$
302

58. $P(z) = 2z^4 + z^2 - 3; P(-4)$
525

59. $Q(x) = x^5 - 4x^3 - 2x^2 + 5x - 2; Q(2)$
0

60. $T(x) = 2x^5 + 4x^4 - x^2 + 4; T(3)$
805

61. $R(x) = 2x^5 - x^3 + 4x - 1; R(-2)$
-65

62. $P(x) = x^5 - x^3 + 4x + 1; P(-3)$
-227

APPLYING THE CONCEPTS

63. Divide by using long division.

a. $\dfrac{a^3 + b^3}{a + b}$
$a^2 - ab + b^2$

b. $\dfrac{x^5 + y^5}{x + y}$
$x^4 - x^3y + x^2y^2 - xy^3 + y^4$

c. $\dfrac{x^6 - y^6}{x + y}$
$x^5 - x^4y + x^3y^2 - x^2y^3 + xy^4 - y^5$

64. For what value of k will the remainder be zero?

a. $(x^3 - x^2 - 3x + k) \div (x + 3)$
$k = 27$

b. $(2x^3 - x + k) \div (x - 1)$
$k = -1$

65. Divide.

a. $(2x^3 + 7x^2 + 2x - 8) \div (4x + 8)$
$\dfrac{1}{2}x^2 + \dfrac{3}{4}x - 1$

b. $(4x^3 + 13x^2 - 22x + 24) \div (6x - 12)$
$\dfrac{2}{3}x^2 + \dfrac{7}{2}x + \dfrac{10}{3} + \dfrac{64}{6x - 12}$

c. $(2x^4 - 3x^3 + 4x^2 + x - 10) \div (x^2 - x + 1)$
$2x^2 - x + 1 + \dfrac{3x - 11}{x^2 - x + 1}$

d. $(x^4 + 4x^3 + 2x^2 - x + 5) \div (x^2 - 2x - 3)$
$x^2 + 6x + 17 + \dfrac{51x + 56}{x^2 - 2x - 3}$

66. Show how synthetic division can be modified so that the divisor can be of the form $ax + b$.

Focus on Problem Solving

Dimensional Analysis

In solving application problems, it may be useful to include the units in order to organize the problem so that the answer is in the proper units. Using units to organize and check the correctness of an application is called **dimensional analysis**. We use the operations of multiplying units and dividing units in applying dimensional analysis to application problems.

The Rule for Multiplying Exponential Expressions states that we multiply two expressions with the same base by adding the exponents.

$$x^4 \cdot x^6 = x^{4+6} = x^{10}$$

In calculations that involve quantities, the units are operated on algebraically.

➡ A rectangle measures 3 m by 5 m. Find the area of the rectangle.

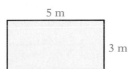

$$A = LW = (3 \text{ m})(5 \text{ m}) = (3 \cdot 5)(\text{m} \cdot \text{m}) = 15 \text{ m}^2$$

The area of the rectangle is 15 m² (square meters).

➡ A box measures 10 cm by 5 cm by 3 cm. Find the volume of the box.

$$V = LWH = (10 \text{ cm})(5 \text{ cm})(3 \text{ cm}) = (10 \cdot 5 \cdot 3)(\text{cm} \cdot \text{cm} \cdot \text{cm}) = 150 \text{ cm}^3$$

The volume of the box is 150 cm³ (cubic centimeters).

➡ Find the area of a square whose side measures $(3x + 5)$ in.

$$A = s^2 = [(3x + 5) \text{ in.}]^2 = (3x + 5)^2 \text{ in}^2 = (9x^2 + 30x + 25) \text{ in}^2$$

The area of the square is $(9x^2 + 30x + 25)$ in² (square inches).

Dimensional analysis is used in the conversion of units.

The following example converts the unit miles to feet. The equivalent measures 1 mi = 5280 ft are used to form the following rates, which are called conversion factors: $\dfrac{1 \text{ mi}}{5280 \text{ ft}}$ and $\dfrac{5280 \text{ ft}}{1 \text{ mi}}$. Because 1 mi = 5280 ft, both of the conversion factors $\dfrac{1 \text{ mi}}{5280 \text{ ft}}$ and $\dfrac{5280 \text{ ft}}{1 \text{ mi}}$ are equal to 1.

To convert 3 mi to feet, multiply 3 mi by the conversion factor $\dfrac{5280 \text{ ft}}{1 \text{ mi}}$.

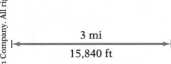

$$3 \text{ mi} = 3 \text{ mi} \cdot 1 = \frac{3 \text{ mi}}{1} \cdot \frac{5280 \text{ ft}}{1 \text{ mi}} = \frac{3 \text{ mi} \cdot 5280 \text{ ft}}{1 \text{ mi}} = 3 \cdot 5280 \text{ ft} = 15{,}840 \text{ ft}$$

There are two important points in the above illustration. First, you can think of dividing the numerator and denominator by the common unit "mile" just as you would divide the numerator and denominator of a fraction by a common factor.

Second, the conversion factor $\dfrac{5280 \text{ ft}}{1 \text{ mi}}$ is equal to 1, and multiplying an expression by 1 does not change the value of the expression.

In the application problem that follows, the units are kept in the problem while the problem is worked.

In 1980, a horse named Fiddle Isle ran a 1.5-mile race in 2.38 min. Find Fiddle Isle's average speed for that race in miles per hour. Round to the nearest tenth.

Strategy   To find the average speed, use the formula $r = \dfrac{d}{t}$, where r is the speed, d is the distance, and t is the time. Use the conversion factor $\dfrac{60 \text{ min}}{1 \text{ h}}$.

Solution $r = \dfrac{d}{t} = \dfrac{1.5 \text{ mi}}{2.38 \text{ min}} = \dfrac{1.5 \text{ mi}}{2.38 \text{ min}} \cdot \dfrac{60 \text{ min}}{1 \text{ h}}$

$= \dfrac{90 \text{ mi}}{2.38 \text{ h}} \approx 37.8 \text{ mph}$

Fiddle Isle's average speed was 37.8 mph.

Try each of the following problems. Round to the nearest tenth.

1. Convert 88 ft/s to miles per hour.

2. Convert 8 m/s to kilometers per hour (1 km = 1000 m).

3. A carpet is to be placed in a meeting hall that is 36 ft wide and 80 ft long. At $21.50 per square yard, how much will it cost to carpet the meeting hall?

4. A carpet is to be placed in a room that is 20 ft wide and 30 ft long. At $22.25 per square yard, how much will it cost to carpet the area?

5. Find the number of gallons of water in a fish tank that is 36 in. long and 24 in. wide and is filled to a depth of 16 in. (1 gal = 231 in^3).

6. Find the number of gallons of water in a fish tank that is 24 in. long and 18 in. wide and is filled to a depth of 12 in. (1 gal = 231 in^3).

7. A $\frac{1}{4}$-acre commercial lot is on sale for $2.15 per square foot. Find the sale price of the commercial lot (1 acre = 43,560 ft^2).

8. A 0.75-acre industrial parcel was sold for $98,010. Find the parcel's price per square foot (1 acre = 43,560 ft^2).

9. A new driveway will require 800 ft^3 of concrete. Concrete is ordered by the cubic yard. How much concrete should be ordered?

10. A piston-engined dragster traveled 440 yd in 4.936 s at Ennis, Texas, on October 9, 1988. Find the average speed of the dragster in miles per hour.

11. The Marianas Trench in the Pacific Ocean is the deepest part of the ocean. The depth is 6.85 mi. The speed of sound under water is 4700 ft/s. Find the time it takes sound to travel from the surface to the bottom of the Marianas Trench and back.

Projects and Group Activities

Pascal's Triangle

Simplifying the power of a binomial is called *expanding the binomial*. The expansion of the first three powers of a binomial is shown below.

$$(a + b)^1 = a + b$$

$$(a + b)^2 = (a + b)(a + b) = a^2 + 2ab + b^2$$

$$(a + b)^3 = (a + b)^2(a + b) = (a^2 + 2ab + b^2)(a + b) = a^3 + 3a^2b + 3ab^2 + b^3$$

Find $(a + b)^4$. [*Hint*: $(a + b)^4 = (a + b)^3(a + b)$]

Find $(a + b)^5$. [*Hint*: $(a + b)^5 = (a + b)^4(a + b)$]

If we continue in this way, the results for $(a + b)^6$ are

$$(a + b)^6 = a^6 + 6a^5b + 15a^4b^2 + 20a^3b^3 + 15a^2b^4 + 6ab^5 + b^6$$

Now expand $(a + b)^8$. Before you begin, see if you can find a pattern that will assist in writing the expansion of $(a + b)^8$ without having to multiply it out. Here are some hints.

1. Write out the variable terms of each binomial expansion from $(a + b)^1$ through $(a + b)^6$. Observe how the exponents on the variables change.

2. Write out the coefficients of all the terms without the variable parts. It will be helpful to make a triangular arrangement as shown at the left. Note that each row begins and ends with a 1. Also note in the two shaded regions that any number in a row is the sum of the two closest numbers above it. For instance, $1 + 5 = 6$ and $6 + 4 = 10$.

```
      1   1
    1   2   1
  1   3   3   1
1   4   6   4   1
1   5  10  10   5   1
1   6  15  20  15   6   1
```

The triangle of numbers shown at the left is called Pascal's Triangle. To find the expansion of $(a + b)^8$, you need to find the eighth row of Pascal's Triangle. First find row seven. Then find row eight and use the patterns you have observed to write the expansion $(a + b)^8$.

Pascal's Triangle has been the subject of extensive analysis, and many patterns have been found. See if you can find some of them. You might check the Internet, where you will find some web sites with information on Pascal's Triangle.

Chapter Summary

Key Words

A *monomial* is a number, a variable, or a product of a number and variables. The *degree of a monomial* is the sum of the exponents of the variables.

An *exponential expression is in simplest form* when it is written with only positive exponents.

A number written in *scientific notation* is a number written in the form $a \times 10^n$, where $1 \leq a < 10$.

A *polynomial* is a variable expression in which the terms are monomials. A polynomial of two terms is a *binomial*. A polynomial of three terms is a *trinomial*. The *degree of a polynomial* is the greatest of the degrees of any of its terms. A polynomial in one variable is usually written in *descending order,* which means that the terms are arranged so that the exponents of the variable decrease from left to right.

A *polynomial function* is an expression whose terms are monomials. A *linear function* is given by the equation $f(x) = mx + b$. A second-degree polynomial function, called a *quadratic function,* is given by the equation $f(x) = ax^2 + bx + c, a \neq 0$. A third-degree polynomial function is called a *cubic function*. The *leading coefficient* of a polynomial function is the coefficient of the variable with the largest exponent.

The product of two binomials can be found using the *FOIL* method, which is based on the Distributive Property. The letters of FOIL stand for First, Outer, Inner, and Last.

Synthetic division is a shorter method of dividing a polynomial by a binomial of the form $x - a$. This method uses only the coefficients of the variable terms.

Essential Rules

Rule for Multiplying Exponential Expressions	$x^m \cdot x^n = x^{m+n}$
Rule for Simplifying Powers of Exponential Expressions	$(x^m)^n = x^{mn}$
Rule for Simplifying Powers of Products	$(x^m y^n)^p = x^{mp} y^{np}$
Definition of Zero as an Exponent	If $x \neq 0$, then $x^0 = 1$.
Definition of a Negative Exponent	$x^{-n} = \dfrac{1}{x^n}$ and $\dfrac{1}{x^{-n}} = x^n$, $x \neq 0$
Rule for Dividing Exponential Expressions	$\dfrac{x^m}{x^n} = x^{m-n}, x \neq 0$
Rule for Simplifying Powers of Quotients	$\left(\dfrac{x^m}{y^n}\right)^p = \dfrac{x^{mp}}{y^{np}}, y \neq 0$
The Sum and Difference of Two Terms	$(a + b)(a - b) = a^2 - b^2$
The Square of a Binomial	$(a + b)^2 = a^2 + 2ab + b^2$
Remainder Theorem	If the polynomial $P(x)$ is divided by $x - a$, then the remainder is $P(a)$.

Dividend = (quotient × divisor) + remainder

Chapter Review

1. Multiply: $(-2a^2b^4)(3ab^2)$

    $-6a^3b^6$ [6.1A]

2. Simplify: $(-3x^2y^3)^2$

    $9x^4y^6$ [6.1A]

3. Simplify: $\dfrac{(2a^4b^{-3}c^2)^3}{(2a^3b^2c^{-1})^4}$

    $\dfrac{c^{10}}{2b^{17}}$ [6.1B]

4. Write 2.54×10^{-3} in decimal notation.

    0.00254   [6.1C]

5. Given $P(x) = 2x^3 - x + 7$, find $P(-2)$.

    -7 [6.2A]

6. Subtract: $(5x^2 - 8xy + 2y^2) - (x^2 - 3y^2)$

    $4x^2 - 8xy + 5y^2$ [6.2B]

7. Simplify: $(2x^{-1}y^2z^5)(-3x^3yz^{-3})^2$

    $\dfrac{18x^5y^4}{z}$ [6.1B]

8. Multiply: $(2a^{12}b^3)(-9b^2c^6)(3ac)$

    $-54a^{13}b^5c^7$ [6.1A]

9. Graph: $f(x) = x^2 + 1$

    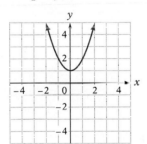

    [6.2A]

10. Identify (a) the leading coefficient, (b) the constant term, and (c) the degree of the polynomial $P(x) = 3x^5 - 3x^2 + 7x + 8$.

    a. 3
    b. 8
    c. 5   [6.2A]

11. Use the Remainder Theorem to evaluate $P(x) = x^3 - 2x^2 + 3x - 5$ when $x = 2$.

    1   [6.4C]

12. Multiply: $-2x(4x^2 + 7x - 9)$

    $-8x^3 - 14x^2 + 18x$ [6.3A]

13. Multiply: $2ab^3(4a^2 - 2ab + 3b^2)$

    $8a^3b^3 - 4a^2b^4 + 6ab^5$ [6.3A]

14. Multiply: $(3y^2 + 4y - 7)(2y + 3)$

    $6y^3 + 17y^2 - 2y - 21$ [6.3B]

15. Multiply: $(5a - 7)(2a + 9)$

    $10a^2 + 31a - 63$ [6.3C]

16. Write 0.000000127 in scientific notation.

    1.27×10^{-7} [6.1C]

17. Simplify: $(5y - 7)^2$

$25y^2 - 70y + 49$ [6.3D]

18. Divide: $\dfrac{15x^2 + 2x - 2}{3x - 2}$

$5x + 4 + \dfrac{6}{3x - 2}$ [6.4A]

19. Divide: $\dfrac{4x^3 + 27x^2 + 10x + 2}{x + 6}$

$4x^2 + 3x - 8 + \dfrac{50}{x + 6}$ [6.4B]

20. Divide: $\dfrac{x^4 - 4}{x - 4}$

$x^3 + 4x^2 + 16x + 64 + \dfrac{252}{x - 4}$ [6.4B]

21. Write 8.1×10^9 in decimal notation.

8,100,000,000   [6.1C]

22. Simplify: $\dfrac{-18a^6b}{27a^3b^4}$

$-\dfrac{2a^3}{3b^3}$ [6.1B]

23. Multiply: $(5a + 2b)(5a - 2b)$

$25a^2 - 4b^2$ [6.3D]

24. Use the Remainder Theorem to evaluate $P(x) = -2x^3 + 2x^2 - 4$ when $x = -3$.

68   [6.4C]

25. Add: $(12y^2 + 17y - 4) + (9y^2 - 13y + 3)$

$21y^2 + 4y - 1$ [6.2B]

26. Multiply: $(6b^3 - 2b^2 - 5)(2b^2 - 1)$

$12b^5 - 4b^4 - 6b^3 - 8b^2 + 5$ [6.3B]

27. Multiply: $(a + 7)(a - 7)$

$a^2 - 49$ [6.3D]

28. Write 765,000,000,000 in scientific notation.

7.65×10^{11} [6.1C]

29. The length of a Ping-Pong table is 1 ft less than twice the width of the table. Let w represent the width of the Ping-Pong table. Express the area of the table in terms of the variable w.
$(2w^2 - w)$ ft^2 [6.3E]

30. The most distant object visible from Earth without the aid of a telescope is the Great Galaxy of Andromeda. It takes light from this galaxy 2.2×10^6 years to travel to Earth. Light travels about 6.7×10^8 mph. How far from Earth is the Great Galaxy of Andromeda? Use a 365-day year.
1.291224×10^{19} mi   [6.1D]

31. Write the number of seconds in one week in scientific notation.
6.048×10^5 s   [6.1D]

32. The length of a side of a square checkerboard is $(3x - 2)$ in. Express the area of the checkerboard in terms of the variable x.
$(9x^2 - 12x + 4)$ in^2 [6.3E]

33. The length of a rectangle is $(5x + 3)$ cm. The width is $(2x - 7)$ cm. Find the area of the rectangle in terms of the variable x.
$(10x^2 - 29x - 21)$ cm^2 [6.3E]

Chapter Test

1. Multiply: $2x(2x^2 - 3x)$

$4x^3 - 6x^2$ [6.3A]

2. Use the Remainder Theorem to evaluate $P(x) = -x^3 + 4x - 8$ when $x = -2$.

-8 [6.4C]

3. Simplify: $\frac{12x^2}{-3x^8}$

$-\dfrac{4}{x^6}$ [6.1B]

4. Simplify: $(-2xy^2)(3x^2y^4)$

$-6x^3y^6$ [6.1A]

5. Divide: $(x^2 + 1) \div (x + 1)$

$x - 1 + \dfrac{2}{x - 1}$ [6.4A/6.4B]

6. Multiply: $(x - 3)(x^2 - 4x + 5)$

$x^3 - 7x^2 + 17x - 15$ [6.3B]

7. Simplify: $(-2a^2b)^3$

$-8a^6b^3$ [6.1A]

8. Simplify: $\frac{(3x^{-2}y^5)^3}{3x^4y^{-1}}$

$\dfrac{9y^{10}}{x^{10}}$ [6.1B]

9. Multiply: $(a - 2b)(a + 5b)$

$a^2 + 3ab - 10b^2$ [6.3B]

10. Given $P(x) - 3x^2 - 8x + 1$, evaluate $P(2)$.

-3 [6.2A]

11. Divide: $(x^2 + 6x - 7) \div (x - 1)$

$x + 7$ [6.4A/6.4B]

12. Multiply: $-3y^2(-2y^2 + 3y - 6)$

$6y^4 - 9y^3 + 18y^2$ [6.3A]

13. Multiply: $(-2x^3 + x^2 - 7)(2x - 3)$

$-4x^4 + 8x^3 - 3x^2 - 14x + 21$ [6.3B]

14. Simplify: $(4y - 3)(4y + 3)$

$16y^2 - 9$ [6.3D]

15. Simplify: $(ab^2)(a^3b^5)$

a^4b^7 [6.1A]

16. Simplify: $\dfrac{2a^{-1}b}{2^{-2}a^{-2}b^{-3}}$

$8ab^4$ [6.1B]

17. Simplify: $\dfrac{(2a^{-4}b^2)^3}{4a^{-2}b^{-1}}$

$\dfrac{2b^7}{a^{10}}$ [6.1B]

18. Subtract: $(3a^2 - 2a - 7) - (5a^3 + 2a - 10)$

$-5a^3 + 3a^2 - 4a + 3$ [6.2B]

19. Simplify: $(2x - 5)^2$

$4x^2 - 20x + 25$ [6.3D]

20. Divide: $\dfrac{x^3 - 2x^2 - 5x + 7}{x + 3}$

$x^2 - 5x + 10 - \dfrac{23}{x + 3}$ [6.4A/6.4B]

21. Multiply: $(2x - 7y)(5x - 4y)$

$10x^2 - 43xy + 28y^2$ [6.3C]

22. Add: $(3x^3 - 2x^2 - 4) + (8x^2 - 8x + 7)$

$3x^3 + 6x^2 - 8x + 3$ [6.2B]

23. Write 0.00000000302 in scientific notation.
3.02×10^{-9} [6.1C]

24. The mass of the moon is 3.7×10^{-8} times the mass of the sun. The mass of the sun is 2.19×10^{27} tons. Find the mass of the moon. Write the answer in scientific notation.
8.103×10^{19} tons [6.1D]

25. The radius of a circle is $(x - 5)$ m. Use the equation $A = \pi r^2$, where r is the radius, to find the area of the circle in terms of the variable x. Leave the answer in terms of π.
$(\pi x^2 - 10\pi x + 25\pi)$ m^2 [6.3E]

Cumulative Review

1. Let $x \in \{-8, -3, 3\}$. For what values of x is the inequality $x \geq -3$ a true statement?

   $-3, 3$ [1.1A]

2. Find the additive inverse of 83.

   -83 [1.1B]

3. Simplify: $8 - 2[-3 - (-1)]^2 \div 4$

   6 [1.3A]

4. Evaluate $\dfrac{2a - b}{b - c}$ when $a = 4, b = -2$, and $c = 6$.

   $-\dfrac{5}{4}$ [1.4A]

5. Simplify: $-5\sqrt{300}$

   $-50\sqrt{3}$ [1.2F]

6. Identify the property that justifies the statement $2x + (-2x) = 0$.

   The Inverse Property of Addition   [1.4B]

7. Simplify: $2x - 4[x - 2(3 - 23x) + 4]$

   $-186x + 8$ [1.4D]

8. Solve: $\dfrac{2}{3} - y = \dfrac{5}{6}$

   $-\dfrac{1}{6}$ [2.2A]

9. Solve: $8x - 3 - x = -6 + 3x - 8$

   $-\dfrac{11}{4}$ [2.2B]

10. Solve: $3 - |2 - 3x| = -2$

    $-1, \dfrac{7}{3}$ [2.5A]

11. Given $P(x) = 3x^2 - 2x + 2$, find $P(-2)$.

    18 [4.1D]

12. Is the relation $\{(-1, 0), (0, 0), (1, 0)\}$ a function?

    yes   [4.1C]

13. Find the slope of the line containing the points $(-2, 3)$ and $(4, 2)$

    $-\dfrac{1}{6}$ [4.3A]

14. Find the equation of the line that contains the point $(-1, 2)$ and has slope $-\dfrac{3}{2}$.

    $y = -\dfrac{3}{2}x + \dfrac{1}{2}$ [4.4A]

15. Find the equation of the line that contains the point $(-2, 4)$ and is perpendicular to the line $3x + 2y = 4$.

    $y = \dfrac{2}{3}x + \dfrac{16}{3}$ [4.5A]

16. Solve by using Cramer's Rule:
    $2x - 3y = 2$
    $x + y = -3$

    $\left(-\dfrac{7}{5}, -\dfrac{8}{5}\right)$ [5.4B]

17. Solve by the addition method:
    $x - y + z = 0$
    $2x + y - 3z = -7$
    $-x + 2y + 2z = 5$

    $\left(-\dfrac{9}{7}, \dfrac{2}{7}, \dfrac{11}{7}\right)$ [5.3B]

18. Simplify: $-2x - (-xy) + 7x - 4xy$

    $5x - 3xy$ [1.4B]

19. Multiply: $(2x + 3)(2x^2 - 3x + 1)$

    $4x^3 - 7x + 3$ [6.3B]

20. Write the number 0.00000501 in scientific notation.

    5.01×10^{-6} [6.1C]

21. Graph: $3x - 4y = 12$

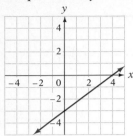

[4.2B]

22. Graph: $-3x + 2y < 6$

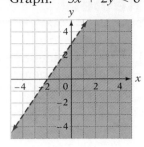

[4.6A]

23. Solve by graphing:
$$x - 2y = 3$$
$$-2x + y = -3$$

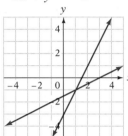

$(1, -1)$ [5.1A]

24. Graph the solution set:
$$2x + y < 2$$
$$-6x + 3y \geq 6$$

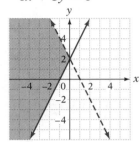

[5.6A]

25. Simplify: $(4a^{-2}b^3)(2a^3b^{-1})^{-2}$ $\dfrac{b^5}{a^8}$ [6.1B]

26. Simplify: $\dfrac{(5x^3y^{-3}z)^{-2}}{y^4z^{-2}}$ $\dfrac{y^2}{25x^6}$ [6.1B]

27. The sum of two integers is twenty-four. The difference between four times the smaller integer and nine is three less than twice the larger integer. Find the integers.   9, 15   [2.2D]

28. How many ounces of pure gold that costs $360 per ounce must be mixed with 80 oz of an alloy that costs $120 per ounce to make a mixture that costs $200 per ounce?   40 oz   [2.3A]

29. Two bicycles are 25 mi apart and traveling toward each other. One cyclist is traveling at 1.5 times the rate of the other cyclist. They meet in 2 h. Find the rate of each cyclist.   slower cyclist: 5 mph; faster cyclist: 7.5 mph   [2.3D]

30. If $3000 is invested at an annual simple interest rate of 7.5%, how much additional money must be invested at an annual simple interest rate of 10% so that the total interest earned in one year is 9% of the total investment? $4500   [2.3C]

31. The graph shows the relationship between the distance traveled and the time of travel. Find the slope of the line between the two points on the graph. Write a sentence that states the meaning of the slope. $m = 50$. The slope represents the average speed of travel in miles per hour.   [4.3A]

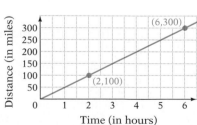

32. The width of a rectangle is 40% of the length. The perimeter of the rectangle is 42 m. Find the length and width of the rectangle. length: 15 m; width: 6 m   [3.2A]

33. The length of a side of a square is $(2x + 3)$ m. Find the area of the square in terms of the variable x. $(4x^2 + 12x + 9)$ m^2 [6.3E]

7

Factoring

Technical writers translate technological information into easily understood language for use in training manuals, public relations brochures, and the like. The computer industry uses software technical writers to explain the programs that computers run. Generally these technical writers need to learn from programmers how things work before they write the descriptions. It is common for software technical writers to have a liberal arts degree with some courses in mathematics and science, which enable them to better understand technical instructions.

Objectives

Section 7.1
To factor a monomial from a polynomial
To factor by grouping

Section 7.2
To factor a trinomial of the form $x^2 + bx + c$
To factor completely

Section 7.3
To factor a trinomial of the form $ax^2 + bx + c$ by using trial factors
To factor a trinomial of the form $ax^2 + bx + c$ by grouping

Section 7.4
To factor the difference of two perfect squares or a perfect-square trinomial
To factor the sum or the difference of two cubes
To factor a trinomial that is quadratic in form
To factor completely

Section 7.5
To solve equations by factoring
To solve application problems

Algebra from Geometry

The early Babylonians made substantial progress in both algebra and geometry. Often the progress they made in algebra was based on geometric concepts.

Here are some geometric proofs of algebraic identities the Babylonians understood.

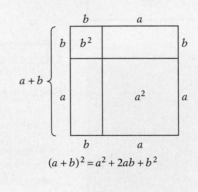

$$(a+b)^2 = a^2 + 2ab + b^2$$

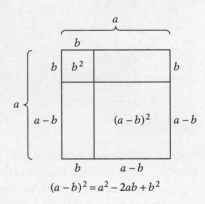

$$(a-b)^2 = a^2 - 2ab + b^2$$

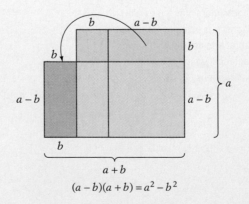

$$(a-b)(a+b) = a^2 - b^2$$

7.1 Common Factors

Objective A   *To factor a monomial from a polynomial* ....

The **greatest common factor (GCF)** of two or more monomials is the product of the GCF of the coefficients and the common variable factors.

$6x^3y = 2 \cdot 3 \cdot x \cdot x \cdot x \cdot y$
$8x^2y^2 = 2 \cdot 2 \cdot 2 \cdot x \cdot x \cdot y \cdot y$
$\text{GCF} = 2 \cdot x \cdot x \cdot y = 2x^2y$

Note that the exponent of each variable in the GCF is the same as the *smallest* exponent of that variable in either of the monomials.

The GCF of $6x^3y$ and $8x^2y^2$ is $2x^2y$.

⇒ Find the GCF of $12a^4b$ and $18a^2b^2c$.

The common variable factors are a^2 and b; c is not a common variable factor.

$12a^4b = 2 \cdot 2 \cdot 3 \cdot a^4 \cdot b$
$18a^2b^2c = 2 \cdot 3 \cdot 3 \cdot a^2 \cdot b^2 \cdot c$
$\text{GCF} = 2 \cdot 3 \cdot a^2 \cdot b = 6a^2b$

To **factor** a polynomial means to write the polynomial as a product of other polynomials.

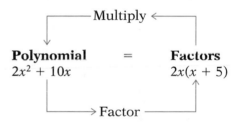

In the example above, $2x$ is the GCF of the terms $2x^2$ and $10x$. It is a **common factor** of the terms.

⇒ Factor: $5x^3 - 35x^2 + 10x$

Find the GCF of the terms of the polynomial.

$5x^3 = 5 \cdot x^3 \qquad 35x^2 = 5 \cdot 7 \cdot x^2 \qquad 10x = 2 \cdot 5 \cdot x$

The GCF is $5x$.

Rewrite the polynomial, expressing each term as a product with the GCF as one of the factors.

$5x^3 - 35x^2 + 10x = 5x(x^2) + 5x(-7x) + 5x(2)$
$\qquad\qquad\qquad = 5x(x^2 - 7x + 2)$

• **Use the Distributive Property to write the polynomial as a product of factors.**

Example 1

Factor: $8x^2 + 2xy$

Solution

The GCF is $2x$.

$8x^2 + 2xy = 2x(4x) + 2x(y) = 2x(4x + y)$

You Try It 1

Factor: $14a^2 - 21a^4b$

Your solution

$7a^2(2 - 3a^2b)$

Example 2

Factor: $n^3 - 5n^2 + 2n$

Solution

The GCF is n.

$n^3 - 5n^2 + 2n = n(n^2) + n(-5n) + n(2)$
$= n(n^2 - 5n + 2)$

You Try It 2

Factor: $27b^2 + 18b + 9$

Your solution

$9(3b^2 + 2b + 1)$

Example 3

Factor: $16x^2y + 8x^4y^2 - 12x^4y^5$

Solution

The GCF is $4x^2y$.

$16x^2y + 8x^4y^2 - 12x^4y^5$
$= 4x^2y(4) + 4x^2y(2x^2y) + 4x^2y(-3x^2y^4)$
$= 4x^2y(4 + 2x^2y - 3x^2y^4)$

You Try It 3

Factor: $6x^4y^2 - 9x^3y^2 + 12x^2y^4$

Your solution

$3x^2y^2(2x^2 - 3x + 4y^2)$

Example 4

Factor: $x^{5n} - 2x^{3n}$

Solution

The GCF is x^{3n}.

$x^{5n} - 2x^{3n} = x^{3n}(x^{2n}) - x^{3n}(2)$
$= x^{3n}(x^{2n} - 2)$

You Try It 4

Factor: $a^{n+4} + a^2$

Your solution

$a^2(a^{n+2} + 1)$

Solutions on p. S18

Objective B   *To factor by grouping* ....

In the examples at the right, the binomials in parentheses are called **binomial factors**.

$$2a(a + b)^2$$
$$3xy(x - y)$$

The Distributive Property is used to factor a common binomial factor from an expression.

The common binomial factor of the expression $6x(x - 3) + y^2(x - 3)$ is $(x - 3)$. To factor that expression, use the Distributive Property to write the expression as a product of factors.

$$6x(x - 3) + y^2(x - 3) = (x - 3)(6x + y^2)$$

Consider the following simplification of $-(a - b)$.

$$-(a - b) = -1(a - b) = -a + b = b - a$$

Thus, $$b - a = -(a - b)$$

This equation is sometimes used to factor a common binomial from an expression.

➡ Factor: $2x(x - y) + 5(y - x)$

$$2x(x - y) + 5(y - x) = 2x(x - y) - 5(x - y)$$
$$= (x - y)(2x - 5)$$

• $5(y - x) = 5[(-1)(x - y)]$
  $= -5(x - y)$

Some polynomials can be factored by grouping terms in such a way that a common binomial factor is found.

➡ Factor: $ax + bx - ay - by$

$$ax + bx - ay - by = (ax + bx) - (ay + by)$$

• Group the first two terms and the last two terms. Note that $-ay - by = -(ay + by)$.

$$= x(a + b) - y(a + b)$$
$$= (a + b)(x - y)$$

• Factor the GCF from each group.

➡ Factor: $6x^2 - 9x - 4xy + 6y$

$$6x^2 - 9x - 4xy + 6y = (6x^2 - 9x) - (4xy - 6y)$$

• Group the first two terms and the last two terms. Note that $-4xy + 6y = -(4xy - 6y)$.

$$= 3x(2x - 3) - 2y(2x - 3)$$
$$= (2x - 3)(3x - 2y)$$

• Factor the GCF from each group.

Example 5

Factor: $4x(3x - 2) - 7(3x - 2)$

Solution

$4x(3x - 2) - 7(3x - 2)$

$= (3x - 2)(4x - 7)$

You Try It 5

Factor: $2y(5x - 2) - 3(2 - 5x)$

Your solution

$(5x - 2)(2y + 3)$

Example 6

Factor: $9x^2 - 15x - 6xy + 10y$

Solution

$9x^2 - 15x - 6xy + 10y$

$= (9x^2 - 15x) - (6xy - 10y)$

$= 3x(3x - 5) - 2y(3x - 5)$

$= (3x - 5)(3x - 2y)$

You Try It 6

Factor: $a^2 - 3a + 2ab - 6b$

Your solution

$(a - 3)(a + 2b)$

Example 7

Factor: $3x^2y - 4x - 15xy + 20$

Solution

$3x^2y - 4x - 15xy + 20$

$= (3x^2y - 4x) - (15xy - 20)$

$= x(3xy - 4) - 5(3xy - 4)$

$= (3xy - 4)(x - 5)$

You Try It 7

Factor: $2mn^2 - n + 8mn - 4$

Your solution

$(2mn - 1)(n + 4)$

Example 8

Factor: $4ab - 6 + 3b - 2ab^2$

Solution

$4ab - 6 + 3b - 2ab^2$

$= (4ab - 6) + (3b - 2ab^2)$

$= 2(2ab - 3) + b(3 - 2ab)$

$= 2(2ab - 3) - b(2ab - 3)$

$= (2ab - 3)(2 - b)$

You Try It 8

Factor: $2xy - 6y - 12 + 4x$

Your solution

$(x - 3)(2y + 4)$

Solutions on p. S19

7.1 Exercises

. . . .

Objective A

Factor.

1. $5a + 5$
$5(a + 1)$

2. $7b - 7$
$7(b - 1)$

3. $16 - 8a^2$
$8(2 - a^2)$

4. $12 + 12y^2$
$12(1 + y^2)$

5. $8x + 12$
$4(2x + 3)$

6. $16a - 24$
$8(2a - 3)$

7. $30a - 6$
$6(5a - 1)$

8. $20b + 5$
$5(4b + 1)$

9. $7x^2 - 3x$
$x(7x - 3)$

10. $12y^2 - 5y$
$y(12y - 5)$

11. $3a^2 + 5a^5$
$a^2(3 + 5a^3)$

12. $9x - 5x^2$
$x(9 - 5x)$

13. $14y^2 + 11y$
$y(14y + 11)$

14. $6b^3 - 5b^2$
$b^2(6b - 5)$

15. $2x^4 - 4x$
$2x(x^3 - 2)$

16. $3y^4 - 9y$
$3y(y^3 - 3)$

17. $10x^4 - 12x^2$
$2x^2(5x^2 - 6)$

18. $12a^5 - 32a^2$
$4a^2(3a^3 - 8)$

19. $8a^8 - 4a^5$
$4a^5(2a^3 - 1)$

20. $16y^4 - 8y^7$
$8y^4(2 - y^3)$

21. $x^2y^2 - xy$
$xy(xy - 1)$

22. $a^2b^2 + ab$
$ab(ab + 1)$

23. $3x^2y^4 - 6xy$
$3xy(xy^3 - 2)$

24. $12a^2b^5 - 9ab$
$3ab(4ab^4 - 3)$

25. $x^2y - xy^3$
$xy(x - y^2)$

26. $3x^3 + 6x^2 + 9x$
$3x(x^2 + 2x + 3)$

27. $5y^3 - 20y^2 + 10y$
$5y(y^2 - 4y + 2)$

28. $2x^4 - 4x^3 + 6x^2$
$2x^2(x^2 - 2x + 3)$

29. $3y^4 - 9y^3 - 6y^2$
$3y^2(y^2 - 3y - 2)$

30. $2x^3 + 6x^2 - 14x$
$2x(x^2 + 3x - 7)$

31. $3y^3 - 9y^2 + 24y$
$3y(y^2 - 3y + 8)$

32. $2y^5 - 3y^4 + 7y^3$
$y^3(2y^2 - 3y + 7)$

33. $6a^5 - 3a^3 - 2a^2$
$a^2(6a^3 - 3a - 2)$

34. $x^3y - 3x^2y^2 + 7xy^3$
$xy(x^2 - 3xy + 7y^2)$

35. $2a^2b - 5a^2b^2 + 7ab^2$
$ab(2a - 5ab + 7b)$

36. $5y^3 + 10y^2 - 25y$
$5y(y^2 + 2y - 5)$

37. $4b^5 + 6b^3 - 12b$
$2b(2b^4 + 3b^2 - 6)$

38. $3a^2b^2 - 9ab^2 + 15b^2$
$3b^2(a^2 - 3a + 5)$

39. $8x^2y^2 - 4x^2y + x^2$
$x^2(8y^2 - 4y + 1)$

40. $x^{2n} - x^n$
$x^n(x^n - 1)$

41. $2a^{5n} + a^{2n}$
$a^{2n}(2a^{3n} + 1)$

42. $x^{3n} - x^{2n}$
$x^{2n}(x^n - 1)$

43. $y^{4n} + y^{2n}$
$y^{2n}(y^{2n} + 1)$

44. $a^{2n+2} + a^2$
$a^2(a^{2n} + 1)$

45. $b^{n+5} - b^5$
$b^5(b^n - 1)$

___

Objective B

Factor.

46. $x(b + 4) + 3(b + 4)$
$(b + 4)(x + 3)$

47. $y(a + z) + 7(a + z)$
$(a + z)(y + 7)$

48. $a(y - x) - b(y - x)$
$(y - x)(a - b)$

49. $3r(a - b) + s(a - b)$
$(a - b)(3r + s)$

50. $x(x - 2) + y(2 - x)$
$(x - 2)(x - y)$

51. $t(m - 7) + 7(7 - m)$
$(m - 7)(t - 7)$

52. $2x(7 + b) - y(b + 7)$
$(b + 7)(2x - y)$

53. $2y(4a - b) - (b - 4a)$
$(4a - b)(2y + 1)$

54. $8c(2m - 3n) + (3n - 2m)$
$(2m - 3n)(8c - 1)$

55. $x^2 + 2x + 2xy + 4y$
$(x + 2)(x + 2y)$

56. $x^2 - 3x + 4ax - 12a$
$(x - 3)(x + 4a)$

57. $p^2 - 2p - 3rp + 6r$
$(p - 2)(p - 3r)$

58. $t^2 + 4t - st - 4s$
$(t + 4)(t - s)$

59. $ab + 6b - 4a - 24$
$(a + 6)(b - 4)$

60. $xy - 5y - 2x + 10$
$(x - 5)(y - 2)$

61. $2z^2 - z + 2yz - y$
$(2z - 1)(z + y)$

62. $2y^2 - 10y + 7xy - 35x$
$(y - 5)(2y + 7x)$

63. $8v^2 - 12vy + 14v - 21y$
$(4v + 7)(2v - 3y)$

64. $21x^2 + 6xy - 49x - 14y$
$(7x + 2y)(3x - 7)$

65. $2x^2 - 5x - 6xy + 15y$
$(2x - 5)(x - 3y)$

66. $4a^2 + 5ab - 10b - 8a$
$(4a + 5b)(a - 2)$

67. $3y^2 - 6y - ay + 2a$
$(y - 2)(3y - a)$

68. $2ra + a^2 - 2r - a$
$(2r + a)(a - 1)$

69. $3xy - y^2 - y + 3x$
$(3x - y)(y + 1)$

70. $2ab - 3b^2 - 3b + 2a$
$(2a - 3b)(b + 1)$

71. $3st + t^2 - 2t - 6s$
$(3s + t)(t - 2)$

72. $4x^2 + 3xy - 12y - 16x$
$(4x + 3y)(x - 4)$

___

APPLYING THE CONCEPTS

A whole number is a perfect number if it is the sum of all of its factors less than itself. For example, 6 is a perfect number because all the factors of 6 that are less than 6 are 1, 2, and 3, and $1 + 2 + 3 = 6$.

73. Find the one perfect number between 20 and 30.
28

74. Find the one perfect number between 490 and 500.
496

75. In the equation $P = 2L + 2W$, what is the effect on P when the quantity $L + W$ doubles?
P doubles.

76. Write the area of the shaded portion of each diagram in factored form.

a.
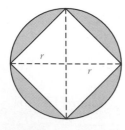
$r^2(\pi - 2)$

b.
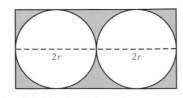
$2r^2(4 - \pi)$

c.

$r^2(4 - \pi)$

7.2 Factoring Polynomials of the Form $x^2 + bx + c$

Objective A   To factor a trinomial of the form $x^2 + bx + c$ ....

Trinomials of the form $x^2 + bx + c$, where b and c are integers, are shown at the right.

$$x^2 + 8x + 12; b = 8, c = 12$$
$$x^2 - 7x + 12; b = -7, c = 12$$
$$x^2 - 2x - 15; b = -2, c = -15$$

To factor a trinomial of this form means to express the trinomial as the product of two binomials.

Trinomials expressed as the product of binomials are shown at the right.

$$x^2 + 8x + 12 = (x + 6)(x + 2)$$
$$x^2 - 7x + 12 = (x - 3)(x - 4)$$
$$x^2 - 2x - 15 = (x + 3)(x - 5)$$

The method by which factors of a trinomial are found is based on FOIL. Consider the following binomial products, noting the relationship between the constant terms of the binomials and the terms of the trinomials.

Signs in the binomials are the same.

$$(x + 6)(x + 2) = x^2 + 2x + 6x + (6)(2) = x^2 + 8x + 12$$
sum of 6 and 2
product of 6 and 2

$$(x - 3)(x - 4) = x^2 - 4x - 3x + (-3)(-4) = x^2 - 7x + 12$$
sum of -3 and -4
product of -3 and -4

Signs in the binomials are opposite.

$$(x + 3)(x - 5) = x^2 - 5x + 3x + (3)(-5) = x^2 - 2x - 15$$
sum of 3 and -5
product of 3 and -5

$$(x - 4)(x + 6) = x^2 + 6x - 4x + (-4)(6) = x^2 + 2x - 24$$
sum of -4 and 6
product of -4 and 6

INSTRUCTOR NOTE

Students sometimes see factoring as unrelated to multiplication. Remind students that the relationships between the binomial factors and the terms of the polynomial are based on multiplying binomials.

IMPORTANT RELATIONSHIPS

1. When the constant term of the trinomial is positive, the constant terms of the binomials have the same sign. They are both positive when the coefficient of the x term in the trinomial is positive. They are both negative when the coefficient of the x term in the trinomial is negative.

2. When the constant term of the trinomial is negative, the constant terms of the binomials have opposite signs.

3. In the trinomial, the coefficient of x is the sum of the constant terms of the binomials.

4. In the trinomial, the constant term is the product of the constant terms of the binomials.

➡ Factor: $x^2 - 7x + 10$

Because the constant term is positive and the coefficient of x is negative, the binomial constants will be negative. Find two negative factors of 10 whose sum is -7. The results can be recorded in a table.

Negative Factors of 10	*Sum*	
$-1, -10$	-11	
$-2, -5$	-7	• These are the correct factors.

$x^2 - 7x + 10 = (x - 2)(x - 5)$ • Write the trinomial as a product of its factors.

Check: $(x - 2)(x - 5) = x^2 - 5x - 2x + 10$ • Check the proposed
$= x^2 - 7x + 10$ factorization by multiplying the two binomials.

➡ Factor: $x^2 - 9x - 36$

The constant term is negative. The binomial constants will have opposite signs. Find two factors of -36 whose sum is -9.

Factors of -36	*Sum*	
$+1, -36$	-35	
$-1, +36$	35	
$+2, -18$	-16	
$-2, +18$	16	
$+3, -12$	-9	• Once the correct factors are found, it is not necessary to try the remaining factors.

$x^2 - 9x - 36 = (x + 3)(x - 12)$ • Write the trinomial as a product of its factors.

➡ Factor: $x^2 + 7x + 8$

Because the constant term is positive and the coefficient of x is positive, the binomial constants will be positive. Find two positive factors of 8 whose sum is 7.

Positive Factors of 8	*Sum*
1, 8	9
2, 4	6

There are no positive integer factors of 8 whose sum is 7. The trinomial $x^2 + 7x + 8$ is said to be **nonfactorable over the integers**. Just as 17 is a prime number, $x^2 + 7x + 8$ is a **prime polynomial**. Binomials of the form $x - a$ and $x + a$ are also prime polynomials.

Example 1
Factor: $x^2 - 8x + 15$

Solution

Factors	*Sum*	• Find two negative
$-1, -15$	-16	factors of 15 whose
$-3, -5$	-8	sum is -8.

$x^2 - 8x + 15 = (x - 3)(x - 5)$

You Try It 1
Factor: $x^2 + 9x + 20$

Your solution
$(x + 4)(x + 5)$

Solution on p. S19

Example 2

Factor: $x^2 + 6x - 27$

Solution

Factors	Sum
$+1, -27$	-26
$-1, +27$	26
$+3, -9$	-6
$-3, +9$	6

• Find two factors of -27 whose sum is 6.

$x^2 + 6x - 27 = (x - 3)(x + 9)$

You Try It 2

Factor: $x^2 + 7x - 18$

Your solution

$(x + 9)(x - 2)$

Solution on p. S19

Objective B   To factor completely ....

A polynomial is factored completely when it is written as a product of factors that are nonfactorable over the integers.

➡ Factor: $4y^3 - 4y^2 - 24y$

$$4y^3 - 4y^2 - 24y = \boxed{4y(y^2) - 4y(y) - 4y(6)}$$

$$= 4y(y^2 - y - 6)$$

$$= 4y(y + 2)(y - 3)$$

• The GCF is $4y$. Do this step mentally.

• Use the Distributive Property to factor out the GCF.

• Factor $y^2 - y - 6$. The two factors of -6 whose sum is -1 are 2 and -3.

It is always possible to check the proposed factorization by multiplying the polynomials. Here is the check for the last example.

Check: $4y(y + 2)(y - 3) = 4y(y^2 - 3y + 2y - 6)$

$$= 4y(y^2 - y - 6)$$

$$= 4y^3 - 4y^2 - 24y$$ • This is the original polynomial.

➡ Factor: $5x^2 + 60xy + 100y^2$

$$5x^2 + 60xy + 100y^2 = \boxed{5(x^2) + 5(12xy) + 5(20y^2)}$$

$$= 5(x^2 + 12xy + 20y^2)$$

$$= 5(x + 2y)(x + 10y)$$

• The GCF is 5. Do this step mentally.

• Use the Distributive Property to factor out the GCF.

• Factor $x^2 + 12xy + 20y^2$. The two factors of 20 whose sum is 12 are 2 and 10.

Note that $2y$ and $10y$ were placed in the binomials. The following check shows that this was necessary.

Check: $5(x + 2y)(x + 10y) = 5(x^2 + 10xy + 2xy + 20y^2)$

$$= 5(x^2 + 12xy + 20y^2)$$

$$= 5x^2 + 60xy + 100y^2$$ • The original polynomial

➡ Factor: $15 - 2x - x^2$

Because the coefficient of x^2 is -1, factor -1 from the trinomial and then write the resulting trinomial in descending order.

$$15 - 2x - x^2 = -(x^2 + 2x - 15)$$

• $15 - 2x - x^2 = -1(-15 + 2x + x^2)$
  $$= -(x^2 + 2x - 15)$$

$$= -(x + 5)(x - 3)$$

• Factor $x^2 + 2x - 15$. The two factors of -15 whose sum is 2 are 5 and -3.

Check: $-(x + 5)(x - 3) = -(x^2 + 2x - 15)$
$$= -x^2 - 2x + 15$$
$$= 15 - 2x - x^2$$

• The original polynomial

TAKE NOTE

When the coefficient of the highest power in a polynomial is negative, consider factoring out a negative GCF. Example 3 below is another example of this technique.

Example 3
Factor: $-3x^3 + 9x^2 + 12x$

Solution
The GCF is $-3x$.

$$-3x^3 + 9x^2 + 12x = -3x(x^2 - 3x - 4)$$

Factor the trinomial $x^2 - 3x - 4$. Find two factors of -4 whose sum is -3.

Factors	Sum
$-2, +2$	0
$+1, -4$	-3

$$-3x^3 + 9x^2 + 12x = -3x(x + 1)(x - 4)$$

You Try It 3
Factor: $-2x^3 + 14x^2 - 12x$

Your solution
$-2x(x - 6)(x - 1)$

Example 4
Factor: $4x^2 - 40xy + 84y^2$

Solution
The GCF is 4.

$$4x^2 - 40xy + 84y^2 = 4(x^2 - 10xy + 21y^2)$$

Factor the trinomial $x^2 - 10xy + 21y^2$. Find two negative factors of 21 whose sum is -10.

Factors	Sum
$-1, -21$	-22
$-3, -7$	-10

$$4x^2 - 40xy + 84y^2 = 4(x - 3y)(x - 7y)$$

You Try It 4
Factor: $3x^2 - 9xy - 12y^2$

Your solution
$3(x + y)(x - 4y)$

Solutions on p. S19

7.2 Exercises

· ·

Objective A

Factor.

1. $x^2 + 3x + 2$
   $(x + 1)(x + 2)$

2. $x^2 + 5x + 6$
   $(x + 2)(x + 3)$

3. $x^2 - x - 2$
   $(x + 1)(x - 2)$

4. $x^2 + x - 6$
   $(x + 3)(x - 2)$

5. $a^2 + a - 12$
   $(a + 4)(a - 3)$

6. $a^2 - 2a - 35$
   $(a + 5)(a - 7)$

7. $a^2 - 3a + 2$
   $(a - 1)(a - 2)$

8. $a^2 - 5a + 4$
   $(a - 1)(a - 4)$

9. $a^2 + a - 2$
   $(a + 2)(a - 1)$

10. $a^2 - 2a - 3$
    $(a + 1)(a - 3)$

11. $b^2 - 6b + 9$
    $(b - 3)(b - 3)$

12. $b^2 + 8h + 16$
    $(b + 4)(b + 4)$

13. $b^2 + 7b - 8$
    $(b + 8)(b - 1)$

14. $y^2 - y - 6$
    $(y + 2)(y - 3)$

15. $y^2 + 6y - 55$
    $(y + 11)(y - 5)$

16. $z^2 - 4z - 45$
    $(z + 5)(z - 9)$

17. $y^2 - 5y + 6$
    $(y - 2)(y - 3)$

18. $y^2 - 8y + 15$
    $(y - 3)(y - 5)$

19. $z^2 - 14z + 45$
    $(z - 5)(z - 9)$

20. $z^2 - 14z + 49$
    $(z - 7)(z - 7)$

21. $z^2 - 12z - 160$
    $(z + 8)(z - 20)$

22. $p^2 + 2p - 35$
    $(p + 7)(p - 5)$

23. $p^2 + 12p + 27$
    $(p + 3)(p + 9)$

24. $p^2 - 6p + 8$
    $(p - 2)(p - 4)$

25. $x^2 + 20x + 100$
    $(x + 10)(x + 10)$

26. $x^2 + 18x + 81$
    $(x + 9)(x + 9)$

27. $b^2 + 9b + 20$
    $(b + 4)(b + 5)$

28. $b^2 + 13b + 40$
    $(b + 5)(b + 8)$

29. $x^2 - 11x - 42$
    $(x + 3)(x - 14)$

30. $x^2 + 9x - 70$
    $(x + 14)(x - 5)$

31. $b^2 - b - 20$
    $(b + 4)(b - 5)$

32. $b^2 + 3b - 40$
    $(b + 8)(b - 5)$

33. $y^2 - 14y - 51$
    $(y + 3)(y - 17)$

34. $y^2 - y - 72$
    $(y + 8)(y - 9)$

35. $p^2 - 4p - 21$
    $(p + 3)(p - 7)$

36. $p^2 + 16p + 39$
    $(p + 3)(p + 13)$

37. $y^2 - 8y + 32$
    nonfactorable over
    the integers

38. $y^2 - 9y + 81$
    nonfactorable over
    the integers

39. $x^2 - 20x + 75$
    $(x - 5)(x - 15)$

40. $p^2 + 24p + 63$
    $(p + 3)(p + 21)$

41. $x^2 - 15x + 56$
$(x - 7)(x - 8)$

42. $x^2 + 21x + 38$
$(x + 2)(x + 19)$

43. $x^2 + x - 56$
$(x + 8)(x - 7)$

44. $x^2 + 5x - 36$
$(x + 9)(x - 4)$

45. $a^2 - 21a - 72$
$(a + 3)(a - 24)$

46. $a^2 - 7a - 44$
$(a + 4)(a - 11)$

47. $a^2 - 15a + 36$
$(a - 3)(a - 12)$

48. $a^2 - 21a + 54$
$(a - 3)(a - 18)$

49. $z^2 - 9z - 136$
$(z + 8)(z - 17)$

50. $z^2 + 14z - 147$
$(z + 21)(z - 7)$

51. $c^2 - c - 90$
$(c + 9)(c - 10)$

52. $c^2 - 3c - 180$
$(c + 12)(c - 15)$

53. $z^2 + 15z + 44$
$(z + 4)(z + 11)$

54. $p^2 + 24p + 135$
$(p + 9)(p + 15)$

55. $c^2 + 19c + 34$
$(c + 2)(c + 17)$

56. $c^2 + 11c + 18$
$(c + 2)(c + 9)$

57. $x^2 - 4x - 96$
$(x + 8)(x - 12)$

58. $x^2 + 10x - 75$
$(x + 15)(x - 5)$

59. $x^2 - 22x + 112$
$(x - 8)(x - 14)$

60. $x^2 + 21x - 100$
$(x + 25)(x - 4)$

61. $b^2 + 8b - 105$
$(b + 15)(b - 7)$

62. $b^2 - 22b + 72$
$(b - 4)(b - 18)$

63. $a^2 - 9a - 36$
$(a + 3)(a - 12)$

64. $a^2 + 42a - 135$
$(a + 45)(a - 3)$

65. $b^2 - 23b + 102$
$(b - 6)(b - 17)$

66. $b^2 - 25b + 126$
$(b - 7)(b - 18)$

67. $a^2 + 27a + 72$
$(a + 3)(a + 24)$

68. $z^2 + 24z + 144$
$(z + 12)(z + 12)$

69. $x^2 + 25x + 156$
$(x + 12)(x + 13)$

70. $x^2 - 29x + 100$
$(x - 4)(x - 25)$

71. $x^2 - 10x - 96$
$(x + 6)(x - 16)$

72. $x^2 + 9x - 112$
$(x + 16)(x - 7)$

Objective B

Factor.

73. $2x^2 + 6x + 4$
$2(x + 1)(x + 2)$

74. $3x^2 + 15x + 18$
$3(x + 2)(x + 3)$

75. $18 + 7x - x^2$
$-(x + 2)(x - 9)$

76. $12 - 4x - x^2$
$-(x - 2)(x + 6)$

77. $ab^2 + 2ab - 15a$
$a(b + 5)(b - 3)$

78. $ab^2 + 7ab - 8a$
$a(b + 8)(b - 1)$

79. $xy^2 - 5xy + 6x$
$x(y - 2)(y - 3)$

80. $xy^2 + 8xy + 15x$
$x(y + 3)(y + 5)$

81. $z^3 - 7z^2 + 12z$
$z(z - 3)(z - 4)$

82. $-2a^3 - 6a^2 - 4a$
$-2a(a + 1)(a + 2)$

83. $-3y^3 + 15y^2 - 18y$
$-3y(y - 2)(y - 3)$

84. $4y^3 + 12y^2 - 72y$
$4y(y + 6)(y - 3)$

85. $3x^2 + 3x - 36$
$3(x + 4)(x - 3)$

86. $2x^3 - 2x^2 + 4x$
$2x(x^2 - x + 2)$

87. $5z^2 - 15z - 140$
$5(z + 4)(z - 7)$

88. $6z^2 + 12z - 90$
$6(z + 5)(z - 3)$

89. $2a^3 + 8a^2 - 64a$
$2a(a + 8)(a - 4)$

90. $3a^3 - 9a^2 - 54a$
$3a(a + 3)(a - 6)$

91. $x^2 - 5xy + 6y^2$
$(x - 2y)(x - 3y)$

92. $x^2 + 4xy - 21y^2$
$(x + 7y)(x - 3y)$

93. $a^2 - 9ab + 20b^2$
$(a - 4b)(a - 5b)$

94. $a^2 - 15ab + 50b^2$
$(a - 5b)(a - 10b)$

95. $x^2 - 3xy - 28y^2$
$(x + 4y)(x - 7y)$

96. $s^2 + 2st - 48t^2$
$(s + 8t)(s - 6t)$

97. $y^2 - 15yz - 41z^2$
nonfactorable over
the integers

98. $y^2 + 85yz + 36z^2$
nonfactorable over
the integers

99. $z^4 - 12z^3 + 35z^2$
$z^2(z - 5)(z - 7)$

100. $z^4 + 2z^3 - 80z^2$
$z^2(z + 10)(z - 8)$

101. $b^4 - 22b^3 + 120b^2$
$b^2(b - 10)(b - 12)$

102. $b^4 - 3b^3 - 10b^2$
$b^2(b + 2)(b - 5)$

103. $2y^4 - 26y^3 - 96y^2$
$2y^2(y + 3)(y - 16)$

104. $3y^4 + 54y^3 + 135y^2$
$3y^2(y + 3)(y + 15)$

105. $-x^4 - 7x^3 + 8x^2$
$-x^2(x + 8)(x - 1)$

106. $-x^4 + 11x^3 + 12x^2$
$-x^2(x + 1)(x - 12)$

107. $4x^2y + 20xy - 56y$
$4y(x + 7)(x - 2)$

108. $3x^2y - 6xy - 45y$
$3y(x + 3)(x - 5)$

109. $c^3 + 18c^2 - 40c$
$c(c + 20)(c - 2)$

110. $-3x^3 + 36x^2 - 81x$
$-3x(x - 3)(x - 9)$

111. $-4x^3 - 4x^2 + 24x$
$-4x(x + 3)(x - 2)$

112. $x^2 - 8xy + 15y^2$
$(x - 3y)(x - 5y)$

113. $y^2 - 7xy - 8x^2$
$(y + x)(y - 8x)$

114. $a^2 - 13ab + 42b^2$
$(a - 6b)(a - 7b)$

115. $y^2 + 4yz - 21z^2$
$(y + 7z)(y - 3z)$

116. $y^2 + 8yz + 7z^2$
$(y + z)(y + 7z)$

117. $y^2 - 16yz + 15z^2$
$(y - z)(y - 15z)$

118. $3x^2y + 60xy - 63y$
$3y(x + 21)(x - 1)$

119. $4x^2y - 68xy - 72y$
$4y(x + 1)(x - 18)$

120. $3x^3 + 3x^2 - 36x$
$3x(x + 4)(x - 3)$

121. $4x^3 + 12x^2 - 160x$
$4x(x + 8)(x - 5)$

122. $4z^3 + 32z^2 - 132z$
$4z(z + 11)(z - 3)$

123. $5z^3 - 50z^2 - 120z$
$5z(z + 2)(z - 12)$

124. $4x^3 + 8x^2 - 12x$
$4x(x + 3)(x - 1)$

125. $5x^3 + 30x^2 + 40x$
$5x(x + 2)(x + 4)$

126. $5p^2 + 25p - 420$
$5(p + 12)(p - 7)$

127. $4p^2 - 28p - 480$
$4(p + 8)(p - 15)$

128. $p^4 + 9p^3 - 36p^2$
$p^2(p + 12)(p - 3)$

129. $p^4 + p^3 - 56p^2$
$p^2(p + 8)(p - 7)$

130. $t^2 - 12ts + 35s^2$
$(t - 5s)(t - 7s)$

131. $a^2 - 10ab + 25b^2$
$(a - 5b)(a - 5b)$

132. $a^2 - 8ab - 33b^2$
$(a + 3b)(a - 11b)$

133. $x^2 + 4xy - 60y^2$
$(x + 10y)(x - 6y)$

134. $5x^4 - 30x^3 + 40x^2$
$5x^2(x - 2)(x - 4)$

135. $6x^3 - 6x^2 - 120x$
$6x(x - 5)(x + 4)$

APPLYING THE CONCEPTS

Factor.

136. $2 + c^2 + 9c$
nonfactorable over
the integers

137. $x^2y - 54y - 3xy$
$y(x + 6)(x - 9)$

138. $45a^2 + a^2b^2 - 14a^2b$
$a^2(b - 5)(b - 9)$

Find all integers k such that the trinomial can be factored over the integers.

139. $x^2 + kx + 35$
$-36, 36, -12, 12$

140. $x^2 + kx + 18$
$-19, 19, -11, 11, -9, 9$

141. $x^2 + kx + 21$
$22, -22, 10, -10$

Determine the positive integer values of k for which the following polynomials
are factorable over the integers.

142. $y^2 + 4y + k$
$3, 4$

143. $z^2 + 7z + k$
$6, 10, 12$

144. $a^2 - 6a + k$
$5, 8, 9$

145. $c^2 - 7c + k$
$6, 10, 12$

146. $x^2 - 3x + k$
2

147. $y^2 + 5y + k$
$4, 6$

148. In Exercises 142–147, there was the stated requirement that $k > 0$. If k
is allowed to be any integer, how many different values of k are possible for each polynomial?
an infinite number

7.3 Factoring Polynomials of the Form $ax^2 + bx + c$

Objective A   *To factor a trinomial of the form $ax^2 + bx + c$ by using trial factors* ....

INSTRUCTOR NOTE

The first objective of this section is to factor by using trial factors. The second objective is to use grouping. You may skip one of these objectives or do both.

Trinomials of the form $ax^2 + bx + c$, where a, b, and c are integers, are shown at the right.

$3x^2 - x + 4$; $a = 3, b = -1, c = 4$
$6x^2 + 2x - 3$; $a = 6, b = 2,$ $c = -3$

These trinomials differ from those in the previous section in that the coefficient of x^2 is not 1. There are various methods of factoring these trinomials. The method described in this objective is factoring polynomials using trial factors.

To reduce the number of trial factors that must be considered, remember the following:

1. Use the signs of the constant term and the coefficient of x in the trinomial to determine the signs of the binomial factors. If the constant term is positive, the signs of the binomial factors will be the same as the sign of the coefficient of x in the trinomial. If the sign of the constant term is negative, the constant terms in the binomials have opposite signs.

2. If the terms of the trinomial do not have a common factor, then the terms of neither of the binomial factors will have a common factor.

➡ Factor: $2x^2 - 7x + 3$

The terms have no common factor. The constant term is positive. The coefficient of x is negative. The binomial constants will be negative.

Positive
Factors of 2
(coefficient of x^2)

  1, 2

Negative
Factors of 3
(constant term)

  $-1, -3$

Write trial factors. Use the **O**uter and **I**nner products of FOIL to determine the middle term, $-7x$, of the trinomial.

Trial Factors

$(x - 1)(2x - 3)$
$(x - 3)(2x - 1)$

Middle Term

$-3x - 2x = -5x$
$-x - 6x = -7x$

Write the factors of the trinomial. $2x^2 - 7x + 3 = (x - 3)(2x - 1)$

➡ Factor: $3x^2 - 8x + 4$

The terms have no common factor. The constant term is positive. The coefficient of x is negative. The binomial constants will be negative.

Positive
Factors of 3
(coefficient of x^2)

  1, 3

Negative
Factors of 4
(constant term)

  $-1, -4$
  $-2, -2$

Write trial factors. Use the **O**uter and **I**nner products of FOIL to determine the middle term, $-8x$, of the trinomial.

Trial Factors

$(x - 1)(3x - 4)$
$(x - 4)(3x - 1)$
$(x - 2)(3x - 2)$

Middle Term

$-4x - 3x = -7x$
$-x - 12x = -13x$
$-2x - 6x = -8x$

Write the factors of the trinomial. $3x^2 - 8x + 4 = (x - 2)(3x - 2)$

➡ Factor: $6x^3 + 14x^2 - 12x$

Factor the GCF, $2x$, from the terms.

$$6x^3 + 14x^2 - 12x = 2x(3x^2 + 7x - 6)$$

Factor the trinomial $3x^2 + 7x - 6$. The constant term is negative. The binomial constants will have opposite signs.

Positive *Factors of 3*	*Factors of -6*
1, 3	-1, 6
	1, -6
	-2, 3
	2, -3

Write trial factors. Use the **O**uter and **I**nner products of FOIL to determine the middle term, $7x$, of the trinomial.

It is not necessary to test trial factors that have a common factor.

Trial Factors	*Middle Term*
$(x - 1)(3x + 6)$	Common factor
$(x + 6)(3x - 1)$	$-x + 18x = 17x$
$(x + 1)(3x - 6)$	Common factor
$(x - 6)(3x + 1)$	$x - 18x = -17x$
$(x - 2)(3x + 3)$	Common factor
$(x + 3)(3x - 2)$	$-2x + 9x = 7x$
$(x + 2)(3x - 3)$	Common factor
$(x - 3)(3x + 2)$	$2x - 9x = -7x$

Write the factors of the trinomial.

$$6x^3 + 14x^2 - 12x = 2x(x + 3)(3x - 2)$$

TAKE NOTE

The binomial factor $3x + 6$ has a common factor of 3: $3x + 6 = 3(x + 2)$. Because $3x^2 + 7x - 6$ does not have a common factor, one of its binomial factors cannot have a common factor.

For this example, all the trial factors were listed. Once the correct factors have been found, however, the remaining trial factors can be omitted. For the examples and solutions in this text, all trial factors except those that have a common factor will be listed.

Example 1
Factor: $3x^2 + x - 2$

Solution

Positive	Factors of -2:	1, -2
factors of 3: 1, 3		-1, 2

Trial Factors	*Middle Term*
$(1x + 1)(3x - 2)$	$-2x + 3x = x$
$(1x - 2)(3x + 1)$	$x - 6x = -5x$
$(1x - 1)(3x + 2)$	$2x - 3x = -x$
$(1x + 2)(3x - 1)$	$-x + 6x = 5x$

$$3x^2 + x - 2 = (x + 1)(3x - 2)$$

You Try It 1
Factor: $2x^2 - x - 3$

Your solution
$(x + 1)(2x - 3)$

Example 2
Factor: $-12x^3 - 32x^2 + 12x$

Solution
The GCF is $-4x$.
$$-12x^3 - 32x^2 + 12x = -4x(3x^2 + 8x - 3)$$
Factor the trinomial.

Positive	Factors of -3:	1, -3
factors of 3: 1, 3		-1, 3

Trial Factors	*Middle Term*
$(x - 3)(3x + 1)$	$x - 9x = -8x$
$(x + 3)(3x - 1)$	$-x + 9x = 8x$

$$-12x^3 - 32x^2 + 12x = -4x(x + 3)(3x - 1)$$

You Try It 2
Factor: $-45y^3 + 12y^2 + 12y$

Your solution
$-3y(3y - 2)(5y + 2)$

Solutions on p. S19

Objective B ***To factor a trinomial of the form $ax^2 + bx + c$ by grouping........***

In the previous objective, trinomials of the form $ax^2 + bx + c$ were factored by using trial factors. In this objective, these trinomials will be factored by grouping.

To factor $ax^2 + bx + c$, first find two factors of $a \cdot c$ whose sum is b. Then use factoring by grouping to write the factorization of the trinomial.

➡ Factor: $2x^2 + 13x + 15$

Find two positive factors of 30 ($2 \cdot 15$) whose sum is 13.

Positive Factors of 30	*Sum*
1, 30	31
2, 15	17
3, 10	13

• When the required sum has been found, the remaining factors need not be checked.

$$2x^2 + 13x + 15 = 2x^2 + 3x + 10x + 15$$

• Use the factors of 30 whose sum is 13 to write $13x$ as $3x + 10x$.

$$= (2x^2 + 3x) + (10x + 15)$$
$$= x(2x + 3) + 5(2x + 3)$$
$$= (2x + 3)(x + 5)$$

• Factor by grouping.

Check: $(2x + 3)(x + 5) = 2x^2 + 10x + 3x + 15$
$$= 2x^2 + 13x + 15$$

➡ Factor: $6x^2 - 11x - 10$

Find two factors of -60 [$6 \cdot (-10)$] whose sum is -11.

Factors of -60	*Sum*
1, -60	-59
-1, 60	59
2, -30	-28
-2, 30	28
3, -20	-17
-3, 20	17
4, -15	-11

$$6x^2 - 11x - 10 = 6x^2 + 4x - 15x - 10$$

• Use the factors of -60 whose sum is -11 to write $-11x$ as $4x - 15x$.

$$= (6x^2 + 4x) - (15x + 10)$$
$$= 2x(3x + 2) - 5(3x + 2)$$
$$= (3x + 2)(2x - 5)$$

• Factor by grouping. Recall that $-15x - 10 = -(15x + 10)$.

Check: $(3x + 2)(2x - 5) = 6x^2 - 15x + 4x - 10$
$$= 6x^2 - 11x - 10$$

➡ Factor: $3x^2 - 2x - 4$

Find two factors of -12 $[3 \cdot (-4)]$ whose sum is -2.

Factors of -12	Sum
1, -12	-11
-1, 12	11
2, -6	-4
-2, 6	4
3, -4	-1
-3, 4	1

Because no integer factors of -12 have a sum of -2, $3x^2 - 2x - 4$ is nonfactorable over the integers. $3x^2 - 2x - 4$ is a prime polynomial.

Example 3
Factor: $2x^2 + 19x - 10$

Solution

Factors of -20 $[2(-10)]$	Sum
-1, 20	19

$$
\begin{aligned}
2x^2 + 19x - 10 &= 2x^2 - x + 20x - 10 \\
&= (2x^2 - x) + (20x - 10) \\
&= x(2x - 1) + 10(2x - 1) \\
&= (2x - 1)(x + 10)
\end{aligned}
$$

You Try It 3
Factor: $2a^2 + 13a - 7$

Your solution
$(2a - 1)(a + 7)$

Example 4
Factor: $24x^2y - 76xy + 40y$

Solution
The GCF is $4y$.

$$24x^2y - 76xy + 40y = 4y(6x^2 - 19x + 10)$$

Negative Factors of 60 $[6(10)]$	Sum
-1, -60	-61
-2, -30	-32
-3, -20	-23
-4, -15	-19

$$
\begin{aligned}
6x^2 - 19x + 10 &= 6x^2 - 4x - 15x + 10 \\
&= (6x^2 - 4x) - (15x - 10) \\
&= 2x(3x - 2) - 5(3x - 2) \\
&= (3x - 2)(2x - 5)
\end{aligned}
$$

$$
\begin{aligned}
24x^2y - 76xy + 40y &= 4y(6x^2 - 19x + 10) \\
&= 4y(3x - 2)(2x - 5)
\end{aligned}
$$

You Try It 4
Factor: $15x^3 + 40x^2 - 80x$

Your solution
$5x(3x - 4)(x + 4)$

Solutions on p. S20

7.3 Exercises

· ·

Objective A

Factor by using trial factors.

1. $2x^2 + 3x + 1$
$(x + 1)(2x + 1)$

2. $5x^2 + 6x + 1$
$(x + 1)(5x + 1)$

3. $2y^2 + 7y + 3$
$(y + 3)(2y + 1)$

4. $3y^2 + 7y + 2$
$(y + 2)(3y + 1)$

5. $2a^2 - 3a + 1$
$(a - 1)(2a - 1)$

6. $3a^2 - 4a + 1$
$(a - 1)(3a - 1)$

7. $2b^2 - 11b + 5$
$(b - 5)(2b - 1)$

8. $3b^2 - 13b + 4$
$(b - 4)(3b - 1)$

9. $2x^2 + x - 1$
$(x + 1)(2x - 1)$

10. $4x^2 - 3x - 1$
$(x - 1)(4x + 1)$

11. $2x^2 - 5x - 3$
$(x - 3)(2x + 1)$

12. $3x^2 + 5x - 2$
$(x + 2)(3x - 1)$

13. $2t^2 - t - 10$
$(t + 2)(2t - 5)$

14. $2t^2 + 5t - 12$
$(t + 4)(2t - 3)$

15. $3p^2 - 16p + 5$
$(p - 5)(3p - 1)$

16. $6p^2 + 5p + 1$
$(2p + 1)(3p + 1)$

17. $12y^2 - 7y + 1$
$(3y - 1)(4y - 1)$

18. $6y^2 - 5y + 1$
$(2y - 1)(3y - 1)$

19. $6z^2 - 7z + 3$
nonfactorable over
the integers

20. $9z^2 + 3z + 2$
nonfactorable over
the integers

21. $6t^2 - 11t + 4$
$(2t - 1)(3t - 4)$

22. $10t^2 + 11t + 3$
$(2t + 1)(5t + 3)$

23. $8x^2 + 33x + 4$
$(x + 4)(8x + 1)$

24. $7x^2 + 50x + 7$
$(x + 7)(7x + 1)$

25. $5x^2 - 62x - 7$
nonfactorable over
the integers

26. $9x^2 - 13x - 4$
nonfactorable over
the integers

27. $12y^2 + 19y + 5$
$(3y + 1)(4y + 5)$

28. $5y^2 - 22y + 8$
$(y - 4)(5y - 2)$

29. $7a^2 + 47a - 14$
$(a + 7)(7a - 2)$

30. $11a^2 - 54a - 5$
$(a - 5)(11a + 1)$

31. $3b^2 - 16b + 16$
$(b - 4)(3b - 4)$

32. $6b^2 - 19b + 15$
$(2b - 3)(3b - 5)$

33. $2z^2 - 27z - 14$
$(z - 14)(2z + 1)$

34. $4z^2 + 5z - 6$
$(z + 2)(4z - 3)$

35. $3p^2 + 22p - 16$
$(p + 8)(3p - 2)$

36. $7p^2 + 19p + 10$
$(p + 2)(7p + 5)$

37. $4x^2 + 6x + 2$
$2(x + 1)(2x + 1)$

38. $12x^2 + 33x - 9$
$3(x + 3)(4x - 1)$

39. $15y^2 - 50y + 35$
$5(y - 1)(3y - 7)$

40. $30y^2 + 10y - 20$
$10(y + 1)(3y - 2)$

41. $2x^3 - 11x^2 + 5x$
$x(x - 5)(2x - 1)$

42. $2x^3 - 3x^2 - 5x$
$x(x + 1)(2x - 5)$

43. $3a^2b - 16ab + 16b$
$b(a - 4)(3a - 4)$

44. $2a^2b - ab - 21b$
$b(a + 3)(2a - 7)$

45. $3z^2 + 95z + 10$
nonfactorable over the integers

46. $8z^2 - 36z + 1$
nonfactorable over the integers

47. $36x - 3x^2 - 3x^3$
$-3x(x - 3)(x + 4)$

48. $-2x^3 + 2x^2 + 4x$
$-2x(x + 1)(x - 2)$

49. $80y^2 - 36y + 4$
$4(4y - 1)(5y - 1)$

50. $24y^2 - 24y - 18$
$6(2y + 1)(2y - 3)$

51. $8z^3 + 14z^2 + 3z$
$z(2z + 3)(4z + 1)$

52. $6z^3 - 23z^2 + 20z$
$z(2z - 5)(3z - 4)$

53. $6x^2y - 11xy - 10y$
$y(2x - 5)(3x + 2)$

54. $8x^2y - 27xy + 9y$
$y(x - 3)(8x - 3)$

55. $10t^2 - 5t - 50$
$5(t + 2)(2t - 5)$

56. $16t^2 + 40t - 96$
$8(t + 4)(2t - 3)$

57. $3p^3 - 16p^2 + 5p$
$p(p - 5)(3p - 1)$

58. $6p^3 + 5p^2 + p$
$p(2p + 1)(3p + 1)$

59. $26z^2 + 98z - 24$
$2(z + 4)(13z - 3)$

60. $30z^2 - 87z + 30$
$3(2z - 5)(5z - 2)$

61. $10y^3 - 44y^2 + 16y$
$2y(y - 4)(5y - 2)$

62. $14y^3 + 94y^2 - 28y$
$2y(y + 7)(7y - 2)$

63. $4yz^3 + 5yz^2 - 6yz$
$yz(z + 2)(4z - 3)$

64. $12a^3 + 14a^2 - 48a$
$2a(2a - 3)(3a + 8)$

65. $42a^3 + 45a^2 - 27a$
$3a(2a + 3)(7a - 3)$

66. $36p^2 - 9p^3 - p^4$
$p^2(3 - p)(12 + p)$

67. $9x^2y - 30xy^2 + 25y^3$
$y(3x - 5y)(3x - 5y)$

68. $8x^2y - 38xy^2 + 35y^3$
$y(2x - 7y)(4x - 5y)$

69. $9x^3y - 24x^2y^2 + 16xy^3$
$xy(3x - 4y)(3x - 4y)$

70. $9x^3y + 12x^2y + 4xy$
$xy(3x + 2)(3x + 2)$

Objective B

Factor by grouping.

71. $6x^2 - 17x + 12$
$(2x - 3)(3x - 4)$

72. $15x^2 - 19x + 6$
$(3x - 2)(5x - 3)$

73. $5b^2 + 33b - 14$
$(b + 7)(5b - 2)$

74. $8x^2 - 30x + 25$
$(2x - 5)(4x - 5)$

75. $6a^2 + 7a - 24$
$(3a + 8)(2a - 3)$

76. $14a^2 + 15a - 9$
$(2a + 3)(7a - 3)$

77. $4z^2 + 11z + 6$
$(z + 2)(4z + 3)$

78. $6z^2 - 25z + 14$
$(2z - 7)(3z - 2)$

79. $22p^2 + 51p - 10$
$(2p + 5)(11p - 2)$

80. $14p^2 - 41p + 15$
$(2p - 5)(7p - 3)$

81. $8y^2 + 17y + 9$
$(y + 1)(8y + 9)$

82. $12y^2 - 145y + 12$
$(y - 12)(12y - 1)$

83. $18t^2 - 9t - 5$
$(6t - 5)(3t + 1)$

84. $12t^2 + 28t - 5$
$(2t + 5)(6t - 1)$

85. $6b^2 + 71b - 12$
$(b + 12)(6b - 1)$

86. $8b^2 + 65b + 8$
$(b + 8)(8b + 1)$

87. $9x^2 + 12x + 4$
$(3x + 2)(3x + 2)$

88. $25x^2 - 30x + 9$
$(5x - 3)(5x - 3)$

89. $6b^2 - 13b + 6$
$(2b - 3)(3b - 2)$

90. $20b^2 + 37b + 15$
$(4b + 5)(5b + 3)$

91. $33b^2 + 34b - 35$
$(3b + 5)(11b - 7)$

92. $15b^2 - 43b + 22$
$(3b - 2)(5b - 11)$

93. $18y^2 - 39y + 20$
$(3y - 4)(6y - 5)$

94. $24y^2 + 41y + 12$
$(3y + 4)(8y + 3)$

95. $15a^2 + 26a - 21$
$(3a + 7)(5a - 3)$

96. $6a^2 + 23a + 21$
$(2a + 3)(3a + 7)$

97. $8y^2 - 26y + 15$
$(2y - 5)(4y - 3)$

98. $18y^2 - 27y + 4$
$(3y - 4)(6y - 1)$

99. $8z^2 + 2z - 15$
$(2z + 3)(4z - 5)$

100. $10z^2 + 3z - 4$
$(5z + 4)(2z - 1)$

101. $15x^2 - 82x + 24$
nonfactorable over
the integers

102. $13z^2 + 49z - 8$
nonfactorable over
the integers

103. $10z^2 - 29z + 10$
$(2z - 5)(5z - 2)$

104. $15z^2 - 44z + 32$
$(3z - 4)(5z - 8)$

105. $36z^2 + 72z + 35$
$(6z + 5)(6z + 7)$

106. $16z^2 + 8z - 35$
$(4z + 7)(4z - 5)$

107. $3x^2 + xy - 2y^2$
$(x + y)(3x - 2y)$

108. $6x^2 + 10xy + 4y^2$
$2(3x + 2y)(x + y)$

109. $3a^2 + 5ab - 2b^2$
$(a + 2b)(3a - b)$

110. $2a^2 - 9ab + 9b^2$
$(a - 3b)(2a - 3b)$

111. $4y^2 - 11yz + 6z^2$
$(y - 2z)(4y - 3z)$

112. $2y^2 + 7yz + 5z^2$
$(2y + 5z)(y + z)$

113. $28 + 3z - z^2$
$-(z - 7)(z + 4)$

114. $15 - 2z - z^2$
$-(z + 5)(z - 3)$

115. $8 - 7x - x^2$
$-(x - 1)(x + 8)$

116. $12 + 11x - x^2$
$-(x + 1)(x - 12)$

117. $9x^2 + 33x - 60$
$3(x + 5)(3x - 4)$

118. $16x^2 - 16x - 12$
$4(2x - 3)(2x + 1)$

119. $24x^2 - 52x + 24$
$4(2x - 3)(3x - 2)$

120. $60x^2 + 95x + 20$
$5(3x + 4)(4x + 1)$

121. $35a^4 + 9a^3 - 2a^2$
$a^2(5a + 2)(7a - 1)$

122. $15a^4 + 26a^3 + 7a^2$
$a^2(5a + 7)(3a + 1)$

123. $15b^2 - 115b + 70$
$5(b - 7)(3b - 2)$

124. $25b^2 + 35b - 30$
$5(b + 2)(5b - 3)$

125. $3x^2 - 26xy + 35y^2$
$(x - 7y)(3x - 5y)$

126. $4x^2 + 16xy + 15y^2$
$(2x + 5y)(2x + 3y)$

127. $216y^2 - 3y - 3$
$3(8y - 1)(9y + 1)$

128. $360y^2 + 4y - 4$
$4(9y + 1)(10y - 1)$

129. $21 - 20x - x^2$
$-(x - 1)(x + 21)$

130. $18 + 17x - x^2$
$-(x + 1)(x - 18)$

131. $15a^2 + 11ab - 14b^2$
$(5a + 7b)(3a - 2b)$

132. $15a^2 - 31ab + 10b^2$
$(3a - 5b)(5a - 2b)$

133. $33z - 8z^2 - z^3$
$-z(z + 11)(z - 3)$

APPLYING THE CONCEPTS

Factor.

134. $2(y + 2)^2 - (y + 2) - 3$
$(2y + 1)(y + 3)$

135. $3(a + 2)^2 - (a + 2) - 4$
$(3a + 2)(a + 3)$

136. $4(y - 1)^2 - 7(y - 1) - 2$
$(4y - 3)(y - 3)$

Find all integers k such that the trinomial can be factored over the integers.

137. $2x^2 + kx + 3$
$7, -7, 5, -5$

138. $2x^2 + kx - 3$
$-5, 5, -1, 1$

139. $3x^2 + kx + 2$
$7, -7, 5, -5$

140. Write the area of the shaded portion of each diagram in factored form.

a.
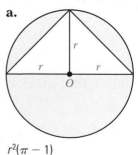
$r^2(\pi - 1)$

b.
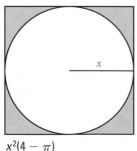
$x^2(4 - \pi)$

c.
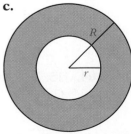
$\pi(R - r)(R + r)$

d.
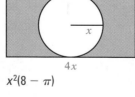
$x^2(8 - \pi)$

141. In your own words, explain how the signs of the last terms of the two binomial factors of a trinomial are determined.

7.4 Special Factoring

Objective A   *To factor the difference of two perfect squares or a perfect-square trinomial* ....

The product of a term and itself is called a **perfect square**. The exponents on variables of perfect squares are always even numbers.

Term		Perfect Square
5	$5 \cdot 5 =$	25
x	$x \cdot x =$	x^2
$3y^4$	$3y^4 \cdot 3y^4 =$	$9y^8$
x^n	$x^n \cdot x^n =$	x^{2n}

The **square root** of a perfect square is one of the two equal factors of the perfect square. "$\sqrt{\ }$" is the symbol for square root. To find the exponent of the square root of a variable term, divide the exponent by 2.

$$\sqrt{25} = 5$$
$$\sqrt{x^2} = x$$
$$\sqrt{9y^8} = 3y^4$$
$$\sqrt{x^{2n}} = x^n$$

The difference of two perfect squares is the product of the sum and difference of two terms. The factors of the difference of two perfect squares are the sum and difference of the square roots of the perfect squares.

> **Factors of the Difference of Two Perfect Squares**
>
> $a^2 - b^2 = (a + b)(a - b)$

The sum of two perfect squares, $a^2 + b^2$, is nonfactorable over the integers.

➡ Factor: $4x^2 - 81y^2$

$4x^2 - 81y^2 = (2x)^2 - (9y)^2$ • Write the binomial as the difference of two perfect squares.

$\qquad\qquad = (2x + 9y)(2x - 9y)$ • The factors are the sum and difference of the square roots of the perfect squares.

A perfect-square trinomial is the square of a binomial.

> **Factors of a Perfect-Square Trinomial**
>
> $a^2 + 2ab + b^2 = (a + b)^2$
> $a^2 - 2ab + b^2 = (a - b)^2$

In factoring a perfect-square trinomial, remember that the terms of the binomial are the square roots of the perfect squares of the trinomial. The sign in the binomial is the sign of the middle term of the trinomial.

➡ Factor: $4x^2 + 12x + 9$

Because $4x^2$ is a perfect square $[4x^2 = (2x)^2]$ and 9 is a perfect square $(9 = 3^2)$, try factoring $4x^2 + 12x + 9$ as the square of a binomial.

$4x^2 + 12x + 9 \overset{2}{=} (2x + 3)^2$

Check: $(2x + 3)^2 = (2x + 3)(2x + 3) = 4x^2 + 6x + 6x + 9 = 4x^2 + 12x + 9$

The check verifies that $4x^2 + 12x + 9 = (2x + 3)^2$.

It is important to check a proposed factorization as we did above. The next example illustrates the importance of this check.

➡ Factor: $x^2 + 13x + 36$

Because x^2 is a perfect square and 36 is a perfect square, try factoring $x^2 + 13x + 36$ as the square of a binomial.

$x^2 + 13x + 36 \overset{2}{=} (x + 6)^2$

Check: $(x + 6)^2 = (x + 6)(x + 6) = x^2 + 6x + 6x + 36 = x^2 + 12x + 36$

INSTRUCTOR NOTE

Another example of what appears to be a perfect square trinomial, but does not factor, is $4x^2 - 17x + 25$.

In this case, the proposed factorization of $x^2 + 13x + 36$ does *not* check. Try another factorization. The numbers 4 and 9 are factors of 36 whose sum is 13.

$x^2 + 13x + 36 = (x + 4)(x + 9)$

Example 1
Factor: $25x^2 - 1$

Solution
$25x^2 - 1 = (5x)^2 - (1)^2$
$\quad\quad\quad = (5x + 1)(5x - 1)$

You Try It 1
Factor: $x^2 - 36y^4$

Your solution
$(x + 6y^2)(x - 6y^2)$

Example 2
Factor: $4x^2 - 20x + 25$

Solution
$4x^2 - 20x + 25 = (2x - 5)^2$

You Try It 2
Factor: $9x^2 + 12x + 4$

Your solution
$(3x + 2)^2$

Example 3
Factor: $(x + y)^2 - 4$

Solution
$(x + y)^2 - 4 = (x + y)^2 - (2)^2$
$\quad\quad\quad\quad\quad = (x + y + 2)(x + y - 2)$

You Try It 3
Factor: $(a + b)^2 - (a - b)^2$

Your solution
$4ab$

Solutions on p. S20

Objective B **To factor the sum or the difference of two cubes**......................... (21) HM³

The product of the same three factors is called a **perfect cube**. The exponents on variables of perfect cubes are always divisible by 3.

Term		*Perfect Cube*
2	$2 \cdot 2 \cdot 2 = 2^3 =$	8
$3y$	$3y \cdot 3y \cdot 3y = (3y)^3 =$	$27y^3$
y^2	$y^2 \cdot y^2 \cdot y^2 = (y^2)^3 =$	y^6

The **cube root** of a perfect cube is one of the three equal factors of the perfect cube. "$\sqrt[3]{}$" is the symbol for cube root. To find the exponent of the cube root of a variable term, divide the exponent by 3.

$$\sqrt[3]{8} = 2$$
$$\sqrt[3]{27y^3} = 3y$$
$$\sqrt[3]{y^6} = y^2$$

The following rules are used to factor the sum or difference of two perfect cubes.

Factors of the Sum or Difference of Two Cubes

$$a^3 + b^3 = (a + b)(a^2 - ab + b^2)$$
$$a^3 - b^3 = (a - b)(a^2 + ab + b^2)$$

➡ Factor: $8x^3 - 27$

Write the binomial as the difference of two perfect cubes.

$$8x^3 - 27 = (2x)^3 - 3^3$$

The terms of the binomial factor are the cube roots of the perfect cubes. The sign of the binomial factor is the same sign as in the given binomial. The trinomial factor is obtained from the binomial factor.

$$= (2x - 3)(4x^2 + 6x + 9)$$

Square of the first term ⟶
Opposite of the product of the two terms ⟶
Square of the last term ⟶

Check:

$$\begin{array}{r} 4x^2 + 6x + 9 \\ 2x - 3 \\ \hline -12x^2 - 18x - 27 \\ 8x^3 + 12x^2 + 18x \\ \hline 8x^3 - 27 \end{array}$$

• The original polynomial

➡ Factor: $a^3 + 64y^3$

$$a^3 + 64y^3 = a^3 + (4y)^3$$

• Write the binomial as the sum of two perfect cubes.

$$= (a + 4y)(a^2 - 4ay + 16y^2)$$

• Factor.

➡ Factor: $64y^4 - 125y$

$$64y^4 - 125y = y(64y^3 - 125)$$

• Factor out y, the GCF.

$$= y[(4y)^3 - 5^3]$$

• Write the binomial as the difference of two cubes.

$$= y(4y - 5)(16y^2 + 20y + 25)$$

• Factor.

Example 4

Factor: $x^3y^3 - 1$

Solution

$x^3y^3 - 1 = (xy)^3 - 1^3$
$\qquad\quad = (xy - 1)(x^2y^2 + xy + 1)$

You Try It 4

Factor: $8x^3 + y^3z^3$

Your solution

$(2x + yz)(4x^2 - 2xyz + y^2z^2)$

Example 5

Factor: $(x + y)^3 - x^3$

Solution

$(x + y)^3 - x^3$
$\quad = [(x + y) - x][(x + y)^2 + x(x + y) + x^2]$
$\quad = y(x^2 + 2xy + y^2 + x^2 + xy + x^2)$
$\quad = y(3x^2 + 3xy + y^2)$

You Try It 5

Factor: $(x - y)^3 + (x + y)^3$

Your solution

$2x(x^2 + 3y^2)$

Solutions on p. S20

Objective C   **To factor a trinomial that is quadratic in form** ....

Certain trinomials that are not quadratic can be expressed in the form $ax^2 + bx + c$ by making suitable variable substitutions. A trinomial is *quadratic in form* if it can be written as $au^2 + bu + c$.

Each of the trinomials shown below is quadratic in form.

$$x^4 + 5x^2 + 6 \qquad\qquad\qquad 2x^2y^2 + 3xy - 9$$

$$(x^2)^2 + 5(x^2) + 6 \qquad\qquad\qquad 2(xy)^2 + 3(xy) - 9$$

Let $u = x^2$. $u^2 + 5u + 6$ Let $u = xy$. $2u^2 + 3u - 9$

When we use this method to factor a trinomial that is quadratic in form, the variable part of the first term in each binomial will be u.

For example, $x^4 + 5x^2 + 6$ is quadratic in form by letting $u = x^2$. Thus,

$x^4 + 5x^2 + 6 = (x^2)^2 + 5(x^2) + 6 = u^2 + 5u + 6$.

➡ Factor: $x^4 + 5x^2 + 6$

$\quad x^4 + 5x^2 + 6 = u^2 + 5u + 6$ • Let $u = x^2$.

$\qquad\qquad\qquad = (u + 3)(u + 2)$ • Factor.

$\qquad\qquad\qquad = (x^2 + 3)(x^2 + 2)$ • Replace u by x^2.

Example 6

Factor: $6x^2y^2 - xy - 12$

Solution

Let $u = xy$.

$6x^2y^2 - xy - 12 = 6u^2 - u - 12$
$= (3u + 4)(2u - 3)$
$= (3xy + 4)(2xy - 3)$

You Try It 6

Factor: $6x^2y^2 - 19xy + 10$

Your solution

$(2xy - 5)(3xy - 2)$

Example 7

Factor: $2x^4 + 5x^2 - 12$

Solution

Let $u = x^2$.

$2x^4 + 5x^2 - 12 = 2u^2 + 5u - 12$
$= (2u - 3)(u + 4)$
$= (2x^2 - 3)(x^2 + 4)$

You Try It 7

Factor: $3x^4 + 4x^2 - 4$

Your solution

$(x^2 + 2)(3x^2 - 2)$

Example 8

Factor: $x^4y^4 + 3x^2y^2 - 10$

Solution

Let $u = x^2y^2$.

$x^4y^4 + 3x^2y^2 - 10 = u^2 + 3u - 10$
$= (u + 5)(u - 2)$
$= (x^2y^2 + 5)(x^2y^2 - 2)$

You Try It 8

Factor: $a^4b^4 + 6a^2b^2 - 7$

Your solution

$(a^2b^2 + 7)(a^2b^2 - 1)$

Solutions on p. S20

Objective D *To factor completely* ....

When factoring a polynomial completely, ask the following questions about the polynomial.

1. Is there a common factor? If so, factor out the GCF.

2. If the polynomial is a binomial, is it the difference of two perfect squares, the sum of two cubes, or the difference of two cubes? If so, factor.

3. If the polynomial is a trinomial, is it a perfect-square trinomial or the product of two binomials? If so, factor.

4. If the polynomial has four terms, can it be factored by grouping? If so, factor.

5. Is each factor nonfactorable over the integers? If not, factor.

Example 9

Factor: $6a^3 + 15a^2 - 36a$

Solution

$$6a^3 + 15a^2 - 36a = 3a(2a^2 + 5a - 12)$$
$$= 3a(2a - 3)(a + 4)$$

You Try It 9

Factor: $18x^3 - 6x^2 - 60x$

Your solution

$6x(3x + 5)(x - 2)$

Example 10

Factor: $x^2y + 2x^2 - y - 2$

Solution

$$x^2y + 2x^2 - y - 2 = (x^2y + 2x^2) - (y + 2)$$
$$= x^2(y + 2) - 1(y + 2)$$
$$= (y + 2)(x^2 - 1)$$
$$= (y + 2)(x + 1)(x - 1)$$

You Try It 10

Factor: $4x - 4y - x^3 + x^2y$

Your solution

$(x - y)(2 + x)(2 - x)$

Example 11

Factor: $x^{4n} - y^{4n}$

Solution

$$x^{4n} - y^{4n} = (x^{2n})^2 - (y^{2n})^2$$
$$= (x^{2n} + y^{2n})(x^{2n} - y^{2n})$$
$$= (x^{2n} + y^{2n})[(x^n)^2 - (y^n)^2]$$
$$= (x^{2n} + y^{2n})(x^n + y^n)(x^n - y^n)$$

You Try It 11

Factor: $x^{4n} - x^{2n}y^{2n}$

Your solution

$x^{2n}(x^n + y^n)(x^n - y^n)$

Example 12

Factor: $x^{n+3} + x^n y^3$

Solution

$$x^{n+3} + x^n y^3 = x^n(x^3 + y^3)$$
$$= x^n(x + y)(x^2 - xy + y^2)$$

You Try It 12

Factor: $ax^5 - ax^2y^6$

Your solution

$ax^2(x - y^2)(x^2 + xy^2 + y^4)$

Solutions on p. S20

7.4 Exercises

· ·

Objective A

Factor.

1. $x^2 - 16$
$(x + 4)(x - 4)$

2. $y^2 - 49$
$(y + 7)(y - 7)$

3. $4x^2 - 1$
$(2x + 1)(2x - 1)$

4. $81x^2 - 4$
$(9x + 2)(9x - 2)$

5. $16x^2 - 121$
$(4x + 11)(4x - 11)$

6. $49y^2 - 36$
$(7y + 6)(7y - 6)$

7. $1 - 9a^2$
$(1 + 3a)(1 - 3a)$

8. $16 - 81y^2$
$(4 + 9y)(4 - 9y)$

9. $x^2y^2 - 100$
$(xy + 10)(xy - 10)$

10. $a^2b^2 - 25$
$(ab + 5)(ab - 5)$

11. $x^2 + 4$
nonfactorable over
the integers

12. $a^2 + 16$
nonfactorable over
the integers

13. $25 - a^2b^2$
$(5 + ab)(5 - ab)$

14. $64 - x^2y^2$
$(8 + xy)(8 - xy)$

15. $a^{2n} - 1$
$(a^n + 1)(a^n - 1)$

16. $b^{2n} - 16$
$(b^n + 4)(b^n - 4)$

17. $x^2 - 12x + 36$
$(x - 6)^2$

18. $y^2 - 6y + 9$
$(y - 3)^2$

19. $b^2 - 2b + 1$
$(b - 1)^2$

20. $a^2 + 14a + 49$
$(a + 7)^2$

21. $16x^2 - 40x + 25$
$(4x - 5)^2$

22. $49x^2 + 28x + 4$
$(7x + 2)^2$

23. $4a^2 + 4a - 1$
nonfactorable over
the integers

24. $9x^2 + 12x - 4$
nonfactorable over
the integers

25. $b^2 + 7b + 14$
nonfactorable over
the integers

26. $y^2 - 5y + 25$
nonfactorable over
the integers

27. $x^2 + 6xy + 9y^2$
$(x + 3y)^2$

28. $4x^2y^2 + 12xy + 9$
$(2xy + 3)^2$

29. $25a^2 - 40ab + 16b^2$
$(5a - 4b)^2$

30. $4a^2 - 36ab + 81b^2$
$(2a - 9b)^2$

31. $x^{2n} + 6x^n + 9$
$(x^n + 3)^2$

32. $y^{2n} - 16y^n + 64$
$(y^n - 8)^2$

33. $(x - 4)^2 - 9$
$(x - 7)(x - 1)$

34. $16 - (a - 3)^2$
$(7 - a)(1 + a)$

35. $(x - y)^2 - (a + b)^2$
$(x - y + a + b)(x - y - a - b)$

36. $(x - 2y)^2 - (x + y)^2$
$(-3y)(2x - y)$

Objective B

Factor.

37. $x^3 - 27$
$(x - 3)(x^2 + 3x + 9)$

38. $y^3 + 125$
$(y + 5)(y^2 - 5y + 25)$

39. $8x^3 - 1$
$(2x - 1)(4x^2 + 2x + 1)$

40. $64a^3 + 27$
$(4a + 3)(16a^2 - 12a + 9)$

41. $x^3 - y^3$
$(x - y)(x^2 + xy + y^2)$

42. $x^3 - 8y^3$
$(x - 2y)(x^2 + 2xy + 4y^2)$

43. $m^3 + n^3$
$(m + n)(m^2 - mn + n^2)$

44. $27a^3 + b^3$
$(3a + b)(9a^2 - 3ab + b^2)$

45. $64x^3 + 1$
$(4x + 1)(16x^2 - 4x + 1)$

46. $1 - 125b^3$
$(1 - 5b)(1 + 5b + 25b^2)$

47. $27x^3 - 8y^3$
$(3x - 2y)(9x^2 + 6xy + 4y^2)$

48. $64x^3 + 27y^3$
$(4x + 3y)(16x^2 - 12xy + 9y^2)$

49. $x^3y^3 + 64$
$(xy + 4)(x^2y^2 - 4xy + 16)$

50. $8x^3y^3 + 27$
$(2xy + 3)(4x^2y^2 - 6xy + 9)$

51. $16x^3 - y^3$
nonfactorable over
the integers

52. $27x^3 - 8y^2$
nonfactorable over
the integers

53. $8x^3 - 9y^3$
nonfactorable over
the integers

54. $27a^3 - 16$
nonfactorable over
the integers

55. $(a - b)^3 - b^3$
$(a - 2b)(a^2 - ab + b^2)$

56. $a^3 + (a + b)^3$
$(2a + b)(a^2 + ab + b^2)$

57. $x^{6n} + y^{3n}$
$(x^{2n} + y^n)(x^{4n} - x^{2n}y^n + y^{2n})$

58. $x^{3n} + y^{3n}$
$(x^n + y^n)(x^{2n} - x^ny^n + y^{2n})$

59. $x^{3n} + 8$
$(x^n + 2)(x^{2n} - 2x^n + 4)$

60. $a^{3n} + 64$
$(a^n + 4)(a^{2n} - 4a^n + 16)$

Objective C

Factor.

61. $x^2y^2 - 8xy + 15$
$(xy - 3)(xy - 5)$

62. $x^2y^2 - 8xy - 33$
$(xy + 3)(xy - 11)$

63. $x^2y^2 - 17xy + 60$
$(xy - 5)(xy - 12)$

64. $a^2b^2 + 10ab + 24$
$(ab + 6)(ab + 4)$

65. $x^4 - 9x^2 + 18$
$(x^2 - 3)(x^2 - 6)$

66. $y^4 - 6y^2 - 16$
$(y^2 + 2)(y^2 - 8)$

67. $b^4 - 13b^2 - 90$
$(b^2 + 5)(b^2 - 18)$

68. $a^4 + 14a^2 + 45$
$(a^2 + 5)(a^2 + 9)$

69. $x^4y^4 - 8x^2y^2 + 12$
$(x^2y^2 - 2)(x^2y^2 - 6)$

70. $a^4b^4 + 11a^2b^2 - 26$
$(a^2b^2 + 13)(a^2b^2 - 2)$

71. $x^{2n} + 3x^n + 2$
$(x^n + 1)(x^n + 2)$

72. $a^{2n} - a^n - 12$
$(a^n + 3)(a^n - 4)$

73. $3x^2y^2 - 14xy + 15$
$(3xy - 5)(xy - 3)$

74. $5x^2y^2 - 59xy + 44$
$(5xy - 4)(xy - 11)$

75. $6a^2b^2 - 23ab + 21$
$(2ab - 3)(3ab - 7)$

76. $10a^2b^2 + 3ab - 7$
$(ab + 1)(10ab - 7)$

77. $2x^4 - 13x^2 - 15$
$(2x^2 - 15)(x^2 + 1)$

78. $3x^4 + 20x^2 + 32$
$(x^2 + 4)(3x^2 + 8)$

79. $2x^{2n} - 7x^n + 3$
$(2x^n - 1)(x^n - 3)$

80. $4x^{2n} + 8x^n - 5$
$(2x^n + 5)(2x^n - 1)$

81. $6a^{2n} + 19a^n + 10$
$(2a^n + 5)(3a^n + 2)$

Objective D

Factor.

82. $5x^2 + 10x + 5$
$5(x + 1)^2$

83. $12x^2 - 36x + 27$
$3(2x - 3)^2$

84. $3x^4 - 81x$
$3x(x - 3)(x^2 + 3x + 9)$

85. $27a^4 - a$
$a(3a - 1)(9a^2 + 3a + 1)$

86. $7x^2 - 28$
$7(x + 2)(x - 2)$

87. $20x^2 - 5$
$5(2x + 1)(2x - 1)$

88. $y^4 - 10y^3 + 21y^2$
$y^2(y - 7)(y - 3)$

89. $y^5 + 6y^4 - 55y^3$
$y^3(y + 11)(y - 5)$

90. $x^4 - 16$
$(x^2 + 4)(x + 2)(x - 2)$

91. $16x^4 - 81$
$(4x^2 + 9)(2x + 3)(2x - 3)$

92. $8x^5 - 98x^3$
$2x^3(2x + 7)(2x - 7)$

93. $16a - 2a^4$
$2a(2 - a)(4 + 2a + a^2)$

94. $x^3y^3 - x^3$
$x^3(y - 1)(y^2 + y + 1)$

95. $a^3b^6 - b^3$
$b^3(ab - 1)(a^2b^2 + ab + 1)$

96. $x^6y^6 - x^3y^3$
$x^3y^3(xy - 1)(x^2y^2 + xy + 1)$

97. $8x^4 - 40x^3 + 50x^2$
$2x^2(2x - 5)^2$

98. $6x^5 + 74x^4 + 24x^3$
$2x^3(3x + 1)(x + 12)$

99. $x^4 - y^4$
$(x^2 + y^2)(x + y)(x - y)$

100. $16a^4 - b^4$
$(4a^2 + b^2)(2a + b)(2a - b)$

101. $x^6 + y^6$
$(x^2 + y^2)(x^4 - x^2y^2 + y^4)$

102. $x^4 - 5x^2 - 4$
nonfactorable over
the integers

103. $a^4 - 25a^2 - 144$
nonfactorable over
the integers

104. $3b^5 - 24b^2$
$3b^2(b - 2)(b^2 + 2b + 4)$

105. $16a^4 - 2a$
$2a(2a - 1)(4a^2 + 2a + 1)$

106. $x^4y^2 - 5x^3y^3 + 6x^2y^4$
$x^2y^2(x - 2y)(x - 3y)$

107. $a^4b^2 - 8a^3b^3 - 48a^2b^4$
$a^2b^2(a + 4b)(a - 12b)$

108. $16x^3y + 4x^2y^2 - 42xy^3$
$2xy(4x + 7y)(2x - 3y)$

109. $24a^2b^2 - 14ab^3 - 90b^4$
$2b^2(3a + 5b)(4a - 9b)$

110. $x^3 - 2x^2 - x + 2$
$(x - 2)(x + 1)(x - 1)$

111. $x^3 - 2x^2 - 4x + 8$
$(x - 2)^2(x + 2)$

112. $4x^2y^2 - 4x^2 - 9y^2 + 9$
$(y + 1)(y - 1)(2x + 3)(2x - 3)$

113. $4x^4 - x^2 - 4x^2y^2 + y^2$
$(x + y)(x - y)(2x + 1)(2x - 1)$

114. $x^5 - 4x^3 - 8x^2 + 32$
$(x + 2)(x - 2)^2(x^2 + 2x + 4)$

115. $x^6y^3 + x^3 - x^3y^3 - 1$
$(x - 1)(x^2 + x + 1)(xy + 1)(x^2y^2 - xy + 1)$

116. $a^{2n+2} - 6a^{n+2} + 9a^2$
$a^2(a^n - 3)^2$

117. $x^{2n+1} + 2x^{n+1} + x$
$x(x^n + 1)^2$

118. $2x^{n+2} - 7x^{n+1} + 3x^n$
$x^n(2x - 1)(x - 3)$

119. $3b^{n+2} + 4b^{n+1} - 4b^n$
$b^n(3b - 2)(b + 2)$

APPLYING THE CONCEPTS

120. Find all integers k such that the trinomial is a perfect square.
   a. $x^2 + kx + 36$ **b.** $4x^2 - kx + 25$ **c.** $49x^2 + kxy + 64y^2$
     $-12, 12$ $-20, 20$ $-112, 112$

   d. $x^2 + 8x + k$ **e.** $x^2 - 12x + k$ **f.** $x^2 + 4xy + ky^2$
     16   36   4

121. Factor: $x^2(x - 3) - 3x(x - 3) + 2(x - 3)$
$(x - 3)(x - 2)(x - 1)$

122. Factor $x^4 + 64$. *Suggestion:* Add and subtract $16x^2$ so that the expression becomes $(x^4 + 16x^2 + 64) - 16x^2$. Now factor by grouping.
$(x^2 - 4x + 8)(x^2 + 4x + 8)$

123. The area of a square is $(16x^2 + 24x + 9)$ m². Find the dimensions of the square in terms of the variable x. Can $x = 0$? What are the possible values of x?
$(4x + 3)$ m by $(4x + 3)$ m. Yes. $x > -\dfrac{3}{4}$

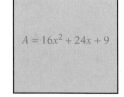

$A = 16x^2 + 24x + 9$

124. Can a third-degree polynomial have factors $(x - 1)$, $(x + 1)$, $(x - 3)$, and $(x + 4)$? Why or why not?

125. Given that $(x - 3)$ and $(x + 4)$ are factors of $x^3 + 6x^2 - 7x - 60$, explain how you can find a third *first-degree* factor of $x^3 + 6x^2 - 7x - 60$. Then find the factor.

7.5 Solving Equations

Objective A *To solve equations by factoring* ....

The Multiplication Property of Zero states that the product of a number and zero is zero. This property is stated below.

If a is a real number, then $a \cdot 0 = 0 \cdot a = 0$.

Now consider $x \cdot y = 0$. For this to be a true equation, then either $x = 0$ or $y = 0$.

> **Principle of Zero Products**
>
> If the product of two factors is zero, then at least one of the factors must be zero.
>
> If $a \cdot b = 0$, then $a = 0$ or $b = 0$.

The Principle of Zero Products is used to solve some equations.

➡ Solve: $(x - 2)(x - 3) = 0$

By the Principle of Zero Products, if $(x - 2)(x - 3) = 0$, then $x - 2 = 0$ or $x - 3 = 0$.

$(x - 2)(x - 3) = 0$

$x - 2 = 0 \qquad x - 3 = 0$ • Let each factor equal zero (the Principle of Zero Products).

$x = 2 \qquad\quad x = 3$ • Solve each equation for x.

Check:

$$\frac{(x - 2)(x - 3) = 0}{(2 - 2)(2 - 3) \mid 0}$$
$$0(-1) \mid 0$$
$$0 = 0 \quad \text{True}$$

$$\frac{(x - 2)(x - 3) = 0}{(3 - 2)(3 - 3) \mid 0}$$
$$(1)(0) \mid 0$$
$$0 = 0 \quad \text{True}$$

The solutions are 2 and 3.

An equation of the form $ax^2 + bx + c = 0$, $a \neq 0$, is a **quadratic equation**. A quadratic equation is in **standard form** when the polynomial is in descending order and equal to zero. The quadratic equations at the right are in standard form.

$3x^2 + 2x + 1 = 0$

$4x^2 - 3x + 2 = 0$

➡ Solve: $2x^2 + x = 6$

$$2x^2 + x = 6$$
$$2x^2 + x - 6 = 0$$ • Write the equation in standard form.
$$(2x - 3)(x + 2) = 0$$ • Factor.
$$2x - 3 = 0 \qquad x + 2 = 0$$ • Use the Principle of Zero Products.
$$2x = 3 \qquad\qquad x = -2$$ • Solve each equation for x.
$$x = \frac{3}{2}$$

$\frac{3}{2}$ and -2 check as solutions. The solutions are $\frac{3}{2}$ and -2.

Example 1

Solve: $x(x - 3) = 0$

Solution

$x(x - 3) = 0$

$x = 0 \qquad x - 3 = 0$
$\qquad\qquad x = 3$

The solutions are 0 and 3.

You Try It 1

Solve: $2x(x + 7) = 0$

Your solution

0 and -7

Example 2

Solve: $2x^2 - 50 = 0$

Solution

$$2x^2 - 50 = 0$$
$$2(x^2 - 25) = 0$$
$$2(x + 5)(x - 5) = 0$$

$x + 5 = 0 \qquad x - 5 = 0$
$\quad x = -5 \qquad\quad x = 5$

The solutions are -5 and 5.

You Try It 2

Solve: $4x^2 - 9 = 0$

Your solution

$\dfrac{3}{2}$ and $-\dfrac{3}{2}$

Example 3

Solve: $(x - 3)(x - 10) = -10$

Solution

$(x - 3)(x - 10) = -10$
$x^2 - 13x + 30 = -10$ • Multiply $(x - 3)(x - 10)$.
$x^2 - 13x + 40 = 0$ • Add 10 to each side of
$(x - 8)(x - 5) = 0$ the equation. The equation
                        is now in standard form.

$x - 8 = 0 \qquad x - 5 = 0$
$\quad x = 8 \qquad\quad x = 5$

The solutions are 8 and 5.

You Try It 3

Solve: $(x + 2)(x - 7) = 52$

Your solution

-6 and 11

Solutions on pp. S20–S21

Objective B   To solve application problems...

Recall that the integers are the numbers . . . , $-3, -2, -1, 0, 1, 2, 3, \ldots$.

An **even integer** is an integer that is divisible by 2. Examples of even integers are -8, 0, and 22. An **odd integer** is an integer that is not divisible by 2. Examples of odd integers are -17, 1, and 39.

Consecutive integers are integers that follow one another in order. Examples of consecutive integers are shown at the right. (Assume that the variable n represents an integer.)	11, 12, 13 $-8, -7, -6$ $n, n + 1, n + 2$
Examples of **consecutive even integers** are shown at the right. (Assume that the variable n represents an even integer.)	24, 26, 28 $-10, -8, -6$ $n, n + 2, n + 4$
Examples of **consecutive odd integers** are shown at the right. (Assume that the variable n represents an odd integer.)	19, 21, 23 $-1, 1, 3$ $n, n + 2, n + 4$

Example 4

The sum of the squares of two consecutive positive even integers is equal to 100. Find the two integers.

Strategy

First positive even integer: n
Second positive even integer: $n + 2$

The sum of the square of the first positive even integer and the square of the second positive even integer is 100.

Solution

$$n^2 + (n + 2)^2 = 100$$
$$n^2 + n^2 + 4n + 4 = 100$$
$$2n^2 + 4n + 4 = 100$$
$$2n^2 + 4n - 96 = 0$$
$$2(n^2 + 2n - 48) = 0$$
$$n^2 + 2n - 48 = 0 \qquad \bullet \text{ Divide each side of the equation by 2.}$$

$$(n - 6)(n + 8) = 0$$

$$n - 6 = 0 \qquad n + 8 = 0$$
$$n = 6 \qquad\quad n = -8$$

Because -8 is not a positive even integer, it is not a solution.

$$n = 6$$
$$n + 2 = 6 + 2 = 8$$

The two integers are 6 and 8.

You Try It 4

The sum of the squares of two positive consecutive integers is 61. Find the two integers.

Your strategy

Your solution

5 and 6

Solution on p. S21

Example 5

A stone is thrown into a well with an initial speed of 4 ft/s. The well is 420 ft deep. How many seconds later will the stone hit the bottom of the well? Use the equation $d = vt + 16t^2$, where d is the distance in feet, v is the initial speed, and t is the time in seconds.

Strategy

To find the time for the stone to drop to the bottom of the well, replace the variables d and v by their given values and solve for t.

Solution

$$d = vt + 16t^2$$
$$420 = 4t + 16t^2$$
$$0 = -420 + 4t + 16t^2$$
$$16t^2 + 4t - 420 = 0$$
$$4(4t^2 + t - 105) = 0$$
$$4t^2 + t - 105 = 0 \quad \bullet \text{ Divide each side of the equation by 4.}$$

$$(4t + 21)(t - 5) = 0$$

$$4t + 21 = 0 \qquad t - 5 = 0$$
$$4t = -21 \qquad t = 5$$
$$t = -\frac{21}{4}$$

Because the time cannot be a negative number, $-\frac{21}{4}$ is not a solution.

The time is 5 s.

You Try It 5

The length of a rectangle is 4 in. longer than twice the width. The area of the rectangle is 96 in². Find the length and width of the rectangle.

Your strategy

Your solution

width: 6 in.;
length: 16 in.

Solution on p. S21

7.5 Exercises

· ·

Objective A

1. In your own words, explain why it is possible to solve a quadratic equation using the Principle of Zero Products.

Solve.

2. $(y + 3)(y + 2) = 0$
$-3, -2$

3. $(y - 3)(y - 5) = 0$
$3, 5$

4. $(z - 7)(z - 3) = 0$
$7, 3$

5. $(z + 8)(z - 9) = 0$
$-8, 9$

6. $x(x - 5) = 0$
$0, 5$

7. $x(x + 2) = 0$
$0, -2$

8. $a(a - 9) = 0$
$0, 9$

9. $a(a + 12) = 0$
$0, -12$

10. $y(2y + 3) = 0$
$0, -\dfrac{3}{2}$

11. $t(4t - 7) = 0$
$0, \dfrac{7}{4}$

12. $2a(3a - 2) = 0$
$0, \dfrac{2}{3}$

13. $4b(2b + 5) = 0$
$0, -\dfrac{5}{2}$

14. $(b + 2)(b - 5) = 0$
$-2, 5$

15. $(b - 8)(b + 3) - 0$
$8, -3$

16. $x^2 - 81 = 0$
$9, -9$

17. $x^2 - 121 = 0$
$11, -11$

18. $4x^2 - 49 = 0$
$\dfrac{7}{2}, -\dfrac{7}{2}$

19. $16x^2 - 1 = 0$
$\dfrac{1}{4}, -\dfrac{1}{4}$

20. $9x^2 - 1 = 0$
$\dfrac{1}{3}, -\dfrac{1}{3}$

21. $16x^2 - 49 = 0$
$\dfrac{7}{4}, -\dfrac{7}{4}$

22. $x^2 + 6x + 8 = 0$
$-4, -2$

23. $x^2 - 8x + 15 - 0$
$3, 5$

24. $z^2 + 5z - 14 = 0$
$2, -7$

25. $z^2 + z - 72 = 0$
$8, -9$

26. $2a^2 - 9a - 5 = 0$
$-\dfrac{1}{2}, 5$

27. $3a^2 + 14a + 8 = 0$
$-\dfrac{2}{3}, -4$

28. $6z^2 + 5z + 1 = 0$
$-\dfrac{1}{3}, -\dfrac{1}{2}$

29. $6y^2 - 19y + 15 = 0$
$\dfrac{5}{3}, \dfrac{3}{2}$

30. $x^2 - 3x = 0$
$0, 3$

31. $a^2 - 5a = 0$
$0, 5$

32. $x^2 - 7x = 0$
$0, 7$

33. $2a^2 - 8a = 0$
$0, 4$

34. $a^2 + 5a = -4$
$-1, -4$

35. $a^2 - 5a = 24$
$-3, 8$

36. $y^2 - 5y = -6$
$2, 3$

37. $y^2 - 7y = 8$
$-1, 8$

38. $2t^2 + 7t = 4$
$\dfrac{1}{2}, -4$

39. $3t^2 + t = 10$
$\dfrac{5}{3}, -2$

40. $3t^2 - 13t = -4$
$\dfrac{1}{3}, 4$

41. $5t^2 - 16t = -12$
$\dfrac{6}{5}, 2$

42. $x(x - 12) = -27$ **43.** $x(x - 11) = 12$ **44.** $y(y - 7) = 18$ **45.** $y(y + 8) = -15$
 3, 9   12, −1   9, −2   −3, −5

46. $p(p + 3) = -2$ **47.** $p(p - 1) = 20$ **48.** $y(y + 4) = 45$ **49.** $y(y - 8) = -15$
 −1, −2   5, −4   5, −9   3, 5

50. $x(x + 3) = 28$ **51.** $p(p - 14) = 15$ **52.** $(x + 8)(x - 3) = -30$ **53.** $(x + 4)(x - 1) = 14$
 4, −7   15, −1   −2, −3   −6, 3

54. $(z - 5)(z + 4) = 52$ **55.** $(z - 8)(z + 4) = -35$ **56.** $(z - 6)(z + 1) = -10$
 −8, 9   1, 3   1, 4

57. $(a + 3)(a + 4) = 72$ **58.** $(a - 4)(a + 7) = -18$ **59.** $(2x + 5)(x + 1) = -1$

 −12, 5   −5, 2 $-\dfrac{3}{2}, -2$

Objective B *Application Problems*

60. The square of a positive number is six more than five times the positive number. Find the number.
6

61. The square of a negative number is fifteen more than twice the negative number. Find the number.
−3

62. The sum of two numbers is six. The sum of the squares of the two numbers is twenty. Find the two numbers.
2, 4

63. The sum of two numbers is eight. The sum of the squares of the two numbers is thirty-four. Find the two numbers.
3, 5

64. The sum of the squares of two consecutive positive integers is forty-one. Find the two integers.
4, 5

65. The sum of the squares of two consecutive positive even integers is one hundred sixty-four. Find the two integers.
8, 10

66. The length of a rectangle is 2 ft more than twice the width. The area of the rectangle is 84 ft². Find the length and width of the rectangle.
length: 14 ft; width: 6 ft

w

$2w + 2$

67. The length of a rectangle is 8 cm more than three times the width. The area of the rectangle is 380 cm². Find the length and width of the rectangle.
length: 38 cm; width: 10 cm

The formula $S = \frac{n^2 + n}{2}$ gives the sum, S, of the first n natural numbers. Use this formula for Exercises 68 and 69.

68. How many consecutive natural numbers beginning with 1 will give a sum of 78?
12

69. How many consecutive natural numbers beginning with 1 will give a sum of 171?
18

The formula $N = \frac{t^2 - t}{2}$ gives the number, N, of football games that must be scheduled in a league with t teams if each team is to play every other team once. Use this formula for Exercises 70 and 71.

70. How many teams are in a league that schedules 15 games in such a way that each team plays every other team once?
6 teams

71. How many teams are in a league that schedules 45 games in such a way that each team plays every other team once?
10 teams

The distance, s, in feet, that an object will fall (neglecting air resistance) in t seconds is given by $s = vt + 16t^2$, where v is the initial velocity of the object in feet per second. Use this formula for Exercises 72 and 73.

72. An object is released from the top of a building 192 ft high. The initial velocity is 16 ft/s, and air resistance is neglected. How many seconds later will the object hit the ground?
3 s

73. An object is released from the top of a building 320 ft high. The initial velocity is 16 ft/s, and air resistance is neglected. How many seconds later will the object hit the ground?
4 s

The height, h, in feet, an object will attain (neglecting air resistance) in t seconds is given by $h = vt - 16t^2$, where v is the initial velocity of the object in feet per second. Use this formula for Exercises 74 and 75.

74. A golf ball is thrown onto a cement surface and rebounds straight up. The initial velocity of the rebound is 60 ft/s. How many seconds later will the golf ball return to the ground?
3.75 s

75. A foul ball leaves a bat and travels straight up with an initial velocity of 64 ft/s. How many seconds later will the ball be 64 ft above the ground?
2 s

76. The height of a triangle is 8 cm more than the length of the base. The area of the triangle is 64 cm². Find the base and height of the triangle.
base: 8 cm; height: 16 cm

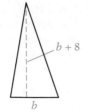

77. The height of a triangle is 4 m more than twice the length of the base. The area of the triangle is 35 m². Find the height of the triangle.
14 m

78. The length of each side of a square is extended 5 in. The area of the resulting square is 64 in². Find the length of a side of the original square.
3 in.

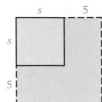

79. A small garden measures 8 ft by 10 ft. A uniform border around the garden increases the total area to 143 ft². What is the width of the border?
1.5 ft

80. The page of a book measures 6 in. by 9 in. A uniform border around the page leaves 28 in² for type. What are the dimensions of the type area?
4 in. by 7 in.

81. The radius of a circle is increased by 3 in.; this increases the area by 100 in². Find the radius of the original circle. Round to the nearest hundredth.
3.81 in.

APPLYING THE CONCEPTS

82. The length of a rectangle is 7 cm, and the width is 4 cm. If both the length and the width are increased by equal amounts, the area of the rectangle is increased by 42 cm². Find the length and width of the larger rectangle.
length: 10 cm; width: 7 cm

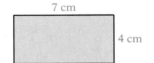

83. A rectangular piece of cardboard is 10 in. longer than it is wide. Squares 2 in. on a side are to be cut from each corner, and then the sides will be folded up to make an open box with a volume of 192 in³. Find the length and width of the piece of cardboard.
length: 20 in.; width: 10 in.

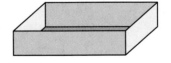

84. Solve: $p^3 = 9p^2$ 0, 9

85. Solve: $(x + 3)(2x - 1) = (3 - x)(5 - 3x)$ 1, 18

86. Find $3n^2$ if $n(n + 5) = -4$.   3, 48

87. Explain the error made in solving the equation at the right. Solve the equation correctly.

$$(x + 2)(x - 3) = 6$$
$$x + 2 = 6 \quad x - 3 = 6$$
$$x = 4 \quad\quad x = 9$$

Focus on Problem Solving

Polya's Four-Step Process

Your success in mathematics and your success in the workplace are heavily dependent on your ability to solve problems. One of the foremost mathematicians to study problem solving was George Polya (1887–1985). The basic structure that Polya advocated for problem solving has four steps, as outlined below.

 (For more information on Polya and his work, conduct a search on the Internet for "Polya." You can also search the Math Forum at *www.forum.swarthmore.edu*.)

1. Understand the Problem

You must have a clear understanding of the problem. To help you focus on understanding the problem, here are some questions to think about.

- Can you restate the problem in your own words?
- Can you determine what is known about these types of problems?
- Is there missing information that you need in order to solve the problem?
- Is there information given that is not needed?
- What is the goal?

2. Devise a Plan

Successful problem solvers use a variety of techniques when they attempt to solve a problem. Here are some frequently used strategies.

- Make a list of the known information.
- Make a list of information that is needed to solve the problem.
- Make a table or draw a diagram.
- Work backwards.
- Try to solve a similar but simpler problem.
- Research the problem to determine whether there are known techniques for solving problems of its kind.
- Try to determine whether some pattern exists.
- Write an equation.

3. Carry out the Plan

Once you have devised a plan, you must carry it out.

- Work carefully.
- Keep an accurate and neat record of all your attempts.
- Realize that some of your initial plans will not work and that you may have to return to Step 2 and devise another plan or modify your existing plan.

4. Review your Solution

Once you have found a solution, check the solution against the known facts.

- Ensure that the solution is consistent with the facts of the problem.
- Interpret the solution in the context of the problem.
- Ask yourself whether there are generalizations of the solution that could apply to other problems.
- Determine the strengths and weaknesses of your solution. For instance, is your solution only an approximation to the actual solution?
- Consider the possibility of alternative solutions.

We will use Polya's four-step process to solve the following problem.

A large soft drink costs $1.25 at a college cafeteria. The dimensions of the cup are shown at the left. Suppose you don't put any ice in the cup. Determine the cost per ounce for the soft drink.

1.5 in.

6 in.

1 in.

1. *Understand the problem.* We must determine the cost per ounce for the soda. To do this, we need the dimensions of the cup (which are given), the cost of the drink (given), and a formula for the volume of the cup (unknown). Also, because the dimensions are given in inches, the volume will be in cubic inches; we need a conversion factor that will convert cubic inches to fluid ounces.

2. *Devise a plan.* Consult a resource book that gives the volume of the figure, which is called a **frustrum**. The formula for the volume is

$$V = \frac{\pi h}{3}(r^2 + rR + R^2)$$

where h is the height, r is the radius of the base, and R is the radius of the top. Also from a reference book, 1 in$^3 \approx 0.55$ fl oz. The general plan is to calculate the volume, convert the answer to fluid ounces, and then divide the cost by the number of fluid ounces.

3. *Carry out the plan.* Using the information from the drawing, evaluate the formula for the volume.

$$V = \frac{6\pi}{3}[1^2 + 1(1.5) + 1.5^2] = 9.5\pi \approx 29.8451 \text{ in}^3$$

$V \approx 29.8451(0.55) \approx 16.4148$ fl oz   • Convert to fluid ounces.

Cost per ounce $\approx \dfrac{1.25}{16.4148} \approx 0.07615$ • Divide the cost by the volume.

The cost of the soft drink is approximately 7.62 cents per ounce.

4. *Review the solution.* The cost of a 12-ounce can of soda from a vending machine is generally about 75¢. Therefore, the cost of canned soda is 75¢ ÷ 12 = 6.25¢ per ounce. This is consistent with our solution. This does not mean our solution is correct, but it does indicate that it is at least reasonable. Why might soda from a cafeteria be more expensive per ounce than soda from a vending machine?

Is there an alternative way to obtain the solution? There are probably many, but one possibility is to get a measuring cup, pour the soft drink into it, and read the number of ounces. Name an advantage and a disadvantage of this method.

Use the four-step solution process for the following problems.

1. A cup dispenser next to a water cooler holds cups that have the shape of a right circular cone. The height of the cone is 4 in., and the radius of the circular top is 1.5 in. How many ounces of water can the cup hold?

2. Soft drink manufacturers do research into the preferences of consumers with regard to the look and feel and size of a soft drink can. Suppose that a manufacturer has determined that people want to have their hand reach around approximately 75% of the can. If this preference is to be achieved, how tall should the can be if it contains 12 oz of fluid? Assume the can is a right circular cylinder.

Projects and Group Activities

Water Displacement   When an object is placed in water, the object displaces an amount of water that is equal to the volume of the object.

➡ A sphere with a diameter of 4 in. is placed in a rectangular tank of water that is 6 in. long and 5 in. wide. How much does the water level rise? Round to the nearest hundredth.

$V = \dfrac{4}{3}\pi r^3$ • Use the formula for the volume of a sphere.

$V = \dfrac{4}{3}\pi (2^3) = \dfrac{32}{3}\pi$ • $r = \dfrac{1}{2}d = \dfrac{1}{2}(4) = 2$

Let x represent the amount of the rise in water level. The volume of the sphere will equal the volume displaced by the water. As shown at the left, this volume is the rectangular solid with width 5 in., length 6 in., and height x in.

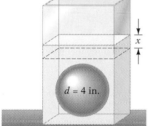

5 in

x

$d = 4$ in.

6 in.

$V = LWH$ • Use the formula for the volume of a rectangular solid.

$\dfrac{32}{3}\pi = (6)(5)x$ • Substitute $\dfrac{32}{3}\pi$ for V, 5 for W, and 6 for L.

$\dfrac{32}{90}\pi = x$ • The exact height that the water will fill is $\dfrac{32}{90}\pi$.

$1.12 \approx x$ • Use a calculator to find an approximation.

The water will rise approximately 1.12 in.

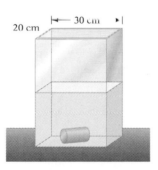

20 cm   ← 30 cm →

Figure 1

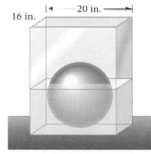

16 in.   ← 20 in. →

Figure 2

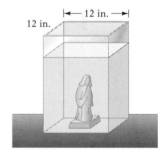

12 in.   ← 12 in. →

Figure 3

1. A cylinder with a 2-centimeter radius and a height of 10 cm is submerged in a tank of water that is 20 cm wide and 30 cm long (see Figure 1). How much does the water level rise? Round to the nearest hundredth.

2. A sphere with a radius of 6 in. is placed in a rectangular tank of water that is 16 in. wide and 20 in. long (see Figure 2). The sphere displaces water until two-thirds of the sphere is submerged. How much does the water level rise? Round to the nearest hundredth.

3. A chemist wants to know the density of a statue that weighs 15 lb. The statue is placed in a rectangular tank of water that is 12 in. long and 12 in. wide (see Figure 3). The water level rises 0.42 in. Find the density of the statue. Round to the nearest hundredth. (*Hint*: Density = weight ÷ volume)

Chapter Summary

Key Words The *greatest common factor* (GCF) of two or more monomials is the product of the GCF of the coefficients and the common variable factors.

To *factor* a polynomial means to write the polynomial as a product of other polynomials.

To *factor* a trinomial of the form $ax^2 + bx + c$ means to express the trinomial as the product of two binomials.

A polynomial is *nonfactorable over the integers* if it does not factor using only integers. Such a polynomial is called a *prime polynomial*.

A product of a term and itself is a *perfect square.*

The product of the same three factors is a *perfect cube.*

An equation of the form $ax^2 + bx + c = 0, a \neq 0$, is a *quadratic equation.*

A quadratic equation is in *standard form* when the polynomial is in descending order and equal to zero. The quadratic equation $ax^2 + bx + c = 0$ is in standard form.

Essential Rules *Factors of the Difference of Two Perfect Squares* $a^2 - b^2 = (a + b)(a - b)$

Factors of a Perfect-Square Trinomial
$$a^2 + 2ab + b^2 = (a + b)^2$$
$$a^2 - 2ab + b^2 = (a - b)^2$$

Factors of the Sum or Difference of Two Cubes
$$a^3 + b^3 = (a + b)(a^2 - ab + b^2)$$
$$a^3 - b^3 = (a - b)(a^2 + ab + b^2)$$

Principle of Zero Products

If the product of two factors is zero, then at least one of the factors must be zero.

If $a \cdot b = 0$, then $a = 0$ or $b = 0$.

General Factoring Strategy

1. Is there a common factor? If so, factor out the GCF.
2. If the polynomial is a binomial, is it the difference of two perfect squares, the sum of two cubes, or the difference of two cubes? If so, factor.
3. If the polynomial is a trinomial, is it a perfect-square trinomial or the product of two binomials? If so, factor.
4. If the polynomial has four terms, can it be factored by grouping? If so, factor.
5. Is each factor nonfactorable over the integers? If not, factor.

Chapter Review

1. Factor: $5x^3 + 10x^2 + 35x$

$5x(x^2 + 2x + 7)$ [7.1A]

2. Factor: $12a^2b + 3ab^2$

$3ab(4a + b)$ [7.1A]

3. Factor: $14y^9 - 49y^6 + 7y^3$

$7y^3(2y^6 - 7y^3 + 1)$ [7.1A]

4. Factor: $4x(x - 3) - 5(3 - x)$

$(x - 3)(4x + 5)$ [7.1B]

5. Factor: $10x^2 + 25x + 4xy + 10y$

$(2x + 5)(5x + 2y)$ [7.1B]

6. Factor: $21ax - 35bx - 10by + 6ay$

$(3a - 5b)(7x + 2y)$ [7.1B]

7. Factor: $b^2 - 13b + 30$

$(b - 3)(b \quad 10)$ [7.2A]

8. Factor: $c^2 + 8c + 12$

$(c + 6)(c + 2)$ [7.2A]

9. Factor: $y^2 + 5y - 36$

$(y - 4)(y + 9)$ [7.2A]

10. Factor: $3a^2 - 15a - 42$

$3(a + 2)(a - 7)$ [7.2B]

11. Factor: $4x^3 - 20x^2 - 24x$

$4x(x - 6)(x + 1)$ [7.2B]

12. Factor: $n^4 - 2n^3 - 3n^2$

$n^2(n + 1)(n - 3)$ [7.2B]

13. Factor $6x^2 - 29x + 28$ by using trial factors.

$(2x - 7)(3x - 4)$ [7.3A]

14. Factor $12y^2 + 16y - 3$ by using trial factors.

$(6y - 1)(2y + 3)$ [7.3A]

15. Factor $2x^2 - 5x + 6$ by using trial factors.

nonfactorable over the integers   [7.3A]

16. Factor $3x^2 - 17x + 10$ by grouping.

$(3x - 2)(x - 5)$ [7.3B]

17. Factor $2a^2 - 19a - 60$ by grouping.

$(2a + 5)(a - 12)$ [7.3B]

18. Factor $18a^2 - 3a - 10$ by grouping.

$(6a - 5)(3a + 2)$ [7.3B]

19. Factor: $x^2y^2 - 9$

$(xy + 3)(xy - 3)$ [7.4A]

20. Factor: $4x^2 + 12xy + 9y^2$

$(2x + 3y)^2$ [7.4A]

21. Factor: $x^{2n} - 12x^n + 36$

$(x^n - 6)^2$ [7.4A]

22. Factor: $64a^3 - 27b^3$

$(4a - 3b)(16a^2 + 12ab + 9b^2)$ [7.4B]

23. Factor: $15x^4 + x^2 - 6$

$(3x^2 + 2)(5x^2 - 3)$ [7.4C]

24. Factor: $21x^4y^4 + 23x^2y^2 + 6$

$(7x^2y^2 + 3)(3x^2y^2 + 2)$ [7.4C]

25. Factor: $3a^6 - 15a^4 - 18a^2$

$3a^2(a^2 + 1)(a^2 - 6)$ [7.4D]

26. Solve: $4x^2 + 27x = 7$

$\frac{1}{4}, -7$ [7.5A]

27. Solve: $(x + 1)(x - 5) = 16$

$7, -3$ [7.5A]

28. The length of a hockey field is 20 yd less than twice the width of the hockey field. The area of the hockey field is 6000 yd². Find the length and width of the hockey field.

width: 60 yd; length: 100 yd [7.5B]

29. A rectangular photograph has dimensions 15 in. by 12 in. A picture frame around the photograph increases the total area to 270 in². What is the width of the frame?

1.5 in. [7.5B]

30. The length of each side of a square garden plot is extended 4 ft. The area of the resulting square is 576 ft². Find the length of a side of the original garden plot.

20 ft [7.5B]

Chapter Test

1. Factor: $ab + 6a - 3b - 18$

   $(b + 6)(a - 3)$ [7.1B]

2. Factor: $2y^4 - 14y^3 - 16y^2$

   $2y^2(y + 1)(y - 8)$ [7.2B]

3. Factor $8x^2 + 20x - 48$ by grouping.

   $4(x + 4)(2x - 3)$ [7.3B]

4. Factor $6x^2 + 19x + 8$ by using trial factors.

   $(2x + 1)(3x + 8)$ [7.3A]

5. Factor: $a^2 - 19a + 48$

   $(a - 3)(a - 16)$ [7.2A]

6. Factor: $6x^3 - 8x^2 + 10x$

   $2x(3x^2 - 4x + 5)$ [7.1A]

7. Factor: $x^2 + 2x - 15$

   $(x + 5)(x - 3)$ [7.2A]

8. Solve: $4x^2 - 1 = 0$

   $\frac{1}{2}, -\frac{1}{2}$ [7.5A]

9. Factor: $5x^2 - 45x - 15$

   $5(x^2 - 9x - 3)$ [7.1A]

10. Factor: $p^2 + 12p + 36$

    $(p + 6)^2$ [7.4A]

11. Solve: $x(x - 8) = -15$

    $3, 5$ [7.5A]

12. Factor: $3x^2 + 12xy + 12y^2$

    $3(x + 2y)^2$ [7.4D]

13. Factor: $27x^3 - 8$

    $(3x - 2)(9x^2 + 6x + 4)$ [7.4B]

14. Factor $6x^2y^2 + 9xy^2 + 3y^2$ by grouping.

    $3y^2(2x + 1)(x + 1)$ [7.3B]

15. Factor: $6a^4 - 13a^2 - 5$

$(2a^2 - 5)(3a^2 + 1)$ [7.4C]

16. Factor: $a(x - 2) + b(x - 2)$

$(x - 2)(a + b)$ [7.1B]

17. Factor: $x(p + 1) - (p + 1)$

$(p + 1)(x - 1)$ [7.1B]

18. Factor: $3a^2 - 75$

$3(a + 5)(a - 5)$ [7.4D]

19. Factor $2x^2 + 4x - 5$ by using trial factors.

nonfactorable over the integers   [7.3A]

20. Factor: $x^2 - 9x - 36$

$(x + 3)(x - 12)$ [7.2A]

21. Factor: $4a^2 - 12ab + 9b^2$

$(2a - 3b)^2$ [7.4A]

22. Factor: $4x^2 - 49y^2$

$(2x + 7y)(2x - 7y)$ [7.4A]

23. Solve: $(2a - 3)(a + 7) = 0$

$\frac{3}{2}, -7$ [7.5A]

24. The sum of two numbers is ten. The sum of the squares of the two numbers is fifty-eight. Find the two numbers.

3, 7   [7.5B]

25. The length of a rectangle is 3 cm longer than twice its width. The area of the rectangle is 90 cm². Find the length and width of the rectangle.

length: 15 cm; width: 6 cm   [7.5B]

Cumulative Review

1. Subtract: $-2 - (-3) - 5 - (-11)$

   7 [1.1C]

2. Simplify: $(3 - 7)^2 \div (-2) - 3(-4)$

   4 [1.3A]

3. Evaluate $-2a^2 \div (2b) - c$ when $a = -4$, $b = 2$, and $c = -1$.

   -7 [1.4A]

4. Multiply: $-\frac{3}{4}(-20x^2)$

   $15x^2$ [1.4C]

5. Simplify: $-2[4x - 2(3 - 2x) - 8x]$

   12 [1.4D]

6. Solve: $-\frac{5}{7}x = -\frac{10}{21}$

   $\frac{2}{3}$ [2.1C]

7. Solve: $3x - 2 = 12 - 5x$

   $\frac{7}{4}$ [2.2B]

8. Solve: $-2 + 4[3x - 2(4 - x) - 3] = 4x + 2$

   3 [2.2C]

9. 120% of what number is 54?

   45 [2.1D]

10. Given $f(x) = -x^2 + 3x - 1$, find $f(2)$.

    1 [4.1D]

11. Graph $y = \frac{1}{4}x + 3$.

    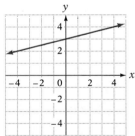

    [4.2A]

12. Graph $5x + 3y = 15$.

    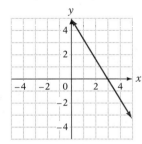

    [4.2B]

13. Find the equation of the line that contains the point $(-3, 4)$ and has slope $\frac{2}{3}$.

    $y = \frac{2}{3}x + 6$ [4.4A]

14. Solve by substitution: $8x - y = 2$
    $y = 5x + 1$

    $(1, 6)$ [5.2A]

15. Solve by the addition method:
$$5x + 2y = -9$$
$$12x - 7y = 2$$

$(-1, -2)$ [5.3A]

16. Simplify: $(-3a^3b^2)^2$

$9a^6b^4$ [6.1A]

17. Multiply: $(x + 2)(x^2 - 5x + 4)$

$x^3 - 3x^2 - 6x + 8$ [6.3B]

18. Divide: $(8x^2 + 4x - 3) \div (2x - 3)$

$4x + 8 + \dfrac{21}{2x - 3}$ [6.4A]

19. Simplify: $(x^{-4}y^3)^2$

$\dfrac{y^6}{x^8}$ [6.1B]

20. Factor: $3a - 3b - ax + bx$

$(a - b)(3 - x)$ [7.1B]

21. Factor: $15xy^2 - 20xy^4$

$5xy^2(3 - 4y^2)$ [7.1A]

22. Factor: $x^2 - 5xy - 14y^2$

$(x - 7y)(x + 2y)$ [7.2A]

23. Solve: $3x^2 + 19x - 14 = 0$

$\dfrac{2}{3}, -7$ [7.5A]

24. Solve: $6x^2 + 60 = 39x$

$\dfrac{5}{2}, 4$ [7.5A]

25. A triangle has a 31° angle and a right angle. Find the measure of the third angle.
59°   [3.1C]

26. A rectangular flower garden has a perimeter of 86 ft. The length of the garden is 28 ft. What is the width of the garden?
15 ft   [3.2A]

27. A board 10 ft long is cut into two pieces. Four times the length of the shorter piece is 2 ft less than three times the length of the longer piece. Find the length of each piece.
shorter piece: 4 ft; longer piece: 6 ft   [2.2D]

28. An investment of $4000 was made at an annual simple interest rate of 8%. How much more money was invested at an annual simple interest rate of 11% if the total interest earned in one year was $1035?
$6500   [2.3C]

29. A family drove to a resort at an average speed of 42 mph and later returned over the same road at an average speed of 56 mph. Find the distance to the resort if the total driving time was 7 h.
168 mi   [2.3D]

30. The length of the base of a triangle is three times the height. The area of the triangle is 24 in². Find the length of the base of the triangle.
12 in.   [7.5B]

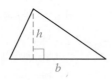

8

Rational Expressions

Geophysicists study the composition and physical characteristics of Earth and its magnetic, electric, and gravitational fields. A main responsibility of an *exploration geophysicist* is to use techniques to locate oil and other minerals. *Hydrologists* study the waters underground and on the surface of our planet. *Geomagneticians* study Earth's magnetic field. Although these are only a few of the careers within geophysics, all physicists use equations containing rational expressions. The exercises for Sections 4 and 6 provide a few examples.

Objectives

Section 8.1
To simplify a rational expression
To multiply rational expressions
To divide rational expressions

Section 8.2
To find the least common multiple (LCM) of two or more polynomials
To express two fractions in terms of the LCM of their denominators
To add or subtract rational expressions with the same denominator
To add or subtract rational expressions with different denominators

Section 8.3
To simplify a complex fraction

Section 8.4
To solve rational equations
To solve proportions
To solve problems involving similar triangles
To solve application problems

Section 8.5
To solve a literal equation for one of the variables

Section 8.6
To solve work problems
To solve uniform motion problems

Section 8.7
To solve variation problems

Syrene

Alexandria   520 mi

$7\frac{1}{2}°$

$$\frac{7\frac{1}{2}°}{360°} = \frac{520 \text{ mi}}{C}$$

$C = 24{,}960$ miles

Measurement of the Circumference of the Earth

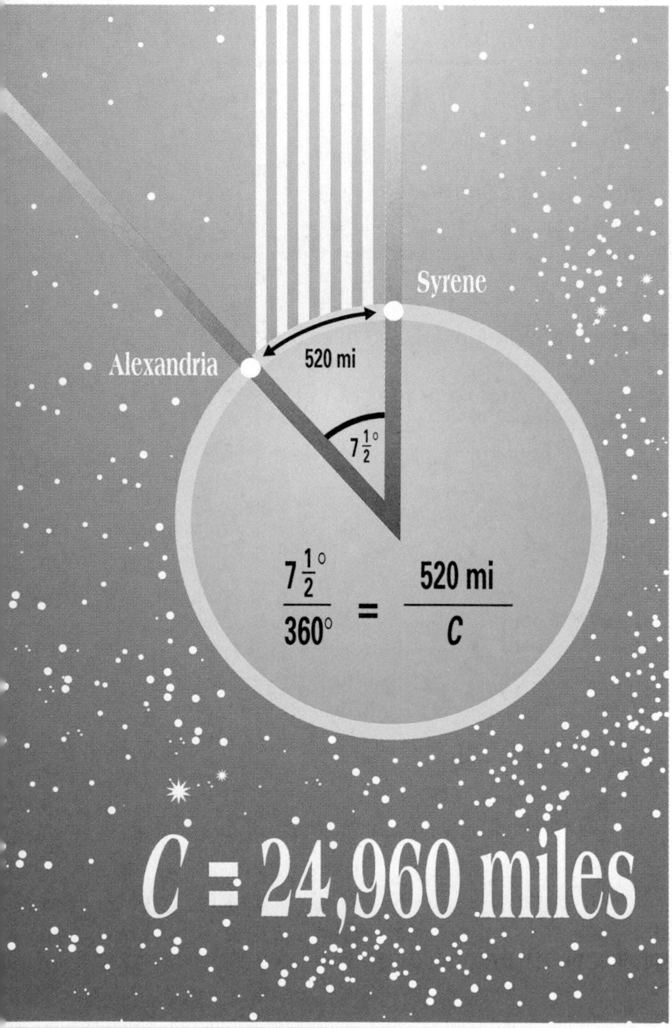

Distances on Earth, the circumference of Earth, and the distance to the moon and stars are known to great precision. Eratosthenes, the fifth librarian of Alexandria (230 B.C.), laid the foundation of scientific geography with his determination of the circumference of Earth.

Eratosthenes was familiar with certain astronomical data that enabled him to calculate the circumference of Earth by using a proportion statement.

Eratosthenes knew that on a midsummer day, the sun was directly overhead at Syrene, as shown in the diagram. At the same time, at Alexandria the sun was at a $7\frac{1}{2}°$ angle from the zenith. The distance from Syrene to Alexandria was 5000 stadia (about 520 mi).

Knowing that the ratio of the $7\frac{1}{2}°$ angle to one revolution (360°) is equal to the ratio of the arc length (520 mi) to the circumference, Eratosthenes was able to write and solve a proportion.

This result, calculated over 2000 years ago, is very close to the accepted value of 24,800 miles.

8.1 Multiplication and Division of Rational Expressions

Objective A   *To simplify a rational expression*...

A fraction in which the numerator and denominator are polynomials is called a **rational expression**. Examples of rational expressions are shown at the right.

$$\frac{5}{z}, \qquad \frac{x^2 + 1}{2x - 1}, \qquad \frac{y^2 + y - 1}{4y^2 + 1}$$

Care must be exercised with a rational expression to ensure that when the variables are replaced with numbers, the resulting denominator is not zero.

Consider the rational expression at the right. The value of x cannot be 3, because the denominator would then be zero.

$$\frac{4x^2 - 9}{2x - 6}$$

$$\frac{4(3)^2 - 9}{2(3) - 6} = \frac{27}{0} \quad \text{Not a real number}$$

A rational expression is in simplest form when the numerator and denominator have no common factors. The Multiplication Property of One is used to write a rational expression in simplest form.

➡ Simplify: $\frac{x^2 - 4}{x^2 - 2x - 8}$

$$\frac{x^2 - 4}{x^2 - 2x - 8} = \frac{(x - 2)(x + 2)}{(x - 4)(x + 2)}$$

- Factor the numerator and denominator.

$$\frac{x - 2}{x - 4} \cdot \boxed{\frac{x + 2}{x + 2}} = \frac{x - 2}{x - 4} \cdot 1$$

$$= \frac{x - 2}{x - 4}, \qquad x \neq -2, 4$$

- The restrictions $x \neq -2, 4$ are necessary to prevent division by zero.

This simplification is usually shown with slashes through the common factors. The last simplification would be shown as follows:

$$\frac{x^2 - 4}{x^2 - 2x - 8} = \frac{(x - 2)(x \overset{1}{\cancel{+ 2}})}{(x - 4)(x \underset{1}{\cancel{+ 2}})}$$

- Factor the numerator and denominator.

$$= \frac{x - 2}{x - 4}, \; x \neq -2, 4$$

- Divide by the common factors. The restrictions $x \neq -2, 4$ are necessary to prevent division by zero.

➡ Simplify: $\frac{10 + 3x - x^2}{x^2 - 4x - 5}$

$$\frac{10 + 3x - x^2}{x^2 - 4x - 5} = \frac{(5 - x)(2 + x)}{(x - 5)(x + 1)}$$

- Factor the numerator and denominator.

$$= \frac{\overset{-1}{\cancel{(5 - x)}}(2 + x)}{\underset{1}{\cancel{(x - 5)}}(x + 1)}$$

- Recall that $5 - x = -(x - 5)$. Therefore, $\frac{5 - x}{x - 5} = \frac{-(x - 5)}{x - 5} = \frac{-1}{1} = -1$.

$$= -\frac{x + 2}{x + 1}, \; x \neq -1, 5$$

For the remaining examples, we will omit the restrictions on the variables that prevent division by zero and assume that the values of the variables are such that division by zero is not possible.

Example 1

Simplify: $\dfrac{4x^3y^4}{6x^4y}$

Solution

$\dfrac{4x^3y^4}{6x^4y} = \dfrac{2y^3}{3x}$ • Use rules of exponents.

You Try It 1

Simplify: $\dfrac{6x^5y}{12x^2y^3}$

Your solution

$\dfrac{x^3}{2y^2}$

Example 2

Simplify: $\dfrac{9 - x^2}{x^2 + x - 12}$

Solution

$\dfrac{9 - x^2}{x^2 + x - 12} = \dfrac{\overset{-1}{\cancel{(3 - x)}}(3 + x)}{\underset{1}{\cancel{(x - 3)}}(x + 4)} = -\dfrac{x + 3}{x + 4}$

You Try It 2

Simplify: $\dfrac{x^2 + 2x - 24}{16 - x^2}$

Your solution

$-\dfrac{x + 6}{x + 4}$

Example 3

Simplify: $\dfrac{x^2 + 2x - 15}{x^2 - 7x + 12}$

Solution

$\dfrac{x^2 + 2x - 15}{x^2 - 7x + 12} = \dfrac{(x + 5)\overset{1}{\cancel{(x - 3)}}}{\underset{1}{\cancel{(x - 3)}}(x - 4)} = \dfrac{x + 5}{x - 4}$

You Try It 3

Simplify: $\dfrac{x^2 + 4x - 12}{x^2 - 3x + 2}$

Your solution

$\dfrac{x + 6}{x - 1}$

Solutions on p. S22

Objective B   ***To multiply rational expressions*** ....

The product of two fractions is a fraction whose numerator is the product of the numerators of the two fractions and whose denominator is the product of the denominators of the two fractions.

> **Rule for Multiplying Fractions**
>
> If $\dfrac{a}{b}$ and $\dfrac{c}{d}$ are fractions and $b \neq 0$, $d \neq 0$, then $\dfrac{a}{b} \cdot \dfrac{c}{d} = \dfrac{ac}{bd}$.

$$\dfrac{2}{3} \cdot \dfrac{4}{5} = \dfrac{8}{15} \qquad \dfrac{3x}{y} \cdot \dfrac{2}{z} = \dfrac{6x}{yz} \qquad \dfrac{x + 2}{x} \cdot \dfrac{3}{x - 2} = \dfrac{3x + 6}{x^2 - 2x}$$

➡ Multiply: $\dfrac{x^2 + 3x}{x^2 - 3x - 4} \cdot \dfrac{x^2 - 5x + 4}{x^2 + 2x - 3}$

$$\dfrac{x^2 + 3x}{x^2 - 3x - 4} \cdot \dfrac{x^2 - 5x + 4}{x^2 + 2x - 3}$$

$$= \dfrac{x(x + 3)}{(x - 4)(x + 1)} \cdot \dfrac{(x - 4)(x - 1)}{(x + 3)(x - 1)}$$

• Factor the numerator and denominator of each fraction.

$$= \dfrac{x(x + 3)(x - 4)(x - 1)}{(x - 4)(x + 1)(x + 3)(x - 1)}$$

• Multiply.

$$= \dfrac{x}{x + 1}$$

• Write the answer in simplest form.

Example 4

Multiply: $\dfrac{10x^2 - 15x}{12x - 8} \cdot \dfrac{3x - 2}{20x - 25}$

Solution

$$\dfrac{10x^2 - 15x}{12x - 8} \cdot \dfrac{3x - 2}{20x - 25}$$

$$= \dfrac{5x(2x - 3)}{4(3x - 2)} \cdot \dfrac{(3x - 2)}{5(4x - 5)}$$

$$= \dfrac{5x(2x - 3)(3x - 2)}{4(3x - 2)5(4x - 5)} = \dfrac{x(2x - 3)}{4(4x - 5)}$$

You Try It 4

Multiply: $\dfrac{12x^2 + 3x}{10x - 15} \cdot \dfrac{8x - 12}{9x + 18}$

Your solution

$$\dfrac{4x(4x + 1)}{15(x + 2)}$$

Example 5

Multiply: $\dfrac{x^2 + x - 6}{x^2 + 7x + 12} \cdot \dfrac{x^2 + 3x - 4}{4 - x^2}$

Solution

$$\dfrac{x^2 + x - 6}{x^2 + 7x + 12} \cdot \dfrac{x^2 + 3x - 4}{4 - x^2}$$

$$= \dfrac{(x + 3)(x - 2)}{(x + 3)(x + 4)} \cdot \dfrac{(x + 4)(x - 1)}{(2 - x)(2 + x)}$$

$$= \dfrac{(x + 3)(x - 2)(x + 4)(x - 1)}{(x + 3)(x + 4)(2 - x)(2 + x)} = -\dfrac{x - 1}{x + 2}$$

You Try It 5

Multiply: $\dfrac{x^2 + 2x - 15}{9 - x^2} \cdot \dfrac{x^2 - 3x - 18}{x^2 - 7x + 6}$

Your solution

$$-\dfrac{x + 5}{x - 1}$$

Solutions on p. S22

Objective C **To divide rational expressions**..

The reciprocal of a fraction is a fraction with the numerator and denominator interchanged.

$$\text{Fraction} \left\{ \begin{array}{cc} \dfrac{a}{b} & \dfrac{b}{a} \\[2mm] x^2 = \dfrac{x^2}{1} & \dfrac{1}{x^2} \\[2mm] \dfrac{x+2}{x} & \dfrac{x}{x+2} \end{array} \right\} \text{Reciprocal}$$

Rule for Dividing Fractions

Divide fractions by multiplying the dividend by the reciprocal of the divisor.

$$\dfrac{a}{b} \div \dfrac{c}{d} = \dfrac{a}{b} \cdot \dfrac{d}{c} = \dfrac{ad}{bc}$$

$$\dfrac{4}{x} \div \dfrac{y}{5} = \dfrac{4}{x} \cdot \dfrac{5}{y} = \dfrac{20}{xy}$$

$$\dfrac{x+4}{x} \div \dfrac{x-2}{4} = \dfrac{x+4}{x} \cdot \dfrac{4}{x-2} = \dfrac{4(x+4)}{x(x-2)}$$

The basis for the division rule is shown at the right.

$$\dfrac{a}{b} \div \dfrac{c}{d} = \dfrac{\dfrac{a}{b}}{\dfrac{c}{d}} = \dfrac{\dfrac{a}{b} \cdot \dfrac{d}{c}}{\dfrac{c}{d} \cdot \dfrac{d}{c}} = \dfrac{\dfrac{a}{b} \cdot \dfrac{d}{c}}{1} = \dfrac{a}{b} \cdot \dfrac{d}{c}$$

Example 6

Divide: $\dfrac{xy^2 - 3x^2y}{z^2} \div \dfrac{6x^2 - 2xy}{z^3}$

Solution

$$\dfrac{xy^2 - 3x^2y}{z^2} \div \dfrac{6x^2 - 2xy}{z^3}$$

$$= \dfrac{xy^2 - 3x^2y}{z^2} \cdot \dfrac{z^3}{6x^2 - 2xy}$$

$$= \dfrac{xy(y - 3x) \cdot z^3}{z^2 \cdot 2x(3x - y)} = -\dfrac{yz}{2}$$

You Try It 6

Divide: $\dfrac{a^2}{4bc^2 - 2b^2c} \div \dfrac{a}{6bc - 3b^2}$

Your solution

$$\dfrac{3a}{2c}$$

Example 7

Divide: $\dfrac{2x^2 + 5x + 2}{2x^2 + 3x - 2} \div \dfrac{3x^2 + 13x + 4}{2x^2 + 7x - 4}$

Solution

$$\dfrac{2x^2 + 5x + 2}{2x^2 + 3x - 2} \div \dfrac{3x^2 + 13x + 4}{2x^2 + 7x - 4}$$

$$= \dfrac{2x^2 + 5x + 2}{2x^2 + 3x - 2} \cdot \dfrac{2x^2 + 7x - 4}{3x^2 + 13x + 4}$$

$$= \dfrac{(2x + 1)(x + 2)(2x - 1)(x + 4)}{(2x - 1)(x + 2)(3x + 1)(x + 4)} = \dfrac{2x + 1}{3x + 1}$$

You Try It 7

Divide: $\dfrac{3x^2 + 26x + 16}{3x^2 - 7x - 6} \div \dfrac{2x^2 + 9x - 5}{x^2 + 2x - 15}$

Your solution

$$\dfrac{x + 8}{2x - 1}$$

Solutions on p. S22

8.1 Exercises

. . . .

Objective A

Simplify.

1. $\dfrac{9x^3}{12x^4}$

$\dfrac{3}{4x}$

2. $\dfrac{16x^2y}{24xy^3}$

$\dfrac{2x}{3y^2}$

3. $\dfrac{(x+3)^2}{(x+3)^3}$

$\dfrac{1}{x+3}$

4. $\dfrac{(2x-1)^5}{(2x-1)^4}$

$2x-1$

5. $\dfrac{3n-4}{4-3n}$

-1

6. $\dfrac{5-2x}{2x-5}$

-1

7. $\dfrac{6y(y+2)}{9y^2(y+2)}$

$\dfrac{2}{3y}$

8. $\dfrac{12x^2(3-x)}{18x(3-x)}$

$\dfrac{2x}{3}$

9. $\dfrac{6x(x-5)}{8x^2(5-x)}$

$-\dfrac{3}{4x}$

10. $\dfrac{14x^3(7-3x)}{21x(3x-7)}$

$-\dfrac{2x^2}{3}$

11. $\dfrac{a^2+4a}{ab+4b}$

$\dfrac{a}{b}$

12. $\dfrac{x^2-3x}{2x-6}$

$\dfrac{x}{2}$

13. $\dfrac{4-6x}{3x^2-2x}$

$-\dfrac{2}{x}$

14. $\dfrac{5xy-3y}{9-15x}$

$-\dfrac{y}{3}$

15. $\dfrac{y^2-3y+2}{y^2-4y+3}$

$\dfrac{y-2}{y-3}$

16. $\dfrac{x^2+5x+6}{x^2+8x+15}$

$\dfrac{x+2}{x+5}$

17. $\dfrac{x^2+3x-10}{x^2+2x-8}$

$\dfrac{x+5}{x+4}$

18. $\dfrac{a^2+7a-8}{a^2+6a-7}$

$\dfrac{a+8}{a+7}$

19. $\dfrac{x^2+x-12}{x^2-6x+9}$

$\dfrac{x+4}{x-3}$

20. $\dfrac{x^2+8x+16}{x^2-2x-24}$

$\dfrac{x+4}{x-6}$

21. $\dfrac{x^2-3x-10}{25-x^2}$

$-\dfrac{x+2}{x+5}$

22. $\dfrac{4-y^2}{y^2-3y-10}$

$\dfrac{2-y}{y-5}$

23. $\dfrac{2x^3+2x^2-4x}{x^3+2x^2-3x}$

$\dfrac{2(x+2)}{x+3}$

24. $\dfrac{3x^3-12x}{6x^3-24x^2+24x}$

$\dfrac{x+2}{2(x-2)}$

25. $\dfrac{6x^2-7x+2}{6x^2+5x-6}$

$\dfrac{2x-1}{2x+3}$

26. $\dfrac{2n^2-9n+4}{2n^2-5n-12}$

$\dfrac{2n-1}{2n+3}$

27. $\dfrac{x^2+3x-28}{24-2x-x^2}$

$-\dfrac{x+7}{x+6}$

Objective B

Multiply.

28. $\dfrac{8x^2}{9y^3} \cdot \dfrac{3y^2}{4x^3}$

$\dfrac{2}{3xy}$

29. $\dfrac{14a^2b^3}{15x^5y^2} \cdot \dfrac{25x^3y}{16ab}$

$\dfrac{35ab^2}{24x^2y}$

30. $\dfrac{12x^3y^4}{7a^2b^3} \cdot \dfrac{14a^3b^4}{9x^2y^2}$

$\dfrac{8xy^2ab}{3}$

31. $\dfrac{18a^4b^2}{25x^2y^3} \cdot \dfrac{50x^5y^6}{27a^6b^2}$

$\dfrac{4x^3y^3}{3a^2}$

32. $\dfrac{3x - 6}{5x - 20} \cdot \dfrac{10x - 40}{27x - 54}$

$\dfrac{2}{9}$

33. $\dfrac{8x - 12}{14x + 7} \cdot \dfrac{42x + 21}{32x - 48}$

$\dfrac{3}{4}$

34. $\dfrac{3x^2 + 2x}{2xy - 3y} \cdot \dfrac{2xy^3 - 3y^3}{3x^3 + 2x^2}$

$\dfrac{y^2}{x}$

35. $\dfrac{4a^2x - 3a^2}{2by + 5b} \cdot \dfrac{2b^3y + 5b^3}{4ax - 3a}$

ab^2

36. $\dfrac{x^2 + 5x + 4}{x^3y^2} \cdot \dfrac{x^2y^3}{x^2 + 2x + 1}$

$\dfrac{y(x + 4)}{x(x + 1)}$

37. $\dfrac{x^2 + x - 2}{xy^2} \cdot \dfrac{x^3y}{x^2 + 5x + 6}$

$\dfrac{x^2(x - 1)}{y(x + 3)}$

38. $\dfrac{x^4y^2}{x^2 + 3x - 28} \cdot \dfrac{x^2 - 49}{xy^4}$

$\dfrac{x^3(x - 7)}{y^2(x - 4)}$

39. $\dfrac{x^5y^3}{x^2 + 13x + 30} \cdot \dfrac{x^2 + 2x - 3}{x^7y^2}$

$\dfrac{y(x - 1)}{x^2(x + 10)}$

40. $\dfrac{2x^2 - 5x}{2xy + y} \cdot \dfrac{2xy^2 + y^2}{5x^2 - 2x^3}$

$-\dfrac{y}{x}$

41. $\dfrac{3a^3 + 4a^2}{5ab - 3b} \cdot \dfrac{3b^3 - 5ab^3}{3a^2 + 4a}$

$-ab^2$

42. $\dfrac{x^2 - 2x - 24}{x^2 - 5x - 6} \cdot \dfrac{x^2 + 5x + 6}{x^2 + 6x + 8}$

$\dfrac{x + 3}{x + 1}$

43. $\dfrac{x^2 - 8x + 7}{x^2 + 3x - 4} \cdot \dfrac{x^2 + 3x - 10}{x^2 - 9x + 14}$

$\dfrac{x + 5}{x + 4}$

44. $\dfrac{x^2 + 2x - 35}{x^2 + 4x - 21} \cdot \dfrac{x^2 + 3x - 18}{x^2 + 9x + 18}$

$\dfrac{x - 5}{x + 3}$

45. $\dfrac{y^2 + y - 20}{y^2 + 2y - 15} \cdot \dfrac{y^2 + 4y - 21}{y^2 + 3y - 28}$

1

46. $\dfrac{x^2 - 3x - 4}{x^2 + 6x + 5} \cdot \dfrac{x^2 + 5x + 6}{8 + 2x - x^2}$

$-\dfrac{x + 3}{x + 5}$

47. $\dfrac{25 - n^2}{n^2 - 2n - 35} \cdot \dfrac{n^2 - 8n - 20}{n^2 - 3n - 10}$

$-\dfrac{n - 10}{n - 7}$

48. $\dfrac{12x^2 - 6x}{x^2 + 6x + 5} \cdot \dfrac{2x^4 + 10x^3}{4x^2 - 1}$

$\dfrac{12x^4}{(x + 1)(2x + 1)}$

49. $\dfrac{8x^3 + 4x^2}{x^2 - 3x + 2} \cdot \dfrac{x^2 - 4}{16x^2 + 8x}$

$\dfrac{x(x + 2)}{2(x - 1)}$

50. $\dfrac{16 + 6x - x^2}{x^2 - 10x - 24} \cdot \dfrac{x^2 - 6x - 27}{x^2 - 17x + 72}$

$-\dfrac{x + 3}{x - 12}$

51. $\dfrac{x^2 - 11x + 28}{x^2 - 13x + 42} \cdot \dfrac{x^3 + 7x + 10}{20 - x - x^2}$

$-\dfrac{x + 2}{x - 6}$

52. $\dfrac{2x^2 + 5x + 2}{2x^2 + 7x + 3} \cdot \dfrac{x^2 - 7x - 30}{x^2 - 6x - 40}$

$\dfrac{x + 2}{x + 4}$

53. $\dfrac{x^2 - 4x - 32}{x^2 - 8x - 48} \cdot \dfrac{3x^2 + 17x + 10}{3x^2 - 22x - 16}$

$\dfrac{x + 5}{x - 12}$

Objective C

Divide.

54. $\dfrac{4x^2y^3}{15a^2b^3} \div \dfrac{6xy}{5a^3b^5}$

$\dfrac{2xy^2ab^2}{9}$

55. $\dfrac{9x^3y^4}{16a^4b^2} \div \dfrac{45x^4y^2}{14a^7b}$

$\dfrac{7a^3y^2}{40bx}$

56. $\dfrac{6x - 12}{8x + 32} \div \dfrac{18x - 36}{10x + 40}$

$\dfrac{5}{12}$

57. $\dfrac{28x + 14}{45x - 30} \div \dfrac{14x + 7}{30x - 20}$

$\dfrac{4}{3}$

58. $\dfrac{6x^3 + 7x^2}{12x - 3} \div \dfrac{6x^2 + 7x}{36x - 9}$

$3x$

59. $\dfrac{5a^2y + 3a^2}{2x^3 + 5x^2} \div \dfrac{10ay + 6a}{6x^3 + 15x^2}$

$\dfrac{3a}{2}$

60. $\dfrac{x^2 + 4x + 3}{x^2y} \div \dfrac{x^2 + 2x + 1}{xy^2}$

$\dfrac{y(x + 3)}{x(x + 1)}$

61. $\dfrac{x^3y^2}{x^2 - 3x - 10} \div \dfrac{xy^4}{x^2 - x - 20}$

$\dfrac{x^2(x + 4)}{y^2(x + 2)}$

62. $\dfrac{x^2 - 49}{x^4y^3} \div \dfrac{x^2 - 14x + 49}{x^4y^3}$

$\dfrac{x + 7}{x - 7}$

63. $\dfrac{x^2y^5}{x^2 - 11x + 30} \div \dfrac{xy^6}{x^2 - 7x + 10}$

$\dfrac{x(x - 2)}{y(x - 6)}$

64. $\dfrac{4ax - 8a}{c^2} \div \dfrac{2y - xy}{c^3}$

$-\dfrac{4ac}{y}$

65. $\dfrac{3x^2y - 9xy}{a^2b} \div \dfrac{3x^2 - x^3}{ab^2}$

$-\dfrac{3by}{ax}$

66. $\dfrac{x^2 - 5x + 6}{x^2 - 9x + 18} \div \dfrac{x^2 - 6x + 8}{x^2 - 9x + 20}$

$\dfrac{x - 5}{x - 6}$

67. $\dfrac{x^2 + 3x - 40}{x^2 + 2x - 35} \div \dfrac{x^2 + 2x - 48}{x^2 + 3x - 18}$

$\dfrac{(x - 3)(x + 6)}{(x + 7)(x - 6)}$

68. $\dfrac{x^2 + 2x - 15}{x^2 - 4x - 45} \div \dfrac{x^2 + x - 12}{x^2 - 5x - 36}$

1

69. $\dfrac{y^2 - y - 56}{y^2 + 8y + 7} \div \dfrac{y^2 - 13y + 40}{y^2 - 4y - 5}$

1

70. $\dfrac{8 + 2x - x^2}{x^2 + 7x + 10} \div \dfrac{x^2 - 11x + 28}{x^2 - x - 42}$

$-\dfrac{x + 6}{x + 5}$

71. $\dfrac{x^2 - x - 2}{x^2 - 7x + 10} \div \dfrac{x^2 - 3x - 4}{40 - 3x - x^2}$

$-\dfrac{x + 8}{x - 4}$

72. $\dfrac{2x^2 - 3x - 20}{2x^2 - 7x - 30} \div \dfrac{2x^2 - 5x - 12}{4x^2 + 12x + 9}$

$\dfrac{2x + 3}{x - 6}$

73. $\dfrac{6n^2 + 13n + 6}{4n^2 - 9} \div \dfrac{6n^2 + n - 2}{4n^2 - 1}$

$\dfrac{2n + 1}{2n - 3}$

APPLYING THE CONCEPTS

74. Given the expression $\dfrac{9}{x^2 + 1}$, choose some values of x and evaluate the expression for those values. Is it possible to choose a value of x for which the value of the expression is greater than 10? If so, what is that value of x? If not, explain why it is not possible.
No. The denominator is always equal to or greater than 1.

75. Given the expression $\dfrac{1}{y - 3}$, choose some values of y and evaluate the expression for those values. Is it possible to choose a value of y for which the value of the expression is greater than 10,000,000? If so, what is that value of y? If not, explain why it is not possible.
Yes. Answers will vary. For example, 3.00000001.

For what values of x is the algebraic fraction undefined?

76. $\dfrac{x}{(x - 2)(x + 5)}$ $2, -5$

77. $\dfrac{7}{x^2 - 25}$ $5, -5$

78. $\dfrac{3x - 8}{3x^2 - 10x - 8}$ $-\dfrac{2}{3}, 4$

Simplify.

79. $\dfrac{xy}{3} \cdot \dfrac{x}{y^2} \div \dfrac{x}{4}$ $\dfrac{4x}{3y}$

80. $\left(\dfrac{y}{3}\right) \div \left(\dfrac{y}{2} \cdot \dfrac{y}{4}\right)$ $\dfrac{8}{3y}$

81. $\left(\dfrac{x - 4}{y^2}\right)^3 \cdot \left(\dfrac{y}{4 - x}\right)^3$ $-\dfrac{1}{y^3}$

82. $\dfrac{x - 2}{x + 5} \div \dfrac{x - 3}{x + 5} \cdot \dfrac{x - 3}{x - 2}$ 1

8.2 Addition and Subtraction of Rational Expressions

Objective A   *To find the least common multiple (LCM) of two or more polynomials* ....

The **least common multiple (LCM)** of two or more numbers is the smallest number that contains the prime factorization of each number.

The LCM of 12 and 18 is 36 because 36 contains the prime factors of 12 and the prime factors of 18.

$$12 = 2 \cdot 2 \cdot 3$$
$$18 = 2 \cdot 3 \cdot 3$$

$$\overbrace{\phantom{\text{Factors of 12}}}^{\text{Factors of 12}}$$
$$\text{LCM} = 36 = 2 \cdot \underbrace{2 \cdot 3 \cdot 3}_{\text{Factors of 18}}$$

The least common multiple of two or more polynomials is the polynomial of least degree that contains the factors of each polynomial.

To find the LCM of two or more polynomials, first factor each polynomial completely. The LCM is the product of each factor the greatest number of times it occurs in any one factorization.

⟹ Find the LCM of $4x^2 + 4x$ and $x^2 + 2x + 1$.

The LCM of the polynomials is the product of the LCM of the numerical coefficients and each variable factor the greatest number of times it occurs in any one factorization.

$$4x^2 + 4x = 4x(x + 1) = 2 \cdot 2 \cdot x(x + 1)$$
$$x^2 + 2x + 1 = (x + 1)(x + 1)$$

$$\overbrace{\phantom{\text{Factors of } 4x^2 + 4x}}^{\text{Factors of } 4x^2 + 4x}$$
$$\text{LCM} = 2 \cdot 2 \cdot \underbrace{x(x + 1)(x + 1)}_{\text{Factors of } x^2 + 2x + 1} = 4x(x + 1)(x + 1)$$

Example 1
Find the LCM of $4x^2y$ and $6xy^2$.

Solution
$4x^2y = 2 \cdot 2 \cdot x \cdot x \cdot y$
$6xy^2 = 2 \cdot 3 \cdot x \cdot y \cdot y$
$\text{LCM} = 2 \cdot 2 \cdot 3 \cdot x \cdot x \cdot y \cdot y = 12x^2y^2$

Example 2
Find the LCM of $x^2 - x - 6$ and $9 - x^2$.

Solution
$x^2 - x - 6 = (x - 3)(x + 2)$
$9 - x^2 = -(x^2 - 9) = -(x + 3)(x - 3)$
$\text{LCM} = (x - 3)(x + 2)(x + 3)$

You Try It 1
Find the LCM of $8uv^2$ and $12uw$.

Your solution
$24uv^2w$

You Try It 2
Find the LCM of $m^2 - 6m + 9$ and $m^2 - 2m - 3$.

Your solution
$(m - 3)(m - 3)(m + 1)$

Solutions on p. S22

Objective B **To express two fractions in terms of the LCM of their denominators** ....

INSTRUCTOR NOTE
This objective allows students to practice writing fractions in terms of the common denominator (LCM) without having to then add or subtract the fractions.

TAKE NOTE
$\dfrac{3(x-2)}{3(x-2)} = 1$ and $\dfrac{2x}{2x} = 1$. We are multiplying each fraction by 1, so we are not changing the value of either fraction.

When adding and subtracting fractions, it is frequently necessary to express two or more fractions in terms of a common denominator. This common denominator is the LCM of the denominators of the fractions.

➡ Write the fractions $\dfrac{x+1}{4x^2}$ and $\dfrac{x-3}{6x^2-12x}$ in terms of the LCM of the denominators.

Find the LCM of the denominators.

The LCM is $12x^2(x-2)$.

For each fraction, multiply the numerator and denominator by the factors whose product with the denominator is the LCM.

$$\frac{x+1}{4x^2} = \frac{x+1}{4x^2} \cdot \frac{3(x-2)}{3(x-2)} = \frac{3x^2-3x-6}{12x^2(x-2)} \leftarrow$$

$$\frac{x-3}{6x^2-12x} = \frac{x-3}{6x(x-2)} \cdot \frac{2x}{2x} = \frac{2x^2-6x}{12x^2(x-2)} \leftarrow$$

LCM

Example 3

Write the fractions $\dfrac{x+2}{3x^2}$ and $\dfrac{x-1}{8xy}$ in terms of the LCM of the denominators.

Solution
The LCM is $24x^2y$.

$$\frac{x+2}{3x^2} = \frac{x+2}{3x^2} \cdot \frac{8y}{8y} = \frac{8xy+16y}{24x^2y}$$

$$\frac{x-1}{8xy} = \frac{x-1}{8xy} \cdot \frac{3x}{3x} = \frac{3x^2-3x}{24x^2y}$$

You Try It 3

Write the fractions $\dfrac{x-3}{4xy^2}$ and $\dfrac{2x+1}{9y^2z}$ in terms of the LCM of the denominators.

Your solution
$$\frac{9xz-27z}{36xy^2z} , \frac{8x^2+4x}{36xy^2z}$$

Example 4

Write the fractions $\dfrac{2x-1}{2x-x^2}$ and $\dfrac{x}{x^2+x-6}$ in terms of the LCM of the denominators.

Solution
$$\frac{2x-1}{2x-x^2} = \frac{2x-1}{-(x^2-2x)} = -\frac{2x-1}{x^2-2x}$$

The LCM is $x(x-2)(x+3)$.

$$\frac{2x-1}{2x-x^2} = -\frac{2x-1}{x(x-2)} \cdot \frac{x+3}{x+3} = -\frac{2x^2+5x-3}{x(x-2)(x+3)}$$

$$\frac{x}{x^2+x-6} = \frac{x}{(x-2)(x+3)} \cdot \frac{x}{x} = \frac{x^2}{x(x-2)(x+3)}$$

You Try It 4

Write the fractions $\dfrac{x+4}{x^2-3x-10}$ and $\dfrac{2x}{25-x^2}$ in terms of the LCM of the denominators.

Your solution
$$\frac{x^2+9x+20}{(x+2)(x-5)(x+5)} , -\frac{2x^2+4x}{(x+2)(x-5)(x+5)}$$

Solutions on p. S22

Objective C **To add or subtract rational expressions with the same denominator**...

When adding rational expressions in which the denominators are the same, add the numerators. The denominator of the sum is the common denominator.

$$\frac{a}{b} + \frac{c}{b} = \frac{a+c}{b}$$

$$\frac{5x}{18} + \frac{7x}{18} = \frac{5x+7x}{18} = \frac{12x}{18} = \frac{2x}{3}$$

$$\frac{x}{x^2-1} + \frac{1}{x^2-1} = \frac{x+1}{x^2-1} = \frac{\overset{1}{\cancel{(x+1)}}}{(x-1)\underset{1}{\cancel{(x+1)}}} = \frac{1}{x-1}$$

Note that the sum is written in simplest form.

When subtracting rational expressions with the same denominators, subtract the numerators. The denominator of the difference is the common denominator. Write the answer in simplest form.

TAKE NOTE

Be careful with signs when subtracting algebraic fractions. Note that we must subtract the *entire* numerator $2x + 3$.
$(3x - 1) - (2x + 3) = 3x - 1 - 2x - 3$.

$$\frac{2x}{x-2} - \frac{4}{x-2} = \frac{2x-4}{x-2} = \frac{2\overset{1}{\cancel{(x-2)}}}{\underset{1}{\cancel{x-2}}} = 2$$

$$\frac{3x-1}{x^2-5x+4} - \frac{2x+3}{x^2-5x+4} = \frac{(3x-1)-(2x+3)}{x^2-5x+4} = \frac{3x-1-2x-3}{x^2-5x+4}$$

$$= \frac{x-4}{x^2-5x+4} = \frac{\overset{1}{\cancel{(x-4)}}}{\underset{1}{\cancel{(x-4)}}(x-1)} = \frac{1}{x-1}$$

Example 5

Add: $\dfrac{7}{x^2} + \dfrac{9}{x^2}$

Solution

$$\frac{7}{x^2} + \frac{9}{x^2} = \frac{7+9}{x^2} = \frac{16}{x^2}$$

You Try It 5

Add: $\dfrac{3}{xy} + \dfrac{12}{xy}$

Your solution

$$\frac{15}{xy}$$

Example 6

Subtract: $\dfrac{3x^2}{x^2-1} - \dfrac{x+4}{x^2-1}$

Solution

$$\frac{3x^2}{x^2-1} - \frac{x+4}{x^2-1} = \frac{3x^2-(x+4)}{x^2-1}$$

$$= \frac{3x^2-x-4}{x^2-1}$$

$$= \frac{(3x-4)\overset{1}{\cancel{(x+1)}}}{(x-1)\underset{1}{\cancel{(x+1)}}} = \frac{3x-4}{x-1}$$

You Try It 6

Subtract: $\dfrac{2x^2}{x^2-x-12} - \dfrac{7x+4}{x^2-x-12}$

Your solution

$$\frac{2x+1}{x+3}$$

Solutions on p. S22

Example 7
Simplify:

$$\frac{2x^2 + 5}{x^2 + 2x - 3} - \frac{x^2 - 3x}{x^2 + 2x - 3} + \frac{x - 2}{x^2 + 2x - 3}$$

Solution

$$\frac{2x^2 + 5}{x^2 + 2x - 3} - \frac{x^2 - 3x}{x^2 + 2x - 3} + \frac{x - 2}{x^2 + 2x - 3}$$

$$= \frac{(2x^2 + 5) - (x^2 - 3x) + (x - 2)}{x^2 + 2x - 3}$$

$$= \frac{2x^2 + 5 - x^2 + 3x + x - 2}{x^2 + 2x - 3}$$

$$= \frac{x^2 + 4x + 3}{x^2 + 2x - 3} = \frac{\overset{1}{\cancel{(x + 3)}}(x + 1)}{\underset{1}{\cancel{(x + 3)}}(x - 1)} = \frac{x + 1}{x - 1}$$

You Try It 7
Simplify:

$$\frac{x^2 - 1}{x^2 - 8x + 12} - \frac{2x + 1}{x^2 - 8x + 12} + \frac{x}{x^2 - 8x + 12}$$

Your solution

$$\frac{x + 1}{x - 6}$$

Solution on p. S22

Objective D   To add or subtract rational expressions with different denominators ....

TAKE NOTE

This objective requires using the skills learned in Objective 8.2B (writing two fractions in terms of the LCM of their denominators) and 8.2C (adding and subtracting algebraic fractions with the same denominator).

Before two fractions with unlike denominators can be added or subtracted, each fraction must be expressed in terms of a common denominator. This common denominator is the LCM of the denominators of the fractions.

➡ Add: $\dfrac{x - 3}{x^2 - 2x} + \dfrac{6}{x^2 - 4}$

Find the LCM of the denominators.   The LCM is $x(x - 2)(x + 2)$.

$$\frac{x - 3}{x^2 - 2x} + \frac{6}{x^2 - 4} = \frac{x - 3}{x(x - 2)} \cdot \frac{x + 2}{x + 2} + \frac{6}{(x - 2)(x + 2)} \cdot \frac{x}{x}$$

• Rewrite each fraction with $x(x - 2)(x + 2)$ as the denominator.

$$= \frac{x^2 - x - 6}{x(x - 2)(x + 2)} + \frac{6x}{x(x - 2)(x + 2)}$$

$$= \frac{(x^2 - x - 6) + 6x}{x(x - 2)(x + 2)}$$

• Add the fractions.

$$= \frac{x^2 + 5x - 6}{x(x - 2)(x + 2)}$$

$$= \frac{(x + 6)(x - 1)}{x(x - 2)(x + 2)}$$

INSTRUCTOR NOTE

Have students write down a list of the basic steps that are used to simplify sums or differences of rational expressions. Here is a suggested list.
• Find the LCM of the denominators.
• Write each fraction as a fraction with the LCM as a denominator.
• Add or subtract the fractions.
• Write the answer in factored form and express the answer in simplest form.

The last step is to factor the numerator to determine whether there are common factors in the numerator and denominator. For this example there are no common factors, so the answer is in simplest form.

Example 8

Simplify: $\dfrac{y}{x} - \dfrac{4y}{3x} + \dfrac{3y}{4x}$

Solution

The LCM of the denominators is $12x$.

$$\dfrac{y}{x} - \dfrac{4y}{3x} + \dfrac{3y}{4x} = \dfrac{y}{x} \cdot \dfrac{12}{12} - \dfrac{4y}{3x} \cdot \dfrac{4}{4} + \dfrac{3y}{4x} \cdot \dfrac{3}{3}$$

$$= \dfrac{12y}{12x} - \dfrac{16y}{12x} + \dfrac{9y}{12x}$$

$$= \dfrac{12y - 16y + 9y}{12x} = \dfrac{5y}{12x}$$

You Try It 8

Simplify: $\dfrac{z}{8y} - \dfrac{4z}{3y} + \dfrac{5z}{4y}$

Your solution

$\dfrac{z}{24y}$

Example 9

Subtract: $\dfrac{2x}{x-3} - \dfrac{5}{3-x}$

Solution

Remember: $3 - x = -(x - 3)$.

Therefore, $\dfrac{5}{3-x} = \dfrac{5}{-(x-3)} = \dfrac{-5}{x-3}$.

$$\dfrac{2x}{x-3} - \dfrac{5}{3-x} = \dfrac{2x}{x-3} - \dfrac{-5}{x-3}$$

$$= \dfrac{2x - (-5)}{x-3} = \dfrac{2x+5}{x-3}$$

You Try It 9

Subtract: $\dfrac{5x}{x-2} - \dfrac{3}{2-x}$

Your solution

$\dfrac{5x+3}{x-2}$

Example 10

Subtract: $\dfrac{2x}{2x-3} - \dfrac{1}{x+1}$

Solution

The LCM is $(2x - 3)(x + 1)$.

$$\dfrac{2x}{2x-3} - \dfrac{1}{x+1}$$

$$= \dfrac{2x}{2x-3} \cdot \dfrac{x+1}{x+1} - \dfrac{1}{x+1} \cdot \dfrac{2x-3}{2x-3}$$

$$= \dfrac{2x^2 + 2x}{(2x-3)(x+1)} - \dfrac{2x-3}{(2x-3)(x+1)}$$

$$= \dfrac{(2x^2 + 2x) - (2x - 3)}{(2x-3)(x+1)} = \dfrac{2x^2 + 3}{(2x-3)(x+1)}$$

You Try It 10

Subtract: $\dfrac{4x}{3x-1} - \dfrac{9}{x+4}$

Your solution

$\dfrac{4x^2 - 11x + 9}{(3x-1)(x+4)}$

Solutions on pp. S22–S23

Example 11

Add: $1 + \dfrac{3}{x^2}$

Solution

The LCM is x^2.

$$1 + \dfrac{3}{x^2} = 1 \cdot \dfrac{x^2}{x^2} + \dfrac{3}{x^2}$$

$$= \dfrac{x^2}{x^2} + \dfrac{3}{x^2} = \dfrac{x^2 + 3}{x^2}$$

You Try It 11

Subtract: $2 - \dfrac{1}{x - 3}$

Your solution

$\dfrac{2x - 7}{x - 3}$

Example 12

Subtract: $\dfrac{x}{2x - 4} - \dfrac{4 - x}{x^2 - 2x}$

Solution

$2x - 4 = 2(x - 2); \; x^2 - 2x = x(x - 2)$

The LCM is $2x(x - 2)$.

$$\dfrac{x}{2x - 4} - \dfrac{4 - x}{x^2 - 2x} = \dfrac{x}{2(x - 2)} \cdot \dfrac{x}{x} - \dfrac{4 - x}{x(x - 2)} \cdot \dfrac{2}{2}$$

$$= \dfrac{x^2 - (4 - x)2}{2x(x - 2)}$$

$$= \dfrac{x^2 - (8 - 2x)}{2x(x - 2)} = \dfrac{x^2 + 2x - 8}{2x(x - 2)}$$

$$= \dfrac{(x + 4)\overset{1}{\cancel{(x - 2)}}}{2x\underset{1}{\cancel{(x - 2)}}} = \dfrac{x + 4}{2x}$$

You Try It 12

Add: $\dfrac{a - 3}{a^2 - 5a} + \dfrac{a - 9}{a^2 - 25}$

Your solution

$\dfrac{2a + 3}{a(a + 5)}$

Example 13

Simplify: $\dfrac{3x + 2}{2x^2 - x - 1} - \dfrac{3}{2x + 1} + \dfrac{4}{x - 1}$

Solution

The LCM is $(2x + 1)(x - 1)$.

$$\dfrac{3x + 2}{2x^2 - x - 1} - \dfrac{3}{2x + 1} + \dfrac{4}{x - 1}$$

$$= \dfrac{3x + 2}{(2x + 1)(x - 1)} - \dfrac{3}{2x + 1} \cdot \dfrac{x - 1}{x - 1} + \dfrac{4}{x - 1} \cdot \dfrac{2x + 1}{2x + 1}$$

$$= \dfrac{3x + 2}{(2x + 1)(x - 1)} - \dfrac{3x - 3}{(2x + 1)(x - 1)} + \dfrac{8x + 4}{(2x + 1)(x - 1)}$$

$$= \dfrac{(3x + 2) - (3x - 3) + (8x + 4)}{(2x + 1)(x - 1)}$$

$$= \dfrac{3x + 2 - 3x + 3 + 8x + 4}{(2x + 1)(x - 1)} = \dfrac{8x + 9}{(2x + 1)(x - 1)}$$

You Try It 13

Simplify: $\dfrac{2x - 3}{3x^2 - x - 2} + \dfrac{5}{3x + 2} - \dfrac{1}{x - 1}$

Your solution

$\dfrac{2(2x - 5)}{(3x + 2)(x - 1)}$

Solutions on pp. S23

8.2 Exercises

· ·

Objective A

Find the LCM of the expressions.

1. $8x^3y$
$12xy^2$
$24x^3y^2$

2. $6ab^2$
$18ab^3$
$18ab^3$

3. $10x^4y^2$
$15x^3y$
$30x^4y^2$

4. $12a^2b$
$18ab^3$
$36a^2b^3$

5. $8x^2$
$4x^2 + 8x$
$8x^2(x + 2)$

6. $6y^2$
$4y + 12$
$12y^2(y + 3)$

7. $2x^2y$
$3x^2 + 12x$
$6x^2y(x + 4)$

8. $4xy^2$
$6xy^2 + 12y^2$
$12xy^2(x + 2)$

9. $9x(x + 2)$
$12(x + 2)^2$
$36x(x + 2)^2$

10. $8x^2(x - 1)^2$
$10x^3(x - 1)$
$40x^3(x - 1)^2$

11. $3x + 3$
$2x^2 + 4x + 2$
$6(x + 1)^2$

12. $4x - 12$
$2x^2 - 12x + 18$
$4(x - 3)^2$

13. $(x - 1)(x + 2)$
$(x - 1)(x + 3)$
$(x - 1)(x + 2)(x + 3)$

14. $(2x - 1)(x + 4)$
$(2x + 1)(x + 4)$
$(2x - 1)(x + 4)(2x + 1)$

15. $(2x + 3)^2$
$(2x + 3)(x - 5)$
$(2x + 3)^2(x - 5)$

16. $(x - 7)(x + 2)$
$(x - 7)^2$

$(x - 7)^2(x + 2)$

17. $x - 1$
$x - 2$
$(x - 1)(x - 2)$
$(x - 1)(x - 2)$

18. $(x + 4)(x - 3)$
$x + 4$
$x - 3$
$(x + 4)(x - 3)$

19. $x^2 - x - 6$
$x^2 + x - 12$
$(x - 3)(x + 2)(x + 4)$

20. $x^2 + 3x - 10$
$x^2 + 5x - 14$
$(x + 5)(x + 7)(x - 2)$

21. $x^2 + 5x + 4$
$x^2 - 3x - 28$
$(x + 4)(x + 1)(x - 7)$

22. $x^2 - 10x + 21$
$x^2 - 8x + 15$
$(x - 7)(x - 3)(x - 5)$

23. $x^2 - 2x - 24$
$x^2 - 36$
$(x - 6)(x + 6)(x + 4)$

24. $x^2 + 7x + 10$
$x^2 - 25$
$(x + 5)(x - 5)(x + 2)$

25. $x^2 - 7x - 30$
$x^2 - 5x - 24$
$(x - 10)(x - 8)(x + 3)$

26. $2x^2 - 7x + 3$
$2x^2 + x - 1$
$(2x - 1)(x - 3)(x + 1)$

27. $3x^2 - 11x + 6$
$3x^2 + 4x - 4$
$(3x - 2)(x - 3)(x + 2)$

28. $2x^2 - 9x + 10$
$2x^2 + x - 15$

$(2x - 5)(x - 2)(x + 3)$

29. $6 + x - x^2$
$x + 2$
$x - 3$
$(x + 2)(x - 3)$

30. $15 + 2x - x^2$
$x - 5$
$x + 3$
$(x + 3)(x - 5)$

31. $5 + 4x - x^2$
$x - 5$
$x + 1$
$(x - 5)(x + 1)$

32. $x^2 + 3x - 18$
$3 - x$
$x + 6$
$(x + 6)(x - 3)$

33. $x^2 - 5x + 6$
$1 - x$
$x - 6$
$(x - 3)(x - 2)(x - 1)(x - 6)$

Objective B

Write each fraction in terms of the LCM of the denominators.

34. $\dfrac{4}{x}, \dfrac{3}{x^2}$

$\dfrac{4x}{x^2}, \dfrac{3}{x^2}$

35. $\dfrac{5}{ab^2}, \dfrac{6}{ab}$

$\dfrac{5}{ab^2}, \dfrac{6b}{ab^2}$

36. $\dfrac{x}{3y^2}, \dfrac{z}{4y}$

$\dfrac{4x}{12y^2}, \dfrac{3yz}{12y^2}$

37. $\dfrac{5y}{6x^2}, \dfrac{7}{9xy}$

$\dfrac{15y^2}{18x^2y}, \dfrac{14x}{18x^2y}$

38. $\dfrac{y}{x(x-3)}, \dfrac{6}{x^2}$

$\dfrac{xy}{x^2(x-3)}, \dfrac{6x-18}{x^2(x-3)}$

39. $\dfrac{a}{y^2}, \dfrac{6}{y(y+5)}$

$\dfrac{ay+5a}{y^2(y+5)}, \dfrac{6y}{y^2(y+5)}$

40. $\dfrac{9}{(x-1)^2}, \dfrac{6}{x(x-1)}$

$\dfrac{9x}{x(x-1)^2}, \dfrac{6x-6}{x(x-1)^2}$

41. $\dfrac{a^2}{y(y+7)}, \dfrac{a}{(y+7)^2}$

$\dfrac{a^2y+7a^2}{y(y+7)^2}, \dfrac{ay}{y(y+7)^2}$

42. $\dfrac{3}{x-3}, \dfrac{5}{x(3-x)}$

$\dfrac{3x}{x(x-3)}, -\dfrac{5}{x(x-3)}$

43. $\dfrac{b}{y(y-4)}, \dfrac{b^2}{4-y}$

$\dfrac{b}{y(y-4)}, -\dfrac{b^2y}{y(y-4)}$

44. $\dfrac{3}{(x-5)^2}, \dfrac{2}{5-x}$

$\dfrac{3}{(x-5)^2}, -\dfrac{2x-10}{(x-5)^2}$

45. $\dfrac{3}{7-y}, \dfrac{2}{(y-7)^2}$

$\dfrac{3y-21}{(y-7)^2}, \dfrac{2}{(y-7)^2}$

46. $\dfrac{3}{x^2+2x}, \dfrac{4}{x^2}$

$\dfrac{3x}{x^2(x+2)}, \dfrac{4x+8}{x^2(x+2)}$

47. $\dfrac{2}{y-3}, \dfrac{3}{y^3-3y^2}$

$\dfrac{2y^2}{y^2(y-3)}, \dfrac{3}{y^2(y-3)}$

48. $\dfrac{x-2}{x+3}, \dfrac{x}{x-4}$

$\dfrac{x^2-6x+8}{(x+3)(x-4)}, \dfrac{x^2+3x}{(x+3)(x-4)}$

49. $\dfrac{x^2}{2x-1}, \dfrac{x+1}{x+4}$

$\dfrac{x^3+4x^2}{(2x-1)(x+4)}, \dfrac{2x^2+x-1}{(2x-1)(x+4)}$

50. $\dfrac{3}{x^2+x-2}, \dfrac{x}{x+2}$

$\dfrac{3}{(x+2)(x-1)}, \dfrac{x^2-x}{(x+2)(x-1)}$

51. $\dfrac{3x}{x-5}, \dfrac{4}{x^2-25}$

$\dfrac{3x^2+15x}{(x-5)(x+5)}, \dfrac{4}{(x-5)(x+5)}$

52. $\dfrac{5}{2x^2-9x+10}, \dfrac{x-1}{2x-5}$

$\dfrac{5}{(2x-5)(x-2)}, \dfrac{x^2-3x+2}{(2x-5)(x-2)}$

53. $\dfrac{x-3}{3x^2+4x-4}, \dfrac{2}{x+2}$

$\dfrac{x-3}{(3x-2)(x+2)}, \dfrac{6x-4}{(3x-2)(x+2)}$

54. $\dfrac{x}{x^2+x-6}, \dfrac{2x}{x^2-9}$

$\dfrac{x^2-3x}{(x+3)(x-2)(x-3)}, \dfrac{2x^2-4x}{(x+3)(x-2)(x-3)}$

55. $\dfrac{x-1}{x^2+2x-15}, \dfrac{x}{x^2+6x+5}$

$\dfrac{x^2-1}{(x-3)(x+5)(x+1)}, \dfrac{x^2-3x}{(x-3)(x+5)(x+1)}$

Objective C

56. Explain the procedure for subtracting rational expressions with the same denominator.

Add or subtract.

57. $\dfrac{3}{y^2} + \dfrac{8}{y^2}$

$\dfrac{11}{y^2}$

58. $\dfrac{6}{ab} - \dfrac{2}{ab}$

$\dfrac{4}{ab}$

59. $\dfrac{3}{x+4} - \dfrac{10}{x+4}$

$-\dfrac{7}{x+4}$

60. $\dfrac{x}{x+6} - \dfrac{2}{x+6}$

$\dfrac{x-2}{x+6}$

61. $\dfrac{3x}{2x+3} + \dfrac{5x}{2x+3}$

$\dfrac{8x}{2x+3}$

62. $\dfrac{6y}{4y+1} - \dfrac{11y}{4y+1}$

$-\dfrac{5y}{4y+1}$

63. $\dfrac{2x+1}{x-3} + \dfrac{3x+6}{x-3}$

$\dfrac{5x+7}{x-3}$

64. $\dfrac{4x+3}{2x-7} + \dfrac{3x-8}{2x-7}$

$\dfrac{7x-5}{2x-7}$

65. $\dfrac{5x-1}{x+9} - \dfrac{3x+4}{x+9}$

$\dfrac{2x-5}{x+9}$

66. $\dfrac{6x-5}{x-10} - \dfrac{3x-4}{x-10}$

$\dfrac{3x-1}{x-10}$

67. $\dfrac{x-7}{2x+7} - \dfrac{4x-3}{2x+7}$

$\dfrac{-3x-4}{2x+7}$

68. $\dfrac{2n}{3n+4} - \dfrac{5n-3}{3n+4}$

$\dfrac{-3n+3}{3n+4}$

69. $\dfrac{x}{x^2+2x-15} - \dfrac{3}{x^2+2x-15}$

$\dfrac{1}{x+5}$

70. $\dfrac{3x}{x^2+3x-10} - \dfrac{6}{x^2+3x-10}$

$\dfrac{3}{x+5}$

71. $\dfrac{2x+3}{x^2-x-30} - \dfrac{x-2}{x^2-x-30}$

$\dfrac{1}{x-6}$

72. $\dfrac{3x-1}{x^2+5x-6} - \dfrac{2x-7}{x^2+5x-6}$

$\dfrac{1}{x-1}$

73. $\dfrac{4y+7}{2y^2+7y-4} - \dfrac{y-5}{2y^2+7y-4}$

$\dfrac{3}{2y-1}$

74. $\dfrac{x+1}{2x^2-5x-12} + \dfrac{x+2}{2x^2-5x-12}$

$\dfrac{1}{x-4}$

75. $\dfrac{2x^2+3x}{x^2-9x+20} + \dfrac{2x^2-3}{x^2-9x+20} - \dfrac{4x^2+2x+1}{x^2-9x+20}$

$\dfrac{1}{x-5}$

76. $\dfrac{2x^2+3x}{x^2-2x-63} - \dfrac{x^2-3x+21}{x^2-2x-63} - \dfrac{x-7}{x^2-2x-63}$

$\dfrac{x-2}{x-9}$

Objective D

77. Explain the procedure for adding rational expressions with different denominators.

Add or subtract.

78. $\dfrac{4}{x} + \dfrac{5}{y}$

$\dfrac{4y+5x}{xy}$

79. $\dfrac{7}{a} + \dfrac{5}{b}$

$\dfrac{7b+5a}{ab}$

80. $\dfrac{12}{x} - \dfrac{5}{2x}$

$\dfrac{19}{2x}$

81. $\dfrac{5}{3a} - \dfrac{3}{4a}$

$\dfrac{11}{12a}$

82. $\dfrac{1}{2x} - \dfrac{5}{4x} + \dfrac{7}{6x}$

$\dfrac{5}{12x}$

83. $\dfrac{7}{4y} + \dfrac{11}{6y} - \dfrac{8}{3y}$

$\dfrac{11}{12y}$

84. $\dfrac{5}{3x} - \dfrac{2}{x^2} + \dfrac{3}{2x}$

$\dfrac{19x - 12}{6x^2}$

85. $\dfrac{6}{y^2} + \dfrac{3}{4y} - \dfrac{2}{5y}$

$\dfrac{120 + 7y}{20y^2}$

86. $\dfrac{2}{x} - \dfrac{3}{2y} + \dfrac{3}{5x} - \dfrac{1}{4y}$

$\dfrac{52y - 35x}{20xy}$

87. $\dfrac{5}{2a} + \dfrac{7}{3b} - \dfrac{2}{b} - \dfrac{3}{4a}$

$\dfrac{21b + 4a}{12ab}$

88. $\dfrac{2x + 1}{3x} + \dfrac{x - 1}{5x}$

$\dfrac{13x + 2}{15x}$

89. $\dfrac{4x - 3}{6x} + \dfrac{2x + 3}{4x}$

$\dfrac{14x + 3}{12x}$

90. $\dfrac{x - 3}{6x} + \dfrac{x + 4}{8x}$

$\dfrac{7}{24}$

91. $\dfrac{2x - 3}{2x} + \dfrac{x + 3}{3x}$

$\dfrac{8x - 3}{6x}$

92. $\dfrac{2x + 9}{9x} - \dfrac{x - 5}{5x}$

$\dfrac{x + 90}{45x}$

93. $\dfrac{3y - 2}{12y} - \dfrac{y - 3}{18y}$

$\dfrac{7}{36}$

94. $\dfrac{x + 4}{2x} - \dfrac{x - 1}{x^2}$

$\dfrac{x^2 + 2x + 2}{2x^2}$

95. $\dfrac{x - 2}{3x^2} - \dfrac{x + 4}{x}$

$\dfrac{-3x^2 - 11x - 2}{3x^2}$

96. $\dfrac{x - 10}{4x^2} + \dfrac{x + 1}{2x}$

$\dfrac{2x^2 + 3x - 10}{4x^2}$

97. $\dfrac{x + 5}{3x^2} + \dfrac{2x + 1}{2x}$

$\dfrac{6x^2 + 5x + 10}{6x^2}$

98. $\dfrac{4}{x + 4} - x$

$\dfrac{-x^2 - 4x + 4}{x + 4}$

99. $2x + \dfrac{1}{x}$

$\dfrac{2x^2 + 1}{x}$

100. $5 - \dfrac{x - 2}{x + 1}$

$\dfrac{4x + 7}{x + 1}$

101. $3 + \dfrac{x - 1}{x + 1}$

$\dfrac{4x + 2}{x + 1}$

102. $\dfrac{x + 3}{6x} - \dfrac{x - 3}{8x^2}$

$\dfrac{4x^2 + 9x + 9}{24x^2}$

103. $\dfrac{x + 2}{xy} - \dfrac{3x - 2}{x^2y}$

$\dfrac{x^2 - x + 2}{x^2y}$

104. $\dfrac{3x - 1}{xy^2} - \dfrac{2x + 3}{xy}$

$\dfrac{3x - 1 - 2xy - 3y}{xy^2}$

105. $\dfrac{4x - 3}{3x^2y} + \dfrac{2x + 1}{4xy^2}$

$\dfrac{16xy - 12y + 6x^2 + 3x}{12x^2y^2}$

106. $\dfrac{5x + 7}{6xy^2} - \dfrac{4x - 3}{8x^2y}$

$\dfrac{20x^2 + 28x - 12xy + 9y}{24x^2y^2}$

107. $\dfrac{x - 2}{8x^2} - \dfrac{x + 7}{12xy}$

$\dfrac{3xy - 6y - 2x^2 - 14x}{24x^2y}$

8.3 Complex Fractions

Objective A   *To simplify a complex fraction* ....

POINT OF INTEREST

There are many instances of complex fractions in application problems. The fraction $\dfrac{1}{\dfrac{1}{R_1} + \dfrac{1}{R_2}}$ is used to determine the total resistance in certain electric circuits.

A **complex fraction** is a fraction whose numerator or denominator contains one or more fractions. Examples of complex fractions are shown at the right.

$$\frac{3}{2 - \dfrac{1}{2}}, \quad \frac{4 + \dfrac{1}{x}}{3 + \dfrac{2}{x}}, \quad \frac{\dfrac{1}{x - 1} + x + 3}{x - 3 + \dfrac{1}{x + 4}}$$

➡ Simplify: $\dfrac{1 - \dfrac{4}{x^2}}{1 + \dfrac{2}{x}}$

Find the LCM of the denominators of the fractions in the numerator and denominator. The LCM of x and x^2 is x^2.

TAKE NOTE

First of all, we are multiplying the complex fraction by $\dfrac{x^2}{x^2}$, which equals 1, so we are not changing the value of the fraction.

Second, we are using the Distributive Property to multiply $\left(1 - \dfrac{4}{x^2}\right)x^2$ and $\left(1 + \dfrac{2}{x}\right)x^2$.

$$\frac{1 - \dfrac{4}{x^2}}{1 + \dfrac{2}{x}} = \frac{1 - \dfrac{4}{x^2}}{1 + \dfrac{2}{x}} \cdot \frac{x^2}{x^2}$$

• Multiply the numerator and denominator by the LCM.

$$= \frac{1 \cdot x^2 - \dfrac{4}{x^2} \cdot x^2}{1 \cdot x^2 + \dfrac{2}{x} \cdot x^2}$$

• Simplify.

$$= \frac{x^2 - 4}{x^2 + 2x} = \frac{(x - 2)\overset{1}{\cancel{(x + 2)}}}{x\underset{1}{\cancel{(x + 2)}}}$$

$$= \frac{x - 2}{x}$$

Example 1

Simplify: $\dfrac{\dfrac{1}{x} + \dfrac{1}{2}}{\dfrac{1}{x^2} - \dfrac{1}{4}}$

Solution

The LCM of x, 2, x^2, and 4 is $4x^2$.

$$\frac{\dfrac{1}{x} + \dfrac{1}{2}}{\dfrac{1}{x^2} - \dfrac{1}{4}} = \frac{\dfrac{1}{x} + \dfrac{1}{2}}{\dfrac{1}{x^2} - \dfrac{1}{4}} \cdot \frac{4x^2}{4x^2} = \frac{\dfrac{1}{x} \cdot 4x^2 + \dfrac{1}{2} \cdot 4x^2}{\dfrac{1}{x^2} \cdot 4x^2 - \dfrac{1}{4} \cdot 4x^2}$$

$$= \frac{4x + 2x^2}{4 - x^2} = \frac{2x\overset{1}{\cancel{(2 + x)}}}{(2 - x)\underset{1}{\cancel{(2 + x)}}} = \frac{2x}{2 - x}$$

You Try It 1

Simplify: $\dfrac{\dfrac{1}{3} - \dfrac{1}{x}}{\dfrac{1}{9} - \dfrac{1}{x^2}}$

Your solution

$\dfrac{3x}{x + 3}$

Solution on p. S23

Example 2

Simplify: $\dfrac{1 - \dfrac{2}{x} - \dfrac{15}{x^2}}{1 - \dfrac{11}{x} + \dfrac{30}{x^2}}$

Solution

The LCM of x and x^2 is x^2.

$$\dfrac{1 - \dfrac{2}{x} - \dfrac{15}{x^2}}{1 - \dfrac{11}{x} + \dfrac{30}{x^2}} = \dfrac{1 - \dfrac{2}{x} - \dfrac{15}{x^2}}{1 - \dfrac{11}{x} + \dfrac{30}{x^2}} \cdot \dfrac{x^2}{x^2}$$

$$= \dfrac{1 \cdot x^2 - \dfrac{2}{x} \cdot x^2 - \dfrac{15}{x^2} \cdot x^2}{1 \cdot x^2 - \dfrac{11}{x} \cdot x^2 + \dfrac{30}{x^2} \cdot x^2}$$

$$= \dfrac{x^2 - 2x - 15}{x^2 - 11x + 30}$$

$$= \dfrac{(\overset{1}{\cancel{x - 5}})(x + 3)}{(\underset{1}{\cancel{x - 5}})(x - 6)} = \dfrac{x + 3}{x - 6}$$

You Try It 2

Simplify: $\dfrac{1 + \dfrac{4}{x} + \dfrac{3}{x^2}}{1 + \dfrac{10}{x} + \dfrac{21}{x^2}}$

Your solution

$\dfrac{x + 1}{x + 7}$

Example 3

Simplify: $\dfrac{x - 8 + \dfrac{20}{x + 4}}{x - 10 + \dfrac{24}{x + 4}}$

Solution

The LCM is $x + 4$.

$$\dfrac{x - 8 + \dfrac{20}{x + 4}}{x - 10 + \dfrac{24}{x + 4}}$$

$$= \dfrac{x - 8 + \dfrac{20}{x + 4}}{x - 10 + \dfrac{24}{x + 4}} \cdot \dfrac{x + 4}{x + 4}$$

$$= \dfrac{x(x + 4) - 8(x + 4) + \dfrac{20}{x + 4} \cdot (x + 4)}{x(x + 4) - 10(x + 4) + \dfrac{24}{x + 4} \cdot (x + 4)}$$

$$= \dfrac{x^2 + 4x - 8x - 32 + 20}{x^2 + 4x - 10x - 40 + 24} = \dfrac{x^2 - 4x - 12}{x^2 - 6x - 16}$$

$$= \dfrac{(x - 6)(\overset{1}{\cancel{x + 2}})}{(x - 8)(\underset{1}{\cancel{x + 2}})} = \dfrac{x - 6}{x - 8}$$

You Try It 3

Simplify: $\dfrac{x + 3 - \dfrac{20}{x - 5}}{x + 8 + \dfrac{30}{x - 5}}$

Your solution

$\dfrac{x - 7}{x - 2}$

Solutions on p. S23

8.3 Exercises

. . . .

Objective A

Simplify.

1. $\dfrac{1 + \dfrac{3}{x}}{1 - \dfrac{9}{x^2}}$

$\dfrac{x}{x-3}$

2. $\dfrac{1 + \dfrac{4}{x}}{1 - \dfrac{16}{x^2}}$

$\dfrac{x}{x-4}$

3. $\dfrac{2 - \dfrac{8}{x+4}}{3 - \dfrac{12}{x+4}}$

$\dfrac{2}{3}$

4. $\dfrac{5 - \dfrac{25}{x+5}}{1 - \dfrac{3}{x+5}}$

$\dfrac{5x}{x+2}$

5. $\dfrac{1 + \dfrac{5}{y-2}}{1 - \dfrac{2}{y-2}}$

$\dfrac{y+3}{y-4}$

6. $\dfrac{2 - \dfrac{11}{2x-1}}{3 - \dfrac{17}{2x-1}}$

$\dfrac{4x-13}{2(3x-10)}$

7. $\dfrac{4 - \dfrac{2}{x+7}}{5 + \dfrac{1}{x+7}}$

$\dfrac{2(2x+13)}{5x+36}$

8. $\dfrac{5 + \dfrac{3}{x-8}}{2 - \dfrac{1}{x-8}}$

$\dfrac{5x-37}{2x-17}$

9. $\dfrac{1 - \dfrac{1}{x} - \dfrac{6}{x^2}}{1 - \dfrac{9}{x^2}}$

$\dfrac{x+2}{x+3}$

10. $\dfrac{1 + \dfrac{4}{x} + \dfrac{4}{x^2}}{1 - \dfrac{2}{x} - \dfrac{8}{x^2}}$

$\dfrac{x+2}{x-4}$

11. $\dfrac{1 - \dfrac{5}{x} - \dfrac{6}{x^2}}{1 + \dfrac{6}{x} + \dfrac{5}{x^2}}$

$\dfrac{x-6}{x+5}$

12. $\dfrac{1 - \dfrac{7}{a} + \dfrac{12}{a^2}}{1 + \dfrac{1}{a} - \dfrac{20}{a^2}}$

$\dfrac{a-3}{a+5}$

13. $\dfrac{1 - \dfrac{6}{x} + \dfrac{8}{x^2}}{\dfrac{4}{x^2} + \dfrac{3}{x} - 1}$

$-\dfrac{x-2}{x+1}$

14. $\dfrac{1 + \dfrac{3}{x} - \dfrac{18}{x^2}}{\dfrac{21}{x^2} - \dfrac{4}{x} - 1}$

$-\dfrac{x+6}{x+7}$

15. $\dfrac{x - \dfrac{4}{x+3}}{1 + \dfrac{1}{x+3}}$

$x-1$

16. $\dfrac{y + \dfrac{1}{y-2}}{1 + \dfrac{1}{y-2}}$

$y-1$

17. $\dfrac{1 - \dfrac{x}{2x+1}}{x - \dfrac{1}{2x+1}}$

$\dfrac{1}{2x-1}$

18. $\dfrac{1 - \dfrac{2x-2}{3x-1}}{x - \dfrac{4}{3x-1}}$

$\dfrac{1}{3x-4}$

19. $\dfrac{x - 5 + \dfrac{14}{x + 4}}{x + 3 - \dfrac{2}{x + 4}}$

$\dfrac{x - 3}{x + 5}$

20. $\dfrac{a + 4 + \dfrac{5}{a - 2}}{a + 6 + \dfrac{15}{a - 2}}$

$\dfrac{a - 1}{a + 1}$

21. $\dfrac{x + 3 - \dfrac{10}{x - 6}}{x + 2 - \dfrac{20}{x - 6}}$

$\dfrac{x - 7}{x - 8}$

22. $\dfrac{x - 7 + \dfrac{5}{x - 1}}{x - 3 + \dfrac{1}{x - 1}}$

$\dfrac{x - 6}{x - 2}$

23. $\dfrac{y - 6 + \dfrac{22}{2y + 3}}{y - 5 + \dfrac{11}{2y + 3}}$

$\dfrac{2y - 1}{2y + 1}$

24. $\dfrac{x + 2 - \dfrac{12}{2x - 1}}{x + 1 - \dfrac{9}{2x - 1}}$

$\dfrac{2x + 7}{2x + 5}$

25. $\dfrac{x - \dfrac{2}{2x - 3}}{2x - 1 - \dfrac{8}{2x - 3}}$

$\dfrac{x - 2}{2x - 5}$

26. $\dfrac{x + 3 - \dfrac{18}{2x + 1}}{x - \dfrac{6}{2x + 1}}$

$\dfrac{x + 5}{x + 2}$

27. $\dfrac{\dfrac{1}{x} - \dfrac{2}{x - 1}}{\dfrac{3}{x} + \dfrac{1}{x - 1}}$

$-\dfrac{x + 1}{4x - 3}$

28. $\dfrac{\dfrac{3}{n + 1} + \dfrac{1}{n}}{\dfrac{2}{n + 1} + \dfrac{3}{n}}$

$\dfrac{4n + 1}{5n + 3}$

29. $\dfrac{\dfrac{3}{2x - 1} - \dfrac{1}{x}}{\dfrac{4}{x} + \dfrac{2}{2x - 1}}$

$\dfrac{x + 1}{2(5x - 2)}$

30. $\dfrac{\dfrac{4}{3x + 1} + \dfrac{3}{x}}{\dfrac{6}{x} - \dfrac{2}{3x + 1}}$

$\dfrac{13x + 3}{2(8x + 3)}$

APPLYING THE CONCEPTS

Simplify.

31. $1 + \dfrac{1}{1 + \dfrac{1}{2}}$

$\dfrac{5}{3}$

32. $1 + \dfrac{1}{1 + \dfrac{1}{1 + \dfrac{1}{2}}}$

$\dfrac{8}{5}$

33. $1 - \dfrac{1}{1 - \dfrac{1}{x}}$

$-\dfrac{1}{x - 1}$

34. $\dfrac{a^{-1} - b^{-1}}{a^{-2} - b^{-2}}$

$\dfrac{ab}{a + b}$

35. $\left(\dfrac{y}{4} - \dfrac{4}{y}\right) \div \left(\dfrac{4}{y} - 3 + \dfrac{y}{2}\right)$

$\dfrac{y + 4}{2(y - 2)}$

36. $\dfrac{1 + x^{-1}}{1 - x^{-1}}$

$\dfrac{x + 1}{x - 1}$

37. How would you explain to a classmate why we multiply the numerator and denominator of a complex fraction by the LCM of the denominators of the fractions in the numerator and denominator?

8.4 Rational Equations

Objective A   *To solve rational equations* ....

To solve an equation containing fractions, **clear denominators** by multiplying each side of the equation by the LCM of the denominators. Then solve for the variable.

➡ Solve: $\dfrac{3x - 1}{4x} + \dfrac{2}{3x} = \dfrac{7}{6x}$

$$\dfrac{3x - 1}{4x} + \dfrac{2}{3x} = \dfrac{7}{6x}$$

- The LCM of 4*x*, 3*x*, and 6*x* is 12*x*.

$$12x\left(\dfrac{3x - 1}{4x} + \dfrac{2}{3x}\right) = 12x\left(\dfrac{7}{6x}\right)$$

- Multiply each side of the equation by the LCM of the denominators.

$$12x\left(\dfrac{3x - 1}{4x}\right) + 12x\left(\dfrac{2}{3x}\right) = 12x\left(\dfrac{7}{6x}\right)$$

- Simplify using the Distributive Property.

$$\dfrac{12x}{1}\left(\dfrac{3x - 1}{4x}\right) + \dfrac{12x}{1}\left(\dfrac{2}{3x}\right) = \dfrac{12x}{1}\left(\dfrac{7}{6x}\right)$$

$$3(3x - 1) + 4(2) = 2(7)$$

- Solve for *x*.

$$9x - 3 + 8 = 14$$
$$9x + 5 = 14$$
$$9x = 9$$
$$x = 1$$

1 checks as a solution. The solution is 1.

Occasionally, a value of the variable that appears to be a solution of an equation will make one of the denominators zero. In this case, the equation has no solution for that value of the variable.

➡ Solve: $\dfrac{2x}{x - 2} = 1 + \dfrac{4}{x - 2}$

$$\dfrac{2x}{x - 2} = 1 + \dfrac{4}{x - 2}$$

$$(x - 2)\dfrac{2x}{x - 2} = (x - 2)\left(1 + \dfrac{4}{x - 2}\right)$$

- The LCM is *x* − 2. Multiply each side of the equation by the LCM.

$$(x - 2)\dfrac{2x}{x - 2} = (x - 2) \cdot 1 + (x - 2)\dfrac{4}{x - 2}$$

- Simplify using the Distributive Property and the Properties of Fractions.

$$\dfrac{\overset{1}{\cancel{(x - 2)}}}{1} \cdot \dfrac{2x}{\cancel{x - 2}} = (x - 2) \cdot 1 + \dfrac{\overset{1}{\cancel{(x - 2)}}}{1} \cdot \dfrac{4}{\cancel{x - 2}}$$

$$2x = x - 2 + 4$$

- Solve for *x*.

$$2x = x + 2$$
$$x = 2$$

When *x* is replaced by 2, the denominators of $\dfrac{2x}{x - 2}$ and $\dfrac{4}{x - 2}$ are zero. Therefore, the equation has no solution.

Example 1

Solve: $\dfrac{x}{x+4} = \dfrac{2}{x}$

Solution

The LCM is $x(x+4)$.

$$\frac{x}{x+4} = \frac{2}{x}$$

$$x(x+4)\left(\frac{x}{x+4}\right) = x(x+4)\left(\frac{2}{x}\right)$$

$$\frac{x(x+4)}{1} \cdot \frac{x}{x+4} = \frac{\overset{1}{x}(x+4)}{1} \cdot \frac{2}{\underset{1}{x}}$$

$$x^2 = (x+4)2$$
$$x^2 = 2x + 8$$

Solve the quadratic equation by factoring.

$$x^2 - 2x - 8 = 0$$
$$(x-4)(x+2) = 0$$
$$x - 4 = 0 \qquad x + 2 = 0$$
$$x = 4 \qquad\quad x = -2$$

Both 4 and -2 check as solutions.
The solutions are 4 and -2.

You Try It 1

Solve: $\dfrac{x}{x+6} = \dfrac{3}{x}$

Your solution

$-3, 6$

Example 2

Solve: $\dfrac{3x}{x-4} = 5 + \dfrac{12}{x-4}$

Solution

The LCM is $x - 4$.

$$\frac{3x}{x-4} = 5 + \frac{12}{x-4}$$

$$(x-4)\left(\frac{3x}{x-4}\right) = (x-4)\left(5 + \frac{12}{x-4}\right)$$

$$\frac{(x-4)}{1} \cdot \frac{3x}{x-4} = (x-4)5 + \frac{(x-4)}{1} \cdot \frac{12}{x-4}$$

$$3x = (x-4)5 + 12$$
$$3x = 5x - 20 + 12$$
$$3x = 5x - 8$$
$$-2x = -8$$
$$x = 4$$

4 does not check as a solution.
The equation has no solution.

You Try It 2

Solve: $\dfrac{5x}{x+2} = 3 - \dfrac{10}{x+2}$

Your solution

no solution

Solutions on p. S24

Objective B   **To solve proportions**...

Quantities such as 4 meters, 15 seconds, and 8 gallons are number quantities written with units. In these examples, the units are meters, seconds, and gallons.

A **ratio** is the quotient of two quantities that have the same unit.

The length of a living room is 16 ft and the width is 12 ft. The ratio of the length to the width is written

$$\frac{16 \text{ ft}}{12 \text{ ft}} = \frac{16}{12} = \frac{4}{3}$$ A ratio is in simplest form when the two numbers do not have a common factor. Note that the units are not written.

A **rate** is the quotient of two quantities that have different units.

There are 2 lb of salt in 8 gal of water. The salt-to-water rate is

$$\frac{2 \text{ lb}}{8 \text{ gal}} = \frac{1 \text{ lb}}{4 \text{ gal}}$$ A rate is in simplest form when the two numbers do not have a common factor. The units are written as part of the rate.

A **proportion** is an equation that states the equality of two ratios or rates. Examples of proportions are shown at the right.

$$\frac{30 \text{ mi}}{4 \text{ h}} = \frac{15 \text{ mi}}{2 \text{ h}}$$

$$\frac{4}{6} = \frac{8}{12}$$

$$\frac{3}{4} = \frac{x}{8}$$

➡ Solve: $\frac{4}{x} = \frac{2}{3}$

$$\frac{4}{x} = \frac{2}{3}$$ • The LCM of x and 3 is $3x$.

$$3x\left(\frac{4}{x}\right) = 3x\left(\frac{2}{3}\right)$$ • Multiply each side of the proportion by $3x$.

$$12 = 2x$$ • Solve the equation.

$$6 = x$$

The solution is 6.

Example 3

Solve: $\dfrac{8}{x+3} = \dfrac{4}{x}$

Solution

$$\frac{8}{x+3} = \frac{4}{x}$$

$$x(x+3)\frac{8}{x+3} = x(x+3)\frac{4}{x}$$

$$8x = 4(x+3)$$
$$8x = 4x + 12$$
$$4x = 12$$
$$x = 3$$

The solution is 3.

You Try It 3

Solve: $\dfrac{2}{x+3} = \dfrac{6}{5x+5}$

Your solution

2

Solution on p. S24

Objective C   **To solve problems involving similar triangles** ....

Similar objects have the same shape but not necessarily the same size. A tennis ball is similar to a basketball. A model ship is similar to an actual ship.

Similar objects have corresponding parts; for example, the rudder on the model ship corresponds to the rudder on the actual ship. The relationship between the sizes of each of the corresponding parts can be written as a ratio, and each ratio will be the same. If the rudder on the model ship is $\frac{1}{100}$ the size of the rudder on the actual ship, then the model wheelhouse is $\frac{1}{100}$ the size of the actual wheelhouse, the width of the model is $\frac{1}{100}$ the width of the actual ship, and so on.

The two triangles *ABC* and *DEF* shown at the right are similar. Side *AB* corresponds to *DE*, side *BC* corresponds to *EF*, and side *AC* corresponds to *DF*. The height *CH* corresponds to the height *FK*. The ratios of corresponding parts are equal.

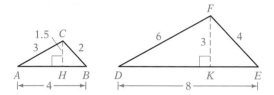

$$\frac{AB}{DE} = \frac{4}{8} = \frac{1}{2}, \qquad \frac{AC}{DF} = \frac{3}{6} = \frac{1}{2}, \qquad \frac{BC}{EF} = \frac{2}{4} = \frac{1}{2}, \qquad \text{and} \qquad \frac{CH}{FK} = \frac{1.5}{3} = \frac{1}{2}$$

Since the ratios of corresponding parts are equal, three proportions can be formed using the sides of the triangles.

$$\frac{AB}{DE} = \frac{AC}{DF}, \qquad \frac{AB}{DE} = \frac{BC}{EF}, \qquad \text{and} \qquad \frac{AC}{DF} = \frac{BC}{EF}$$

Three proportions can also be formed by using the sides and height of the triangles.

$$\frac{AB}{DE} = \frac{CH}{FK}, \qquad \frac{AC}{DF} = \frac{CH}{FK}, \qquad \text{and} \qquad \frac{BC}{EF} = \frac{CH}{FK}$$

➡ Triangles *ABC* and *DEF* at the right are similar. Find the height of triangle *ABC*.

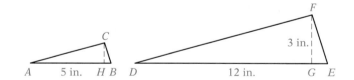

$$\frac{AB}{DE} = \frac{CH}{FG}$$

• Solve a proportion to find the height of triangle *ABC*.

$$\frac{5}{12} = \frac{CH}{3}$$

$$12 \cdot \frac{5}{12} = 12 \cdot \frac{CH}{3}$$

$$5 = 4(CH)$$

$$1.25 = CH$$

The height of triangle *ABC* is 1.25 in.

The corresponding angles in similar triangles are equal. Therefore, for the triangles in the last example,

$$\angle A = \angle D, \qquad \angle B = \angle E, \qquad \text{and} \qquad \angle C = \angle F$$

It is also true that if the three angles of one triangle are equal respectively to the three angles of another triangle, then the two triangles are similar.

A line *DE* is drawn parallel to the base *AB* in the triangle at the right. $\angle x = \angle m$ and $\angle y = \angle n$ because corresponding angles are equal. Angle *C* = angle *C*, and thus the three angles of triangle *DEC* are equal respectively to the three angles of triangle *ABC*. The triangle *DEC* is similar to the triangle *ABC*.

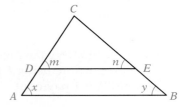

The sum of the three angles of a triangle is 180°. If two angles of one triangle are equal to two angles of another triangle, then the third angles must be equal. Thus we can say that if two angles of one triangle are equal to two angles of another triangle, then the two triangles are similar. This fact is used in Example 4.

Example 4

In the figure at the right, *AC* is parallel to *BD* and angles *C* and *D* are right angles. Find the length of *DO*.

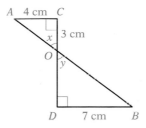

Strategy

$\angle C = \angle D$ because they are right angles. $\angle x = \angle y$ because they are vertical angles. Therefore, triangle *AOC* is similar to triangle *BOD* because two angles of one triangle are equal to two angles of the other. Use a proportion to find the length of *DO*.

Solution

$$\frac{AC}{DB} = \frac{CO}{DO}$$

$$\frac{4}{7} = \frac{3}{DO}$$

$$7(DO)\frac{4}{7} = 7(DO)\frac{3}{DO}$$

$$4(DO) = 7(3)$$

$$4(DO) = 21$$

$$DO = 5.25$$

The length of *DO* is 5.25 cm.

You Try It 4

In the figure at the right, *AB* is parallel to *DC* and angles *A* and *D* are right angles. Find the area of triangle *AOB*.

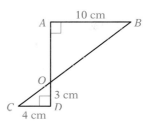

Your strategy

Your solution   37.5 cm²

Solution on p. S24

Objective D   To solve application problems...

Example 5
The monthly loan payment for a car is
$28.35 for each $1000 borrowed. At this
rate, find the monthly payment for a
$6000 car loan.

Strategy
To find the monthly payment, write and
solve a proportion, using P to represent
the monthly car payment.

Solution
$$\frac{28.35}{1000} = \frac{P}{6000}$$
$$6000\left(\frac{28.35}{1000}\right) = 6000\left(\frac{P}{6000}\right)$$
$$170.10 = P$$

The monthly payment is $170.10.

You Try It 5
Sixteen ceramic tiles are needed to tile an
area of 9 ft². At this rate, how many square
feet can be tiled using 256 ceramic tiles?

Your strategy

Your solution
144 ft²

Example 6
An investment of $500 earns $60 each
year. At the same rate, how much
additional money must be invested to
earn $90 each year?

Strategy
To find the additional amount of money
that must be invested, write and solve a
proportion, using x to represent the
additional money. Then $500 + x$ is the
total amount invested.

Solution
$$\frac{60}{500} = \frac{90}{500 + x}$$
$$\frac{3}{25} = \frac{90}{500 + x}$$
$$25(500 + x)\left(\frac{3}{25}\right) = 25(500 + x)\left(\frac{90}{500 + x}\right)$$
$$(500 + x)3 = 25(90)$$
$$1500 + 3x = 2250$$
$$3x = 750$$
$$x = 250$$

An additional $250 must be invested.

You Try It 6
Three ounces of a certain medication are
required for a 150-pound adult. At the
same rate, how many additional ounces of
this medication are required for a
200-pound adult?

Your strategy

Your solution
1 additional ounce

Solutions on p. S24

8.4 Exercises

Objective A

Solve.

1. $\dfrac{2x}{3} - \dfrac{5}{2} = -\dfrac{1}{2}$
3

2. $\dfrac{x}{3} - \dfrac{1}{4} = \dfrac{1}{12}$
1

3. $\dfrac{x}{3} - \dfrac{1}{4} = \dfrac{x}{4} - \dfrac{1}{6}$
1

4. $\dfrac{2y}{9} - \dfrac{1}{6} = \dfrac{y}{9} + \dfrac{1}{6}$
3

5. $\dfrac{2x-5}{8} + \dfrac{1}{4} = \dfrac{x}{8} + \dfrac{3}{4}$
9

6. $\dfrac{3x+4}{12} - \dfrac{1}{3} = \dfrac{5x+2}{12} - \dfrac{1}{2}$
2

7. $\dfrac{6}{2a+1} = 2$
1

8. $\dfrac{12}{3x-2} = 3$
2

9. $\dfrac{9}{2x-5} = -2$
$\dfrac{1}{4}$

10. $\dfrac{6}{4-3x} = 3$
$\dfrac{2}{3}$

11. $2 + \dfrac{5}{x} = 7$
1

12. $3 + \dfrac{8}{n} = 5$
4

13. $1 - \dfrac{9}{x} = 4$
-3

14. $3 - \dfrac{12}{x} = 7$
-3

15. $\dfrac{2}{y} + 5 = 9$
$\dfrac{1}{2}$

16. $\dfrac{6}{x} + 3 = 11$
$\dfrac{3}{4}$

17. $\dfrac{3}{x-2} = \dfrac{4}{x}$
8

18. $\dfrac{5}{x+3} = \dfrac{3}{x-1}$
7

19. $\dfrac{2}{3x-1} = \dfrac{3}{4x+1}$
5

20. $\dfrac{5}{3x-4} = \dfrac{-3}{1-2x}$
-7

21. $\dfrac{-3}{2x+5} = \dfrac{2}{x-1}$
-1

22. $\dfrac{4}{5y-1} = \dfrac{2}{2y-1}$
-1

23. $\dfrac{4x}{x-4} + 5 = \dfrac{5x}{x-4}$
5

24. $\dfrac{2x}{x+2} - 5 = \dfrac{7x}{x+2}$
-1

25. $2 + \dfrac{3}{a-3} = \dfrac{a}{a-3}$
no solution

26. $\dfrac{x}{x+4} = 3 - \dfrac{4}{x+4}$
no solution

27. $\dfrac{x}{x-1} = \dfrac{8}{x+2}$
2, 4

28. $\dfrac{x}{x+12} = \dfrac{1}{x+5}$
−6, 2

29. $\dfrac{2x}{x+4} = \dfrac{3}{x-1}$
$-\dfrac{3}{2}$, 4

30. $\dfrac{5}{3n-8} = \dfrac{n}{n+2}$
$-\dfrac{2}{3}$, 5

31. $x + \dfrac{6}{x-2} = \dfrac{3x}{x-2}$
3

32. $x - \dfrac{6}{x-3} = \dfrac{2x}{x-3}$
6, −1

33. $\dfrac{8}{y} = \dfrac{2}{y-2} + 1$
4

Objective B

Solve.

34. $\dfrac{x}{12} = \dfrac{3}{4}$
9

35. $\dfrac{6}{x} = \dfrac{2}{3}$
9

36. $\dfrac{4}{9} = \dfrac{x}{27}$
12

37. $\dfrac{16}{9} = \dfrac{64}{x}$
36

38. $\dfrac{x+3}{12} = \dfrac{5}{6}$
7

39. $\dfrac{3}{5} = \dfrac{x-4}{10}$
10

40. $\dfrac{18}{x+4} = \dfrac{9}{5}$
6

41. $\dfrac{2}{11} = \dfrac{20}{x-3}$
113

42. $\dfrac{2}{x} = \dfrac{4}{x+1}$
1

43. $\dfrac{16}{x-2} = \dfrac{8}{x}$
−2

44. $\dfrac{x+3}{4} = \dfrac{x}{8}$
−6

45. $\dfrac{x-6}{3} = \dfrac{x}{5}$
15

46. $\dfrac{2}{x-1} = \dfrac{6}{2x+1}$
4

47. $\dfrac{9}{x+2} = \dfrac{3}{x-2}$
4

48. $\dfrac{2x}{7} = \dfrac{x-2}{14}$
$-\dfrac{2}{3}$

___

Objective C

Triangles *ABC* and *DEF* in Exercises 49 to 56 are similar. Round answers to the nearest tenth.

49. Find side *AC*.

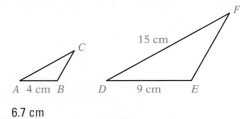

6.7 cm

50. Find side *DE*.

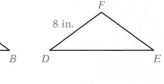

12.8 in.

51. Find the height of triangle *ABC*.

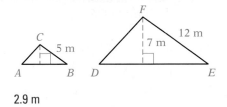

2.9 m

52. Find the height of triangle *DEF*.

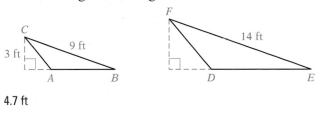

4.7 ft

53. Find the perimeter of triangle *DEF*.

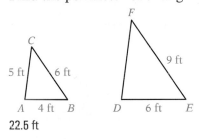

22.5 ft

54. Find the perimeter of triangle *ABC*.

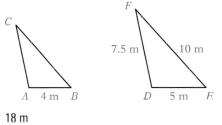

18 m

55. Find the area of triangle *ABC*.

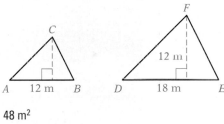

48 m²

56. Find the area of triangle *ABC*.

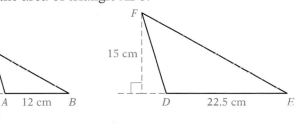

48 cm²

57. Given *BD* ∥ *AE*, *BD* measures 5 cm, *AE* measures 8 cm, and *AC* measures 10 cm, find the length of *BC*.

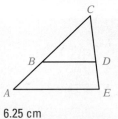

6.25 cm

58. Given *AC* ∥ *DE*, *BD* measures 8 m, *AD* measures 12 m, and *BE* measures 6 m, find the length of *BC*.

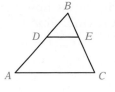

15 m

59. Given $DE \parallel AC$, DE measures 6 in., AC measures 10 in., and AB measures 15 in., find the length of DA.

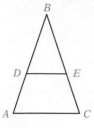

6 in.

60. Given MP and NQ intersect at O, NO measures 25 ft, MO measures 20 ft, and PO measures 8 ft, find the length of QO.

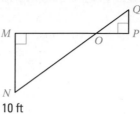

10 ft

61. Given MP and NQ intersect at O, NO measures 24 cm, MN measures 10 cm, MP measures 39 cm, and QO measures 12 cm, find the length of OP.

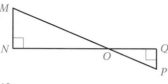

13 cm

62. Given MQ and NP intersect at O, NO measures 12 m, MN measures 9 m, PQ measures 3 m, and MQ measures 20 m, find the perimeter of triangle OPQ.

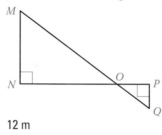

12 m

63. The sun's rays cast a shadow as shown in the diagram at the right. Find the height of the flagpole. Write the answer in terms of feet.

14.375 ft

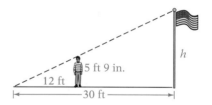

64. Similar triangles can be used as an indirect way to measure inaccessible distances. The diagram at the right represents a river of width DC. The triangles AOB and DOC are similar. The distances AB, BO, and OC can be measured. Find the width of the river.

35 m

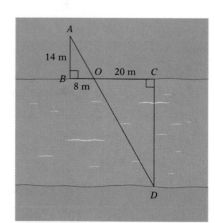

65. The diagram at the right shows how surveyors laid out similar triangles along a ravine. Find the width, w, of the ravine.

82.5 ft

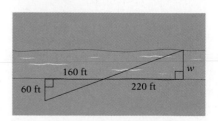

Objective D *Application Problems*

66. Simple syrup used in making some desserts requires 2 cups (c) of sugar for every $\frac{2}{3}$ c of boiling water. At this rate, how many cups of sugar are required for 2 c boiling water?
6 c

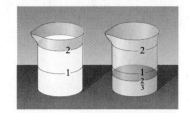

67. An exit poll survey showed that 4 out of every 7 voters cast a ballot in favor of an amendment to a city charter. At this rate, how many voters voted in favor of the amendment if 35,000 people voted?
20,000 voters

68. In a city of 25,000 homes, a survey was taken to determine the number with cable television. Of the 300 homes surveyed, 210 had cable television. Estimate the number of homes in the city that have cable television.
17,500 homes

69. On a map, two cities are $2\frac{5}{8}$ in. apart. If $\frac{3}{8}$ in. on the map represents 25 mi, find the number of miles between the two cities.
175 mi

70. The lighting for some billboards is provided by using solar energy. If 3 small solar energy panels can generate 10 W of power, how many panels are necessary to provide 600 W of power?
180 panels

71. A soft drink is made by mixing 4 parts carbonated water with every 3 parts syrup. How many milliliters of water are in 280 ml of soft drink?
160 ml

72. An air conditioning specialist recommends 2 air vents for each 300 ft² of floor space. At this rate, how many air vents are required for a 21,000-square-foot office building?
140 air vents

73. A laser printer is rated by the number of pages per minute it can print. An inexpensive laser printer can print 5 pages every 2 min. At this rate, how long would it take to print a document 45 pages long?
18 min

74. As part of a conservation effort for a lake, 40 fish are caught, tagged, and then released. Later 80 fish are caught. Four of the 80 fish are found to have tags. Estimate the number of fish in the lake.
800 fish

75. To conserve energy and still allow for as much natural lighting as possible, an architect suggests that the ratio of the area of a window to the area of the total wall surface be 5 to 12. Using this ratio, determine the recommended area of a window to be installed in a wall that measures 8 ft by 12 ft.
40 ft²

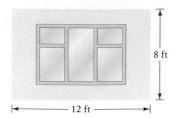

76. The engine of a small rocket burns 170,000 lb of fuel in 1 min. At this rate, how many pounds of fuel does the rocket burn in 45 s?
127,500 lb

77. A company decides to accept a large shipment of 10,000 computer chips if there are 2 or fewer defects in a sample of 100 randomly chosen chips. Assuming that there are 300 defective chips in the shipment and that the rate of defective chips in the sample is the same as the rate in the shipment, will the shipment be accepted?
no

78. The sales tax on a car that sold for $12,000 is $780. At this rate, how much higher is the sales tax on a car that sells for $13,500?
$97.50

79. A painter estimates that 5 gal of paint will cover 1200 ft² of wall space. At this rate, how many additional gallons will be necessary to cover 1680 ft²?
2 additional gallons

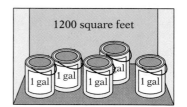

APPLYING THE CONCEPTS

80. Three people put their money together to buy lottery tickets. The first person put in $25, the second person put in $30, and the third person put in $35. One of their tickets was a winning ticket. If they won $4.5 million, what was the first person's share of the winnings?
$1.25 million

81. No one belongs to both the Math Club and the Photography Club, but the two clubs join to hold a car wash. Ten members of the Math Club and 6 members of the Photography Club participate. The profits from the car wash are $120. If each club's profits are proportional to the number of members participating, what share of the profits does the Math Club receive?
$75

82. A basketball player has made 5 out of every 6 foul shots attempted in one year of play. If 42 foul shots were missed that year, how many shots did the basketball player make?
210 shots

83. Explain the procedure for solving an equation that contains fractions. Include in your discussion how the LCM of the denominators is used to eliminate fractions in the equation.

8.5 Literal Equations

Objective A   *To solve a literal equation for one of the variables*.....................

A **literal equation** is an equation that contains more than one variable. Examples of literal equations are shown at the right.

$$2x + 3y = 6$$
$$4w - 2x + z = 0$$

Formulas are used to express a relationship among physical quantities. A **formula** is a literal equation that states rules about measurements. Examples of formulas are shown at the right.

$$\frac{1}{R_1} + \frac{1}{R_2} = \frac{1}{R} \quad \text{(Physics)}$$
$$s = a + (n - 1)d \quad \text{(Mathematics)}$$
$$A = P + Prt \quad \text{(Business)}$$

The Addition and Multiplication Properties can be used to solve a literal equation for one of the variables. The goal is to rewrite the equation so that the variable being solved for is alone on one side of the equation and all the other numbers and variables are on the other side.

➡ Solve $A = P(1 + i)$ for i.

The goal is to rewrite the equation so that i is on one side of the equation and all other variables are on the other side.

$$A = P(1 + i)$$
$$A = P + Pi \qquad \text{• Use the Distributive Property to remove parentheses.}$$
$$A - P = P - P + Pi \qquad \text{• Subtract } P \text{ from each side of the equation.}$$
$$A - P = Pi$$
$$\frac{A - P}{P} = \frac{Pi}{P} \qquad \text{• Divide each side of the equation by } P.$$
$$\frac{A - P}{P} = i$$

Example 1

Solve $s = a + (n - 1)d$ for d.

Solution

$$s = a + (n - 1)d$$
$$s - a = a - a + (n - 1)d$$
$$s - a = (n - 1)d$$
$$\frac{s - a}{n - 1} = \frac{(n - 1)d}{n - 1}$$
$$\frac{s - a}{n - 1} = d$$

You Try It 1

Solve $A = P + Prt$ for r.

Your solution

$$r = \frac{A - P}{Pt}$$

Solution on p. S25

Example 2

Solve $I = \dfrac{E}{R + r}$ for R.

Solution

$$I = \frac{E}{R + r}$$

$$(R + r)I = (R + r)\frac{E}{R + r}$$

$$RI + rI = E$$

$$RI + rI - rI = E - rI$$

$$RI = E - rI$$

$$\frac{RI}{I} = \frac{E - rI}{I}$$

$$R = \frac{E - rI}{I}$$

You Try It 2

Solve $s = \dfrac{A + L}{2}$ for L.

Your solution

$L = 2s - A$

Example 3

Solve $L = a(1 + ct)$ for c.

Solution

$$L = a(1 + ct)$$

$$L = a + act$$

$$L - a = a - a + act$$

$$L - a = act$$

$$\frac{L - a}{at} = \frac{act}{at}$$

$$\frac{L - a}{at} = c$$

You Try It 3

Solve $s = a + (n - 1)d$ for n.

Your solution

$n = \dfrac{s - a + d}{d}$

Example 4

Solve $S = C - rC$ for C.

Solution

$$S = C - rC$$

$$S = (1 - r)C$$

$$\frac{S}{1 - r} = \frac{(1 - r)C}{1 - r}$$

$$\frac{S}{1 - r} = C$$

You Try It 4

Solve $S = C + rC$ for C.

Your solution

$C = \dfrac{S}{1 + r}$

Solutions on p. S25

8.5 Exercises

· ·

Objective A

Solve the formula for the given variable.

1. $A = \dfrac{1}{2}bh; h$ (Geometry)

$h = \dfrac{2A}{b}$

2. $P = a + b + c; b$ (Geometry)

$b = P - a - c$

3. $d = rt; t$ (Physics)

$t = \dfrac{d}{r}$

4. $E = IR; R$ (Physics)

$R = \dfrac{E}{I}$

5. $PV = nRT; T$ (Chemistry)

$T = \dfrac{PV}{nR}$

6. $A = bh; h$ (Geometry)

$h = \dfrac{A}{b}$

7. $P = 2L + 2W; L$ (Geometry)

$L = \dfrac{P - 2W}{2}$

8. $F = \dfrac{9}{5}C + 32; C$ (Temperature conversion)

$C = \dfrac{5F - 160}{9}$

9. $A = \dfrac{1}{2}h(b_1 + b_2); b_1$ (Geometry)

$b_1 = \dfrac{2A - hb_2}{h}$

10. $C = \dfrac{5}{9}(F - 32); F$ (Temperature conversion)

$F = \dfrac{9C + 160}{5}$

11. $V = \dfrac{1}{3}Ah; h$ (Geometry)

$h = \dfrac{3V}{A}$

12. $P = R - C; C$ (Business)

$C = R - P$

13. $R = \dfrac{C - S}{t}; S$ (Business)

$S = C - Rt$

14. $P = \dfrac{R - C}{n}; R$ (Business)

$R = Pn + C$

15. $A = P + Prt; P$ (Business)

$P = \dfrac{A}{1 + rt}$

16. $T = fm - gm; m$ (Engineering)

$m = \dfrac{T}{f - g}$

17. $A = Sw + w; w$ (Physics)

$w = \dfrac{A}{S + 1}$

18. $a = S - Sr; S$ (Mathematics)

$S = \dfrac{a}{1 - r}$

APPLYING THE CONCEPTS

The surface area of a right circular cylinder is given by the formula $S = 2\pi rh + 2\pi r^2$, where r is the radius of the base, and h is the height of the cylinder.

19. a. Solve the formula $S = 2\pi rh + 2\pi r^2$ for h. $h = \dfrac{S - 2\pi r^2}{2\pi r}$

    b. Use your answer to part **a** to find the height of a right circular cylinder when the surface area is 12π in^2 and the radius is 1 in.   5 in.

    c. Use your answer to part **a** to find the height of a right circular cylinder when the surface area is 24π in^2 and the radius is 2 in.   4 in.

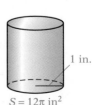

$S = 12\pi$ in^2

1 in.

When markup is based on selling price, the selling price of a product is given by the formula $S = \dfrac{C}{1-r}$, where C is the cost of the product, and r is the markup rate.

20. **a.** Solve the formula $S = \dfrac{C}{1-r}$ for r. $r = \dfrac{S-C}{S}$

   b. Use your answer to part **a** to find the markup rate on a tennis racket when the cost is \$112 and the selling price is \$140.   20%

   c. Use your answer to part **a** to find the markup rate on a radio when the cost is \$50.40 and the selling price is \$72.   30%

Break-even analysis is a method used to determine the sales volume required for a company to break even, or experience neither a profit nor a loss on the sale of a product. The break-even point represents the number of units that must be made and sold for income from sales to equal the cost of the product. The break-even point can be calculated using the formula $B = \dfrac{F}{S-V}$, where F is the fixed costs, S is the selling price per unit, and V is the variable costs per unit.

21. **a.** Solve the formula $B = \dfrac{F}{S-V}$ for S. $S = \dfrac{F + BV}{B}$

   b. Use your answer to part **a** to find the required selling price per desk for a company to break even. The fixed costs are \$20,000, the variable costs per desk are \$80, and the company plans to make and sell 200 desks.   \$180

   c. Use your answer to part **a** to find the required selling price per camera for a company to break even. The fixed costs are \$15,000, the variable costs per camera are \$50, and the company plans to make and sell 600 cameras.   \$75

Resistors are used to control the flow of current. The total resistance of two resistors in a circuit can be given by the formula $R = \dfrac{1}{\dfrac{1}{R_1} + \dfrac{1}{R_2}}$, where R_1 and R_2 are the two resistors in the circuit. Resistance is measured in ohms.

22. **a.** Solve the formula $R = \dfrac{1}{\dfrac{1}{R_1} + \dfrac{1}{R_2}}$ for R_1. $R_1 = \dfrac{R_2 R}{R_2 - R}$

   b. Use your answer to part **a** to find the resistance in R_1 if the resistance in R_2 is 30 ohms and the total resistance is 12 ohms.   20 ohms

   c. Use your answer to part **a** to find the resistance in R_1 if the resistance in R_2 is 15 ohms and the total resistance is 6 ohms.   10 ohms

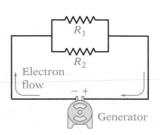

8.6 Work and Uniform Motion Problems

Objective A   *To solve work problems* .... 📼 HM³

POINT OF INTEREST

The following problem was recorded in the *Jiuzhang*, a Chinese text that dates to the Han dynasty (about 200 B.C. to A.D. 200). "A reservoir has 5 channels bringing water to it. The first can fill the reservoir in $\frac{1}{3}$ day, the second in 1 day, the third in $2\frac{1}{2}$ days, the fourth in 3 days, and the fifth in 5 days. If all channels are open, how long does it take to fill the reservoir?" This problem is the earliest known work problem. The answer is $\frac{15}{74}$ day.

If a painter can paint a room in 4 h, then in 1 h the painter can paint $\frac{1}{4}$ of the room. The painter's rate of work is $\frac{1}{4}$ of the room each hour. The **rate of work** is the part of a task that is completed in one unit of time.

A pipe can fill a tank in 30 min. This pipe can fill $\frac{1}{30}$ of the tank in 1 min. The rate of work is $\frac{1}{30}$ of the tank each minute. If a second pipe can fill the tank in x min, the rate of work for the second pipe is $\frac{1}{x}$ of the tank each minute.

In solving a work problem, the goal is to determine the time it takes to complete a task. The basic equation that is used to solve work problems is

Rate of work × time worked = part of task completed

For example, if a faucet can fill a sink in 6 min, then in 5 min the faucet can fill $\frac{1}{6} \times 5 = \frac{5}{6}$ of the sink. In 5 min the faucet completes $\frac{5}{6}$ of the task.

➡ A painter can paint a wall in 20 min. The painter's apprentice can paint the same wall in 30 min. How long will it take them to paint the wall when they work together?

Strategy for Solving a Work Problem

1. For each person or machine, write a numerical or variable expression for the rate of work, the time worked, and the part of the task completed. The results can be recorded in a table.

TAKE NOTE

Use the information given in the problem to fill in the "Rate" and "Time" columns of the table. Fill in the "Part Completed" column by multiplying the two expressions you wrote in each row.

Unknown time to paint the wall working together: t

	Rate of Work	·	*Time Worked*	=	*Part of Task Completed*
Painter	$\frac{1}{20}$	·	t	=	$\frac{t}{20}$
Apprentice	$\frac{1}{30}$	·	t	=	$\frac{t}{30}$

---

2. Determine how the parts of the task completed are related. Use the fact that the sum of the parts of the task completed must equal 1; the complete task.

$$\frac{t}{20} + \frac{t}{30} = 1$$

- The sum of the part of the task completed by the painter and the part of the task completed by the apprentice is 1.

$$60\left(\frac{t}{20} + \frac{t}{30}\right) = 60 \cdot 1$$

- Multiply by the LCM of 20 and 30.

$$3t + 2t = 60$$
$$5t = 60$$
$$t = 12$$

Working together, they will paint the wall in 12 min.

Example 1

A small water pipe takes three times longer to fill a tank than does a large water pipe. With both pipes open, it takes 4 h to fill the tank. Find the time it would take the small pipe, working alone, to fill the tank.

Strategy

• Time for large pipe to fill the tank: t
  Time for small pipe to fill the tank: $3t$

Fills tank
in $3t$ hours

Fills tank
in t hours

Fills $\frac{4}{3t}$ of the
tank in 4 hours

Fills $\frac{4}{t}$ of the
tank in 4 hours

	Rate	*Time*	*Part*
Small pipe	$\frac{1}{3t}$	4	$\frac{4}{3t}$
Large pipe	$\frac{1}{t}$	4	$\frac{4}{t}$

• The sum of the parts of the task completed by each pipe must equal 1.

Solution

$$\frac{4}{3t} + \frac{4}{t} = 1$$

$$3t\left(\frac{4}{3t} + \frac{4}{t}\right) = 3t \cdot 1$$

$$4 + 12 = 3t$$

$$16 = 3t$$

$$\frac{16}{3} = t$$

$$3t = 3\left(\frac{16}{3}\right) = 16$$

The small pipe working alone takes 16 h to fill the tank.

You Try It 1

Two computer printers that work at the same rate are working together to print the payroll checks for a large corporation. After they work together for 2 h, one of the printers quits. The second requires 3 h more to complete the payroll checks. Find the time it would take one printer, working alone, to print the payroll.

Your strategy

Your solution

7 h

Solution on p. S25

Objective B **To solve uniform motion problems**..................................... ▢26▢ ▢HM³

INSTRUCTOR NOTE

Here is a challenge problem for students to try.

Two trains on the same track are heading toward each other. One is traveling at 40 mph; the other is traveling at 50 mph. How far apart are they 1 min before they would meet?

Ans: 1.5 mi

A car that travels constantly in a straight line at 30 mph is in uniform motion. **Uniform motion** means that the speed or direction of an object does not change.

The basic equation used to solve uniform motion problems is

$$\textbf{Distance} = \textbf{rate} \times \textbf{time}$$

An alternative form of this equation can be written by solving the equation for time.

$$\frac{\textbf{Distance}}{\textbf{Rate}} = \textbf{time}$$

This form of the equation is useful when the total time of travel for two objects or the time of travel between two points is known.

➡ The speed of a boat in still water is 20 mph. The boat traveled 75 mi down a river in the same amount of time it took to travel 45 mi up the river. Find the rate of the river's current.

> **Strategy for Solving a Uniform Motion Problem**
>
> 1. For each object, write a numerical or variable expression for the distance, rate, and time. The results can be recorded in a table.

TAKE NOTE

Use the information given in the problem to fill in the "Distance" and "Rate" columns of the table. Fill in the "Time" column by dividing the two expressions you wrote in each row.

The unknown rate of the river's current: r

	Distance	÷	*Rate*	=	*Time*
Down river	75	÷	$20 + r$	=	$\dfrac{75}{20 + r}$
Up river	45	÷	$20 - r$	=	$\dfrac{45}{20 - r}$

> 2. Determine how the times traveled by each object are related. For example, it may be known that the times are equal, or the total time may be known.

$$\frac{75}{20 + r} = \frac{45}{20 - r}$$

• The time down the river is equal to the time up the river.

$$(20 + r)(20 - r)\frac{75}{20 + r} = (20 + r)(20 - r)\frac{45}{20 - r}$$
$$(20 - r)75 = (20 + r)45$$
$$1500 - 75r = 900 + 45r$$
$$-120r = -600$$
$$r = 5$$

• Multiply by the LCM of the denominators.

The rate of the river's current is 5 mph.

Example 2

A cyclist rode the first 20 mi of a trip at a constant rate. For the next 16 mi, the cyclist reduced the speed by 2 mph. The total time for the 36 mi was 4 h. Find the rate of the cyclist for each leg of the trip.

Strategy

- Rate for the first 20 mi: r
  Rate for the next 16 mi: $r - 2$

	Distance	Rate	Time
First 20 mi	20	r	$\dfrac{20}{r}$
Next 16 mi	16	$r - 2$	$\dfrac{16}{r - 2}$

- The total time for the trip was 4 h.

Solution

$$\frac{20}{r} + \frac{16}{r - 2} = 4$$

$$r(r - 2)\left[\frac{20}{r} + \frac{16}{r - 2}\right] = r(r - 2) \cdot 4$$

$$(r - 2)20 + 16r = 4r^2 - 8r$$

$$20r - 40 + 16r = 4r^2 - 8r$$

$$36r - 40 = 4r^2 - 8r$$

Solve the quadratic equation by factoring.

$$0 = 4r^2 - 44r + 40$$

$$0 = 4(r^2 - 11r + 10)$$

$$0 = 4(r - 10)(r - 1)$$

$$r - 10 = 0 \qquad r - 1 = 0$$

$$r = 10 \qquad r = 1$$

The solution $r = 1$ mph is not possible, because the rate on the last 16 mi would then be -1 mph.

10 mph was the rate for the first 20 mi.
8 mph was the rate for the next 16 mi.

You Try It 2

The total time it took for a sailboat to sail back and forth across a lake 6 km wide was 2 h. The rate sailing back was three times the rate sailing across. Find the rate sailing out across the lake.

Your strategy

Your solution

4 km/h

Solution on p. S25

8.6 Exercises

· ·

Objective A   *Application Problems*

1. A park has two sprinklers that are used to fill a fountain. One sprinkler can fill the fountain in 3 h, whereas the second sprinkler can fill the fountain in 6 h. How long will it take to fill the fountain with both sprinklers operating?
    2 h

2. One grocery clerk can stock a shelf in 20 min, whereas a second clerk requires 30 min to stock the same shelf. How long would it take to stock the shelf if the two clerks worked together?
    12 min

3. One person with a skiploader requires 12 h to remove a large quantity of earth. A second, larger skiploader can remove the same amount of earth in 4 h. How long would it take to remove the earth with both skiploaders working together?
    3 h

4. An experienced painter can paint a fence twice as fast as an inexperienced painter. Working together, the painters require 4 h to paint the fence. How long would it take the experienced painter working alone to paint the fence?
    6 h

5. One computer can solve a complex prime factorization problem in 75 h. A second computer can solve the same problem in 50 h. How long would it take both computers, working together, to solve the problem?
    30 h

6. A new machine can make 10,000 aluminum cans three times as fast as an older machine. With both machines working, 10,000 cans can be made in 9 h. How long would it take the new machine, working alone, to make the 10,000 cans?
    12 h

7. A small air conditioner can cool a room 5° in 75 min. A larger air conditioner can cool the room 5° in 50 min. How long would it take to cool the room 5° with both air conditioners working?
    30 min

8. One printing press can print the first edition of a book in 55 min, whereas a second printing press requires 66 min to print the same number of copies. How long would it take to print the first edition with both presses operating?
    30 min

9. Two oil pipelines can fill a small tank in 30 min. Using one of the pipelines would require 45 min to fill the tank. How long would it take the second pipeline alone to fill the tank?
    90 min

10. Working together, two dock workers can load a crate in 6 min. One dock worker, working alone, can load the crate in 15 min. How long would it take the second dock worker, working alone, to load the crate?
10 min

11. A mason can construct a retaining wall in 10 h. With the mason's apprentice assisting, the task would take 6 h. How long would it take the apprentice working alone to construct the wall?
15 h

12. A mechanic requires 2 h to repair a transmission, whereas an apprentice requires 6 h to make the same repairs. The mechanic worked alone for 1 h and then stopped. How long will it take the apprentice, working alone, to complete the repairs?
3 h

13. One computer technician can wire a modem in 4 h, whereas it takes 6 h for a second technician to do the same job. After working alone for 2 h, the first technician quit. How long will it take the second technician to complete the wiring?
3 h

14. A wallpaper hanger requires 2 h to hang the wallpaper on one wall of a room. A second wallpaper hanger requires 4 h to hang the same amount of paper. The first wallpaper hanger worked alone for 1 h and then quit. How long will it take the second wallpaper hanger, working alone, to complete the wall?
2 h

15. Two welders who work at the same rate are welding the girders of a building. After they work together for 10 h, one of the welders quits. The second welder requires 20 more hours to complete the welds. Find the time it would have taken one of the welders, working alone, to complete the welds.
40 h

16. A large and a small heating unit are being used to heat the water of a pool. The larger unit, working alone, requires 8 h to heat the pool. After both units have been operating for 2 h, the larger unit is turned off. The small unit requires 9 h more to heat the pool. How long would it take the small unit, working alone, to heat the pool?
$14\frac{2}{3}$ h

17. Two machines that fill cereal boxes work at the same rate. After they work together for 7 h, one machine breaks down. The second machine requires 14 h more to finish filling the boxes. How long would it have taken one of the machines, working alone, to fill the boxes?
28 h

18. A large and a small drain are opened to drain a pool. The large drain can empty the pool in 6 h. After both drains have been open for 1 h, the large drain becomes clogged and is closed. The smaller drain remains open and requires 9 h more to empty the pool. How long would it have taken the small drain, working alone, to empty the pool?
12 h

Objective B   *Application Problems*

19. Commuting from work to home, a lab technician traveled 10 mi at a constant rate through congested traffic. On reaching the expressway, the technician increased the speed by 20 mph. An additional 20 mi was traveled at the increased speed. The total time for the trip was 1 h. Find the rate of travel through the congested traffic.
20 mph

20. The president of a company traveled 1800 mi by jet and 300 mi on a prop plane. The rate of the jet was four times the rate of the prop plane. The entire trip took a total of 5 h. Find the rate of the jet plane.
600 mph

21. As part of a conditioning program, a jogger ran 8 mi in the same time a cyclist rode 20 mi. The rate of the cyclist was 12 mph faster than the rate of the jogger. Find the rate of the jogger and that of the cyclist.
jogger: 8 mph; cyclist: 20 mph

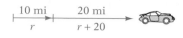

22. An express train travels 600 mi in the same amount of time it takes a freight train to travel 360 mi. The rate of the express train is 20 mph faster than that of the freight train. Find the rate of each train.
freight train: 30 mph; express train: 50 mph

23. To assess the damage done by a fire, a forest ranger traveled 1080 mi by jet and then an additional 180 mi by helicopter. The rate of the jet was 4 times the rate of the helicopter. The entire trip took a total of 5 h. Find the rate of the jet.
360 mph

24. A twin-engine plane can fly 800 mi in the same time that it takes a single-engine plane to fly 600 mi. The rate of the twin-engine plane is 50 mph faster than that of the single-engine plane. Find the rate of the twin-engine plane.
200 mph

25. The rate of a motorcycle is 36 mph faster than the rate of a bicycle. The motorcycle travels 192 mi in the same amount of time as the bicycle travels 48 mi. Find the rate of the motorcycle.
48 mph

26. A car and a bus leave a town at 1 P.M. and head for a town 300 mi away. The rate of the car is twice the rate of the bus. The car arrives 5 h ahead of the bus. Find the rate of the car.
60 mph

27. A car is traveling at a rate that is 36 mph faster than the rate of a cyclist. The car travels 384 mi in the same time it takes the cyclist to travel 96 mi. Find the rate of the car.
48 mph

28. A backpacker hiking into a wilderness area walked 9 mi at a constant rate and then reduced this rate by 1 mph. Another 4 mi was hiked at this reduced rate. The time required to hike the 4 mi was 1 h less than the time required to walk the 9 mi. Find the rate at which the hiker walked the first 9 mi.
3 mph

29. A plane can fly 180 mph in calm air. Flying with the wind, the plane can fly 600 mi in the same amount of time it takes to fly 480 mi against the wind. Find the rate of the wind.
20 mph

30. A commercial jet can fly 550 mph in calm air. Traveling with the jet stream, the plane flew 2400 mi in the same amount of time it takes to fly 2000 mi against the jet stream. Find the rate of the jet stream.
50 mph

$$\overset{2400 \text{ mi}}{\underset{550 + r}{\vert\longrightarrow}}$$

$$\overset{2000 \text{ mi}}{\underset{550 - r}{\longleftarrow\vert}}$$

31. A cruise ship can sail at 28 mph in calm water. Sailing with the gulf current, the ship can sail 170 mi in the same amount of time that it can sail 110 mi against the gulf current. Find the rate of the gulf current.
6 mph

32. Rowing with the current of a river, a rowing team can row 25 mi in the same amount of time it takes to row 15 mi against the current. The rate of the rowing team in calm water is 20 mph. Find the rate of the current.
5 mph

33. On a recent trip, a trucker traveled 330 mi at a constant rate. Because of road construction, the trucker then had to reduce the speed by 25 mph. An additional 30 mi was traveled at the reduced rate. The total time for the entire trip was 7 h. Find the rate of the trucker for the first 330 mi.
55 mph

APPLYING THE CONCEPTS

34. One pipe can fill a tank in 2 h, a second pipe can fill the tank in 4 h, and a third pipe can fill the tank in 5 h. How long will it take to fill the tank with all three pipes working?
$1\frac{1}{19}$ h

35. A mason can construct a retaining wall in 10 h. The mason's more-experienced apprentice can do the same job in 15 h. How long would it take the mason's less-experienced apprentice to do the job if, working together, all three can complete the job in 5 h?
30 h

36. A surveyor traveled 32 mi by canoe and then hiked 4 mi. The rate of speed by boat was four times the rate on foot. If the time spent walking was 1 h less than the time spent canoeing, find the amount of time spent traveling by canoe.
2 h

37. Because of bad weather, a bus driver reduced the usual speed along a 150-mile bus route by 10 mph. The bus arrived only 30 min later than its usual arrival time. How fast does the bus usually travel?
60 mph

8.7   Variation

Objective A   *To solve variation problems*....................................

Direct variation is a special function that can be expressed as the equation $y = kx$, where k is a constant. The equation $y = kx$ is read "*y* varies directly as *x*" or "*y* is proportional to *x*." The constant k is called the **constant of variation** or the **constant of proportionality**.

The circumference (C) of a circle varies directly as the diameter (d). The direct variation equation is written $C = \pi d$. The constant of variation is π.

A nurse makes \$20 per hour. The total wage (w) of the nurse is directly proportional to the number of hours (h) worked. The equation of variation is $w = 20h$. The constant of proportionality is 20.

A direct variation equation can be written in the form $y = kx^n$, where n is a positive number. For example, the equation $y = kx^2$ is read "*y* varies directly as the square of *x*."

The area (A) of a circle varies directly as the square of the radius (r) of the circle. The direct variation equation is $A = \pi r^2$. The constant of variation is π.

⟹ Given that V varies directly as r and that $V = 20$ when $r = 4$, find the constant of variation and the equation of variation.

$V = kr$ • Write the basic direct variation equation.

$20 = k \cdot 4$ • Replace V and r by the given values. Then solve for k.

$5 = k$ • This is the constant of variation.

$V = 5r$ • Write the direct variation equation by substituting the value of k into the basic direct variation equation.

⟹ The tension (T) in a spring varies directly as the distance (x) it is stretched. If $T = 8$ lb when $x = 2$ in., find T when $x = 4$ in.

$T = kx$ • Write the basic direct variation equation.

$8 = k \cdot 2$ • Replace T and x by the given values.

$4 = k$ • Solve for the constant of variation.

$T = 4x$ • Write the direct variation equation.

$T = 4x = 4 \cdot 4 = 16$ • To find T when $x = 4$, substitute 4 for x in the equation and solve for T.

The tension is 16 lb.

Inverse variation is a function that can be expressed as the equation $y = \frac{k}{x}$, where k is a constant. The equation $y = \frac{k}{x}$ is read "y varies inversely as x" or "y is inversely proportional to x."

In general, an inverse variation equation can be written $y = \frac{k}{x^n}$, where n is a positive number. For example, the equation $y = \frac{k}{x^2}$ is read "y varies inversely as the square of x."

➡ Given that P varies inversely as the square of x and that $P = 5$ when $x = 2$, find the variation constant and the equation of variation.

$P = \dfrac{k}{x^2}$ • Write the basic inverse variation equation.

$5 = \dfrac{k}{2^2}$ • Replace *P* and *x* by the given values. Then solve for *k*.

$5 = \dfrac{k}{4}$

$20 = k$ • This is the constant of variation.

$P = \dfrac{20}{x^2}$ • Write the inverse variation equation by substituting the value of *k* into the basic inverse variation equation.

➡ The length (L) of a rectangle with fixed area is inversely proportional to the width (W). If $L = 6$ ft when $W = 2$ ft, find L when $W = 3$ ft.

$L = \dfrac{k}{W}$ • Write the basic inverse variation equation.

$6 = \dfrac{k}{2}$ • Replace *L* and *W* by the given values.

$12 = k$ • Solve for the constant of variation.

$L = \dfrac{12}{W}$ • Write the inverse variation equation.

$L = \dfrac{12}{W} = \dfrac{12}{3} = 4$ • To find *L* when *W* = 3 ft, substitute 3 for *W* in the equation and solve for *L*.

The length is 4 ft.

Joint variation is a variation in which a variable varies directly as the product of two or more other variables. A joint variation can be expressed as the equation $z = kxy$, where k is a constant. The equation $z = kxy$ is read "z varies jointly as x and y."

The area (A) of a triangle varies jointly as the base (b) and the height (h). The joint variation equation is written $A = \frac{1}{2}bh$. The constant of variation is $\frac{1}{2}$.

A **combined variation** is a variation in which two or more types of variation occur at the same time. For example, in physics, the volume (V) of a gas varies directly as the temperature (T) and inversely as the pressure (P). This combined variation is written $V = \frac{kT}{P}$.

➡️ A ball is being twirled on the end of a string. The tension (T) in the string is directly proportional to the square of the speed (v) of the ball and inversely proportional to the length (r) of the string. The tension is 96 lb when the length of the string is 0.5 ft and the speed is 4 ft/s. Find the tension when the length of the string is 1 ft and the speed is 5 ft/s.

$$T = \frac{kv^2}{r}$$ • Write the basic combined variation equation.

$$96 = \frac{k \cdot 4^2}{0.5}$$ • Replace *T*, *v*, and *r* by the given values.

$$96 = \frac{k \cdot 16}{0.5}$$

$$96 = k \cdot 32$$ • Solve for the contant of variation.
$$3 = k$$

$$T = \frac{3v^2}{r}$$ • Write the combined variation equation.

$$T = \frac{3v^2}{r} = \frac{3 \cdot 5^2}{1} = 3 \cdot 25 = 75$$ • To find *T* when *r* = 1 ft and *v* = 5 ft/s, substitute 1 for *r* and 5 for *v* and solve for *T*.

The tension is 75 lb.

Example 1

The amount (A) of medication prescribed for a person is directly related to the person's weight (W). For a 50-kilogram person, 2 ml of medication are prescribed. How many milliliters of medication are required for a person who weighs 75 kg?

Strategy

To find the required amount of medication:

* Write the basic direct variation equation, replace the variables by the given values, and solve for k.
* Write the direct variation equation, replacing k by its value. Substitute 75 for W and solve for A.

Solution

$$A = kW$$
$$2 = k \cdot 50$$
$$\frac{1}{25} = k$$

$$A = \frac{1}{25}W = \frac{1}{25} \cdot 75 = 3$$

The required amount of medication is 3 ml.

You Try It 1

The distance (s) a body falls from rest varies directly as the square of the time (t) of the fall. An object falls 64 ft in 2 s. How far will it fall in 5 s?

Your strategy

Your solution
400 ft

Solution on p. S25

Example 2

A company that produces personal computers has determined that the number of computers it can sell (s) is inversely proportional to the price (P) of the computer. Two thousand computers can be sold when the price is $2500. How many computers can be sold when the price of a computer is $2000?

Strategy

To find the number of computers:

* Write the basic inverse variation equation, replace the variables by the given values, and solve for k.
* Write the inverse variation equation, replacing k by its value. Substitute 2000 for P and solve for s.

Solution $s = \dfrac{k}{P}$

$$2000 = \dfrac{k}{2500}$$
$$5{,}000{,}000 = k$$
$$s = \dfrac{5{,}000{,}000}{P} = \dfrac{5{,}000{,}000}{2000} = 2500$$

At $2000 each, 2500 computers can be sold.

Example 3

The pressure (P) of a gas varies directly as the temperature (T) and inversely as the volume (V). When $T = 50°$ and $V = 275$ in^3, $P = 20$ lb/in^2. Find the pressure of a gas when $T = 60°$ and $V = 250$ in^3.

Strategy

To find the pressure:

* Write the basic combined variation equation, replace the variables by the given values, and solve for k.
* Write the combined variation equation, replacing k by its value. Substitute 60 for T and 250 for V, and solve for P.

Solution $P = \dfrac{kT}{V}$

$$20 = \dfrac{k \cdot 50}{275}$$
$$110 = k$$
$$P = \dfrac{110T}{V} = \dfrac{110 \cdot 60}{250} = 26.4$$

The pressure is 26.4 lb/in^2.

You Try It 2

The resistance (R) to the flow of electric current in a wire of fixed length is inversely proportional to the square of the diameter (d) of a wire. If a wire of diameter 0.01 cm has a resistance of 0.5 ohm, what is the resistance in a wire that is 0.02 cm in diameter?

Your strategy

Your solution

0.125 ohm

You Try It 3

The strength (s) of a rectangular beam varies jointly as its width (w) and the square of its depth (d) and inversely as its length (L). If the strength of a beam 2 in. wide, 12 in. deep, and 12 ft long is 1200 lb, find the strength of a beam that is 4 in. wide, 8 in. deep, and 16 ft long.

Your strategy

Your solution

800 lb

Solutions on p. S26

8.7 Exercises

· ·

Objective A   *Application Problems*

1. The profit (P) realized by a company varies directly as the number of products it sells (s). If a company makes a profit of $4000 on the sale of 250 products, what is the profit when the company sells 5000 products?
    $80,000

2. The income (I) of a computer analyst varies directly as the number of hours (h) worked. If the analyst earns $256 for working 8 h, how much will the analyst earn by working 36 h?
    $1152

3. The pressure (p) on a diver in the water varies directly as the depth (d). If the pressure is 4.5 lb/in^2 when the depth is 10 ft, what is the pressure when the depth is 15 ft?
    6.75 lb/in^2

4. The distance (d) a spring will stretch varies directly as the force (f) applied to the spring. If a force of 6 lb is required to stretch a spring 3 in., what force is required to stretch the spring 4 in.?
    8 lb

5. The distance (d) an object will fall is directly proportional to the square of the time (t) of the fall. If an object falls 144 ft in 3 s, how far will the object fall in 10 s?
    1600 ft

6. The period (p) of a pendulum, or the time it takes the pendulum to make one complete swing, varies directly as the square root of the length (L) of the pendulum. If the period of a pendulum is 1.5 s when the length is 2 ft, find the period when the length is 5 ft. Round to the nearest hundredth.
    2.37 s

7. The distance (s) a ball will roll down an inclined plane is directly proportional to the square of the time (t). If the ball rolls 6 ft in 1 s, how far will it roll in 3 s?
    54 ft

8. The stopping distance (s) of a car varies directly as the square of its speed (v). If a car traveling 30 mph requires 63 ft to stop, find the stopping distance for a car traveling 55 mph.
    211.75 ft

9. The length (L) of a rectangle of fixed area varies inversely as the width (w). If the length of a rectangle is 8 ft when the width is 5 ft, find the length of the rectangle when the width is 4 ft.
    10 ft

10. The time (t) for a car to travel between two cities is inversely proportional to the rate (r) of travel. If it takes 5 h to travel between the cities at a rate of 55 mph, find the time to travel between the two cities at a rate of 65 mph. Round to the nearest tenth.
4.2 h

11. The speed (v) of a gear varies inversely as the number of teeth (t). If a gear that has 45 teeth makes 24 revolutions per minute, how many revolutions per minute will a gear that has 36 teeth make?
30 revolutions/min

12. The pressure (p) in a liquid varies directly as the product of the depth (d) and the density (D) of the liquid. If the pressure is 150 lb/in² when the depth is 100 in. and the density is 1.2, find the pressure when the density remains the same and the depth is 75 in.
112.5 lb/in²

13. The current (I) in a wire varies directly as the voltage (V) and inversely as the resistance (R). If the current is 10 amps when the voltage is 110 volts and the resistance is 11 ohms, find the current when the voltage is 180 volts and the resistance is 24 ohms.
7.5 amps

14. The repulsive force (f) between the north poles of two magnets is inversely proportional to the square of the distance (d) between them. If the repulsive force is 20 lb when the distance is 4 in., find the repulsive force when the distance is 2 in.
80 lb

15. The intensity (I) of a light source is inversely proportional to the square of the distance (d) from the source. If the intensity is 12 foot-candles at a distance of 10 ft, what is the intensity when the distance is 5 ft?
48 foot-candles

APPLYING THE CONCEPTS

16. In the inverse variation equation $y = \dfrac{k}{x}$, what is the effect on x if y doubles?
x is halved.

17. In the direct variation equation $y = kx$, what is the effect on y when x doubles?
y is doubled.

Complete using the word *directly* or *inversely*.

18. If a varies directly as b and inversely as c, then c varies _____directly_____ as b and _____inversely_____ as a.

19. If a varies _____inversely_____ as b and c, then abc is constant.

20. If the length of a rectangle is held constant, the area of the rectangle varies _____directly_____ as the width.

21. If the area of a rectangle is held constant, the length of the rectangle varies _____inversely_____ as the width.

Focus on Problem Solving

Find a Pattern   Polya's four recommended problem-solving steps are stated below.

1. Understand the problem.   **3.** Carry out the plan.

2. Devise a plan.   **4.** Review your solution.

One of the several ways of devising a plan is first to try to find a pattern. Karl Friedrich Gauss supposedly used this method to solve a problem that was given to his math class when he was in elementary school. As the story goes, his teacher wanted to grade some papers while the class worked on a math problem. The problem given to the class was to find the sum

$$1 + 2 + 3 + 4 + \cdots + 100$$

Gauss quickly solved the problem by seeing a pattern. Here is what he saw.

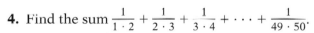

Note that

$1 + 100 = 101$
$2 + 99 = 101$
$3 + 98 = 101$
$4 + 97 = 101$

Gauss noted that there were 50 sums of 101. Therefore, the sum of the first 100 natural numbers is

$$1 + 2 + 3 + 4 + \cdots + 97 + 98 + 99 + 100 = 50(101) = 5050$$

Try to solve the following problems by finding a pattern.

1. Find the sum $2 + 4 + 6 + \cdots + 96 + 98 + 100$.

2. Find the sum $1 + 3 + 5 + \cdots + 97 + 99 + 101$.

3. Find another method of finding the sum $1 + 3 + 5 + \cdots + 97 + 99 + 101$ given in the previous exercise.

4. Find the sum $\dfrac{1}{1 \cdot 2} + \dfrac{1}{2 \cdot 3} + \dfrac{1}{3 \cdot 4} + \cdots + \dfrac{1}{49 \cdot 50}$.

Hint: $\dfrac{1}{1 \cdot 2} = \dfrac{1}{2}, \dfrac{1}{1 \cdot 2} + \dfrac{1}{2 \cdot 3} = \dfrac{2}{3}, \dfrac{1}{1 \cdot 2} + \dfrac{1}{2 \cdot 3} + \dfrac{1}{3 \cdot 4} = \dfrac{3}{4}$

5. The following problem shows that checking a few cases does not always result in a conjecture that is true for *all* cases. Select any two points on a circle and draw a *chord* (see the drawing in the left margin), the line connecting the points. The chord divides the circle into 2 regions. Now select 3 different points and draw chords connecting each of the three points with every other point. The chords divide the circle into 4 regions. Now select 4 points and connect each of the points with every other point. Make a conjecture about the relationship between the number of regions and the number of points on the circle. Does your conjecture work for 5 points? 6 points?

6. A *polygonal number* is a number that can be represented by arranging that number of dots in rows to form a geometric figure such as a triangle, square, pentagon, or hexagon. For instance, the first four *triangular* numbers, 3, 6, 10, and 15, are given (and shown) below. What are the next two triangular numbers?

2 points, 2 regions

3 points, 4 regions

4 points, 8 regions

5 points, ? regions

3   6   10   15

Projects and Group Activities

Continued Fractions

The following complex fraction is called a **continued fraction**.

$$1 + \cfrac{1}{1 + \cfrac{1}{1 + \cfrac{1}{1 + \cfrac{1}{1 + \cdots}}}}$$

The dots indicate that the pattern continues to repeat forever.

A **convergent** for a continued fraction is an approximation of the repeated pattern. For instance,

$$c_2 = 1 + \cfrac{1}{1 + \cfrac{1}{1 + 1}} \qquad c_3 = 1 + \cfrac{1}{1 + \cfrac{1}{1 + \cfrac{1}{1 + 1}}} \qquad c_4 = 1 + \cfrac{1}{1 + \cfrac{1}{1 + \cfrac{1}{1 + \cfrac{1}{1 + 1}}}}$$

1. Calculate c_5 for the continued fraction above.

This particular continued fraction is related to the golden rectangle, which has been used in architectural designs as diverse as the Parthenon in Athens, built around 440 B.C., and the United Nations building. A golden rectangle is one for which

$$\frac{\text{length}}{\text{width}} = \frac{\text{length} + \text{width}}{\text{length}}$$

An example of a golden rectangle is shown at the right.

Here is another continued fraction that was discovered by Leonhard Euler (1707–1793). Calculating the convergents of this continued fraction yields approximations that are closer and closer to π.

$$\pi = 3 + \cfrac{1^2}{6 + \cfrac{3^2}{6 + \cfrac{5^2}{6 + \cfrac{7^2}{6 + \cdots}}}}$$

2. Calculate $c_5 = 3 + \cfrac{1^2}{6 + \cfrac{3^2}{6 + \cfrac{5^2}{6 + \cfrac{7^2}{6 + \cfrac{9^2}{6 + 11^2}}}}}$

Graphing Rational Functions

The domain of a function is the set of the first coordinates of all the ordered pairs of the function. When a function is given by an equation, the domain of the function is all real numbers for which the function evaluates to a real number. For rational functions, we must exclude from the domain all those values of the variable for which the denominator of the rational function is zero. The graphing calculator is a useful tool to show the graphs of functions with excluded values in the domain of the function.

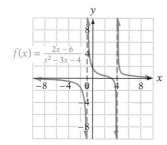

The graph of the function $f(x) = \dfrac{2x - 6}{x^2 - 3x - 4}$ is shown at the left. Note that the graph never intersects the lines $x = -1$ and $x = 4$ (shown as dashed lines). These are the two values excluded from the domain of f. The graph of the function f gets closer to the dashed line $x = 4$ as x gets closer to 4. The graph of the function f also gets closer to $x = -1$ as x gets closer to -1. The lines that are "approached" by the function are called **asymptotes**.

The domain is
$\{x \mid x \neq -1, x \neq 4\}$.

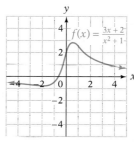

The graph of the function $f(x) = \dfrac{3x + 2}{x^2 + 1}$ is shown at the left. The domain must exclude values of x for which $x^2 + 1 = 0$. It is not possible that $x^2 + 1 = 0$, because $x^2 \geq 0$, and a positive number added to a number equal to or greater than zero cannot equal zero. Therefore, there are no real numbers that must be excluded from the domain of f.

The domain is
$\{x \mid x \in \text{real numbers}\}$.

Use a graphing calculator to find the domain of the rational function.

1. $h(x) = \dfrac{5x}{3x + 9}$ **2.** $f(x) = \dfrac{-2x}{6 - 2x}$ **3.** $q(x) = \dfrac{2x - 1}{x^2 + x - 6}$

4. $G(x) = \dfrac{3 - 4x}{x^2 + 4x - 5}$ **5.** $H(x) = \dfrac{x + 3}{x^2 + 2}$ **6.** $g(x) = \dfrac{x^2 + 1}{x^2}$

Graphing Variation Equations

1. Graph $y = kx$ when $k = 2$.
What kind of function does the graph represent?

2. Graph $y = kx$ when $k = \dfrac{1}{2}$.
What kind of function does the graph represent?

3. Graph $y = \dfrac{k}{x}$ when $k = 2$ and $x > 0$.
Is this the graph of a function?

Chapter Summary

Key Words   A *rational expression* is a fraction in which the numerator and denominator are polynomials. A rational expression is in *simplest form* when the numerator and denominator have no common factors.

The *least common multiple* (LCM) of two or more polynomials is the simplest polynomial that contains the factors of each polynomial.

The *reciprocal* of a rational expression is the rational expression with the numerator and denominator interchanged.

A *complex fraction* is a fraction whose numerator or denominator contains one or more fractions.

A *ratio* is the quotient of two quantities that have the same unit.

A *rate* is the quotient of two quantities that have different units.

A *proportion* is an equation that states the equality of two ratios or rates.

A *literal equation* is an equation that contains more than one variable.

Direct variation is a special function that can be expressed as the equation $y = kx$, where k is a constant called the *constant of variation* or the *constant of proportionality*.

Inverse variation is a function that can be expressed as the equation $y = \dfrac{k}{x}$, where k is a constant.

Joint variation is a variation in which a variable varies directly as the product of two or more variables. A joint variation can be expressed as the equation $z = kxy$, where k is a constant.

Combined variation is a variation in which two or more types of variation occur at the same time.

Essential Rules   *To Multiply Fractions*

$$\frac{a}{b} \cdot \frac{c}{d} = \frac{ac}{bd}$$

To Divide Fractions

$$\frac{a}{b} \div \frac{c}{d} = \frac{a}{b} \cdot \frac{d}{c} = \frac{ad}{bc}$$

To Add Fractions

$$\frac{a}{c} + \frac{b}{c} = \frac{a+b}{c}$$

To Subtract Fractions

$$\frac{a}{c} - \frac{b}{c} = \frac{a-b}{c}$$

Equation for Work Problems

$$\text{Rate of work} \times \text{time worked} = \text{part of task completed}$$

Uniform Motion Equation

$$\text{Distance} = \text{rate} \times \text{time}$$

Chapter Review

1. Divide: $\dfrac{6a^2b^7}{25x^3y} \div \dfrac{12a^3b^4}{5x^2y^2}$

$\dfrac{b^3y}{10ax}$ [8.1C]

2. Add: $\dfrac{x+7}{15x} + \dfrac{x-2}{20x}$

$\dfrac{7x+22}{60x}$ [8.2D]

3. Simplify: $\dfrac{x - \dfrac{16}{5x-2}}{3x-4 - \dfrac{88}{5x-2}}$

$\dfrac{x-2}{3x-10}$ [8.3A]

4. Simplify: $\dfrac{x^2+x-30}{15+2x-x^2}$

$-\dfrac{x+6}{x+3}$ [8.1A]

5. Simplify: $\dfrac{16x^5y^3}{24xy^{10}}$

$\dfrac{2x^4}{3y^7}$ [8.1A]

6. Solve: $\dfrac{20}{x+2} = \dfrac{5}{16}$

62 [8.4B]

7. Divide: $\dfrac{10-23y+12y^2}{6y^2-y-5} \div \dfrac{4y^2-13y+10}{18y^2+3y-10}$

$\dfrac{(3y-2)^2}{(y-1)(y-2)}$ [8.1C]

8. Multiply: $\dfrac{8ab^2}{15x^3y} \cdot \dfrac{5xy^4}{16a^2b}$

$\dfrac{by^3}{6ax^2}$ [8.1B]

9. Simplify: $\dfrac{1-\dfrac{1}{x}}{1-\dfrac{8x-7}{x^2}}$

$\dfrac{x}{x-7}$ [8.3A]

10. Write each fraction in terms of the LCM of the denominators.

$\dfrac{x}{12x^2+16x-3}, \dfrac{4x^2}{6x^2+7x-3}$

$\dfrac{3x^2-x}{(2x+3)(6x-1)(3x-1)}, \dfrac{24x^3-4x^2}{(2x+3)(6x-1)(3x-1)}$ [8.2B]

11. Solve $T = 2(ab + bc + ca)$ for a.

$a = \dfrac{T-2bc}{2b+2c}$ [8.5A]

12. Solve: $\dfrac{5}{7} + \dfrac{x}{2} = 2 - \dfrac{x}{7}$

2 [8.4A]

13. Solve $i = \dfrac{100m}{c}$ for c.

$c = \dfrac{100m}{i}$ [8.5A]

14. Solve: $\dfrac{x+8}{x+4} = 1 + \dfrac{5}{x+4}$

no solution [8.4A]

15. Divide: $\dfrac{20x^2-45x}{6x^3+4x^2} \div \dfrac{40x^3-90x^2}{12x^2+8x}$

$\dfrac{1}{x^2}$ [8.1C]

16. Add: $\dfrac{2y}{5y-7} + \dfrac{3}{7-5y}$

$\dfrac{2y-3}{5y-7}$ [8.2D]

17. Subtract: $\dfrac{5x + 3}{2x^2 + 5x - 3} - \dfrac{3x + 4}{2x^2 + 5x - 3}$

$\dfrac{1}{x + 3}$ [8.2C]

18. Find the LCM of $10x^2 - 11x + 3$ and $20x^2 - 17x + 3$.

$(5x - 3)(2x - 1)(4x - 1)$ [8.2A]

19. Solve $4x + 9y = 18$ for y.

$y = -\dfrac{4}{9}x + 2$ [8.5A]

20. Multiply: $\dfrac{24x^2 - 94x + 15}{12x^2 - 49x + 15} \cdot \dfrac{24x^2 + 7x - 5}{4 - 27x + 18x^2}$

$\dfrac{8x + 5}{3x - 4}$ [8.1B]

21. Solve: $\dfrac{20}{2x + 3} = \dfrac{17x}{2x + 3} - 5$

5 [8.4A]

22. Add: $\dfrac{x - 1}{x + 2} + \dfrac{3x - 2}{5 - x} + \dfrac{5x^2 + 15x - 11}{x^2 - 3x - 10}$

$\dfrac{3x - 1}{x - 5}$ [8.2D]

23. Solve: $\dfrac{6}{x - 7} = \dfrac{8}{x - 6}$

10 [8.4B]

24. Solve: $\dfrac{3}{20} = \dfrac{x}{80}$

12 [8.4B]

25. Triangles *ABC* and *DEF* are similar. Find the perimeter of triangle *ABC*.
24 in. [8.4C]

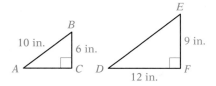

26. One hose can fill a pool in 15 h. The second hose can fill the pool in 10 h. How long would it take to fill the pool using both hoses?
6 h [8.6A]

27. A car travels 315 mi in the same amount of time that a bus travels 245 mi. The rate of the car is 10 mph faster than that of the bus. Find the rate of the car.
45 mph [8.6B]

28. The rate of a jet is 400 mph in calm air. Traveling with the wind, the jet can fly 2100 mi in the same amount of time it takes to fly 1900 mi against the wind. Find the rate of the wind.
20 mph [8.6B]

29. A pitcher's earned run average (ERA) is the average number of runs allowed in 9 innings of pitching. If a pitcher allows 15 runs in 100 innings, find the pitcher's ERA.
1.35 [8.4D]

30. The current (*I*) in an electric circuit varies inversely as the resistance (*R*). If the current in the circuit is 4 amps when the resistance is 50 ohms, find the current in the circuit when the resistance is 100 ohms.
2 amps [8.7A]

Chapter Test

1. Simplify: $\dfrac{16x^5y}{24x^2y^4}$

   $\dfrac{2x^3}{3y^3}$ [8.1A]

2. Simplify: $\dfrac{x^2 + 4x - 5}{1 - x^2}$

   $-\dfrac{x + 5}{x + 1}$ [8.1A]

3. Multiply: $\dfrac{x^3y^4}{x^2 - 4x + 4} \cdot \dfrac{x^2 - x - 2}{x^6y^4}$

   $\dfrac{x + 1}{x^3(x - 2)}$ [8.1B]

4. Multiply: $\dfrac{x^2 + 2x - 3}{x^2 + 6x + 9} \cdot \dfrac{2x^2 - 11x + 5}{2x^2 + 3x - 5}$

   $\dfrac{(x - 5)(2x - 1)}{(x + 3)(2x + 5)}$ [8.1B]

5. Divide: $\dfrac{x^2 + 3x + 2}{x^2 + 5x + 4} \div \dfrac{x^2 - x - 6}{x^2 + 2x - 15}$

   $\dfrac{x + 5}{x + 4}$ [8.1C]

6. Find the LCM of $6x - 3$ and $2x^2 + x - 1$.

   $3(2x - 1)(x + 1)$ [8.2A]

7. Write each fraction in terms of the LCM of the denominators.

   $\dfrac{3}{x^2 - 2x}, \dfrac{x}{x^2 - 4}$

   $\dfrac{3(x + 2)}{x(x + 2)(x - 2)}, \dfrac{x^2}{x(x + 2)(x - 2)}$ [8.2B]

8. Subtract: $\dfrac{2x}{x^2 + 3x - 10} - \dfrac{4}{x^2 + 3x - 10}$

   $\dfrac{2}{x + 5}$ [8.2C]

9. Subtract: $\dfrac{2}{2x - 1} - \dfrac{3}{3x + 1}$

   $\dfrac{5}{(2x - 1)(3x + 1)}$ [8.2D]

10. Subtract: $\dfrac{x}{x + 3} - \dfrac{2x - 5}{x^2 + x - 6}$

    $\dfrac{x^2 - 4x + 5}{(x - 2)(x + 3)}$ [8.2D]

11. Simplify: $\dfrac{1 + \dfrac{1}{x} - \dfrac{12}{x^2}}{1 + \dfrac{2}{x} - \dfrac{8}{x^2}}$

    $\dfrac{x - 3}{x - 2}$ [8.3A]

12. Solve: $\dfrac{6}{x} - 2 = 1$

    2 [8.4A]

13. Solve: $\dfrac{2x}{x+1} - 3 = \dfrac{-2}{x+1}$

no solution   [8.4A]

14. Solve: $\dfrac{3}{x+4} = \dfrac{5}{x+6}$

−1   [8.4B]

15. Triangles *ABC* and *DEF* are similar. Find the area of triangle *DEF*.   64.8 m²   [8.4C]

16. Solve $d = s + rt$ for t.

$t = \dfrac{d-s}{r}$ [8.5A]

17. An interior designer uses 2 rolls of wallpaper for every 45 ft² of wall space in an office. At this rate, how many rolls of wallpaper are needed for an office that has 315 ft² of wall space?

14 rolls   [8.4D]

18. One landscaper can till the soil for a lawn in 30 min, whereas it takes a second landscaper 15 min to do the same job. How long would it take to till the soil for the lawn with both landscapers working together?

10 min   [8.6A]

19. A cyclist travels 20 mi in the same amount of time as it takes a hiker to walk 6 mi. The rate of the cyclist is 7 mph faster than the rate of the hiker. Find the rate of the cyclist.

10 mph   [8.6B]

20. The electrical resistance (r) of a cable varies directly as its length (l) and inversely as the square of its diameter (d). If a cable 16,000 ft long and $\frac{1}{4}$ in. in diameter has a resistance of 3.2 ohms, what is the resistance of a cable that is 8000 ft long and $\frac{1}{2}$ in. in diameter?

0.4 ohm   [8.7A]

Cumulative Review

1. Simplify: $\left(\frac{2}{3}\right)^2 \div \left(\frac{3}{2} - \frac{2}{3}\right) + \frac{1}{2}$

   $\frac{31}{30}$ [1.3A]

2. Evaluate $-a^2 + (a - b)^2$ when $a = -2$ and $b = 3$.

   21 [1.4A]

3. Simplify: $-2x - (-3y) + 7x - 5y$

   $5x - 2y$ [1.4B]

4. Simplify: $2[3x - 7(x - 3) - 8]$

   $-8x + 26$ [1.4D]

5. Solve: $4 - \frac{2}{3}x = 7$

   $-\frac{9}{2}$ [2.2A]

6. Solve: $3[x - 2(x - 3)] = 2(3 - 2x)$

   -12 [2.2C]

7. Find $16\frac{2}{3}\%$ of 60.

   10 [2.1D]

8. Solve: $x - 3(1 - 2x) \geq 1 - 4(3 - 2x)$

   $\{x \mid x \leq 8\}$ [2.4A]

9. Find the volume of the rectangular solid shown in the figure.

   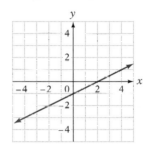

   200 ft^3 [3.3A]

10. Graph: $x - 2y = 2$

    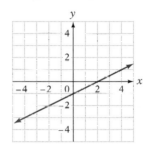

    [4.2B]

11. Given $P(x) = \frac{x - 1}{2x - 3}$, find $P(-2)$.

    $\frac{3}{7}$ [4.1D]

12. Find the equation of the line that contains the point $(-2, -1)$ and is parallel to the line $3x - 2y = 6$.

    $y = \frac{3}{2}x + 2$ [4.5A]

13. Evaluate the determinant:

    $\begin{vmatrix} 6 & 5 \\ 2 & -3 \end{vmatrix}$

    -28 [5.4A]

14. Multiply: $(a^2b^5)(ab^2)$

    a^3b^7 [6.1A]

15. Simplify: $\frac{(2a^{-2}b^3)^{-2}}{(4a)^{-1}}$

    $\frac{a^5}{b^6}$ [6.1B]

16. Write 0.000000035 in scientific notation.

    3.5×10^{-8} [6.1C]

17. Multiply: $(2a^2 - 3a + 1)(-2a^2)$

    $-4a^4 + 6a^3 - 2a^2$ [6.3A]

18. Multiply: $(a - 3b)(a + 4b)$

    $a^2 + ab - 12b^2$ [6.3C]

19. Divide: $(x^3 - 8) \div (x - 2)$
$x^2 + 2x + 4$ [6.4B]

20. Factor: $y^2 - 7y + 6$
$(y - 6)(y - 1)$ [7.2A]

21. Factor: $12x^2 - x - 1$
$(4x + 1)(3x - 1)$ [7.3A/7.3B]

22. Factor: $2a^3 + 7a^2 - 15a$
$a(2a - 3)(a + 5)$ [7.3A/7.3B]

23. Factor: $4b^2 - 100$
$4(b + 5)(b - 5)$ [7.4D]

24. Solve: $(x + 3)(2x - 5) = 0$
$-3, \dfrac{5}{2}$ [7.5A]

25. Simplify: $\dfrac{12x^4y^2}{18xy^7}$
$\dfrac{2x^3}{3y^5}$ [8.1A]

26. Simplify: $\dfrac{x^2 - 7x + 10}{25 - x^2}$
$-\dfrac{x - 2}{x + 5}$ [8.1A]

27. Divide: $\dfrac{x^2 - x - 56}{x^2 + 8x + 7} \div \dfrac{x^2 - 13x + 40}{x^2 - 4x - 5}$
1 [8.1C]

28. Subtract: $\dfrac{2}{2x - 1} - \dfrac{1}{x + 1}$
$\dfrac{3}{(2x - 1)(x + 1)}$ [8.2D]

29. Simplify: $\dfrac{1 - \dfrac{2}{x} - \dfrac{15}{x^2}}{1 - \dfrac{25}{x^2}}$
$\dfrac{x + 3}{x + 5}$ [8.3A]

30. Solve: $\dfrac{3x}{x - 3} - 2 = \dfrac{10}{x - 3}$
4 [8.4A]

31. A silversmith mixes 60 g of an alloy that is 40% silver with 120 g of another silver alloy. The resulting alloy is 60% silver. Find the percent of silver in the 120 g of alloy.
70%   [2.3B]

32. A life insurance policy costs $16 for every $1000 of coverage. At this rate, how much money would a policy of $5000 cost?
$80   [8.4D]

33. One water pipe can fill a tank in 9 min, whereas a second pipe requires 18 min to fill the tank. How long would it take both pipes, working together, to fill the tank?
6 min   [8.6A]

9

Rational Exponents and Radicals

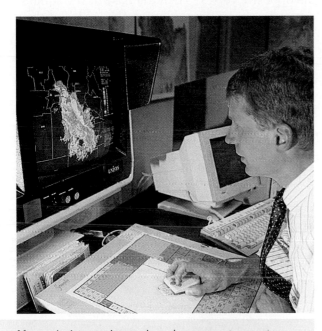

Objectives

Section 9.1
To simplify expressions with rational exponents

To write exponential expressions as radical expressions and to write radical expressions as exponential expressions

To simplify radical expressions that are roots of perfect powers

Section 9.2
To simplify radical expressions

To add or subtract radical expressions

To multiply radical expressions

To divide radical expressions

Section 9.3
To simplify a complex number

To add or subtract complex numbers

To multiply complex numbers

To divide complex numbers

Section 9.4
To solve a radical equation

To solve application problems

Meteorologists use data such as air pressure, temperature, humidity, and wind velocity to predict the weather. Today meteorologists are aided by computers and weather satellites. For example, weather satellites can measure the diameter of a storm. Then a meteorologist can use the formula $t = \left(\dfrac{d}{2}\right)^{3/2}$, where d is the diameter of a storm in miles, to approximate t, the duration of the storm in hours. The expression $\left(\dfrac{d}{2}\right)^{3/2}$ is an exponential expression with a rational exponent.

Golden Rectangle

The golden rectangle fascinated the early Greeks and appeared in much of their architecture. They considered this particular rectangle the most pleasing to the eye and believed that when it was used in the design of a building, it would make the structure pleasant to look at.

The golden rectangle is constructed from a square by drawing a line from the midpoint of the base of the square to the opposite vertex. Then the base of the square is extended, starting from the midpoint, the length of the line. The resulting rectangle is called the golden rectangle.

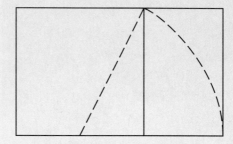

The Parthenon in Athens, Greece, is the classic example of the use of the golden rectangle in Greek architecture. A rendering of the Parthenon is shown here.

9.1 Rational Exponents and Radical Expressions

Objective A   *To simplify expressions with rational exponents* ....

In this section, the definition of an exponent is extended beyond integers so that any rational number can be used as an exponent. The definition is expressed in such a way that the Rules of Exponents hold true for rational exponents.

Consider the expression $(a^{1/n})^n$ for $a > 0$ and n a positive integer. Now simplify, assuming that the Rule for Simplifying Powers of Exponential Expressions is true.

$$(a^{1/n})^n = a^{\frac{1}{n} \cdot n} = a^1 = a$$

Because $(a^{1/n})^n = a$, the number $a^{1/n}$ is the number whose nth power is a.

If $a > 0$ and n is a positive number, then $a^{1/n}$ is called the *nth root of a.*

$25^{1/2} = 5$ because $(5)^2 = 25$. $8^{1/3} = 2$ because $(2)^3 = 8$.

In the expression $a^{1/n}$, if a is a negative number and n is a positive even integer, then $a^{1/n}$ is not a real number.

$(-4)^{1/2}$ is not a real number, because there is no real number whose second power is 4.

When n is a positive odd integer, a can be a positive or a negative number.

$(-27)^{1/3} = -3$ because $(-3)^3 = -27$.

Using the definition of $a^{1/n}$ and the Rules of Exponents, it is possible to define any exponential expression that contains a rational exponent.

> **Rule for Rational Exponents**
>
> If m and n are positive integers and $a^{1/n}$ is a real number, then
>
> $$a^{m/n} = (a^{1/n})^m$$

The expression $a^{m/n}$ can also be written $a^{m/n} = a^{m \cdot \frac{1}{n}} = (a^m)^{1/n}$.

As shown above, expressions that contain rational exponents do not always represent real numbers when the base of the exponential expression is a negative number. For this reason, all variables in this chapter represent positive numbers unless otherwise stated.

➡ Simplify: $27^{2/3}$

$$27^{2/3} = (3^3)^{2/3}$$ • **Rewrite 27 as 3^3.**

$$= 3^{3(2/3)}$$ • **Multiply the exponents.**

$$= 3^2$$ • **Simplify.**

$$= 9$$

➡ Simplify: $32^{-2/5}$

$$32^{-2/5} = (2^5)^{-2/5}$$ • **Rewrite 32 as 2^5.**

$$= 2^{-2}$$ • **Multiply the exponents.**

$$= \frac{1}{2^2}$$ • **Use the Rule of Negative Exponents.**

$$= \frac{1}{4}$$ • **Simplify.**

➡ Simplify: $a^{1/2} \cdot a^{2/3} \cdot a^{-1/4}$

$$a^{1/2} \cdot a^{2/3} \cdot a^{-1/4} = a^{1/2+2/3-1/4}$$ • **Use the Rule for Multiplying Exponential Expressions.**

$$= a^{6/12+8/12-3/12}$$

$$= a^{11/12}$$ • **Simplify.**

➡ Simplify: $(x^6y^4)^{3/2}$

$$(x^6y^4)^{3/2} = x^{6(3/2)}y^{4(3/2)}$$ • **Use the Rule for Simplifying Powers of Products.**

$$= x^9y^6$$ • **Simplify.**

➡ Simplify: $\left(\dfrac{8a^3b^{-4}}{64a^{-9}b^2}\right)^{2/3}$

$$\left(\frac{8a^3b^{-4}}{64a^{-9}b^2}\right)^{2/3} = \left(\frac{2^3a^3b^{-4}}{2^6a^{-9}b^2}\right)^{2/3}$$ • **Rewrite 8 as 2^3 and 64 as 2^6.**

$$= (2^{-3}a^{12}b^{-6})^{2/3}$$ • **Use the Rule for Dividing Exponential Expressions.**

$$= 2^{-2}a^8b^{-4}$$ • **Use the Rule for Simplifying Powers of Products.**

$$= \frac{a^8}{2^2b^4} = \frac{a^8}{4b^4}$$ • **Use the Rule of Negative Exponents and simplify.**

Example 1   Simplify: $64^{-2/3}$

Solution $64^{-2/3} = (2^6)^{-2/3} = 2^{-4}$
$$= \frac{1}{2^4} = \frac{1}{16}$$

You Try It 1   Simplify: $16^{-3/4}$

Your solution $\dfrac{1}{8}$

Example 2   Simplify: $(-49)^{3/2}$

Solution   The base of the exponential expression is a negative number, while the denominator of the exponent is a positive even number.

Therefore, $(-49)^{3/2}$ is not a real number.

You Try It 2   Simplify: $(-81)^{3/4}$

Your solution   not a real number

Example 3   Simplify: $(x^{1/2}y^{-3/2}z^{1/4})^{-3/2}$

Solution $(x^{1/2}y^{-3/2}z^{1/4})^{-3/2}$
$$= x^{-3/4}y^{9/4}z^{-3/8}$$
$$= \frac{y^{9/4}}{x^{3/4}z^{3/8}}$$

You Try It 3   Simplify: $(x^{3/4}y^{1/2}z^{-2/3})^{-4/3}$

Your solution $\dfrac{z^{8/9}}{xy^{2/3}}$

Example 4   Simplify: $\dfrac{x^{1/2}y^{-5/4}}{x^{-4/3}y^{1/3}}$

Solution $\dfrac{x^{1/2}y^{-5/4}}{x^{-4/3}y^{1/3}}$
$$= x^{3/6 - (-8/6)}y^{-15/12 - 4/12}$$
$$= x^{11/6}y^{-19/12} = \frac{x^{11/6}}{y^{19/12}}$$

You Try It 4   Simplify: $\left(\dfrac{16a^{-2}b^{4/3}}{9a^4b^{-2/3}}\right)^{-1/2}$

Your solution $\dfrac{3a^3}{4b}$

Solutions on p. S26

Objective B   **To write exponential expressions as radical expressions and to write radical expressions as exponential expressions** ....

POINT OF INTEREST

The radical sign was introduced in 1525 in a book by Christoff Rudolff called *Coss*. He modified the symbol to indicate square roots, cube roots, and fourth roots. The idea of using an index, as we do in our modern notation, did not occur until some years later.

Recall that $a^{1/n}$ is the nth root of a. The expression $\sqrt[n]{a}$ is another symbol for the nth root of a.

If a is a real number, then $a^{1/n} = \sqrt[n]{a}$.

In the expression $\sqrt[n]{a}$, the symbol $\sqrt{}$ is called a **radical sign**, n is the **index** of the radical, and a is the **radicand**. When $n = 2$, the radical expression represents a square root and the index 2 is usually not written.

An exponential expression with a rational exponent can be written as a radical expression.

> **Rule for Writing Exponential Expressions as Radical Expressions**
>
> If $a^{1/n}$ is a real number, then $a^{m/n} = a^{m \cdot 1/n} = (a^m)^{1/n} = \sqrt[n]{a^m}$.

The expression $a^{m/n}$ can also be written $a^{m/n} = (a^{1/n})^m = (\sqrt[n]{a})^m$.

The exponential expression at the right has been written as a radical expression.

$$y^{2/3} = (y^2)^{1/3}$$
$$= \sqrt[3]{y^2}$$

The radical expressions at the right have been written as exponential expressions.

$$\sqrt[5]{x^6} = (x^6)^{1/5} = x^{6/5}$$
$$\sqrt{17} = (17)^{1/2} = 17^{1/2}$$

➡ Write $(5x)^{2/5}$ as a radical expression.

$$(5x)^{2/5} = \sqrt[5]{(5x)^2}$$

• The denominator of the rational exponent is the index of the radical. The numerator is the power of the radicand.

$$= \sqrt[5]{25x^2}$$

• Simplify.

➡ Write $\sqrt[3]{x^4}$ as an exponential expression with a rational exponent.

$$\sqrt[3]{x^4} = (x^4)^{1/3}$$

• The index of the radical is the denominator of the rational exponent. The power of the radicand is the numerator of the rational exponent.

$$= x^{4/3}$$

• Simplify.

➡ Write $\sqrt[3]{a^3 + b^3}$ as an exponential expression with a rational exponent.

$$\sqrt[3]{a^3 + b^3} = (a^3 + b^3)^{1/3}$$

Note that $(a^3 + b^3)^{1/3} \neq a + b$.

Example 5 Write $(3x)^{5/4}$ as a radical expression.

Solution $(3x)^{5/4} = \sqrt[4]{(3x)^5} = \sqrt[4]{243x^5}$

You Try It 5 Write $(2x^3)^{3/4}$ as a radical expression.

Your solution $\sqrt[4]{8x^9}$

Example 6 Write $-2x^{2/3}$ as a radical expression.

Solution $-2x^{2/3} = -2(x^2)^{1/3} = -2\sqrt[3]{x^2}$

You Try It 6 Write $-5a^{5/6}$ as a radical expression.

Your solution $-5\sqrt[6]{a^5}$

Example 7 Write $\sqrt[4]{3a}$ as an exponential expression.

Solution $\sqrt[4]{3a} = (3a)^{1/4}$

You Try It 7 Write $\sqrt[3]{3ab}$ as an exponential expression.

Your solution $(3ab)^{1/3}$

Example 8 Write $\sqrt{a^2 - b^2}$ as an exponential expression.

Solution $\sqrt{a^2 - b^2} = (a^2 - b^2)^{1/2}$

You Try It 8 Write $\sqrt[4]{x^4 + y^4}$ as an exponential expression.

Your solution $(x^4 + y^4)^{1/4}$

Solutions on p. S26

Objective C   **To simplify radical expressions that
are roots of perfect powers** ....

Every positive number has two square roots, one a positive and one a negative number. For example, because $(5)^2 = 25$ and $(-5)^2 = 25$, there are two square roots of 25: 5 and -5.

The symbol $\sqrt{}$ is used to indicate the positive or **principal square root**. To indicate the negative square root of a number, a negative sign is placed in front of the radical.

$$\sqrt{25} = 5$$

$$-\sqrt{25} = -5$$

The square root of zero is zero.

$$\sqrt{0} = 0$$

The square root of a negative number is not a real number, because the square of a real number must be positive.

$\sqrt{-25}$ is not a real number.

Note that

$$\sqrt{(-5)^2} = \sqrt{25} = 5 \text{ and } \sqrt{5^2} = \sqrt{25} = 5$$

This is true for all real numbers and is stated as the following result.

For any real number a, $\sqrt{a^2} = |a|$ and $-\sqrt{a^2} = -|a|$. If a is a positive real number, then $\sqrt{a^2} = a$ and $(\sqrt{a})^2 = a$.

Besides square roots, we can also determine cube roots, fourth roots, and so on.

$\sqrt[3]{8} = 2$, because $2^3 = 8$.

 • **The cube root of a positive number is positive.**

$\sqrt[3]{-8} = -2$, because $(-2)^3 = -8$.

 • **The cube root of a negative number is negative.**

$\sqrt[4]{625} = 5$, because $5^4 = 625$.

$\sqrt[5]{243} = 3$, because $3^5 = 243$.

The following properties hold true for finding the nth root of a real number.

If n is an even integer, then $\sqrt[n]{a^n} = |a|$ and $-\sqrt[n]{a^n} = -|a|$. If n is an odd integer, then $\sqrt[n]{a^n} = a$.

For example,

$$\sqrt[6]{y^6} = |y| \qquad -\sqrt[12]{x^{12}} = -|x| \qquad \sqrt[5]{b^5} = b$$

We have agreed that all variables in this chapter represent positive numbers unless otherwise stated, so it is not necessary to use the absolute value signs.

➡ Simplify: $\sqrt[3]{64}$

$$\sqrt[3]{64} = \sqrt[3]{2^6}$$
$$= (2^6)^{1/3}$$
$$= 2^2 = 4$$

- Write the prime factorization of the radicand in simplest form.
- Write the radical expression as an exponential expression.
- Use the Rule for Simplifying the Power of an Exponential Expression.

➡ Simplify: $\sqrt[4]{x^4y^8}$

The radicand is a perfect fourth power because the exponents on the variables are divisible by 4.

$$\sqrt[4]{x^4y^8} = (x^4y^8)^{1/4}$$
$$= xy^2$$

- Write the radical expression as an exponential expression.
- Use the Rule for Simplifying Powers of Products.

➡ Simplify: $\sqrt[5]{32x^{15}}$

$$\sqrt[5]{32x^{15}} = (2^5x^{15})^{1/5}$$
$$= 2x^3$$

- Write the prime factorization of 32. Write the radical expression as an exponential expression.
- Use the Rule for Simplifying Powers of Products.

Example 9
Simplify: $\sqrt{49x^2y^{12}}$

Solution
$$\sqrt{49x^2y^{12}} = \sqrt{7^2x^2y^{12}}$$
$$= (7^2x^2y^{12})^{1/2}$$
$$= 7xy^6$$

You Try It 9
Simplify: $\sqrt{121x^{10}y^4}$

Your solution
$11x^5y^2$

Example 10
Simplify: $\sqrt[3]{-125a^6b^9}$

Solution
$$\sqrt[3]{-125a^6b^9} = \sqrt[3]{(-5)^3a^6b^9}$$
$$= [(-5)^3a^6b^9]^{1/3}$$
$$= -5a^2b^3$$

You Try It 10
Simplify: $\sqrt[3]{-8x^{12}y^3}$

Your solution
$-2x^4y$

Example 11
Simplify: $-\sqrt[4]{16a^4b^8}$

Solution
$$-\sqrt[4]{16a^4b^8} = -\sqrt[4]{2^4a^4b^8}$$
$$= -(2^4a^4b^8)^{1/4}$$
$$= -2ab^2$$

You Try It 11
Simplify: $-\sqrt[4]{81x^{12}y^8}$

Your solution
$-3x^3y^2$

Solutions on p. S26

9.1 Exercises

· ·

Objective A

Simplify.

1. $8^{1/3}$

2

2. $16^{1/2}$

4

3. $9^{3/2}$

27

4. $25^{3/2}$

125

5. $27^{-2/3}$

$\dfrac{1}{9}$

6. $64^{-1/3}$

$\dfrac{1}{4}$

7. $32^{2/5}$

4

8. $16^{3/4}$

8

9. $(-25)^{5/2}$

not a real number

10. $(-36)^{1/4}$

not a real number

11. $\left(\dfrac{25}{49}\right)^{-3/2}$

$\dfrac{343}{125}$

12. $\left(\dfrac{8}{27}\right)^{-2/3}$

$\dfrac{9}{4}$

13. $x^{1/2}x^{1/2}$

x

14. $a^{1/3}a^{5/3}$

a^2

15. $y^{-1/4}y^{3/4}$

$y^{1/2}$

16. $x^{2/5} \cdot x^{-4/5}$

$\dfrac{1}{x^{2/5}}$

17. $x^{-2/3} \cdot x^{3/4}$

$x^{1/12}$

18. $x \cdot x^{-1/2}$

$x^{1/2}$

19. $a^{1/3} \cdot a^{3/4} \cdot a^{-1/2}$

$a^{7/12}$

20. $y^{-1/6} \cdot y^{2/3} \cdot y^{1/2}$

y

21. $\dfrac{a^{1/2}}{a^{3/2}}$

$\dfrac{1}{a}$

22. $\dfrac{b^{1/3}}{b^{4/3}}$

$\dfrac{1}{b}$

23. $\dfrac{y^{-3/4}}{y^{1/4}}$

$\dfrac{1}{y}$

24. $\dfrac{x^{-3/5}}{x^{1/5}}$

$\dfrac{1}{x^{4/5}}$

25. $\dfrac{y^{2/3}}{y^{-5/6}}$

$y^{3/2}$

26. $\dfrac{b^{3/4}}{b^{-3/2}}$

$b^{9/4}$

27. $(x^2)^{-1/2}$

$\dfrac{1}{x}$

28. $(a^8)^{-3/4}$

$\dfrac{1}{a^6}$

29. $(x^{-2/3})^6$

$\dfrac{1}{x^4}$

30. $(y^{-5/6})^{12}$

$\dfrac{1}{y^{10}}$

31. $(a^{-1/2})^{-2}$

a

32. $(b^{-2/3})^{-6}$

b^4

33. $(x^{-3/8})^{-4/5}$

$x^{3/10}$

34. $(y^{-3/2})^{-2/9}$

$y^{1/3}$

35. $(a^{1/2} \cdot a)^2$

a^3

36. $(b^{2/3} \cdot b^{1/6})^6$

b^5

37. $(x^{-1/2} \cdot x^{3/4})^{-2}$

$\dfrac{1}{x^{1/2}}$

38. $(a^{1/2} \cdot a^{-2})^3$

$\dfrac{1}{a^{9/2}}$

39. $(y^{-1/2} \cdot y^{2/3})^{2/3}$
$y^{1/9}$

40. $(b^{-2/3} \cdot b^{1/4})^{-4/3}$
$b^{5/9}$

41. $(x^8y^2)^{1/2}$
x^4y

42. $(a^3b^9)^{2/3}$
a^2b^6

43. $(x^4 y^2 z^6)^{3/2}$

$x^6 y^3 z^9$

44. $(a^8 b^4 c^4)^{3/4}$

$a^6 b^3 c^3$

45. $(x^{-3} y^6)^{-1/3}$

$\dfrac{x}{y^2}$

46. $(a^2 b^{-6})^{-1/2}$

$\dfrac{b^3}{a}$

47. $(x^{-2} y^{1/3})^{-3/4}$

$\dfrac{x^{3/2}}{y^{1/4}}$

48. $(a^{-2/3} b^{2/3})^{3/2}$

$\dfrac{b}{a}$

49. $\left(\dfrac{x^{1/2}}{y^2}\right)^4$

$\dfrac{x^2}{y^8}$

50. $\left(\dfrac{b^{-3/4}}{a^{-1/2}}\right)^8$

$\dfrac{a^4}{b^6}$

51. $\dfrac{x^{1/4} \cdot x^{-1/2}}{x^{2/3}}$

$\dfrac{1}{x^{11/12}}$

52. $\dfrac{b^{1/2} \cdot b^{-3/4}}{b^{1/4}}$

$\dfrac{1}{b^{1/2}}$

53. $\left(\dfrac{y^{2/3} \cdot y^{-5/6}}{y^{1/9}}\right)^9$

$\dfrac{1}{y^{5/2}}$

54. $\left(\dfrac{a^{1/3} \cdot a^{-2/3}}{a^{1/2}}\right)^4$

$\dfrac{1}{a^{10/3}}$

55. $\left(\dfrac{b^2 \cdot b^{-3/4}}{b^{-1/2}}\right)^{-1/2}$

$\dfrac{1}{b^{7/8}}$

56. $\dfrac{(x^{-5/6} \cdot x^3)^{-2/3}}{x^{4/3}}$

$\dfrac{1}{x^{25/9}}$

57. $(a^{2/3} b^2)^6 (a^3 b^3)^{1/3}$

$a^5 b^{13}$

58. $(x^3 y^{-1/2})^{-2} (x^{-3} y^2)^{1/6}$

$\dfrac{y^{4/3}}{x^{13/2}}$

59. $(16 m^{-2} n^4)^{-1/2} (m n^{1/2})$

$\dfrac{m^2}{4 n^{3/2}}$

60. $(27 m^3 n^{-6})^{1/3} (m^{-1/3} n^{5/6})^6$

$\dfrac{3 n^3}{m}$

61. $\left(\dfrac{x^{1/2} y^{-3/4}}{y^{2/3}}\right)^{-6}$

$\dfrac{y^{17/2}}{x^3}$

62. $\left(\dfrac{x^{1/2} y^{-5/4}}{y^{-3/4}}\right)^{-4}$

$\dfrac{y^2}{x^2}$

63. $\left(\dfrac{2^{-6} b^{-3}}{a^{-1/2}}\right)^{-2/3}$

$\dfrac{16 b^2}{a^{1/3}}$

64. $\left(\dfrac{49 c^{5/3}}{a^{-1/4} b^{5/6}}\right)^{-3/2}$

$\dfrac{b^{5/4}}{343 a^{3/8} c^{5/2}}$

65. $y^{3/2}(y^{1/2} - y^{-1/2})$

$y^2 - y$

66. $y^{3/5}(y^{2/5} + y^{-3/5})$

$y + 1$

67. $a^{-1/4}(a^{5/4} - a^{9/4})$

$a - a^2$

68. $x^{4/3}(x^{2/3} + x^{-1/3})$

$x^2 + x$

69. $x^n \cdot x^{3n}$

x^{4n}

70. $a^{2n} \cdot a^{-5n}$

$\dfrac{1}{a^{3n}}$

71. $x^n \cdot x^{n/2}$

$x^{3n/2}$

72. $a^{n/2} \cdot a^{-n/3}$

$a^{n/6}$

73. $\dfrac{y^{n/2}}{y^{-n}}$

$y^{3n/2}$

74. $\dfrac{b^{m/3}}{b^m}$

$\dfrac{1}{b^{2m/3}}$

75. $(x^{2n})^n$

x^{2n^2}

76. $(x^{5n})^{2n}$

x^{10n^2}

77. $(x^{n/4} y^{n/8})^8$

$x^{2n} y^n$

78. $(x^{n/2} y^{n/3})^6$

$x^{3n} y^{2n}$

79. $(x^{n/5} y^{n/10})^{20}$

$x^{4n} y^{2n}$

80. $(x^{n/2} y^{n/5})^{10}$

$x^{5n} y^{2n}$

_____

Objective B

Rewrite the exponential expression as a radical expression.

81. $3^{1/4}$
$\sqrt[4]{3}$

82. $5^{1/2}$
$\sqrt{5}$

83. $a^{3/2}$
$\sqrt{a^3}$

84. $b^{4/3}$
$\sqrt[3]{b^4}$

85. $(2t)^{5/2}$
$\sqrt{32t^5}$

86. $(3x)^{2/3}$
$\sqrt[3]{9x^2}$

87. $-2x^{2/3}$
$-2\sqrt[3]{x^2}$

88. $-3a^{2/5}$
$-3\sqrt[5]{a^2}$

89. $(a^2b)^{2/3}$
$\sqrt[3]{a^4b^2}$

90. $(x^2y^3)^{3/4}$
$\sqrt[4]{x^6y^9}$

91. $(a^2b^4)^{3/5}$
$\sqrt[5]{a^6b^{12}}$

92. $(a^3b^7)^{3/2}$
$\sqrt{a^9b^{21}}$

93. $(4x-3)^{3/4}$

$\sqrt[4]{(4x-3)^3}$

94. $(3x-2)^{1/3}$

$\sqrt[3]{3x-2}$

95. $x^{-2/3}$

$\dfrac{1}{\sqrt[3]{x^2}}$

96. $b^{-3/4}$

$\dfrac{1}{\sqrt[4]{b^3}}$

Rewrite the radical expression as an exponential expression.

97. $\sqrt{14}$
$14^{1/2}$

98. $\sqrt{7}$
$7^{1/2}$

99. $\sqrt[3]{x}$
$x^{1/3}$

100. $\sqrt[4]{x}$
$y^{1/4}$

101. $\sqrt[3]{x^4}$
$x^{4/3}$

102. $\sqrt[4]{a^3}$
$a^{3/4}$

103. $\sqrt[5]{b^3}$
$b^{3/5}$

104. $\sqrt[4]{b^5}$
$b^{5/4}$

105. $\sqrt[3]{2x^2}$
$(2x^2)^{1/3}$

106. $\sqrt[5]{4y^7}$
$(4y^7)^{1/5}$

107. $-\sqrt{3x^5}$
$-(3x^5)^{1/2}$

108. $-\sqrt[4]{4x^5}$
$-(4x^5)^{1/4}$

109. $3x\sqrt[3]{y^2}$
$3xy^{2/3}$

110. $2y\sqrt{x^3}$
$2x^{3/2}y$

111. $\sqrt{a^2-2}$
$(a^2-2)^{1/2}$

112. $\sqrt{3-y^2}$
$(3-y^2)^{1/2}$

Objective C

Simplify.

113. $\sqrt{x^{16}}$
x^8

114. $\sqrt{y^{14}}$
y^7

115. $-\sqrt{x^8}$
$-x^4$

116. $-\sqrt{a^6}$
$-a^3$

117. $\sqrt[3]{x^3y^9}$
xy^3

118. $\sqrt[3]{a^6b^{12}}$
a^2b^4

119. $-\sqrt[3]{x^{15}y^3}$
$-x^5y$

120. $-\sqrt[3]{a^9b^9}$
$-a^3b^3$

121. $\sqrt{16a^4b^{12}}$
$4a^2b^6$

122. $\sqrt{25x^8y^2}$
$5x^4y$

123. $\sqrt{-16x^4y^2}$
not a real
number

124. $\sqrt{-9a^4b^8}$
not a real
number

125. $\sqrt[3]{27x^9}$
$3x^3$

126. $\sqrt[3]{8a^{21}b^6}$
$2a^7b^2$

127. $\sqrt[3]{-64x^9y^{12}}$
$-4x^3y^4$

128. $\sqrt[3]{-27a^3b^{15}}$
$-3ab^5$

129. $-\sqrt[4]{x^8y^{12}}$
$-x^2y^3$

130. $-\sqrt[4]{a^{16}b^4}$
$-a^4b$

131. $\sqrt[5]{x^{20}y^{10}}$
x^4y^2

132. $\sqrt[5]{a^5b^{25}}$
ab^5

133. $\sqrt[4]{81x^4y^{20}}$
$3xy^5$

134. $\sqrt[4]{16a^8b^{20}}$
$2a^2b^5$

135. $\sqrt[5]{32a^5b^{10}}$
$2ab^2$

136. $\sqrt[5]{-32x^{15}y^{20}}$
$-2x^3y^4$

APPLYING THE CONCEPTS

137. Determine whether the following statements are true or false. If the statement is false, correct the right-hand side of the equation.

a. $\sqrt{(-2)^2} = -2$
false; 2

b. $\sqrt[3]{(-3)^3} = -3$
true

c. $\sqrt[n]{a} = a^{1/n}$
true

d. $\sqrt[n]{a^n + b^n} = a + b$
false; $(a^n + b^n)^{1/n}$

e. $(a^{1/2} + b^{1/2})^2 = a + b$
false; $a + 2a^{1/2}b^{1/2} + b$

f. $\sqrt[m]{a^n} = a^{mn}$
false: $a^{n/m}$

138. Simplify.

a. $\sqrt[3]{\sqrt{x^6}}$ x

b. $\sqrt[4]{\sqrt{a^8}}$ a

c. $\sqrt{\sqrt{81y^8}}$ $3y^2$

d. $\sqrt{\sqrt[n]{a^{4n}}}$ a^2

e. $\sqrt[n]{\sqrt{b^{6n}}}$ b^3

f. $\sqrt{\sqrt[3]{x^{12}y^{24}}}$ x^2y^4

139. Show how to locate $\sqrt{2}$ on the number line.

140. If x is any real number, is $\sqrt{x^2} = x$ always true? Show why or why not.

9.2 Operations on Radical Expressions

Objective A   *To simplify radical expressions* ....

If a number is not a perfect power, its root can only be approximated; examples include $\sqrt{5}$ and $\sqrt[3]{3}$. These numbers are **irrational numbers**. Their decimal representations never terminate or repeat.

$$\sqrt{5} = 2.2360679 \ldots \qquad \sqrt[3]{3} = 1.4422495 \ldots$$

A radical expression is in simplest form when the radicand contains no factor that is a perfect power. The Product Property of Radicals is used to simplify radical expressions whose radicands are not perfect powers.

The Product Property of Radicals

If $\sqrt[n]{a}$ and $\sqrt[n]{b}$ are positive real numbers, then $\sqrt[n]{ab} = \sqrt[n]{a} \cdot \sqrt[n]{b}$ and $\sqrt[n]{a} \cdot \sqrt[n]{b} = \sqrt[n]{ab}$.

➡ Simplify: $\sqrt[3]{x^7}$

$\sqrt[3]{x^7} = \sqrt[3]{x^6 \cdot x}$
- Write the radicand as the product of a perfect cube and a factor that does not contain a perfect cube.

$\qquad = \sqrt[3]{x^6}\,\sqrt[3]{x}$
- Use the Product Property of Radicals to write the expression as a product.

$\qquad = x^2\sqrt[3]{x}$
- Simplify.

➡ Simplify: $\sqrt[4]{32x^7}$

$\sqrt[4]{32x^7} = \sqrt[4]{2^5x^7}$
- Write the prime factorization of the coefficient of the radicand in exponential form.

$\qquad = \sqrt[4]{2^4x^4(2x^3)}$
- Write the radicand as the product of a perfect fourth power and factors that do not contain a perfect fourth power.

$\qquad = \sqrt[4]{2^4x^4}\,\sqrt[4]{2x^3}$
- Use the Product Property of Radicals to write the expression as a product.

$\qquad = 2x\sqrt[4]{2x^3}$
- Simplify.

Example 1   Simplify: $\sqrt[4]{x^9}$

Solution $\sqrt[4]{x^9} = \sqrt[4]{x^8 \cdot x} = \sqrt[4]{x^8}\,\sqrt[4]{x}$
$\qquad = x^2\sqrt[4]{x}$

You Try It 1   Simplify: $\sqrt[5]{x^7}$

Your solution $x\sqrt[5]{x^2}$

Solution on p. S26

Example 2

Simplify: $\sqrt[3]{-27a^5b^{12}}$

Solution

$$\sqrt[3]{-27a^5b^{12}} = \sqrt[3]{(-3)^3a^5b^{12}}$$
$$= \sqrt[3]{(-3)^3a^3b^{12}(a^2)}$$
$$= \sqrt[3]{(-3)^3a^3b^{12}}\sqrt[3]{a^2}$$
$$= -3ab^4\sqrt[3]{a^2}$$

You Try It 2

Simplify: $\sqrt[3]{-64x^8y^{18}}$

Your solution

$-4x^2y^6\sqrt[3]{x^2}$

Solution on p. S27

Objective B To add or subtract radical expressions..................................

The Distributive Property is used to simplify the sum or difference of radical expressions that have the same radicand and the same index. For example,

$$3\sqrt{5} + 8\sqrt{5} = (3 + 8)\sqrt{5} = 11\sqrt{5}$$
$$2\sqrt[3]{3x} - 9\sqrt[3]{3x} = (2 - 9)\sqrt[3]{3x} = -7\sqrt[3]{3x}$$

Radical expressions that are in simplest form and have unlike radicands or different indices cannot be simplified by the Distributive Property. The expressions below cannot be simplified by the Distributive Property.

$$3\sqrt[4]{2} - 6\sqrt[4]{3} \qquad\qquad 2\sqrt[4]{4x} + 3\sqrt[3]{4x}$$

➡ Simplify: $3\sqrt{32x^2} - 2x\sqrt{2} + \sqrt{128x^2}$

First simplify each term. Then combine like terms by using the Distributive Property.

$$3\sqrt{32x^2} - 2x\sqrt{2} + \sqrt{128x^2} = 3\sqrt{2^5x^2} - 2x\sqrt{2} + \sqrt{2^7x^2}$$
$$= 3\sqrt{2^4x^2}\sqrt{2} - 2x\sqrt{2} + \sqrt{2^6x^2}\sqrt{2}$$
$$= 3 \cdot 2^2x\sqrt{2} - 2x\sqrt{2} + 2^3x\sqrt{2}$$
$$= 12x\sqrt{2} - 2x\sqrt{2} + 8x\sqrt{2}$$
$$= 18x\sqrt{2}$$

Example 3

Subtract: $5b\sqrt[4]{32a^7b^5} - 2a\sqrt[4]{162a^3b^9}$

Solution

$5b\sqrt[4]{32a^7b^5} - 2a\sqrt[4]{162a^3b^9}$

$= 5b\sqrt[4]{2^5a^7b^5} - 2a\sqrt[4]{3^4 \cdot 2a^3b^9}$

$= 5b\sqrt[4]{2^4a^4b^4}\sqrt[4]{2a^3b} - 2a\sqrt[4]{3^4b^8}\sqrt[4]{2a^3b}$

$= 5b \cdot 2ab\sqrt[4]{2a^3b} - 2a \cdot 3b^2\sqrt[4]{2a^3b}$

$= 10ab^2\sqrt[4]{2a^3b} - 6ab^2\sqrt[4]{2a^3b}$

$= 4ab^2\sqrt[4]{2a^3b}$

You Try It 3

Subtract: $3xy\sqrt[3]{81x^5y} - \sqrt[3]{192x^8y^4}$

Your solution

$5x^2y\sqrt[3]{3x^2y}$

Solution on p. S27

Objective C   *To multiply radical expressions*......................................

The Product Property of Radicals is used to multiply radical expressions with the same index.

$$\sqrt{3x} \cdot \sqrt{5y} = \sqrt{3x \cdot 5y}$$
$$= \sqrt{15xy}$$

When the expression $(\sqrt{x})^2$ is simplified using the Product Property of Radicals, the result is x.

$$(\sqrt{x})^2 = \sqrt{x} \cdot \sqrt{x} = \sqrt{x \cdot x}$$
$$= \sqrt{x^2} = x$$

➡ Multiply: $\sqrt[3]{2a^5b}\,\sqrt[3]{16a^2b^2}$

$$\sqrt[3]{2a^5b}\,\sqrt[3]{16a^2b^2} = \sqrt[3]{32a^7b^3}$$

- Use the Product Property of Radicals to multiply the radicands.

$$= \sqrt[3]{2^5a^7b^3}$$

- Simplify.

$$= \sqrt[3]{2^3a^6b^3}\,\sqrt[3]{2^2a}$$
$$= 2a^2b\,\sqrt[3]{4a}$$

➡ Multiply: $\sqrt{2x}(\sqrt{8x} - \sqrt{3})$

$$\sqrt{2x}(\sqrt{8x} - \sqrt{3}) = \sqrt{2x}(\sqrt{8x}) - \sqrt{2x}(\sqrt{3})$$

- Use the Distributive Property.

$$= \sqrt{16x^2} - \sqrt{6x}$$

- Simplify.

$$= \sqrt{2^4x^2} - \sqrt{6x}$$
$$= 2^2x - \sqrt{6x}$$
$$= 4x - \sqrt{6x}$$

➡ Multiply: $(2\sqrt{5} - 3)(3\sqrt{5} + 4)$

$$(2\sqrt{5} - 3)(3\sqrt{5} + 4) = 6(\sqrt{5})^2 + 8\sqrt{5} - 9\sqrt{5} - 12$$

- Use the FOIL method to multiply the numbers.

$$= 30 + 8\sqrt{5} - 9\sqrt{5} - 12$$
$$= 18 - \sqrt{5}$$

- Combine like terms.

➡ Multiply: $(4\sqrt{a} - \sqrt{b})(2\sqrt{a} + 5\sqrt{b})$

$$(4\sqrt{a} - \sqrt{b})(2\sqrt{a} + 5\sqrt{b})$$
$$= 8(\sqrt{a})^2 + 20\sqrt{ab} - 2\sqrt{ab} - 5(\sqrt{b})^2$$

- Use the FOIL method.

$$= 8a + 18\sqrt{ab} - 5b$$

TAKE NOTE

The concept of conjugate is used in a number of different instances. Make sure you understand this idea.

The conjugate of $\sqrt{3} - 4$ is $\sqrt{3} + 4$.

The conjugate of $\sqrt{3} + 4$ is $\sqrt{3} - 4$.

The conjugate of $\sqrt{5a} + \sqrt{b}$ is $\sqrt{5a} - \sqrt{b}$.

The expressions $a + b$ and $a - b$ are **conjugates** of each other. Recall that $(a + b)(a - b) = a^2 - b^2$.

➡ Multiply: $(\sqrt{11} - 3)(\sqrt{11} + 3)$

$$(\sqrt{11} - 3)(\sqrt{11} + 3) = (\sqrt{11})^2 - 3^2$$

- The expressions are conjugates.

$$= 11 - 9 = 2$$

Example 4

Multiply: $\sqrt{3x}(\sqrt{27x^2} - \sqrt{3x})$

Solution

$$\sqrt{3x}(\sqrt{27x^2} - \sqrt{3x}) = \sqrt{81x^3} - (\sqrt{3x})^2$$

$$= \sqrt{3^4x^3} - 3x$$

$$= \sqrt{3^4x^2}\sqrt{x} - 3x$$

$$= 3^2x\sqrt{x} - 3x$$

$$= 9x\sqrt{x} - 3x$$

You Try It 4

Multiply: $\sqrt{5b}(\sqrt{3b} - \sqrt{10})$

Your solution

$b\sqrt{15} - 5\sqrt{2b}$

Example 5

Multiply: $(2\sqrt[3]{x} - 3)(3\sqrt[3]{x} - 4)$

Solution

$(2\sqrt[3]{x} - 3)(3\sqrt[3]{x} - 4)$

$= 6\sqrt[3]{x^2} - 8\sqrt[3]{x} - 9\sqrt[3]{x} + 12$

$= 6\sqrt[3]{x^2} - 17\sqrt[3]{x} + 12$

You Try It 5

Multiply: $(2\sqrt[3]{2x} - 3)(\sqrt[3]{2x} - 5)$

Your solution

$2\sqrt[3]{4x^2} - 13\sqrt[3]{2x} + 15$

Example 6

Multiply: $(2\sqrt{x} - \sqrt{2y})(2\sqrt{x} + \sqrt{2y})$

Solution

$(2\sqrt{x} - \sqrt{2y})(2\sqrt{x} + \sqrt{2y})$

$= (2\sqrt{x})^2 - (\sqrt{2y})^2$

$= 4x - 2y$

You Try It 6

Multiply: $(\sqrt{a} - 3\sqrt{y})(\sqrt{a} + 3\sqrt{y})$

Your solution

$a - 9y$

Solutions on p. S27

Objective D *To divide radical expressions*...

The Quotient Property of Radicals is used to divide radical expressions with the same index.

> **The Quotient Property of Radicals**
>
> If $\sqrt[n]{a}$ and $\sqrt[n]{b}$ are real numbers, and $b \neq 0$, then
>
> $$\sqrt[n]{\frac{a}{b}} = \frac{\sqrt[n]{a}}{\sqrt[n]{b}} \quad \text{and} \quad \frac{\sqrt[n]{a}}{\sqrt[n]{b}} = \sqrt[n]{\frac{a}{b}}$$

➡ Simplify: $\sqrt[3]{\dfrac{81x^5}{y^6}}$

$$\sqrt[3]{\frac{81x^5}{y^6}} = \frac{\sqrt[3]{81x^5}}{\sqrt[3]{y^6}}$$

• Use the Quotient Property of Radicals.

$$= \frac{\sqrt[3]{3^4 x^5}}{\sqrt[3]{y^6}}$$

• Simplify each radical expression.

$$= \frac{\sqrt[3]{3^3 x^3}\sqrt[3]{3x^2}}{\sqrt[3]{y^6}}$$

$$= \frac{3x\sqrt[3]{3x^2}}{y^2}$$

➡ Simplify: $\dfrac{\sqrt{5a^4b^7c^2}}{\sqrt{ab^3c}}$

$$\frac{\sqrt{5a^4b^7c^2}}{\sqrt{ab^3c}} = \sqrt{\frac{5a^4b^7c^2}{ab^3c}}$$

• Use the Quotient Property of Radicals.

$$= \sqrt{5a^3b^4c}$$

• Simplify the radicand.

$$= \sqrt{a^2b^4}\sqrt{5ac}$$

$$= ab^2\sqrt{5ac}$$

A radical expression is in simplest form when no radical remains in the denominator of the radical expression. The procedure used to remove a radical from the denominator is called **rationalizing the denominator**.

➡ Simplify: $\dfrac{5}{\sqrt{2}}$

Multiply by $\dfrac{\sqrt{2}}{\sqrt{2}}$, which equals 1.

$$\frac{5}{\sqrt{2}} = \frac{5}{\sqrt{2}} \cdot 1 = \frac{5}{\sqrt{2}} \cdot \frac{\sqrt{2}}{\sqrt{2}}$$

• $\dfrac{\sqrt{2}}{\sqrt{2}} = 1$

$$= \frac{5\sqrt{2}}{2}$$

• $\sqrt{2} \cdot \sqrt{2} = (\sqrt{2})^2 = 2$

➡ Simplify: $\dfrac{3x}{\sqrt[3]{4x}}$

$$\frac{3x}{\sqrt[3]{4x}} = \frac{3x}{\sqrt[3]{2^2 x}} \cdot \frac{\sqrt[3]{2x^2}}{\sqrt[3]{2x^2}}$$

• $\sqrt[3]{2^2 x} \cdot \sqrt[3]{2x^2} = \sqrt[3]{2^3 x^3}$, the cube root of a perfect cube. Multiply the numerator and denominator by $\dfrac{\sqrt[3]{2x^2}}{\sqrt[3]{2x^2}}$, which equals 1.

$$= \frac{3x\sqrt[3]{2x^2}}{\sqrt[3]{2^3 x^3}} = \frac{3x\sqrt[3]{2x^2}}{2x}$$

• Simplify.

$$= \frac{3\sqrt[3]{2x^2}}{2}$$

➡ Simplify: $\dfrac{\sqrt{x} - \sqrt{y}}{\sqrt{x} + \sqrt{y}}$

To simplify a fraction that has a radical expression with two terms in the denominator, multiply the numerator and denominator by the conjugate of the denominator. Then simplify.

$$\frac{\sqrt{x} - \sqrt{y}}{\sqrt{x} + \sqrt{y}} = \frac{\sqrt{x} - \sqrt{y}}{\sqrt{x} + \sqrt{y}} \cdot \frac{\sqrt{x} - \sqrt{y}}{\sqrt{x} - \sqrt{y}} = \frac{(\sqrt{x} - \sqrt{y})(\sqrt{x} - \sqrt{y})}{(\sqrt{x} + \sqrt{y})(\sqrt{x} - \sqrt{y})}$$

$$= \frac{(\sqrt{x})^2 - \sqrt{xy} - \sqrt{xy} + (\sqrt{y})^2}{(\sqrt{x})^2 - (\sqrt{y})^2}$$

$$= \frac{x - 2\sqrt{xy} + y}{x - y}$$

Example 7   Simplify: $\dfrac{5}{\sqrt{5x}}$

Solution $\dfrac{5}{\sqrt{5x}} = \dfrac{5}{\sqrt{5x}} \cdot \dfrac{\sqrt{5x}}{\sqrt{5x}}$

$= \dfrac{5\sqrt{5x}}{(\sqrt{5x})^2}$

$= \dfrac{5\sqrt{5x}}{5x}$

$= \dfrac{\sqrt{5x}}{x}$

You Try It 7   Simplify: $\dfrac{y}{\sqrt{3y}}$

Your solution $\dfrac{\sqrt{3y}}{3}$

Example 8   Simplify: $\dfrac{3}{\sqrt[4]{2x}}$

Solution $\dfrac{3}{\sqrt[4]{2x}} = \dfrac{3}{\sqrt[4]{2x}} \cdot \dfrac{\sqrt[4]{2^3x^3}}{\sqrt[4]{2^3x^3}}$

$= \dfrac{3\sqrt[4]{8x^3}}{\sqrt[4]{2^4x^4}}$

$= \dfrac{3\sqrt[4]{8x^3}}{2x}$

You Try It 8   Simplify: $\dfrac{3}{\sqrt[3]{3x^2}}$

Your solution $\dfrac{\sqrt[3]{9x}}{x}$

Example 9   Simplify: $\dfrac{3}{5 - 2\sqrt{3}}$

Solution $\dfrac{3}{5 - 2\sqrt{3}} \cdot \dfrac{5 + 2\sqrt{3}}{5 + 2\sqrt{3}} = \dfrac{15 + 6\sqrt{3}}{5^2 - (2\sqrt{3})^2}$

$= \dfrac{15 + 6\sqrt{3}}{25 - 12}$

$= \dfrac{15 + 6\sqrt{3}}{13}$

You Try It 9   Simplify: $\dfrac{3 + \sqrt{6}}{2 - \sqrt{6}}$

Your solution $-\dfrac{12 + 5\sqrt{6}}{2}$

Solutions on p. S27

9.3 Complex Numbers

Objective A   *To simplify a complex number* ....

The radical expression $\sqrt{-4}$ is not a real number, because there is no real number whose square is -4. However, the solution of an algebraic equation is sometimes the square root of a negative number.

For example, the equation $x^2 + 1 = 0$ does not have a real number solution, because there is no real number whose square is a negative number.

$$x^2 + 1 = 0$$
$$x^2 = -1$$

Around the 17th century, a new number, called an **imaginary number**, was defined so that a negative number would have a square root. The letter i was chosen to represent the number whose square is -1.

$$i^2 = -1$$

An imaginary number is defined in terms of i.

> If a is a positive real number, then the principal square root of negative a is the imaginary number $i\sqrt{a}$.
> $$\sqrt{-a} = i\sqrt{a}$$

Here are some examples.

$$\sqrt{-16} = i\sqrt{16} = 4i$$
$$\sqrt{-12} = i\sqrt{12} = 2i\sqrt{3}$$
$$\sqrt{-21} = i\sqrt{21}$$
$$\sqrt{-1} = i\sqrt{1} = i$$

It is customary to write i in front of a radical to avoid confusing $\sqrt{a}\,i$ with $\sqrt{ai}$.

The real numbers and imaginary numbers make up the complex numbers.

> **Complex Number**
>
> A **complex number** is a number of the form $a + bi$, where a and b are real numbers and $i = \sqrt{-1}$. The number a is the **real part** of $a + bi$, and b is the **imaginary part**.

Examples of complex numbers are shown at the right.

Real Part	Imaginary Part
a +	bi
3 +	$2i$
8 −	$10i$

$$
\text{Complex numbers} \atop a + bi
\begin{cases}
\text{Real Numbers} \\
\quad a + 0i \\
\\
\text{Imaginary Numbers} \\
\quad 0 + bi
\end{cases}
$$

A *real number* is a complex number in which $b = 0$.

An *imaginary number* is a complex number in which $a = 0$.

➡ Simplify: $\sqrt{20} - \sqrt{-50}$

$$
\sqrt{20} - \sqrt{-50} = \sqrt{20} - i\sqrt{50}
$$

$$
= \sqrt{2^2 \cdot 5} - i\sqrt{5^2 \cdot 2}
$$

$$
= 2\sqrt{5} - 5i\sqrt{2}
$$

- Write the complex number in the form $a + bi$.
- Use the Product Property of Radicals to simplify each radical.

Example 1
Simplify: $\sqrt{-80}$

Solution
$\sqrt{-80} = i\sqrt{80} = i\sqrt{2^4 \cdot 5} = 4i\sqrt{5}$

Example 2
Simplify: $\sqrt{25} + \sqrt{-40}$

Solution
$$\sqrt{25} + \sqrt{-40} = \sqrt{25} + i\sqrt{40}$$
$$= \sqrt{5^2} + i\sqrt{2^2 \cdot 2 \cdot 5}$$
$$= 5 + 2i\sqrt{10}$$

You Try It 1
Simplify: $\sqrt{-45}$

Your solution
$3i\sqrt{5}$

You Try It 2
Simplify: $\sqrt{98} - \sqrt{-60}$

Your solution
$7\sqrt{2} - 2i\sqrt{15}$

Solutions on p. S27

Objective B   To add or subtract complex numbers...

The Addition and Subtraction of Complex Numbers

To add two complex numbers, add the real parts and add the imaginary parts. To subtract two complex numbers, subtract the real parts and subtract the imaginary parts.

$$(a + bi) + (c + di) = (a + c) + (b + d)i$$

$$(a + bi) - (c + di) = (a - c) + (b - d)i$$

➡ Subtract: $(3 - 7i) - (4 - 2i)$

$$
(3 - 7i) - (4 - 2i) = (3 - 4) + [-7 - (-2)]i
$$

$$
= -1 - 5i
$$

- Subtract the real parts and subtract the imaginary parts of the complex numbers.

⮕ Add: $(3 + \sqrt{-12}) + (7 - \sqrt{-27})$

$(3 + \sqrt{-12}) + (7 - \sqrt{-27})$

$= (3 + i\sqrt{12}) + (7 - i\sqrt{27})$ • Write each complex number in the form $a + bi$.

$= (3 + i\sqrt{2^2 \cdot 3}) + (7 - i\sqrt{3^2 \cdot 3})$ • Use the Product Property of Radicals to simplify each radical.

$= (3 + 2i\sqrt{3}) + (7 - 3i\sqrt{3})$

$= 10 - i\sqrt{3}$ • Add the complex numbers.

Example 3
Add: $(3 + 2i) + (6 - 5i)$

Solution
$(3 + 2i) + (6 - 5i) = 9 - 3i$

You Try It 3
Subtract: $(-4 + 2i) - (6 - 8i)$

Your solution
$-10 + 10i$

Example 4
Subtract: $(9 - \sqrt{-8}) - (5 + \sqrt{-32})$

Solution
$(9 - \sqrt{-8}) - (5 + \sqrt{-32})$

$= (9 - i\sqrt{8}) - (5 + i\sqrt{32})$

$= (9 - i\sqrt{2^2 \cdot 2}) - (5 + i\sqrt{2^4 \cdot 2})$

$= (9 - 2i\sqrt{2}) - (5 + 4i\sqrt{2})$

$= 4 - 6i\sqrt{2}$

You Try It 4
Subtract: $(16 - \sqrt{-45}) - (3 + \sqrt{-20})$

Your solution
$13 - 5i\sqrt{5}$

Example 5
Add: $(6 + 4i) + (-6 - 4i)$

Solution
$(6 + 4i) + (-6 - 4i) = 0 + 0i = 0$

This illustrates that the additive inverse of $a + bi$ is $-a - bi$.

You Try It 5
Add: $(3 - 2i) + (-3 + 2i)$

Your solution
0

Solutions on p. S27

Objective C   *To multiply complex numbers*..

When multiplying complex numbers, we often find that i^2 is a part of the product. Recall that $i^2 = -1$.

⮕ Multiply: $2i \cdot 3i$

$2i \cdot 3i = 6i^2$ • Multiply the imaginary numbers.

$= 6(-1)$ • Replace i^2 by -1.

$= -6$ • Simplify.

➡ Multiply: $\sqrt{-6} \cdot \sqrt{-24}$

$\sqrt{-6} \cdot \sqrt{-24} = i\sqrt{6} \cdot i\sqrt{24}$
- Write each radical as the product of a real number and i.

$= i^2\sqrt{144}$
- Multiply the imaginary numbers.

$= -\sqrt{144}$
- Replace i^2 by -1.

$= -12$
- Simplify the radical expression.

Note from the last example that it would have been incorrect to multiply the radicands of the two radical expressions. To illustrate,

$$\sqrt{-6} \cdot \sqrt{-24} = \sqrt{(-6)(-24)} = \sqrt{144} = 12, \, not \, -12$$

➡ Multiply: $4i(3 - 2i)$

$4i(3 - 2i) = 12i - 8i^2$
- Use the Distributive Property to remove parentheses.

$= 12i - 8(-1)$
- Replace i^2 by -1.

$= 8 + 12i$
- Write the answer in the form $a + bi$.

The product of two complex numbers is defined as follows.

Product of Complex Numbers

$(a + bi)(c + di) = (ac - bd) + (ad + bc)i$

One way to remember this rule is to use the FOIL method.

➡ Multiply: $(2 + 4i)(3 - 5i)$

$(2 + 4i)(3 - 5i) = 6 - 10i + 12i - 20i^2$
- Use the FOIL method to find the product.

$= 6 + 2i - 20i^2$

$= 6 + 2i - 20(-1)$
- Replace i^2 by -1.

$= 26 + 2i$
- Write the answer in the form $a + bi$.

The conjugate of $a + bi$ is $a - bi$. The product of conjugates, $(a + bi)(a - bi)$, is the real number $a^2 + b^2$.

$$(a + bi)(a - bi) = a^2 - b^2i^2$$
$$= a^2 - b^2(-1)$$
$$= a^2 + b^2$$

➡ Multiply: $(2 + 3i)(2 - 3i)$

$(2 + 3i)(2 - 3i) = 2^2 + 3^2$
- The product of conjugates is $a^2 + b^2$.

$= 4 + 9$

$= 13$

Note that the product of a complex number and its conjugate is a real number.

Example 6
Multiply: $(2i)(-5i)$

Solution
$(2i)(-5i) = -10i^2 = (-10)(-1) = 10$

You Try It 6
Multiply: $(-3i)(-10i)$

Your solution
-30

Example 7
Multiply: $\sqrt{-10} \cdot \sqrt{-5}$

Solution
$\sqrt{-10} \cdot \sqrt{-5} = i\sqrt{10} \cdot i\sqrt{5}$
$= i^2\sqrt{50} = -\sqrt{5^2 \cdot 2} = -5\sqrt{2}$

You Try It 7
Multiply: $-\sqrt{-8} \cdot \sqrt{-5}$

Your solution
$2\sqrt{10}$

Example 8
Multiply: $3i(2 - 4i)$

Solution:
$3i(2 - 4i) = 6i - 12i^2 = 6i - 12(-1)$
$= 12 + 6i$

You Try It 8
Multiply: $-6i(3 + 4i)$

Your solution
$24 - 18i$

Example 9
Multiply: $\sqrt{-8}(\sqrt{6} - \sqrt{-2})$

Solution
$\sqrt{-8}(\sqrt{6} - \sqrt{-2}) = i\sqrt{8}(\sqrt{6} - i\sqrt{2})$
$= i\sqrt{48} - i^2\sqrt{16}$
$= i\sqrt{2^4 \cdot 3} - (-1)\sqrt{2^4}$
$= 4i\sqrt{3} + 4 = 4 + 4i\sqrt{3}$

You Try It 9
Multiply: $\sqrt{-3}(\sqrt{27} - \sqrt{-6})$

Your solution
$3\sqrt{2} + 9i$

Example 10
Multiply: $(3 - 4i)(2 + 5i)$

Solution
$(3 - 4i)(2 + 5i) = 6 + 15i - 8i - 20i^2$
$= 6 + 7i - 20i^2$
$= 6 + 7i - 20(-1) = 26 + 7i$

You Try It 10
Multiply: $(4 - 3i)(2 - i)$

Your solution
$5 - 10i$

Example 11
Multiply: $(4 + 5i)(4 - 5i)$

Solution
$(4 + 5i)(4 - 5i) = 4^2 + 5^2 = 16 + 25 = 41$

You Try It 11
Multiply: $(3 + 6i)(3 - 6i)$

Your solution
45

Example 12
Multiply: $\left(\dfrac{9}{10} + \dfrac{3}{10}i\right)\left(1 - \dfrac{1}{3}i\right)$

Solution
$\left(\dfrac{9}{10} + \dfrac{3}{10}i\right)\left(1 - \dfrac{1}{3}i\right) = \dfrac{9}{10} - \dfrac{3}{10}i + \dfrac{3}{10}i - \dfrac{1}{10}i^2$
$= \dfrac{9}{10} - \dfrac{1}{10}i^2 = \dfrac{9}{10} - \dfrac{1}{10}(-1)$
$= \dfrac{9}{10} + \dfrac{1}{10} = 1$

You Try It 12
Multiply: $(3 - i)\left(\dfrac{3}{10} + \dfrac{1}{10}i\right)$

Your solution
1

Solutions on p. S27

Objective D **To divide complex numbers** ....

A rational expression containing one or more complex numbers is in simplest form when no imaginary number remains in the denominator.

➡ Simplify: $\dfrac{2 - 3i}{2i}$

$$\dfrac{2 - 3i}{2i} = \dfrac{2 - 3i}{2i} \cdot \dfrac{i}{i}$$

• Multiply the expression by $\dfrac{i}{i}$.

$$= \dfrac{2i - 3i^2}{2i^2}$$

$$= \dfrac{2i - 3(-1)}{2(-1)}$$

• Replace i^2 by -1.

$$= \dfrac{3 + 2i}{-2}$$

• Simplify.

$$= -\dfrac{3}{2} - i$$

• Write the answer in the form $a + bi$.

INSTRUCTOR NOTE

Students think that division of complex numbers is somehow different from division of other numbers. Show them that just as

$\dfrac{12}{4} = 3$ because $4 \cdot 3 = 12$,

$\dfrac{3 + 2i}{1 + i} = \dfrac{5}{2} - \dfrac{1}{2}i$ because

$(1 + i)\left(\dfrac{5}{2} - \dfrac{1}{2}i\right) = 3 + 2i.$

➡ Simplify: $\dfrac{3 + 2i}{1 + i}$

$$\dfrac{3 + 2i}{1 + i} = \dfrac{3 + 2i}{1 + i} \cdot \dfrac{1 - i}{1 - i}$$

• Multiply the numerator and denominator by the conjugate of $1 + i$.

$$= \dfrac{3 - 3i + 2i - 2i^2}{1^2 + 1^2}$$

• In $1 + i$, $a = 1$ and $b = 1$.
  $a^2 + b^2 = 1^2 + 1^2$.

$$= \dfrac{3 - i - 2(-1)}{2}$$

• Replace i^2 by -1 and simplify.

$$= \dfrac{5 - i}{2} = \dfrac{5}{2} - \dfrac{1}{2}i$$

• Write the answer in the form $a + bi$.

Example 13

Simplify: $\dfrac{5 + 4i}{3i}$

Solution

$$\dfrac{5 + 4i}{3i} = \dfrac{5 + 4i}{3i} \cdot \dfrac{i}{i} = \dfrac{5i + 4i^2}{3i^2}$$

$$= \dfrac{5i + 4(-1)}{3(-1)} = \dfrac{-4 + 5i}{-3} = \dfrac{4}{3} - \dfrac{5}{3}i$$

You Try It 13

Simplify: $\dfrac{2 - 3i}{4i}$

Your solution

$-\dfrac{3}{4} - \dfrac{1}{2}i$

Example 14

Simplify: $\dfrac{5 - 3i}{4 + 2i}$

Solution

$$\dfrac{5 - 3i}{4 + 2i} = \dfrac{5 - 3i}{4 + 2i} \cdot \dfrac{4 - 2i}{4 - 2i}$$

$$= \dfrac{20 - 10i - 12i + 6i^2}{4^2 + 2^2}$$

$$= \dfrac{20 - 22i + 6(-1)}{20}$$

$$= \dfrac{14 - 22i}{20} = \dfrac{14}{20} - \dfrac{22}{20}i = \dfrac{7}{10} - \dfrac{11}{10}i$$

You Try It 14

Simplify: $\dfrac{2 + 5i}{3 - 2i}$

Your solution

$-\dfrac{4}{13} + \dfrac{19}{13}i$

Solutions on p. S28

9.3 Exercises

. . . .

Objective A

Simplify.

1. $\sqrt{-4}$
$2i$

2. $\sqrt{-64}$
$8i$

3. $\sqrt{-98}$
$7i\sqrt{2}$

4. $\sqrt{-72}$
$6i\sqrt{2}$

5. $\sqrt{-27}$
$3i\sqrt{3}$

6. $\sqrt{-75}$
$5i\sqrt{3}$

7. $\sqrt{16} + \sqrt{-4}$
$4 + 2i$

8. $\sqrt{25} + \sqrt{-9}$
$5 + 3i$

9. $\sqrt{12} - \sqrt{-18}$
$2\sqrt{3} - 3i\sqrt{2}$

10. $\sqrt{60} - \sqrt{-48}$
$2\sqrt{15} - 4i\sqrt{3}$

11. $\sqrt{160} - \sqrt{-147}$
$4\sqrt{10} - 7i\sqrt{3}$

12. $\sqrt{96} - \sqrt{-125}$
$4\sqrt{6} - 5i\sqrt{5}$

Objective B

Add or subtract.

13. $(2 + 4i) + (6 - 5i)$
$8 - i$

14. $(6 - 9i) + (4 + 2i)$
$10 - 7i$

15. $(-2 - 4i) - (6 - 8i)$
$-8 + 4i$

16. $(3 - 5i) + (8 - 2i)$
$11 - 7i$

17. $(8 - \sqrt{-4}) - (2 + \sqrt{-16})$
$6 - 6i$

18. $(5 - \sqrt{-25}) - (11 - \sqrt{-36})$
$-6 + i$

19. $(12 - \sqrt{-50}) + (7 - \sqrt{-8})$
$19 - 7i\sqrt{2}$

20. $(5 - \sqrt{-12}) - (9 + \sqrt{-108})$
$-4 - 8i\sqrt{3}$

21. $(\sqrt{8} + \sqrt{-18}) + (\sqrt{32} - \sqrt{-72})$
$6\sqrt{2} - 3i\sqrt{2}$

22. $(\sqrt{40} - \sqrt{-98}) - (\sqrt{90} + \sqrt{-32})$
$-\sqrt{10} - 11i\sqrt{2}$

Objective C

Multiply.

23. $(7i)(-9i)$
63

24. $(-6i)(-4i)$
-24

25. $\sqrt{-2}\sqrt{-8}$
-4

26. $\sqrt{-5}\sqrt{-45}$
-15

27. $\sqrt{-3}\sqrt{-6}$
$-3\sqrt{2}$

28. $\sqrt{-5}\sqrt{-10}$
$-5\sqrt{2}$

29. $2i(6 + 2i)$

$-4 + 12i$

30. $-3i(4 - 5i)$

$-15 - 12i$

31. $\sqrt{-2}(\sqrt{8} + \sqrt{-2})$

$-2 + 4i$

32. $\sqrt{-3}(\sqrt{12} - \sqrt{-6})$

$3\sqrt{2} + 6i$

33. $(5 - 2i)(3 + i)$

$17 - i$

34. $(2 - 4i)(2 - i)$

$-10i$

35. $(6 + 5i)(3 + 2i)$

$8 + 27i$

36. $(4 - 7i)(2 + 3i)$

$29 - 2i$

37. $(1 - i)\left(\dfrac{1}{2} + \dfrac{1}{2}i\right)$

1

38. $\left(\dfrac{4}{5} - \dfrac{2}{5}i\right)\left(1 + \dfrac{1}{2}i\right)$

1

39. $\left(\dfrac{6}{5} + \dfrac{3}{5}i\right)\left(\dfrac{2}{3} - \dfrac{1}{3}i\right)$

1

40. $(2 - i)\left(\dfrac{2}{5} + \dfrac{1}{5}i\right)$

1

Objective D

Simplify.

41. $\dfrac{3}{i}$

$-3i$

42. $\dfrac{4}{5i}$

$-\dfrac{4}{5}i$

43. $\dfrac{2 - 3i}{-4i}$

$\dfrac{3}{4} + \dfrac{1}{2}i$

44. $\dfrac{16 + 5i}{-3i}$

$-\dfrac{5}{3} + \dfrac{16}{3}i$

45. $\dfrac{4}{5 + i}$

$\dfrac{10}{13} - \dfrac{2}{13}i$

46. $\dfrac{6}{5 + 2i}$

$\dfrac{30}{29} - \dfrac{12}{29}i$

47. $\dfrac{2}{2 - i}$

$\dfrac{4}{5} + \dfrac{2}{5}i$

48. $\dfrac{5}{4 - i}$

$\dfrac{20}{17} + \dfrac{5}{17}i$

49. $\dfrac{1 - 3i}{3 + i}$

$-i$

50. $\dfrac{2 + 12i}{5 + i}$

$\dfrac{11}{13} + \dfrac{29}{13}i$

51. $\dfrac{\sqrt{-10}}{\sqrt{8} - \sqrt{-2}}$

$-\dfrac{\sqrt{5}}{5} + \dfrac{2\sqrt{5}}{5}i$

52. $\dfrac{\sqrt{-2}}{\sqrt{12} - \sqrt{-8}}$

$-\dfrac{1}{5} + \dfrac{\sqrt{6}}{10}i$

53. $\dfrac{2 - 3i}{3 + i}$

$\dfrac{3}{10} - \dfrac{11}{10}i$

54. $\dfrac{3 + 5i}{1 - i}$

$-1 + 4i$

55. $\dfrac{5 + 3i}{3 - i}$

$\dfrac{6}{5} + \dfrac{7}{5}i$

56. $\dfrac{3 - 2i}{2i + 3}$

$\dfrac{5}{13} - \dfrac{12}{13}i$

APPLYING THE CONCEPTS

57. The property that the product of conjugates of the form $(a + bi)(a - bi) = a^2 + b^2$ can be used to factor the sum of two perfect squares over the set of complex numbers. For instance, $x^2 + 4 = (x + 2i)(x - 2i)$. Factor the following expressions over the set of complex numbers.

  a. $y^2 + 1$

    $(y + i)(y - i)$

  b. $49x^2 + 16$

    $(7x + 4i)(7x - 4i)$

  c. $9a^2 + 64$

    $(3a + 8i)(3a - 8i)$

58. **a.** Is $3i$ a solution of $2x^2 + 18 = 0$? yes

    b. Is $3 + i$ a solution of $x^2 - 6x + 10 = 0$? yes

59. Given $\sqrt{i} = \dfrac{\sqrt{2}}{2} + \dfrac{\sqrt{2}}{2}i$, find $\sqrt{-i}$. $-\dfrac{\sqrt{2}}{2} + \dfrac{\sqrt{2}}{2}i$

60. Evaluate i^n for $n = 0, 1, 2, 3, 4, 5, 6$, and 7. Make a conjecture for the value of i^n for any natural number. Using your conjecture, evaluate i^{76}. $i^{76} = 1$

9.4 Solving Equations Containing Radical Expressions

Objective A   *To solve a radical equation* ....

An equation that contains a variable expression in a radicand is a **radical equation**.

$$\sqrt[3]{2x - 5} + x = 7$$
$$\sqrt{x + 1} - \sqrt{x} = 4$$ } Radical Equations

The following property is used to solve a radical equation.

The Property of Raising Each Side of an Equation to a Power

If two numbers are equal, then the same powers of the numbers are equal.

If $a = b$, then $a^n = b^n$.

➡ Solve: $\sqrt{x - 2} - 6 = 0$

$$\sqrt{x - 2} - 6 = 0$$

$$\sqrt{x - 2} = 6$$ • Isolate the radical by adding 6 to each side of the equation.

$$(\sqrt{x - 2})^2 = 6^2$$ • Square each side of the equation.

$$x - 2 = 36$$ • Simplify and solve for *x*.

$$x = 38$$

Check: $$\frac{\sqrt{x - 2} - 6 = 0}{\sqrt{38 - 2} - 6 \;\big|\; 0}$$
$$\sqrt{36} - 6 \;\big|\; 0$$
$$6 - 6 \;\big|\; 0$$
$$0 = 0$$

38 checks as a solution. The solution is 38.

➡ Solve: $\sqrt[3]{x + 2} = -3$

$$\sqrt[3]{x + 2} = -3$$

$$(\sqrt[3]{x + 2})^3 = (-3)^3$$ • Cube each side of the equation.

$$x + 2 = -27$$ • Solve the resulting equation.

$$x = -29$$

Check: $$\frac{\sqrt[3]{x + 2} = -3}{\sqrt[3]{-29 + 2} \;\big|\; -3}$$
$$\sqrt[3]{-27} \;\big|\; -3$$
$$-3 = -3$$

−29 checks as a solution. The solution is −29.

Raising each side of an equation to an even power may result in an equation that has a solution that is not a solution of the original equation. This is called an **extraneous solution**. Here is an example:

➡ Solve: $\sqrt{2x - 1} + \sqrt{x} = 2$

$$\sqrt{2x - 1} + \sqrt{x} = 2$$
$$\sqrt{2x - 1} = 2 - \sqrt{x}$$ • Solve for one of the radical expressions.
$$(\sqrt{2x - 1})^2 = (2 - \sqrt{x})^2$$ • Square each side. Recall that $(a - b)^2 = a^2 - 2ab + b^2$.
$$2x - 1 = 4 - 4\sqrt{x} + x$$
$$x - 5 = -4\sqrt{x}$$
$$(x - 5)^2 = (-4\sqrt{x})^2$$ • Square each side.
$$x^2 - 10x + 25 = 16x$$
$$x^2 - 26x + 25 = 0$$ • Solve the quadratic equation by factoring.
$$(x - 25)(x - 1) = 0$$
$$x = 25 \quad \text{or} \quad x = 1$$

TAKE NOTE

Note that
$(2 - \sqrt{x})^2 =$
$(2 - \sqrt{x})(2 - \sqrt{x})$
$= 4 - 4\sqrt{x} + x$

TAKE NOTE

You must check the proposed solutions to radical equations. The proposed solutions of the equation on the right were 1 and 25. However, 25 did not check as a solution. Here 25 is an extraneous solution.

Check:

$$\frac{\sqrt{2x - 1} + \sqrt{x} = 2}{\sqrt{2(25) - 1} + \sqrt{25} \ \Big| \ 2}$$
$$7 + 5 \ \Big| \ 2$$
$$12 \neq 2$$

$$\frac{\sqrt{2x - 1} + \sqrt{x} = 2}{\sqrt{2(1) - 1} + \sqrt{1} \ \Big| \ 2}$$
$$1 + 1 \ \Big| \ 2$$
$$2 = 2$$

25 does not check as a solution. 1 checks as a solution. The solution is 1.

Example 1
Solve: $\sqrt[3]{3x - 1} = -4$

Solution
$$\sqrt[3]{3x - 1} = -4$$
$$(\sqrt[3]{3x - 1})^3 = (-4)^3$$
$$3x - 1 = -64$$
$$3x = -63$$
$$x = -21$$

Check:
$$\frac{\sqrt[3]{3x - 1} = -4}{\sqrt[3]{3(-21) - 1} \ \Big| \ -4}$$
$$\sqrt[3]{-64} \ \Big| \ -4$$
$$-4 = -4$$

The solution is -21.

You Try It 1
Solve: $\sqrt[4]{x - 8} = 3$

Your solution
89

Example 2
Solve: $\sqrt{x - 1} + \sqrt{x + 4} = 5$

Solution
$$\sqrt{x - 1} + \sqrt{x + 4} = 5$$
$$\sqrt{x + 4} = 5 - \sqrt{x - 1}$$
$$(\sqrt{x + 4})^2 = (5 - \sqrt{x - 1})^2$$
$$x + 4 = 25 - 10\sqrt{x - 1} + x - 1$$
$$2 = \sqrt{x - 1}$$
$$2^2 = (\sqrt{x - 1})^2$$
$$4 = x - 1$$
$$5 = x$$

5 checks as a solution. The solution is 5.

You Try It 2
Solve: $\sqrt{x} - \sqrt{x + 5} = 1$

Your solution
no solution

Solutions on p. S28

Objective B **To solve application problems**.....................................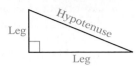

A right triangle contains one 90° angle. The side opposite the 90° angle is called the **hypotenuse**. The other two sides are called **legs**.

Pythagoras, a Greek mathematician, discovered that the square of the hypotenuse of a right triangle is equal to the sum of the squares of the two legs. This is called the **Pythagorean Theorem**.

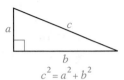

$$c^2 = a^2 + b^2$$

Example 3
A ladder 20 ft long is leaning against a building. How high on the building will the ladder reach when the bottom of the ladder is 8 ft from the building? Round to the nearest tenth.

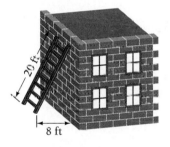

Strategy
To find the distance, use the Pythagorean Theorem. The hypotenuse is the length of thc ladder. One leg is the distance from the bottom of the ladder to the base of the building. The distance along the building from the ground to the top of the ladder is the unknown leg.

Solution
$$c^2 = a^2 + b^2$$
$$20^2 = 8^2 + b^2$$
$$400 = 64 + b^2$$
$$336 = b^2$$
$$(336)^{1/2} = (b^2)^{1/2}$$
$$\sqrt{336} = b$$
$$18.3 \approx b$$

The distance is 18.3 ft.

You Try It 3
Find the diagonal of a rectangle that is 6 cm long and 3 cm wide. Round to the nearest tenth.

Your strategy

Your solution
6.7 cm

Solution on p. S28

Example 4

An object is dropped from a high building. Find the distance the object has fallen when the speed reaches 96 ft/s. Use the equation $v = \sqrt{64d}$, where v is the speed of the object and d is the distance.

Strategy

To find the distance the object has fallen, replace v in the equation with the given value and solve for d.

Solution

$$v = \sqrt{64d}$$
$$96 = \sqrt{64d}$$
$$(96)^2 = (\sqrt{64d})^2$$
$$9216 = 64d$$
$$144 = d$$

The object has fallen 144 ft.

Example 5

Find the length of a pendulum that makes one swing in 1.5 s. The equation for the time of one swing is given by $T = 2\pi\sqrt{\dfrac{L}{32}}$, where T is the time in seconds and L is the length in feet. Round to the nearest hundredth.

Strategy

To find the length of the pendulum, replace T in the equation with the given value and solve for L.

Solution

$$T = 2\pi\sqrt{\frac{L}{32}}$$

$$1.5 = 2\pi\sqrt{\frac{L}{32}}$$

$$\frac{1.5}{2\pi} = \sqrt{\frac{L}{32}} \qquad \bullet \text{ Divide each side by } 2\pi.$$

$$\left(\frac{1.5}{2\pi}\right)^2 = \frac{L}{32} \qquad \bullet \text{ Square each side.}$$

$$32\left(\frac{1.5}{2\pi}\right)^2 = L \qquad \bullet \text{ Multiply each side by 32.}$$

$$1.82 \approx L \qquad \bullet \text{ Use the } \pi \text{ key on your} \\ \text{calculator.}$$

The length of the pendulum is 1.82 ft.

You Try It 4

How far would a submarine periscope have to be above the water for the lookout to locate a ship 5.5 mi away? The equation for the distance in miles that the lookout can see is $d = \sqrt{1.5h}$, where h is the height in feet above the surface of the water. Round to the nearest hundredth.

Your strategy

Your solution
20.17 ft

You Try It 5

Find the distance required for a car to reach a velocity of 88 ft/s when the acceleration is 22 ft/s². Use the equation $v = \sqrt{2as}$, where v is the velocity, a is the acceleration, and s is the distance.

Your strategy

Your solution
176 ft

Solutions on p. S28

9.4 Exercises

. . . .

Objective A

Solve.

1. $\sqrt{x} = 5$
25

2. $\sqrt{y} = 2$
4

3. $\sqrt[3]{a} = 3$
27

4. $\sqrt[3]{y} = 5$
125

5. $\sqrt{3x} = 12$
48

6. $\sqrt{5x} = 10$
20

7. $\sqrt[3]{4x} = -2$
-2

8. $\sqrt[3]{6x} = -3$
$-\dfrac{9}{2}$

9. $\sqrt{2x} = -4$
no solution

10. $\sqrt{5x} = -5$
no solution

11. $\sqrt{3x - 2} = 5$
9

12. $\sqrt{5x - 4} = 9$
17

13. $\sqrt{3 - 2x} = 7$
-23

14. $\sqrt{9 - 4x} = 4$
$-\dfrac{7}{4}$

15. $7 = \sqrt{1 - 3x}$
-16

16. $6 = \sqrt{8 - 7x}$
-4

17. $\sqrt[3]{4x - 1} = 2$
$\dfrac{9}{4}$

18. $\sqrt[3]{5x + 2} = 3$
5

19. $\sqrt[3]{1 - 2x} = -3$
14

20. $\sqrt[3]{3 - 2x} = -2$
$\dfrac{11}{2}$

21. $\sqrt[3]{9x + 1} = 4$
7

22. $\sqrt{3x + 9} - 12 = 0$
45

23. $\sqrt{4x - 3} - 5 = 0$
7

24. $\sqrt{x - 2} = 4$
18

25. $\sqrt[3]{x - 3} + 5 = 0$
-122

26. $\sqrt[3]{x - 2} = 3$
29

27. $\sqrt[3]{2x - 6} = 4$
35

28. $\sqrt{x^2 - 8x} = 3$
$-1, 9$

29. $\sqrt{x^2 + 7x + 11} = 1$
$-5, -2$

30. $\sqrt[4]{4x + 1} = 2$
$\dfrac{15}{4}$

31. $\sqrt[4]{2x - 9} = 3$
45

32. $\sqrt{2x - 3} - 2 = 1$
6

33. $\sqrt{3x - 5} - 5 = 3$
23

34. $\sqrt[3]{2x - 3} + 5 = 2$
−12

35. $\sqrt[3]{x - 4} + 7 = 5$
−4

36. $\sqrt{5x - 16} + 1 = 4$
5

37. $\sqrt{3x - 5} - 2 = 3$
10

38. $\sqrt{2x - 1} - 8 = -5$
5

39. $\sqrt{7x + 2} - 10 = -7$
1

40. $\sqrt[3]{4x - 3} - 2 = 3$
32

41. $\sqrt[3]{1 - 3x} + 5 = 3$
3

42. $1 - \sqrt{4x + 3} = -5$
$\dfrac{33}{4}$

43. $7 - \sqrt{3x + 1} = -1$
21

44. $\sqrt{x + 1} = 2 - \sqrt{x}$
$\dfrac{9}{16}$

45. $\sqrt{2x + 4} = 3 - \sqrt{2x}$
$\dfrac{25}{72}$

46. $\sqrt{x^2 + 3x - 2} - x = 1$
3

47. $\sqrt{x^2 - 4x - 1} + 3 = x$
5

48. $\sqrt{x^2 - 3x - 1} = 3$
5, −2

49. $\sqrt{x^2 - 2x + 1} = 3$
4, −2

50. $\sqrt{2x + 5} - \sqrt{3x - 2} = 1$
2

51. $\sqrt{4x + 1} - \sqrt{2x + 4} = 1$
6

52. $\sqrt{5x - 1} - \sqrt{3x - 2} = 1$
2, 1

53. $\sqrt{5x + 4} - \sqrt{3x + 1} = 1$
0, 1

54. $\sqrt[3]{x^2 + 2} - 3 = 0$
5, −5

55. $\sqrt[3]{x^2 + 4} - 2 = 0$
−2, 2

56. $\sqrt[4]{x^2 + 2x + 8} - 2 = 0$
−4, 2

57. $\sqrt[4]{x^2 + x - 1} - 1 = 0$
−2, 1

58. $4\sqrt{x + 1} - x = 1$
15, −1

59. $3\sqrt{x - 2} + 2 = x$
2, 11

60. $x + 3\sqrt{x - 2} = 12$
6

Objective B   *Application Problems*

61. Find the width of a rectangle that has a diagonal of 10 ft and a length of 8 ft.
6 ft

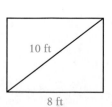
10 ft

8 ft

62. Find the length of a rectangle that has a diagonal of 15 m and a width of 9 m.
12 m

63. A 26-foot ladder is leaning against a building. How far is the bottom of the ladder from the building when the ladder reaches a height of 24 ft on the building?
10 ft

64. A 16-foot ladder is leaning against a building. How high on the building will the ladder reach when the bottom of the ladder is 5 ft from the building? Round to the nearest tenth.
15.2 ft

16 ft

5 ft

65. An object is dropped from an airplane. Find the distance the object has fallen when the speed reaches 400 ft/s. Use the equation $v = \sqrt{64d}$, where v is the speed of the object and d is the distance.
2500 ft

66. An object is dropped from a bridge. Find the distance the object has fallen when the speed reaches 100 ft/s. Use the equation $v = \sqrt{64d}$, where v is the speed of the object and d is the distance.
156.25 ft

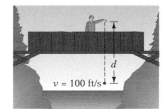

d

$v = 100$ ft/s

67. How far would a submarine periscope have to be above the water for the lookout to locate a ship 3.6 mi away? The equation for the distance in miles that the lookout can see is $d = \sqrt{1.5h}$, where h is the height in feet above the surface of the water.
8.64 ft

68. How far would a submarine periscope have to be above the water for the lookout to locate a ship 4.2 mi away? The equation for the distance in miles that the lookout can see is $d = \sqrt{1.5h}$, where h is the height in feet above the surface of the water.
11.76 ft

69. Find the length of a pendulum on a clock that makes one swing in 2.4 s. The equation for the time of one swing of a pendulum is given by $T = 2\pi\sqrt{\dfrac{L}{32}}$, where T is the time in seconds and L is the length in feet. Round to the nearest hundredth.
4.67 ft

70. Find the length of a pendulum that makes one swing in 3 s. The equation for the time of one swing of a pendulum is given by $T = 2\pi\sqrt{\dfrac{L}{32}}$, where T is the time in seconds and L is the length in feet. Round to the nearest hundredth.
7.30 ft

L

3 s

71. Find the distance required for a car to reach a velocity of 60 m/s when the acceleration is 10 m/s^2. Use the equation $v = \sqrt{2as}$, where v is the velocity, a is the acceleration, and s is the distance.
180 m

72. The time it takes for an object to fall a certain distance is given by the equation $t = \sqrt{\dfrac{2d}{g}}$, where t is the time in seconds, d is the distance in feet, and g is the acceleration due to gravity. The acceleration due to gravity on Earth is 32 feet per second. If an object is dropped from the top of a tall building, how far will it fall in 6 s?
576 ft

73. High definition television (HDTV) gives consumers a wider viewing area, more like a film seen in a theater. A regular television with a 27-inch diagonal measurement has a screen 16.2 in. tall. An HDTV screen with the same 16.2-inch height would have a diagonal measuring 33 in. How many inches wider is the HDTV screen? Round to the nearest hundredth.
7.15 in.

74. At what height above Earth's surface would a satellite be in orbit if it is traveling at a speed of 7500 m/s? Use the equation $v = \sqrt{\dfrac{4 \times 10^{14}}{h + 6.4 \times 10^6}}$, where v is the speed of the satellite in meters and h is the height above Earth's surface in meters. Round to the nearest thousand.
711,000 m

APPLYING THE CONCEPTS

75. Solve the following equations. Describe the solution by using the following terms: integer, rational number, irrational number, real number, and imaginary number. Note that more than one term may be used to describe the answer.

a. $x^2 + 3 = 7$
2, −2; integer, rational number, real number

b. $x^2 + 1 = 0$
$i, -i$; imaginary

c. $x^{3/4} = 8$
16; integer, rational number, real number

76. Solve: $\sqrt{3x - 2} = \sqrt{2x - 3} + \sqrt{x - 1}$
2

77. Solve $a^2 + b^2 = c^2$ for a.
$a = \sqrt{c^2 - b^2}$ or $a = -\sqrt{c^2 - b^2}$

78. Solve $V = \dfrac{4}{3}\pi r^3$ for r.
$r = \sqrt[3]{\dfrac{3V}{4\pi}}$

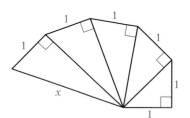

79. Find the length of the side labeled x.
$x = \sqrt{6}$

Focus on Problem Solving

Another Look at Polya's Four-Step Process

Polya's four general steps to follow when attempting to solve a problem are to understand the problem, devise a plan, carry out the plan, and review the solution. (See the Focus on Problem Solving in the chapter entitled "Factoring.") In the process of devising a plan (Step 2), it may be appropriate to write a mathematical expression or an equation. We will illustrate this with the following problem.

Number the letters of the alphabet in sequence from 1 to 26. (See the list at the left.) Find a word for which the product of the numerical values of the letters of the word equals 1,000,000. We will agree that a "word" is any sequence of letters that contains at least one vowel; it need not be in the dictionary.

A = 1
B = 2
C = 3
D = 4
E = 5
F = 6
G = 7
H = 8
I = 9
J = 10
K = 11
L = 12
M = 13
N = 14
O = 15
P = 16
Q = 17
R = 18
S = 19
T = 20
U = 21
V = 22
W = 23
X = 24
Y = 25
Z = 26

Understand the Problem

Consider REZB. The product of the letters is $18 \cdot 5 \cdot 26 \cdot 2 = 4680$. This "word" is a sequence of letters with at least one vowel. However, the product of the numerical values of the letters is not 1,000,000. Thus this word does not solve our problem.

Devise a Plan

Actually, we should have known that the product of the letters in REZB could not equal 1,000,000. The letter R has a factor of 9, and the letter Z has a factor of 13. Neither of these two numbers is a factor of 1,000,000. Consequently, R and Z cannot be letters in the word we are trying to find. This observation leads to an important observation: Each of the letters that make up our word must be a factor of 1,000,000. To find these letters, consider the prime factorization of 1,000,000.

$$1,000,000 = 2^6 \cdot 5^6$$

Looking at the prime factorization, we note that only letters that contain 2 or 5 as factors are possible candidates. These letters are B, D, E, H, J, P, T, and Y. One additional point: Because 1 times any number is the number, the letter A can be part of any word we construct.

Our task is now to construct a word from these letters such that the product is 1,000,000. From the prime factorization above, we must have 2 as a factor six times and 5 as a factor six times.

Carry Out the Plan

We must construct a word with the characteristics described in our plan. Here is a possibility:

THEBEYE

Review the Solution

You should multiply the values of all the letters and verify that the product is 1,000,000. To ensure that you have an understanding of the problem, try to find other "words" that satisfy the conditions of the problem.

Projects and Group Activities

Distance to the Horizon   In Section 9.4, we used the formula $d = \sqrt{1.5h}$ to calculate the approximate distance d (in miles) that a person using a periscope h feet above the water could see. That formula is derived by using the Pythagorean Theorem.

Consider the diagram (not to scale) at the right, which shows Earth as a sphere and the periscope extending h feet above the surface. From geometry, because AB is tangent to the circle and OA is a radius, triangle AOB is a right triangle. Therefore,

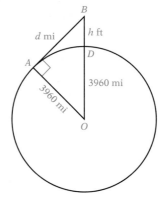

$$(OA)^2 + (AB)^2 = (OB)^2$$

Substituting into this formula, we have

$$3960^2 + d^2 = \left(3960 + \frac{h}{5280}\right)^2$$

• Because h is in feet, $\dfrac{h}{5280}$ is in miles.

$$3960^2 + d^2 = 3960^2 + \frac{2 \cdot 3960}{5280}h + \left(\frac{h}{5280}\right)^2$$

$$d^2 = \frac{3}{2}h + \left(\frac{h}{5280}\right)^2$$

$$d = \sqrt{\frac{3}{2}h + \left(\frac{h}{5280}\right)^2}$$

At this point, an assumption is made that $\sqrt{\frac{3}{2}h + \left(\frac{h}{5280}\right)^2} \approx \sqrt{1.5h}$, where we have written $\frac{3}{2}$ as 1.5. Thus $d \approx \sqrt{1.5h}$ is used to approximate the distance that can be seen using a periscope h feet above the water.

1. Write a paragraph that justifies the assumption that

$$\sqrt{\frac{3}{2}h + \left(\frac{h}{5280}\right)^2} \approx \sqrt{1.5h}$$

   (*Suggestion:* Evaluate each expression for various values of h. Because h is the height of a periscope above the water, it is unlikely that $h > 25$ ft.)

2. The distance d is the distance from the top of the periscope to A. The distance along the surface of the water is given by arc AD. This distance, D, can be approximated by the equation

$$D \approx \sqrt{1.5h} + 0.306186\left(\sqrt{\frac{h}{5280}}\right)^3$$

   Using this formula, calculate D when $h = 10$.

Pythagorean Triples   The Pythagorean Theorem states that if a and b are the legs of a right triangle and c is the length of the hypotenuse, then $a^2 + b^2 = c^2$.

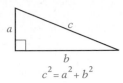

For instance, the triangle with legs 3 and 4 and hypotenuse 5 is a right triangle because $3^2 + 4^2 = 5^2$. The numbers 3, 4, and 5 are called a **Pythagorean triple** because they are natural numbers that satisfy the equation of the Pythagorean Theorem.

1. Determine if the numbers are a Pythagorean triple.
   a. 5, 7, and 9   **b.** 8, 15, and 17
   c. 11, 60, and 61   **d.** 28, 45, and 53

Mathematicians have investigated Pythagorean triples and have found formulas that will generate these triples. One such formula is

$$a = m^2 - n^2 \qquad b = 2mn \qquad c = m^2 + n^2, \text{ where } m > n$$

For instance, let $m = 2$ and $n = 1$. Then $a = 2^2 - 1^2 = 3$, $b = 2(2)(1) = 4$, and $c = 2^2 + 1^2 = 5$. This is the Pythagorean triple given above.

2. Find the Pythagorean triple produced by each of the following.
   a. $m = 3$ and $n = 1$ **b.** $m = 5$ and $n = 2$
   c. $m = 4$ and $n = 2$ **d.** $m = 6$ and $n = 1$

3. Find values of m and n that yield the Pythagorean triple 11, 60, 61.

4. Verify that $a^2 + b^2 = c^2$ when $a = m^2 - n^2$, $b = 2mn$, and $c = m^2 + n^2$.

5. The early Greek builders used a rope with 12 equally spaced knots to make right-angle corners for buildings. Explain how they used the rope.

6. Find three odd integers, a, b, c, such that $a^2 + b^2 = c^2$.

Chapter Summary

Key Words   The *nth root of* a is $a^{1/n}$. The expression $\sqrt[n]{a}$ is another symbol for the *n*th root of a. In the expression $\sqrt[n]{a}$, the symbol $\sqrt{}$ is called a *radical sign*, n is the *index*, and a is the *radicand*.

If $a^{1/n}$ is a real number, then $a^{m/n} = \sqrt[n]{a^m} = (\sqrt[n]{a})^m$.

The symbol $\sqrt{}$ is used to indicate the positive or *principal square root* of a number.

The expressions $a + b$ and $a - b$ are called *conjugates* of each other. The product of conjugates of the form $(a + b)(a - b)$ is $a^2 - b^2$.

The procedure used to remove a radical from the denominator of a radical expression is called *rationalizing the denominator*.

A *complex number* is a number of the form $a + bi$, where a and b are real numbers and $i = \sqrt{-1}$. For the complex number $a + bi$, a is the *real part* of the complex number, and b is the *imaginary part* of the complex number.

A *radical equation* is an equation that contains a variable expression in a radicand.

Essential Rules   ***The Product Property of Radicals***

If a and b are positive real numbers, then $\sqrt[n]{ab} = \sqrt[n]{a}\sqrt[n]{b}$.

The Quotient Property of Radicals

If a and b are positive real numbers, then $\sqrt[n]{\dfrac{a}{b}} = \dfrac{\sqrt[n]{a}}{\sqrt[n]{b}}$.

Addition of Complex Numbers

If $a + bi$ and $c + di$ are complex numbers, then
$(a + bi) + (c + di) = (a + c) + (b + d)i$.

Subtraction of Complex Numbers

If $a + bi$ and $c + di$ arc complex numbers, then
$(a + bi) - (c + di) = (a - c) + (b - d)i$.

The Property of Raising Each Side of an Equation to a Power

If a and b are real numbers and $a = b$, then $a^n = b^n$.

The Pythagorean Theorem

The square of the hypotenuse of a right triangle is equal to the sum of the squares of the two legs.
$c^2 = a^2 + b^2$

Chapter Review

1. Simplify: $(16x^{-4}y^{12})^{1/4}(100x^6y^{-2})^{1/2}$
$20x^2y^2$ [9.1A]

2. Solve: $\sqrt[4]{3x-5}=2$
7 [9.4A]

3. Multiply: $(6-5i)(4+3i)$
$39-2i$ [9.3C]

4. Rewrite $7y\sqrt[3]{x^2}$ as an exponential expression.
$7x^{2/3}y$ [9.1B]

5. Multiply: $(\sqrt{3}+8)(\sqrt{3}-2)$
$6\sqrt{3}-13$ [9.2C]

6. Solve: $\sqrt{4x+9}+10=11$
-2 [9.4A]

7. Simplify: $\dfrac{x^{-3/2}}{x^{7/2}}$

$\dfrac{1}{x^5}$ [9.1A]

8. Simplify: $\dfrac{8}{\sqrt{3y}}$

$\dfrac{8\sqrt{3y}}{3y}$ [9.2D]

9. Simplify: $\sqrt[3]{-8a^6b^{12}}$
$-2a^2b^4$ [9.1C]

10. Subtract: $\sqrt{50a^4b^3}-ab\sqrt{18a^2b}$
$2a^2b\sqrt{2b}$ [9.2B]

11. Simplify: $\dfrac{x+2}{\sqrt{x}+\sqrt{2}}$
$\dfrac{x\sqrt{x}-x\sqrt{2}+2\sqrt{x}-2\sqrt{2}}{x-2}$ [9.2D]

12. Simplify: $\dfrac{5+2i}{3i}$

$\dfrac{2}{3}-\dfrac{5}{3}i$ [9.3D]

13. Simplify: $\sqrt{18a^3b^6}$
$3ab^3\sqrt{2a}$ [9.2A]

14. Subtract: $(\sqrt{50}+\sqrt{-72})-(\sqrt{162}-\sqrt{-8})$
$-4\sqrt{2}+8i\sqrt{2}$ [9.3B]

15. Subtract: $3x\sqrt[3]{54x^8y^{10}}-2x^2y\sqrt[3]{16x^5y^7}$
$5x^3y^3\sqrt[3]{2x^2y}$ [9.2B]

16. Multiply: $\sqrt[3]{16x^4y}\,\sqrt[3]{4xy^5}$
$4xy^2\sqrt[3]{x^2}$ [9.2C]

17. Multiply: $i(3-7i)$
$7+3i$ [9.3C]

18. Rewrite $3x^{3/4}$ as a radical expression.
$3\sqrt[4]{x^3}$ [9.1B]

19. Simplify: $\sqrt[5]{-64a^8b^{12}}$

$-2ab^2\sqrt[5]{2a^3b^2}$ [9.2A]

20. Simplify: $\dfrac{5 + 9i}{1 - i}$

$-2 + 7i$ [9.3D]

21. Multiply: $\sqrt{-12}\sqrt{-6}$

$-6\sqrt{2}$ [9.3C]

22. Solve: $\sqrt{x - 5} + \sqrt{x + 6} = 11$

30 [9.4A]

23. Simplify: $\sqrt[4]{81a^8b^{12}}$

$3a^2b^3$ [9.1C]

24. Simplify: $\sqrt{-50}$

$5i\sqrt{2}$ [9.3A]

25. Subtract: $(-8 + 3i) - (4 - 7i)$

$-12 + 10i$ [9.3B]

26. Simplify: $(5 - \sqrt{6})^2$

$31 - 10\sqrt{6}$ [9.2C]

27. Simplify: $4x\sqrt{12x^2y} + \sqrt{3x^4y} - x^2\sqrt{27y}$

$6x^2\sqrt{3y}$ [9.2B]

28. The velocity of the wind determines the amount of power generated by a windmill. A typical equation for this relationship is $v = 4.05\sqrt[3]{P}$, where v is the velocity in miles per hour and P is the power in watts. Find the amount of power generated by a 20-mph wind. Round to the nearest whole number.

120 watts [9.4B]

29. Find the distance required for a car to reach a velocity of 88 ft/s when the acceleration is 16 ft/s². Use the equation $v = \sqrt{2as}$, where v is the velocity, a is the acceleration, and s is the distance.

242 ft [9.4B]

30. A 12-foot ladder is leaning against a building. How far from the building is the bottom of the ladder when the top of the ladder touches the building 10 ft above the ground? Round to the nearest hundredth.

6.63 ft [9.4B]

Chapter Test

1. Write $\frac{1}{2}\sqrt[4]{x^3}$ as an exponential expression.

$\frac{1}{2}x^{3/4}$ [9.1B]

2. Subtract: $\sqrt[3]{54x^7y^3} - x\sqrt[3]{128x^4y^3} - x^2\sqrt[3]{2xy^3}$

$-2x^2y\sqrt[3]{2x}$ [9.2B]

3. Write $3y^{2/5}$ as a radical expression.

$3\sqrt[5]{y^2}$ [9.1B]

4. Multiply: $(2 + 5i)(4 - 2i)$

$18 + 16i$ [9.3C]

5. Simplify: $(2\sqrt{x} + \sqrt{y})^2$

$4x + 4\sqrt{xy} + y$ [9.2C]

6. Simplify: $\frac{r^{2/3}r^{-1}}{r^{-1/2}}$

$r^{1/6}$ [9.1A]

7. Solve: $\sqrt{x + 12} - \sqrt{x} = 2$

4 [9.4A]

8. Simplify: $\sqrt[3]{8x^3y^6}$

$2xy^2$ [9.1C]

9. Multiply: $\sqrt{3x}(\sqrt{x} - \sqrt{25x})$

$-4x\sqrt{3}$ [9.2C]

10. Subtract: $(5 - 2i) - (8 - 4i)$

$-3 + 2i$ [9.3B]

11. Simplify: $\sqrt{32x^4y^7}$

$4x^2y^3\sqrt{2y}$ [9.2A]

12. Multiply: $(2\sqrt{3} + 4)(3\sqrt{3} - 1)$

$14 + 10\sqrt{3}$ [9.2C]

13. Add: $(2 + i) + (2 - i)$

4 [9.3B]

14. Simplify: $\frac{4 - 2\sqrt{5}}{2 - \sqrt{5}}$

2 [9.2D]

15. Add: $\sqrt{18a^3} + a\sqrt{50a}$

$8a\sqrt{2a}$ [9.2B]

16. Multiply: $(\sqrt{a} - 3\sqrt{b})(2\sqrt{a} + 5\sqrt{b})$

$2a - \sqrt{ab} - 15b$ [9.2C]

17. Simplify: $\dfrac{(2x^{1/3}y^{-2/3})^6}{(x^{-4}y^8)^{1/4}}$

$\dfrac{64x^3}{y^6}$ [9.1A]

18. Simplify: $\dfrac{\sqrt{x}}{\sqrt{x} - \sqrt{y}}$

$\dfrac{x + \sqrt{xy}}{x - y}$ [9.2D]

19. Simplify: $\dfrac{2 + 3i}{1 - 2i}$

$-\dfrac{4}{5} + \dfrac{7}{5}i$ [9.3D]

20. Solve: $\sqrt[3]{2x - 2} + 4 = 2$

-3 [9.4A]

21. Simplify: $\left(\dfrac{4a^4}{b^2}\right)^{-3/2}$

$\dfrac{b^3}{8a^6}$ [9.1A]

22. Simplify: $\sqrt[3]{27a^4b^3c^7}$

$3abc^2\sqrt[3]{ac}$ [9.2A]

23. Simplify: $\dfrac{\sqrt{32x^5y}}{\sqrt{2xy^3}}$

$\dfrac{4x^2}{y}$ [9.2D]

24. Multiply: $(\sqrt{-8})(\sqrt{-2})$

-4 [9.3C]

25. An object is dropped from a high building. Find the distance the object has fallen when the speed reaches 192 ft/s. Use the equation $v = \sqrt{64d}$, where v is the speed of the object and d is the distance.

576 ft   [9.4B]

Cumulative Review

1. Simplify: $2^3 \cdot 3 - 4(3 - 4 \cdot 5)$
   92   [1.3A]

2. Evaluate $4a^2b - a^3$ when $a = -2$ and $b = 3$.
   56   [1.4A]

3. Simplify: $-3(4x - 1) - 2(1 - x)$

   $-10x + 1$ [1.4D]

4. Solve: $5 - \frac{2}{3}x = 4$

   $\frac{3}{2}$ [2.2A]

5. Solve: $2[4 - 2(3 - 2x)] = 4(1 - x)$

   $\frac{2}{3}$ [2.2C]

6. Solve: $6x - 3(2x + 2) > 3 - 3(x + 2)$

   $\{x | x > 1\}$ [2.4A]

7. Solve: $2 + |4 - 3x| = 5$

   $\frac{1}{3}, \frac{7}{3}$ [2.5A]

8. Solve: $|2x + 3| \le 9$

   $\{x | -6 \le x \le 3\}$ [2.5B]

9. Find the area of the triangle shown in the figure below.

   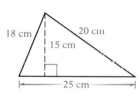

   18 cm   20 cm   15 cm   25 cm

   187.5 cm²   [3.2 B]

10. Find the value of the determinant:

    $$\begin{vmatrix} 1 & 2 & -3 \\ 0 & -1 & 2 \\ 3 & 1 & -2 \end{vmatrix}$$

    3   [5.4A]

11. Find the slope and y-intercept and graph $3x - 2y = -6$.

    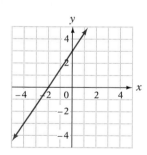

    $m = \frac{3}{2}, b = 3$ [4.2B]

12. Graph the solution set of $3x + 2y \le 4$.

    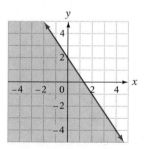

    [4.6A]

13. Find the equation of the line that passes through the points $(2, 3)$ and $(-1, 2)$.

    $y = \frac{1}{3}x + \frac{7}{3}$ [4.4B]

14. Solve by using Cramer's Rule:
    $$2x - y = 4$$
    $$-2x + 3y = 5$$
    $\left(\frac{17}{4}, \frac{9}{2}\right)$ [5.4B]

15. Simplify: $(2^{-1}x^2y^{-6})(2^{-1}y^{-4})^{-2}$
    $2x^2y^2$ [6.1B]

16. Factor: $81x^2 - y^2$
    $(9x + y)(9x - y)$ [7.4A]

17. Factor: $x^5 + 2x^3 - 3x$

$x(x^2 + 3)(x + 1)(x - 1)$ [7.4D]

18. Solve $P = \dfrac{R - C}{n}$ for C.

$C = R - nP$ [8.5A]

19. Simplify: $\left(\dfrac{x^{-2/3}y^{1/2}}{y^{-1/3}}\right)^6$

$\dfrac{y^5}{x^4}$ [9.1A]

20. Subtract: $\sqrt{40x^3} - x\sqrt{90x}$

$-x\sqrt{10x}$ [9.2B]

21. Multiply: $(\sqrt{3} - 2)(\sqrt{3} - 5)$

$13 - 7\sqrt{3}$ [9.2C]

22. Simplify: $\dfrac{4}{\sqrt{6} - \sqrt{2}}$

$\sqrt{6} + \sqrt{2}$ [9.2D]

23. Simplify: $\dfrac{2i}{3 - i}$

$-\dfrac{1}{5} + \dfrac{3}{5}i$ [9.3D]

24. Solve: $\sqrt[3]{3x - 4} + 5 = 1$

-20 [9.4A]

25. The two triangles are similar triangles. Find the length of side DE.

27 m   [8.4C]

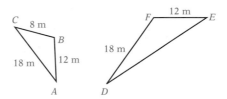

26. An investment of $2500 is made an at annual simple interest rate of 7.2%. How much additional money must be invested at an annual simple interest rate of 8.4% so that the total interest earned is $516?

$4000   [2.3C]

27. A sales executive traveled 25 mi by car and then an additional 625 mi by plane. The rate of the plane was five times the rate of the car. The total time of the trip was 3 h. Find the rate of the plane.

250 mph   [8.6B]

28. How long does it take light to travel to Earth from the moon when the moon is 232,500 mi from Earth? Light travels 1.86×10^5 mi/s.

1.25 s   [6.1D]

29. The graph shows the amount invested and the annual income from the investment. Find the slope of the line between the two points shown on the graph. Then write a sentence that states the meaning of the slope.

$m = 0.08$. The slope represents the simple interest rate on an investment. The interest rate is 8%.   [4.3A]

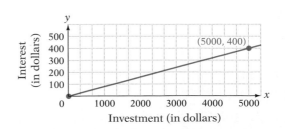

30. How far would a submarine periscope have to be above the water for the lookout to locate a ship 7 mi away? The equation for the distance in miles that the lookout can see is $d = \sqrt{1.5h}$, where h is the height in feet above the surface of the water. Round to the nearest tenth of a foot.

32.7 ft   [9.4B]

10

Quadratic Equations

Building inspectors evaluate the structural integrity of buildings. Inspectors may specialize in structural steel or reinforced concrete structures. Before construction begins, plan examiners determine whether the plans for the building or other structure comply with building code regulations and are suited to the engineering and environmental demands of the building site. Some of the equations that determine the loads various beams can safely carry are quadratic equations, the subject of this chapter.

Objectives

Section 10.1
To solve a quadratic equation by factoring
To write a quadratic equation given its solutions
To solve a quadratic equation by taking square roots

Section 10.2
To solve a quadratic equation by completing the square

Section 10.3
To solve a quadratic equation by using the quadratic formula

Section 10.4
To solve an equation that is quadratic in form
To solve a radical equation that is reducible to a quadratic equation
To solve a fractional equation that is reducible to a quadratic equation

Section 10.5
To solve application problems

Section 10.6
To solve a nonlinear inequality

$$(x - a)^2(x^2 + y^2) - bx^2 = 0$$

x

y

0

Algebraic Symbolism

The way in which an algebraic expression or equation is written has gone through several stages of development. First there was the *rhetoric*, which was in vogue until the late 13th century. In this method, expressions were written out in sentences. The word *res* was used to represent an unknown.

Rhetoric: From the additive *res* in the additive *res* results in a square *res*. From the three in an additive *res* comes three additive *res* and from the subtractive four in the additive *res* comes subtractive four *res*. From three in subtractive four comes subtractive twelve.

$$\text{Modern: } (x + 3)(x - 4) = x^2 - x - 12$$

The second stage was *syncoptic*, which was a shorthand in which abbreviations were used for words.

Syncoptic: a 6 in b quad $- c$ plano 4 in $b + b$ cub

Modern: $6ab^2 - 4cb + b^3$

The current modern stage, called the *symbolic* stage, began with the use of exponents rather than words to symbolize exponential expressions. This occurred near the beginning of the 17th century with the publication of the book *La Geometrie* by René Descartes. Modern notation is still evolving as mathematicians continue to search for convenient methods to symbolize concepts.

10.1 Solving Quadratic Equations by Factoring or by Taking Square Roots

Objective A *To solve a quadratic equation by factoring* ....

Recall that a **quadratic equation** is an equation of the form $ax^2 + bx + c = 0$, where a, b, and c are constants and $a \neq 0$.

Quadratic Equations $\begin{cases} 3x^2 - x + 2 = 0, & a = 3, & b = -1, & c = 2 \\ -x^2 + 4 = 0, & a = -1, & b = 0, & c = 4 \\ 6x^2 - 5x = 0, & a = 6, & b = -5, & c = 0 \end{cases}$

A quadratic equation is in **standard form** when the polynomial is in descending order and equal to zero. Because the degree of the polynomial $ax^2 + bx + c$ is 2, a quadratic equation is also called a **second-degree equation**.

As we discussed earlier, quadratic equations sometimes can be solved by using the Principle of Zero Products. This method is reviewed here.

The Principle of Zero Products

If a and b are real numbers and $ab = 0$, then $a = 0$ or $b = 0$.

The Principle of Zero Products states that if the product of two factors is zero, then at least one of the factors must be zero.

➡ Solve by factoring: $3x^2 = 2 - 5x$

$$3x^2 = 2 - 5x$$
$$3x^2 + 5x - 2 = 0 \qquad \text{• Write the equation in standard form.}$$
$$(3x - 1)(x + 2) = 0 \qquad \text{• Factor.}$$
$$3x - 1 = 0 \qquad\qquad x + 2 = 0 \qquad \text{• Use the Principle of Zero Products to write two equations.}$$
$$3x = 1 \qquad\qquad\qquad x = -2 \qquad \text{• Solve each equation.}$$
$$x = \frac{1}{3}$$

$\frac{1}{3}$ and -2 check as solutions. The solutions are $\frac{1}{3}$ and -2.

➡ Solve by factoring: $x^2 - 6x = -9$

$$x^2 - 6x = -9$$
$$x^2 - 6x + 9 = 0 \qquad \text{• Write the equation in standard form.}$$
$$(x - 3)(x - 3) = 0 \qquad \text{• Factor.}$$
$$x - 3 = 0 \qquad\qquad x - 3 = 0 \qquad \text{• Use the Principle of Zero Products.}$$
$$x = 3 \qquad\qquad\qquad x = 3 \qquad \text{• Solve each equation.}$$

3 checks as a solution. The solution is 3.

Example 1

Solve by factoring: $2x(x - 3) = x + 4$

Solution

$$2x(x - 3) = x + 4$$
$$2x^2 - 6x = x + 4$$
$$2x^2 - 7x - 4 = 0$$
$$(2x + 1)(x - 4) = 0$$

$$2x + 1 = 0 \qquad x - 4 = 0$$
$$2x = -1 \qquad x = 4$$
$$x = -\frac{1}{2}$$

The solutions are $-\frac{1}{2}$ and 4.

You Try It 1

Solve by factoring: $2x^2 = 7x - 3$

Your solution

$\frac{1}{2}, 3$

Example 2

Solve for x by factoring: $x^2 - 4ax - 5a^2 = 0$

Solution

This is a literal equation. Solve for x in terms of a.

$$x^2 - 4ax - 5a^2 = 0$$
$$(x + a)(x - 5a) = 0$$
$$x + a = 0 \qquad x - 5a = 0$$
$$x = -a \qquad x = 5a$$

The solutions are $-a$ and $5a$.

You Try It 2

Solve for x by factoring: $x^2 - 3ax - 4a^2 = 0$

Your solution

$-a, 4a$

Solutions on p. S29

Objective B   ***To write a quadratic equation given its solutions*** ....

As shown below, the solutions of the equation $(x - r_1)(x - r_2) = 0$ are r_1 and r_2.

$$(x - r_1)(x - r_2) = 0$$

$$x - r_1 = 0 \qquad\qquad x - r_2 = 0$$
$$x = r_1 \qquad\qquad x = r_2$$

Check:

$$\frac{(x - r_1)(x - r_2) = 0}{\begin{array}{c}(r_1 - r_1)(r_1 - r_2) \\ 0 \cdot (r_1 - r_2) \\ 0 = 0\end{array}} \qquad \frac{(x - r_1)(x - r_2) = 0}{\begin{array}{c}(r_2 - r_1)(r_2 - r_2) \\ (r_2 - r_1) \cdot 0 \\ 0 = 0\end{array}}$$

Using the equation $(x - r_1)(x - r_2) = 0$ and the fact that r_1 and r_2 are solutions of this equation, it is possible to write a quadratic equation given its solutions.

➡ Write a quadratic equation that has solutions 4 and -5.

$$(x - r_1)(x - r_2) = 0$$
$$(x - 4)[x - (-5)] = 0$$
$$(x - 4)(x + 5) = 0$$
$$x^2 + x - 20 = 0$$

• Replace r_1 by 4 and r_2 by -5.
• Simplify.
• Multiply.

⟹ Write a quadratic equation with integer coefficients and solutions $\frac{2}{3}$ and $\frac{1}{2}$.

$$(x - r_1)(x - r_2) = 0$$

$$\left(x - \frac{2}{3}\right)\left(x - \frac{1}{2}\right) = 0$$ • Replace r_1 by $\frac{2}{3}$ and r_2 by $\frac{1}{2}$.

$$x^2 - \frac{7}{6}x + \frac{1}{3} = 0$$ • Multiply.

$$6\left(x^2 - \frac{7}{6}x + \frac{1}{3}\right) = 6 \cdot 0$$ • Multiply each side of the equation by the LCM of the denominators.

$$6x^2 - 7x + 2 = 0$$

Example 3

Write a quadratic equation with integer coefficients and solutions $\frac{1}{2}$ and -4.

Solution

$$(x - r_1)(x - r_2) = 0$$

$$\left(x - \frac{1}{2}\right)[x - (-4)] = 0$$

$$\left(x - \frac{1}{2}\right)(x + 4) = 0$$

$$x^2 + \frac{7}{2}x - 2 = 0$$

$$2\left(x^2 + \frac{7}{2}x - 2\right) = 2 \cdot 0$$

$$2x^2 + 7x - 4 = 0$$

You Try It 3

Write a quadratic equation with integer coefficients and solutions 3 and $-\frac{1}{2}$.

Your solution

$2x^2 - 5x - 3 = 0$

Solution on p. S29

Objective C   *To solve a quadratic equation by taking square roots*................

The solution of the quadratic equation $x^2 = 16$ is shown at the right.

$$x^2 - 16$$
$$x^2 - 16 = 0$$
$$(x - 4)(x + 4) = 0$$
$$x - 4 = 0 \qquad x + 4 = 0$$
$$x = 4 \qquad x = -4$$

INSTRUCTOR NOTE

Another demonstration that $x^2 = a$ implies that $x = \pm\sqrt{a}$ is to rely on the fact that $\sqrt{x^2} = |x|$. Thus $x^2 = a$ implies that $|x| = \sqrt{a}$, or that $x = \pm\sqrt{a}$.

As shown below, the solutions can also be found by taking the square root of each side of the equation and writing the positive and negative square roots of the number. The notation $x = \pm 4$ means $x = 4$ or $x = -4$.

$$x^2 = 16$$
$$\sqrt{x^2} = \sqrt{16}$$
$$x = \pm 4$$

The solutions are 4 and -4.

⟹ Solve by taking square roots: $3x^2 = 54$

$$3x^2 = 54$$
$$x^2 = 18$$ • Solve for x^2.
$$\sqrt{x^2} = \sqrt{18}$$ • Take the square root of each side of the equation.
$$x = \pm\sqrt{18} = \pm 3\sqrt{2}$$ • Simplify.

$3\sqrt{2}$ and $-3\sqrt{2}$ check as solutions. The solutions are $3\sqrt{2}$ and $-3\sqrt{2}$.

Solving a quadratic equation by taking the square root of each side of the equation can lead to solutions that are complex numbers.

➡ Solve by taking square roots: $2x^2 + 18 = 0$

$$2x^2 + 18 = 0$$
$$2x^2 = -18 \qquad \text{• Solve for } x^2$$
$$x^2 = -9$$
$$\sqrt{x^2} = \sqrt{-9} \qquad \text{• Take the square root of each side of the equation.}$$
$$x = \pm\sqrt{-9} = \pm 3i \qquad \text{• Simplify.}$$

Check:

$2x^2 + 18 = 0$		$2x^2 + 18 = 0$	
$2(3i)^2 + 18$	0	$2(-3i)^2 + 18$	0
$2(-9) + 18$	0	$2(-9) + 18$	0
$-18 + 18$	0	$-18 + 18$	0
	$0 = 0$		$0 = 0$

The solutions are $3i$ and $-3i$.

An equation containing the square of a binomial can be solved by taking square roots.

➡ Solve by taking square roots: $(x + 2)^2 - 24 = 0$

$$(x + 2)^2 - 24 = 0$$
$$(x + 2)^2 = 24 \qquad \text{• Solve for } (x + 2)^2.$$
$$\sqrt{(x + 2)^2} = \sqrt{24} \qquad \text{• Take the square root of each side of the equation.}$$
$$x + 2 = \pm\sqrt{24} = \pm 2\sqrt{6} \qquad \text{• Simplify.}$$
$$x + 2 = 2\sqrt{6} \qquad x + 2 = -2\sqrt{6} \qquad \text{• Solve for } x.$$
$$x = -2 + 2\sqrt{6} \qquad x = -2 - 2\sqrt{6}$$

The solutions are $-2 + 2\sqrt{6}$ and $-2 - 2\sqrt{6}$.

Example 4
Solve by taking square roots:
$3(x - 2)^2 + 12 = 0$

Solution
$$3(x - 2)^2 + 12 = 0$$
$$3(x - 2)^2 = -12$$
$$(x - 2)^2 = -4$$
$$\sqrt{(x - 2)^2} = \sqrt{-4}$$
$$x - 2 = \pm\sqrt{-4} = \pm 2i$$
$$x - 2 = 2i \qquad x - 2 = -2i$$
$$x = 2 + 2i \qquad x = 2 - 2i$$

The solutions are $2 + 2i$ and $2 - 2i$.

You Try It 4
Solve by taking square roots:
$2(x + 1)^2 - 24 = 0$

Your solution
$-1 + 2\sqrt{3}, -1 - 2\sqrt{3}$

Solution on p. S29

10.1 Exercises

. . . .

Objective A

Solve by factoring.

1. $x^2 - 4x = 0$
0, 4

2. $y^2 + 6y = 0$
0, −6

3. $t^2 - 25 = 0$
5, −5

4. $p^2 - 81 = 0$
9, −9

5. $s^2 - s - 6 = 0$
3, −2

6. $v^2 + 4v - 5 = 0$
1, −5

7. $y^2 - 6y + 9 = 0$
3

8. $x^2 + 10x + 25 = 0$
−5

9. $9z^2 - 18z = 0$
0, 2

10. $4y^2 + 20y = 0$
0, −5

11. $r^2 - 3r = 10$
5, −2

12. $p^2 + 5p = 6$
1, −6

13. $v^2 + 10 = 7v$
2, 5

14. $t^2 - 16 = 15t$
16, −1

15. $2x^2 - 9x - 18 = 0$
$6, -\dfrac{3}{2}$

16. $3y^2 - 4y - 4 = 0$
$-\dfrac{2}{3}, 2$

17. $4z^2 - 9z + 2 = 0$
$2, \dfrac{1}{4}$

18. $2s^2 - 9s + 9 = 0$
$\dfrac{3}{2}, 3$

19. $3w^2 + 11w = 4$
$\dfrac{1}{3}, -4$

20. $2r^2 + r = 6$
$\dfrac{3}{2}, -2$

21. $6x^2 = 23x + 18$
$\dfrac{9}{2}, -\dfrac{2}{3}$

22. $6x^2 = 7x - 2$
$\dfrac{2}{3}, \dfrac{1}{2}$

23. $4 - 15u - 4u^2 = 0$
$\dfrac{1}{4}, -4$

24. $3 - 2y - 8y^2 = 0$
$-\dfrac{3}{4}, \dfrac{1}{2}$

25. $x + 18 = x(x - 6)$
9, −2

26. $t + 24 = t(t + 6)$
3, −8

27. $4s(s + 3) = s - 6$
$-2, -\dfrac{3}{4}$

28. $3v(v - 2) = 11v + 6$
$-\dfrac{1}{3}, 6$

29. $u^2 - 2u + 4 = (2u - 3)(u + 2)$
2, −5

30. $(3v - 2)(2v + 1) = 3v^2 - 11v - 10$
$-2, -\dfrac{4}{3}$

31. $(3x - 4)(x + 4) = x^2 - 3x - 28$
$-4, -\dfrac{3}{2}$

Solve for x by factoring.

32. $x^2 + 14ax + 48a^2 = 0$
$-6a, -8a$

33. $x^2 - 9bx + 14b^2 = 0$
$2b, 7b$

34. $x^2 + 9xy - 36y^2 = 0$
$-12y, 3y$

35. $x^2 - 6cx - 7c^2 = 0$
$7c, -c$

36. $x^2 - ax - 20a^2 = 0$
$-4a, 5a$

37. $2x^2 + 3bx + b^2 = 0$
$-\dfrac{b}{2}, -b$

38. $3x^2 - 4cx + c^2 = 0$
$\dfrac{c}{3}, c$

39. $3x^2 - 14ax + 8a^2 = 0$
$4a, \dfrac{2a}{3}$

40. $3x^2 - 11xy + 6y^2 = 0$
$\dfrac{2y}{3}, 3y$

41. $3x^2 - 8ax - 3a^2 = 0$
$-\dfrac{a}{3}, 3a$

42. $3x^2 - 4bx - 4b^2 = 0$
$-\dfrac{2b}{3}, 2b$

43. $4x^2 + 8xy + 3y^2 = 0$
$-\dfrac{3y}{2}, -\dfrac{y}{2}$

44. $6x^2 - 11cx + 3c^2 = 0$
$\dfrac{c}{3}, \dfrac{3c}{2}$

45. $6x^2 + 11ax + 4a^2 = 0$
$-\dfrac{a}{2}, -\dfrac{4a}{3}$

46. $12x^2 - 5xy - 2y^2 = 0$
$-\dfrac{y}{4}, \dfrac{2y}{3}$

Objective B

Write a quadratic equation that has integer coefficients and has as solutions the given pair of numbers.

47. 2 and 5
$x^2 - 7x + 10 = 0$

48. 3 and 1
$x^2 - 4x + 3 = 0$

49. -2 and -4
$x^2 + 6x + 8 = 0$

50. -1 and -3
$x^2 + 4x + 3 = 0$

51. 6 and -1
$x^2 - 5x - 6 = 0$

52. -2 and 5
$x^2 - 3x - 10 = 0$

53. 3 and -3
$x^2 - 9 = 0$

54. 5 and -5
$x^2 - 25 = 0$

55. 4 and 4
$x^2 - 8x + 16 = 0$

56. 2 and 2
$x^2 - 4x + 4 = 0$

57. 0 and 5
$x^2 - 5x = 0$

58. 0 and -2
$x^2 + 2x = 0$

59. 0 and 3
$x^2 - 3x = 0$

60. 0 and -1
$x^2 + x = 0$

61. 3 and $\dfrac{1}{2}$
$2x^2 - 7x + 3 = 0$

62. 2 and $\frac{2}{3}$

$3x^2 - 8x + 4 = 0$

63. $-\frac{3}{4}$ and 2

$4x^2 - 5x - 6 = 0$

64. $-\frac{1}{2}$ and 5

$2x^2 - 9x - 5 = 0$

65. $-\frac{5}{3}$ and -2

$3x^2 + 11x + 10 = 0$

66. $-\frac{3}{2}$ and -1

$2x^2 + 5x + 3 = 0$

67. $-\frac{2}{3}$ and $\frac{2}{3}$

$9x^2 - 4 = 0$

68. $-\frac{1}{2}$ and $\frac{1}{2}$

$4x^2 - 1 = 0$

69. $\frac{1}{2}$ and $\frac{1}{3}$

$6x^2 - 5x + 1 = 0$

70. $\frac{3}{4}$ and $\frac{2}{3}$

$12x^2 - 17x + 6 = 0$

71. $\frac{6}{5}$ and $-\frac{1}{2}$

$10x^2 - 7x - 6 = 0$

72. $\frac{3}{4}$ and $-\frac{3}{2}$

$8x^2 + 6x - 9 = 0$

73. $-\frac{1}{4}$ and $-\frac{1}{2}$

$8x^2 + 6x + 1 = 0$

74. $-\frac{5}{6}$ and $-\frac{2}{3}$

$18x^2 + 27x + 10 = 0$

75. $\frac{3}{5}$ and $-\frac{1}{10}$

$50x^2 - 25x - 3 = 0$

76. $\frac{7}{2}$ and $-\frac{1}{4}$

$8x^2 - 26x - 7 = 0$

Objective C

Solve by taking square roots.

77. $y^2 = 49$
7, -7

78. $x^2 = 64$
8, -8

79. $z^2 = -4$
$2i$, $-2i$

80. $v^2 = -16$
$4i$, $-4i$

81. $s^2 - 4 = 0$
2, -2

82. $r^2 - 36 = 0$
6, -6

83. $4x^2 - 81 = 0$
$\frac{9}{2}, -\frac{9}{2}$

84. $9x^2 - 16 = 0$
$\frac{4}{3}, -\frac{4}{3}$

85. $y^2 + 49 = 0$

$7i$, $-7i$

86. $z^2 + 16 = 0$
$4i$, $-4i$

87. $v^2 - 48 = 0$
$4\sqrt{3}, -4\sqrt{3}$

88. $s^2 - 32 = 0$
$4\sqrt{2}, -4\sqrt{2}$

89. $r^2 - 75 = 0$
$5\sqrt{3}, -5\sqrt{3}$

90. $u^2 - 54 = 0$
$3\sqrt{6}, -3\sqrt{6}$

91. $z^2 + 18 = 0$
$3i\sqrt{2}, -3i\sqrt{2}$

92. $t^2 + 27 = 0$
$3i\sqrt{3}, -3i\sqrt{3}$

93. $(x - 1)^2 = 36$
$7, -5$

94. $(x + 2)^2 = 25$
$3, -7$

95. $3(y + 3)^2 = 27$
$0, -6$

96. $4(s - 2)^2 = 36$
$5, -1$

97. $5(z + 2)^2 = 125$
$3, -7$

98. $2(y - 3)^2 = 18$
$6, 0$

99. $\left(v - \dfrac{1}{2}\right)^2 = \dfrac{1}{4}$
$1, 0$

100. $\left(r + \dfrac{2}{3}\right)^2 = \dfrac{1}{9}$
$-\dfrac{1}{3}, -1$

101. $(x + 5)^2 - 6 = 0$
$-5 + \sqrt{6}, -5 - \sqrt{6}$

102. $(t - 1)^2 - 15 = 0$
$1 + \sqrt{15}, 1 - \sqrt{15}$

103. $(v - 3)^2 + 45 = 0$
$3 + 3i\sqrt{5}, 3 - 3i\sqrt{5}$

104. $(x + 5)^2 + 32 = 0$
$-5 + 4i\sqrt{2}, -5 - 4i\sqrt{2}$

105. $\left(u - \dfrac{2}{3}\right)^2 - 18 = 0$
$-\dfrac{2 - 9\sqrt{2}}{3}, -\dfrac{2 + 9\sqrt{2}}{3}$

106. $\left(z - \dfrac{1}{2}\right)^2 - 20 = 0$
$\dfrac{1 + 4\sqrt{5}}{2}, \dfrac{1 - 4\sqrt{5}}{2}$

APPLYING THE CONCEPTS

Write a quadratic equation that has as solutions the given pair of numbers.

107. $\sqrt{2}$ and $-\sqrt{2}$
$x^2 - 2 = 0$

108. $2i$ and $-2i$
$x^2 + 4 = 0$

109. $3\sqrt{2}$ and $-3\sqrt{2}$
$x^2 - 18 = 0$

110. $2i\sqrt{3}$ and $-2i\sqrt{3}$
$x^2 + 12 = 0$

Solve for x.

111. $4a^2x^2 = 36b^2, a > 0, b > 0$
$\dfrac{3b}{a}, -\dfrac{3b}{a}$

112. $(x + a)^2 - 4 = 0$
$2 - a, -2 - a$

113. $(2x - 1)^2 = (2x + 3)^2$
$-\dfrac{1}{2}$

114. Show that the solutions of the equation $ax^2 + bx = 0, a > 0, b > 0$,
are 0 and $-\dfrac{b}{a}$.

115. Show that the solutions of the equation $ax^2 + c = 0, a > 0, c > 0$,
are $\dfrac{\sqrt{ca}}{a}i$ and $-\dfrac{\sqrt{ca}}{a}i$.

116. Explain why the restriction that $a \neq 0$ is given in the definition of a
quadratic equation.

10.2 Solving Quadratic Equations by Completing the Square

Objective A *To solve a quadratic equation by completing the square* ....

Recall that a perfect-square trinomial is the square of a binomial.

Perfect-Square Trinomial		Square of a Binomial
$x^2 + 8x + 16$	$=$	$(x + 4)^2$
$x^2 - 10x + 25$	$=$	$(x - 5)^2$
$x^2 + 2ax + a^2$	$=$	$(x + a)^2$

For each perfect-square trinomial, the square of $\frac{1}{2}$ of the coefficient of x equals the constant term.

$$\left(\frac{1}{2} \text{ coefficient of } x\right)^2 = \text{constant term}$$

$$x^2 + 8x + 16, \quad \left(\frac{1}{2} \cdot 8\right)^2 = 16$$

$$x^2 - 10x + 25, \quad \left[\frac{1}{2}(-10)\right]^2 = 25$$

$$x^2 + 2ax + a^2, \quad \left(\frac{1}{2} \cdot 2a\right)^2 = a^2$$

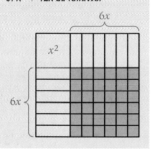

This relationship can be used to write the constant term for a perfect-square trinomial. Adding to a binomial the constant term that makes it a perfect-square trinomial is called **completing the square**.

➡ Complete the square on $x^2 + 12x$. Write the resulting perfect-square trinomial as the square of a binomial.

$$\left[\frac{1}{2}(12)\right]^2 = (6)^2 = 36$$ • Find the constant term.

$$x^2 + 12x + 36$$ • Complete the square on $x^2 + 12x$ by adding the constant term.

$$x^2 + 12x + 36 = (x + 6)^2$$ • Write the resulting perfect-square trinomial as the square of a binomial.

➡ Complete the square on $z^2 - 3z$. Write the resulting perfect-square trinomial as the square of a binomial.

$$\left[\frac{1}{2} \cdot (-3)\right]^2 = \left(-\frac{3}{2}\right)^2 = \frac{9}{4}$$ • Find the constant term.

$$z^2 - 3z + \frac{9}{4}$$ • Complete the square on $z^2 - 3z$ by adding the constant term.

$$z^2 - 3z + \frac{9}{4} = \left(z - \frac{3}{2}\right)^2$$ • Write the resulting perfect-square trinomial as the square of a binomial.

Any quadratic equation can be solved by completing the square. Add to each side of the equation the term that completes the square. Rewrite the equation in the form $(x + a)^2 = b$. Take the square root of each side of the equation.

INSTRUCTOR NOTE
To say that students will find completing the square a daunting task is an understatement. The positive note is that the procedure is the same each time.

- Isolate $ax^2 + bx$.
- Multiply by $\frac{1}{a}$.
- Complete the square.
- Factor.
- Take the square root.
- Solve for x.

➡ Solve by completing the square: $x^2 - 6x - 15 = 0$

$$x^2 - 6x - 15 = 0$$

$$x^2 - 6x = 15$$ • Add 15 to each side of the equation.

$$x^2 - 6x + 9 = 15 + 9$$ • Complete the square. Add $\left[\frac{1}{2}(-6)\right]^2 = (-3)^2 = 9$ to each side of the equation.

$$(x - 3)^2 = 24$$ • Factor the trinomial.

$$\sqrt{(x - 3)^2} = \sqrt{24}$$ • Take the square root of each side of the equation.

$$x - 3 = \pm\sqrt{24}$$ • Solve for x.

$$x - 3 = \pm2\sqrt{6}$$

$$x - 3 = 2\sqrt{6} \qquad x - 3 = -2\sqrt{6}$$

$$x = 3 + 2\sqrt{6} \qquad x = 3 - 2\sqrt{6}$$

Check:

$$x^2 - 6x - 15 = 0$$

$$\frac{(3 + 2\sqrt{6})^2 - 6(3 + 2\sqrt{6}) - 15 \mid 0}{9 + 12\sqrt{6} + 24 - 18 - 12\sqrt{6} - 15 \mid 0}$$

$$0 = 0$$

$$x^2 - 6x - 15 = 0$$

$$\frac{(3 - 2\sqrt{6})^2 - 6(3 - 2\sqrt{6}) - 15 \mid 0}{9 - 12\sqrt{6} + 24 - 18 + 12\sqrt{6} - 15 \mid 0}$$

$$0 = 0$$

The solutions are $3 + 2\sqrt{6}$ and $3 - 2\sqrt{6}$.

INSTRUCTOR NOTE
An Instructor Note in the previous section suggested an alternative method of checking the solutions of a quadratic equation. You may want to use it to check the solutions here.

➡ Solve by completing the square: $2x^2 - x - 2 = 0$

In order for us to complete the square on an expression, the coefficient of the squared term must be 1. After adding the opposite of the constant term to each side of the equation, multiply each side of the equation by $\frac{1}{2}$.

$$2x^2 - x - 2 = 0$$

$$2x^2 - x = 2$$ • Add 2 to each side of the equation.

$$\frac{1}{2}(2x^2 - x) = \frac{1}{2} \cdot 2$$ • Multiply each side of the equation by $\frac{1}{2}$.

$$x^2 - \frac{1}{2}x = 1$$ • The coefficient of x^2 is now 1.

$$x^2 - \frac{1}{2}x + \frac{1}{16} = 1 + \frac{1}{16}$$

- Complete the square. Add $\left[\frac{1}{2}\left(-\frac{1}{2}\right)\right]^2 = \left(-\frac{1}{4}\right)^2 = \frac{1}{16}$ to each side of the equation.

$$\left(x - \frac{1}{4}\right)^2 = \frac{17}{16}$$

- Factor the perfect-square trinomial.

$$\sqrt{\left(x - \frac{1}{4}\right)^2} = \sqrt{\frac{17}{16}}$$

- Take the square root of each side of the equation.

$$x - \frac{1}{4} = \pm\frac{\sqrt{17}}{4}$$

- Solve for x.

$$x - \frac{1}{4} = \frac{\sqrt{17}}{4} \qquad x - \frac{1}{4} = -\frac{\sqrt{17}}{4}$$

$$x = \frac{1}{4} + \frac{\sqrt{17}}{4} \qquad x = \frac{1}{4} - \frac{\sqrt{17}}{4}$$

The solutions are $\frac{1 + \sqrt{17}}{4}$ and $\frac{1 - \sqrt{17}}{4}$.

The solutions of the quadratic equation in the example below are complex numbers.

POINT OF INTEREST

Mathematicians have studied quadratic equations for centuries. Many of the initial equations were a result of trying to solve a geometry problem. One of the most famous, which dates from around 500 B.C., is "squaring the circle." The question was "Is it possible to construct a square whose area is that of a given circle?" For these early mathematicians, to *construct* meant to draw with only a straightedge and a compass. It was approximately 2300 years later that mathematicians were able to prove that such a construction is impossible.

➡ Solve by completing the square: $x^2 - 3x + 5 = 0$

$$x^2 - 3x + 5 = 0$$

$$x^2 - 3x = -5$$

- Add the opposite of the constant term to each side of the equation.

$$x^2 - 3x + \frac{9}{4} = -5 + \frac{9}{4}$$

- Add to each side of the equation the term that completes the square on $x^2 - 3x$.

$$\left(x - \frac{3}{2}\right)^2 = -\frac{11}{4}$$

- Factor the perfect-square trinomial.

$$\sqrt{\left(x - \frac{3}{2}\right)^2} = \sqrt{-\frac{11}{4}}$$

- Take the square root of each side of the equation.

$$x - \frac{3}{2} = \pm\frac{i\sqrt{11}}{2}$$

- Simplify.

$$x - \frac{3}{2} = \frac{i\sqrt{11}}{2} \qquad x - \frac{3}{2} = -\frac{i\sqrt{11}}{2}$$

- Solve for x.

$$x = \frac{3}{2} + \frac{i\sqrt{11}}{2} \qquad x = \frac{3}{2} - \frac{i\sqrt{11}}{2}$$

$\frac{3}{2} + \frac{\sqrt{11}}{2}i$ and $\frac{3}{2} - \frac{\sqrt{11}}{2}i$ check as solutions.

The solutions are $\frac{3}{2} + \frac{\sqrt{11}}{2}i$ and $\frac{3}{2} - \frac{\sqrt{11}}{2}i$.

Example 1
Solve by completing the square:
$4x^2 - 8x + 1 = 0$

Solution

$4x^2 - 8x + 1 = 0$

$\qquad 4x^2 - 8x = -1$

$\frac{1}{4}(4x^2 - 8x) = \frac{1}{4}(-1)$ • The coefficient of x^2 must be 1.

$\qquad x^2 - 2x = -\frac{1}{4}$

$x^2 - 2x + 1 = -\frac{1}{4} + 1$ • Complete the square.

$\qquad (x - 1)^2 = \frac{3}{4}$

$\qquad \sqrt{(x-1)^2} = \sqrt{\frac{3}{4}}$

$\qquad x - 1 = \pm\frac{\sqrt{3}}{2}$

$x - 1 = \frac{\sqrt{3}}{2} \qquad\qquad x - 1 = -\frac{\sqrt{3}}{2}$

$\quad x = 1 + \frac{\sqrt{3}}{2} \qquad\qquad x = 1 - \frac{\sqrt{3}}{2}$

$\quad\;\; = \frac{2 + \sqrt{3}}{2} \qquad\qquad\;\; = \frac{2 - \sqrt{3}}{2}$

The solutions are $\frac{2 + \sqrt{3}}{2}$ and $\frac{2 - \sqrt{3}}{2}$.

You Try It 1
Solve by completing the square:
$4x^2 - 4x - 1 = 0$

Your solution

$\frac{1 + \sqrt{2}}{2}, \frac{1 - \sqrt{2}}{2}$

Example 2
Solve by completing the square:
$x^2 + 4x + 5 = 0$

Solution

$x^2 + 4x + 5 = 0$

$\quad x^2 + 4x = -5$

$x^2 + 4x + 4 = -5 + 4$ • Complete the square.

$\quad (x + 2)^2 = -1$

$\sqrt{(x + 2)^2} = \sqrt{-1}$

$\qquad x + 2 = \pm i$

$x + 2 = i \qquad\qquad x + 2 = -i$

$\quad x = -2 + i \qquad\qquad x = -2 - i$

The solutions are $-2 + i$ and $-2 - i$.

You Try It 2
Solve by completing the square:
$2x^2 + x - 5 = 0$

Your solution

$\frac{-1 + \sqrt{41}}{4}, \frac{-1 - \sqrt{41}}{4}$

Solutions on p. S29

10.2 Exercises
· ·

Objective A

1. What is the meaning of the phrase "complete the square"?

2. Write out the steps for solving a quadratic equation by completing the square.

Solve by completing the square.

3. $x^2 - 4x - 5 = 0$
   5, −1

4. $y^2 + 6y + 5 = 0$
   −1, −5

5. $v^2 + 8v - 9 = 0$
   −9, 1

6. $w^2 - 2w - 24 = 0$
   6, −4

7. $z^2 - 6z + 9 = 0$
   3

8. $u^2 + 10u + 25 = 0$
   −5

9. $r^2 + 4r - 7 = 0$
   $-2 + \sqrt{11}, -2 - \sqrt{11}$

10. $s^2 + 6s - 1 = 0$
    $-3 + \sqrt{10}, -3 - \sqrt{10}$

11. $x^2 - 6x + 7 = 0$
    $3 + \sqrt{2}, 3 - \sqrt{2}$

12. $y^2 + 8y + 13 = 0$
    $-4 + \sqrt{3}, -4 - \sqrt{3}$

13. $z^2 - 2z + 2 = 0$
    $1 + i, 1 - i$

14. $t^2 - 4t + 8 = 0$
    $2 + 2i, 2 - 2i$

15. $s^2 - 5s - 24 = 0$
    8, −3

16. $v^2 + 7v - 44 = 0$
    4, −11

17. $x^2 + 5x - 36 = 0$
    4, −9

18. $y^2 - 9y + 20 = 0$

    5, 4

19. $p^2 - 3p + 1 = 0$
    $\dfrac{3 + \sqrt{5}}{2}, \dfrac{3 - \sqrt{5}}{2}$

20. $r^2 - 5r - 2 = 0$
    $\dfrac{5 + \sqrt{33}}{2}, \dfrac{5 - \sqrt{33}}{2}$

21. $t^2 - t - 1 = 0$
    $\dfrac{1 + \sqrt{5}}{2}, \dfrac{1 - \sqrt{5}}{2}$

22. $u^2 - u - 7 = 0$
    $\dfrac{1 + \sqrt{29}}{2}, \dfrac{1 - \sqrt{29}}{2}$

23. $y^2 - 6y = 4$

    $3 + \sqrt{13}, 3 - \sqrt{13}$

24. $w^2 + 4w = 2$
    $-2 + \sqrt{6}, -2 - \sqrt{6}$

25. $x^2 = 8x - 15$
    5, 3

26. $z^2 = 4z - 3$
    3, 1

27. $v^2 = 4v - 13$
    $2 + 3i, 2 - 3i$

28. $x^2 = 2x - 17$
    $1 + 4i, 1 - 4i$

29. $p^2 + 6p = -13$
    $-3 + 2i, -3 - 2i$

30. $x^2 + 4x = -20$
    $-2 + 4i, -2 - 4i$

31. $y^2 - 2y = 17$
    $1 + 3\sqrt{2}, 1 - 3\sqrt{2}$

32. $x^2 + 10x = 7$
    $-5 + 4\sqrt{2}, -5 - 4\sqrt{2}$

33. $z^2 = z + 4$
$\dfrac{1 + \sqrt{17}}{2}, \dfrac{1 - \sqrt{17}}{2}$

34. $r^2 = 3r - 1$
$\dfrac{3 + \sqrt{5}}{2}, \dfrac{3 - \sqrt{5}}{2}$

35. $x^2 + 13 = 2x$
$1 + 2i\sqrt{3}, 1 - 2i\sqrt{3}$

36. $6v^2 - 7v = 3$
$\dfrac{3}{2}, -\dfrac{1}{3}$

37. $4x^2 - 4x + 5 = 0$
$\dfrac{1}{2} + i, \dfrac{1}{2} - i$

38. $4t^2 - 4t + 17 = 0$
$\dfrac{1}{2} + 2i, \dfrac{1}{2} - 2i$

39. $9x^2 - 6x + 2 = 0$
$\dfrac{1}{3} + \dfrac{1}{3}i, \dfrac{1}{3} - \dfrac{1}{3}i$

40. $9y^2 - 12y + 13 = 0$
$\dfrac{2}{3} + i, \dfrac{2}{3} - i$

41. $2s^2 = 4s + 5$
$\dfrac{2 + \sqrt{14}}{2}, \dfrac{2 - \sqrt{14}}{2}$

42. $3u^2 = 6u + 1$
$\dfrac{3 + 2\sqrt{3}}{3}, \dfrac{3 - 2\sqrt{3}}{3}$

43. $2r^2 = 3 - r$
$1, -\dfrac{3}{2}$

44. $2x^2 = 12 - 5x$
$\dfrac{3}{2}, -4$

45. $y - 2 = (y - 3)(y + 2)$
$1 + \sqrt{5}, 1 - \sqrt{5}$

46. $8s - 11 = (s - 4)(s - 2)$
$7 + \sqrt{30}, 7 - \sqrt{30}$

47. $6t - 2 = (2t - 3)(t - 1)$
$\dfrac{1}{2}, 5$

48. $2z + 9 = (2z + 3)(z + 2)$
$\dfrac{1}{2}, -3$

49. $(x - 4)(x + 1) = x - 3$
$2 + \sqrt{5}, 2 - \sqrt{5}$

50. $(y - 3)^2 = 2y + 10$
$4 + \sqrt{17}, 4 - \sqrt{17}$

APPLYING THE CONCEPTS

Solve by completing the square. Approximate the solutions to the nearest thousandth.

51. $z^2 + 2z = 4$
1.236, −3.236

52. $t^2 - 4t = 7$
5.317, −1.317

53. $2x^2 = 4x - 1$
1.707, 0.293

Solve for x by completing the square.

54. $x^2 - ax - 2a^2 = 0$
$x = 2a, x = -a$

55. $x^2 + 3ax - 4a^2 = 0$
$x = a, x = -4a$

56. $x^2 + 3ax - 10a^2 = 0$
$x = 2a, x = -5a$

57. After a baseball is hit, the height h (in feet) of the ball above the ground t seconds after it is hit can be approximated by the equation $h = -16t^2 + 70t + 4$. Using this equation, determine when the ball will hit the ground. (*Hint:* The ball hits the ground when $h = 0$.)
4.43 s

58. After a baseball is hit, there are two equations that can be considered. One gives the height h (in feet) the ball is above the ground t seconds after it is hit. The second is the distance s (in feet) the ball is from home plate t seconds after it is hit. A model of this situation is given by $h = -16t^2 + 70t + 4$ and $s = 44.5t$. Using this model, determine whether the ball will clear a 6-foot fence 325 ft from home plate.
No. The ball will have gone only 197.2 ft when it hits the ground.

10.3 Solving Quadratic Equations by Using the Quadratic Formula

Objective A *To solve a quadratic equation by using the quadratic formula* ....

A general formula known as the **quadratic formula** can be derived by applying the method of completing the square to the standard form of a quadratic equation. This formula can be used to solve any quadratic equation.

Solve $ax^2 + bx + c = 0$ by completing the square.

$$ax^2 + bx + c = 0$$

Add the opposite of the constant term to each side of the equation.

$$ax^2 + bx + c + (-c) = 0 + (-c)$$

$$ax^2 + bx = -c$$

Multiply each side of the equation by the reciprocal of a, the coefficient of x^2.

$$\frac{1}{a}(ax^2 + bx) = \frac{1}{a}(-c)$$

$$x^2 + \frac{b}{a}x = -\frac{c}{a}$$

Complete the square by adding $\left(\frac{1}{2} \cdot \frac{b}{a}\right)^2 = \frac{b^2}{4a^2}$ to each side of the equation.

$$x^2 + \frac{b}{a}x + \frac{b^2}{4a^2} = \frac{b^2}{4a^2} - \frac{c}{a}$$

Simplify the right side of the equation.

$$x^2 + \frac{b}{a}x + \frac{b^2}{4a^2} = \frac{b^2}{4a^2} - \left(\frac{c}{a} \cdot \frac{4a}{4a}\right)$$

$$x^2 + \frac{b}{a}x + \frac{b^2}{4a^2} = \frac{b^2}{4a^2} - \frac{4ac}{4a^2}$$

$$x^2 + \frac{b}{a}x + \frac{b^2}{4a^2} = \frac{b^2 - 4ac}{4a^2}$$

Factor the perfect-square trinomial on the left side of the equation.

$$\left(x + \frac{b}{2a}\right)^2 = \frac{b^2 - 4ac}{4a^2}$$

Take the square root of each side of the equation.

$$\sqrt{\left(x + \frac{b}{2a}\right)^2} = \sqrt{\frac{b^2 - 4ac}{4a^2}}$$

$$x + \frac{b}{2a} = \pm\frac{\sqrt{b^2 - 4ac}}{2a}$$

Solve for x.

$$x + \frac{b}{2a} = \frac{\sqrt{b^2 - 4ac}}{2a}$$

$$x = -\frac{b}{2a} + \frac{\sqrt{b^2 - 4ac}}{2a}$$

$$= \frac{-b + \sqrt{b^2 - 4ac}}{2a}$$

$$x + \frac{b}{2a} = -\frac{\sqrt{b^2 - 4ac}}{2a}$$

$$x = -\frac{b}{2a} - \frac{\sqrt{b^2 - 4ac}}{2a}$$

$$= \frac{-b - \sqrt{b^2 - 4ac}}{2a}$$

POINT OF INTEREST

Although mathematicians have studied quadratic equations since around 500 B.C., it was not until the 18th century that the formula was written as it is today. Of further note, the word *quadratic* has the same Latin root as does the word *square*.

The Quadratic Formula

The solutions of $ax^2 + bx + c = 0$, $a \neq 0$, are

$$\frac{-b + \sqrt{b^2 - 4ac}}{2a} \quad \text{and} \quad \frac{-b - \sqrt{b^2 - 4ac}}{2a}$$

The quadratic formula is frequently written as $x = \dfrac{-b \pm \sqrt{b^2 - 4ac}}{2a}$.

➡ Solve by using the quadratic formula: $2x^2 + 5x + 3 = 0$

From the standard form of the equation, $a = 2$, $b = 5$, and $c = 3$. Replace a, b, and c in the quadratic formula with these values.

$$
\begin{aligned}
x &= \frac{-b \pm \sqrt{b^2 - 4ac}}{2a} \\
&= \frac{-(5) \pm \sqrt{(5)^2 - 4(2)(3)}}{2(2)} \\
&= \frac{-5 \pm \sqrt{25 - 24}}{4} \\
&= \frac{-5 \pm \sqrt{1}}{4} = \frac{-5 \pm 1}{4}
\end{aligned}
$$

$\bullet$ $a = 2$, $b = 5$, $c = 3$

$$
x = \frac{-5 + 1}{4} = -1 \qquad x = \frac{-5 - 1}{4} = \frac{-6}{4} = -\frac{3}{2}
$$

The solutions are -1 and $-\dfrac{3}{2}$.

➡ Solve by using the quadratic formula: $3x^2 = 4x + 6$

Write the equation in standard form.

$$
\begin{aligned}
3x^2 &= 4x + 6 \\
3x^2 - 4x - 6 &= 0
\end{aligned}
$$

$\bullet$ Subtract $4x$ and 6 from each side of the equation.

From the standard form of the equation, $a = 3$, $b = -4$, and $c = -6$. Replace a, b, and c in the quadratic formula with these values.

$$
\begin{aligned}
x &= \frac{-b \pm \sqrt{b^2 - 4ac}}{2a} \\
&= \frac{-(-4) \pm \sqrt{(-4)^2 - 4(3)(-6)}}{2(3)} \\
&= \frac{4 \pm \sqrt{16 - (-72)}}{6} \\
&= \frac{4 \pm \sqrt{88}}{6} = \frac{4 \pm 2\sqrt{22}}{6} \\
&= \frac{2(2 \pm \sqrt{22})}{2 \cdot 3} = \frac{2 \pm \sqrt{22}}{3}
\end{aligned}
$$

$\bullet$ $a = 3$, $b = -4$, $c = -6$

Check:

$$
\begin{array}{c|c}
\hline
\multicolumn{2}{c}{3x^2 = 4x + 6} \\
\hline
3\left(\dfrac{2 + \sqrt{22}}{3}\right)^2 & 4\left(\dfrac{2 + \sqrt{22}}{3}\right) + 6 \\
3\left(\dfrac{4 + 4\sqrt{22} + 22}{9}\right) & \dfrac{8}{3} + \dfrac{4\sqrt{22}}{3} + \dfrac{18}{3} \\
3\left(\dfrac{26 + 4\sqrt{22}}{9}\right) & \dfrac{26}{3} + \dfrac{4\sqrt{22}}{3} \\
\dfrac{26 + 4\sqrt{22}}{3} & = \dfrac{26 + 4\sqrt{22}}{3} \\
\end{array}
\qquad
\begin{array}{c|c}
\hline
\multicolumn{2}{c}{3x^2 = 4x + 6} \\
\hline
3\left(\dfrac{2 - \sqrt{22}}{3}\right)^2 & 4\left(\dfrac{2 - \sqrt{22}}{3}\right) + 6 \\
3\left(\dfrac{4 - 4\sqrt{22} + 22}{9}\right) & \dfrac{8}{3} - \dfrac{4\sqrt{22}}{3} + \dfrac{18}{3} \\
3\left(\dfrac{26 - 4\sqrt{22}}{9}\right) & \dfrac{26}{3} - \dfrac{4\sqrt{22}}{3} \\
\dfrac{26 - 4\sqrt{22}}{3} & = \dfrac{26 - 4\sqrt{22}}{3} \\
\end{array}
$$

The solutions are $\dfrac{2 + \sqrt{22}}{3}$ and $\dfrac{2 - \sqrt{22}}{3}$.

➡ Solve by using the quadratic formula: $4x^2 = 8x - 13$

$$4x^2 = 8x - 13$$

$$4x^2 - 8x + 13 = 0$$ • Write the equation in standard form.

$$x = \frac{-b \pm \sqrt{b^2 - 4ac}}{2a}$$ • Use the quadratic formula.

$$= \frac{-(-8) \pm \sqrt{(-8)^2 - 4 \cdot 4 \cdot 13}}{2 \cdot 4}$$ • $a = 4, b = -8, c = 13$

$$= \frac{8 \pm \sqrt{64 - 208}}{8} = \frac{8 \pm \sqrt{-144}}{8}$$

$$= \frac{8 \pm 12i}{8} = \frac{2 + 3i}{2}$$

The solutions are $1 + \frac{3}{2}i$ and $1 - \frac{3}{2}i$.

Of the three preceding examples, the first two had real number solutions; the last one had complex number solutions.

In the quadratic formula, the quantity $b^2 - 4ac$ is called the **discriminant**. When a, b, and c are real numbers, the discriminant determines whether a quadratic equation will have a double root, two real number solutions that are not equal, or two complex number solutions.

THE EFFECT OF THE DISCRIMINANT ON THE SOLUTIONS OF A QUADRATIC EQUATION

1. If $b^2 - 4ac = 0$, the equation has one real number solution, a double root.
2. If $b^2 - 4ac > 0$, the equation has two unequal real number solutions.
3. If $b^2 - 4ac < 0$, the equation has two complex number solutions.

➡ Use the discriminant to determine whether $x^2 - 4x - 5 = 0$ has one real number solution, two real number solutions, or two complex number solutions.

$b^2 - 4ac$ • Evaluate the discriminant. $a = 1, b = -4, c = -5$

$(-4)^2 - 4(1)(-5) = 16 + 20 = 36$

$36 > 0$

Because $b^2 - 4ac > 0$, the equation has two real number solutions.

Example 1 Solve by using the quadratic formula: $2x^2 - x + 5 = 0$

Solution $2x^2 - x + 5 = 0$
$a = 2, b = -1, c = 5$

$$x = \frac{-b \pm \sqrt{b^2 - 4ac}}{2a}$$

$$= \frac{-(-1) \pm \sqrt{(-1)^2 - 4(2)(5)}}{2 \cdot 2}$$

$$= \frac{1 \pm \sqrt{1 - 40}}{4} = \frac{1 \pm \sqrt{-39}}{4}$$

$$= \frac{1 \pm i\sqrt{39}}{4}$$

The solutions are $\frac{1}{4} + \frac{\sqrt{39}}{4}i$ and $\frac{1}{4} - \frac{\sqrt{39}}{4}i$.

You Try It 1 Solve by using the quadratic formula: $x^2 - 2x + 10 = 0$

Your solution $1 + 3i, 1 - 3i$

Solution on p. S29

Example 2

Solve by using the quadratic formula:
$2x^2 = (x - 2)(x - 3)$

Solution

$2x^2 = (x - 2)(x - 3)$
$2x^2 = x^2 - 5x + 6$

$x^2 + 5x - 6 = 0$
$a = 1, b = 5, c = -6$

$$x = \frac{-b \pm \sqrt{b^2 - 4ac}}{2a}$$

$$= \frac{-5 \pm \sqrt{5^2 - 4(1)(-6)}}{2 \cdot 1}$$

$$= \frac{-5 \pm \sqrt{25 + 24}}{2} = \frac{-5 \pm \sqrt{49}}{2}$$

$$= \frac{-5 \pm 7}{2}$$

$$x = \frac{-5 + 7}{2} \qquad x = \frac{-5 - 7}{2}$$

$$= \frac{2}{2} = 1 \qquad\quad = \frac{-12}{2} = -6$$

The solutions are 1 and −6.

You Try It 2

Solve by using the quadratic formula:
$4x^2 = 4x - 1$

Your solution

$\dfrac{1}{2}$

Example 3

Use the discriminant to determine whether $4x^2 - 2x + 5 = 0$ has one real number solution, two real number solutions, or two complex number solutions.

Solution

$a = 4, b = -2, c = 5$

$$b^2 - 4ac = (-2)^2 - 4(4)(5)$$
$$= 4 - 80$$
$$= -76$$

$-76 < 0$

Because the discriminant is less than zero, the equation has two complex number solutions.

You Try It 3

Use the discriminant to determine whether $3x^2 - x - 1 = 0$ has one real number solution, two real number solutions, or two complex number solutions.

Your solution

two real number solutions

Solutions on p. S30

10.3 Exercises

· ·

Objective A

Solve by using the quadratic formula.

1. $x^2 - 3x - 10 = 0$
$5, -2$

2. $z^2 - 4z - 8 = 0$
$2 + 2\sqrt{3}, 2 - 2\sqrt{3}$

3. $y^2 + 5y - 36 = 0$
$4, -9$

4. $z^2 - 3z - 40 = 0$
$8, -5$

5. $w^2 = 8w + 72$
$4 + 2\sqrt{22}, 4 - 2\sqrt{22}$

6. $t^2 = 2t + 35$
$7, -5$

7. $v^2 = 24 - 5v$
$3, -8$

8. $x^2 = 18 - 7x$
$2, -9$

9. $2y^2 + 5y - 3 = 0$
$-3, \dfrac{1}{2}$

10. $4p^2 - 7p + 3 = 0$
$1, \dfrac{3}{4}$

11. $8s^2 = 10s + 3$
$\dfrac{3}{2}, -\dfrac{1}{4}$

12. $12t^2 = 5t + 2$
$\dfrac{2}{3}, -\dfrac{1}{4}$

13. $x^2 = 14x - 24$
$2, 12$

14. $v^2 = 12v - 24$
$6 + 2\sqrt{3}, 6 - 2\sqrt{3}$

15. $2z^2 - 2z - 1 = 0$
$\dfrac{1 + \sqrt{3}}{2}, \dfrac{1 - \sqrt{3}}{2}$

16. $6w^2 = 19w - 10$
$\dfrac{5}{2}, \dfrac{2}{3}$

17. $z^2 + 2z + 2 = 0$
$-1 + i, -1 - i$

18. $p^2 - 4p + 5 = 0$
$2 + i, 2 - i$

19. $y^2 - 2y + 5 = 0$
$1 + 2i, 1 - 2i$

20. $x^2 + 6x + 13 = 0$
$-3 + 2i, -3 - 2i$

21. $s^2 - 4s + 13 = 0$
$2 + 3i, 2 - 3i$

22. $t^2 - 6t + 10 = 0$
$3 + i, 3 - i$

23. $2w^2 - 2w + 5 = 0$
$\dfrac{1}{2} + \dfrac{3}{2}i, \dfrac{1}{2} - \dfrac{3}{2}i$

24. $4v^2 + 8v + 3 = 0$
$-\dfrac{1}{2}, -\dfrac{3}{2}$

25. $2x^2 + 6x + 5 = 0$
$-\dfrac{3}{2} + \dfrac{1}{2}i, -\dfrac{3}{2} - \dfrac{1}{2}i$

26. $2y^2 + 2y + 13 = 0$
$-\dfrac{1}{2} + \dfrac{5}{2}i, -\dfrac{1}{2} - \dfrac{5}{2}i$

27. $4t^2 - 6t + 9 = 0$
$\dfrac{3}{4} + \dfrac{3\sqrt{3}}{4}i, \dfrac{3}{4} - \dfrac{3\sqrt{3}}{4}i$

Use the discriminant to determine whether the quadratic equation has one real number solution, two real number solutions, or two complex number solutions.

28. $2z^2 - z + 5 = 0$
two complex

29. $3y^2 + y + 1 = 0$
two complex

30. $9x^2 - 12x + 4 = 0$
one real

31. $4x^2 + 20x + 25 = 0$
one real

32. $2v^2 - 3v - 1 = 0$
two real

33. $3w^2 + 3w - 2 = 0$
two real

APPLYING THE CONCEPTS

34. Name the three methods of solving a quadratic equation that have been discussed. What are the advantages and disadvantages of each?

For what values of p does the quadratic equation have two real number solutions that are not equal? Write the answer in set-builder notation.

35. $x^2 - 6x + p = 0$
  $\{p|p < 9\}$

36. $x^2 + 10x + p = 0$
  $\{p|p < 25\}$

For what values of p does the quadratic equation have two complex number solutions? Write the answer in set-builder notation.

37. $x^2 - 2x + p = 0$
  $\{p|p > 1\}$

38. $x^2 + 4x + p = 0$
  $\{p|p > 4\}$

39. Show that the equation $x^2 + bx - 1 = 0$ always has real number solutions regardless of the value of b.
  The complete solution is in the *Solutions Manual.*

40. Can the quadratic formula be used to solve *any* quadratic equation? If so, explain why. If not, give an example of a quadratic equation that cannot be solved by using the quadratic formula.

41. One of the steps in the derivation of the quadratic formula is $x + \frac{b}{2a} = \pm\sqrt{\frac{b^2 - 4ac}{2a}}$. Carefully explain the occurrence of the $\pm$ sign. (*Hint:* Recall that $\sqrt{x^2} = |x|$.)

42. *Survival of the Spotted Owl*   The National Forest Management Act of 1976 specifies that harvesting timber in national forests must be accomplished in conjunction with environmental considerations. One such consideration is providing a habitat for the spotted owl. One model of the survival of the spotted owl requires the solution of the equation $x^2 - s_a x - s_j s_s f = 0$ for x. Different values of s_a, s_j, s_s, and f are given in the table at the right. The values are particularly important because they are related to the survival of the owl. If $x > 1$, then the model predicts a growth in the population; if $x = 1$, the population remains steady; for $x < 1$, the population decreases. The important solution of the equation is the larger of the two roots of the equation.

	U.S. Forest Service	Lande
s_j	0.34	0.11
s_s	0.97	0.71
s_a	0.97	0.94
f	0.24	0.24

Source: Biles, Charles and Barry Noon. "The Spotted Owl." *The Journal of Undergraduate Mathematics and Its Application* vol.11, no. 2, 1990.

  a. Determine the larger root of this equation for values provided by the U.S. Forest Service. Round to the nearest hundredth. Does it predict that the population will increase, remain steady, or decrease?
    $x = 1.05$; increases

  b. Determine the larger root of this equation for the values provided by R. Lande in *Oecologia* (vol. 75, 1988). Round to the nearest hundredth. Does it predict that the population will increase, remain steady, or decrease?
    $x = 0.96$; decreases

10.4 Solving Equations That Are Reducible to Quadratic Equations

Objective A ***To solve an equation that is quadratic in form*** ....

Certain equations that are not quadratic can be expressed in quadratic form by making suitable substitutions. An equation is quadratic in form if it can be written as $au^2 + bu + c = 0$.

The equation $x^4 - 4x^2 - 5 = 0$ is quadratic in form.

$$x^4 - 4x^2 - 5 = 0$$
$$(x^2)^2 - 4(x^2) - 5 = 0 \qquad \bullet \text{ Let } x^2 = u.$$
$$u^2 - 4u - 5 = 0$$

The equation $y - y^{1/2} - 6 = 0$ is quadratic in form.

$$y - y^{1/2} - 6 = 0$$
$$(y^{1/2})^2 - (y^{1/2}) - 6 = 0 \qquad \bullet \text{ Let } y^{1/2} = u.$$
$$u^2 - u - 6 = 0$$

Here is the key to recognizing equations that are quadratic in form: When the equation is written in standard form, the exponent on one variable term is $\frac{1}{2}$ the exponent on the other variable term.

➡ Solve: $z + 7z^{1/2} - 18 = 0$

$$\begin{aligned} z + 7z^{1/2} - 18 &= 0 \\ (z^{1/2})^2 + 7(z^{1/2}) - 18 &= 0 \qquad &\bullet \text{ The equation is quadratic in form.} \\ u^2 + 7u - 18 &= 0 \qquad &\bullet \text{ Let } z^{1/2} = u. \\ (u - 2)(u + 9) &= 0 \qquad &\bullet \text{ Solve by factoring.} \end{aligned}$$

$$\begin{array}{ll} u - 2 = 0 & u + 9 = 0 \\ u = 2 & u = -9 \end{array}$$

$$\begin{array}{ll} z^{1/2} = 2 & z^{1/2} = -9 \qquad \bullet \text{ Replace } u \text{ by } z^{1/2}. \\ \sqrt{z} = 2 & \sqrt{z} = -9 \end{array}$$

$$\begin{array}{ll} (\sqrt{z})^2 = 2^2 & (\sqrt{z})^2 = (-9)^2 \qquad \bullet \text{ Solve for } z. \\ z = 4 & z = 81 \end{array}$$

Check each solution.

Check:

$$\begin{array}{c|c} z + 7z^{1/2} - 18 = 0 \\ \hline 4 + 7(4)^{1/2} - 18 & 0 \\ 4 + 7 \cdot 2 - 18 \\ 4 + 14 - 18 \\ & 0 = 0 \end{array} \qquad \begin{array}{c|c} z + 7z^{1/2} - 18 = 0 \\ \hline 81 + 7(81)^{1/2} - 18 & 0 \\ 81 + 7 \cdot 9 - 18 \\ 81 + 63 - 18 \\ & 126 \neq 0 \end{array}$$

4 checks as a solution, but 81 does not check as a solution.
The solution is 4.

TAKE NOTE

When each side of an equation is squared, the resulting equation may have a solution that is not a solution of the original equation.

Example 1   Solve: $x^4 + x^2 - 12 = 0$

Solution
$$x^4 + x^2 - 12 = 0$$
$$(x^2)^2 + (x^2) - 12 = 0$$
$$u^2 + u - 12 = 0$$
$$(u - 3)(u + 4) = 0$$

$$u - 3 = 0 \qquad u + 4 = 0$$
$$u = 3 \qquad\quad u = -4$$

Replace u by x^2.

$$x^2 = 3 \qquad\qquad x^2 = -4$$
$$\sqrt{x^2} = \sqrt{3} \qquad \sqrt{x^2} = \sqrt{-4}$$
$$x = \pm\sqrt{3} \qquad\quad x = \pm 2i$$

The solutions are $\sqrt{3}$, $-\sqrt{3}$, $2i$, and $-2i$.

You Try It 1   Solve: $x - 5x^{1/2} + 6 = 0$

Your solution $4, 9$

Solution on p. S30

Objective B   *To solve a radical equation that is reducible to a quadratic equation* ....

Certain equations that contain radicals can be expressed as quadratic equations.

➡ Solve: $\sqrt{x + 2} + 4 = x$

$$\sqrt{x + 2} + 4 = x$$
$$\sqrt{x + 2} = x - 4 \qquad\qquad \bullet \text{ Solve for the radical expression.}$$
$$(\sqrt{x + 2})^2 = (x - 4)^2 \qquad \bullet \text{ Square each side of the equation.}$$
$$x + 2 = x^2 - 8x + 16 \qquad \bullet \text{ Simplify.}$$
$$0 = x^2 - 9x + 14 \qquad\quad \bullet \text{ Write the equation in standard form.}$$
$$0 = (x - 7)(x - 2) \qquad\quad \bullet \text{ Solve for } x.$$

$$x - 7 = 0 \qquad x - 2 = 0$$
$$x = 7 \qquad\quad x = 2$$

TAKE NOTE

You should always check your solutions by substituting the proposed solutions back into the *original* equation.

Check:
$$\begin{array}{c|c} \sqrt{x + 2} + 4 = x \\ \hline \sqrt{7 + 2} + 4 \mid 7 \\ \sqrt{9} + 4 \\ 3 + 4 \\ 7 = 7 \end{array}$$
$$\begin{array}{c|c} \sqrt{x + 2} + 4 = x \\ \hline \sqrt{2 + 2} + 4 \mid 2 \\ \sqrt{4} + 4 \\ 2 + 4 \\ 6 \neq 2 \end{array}$$

7 checks as a solution, but 2 does not check as a solution.
The solution is 7.

Example 2

Solve: $\sqrt{7y - 3} + 3 = 2y$

Solution

$$\sqrt{7y - 3} + 3 = 2y$$
$$\sqrt{7y - 3} = 2y - 3$$
$$(\sqrt{7y - 3})^2 = (2y - 3)^2$$
$$7y - 3 = 4y^2 - 12y + 9$$
$$0 = 4y^2 - 19y + 12$$
$$0 = (4y - 3)(y - 4)$$

$$4y - 3 = 0 \qquad y - 4 = 0$$
$$4y = 3 \qquad\qquad y = 4$$
$$y = \frac{3}{4}$$

4 checks as a solution.

$\frac{3}{4}$ does not check as a solution.

The solution is 4.

You Try It 2

Solve: $\sqrt{2x + 1} + x = 7$

Your solution

4

Example 3

Solve: $\sqrt{2y + 1} - \sqrt{y} = 1$

Solution

$$\sqrt{2y + 1} - \sqrt{y} = 1$$

Solve for one of the radical expressions.

$$\sqrt{2y + 1} = \sqrt{y} + 1$$
$$(\sqrt{2y + 1})^2 = (\sqrt{y} + 1)^2$$
$$2y + 1 = y + 2\sqrt{y} + 1$$
$$y = 2\sqrt{y}$$

Square each side of the equation.

$$y^2 = (2\sqrt{y})^2$$
$$y^2 = 4y$$
$$y^2 - 4y = 0$$
$$y(y - 4) = 0$$
$$y = 0 \qquad y - 4 = 0$$
$$y = 4$$

0 and 4 check as solutions.

The solutions are 0 and 4.

You Try It 3

Solve: $\sqrt{2x - 1} + \sqrt{x - 2}$

Your solution

1

Solutions on p. S30

Objective C *To solve a fractional equation that is reducible to a quadratic equation*...

After each side of a fractional equation has been multiplied by the LCM of the denominators, the resulting equation may be a quadratic equation.

➡ Solve: $\dfrac{1}{r} + \dfrac{1}{r+1} = \dfrac{3}{2}$

$$\dfrac{1}{r} + \dfrac{1}{r+1} = \dfrac{3}{2}$$

$$2r(r+1)\left(\dfrac{1}{r} + \dfrac{1}{r+1}\right) = 2r(r+1)\cdot\dfrac{3}{2}$$

• Multiply each side of the equation by the LCM of the denominators.

$$2(r+1) + 2r = r(r+1)\cdot 3$$
$$2r + 2 + 2r = 3r(r+1)$$
$$4r + 2 = 3r^2 + 3r$$
$$0 = 3r^2 - r - 2$$

• Write the equation in standard form.

$$0 = (3r+2)(r-1)$$

• Solve for *r* by factoring.

$$3r + 2 = 0 \qquad r - 1 = 0$$
$$3r = -2 \qquad\quad r = 1$$
$$r = -\dfrac{2}{3}$$

$-\dfrac{2}{3}$ and 1 check as solutions. The solutions are $-\dfrac{2}{3}$ and 1.

Example 4

Solve: $\dfrac{9}{x-3} = 2x + 1$

Solution

$$\dfrac{9}{x-3} = 2x + 1$$

$$(x-3)\dfrac{9}{x-3} = (x-3)(2x+1)$$
$$9 = 2x^2 - 5x - 3$$
$$0 = 2x^2 - 5x - 12$$
$$0 = (2x+3)(x-4)$$

$$2x + 3 = 0 \qquad x - 4 = 0$$
$$2x = -3 \qquad\quad x = 4$$
$$x = -\dfrac{3}{2}$$

$-\dfrac{3}{2}$ and 4 check as solutions.

The solutions are $-\dfrac{3}{2}$ and 4.

You Try It 4

Solve: $3y + \dfrac{25}{3y-2} = -8$

Your solution

-1

Solution on p. S30

10.4 Exercises

· ·

Objective A

Solve.

1. $x^4 - 13x^2 + 36 = 0$
2, −2, 3, −3

2. $y^4 - 5y^2 + 4 = 0$
1, −1, 2, −2

3. $z^4 - 6z^2 + 8 = 0$
2, −2, $\sqrt{2}$, −$\sqrt{2}$

4. $t^4 - 12t^2 + 27 = 0$
3, −3, $\sqrt{3}$, −$\sqrt{3}$

5. $p - 3p^{1/2} + 2 = 0$
1, 4

6. $v - 7v^{1/2} + 12 = 0$
9, 16

7. $x - x^{1/2} - 12 = 0$
16

8. $w - 2w^{1/2} - 15 = 0$
25

9. $z^4 + 3z^2 - 4 = 0$
2i, −2i, 1, −1

10. $y^4 + 5y^2 - 36 = 0$
2, −2, 3i, −3i

11. $x^4 + 12x^2 - 64 = 0$
4i, −4i, 2, −2

12. $x^4 - 81 = 0$
3i, −3i, 3, −3

13. $p + 2p^{1/2} - 24 = 0$
16

14. $v + 3v^{1/2} - 4 = 0$
1

15. $y^{2/3} - 9y^{1/3} + 8 = 0$
1, 512

16. $z^{2/3} - z^{1/3} - 6 = 0$
−8, 27

17. $9w^4 - 13w^2 + 4 = 0$
$\frac{2}{3}, -\frac{2}{3}, 1, -1$

18. $4y^4 - 7y^2 - 36 = 0$
$\frac{3}{2}i, -\frac{3}{2}i, 2, -2$

Objective B

Solve.

19. $\sqrt{x + 1} + x = 5$
3

20. $\sqrt{x - 4} + x = 6$
5

21. $x = \sqrt{x} + 6$
9

22. $\sqrt{2y - 1} = y - 2$
5

23. $\sqrt{3w + 3} = w + 1$
2, −1

24. $\sqrt{2s + 1} = s - 1$
4

25. $\sqrt{4y + 1} - y = 1$
0, 2

26. $\sqrt{3s + 4} + 2s = 12$
4

27. $\sqrt{10x + 5} - 2x = 1$
$-\frac{1}{2}, 2$

28. $\sqrt{t + 8} = 2t + 1$

1

29. $\sqrt{p + 11} = 1 - p$

−2

30. $x - 7 = \sqrt{x - 5}$

9

31. $\sqrt{x - 1} - \sqrt{x} = -1$

1

32. $\sqrt{y + 1} = \sqrt{y + 5}$

4

33. $\sqrt{2x - 1} = 1 - \sqrt{x - 1}$

1

34. $\sqrt{x + 6} + \sqrt{x + 2} = 2$

−2

35. $\sqrt{t + 3} + \sqrt{2t + 7} = 1$

−3

36. $\sqrt{5 - 2x} = \sqrt{2 - x} + 1$

2, −2

Objective C

Solve.

37. $x = \dfrac{10}{x - 9}$

10, −1

38. $z = \dfrac{5}{z - 4}$

5, −1

39. $\dfrac{t}{t + 1} = \dfrac{-2}{t - 1}$

$-\dfrac{1}{2} + \dfrac{\sqrt{7}}{2}i, -\dfrac{1}{2} - \dfrac{\sqrt{7}}{2}i$

40. $\dfrac{2v}{v - 1} = \dfrac{5}{v + 2}$

$\dfrac{1}{4} + \dfrac{\sqrt{39}}{4}i, \dfrac{1}{4} - \dfrac{\sqrt{39}}{4}i$

41. $\dfrac{y - 1}{y + 2} + y = 1$

−3, 1

42. $\dfrac{2p - 1}{p - 2} + p = 8$

5, 3

43. $\dfrac{3r + 2}{r + 2} - 2r = 1$

0, −1

44. $\dfrac{2v + 3}{v + 4} + 3v = 4$

$-\dfrac{13}{3}, 1$

45. $\dfrac{2}{2x + 1} + \dfrac{1}{x} = 3$

$\dfrac{1}{2}, -\dfrac{1}{3}$

46. $\dfrac{3}{s} - \dfrac{2}{2s - 1} = 1$

$\dfrac{3}{2}, 1$

47. $\dfrac{16}{z - 2} + \dfrac{16}{z + 2} = 6$

$-\dfrac{2}{3}, 6$

48. $\dfrac{2}{y + 1} + \dfrac{1}{y - 1} = 1$

0, 3

49. $\dfrac{t}{t - 2} + \dfrac{2}{t - 1} = 4$

$\dfrac{4}{3}, 3$

50. $\dfrac{4t + 1}{t + 4} + \dfrac{3t - 1}{t + 1} = 2$

$-\dfrac{11}{5}, 1$

51. $\dfrac{5}{2p - 1} + \dfrac{4}{p + 1} = 2$

$-\dfrac{1}{4}, 3$

APPLYING THE CONCEPTS

Solve.

52. $(\sqrt{x} - 2)^2 - 5\sqrt{x} + 14 = 0$
Hint: Let $u = \sqrt{x} - 2$.
9, 36

53. $(\sqrt{x} + 3)^2 - 4\sqrt{x} - 17 = 0$
Hint: Let $u = \sqrt{x} + 3$.
4

10.5 Applications of Quadratic Equations

Objective A   *To solve application problems* ....

The application problems in this section are similar to problems solved earlier in the text. Each of the strategies for the problems in this section will result in a quadratic equation.

→ A small pipe takes 16 min longer to empty a tank than does a larger pipe. Working together, the pipes can empty the tank in 6 min. How long would it take the smaller pipe working alone to empty the tank?

> **Strategy for Solving an Application Problem**
>
> 1. Determine the type of problem. Is it a uniform motion problem, a geometry problem, an integer problem, or a work problem?

The problem is a work problem.

> 2. Choose a variable to represent the unknown quantity. Write numerical or variable expressions for all the remaining quantities. These results can be recorded in a table.

The unknown time of the larger pipe: t
The unknown time of the smaller pipe: $t + 16$

	Rate of Work	·	Time Worked	=	Part of Task Completed
Larger pipe	$\dfrac{1}{t}$	·	6	=	$\dfrac{6}{t}$
Smaller pipe	$\dfrac{1}{t + 16}$	·	6	=	$\dfrac{6}{t + 16}$

> 3. Determine how the quantities are related.

$$\frac{6}{t} + \frac{6}{t + 16} = 1$$

• The sum of the parts of the task completed must equal 1.

$$t(t + 16)\left(\frac{6}{t} + \frac{6}{t + 16}\right) = t(t + 16) \cdot 1$$
$$(t + 16)6 + 6t = t^2 + 16t$$
$$6t + 96 + 6t = t^2 + 16t$$
$$0 = t^2 + 4t - 96$$
$$0 = (t + 12)(t - 8)$$

$$t + 12 = 0 \qquad t - 8 = 0$$
$$t = -12 \qquad t = 8$$

Because time cannot be negative, the solution $t = -12$ is not possible.

The time for the smaller pipe is $t + 16$.

$t + 16 = 8 + 16 = 24$ • Replace t by 8 and evaluate.

The smaller pipe requires 24 min to empty the tank.

Example 1

In 8 h, two campers rowed 15 mi down a river and then rowed back to their campsite. The rate of the river's current was 1 mph. Find the rate at which the campers rowed.

Strategy

- This is a uniform motion problem.
- Unknown rowing rate of the campers: r

	Distance	Rate	Time
Down river	15	$r + 1$	$\dfrac{15}{r + 1}$
Up river	15	$r - 1$	$\dfrac{15}{r - 1}$

- The total time of the trip was 8 h.

Solution

$$\frac{15}{r + 1} + \frac{15}{r - 1} = 8$$

$$(r + 1)(r - 1)\left(\frac{15}{r + 1} + \frac{15}{r - 1}\right) = (r + 1)(r - 1)8$$

$$(r - 1)15 + (r + 1)15 = (r^2 - 1)8$$

$$15r - 15 + 15r + 15 = 8r^2 - 8$$

$$30r = 8r^2 - 8$$

$$0 = 8r^2 - 30r - 8$$

$$0 = 2(4r^2 - 15r - 4)$$

$$0 = 2(4r + 1)(r - 4)$$

$$4r + 1 = 0 \qquad r - 4 = 0$$
$$4r = -1 \qquad r = 4$$
$$r = -\frac{1}{4}$$

The solution $r = -\frac{1}{4}$ is not possible, because the rate cannot be a negative number.

The rowing rate was 4 mph.

You Try It 1

The length of a rectangle is 3 m more than the width. The area is 54 m². Find the length of the rectangle.

Your strategy

Your solution

9 m

Solution on p. S30

10.5 Exercises

· ·

Objective A   Application Problems

1. The base of a triangle is one less than five times the height of the trian-gle. The area of the triangle is 21 cm². Find the height and the length of the base of the triangle.   height: 3 cm; base: 14 cm

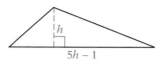

2. The height of a triangle is 3 in. less than the base of the triangle. The area of the triangle is 90 in². Find the height and the length of the base of the triangle.   height: 12 in.; base: 15 in.

3. The length of a rectangle is 2 ft less than three times the width of the rectangle. The area of the rectangle is 65 ft². Find the length and width of the rectangle.   length: 13 ft; width: 5 ft

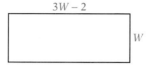

4. The length of a rectangle is 2 cm less than twice the width. The area of the rectangle is 180 cm². Find the length and width of the rectangle.
length: 18 cm; width: 10 cm

5. The state of Colorado is almost perfectly rectangular, with its north border 111 mi longer than its west border. If the state en-compasses 104,000 mi², estimate the dimensions of Colorado. Round to the nearest mile.   272 mi by 383 mi

6. A car with good tire tread can stop in less distance than a car with poor tread. The formula for the stopping distance, d, of a car with good tread on dry cement is approximated by $d = 0.04v^2 + 0.5v$, where v is the speed of the car. If the driver must be able to stop within 60 ft, what is the maximum safe speed, to the nearest mile per hour, of the car?   33 mph

7. A square piece of cardboard is formed into a box by cutting 10-centimeter squares from each of the four corners and then folding up the sides, as shown in the figure. If the volume, V, of the box is to be 49,000 cm³, what size square piece of cardboard is needed? Recall that $V = LWH$.   90 cm by 90 cm

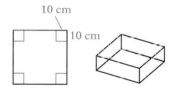

8. The height of a projectile fired upward is given by the formula $s = v_0t - 16t^2$, where s is the height, v_0 is the initial velocity, and t is the time. Find the time for a projectile to return to Earth if it has an initial velocity of 200 ft/s.   12.5 s

9. The height of a projectile fired upward is given by the formula $s = v_0t - 16t^2$, where s is the height, v_0 is the initial velocity, and t is the time. Find the time for a projectile to reach a height of 64 ft if it has an initial velocity of 128 ft/s. Round to the nearest hundredth of a second.
0.54 s (on the way up) or 7.46 s (on the way down)

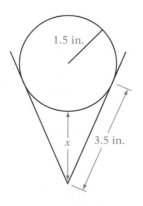

10. A perfectly spherical scoop of mint chocolate chip ice cream is placed in a cone, as shown in the figure. How far is the bottom of the scoop of ice cream from the bottom of the cone? (*Hint:* A line segment from the center of the ice cream to the point at which the ice cream touches the cone is perpendicular to the edge of the cone.)   2.3 in.

11. A small pipe can fill a tank in 6 min more time than it takes a larger pipe to fill the same tank. Working together, both pipes can fill the tank in 4 min. How long would it take each pipe working alone to fill the tank?   smaller pipe: 12 min; larger pipe: 6 min

12. A cruise ship made a trip of 100 mi in 8 h. The ship traveled the first 40 mi at a constant rate before increasing its speed by 5 mph. Then it traveled another 60 mi at the increased speed. Find the rate of the cruise ship for the first 40 mi.   10 mph

13. The Concorde's speed in calm air is 1320 mph. Flying with the wind, the Concorde can fly from New York to London, a distance of approximately 4000 mi, in 0.5 h less than the time required to make the return trip. Find the rate of the wind to the nearest mile per hour.   108 mph

14. A car travels 120 mi. A second car, traveling 10 mph faster than the first car, makes the same trip in 1 h less time. Find the speed of each car.
first car: 30 mph; second car: 40 mph

15. For a portion of the Green River in Utah, the rate of the river's current is 4 mph. A tour guide can row 5 mi down this river and back in 3 h. Find the rowing rate of the guide in calm water.   6 mph

16. The height of an arch is given by the equation $h(x) = -\frac{3}{64}x^2 + 27$, where $|x|$ is the distance in feet from the center of the arch.

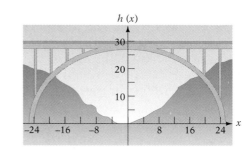

   a. What is the maximum height of the arch?   27 ft
   b. What is the height of the arch 8 ft to the right of the center?   24 ft
   c. How far from the center is the arch 8 ft tall?   20.13 ft

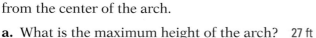

APPLYING THE CONCEPTS

17. Some forecasters are predicting the revenue generated by business on the Internet from 1997 to 2002 will expand to values that can be approximated by the model $R(t) = 15.8t^2 - 17.2t + 10.2$, where R is the annual revenue in billions of dollars and t is the time in years, with $t = 0$ corresponding to 1997. According to this model, in what year will the revenue reach $200 billion? Round to the nearest year. Explain why there is just one answer to this problem. (Source: Forrester Research)
2001; the negative value of t corresponds to a year before 1997, which is not between 1997 and 2002.

18. Using Torricelli's Principle, it can be shown that the depth, d, of a liquid in a bottle with a hole of area 0.5 cm² in its side can be approximated by $d = 0.0034t^2 - 0.52518t + 20$, where t is the time since a stopper was removed from the hole. When will the depth be 10 cm? Round to the nearest tenth of a second.   22.2 s

10.6 Quadratic Inequalities and Rational Inequalities

Objective A   *To solve a nonlinear inequality*..

A **quadratic inequality** is one that can be written in the form $ax^2 + bx + c < 0$ or $ax^2 + bx + c > 0$, where $a \neq 0$. The symbols $\leq$ and $\geq$ can also be used. The solution set of a quadratic inequality can be found by solving a compound inequality.

To solve $x^2 - 3x - 10 > 0$, first factor the trinomial.

$$x^2 - 3x - 10 > 0$$
$$(x + 2)(x - 5) > 0$$

There are two cases for which the product of the factors will be positive: (1) both factors are positive, or (2) both factors are negative.

(1) $x + 2 > 0$ and $x - 5 > 0$
(2) $x + 2 < 0$ and $x - 5 < 0$

Solve each pair of compound inequalities.

(1) $x + 2 > 0$ and $x - 5 > 0$
$x > -2$ $x > 5$
$\{x | x > -2\} \cap \{x | x > 5\} = \{x | x > 5\}$

(2) $x + 2 < 0$ and $x - 5 < 0$
$x < -2$ $x < 5$
$\{x | x < -2\} \cap \{x | x < 5\} = \{x | x < -2\}$

Because the two cases for which the product will be positive are connected by *or*, the solution set is the union of the solution sets of the individual inequalities.

$$\{x | x > 5\} \cup \{x | x < -2\} = \{x | x > 5 \text{ or } x < -2\}$$

Although the solution set of any quadratic inequality can be found by using the method outlined above, frequently a graphical method is easier to use.

⇒ Solve and graph the solution set of $x^2 - x - 6 < 0$.

Factor the trinomial.

$$x^2 - x - 6 < 0$$
$$(x - 3)(x + 2) < 0$$

On a number line, draw lines indicating the numbers that make each factor equal to zero.

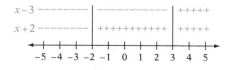

$x - 3 = 0$ $x + 2 = 0$
$x = 3$ $x = -2$

For each factor, place plus signs above the number line for those regions where the factor is positive and negative signs where the factor is negative.

Because $x^2 - x - 6 < 0$, the solution set will be the regions where one factor is positive and the other factor is negative.

Write the solution set.

$$\{x | -2 < x < 3\}$$

The graph of the solution set of $x^2 - x - 6 < 0$ is shown at the right.

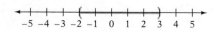

➡ Solve and graph the solution set of $(x - 2)(x + 1)(x - 4) > 0$.

On a number line, identify for each factor the regions where the factor is positive and those where the factor is negative.

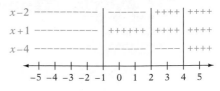

There are two regions where the product of the three factors is positive.

Write the solution set.
$\{x \mid -1 < x < 2 \text{ or } x > 4\}$

The graph of the solution set of $(x - 2)(x + 1)(x - 4) > 0$ is shown at the right.

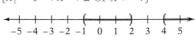

➡ Solve: $\dfrac{2x - 5}{x - 4} \leq 1$

$$\frac{2x - 5}{x - 4} \leq 1$$

Rewrite the inequality so that 0 appears on the right side of the inequality.

$$\frac{2x - 5}{x - 4} - 1 \leq 0$$

Simplify.

$$\frac{2x - 5}{x - 4} - \frac{x - 4}{x - 4} \leq 0$$

$$\frac{x - 1}{x - 4} \leq 0$$

On a number line, identify for each factor of the numerator and each factor of the denominator the regions where the factor is positive and those where the factor is negative.

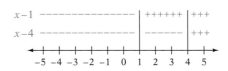

The region where the quotient of the two factors is negative is between 1 and 4.

Write the solution set.
$\{x \mid 1 \leq x < 4\}$

Note that 1 is part of the solution set but that 4 is not because the denominator of the rational expression is zero when $x = 4$.

Example 1
Solve and graph the solution set of
$2x^2 - x - 3 \geq 0$.

Solution
$$2x^2 - x - 3 \geq 0$$
$$(2x - 3)(x + 1) \geq 0$$

$$\left\{ x \mid x \leq -1 \text{ or } x \geq \frac{3}{2} \right\}$$

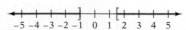

You Try It 1
Solve and graph the solution set of
$2x^2 - x - 10 \leq 0$.

Your solution
$$\left\{ x \mid -2 \leq x \leq \frac{5}{2} \right\}$$

Solution on p. S31

10.6 Exercises

· ·

Objective A

Solve and graph the solution set.

1. $(x - 4)(x + 2) > 0$

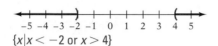

$\{x | x < -2 \text{ or } x > 4\}$

2. $(x + 1)(x - 3) > 0$

$\{x | x < -1 \text{ or } x > 3\}$

3. $x^2 - 3x + 2 \geq 0$

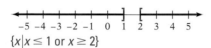

$\{x | x \leq 1 \text{ or } x \geq 2\}$

4. $x^2 + 5x + 6 > 0$

$\{x | x < -3 \text{ or } x > -2\}$

5. $x^2 - x - 12 < 0$

$\{x | -3 < x < 4\}$

6. $x^2 + x - 20 < 0$

$\{x | -5 < x < 4\}$

7. $(x - 1)(x + 2)(x - 3) < 0$

$\{x | x < -2 \text{ or } 1 < x < 3\}$

8. $(x + 4)(x - 2)(x + 1) > 0$

$\{x | -4 < x < -1 \text{ or } x > 2\}$

9. $(x + 4)(x - 2)(x - 1) \geq 0$

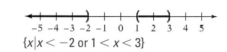

$\{x | -4 \leq x \leq 1 \text{ or } x \geq 2\}$

10. $(x - 1)(x + 5)(x - 2) \leq 0$

$\{x | x \leq -5 \text{ or } 1 \leq x \leq 2\}$

11. $\dfrac{x - 4}{x + 2} > 0$

$\{x | x < -2 \text{ or } x > 4]$

12. $\dfrac{x + 2}{x - 3} > 0$

$\{x | x < -2 \text{ or } x > 3\}$

13. $\dfrac{x - 3}{x + 1} \leq 0$

$\{x | -1 < x \leq 3\}$

14. $\dfrac{x - 1}{x} > 0$

$\{x | x < 0 \text{ or } x > 1\}$

15. $\dfrac{(x - 1)(x + 2)}{x - 3} \leq 0$

$\{x | x \leq -2 \text{ or } 1 \leq x < 3\}$

16. $\dfrac{(x + 3)(x - 1)}{x - 2} \geq 0$

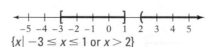

$\{x | -3 \leq x \leq 1 \text{ or } x > 2\}$

Solve.

17. $x^2 - 16 > 0$
$\{x \mid x > 4 \text{ or } x < -4\}$

18. $x^2 - 4 \geq 0$
$\{x \mid x \leq -2 \text{ or } x \geq 2\}$

19. $x^2 - 9x \leq 36$
$\{x \mid -3 \leq x \leq 12\}$

20. $x^2 + 4x > 21$
$\{x \mid x < -7 \text{ or } x > 3\}$

21. $4x^2 - 8x + 3 < 0$
$\left\{x \mid \dfrac{1}{2} < x < \dfrac{3}{2}\right\}$

22. $2x^2 + 11x + 12 \geq 0$
$\left\{x \mid x \leq -4 \text{ or } x \geq -\dfrac{3}{2}\right\}$

23. $\dfrac{3}{x-1} < 2$
$\left\{x \mid x < 1 \text{ or } x > \dfrac{5}{2}\right\}$

24. $\dfrac{x}{(x-1)(x+2)} \geq 0$
$\{x \mid x > 1 \text{ or } -2 < x \leq 0\}$

25. $\dfrac{x-2}{(x+1)(x-1)} \leq 0$
$\{x \mid x < -1 \text{ or } 1 < x \leq 2\}$

26. $\dfrac{1}{x} < 2$
$\left\{x \mid x > \dfrac{1}{2} \text{ or } x < 0\right\}$

27. $\dfrac{x}{2x-1} \geq 1$
$\left\{x \mid \dfrac{1}{2} < x \leq 1\right\}$

28. $\dfrac{x}{2x-3} \leq 1$
$\left\{x \mid x < \dfrac{3}{2} \text{ or } x \geq 3\right\}$

29. $\dfrac{x}{2-x} \leq -3$
$\{x \mid 2 < x \leq 3\}$

30. $\dfrac{3}{x-2} > \dfrac{2}{x+2}$
$\{x \mid x > 2 \text{ or } -10 < x < -2\}$

31. $\dfrac{3}{x-5} > \dfrac{1}{x+1}$
$\{x \mid x > 5 \text{ or } -4 < x < -1\}$

APPLYING THE CONCEPTS

Graph the solution set.

32. $(x+2)(x-3)(x+1)(x+4) > 0$

33. $(x-1)(x+3)(x-2)(x-4) \geq 0$

34. $(x^2 + 2x - 8)(x^2 - 2x - 3) < 0$

35. $(x^2 + 2x - 3)(x^2 + 3x + 2) \geq 0$

36. $(x^2 + 1)(x^2 - 3x + 2) > 0$

37. $(x-4)^2 > -2$

38. $x < x^2$

39. $x^3 > x$

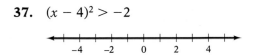

Focus on Problem Solving

**Use a Variety of
Problem-Solving
Techniques**

We have examined several problem-solving strategies throughout the text. See if you can apply those techniques to the following problems. (There are many sites on the Internet dealing with problem solving. Two such sites are www.askdrmath.com and www.mcallister.org. You can also conduct a search for "problem solving.")

1. Eight coins look exactly alike, but one is lighter than the others. Explain how the different coin can be found in two weighings on a balance scale.

2. For the sequence of numbers 1, 1, 2, 3, 5, 8, 13, . . . , identify a possible pattern and then use that pattern to determine the next number in the sequence.

3. Arrange the numbers 1, 2, 3, 4, 5, 6, 7, 8, and 9 in the squares at the right so that the sum of any row, column, or diagonal is 15. (*Suggestion:* Note that 1, 5, 9; 2, 5, 8; 3, 5, 7; and 4, 5, 6 all add to 15. Because 5 is part of each sum, this suggests that 5 be placed in the center of the squares.)

4. A restaurant charges $10.00 for a pizza that has a diameter of 9 in. Determine the selling price of a pizza with a diameter of 18 in. so that the selling price per square inch is the same as for the 9-inch pizza.

5. You have a balance scale and weights of 1 g, 4 g, 8 g, and 16 g. Using only these weights, can you weigh something that weighs 7 g? 12 g? 14 g? 19 g?

6. Determine the number of possible paths from *A* to *B* for the grid at the right. A path consists of moves right or up along one of the grid lines.

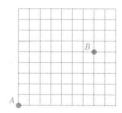

7. Can the checkerboard at the right be covered with dominos (which look like 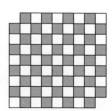) so that every square on the board is covered by a domino? Why or why not? (*Note:* The dominos cannot overlap.)

Projects and Group Activities

Completing the Square

Essentially all of the investigations into mathematics before the Renaissance were geometric. The solutions of quadratic equations were calculated from a construction of a certain area. Proofs of theorems, even theorems about numbers, were based entirely on geometry. In this project, we will examine the geometric solution of a quadratic equation.

➡ Solve: $x^2 + 6x = 7$

Begin with a line of unknown length, x, and one of length 6, the coefficient of x. Using these lines, construct a rectangle as shown.

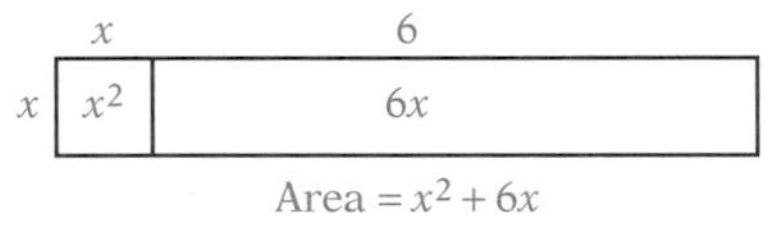

Figure 1

Area $= x^2 + 6x$

Now draw another area that has exactly the same area as Figure 1 by cutting off one-half of the rectangle of area $6x$ and placing it on the bottom of the square labeled x^2. See Figure 2.

The unshaded area in Figure 2 has exactly the same area as Figure 1. However, when the shaded area is added to Figure 2 to make a square, the total area is 9 square units larger than that of Figure 1. In equation form,

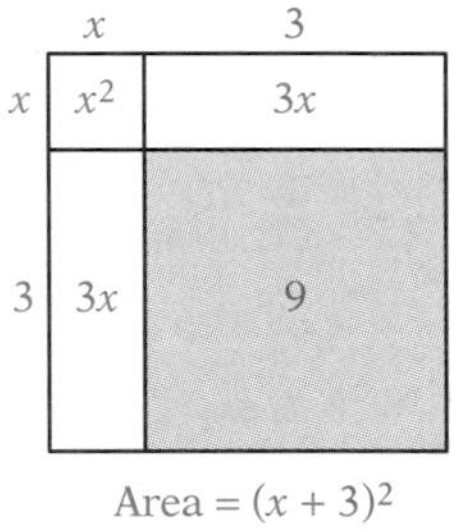

Area $= (x + 3)^2$

Figure 2

(Area of Figure 1) $+ 9 =$ area of Figure 2

or

$$x^2 + 6x + 9 = (x + 3)^2$$

From the original equation, $x^2 + 6x = 7$. Thus,

$$
\begin{aligned}
x^2 + 6x + 9 &= (x + 3)^2 \\
7 + 9 &= (x + 3)^2 \qquad \bullet\ \boldsymbol{x^2 + 6x = 7} \\
16 &= (x + 3)^2 \\
4 &= x + 3 \qquad\quad \bullet\ \textbf{See note below.} \\
1 &= x
\end{aligned}
$$

Note: Although early mathematicians knew that a quadratic equation may have two solutions, both solutions were allowed only if they were positive. After all, a geometric construction could not have a negative length. Therefore, the solution of this equation was 1; the solution -7 would have been dismissed as *fictitious*, the actual word that was frequently used through the 15th century for negative-number solutions of an equation.

Try to solve the quadratic equation $x^2 + 4x = 12$ by geometrically completing the square.

**Using a Graphing
Calculator to Solve a
Quadratic Equation**

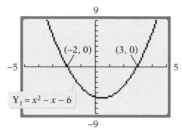

Figure 3

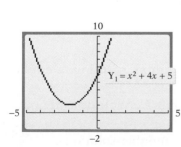

Figure 4

Recall that an x-intercept of the graph of an equation is a point at which the graph crosses the x-axis. For the graph in Figure 3, the x-intercepts are $(-2, 0)$ and $(3, 0)$.

Recall also that to find the x-intercept of a graph, set $y = 0$ and then solve for x. For the equation in Figure 3, if we set $y = 0$, the resulting equation is $0 = x^2 - x - 6$, which is a quadratic equation. Solving this equation by factoring, we have

$$0 = x^2 - x - 6$$
$$0 = (x + 2)(x - 3)$$

$$x + 2 = 0 \qquad\qquad x - 3 = 0$$
$$x = -2 \qquad\qquad\quad x = 3$$

Thus the solutions of the equation are the x-coordinates of the x-intercepts of the graph.

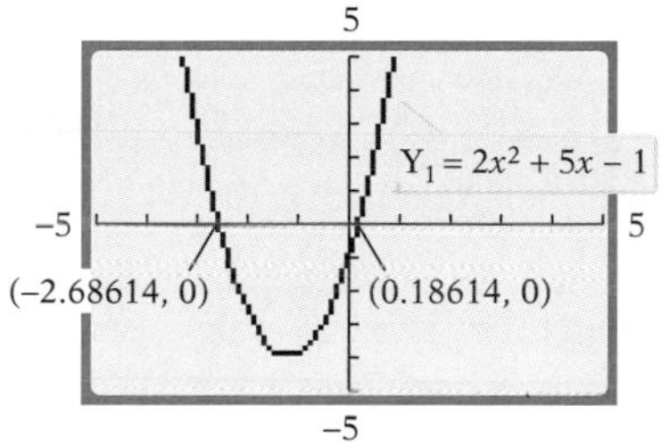

This connection between the solutions of an equation and the x-intercepts of a graph allows us to graphically find the real number solutions of an equation. Using a graphing calculator, graph the equation and estimate the x-intercepts. For instance, to graphically approximate the solutions of $2x^2 + 5x - 1 = 0$, graph $y = 2x^2 + 5x - 1$ and approximate the x-coordinates of the x-intercepts. You can use the following keystrokes to graph the equation and approximate the solutions of the equation. The result is the graph in Figure 4.

TI-83 ⎣Y =⎦ ⎣CLEAR⎦ 2 ⎣X, T, θ, n⎦ ⎣∧⎦ 2 ⎣+⎦
5 ⎣X, T, θ, n⎦ ⎣−⎦ 1 ⎣2nd⎦ QUIT ⎣ZOOM⎦ 5 ⎣ENTER⎦ ⎣2nd⎦ CALC 2
Use the arrow keys to move to the left of the leftmost x-intercept. Then press ENTER. Now use the arrow keys to move to a point just to the right of the leftmost x-intercept. Then press ENTER. Press ENTER again. The x-coordinate at the bottom of the screen is one approximate solution of the equation. To find the other solution, proceed in the same manner for the next x-intercept.

SHARP EL-9360 ⎣Y =⎦ ⎣CL⎦ 2 ⎣X/θ/T/n⎦ ⎣a^b⎦ 2 ⎣▶⎦ ⎣+⎦ 5 ⎣X/θ/T/n⎦ ⎣−⎦ 1 ⎣ZOOM⎦ 5.
This will produce the graph. Now press ⎣2nd⎦ CALC 5 ⎣ENTER⎦. After pressing 5, the x-intercept will show on the bottom of the screen. Now press ⎣2nd⎦ CALC 5 ⎣ENTER⎦ to find the other x-intercept.

CASIO CFX-9850 ⎣MENU⎦ 5 ⎣F2⎦ ⎣F1⎦ 2 ⎣X/θ/T⎦ ⎣x^2⎦ ⎣+⎦ 5 ⎣X/θ/T⎦ ⎣−⎦ 1 ⎣EXE⎦
⎣F6⎦ ⎣SHIFT⎦ G-Solv ⎣F1⎦. Now press ⎣▶⎦ to find the other x-intercept.

Attempting to find the solutions of an equation graphically will not necessarily find all the solutions. Because the x-coordinates of the x-intercepts of a graph are *real* numbers, only real number solutions can be found. For instance, consider the equation $x^2 + 4x + 5 = 0$. The graph of $y = x^2 + 4x + 5$ is shown in Figure 5. Note that the graph has no x-intercepts and, consequently, no real number solutions. However, $x^2 + 4x + 5 = 0$ does have complex number solutions that can be obtained by using the quadratic formula. They are $-2 + i$ and $-2 - i$.

Figure 5

Chapter Summary

Key Words A *quadratic equation* is an equation of the form $ax^2 + bx + c = 0$, $a \neq 0$. A quadratic equation is also called a *second-degree equation*.

A quadratic equation is in *standard form* when the polynomial is in descending order and equal to zero.

When a quadratic equation has two solutions that are the same number, the solution is called a *double root* of the equation.

Adding to a binomial the constant term that makes it a perfect-square trinomial is called *completing the square*.

For an equation of the form $ax^2 + bx + c = 0$, the quantity $b^2 - 4ac$ is called the *discriminant*.

An equation is quadratic in form if it can be written as $au^2 + bu + c = 0$.

A *quadratic inequality* is one that can be written in the form $ax^2 + bx + c > 0$ or $ax^2 + bx + c < 0$, where $a \neq 0$. The symbols $\leq$ and $\geq$ can also be used.

Essential Rules *The Principle of Zero Products*

If $ab = 0$, then $a = 0$ or $b = 0$.

Completing the Square

To complete the square on $x^2 + bx$,

add ($\frac{1}{2}$ the coefficient of x)^2 to the binomial.

The Quadratic Formula

$$x = \frac{-b \pm \sqrt{b^2 - 4ac}}{2a}$$

The Effect of the Discriminant on the Solutions of a Quadratic Equation

1. If $b^2 - 4ac = 0$, then the equation has one real number solution, a double root.
2. If $b^2 - 4ac > 0$, then the equation has two real number solutions that are not equal.
3. If $b^2 - 4ac < 0$, then the equation has two complex number solutions.

Chapter Review

1. Solve by factoring: $2x^2 - 3x = 0$

   $0, \dfrac{3}{2}$ [10.1A]

2. Solve by factoring: $6x^2 + 9cx = 6c^2$

   $\dfrac{c}{2}, -2c$ [10.1A]

3. Solve by taking square roots:
   $x^2 = 48$
   $4\sqrt{3}, -4\sqrt{3}$ [10.1C]

4. Solve by taking square roots:
   $\left(x + \dfrac{1}{2}\right)^2 + 4 = 0$

   $-\dfrac{1}{2} + 2i, -\dfrac{1}{2} - 2i$ [10.1C]

5. Solve by completing the square:
   $x^2 + 4x + 3 = 0$
   $-3, -1$ [10.2A]

6. Solve by completing the square:
   $7x^2 - 14x + 3 = 0$
   $\dfrac{7 + 2\sqrt{7}}{7}, \dfrac{7 - 2\sqrt{7}}{7}$ [10.2A]

7. Solve by using the quadratic formula:
   $12x^2 - 25x + 12 = 0$
   $\dfrac{3}{4}, \dfrac{4}{3}$ [10.3A]

8. Solve by using the quadratic formula:
   $x^2 - x + 8 = 0$
   $\dfrac{1}{2} + \dfrac{\sqrt{31}}{2}i, \dfrac{1}{2} - \dfrac{\sqrt{31}}{2}i$ [10.3A]

9. Write a quadratic equation that has integer coefficients and has solutions 0 and -3.
   $x^2 + 3x = 0$ [10.1B]

10. Write a quadratic equation that has integer coefficients and has solutions $\dfrac{3}{4}$ and $-\dfrac{2}{3}$.
    $12x^2 - x - 6 = 0$ [10.1B]

11. Solve by completing the square:
    $x^2 - 2x + 8 = 0$
    $1 + i\sqrt{7}, 1 - i\sqrt{7}$ [10.2A]

12. Solve by completing the square:
    $(x - 2)(x + 3) = x - 10$
    $2i, -2i$ [10.2A]

13. Solve by using the quadratic formula:
    $3x(x - 3) = 2x - 4$
    $\dfrac{11 + \sqrt{73}}{6}, \dfrac{11 - \sqrt{73}}{6}$ [10.3A]

14. Using the discriminant, determine the number and type of solutions for $3x^2 - 5x + 1 = 0$.
    two real number solutions [10.3A]

15. Solve: $(x + 3)(2x - 5) < 0$
    $\left\{x \mid -3 < x < \dfrac{5}{2}\right\}$ [10.6A]

16. Solve: $(x - 2)(x + 4)(2x + 3) \le 0$
    $\left\{x \mid x \le -4 \text{ or } -\dfrac{3}{2} \le x \le 2\right\}$ [10.6A]

17.   Solve: $x^{2/3} + x^{1/3} - 12 = 0$

27, −64   [10.4A]

18.   Solve: $2(x - 1) + 3\sqrt{x - 1} - 2 = 0$

$\dfrac{5}{4}$ [10.4B]

19.   Solve: $3x = \dfrac{9}{x - 2}$

−1, 3   [10.4C]

20.   Solve: $\dfrac{3x + 7}{x + 2} + x = 3$

−1   [10.4C]

21.   Solve and graph the solution set:

$\dfrac{x - 2}{2x - 3} \geq 0$

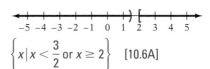

$\left\{ x \,\middle|\, x < \dfrac{3}{2} \text{ or } x \geq 2 \right\}$ [10.6A]

22.   Solve and graph the solution set:

$\dfrac{(2x - 1)(x + 3)}{x - 4} \leq 0$

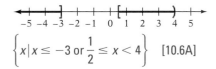

$\left\{ x \,\middle|\, x \leq -3 \text{ or } \dfrac{1}{2} \leq x < 4 \right\}$ [10.6A]

23.   Solve: $x = \sqrt{x} + 2$

4   [10.4B]

24.   Solve: $2x = \sqrt{5x + 24} + 3$

5   [10.4B]

25.   Solve: $\dfrac{x - 2}{2x + 3} - \dfrac{x - 4}{x} = 2$

$\dfrac{-3 + \sqrt{249}}{10}, \dfrac{-3 - \sqrt{249}}{10}$ [10.4C]

26.   Solve: $1 - \dfrac{x + 4}{2 - x} = \dfrac{x - 3}{x + 2}$

$\dfrac{-11 + \sqrt{129}}{2}, \dfrac{-11 - \sqrt{129}}{2}$ [10.4C]

27.   The length of a rectangle is two more than twice the width. The area of the rectangle is 60 cm². Find the length and width of the rectangle.
length: 12 cm; width: 5 cm   [10.5A]

28.   The sum of the squares of three consecutive even integers is fifty-six. Find the three integers.
2, 4, and 6 or −6, −4, and −2   [10.5A]

29.   An older computer requires 12 min longer to print the payroll than does a newer computer. Together the computers can print the payroll in 8 min. Find the time for the new computer working alone to print the payroll.
12 min   [10.5A]

30.   A car travels 200 mi. A second car, making the same trip, travels 10 mph faster than the first car and makes the trip in 1 h less. Find the speed of each car.
first car: 40 mph; second car: 50 mph   [10.5A]

Chapter Test

1. Solve by factoring: $3x^2 + 10x = 8$
   $\frac{2}{3}, -4$ [10.1A]

2. Solve by factoring: $6x^2 - 5x - 6 = 0$
   $\frac{3}{2}, -\frac{2}{3}$ [10.1A]

3. Write a quadratic equation that has integer coefficients and has solutions 3 and -3.
   $x^2 - 9 = 0$ [10.1B]

4. Write a quadratic equation that has integer coefficients and has solutions $\frac{1}{2}$ and -4.
   $2x^2 + 7x - 4 = 0$ [10.1B]

5. Solve by taking square roots:
   $3(x - 2)^2 - 24 = 0$
   $2 + 2\sqrt{2}, 2 - 2\sqrt{2}$ [10.1C]

6. Solve by completing the square:
   $x^2 - 6x - 2 = 0$
   $3 + \sqrt{11}, 3 - \sqrt{11}$ [10.2A]

7. Solve by completing the square:
   $3x^2 - 6x = 2$
   $\frac{3 + \sqrt{15}}{3}, \frac{3 - \sqrt{15}}{3}$ [10.2A]

8. Solve by using the quadratic formula:
   $2x^2 - 2x - 1$
   $\frac{1 + \sqrt{3}}{2}, \frac{1 - \sqrt{3}}{2}$ [10.3A]

9. Solve by using the quadratic formula:
   $x^2 + 4x + 12 = 0$
   $-2 + 2i\sqrt{2}, -2 - 2i\sqrt{2}$ [10.3A]

10. Use the discriminant to determine whether $3x^2 - 4x = 1$ has one real number solution, two real number solutions, or two complex number solutions.
    two real number solutions   [10.3A]

11. Use the discriminant to determine whether $x^2 - 6x = -15$ has one real number solution, two real number solutions, or two complex number solutions.
    two complex number solutions   [10.3A]

12. Solve: $2x + 7x^{1/2} - 4 = 0$
    $\frac{1}{4}$ [10.4A]

13. Solve: $x^4 - 4x^2 + 3 = 0$
$1, -1, \sqrt{3}, -\sqrt{3}$ [10.4A]

14. Solve: $\sqrt{2x + 1} + 5 = 2x$
4 [10.4B]

15. Solve: $\sqrt{x - 2} = \sqrt{x} - 2$
no solution   [10.4B]

16. Solve: $\dfrac{2x}{x - 3} + \dfrac{5}{x - 1} = 1$
$2, -9$ [10.4C]

17. Solve and graph the solution set of $(x - 2)(x + 4)(x - 4) < 0$.

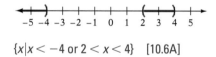

$\{x \mid x < -4 \text{ or } 2 < x < 4\}$ [10.6A]

18. Solve and graph the solution set of $\dfrac{2x - 3}{x + 4} \le 0$.

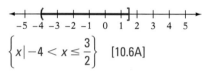

$\left\{ x \mid -4 < x \le \dfrac{3}{2} \right\}$ [10.6A]

19. The base of a triangle is 3 ft more than three times the height. The area of the triangle is 30 ft^2. Find the base and height of the triangle.
base: 15 ft; height: 4 ft   [10.5A]

20. The rate of a river's current is 2 mph. A canoe was rowed 6 mi down the river and back in 4 h. Find the rowing rate in calm water.
4 mph   [10.5A]

Cumulative Review

1. Evaluate $2a^2 - b^2 \div c^2$ when $a = 3$, $b = -4$, and $c = -2$.
   14 [1.4A]

2. Solve: $|3x - 2| < 8$
   $\left\{ x | -2 < x < \dfrac{10}{3} \right\}$ [2.5B]

3. Find the volume of a cylinder with a height of 6 m and a radius of 3 m. Give the exact measure.
   54π m³ [3.3A]

4. Given $f(x) = \dfrac{2x - 3}{x^2 - 1}$, find $f(-2)$.
   $-\dfrac{7}{3}$ [4.1D]

5. Find the slope of the line containing the points $(3, -4)$ and $(-1, 2)$.
   $-\dfrac{3}{2}$ [4.3A]

6. Find the x- and y-intercepts of the graph of $6x - 5y = 15$.
   $\left(\dfrac{5}{2}, 0 \right)$, $(0, -3)$ [4.2B]

7. Find the equation of the line that contains the point $(1, 2)$ and is parallel to the line $x - y = 1$.
   $y = x + 1$ [4.5A]

8. Solve the system of equations.
   $x + y + z = 2$
   $-x + 2y - 3z = -9$
   $x - 2y - 2z = -1$
   $(1, -1, 2)$ [5.3B]

9. Graph the solution set:
   $x + y \le 3$
   $2x - y < 4$

   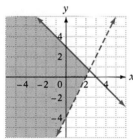

   [5.6A]

10. Triangles ABC and DEF are similar. Find the height of triangle DEF.

    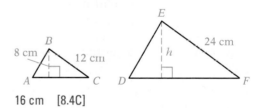

    16 cm [8.4C]

11. Divide: $(3x^3 - 13x^2 + 10) \div (3x - 4)$
    $x^2 - 3x - 4 - \dfrac{6}{3x - 4}$ [6.4A]

12. Factor: $-3x^3y + 6x^2y^2 - 9xy^3$
    $-3xy(x^2 - 2xy + 3y^2)$ [7.1A]

13. Factor: $6x^2 - 7x - 20$
    $(2x - 5)(3x + 4)$ [7.3A/7.3B]

14. Multiply: $\dfrac{x^2 + 2x + 1}{8x^2 + 8x} \cdot \dfrac{4x^3 - 4x^2}{x^2 - 1}$
    $\dfrac{x}{2}$ [8.1B]

15. Solve: $\dfrac{x}{x+2} - \dfrac{4x}{x+3} = 1$

$-\dfrac{3}{2}, -1$ [8.4A]

16. Solve $S = \dfrac{n}{2}(a+b)$ for b.

$b = \dfrac{2S - an}{n}$ [8.5A]

17. Multiply: $a^{-1/2}(a^{1/2} - a^{3/2})$

$1 - a$ [9.1A]

18. Multiply: $-2i(7 - 4i)$

$-8 - 14i$ [9.3C]

19. Solve: $\sqrt{3x + 1} - 1 = x$

$0, 1$ [9.4A]

20. Solve: $x^4 - 6x^2 + 8 = 0$

$2, -2, \sqrt{2}, -\sqrt{2}$ [10.4A]

21. A piston rod for an automobile is $9\dfrac{3}{8}$ in. with a tolerance of $\dfrac{1}{64}$ in. Find the lower and upper limits of the length of the piston rod.

lower limit: $9\dfrac{23}{64}$ in.;

upper limit: $9\dfrac{25}{64}$ in.   [2.5C]

22. The base of a triangle is $(x + 8)$ ft. The height is $(2x - 4)$ ft. Find the area of the triangle in terms of the variable x.

$(x^2 + 6x - 16)$ ft^2 [6.3E]

23. The graph shows the relationship between the value of a building and the time, in years, since depreciation began. Find the slope of the line between the two points shown on the graph. Write a sentence that states the meaning of the slope.

$m = -\dfrac{25,000}{3}$. The building depreciates $8333.33 in value each year.   [4.3A]

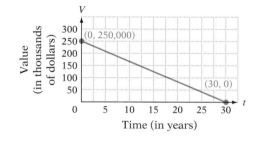

24. How high on a building will a 17-foot ladder reach when the bottom of the ladder is 8 ft from the building?

15 ft   [9.4B]

25. Use the discriminant to determine whether $2x^2 + 4x + 3 = 0$ has one real number solution, two real number solutions, or two complex number solutions.

two complex number solutions   [10.3A]

11

Functions and Relations

Forestry technicians compile data on the characteristics of forest land tracts, such as species and population of trees, disease and insect damage, tree seedling mortality, and conditions that may cause fire danger. They also train and lead conservation workers in seasonal activities such as planting tree seedlings, putting out forest fires, and maintaining recreational facilities. These technicians may use functions to model, for instance, the progress of a tree disease as it spreads through a tract of forest.

Objectives

Section 11.1
To graph a linear function
To solve application problems

Section 11.2
To graph a quadratic function
To find the x-intercepts of a parabola
To find the minimum or maximum of a quadratic function
To solve application problems

Section 11.3
To graph functions

Section 11.4
To perform operations on functions
To find the composition of two functions

Section 11.5
To determine whether a function is one-to-one
To find the inverse of a function

Section 11.6
To graph a parabola
To find the equation of a circle and to graph a circle
To graph an ellipse with center at the origin
To graph a hyperbola with center at the origin

Conic Sections

The graphs of four curves—the circle, the ellipse, the parabola, and the hyperbola—are discussed in this chapter. These curves were studied by the Greeks and were known prior to 400 B.C. Their names were first used by Apollonius around 250 B.C. in *Conic Sections,* the most authoritative Greek discussion of these curves. Apollonius borrowed the names from a school founded by Pythagoras.

The diagram at the right shows the path of a planet around the sun. The curve traced out by the planet is an ellipse. The **aphelion** is the position of the planet when it is farthest from the sun. The **perihelion** is the planet's position when it is nearest to the sun.

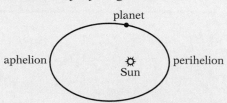

A telescope, like the one at the Palomar Observatory, has a cross section that is in the shape of a parabola. A parabolic mirror has the unusual property that all light rays parallel to the axis of symmetry that hit the mirror are reflected to the same point. This point is called the **focus of the parabola**.

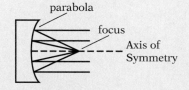

Some comets, unlike Halley's Comet, travel with such speed that they are not captured by the sun's gravitational field. The path of the comet as it comes around the sun is in the shape of a hyperbola.

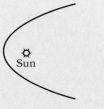

11.1 Linear Functions

Objective A   *To graph a linear function* ....

The graph of a function is the graph of the ordered pairs (x, y) that belong to the function. Because y and $f(x)$ are interchangeable, the ordered pairs of a function can be written as (x, y) or $(x, f(x))$. A function that can be written in the form $y = mx + b$ or $f(x) = mx + b$ is called a **linear function**. The graph of a linear function has certain characteristics. It is a straight line with slope m and y-intercept $(0, b)$.

➡ Graph: $f(x) = 2x + 1$.

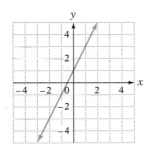

This is a linear function. You can think of the function as the equation $y = 2x + 1$. The y-intercept is $(0, 1)$. The slope is 2.

Beginning at the y-intercept, move right 1 and up 2. The point $(1, 3)$ is another point on the graph. Draw a straight line through the points $(0, 1)$ and $(1, 3)$.

When a function is given by an equation, the domain of the function is all real numbers for which the function evaluates to a real number. For instance,

• The domain of $f(x) = 2x + 1$ is all real numbers because the value of $2x + 1$ is a real number for any value of x.

• The domain of $g(x) = \dfrac{1}{x - 2}$ is all real numbers except 2; when $x = 2$, $g(2) = \dfrac{1}{2 - 2} = \dfrac{1}{0}$, which is not a real number.

Example 1   Graph: $f(x) = \dfrac{2}{3}x$

Solution

$b = 0$
y-intercept: $(0, 0)$
$m = \dfrac{2}{3}$

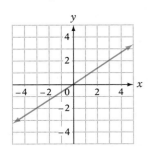

You Try It 1   Graph: $f(x) = \dfrac{3}{5}x - 4$

Your solution

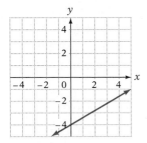

Solution on p. S31

Objective B   *To solve application problems*..

Linear functions can be used to model a variety of applications in science and business. For each application, data are collected and the independent and dependent variables are selected. Then a linear function is determined that models the data.

Example 2

Suppose a manufacturer has determined that at a price of $115, consumers will purchase 1 million portable CD players and that at a price of $90, consumers will purchase 1.25 million portable CD players. Describe this situation with a linear function. Use this function to predict how many portable CD players consumers will purchase if the price is $80.

Strategy

• Select the independent and dependent variables. Because you are trying to determine the number of CD players, that quantity is the *dependent* variable, y. The price of CD players is the *independent* variable, x. From the given data, two ordered pairs are (115, 1) and (90, 1.25). (The ordinates are in millions of units.) Use these ordered pairs to determine the linear function.

• Evaluate the function for $x = 80$ to predict how many CD players consumers will purchase if the price is $80.

Solution

Let $(x_1, y_1) = (115, 1)$ and $(x_2, y_2) = (90, 1.25)$.

$$m = \frac{y_2 - y_1}{x_2 - x_1} = \frac{1.25 - 1}{90 - 115} = -\frac{0.25}{25} = -0.01$$

$$y - y_1 = m(x - x_1)$$
$$y - 1 = -0.01(x - 115)$$
$$y - 1 = -0.01x + 1.15$$
$$y = -0.01x + 2.15$$

The linear function is
$f(x) = -0.01x + 2.15$.

$f(80) = -0.01(80) + 2.15 = 1.35$

Consumers will purchase 1.35 million CD players at a price of $80.

You Try It 2

Gabriel Daniel Fahrenheit invented the mercury thermometer in 1717. In terms of readings on this thermometer, water freezes at 32°F and boils at 212°F. In 1742 Anders Celsius invented the Celsius temperature scale. On this scale, water freezes at 0°C and boils at 100°C. Determine a linear function that can be used to predict the Celsius temperature when the Fahrenheit temperature is known.

Your strategy

Your solution

$$f(F) = \frac{5}{9}(F - 32)$$

Solution on p. S31

11.1 Exercises

· ·

Objective A

Graph.

1. $f(x) = 3x - 4$

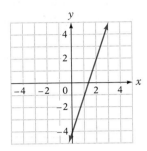

2. $f(x) = -2x + 3$

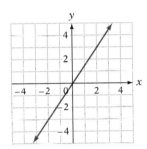

3. $f(x) = -\frac{2}{3}x$

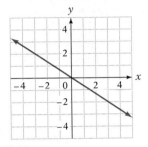

4. $f(x) = \frac{3}{2}x$

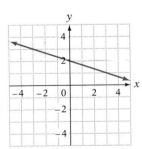

5. $f(x) = \frac{2}{3}x - 4$

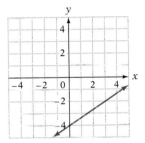

6. $f(x) = \frac{3}{4}x + 2$

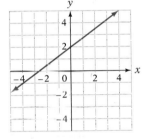

7. $f(x) = -\frac{1}{3}x + 2$

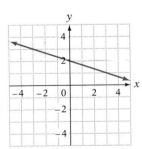

8. $f(x) = -\frac{3}{2}x - 3$

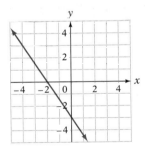

9. $f(x) = \frac{3}{5}x - 1$

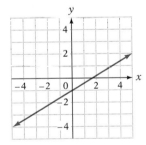

Objective B   *Application Problems*

10. The sale price of an item is a function, *s*, of the original price, *p*, where $s(p) = 0.80p$. If an item's original price is $200, what is the sale price of the item?
$160

11. The markup on an item is a function, *m*, of its cost, *c*, where $m(c) = 0.25c$. If the cost of an item is $150, what is the markup on the item?
$37.50

12. A manufacturer of graphing calculators has determined that 10,000 calculators per week will be sold at a price of $95. At a price of $90, it is estimated that 12,000 calculators would be sold. Determine a linear function that will predict the number of calculators that would be sold at a given price. Use this method to predict the number of calculators per week that would be sold at a price of $75.
$y = -400x + 48{,}000$; 18,000 calculators

13. The operator of a hotel estimates that 500 rooms per night will be rented if the room rate per night is $75. For each $10 increase in the price of a room, 6 fewer rooms will be rented. Determine a linear function that will predict the number of rooms that will be rented for a given price per room. Use this model to predict the number of rooms that will be rented if the room rate is $100.

$y = -\dfrac{3}{5}x + 545$; 485 rooms

14. A general building contractor estimates that the cost to build a new home is $30,000 plus $85 for each square foot of floor space in the house. Determine a linear function that will give the cost of building a house that contains a given number of square feet. Use this model to determine the cost to build a house that contains 1800 ft².
$y = 85x + 30{,}000$; $183,000

APPLYING THE CONCEPTS

15. A child's height is a function of the child's age. The graph of this function is not linear, as children go through growth spurts as they develop. However, for the graph to be reasonable, the function must be an increasing function (that is, as the age increases, the height increases) because children do not get shorter as they grow older. Match each function described below with a reasonable graph of the function.

a. The height of a plane above the ground during take-off depends on how long it has been since the plane left the gate.

b. The height of a football above the ground is related to the number of seconds that have passed since it was punted.

c. A basketball player is dribbling a basketball. The basketball's distance from the floor is related to the number of seconds that have passed since the player began dribbling the ball.

d. Two children are seated together on a roller coaster. The height of the children above the ground depends on how long they have been on the ride.

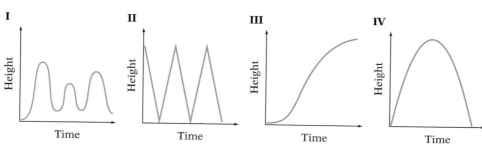

a. III; b. IV; c. II; d. I

11.2 Quadratic Functions

Objective A   ***To graph a quadratic function*** ·······························

Recall that a linear function is one that can be expressed by the equation $f(x) = mx + b$. The graph of a linear function has certain characteristics. It is a straight line with slope m and y-intercept $(0, b)$. A **quadratic function** is one that can be expressed by the equation $f(x) = ax^2 + bx + c$, $a \neq 0$. The graph of this function, called a **parabola**, also has certain characteristics. The graph of a quadratic function can be drawn by finding ordered pairs that belong to the function.

→ Graph $f(x) = x^2 - 2x - 3$.

By evaluating the function for various values of x, find enough ordered pairs to determine the shape of the graph.

x	$f(x) = x^2 - 2x - 3$	$f(x)$	(x, y)
-2	$f(-2) = (-2)^2 - 2(-2) - 3$	5	$(-2, 5)$
-1	$f(-1) = (-1)^2 - 2(-1) - 3$	0	$(-1, 0)$
0	$f(0) = (0)^2 - 2(0) - 3$	-3	$(0, -3)$
1	$f(1) = (1)^2 - 2(1) - 3$	-4	$(1, -4)$
2	$f(2) = (2)^2 - 2(2) - 3$	-3	$(2, -3)$
3	$f(3) = (3)^2 - 2(3) - 3$	0	$(3, 0)$
4	$f(4) = (4)^2 - 2(4) - 3$	5	$(4, 5)$

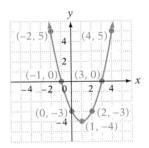

Because the value of $f(x) = x^2 - 2x - 3$ is a real number for all values of x, the domain of f is all real numbers. From the graph, it appears that no value of y is less than -4. Thus the range is $\{y | y \geq -4\}$. The range can also be determined algebraically, as shown below, by completing the square.

TAKE NOTE

In completing the square, 1 is both added and subtracted. Because $1 - 1 = 0$, the expression $x^2 - 2x - 3$ is not changed. Note that

$(x - 1)^2 - 4$
$= (x^2 - 2x + 1) - 4$
$= x^2 - 2x - 3$

which is the original expression.

$f(x) = x^2 - 2x - 3$

$\quad = (x^2 - 2x) - 3$ • Group the variable terms.

$\quad = (x^2 - 2x + 1) - 1 - 3$ • Complete the square of $x^2 - 2x$. Add and

$\qquad\qquad\qquad\qquad$ subtract $\left[\dfrac{1}{2}(-2)\right]^2 = 1$.

$\quad = (x - 1)^2 - 4$ • Factor and combine like terms.

Because the square of a positive number is always positive, we have

$\qquad (x - 1)^2 \geq 0$

$(x - 1)^2 - 4 \geq -4$ • Subtract 4 from each side of the inequality.

$\qquad\quad f(x) \geq -4$ • $f(x) = x^2 - 2x - 3 = (x - 1)^2 - 4$

$\qquad\qquad y \geq -4$

From the last inequality, the range is $\{y | y \geq -4\}$.

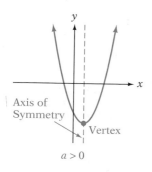

Axis of Symmetry

Vertex

$a > 0$

In general, the graph of $f(x) = ax^2 + bx + c, a \neq 0$, resembles a "cup" shape as shown at the left. The parabola opens up when $a > 0$ (a is positive) and opens down when $a < 0$ (a is negative). When the parabola opens up, the **vertex** of the parabola is the point with the smallest y-coordinate. When the parabola opens down, the vertex is the point with the largest y-coordinate.

The **axis of symmetry** is a line that passes through the vertex of the parabola and is parallel to the y-axis. To understand the axis of symmetry, think of folding the graph along that line. The two portions of the graph will match up.

The following formulas can be used to find the axis of symmetry and the vertex of a parabola.

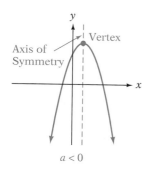

Axis of Symmetry

Vertex

$a < 0$

The Axis of Symmetry and Vertex of a Parabola

Let $f(x) = ax^2 + bx + c$ be the equation of a parabola.

The equation of the axis of symmetry is $x = -\dfrac{b}{2a}$.

The coordinates of the vertex are $\left(-\dfrac{b}{2a}, f\left(-\dfrac{b}{2a}\right)\right)$.

➡ Find the axis of symmetry and the vertex of the parabola whose equation is $g(x) = -2x^2 + 3x + 1$. Then graph the equation.

From the equation $g(x) = -2x^2 + 3x + 1$, $a = -2$, $b = 3$, and $c = 1$.

Axis of symmetry: $x = -\dfrac{b}{2a} = -\dfrac{3}{2(-2)} = \dfrac{3}{4}$

The axis of symmetry is a vertical line passing through the point $\left(\dfrac{3}{4}, 0\right)$.

The x-coordinate of the vertex is $\dfrac{3}{4}$.

Find the y-coordinate of the vertex by replacing x with $\dfrac{3}{4}$ and evaluating.

$$y = -2x^2 + 3x + 1$$
$$= -2\left(\frac{3}{4}\right)^2 + 3\left(\frac{3}{4}\right) + 1 = \frac{17}{8}$$

The vertex is $\left(\dfrac{3}{4}, \dfrac{17}{8}\right)$.

Because a is negative ($a = -2$), the graph opens down. Find a few ordered pairs that belong to the function, and then sketch the graph.

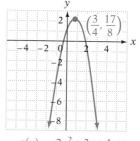

$g(x) = -2x^2 + 3x + 1$

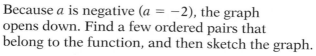

TAKE NOTE

Once the coordinates of the vertex are found, the range of a quadratic function can be determined.

Once the y-coordinate of the vertex is known, the range of the function can be determined. Here, the graph of g opens down, so the y-coordinate of the vertex is the largest value of y. Therefore, the range of g is $\left\{y \,|\, y \leq \dfrac{17}{8}\right\}$. The value of $-2x^2 + 3x + 1$ is a real number for all values of x; the domain is all real numbers.

Example 1

Find the vertex and axis of symmetry of the parabola whose equation is $y = -x^2 + 4x + 1$. Then graph the equation.

Solution

x-coordinate of vertex:

$$-\frac{b}{2a} = -\frac{4}{2(-1)} = 2$$

y-coordinate of vertex:

$$\begin{aligned} y &= -x^2 + 4x + 1 \\ &= -(2)^2 + 4(2) + 1 \\ &= 5 \end{aligned}$$

vertex: $(2, 5)$
axis of symmetry: $x = 2$

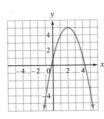

You Try It 1

Find the vertex and axis of symmetry of the parabola whose equation is $y = 4x^2 + 4x + 1$. Then graph the equation.

Your solution

vertex: $\left(-\frac{1}{2}, 0\right)$

axis of symmetry: $x = -\frac{1}{2}$

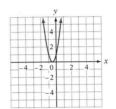

Solution on p. S31

Objective B   **To find the x-intercepts of a parabola** ....

Recall that a point at which a graph crosses the x- or y-axis is called an *intercept* of the graph. The x-intercepts of the graph of an equation occur when $y = 0$; the y-intercepts occur when $x = 0$.

The graph of $y = x^2 + 3x - 4$ is shown at the right. The points whose coordinates are $(-4, 0)$ and $(1, 0)$ are x-intercepts of the graph.

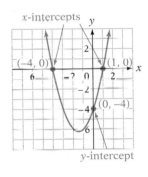

⇒ Find the x-intercepts for the parabola whose equation is $y = 4x^2 - 4x + 1$.

To find the x-intercepts, let $y = 0$ and then solve for x.

$$\begin{aligned} y &= 4x^2 - 4x + 1 \\ 0 &= 4x^2 - 4x + 1 \end{aligned}$$ • Let $y = 0$.

$$0 = (2x - 1)(2x - 1)$$ • Solve for x by factoring.

$$\begin{array}{ll} 2x - 1 = 0 & 2x - 1 = 0 \\ 2x = 1 & 2x = 1 \\ x = \dfrac{1}{2} & x = \dfrac{1}{2} \end{array}$$

The x-intercept is $\left(\frac{1}{2}, 0\right)$.

In this last example, the parabola has only one x-intercept. In this case, the parabola is said to be **tangent** to the x-axis at $x = \frac{1}{2}$.

➡ Find the x-intercepts of $y = x^2 - 2x - 1$.

To find the x-intercepts, let $y = 0$ and solve for x.

$y = x^2 - 2x - 1$

$0 = x^2 - 2x - 1$

$$x = \frac{-b \pm \sqrt{b^2 - 4ac}}{2a}$$

• Because $x^2 - 2x - 1$ does not easily factor, use the quadratic formula to solve for x.

$$= \frac{-(-2) \pm \sqrt{(-2)^2 - 4(1)(-1)}}{2(1)}$$

• $a = 1, b = -2, c = -1$

$$= \frac{2 \pm \sqrt{4 + 4}}{2} = \frac{2 \pm \sqrt{8}}{2}$$

$$= \frac{2 \pm 2\sqrt{2}}{2} = 1 \pm \sqrt{2}$$

The x-intercepts are $(1 - \sqrt{2}, 0)$ and $(1 + \sqrt{2}, 0)$.

The graph of a parabola may not have x-intercepts. The graph of $y = -x^2 + 2x - 2$ is shown at the right. Note that the graph does not pass through the x-axis and thus there are no x-intercepts. This means there are no real number solutions of $-x^2 + 2x - 2 = 0$.

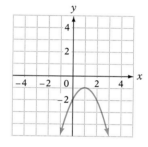

Using the quadratic formula, we find that the solutions of the equation $-x^2 + 2x - 2 = 0$ are the complex numbers $1 - i$ and $1 + i$.

Recall that the discriminant of the quadratic formula is the expression $b^2 - 4ac$ and that this expression can be used to determine whether $ax^2 + bx + c = 0$ has zero, one, or two real number solutions. Because there is a connection between the solutions of $ax^2 + bx + c = 0$ and the x-intercepts of the graph of $y = ax^2 + bx + c$, the discriminant can be used to determine the number of x-intercepts of a parabola.

> **The Effect of the Discriminant on the Number of x-Intercepts of a Parabola**
>
> 1. If $b^2 - 4ac = 0$, the parabola has one x-intercept.
> 2. If $b^2 - 4ac > 0$, the parabola has two x-intercepts.
> 3. If $b^2 - 4ac < 0$, the parabola has no x-intercepts.

➡ Use the discriminant to determine the number of x-intercepts of the parabola whose equation is $y = 2x^2 - x + 2$.

$b^2 - 4ac$

$(-1)^2 - 4(2)(2) = 1 - 16 = -15$

$-15 < 0$

• Evaluate the discriminant.
  $a = 2, b = -1, c = 2$

The discriminant is less than zero, so the parabola has no x-intercepts.

Example 2
Find the x-intercepts of
$y = 2x^2 - 5x + 2$.

Solution
$y = 2x^2 - 5x + 2$
$0 = 2x^2 - 5x + 2$
$0 = (2x - 1)(x - 2)$

$2x - 1 = 0 \qquad x - 2 = 0$
$\quad\; 2x = 1 \qquad\quad\; x = 2$
$\quad\;\; x = \dfrac{1}{2}$

The x-intercepts are $\left(\dfrac{1}{2}, 0\right)$ and $(2, 0)$.

You Try It 2
Find the x-intercepts of
$y = x^2 + 3x + 4$.

Your solution
no x-intercepts

Example 3
Use the discriminant to determine the
number of x-intercepts of
$y = x^2 - 6x + 9$.

Solution
$a = 1, b = -6, c = 9$
$b^2 - 4ac = (-6)^2 - 4(1)(9) = 36 - 36 = 0$

Because the discriminant is equal to zero,
the parabola has one x-intercept.

You Try It 3
Use the discriminant to determine the
number of x-intercepts of $y = x^2 - x - 6$.

Your solution
two x-intercepts

Solutions on pp. S31–S32

Objective C   *To find the minimum or maximum of a quadratic function* ....

POINT OF INTEREST

Calculus is a branch of mathematics that demonstrates, among other things, how to find the maximum or minimum of functions other than quadratic functions. These are very important problems in applied mathematics. For instance, an automotive engineer wants to design a car whose shape will *minimize* the effects of air flow. The same engineer tries to *maximize* the efficiency of a car's engine. Similarly, an economist may try to determine what business practices will *minimize* cost and *maximize* profit.

The graph of $f(x) = x^2 - 2x + 3$ is shown at the right. Because a is positive, the parabola opens up. The vertex of the parabola is the lowest point on the parabola. It is the point that has the minimum y-coordinate. Therefore, the value of the function at this point is a **minimum**.

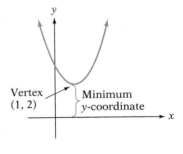

The graph of $f(x) = -x^2 + 2x + 1$ is shown at the right. Because a is negative, the parabola opens down. The vertex of the parabola is the highest point on the parabola. It is the point that has the maximum y-coordinate. Therefore, the value of the function at this point is a **maximum**.

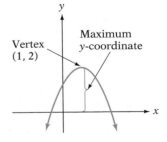

To find the minimum or maximum value of a quadratic function, first find the x-coordinate of the vertex. Then evaluate the function at that value.

Example 4

Find the minimum value of
$f(x) = 2x^2 - 3x + 1$.

Solution

$x = -\dfrac{b}{2a} = -\dfrac{-3}{2(2)} = \dfrac{3}{4}$

$f(x) = 2x^2 - 3x + 1$

$f\left(\dfrac{3}{4}\right) = 2\left(\dfrac{3}{4}\right)^2 - 3\left(\dfrac{3}{4}\right) + 1$

$\qquad = \dfrac{9}{8} - \dfrac{9}{4} + 1 = -\dfrac{1}{8}$

Because a is positive, the graph opens up.
The function has a minimum value.

The minimum value of the function is $-\dfrac{1}{8}$.

You Try It 4

Find the maximum value of
$f(x) = -3x^2 + 4x - 1$.

Your solution

$\dfrac{1}{3}$

Solution on p. S32

Objective D   To solve application problems ....

Example 5

A mining company has determined that
the cost (*C*) in dollars per ton of mining
a mineral is given by the equation
$C(x) = 0.2x^2 - 2x + 12$, where x is the
number of tons of the mineral that
are mined. Find the number of tons of
the mineral that should be mined to
minimize the cost. What is the
minimum cost?

Strategy

- To find the number of tons that will
  minimize the cost, find the
  x-coordinate of the vertex.
- To find the minimum cost, evaluate
  the function at the x-coordinate of the
  vertex.

Solution

$x = -\dfrac{b}{2a} = -\dfrac{-2}{2(0.2)} = 5$

To minimize cost, 5 tons should be mined.

$C(x) = 0.2x^2 - 2x + 12$
$C(5) = 0.2(5)^2 - 2(5) + 12 = 5 - 10 + 12 = 7$

The minimum cost per ton is $7.

You Try It 5

The height (*s*) in feet of a ball thrown
straight up is given by the equation
$s(t) = -16t^2 + 64t$, where t is the time in
seconds. Find the time it takes the ball to
reach its maximum height. What is the
maximum height?

Your strategy

Your solution

2 s; 64 ft

Solution on p. S32

11.2 Exercises

Objective A

1. Describe (a) the vertex and (b) the axis of symmetry of a parabola.

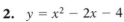

Find the vertex and axis of symmetry of the parabola. Then sketch its graph.

2. $y = x^2 - 2x - 4$

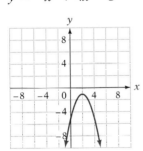

$(1, -5);$
$x = 1$

3. $y = x^2 + 4x - 4$

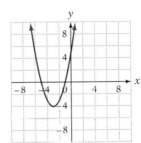

$(-2, -8);$
$x = -2$

4. $y = -x^2 + 2x - 3$

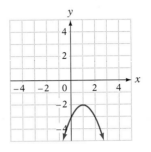

$(1, -2);$
$x = 1$

5. $y = -x^2 + 4x - 5$

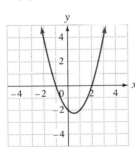

$(2, -1);$
$x = 2$

6. $f(x) = x^2 + 6x + 5$

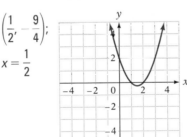

$(-3, -4);$
$x = -3$

7. $f(x) = x^2 - x - 6$

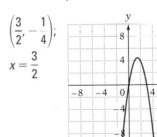

$\left(\dfrac{1}{2}, -\dfrac{25}{4}\right);$

$x = \dfrac{1}{2}$

8. $G(x) = x^2 - x - 2$

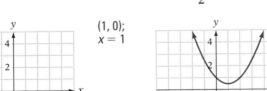

$\left(\dfrac{1}{2}, -\dfrac{9}{4}\right);$

$x = \dfrac{1}{2}$

9. $F(x) = x^2 - 3x + 2$

$\left(\dfrac{3}{2}, -\dfrac{1}{4}\right);$

$x = \dfrac{3}{2}$

10. $y = -2x^2 + 6x$

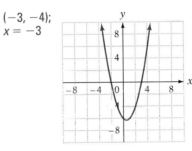

$\left(\dfrac{3}{2}, \dfrac{9}{2}\right);$

$x = \dfrac{3}{2}$

11. $y = -x^2 + 2x - 1$

$(1, 0);$
$x = 1$

12. $h(x) = \dfrac{1}{2}x^2 - x + 1$

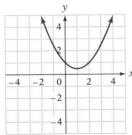

$\left(1, \dfrac{1}{2}\right);$

$x = 1$

13. $P(x) = -\dfrac{1}{2}x^2 + 2x - 3$

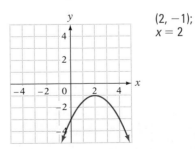

$(2, -1);$
$x = 2$

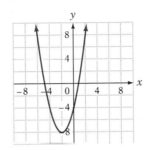

Objective B

14. What are the x-intercepts of a parabola?

Find the x-intercepts of the graph of the parabola.

15. $y = x^2 - 4$
(2, 0), (−2, 0)

16. $y = x^2 - 9$
(3, 0), (−3, 0)

17. $y = 2x^2 - 4x$
(0, 0), (2, 0)

18. $y = 3x^2 + 6x$
(0, 0), (−2, 0)

19. $y = x^2 - x - 2$
(2, 0), (−1, 0)

20. $y = x^2 - 2x - 8$
(4, 0), (−2, 0)

21. $y = 2x^2 - x - 1$
$\left(-\dfrac{1}{2}, 0\right)$, (1, 0)

22. $y = 2x^2 - 5x - 3$
$\left(-\dfrac{1}{2}, 0\right)$, (3, 0)

23. $y = x^2 + 2x - 1$
$(-1 + \sqrt{2}, 0)$, $(-1 - \sqrt{2}, 0)$

24. $y = x^2 + 4x - 3$
$(-2 + \sqrt{7}, 0)$, $(-2 - \sqrt{7}, 0)$

25. $y = x^2 + 6x + 10$
no x-intercepts

26. $y = -x^2 - 4x - 5$
no x-intercepts

27. $y = x^2 - 2x - 2$
$(1 + \sqrt{3}, 0)$, $(1 - \sqrt{3}, 0)$

28. $y = -x^2 - 2x + 1$
$(-1 + \sqrt{2}, 0)$, $(-1 - \sqrt{2}, 0)$

29. $y = -x^2 + 4x + 1$
$(2 + \sqrt{5}, 0)$, $(2 - \sqrt{5}, 0)$

Use the discriminant to determine the number of x-intercepts of the graph.

30. $y = 2x^2 + x + 1$
no x-intercepts

31. $y = 2x^2 + 2x - 1$
two x-intercepts

32. $y = -x^2 - x + 3$
two x-intercepts

33. $y = -2x^2 + x + 1$
two x-intercepts

34. $y = x^2 - 8x + 16$
one x-intercept

35. $y = x^2 - 10x + 25$
one x-intercept

36. $y = -3x^2 - x - 2$
no x-intercepts

37. $y = -2x^2 + x - 1$
no x-intercepts

38. $y = 4x^2 - x - 2$
two x-intercepts

39. $y = 2x^2 + x + 4$
no x-intercepts

40. $y = -2x^2 - x - 5$
no x-intercepts

41. $y = -3x^2 + 4x - 5$
no x-intercepts

Objective C

42. When does a quadratic function have a minimum value and when does it have a maximum value?

Find the minimum or maximum value of the quadratic function.

43. $f(x) = x^2 - 2x + 3$

    minimum: 2

44. $f(x) = x^2 + 3x - 4$

    minimum: $-\dfrac{25}{4}$

45. $f(x) = -2x^2 + 4x - 3$

    maximum: -1

46. $f(x) = -2x^2 - 3x + 4$

    maximum: $\dfrac{41}{8}$

47. $f(x) = 2x^2 + 4x$

    minimum: -2

48. $f(x) = -2x^2 - 3x$

    maximum: $\dfrac{9}{8}$

49. $f(x) = -2x^2 + 4x - 5$

    maximum: -3

50. $f(x) = -3x^2 + x - 6$

    maximum: $-\dfrac{71}{12}$

51. $f(x) = 2x^2 + 3x - 8$

    minimum: $-\dfrac{73}{8}$

52. $f(x) = -x^2 - x + 2$

    maximum: $\dfrac{9}{4}$

53. $f(x) = 3x^2 + 3x - 2$

    minimum: $-\dfrac{11}{4}$

54. $f(x) = x^2 - 5x + 3$

    minimum: $-\dfrac{13}{4}$

55. $f(x) = -3x^2 + 4x - 2$

    maximum: $-\dfrac{2}{3}$

56. $f(x) = -2x^2 - 5x + 1$

    maximum: $\dfrac{33}{8}$

57. $f(x) = 3x^2 + 5x + 2$

    minimum: $-\dfrac{1}{12}$

Objective D   *Application Problems*

58. The height in feet, s, of a rock thrown upward at an initial speed of 64 ft/s from a cliff 50 ft above an ocean beach is given by $s(t) = -16t^2 + 64t + 50$, where t is the time in seconds. Find the maximum height the rock will attain above the beach.
    114 ft

59. An event in the Summer Olympics is 10-meter springboard diving. The height, s, of a diver in this event above the water t seconds after jumping is given by $s(t) = -4.9t^2 + 7.8t + 10$. What is the maximum height, to the nearest tenth of a meter, that the diver will be above the water?
    13.1 m

60. A tour operator believes that the profit, P, from selling x tickets is given by $P(x) = 40x - 0.25x^2$. Using this model, what is the maximum profit the tour operator can expect?
    $1600

61. A manufacturer of microwave ovens believes that the revenue the company receives is related to the price, P, of an oven by $R(P) = 125P - \dfrac{1}{4}P^2$. What price will give the maximum revenue?
    $250

62. The suspension cable that supports a small footbridge hangs in the shape of a parabola. The height in feet of the cable above the bridge is given by the function $h(x) = 0.25x^2 - 0.8x + 25$, where x is the distance from one end of the bridge. What is the minimum height of the cable above the bridge?
    24.36 ft

63. A pool is treated with a chemical to reduce the amount of algae. The amount of algae in the pool t days after the treatment can be approximated by the function $A(t) = 40t^2 - 400t + 1500$. How many days after treatment will the pool have the least amount of algae?
5 days

64. An equation of the thickness (in inches), h, of the mirror at the Palomar Mountain Observatory is given by $h(x) = 0.000379x^2 - 0.0758x + 24$, where x is measured from the edge of the mirror. Find the minimum thickness of the mirror.
20.21 in.

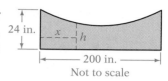

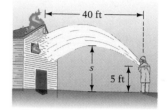

24 in.

200 in.

Not to scale

65. The height, s, of water squirting from a fire hose nozzle is given by the equation $s(x) = -\frac{1}{30}x^2 + 2x + 5$, where x is the horizontal distance from the nozzle. How high on a building 40 ft from the fire hose will the water land?
$31\frac{2}{3}$ ft

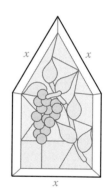

40 ft

s

5 ft

66. The height, h, of a baseball hit by Tony Gwinn that is a distance of d feet from him can be given by $h(d) = -0.0015d^2 + 0.52d + 5$. Will this ball clear a 5-foot wall 340 ft from where it was hit?
yes

67. A designer of stained glass windows has 26 ft of wire that is to be bent so that the bottom portion is a rectangle and the top is an equilateral triangle. The enclosed area of this figure depends on the length of the base and is given by $A(x) = \frac{1}{4}(\sqrt{3} - 6)x^2 + 13x$. What is the maximum area, to the nearest tenth, that can be enclosed by this shape?
39.6 ft²

68. The perimeter of a rectangular window is 24 ft. Find the dimensions of the window that will enclose the largest area. What is the maximum area?
6 ft by 6 ft; 36 ft²

APPLYING THE CONCEPTS

69. Determine whether the following statements are always true, sometimes true, or never true.
a. An axis of symmetry of a parabola passes through the vertex.   always true
b. A parabola has two x-intercepts.   sometimes true
c. A quadratic function has a minimum value.   sometimes true

70. An equation of the form $y = x^2 + bx + c$ can be written in the form $y = (x - h)^2 + k$, where (h, k) are the coordinates of the vertex of the parabola. Use the process of completing the square to rewrite the equation in the form $y = a(x - h)^2 + k$. Find the vertex.
a. $y = x^2 - 4x + 7$
　　$y = (x - 2)^2 + 3; (2, 3)$
b. $y = x^2 - 2x - 2$
　　$y = (x - 1)^2 - 3; (1, -3)$
c. $y = x^2 - 6x + 3$
　　$y = (x - 3)^2 - 6; (3, -6)$
d. $y = x^2 + 4x - 1$
　　$y = (x + 2)^2 - 5; (-2, -5)$
e. $y = x^2 + x + 2$
　　$y = \left(x + \frac{1}{2}\right)^2 + \frac{7}{4}; \left(-\frac{1}{2}, \frac{7}{4}\right)$
f. $y = x^2 - x - 3$
　　$y = \left(x - \frac{1}{2}\right)^2 - \frac{13}{4}; \left(\frac{1}{2}, -\frac{13}{4}\right)$

11.3 Graphs of Functions

Objective A *To graph functions* ....

The graphs of the polynomial functions $f(x) = mx + b$ (a straight line) and $f(x) = ax^2 + bx + c$, $a \neq 0$ (a parabola) have been discussed. The graphs of other functions can be drawn by finding ordered pairs that belong to the function, plotting the points that correspond to the ordered pairs, and then drawing a curve through the points.

➡ Graph: $F(x) = x^3$

Select several values of x and evaluate the function.

x	$F(x) = x^3$	$F(x)$	(x, y)
-2	$(-2)^3$	-8	$(-2, -8)$
-1	$(-1)^3$	-1	$(-1, -1)$
0	0^3	0	$(0, 0)$
1	1^3	1	$(1, 1)$
2	2^3	8	$(2, 8)$

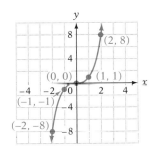

Plot the ordered pairs and draw a graph through the points.

➡ Graph: $g(x) = x^3 - 4x + 5$

Select several values of x and evaluate the function.

x	$g(x) = x^3 - 4x + 5$	$g(x)$	(x, y)
-3	$(-3)^3 - 4(-3) + 5$	-10	$(-3, -10)$
-2	$(-2)^3 - 4(-2) + 5$	5	$(-2, 5)$
-1	$(-1)^3 - 4(-1) + 5$	8	$(-1, 8)$
0	$(0)^3 - 4(0) + 5$	5	$(0, 5)$
1	$(1)^3 - 4(1) + 5$	2	$(1, 2)$
2	$(2)^3 - 4(2) + 5$	5	$(2, 5)$

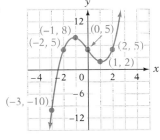

Plot the ordered pairs and draw a graph through the points.

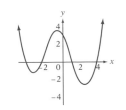

Note from the graphs of the two different cubic functions that the shapes of the graphs can be different. The following graphs of typical cubic polynomial functions show their general shapes.

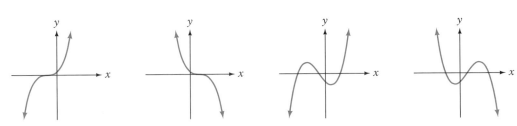

As the degree of a polynomial increases, the graph of the polynomial function can change significantly. In these cases, it may be necessary to plot many points before an accurate graph can be drawn. Only polynomials of degree 3 are considered here.

Example 1
Use the vertical-line test to determine whether the graph shown is the graph of a function.

Solution

A vertical line intersects the graph more than once. The graph is not the graph of a function.

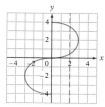

You Try It 1
Use the vertical-line test to determine whether the graph shown is the graph of a function.

Your solution

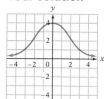 yes

Example 2
Graph $f(x) = x^3 - 3x$. State the domain and range of the function.

Solution

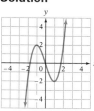

domain:
$\{x \mid x \in \text{real numbers}\}$
range:
$\{y \mid y \in \text{real numbers}\}$

You Try It 2
Graph $f(x) = -\frac{1}{2}x^3 + 2x$. State the domain and range of the function.

Your solution

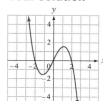

domain: $\{x \mid x \in \text{real numbers}\}$
range: $\{y \mid y \in \text{real numbers}\}$

Example 3
Graph $f(x) = |x| + 2$. State the domain and range of the function.

Solution

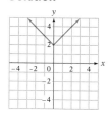

domain:
$\{x \mid x \in \text{real numbers}\}$
range:
$\{y \mid y \geq 2\}$

You Try It 3
Graph $f(x) = |x + 2|$. State the domain and range of the function.

Your solution

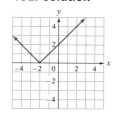

domain: $\{x \mid x \in \text{real numbers}\}$
range: $\{y \mid y \geq 0\}$

Example 4
Graph $f(x) = \sqrt{2 - x}$. State the domain and range of the function.

Solution

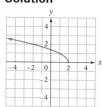

domain: $\{x \mid x \leq 2\}$
range: $\{y \mid y \geq 0\}$

You Try It 4
Graph $f(x) = -\sqrt{x - 1}$. State the domain and range of the function.

Your solution

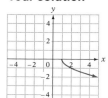

domain: $\{x \mid x \geq 1\}$
range: $\{y \mid y \leq 0\}$

Solutions on p. S32

11.3 Graphs of Functions

Objective A   *To graph functions* ....

The graphs of the polynomial functions $f(x) = mx + b$ (a straight line) and $f(x) = ax^2 + bx + c$, $a \neq 0$ (a parabola) have been discussed. The graphs of other functions can be drawn by finding ordered pairs that belong to the function, plotting the points that correspond to the ordered pairs, and then drawing a curve through the points.

➡ Graph: $F(x) = x^3$

Select several values of x and evaluate the function.

x	$F(x) = x^3$	$F(x)$	(x, y)
-2	$(-2)^3$	-8	$(-2, -8)$
-1	$(-1)^3$	-1	$(-1, -1)$
0	0^3	0	$(0, 0)$
1	1^3	1	$(1, 1)$
2	2^3	8	$(2, 8)$

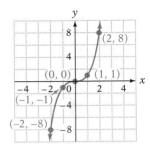

Plot the ordered pairs and draw a graph through the points.

➡ Graph: $g(x) = x^3 - 4x + 5$

Select several values of x and evaluate the function.

x	$g(x) = x^3 - 4x + 5$	$g(x)$	(x, y)
-3	$(-3)^3 - 4(-3) + 5$	-10	$(-3, -10)$
-2	$(-2)^3 - 4(-2) + 5$	5	$(-2, 5)$
-1	$(-1)^3 - 4(-1) + 5$	8	$(-1, 8)$
0	$(0)^3 - 4(0) + 5$	5	$(0, 5)$
1	$(1)^3 - 4(1) + 5$	2	$(1, 2)$
2	$(2)^3 - 4(2) + 5$	5	$(2, 5)$

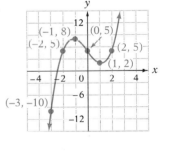

Plot the ordered pairs and draw a graph through the points.

Note from the graphs of the two different cubic functions that the shapes of the graphs can be different. The following graphs of typical cubic polynomial functions show their general shapes.

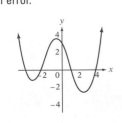

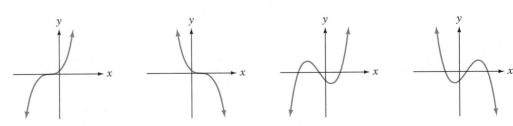

As the degree of a polynomial increases, the graph of the polynomial function can change significantly. In these cases, it may be necessary to plot many points before an accurate graph can be drawn. Only polynomials of degree 3 are considered here.

➡ Graph: $f(x) = |x + 2|$

This is an absolute value function.

x	$f(x) = |x + 2|$	$f(x)$	(x, y)
-3	$|-3 + 2|$	1	$(-3, 1)$
-2	$|-2 + 2|$	0	$(-2, 0)$
-1	$|-1 + 2|$	1	$(-1, 1)$
0	$|0 + 2|$	2	$(0, 2)$
1	$|1 + 2|$	3	$(1, 3)$
2	$|2 + 2|$	4	$(2, 4)$

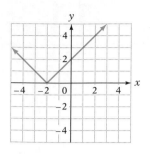

In general, the graph of the absolute value of a linear polynomial is V-shaped.

➡ Graph: $R(x) = \sqrt{2x - 4}$

This is a radical function. Because the square root of a negative number is not a real number, the domain of this function requires that $2x - 4 \geq 0$. Solve this inequality for x.

$$2x - 4 \geq 0$$
$$2x \geq 4$$
$$x \geq 2$$

The domain is $\{x | x \geq 2\}$. This means that only values of x that are greater than or equal to 2 can be chosen as values at which to evaluate the function. In this case, some of the y-coordinates must be approximated.

x	$R(x) = \sqrt{2x - 4}$	$R(x)$	(x, y)
2	$\sqrt{2(2) - 4}$	0	$(2, 0)$
3	$\sqrt{2(3) - 4}$	1.41	$(3, 1.41)$
4	$\sqrt{2(4) - 4}$	2	$(4, 2)$
5	$\sqrt{2(5) - 4}$	2.45	$(5, 2.45)$
6	$\sqrt{2(6) - 4}$	2.83	$(6, 2.83)$

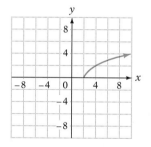

Recall that a function is a special type of relation, one for which no two ordered pairs have the same first coordinate. Graphically, this means that the graph of a function cannot pass through two points that have the same x-coordinate and different y-coordinates. For instance, the graph at the right is not the graph of a function because there are ordered pairs with the same x-coordinate and different y-coordinates.

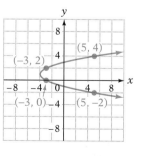

This last graph illustrates a general statement that can be made about whether a graph defines a function. It is called the *vertical-line test*.

Vertical-Line Test

A graph defines a function if any vertical line intersects the graph at no more than one point.

For example, the graph of a nonvertical straight line is the graph of a function. Any vertical line intersects the graph no more than once. The graph of a circle, however, is not the graph of a function. There are vertical lines that intersect the graph at more than one point.

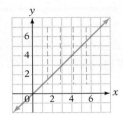 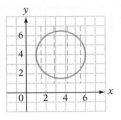

There may be practical situations in which a graph is not the graph of a function. The problem below is an example.

One of the causes of smog is an inversion layer where temperatures at higher altitudes are warmer than those at lower altitudes. The graph at the right shows the altitudes at which various temperatures were recorded. As shown by the dashed lines in the graph, there are two altitudes at which the temperature was 25°C. This means that there are two ordered pairs (shown in the graph) with the same first coordinate but different second coordinates. The graph does not define a function.

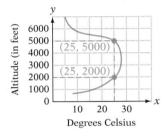

When a graph does define a function, the domain and range can be estimated from the graph.

➡ Determine the domain and range of the function given by the graph at the right.

The solid dots on the graph indicate its beginning and ending points.

The domain is the set of x-coordinates.
Domain: $\{x \mid 1 \le x \le 6\}$

The range is the set of y-coordinates.
Range: $\{y \mid 2 \le y \le 5\}$

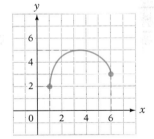

➡ Determine the domain and range of the function given by the graph at the right.

The arrows on the graph indicate that the graph continues in the same manner.

The domain is the set of x-coordinates.
Domain: $\{x \mid x \in \text{real numbers}\}$

The range is the set of y-coordinates.
Range: $\{y \mid -4 \le y \le 4\}$

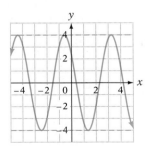

Example 1

Use the vertical-line test to determine whether the graph shown is the graph of a function.

Solution

A vertical line intersects the graph more than once. The graph is not the graph of a function.

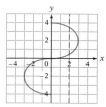

You Try It 1

Use the vertical-line test to determine whether the graph shown is the graph of a function.

Your solution

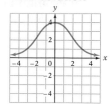   yes

Example 2

Graph $f(x) = x^3 - 3x$. State the domain and range of the function.

Solution

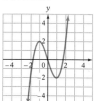

domain:
$\{x \mid x \in \text{real numbers}\}$
range:
$\{y \mid y \in \text{real numbers}\}$

You Try It 2

Graph $f(x) = -\frac{1}{2}x^3 + 2x$. State the domain and range of the function.

Your solution

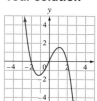

domain: $\{x \mid x \in \text{real numbers}\}$
range: $\{y \mid y \in \text{real numbers}\}$

Example 3

Graph $f(x) = |x| + 2$. State the domain and range of the function.

Solution

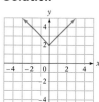

domain:
$\{x \mid x \in \text{real numbers}\}$
range:
$\{y \mid y \geq 2\}$

You Try It 3

Graph $f(x) = |x + 2|$. State the domain and range of the function.

Your solution

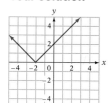

domain: $\{x \mid x \in \text{real numbers}\}$
range: $\{y \mid y \geq 0\}$

Example 4

Graph $f(x) = \sqrt{2 - x}$. State the domain and range of the function.

Solution

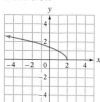

domain: $\{x \mid x \leq 2\}$
range: $\{y \mid y \geq 0\}$

You Try It 4

Graph $f(x) = -\sqrt{x - 1}$. State the domain and range of the function.

Your solution

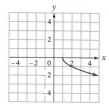

domain: $\{x \mid x \geq 1\}$
range: $\{y \mid y \leq 0\}$

Solutions on p. S32

11.3 Exercises

Objective A

Use the vertical-line test to determine whether the graph is the graph of a function.

1.

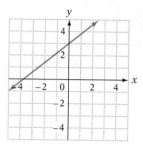

yes

2.

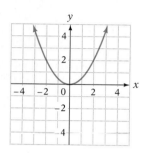

yes

3.

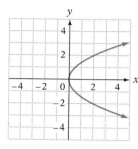

no

4.

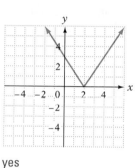

yes

5.

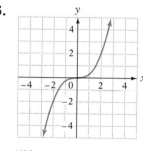

yes

6.

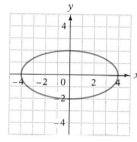

no

Graph the function and state its domain and range.

7. $f(x) = 3|2 - x|$

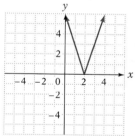

domain: $\{x \mid x \in \text{real numbers}\}$
range: $\{y \mid y \geq 0\}$

8. $f(x) = x^3 - 1$

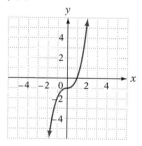

domain: $\{x \mid x \in \text{real numbers}\}$
range: $\{y \mid y \in \text{real numbers}\}$

9. $f(x) = 1 - x^3$

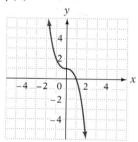

domain: $\{x \mid x \in \text{real numbers}\}$
range: $\{y \mid y \in \text{real numbers}\}$

10. $f(x) = \sqrt{1 + x}$

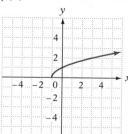

domain: $\{x \mid x \geq -1\}$
range: $\{y \mid y \geq 0\}$

11. $f(x) = \sqrt{4 - x}$

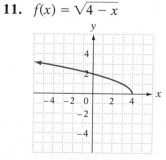

domain: $\{x \mid x \leq 4\}$
range: $\{y \mid y \geq 0\}$

12. $f(x) = |2x - 1|$

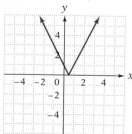

domain: $\{x \mid x \in \text{real numbers}\}$
range: $\{y \mid y \geq 0\}$

13. $f(x) = x^3 + 4x^2 + 4x$

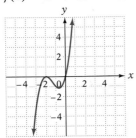

domain: $\{x \mid x \in \text{real numbers}\}$
range: $\{y \mid y \in \text{real numbers}\}$

14. $f(x) = x^3 - x^2 - x + 1$

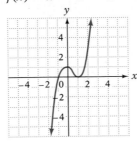

domain: $\{x \mid x \in \text{real numbers}\}$
range: $\{y \mid y \in \text{real numbers}\}$

15. $f(x) = -\sqrt{x + 2}$

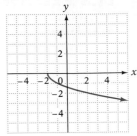

domain: $\{x \mid x \geq -2\}$
range: $\{y \mid y \leq 0\}$

16. $f(x) = -\sqrt{x - 3}$

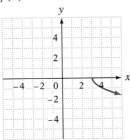

domain: $\{x \mid x \geq 3\}$
range: $\{y \mid y \leq 0\}$

17. $f(x) = |2x + 2|$

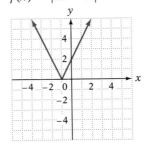

domain: $\{x \mid x \in \text{real numbers}\}$
range: $\{y \mid y \geq 0\}$

18. $f(x) = 2|x + 1|$

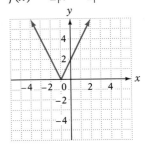

domain: $\{x \mid x \in \text{real numbers}\}$
range: $\{y \mid y \geq 0\}$

APPLYING THE CONCEPTS

19. If $f(x) = \sqrt{x - 2}$ and $f(a) = 4$, find a. $a = 18$

20. If $f(x) = \sqrt{x + 5}$ and $f(a) = 3$, find a. $a = 4$

21. $f(a, b) = $ the sum of a and b
$g(a, b) = $ the product of a and b
Find $f(2, 5) + g(2, 5)$.   17

22. $f(a, b) = $ the greatest common divisor of a and b
$g(a, b) = $ the least common multiple of a and b
Find $f(14, 35) + g(14, 35)$.   77

23. Let $f(x)$ be the digit in the xth decimal place of the repeating decimal $0.\overline{387}$. For example, $f(3) = 7$ because 7 is the digit in the third decimal place. Find $f(14)$. $f(14) = 8$

24. Given $f(x) = (x + 1)(x - 1)$, for what values of x is $f(x)$ negative? Write your answer in set-builder notation. $\{x \mid -1 < x < 1\}$

25. Given $f(x) = -|x + 3|$, for what value of x is $f(x)$ greatest? $x = -3$

26. Given $f(x) = |2x - 2|$, for what value of x is $f(x)$ smallest? $x = 1$

➡ Given $f(x) = 2x^2 - 5x + 3$ and $g(x) = x^2 - 1$, find $\left(\dfrac{f}{g}\right)(1)$.

$$\left(\frac{f}{g}\right)(1) = \frac{f(1)}{g(1)}$$

$$= \frac{2(1)^2 - 5(1) + 3}{(1)^2 - 1}$$

$$= \frac{0}{0} \qquad \bullet \text{ Not a real number}$$

Because $\dfrac{0}{0}$ is not defined, the expression $\left(\dfrac{f}{g}\right)(1)$ cannot be evaluated.

Example 1
Given $f(x) = x^2 - x + 1$ and $g(x) = x^3 - 4$,
find $(f - g)(3)$.

Solution
$$(f - g)(3) = f(3) - g(3)$$
$$= (3^2 - 3 + 1) - (3^3 - 4)$$
$$= 7 - 23$$
$$= -16$$

$(f - g)(3) = -16$

Example 2
Given $f(x) = x^2 + 2$ and $g(x) = 2x + 3$, find
$(f \cdot g)(-2)$.

Solution
$$(f \cdot g)(-2) = f(-2) \cdot g(-2)$$
$$= [(-2)^2 + 2] \cdot [2(-2) + 3]$$
$$= 6 \cdot (-1)$$
$$= -6$$

$(f \cdot g)(-2) = -6$

Example 3
Given $f(x) = x^2 + 4x + 4$ and $g(x) = x^3 - 2$,
find $\left(\dfrac{f}{g}\right)(3)$.

Solution
$$\left(\frac{f}{g}\right)(3) = \frac{f(3)}{g(3)}$$
$$= \frac{3^2 + 4(3) + 4}{3^3 - 2}$$
$$= \frac{25}{25}$$
$$= 1$$

$\left(\dfrac{f}{g}\right)(3) = 1$

You Try It 1
Given $f(x) = x^2 + 2x$ and $g(x) = 5x - 2$,
find $(f + g)(-2)$.

Your solution
-12

You Try It 2
Given $f(x) = 4 - x^2$ and $g(x) = 3x - 4$,
find $(f \cdot g)(3)$.

Your solution
-25

You Try It 3
Given $f(x) = x^2 - 4$ and $g(x) = x^2 + 2x + 1$,
find $\left(\dfrac{f}{g}\right)(4)$.

Your solution
$\dfrac{12}{25}$

Solutions on p. S32

11.4 Algebra of Functions

Objective A   *To perform operations on functions* ....

The operations of addition, subtraction, multiplication, and division of functions are defined as follows.

Operations on Functions

If f and g are functions and x is an element of the domain of each function, then

$$(f + g)(x) = f(x) + g(x) \qquad (f \cdot g)(x) = f(x) \cdot g(x)$$

$$(f - g)(x) = f(x) - g(x) \qquad \left(\frac{f}{g}\right)(x) = \frac{f(x)}{g(x)}, \; g(x) \neq 0$$

➡ Given $f(x) = x^2 + 1$ and $g(x) = 3x - 2$, find $(f + g)(3)$ and $(f \cdot g)(-1)$.

$$(f + g)(3) = f(3) + g(3)$$
$$= [(3)^2 + 1] + [3(3) - 2]$$
$$= 10 + 7 = 17$$

$$(f \cdot g)(-1) = f(-1) \cdot g(-1)$$
$$= [(-1)^2 + 1] \cdot [3(-1) - 2]$$
$$= 2 \cdot (-5) = -10$$

Consider the functions f and g from the last example. Let $S(x)$ be the sum of the two functions. Then

$$S(x) = (f + g)(x) = f(x) + g(x)$$
$$= (x^2 + 1) + (3x - 2)$$
$$S(x) = x^2 + 3x - 1$$

• The definition of addition of functions
• $f(x) = x^2 + 1$, $g(x) = 3x - 2$

Now evaluate $S(3)$.

$$S(3) = (3)^2 + 3(3) - 1$$
$$= 9 + 9 - 1$$
$$= 17 = (f + g)(3)$$

Note that $S(3) = 17$ and $(f + g)(3) = 17$. This shows that adding $f(x) + g(x)$ and then evaluating is the same as evaluating $f(x)$ and $g(x)$ and then adding. The same is true for the other operations on functions. For instance, let $P(x)$ be the product of the functions f and g. Then

$$P(x) = (f \cdot g)(x) = f(x) \cdot g(x)$$
$$= (x^2 + 1)(3x - 2)$$
$$= 3x^3 - 2x^2 + 3x - 2$$
$$P(-1) = 3(-1)^3 - 2(-1)^2 + 3(-1) - 2$$
$$= -3 - 2 - 3 - 2$$
$$= -10 = (f \cdot g)(-1)$$

11.4 Exercises

· ·

Objective A

For $f(x) = 2x^2 - 3$ and $g(x) = -2x + 4$, find:

1. $(f - g)(2)$
5

2. $(f - g)(3)$
17

3. $(f + g)(0)$
1

4. $(f + g)(1)$
1

5. $(f \cdot g)(2)$
0

6. $(f \cdot g)(-1)$
-6

7. $\left(\dfrac{f}{g}\right)(4)$

$-\dfrac{29}{4}$

8. $\left(\dfrac{f}{g}\right)(-1)$

$-\dfrac{1}{6}$

9. $\left(\dfrac{g}{f}\right)(-3)$

$\dfrac{2}{3}$

For $f(x) = 2x^2 + 3x - 1$ and $g(x) = 2x - 4$, find:

10. $(f + g)(-3)$
-2

11. $(f + g)(1)$
2

12. $(f - g)(-2)$
9

13. $(f - g)(4)$
39

14. $(f \cdot g)(-2)$
-8

15. $(f \cdot g)(1)$
-8

16. $\left(\dfrac{f}{g}\right)(2)$

undefined

17. $\left(\dfrac{f}{g}\right)(-3)$

$-\dfrac{4}{5}$

18. $(f \cdot g)\left(\dfrac{1}{2}\right)$

-3

For $f(x) = x^2 + 3x - 5$ and $g(x) = x^3 - 2x + 3$, find:

19. $(f - g)(2)$

-2

20. $(f \cdot g)(-3)$

90

21. $\left(\dfrac{f}{g}\right)(-2)$

7

Objective B

Given $f(x) = 2x - 3$ and $g(x) = 4x - 1$, evaluate the composite function.

22. $f[g(0)]$
-5

23. $g[f(0)]$
-13

24. $f[g(2)]$
11

25. $g[f(-2)]$
-29

26. $f[g(x)]$
$8x - 5$

27. $g[f(x)]$
$8x - 13$

Given $h(x) = 2x + 4$ and $f(x) = \frac{1}{2}x + 2$, evaluate the composite function.

28. $(h \circ f)(0)$
8

29. $(f \circ h)(0)$
4

30. $(h \circ f)(2)$
10

31. $(f \circ h)(-1)$
3

32. $(h \circ f)(x)$
$x + 8$

33. $(f \circ h)(x)$
$x + 4$

Given $f(x) = x^2 + x + 1$ and $h(x) = 3x + 2$, evaluate the composite function.

34. $(f \circ h)(0)$
7

35. $(h \circ f)(0)$
5

36. $(f \circ h)(-1)$
1

37. $(h \circ f)(-2)$
11

38. $(f \circ h)(x)$
$9x^2 + 15x + 7$

39. $(h \circ f)(x)$
$3x^2 + 3x + 5$

Given $f(x) = x - 2$ and $g(x) = x^3$, evaluate the composite function.

40. $(f \circ g)(2)$
6

41. $(f \circ g)(-1)$
-3

42. $(g \circ f)(2)$
0

43. $(g \circ f)(-1)$
-27

44. $(f \circ g)(x)$
$x^3 - 2$

45. $(g \circ f)(x)$
$x^3 - 6x^2 + 12x - 8$

APPLYING THE CONCEPTS

For the function $g(x) = x^2 - 1$, find:

46. $g(2 + h)$
$h^2 + 4h + 3$

47. $g(3 + h) - g(3)$
$h^2 + 6h$

48. $g(-1 + h) - g(-1)$
$h^2 - 2h$

49. $\dfrac{g(1 + h) - g(1)}{h}$
$2 + h$

50. $\dfrac{g(-2 + h) - g(-2)}{h}$
$-4 + h$

51. $\dfrac{g(a + h) - g(a)}{h}$
$2a + h$

Given $f(x) = 2x$, $g(x) = 3x - 1$, and $h(x) = x - 2$, find:

52. $f(g[h(2)])$
-2

53. $g(h[f(1)])$
-1

54. $h(g[f(-1)])$
-9

55. $f(h[g(0)])$
-6

56. $f(g[h(x)])$
$6x - 14$

57. $g(f[h(x)])$
$6x - 13$

11.5 One-to-One and Inverse Functions

Objective A   *To determine whether a function is one-to-one* ....

Recall that a function is a set of ordered pairs in which no two ordered pairs that have the same first coordinate have different second coordinates. This means that given any x, there is only one y that can be paired with that x. A *one-to-one* function satisfies the additional condition that given any y, there is only one x that can be paired with the given y. One-to-one functions are commonly written as 1–1.

> **One-to-One Function**
>
> A function f is a 1–1 function if, for any a and b in the domain of f, $f(a) = f(b)$ implies that $a = b$.

This definition states that if the y-coordinates of an ordered pair are equal, $f(a) = f(b)$, then the x-coordinates must be equal, $a = b$.

The function defined by $f(x) = 2x + 1$ is a 1–1 function. To show this, determine $f(a)$ and $f(b)$. Then form the equation $f(a) = f(b)$.

$$f(a) = 2a + 1 \qquad f(b) = 2b + 1$$

$$f(a) = f(b)$$
$$2a + 1 = 2b + 1$$
$$2a = 2b \qquad \bullet \text{ Subtract 1 from each side of the equation.}$$
$$a = b \qquad \bullet \text{ Divide each side of the equation by 2.}$$

Because $f(a) = f(b)$ implies that $a = b$, the function is a 1–1 function.

Consider the function defined by $g(x) = x^2 - x$. Evaluate the function at -2 and 3.

$$g(-2) = (-2)^2 - (-2) = 6 \qquad\qquad g(3) = 3^2 - 3 = 6$$

From this evaluation, $g(-2) = 6$ and $g(3) = 6$, but $-2 \neq 3$. Thus f is not a 1–1 function.

The graphs of $f(x) = 2x + 1$ and $g(x) = x^2 - x$ are shown below. Note that a horizontal line intersects the graph of f at no more than one point. However, a horizontal line intersects the graph of g at more than one point.

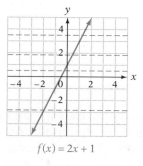

$$f(x) = 2x + 1$$

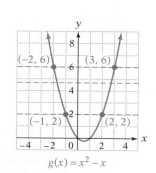

$$g(x) = x^2 - x$$

Looking at the graph of f on the previous page, note that for each y-coordinate there is only one x-coordinate. Thus f is a 1–1 function. From the graph of g, however, there are *two* x-coordinates for a given y-coordinate. For instance, $(-2, 6)$ and $(3, 6)$ are the coordinates of two points on the graph for which the y-coordinates are the same and the x-coordinates are different. Therefore, g is not a 1–1 function.

Horizontal-Line Test

The graph of a function represents the graph of a 1–1 function if any horizontal line intersects the graph at no more than one point.

Example 1

Determine whether the graph is the graph of a 1–1 function.

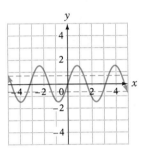

Solution

Because a horizontal line intersects the graph more than once, the graph is not the graph of a 1–1 function.

You Try It 1

Determine whether the graph is the graph of a 1–1 function.

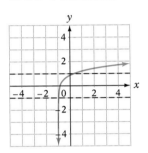

Your solution

Because any horizontal line intersects the graph at most once, the graph is the graph of a 1–1 function.

Solution on p. S33

Objective B   To find the inverse of a function..

The **inverse of a function** is the set of ordered pairs formed by reversing the coordinates of each ordered pair of the function.

For example, the set of ordered pairs of the function defined by $f(x) = 2x$ with domain $\{-2, -1, 0, 1, 2\}$ is $\{(-2, -4), (-1, -2), (0, 0), (1, 2), (2, 4)\}$. The set of ordered pairs of the inverse function is $\{(-4, -2), (-2, -1), (0, 0), (2, 1), (4, 2)\}$.

From the ordered pairs of f, we have

$$\text{domain} = \{-2, -1, 0, 1, 2\} \quad \text{and} \quad \text{range} = \{-4, -2, 0, 2, 4\}$$

From the ordered pairs of the inverse function, we have

$$\text{domain} = \{-4, -2, 0, 2, 4\} \quad \text{and} \quad \text{range} = \{-2, -1, 0, 1, 2\}$$

Note that the domain of the inverse function is the range of the function, and the range of the inverse function is the domain of the function.

Now consider the function defined by $g(x) = x^2$ with domain $\{-2, -1, 0, 1, 2\}$. The set of ordered pairs of this function is $\{(-2, 4), (-1, 1), (0, 0), (1, 1), (2, 4)\}$. Reversing the ordered pairs gives $\{(4, -2), (1, -1), (0, 0), (1, 1), (4, 2)\}$. These ordered pairs do not satisfy the condition of a function, because there are ordered pairs with the same first coordinate and different second coordinates. This example illustrates that not all functions have an inverse function.

INSTRUCTOR NOTE

It may be necessary to remind students of the definition of domain and range before discussing this material.

11.5 Exercises

· ·

Objective A

Determine whether the graph represents the graph of a 1–1 function.

1.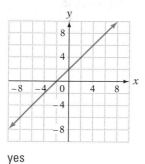

yes

2.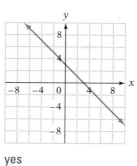

yes

3.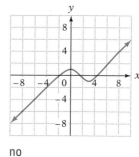

no

4.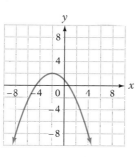

no

5.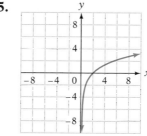

yes

6.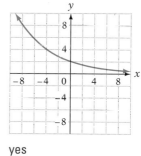

yes

7.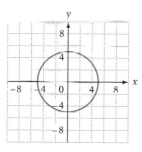

no

8.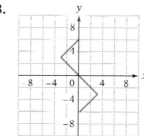

no

9.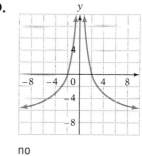

no

10.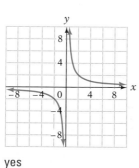

yes

11.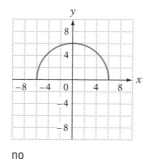

no

12.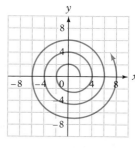

no

Objective B

13. What is the inverse of a function?

14. What does the notation $f^{-1}(x)$ mean?

Find the inverse of the function. If the function does not have an inverse function, write "no inverse."

15. $\{(1, 0), (2, 3), (3, 8), (4, 15)\}$
$\{(0, 1), (3, 2), (8, 3), (15, 4)\}$

16. $\{(1, 0), (2, 1), (-1, 0), (-2, 0)\}$
no inverse

17. $\{(3, 5), (-3, -5), (2, 5), (-2, -5)\}$
no inverse

18. $\{(-5, -5), (-3, -1), (-1, 3), (1, 7)\}$
$\{(-5, -5), (-1, -3), (3, -1), (7, 1)\}$

19. $\{(0, -2), (-1, 5), (3, 3), (-4, 6)\}$
$\{(-2, 0), (5, -1), (3, 3), (6, -4)\}$

20. $\{(-2, -2), (0, 0), (2, 2), (4, 4)\}$
$\{(-2, -2), (0, 0), (2, 2), (4, 4)\}$

21. $\{(-2, -3), (-1, 3), (0, 3), (1, 3)\}$
no inverse

22. $\{(2, 0), (1, 0), (3, 0), (4, 0)\}$
no inverse

Find $f^{-1}(x)$.

23. $f(x) = 4x - 8$
$f^{-1}(x) = \frac{1}{4}x + 2$

24. $f(x) = 3x + 6$
$f^{-1}(x) = \frac{1}{3}x - 2$

25. $f(x) = 2x + 4$
$f^{-1}(x) = \frac{1}{2}x - 2$

26. $f(x) = x - 5$
$f^{-1}(x) = x + 5$

27. $f(x) = \frac{1}{2}x - 1$
$f^{-1}(x) = 2x + 2$

28. $f(x) = \frac{1}{3}x + 2$
$f^{-1}(x) = 3x - 6$

29. $f(x) = -2x + 2$
$f^{-1}(x) = -\frac{1}{2}x + 1$

30. $f(x) = -3x - 9$
$f^{-1}(x) = -\frac{1}{3}x - 3$

31. $f(x) = \frac{2}{3}x + 4$
$f^{-1}(x) = \frac{3}{2}x - 6$

32. $f(x) = \frac{3}{4}x - 4$
$f^{-1}(x) = \frac{1}{2}x + \frac{5}{2}$

33. $f(x) = -\frac{1}{3}x + 1$
$f^{-1}(x) = -3x + 3$

34. $f(x) = -\frac{1}{2}x + 2$
$f^{-1}(x) = -2x + 4$

35. $f(x) = 2x - 5$
$f^{-1}(x) = \frac{1}{2}x + \frac{5}{2}$

36. $f(x) = 3x + 4$
$f^{-1}(x) = \frac{1}{3}x - \frac{4}{3}$

37. $f(x) = 5x - 2$
$f^{-1}(x) = \frac{1}{5}x + \frac{2}{5}$

38. $f(x) = 4x - 2$
$f^{-1}(x) = \frac{1}{4}x + \frac{1}{2}$

39. $f(x) = 6x - 3$
$f^{-1}(x) = \frac{1}{6}x + \frac{1}{2}$

40. $f(x) = -8x + 4$
$f^{-1}(x) = -\frac{1}{8}x + \frac{1}{2}$

41. $f(x) = -6x + 2$

$f^{-1}(x) = -\dfrac{1}{6}x + \dfrac{1}{3}$

42. $f(x) = 8x + 6$

$f^{-1}(x) = \dfrac{1}{8}x - \dfrac{3}{4}$

43. $f(x) = 3x - 4$

$f^{-1}(x) = \dfrac{1}{3}x + \dfrac{4}{3}$

44. $f(x) = \dfrac{5}{8}x + 5$

$f^{-1}(x) = \dfrac{8}{5}x - 8$

45. $f(x) = -\dfrac{2}{3}x + 4$

$f^{-1}(x) = -\dfrac{3}{2}x + 6$

46. $f(x) = 5x + 5$

$f^{-1}(x) = \dfrac{1}{5}x - 1$

47. $f(x) = 3x - 2$

$f^{-1}(x) = \dfrac{1}{3}x + \dfrac{2}{3}$

48. $f(x) = \dfrac{1}{4}x + 4$

$f^{-1}(x) = 4x - 16$

49. $f(x) = -\dfrac{3}{4}x - 2$

$f^{-1}(x) = -\dfrac{4}{3}x - \dfrac{8}{3}$

Use the Property of the Composition of Inverse Functions to determine whether the functions are inverses of each other.

50. $f(x) = 4x; g(x) = \dfrac{x}{4}$

yes

51. $g(x) = x + 5; h(x) = x - 5$

yes

52. $f(x) = 3x; h(x) = \dfrac{1}{3x}$

no

53. $h(x) = x + 2; g(x) = 2 - x$

no

54. $g(x) = 3x + 2; f(x) = \dfrac{1}{3}x - \dfrac{2}{3}$

yes

55. $h(x) = 4x - 1; f(x) = \dfrac{1}{4}x + \dfrac{1}{4}$

yes

56. $f(x) = \dfrac{1}{2}x - \dfrac{3}{2}; g(x) = 2x + 3$

yes

57. $g(x) = -\dfrac{1}{2}x - \dfrac{1}{2}; h(x) = -2x + 1$

no

58. $f(x) = \dfrac{3}{2}x + 2; g(x) = \dfrac{2}{3}x - \dfrac{4}{3}$

yes

59. $f(x) = 3x - 2; g(x) = 2 - 3x$

no

60. $h(x) = \dfrac{3}{2}x + \dfrac{4}{3}; g(x) = \dfrac{2}{3}x + \dfrac{3}{4}$

no

61. $g(x) = -\dfrac{1}{2}x - 2; f(x) = -2x - 4$

yes

62. $g(x) = -\dfrac{2}{3}x + 3; h(x) = \dfrac{3}{2}x - \dfrac{9}{2}$

no

63. $f(x) = -\dfrac{1}{2}x + \dfrac{3}{2}; h(x) = -2x + 3$

yes

APPLYING THE CONCEPTS

Given the graph of the 1–1 function, draw the graph of the inverse of the function by using the technique shown in Objective B of this section.

64.

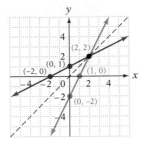

65.

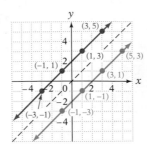

66.

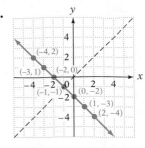

The inverse is the same graph.

67.

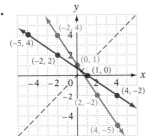

68.

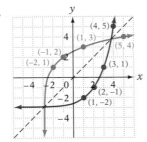

69.

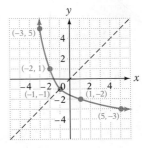

The inverse is the same graph.

Each of the tables below defines a function. Is the inverse of the function a function? Explain your answer.

70. Grading Scale Table

Score	Grade
90–100	A
80–89	B
70–79	C
60–69	D
0–59	F

no

71. First-Class Postage

Weight	Cost
$0 < w < 1$	$.33
$1 < w \leq 2$	$.55
$2 < w \leq 3$	$.77
$3 < w \leq 4$	$.99

no

If f is a 1–1 function and $f(0) = 1$, $f(3) = -1$, and $f(5) = -3$, find:

72. $f^{-1}(-3)$

5

73. $f^{-1}(-1)$

3

74. $f^{-1}(1)$

0

If f is a 1–1 function and $f(-3) = 3$, $f(-4) = 7$, and $f(0) = 8$, find:

75. $f^{-1}(3)$

−3

76. $f^{-1}(7)$

−4

77. $f^{-1}(8)$

0

78. Is the inverse of a constant function a function? Explain your answer.

79. The graphs of all functions given by $f(x) = mx + b$, $m \neq 0$, are straight lines. Are all of these functions 1–1 functions? If so, explain why. If not, give an example of a linear function that is not 1–1.

yes

11.6   Conic Sections

Objective A   *To graph a parabola*..

The **conic sections** are curves that can be constructed from the intersection of a plane and a right circular cone. The parabola, which was introduced earlier, is one of these curves. Here we will review some of that previous discussion and look at equations of parabolas that were not discussed before.

 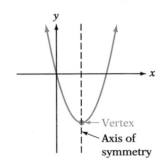

Every parabola has an axis of symmetry and a vertex that is on the axis of symmetry. To understand the axis of symmetry, think of folding the paper along that axis. The two halves of the curve will match up.

The graph of the equation $y = ax^2 + bx + c$, $a \neq 0$, is a parabola with the axis of symmetry parallel to the y-axis. The parabola opens up when $a > 0$ and opens down when $a < 0$. When the parabola opens up, the vertex is the lowest point on the parabola. When the parabola opens down, the vertex is the highest point on the parabola.

INSTRUCTOR NOTE

Some properties of the parabola were covered earlier. Those properties are repeated here for completeness.

The coordinates of the vertex can be found by completing the square.

➡ Find the vertex of the parabola whose equation is $y = x^2 - 4x + 5$.

$y = x^2 - 4x + 5$
$y = (x^2 - 4x) + 5$ • Group the terms involving x.
$y = (x^2 - 4x + 4) - 4 + 5$ • Complete the square of $x^2 - 4x$. Note that 4 is added and subtracted. Because $4 - 4 = 0$, the equation is not changed.

$y = (x - 2)^2 + 1$ • Factor the trinomial and combine like terms.

INSTRUCTOR NOTE

This argument is particularly difficult for students. You might have students evaluate the expression $(x - 2)^2$ for various values of x to illustrate that the quantity is always nonnegative and is zero when $x = 2$.

The coefficient of x^2 is positive, so the parabola opens up. The vertex is the lowest point on the parabola, or the point that has the least y-coordinate.

Because $(x - 2)^2 \geq 0$ for all x, the least y-coordinate occurs when $(x - 2)^2 = 0$, which occurs when $x = 2$. This means the x-coordinate of the vertex is 2.

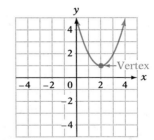

To find the y-coordinate of the vertex, replace x in $y = (x - 2)^2 + 1$ by 2 and solve for y.

$y = (x - 2)^2 + 1$
$\quad = (2 - 2)^2 + 1 = 1$

The vertex is (2, 1).

POINT OF INTEREST

The suspension cables for some bridges, such as the Golden Gate bridge, hang in the shape of a parabola. Parabolic shapes are also used for mirrors in telescopes and in certain antenna designs.

By following the procedure of the last example and completing the square on the equation $y = ax^2 + bx + c$, we find that the **x-coordinate of the vertex** is $-\dfrac{b}{2a}$. The y-coordinate of the vertex can then be determined by substituting this value of x into $y = ax^2 + bx + c$ and solving for y.

Because the axis of symmetry is parallel to the y-axis and passes through the vertex, the equation of the **axis of symmetry** is $x = -\dfrac{b}{2a}$.

➡ Find the vertex and axis of symmetry of the parabola whose equation is $y = -3x^2 + 6x + 1$. Then sketch its graph.

x-coordinate: $-\dfrac{b}{2a} = -\dfrac{6}{2(-3)} = 1$ • Find the x-coordinate of the vertex and the axis of symmetry, $a = -3$, $b = 6$.

The x-coordinate of the vertex is 1.
The axis of symmetry is the line $x = 1$.

To find the y-coordinate of the vertex, replace x by 1 and solve for y.

$y = -3x^2 + 6x + 1$
$\;\;= -3(1)^2 + 6(1) + 1 = 4$

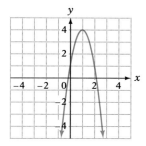

The vertex is $(1, 4)$.

Because a is negative, the parabola opens down.

Find a few ordered pairs and use symmetry to sketch the graph.

➡ Find the vertex and axis of symmetry of the parabola whose equation is $y = x^2 - 2$. Then sketch its graph.

x-coordinate: $-\dfrac{b}{2a} = -\dfrac{0}{2(1)} = 0$ • Find the x-coordinate of the vertex and the axis of symmetry. $a = 1$, $b = 0$

The x-coordinate of the vertex is 0.
The axis of symmetry is the line $x = 0$.

To find the y-coordinate of the vertex, replace x by 0 and solve for y.

$y = x^2 - 2$
$\;\;= 0^2 - 2 = -2$

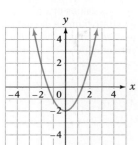

The vertex is $(0, -2)$.

Because a is positive, the parabola opens up.

Find a few ordered pairs and use symmetry to sketch the graph.

The graph of an equation of the form $x = ay^2 + by + c$, $a \neq 0$, is also a parabola. In this case, the parabola opens to the right when a is positive and opens to the left when a is negative.

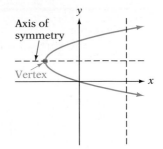

For a parabola of this form, the **y-coordinate of the vertex** is $-\dfrac{b}{2a}$. The **axis of symmetry** is the line $y = -\dfrac{b}{2a}$.

Using the vertical line test, the graph of a parabola of this form is not the graph of a function. The graph of $x = ay^2 + by + c$ is a relation.

⮕ Find the vertex and axis of symmetry of the parabola whose equation is $x = 2y^2 - 8y + 5$. Then sketch its graph.

$$y\text{-coordinate: } -\frac{b}{2a} = -\frac{-8}{2(2)} = 2$$

- Find the y-coordinate of the vertex and the axis of symmetry. $a = 2$, $b = -8$

The y-coordinate of the vertex is 2.
The axis of symmetry is the line $y = 2$.

To find the x-coordinate of the vertex, replace y by 2 and solve for x.

$$x = 2y^2 - 8y + 5$$
$$= 2(2)^2 - 8(2) + 5 = -3$$

The vertex is $(-3, 2)$.

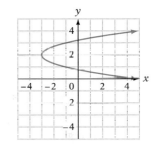

Since a is positive, the parabola opens to the right.

Find a few ordered pairs and use symmetry to sketch the graph.

⮕ Find the vertex and axis of symmetry of the parabola whose equation is $x = -2y^2 - 4y - 3$. Then sketch its graph.

$$y\text{-coordinate: } -\frac{b}{2a} = -\frac{-4}{2(-2)} = -1$$

- Find the y-coordinate of the vertex and the axis of symmetry. $a = -2$, $b = -4$

The y-coordinate of the vertex is -1.
The axis of symmetry is the line $y = -1$.

To find the x-coordinate of the vertex, replace y by -1 and solve for x.

$$x = -2y^2 - 4y - 3$$
$$= -2(-1)^2 - 4(-1) - 3 = -1$$

The vertex is $(-1, -1)$.

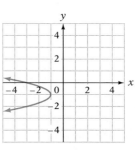

Because a is negative, the parabola opens to the left.

Find a few ordered pairs and use symmetry to sketch the graph.

Example 1

Find the vertex and axis of symmetry of the parabola whose equation is $y = x^2 - 4x + 3$. Then sketch its graph.

Solution

$$-\frac{b}{2a} = -\frac{-4}{2(1)} = 2$$

axis of symmetry:
$$x = 2$$

$$y = 2^2 - 4(2) + 3$$
$$= -1$$

vertex: $(2, -1)$

You Try It 1

Find the vertex and axis of symmetry of the parabola whose equation is $y = x^2 + 2x + 1$. Then sketch its graph.

Your solution

vertex: $(-1, 0)$

axis of symmetry:
$$x = -1$$

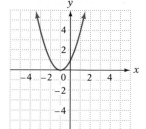

Example 2

Find the vertex and axis of symmetry of the parabola whose equation is $x = 2y^2 - 4y + 1$. Then sketch its graph.

Solution

$$-\frac{b}{2a} = -\frac{-4}{2(2)} = 1$$

axis of symmetry:
$$y = 1$$

$$x = 2(1)^2 - 4(1) + 1$$
$$= -1$$

vertex: $(-1, 1)$

You Try It 2

Find the vertex and axis of symmetry of the parabola whose equation is $x = -y^2 - 2y + 2$. Then sketch its graph.

Your solution

vertex: $(3, -1)$

axis of symmetry:
$$y = -1$$

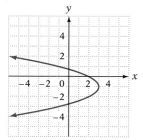

Example 3

Find the vertex and axis of symmetry of the parabola whose equation is $y = x^2 + 1$. Then sketch its graph.

Solution

$$-\frac{b}{2a} = -\frac{0}{2(1)} = 0$$

axis of symmetry:
$$x = 0$$

$$y = 0^2 + 1$$
$$= 1$$

vertex: $(0, 1)$

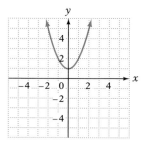

You Try It 3

Find the vertex and axis of symmetry of the parabola whose equation is $y = x^2 - 2x - 1$. Then sketch its graph.

Your solution

vertex: $(1, -2)$

axis of symmetry:
$$x = 1$$

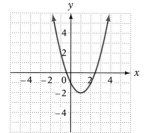

Solutions on p. S33

Objective B **To find the equation of a circle and to graph a circle** ....

A **circle** is a conic section formed by the intersection of a cone and a plane parallel to the base of the cone.

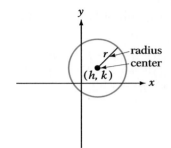

A **circle** can be defined as all the points (x, y) in the plane that are a fixed distance from a given point (h, k) called the **center**. The fixed distance is the **radius** of the circle.

The Standard Form of the Equation of a Circle

Let r be the radius of a circle and let (h, k) be the coordinates of the center of the circle. Then the equation of the circle is given by

$$(x - h)^2 + (y - k)^2 = r^2$$

➡ Sketch a graph of $(x - 1)^2 + (y + 2)^2 = 9$.

$(x - 1)^2 + [y - (-2)]^2 = 3^2$ • Rewrite the equation in standard form.

center: $(1, -2)$ radius: 3

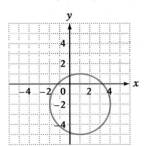

➡ Find the equation of the circle with radius 4 and center $(-1, 2)$. Then sketch its graph.

$(x - h)^2 + (y - k)^2 = r^2$ • Use the standard form of the equation of a circle.

$[x - (-1)]^2 + (y - 2)^2 = 4^2$ • Replace r by 4, h by -1, and k by 2.

$(x + 1)^2 + (y - 2)^2 = 16$

     • Sketch the graph by drawing a circle with center $(-1, 2)$ and radius 4.

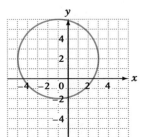

Applying the vertical-line test reveals that the graph of a circle is not the graph of a function. The graph of a circle is the graph of a relation.

Example 4
Sketch a graph of $(x + 2)^2 + (y - 1)^2 = 4$.

Solution

$$(x - h)^2 + (y - k)^2 = r^2$$
$$[x - (-2)]^2 + (y - 1)^2 = 2^2$$
center: $(h, k) = (-2, 1)$
radius: $r = 2$

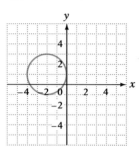

You Try It 4
Sketch a graph of $(x - 2)^2 + (y + 3)^2 = 9$.

Your solution

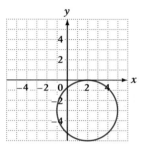

Example 5
Find the equation of the circle with radius 5 and center $(-1, 3)$. Then sketch its graph.

Solution

$$(x - h)^2 + (y - k)^2 = r^2$$
$$[x - (-1)]^2 + (y - 3)^2 = 5^2$$
$$(x + 1)^2 + (y - 3)^2 = 25$$

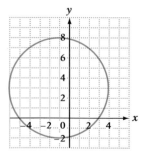

You Try It 5
Find the equation of the circle with radius 4 and center $(2, -3)$. Then sketch its graph.

Your solution
$(x - 2)^2 + (y + 3)^2 = 16$

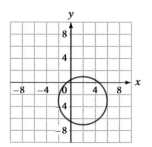

Solutions on p. S33

Objective C   *To graph an ellipse with center at the origin* ....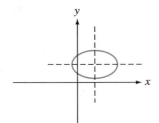

The orbits of the planets around the sun are "oval" shaped. This oval shape can be described as an **ellipse**, which is another of the conic sections.

There are two **axes of symmetry** for an ellipse. The intersection of these two axes is the **center** of the ellipse.

An ellipse with center at the origin is shown at the right. Note that there are two *x*-intercepts and two *y*-intercepts.

> **The Standard Form of the Equation of an Ellipse with Center at the Origin**
>
> The equation of an ellipse with center at the origin is $\dfrac{x^2}{a^2} + \dfrac{y^2}{b^2} = 1$.
>
> The *x*-intercepts are $(a, 0)$ and $(-a, 0)$. The *y*-intercepts are $(0, b)$ and $(0, -b)$.

By finding the *x*- and *y*-intercepts for an ellipse and using the fact that the ellipse is "oval" shaped, we can sketch a graph of an ellipse.

➡ Sketch the graph of the ellipse whose equation is $\dfrac{x^2}{9} + \dfrac{y^2}{4} = 1$.

Comparing $\dfrac{x^2}{9} + \dfrac{y^2}{4} = 1$ with $\dfrac{x^2}{a^2} + \dfrac{y^2}{b^2} = 1$, we have $a^2 = 9$ and $b^2 = 4$.

Therefore, $a = 3$ and $b = 2$.

The *x*-intercepts are $(3, 0)$ and $(-3, 0)$.
The *y*-intercepts are $(0, 2)$ and $(0, -2)$.

Use the intercepts to sketch a graph of the ellipse.

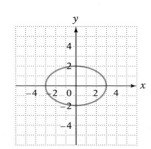

Using the vertical-line test, we find that the graph of an ellipse is not the graph of a function. The graph of an ellipse is the graph of a relation.

➡️ Sketch a graph of the ellipse whose equation is $\frac{x^2}{16} + \frac{y^2}{16} = 1$.

POINT OF INTEREST

For a circle, $a = b$ and thus $\frac{a}{b} = 1$. Early Greek astronomers thought that each planet had a circular orbit. Today we know that the planets have elliptical orbits. However, in most cases the ellipse is very nearly a circle.

For Earth, $\frac{a}{b} \approx 1.00014$. The most elliptical orbit is Pluto's, for which $\frac{a}{b} \approx 1.0328$.

The x-intercepts are $(4, 0)$ and $(-4, 0)$.　　• $a^2 = 16$, $b^2 = 16$

The y-intercepts are $(0, 4)$ and $(0, -4)$.

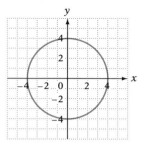

• **Use the intercepts and symmetry to sketch the graph of the ellipse.**

The graph in this example is the graph of a circle. A circle is a special case of an ellipse. It occurs when $a^2 = b^2$ in the equation $\frac{x^2}{a^2} + \frac{y^2}{b^2} = 1$

Example 6
Sketch a graph of the ellipse whose equation is $\frac{x^2}{9} + \frac{y^2}{16} = 1$.

Solution
x-intercepts:
$(3, 0)$ and $(-3, 0)$

y-intercepts:
$(0, 4)$ and $(0, -4)$

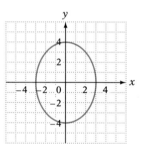

You Try It 6
Sketch a graph of the ellipse whose equation is $\frac{x^2}{4} + \frac{y^2}{25} = 1$.

Your solution

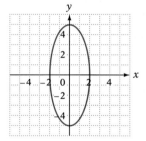

Example 7
Sketch a graph of the ellipse whose equation is $\frac{x^2}{16} + \frac{y^2}{12} = 1$.

Solution
x-intercepts:
$(4, 0)$ and $(-4, 0)$

y-intercepts:
$(0, 2\sqrt{3})$
and $(0, -2\sqrt{3})$
$(2\sqrt{3} \approx 3.5)$

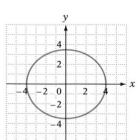

You Try It 7
Sketch a graph of the ellipse whose equation is $\frac{x^2}{18} + \frac{y^2}{9} = 1$.

Your solution

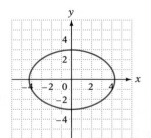

Solutions on p. S33

Objective D   ***To graph a hyperbola with center at the origin*** ....

A **hyperbola** is a conic section that is formed by the intersection of a cone and a plane perpendicular to the base of the cone.

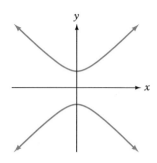 

The hyperbola has two **vertices** and an **axis of symmetry** that passes through the vertices. The **center** of a hyperbola is the point halfway between the two vertices.

The graphs at the right show two possible graphs of a hyperbola with center at the origin.

In the first graph, an axis of symmetry is the x-axis and the vertices are x-intercepts.

In the second graph, an axis of symmetry is the y-axis and the vertices are y-intercepts.

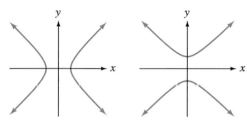

Note that in either case, the graph of a hyperbola is not the graph of a function. The graph of a hyperbola is the graph of a relation.

> **The Standard Form of the Equation of a Hyperbola with Center at the Origin**
>
> The equation of a hyperbola for which an axis of symmetry is the
> x-axis is $\dfrac{x^2}{a^2} - \dfrac{y^2}{b^2} = 1$. The vertices are $(a, 0)$ and $(-a, 0)$.
>
> The equation of a hyperbola for which an axis of symmetry is the
> y-axis is $\dfrac{y^2}{b^2} - \dfrac{x^2}{a^2} = 1$. The vertices are $(0, b)$ and $(0, -b)$.

To sketch a hyperbola, it is helpful to draw two lines that are "approached" by the hyperbola. These two lines are called **asymptotes**. As the hyperbola gets farther from the origin, the hyperbola "gets closer to" the asymptotes.

Because the asymptotes are straight lines, their equations are linear equations. The equations of the asymptotes for a hyperbola with center at the origin are $y = \dfrac{b}{a}x$ and $y = -\dfrac{b}{a}x$.

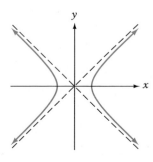

➡ Sketch a graph of the hyperbola whose equation is $\frac{y^2}{9} - \frac{x^2}{4} = 1$.

An axis of symmetry is the *y*-axis.

$b^2 = 9, a^2 = 4$

The vertices are (0, 3) and (0, −3).

The asymptotes are $y = \frac{3}{2}x$ and $y = -\frac{3}{2}x$.

- The vertices are (0, *b*) and (0, −*b*).
- The asymptotes are $y = \frac{b}{a}x$ and $y = -\frac{b}{a}x$.

- Sketch the asymptotes. Use symmetry and the fact that the hyperbola will approach the asymptotes to sketch its graph.

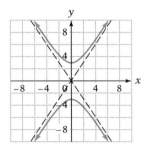

Example 8
Sketch a graph of the hyperbola whose equation is $\frac{x^2}{16} - \frac{y^2}{4} = 1$.

Solution
axis of symmetry:
x-axis

vertices:
(4, 0) and (−4, 0)

asymptotes:
$y = \frac{1}{2}x$ and $y = -\frac{1}{2}x$

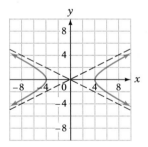

You Try It 8
Sketch a graph of the hyperbola whose equation is $\frac{x^2}{9} - \frac{y^2}{25} = 1$.

Your solution

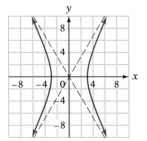

Example 9
Sketch a graph of the hyperbola whose equation is $\frac{y^2}{16} - \frac{x^2}{25} = 1$.

Solution
axis of symmetry:
y-axis

vertices:
(0, 4) and (0, −4)

asymptotes:
$y = \frac{4}{5}x$ and $y = -\frac{4}{5}x$

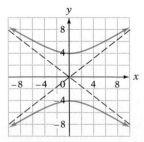

You Try It 9
Sketch a graph of the hyperbola whose equation is $\frac{y^2}{9} - \frac{x^2}{9} = 1$.

Your solution

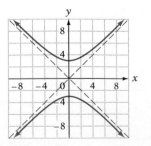

Solutions on p. S34

11.6 Exercises

Objective A

Find the vertex and axis of symmetry of the parabola given by each equation. Then sketch its graph.

1. $x = y^2 - 3y - 4$

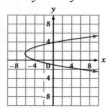

vertex: $\left(-\dfrac{25}{4}, \dfrac{3}{2}\right)$

axis of symmetry: $y = \dfrac{3}{2}$

2. $y = x^2 - 2$

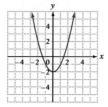

vertex: $(0, -2)$
axis of symmetry: $x = 0$

3. $y = x^2 + 2$

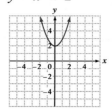

vertex: $(0, 2)$
axis of symmetry: $x = 0$

4. $x = -\dfrac{1}{2}y^2 + 4$

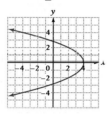

vertex: $(4, 0)$
axis of symmetry: $y = 0$

5. $x = -\dfrac{1}{4}y^2 - 1$

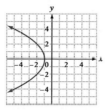

vertex: $(-1, 0)$
axis of symmetry: $y = 0$

6. $x = \dfrac{1}{2}y^2 - y + 1$

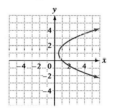

vertex: $\left(\dfrac{1}{2}, 1\right)$

axis of symmetry: $y - 1$

7. $x = -\dfrac{1}{2}y^2 + 2y - 3$

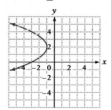

vertex: $(-1, 2)$
axis of symmetry: $y = 2$

8. $y = -\dfrac{1}{2}x^2 + 2x + 6$

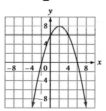

vertex: $(2, 8)$
axis of symmetry: $x = 2$

9. $y = \dfrac{1}{2}x^2 + x - 3$

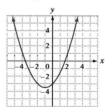

vertex: $\left(-1, -\dfrac{7}{2}\right)$

axis of symmetry: $x = -1$

10. $x = y^2 + 6y + 5$

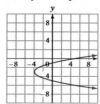

vertex: $(-4, -3)$
axis of symmetry: $y = -3$

11. $x = y^2 - y - 6$

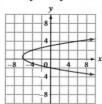

vertex: $\left(-\dfrac{25}{4}, \dfrac{1}{2}\right)$

axis of symmetry: $y = \dfrac{1}{2}$

12. $x = -y^2 + 2y - 3$

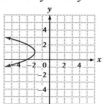

vertex: $(-2, 1)$
axis of symmetry: $y = 1$

Objective B

Sketch a graph of the circle given by the equation.

13. $(x - 2)^2 + (y + 2)^2 = 9$

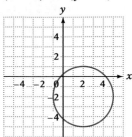

14. $(x + 2)^2 + (y - 3)^2 = 16$

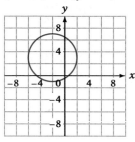

15. $(x + 3)^2 + (y - 1)^2 = 25$

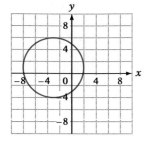

16. $(x - 2)^2 + (y + 3)^2 = 4$

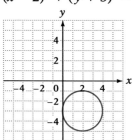

17. $(x + 2)^2 + (y + 2)^2 = 4$

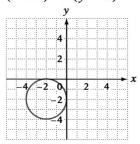

18. $(x - 1)^2 + (y - 2)^2 = 25$

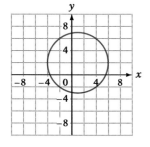

19. Find the equation of the circle with radius 2 and center $(2, -1)$. Then sketch its graph.

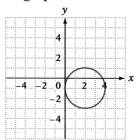

$(x - 2)^2 + (y + 1)^2 = 4$

20. Find the equation of the circle with radius 3 and center $(-1, -2)$. Then sketch its graph.

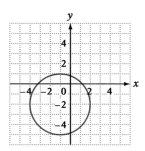

$(x + 1)^2 + (y + 2)^2 = 9$

21. Find the equation of the circle with radius $\sqrt{5}$ and center $(-1, 1)$. Then sketch its graph.

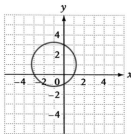

$(x + 1)^2 + (y - 1)^2 = 5$

22. Find the equation of the circle with radius $\sqrt{5}$ and center $(-2, 1)$. Then sketch its graph.

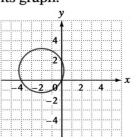

$(x + 2)^2 + (y - 1)^2 = 5$

Objective C

Sketch a graph of the ellipse given by each equation.

23. $\dfrac{x^2}{4} + \dfrac{y^2}{9} = 1$

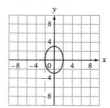

24. $\dfrac{x^2}{25} + \dfrac{y^2}{16} = 1$

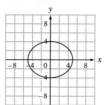

25. $\dfrac{x^2}{25} + \dfrac{y^2}{9} = 1$

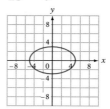

26. $\dfrac{x^2}{16} + \dfrac{y^2}{9} = 1$

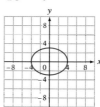

27. $\dfrac{x^2}{36} + \dfrac{y^2}{16} = 1$

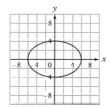

28. $\dfrac{x^2}{49} + \dfrac{y^2}{64} = 1$

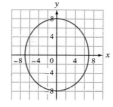

29. $\dfrac{x^2}{16} + \dfrac{y^2}{49} = 1$

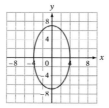

30. $\dfrac{x^2}{25} + \dfrac{y^2}{36} = 1$

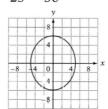

31. $\dfrac{x^2}{4} + \dfrac{y^2}{25} = 1$

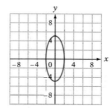

Objective D

Sketch a graph of the hyperbola given by each equation.

32. $\dfrac{x^2}{9} - \dfrac{y^2}{16} = 1$

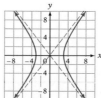

33. $\dfrac{x^2}{25} - \dfrac{y^2}{4} = 1$

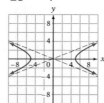

34. $\dfrac{y^2}{16} - \dfrac{x^2}{9} = 1$

35. $\dfrac{y^2}{16} - \dfrac{x^2}{25} = 1$

36. $\dfrac{x^2}{16} - \dfrac{y^2}{4} = 1$

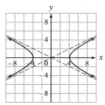

37. $\dfrac{x^2}{9} - \dfrac{y^2}{49} = 1$

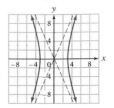

38. $\dfrac{y^2}{25} - \dfrac{x^2}{9} = 1$

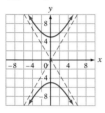

39. $\dfrac{y^2}{4} - \dfrac{x^2}{16} = 1$

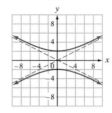

40. $\dfrac{x^2}{4} - \dfrac{y^2}{25} = 1$

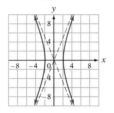

41. $\dfrac{x^2}{36} - \dfrac{y^2}{9} = 1$

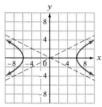

42. $\dfrac{y^2}{9} - \dfrac{x^2}{36} = 1$

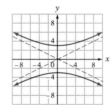

43. $\dfrac{y^2}{25} - \dfrac{x^2}{4} = 1$

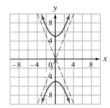

APPLYING THE CONCEPTS

44. Find the equation of a circle that has center (4, 0) and passes through the origin.

$(x - 4)^2 + y^2 = 16$

45. Find the equation of the circle with center at (3, 3) if the circle is tangent to the x-axis.

$(x - 3)^2 + (y - 3)^2 = 9$

For each of the following, write the equation in standard form. Identify the graph, and then graph the equation.

46. $4x^2 + 9y^2 = 36$

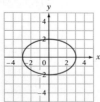

$\dfrac{x^2}{9} + \dfrac{y^2}{4} = 1$ ellipse

47. $16x^2 + 25y^2 = 400$

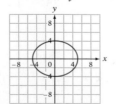

$\dfrac{x^2}{25} + \dfrac{y^2}{16} = 1$ ellipse

48. $9y^2 - 16x^2 = 144$

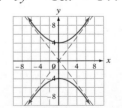

$\dfrac{y^2}{16} - \dfrac{x^2}{9} = 1$ hyperbola

Focus on Problem Solving

Algebraic Manipulation and Graphing Techniques

Problem solving is often easier when we have both algebraic manipulation and graphing techniques at our disposal. Solving quadratic equations and graphing quadratic equations in two variables are used here to solve problems involving profit.

A company's revenue, R, is the total amount of money the company earned by selling its products. The cost, C, is the total amount of money the company spent to manufacture and sell its products. A company's profit, P, is the difference between the revenue and cost: $P = R - C$. A company's revenue and cost may be represented by equations.

A company manufactures and sells woodstoves. The total monthly cost, in dollars, to produce n woodstoves is $C = 30n + 2000$. Write a variable expression for the company's monthly profit if the revenue, in dollars, obtained from selling all n woodstoves is $R = 150n - 0.4n^2$.

$P = R - C$
$P = 150n - 0.4n^2 - (30n + 2000)$
$P = -0.4n^2 + 120n - 2000$

- Replace R by $150n - 0.4n^2$ and C by $30n + 2000$. Then simplify.

How many woodstoves must the company manufacture and sell in order to make a profit of $6000 a month?

$P = -0.4n^2 + 120n - 2000$
$6000 = -0.4n^2 + 120n - 2000$ • Substitute 6000 for P.
$0 = -0.4n^2 + 120n - 8000$ • Write the equation in standard form.

$0 = n^2 - 300n + 20{,}000$ • Divide each side of the equation by -0.4.

$0 = (n - 100)(n - 200)$ • Factor.

$n - 100 = 0$ $n - 200 = 0$ • Solve for n.

$n = 100$ $n = 200$

The company will make a monthly profit of $6000 if either 100 or 200 woodstoves are manufactured and sold.

The graph of $P = -0.4n^2 + 120n - 2000$ is shown at the right. Note that when $P = 6000$, the values of n are 100 and 200.

Also note that the coordinates of the highest point on the graph are (150, 7000). This means that the company makes a *maximum* profit of $7000 per month when 150 woodstoves are manufactured and sold.

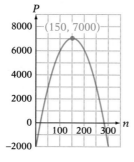

1. The total cost, in dollars, for a company to produce and sell n guitars per month is $C = 240n + 1200$. The company's revenue, in dollars, from selling all n guitars is $R = 400n - 2n^2$.

   a. How many guitars must the company produce and sell each month in order to make a monthly profit of $1200?

   b. Graph the profit equation. What is the maximum monthly profit the company can make?

Projects and Group Activities

Graphing Conic Sections Using a Graphing Utility

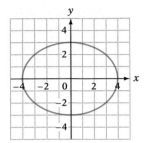

Consider the graph of the ellipse $\frac{x^2}{16} + \frac{y^2}{9} = 1$ shown at the left. Because a vertical line can intersect the graph at more than one point, the graph is not the graph of a function. And because the graph is not the graph of a function, the equation does not represent a function. Consequently, the equation cannot be entered into a graphing utility to be graphed. However, by solving the equation for y, we have

$$\frac{y^2}{9} = 1 - \frac{x^2}{16}$$

$$y^2 = 9\left(1 - \frac{x^2}{16}\right)$$

$$y = +\ \pm 3\sqrt{1 - \frac{x^2}{16}}$$

There are two solutions for y, which can be written

$$y_1 = 3\sqrt{1 - \frac{x^2}{16}} \quad \text{and} \quad y_2 = -3\sqrt{1 - \frac{x^2}{16}}$$

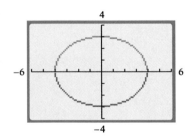

Each of these equations is the equation of a function and therefore can be entered into a graphing utility. The graph of $y_1 = 3\sqrt{1 - \frac{x^2}{16}}$ is shown above the x-axis at the left, and the graph of $y_2 = -3\sqrt{1 - \frac{x^2}{16}}$ is shown below the x-axis. Note that, together, the graphs are the graph of an ellipse.

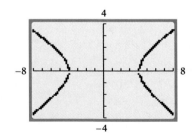

A similar technique can be used to graph a hyperbola. To graph $\frac{x^2}{16} - \frac{y^2}{4} = 1$, solve for y. Then graph each equation, $y_1 = 2\sqrt{\frac{x^2}{16} - 1}$ and $y_2 = -2\sqrt{\frac{x^2}{16} - 1}$.

Guidelines for using graphing calculators are found in the appendix. In working through these examples or the exercises below, consult the appendix or the user's manual for your particular calculator.

Solve each equation for y. Then graph using a graphing utility.

1. $\frac{x^2}{25} + \frac{y^2}{49} = 1$

2. $\frac{x^2}{4} + \frac{y^2}{64} = 1$

3. $\frac{x^2}{16} - \frac{y^2}{4} = 1$

4. $\frac{x^2}{9} - \frac{y^2}{36} = 1$

Properties of Polynomials

The graph of a fifth-degree polynomial with 4 *turning points* is shown at the right. In this project you will graph various polynomials and try to make a conjecture as to the relationship between the degree of a polynomial and the number of turning points in its graph. For each of the following, graph the equation. Record the degree of the equation and the number of turning points.

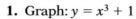

1. Graph: $y = x^3 + 1$
2. Graph: $y = x^3 + 2x^2 - 5x - 6$
3. Graph: $y = x^4 - x^3 - 11x^2 - x - 12$
4. Graph: $y = x^4 - 2x^3 - 13x^2 + 14x + 24$
5. Graph: $y = x^5 - 2$
6. Graph: $y = x^5 - 3x^4 - 11x^3 + 27x^2 + 10x - 24$
7. Graph: $y = x^5 - 2x^4 - 10x^3 + 10x^2 - 11x + 12$

Make a conjecture as to a relationship between the degree of a polynomial and the number of turning points in its graph. Graph a few more polynomials of your choosing and see whether your conjecture is valid for those graphs. If not, refine your conjecture and test it again.

Chapter Summary

Key Words

A function that can be written in the form $y = mx + b$ or $f(x) = mx + b$ is a *linear function*. The graph of a linear function is a straight line with slope m and y-intercept $(0, b)$.

A *quadratic function* is one that can be expressed by the equation $f(x) = ax^2 + bx + c, a \neq 0$. The graph of this function is a *parabola*.

The *inverse of a function* is the set of ordered pairs formed by reversing the coordinates of each ordered pair of the function.

The graph of a *conic section* can be represented by the intersection of a plane and a cone. The four conic sections are the *parabola*, *ellipse*, *hyperbola*, and *circle*.

A *circle* is the set of all points (x, y) in the plane that are a fixed distance from a given point (h, k) called the *center*. The fixed distance is the *radius* of the circle.

The *asymptotes* of a hyperbola are the two straight lines that are "approached" by the hyperbola. As the graph of the hyperbola gets farther from the origin, the hyperbola "gets closer to" the asymptotes.

Essential Rules　*Vertical-Line Test*　A graph defines a function if any vertical line intersects the graph at no more than one point.

Operations on Functions　If f and g are functions and x is an element of the domain of each function, then

$$(f + g)(x) = f(x) + g(x) \qquad (f - g)(x) = f(x) - g(x)$$

$$(f \cdot g)(x) = f(x) \cdot g(x) \qquad \left(\frac{f}{g}\right)(x) = \frac{f(x)}{g(x)}, \, g(x) \neq 0$$

Composition of Two Functions　The composition of two functions, $f \circ g$, is the function whose value at x is given by $(f \circ g)(x) = f[g(x)]$.

One-to-One Function　A function f is a 1–1 function if, for any a and b in the domain of f, $f(a) = f(b)$ implies that $a = b$.

Horizontal-Line Test　The graph of a function represents the graph of a 1–1 function if any horizontal line intersects the graph at no more than one point.

Condition for an Inverse Function　A function f has an inverse function if and only if f is a 1–1 function.

Property of the Composition of Inverse Functions　$f^{-1}[f(x)] = x$ and $f[f^{-1}(x)] = x$

Equation of a Parabola
$y = ax^2 + bx + c$

When $a > 0$, the parabola opens up.
When $a < 0$, the parabola opens down.
The x-coordinate of the vertex is $-\dfrac{b}{2a}$.
The axis of symmetry is the line $x = -\dfrac{b}{2a}$.

$x = ay^2 + by + c$

When $a > 0$, the parabola opens to the right.
When $a < 0$, the parabola opens to the left.
The y-coordinate of the vertex is $-\dfrac{b}{2a}$.
The axis of symmetry is the line $y = -\dfrac{b}{2a}$.

Equation of a Circle
$(x - h)^2 + (y - k)^2 = r^2$　The center is (h, k) and the radius is r.

Equation of an Ellipse
$\dfrac{x^2}{a^2} + \dfrac{y^2}{b^2} = 1$

The x-intercepts are $(a, 0)$ and $(-a, 0)$.
The y-intercepts are $(0, b)$ and $(0, -b)$.

Equation of a Hyperbola
$\dfrac{x^2}{a^2} - \dfrac{y^2}{b^2} = 1$

An axis of symmetry is the x-axis.
The vertices are $(a, 0)$ and $(-a, 0)$.

$\dfrac{y^2}{b^2} - \dfrac{x^2}{a^2} = 1$

An axis of symmetry is the y-axis.
The vertices are $(0, b)$ and $(0, -b)$.

The equations of the asymptotes are $y = \pm\dfrac{b}{a}x$.

Chapter Review

1. Graph: $f(x) = \frac{1}{4}x + 3$

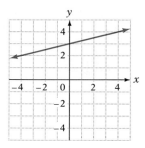

[11.1A]

2. Sketch a graph of $f(x) = x^2 - 2x + 3$.

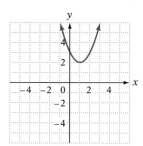

[11.2A]

3. Find the x-intercepts of $y = 2x^2 - 3x + 4$.
no x-intercepts   [11.2B]

4. Find the maximum value of the function $f(x) = -x^2 + 8x - 7$.
9   [11.2C]

5. Graph $f(x) = -\sqrt{3 - x}$. State the domain and range.

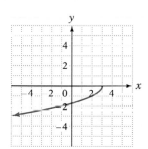

[11.3A]

domain: $\{x \mid x \le 3\}$
range: $\{y \mid y \le 0\}$

6. Graph $f(x) = \left|\frac{1}{2}x\right| - 2$. State the domain and range.

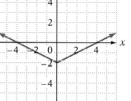

[11.3A]

domain: $\{x \mid x \in$ real numbers$\}$
range: $\{y \mid y \ge -2\}$

7. Graph $f(x) = x^3 - 3x + 2$. State the domain and range.

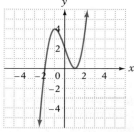

[11.3A]

domain: $\{x \mid x \in$ real numbers$\}$
range: $\{y \mid y \in$ real numbers$\}$

8. Determine whether the graph is the graph of a 1–1 function.

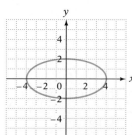

[11.5A]

no

9. Given $f(x) = x^2 + 2x - 3$ and $g(x) = x^3 - 1$, find $(f - g)(2)$.

-2 [11.4A]

10. Given $f(x) = 4x - 5$ and $g(x) = x^2 + 3x + 4$, find $\left(\dfrac{f}{g}\right)(-2)$.

$-\dfrac{13}{2}$ [11.4A]

11. Given $f(x) = 4x + 2$ and $g(x) = \dfrac{x}{x + 1}$, find $f[g(3)]$.

5 [11.4B]

12. Given $f(x) = 2x^2 - 7$ and $g(x) = x - 1$, find $f[g(x)]$.

$2x^2 - 4x - 5$ [11.4B]

13. Find the inverse of the function $\{(2, 6), (3, 5), (4, 4), (5, 3)\}$.

$\{(6, 2), (5, 3), (4, 4), (3, 5)\}$ [11.5B]

14. Find the inverse of the function $f(x) = \dfrac{1}{4}x - 4$.

$f^{-1}(x) = 4x + 16$ [11.5B]

15. Sketch a graph of $x = y^2 - y - 2$.

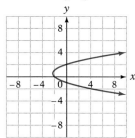

[11.6A]

16. Sketch a graph of $(x - 2)^2 + (y + 1)^2 = 9$.

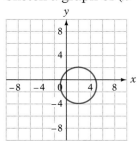

[11.6B]

17. Sketch a graph of $\dfrac{x^2}{9} - \dfrac{y^2}{4} = 1$.

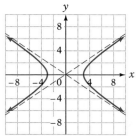

[11.6D]

18. Sketch a graph of $\dfrac{x^2}{16} + \dfrac{y^2}{4} = 1$.

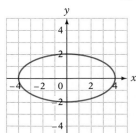

[11.6C]

19. Find the equation of the circle with radius 4 and center $(-3, -3)$.

$(x + 3)^2 + (y + 3)^2 = 16$ [11.6B]

20. The perimeter of a rectangle is 200 cm. What dimensions would give the rectangle a maximum area? What is the maximum area?

length: 50 cm; width: 50 cm; maximum area: 2500 cm² [11.2D]

Chapter Test

1. Graph: $f(x) = 2x - 4$

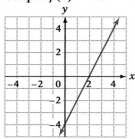

[11.1A]

2. Sketch a graph of $f(x) = -2x^2 + x - 2$.

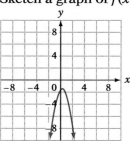

[11.2A]

3. Find the x-intercepts of $y = 3x^2 + 9x$.

$(0, 0), (-3, 0)$ [11.2B]

4. Find the maximum value of $f(x) = -2x^2 + 4x + 1$.

3 [11.2C]

5. Graph $f(x) = \sqrt{x + 4}$. State the domain and range.

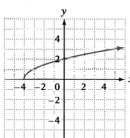

domain: $\{x \mid x \geq -4\}$
range: $\{y \mid y \geq 0\}$ [11.3A]

6. Graph $f(x) = |x| - 3$. State the domain and range.

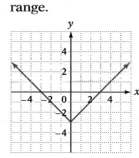

domain:
$\{x \mid x \in \text{real numbers}\}$
range: $\{y \mid y \geq -3\}$

[11.3A]

7. Graph $f(x) = 3x^3 - 2$. State the domain and range.

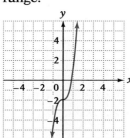

domain:
$\{x \mid x \in \text{real numbers}\}$
range:
$\{y \mid y \in \text{real numbers}\}$

[11.3A]

8. Is the graph below the graph of a 1–1 function?

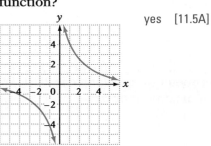

yes [11.5A]

For problems 9 to 12, use $f(x) = x^2 + 2x - 3$ and $g(x) = x^2 - 2$.

9. Evaluate: $(f + g)(2)$
7   [11.4A]

10. Evaluate: $(f - g)(-4)$
-9   [11.4A]

11. Evaluate: $(f \cdot g)(-4)$
70   [11.4A]

12. Evaluate: $\left(\dfrac{f}{g}\right)(3)$
$\dfrac{12}{7}$ [11.4A]

13. Given $f(x) = 2x^2 + x - 5$ and $g(x) = 3x - 1$, find $g[f(x)]$.
$6x^2 + 3x - 16$ [11.4B]

14. Find the inverse of $f(x) = -6x + 4$.
$f^{-1}(x) = -\dfrac{1}{6}x + \dfrac{2}{3}$ [11.5B]

15. Sketch a graph of $x = 2y^2 - 6y + 5$.

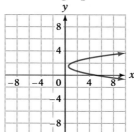

[11.6A]

16. Sketch a graph of $(x + 3)^2 + (y + 1)^2 = 1$.

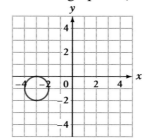

[11.6B]

17. Sketch a graph of $\dfrac{x^2}{1} + \dfrac{y^2}{9} = 1$.

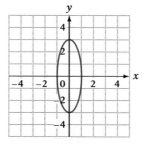

[11.6C]

18. Sketch of graph of $\dfrac{x^2}{25} - \dfrac{y^2}{1} = 1$.

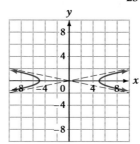

[11.6D]

19. Are the functions given by $f(x) = -\dfrac{1}{4}x + \dfrac{5}{4}$ and $g(x) = -4x + 5$ inverses of each other?
yes   [11.5B]

20. The perimeter of a rectangle is 28 ft. What dimensions would give the rectangle a maximum area?
7 ft by 7 ft   [11.2A]

Cumulative Review

1. Graph the solution set of
   $\{x|x < 4\} \cap \{x|x > 2\}$.

   $[1.5C]$

2. Solve: $\dfrac{5x - 2}{3} - \dfrac{1 - x}{5} = \dfrac{x + 4}{10}$

   $\dfrac{38}{53}$ $[8.4A]$

3. Evaluate the function $f(x) = -x^2 + 3x - 2$ at
   $x = -3$.
   -20 $[4.1D]$

4. Find the equation of the line that contains
   the point $(2, -3)$ and has slope $-\dfrac{3}{2}$.

   $y = -\dfrac{3}{2}x$ $[4.4A]$

5. Find the equation of the line that contains
   the point $(4, -2)$ and is perpendicular to the
   line $y = -x + 5$.
   $y = x - 6$ $[4.5A]$

6. Simplify. $\dfrac{ax - bx}{ax + ay - bx - by}$

   $\dfrac{x}{x + y}$ $[8.1A]$

7. Subtract: $\dfrac{x - 4}{3x - 2} - \dfrac{1 + x}{3x^2 + x - 2}$

   $\dfrac{x - 5}{3x - 2}$ $[8.2D]$

8. Solve: $\dfrac{6x}{2x - 3} - \dfrac{1}{2x - 3} = 7$

   $\dfrac{5}{2}$ $[8.4A]$

9. Simplify: $\left(\dfrac{12a^2b^2}{a^{-3}b^{-4}}\right)^{-1} \left(\dfrac{ab}{4^{-1}a^{-2}b^4}\right)^2$

   $\dfrac{4a}{3b^{12}}$ $[6.1B]$

10. Write $2\sqrt[4]{x^3}$ as an exponential expression.
    $2x^{3/4}$ $[9.1B]$

11. Simplify: $\sqrt{18} - \sqrt{-25}$
    $3\sqrt{2} - 5i$ $[9.3A]$

12. Solve: $2x^2 + 2x - 3 = 0$
    $\dfrac{-1 + \sqrt{7}}{2}, \dfrac{-1 - \sqrt{7}}{2}$ $[10.2A/10.3A]$

13. Solve: $x - \sqrt{2x - 3} = 3$
    6 $[10.4B]$

14. Solve: $\dfrac{3x - 2}{x + 4} \le 1$
    $\{x| - 4 < x \le 3\}$ $[10.6A]$

15. Find the maximum value of the function
    $f(x) = -2x^2 + 4x - 2$.
    0 $[11.2C]$

16. Find the inverse of the function
    $f(x) = 4x + 8$.

    $f^{-1}(x) = \dfrac{1}{4}x - 2$ $[11.5B]$

17. Graph the solution set of $5x + 2y > 10$.

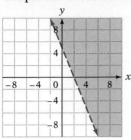

[4.6A]

18. Graph: $x = y^2 - 2y + 3$

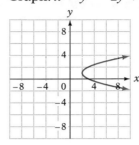

[11.6A]

19. Graph: $\dfrac{x^2}{25} + \dfrac{y^2}{4} = 1$

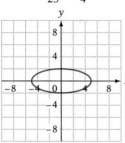

[11.6C]

20. Graph: $\dfrac{y^2}{4} + \dfrac{x^2}{25} = 1$

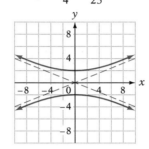

[11.6D]

21. Tickets for a school play sold for $4.00 for each adult and $1.50 for each child. The total receipts for the 192 tickets sold were $493. Find the number of adult tickets sold.

82 adult tickets   [5.5B]

22. A motorcycle travels 180 mi in the same amount of time that it takes a car to travel 144 mi. The rate of the motorcycle is 12 mph faster than the rate of the car. Find the rate of the motorcycle.

60 mph   [8.6B]

23. The rate of a river's current is 1.5 mph. A rowing crew can row 12 mi down this river and 12 mi back in 6 h. Find the rowing rate of the crew in calm water.

4.5 mph   [5.5A]

24. The speed (v) of a gear varies inversely as the number of teeth (t). If a gear that has 36 teeth makes 30 revolutions per minute, how many revolutions per minute will a gear that has 60 teeth make?

18 revolutions per minute   [8.7A]

25. Find the maximum product of two numbers whose sum is 40.

400   [11.2D]

C H A P T E R

12

Exponential and Logarithmic Functions

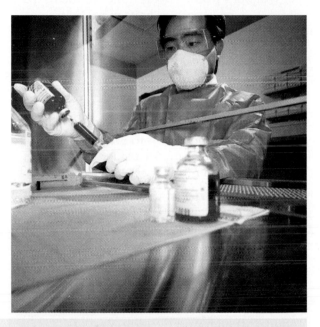

Nuclear medicine technologists operate cameras that detect and map the presence of a radioactive drug in a patient's body. They prepare a dosage of the radiopharmaceutical and administer it to the patient. When preparing radiopharmaceuticals, exponential equations are used to model the amount of radiation in the radiopharmaceutical.

Objectives

Section 12.1
To evaluate an exponential function
To graph an exponential function

Section 12.2
To write equivalent exponential and logarithmic equations
To use the Properties of Logarithms
To use the change-of-base formula

Section 12.3
To graph a logarithmic function

Section 12.4
To solve an exponential equation
To solve a logarithmic equation

Section 12.5
To solve application problems

Napier Rods

The labor involved in calculating the products of large numbers has led many people to devise ways to shorten the procedure. One such short-cut was first described in the early 1600s by John Napier and is based on Napier Rods.

Making a Napier Rod consists of placing a number and the first 9 multiples of that number on a rectangular piece of paper (Napier's Rod). This is done for the first 9 positive integers. It is necessary to have more than one rod for each number. The rod for 7 is shown at the left.

To illustrate how these rods were used to multiply, let's look at an example.

Multiply: 2893
          × 246

Place the rods for 2, 8, 9, and 3 next to one another. The products for 2, 4, and 6 are found by using the numbers along the 2nd, 4th, and 6th rows.

Each number is found by adding the digits diagonally downward on the diagonal and carrying to the next diagonal when necessary. The products for 2 and 6 are shown at the left.

Note that in the product for 6, the sum of the 3rd diagonal is 13, so carrying to the next diagonal is necessary.

The final product is then found by addition.

Before the invention of the electronic calculator, logarithms were used to ease the drudgery of lengthy calculations. John Napier is also credited with the invention of logarithms.

The rod for **7**:

row 1	0 / 7	$1 \times 7 = 7$
row 2	1 / 4	$2 \times 7 = 14$
row 3	2 / 1	$3 \times 7 = 21$
row 4	2 / 8	$4 \times 7 = 28$
row 5	3 / 5	$5 \times 7 = 35$
row 6	4 / 2	$6 \times 7 = 42$
row 7	4 / 9	$7 \times 7 = 49$
row 8	5 / 6	$8 \times 7 = 56$
row 9	6 / 3	$9 \times 7 = 63$

Rods for 2, 8, 9, 3:

	2	8	9	3	
1	0/2	0/8	0/9	0/3	
2	0/4	1/6	1/8	0/6	← 2(2893) = 5786
3	0/6	2/4	2/7	0/9	
4	0/8	3/2	3/6	1/2	← 4(2893) = 11572
5	1/0	4/0	4/5	1/5	
6	1/2	4/8	5/4	1/8	← 6(2893) = 17358
7	1/4	5/6	6/3	2/1	
8	1/6	6/4	7/2	2/4	
9	1/8	7/2	8/1	2/7	

2: 0/4 1/6 1/8 0/6
      5   7   8   6

6: 1/2 4/8 5/4 1/8
      1 6   13   5   8   = 17358

```
  5786
 11572
+17358
711678
```

12.1 **Exponential Functions**

Objective A *To evaluate an exponential function* ....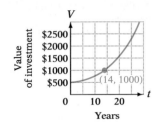

The growth of a $500 savings account that earns 5% annual interest compounded daily is shown at the right. In 14 years, the savings account contains approximately $1000, twice the initial amount. The growth of this savings account is an example of an exponential function.

The pressure of the atmosphere at a certain height is shown in the graph at the right. This is another example of an exponential function. From the graph, we read that the air pressure is approximately 6.5 lb/in² at an altitude of 20,000 ft.

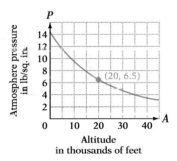

TAKE NOTE

It is important to distinguish between $F(x) = 2^x$ and $P(x) = x^2$. The first is an exponential function; the second is a polynomial function. Exponential functions are characterized by a constant base and a variable exponent. Polynomial functions have a variable base and a constant exponent.

Definition of an Exponential Function

The **exponential function** with base b is defined by

$$f(x) = b^x$$

where $b > 0$, $b \neq 1$, and x is any real number.

In the definition of an exponential function, b, the base, is required to be positive. If the base were a negative number, the value of the function would be a complex number for some values of x. For instance, the value of $f(x) = (-4)^x$ when $x = \frac{1}{2}$ is $f\left(\frac{1}{2}\right) = (-4)^{1/2} = \sqrt{-4} = 2i$. To avoid complex number values of a function, the base of the exponential function is a positive number.

➡ Evaluate $f(x) = 2^x$ at $x = 3$ and $x = -2$.

$f(3) = 2^3 = 8$ • Substitute 3 for x and simplify.

$f(-2) = 2^{-2} = \dfrac{1}{2^2} = \dfrac{1}{4}$ • Substitute -2 for x and simplify.

To evaluate an exponential expression for an irrational number such as $\sqrt{2}$, we obtain an approximation to the value of the function by approximating the irrational number. For instance, the value of $f(x) = 4^x$ when $x = \sqrt{2}$ can be approximated by using an approximation of $\sqrt{2}$.

$$f(\sqrt{2}) = 4^{\sqrt{2}} \approx 4^{1.4142} \approx 7.1029$$

TAKE NOTE

The natural exponential function is an extremely important function. It is used extensively in applied problems in virtually all disciplines from archaeology to zoology. Leonhard Euler (1707–1783) was the first to use the letter e as the base of the natural exponential function.

Because $f(x) = b^x$ ($b > 0$, $b \neq 1$) can be evaluated at both rational and irrational numbers, the domain of f is all real numbers. And because $b^x > 0$ for all values of x, the range of f is the positive real numbers.

A frequently used base in applications of exponential functions is an irrational number designated by e. The number e is approximately 2.71828183. It is an irrational number, so it has a nonterminating, nonrepeating decimal representation.

INSTRUCTOR NOTE

If time permits, show students some of the remarkable relationships that exist between i, e, and π. For instance, $e^{\pi i} = -1$ and $i^{-1} = e^{\pi/2}$.

Natural Exponential Function

The function defined by $f(x) = e^x$ is called the **natural exponential function.**

The e^x key on a calculator can be used to evaluate the natural exponential function.

Example 1

Evaluate $f(x) = \left(\dfrac{1}{2}\right)^x$ at $x = 2$ and $x = -3$.

Solution

$$f(x) = \left(\frac{1}{2}\right)^x$$

$$f(2) = \left(\frac{1}{2}\right)^2 = \frac{1}{4}$$

$$f(-3) = \left(\frac{1}{2}\right)^{-3} = 2^3 = 8$$

You Try It 1

Evaluate $f(x) = \left(\dfrac{2}{3}\right)^x$ at $x = 3$ and $x = -2$.

Your solution

$$f(3) = \frac{8}{27}$$

$$f(-2) = \frac{9}{4}$$

Example 2

Evaluate $f(x) = 2^{3x-1}$ at $x = 1$ and $x = -1$.

Solution

$$f(x) = 2^{3x-1}$$
$$f(1) = 2^{3(1)-1} = 2^2 = 4$$
$$f(-1) = 2^{3(-1)-1} = 2^{-4} = \frac{1}{2^4} = \frac{1}{16}$$

You Try It 2

Evaluate $f(x) = 2^{2x+1}$ at $x = 0$ and $x = -2$.

Your solution

$$f(0) = 2$$
$$f(-2) = \frac{1}{8}$$

Example 3

Evaluate $f(x) = e^{2x}$ at $x = 1$ and $x = -1$. Round to the nearest ten-thousandth.

Solution

$$f(x) = e^{2x}$$
$$f(1) = e^{2 \cdot 1} = e^2 \approx 7.3891$$
$$f(-1) = e^{2(-1)} = e^{-2} \approx 0.1353$$

You Try It 3

Evaluate $f(x) = e^{2x-1}$ at $x = 2$ and $x = -2$. Round to the nearest ten-thousandth.

Your solution

$$f(2) \approx 20.0855$$
$$f(-2) \approx 0.0067$$

Solutions on p. S34

Objective B   ***To graph an exponential function*** ....

Some properties of an exponential function can be seen in its graph.

➡ Graph $f(x) = 2^x$.

Think of this as the equation $y = 2^x$.

Choose values of x and find the corresponding values of y.

Graph the ordered pairs on a rectangular coordinate system.

Connect the points with a smooth curve.

x	$f(x) = y$
-2	$2^{-2} = \frac{1}{4}$
-1	$2^{-1} = \frac{1}{2}$
0	$2^0 = 1$
1	$2^1 = 2$
2	$2^2 = 4$
3	$2^3 = 8$

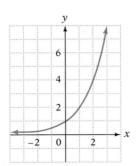

Note that a vertical line would intersect the graph at only one point. Therefore, by the vertical-line test, the graph of $f(x) = 2^x$ is the graph of a function. Also note that a horizontal line would intersect the graph at only one point. Therefore, the graph of $f(x) = 2^x$ is the graph of a one-to-one function.

➡ Graph $f(x) = \left(\frac{1}{2}\right)^x$.

Think of this as the equation $y = \left(\frac{1}{2}\right)^x$.

Choose values of x and find the corresponding values of y.

Graph the ordered pairs on a rectangular coordinate system.

Connect the points with a smooth curve.

x	$f(x) = y$
-3	$\left(\frac{1}{2}\right)^{-3} = 8$
-2	$\left(\frac{1}{2}\right)^{-2} = 4$
-1	$\left(\frac{1}{2}\right)^{-1} = 2$
0	$\left(\frac{1}{2}\right)^0 = 1$
1	$\left(\frac{1}{2}\right)^1 = \frac{1}{2}$
2	$\left(\frac{1}{2}\right)^2 = \frac{1}{4}$

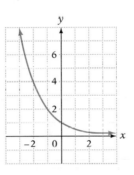

Applying the vertical-line and horizontal-line tests reveals that the graph of $f(x) = \left(\frac{1}{2}\right)^x$ is also the graph of a one-to-one function.

➡ Graph $f(x) = 2^{-x}$.

Think of this as the equation $y = 2^{-x}$.

Choose values of x and find the corresponding values of y.

Graph the ordered pairs on a rectangular coordinate system.

Connect the points with a smooth curve.

x	y
-3	8
-2	4
-1	2
0	1
1	$\frac{1}{2}$
2	$\frac{1}{4}$

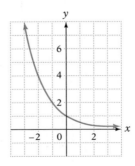

Note that because $2^{-x} = (2^{-1})^x = \left(\frac{1}{2}\right)^x$, the graphs of $f(x) = 2^{-x}$ and $f(x) = \left(\frac{1}{2}\right)^x$ are the same.

Example 4
Graph: $f(x) = 3^{\frac{1}{2}x - 1}$

Solution

x	y
-2	$\frac{1}{9}$
0	$\frac{1}{3}$
2	1
4	3

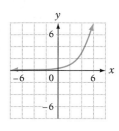

You Try It 4
Graph: $f(x) = 2^{-\frac{1}{2}x}$

Your solution

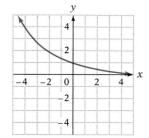

Example 5
Graph: $f(x) = 2^x - 1$

Solution

x	y
-2	$-\frac{3}{4}$
-1	$-\frac{1}{2}$
0	0
1	1
2	3
3	7

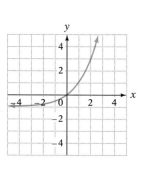

You Try It 5
Graph: $f(x) = 2^x + 1$

Your solution

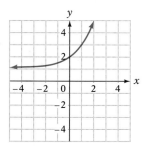

Example 6
Graph: $f(x) = \left(\frac{1}{3}\right)^x - 2$

Solution

x	y
-2	7
-1	1
0	-1
1	$-\frac{5}{3}$
2	$-\frac{17}{9}$

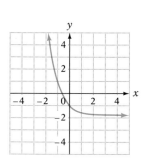

You Try It 6
Graph: $f(x) = 2^{-x} + 2$

Your solution

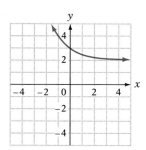

Example 7
Graph: $f(x) = 2^{-\frac{1}{2}x} - 1$

Solution

x	y
-6	7
-4	3
-2	1
0	0
2	$-\frac{1}{2}$
4	$-\frac{3}{4}$

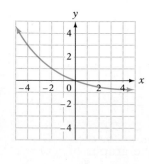

You Try It 7
Graph: $f(x) = \left(\frac{1}{2}\right)^{-\frac{1}{2}x} + 2$

Your solution

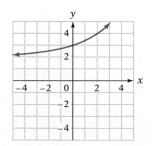

Solutions on p. S34

12.1 Exercises

. . . .

Objective A

1. Given $f(x) = 3^x$, evaluate:
  a. $f(2)$ **b.** $f(0)$ **c.** $f(-2)$
  9   1 $\dfrac{1}{9}$

2. Given $H(x) = 2^x$, evaluate:
  a. $H(-3)$ **b.** $H(0)$ **c.** $H(2)$
  $\dfrac{1}{8}$ 1   4

3. Given $g(x) = 2^{x+1}$, evaluate:
  a. $g(3)$ **b.** $g(1)$ **c.** $g(-3)$
  16   4 $\dfrac{1}{4}$

4. Given $F(x) = 3^{x-2}$, evaluate:
  a. $F(-4)$ **b.** $F(-1)$ **c.** $F(0)$
  $\dfrac{1}{729}$ $\dfrac{1}{27}$ $\dfrac{1}{9}$

5. Given $P(x) = \left(\dfrac{1}{2}\right)^{2x}$, evaluate:
  a. $P(0)$ **b.** $P\left(\dfrac{3}{2}\right)$ **c.** $P(\ 2)$
  1            $\dfrac{1}{8}$ 16

6. Given $R(t) = \left(\dfrac{1}{3}\right)^{3t}$, evaluate:
  a. $R\left(-\dfrac{1}{3}\right)$ **b.** $R(1)$ **c.** $R(-2)$
  3            $\dfrac{1}{27}$ 729

7. Given $G(x) = e^{x/2}$, evaluate the following. Round to the nearest ten-thousandth.
  a. $G(4)$ **b.** $G(-2)$ **c.** $G\left(\dfrac{1}{2}\right)$
  7.3891   0.3679   1.2840

8. Given $f(x) = e^{2x}$, evaluate the following. Round to the nearest ten-thousandth.
  a. $f(-2)$ **b.** $f\left(-\dfrac{2}{3}\right)$ **c.** $f(2)$
  0.0183   0.2636   54.5982

9. Given $H(r) = e^{-r+3}$, evaluate the following. Round to the nearest ten-thousandth.
  a. $H(-1)$ **b.** $H(3)$ **c.** $H(5)$
  54.5982   1   0.1353

10. Given $P(t) = e^{-\frac{1}{2}t}$, evaluate the following. Round to the nearest ten-thousandth.
  a. $P(-3)$ **b.** $P(4)$ **c.** $P\left(\dfrac{1}{2}\right)$
  4.4817   0.1353   0.7788

11. Given $F(x) = 2^{x^2}$, evaluate:
  a. $F(2)$ **b.** $F(-2)$ **c.** $F\left(\dfrac{3}{4}\right)$
  16   16   1.4768

12. Given $Q(x) = 2^{-x^2}$, evaluate:
  a. $Q(3)$ **b.** $Q(-1)$ **c.** $Q(-2)$
  $\dfrac{1}{512}$ $\dfrac{1}{2}$ $\dfrac{1}{16}$

13. Given $f(x) = e^{-x^2/2}$, evaluate the following. Round to the nearest ten-thousandth.
  a. $f(-2)$ **b.** $f(2)$ **c.** $f(-3)$
  0.1353   0.1353   0.0111

14. Given $f(x) = e^{-2x} + 1$, evaluate the following. Round to the nearest ten-thousandth.
  a. $f(-1)$ **b.** $f(3)$ **c.** $f(-2)$
  8.3891   1.0025   55.5982

Objective B

Graph.

15. $f(x) = 3^x$

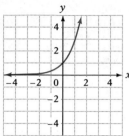

16. $f(x) = 3^{-x}$

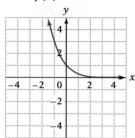

17. $f(x) = 2^{x+1}$

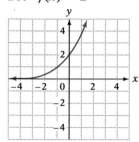

18. $f(x) = 2^{x-1}$

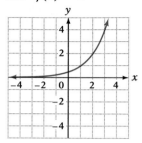

19. $f(x) = \left(\dfrac{1}{3}\right)^x$

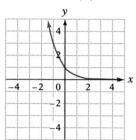

20. $f(x) = \left(\dfrac{2}{3}\right)^x$

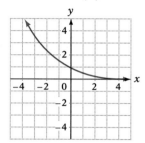

21. $f(x) = 2^{-x} + 1$

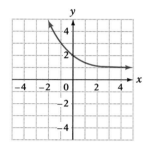

22. $f(x) = 2^x - 3$

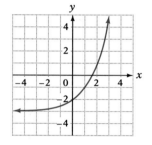

23. $f(x) = \left(\dfrac{1}{3}\right)^{-x}$

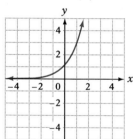

24. $f(x) = \left(\dfrac{3}{2}\right)^{-x}$

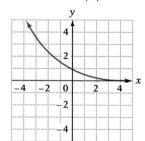

25. $f(x) = \left(\dfrac{1}{2}\right)^{-x} + 2$

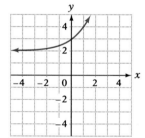

26. $f(x) = \left(\dfrac{1}{2}\right)^x - 1$

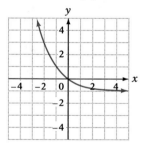

APPLYING THE CONCEPTS

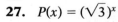 Use a graphing calculator to graph each of the following.

27. $P(x) = (\sqrt{3})^x$

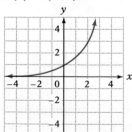

28. $F(x) = (\sqrt{5})^x$

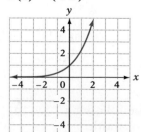

29. $Q(x) = (\sqrt{3})^{-x}$

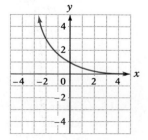

30. $A(x) = (\sqrt{2})^{-x}$

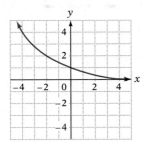

31. $\sinh(x) = \dfrac{e^x - e^{-x}}{2}$

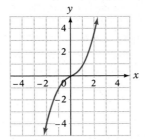

32. $\cosh(x) = \dfrac{e^x + e^{-x}}{2}$

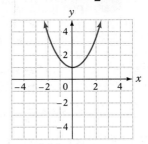

33. $N(x) = e^{-x^2/2}$

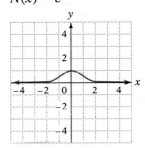

34. $M(x) = xe^{-x^2/2}$

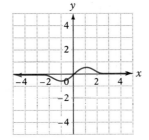

35. $f(x) = 2^x - x^2$

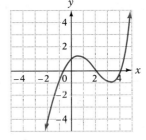

36. $h(x) = 3^x - x^3$

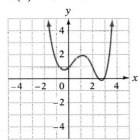

37. $f(x) = \pi^x$

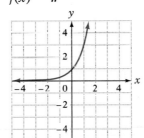

38. $g(x) = \pi^{-x}$

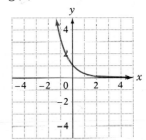

39. According to population studies, the population of China can be approximated by the equation $P(t) = 1.17(1.012)^t$, where $t = 0$ corresponds to 1993 and $P(t)$ is the population, in billions, of China in t years.

a. Graph this equation. *Suggestion:* Use Xmin = 0, Xmax = 19, Ymin = −0.5, Ymax = 1.75, and Yscl = 0.25.

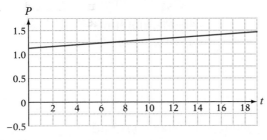

b. The point whose approximate coordinates are (5, 1.242) is on this graph. Write a sentence that explains the meaning of these coordinates.

The point (5, 1.242) means that in the year 1998, the Chinese population was approximately 1.242 billion.

40. The growth of the population of India can be approximated by the equation $P(t) = 0.883(1.017)^t$, where $t = 0$ corresponds to 1993 and $P(t)$ is the population, in billions, of India in t years.

 a. Graph this equation. *Suggestion:* Use Xmin = 0, Xmax = 20, Ymin = −0.5, Ymax = 1.75, and Yscl = 0.25.

b. The point whose approximate coordinates are (8, 1.01) is on this graph. Write a sentence that explains the meaning of these coordinates.

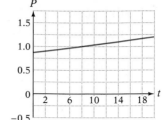

The point (8, 1.01) means that in the year 2001, the population of India will be approximately 1.01 billion.

41. If air resistance is ignored, the speed v, in feet per second, of an object t seconds after it has been dropped is given by $v = 32t$. However, if air resistance is considered, then the speed depends on the mass (and on other things). For a certain mass, the speed t seconds after it has been dropped is given by $v = 32(1 - e^{-t})$.

 a. Graph this equation. *Suggestion:* Use Xmin = 0, Xmax = 5.5, Ymin = 0, Ymax = 40, and Yscl = 5.

b. The point whose approximate coordinates are (2, 27.7) is on this graph. Write a sentence that explains the meaning of these coordinates.

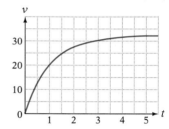

The point (2, 27.7) means that after 2 s, the object is dropping at a speed of 27.7 ft/s.

42. If air resistance is ignored, the speed v, in feet per second, of an object t seconds after it has been dropped is given by $v = 32t$. However, if air resistance is considered, then the speed depends on the mass (and on other things). For a certain mass, the speed t seconds after it has been dropped is given by $v = 64(1 - e^{-t/2})$.

 a. Graph this equation. *Suggestion:* Use Xmin = 0, Xmax = 11, Ymin = 0, Ymax = 80, and Yscl = 10.

b. The point whose approximate coordinates are (4, 55.3) is on this graph. Write a sentence that explains the meaning of these coordinates.

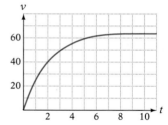

The point (4, 55.3) means that after 4 s, the object is moving at a speed of 55.3 ft/s.

43. If $f(x) = b^x$, determine whether the following statements are always true, sometimes true, or never true.
a. If $b > 0$ and $b \ne 1$, then $f(x) = b^x$ is a one-to-one function.   always true
b. If $b > 0$ and $b \ne 1$, then $f(x) = b^x$ is greater than zero.   always true

44. Evaluate $\left(1 + \dfrac{1}{n}\right)^n$ for $n = 100, 1000, 10{,}000,$ and $100{,}000$ and compare the results with the value of e, the base of the natural exponential function. On the basis of your evaluation, complete the following sentence:

As n increases, $\left(1 + \dfrac{1}{n}\right)^n$ becomes closer to _____ e _____.

45. Evaluate $(1 + x)^{1/x}$ for $x = 0.1, 0.01, 0.001, 0.00001,$ and 0.0000001 and compare the results with the value of e, the base of the natural exponential function. On the basis of your evaluation, complete the following sentence: As x gets closer to 0, $(1 + x)^{1/x}$ becomes closer to _____ e _____.

12.2 Introduction to Logarithms

Objective A   *To write equivalent exponential and logarithmic equations* ....

Because the exponential function is a 1–1 function, it has an inverse function, which is called a *logarithm*. A logarithm is used to answer a question similar to the following one: "If $16 = 2^y$, what is the value of y?" Because $16 = 2^4$, the logarithm, base 2, of 16 is 4. This is written as $\log_2 16 = 4$. Note that a logarithm is an exponent that solves a certain equation.

> **Definition of Logarithm**
>
> For $b > 0$, $b \neq 1$, $y = \log_b x$ is equivalent to $x = b^y$.

Read $\log_b x$ as "the logarithm of x, base b" or "log base b of x."

The table at the right shows equivalent statements written in both exponential and logarithmic form.

Exponential Form	Logarithmic Form
$2^4 = 16$	$\log_2 16 = 4$
$\left(\frac{2}{3}\right)^2 = \frac{4}{9}$	$\log_{2/3}\left(\frac{4}{9}\right) = 2$
$10^{-1} = 0.1$	$\log_{10}(0.1) = -1$

➡ Write $\log_3 81 = 4$ in exponential form.

   $\log_3 81 = 4$ is equivalent to $3^4 = 81$.

➡ Write $10^{-2} = 0.01$ in logarithmic form.

   $10^{-2} = 0.01$ is equivalent to $\log_{10}(0.01) = -2$.

The 1–1 property of exponential functions can be used to evaluate some logarithms.

> **1–1 Property of Exponential Functions**
>
> For $b > 0$, $b \neq 1$, if $b^u = b^v$, then $u = v$.

➡ Evaluate $\log_2 8$.

$\log_2 8 = x$	• Write an equation.
$8 = 2^x$	• Write the equation in its equivalent exponential form.
$2^3 = 2^x$	• Write 8 as 2^3.
$3 = x$	• Use the 1–1 Property of Exponential Functions.
$\log_2 8 = 3$	

➡ Solve $\log_4 x = -2$ for x.

$$\log_4 x = -2$$

$$4^{-2} = x$$ • Write the equation in its equivalent exponential form.

$$\frac{1}{16} = x$$ • Simplify.

The solution is $\frac{1}{16}$.

In this example, $\frac{1}{16}$ is called the *antilogarithm*, base 4, of -2.

INSTRUCTOR NOTE
The concept of antilogarithm is nothing other than a restatement of the equivalence of a logarithmic expression and an exponential expression. This relationship can be illustrated by using a calculator. To solve the equation $\log_{10} x = \frac{1}{2}$, the student uses the 10^x key on a calculator. To solve $10^x = 3$, the student uses the $\log_{10} x$ key. The same is true for the natural exponential function and logarithm. Some students will not have a 10^x key on their calculators but will have an INV (inverse) key instead. This affords a good opportunity to reinforce the fact that the log and exponential functions are inverses of each other.

> **Definition of Antilogarithm**
>
> If $\log_b M = N$, the **antilogarithm**, base b, of N is M. In exponential form, $M = b^N$.

The antilogarithm if a number can be determined by rewriting $\log_b M = N$ in exponential form, $b^N = M$. Thus M, the antilogarithm of N, is b^N. For instance, if $\log_5 x = 3$, then x (the antilogarithm, base 5, of 3) is $5^3 = x = 125$.

Logarithms, base 10, are called **common logarithms**. We usually omit the base, 10, when writing the common logarithm of a number. Therefore, $\log_{10} x$ is written $\log x$. To find the common logarithm of most numbers, a calculator is necessary. Because the logarithms of most numbers are irrational numbers, the value in the display of a calculator is an approximation of the number. Using a calculator reveals that

$$\log 384 \approx \underset{\text{Characteristic}}{\underbrace{2.}}\overset{\text{Mantissa}}{\overbrace{5843312}}$$

The decimal part of a *common logarithm* is called the **mantissa**; the integer part is called the **characteristic**.

When e (the base of the natural exponential function) is used as a base of a logarithm, the logarithm is referred to as the **natural logarithm** and is abbreviated $\ln x$. This is read "el en x." Using a calculator, we learn that

$$\ln 23 \approx 3.135494216$$

The integer and decimal parts of a natural logarithm do not have special names.

Example 1 Evaluate: $\log_3\left(\frac{1}{9}\right)$

Solution $\log_3\left(\frac{1}{9}\right) = x$

$$\frac{1}{9} = 3^x$$

$$3^{-2} = 3^x$$

$$-2 = x$$

$$\log_3\left(\frac{1}{9}\right) = -2$$

You Try It 1 Evaluate: $\log_4 64$

Your solution 3

Solution on p. S34

Example 2   Solve for x: $\log_5 x = 2$

    Solution $\log_5 x = 2$
                  $5^2 = x$
                  $25 = x$

        The solution is 25.

You Try It 2   Solve for x: $\log_2 x = -4$

    Your solution $\dfrac{1}{16}$

Example 3   Solve $\log x = -1.5$ for x.
               Round to the nearest
               ten-thousandth.

    Solution $\log x = -1.5$
            $10^{-1.5} = x$

        $0.0316 \approx x$ • Use a calculator.

You Try It 3   Solve $\ln x = 3$ for x.
               Round to the nearest
               ten-thousandth.

    Your solution   20.0855

                             Solutions on pp. S34–S35

Objective B   To use the Properties of Logarithms..

Because a logarithm is a special kind of exponent, the Properties of Logarithms are similar to the Properties of Exponents.

The property of logarithms that states that the logarithm of the product of two numbers equals the sum of the logarithms of the two numbers is similar to the property of exponents that states that to multiply two exponential expressions with the same base, we add the exponents.

TAKE NOTE

Pay close attention to this theorem. Note, for instance, that this theorem states that
$\log_3(4 \cdot p) = \log_3 4 + \log_3 p$.
It also states that
$\log_5 9 + \log_5 z = \log_5(9z)$.
It does *not* state any relationship that involves $\log_b(x + y)$. **This expression cannot be simplified.**

The Logarithm Property of the Product of Two Numbers

For any positive real numbers x, y, and b, $b \neq 1$,
$\log_b(xy) = \log_b x + \log_b y$.

A proof of this property can be found in the Appendix.

➡ Write $\log_b(6z)$ in expanded form.

    $\log_b(6z) = \log_b 6 + \log_b z$ • Use the Logarithm Property of Products.

➡ Write $\log_b 12 + \log_b r$ as a single logarithm.

    $\log_b 12 + \log_b r = \log_b(12r)$ • Use the Logarithm Property of Products.

The Logarithm Property of Products can be extended to include the logarithm of the product of more than two factors. For instance,

$$\log_b(xyz) = \log_b x + \log_b y + \log_b z$$
$$\log_b(7rt) = \log_b 7 + \log_b r + \log_b t$$

A second property of logarithms involves the logarithm of the quotient of two numbers. This property of logarithms is also based on the fact that a logarithm is an exponent and that to divide two exponential expressions with the same base, we subtract the exponents.

The Logarithm Property of the Quotient of Two Numbers

For any positive real numbers x, y, and b, $b \neq 1$,

$$\log_b \frac{x}{y} = \log_b x - \log_b y.$$

A proof of this property can be found in the Appendix.

➡ Write $\log_b \dfrac{p}{8}$ in expanded form.

$$\log_b \frac{p}{8} = \log_b p - \log_b 8 \qquad \bullet \text{ Use the Logarithm Property of Quotients.}$$

➡ Write $\log_b y - \log_b v$ as a single logarithm.

$$\log_b y - \log_b v = \log_b \frac{y}{v} \qquad \bullet \text{ Use the Logarithm Property of Quotients.}$$

A third property of logarithms is used to simplify powers of a number.

The Logarithm Property of the Power of a Number

For any positive real numbers x and b, $b \neq 1$, and for any real number r, $\log_b x^r = r \log_b x$.

A proof of this property can be found in the Appendix.

➡ Rewrite $\log_b x^3$ in terms of $\log_b x$.

$$\log_b x^3 = 3 \log_b x \qquad \bullet \text{ Use the Logarithm Property of Powers.}$$

➡ Rewrite $\dfrac{2}{3} \log_b x$ with a coefficient of 1.

$$\frac{2}{3} \log_b x = \log_b x^{2/3} \qquad \bullet \text{ Use the Logarithm Property of Powers.}$$

The following table summarizes the properties of logarithms that we have discussed, along with two other properties.

Summary of the Properties of Logarithms

Let x, y, and b be positive real numbers with $b \neq 1$. Then

Product Property	$\log_b(x \cdot y) = \log_b x + \log_b y$
Quotient Property	$\log_b\left(\dfrac{x}{y}\right) = \log_b x - \log_b y$
Power Property	$\log_b x^r = r \log_b x$
Logarithm of One	$\log_b 1 = 0$
1–1 Property	If $\log_b x = \log_b y$, then $x = y$.

➡ Write $\log_b \frac{xy}{z}$ in expanded form.

$$\log_b \frac{xy}{z} = \log_b(xy) - \log_b z$$
• Use the Logarithm Property of Quotients.
$$= \log_b x + \log_b y - \log_b z$$
• Use the Logarithm Property of Products.

➡ Write $\log_b \frac{x^2}{y^3}$ in expanded form.

$$\log_b \frac{x^2}{y^3} = \log_b x^2 - \log_b y^3$$
• Use the Logarithm Property of Quotients.
$$= 2\log_b x - 3\log_b y$$
• Use the Logarithm Property of Powers.

➡ Write $2\log_b x + 4\log_b y$ as a single logarithm with a coefficient of 1.

$$2\log_b x + 4\log_b y = \log_b x^2 + \log_b y^4$$
• Use the Logarithm Property of Powers.
$$= \log_b x^2 y^4$$
• Use the Logarithm Property of Products.

Example 4
Write $\log\sqrt{x^3 y}$ in expanded form.

Solution
$$\log\sqrt{x^3 y} = \log(x^3 y)^{1/2} = \frac{1}{2}\log(x^3 y)$$
$$= \frac{1}{2}(\log x^3 + \log y)$$
$$= \frac{1}{2}(3\log x + \log y)$$
$$= \frac{3}{2}\log x + \frac{1}{2}\log y$$

You Try It 4
Write $\log_8 \sqrt[3]{xy^2}$ in expanded form.

Your solution
$$\frac{1}{3}\log_8 x + \frac{2}{3}\log_8 y$$

Example 5
Write $\frac{1}{2}(\log_3 x - 3\log_3 y + \log_3 z)$ as a single logarithm with a coefficient of 1.

Solution
$$\frac{1}{2}(\log_3 x - 3\log_3 y + \log_3 z)$$
$$= \frac{1}{2}(\log_3 x - \log_3 y^3 + \log_3 z)$$
$$= \frac{1}{2}\left(\log_3 \frac{x}{y^3} + \log_3 z\right)$$
$$= \frac{1}{2}\left(\log_3 \frac{xz}{y^3}\right) = \log_3\left(\frac{xz}{y^3}\right)^{1/2} = \log_3 \sqrt{\frac{xz}{y^3}}$$

You Try It 5
Write $\frac{1}{3}(\log_4 x - 2\log_4 y + \log_4 z)$ as a single logarithm with a coefficient of 1.

Your solution
$$\log_4 \sqrt[3]{\frac{xz}{y^2}}$$

Example 6
Find $\log_4 1$.

Solution
$\log_4 1 = 0$ • Logarithm of One

You Try It 6
Find $\log_9 1$.

Your solution
0

Solutions on p. S35

Although only common logarithms and natural logarithms are programmed into a calculator, the logarithms for other positive bases can be found.

⇒ Evaluate $\log_5 22$.

$\log_5 22 = x$	• Write an equation.
$5^x = 22$	• Write the equation in its equivalent exponential form.
$\log 5^x = \log 22$	• Take the common logarithm of each side of the equation.
$x \log 5 = \log 22$	• Use the Power Property of Logarithms.
$x = \dfrac{\log 22}{\log 5}$	• Divide each side by log 5. This is the exact answer.
$x \approx 1.9206$	• This is an approximate answer.
$\log_5 22 \approx 1.9206$	

In the third step above, the natural logarithm, instead of the common logarithm, could have been applied to each side of the equation. The same result would have been obtained.

Using a procedure similar to the one for $\log_5 22$, a formula for changing bases can be derived.

INSTRUCTOR NOTE

Because graphing calculators only have preprogrammed common and natural logarithms, the change-of-base formula is used to graph logarithms with other bases. For instance, to graph $f(x) = \log_2(x - 3)$, the students must enter $\dfrac{1}{\log 2} \log (x - 3)$ or an equivalent expression using natural logarithms.

Change-of-Base Formula

$$\log_a N = \frac{\log_b N}{\log_b a}$$

⇒ Evaluate $\log_2 14$.

$$\log_2 14 = \frac{\log 14}{\log 2}$$ • Use the Change-of-Base Formula with $N = 14$, $a = 2$, $b = 10$.

$$\approx 3.8074$$

For the last example, common logarithms were used. Here is the same example using natural logarithms. Note that the answers are the same.

$$\log_2 14 = \frac{\ln 14}{\ln 2} \approx 3.8074$$

Example 7

Evaluate $\log_2 90.813$ by using common logarithms.

Solution

$$\log_2 90.813 = \frac{\log 90.813}{\log 2} \approx 6.5048$$

Example 8

Evaluate $\log_8 0.137$ by using natural logarithms.

Solution

$$\log_8 0.137 = \frac{\ln 0.137}{\ln 8} \approx -0.9559$$

You Try It 7

Evaluate $\log_7 6.45$ by using common logarithms.

Your solution

0.95795

You Try It 8

Evaluate $\log_3 0.834$ by using natural logarithms.

Your solution

−0.16523

Solutions on p. S35

12.2 Exercises

· ·

Objective A

Write the exponential equation in logarithmic form.

1. $5^2 = 25$

$\log_5 25 = 2$

2. $10^3 = 1000$

$\log_{10} 1000 = 3$

3. $4^{-2} = \dfrac{1}{16}$

$\log_4\left(\dfrac{1}{16}\right) = -2$

4. $3^{-3} = \dfrac{1}{27}$

$\log_3\left(\dfrac{1}{27}\right) = -3$

5. $10^y = x$
$\log_{10} x = y$

6. $e^y = x$
$\ln x = y$

7. $a^x = w$
$\log_a w = x$

8. $b^y = c$
$\log_b c = y$

Write the logarithmic equation in exponential form.

9. $\log_3 9 = 2$

$3^2 = 9$

10. $\log_2 32 = 5$

$2^5 = 32$

11. $\log 0.01 = -2$

$10^{-2} = 0.01$

12. $\log_5 \dfrac{1}{5} = -1$

$5^{-1} = \dfrac{1}{5}$

13. $\ln x = y$
$e^y = x$

14. $\log x = y$
$10^y = x$

15. $\log_b u - v$
$b^v = u$

16. $\log_c x = y$
$c^y = x$

Evaluate.

17. $\log_3 81$
4

18. $\log_7 49$
2

19. $\log_2 128$
7

20. $\log_5 125$
3

21. $\log 100$
2

22. $\log 0.001$
−3

23. $\ln e^3$
3

24. $\ln e^2$
2

25. $\log_8 1$
0

26. $\log_3 243$
5

27. $\log_5 625$
4

28. $\log_2 64$
6

Solve for x.

29. $\log_3 x = 2$
9

30. $\log_5 x = 1$
5

31. $\log_4 x = 3$
64

32. $\log_2 x = 6$
64

33. $\log_7 x = -1$
$\dfrac{1}{7}$

34. $\log_8 x = -2$
$\dfrac{1}{64}$

35. $\log_6 x = 0$
1

36. $\log_4 x = 0$
1

Solve for x. Round to the nearest hundredth.

37. $\log x = 2.5$
316.23

38. $\log x = 3.2$
1584.89

39. $\log x = -1.75$
0.02

40. $\log x = -2.1$
0.01

41. $\ln x = 2$

7.39

42. $\ln x = 1.4$

4.06

43. $\ln x = -\dfrac{1}{2}$

0.61

44. $\ln x = -1.7$

0.18

Objective B

Express as a single logarithm with a coefficient of 1.

45. $\log_3 x^3 + \log_3 y^2$

$\log_3(x^3 y^2)$

46. $\log_7 x + \log_7 z^2$

$\log_7(xz^2)$

47. $\ln x^4 - \ln y^2$

$\ln\left(\dfrac{x^4}{y^2}\right)$

48. $\ln x^2 - \ln y$

$\ln\left(\dfrac{x^2}{y}\right)$

49. $3 \log_7 x$

$\log_7 x^3$

50. $4 \log_8 y$

$\log_8 y^4$

51. $3 \ln x + 4 \ln y$

$\ln (x^3 y^4)$

52. $2 \ln x - 5 \ln y$

$\ln\left(\dfrac{x^2}{y^5}\right)$

53. $2(\log_4 x + \log_4 y)$

$\log_4(x^2 y^2)$

54. $3(\log_5 r + \log_5 t)$

$\log_5(r^3 t^3)$

55. $\dfrac{1}{2}(\log_6 x - \log_6 y)$

$\log_6 \sqrt{\dfrac{x}{y}}$

56. $\dfrac{1}{3}(\log_8 x - \log_8 y)$

$\log_8 \sqrt[3]{\dfrac{x}{y}}$

57. $2 \log_3 x - \log_3 y + 2 \log_3 z$

$\log_3\left(\dfrac{x^2 z^2}{y}\right)$

58. $4 \log_5 r - 3 \log_5 s + \log_5 t$

$\log_5\left(\dfrac{r^4 t}{s^3}\right)$

59. $\ln x - (2 \ln y + \ln z)$

$\ln\left(\dfrac{x}{y^2 z}\right)$

60. $2 \log_b x - 3(\log_b y + \log_b z)$

$\log_b\left(\dfrac{x^2}{y^3 z^3}\right)$

61. $2(\log_4 s - 2 \log_4 t + \log_4 r)$

$\log_4\left(\dfrac{s^2 r^2}{t^4}\right)$

62. $3(\log_9 x + 2 \log_9 y - 2 \log_9 z)$

$\log_9\left(\dfrac{x^3 y^6}{z^6}\right)$

63. $\ln x - 2(\ln y + \ln z)$

$\ln\left(\dfrac{x}{y^2 z^2}\right)$

64. $\ln t - 3(\ln u + \ln v)$

$\ln\left(\dfrac{t}{u^3 v^3}\right)$

65. $3 \log_2 t - 2(\log_2 r - \log_2 v)$

$\log_2\left(\dfrac{t^3 v^2}{r^2}\right)$

66. $2 \log_{10} x - 3(\log_{10} y - \log_{10} z)$

$\log_{10}\left(\dfrac{x^2 z^3}{y^3}\right)$

67. $\dfrac{1}{2}(3 \log_4 x - 2 \log_4 y + \log_4 z)$

$\log_4 \sqrt{\dfrac{x^3 z}{y^2}}$

68. $\dfrac{1}{3}(4 \log_5 t - 5 \log_5 u - 7 \log_5 v)$

$\log_5 \sqrt[3]{\dfrac{t^4}{u^5 v^7}}$

69. $\dfrac{1}{2}(\ln x - 3 \ln y)$

$\ln \sqrt{\dfrac{x}{y^3}}$

70. $\dfrac{1}{3} \ln a + \dfrac{2}{3} \ln b$

$\ln \sqrt[3]{ab^2}$

71. $\dfrac{1}{2}\log_2 x - \dfrac{2}{3}\log_2 y + \dfrac{1}{2}\log_2 z$

$\log_2\left(\dfrac{\sqrt{xz}}{\sqrt[3]{y^2}}\right)$

72. $\dfrac{2}{3}\log_3 x + \dfrac{1}{3}\log_3 y - \dfrac{1}{2}\log_3 z$

$\log_3\left(\dfrac{\sqrt[3]{x^2 y}}{\sqrt{z}}\right)$

Write the logarithm in expanded form.

73. $\log_8(xz)$

$\log_8 x + \log_8 z$

74. $\log_7(rt)$

$\log_7 r + \log_7 t$

75. $\log_3 x^5$

$5 \log_3 x$

76. $\log_2 y^7$

$7 \log_2 y$

77. $\log_b\left(\dfrac{r}{s}\right)$

$\log_b r - \log_b s$

78. $\log_c\left(\dfrac{z}{4}\right)$

$\log_c z - \log_c 4$

79. $\log_3(x^2 y^6)$

$2 \log_3 x + 6 \log_3 y$

80. $\log_4(t^4 u^2)$

$4 \log_4 t + 2 \log_4 u$

81. $\log_7\left(\dfrac{u^3}{v^4}\right)$

$3 \log_7 u - 4 \log_7 v$

82. $\log\left(\dfrac{s^5}{t^2}\right)$

$5 \log s \quad 2 \log t$

83. $\log_2(rs)^2$

$2 \log_2 r + 2 \log_2 s$

84. $\log_3(x^2 y)^3$

$6 \log_3 x + 3 \log_3 y$

85. $\ln(x^2 yz)$

$2 \ln x + \ln y + \ln z$

86. $\ln(xy^2 z^3)$

$\ln x + 2 \ln y + 3 \ln z$

87. $\log_5\left(\dfrac{xy^2}{z^4}\right)$

$\log_5 x + 2 \log_5 y - 4 \log_5 z$

88. $\log_b\left(\dfrac{r^2 s}{t^3}\right)$

$2 \log_b r + \log_b s - 3 \log_b t$

89. $\log_8\left(\dfrac{x^2}{yz^2}\right)$

$2 \log_8 x - \log_8 y - 2 \log_8 z$

90. $\log_9\left(\dfrac{x}{y^2 z^3}\right)$

$\log_9 x - 2 \log_9 y - 3 \log_9 z$

91. $\log_4 \sqrt{x^3 y}$

$\dfrac{3}{2}\log_4 x + \dfrac{1}{2}\log_4 y$

92. $\log_3 \sqrt{x^5 y^3}$

$\dfrac{5}{2}\log_3 x + \dfrac{3}{2}\log_3 y$

93. $\log_7 \sqrt{\dfrac{x^3}{y}}$

$\dfrac{3}{2}\log_7 x - \dfrac{1}{2}\log_7 y$

94. $\log_b \sqrt[3]{\dfrac{r^2}{t}}$

$\dfrac{2}{3}\log_b r - \dfrac{1}{3}\log_b t$

95. $\ln\left(x \sqrt{\dfrac{y}{z}}\right)$

$\ln x + \dfrac{1}{2}\ln y - \dfrac{1}{2}\ln z$

96. $\ln\left(x \sqrt[3]{\dfrac{r}{s}}\right)$

$\ln y + \dfrac{1}{3}\ln r - \dfrac{1}{3}\ln s$

97. $\log_3 \dfrac{t}{\sqrt{x}}$

$\log_3 t - \dfrac{1}{2}\log_3 x$

98. $\log_4 \dfrac{x}{\sqrt{y^2 z}}$

$\log_4 x - \log_4 y - \dfrac{1}{2}\log_4 z$

99. $\log_7\left(\dfrac{\sqrt{uv}}{x}\right)$

$\dfrac{1}{2}\log_7 u + \dfrac{1}{2}\log_7 v - \log_7 x$

100. $\log_2\left(\dfrac{\sqrt{xy}}{z^2}\right)$

$\dfrac{1}{2}\log_2 x + \dfrac{1}{2}\log_2 y - 2 \log_2 z$

Objective C

Evaluate. Round to the nearest ten-thousandth.

101. $\log_{10} 7$

0.8451

102. $\log_{10} 9$

0.9542

103. $\log_{10}\left(\dfrac{3}{5}\right)$

-0.2218

104. $\log_{10}\left(\dfrac{13}{3}\right)$

0.6368

105. $\ln 4$

1.3863

106. $\ln 6$

1.7918

107. $\ln\left(\dfrac{17}{6}\right)$

1.0415

108. $\ln\left(\dfrac{13}{17}\right)$

-0.2683

109. $\log_8 6$
0.8617

110. $\log_4 8$
1.500

111. $\log_5 30$
2.1133

112. $\log_6 28$
1.8597

113. $\log_3(0.5)$
-0.6309

114. $\log_5(0.6)$
-0.3174

115. $\log_7(1.7)$
0.2727

116. $\log_6(3.2)$
0.6492

117. $\log_5 15$
1.6826

118. $\log_3 25$
2.9299

119. $\log_{12} 120$
1.9266

120. $\log_9 90$
2.0480

121. $\log_4 2.55$
0.6752

122. $\log_8 6.42$
0.8942

123. $\log_5 67$
2.6125

124. $\log_8 35$
1.7098

APPLYING THE CONCEPTS

125. For each of the following, answer True or False. Assume all variables represent positive numbers.

  a. $\log_3(-9) = -2$
  false

  b. $x^y = z$ and $\log_x z = y$ are equivalent equations.
  true

  c. $\log(x^{-1}) = \dfrac{1}{\log x}$
  false

  d. $\log(x + y) = \log x + \log y$
  false

  e. $\log(x \cdot y) = \log x \cdot \log y$
  false

  f. $\log\left(\dfrac{x}{y}\right) = \log x - \log y$
  true

  g. $\dfrac{\log x}{\log y} = \dfrac{x}{y}$
  false

  h. If $\log x = \log y$, then $x = y$.
  true

126. Complete each statement using the equation $\log_a b = c$.

  a. $a^c = \underline{\quad b \quad}$

  b. $\text{antilog}_a(\log_a b) = \underline{\quad b \quad}$

12.3 Graphs of Logarithmic Functions

Objective A **To graph a logarithmic function** .... (46)

The graph of a logarithmic function can be drawn by using the relationship between the exponential and logarithmic functions.

➡ Graph: $f(x) = \log_2 x$

Think of this as the equation $y = \log_2 x$.

$$f(x) = \log_2 x$$
$$y = \log_2 x$$

Write the equivalent exponential equation.

$$x = 2^y$$

Because the equation is solved for x in terms of y, it is easier to choose values of y and find the corresponding values of x. The results can be recorded in a table.

Graph the ordered pairs on a rectangular coordinate system.

Connect the points with a smooth curve.

x	y
$\frac{1}{4}$	-2
$\frac{1}{2}$	-1
1	0
2	1
4	2

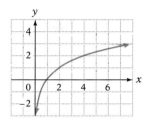

Applying the vertical-line and horizontal-line tests reveals that $f(x) = \log_2 x$ is a 1–1 function.

➡ Graph: $f(x) = \log_2(x) + 1$

Think of $f(x) = \log_2(x) + 1$ as the equation $y = \log_2(x) + 1$.

$$y = \log_2(x) + 1$$
$$y - 1 = \log_2(x)$$ • Solve for $\log_2(x)$.
$$2^{y-1} = x$$ • Write the equivalent exponential equation.

Choose values of y and find the corresponding values of x.

Graph the ordered pairs on a rectangular coordinate system.

Connect the points with a smooth curve.

x	y
$\frac{1}{4}$	-1
$\frac{1}{2}$	0
1	1
2	2
4	3

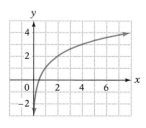

Example 1

Graph: $f(x) = \log_3 x$

Solution

$f(x) = \log_3 x$

$y = \log_3 x$

$3^y = x$ • Write the equivalent exponential equation.

x	y
$\frac{1}{9}$	-2
$\frac{1}{3}$	-1
1	0
3	1

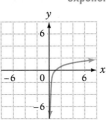

You Try It 1

Graph: $f(x) = \log_2(x - 1)$

Your solution

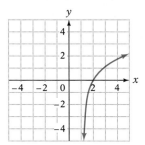

Example 2

Graph: $f(x) = 2 \log_3 x$

Solution

$f(x) = 2 \log_3 x$

$y = 2 \log_3 x$

$\dfrac{y}{2} = \log_3 x$

$3^{y/2} = x$ • Write the equivalent exponential equation.

x	y
$\frac{1}{9}$	-4
$\frac{1}{3}$	-2
1	0
3	2

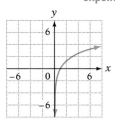

You Try It 2

Graph: $f(x) = \log_3(2x)$

Your solution

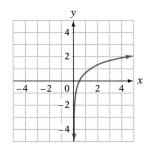

Example 3

Graph: $f(x) = -\log_2(x - 2)$

Solution

$f(x) = -\log_2(x - 2)$

$y = -\log_2(x - 2)$

$-y = \log_2(x - 2)$

$2^{-y} = x - 2$

$2^{-y} + 2 = x$ • Write the equivalent exponential equation.

x	y
6	-2
4	-1
3	0
$\frac{5}{2}$	1
$\frac{9}{4}$	2
$\frac{17}{8}$	3

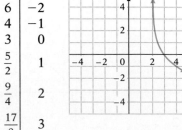

You Try It 3

Graph: $f(x) = -\log_3(x + 1)$

Your solution

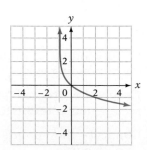

Solutions on p. S35

12.3 Exercises

· ·

Objective A

Graph.

1. $f(x) = \log_4 x$

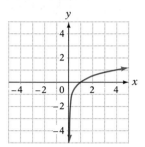

2. $f(x) = \log_2(x + 1)$

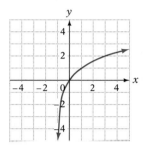

3. $f(x) = \log_3(2x - 1)$

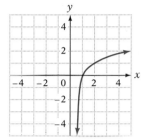

4. $f(x) = \log_2\left(\frac{1}{2}x\right)$

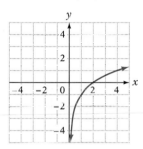

5. $f(x) = 3\log_2 x$

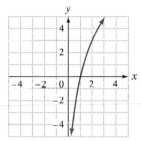

6. $f(x) = \frac{1}{2}\log_2 x$

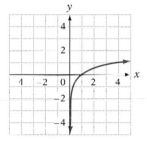

7. $f(x) = -\log_2 x$

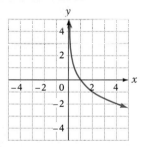

8. $f(x) = -\log_3 x$

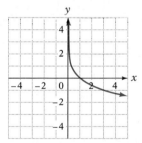

9. $f(x) = \log_2(x - 1)$

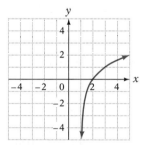

10. $f(x) = \log_3(2 - x)$

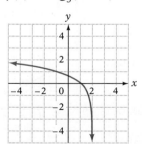

11. $f(x) = -\log_2(x - 1)$

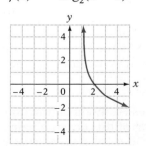

12. $f(x) = -\log_2(1 - x)$

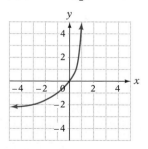

APPLYING THE CONCEPTS

Use a graphing calculator to graph the following.

13. $f(x) = \log_2 x - 3$

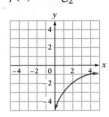

14. $f(x) = \log_3 x + 2$

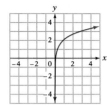

15. $f(x) = -\log_2 x + 2$

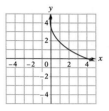

16. $f(x) = -\dfrac{1}{2}\log_2 x - 1$

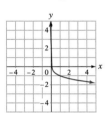

17. $f(x) = x - \log_2(1 - x)$

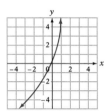

18. $f(x) = x + \log_3(2 - x)$

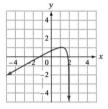

19. $f(x) = \dfrac{x}{2} - 2\log_2(x + 1)$

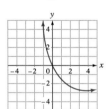

20. $f(x) = \dfrac{x}{3} - 3\log_2(x + 3)$

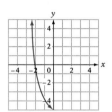

21. $f(x) = x^2 - 10\ln(x - 1)$

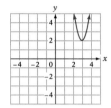

22. The Power Property of Logarithms tells us that $\ln x^2 = 2 \ln x$. Graph $f(x) = \ln x^2$ and $g(x) = 2 \ln x$. Are the graphs the same? Explain.
   No. If $x < 0$, then $\ln x^2$ is a real number but $2 \ln x$ is not a real number.

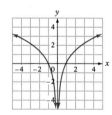

23. Astronomers use the *distance modulus* of a star as a method of determining the star's distance from Earth. The formula is $M = 5 \log s - 5$, where M is the distance modulus and s is the star's distance from the Earth in parsecs. (One parsec $\approx 1.9 \times 10^{13}$ miles.)
   a. Graph the equation.
   b. The point with coordinates (25.1, 2) is on the graph. Write a sentence that describes the meaning of this ordered pair.
      The point (25.1, 2) means that a star that is 25.1 parsecs from Earth has a distance modulus of 2.

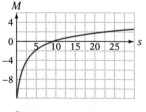

24. Without practice, the proficiency of a typist decreases. The equation $S = 60 - 7 \ln(t + 1)$, where S is the typing speed in words per minute and t is the number of months without typing, approximates this decrease.
   a. Graph the equation.
   b. The point with coordinates (4, 49) is on the graph. Write a sentence that describes the meaning of this ordered pair.
      The point (4, 49) means that after 4 months, the typist's proficiency has dropped to 49 words per minute.

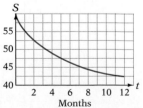
Months

12.4 Exercises

· ·

Objective A

Solve for x. Round to the nearest ten-thousandth.

1. $5^{4x-1} = 5^{x-2}$

$-\dfrac{1}{3}$

2. $7^{4x-3} = 7^{2x+1}$

2

3. $8^{x-4} = 8^{5x+8}$

-3

4. $10^{4x-5} = 10^{x+4}$

3

5. $9^x = 3^{x+1}$

1

6. $2^{x-1} = 4^x$

-1

7. $8^{x+2} = 16^x$

6

8. $9^{3x} = 81^{x-4}$

-8

9. $16^{2-x} = 32^{2x}$

$\dfrac{4}{7}$

10. $27^{2x-3} = 81^{4-x}$

$\dfrac{5}{2}$

11. $25^{3-x} = 125^{2x-1}$

$\dfrac{9}{8}$

12. $8^{4x-7} = 64^{x-3}$

$\dfrac{1}{2}$

13. $5^x = 6$

1.1133

14. $7^x = 10$

1.1833

15. $e^x = 3$

1.0986

16. $e^x = 2$

0.6931

17. $10^x = 21$

1.3222

18. $10^x = 37$

1.5682

19. $2^{-x} = 7$

-2.8074

20. $3^{-x} = 14$

-2.4022

21. $2^{x-1} = 6$

3.5850

22. $4^{x+1} = 9$

0.5850

23. $3^{2x-1} = 4$

1.1309

24. $4^{-x+2} = 12$

0.2075

Objective B

Solve for x.

25. $\log_2(2x - 3) = 3$

$\dfrac{11}{2}$

26. $\log_4(3x + 1) = 2$

5

27. $\log_2(x^2 + 2x) = 3$

$-4, 2$

28. $\log_3(x^2 + 6x) = 3$

$-9, 3$

29. $\log_5\left(\dfrac{2x}{x-1}\right) = 1$

$\dfrac{5}{3}$

30. $\log_6\left(\dfrac{3x}{x+1}\right) = 1$

-2

31. $\log x = \log(1 - x)$

$\dfrac{1}{2}$

32. $\ln(3x - 2) = \ln(x + 1)$

$\dfrac{3}{2}$

33. $\ln 5 = \ln(4x - 13)$

$\dfrac{9}{2}$

34. $\log_3(x - 2) = \log_3(2x)$

no solution

35. $\ln(3x + 2) = 4$

17.5327

36. $\ln(2x + 3) = -1$

-1.3161

37. $\log_2(8x) - \log_2(x^2 - 1) = \log_2 3$
3

38. $\log_5(3x) - \log_5(x^2 - 1) = \log_5 2$
2

39. $\log_9 x + \log_9(2x - 3) = \log_9 2$
2

40. $\log_6 x + \log_6(3x - 5) = \log_6 2$
2

41. $\log_8(6x) = \log_8 2 + \log_8(x - 4)$
no solution

42. $\log_7(5x) = \log_7 3 + \log_7(2x + 1)$
no solution

APPLYING THE CONCEPTS

Solve each equation with a graphing calculator. Round answers to the nearest hundredth.

43. $3^x = -x$
−0.55

44. $2^x = -x + 2$
0.54

45. $2^{-x} = x - 1$
1.38

46. $3^{-x} = 2x$
0.34

47. $\ln x = x^2$
no solution

48. $2 \ln x = -x + 1$
1

49. $\log_3 x = -2x - 2$
0.09

50. $\log_5(2x) = -2x + 1$
0.50

51. A model for the distance s (in feet) that an object that is experiencing air resistance will fall in t seconds is given by $s = 312.5 \ln\left(\dfrac{e^{0.32t} + e^{-0.32t}}{2}\right)$.

 a. Graph this equation. *Suggestion:* Use Xmin = 0, Xmax = 4.5, Ymin = 0, Ymax = 140, and Yscl = 20.
   b. Determine, to the nearest hundredth of a second, the time it takes the object to travel 100 ft.
   It will take the object approximately 2.64 s to fall 100 ft.

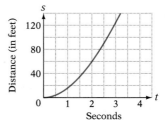

52. A model for the distance s (in feet) that an object that is experiencing air resistance will fall in t seconds is given by $s = 78 \ln\left(\dfrac{e^{0.8t} + e^{-0.8t}}{2}\right)$.

 a. Graph this equation. *Suggestion:* Use Xmin = 0, Xmax = 4.5, Ymin = 0, Ymax = 140, and Yscl = 20.
   b. Determine, to the nearest hundredth of a second, the time it takes the object to travel 125 ft.
   It will take the object approximately 2.86 s to fall 125 ft.

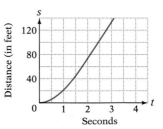

53. The following "proof" shows that $0.5 < 0.25$. Explain the error.

$$1 < 2$$
$$1 \cdot \log 0.5 < 2 \cdot \log 0.5$$
$$\log 0.5 < \log(0.5)^2$$
$$0.5 < (0.5)^2$$
$$0.5 < 0.25$$

12.5

Applications of Exponential and Logarithmic Functions

Objective A   *To solve application problems*.....................................

A biologist places one single-celled bacterium in a culture, and each hour that particular species of bacteria divides into two bacteria. After one hour there will be two bacteria. After two hours, each of the two bacteria will divide and there will be four bacteria. After three hours, each of the four bacteria will divide and there will be eight bacteria.

The table at the right shows the number of bacteria in the culture after various intervals of time, t, in hours. Values in this table could also be found by using the exponential equation $N = 2^t$.

Time, t	Number of Bacteria, N
0	1
1	2
2	4
3	8
4	16

The equation $N = 2^t$ is an example of an **exponential growth equation**. In general, any equation that can be written in the form $A = A_0 b^{kt}$, where A is the size at time t, A_0 is the initial size, $b > 1$, and k is a positive real number, is an exponential growth equation. These equations are important not only in population growth studies but also in physics, chemistry, psychology, and economics.

Recall that interest is the amount of money paid (or received) when borrowing (or investing) money. **Compound interest** is interest that is computed not only on the original principal, but also on the interest already earned. The compound interest formula is an exponential equation.

INSTRUCTOR NOTE

Another exponential function from finance that will be of interest to students is the one that enables them to calculate the amount of an amortized loan payment, such as a car loan.

$$P = B\left[\frac{i/12}{1 - [1 + (i/12)]^{-n}}\right]$$

B is the amount borrowed, i is the annual interest rate as a decimal, and n is the number of months to repay the loan.

The **compound interest formula** is $P = A(1 + i)^n$, where A is the original value of an investment, i is the interest rate per compounding period, n is the total number of compounding periods, and P is the value of the investment after n periods.

➡ An investment broker deposits \$1000 into an account that earns 12% annual interest compounded quarterly. What is the value of the investment after two years?

$i = \dfrac{12\%}{4} = \dfrac{0.12}{4} = 0.03$ • Find i, the interest rate per quarter. The quarterly rate is the annual rate divided by 4, the number of quarters in one year.

$n = 4 \cdot 2 = 8$ • Find n, the number of compounding periods. The investment is compounded quarterly, 4 times a year, for 2 years.

$P = A(1 + i)^n$ • Use the compound interest formula.

$P = 1000(1 + 0.03)^8$ • Replace A, i, and n by their values.

$P \approx 1267$ • Solve for P.

The value of the investment after two years is approximately \$1267.

Exponential decay offers another example of an exponential equation. One of the most common illustrations is the decay of a radioactive substance. For instance, tritium, a radioactive nucleus of hydrogen that has been used in luminous watch dials, has a half-life of approximately 12 years. This means that one-half of any given amount of tritium will disintegrate in 12 years.

The table at the right indicates the amount of an initial 10-microgram sample of tritium that remains after various intervals of time, t, in years. Values in this table could also be found by using the exponential equation $A = 10(0.5)^{t/12}$.

Time, t	Amount, A
0	10
12	5
24	2.5
36	1.25
48	0.625

The equation $A = 10(0.5)^{t/12}$ is an example of an **exponential decay equation**. Comparing this equation to the exponential growth equation, note that for exponential growth, the base of the exponential equation is greater than 1, whereas for exponential decay, the base is between 0 and 1.

A method by which an archaeologist can measure the age of a bone is called carbon dating. Carbon dating is based on a radioactive isotope of carbon called carbon-14, which has a half-life of approximately 5570 years. The exponential decay equation is given by $A = A_0(0.5)^{t/5570}$, where A_0 is the original amount of carbon-14 present in the bone, t is the age of the bone, and A is the amount of carbon-14 present after t years.

⇨ A bone that originally contained 100 mg of carbon-14 now has 70 mg of carbon-14. What is the approximate age of the bone?

$$A = A_0(0.5)^{t/5570}$$ • Use the exponential decay equation.

$$70 = 100(0.5)^{t/5570}$$ • Replace A by 70 and A_0 by 100 and solve for t.

$$0.7 = (0.5)^{t/5570}$$ • Divide each side by 100.

$$\log 0.7 = \log(0.5)^{t/5570}$$ • Take the common logarithm of each side of the equation. Then simplify.

$$\log 0.7 = \frac{t}{5570}\log(0.5)$$

$$\frac{5570 \log 0.7}{\log 0.5} = t$$

$$2866 \approx t$$

The bone is approximately 2866 years old.

A chemist measures the acidity or alkalinity of a solution by the concentration of hydrogen ions, H^+, in the solution using the formula $pH = -\log(H^+)$. A neutral solution such as distilled water has a pH of 7, acids have a pH of less than 7, and alkaline solutions (also called basic solutions) have a pH of greater than 7.

⇨ Find the pH of a certain orange juice that has a hydrogen ion concentration, H^+, of 2.9×10^{-4}. Round to the nearest tenth.

$$pH = -\log(H^+)$$

$$= -\log(2.9 \times 10^{-4})$$ • $H^+ = 2.9 \times 10^{-4}$

$$\approx 3.5376$$

The pH of the orange juice is approximately 3.5.

The **Richter scale** measures the magnitude, M, of an earthquake in terms of the intensity, I, of its shock waves. The relationship between the magnitude and the intensity is given by $M = \log\dfrac{I_1}{I_0}$, where I_0 is a constant.

➡️ How many times as intense is an earthquake that has a magnitude of 6 on the Richter scale than one that has a magnitude of 2?

$$6 = \log\frac{I_1}{I_0}$$

- Use the Richter equation to write a system of equations, one for magnitude 6 and one for magnitude 2.

$$2 = \log\frac{I_2}{I_0}$$

(1) $6 = \log I_1 - \log I_0$
(2) $2 = \log I_2 - \log I_0$

- Rewrite the equations using the Quotient Property of Logarithms.

$$4 = \log I_1 - \log I_2$$

- Solve the system of equations by subtracting Equation (2) from Equation (1).

$$4 = \log\frac{I_1}{I_2}$$

- Rewrite the equation using the Quotient Property of Logarithms.

$$\frac{I_1}{I_2} = 10^4 = 10{,}000$$

- Solve for $\dfrac{I_1}{I_2}$ using the equivalence of $y = \log x$ and $x = 10^y$.

An earthquake that has magnitude 6 on the Richter scale has an intensity that is 10,000 times greater than an earthquake of magnitude 2.

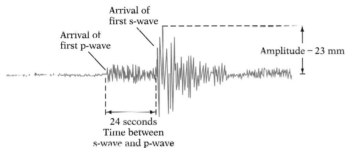

Arrival of first s-wave

Arrival of first p-wave

Amplitude – 23 mm

24 seconds
Time between s-wave and p-wave

The graph at the left is a *seismogram*, which is used to measure the magnitude of an earthquake. The magnitude, M, is determined by the amplitude, A, of the wave and the difference in time, t, between the occurrence of two types of waves, called *s-waves* and *p-waves*. The equation is given by $M = \log A + 3 \log 8t - 2.92$.

➡️ Determine the magnitude of the earthquake for the seismogram given in the figure. Round to the nearest tenth.

$$\begin{aligned}
M &= \log A + 3 \log 8t - 2.92 \\
&= \log 23 + 3 \log[8(24)] - 2.92 \\
&\approx 1.36173 + 6.84990 - 2.92 \\
&\approx 5.3
\end{aligned}$$

- Replace A by 23 and t by 24.
- Simplify.

The earthquake has a magnitude of 5.3 on the Richter scale.

The percent of light that will pass through a substance is given by $\log P = -kd$, where P is the percent of light passing through the substance, k is a constant depending on the substance, and d is the thickness of the substance in meters.

➡️ For certain parts of the ocean, $k = 0.03$. Using this value, at what depth will the percent of light be 50% of the light at the surface of the ocean? Round to the nearest meter.

$$\begin{aligned}
\log P &= -kd \\
\log(0.5) &= -0.03d \\
\frac{\log(0.5)}{-0.03} &= d \\
10.0343 &\approx d
\end{aligned}$$

- Replace P by 0.5 (50%) and k by 0.03.
- Solve for d.

At a depth of about 10 m, the light will be 50% of the light at the surface.

Example 1

An investment of \$3000 is placed into an account that earns 12% annual interest compounded monthly. In approximately how many years will the investment be worth twice the original amount?

Strategy

To find the time, solve the compound interest formula for n. Use $P = 6000$, $A = 3000$, and $i = \frac{12\%}{12} = \frac{0.12}{12} = 0.01$.

Solution

$$P = A(1 + i)^n$$
$$6000 = 3000(1 + 0.01)^n$$
$$6000 = 3000(1.01)^n$$
$$2 = (1.01)^n$$
$$\log 2 = \log(1.01)^n$$
$$\log 2 = n \log 1.01$$
$$\frac{\log 2}{\log 1.01} = n$$
$$70 \approx n$$

70 months ÷ 12 ≈ 5.8 years

In approximately 6 years, the investment will be worth \$6000.

Example 2

The number of words per minute that a student can type will increase with practice and can be approximated by the equation $N = 100[1 - (0.9)^t]$, where N is the number of words typed per minute after t days of instruction. Find the number of words a student will type per minute after 8 days of instruction.

Strategy

To find the number of words per minute, replace t by its given value in the equation and solve for N.

Solution

$$N = 100[1 - (0.9)^t]$$
$$= 100[1 - (0.9)^8]$$
$$\approx 56.95$$

After 8 days of instruction, a student will type approximately 57 words per minute.

You Try It 1

Find the hydrogen ion concentration, H^+, of vinegar that has a pH of 2.9.

Your strategy

Your solution

0.00126

You Try It 2

An earthquake that measures 5 on the Richter scale can cause serious damage to buildings. The San Francisco earthquake of 1906 would have measured about 7.8 on this scale. How many times as strong was the San Francisco earthquake as compared with the least forceful earthquake that can cause serious damage to buildings? Round to the nearest whole number.

Your strategy

Your solution

631 times as strong

Solutions on p. S36

12.5 Exercises

· ·

Objective A

For Exercises 1–4, use the compound interest formula $P = A(1 + i)^n$ given in this section. Round answers to the nearest dollar or year.

1. The Prime Investment Club deposits $5000 into an account that earns 9% annual interest compounded monthly. What is the value of the investment after 2 years?

$5982

2. An insurance broker deposits $4000 into an account that earns 7% annual interest compounded monthly. In approximately how many years will the investment be worth $8000?

10 years

3. A manager estimates that in 4 years the company will need to purchase a new bottling machine at a cost of $25,000. How much money must be deposited in an account that earns 10% annual interest compounded monthly so that the value of the account in 4 years will be $25,000?

$16,786

4. The comptroller of a company has determined that it will be necessary to purchase a new computer in 3 years. The estimated cost of the computer is $10,000. How much money must be deposited in an account that earns 9% annual interest compounded quarterly so that the value of the account in 3 years will be $10,000?

$7657

For Exercises 5–8, use the exponential decay equation $A = A_0(0.5)^{t/k}$ given in this section. Round answers to the nearest tenth.

5. An isotope of technetium is used to prepare images of internal body organs. This isotope has a half-life of approximately 6 h. If a patient is injected with 30 mg of this isotope, how long (in hours) will it take for the technetium level to reach 20 mg?

3.5 h

6. Iodine-131 has a half-life of approximately 8 days and is used to study the functioning of the thyroid gland. If a patient is given an injection that contains 8 micrograms of iodine-131, how long (in days) will it take for the iodine level to reach 5 micrograms?

5.4 days

7. A sample of promethium-147 (used in some luminous paints) contains 25 mg. One year later, the sample contains 18.95 mg. What is the half-life of promethium-147, in years?
2.5 years

8. Francium-223 is a very rare radioactive isotope discovered in 1939 by Marguerite Percy. In a laboratory, a 3-microgram sample of francium-223 will decay to 2.54 micrograms in 5 min. What is the half-life of francium-223, in minutes?
20.8 min

9. The percent, P, of correct welds a student can make increases with practice according to the equation $P = 100(1 - 0.75^t)$, where t is the time in weeks. To the nearest week, how many weeks of practice are necessary before a student will make 80% of the welds correctly?
6 weeks

10. The training division of a large corporation has determined that the percent, P, of correct responses for new employees on a product knowledge test can be modeled by the equation $P = 100(1 - 0.8^t)$, where t is the time in days. To the nearest percent, what percent of the questions will the employee answer correctly after 10 days of training?
89%

For Exercises 11 and 12, use the equation $pH = -\log(H^+)$ studied in this section.

11. Find the pH of the digestive solution of the stomach, for which the hydrogen ion concentration is 0.045.
1.35

12. Find the hydrogen ion concentration of cow's milk, which has an approximate pH of 6.6.
2.5×10^{-7}

For Exercises 13 and 14, use the equation $\log P = -kd$, which gives the relationship between the percent, P (as a decimal), of light passing through a substance and its thickness, d.

13. The value of k for a swimming pool is approximately 0.05. At what depth (in meters) will the percent of light be 75% of the light at the surface of the pool?
2.5 m

14. The constant k for a piece of blue stained glass is 20. What percent of light will pass through a piece of this glass that is 0.005 m thick?
79.4%

For Exercises 15 and 16, use the equation $M = \log\dfrac{I_1}{I_0}$ given in this section.

15. An earthquake that occurred in China in 1978 measured 8.2 on the Richter scale. In 1988, an earthquake in Armenia measured 6.9 on the Richter scale. How many times as strong was China's earthquake?
20 times

16. In October 1989, an earthquake of magnitude 7.1 on the Richter scale struck San Francisco, California. In January 1994, an earthquake measuring 6.6 on the Richter scale occurred in the San Fernando Valley in California. How many times as strong was the San Francisco earthquake as compared with the San Fernando Valley earthquake?
3.2 times

For Exercises 17 and 18, use the equation $M = \log A + 3\log(8t) - 2.92$ given in this section.

17. Find the magnitude of an earthquake that has a seismogram with an amplitude of 30 mm and for which $t = 21$ s.
5.2

18. Find the magnitude of an earthquake that has a seismogram with an amplitude of 28 mm and for which $t = 28$ s.
5.6

For Exercises 19 and 20, use the equation $D = 10(\log I + 16)$, where D is the number of decibels of a sound and I is the power of the sound in watts.

19. Find the number of decibels of normal conversation. The power of the sound of normal conversation is approximately 3.2×10^{-10} watts.
65 decibels

20. The loudest sound made by any animal is made by the blue whale and can be heard over 500 mi away. The power of the sound made by the blue whale is 630 watts. Find the number of decibels of the sound emitted by the blue whale.
188 decibels

Astronomers use the distance modulus formula $M = 5\log r - 5$, where M is the distance modulus of a star and r is the distance from Earth to the star in parsecs (1 parsec = 1.918×10^{13} mi). Use this formula for Exercises 21 to 24.

21. The distance modulus of the star Betelgeuse is 5.89. How many parsecs from Earth is this star?
150.7 parsecs

22. The distance modulus of Alpha Centauri is -1.11. How many parsecs from Earth is this star?
6.0 parsecs

23. The distance modulus of the star Antares is 5.4, which is twice that of the star Pollux. Is Antares twice as far from Earth as Pollux? If not, how many times as far from Earth is Antares as compared with Pollux?

    no; 3.5 times as far

24. If one star has a distance modulus of 2 and a second star has a distance modulus of 6, is the second star three times as far from Earth as the first star?

    no; 6.3 times as far

The formula $T = 14.29 \ln(0.00411r + 1)$ is one model for the time, T (in years), before our natural oil resources, r (in billions of barrels of oil), will be depleted. Use this formula for Exercises 25 and 26.

25. According to this model, how many barrels of oil are necessary for our natural oil resources to last 20 more years?

    742.9 billion barrels

26. According to this model, how many barrels of oil are necessary for our natural oil resources to last 50 more years?

    7,805.5 billion barrels

APPLYING THE CONCEPTS

27. Some banks now use continuous compounding of an amount invested. In this case, the equation that relates the value of an initial investment of A dollars after t years at an annual interest rate of $r\%$ is given by $P = Ae^{rt}$. Using this equation, find the value after 5 years of an investment of $2500 into an account that earns 5% annual interest.

    $3210.06

28. Using the continuous compounding interest formula in Exercise 27, find how many years it will take an investment to double if the annual interest rate is 6%. Does the time it takes the investment to double in value depend on the amount of the initial investment?

    11.6 years; no

29. Solve for r: $T = 14.29 \ln(0.00411r + 1)$

    $r = 243.31(e^{T/14.29} - 1)$

30. Solve for r: $M = 5 \log r - 5$

    $r = 10^{(M + 5)/5}$

31. If $M = 5 \log r_1 - 5$ and $2M = 5 \log r_2 - 5$, express r_1 in terms of r_2.

    $r_1 = \sqrt{10 r_2}$

Focus on Problem Solving

Proof by Contradiction

The four-step plan for solving problems that we have used before is restated here.

1. Understand the problem.
2. Devise a plan.
3. Carry out the plan.
4. Review the solution.

One of the techniques that can be used in the second step is a method called *proof by contradiction*. In this method you assume that the conditions of the problem you are trying to solve can be met and then show that your assumption leads to a condition you already know is not true.

To illustrate this method, suppose we try to prove that $\sqrt{2}$ is a rational number. We begin by recalling that a rational number is one that can be written as the quotient of integers. Therefore, let a and b be two integers with no common factors. If $\sqrt{2}$ is a rational number, then

$$\sqrt{2} = \frac{a}{b}$$

$$(\sqrt{2})^2 = \left(\frac{a}{b}\right)^2 \qquad \bullet \text{ Square each side.}$$

$$2 = \frac{a^2}{b^2}$$

$$2b^2 = a^2 \qquad \bullet \text{ Multiply each side by } b^2.$$

From the last equation, a^2 is an even number. Because a^2 is an even number, a is an even number. Now divide each side of the last equation by 2.

$$2b^2 = a^2 = a \cdot a$$

$$b^2 = a \cdot x \qquad \qquad \bullet \ x = \frac{a}{2}$$

Because a is an even number, $a \cdot x$ is an even number. Because $a \cdot x$ is an even number, b^2 is an even number, and this in turn means that b is an even number. This result, however, contradicts the assumption that a and b are two integers with no common factors. Because this assumption is now known not to be true, we conclude that our original assumption, that $\sqrt{2}$ is a rational number, is false. This proves that $\sqrt{2}$ is an irrational number.

Try a proof by contradiction for the following problem: "Is it possible to write numbers using each of the digits 0, 1, 2, 3, 4, 5, 6, 7, 8, and 9 exactly once so that the sum of the numbers is exactly 100?"* Here are some suggestions. First note that the sum of the 10 digits is 45. This means that some of the digits used must be tens digits. Let x be the sum of those digits.

1. What is the sum of the remaining units digits?
2. Express "the sum of the units digits and the tens digits equals 100" as an equation. (*Note:* Writing an equation is one of the possible problem-solving strategies.)
3. Solve the equation for x.
4. Explain why this result means that it is impossible to satisfy both conditions of the problem.

*G. Polya, *How to Solve It: A New Aspect of Mathematical Method,* copyright © 1957 by G. Polya. Reprinted by permission of Princeton University Press.

Projects and Group Activities

Fractals* Fractals have a wide variety of applications. They have been used to create special effects for movies such as *Star Trek II: The Wrath of Khan* and to explain the behavior of some biological and economic systems. One aspect of fractals that has fascinated mathematicians is that they apparently have *fractional dimension*.

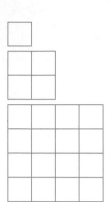

To understand the idea of fractional dimension, one must first understand the terms "scale factor" and "size." Consider a unit square (a square of length 1). By joining four of these squares, we can create another square, the length of which is 2, and the size of which is 4. (Here, size = number of square units.) Four of these larger squares can in turn be put together to make a third square of length 4 and size 16. This process of grouping together four squares can in theory be done an infinite number of times; yet at each step, the following quantities will be the same:

$$\text{scale factor} = \frac{\text{new length}}{\text{old length}} \qquad \text{size ratio} = \frac{\text{new size}}{\text{old size}}$$

Consider the unit square as Step 1, the four unit squares as Step 2, etc.

1. Calculate the scale factor going from **a.** Step 1 to Step 2, **b.** Step 2 to Step 3, and **c.** Step 3 to Step 4.

2. Calculate the size ratio going from **a.** Step 1 to Step 2, **b.** Step 2 to Step 3, and **c.** Step 3 to Step 4.

3. What is **a.** the scale factor and **b.** the size ratio going from Step n to Step $n + 1$?

Mathematicians have defined dimension using the formula $d = \dfrac{\log(\text{size ratio})}{\log(\text{scale factor})}$.

For the squares discussed above, $d = \dfrac{\log(\text{size ratio})}{\log(\text{scale factor})} = \dfrac{\log 4}{\log 2} = 2$.

So by this definition of dimension, squares are two-dimensional figures.

Now consider a unit cube (Step 1). Group eight unit cubes to form a cube that is 2 units on each side (Step 2). Group eight of the cubes from Step 2 to form a cube that is 4 units on each side (Step 3).

4. Calculate **a.** the scale factor and **b.** the size ratio for this process.

5. Show that the cubes are three-dimensional figures.

In each of the above examples, if the process is continued indefinitely, we still have a square or a cube. Consider a process that is more difficult to envision. Let Step 1 be an equilateral triangle whose base has length 1 unit, and let Step 2 be a grouping of three of these equilateral triangles, such that the space between them is another equilateral triangle with a base of length 1 unit. Three shapes from Step 2 are arranged with an equilateral triangle in their center, and so on. It is hard to imagine the result if this is done an infinite number of times, but mathematicians have shown that the result is a single figure of fractional dimension. (Similar processes have been used to create fascinating artistic patterns and to explain scientific phenomena.)

6. Show that for this process **a.** the scale factor is 2 and **b.** the size ratio is 3.

7. Calculate the dimension of the fractal. (Note that it is a *fractional* dimension!)

*Adapted with permission from "Student Math Notes," by Tami Martin, News Bulletin, November 1991.

Graphing Logarithmic Functions Using a Graphing Calculator

A graphing calculator can be used to draw the graphs of logarithmic functions. For the graphs below, a suggested viewing window will be given as [XMIN, XMAX] by [YMIN, YMAX], but the keystrokes for that window will not be shown.

To graph a logarithmic function, first note that there are two logarithm keys, $\boxed{\text{LOG}}$ and $\boxed{\text{LN}}$. The first key gives logarithms to the base 10 and the second gives the values of natural logarithms. The graph of $y = \ln x$ is shown at the left.

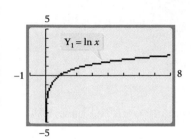

$Y_1 = \ln x$

CALCULATOR NOTE

The Appendix: Guidelines for Using Graphing Calculators contains keystroking suggestions to use with this project.

To graph a logarithmic function other than base 10 or base e, the change of base formula is used. Here is the change of base formula discussed earlier.

$$\log_a N = \frac{\log_b N}{\log_b a}$$

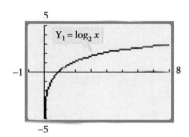

$Y_1 = \log_2 x$

To graph $y = \log_2 x$, we can change from base 2 logarithms to the equivalent base 10 logarithms* as follows.

$$y = \log_2 x = \frac{\log_{10} x}{\log_{10} 2} \qquad \bullet \ a = 2, b = 10, N = x$$

We now graph the equivalent equation $y = \dfrac{\log x}{\log 2}$ using a viewing window of $[-1, 8]$ by $[-5, 5]$.

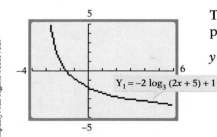

$Y_1 = -2 \log_3 (2x + 5) + 1$

The graphs of more complicated functions involving logarithms are produced in much the same way as was shown above. To graph $y = -2 \log_3(2x + 5) + 1$, enter into the calculator $y = \dfrac{-2 \log(2x + 5)}{\log 3} + 1$.

*We are using base 10 here. You can also produce the graphs by using natural logarithms.

Chapter Summary

Key Words

A function of the form $f(x) = b^x$ is an *exponential function*, where b is a positive real number not equal to one. The number b is the *base* of the exponential function.

For $b > 0$, $b \neq 1$, $y = \log_b x$ is equivalent to $x = b^y$.

$\log_b x$ is the logarithm of x to the base b.

Common logarithms are logarithms to the base 10. (We usually omit the base 10 when writing the common logarithm of a number.)

The *mantissa* is the decimal part of a common logarithm. The *characteristic* is the integer part of a common logarithm.

When e (the base of the natural exponential function) is used as a base of a logarithm, the logarithm is referred to as the natural logarithm and is abbreviated $\ln x$.

An *exponential equation* is an equation in which the variable occurs in the exponent.

Essential Rules

The Logarithm Property of the Product of Two Numbers

For any positive real numbers x, y, and b, $b \neq 1$,
$\log_b(xy) = \log_b x + \log_b y$.

The Logarithm Property of the Quotient of Two Numbers

For any positive real numbers x, y, and b, $b \neq 1$,
$\log_b \frac{x}{y} = \log_b x - \log_b y$.

The Logarithm Property of the Power of a Number

For any positive real numbers x and b, $b \neq 1$, and for any real number r, $\log_b x^r = r \log_b x$.

Additional Properties of Logarithms

Let x, y, and b be positive and real numbers with $b \neq 1$. Then
$\log_b 1 = 0$.
If $\log_b x = \log_b y$, then $x = y$.

Change-of-Base Formula

$\log_a N = \frac{\log_b N}{\log_b a}$

1–1 Property of Exponential Functions

If $b^x = b^y$, then $x = y$.

Chapter Review

1. Evaluate $f(x) = e^{x-2}$ at $x = 2$.
  1   [12.1A]

2. Write $\log_5 25 = 2$ in exponential form.
  $5^2 = 25$ [12.2A]

3. Graph: $f(x) = 3^{-x} + 2$

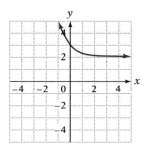

[12.1B]

4. Graph: $f(x) = \log_3(x - 1)$

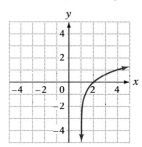

[12.3A]

5. Write $\log_3 \sqrt[5]{x^2 y^4}$ in expanded form.
  $\dfrac{2}{5}\log_3 x + \dfrac{4}{5}\log_3 y$ [12.2B]

6. Write $2\log_3 x - 5\log_3 y$ as a single logarithm with a coefficient of 1.
  $\log_3 \dfrac{x^2}{y^5}$ [12.2B]

7. Solve: $27^{2x+4} = 81^{x-3}$
  -12 [12.4A]

8. Solve: $\log_5 \dfrac{7x+2}{3x} = 1$
  $\dfrac{1}{4}$ [12.4B]

9. Find $\log_6 22$. Round to the nearest ten-thousandth.
  1.7251   [12.2C]

10. Solve: $\log_2 x = 5$
  32   [12.2A]

11. Solve: $\log_3(x + 2) = 4$
  79   [12.4B]

12. Solve: $\log_{10} x = 3$
  1000   [12.2A]

13. Write $\dfrac{1}{3}(\log_7 x + 4\log_7 y)$ as a single logarithm with a coefficient of 1.
  $\log_7 \sqrt[3]{xy^4}$ [12.2B]

14. Write $\log_8 \sqrt{\dfrac{x^5}{y^3}}$ in expanded form.
  $\dfrac{1}{2}(5\log_8 x - 3\log_8 y)$ [12.2B]

15. Write $2^5 = 32$ in logarithmic form.
  $\log_2 32 = 5$ [12.2A]

16. Find $\log_3 1.6$. Round to the nearest ten-thousandth.
  0.4278   [12.2C]

17. Solve $3^{x+2} = 5$ for x. Round to the nearest thousandth.
-0.535 [12.4A]

18. Evaluate $f(x) = \left(\dfrac{2}{3}\right)^{x+2}$ at $x = -3$.
$\dfrac{3}{2}$ [12.1A]

19. Solve: $\log_8(x + 2) - \log_8 x = \log_8 4$
$\dfrac{2}{3}$ [12.4B]

20. Solve: $\log_6(2x) = \log_6 2 + \log_6(3x - 4)$
2 [12.4B]

21. Graph: $f(x) = \left(\dfrac{2}{3}\right)^{x+1}$

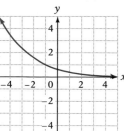

[12.1B]

22. Graph: $f(x) = \log_2(2x - 1)$

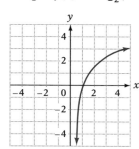

[12.3A]

23. Use the compound interest formula $P = A(1 + i)^n$, where A is the original value of an investment, i is the interest rate per compounding period, and n is the number of compounding periods, to find the value of an investment after 2 years. The amount of the investment is \$4000, and it is invested at 8% compounded monthly.
\$4692 [12.5A]

24. Using the Richter equation $M = \log\dfrac{I}{I_0}$, where M is the magnitude of an earthquake, I is the intensity of its shock waves, and I_0 is a constant, how many times as strong is an earthquake with magnitude 6 on the Richter scale as one with magnitude 3 on the scale?
1000 times [12.5A]

25. Use the exponential decay equation $A = A_0\left(\dfrac{1}{2}\right)^{t/k}$, where A is the amount of a radioactive material present after time t, k is the half-life, and A_0 is the original amount of radioactive material, to find the half-life of a material that decays from 25 mg to 15 mg in 20 days. Round to the nearest whole number.
27 days [12.5A]

26. The number of decibels, D, of a sound can be given by the equation $D = 10(\log I + 16)$, where I is the power of the sound measured in watts. Find the number of decibels of sound emitted from a busy street corner for which the power of the sound is 5×10^{-6} watts.
107 decibels [12.5A]

Chapter Test

1. Evaluate $f(x) = \left(\frac{2}{3}\right)^x$ at $x = 0$.

$f(0) = 1$ [12.1A]

2. Evaluate $f(x) = 3^{x+1}$ at $x = -2$.

$f(-2) = \frac{1}{3}$ [12.1A]

3. Graph: $f(x) = 2^x - 3$

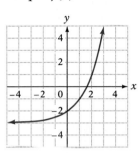

[12.1B]

4. Graph: $f(x) = 2^x + 2$

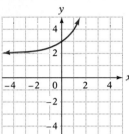

[12.1B]

5. Evaluate: $\log_4 16$

2   [12.2A]

6. Solve for x: $\log_3 x = -2$

$\frac{1}{9}$ [12.2A]

7. Graph: $f(x) = \log_2(2x)$

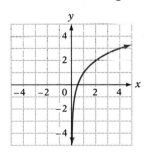

[12.3A]

8. Graph: $f(x) = \log_3(x + 1)$

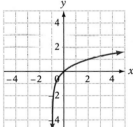

[12.3A]

9. Write $\log_6 \sqrt{xy^3}$ in expanded form.

$\frac{1}{2}(\log_6 x + 3\log_6 y)$ [12.2B]

10. Write $\frac{1}{2}(\log_3 x - \log_3 y)$ as a single logarithm with a coefficient of 1.

$\log_3 \sqrt{\dfrac{x}{y}}$ [12.2B]

11. Write $\ln\left(\dfrac{x}{\sqrt{z}}\right)$ in expanded form.

$\ln x - \dfrac{1}{2}\ln z$ [12.2B]

12. Write $3\ln x - \ln y - \dfrac{1}{2}\ln z$ as a single logarithm with a coefficient of 1.

$\ln\dfrac{x^3}{y\sqrt{z}}$ [12.2B]

13. Solve for x: $3^{7x+1} = 3^{4x-5}$

-2 [12.4A]

14. Solve for x: $8^x = 2^{x-6}$

-3 [12.4A]

15. Solve for x: $3^x = 17$

2.5789 [12.4A]

16. Solve for x: $\log x + \log(x-4) = \log 12$

6 [12.4B]

17. Solve for x: $\log_6 x + \log_6(x-1) = 1$

3 [12.4B]

18. Find $\log_5 9$.

1.3652 [12.2C]

19. Find $\log_3 19$.

2.6801 [12.2C]

20. Use the exponential decay equation $A = A_0\left(\dfrac{1}{2}\right)^{t/k}$, where A is the amount of a radioactive material present after time t, k is the half-life, and A_0 is the original amount of radioactive material, to find the half-life of a material that decays from 10 mg to 9 mg in 5 h. Round to the nearest whole number.

33 h [12.5A]

Cumulative Review

1. Solve: $4 - 2[x - 3(2 - 3x) - 4x] = 2x$
   $\dfrac{8}{7}$ [2.2C]

2. Find the equation of the line that contains the point $(2, -2)$ and is parallel to the line $2x - y = 5$.
   $y = 2x - 6$ [4.5A]

3. Factor: $4x^{2n} + 7x^n + 3$
   $(4x^n + 3)(x^n + 1)$ [7.3A/7.3B]

4. Simplify: $\dfrac{1 - \dfrac{5}{x} + \dfrac{6}{x^2}}{1 + \dfrac{1}{x} - \dfrac{6}{x^2}}$
   $\dfrac{x - 3}{x + 3}$ [8.3A]

5. Simplify: $\dfrac{\sqrt{xy}}{\sqrt{x} - \sqrt{y}}$
   $\dfrac{x\sqrt{y} + y\sqrt{x}}{x - y}$ [9.2D]

6. Solve by completing the square:
   $x^2 - 4x - 6 = 0$
   $2 + \sqrt{10}, 2 - \sqrt{10}$ [10.2A]

7. Find the unknown side of the triangle in the figure below.

   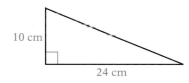

   26 cm   [9.4B]

8. Graph the solution set: $2x - y < 3$
   $x + y < 1$

   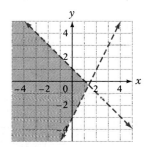

   [5.6A]

9. Solve by the addition method.
   $3x - y + z = 3$
   $x + y + 4z = 7$
   $3x - 2y + 3z = 8$
   $(0, -1, 2)$ [5.3B]

10. Subtract: $\dfrac{x - 4}{2 - x} - \dfrac{1 - 6x}{2x^2 - 7x + 6}$
    $-\dfrac{2x^2 - 17x + 13}{(x - 2)(2x - 3)}$ [8.2D]

11. Solve: $x^2 + 4x - 5 \le 0$
    $\{x | -5 \le x \le 1\}$ [10.6A]

12. Solve: $|2x - 5| \le 3$
    $\{x | 1 \le x \le 4\}$ [2.5B]

13. Graph: $f(x) = \left(\dfrac{1}{2}\right)^x + 1$

    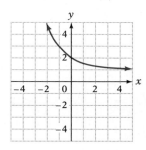

    [12.1B]

14. Graph: $f(x) = \log_2 x - 1$

    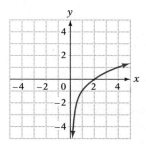

    [12.3A]

15. New carpet is installed in a room measuring 18 ft by 14 ft. Find the area of the room in square yards. ($9 \text{ ft}^2 = 1 \text{ yd}^2$)
28 yd² [3.2B]

16. Solve for x: $\log_5 x = 3$
125 [12.2A]

17. Write $3 \log_b x - 5 \log_b y$ as a single logarithm with a coefficient of 1.
$\log_b \dfrac{x^3}{y^5}$ [12.2B]

18. Find $\log_3 7$. Round to the nearest ten-thousandth.
1.7712 [12.2C]

19. Solve for x: $4^{5x-2} = 4^{3x+2}$
2 [12.4A]

20. Solve for x: $\log x + \log(2x + 3) = \log 2$
$\dfrac{1}{2}$ [12.4B]

21. A bank offers two types of checking accounts. One account has a charge of $5 per month plus 2 cents per check. The second account has a charge of $2 per month plus 8 cents per check. How many checks can a customer who has the second type of account write if it is to cost the customer less than the first type of checking account?
less than 50 checks [2.4C]

22. Find the cost per pound of a mixture made from 16 lb of chocolate that costs $4.00 per pound and 24 lb of chocolate that costs $2.50 per pound.
$3.10 [2.3A]

23. A plane can fly at a rate of 225 mph in calm air. Traveling with the wind, the plane flew 1000 mi in the same amount of time that it took to fly 800 mi against the wind. Find the rate of the wind.
25 mph [5.5A]

24. The distance (d) that a spring stretches varies directly as the force (f) used to stretch the spring. If a force of 20 lb stretches a spring 6 in., how far will a force of 34 lb stretch the spring?
10.2 in. [8.7A]

25. A carpenter purchased 80 ft of redwood and 140 ft of fir for a total cost of $67. A second purchase, at the same prices, included 140 ft of redwood and 100 ft of fir for a total cost of $81. Find the cost of redwood and of fir.
redwood: $.40 per foot; fir: $.25 per foot [5.5B]

26. The compound interest formula is $P = A(1 + i)^n$, where A is the original value of an investment, i is the interest rate per compounding period, n is the total number of compounding periods, and P is the value of the investment after n periods. Use the compound interest formula to find the number of years in which an investment of $5000 will double in value. The investment earns 9% annual interest and is compounded semiannually. Round to the nearest whole number.
8 years [12.5A]

Final Exam

1. Simplify:
   $12 - 8[3 - (-2)]^2 \div 5 - 3$
   -31 [1.3A]

2. Evaluate $\dfrac{a^2 - b^2}{a - b}$ when $a = 3$ and $b = -4$.
   -1 [1.4A]

3. Simplify: $5 - 2[3x - 7(2 - x) - 5x]$
   $-10x + 33$ [1.4D]

4. Solve: $\dfrac{3}{4}x - 2 = 4$
   8   [2.2A]

5. Solve: $8 - |5 - 3x| = 1$
   $-\dfrac{2}{3}, 4$ [2.5A]

6. Find the volume of a sphere with a diameter of 8 ft. Round to the nearest tenth.
   268.1 ft³   [3.3A]

7. Graph $2x - 3y = 9$ using the x- and y-intercepts.

   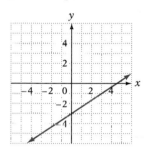

   [4.2B]

8. Find the equation of the line containing the points $(3, -2)$ and $(1, 4)$.
   $y = -3x + 7$ [4.4B]

9. Find the equation of the line that contains the point $(-2, 1)$ and is perpendicular to the line $3x - 2y = 6$.
   $y = -\dfrac{2}{3}x - \dfrac{1}{3}$ [4.5A]

10. Simplify: $2a[5 - a(2 - 3a) - 2a] + 3a^2$
    $6a^3 - 5a^2 + 10a$ [6.3A]

11. Factor: $8 - x^3y^3$
    $(2 - xy)(4 + 2xy + x^2y^2)$ [7.4B]

12. Factor: $x - y - x^3 + x^2y$
    $(x - y)(1 - x)(1 + x)$ [7.4D]

13. Divide: $(2x^3 - 7x^2 + 4) \div (2x - 3)$
    $x^2 - 2x - 3 - \dfrac{5}{2x - 3}$ [6.4A]

14. Divide: $\dfrac{x^2 - 3x}{2x^2 - 3x - 5} \div \dfrac{4x - 12}{4x^2 - 4}$
    $\dfrac{x(x - 1)}{2x - 5}$ [8.1C]

15. Subtract: $\dfrac{x - 2}{x + 2} - \dfrac{x + 3}{x - 3}$
    $\dfrac{-10x}{(x + 2)(x - 3)}$ [8.2D]

16. Simplify: $\dfrac{\dfrac{3}{x} + \dfrac{1}{x + 4}}{\dfrac{1}{x} + \dfrac{3}{x + 4}}$
    $\dfrac{x + 3}{x + 1}$ [8.3A]

17. Solve: $\dfrac{5}{x-2} - \dfrac{5}{x^2-4} = \dfrac{1}{x+2}$

$-\dfrac{7}{4}$ [8.4A]

18. Solve $a_n = a_1 + (n-1)d$ for d.

$d = \dfrac{a_n - a_1}{n-1}$ [8.5A]

19. Simplify: $\left(\dfrac{4x^2y^{-1}}{3x^{-1}y}\right)^{-2}\left(\dfrac{2x^{-1}y^2}{9x^{-2}y^2}\right)^3$

$\dfrac{y^4}{162x^3}$ [6.1B]

20. Simplify: $\left(\dfrac{3x^{2/3}y^{1/2}}{6x^2y^{4/3}}\right)^6$

$\dfrac{1}{64x^8y^5}$ [9.1A]

21. Subtract: $x\sqrt{18x^2y^3} - y\sqrt{50x^4y}$

$-2x^2y\sqrt{2y}$ [9.2B]

22. Simplify: $\dfrac{\sqrt{16x^5y^4}}{\sqrt{32xy^7}}$

$\dfrac{x^2\sqrt{2y}}{2y^2}$ [9.2D]

23. Simplify: $\dfrac{3}{2+i}$

$\dfrac{6}{5} - \dfrac{3}{5}i$ [9.3D]

24. Write a quadratic equation that has integer coefficients and has solution $-\dfrac{1}{2}$ and 2.

$2x^2 - 3x - 2 = 0$ [10.1B]

25. Solve by using the quadratic formula:
$2x^2 - 3x - 1 = 0$

$\dfrac{3+\sqrt{17}}{4}, \dfrac{3-\sqrt{17}}{4}$ [10.3A]

26. Solve: $x^{2/3} - x^{1/3} - 6 = 0$

$-8, 27$ [10.4A]

27. Graph: $f(x) = -x^2 + 4$

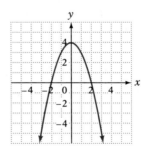

[11.2A]

28. Graph: $\dfrac{x^2}{16} + \dfrac{y^2}{4} = 1$

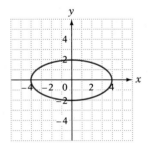

[11.6C]

29. Solve: $\dfrac{2}{x} - \dfrac{2}{2x+3} = 1$

$-2, \dfrac{3}{2}$ [10.4C]

30. Find the inverse of the function
$f(x) = \dfrac{2}{3}x - 4$.

$f^{-1}(x) = \dfrac{3}{2}x + 6$ [11.5B]

31. Solve by the addition method:
$3x - 2y = 1$
$5x - 3y = 3$
$(3, 4)$ [5.3A]

32. Evaluate the determinant:
$\begin{vmatrix} 3 & 4 \\ -1 & 2 \end{vmatrix}$

10 [5.4A]

33. Solve: $2 - 3x < 6$ and $2x + 1 > 4$

$\left\{ x \mid x > \dfrac{3}{2} \right\}$ [2.4B]

34. Solve: $|2x + 5| < 3$

$\{ x \mid -4 < x < -1 \}$ [2.5B]

35. Graph the solution set: $3x + 2y > 6$

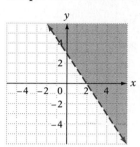

[4.6A]

36. Graph: $f(x) = 3^{-x} - 2$

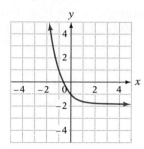

[12.1B]

37. Graph: $f(x) = \log_2(x + 1)$

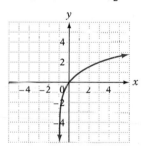

[12.3A]

38. Write $2(\log_2 a - \log_2 b)$ as a single logarithm with a coefficient of 1.

$\log_2 \dfrac{a^2}{b^2}$ [12.2B]

39. Solve for x: $\log_3 x - \log_3(x - 3) = \log_3 2$

6 [12.4B]

40. An average score of 70–79 in a history class receives a C grade. A student has grades of 64, 58, 82, and 77 on four history tests. Find the range of scores on the fifth test that will give the student a C grade for the course.

$69 \le x \le 100$ [2.4C]

41. A jogger and a cyclist set out at 8 A.M. from the same point headed in the same direction. The average speed of the cyclist is two and a half times the average speed of the jogger. In 2 h, the cyclist is 24 mi ahead of the jogger. How far did the cyclist ride in that time?

40 mi [2.3D]

42. You have a total of $12,000 invested in two simple interest accounts. On one account, a money market fund, the annual simple interest rate is 8.5%. On the other account, a tax free bond fund, the annual simple interest rate is 6.4%. The total annual interest earned by the two accounts is $936. How much do you have invested in each account?
    $8000 @ 8.5%; $4000 @ 6.4%   [2.3C]

43. The length of a rectangle is 1 ft less than three times the width. The area of the rectangle is 140 ft². Find the length and width of the rectangle.
    width: 7 ft; length: 20 ft   [10.5A]

44. Three hundred shares of a utility stock earn a yearly dividend of $486. How many additional shares of the utility stock would give a total dividend income of $810?
    200   [8.4B]

45. An account executive traveled 45 mi by car and then an additional 1050 mi by plane. The rate of the plane was seven times the rate of the car. The total time for the trip was $3\frac{1}{4}$ h. Find the rate of the plane.
    420 mph   [8.6B]

46. An object is dropped from the top of a building. Find the distance the object has fallen when the speed reaches 75 ft/s. Use the equation $v = \sqrt{64d}$, where v is the speed of the object and d is the distance. Round to the nearest whole number.
    88 ft   [9.4B]

47. A small plane made a trip of 660 mi in 5 h. The plane traveled the first 360 mi at a constant rate before increasing its speed by 30 mph. Then it traveled another 300 mi at the increased speed. Find the rate of the plane for the first 360 mi.
    120 mph   [8.6B]

48. The intensity (L) of a light source is inversely proportional to the square of the distance (d) from the source. If the intensity is 8 foot-candles at a distance of 20 ft, what is the intensity when the distance is 4 ft?
    200 foot-candles   [8.7A]

49. A motorboat traveling with the current can go 30 mi in 2 h. Against the current, it takes 3 h to go the same distance. Find the rate of the motorboat in calm water and the rate of the current.
    rate of the boat in calm water: 12.5 mph;
    rate of the current: 2.5 mph   [5.5A]

50. An investor deposits $4000 into an account that earns 9% annual interest compounded monthly. Use the compound interest formula $P = A(1 + i)^n$, where A is the original value of the investment, i is the interest rate per compounding period, n is the total number of compounding periods, and P is the value of the investment after n periods, to find the value of the investment after 2 years. Round to the nearest cent.
    $4785.65   [12.5A]

Appendix: Guidelines for Using Graphing Calculators

TEXAS INSTRUMENTS TI-83

To evaluate an expression

a. Press the $\boxed{Y=}$ key. A menu showing $\backslash Y_1 =$ through $\backslash Y_7 =$ will be displayed vertically with a blinking cursor to the right of $\backslash Y_1 =$. Press $\boxed{CLEAR}$, if necessary, to delete an unwanted expression.

b. Input the expression to be evaluated. For example, to input the expression $-3a^2b - 4c$, use the following keystrokes:

$\boxed{(-)}$ 3 $\boxed{ALPHA}$ A $\boxed{\wedge}$ 2 $\boxed{ALPHA}$ B $\boxed{-}$ 4 $\boxed{ALPHA}$ C $\boxed{2nd}$ QUIT

Note the difference between the keys for a negative sign $\boxed{(-)}$ and a *minus* sign $\boxed{-}$.

c. Store the value of each variable that will be used in the expression. For example, to evaluate the expression above when $a = 3$, $b = -2$, and $c = -4$, use the following keystrokes:

3 $\boxed{STO\triangleright}$ $\boxed{ALPHA}$ A $\boxed{ENTER}$ $\boxed{(-)}$ 2 $\boxed{STO\triangleright}$ $\boxed{ALPHA}$ B $\boxed{ENTER}$ $\boxed{(-)}$ 4 $\boxed{STO\triangleright}$ $\boxed{ALPHA}$ C $\boxed{ENTER}$

These steps store the value of each variable.

d. Press $\boxed{VARS}$ $\boxed{\triangleright}$ $\boxed{1}$ $\boxed{1}$ $\boxed{ENTER}$. The value for the expression, Y_1, for the given values is displayed; in this case, $Y_1 = 70$.

To graph a function

a. Press the $\boxed{Y=}$ key. A menu showing $\backslash Y_1 =$ through $\backslash Y_7 =$ will be displayed vertically with a blinking cursor to the right of $\backslash Y_1 =$. Press $\boxed{CLEAR}$, if necessary, to delete an unwanted expression.

b. Input the expression for each function that is to be graphed. Press $\boxed{X,T,\theta,n}$ to input x. For example, to input $y = x^3 + 2x^2 - 5x - 6$, use the following keystrokes:

$\boxed{X,T,\theta,n}$ $\boxed{\wedge}$ 3 $\boxed{+}$ 2 $\boxed{X,T,\theta,n}$ $\boxed{\wedge}$ 2 $\boxed{-}$ 5 $\boxed{X,T,\theta,n}$ $\boxed{-}$ 6

c. Set the domain and range by pressing $\boxed{WINDOW}$. Enter the values for the minimum x-value (Xmin), the maximum x-value (Xmax), the distance between tick marks on the x-axis (Xscl), the minimum y-value (Ymin), the maximum y-value (Ymax), and the distance between tick marks on the y-axis (Yscl). Now press $\boxed{GRAPH}$. For the graph shown at the left, Xmin = -10, Xmax = 10, Xscl = 1, Ymin = -10, Ymax = 10, and Yscl = 1. This is called the standard viewing rectangle. Pressing $\boxed{ZOOM}$ $\boxed{6}$ is a quick way to set the calculator to the standard viewing rectangle. *Note:* This will also immediately graph the function in that window.

d. Press the $\boxed{Y=}$ key. The equal sign has a black rectangle around it. This indicates that the function is active and will be graphed when the $\boxed{GRAPH}$ key is pressed. A function is deactivated by using the arrow keys. Move the cursor over the equal sign and press $\boxed{ENTER}$. When the cursor is moved to the right, the black rectangle will not be present and that equation will not be active.

e. Graphing some radical equations requires special care. To graph the function $y = \sqrt{2x + 3}$, enter the following keystrokes:

$\boxed{Y=}$ $\boxed{2nd}$ $\sqrt{}$ 2 $\boxed{X,T,\theta,n}$ $\boxed{+}$ 3 $\boxed{)}$

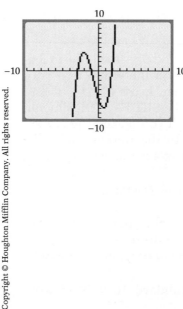

The graph is shown below.

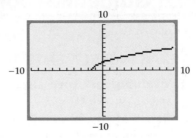

To display the x-coordinates of rectangular coordinates as integers

a. Set the viewing window as follows: Xmin = −47, Xmax = 47, Xscl = 10, Ymin = −31, Ymax = 31, Yscl = 10.

b. Graph the function and use the TRACE feature. Press ⟨TRACE⟩ and then move the cursor with the ◁ and ▷ keys. The values of x and $y = f(x)$ displayed on the bottom of the screen are the coordinates of a point on the graph.

To display the x-coordinates of rectangular coordinates in tenths

a. Set the viewing window as follows: ⟨ZOOM⟩ ⟨4⟩

b. Graph the function and use the ⟨TRACE⟩ feature. Press ⟨TRACE⟩ and then move the cursor with the ◁ and ▷ keys. The values of x and $y = f(x)$ displayed on the bottom of the screen are the coordinates of a point on the graph.

To evaluate a function for a given value of x, or to produce ordered pairs of a function

a. Input the equation; for example, input $Y_1 = 2x^3 − 3x + 2$.

b. Press ⟨2nd⟩ QUIT.

c. Input a value for x; for example, to input 3 press 3 ⟨STO▷⟩ ⟨X,T,θ,n⟩ ⟨ENTER⟩.

d. Press ⟨VARS⟩ ⟨▷⟩ ⟨1⟩ ⟨1⟩ ⟨ENTER⟩. The value for the expression, Y_1, for the given x-value is displayed, in this case, $Y_1 = 47$. An ordered pair of the function is (3, 47).

e. Repeat steps **c.** and **d.** to produce as many pairs as desired. The TABLE feature of the *TI-83* can also be used to determine pairs.

ZOOM FEATURES

To zoom in or out on a graph

a. Here are two methods of using ZOOM. The first method uses the built-in features of the calculator. Move the cursor to a point on the graph that is of interest. Press ⟨ZOOM⟩. The ZOOM menu will appear. Press ⟨2⟩ ⟨ENTER⟩ to zoom in on the graph by the amount shown under the SET FACTORS menu. The center of the new graph is the location at which you placed the cursor. Press ⟨ZOOM⟩ ⟨3⟩ ⟨ENTER⟩ to zoom out on the graph by the amount under the SET FACTORS menu. (The SET FACTORS menu is accessed by pressing ⟨ZOOM⟩ ⟨▷⟩ ⟨4⟩.)

b. The second method uses the ZBOX option under the ZOOM menu. To use this method, press ⟨ZOOM⟩ ⟨1⟩. A cursor will appear on the graph. Use the arrow keys to move the cursor to a portion of the graph that is of interest. Press ⟨ENTER⟩. Now use the arrow keys to draw a box around the portion of the graph you wish to see. Press ⟨ENTER⟩. The portion of the graph defined by the box will be drawn.

c. Pressing ⟨ZOOM⟩ ⟨6⟩ resets the window to the standard 10 × 10 viewing window.

SOLVING EQUATIONS

This discussion is based on the fact that the solution of an equation can be related to the x-intercepts of a graph. For instance, the real solutions of the equation $x^2 = x + 1$ are the x-intercepts of the graph of $f(x) = x^2 - x - 1$, which are the zeros of f.

To solve $x^2 = x + 1$, rewrite the equation with all terms on one side. The equation is now $x^2 - x - 1 = 0$. Think of this equation as $Y_1 = x^2 - x - 1$. The x-intercepts of the graph of Y_1 are the solutions of the equation $x^2 = x + 1$.

a. Enter $x^2 - x - 1$ into Y_1.

b. Graph the equation. You may need to adjust the viewing window so that the x-intercepts are visible.

c. Press $\boxed{\text{2nd}}$ CALC $\boxed{2}$.

d. Move the cursor to a point on the curve that is to the left of an x-intercept. Press $\boxed{\text{ENTER}}$.

e. Move the cursor to a point on the curve that is to the right of an x-intercept. Press $\boxed{\text{ENTER}}$.

f. Press $\boxed{\text{ENTER}}$.

g. The root is shown as the x-coordinate on the bottom of the screen; in this case, the root is approximately -0.618034. To find the next intercept, repeat steps **c.** through **f.** The SOLVER feature under the MATH menu can also be used to find solutions of equations.

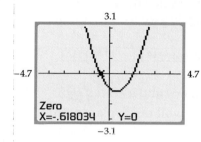

SOLVING SYSTEMS OF EQUATIONS IN TWO VARIABLES

To solve a system of equations

To solve $\quad \begin{aligned} y &= x^2 - 1 \\ \tfrac{1}{2}x + y &= 1 \end{aligned} \quad$,

a. Solve each equation for y.

b. Enter the first equation as Y_1. For instance, $Y_1 = x^2 - 1$.

c. Enter the second equation as Y_2. For instance, $Y_2 = 1 - \tfrac{1}{2}x$.

d. Graph both equations. (*Note:* The point of intersection must appear on the screen. It may be necessary to adjust the viewing window so that the point(s) of intersection are displayed.)

e. Press $\boxed{\text{2nd}}$ CALC $\boxed{5}$.

f. Move the cursor to the left of the first point of intersection. Press $\boxed{\text{ENTER}}$.

g. Move the cursor to the right of the first point of intersection. Press $\boxed{\text{ENTER}}$.

h. Press $\boxed{\text{ENTER}}$.

i. The first point of intersection is $(-1.686141, 1.8430703)$.

j. Repeat steps **e.** through **h.** for each point of intersection.

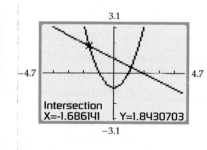

FINDING MINIMUM OR MAXIMUM VALUES OF A FUNCTION

a. Enter the function into Y_1. The equation $y = x^2 - x - 1$ is used here.

b. Graph the equation. You may need to adjust the viewing window so that the maximum or minimum points are visible.

c. Press $\boxed{\text{2nd}}$ CALC $\boxed{3}$ to determine a minimum value or press $\boxed{\text{2nd}}$ CALC $\boxed{4}$ to determine a maximum value.

d. Move the cursor to a point on the curve that is to the left of the minimum (maximum). Press $\boxed{\text{ENTER}}$.

e. Move the cursor to a point on the curve that is to the right of the minimum (maximum). Press ENTER.

f. Press ENTER.

g. The minimum (maximum) is shown as the y-coordinate on the bottom of the screen; in this case the minimum value is -1.25.

SHARP EL-9600

To evaluate an expression

a. The SOLVER mode of the calculator is used to evaluate expressions. To enter SOLVER mode, press 2ndF SOLVER CL. The expression $-3a^2b - 4c$ must be entered as the equation $-3a^2b - 4c = t$. The letter t can be any letter other than one used in the expression. Use the following keystrokes to input $-3a^2b - 4c = t$:

(−) 3 ALPHA A a^b 2 ▷ ALPHA B − 4 ALPHA C ALPHA = ALPHA T ENTER

Note the difference between the keys for a *negative* sign (−) and a *minus* sign.

b. After you press ENTER, variables used in the equation will be displayed on the screen. To evaluate the expression for $a = 3$, $b = -2$, and $c = -4$, input each value, pressing ENTER after each number. When the cursor moves to T, press 2ndF EXE. T = 70 will appear on the screen. This is the value of the expression. To evaluate the expression again for different values of a, b, and c, press 2ndF QUIT and then 2ndF SOLVER.

c. Press [⊞⊟⊠⊘] to return to normal operation.

To graph a function

a. Press the Y= key. The screen will show Y1 through Y8.

b. Input the expression for a function that is to be graphed. Press X/θ/T/n to enter an x. For example, to input $y = \frac{1}{2}x - 3$, use the following keystrokes:

Y= CL (1 ÷ 2) X/θ/T/n − 3 ENTER

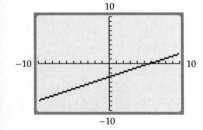

c. Set the viewing window by pressing WINDOW. Enter the values for the minimum x-value (Xmin), the maximum x-value (Xmax), the distance between tick marks on the x-axis (Xscl), the minimum y-value (Ymin), the maximum y-value (Ymax), and the distance between tick marks on the y-axis (Yscl). Press ENTER after each entry. Press GRAPH. For the graph shown at the left, enter Xmin = −10, Xmax = 10, Xscl = 1, Ymin = −10, Ymax = 10, Yscl = 1.

d. Press Y= to return to the equation. The equal sign has a black rectangle around it. This indicates that the function is active and will be graphed when the GRAPH key is pressed. A function is deactivated by using the arrow keys. Move the cursor over the equal sign and press ENTER. When the cursor is moved to the right, the black rectangle will not be present and that equation will not be active.

e. Graphing some radical equations requires special care. To graph the function $y = \sqrt{2x + 3}$, enter the following keystrokes:

Y= CL 2ndF √ 2 X/θ/T/n + 3 ▷ GRAPH

The graph is shown at the left.

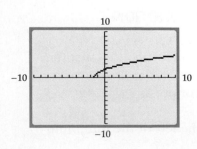

To display the xy-coordinates as integers

a. Press ZOOM ▷ 8.

b. Graph the function. Press TRACE. Use the left and right arrow keys to trace along the graph of the function. The *x*- and *y*-coordinates of the function are shown on the bottom of the screen.

To display the *xy*-coordinates in tenths

a. Press ZOOM ▷ 7.

b. Graph the function. Press TRACE .Use the left and right arrow keys to trace along the graph of the function. The *x*- and *y*-coordinates of the function are shown on the bottom of the screen.

To evaluate a function for a given value of *x*, or to produce ordered pairs of the function

a. Press Y= . Input the expression. For instance, input

Y= CL 2 X/θ/T/*n* ∧ 3 − 3 X/θ/T/*n* + 2. Press ENTER .

b. Press ⊞⊟⊠÷ . Store the *x*-coordinate of the ordered pair you want in X/θ/T/*n* .

For instance, enter 3 STO X/θ/T/*n* ENTER .

c. Press VARS ENTER 1 ENTER . The value of *y*, 47, will be displayed on the screen. The ordered pair is (3, 47). The TABLE feature of the calculator can also be used to find many ordered pairs for a function.

ZOOM FEATURES

To zoom in or out on a graph

a. Here are two methods of using ZOOM. The first method uses the built-in features of the calculator. Move the cursor to a point on the graph that is of interest. Press ZOOM . The ZOOM menu will appear. Press 3 to zoom in on the graph by the amount shown by FACTOR. The center of the new graph is the location at which you placed the cursor. Press ZOOM 4 to zoom out on the graph by the amount shown in FACTOR.

b. The second method uses the BOX option under the ZOOM menu. To use this method, press ZOOM 2. A cursor will appear on the screen. Use the arrow keys to move the cursor to a portion of the graph that is of interest. Press ENTER . Use the arrow keys to draw a box around the portion of the graph you wish to see. Press ENTER .

SOLVING EQUATIONS

This discussion is based on the fact that the real solutions of an equation can be related to the *x*-intercepts of a graph. For instance, the real solutions of $x^2 = x + 1$ are the *x*-intercepts of the graph of $f(x) = x^2 - x - 1$, which are the zeros of *f*.

To solve $x^2 = x + 1$, rewrite the equation with all terms on one side of the equation. The equation is now $x^2 - x - 1 = 0$. Think of this equation as $Y_1 = x^2 - x + 1$ The *x*-intercepts of the graph of Y_1 are the solutions of the equation $x^2 = x + 1$.

a. Enter $x^2 - x - 1$ into Y_1.

b. Graph the equation. You may need to adjust the viewing window so that the *x*-intercepts are visible.

c. Press 2ndF CALC 5.

d. A solution is shown as the *x*-coordinate at the bottom of the screen. To find another intercept, move the cursor to the right of the first *x*-intercept. Then press 2ndF CALC 5.

SOLVING SYSTEMS OF EQUATIONS IN TWO VARIABLES

To solve a system of equations

a. Solve each equation for y.

b. Press $\boxed{Y=}$ and then enter both equations.

c. Graph the equations. You may need to adjust the viewing window so that the point of intersection is visible.

d. Press $\boxed{2ndF}$ CALC 2 to find the point of intersection. Pressing $\boxed{2ndF}$ CALC 2 again will find another point of intersection.

e. The x- and y-coordinates at the bottom of the screen are the coordinates for the point of intersection.

FINDING MAXIMUM AND MINIMUM VALUES OF A FUNCTION

a. Press $\boxed{Y=}$ and then enter the function.

b. Graph the equation. You may need to adjust the viewing window so that the maximum (minimum) are visible.

c. Press $\boxed{2ndF}$ CALC 3 for the minimum value of the function or $\boxed{2ndF}$ CALC 4 for the maximum value of the fuction.

d. The y-coordinate at the bottom of the screen is the maximum (minimum).

CASIO *CFX-9850G*

To evaluate an expression

a. Press $\boxed{MENU}$ $\boxed{5}$. Use the arrow keys to highlight Y₁.

b. Input the expression to be evaluated. For example, to input the expression $-3A^2B - 4C$, use the following keystrokes:

$\boxed{(-)}$ 3 $\boxed{ALPHA}$ A $\boxed{x^2}$ $\boxed{ALPHA}$ B $\boxed{-}$ 4 $\boxed{ALPHA}$ C $\boxed{EXE}$

Note the difference between the keys for a *negative* sign $\boxed{(-)}$ and a *minus* sign $\boxed{-}$.

c. Press $\boxed{MENU}$ 1. Store the value of each variable that will be used in the expression. For example, to evaluate the expression above when $A = 3$, $B = -2$, and $C = -4$, use the following keystrokes:

3 → $\boxed{ALPHA}$ A $\boxed{EXE}$ $\boxed{(-)}$ 2 → $\boxed{ALPHA}$ B $\boxed{EXE}$ $\boxed{(-)}$ 4 → $\boxed{ALPHA}$ C $\boxed{EXE}$

These steps store the value of each variable.

d. Press $\boxed{VARS}$ $\boxed{F4}$ $\boxed{F1}$ 1 $\boxed{EXE}$.

The value of the expression, Y₁, for the given values is displayed; in this case, $Y_1 = 70$.

To graph a function

a. Press Menu $\boxed{5}$ to obtain the GRAPH FUNCTION Menu.

b. Input the function that you desire to graph. Press $\boxed{X,\theta,T}$ to input the variable x. For example, to input $Y_1 = x^3 + 2x^2 - 5x - 6$, use the following keystrokes:

$\boxed{X,\theta,T}$ $\boxed{\wedge}$ 3 $\boxed{+}$ 2 $\boxed{X,\theta,T}$ $\boxed{x^2}$ $\boxed{-}$ 5 $\boxed{X,\theta,T}$ $\boxed{-}$ 6 $\boxed{EXE}$

c. Set the viewing window by pressing $\boxed{SHIFT}$ $\boxed{F3}$ and the Range Parameter Menu will appear. Enter the values for the minimum x-value (Xmin), maximum x-value (Xmax), units between tick marks on the x-axis (Xscl), minimum y-value (Ymin), maximum y-value (Ymax), and the units between tick marks on the y-axis (Yscl). Press $\boxed{EXE}$ after each of the 6 entries above. Press $\boxed{EXIT}$, or $\boxed{SHIFT}$ $\boxed{QUIT}$, to leave the Range Parameter Menu.

d. Press $\boxed{F6}$ to draw the graph. For the graph shown at the left, Xmin = −10, Xmax = 10, Xscl = 1, Ymin = −10, Ymax = 10, Yscl = 1.

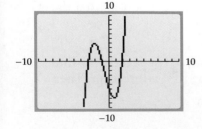

e. In the equation for Y1, there is a rectangle around the equal sign. This indicates that this function is *active* and will be graphed when the [F6] key is pressed. A function is deactivated by using the [F1] key. After using this key once, the rectangle around the equal sign will not be present and that function will not be graphed.

To display the *x*-coordinates of rectangular coordinates as integers

a. Set the Range as follows: For example, set Xmin = −63, Xmax = 63, Xscl = 10, Ymin = −32, Ymax = 32, Yscl = 10.

b. Graph a function and use the Trace feature. Press [F1] and then move the cursor with the [◁] and the [▷] keys. The values of *x* and *y* = *f*(*x*) displayed on the bottom of the screen are the coordinates of a point on the graph. Observe that the *x*-value is given as an integer.

To display the *x*-coordinates of rectangular coordinates in tenths

a. Set the Range as follows: For example, set Xmin = −6.3, Xmax = 6.3. A quick way to choose these range parameter settings is to press [F1] from the V-Window Menu.

b. Graph a function and use the Trace feature. Press [F1] and then move the cursor with the [◁] and the [▷] keys. The values of *x* and *y* = *f*(*x*) displayed on the bottom of the screen are the coordinates of a point on the graph. Observe that the *x*-value is given in tenths.

To evaluate a function for a given value of *x*, or to produce ordered pairs of the function

a. Press [MENU] [5].

b. Input the function to be evaluated. For example, input $2x^3 - 3x + 2$ into Y1.

c. Press [MENU] 1.

d. Input a value for *x*; for example, to input 3 press
$$3 \to [X,\theta,T] \; [EXE]$$

e. Press [VARS] [F4] [F1] 1 [EXE].

The value of Y1 for the given value *x* = 3 is displayed. In this case, Y1 = 47.

ZOOM FEATURES

To zoom in or out on a graph

a. After drawing a graph, press [SHIFT] Zoom to display the Zoom/Auto Range menu. To zoom in on a graph by a factor of 2 on the *x*-axis and a factor of 1.5 on the *y*-axis:
Press [F2] to display the Factor Input Screen. Input the zoom factors for each axis: 2 [EXE] 1 [·] 5 [EXE] [EXIT]. Press [F3] to redraw the graph according to the factors specified above. To specify the center point of the enlarged (reduced) display after pressing [SHIFT] Zoom, use the arrow keys to move the pointer to the position you wish to become the center of the next display. You can repeat the zoom procedures as needed. If you wish to see the original graph, press [F6] [F1]. This procedure resets the range parameters to their original values and redraws the graph.

b. A second method of zooming makes use of the Box Zoom Function. To use this method, first draw a graph. Then press [SHIFT] Zoom [F1]. Now use the arrow (cursor) keys to move the pointer. Once the pointer is located at a portion of the graph that is of interest, press [EXE]. Now use the arrow keys to draw a box around the portion of the graph you wish to see. Press [EXE]. The portion of the graph defined by the box will be drawn.

SOLVING EQUATIONS

This discussion is based on the fact that the real solutions of an equation can be related to the x-intercepts of a graph. For instance, the real solutions of $x^2 = x + 1$ are the x-intercepts of the graph of $f(x) = x^2 - x - 1$, which are the zeros of f.

To solve $x^2 = x + 1$, rewrite the equation with all terms on one side. The equation is now $x^2 - x - 1 = 0$. Think of this equation as $Y_1 = x^2 - x - 1$. The x-intercepts of the graph of Y_1 are the solutions of the equation $x^2 = x + 1$.

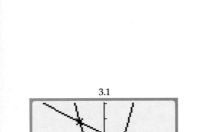

a. Enter $x^2 - x - 1$ into Y_1.

b. Graph the equation. You may need to adjust the viewing window so that the x-intercept is visible.

c. Press $\boxed{\text{SHIFT}}$ G-SOLV $\boxed{\text{F1}}$.

d. The root is shown as the x-coordinate on the bottom of the screen; in this case, the root is approximately -0.618034. To find the next x-intercept, press the right arrow key.

The EQUA Mode (Press $\boxed{\text{MENU}}$ $\boxed{\text{ALPHA}}$ A) can also be used to find solutions of linear, quadratic, and cubic equations.

SOLVING SYSTEMS OF TWO EQUATIONS IN TWO VARIABLES

The following discussion is based on the concept that the solutions of a system of two equations are represented by the point(s) of intersection of the graphs.

The system of equations $\begin{array}{l} y = x^2 - 1 \\ \frac{1}{2}x + y = 1 \end{array}$ will be solved.

a. Solve each equation for y.

b. Enter the first equation in the Graph Menu as Y_1. For instance, let $Y_1 = x^2 - 1$.

c. Enter the second equation as Y_2. For instance, let $Y_2 = 1 - \frac{1}{2}x$.

d. Graph both equations. (*Note:* The point of intersection must appear on the screen. It may be necessary to adjust the viewing window so that the point of intersection that is of interest is the only intersection point that is displayed.)

e. Press $\boxed{\text{SHIFT}}$ G-SOL $\boxed{\text{F5}}$ $\boxed{\text{EXE}}$.

f. The display will show that the graphs intersect at $(-1.686141, 1.8430703)$. To find another point of intersection, repeat step **e**.

FINDING MINIMUM OR MAXIMUM VALUES OF A FUNCTION

a. Enter the function into the graphing menu. For this example we have used $y = x^2 - x - 1$.

b. Graph the function. Adjust the viewing window so that the maximum or minimum is visible.

c. Press $\boxed{\text{SHIFT}}$ G-SOL $\boxed{\text{F2}}$ $\boxed{\text{EXE}}$ for a maximum and $\boxed{\text{F3}}$ $\boxed{\text{EXE}}$ for a minimum.

d. The local maximum (minimum) is shown as the y-coordinate on the bottom of the screen; in this case, the minimum value is -1.25.

Table of Symbols

+	add	$<$	is less than
−	subtract	$\leq$	is less than or equal to
$\cdot$, $\times$, $(a)(b)$	multiply	$>$	is greater than
$\frac{a}{b}$, $\div$, $a\overline{)b}$	divide	$\geq$	is greater than or equal to
( )	parentheses, a grouping symbol	(a, b)	an ordered pair whose first component is a and whose second component is b
[ ]	brackets, a grouping symbol		
π	pi, a number approximately equal to $\frac{22}{7}$ or 3.14	$\circ$	degree (for angles)
		$\sqrt{a}$	the principal square root of a
$-a$	the opposite, or additive inverse, of a	$\varnothing$, { }	the empty set
$\frac{1}{a}$	the reciprocal, or multiplicative inverse, of a	$|a|$	the absolute value of a
=	is equal to	$\cup$	union of two sets
$\approx$	is approximately equal to	$\cap$	intersection of two sets
$\neq$	is not equal to	$\in$	is an element of (for sets)
		$\notin$	is not an element of (for sets)

Table of Measurement Abbreviations

U.S. Customary System

Length		Capacity		Weight		Area	
in.	inches	oz	fluid ounces	oz	ounces	in^2	square inches
ft	feet	c	cups	lb	pounds	ft^2	square feet
yd	yards	qt	quarts			yd^2	square yards
mi	miles	gal	gallons			mi^2	square miles

Metric System

Length		Capacity		Weight/Mass		Area	
mm	millimeter (0.001 m)	ml	milliliter (0.001 L)	mg	milligram (0.001 g)	cm^2	square centimeters
cm	centimeter (0.01 m)	cl	centiliter (0.01 L)	cg	centigram (0.01 g)	m^2	square meters
dm	decimeter (0.1 m)	dl	deciliter (0.1 L)	dg	decigram (0.1 g)		
m	meter	L	liter	g	gram		
dam	decameter (10 m)	dal	decaliter (10 L)	dag	decagram (10 g)		
hm	hectometer (100 m)	hl	hectoliter (100 L)	hg	hectogram (100 g)		
km	kilometer (1000 m)	kl	kiloliter (1000 L)	kg	kilogram (1000 g)		

Time

h	hours	min	minutes	s	seconds

Solutions to Chapter 1 "You Try It"

SECTION 1.1

You Try It 1   Replace y by each of the elements of the set and determine whether the inequality is true.

$$y > -1$$
$$-5 > -1 \text{ False}$$
$$-1 > -1 \text{ False}$$
$$5 > -1 \text{ True}$$

The inequality is true for 5.

You Try It 2   Replace z by each element of the set and determine the value of the expression.

$-z$	$\|z\|$
$-(-11) = 11$	$\|-11\| = 11$
$-(0) = 0$	$\|0\| = 0$
$-(8) = -8$	$\|8\| = 8$

You Try It 3 $100 + (-43) = 57$

You Try It 4 $(-51) + 42 + 17 + (-102)$
$$= -9 + 17 + (-102)$$
$$= 8 + (-102)$$
$$= -94$$

You Try It 5 $19 - (-32) = 19 + 32$
$$= 51$$

You Try It 6 $-9 - (-12) - 17 - 4$
$$= -9 + 12 + (-17) + (-4)$$
$$= 3 + (-17) + (-4)$$
$$= -14 + (-4)$$
$$= -18$$

You Try It 7 $8(-9)10 = -72(10)$
$$= -720$$

You Try It 8 $(-2)3(-8)7 = -6(-8)7$
$$= 48(7)$$
$$= 336$$

You Try It 9 $(-135) \div (-9) = 15$

You Try It 10 $\dfrac{-72}{4} = -18$

You Try It 11 $-\dfrac{36}{-12} = -(-3)$
$$= 3$$

You Try It 12

Strategy   To find the average low temperature:
- Add the seven temperature readings.
- Divide the sum by 7.

Solution
$$-6 + (-7) + 0 + (-5) + (-8) + (-1) + (-1) = -28$$
$$-28 \div 7 = -4$$

The average daily low temperature was $-4°C$.

SECTION 1.2

You Try It 1

$$\begin{array}{r} 0.444 \\ 9\,\overline{)4.000} \\ -3\,6 \\ \hline 40 \\ -36 \\ \hline 40 \\ -36 \\ \hline 4 \end{array}$$

$$\frac{4}{9} = 0.\overline{4}$$

You Try It 2 $125\% = 125\left(\dfrac{1}{100}\right) = \dfrac{125}{100} = \dfrac{5}{4}$

$$125\% = 125(0.01) = 1.25$$

You Try It 3 $\frac{1}{3} = \frac{1}{3}(100\%)$

$$= \frac{100}{3}\% = 33\frac{1}{3}\%$$

You Try It 4 $0.043 = 0.043(100\%) = 4.3\%$

You Try It 5 The LCM of 8, 6, and 4 is 24.

$$-\frac{7}{8} - \frac{5}{6} + \frac{3}{4} = -\frac{21}{24} - \frac{20}{24} + \frac{18}{24}$$

$$= \frac{-21}{24} + \frac{-20}{24} + \frac{18}{24}$$

$$= \frac{-21 - 20 + 18}{24}$$

$$= \frac{-23}{24} = -\frac{23}{24}$$

You Try It 6 $16.127 - 67.91$

$$= 16.127 + (-67.91)$$

$$= -51.783$$

You Try It 7

The quotient is positive.

$$-\frac{3}{8} \div \left(-\frac{5}{12}\right) = \frac{3}{8} \cdot \frac{12}{5}$$

$$= \frac{3 \cdot 12}{8 \cdot 5}$$

$$= \frac{3 \cdot \overset{1}{\cancel{2}} \cdot \overset{1}{\cancel{2}} \cdot 3}{2 \cdot \underset{1}{\cancel{2}} \cdot \underset{1}{\cancel{2}} \cdot 5} = \frac{9}{10}$$

You Try It 8

$$\begin{array}{r} 5.44 \\ \times\ 3.8 \\ \hline 4352 \\ 1632 \\ \hline 20.672 \end{array}$$

$$-5.44(3.8) = -20.672$$

You Try It 9

$$-6^3 = -(6 \cdot 6 \cdot 6) = -216$$

You Try It 10

$$(-3)^4 = (-3)(-3)(-3)(-3) = 81$$

You Try It 11

$$(3^3)(-2)^3 = (3)(3)(3) \cdot (-2)(-2)(-2)$$

$$= 27(-8) = -216$$

You Try It 12

$$\left(-\frac{2}{5}\right)^2 = \left(-\frac{2}{5}\right)\left(-\frac{2}{5}\right) = \frac{4}{25}$$

You Try It 13

$$-3(0.3)^3 = -3(0.3)(0.3)(0.3)$$

$$= -0.9(0.3)(0.3)$$

$$= -0.27(0.3) = -0.081$$

You Try It 14

$$-5\sqrt{32} = -5\sqrt{2^5} = -5\sqrt{2^4 \cdot 2} = -5\sqrt{2^4}\sqrt{2}$$

$$= -5 \cdot 2^2\sqrt{2} = -20\sqrt{2}$$

You Try It 15

$$\sqrt{216} = \sqrt{2^3 \cdot 3^3} = \sqrt{2^2 \cdot 3^2(2 \cdot 3)}$$

$$= \sqrt{2^2 \cdot 3^2}\sqrt{2 \cdot 3} = 2 \cdot 3\sqrt{2 \cdot 3} = 6\sqrt{6}$$

You Try It 16

Strategy To find the percent of the population that is in the baby-boomer generation:

- Find the total population by adding the numbers in all four generations.

- Divide the number of people in the baby-boomer generation (77.6 million) by the total population.

Solution $72.4 + 44.6 + 77.6 + 68.3 = 262.9$

The population of the United States is 262.9 million.

$$\frac{77.6}{262.9} \approx 0.295 \approx 30\%$$

The baby boomers make up about 30% of the population of the United States.

SECTION 1.3

You Try It 1

$$18 - 5[8 - 2(2 - 5)] \div 10$$
$$= 18 - 5[8 - 2(-3)] \div 10$$
$$= 18 - 5[8 + 6] \div 10$$
$$= 18 - 5[14] \div 10$$
$$= 18 - 70 \div 10$$
$$= 18 - 7$$
$$= 11$$

You Try It 2

$$36 \div (8 - 5)^2 - (-3)^2 \cdot 2$$
$$= 36 \div (3)^2 - (-3)^2 \cdot 2$$
$$= 36 \div 9 - 9 \cdot 2$$
$$= 4 - 9 \cdot 2$$
$$= 4 - 18$$
$$= -14$$

You Try It 3

$$(6.97 - 4.72)^2 \cdot 4.5 \div 0.05$$
$$= (2.25)^2 \cdot 4.5 \div 0.05$$
$$- 5.0625 \cdot 4.5 \div 0.05$$
$$= 22.78125 \div 0.05$$
$$= 455.625$$

SECTION 1.4

You Try It 1 $\dfrac{a^2 + b^2}{a + b}$

$$\frac{5^2 + (-3)^2}{5 + (-3)} = \frac{25 + 9}{5 + (-3)}$$
$$= \frac{34}{2}$$
$$= 17$$

You Try It 2 $x^3 - 2(x + y) + z^2$
$$(2)^3 - 2[2 + (-4)] + (-3)^2$$
$$= (2)^3 - 2(-2) + (-3)^2$$
$$= 8 - 2(-2) + 9$$
$$= 8 + 4 + 9$$
$$= 12 + 9$$
$$= 21$$

You Try It 3 $3a - 2b - 5a + 6b = -2a + 4b$

You Try It 4 $-3y^2 + 7 + 8y^2 - 14 = 5y^2 - 7$

You Try It 5 $-5(4y^2) = -20y^2$

You Try It 6 $-7(-2a) = 14a$

You Try It 7 $(-5x)(-2) = 10x$

You Try It 8 $-8(-2a + 7b) = 16a - 56b$

You Try It 9 $(3a - 1)5 = 15a - 5$

You Try It 10 $2(x^2 - x + 7) = 2x^2 - 2x + 14$

You Try It 11 $3y - 2(y - 7x) = 3y - 2y + 14x$
$$= 14x + y$$

You Try It 12

$$-2(x - 2y) - (-x + 3y) = -2x + 4y + x - 3y$$
$$= -x + y$$

You Try It 13

$$3y - 2[x - 4(2 - 3y)] = 3y - 2[x - 8 + 12y]$$
$$= 3y - 2x + 16 - 24y$$
$$= -2x - 21y + 16$$

You Try It 14 the unknown number: x
the difference between
the number and sixty: $x - 60$

$5(x - 60)$; $5x - 300$

You Try It 15 the speed of the older model: s
the speed of the new model: $2s$

You Try It 16 the length of the longer piece: L
the length of the shorter piece:
$6 - L$

SECTION 1.5

You Try It 1 $A = \{-9, -7, -5, -3, -1\}$

You Try It 2 $A = \{1, 3, 5, \ldots\}$

You Try It 3 $A \cup B = \{-2, -1, 0, 1, 2, 3, 4\}$

You Try It 4 $C \cap D = \{10, 16\}$

You Try It 5 $A \cap B = \varnothing$

You Try It 6 $\{x \mid x < 59, x \in \text{positive even integers}\}$

You Try It 7 $\{x \mid x > -3, x \in \text{real numbers}\}$

You Try It 8 The graph is the numbers greater than -2.

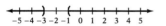

You Try It 9 The graph is the numbers greater than -1 and the numbers less than -3.

You Try It 10 The graph is the numbers less than or equal to 4 and greater than or equal to -4.

You Try It 11 The graph is the real numbers.

Solutions to Chapter 2 "You Try It"

SECTION 2.1

You Try It 1
$$5 - 4x = 8x + 2$$

$5 - 4\left(\dfrac{1}{4}\right)$	$8\left(\dfrac{1}{4}\right) + 2$
$5 - 1$	$2 + 2$
4	$= 4$

Yes, $\dfrac{1}{4}$ is a solution.

You Try It 2
$$10x - x^2 = 3x - 10$$

$10(5) - (5)^2$	$3(5) - 10$
$50 - 25$	$15 - 10$
25	$\neq 5$

No, 5 is not a solution.

You Try It 3
$$\frac{5}{6} = y - \frac{3}{8}$$
$$\frac{5}{6} + \frac{3}{8} = y - \frac{3}{8} + \frac{3}{8}$$
$$\frac{29}{24} = y$$

The solution is $\dfrac{29}{24}$.

You Try It 4
$$-\frac{2x}{5} = 6$$
$$\left(-\frac{5}{2}\right)\left(-\frac{2}{5}x\right) = \left(-\frac{5}{2}\right)(6)$$
$$x = -15$$

The solution is -15.

You Try It 5

$$4x - 8x = 16$$
$$-4x = 16$$
$$\frac{-4x}{-4} = \frac{16}{-4}$$
$$x = -4$$

The solution is -4.

You Try It 6

$$P \cdot B = 108$$
$$\frac{1}{6}B = 18 \qquad \bullet \, 16\frac{2}{3}\% = \frac{1}{6}$$
$$6 \cdot \frac{1}{6}B = 6 \cdot 18$$
$$B = 108$$

18 is $16\frac{2}{3}\%$ of 108.

You Try It 7

Strategy   To find the percent, solve the basic percent equation using $B = 47.1$ and $A = 23.1$. The percent is unknown.

Solution

$$P \cdot B = A$$
$$P(47.1) = 23.1$$
$$\frac{P(47.1)}{47.1} = \frac{23.1}{47.1}$$
$$P \approx 49.0\%$$

The March 1997 deficit was 49.0% of the March 1996 deficit.

SECTION 2.2

You Try It 1

$$5x + 7 = 10$$
$$5x + 7 - 7 = 10 - 7$$
$$5x = 3$$
$$\frac{5x}{5} = \frac{3}{5}$$
$$x = \frac{3}{5}$$

The solution is $\frac{3}{5}$.

You Try It 2

$$2 = 11 + 3x$$
$$2 - 11 = 11 - 11 + 3x$$
$$-9 = 3x$$
$$\frac{-9}{3} = \frac{3x}{3}$$
$$-3 = x$$

The solution is -3.

You Try It 3

$$x - 5 + 4x = 25$$
$$5x - 5 = 25$$
$$5x - 5 + 5 = 25 + 5$$
$$5x = 30$$

$$\frac{5x}{5} = \frac{30}{5}$$
$$x = 6$$

The solution is 6.

You Try It 4

$$5x + 4 = 6 + 10x$$
$$5x - 10x + 4 = 6 + 10x - 10x$$
$$-5x + 4 = 6$$
$$-5x + 4 - 4 = 6 - 4$$
$$-5x = 2$$
$$\frac{-5x}{-5} = \frac{2}{-5}$$
$$x = -\frac{2}{5}$$

The solution is $-\frac{2}{5}$.

You Try It 5

$$5x - 10 - 3x = 6 - 4x$$
$$2x - 10 = 6 - 4x$$
$$2x + 4x - 10 = 6 - 4x + 4x$$
$$6x - 10 = 6$$
$$6x - 10 + 10 = 6 + 10$$
$$6x = 16$$
$$\frac{6x}{6} = \frac{16}{6}$$
$$x = \frac{8}{3}$$

The solution is $\frac{8}{3}$.

You Try It 6

$$5x - 4(3 - 2x) = 2(3x - 2) + 6$$
$$5x - 12 + 8x = 6x - 4 + 6$$
$$13x - 12 = 6x + 2$$
$$13x - 6x - 12 = 6x - 6x + 2$$
$$7x - 12 = 2$$
$$7x - 12 + 12 = 2 + 12$$
$$7x = 14$$
$$\frac{7x}{7} = \frac{14}{7}$$
$$x = 2$$

The solution is 2.

You Try It 7

$$-2[3x - 5(2x - 3)] = 3x - 8$$
$$-2[3x - 10x + 15] = 3x - 8$$
$$-2[-7x + 15] = 3x - 8$$
$$14x - 30 = 3x - 8$$
$$14x - 3x - 30 = 3x - 3x - 8$$
$$11x - 30 = -8$$
$$11x - 30 + 30 = -8 + 30$$
$$11x = 22$$
$$\frac{11x}{11} = \frac{22}{11}$$
$$x = 2$$

The solution is 2.

You Try It 8   the smaller number: n
the larger number: $14 - n$

one more than three times the smaller number	equals	the sum of the larger number and three

$$3n + 1 = (14 - n) + 3$$
$$3n + 1 = 17 - n$$
$$3n + n + 1 = 17 - n + n$$
$$4n + 1 = 17$$
$$4n + 1 - 1 = 17 - 1$$
$$4n = 16$$
$$\frac{4n}{4} = \frac{16}{4}$$
$$n = 4$$

$$14 - n = 14 - 4 = 10$$

These numbers check as solutions.

The smaller number is 4.
The larger number is 10.

SECTION 2.3

You Try It 1

Strategy   • Pounds of $.55 fertilizer: x

	Amount	Cost	Value
$.80 fertilizer	20	0.80	0.80(20)
$.55 fertilizer	x	0.55	0.55x
$.75 fertilizer	$20 + x$	0.75	$0.75(20 + x)$

• The sum of the values before mixing equals the value after mixing.

Solution $0.80(20) + 0.55x = 0.75(20 + x)$
$$16 + 0.55x = 15 + 0.75x$$
$$16 - 0.20x = 15$$
$$-0.20x = -1$$
$$x = 5$$

5 lb of the $.55 fertilizer must be added.

You Try It 2

Strategy   • Liters of the 6% solution: x

	Amount	Percent	Quantity
6%	x	0.06	0.06x
12%	5	0.12	5(0.12)
8%	$x + 5$	0.08	$0.08(x + 5)$

• The sum of the quantities before mixing equals the quantity after mixing.

Solution $0.06x + 5(0.12) = 0.08(x + 5)$
$$0.06x + 0.60 = 0.08x + 0.40$$
$$0.06x + 0.20 = 0.08x$$
$$0.20 = 0.02x$$
$$10 = x$$

The pharmacist adds 10 L of the 6% solution to the 12% solution to get an 8% solution.

You Try It 3

Strategy   • Additional amount: x

	Principal	Rate	Interest
8%	5000	0.08	0.08(5000)
11%	x	0.11	0.11x
9%	$5000 + x$	0.09	$0.09(5000 + x)$

• The sum of the interest earned by the two investments equals 9% of the total investment.

Solution $0.08(5000) + 0.11x = 0.09(5000 + x)$
$$400 + 0.11x = 450 + 0.09x$$
$$400 + 0.02x = 450$$
$$0.02x = 50$$
$$x = 2500$$

$2500 more must be invested at 11%.

You Try It 4

Strategy   • Rate of the first train: r
Rate of the second train: $2r$

	Rate	Time	Distance
1st train	r	3	$3r$
2nd train	$2r$	3	$3(2r)$

• The sum of the distances traveled by the two trains equals 288 mi.

Solution $3r + 3(2r) = 288$
$$3r + 6r = 288$$
$$9r = 288$$
$$r = 32$$

$$2r = 2(32) = 64$$

The first train is traveling at 32 mph.
The second train is traveling at 64 mph.

You Try It 5

Strategy   • Time spent flying out: t
Time spent flying back: $5 - t$

	Rate	Time	Distance
Out	150	t	$150t$
Back	100	$5 - t$	$100(5 - t)$

- The distance out equals the distance back.

Solution $150t = 100(5 - t)$
$150t = 500 - 100t$
$250t = 500$
$t = 2$ (The time out was 2 h.)

The distance out $= 150t = 150(2) =$ 300 mi.

The parcel of land was 300 mi away.

SECTION 2.4

You Try It 1 $2x - 1 < 6x + 7$
$-4x - 1 < 7$
$-4x < 8$
$\dfrac{-4x}{-4} > \dfrac{8}{-4}$
$x > 2$
$\{x \,|\, x > -2\}$

You Try It 2 $5x - 2 \le 4 - 3(x - 2)$
$5x - 2 \le 4 - 3x + 6$
$5x - 2 \le 10 - 3x$
$8x - 2 \le 10$
$8x \le 12$
$\dfrac{8x}{8} \le \dfrac{12}{8}$
$x \le \dfrac{3}{2}$
$\left\{ x \,\middle|\, x \le \dfrac{3}{2} \right\}$

You Try It 3 $-2 \le 5x + 3 \le 13$
$-2 - 3 \le 5x + 3 - 3 \le 13 - 3$
$-5 \le 5x \le 10$
$\dfrac{-5}{5} \le \dfrac{5x}{5} \le \dfrac{10}{5}$
$-1 \le x \le 2$

$\{x \,|\, -1 \le x \le 2\}$

You Try It 4 $2 - 3x > 11$ or $5 + 2x > 7$
$-3x > 9 2x > 2$
$x < -3 x > 1$
$\{x \,|\, x < -3\} \{x \,|\, x > 1\}$
$\{x \,|\, x < -3\} \cup \{x \,|\, x > 1\}$
$ = \{x \,|\, x < -3 \text{ or } x > 1\}$

You Try It 5

Strategy   To find the maximum number of miles:
- Write an expression for the cost of each car, using x to represent the number of miles driven during the week.
- Write and solve an inequality.

Solution

Cost of a Company A car	is less than	Cost of a Company B car

$8(7) + 0.10x < 10(7) + 0.08x$
$56 + 0.10x < 70 + 0.08x$
$56 + 0.10x - 0.08x < 70 + 0.08x - 0.08x$
$56 + 0.02x < 70$
$56 - 56 + 0.02x < 70 - 56$
$0.02x < 14$
$\dfrac{0.02x}{0.02} < \dfrac{14}{0.02}$
$x < 700$

The maximum number of miles is 699.

SECTION 2.5

You Try It 1 $|2x - 3| = 5$
$2x - 3 = 5 2x - 3 = -5$
$2x = 8 2x = -2$
$x = 4 x = -1$

The solutions are 4 and -1.

You Try It 2 $5 - |3x + 5| = 3$
$-|3x + 5| = -2$
$|3x + 5| = 2$
$3x + 5 = 2 3x + 5 = -2$
$3x = -3 3x = -7$
$x = -1 x = -\dfrac{7}{3}$

The solutions are -1 and $-\dfrac{7}{3}$.

You Try It 3 $|3x + 2| < 8$
$-8 < 3x + 2 < 8$
$-8 - 2 < 3x + 2 - 2 < 8 - 2$
$-10 < 3x < 6$
$\dfrac{-10}{3} < \dfrac{3x}{3} < \dfrac{6}{3}$
$-\dfrac{10}{3} < x < 2$
$\left\{ x \,\middle|\, -\dfrac{10}{3} < x < 2 \right\}$

You Try It 4 $|5x + 3| > 8$
$5x + 3 < -8$ or $5x + 3 > 8$
$5x < -11 5x > 5$
$x < -\dfrac{11}{5} x > 1$
$\left\{ x \,\middle|\, x < -\dfrac{11}{5} \right\} \{x \,|\, x > 1\}$

(Continued on page S8)

$$\left\{x \,\middle|\, x < -\frac{11}{5}\right\} \cup \{x \,|\, x > 1\}$$
$$= \left\{x \,\middle|\, x < -\frac{11}{5} \text{ or } x > 1\right\}$$

You Try It 5

Strategy   Let b represent the desired diameter of the bushing, T the tolerance, and d the actual diameter. Solve the absolute value inequality $|d - b| \le T$ for d.

Solution
$$|d - b| \le T$$
$$|d - 2.55| \le 0.003$$
$$-0.003 \le d - 2.55 \le 0.003$$
$$-0.003 + 2.55 \le d - 2.55 + 2.55 \le 0.003 + 2.55$$
$$2.547 \le d \le 2.553$$

The lower and upper limits of the diameter of the bushing are 2.547 in. and 2.553 in.

Solutions to Chapter 3 "You Try It"

SECTION 3.1

You Try It 1
$$QR + RS + ST = QT$$
$$24 + RS + 17 = 62$$
$$41 + RS = 62$$
$$RS = 21$$

$$RS = 21 \text{ cm}$$

You Try It 2
$$AC = AB + BC$$
$$AC = \frac{1}{4}(BC) + BC$$
$$AC = \frac{1}{4}(16) + 16$$
$$AC = 4 + 16$$
$$AC = 20$$

$$AC = 20 \text{ ft}$$

You Try It 3

Strategy   Supplementary angles are two angles whose sum is 180°. To find the supplement, let x represent the supplement of a 129° angle. Write an equation and solve for x.

Solution $x + 129° = 180°$
$$x = 51°$$

The supplement of a 129°angle is a 51° angle.

You Try It 4

Strategy   To find the measure of $\angle a$, write an equation using the fact that the sum of the measure of $\angle a$ and 68° is 118°. Solve for $\angle a$.

Solution $\angle a + 68° = 118°$
$$\angle a = 50°$$

The measure of $\angle a$ is 50°.

You Try It 5

Strategy   The angles labeled are adjacent angles of intersecting lines and are, therefore, supplementary angles. To find x, write an equation and solve for x.

Solution $(x + 16°) + 3x = 180°$
$$4x + 16° = 180°$$
$$4x = 164°$$
$$x = 41°$$

You Try It 6

Strategy $3x = y$ because corresponding angles have the same measure. $y + (x + 40°) = 180°$ because adjacent angles of intersecting lines are supplementary angles. Substitute $3x$ for y and solve for x.

Solution $3x + (x + 40°) = 180°$
$$4x + 40° = 180°$$
$$4x = 140°$$
$$x = 35°$$

You Try It 7

Strategy
- To find the measure of angle b, use the fact that $\angle b$ and $\angle x$ are supplementary angles.
- To find the measure of angle c, use the fact that the sum of the measures of the interior angles of a triangle is 180°.

- To find the measure of angle y, use the fact that $\angle c$ and $\angle y$ are vertical angles.

Solution
$$\angle b + \angle x = 180°$$
$$\angle b + 100° = 180°$$
$$\angle b = 80°$$
$$\angle a + \angle b + \angle c = 180°$$
$$45° + 80° + \angle c = 180°$$
$$125° + \angle c = 180°$$
$$\angle c = 55°$$

$$\angle y = \angle c = 55°$$

You Try It 8

Strategy To find the measure of the third angle, use the facts that the measure of a right angle is 90° and the sum of the measures of the interior angles of a triangle is 180°. Write an equation using x to represent the measure of the third angle. Solve the equation for x.

Solution
$$x + 90° + 34° = 180°$$
$$x + 124° = 180°$$
$$x = 56°$$

The measure of the third angle is 56°.

SECTION 3.2

You Try It 1

Strategy To find the perimeter, use the formula for the perimeter of a square. Substitute 60 for s and solve for P.

Solution
$$P = 4s$$
$$P = 4(60)$$
$$P = 240$$

The perimeter of the infield is 240 ft.

You Try It 2

Strategy To find the perimeter, use the formula for the perimeter of a rectangle. Substitute 11 for L and $8\frac{1}{2}$ for W and solve for P.

Solution
$$P = 2L + 2W$$
$$P = 2(11) + 2\left(8\frac{1}{2}\right)$$
$$P = 2(11) + 2\left(\frac{17}{2}\right)$$
$$P = 22 + 17$$
$$P = 39$$

The perimeter of a standard piece of typing paper is 39 in.

You Try It 3

Strategy To find the circumference, use the circumference formula that involves the diameter. Leave the answer in terms of π.

Solution
$$C = \pi d$$
$$C = \pi(9)$$
$$C = 9\pi$$

The circumference is 9π in.

You Try It 4

Strategy To find the number of rolls of wallpaper to be purchased:

- Use the formula for the area of a rectangle to find the area of one wall.
- Multiply the area of one wall by the number of walls to be covered (2).
- Divide the area of wall to be covered by the area that one roll of wallpaper will cover (30).

Solution
$$A = LW$$
$$A = 12 \cdot 8 = 96 \quad \text{The area of one wall}$$
$$\text{is 96 ft}^2.$$
$$2(96) = 192 \quad \text{The area of the two}$$
$$\text{walls is 192 ft}^2.$$
$$192 \div 30 = 6.4$$

Because a portion of a seventh roll is needed, 7 rolls of wallpaper should be purchased.

You Try It 5

Strategy To find the area, use the formula for the area of a circle. An approximation is asked for; use the π key on a calculator. $r = 11$.

Solution
$$A = \pi r^2$$
$$A = \pi(11)^2$$
$$A = 121\pi$$
$$A \approx 380.13$$

The area is approximately 380.13 cm².

SECTION 3.3

You Try It 1

Strategy To find the volume, use the formula for the volume of a cube. $s = 2.5$.

(Continued on page S10)

Solution $V = s^3$
$V = (2.5)^3 = 15.625$

The volume of the cube is 15.625 m³.

You Try It 2

Strategy To find the volume:

- Find the radius of the base of the cylinder. $d = 8$.
- Use the formula for the volume of a cylinder. Leave the answer in terms of π.

Solution $r = \dfrac{1}{2}d = \dfrac{1}{2}(8) = 4$

$V = \pi r^2 h = \pi(4)^2(22) = \pi(16)(22) = 352\pi$

The volume of the cylinder is 352π ft³.

You Try It 3

Strategy To find the surface area of the cylinder:

- Find the radius of the base of the cylinder. $d = 6$.
- Use the formula for the surface area of a cylinder. An approximation is asked for; use the π key on a calculator.

Solution $r = \dfrac{1}{2}d = \dfrac{1}{2}(6) = 3$

$SA = 2\pi r^2 + 2\pi rh$
$SA = 2\pi(3)^2 + 2\pi(3)(8)$
$SA = 2\pi(9) + 2\pi(3)(8)$
$SA = 18\pi + 48\pi$
$SA = 66\pi$
$SA \approx 207.35$

The surface area of the cylinder is approximately 207.35 ft².

You Try It 4

Strategy To find which solid has the larger surface area:

- Use the formula for the surface area of a cube to find the surface area of the cube. $s = 10$.
- Find the radius of the sphere. $d = 8$.
- Use the formula for the surface area of a sphere to find the surface area of the sphere. Because this number is to be compared to another number, use the π key on a calculator to approximate the surface area.
- Compare the two numbers.

Solution $SA = 6s^2$
$SA = 6(10)^2 = 6(100) = 600$
  The surface area of the cube is 600 cm².

$r = \dfrac{1}{2}d = \dfrac{1}{2}(8) = 4$

$SA = 4\pi r^2$

$SA = 4\pi(4)^2 = 4\pi(16) = 64\pi \approx 201.06$
  The surface area of the sphere is approximately 201.06 cm².

$600 > 201.06$

The cube has a larger surface area than the sphere.

Solutions to Chapter 4 "You Try It"

SECTION 4.1

You Try It 1

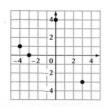

You Try It 2 The coordinates of A are $(4, -2)$.
The coordinates of B are $(-2, 4)$.

The abscissa of D is 0.
The ordinate of C is 0.

You Try It 3

$$x - 3y = -14$$

$$\begin{array}{c|c} -2 - 3(4) & -14 \\ \hline -2 - 12 & -14 \\ -14 = -14 \end{array}$$

Yes, $(-2, 4)$ is a solution of $x - 3y = -14$.

You Try It 4 Replace x by -2 and solve for y.

$$y = \frac{3(-2)}{-2+1} = \frac{-6}{-1} = 6$$

The ordered-pair solution is $(-2, 6)$.

You Try It 5

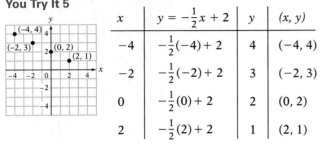

x	$y = -\frac{1}{2}x + 2$	y	(x, y)
-4	$-\frac{1}{2}(-4) + 2$	4	$(-4, 4)$
-2	$-\frac{1}{2}(-2) + 2$	3	$(-2, 3)$
0	$-\frac{1}{2}(0) + 2$	2	$(0, 2)$
2	$-\frac{1}{2}(2) + 2$	1	$(2, 1)$

You Try It 6
{(145, 140), (140, 125), (150, 130), (165, 150), (140, 130), (165, 160)}

No, the relation is not a function. The two ordered pairs (140, 125) and (140, 130) have the same first coordinate but different second coordinates.

You Try It 7 Determine the ordered pairs defined by the equation. Replace x in $y = \frac{1}{2}x + 1$ by the given values and solve for y.
{(−4, −1), (0, 1), (2, 2)}
Yes, y is a function of x.

You Try It 8 $H(x) = \dfrac{x}{x - 4}$

$H(8) = \dfrac{8}{8 - 4}$

$H(8) = \dfrac{8}{4} = 2$

SECTION 4.2

You Try It 1

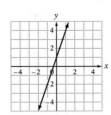

You Try It 2

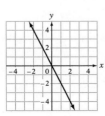

You Try It 3

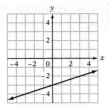

You Try It 4 $5x - 2y = 10$
$$-2y = -5x + 10$$
$$y = \frac{5}{2}x - 5$$

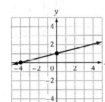

You Try It 5 x-intercept: $x - 4y = -4$
$$x - 4(0) = -4$$
$$x = -4$$
$(-4, 0)$
y-intercept: $x - 4y = -4$
$$0 - 4y = -4$$
$$-4y = -4$$
$$y = 1$$
$(0, 1)$

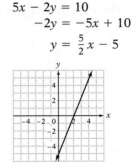

You Try It 6

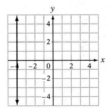

You Try It 7

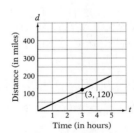

The ordered pair (3, 120) means that in 3 h the car will travel 120 mi.

SECTION 4.3

You Try It 1 Let $P_1 = (4, -3)$ and $P_2 = (2, 7)$.
$$m = \frac{y_2 - y_1}{x_2 - x_1} = \frac{7 - (-3)}{2 - 4} = \frac{10}{-2} = -5$$
The slope is -5.

You Try It 2 Let $P_1 = (6, -1)$ and $P_2 = (6, 7)$.

$$m = \frac{y_2 - y_1}{x_2 - x_1} = \frac{7 - (-1)}{6 - 6}$$

$$m = \frac{8}{0} \quad \text{Division by zero is not defined.}$$

The slope of the line is undefined.

You Try It 3 $m = \dfrac{8650 - 6100}{1 - 4} = \dfrac{2550}{-3}$

$m = -850$

A slope of -850 means that the value of the car is decreasing at a rate of $850 per year.

You Try It 4 y-intercept $= (0, b) = (0, -1)$

$$m = -\frac{1}{4}$$

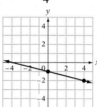

You Try It 5 Solve the equation for y.

$$x - 2y = 4$$
$$-2y = -x + 4$$
$$y = \frac{1}{2}x - 2$$

y-intercept $= (0, b) = (0, -2)$

$$m = \frac{1}{2}$$

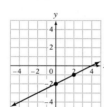

SECTION 4.4

You Try It 1 Because the slope and y-intercept are known, use the slope–intercept formula, $y = mx + b$.

$$y = mx + b$$
$$y = \frac{5}{3}x + 2$$

You Try It 2 $m = \dfrac{3}{4}$ $(x_1, y_1) = (4, -2)$

$$y - y_1 = m(x - x_1)$$
$$y - (-2) = \frac{3}{4}(x - 4)$$
$$y + 2 = \frac{3}{4}x - 3$$
$$y = \frac{3}{4}x - 5$$

The equation of the line is $y = \dfrac{3}{4}x - 5$.

You Try It 3 Find the slope of the line between the two points.

$$m = \frac{y_2 - y_1}{x_2 - x_1} = \frac{1 - (-1)}{3 - (-6)} = \frac{2}{9}$$

Use the point–slope formula.

$$y - y_1 = m(x - x_1)$$
$$y - (-1) = \frac{2}{9}[x - (-6)]$$
$$y + 1 = \frac{2}{9}x + \frac{4}{3}$$
$$y = \frac{2}{9}x + \frac{1}{3}$$

You Try It 4

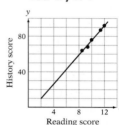

The slope of the line means that the grade on the history test increases 8.3 points for each 1-point increase in the grade on the reading test.

SECTION 4.5

You Try It 1 $m_1 = \dfrac{1 - (-3)}{7 - (-2)} = \dfrac{4}{9}$

$m_2 = \dfrac{-5 - 1}{6 - 4} = \dfrac{-6}{2} = -3$

$m_1 \cdot m_2 = \dfrac{4}{9} \cdot -3 = -\dfrac{4}{3}$

No, the lines are not perpendicular.

You Try It 2 $5x + 2y = 2$
$$2y = -5x + 2$$
$$y = -\frac{5}{2}x + 1$$

$$m_1 = -\frac{5}{2}$$

$5x + 2y = -6$
$$2y = -5x - 6$$
$$y = -\frac{5}{2}x - 3$$

$$m_2 = -\frac{5}{2}$$

$$m_1 = m_2 = -\frac{5}{2}$$

Yes, the lines are parallel.

You Try It 3 $y = \dfrac{1}{4}x - 3$

$$m_1 = \frac{1}{4}$$

$$m_1 \cdot m_2 = -1$$
$$\frac{1}{4} \cdot m_2 = -1$$
$$m_2 = -4$$

$$y - y_1 = m(x - x_1)$$
$$y - 2 = -4[x - (-2)]$$
$$y - 2 = -4(x + 2)$$
$$y - 2 = -4x - 8$$
$$y = -4x - 6$$

The equation of the line is
$y = -4x - 6$.

SECTION 4.6

You Try It 1

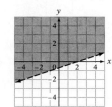

$$x - 3y < 2$$
$$x - x - 3y < -x + 2$$
$$-3y < -x + 2$$
$$\frac{-3y}{-3} > \frac{-x + 2}{-3}$$
$$y > \frac{1}{3}x - \frac{2}{3}$$

Solutions to Chapter 5 "You Try It"

SECTION 5.1

You Try It 1

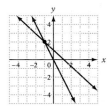

The solution is $(-1, 2)$.

You Try It 2

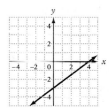

The two equations represent the same line. The system of equations is dependent. The solutions are the ordered pairs $\left(x, \frac{3}{4}x - 3\right)$.

SECTION 5.2

You Try It 1

(1) $7x - y = 4$
(2) $3x + 2y = 9$

Solve Equation (1) for y.

$$7x - y = 4$$
$$-y = -7x + 4$$
$$y = 7x - 4$$

Substitute in Equation (2).

$$3x + 2y = 9$$
$$3x + 2(7x - 4) = 9$$
$$3x + 14x - 8 = 9$$
$$17x - 8 = 9$$
$$17x = 17$$
$$x = 1$$

Substitute in Equation (1).

$$7x - y = 4$$
$$7(1) - y = 4$$
$$7 - y = 4$$
$$-y = -3$$
$$y = 3$$

The solution is $(1, 3)$.

You Try It 2

(1) $3x - y = 4$
(2) $y = 3x + 2$

$$3x - y = 4$$
$$3x - (3x + 2) = 4$$
$$3x - 3x - 2 = 4$$
$$-2 = 4$$

This is not a true equation. The system of equations is inconsistent and therefore does not have a solution.

You Try It 3

(1) $y = -2x + 1$
(2) $6x + 3y = 3$

$$6x + 3y = 3$$
$$6x + 3(-2x + 1) = 3$$
$$6x - 6x + 3 = 3$$
$$3 = 3$$

The system of equations is dependent. The solutions are the ordered pairs $(x, -2x + 1)$.

SECTION 5.3

You Try It 1

(1) $2x + 5y = 6$
(2) $3x - 2y = 6x + 2$

Write Equation (2) in the form $Ax + By = C$.

$3x - 2y = 6x + 2$
$-3x - 2y = 2$

Solve the system: $2x + 5y = 6$
$-3x - 2y = 2$

Eliminate y.

$2(2x + 5y) = 2(6)$
$5(-3x - 2y) = 5(2)$

$4x + 10y = 12$
$-15x - 10y = 10$

Add the equations.

$-11x = 22$
$x = -2$

Replace x in Equation (1).

$2x + 5y = 6$
$2(-2) + 5y = 6$
$-4 + 5y = 6$
$5y = 10$
$y = 2$

The solution is $(-2, 2)$.

You Try It 2

$2x + y = 5$
$4x + 2y = 6$

Eliminate y.

$-2(2x + y) = -2(5)$
$4x + 2y = 6$

$-4x - 2y = -10$
$4x + 2y = 6$

Add the equations.

$0x + 0y = -4$
$0 = -4$

This is not a true equation. The system is inconsistent and therefore has no solution.

You Try It 3

(1) $x - y + z = 6$
(2) $2x + 3y - z = 1$
(3) $x + 2y + 2z = 5$

Eliminate z. Add Equations (1) and (2).

$x - y + z = 6$
$2x + 3y - z = 1$
(4) $3x + 2y = 7$

Multiply Equation (2) by 2 and add to Equation (3).

$4x + 6y - 2z = 2$
$x + 2y + 2z = 5$
(5) $5x + 8y = 7$

Solve the system of two equations.

(4) $3x + 2y = 7$
(5) $5x + 8y = 7$

Multiply Equation (4) by -4 and add to Equation (5).

$-12x - 8y = -28$
$5x + 8y = 7$
$-7x = -21$
$x = 3$

Replace x by 3 in Equation (4).

$3x + 2y = 7$
$3(3) + 2y = 7$
$9 + 2y = 7$
$2y = -2$
$y = -1$

Replace x by 3 and y by -1 in Equation (1).

$x - y + z = 6$
$3 - (-1) + z = 6$
$4 + z = 6$
$z = 2$

The solution is $(3, -1, 2)$.

SECTION 5.4

You Try It 1

$$\begin{vmatrix} -1 & -4 \\ 3 & -5 \end{vmatrix} = -1(-5) - 3(-4) = 5 + 12 = 17$$

The value of the determinant is 17.

You Try It 2 Expand by cofactors of the first row.

$$\begin{vmatrix} 1 & 4 & -2 \\ 3 & 1 & 1 \\ 0 & -2 & 2 \end{vmatrix}$$

$$= 1 \begin{vmatrix} 1 & 1 \\ -2 & 2 \end{vmatrix} - 4 \begin{vmatrix} 3 & 1 \\ 0 & 2 \end{vmatrix} + (-2) \begin{vmatrix} 3 & 1 \\ 0 & -2 \end{vmatrix}$$

$$= 1(2 + 2) - 4(6 - 0) - 2(-6 - 0)$$
$$= 4 - 24 + 12$$
$$= -8$$

The value of the determinant is -8.

You Try It 3

$$\begin{vmatrix} 3 & -2 & 0 \\ 1 & 4 & 2 \\ -2 & 1 & 3 \end{vmatrix}$$

$$= 3\begin{vmatrix} 4 & 2 \\ 1 & 3 \end{vmatrix} - (-2)\begin{vmatrix} 1 & 2 \\ -2 & 3 \end{vmatrix} + 0\begin{vmatrix} 1 & 4 \\ -2 & 1 \end{vmatrix}$$

$$= 3(12 - 2) + 2(3 + 4) + 0$$
$$= 3(10) + 2(7)$$
$$= 30 + 14$$
$$= 44$$

The value of the determinant is 44.

You Try It 4

$$3x - y = 4$$
$$6x - 2y = 5$$

$$D = \begin{vmatrix} 3 & -1 \\ 6 & -2 \end{vmatrix} = -6 + 6 = 0$$

Because $D = 0$, $\frac{D_x}{D}$ is undefined. Therefore, the system of equations is dependent or inconsistent.

It is not possible to solve this system by using Cramer's Rule.

You Try It 5

$$2x - y + z = -1$$
$$3x + 2y - z = 3$$
$$x + 3y + z = -2$$

$$D = \begin{vmatrix} 2 & -1 & 1 \\ 3 & 2 & -1 \\ 1 & 3 & 1 \end{vmatrix} = 21$$

$$D_x = \begin{vmatrix} -1 & -1 & 1 \\ 3 & 2 & -1 \\ -2 & 3 & 1 \end{vmatrix} = 9$$

$$D_y = \begin{vmatrix} 2 & -1 & 1 \\ 3 & 3 & -1 \\ 1 & -2 & 1 \end{vmatrix} = -3$$

$$D_z = \begin{vmatrix} 2 & -1 & -1 \\ 3 & 2 & 3 \\ 1 & 3 & -2 \end{vmatrix} = -42$$

$$x = \frac{D_x}{D} = \frac{9}{21} = \frac{3}{7}$$

$$y = \frac{D_y}{D} = \frac{-3}{21} = -\frac{1}{7}$$

$$z = \frac{D_z}{D} = \frac{-42}{21} = -2$$

The solution is $\left(\frac{3}{7}, -\frac{1}{7}, -2\right)$.

SECTION 5.5

You Try It 1

Strategy • Rate of the rowing team in calm water: t
Rate of the current: c

	Rate	Time	Distance
With current	$t + c$	2	$2(t + c)$
Against current	$t - c$	2	$2(t - c)$

• The distance traveled with the current is 18 mi.
The distance traveled against the current is 10 mi.

Solution

$$2(t + c) = 18 \qquad \frac{1}{2} \cdot 2(t + c) = \frac{1}{2} \cdot 18$$

$$2(t - c) = 10 \qquad \frac{1}{2} \cdot 2(t - c) = \frac{1}{2} \cdot 10$$

$$t + c = 9$$
$$t - c = 5$$
$$2t = 14$$
$$t = 7$$

$$t + c = 9$$
$$7 + c = 9$$
$$c = 2$$

The rate of the rowing team in calm water is 7 mph.

The rate of the current is 2 mph.

You Try It 2

Strategy • Amount invested at 8%: x
Amount invested at 7%: y

Investment	Principal	Interest Rate	Interest Earned
8%	x	0.08	$0.08x$
7%	y	0.07	$0.07y$

• The total amount invested was $15,000.
The total amount of interest earned was $1170.

Solution

$$x + y = 15{,}000$$
$$0.08x + 0.07y = 1170$$

$$-8x - 8y = -120{,}000$$
$$8x + 7y = 117{,}000$$
$$-y = -3000$$
$$y = 3000$$

$$x + y = 15{,}000$$
$$x + 3000 = 15{,}000$$
$$x = 12{,}000$$

(Continued on page S16)

$12,000 was invested in the 8% account.
$3000 was invested in the 7% account.

SECTION 5.6

You Try It 1   Shade above the solid line $y = 2x - 3$.
Shade above the dashed line $y = -3x$.

The solution set of the system is the intersection of the solution sets of the individual inequalities.

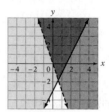

You Try It 2 $3x + 4y > 12$
$$4y > -3x + 12$$
$$y > -\frac{3}{4}x + 3$$

Shade above the dashed line $y = -\frac{3}{4}x + 3$.

Shade below the dashed line $y = \frac{3}{4}x - 1$.

The solution set of the system is the intersection of the solution sets of the individual inequalities.

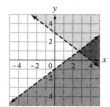

Solutions to Chapter 6 "You Try It"

SECTION 6.1

You Try It 1
$$(-3a^2b^4)(-2ab^3)^4 = (-3a^2b^4)[(-2)^4a^4b^{12}]$$
$$= (-3a^2b^4)(16a^4b^{12})$$
$$= -48a^6b^{16}$$

You Try It 2 $(y^{n-3})^2 = y^{(n-3)2} = y^{2n-6}$

You Try It 3 $[(ab^3)^3]^4 = [a^3b^9]^4 = a^{12}b^{36}$

You Try It 4
$$\frac{20r^{-2}t^{-5}}{-16r^{-3}s^{-2}} = -\frac{4 \cdot 5r^{-2-(-3)}s^2t^{-5}}{4 \cdot 4}$$
$$= -\frac{5rs^2}{4t^5}$$

You Try It 5
$$\frac{(9u^{-6}v^4)^{-1}}{(6u^{-3}v^{-2})^{-2}} = \frac{9^{-1}u^6v^{-4}}{6^{-2}u^6v^4}$$
$$= 9^{-1} \cdot 6^2u^0v^{-8}$$
$$= \frac{36}{9v^8}$$
$$= \frac{4}{v^8}$$

You Try It 6 $\dfrac{a^{2n+1}}{a^{n+3}} = a^{2n+1-(n+3)} = a^{2n+1-n-3} = a^{n-2}$

You Try It 7 $942,000,000 = 9.42 \times 10^8$

You Try It 8 $2.7 \times 10^{-5} = 0.000027$

You Try It 9
$$\frac{5,600,000 \times 0.000000081}{900 \times 0.000000028}$$
$$= \frac{5.6 \times 10^6 \times 8.1 \times 10^{-8}}{9 \times 10^2 \times 2.8 \times 10^{-8}}$$
$$= \frac{(5.6)(8.1) \times 10^{6+(-8)-2-(-8)}}{(9)(2.8)}$$
$$= 1.8 \times 10^4 = 18,000$$

You Try It 10

Strategy   To find the number of arithmetic operations:
- Find the reciprocal of 1×10^{-7}, which is the number of operations performed in one second.
- Write the number of seconds in one minute (60) in scientific notation.
- Multiply the number of arithmetic operations per second by the number of seconds in one minute.

Solution $\dfrac{1}{1 \times 10^{-7}} = 10^7$

$60 = 6 \times 10$

$6 \times 10 \times 10^7 = 6 \times 10^8$

The computer can perform 6×10^8 operations in one minute.

SECTION 6.2

You Try It 1 $R(x) = -2x^4 - 5x^3 + 2x - 8$
$R(2) = -2(2)^4 - 5(2)^3 + 2(2) - 8$
$= -2(16) - 5(8) + 2(2) - 8$
$= -32 - 40 + 4 - 8$
$= -76$

You Try It 2   The leading coefficient is -3, the constant term is -12, and the degree is 4.

You Try It 3
a. This is a polynomial function.
b. This is not a polynomial function. A polynomial function does not have a variable expression raised to a negative power.
c. This is not a polynomial function. A polynomial function does not have a variable expression within a radical.

You Try It 4

x	$y = f(x)$
-3	-25
-2	-6
-1	1
0	2
1	3
2	10
3	29

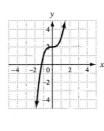

You Try It 5

x	$y = f(x)$
-3	28
-2	9
-1	2
0	1
1	0
2	-7
3	-26

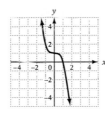

You Try It 6
$$\begin{array}{r} -3x^2 - 4x + 9 \\ -5x^2 - 7x + 1 \\ \hline -8x^2 - 11x + 10 \end{array}$$

You Try It 7   Add the additive inverse of $6x^2 + 3x - 7$ to $-5x^2 + 2x - 3$.

$$\begin{array}{r} -5x^2 + 2x - 3 \\ -6x^2 - 3x + 7 \\ \hline -11x^2 - x + 4 \end{array}$$

You Try It 8
$S(x) = P(x) + R(x)$
$= (4x^3 - 3x^2 + 2) + (-2x^2 + 2x - 3)$
$= 4x^3 - 5x^2 + 2x - 1$

$S(-1) = 4(-1)^3 - 5(-1)^2 + 2(-1) - 1$
$= 4(-1) - 5(1) + 2(-1) - 1$
$= -4 - 5 - 2 - 1$
$= -12$

You Try It 9
$D(x) = P(x) - R(x)$

$D(x) = (5x^{2n} - 3x^n - 7) - (-2x^{2n} - 5x^n + 8)$
$= (5x^{2n} - 3x^n - 7) + (2x^{2n} + 5x^n - 8)$
$= 7x^{2n} + 2x^n - 15$

SECTION 6.3

You Try It 1 $(-2y + 3)(-4y) = 8y^2 - 12y$

You Try It 2 $-a^2(3a^2 + 2a - 7) = -3a^4 - 2a^3 + 7a^2$

You Try It 3
$$\begin{array}{r} 2y^3 + 2y^2 \quad\quad - 3 \\ 3y - 1 \\ \hline -2y^3 - 2y^2 \quad\quad + 3 \\ 6y^4 + 6y^3 \quad\quad - 9y \\ \hline 6y^4 + 4y^3 - 2y^2 - 9y + 3 \end{array}$$

You Try It 4
$(4y - 5)(2y - 3) = 8y^2 - 12y - 10y + 15$
$= 8y^2 - 22y + 15$

You Try It 5
$(3b + 2)(3b - 5) = 9b^2 - 15b + 6b - 10$
$= 9b^2 - 9b - 10$

You Try It 6 $(2a + 5c)(2a - 5c) = 4a^2 - 25c^2$

You Try It 7 $(3x + 2y)^2 = 9x^2 + 12xy + 4y^2$

You Try It 8

Strategy   To find the area, replace the variables b and h in the equation $A = \frac{1}{2}bh$ by the given values and solve for A.

Solution $A = \frac{1}{2}bh$

$A = \frac{1}{2}(2x + 6)(x - 4)$
$A = (x + 3)(x - 4)$
$A = x^2 - 4x + 3x - 12$
$A = x^2 - x - 12$

The area is $(x^2 - x - 12)$ ft^2.

SECTION 6.4

You Try It 1

$$3x + 4 \overline{)\begin{array}{r} 5x - 1 \\ 15x^2 + 17x - 20 \\ \underline{15x^2 + 20x} \\ -3x - 20 \\ \underline{-3x - 4} \\ -16 \end{array}}$$

$$\frac{15x^2 + 17x - 20}{3x + 4} = 5x - 1 - \frac{16}{3x + 4}$$

You Try It 2

$$3x - 1 \overline{)\begin{array}{r} x^2 + 3x - 1 \\ 3x^3 + 8x^2 - 6x + 2 \\ \underline{3x^3 - x^2} \\ 9x^2 - 6x \\ \underline{9x^2 - 3x} \\ -3x + 2 \\ \underline{-3x + 1} \\ 1 \end{array}}$$

$$\frac{3x^3 + 8x^2 - 6x + 2}{3x - 1} = x^2 + 3x - 1 + \frac{1}{3x - 1}$$

You Try It 3

$$x^2 - 3x + 2 \overline{)\begin{array}{r} 3x^2 - 2x + 4 \\ 3x^4 - 11x^3 + 16x^2 - 16x + 8 \\ \underline{3x^4 - 9x^3 + 6x^2} \\ -2x^3 + 10x^2 - 16x \\ \underline{-2x^3 + 6x^2 - 4x} \\ 4x^2 - 12x + 8 \\ \underline{4x^2 - 12x + 8} \\ 0 \end{array}}$$

$$\frac{3x^4 - 11x^3 + 16x^2 - 16x + 8}{x^2 - 3x + 2} = 3x^2 - 2x + 4$$

You Try It 4

$$\begin{array}{r|rrr} -2 & 6 & 8 & -5 \\ & & -12 & 8 \\ \hline & 6 & -4 & 3 \end{array}$$

$$(6x^2 + 8x - 5) \div (x + 2) = 6x - 4 + \frac{3}{x + 2}$$

You Try It 5

$$\begin{array}{r|rrrr} 2 & 5 & -12 & -8 & 16 \\ & & 10 & -4 & -24 \\ \hline & 5 & -2 & -12 & -8 \end{array}$$

$$(5x^3 - 12x^2 - 8x + 16) \div (x - 2)$$
$$= 5x^2 - 2x - 12 - \frac{8}{x - 2}$$

You Try It 6

$$\begin{array}{r|rrrrr} 3 & 2 & -3 & -8 & 0 & -2 \\ & & 6 & 9 & 3 & 9 \\ \hline & 2 & 3 & 1 & 3 & 7 \end{array}$$

$$(2x^4 - 3x^3 - 8x^2 - 2) \div (x - 3)$$
$$= 2x^3 + 3x^2 + x + 3 + \frac{7}{x - 3}$$

You Try It 7

$$\begin{array}{r|rrrr} -3 & 2 & -5 & 0 & 7 \\ & & -6 & 33 & -99 \\ \hline & 2 & -11 & 33 & -92 \end{array}$$

$$P(-3) = -92$$

Solutions to Chapter 7 "You Try It"

SECTION 7.1

You Try It 1
The GCF is $7a^2$.

$$14a^2 - 21a^4b = 7a^2(2) + 7a^2(-3a^2b)$$
$$= 7a^2(2 - 3a^2b)$$

You Try It 2
The GCF is 9.

$$27b^2 + 18b + 9 = 9(3b^2) + 9(2b) + 9(1)$$
$$= 9(3b^2 + 2b + 1)$$

You Try It 3
The GCF is $3x^2y^2$.

$$6x^4y^2 - 9x^3y^2 + 12x^2y^4$$
$$= 3x^2y^2(2x^2) + 3x^2y^2(-3x) + 3x^2y^2(4y^2)$$
$$= 3x^2y^2(2x^2 - 3x + 4y^2)$$

You Try It 4
The GCF is a^2.

$$a^{n+4} + a^2 = a^2(a^{n+2}) + a^2(1)$$
$$= a^2(a^{n+2} + 1)$$

You Try It 5 $2y(5x - 2) - 3(2 - 5x)$
$$= 2y(5x - 2) + 3(5x - 2)$$
$$= (5x - 2)(2y + 3)$$

You Try It 6 $a^2 - 3a + 2ab - 6b$
$$= (a^2 - 3a) + (2ab - 6b)$$
$$= a(a - 3) + 2b(a - 3)$$
$$= (a - 3)(a + 2b)$$

You Try It 7
$2mn^2 - n + 8mn - 4 = (2mn^2 - n) + (8mn - 4)$
$$= n(2mn - 1) + 4(2mn - 1)$$
$$= (2mn - 1)(n + 4)$$

You Try It 8 $2xy - 6y - 12 + 4x$
$$= (2xy - 6y) - (12 - 4x)$$
$$= 2y(x - 3) - 4(3 - x)$$
$$= 2y(x - 3) + 4(x - 3)$$
$$= (x - 3)(2y + 4)$$

SECTION 7.2

You Try It 1

Factors	Sum
1, 20	21
2, 10	12
4, 5	9

● Find the positive factors of 20 whose sum is 9.

$x^2 + 9x + 20 = (x + 4)(x + 5)$

You Try It 2

Factors	Sum
+1, −18	−17
−1, +18	17
+2, −9	−7
−2, +9	7
+3, −6	−3
−3, +6	+3

● Find the factors of −18 whose sum is 7.

$x^2 + 7x - 18 = (x + 9)(x - 2)$

You Try It 3
The GCF is $-2x$.

$-2x^3 + 14x^2 - 12x = -2x(x^2 - 7x + 6)$

Factor the trinomial $x^2 - 7x + 6$. Find two negative factors of 6 whose sum is -7.

Factors	Sum
−1, −6	−7
−2, −3	−5

$-2x^3 + 14x^2 - 12x = -2x(x - 6)(x - 1)$

You Try It 4
The GCF is 3.

$3x^2 - 9xy - 12y^2 = 3(x^2 - 3xy - 4y^2)$

Factor the trinomial. Find the factors of −4 whose sum is −3.

Factors	Sum
+1, −4	−3
−1, +4	3
+2, −2	0

$3x^2 - 9xy - 12y^2 = 3(x + y)(x - 4y)$

SECTION 7.3

You Try It 1
Factor the trinomial $2x^2 - x - 3$.

Positive factors of 2: 1, 2	Factors of −3: 1, −3
	−1, 3

Trial Factors	Middle Term
$(1x + 1)(2x - 3)$	$-3x + 2x = -x$
$(1x - 3)(2x + 1)$	$x - 6x = -5x$
$(1x - 1)(2x + 3)$	$3x - 2x = x$
$(1x + 3)(2x - 1)$	$-x + 6x = 5x$

$2x^2 - x - 3 = (x + 1)(2x - 3)$

You Try It 2
The GCF is $-3y$.

$-45y^3 + 12y^2 + 12y = -3y(15y^2 - 4y - 4)$

Factor the trinomial $15y^2 - 4y - 4$.

Positive factors of 15: 1, 15	Factors of −4: 1, −4
3, 5	−1, 4
	2, −2

Trial Factors	Middle Term
$(1y + 1)(15y - 4)$	$-4y + 15y = 11y$
$(1y - 4)(15y + 1)$	$y - 60y = -59y$
$(1y - 1)(15y + 4)$	$4y - 15y = -11y$
$(1y + 4)(15y - 1)$	$-y + 60y = 59y$
$(1y + 2)(15y - 2)$	$-2y + 30y = 28y$
$(1y - 2)(15y + 2)$	$2y - 30y = -28y$
$(3y + 1)(5y - 4)$	$-12y + 5y = -7y$
$(3y - 4)(5y + 1)$	$3y - 20y = -17y$
$(3y - 1)(5y + 4)$	$12y - 5y = 7y$
$(3y + 4)(5y - 1)$	$-3y + 20y = 17y$
$(3y + 2)(5y - 2)$	$-6y + 10y = 4y$
$(3y - 2)(5y + 2)$	$6y - 10y = -4y$

$-45y^3 + 12y^2 + 12y = -3y(3y - 2)(5y + 2)$

You Try It 3

Factors of -14 $[2(-7)]$	Sum
1, -14	-13
-1, 14	13
2, -7	-5
-2, 7	5

$$\begin{aligned} 2a^2 + 13a - 7 &= 2a^2 - a + 14a - 7 \\ &= (2a^2 - a) + (14a - 7) \\ &= a(2a - 1) + 7(2a - 1) \\ &= (2a - 1)(a + 7) \end{aligned}$$

$$2a^2 + 13a - 7 = (2a - 1)(a + 7)$$

You Try It 4

The GCF is $5x$.

$$15x^3 + 40x^2 - 80x = 5x(3x^2 + 8x - 16)$$

Factors of -48 $[3(-16)]$	Sum
1, -48	-47
-1, 48	47
2, -24	-22
-2, 24	22
3, -16	-13
-3, 16	13
4, -12	-8
-4, 12	8

$$\begin{aligned} 3x^2 + 8x - 16 &= 3x^2 - 4x + 12x - 16 \\ &= (3x^2 - 4x) + (12x - 16) \\ &= x(3x - 4) + 4(3x - 4) \\ &= (3x - 4)(x + 4) \end{aligned}$$

$$\begin{aligned} 15x^3 + 40x^2 - 80x &= 5x(3x^2 + 8x - 16) \\ &= 5x(3x - 4)(x + 4) \end{aligned}$$

SECTION 7.4

You Try It 1

$$\begin{aligned} x^2 - 36y^4 &= x^2 - (6y^2)^2 \\ &= (x + 6y^2)(x - 6y^2) \end{aligned}$$

You Try It 2 $9x^2 + 12x + 4 = (3x + 2)^2$

You Try It 3

$$\begin{aligned} (a + b)^2 &- (a - b)^2 \\ &= [(a + b) + (a - b)][(a + b) - (a - b)] \\ &= (a + b + a - b)(a + b - a + b) \\ &= (2a)(2b) = 4ab \end{aligned}$$

You Try It 4

$$\begin{aligned} 8x^3 + y^3z^3 &= (2x)^3 + (yz)^3 \\ &= (2x + yz)(4x^2 - 2xyz + y^2z^2) \end{aligned}$$

You Try It 5

$$\begin{aligned} (x - y)^3 &+ (x + y)^3 \\ &= [(x - y) + (x + y)][(x - y)^2 - (x - y)(x + y) + (x + y)^2] \\ &= 2x[x^2 - 2xy + y^2 - (x^2 - y^2) + x^2 + 2xy + y^2] \\ &= 2x(x^2 - 2xy + y^2 - x^2 + y^2 + x^2 + 2xy + y^2) \\ &= 2x(x^2 + 3y^2) \end{aligned}$$

You Try It 6

Let $u = xy$.

$$\begin{aligned} 6x^2y^2 - 19xy + 10 &= 6u^2 - 19u + 10 \\ &= (2u - 5)(3u - 2) \\ &= (2xy - 5)(3xy - 2) \end{aligned}$$

You Try It 7

Let $u = x^2$.

$$\begin{aligned} 3x^4 + 4x^2 - 4 &= 3u^2 + 4u - 4 \\ &= (u + 2)(3u - 2) \\ &= (x^2 + 2)(3x^2 - 2) \end{aligned}$$

You Try It 8

Let $u = a^2b^2$.

$$\begin{aligned} a^4b^4 + 6a^2b^2 - 7 &= u^2 + 6u - 7 \\ &= (u + 7)(u - 1) \\ &= (a^2b^2 + 7)(a^2b^2 - 1) \end{aligned}$$

You Try It 9

$$\begin{aligned} 18x^3 - 6x^2 - 60x &= 6x(3x^2 - x - 10) \\ &= 6x(3x + 5)(x - 2) \end{aligned}$$

You Try It 10
$$\begin{aligned} 4x - 4y &- x^3 + x^2y \\ &= (4x - 4y) - (x^3 - x^2y) \\ &= 4(x - y) - x^2(x - y) \\ &= (x - y)(4 - x^2) \\ &= (x - y)(2 + x)(2 - x) \end{aligned}$$

You Try It 11

$$\begin{aligned} x^{4n} - x^{2n}y^{2n} &= x^{2n+2n} - x^{2n}y^{2n} \\ &= x^{2n}(x^{2n} - y^{2n}) \\ &= x^{2n}[(x^n)^2 - (y^n)^2] \\ &= x^{2n}(x^n + y^n)(x^n - y^n) \end{aligned}$$

You Try It 12

$$\begin{aligned} ax^5 - ax^2y^6 &= ax^2(x^3 - y^6) \\ &= ax^2(x - y^2)(x^2 + xy^2 + y^4) \end{aligned}$$

SECTION 7.5

You Try It 1

$$2x(x + 7) = 0$$

$2x = 0$	$x + 7 = 0$
$x = 0$	$x = -7$

The solutions are 0 and -7.

You Try It 2

$$4x^2 - 9 = 0$$
$$(2x - 3)(2x + 3) = 0$$

$$2x - 3 = 0 \qquad 2x + 3 = 0$$
$$2x = 3 \qquad\qquad 2x = -3$$
$$x = \frac{3}{2} \qquad\qquad x = -\frac{3}{2}$$

The solutions are $\frac{3}{2}$ and $-\frac{3}{2}$.

You Try It 3

$$(x + 2)(x - 7) = 52$$
$$x^2 - 5x - 14 = 52$$
$$x^2 - 5x - 66 = 0$$
$$(x + 6)(x - 11) = 0$$

$$x + 6 = 0 \qquad x - 11 = 0$$
$$x = -6 \qquad\quad x = 11$$

The solutions are -6 and 11.

You Try It 4

Strategy   First positive consecutive integer: n
Second positive consecutive integer: $n + 1$

The sum of the squares of the two positive consecutive integers is 61.

Solution
$$n^2 + (n + 1)^2 = 61$$
$$n^2 + n^2 + 2n + 1 = 61$$
$$2n^2 + 2n + 1 = 61$$
$$2n^2 + 2n - 60 = 0$$
$$2(n^2 + n - 30) = 0$$
$$n^2 + n - 30 = 0$$
$$(n - 5)(n + 6) = 0$$

$$n - 5 = 0 \qquad n + 6 = 0$$
$$n = 5 \qquad\quad n = -6$$

Since -6 is not a positive integer, it is not a solution.

$$n = 5$$
$$n + 1 = 5 + 1 = 6$$

The two integers are 5 and 6.

You Try It 5

Strategy   Width $= x$
Length $= 2x + 4$

The area of the rectangle is 96 in². Use the equation $A = L \cdot W$.

Solution
$$A = L \cdot W$$
$$96 = (2x + 4)x$$
$$96 = 2x^2 + 4x$$
$$0 = 2x^2 + 4x - 96$$
$$0 = 2(x^2 + 2x - 48)$$
$$0 = x^2 + 2x - 48$$
$$0 = (x + 8)(x - 6)$$

$$x + 8 = 0 \qquad x - 6 = 0$$
$$x = -8 \qquad\quad x = 6$$

Since the width cannot be a negative number, -8 is not a solution.

$$x = 6$$
$$2x + 4 = 2(6) + 4 = 12 + 4 = 16$$

The width is 6 in.
The length is 16 in.

Solutions to Chapter 8 "You Try It"

SECTION 8.1

You Try It 1 $\dfrac{6x^5y}{12x^2y^3} = \dfrac{\overset{1}{\cancel{2}} \cdot \overset{1}{\cancel{3}} \cdot x^5y}{2 \cdot 2 \cdot 3 \cdot x^2y^3} = \dfrac{x^3}{2y^2}$

You Try It 2 $\dfrac{x^2 + 2x - 24}{16 - x^2} = \dfrac{\overset{-1}{\cancel{(x - 4)}}(x + 6)}{\underset{1}{\cancel{(4 - x)}}(4 + x)} = -\dfrac{x + 6}{x + 4}$

You Try It 3 $\dfrac{x^2 + 4x - 12}{x^2 - 3x + 2} = \dfrac{\overset{1}{\cancel{(x - 2)}}(x + 6)}{(x - 1)\underset{1}{\cancel{(x - 2)}}} = \dfrac{x + 6}{x - 1}$

You Try It 4

$\dfrac{12x^2 + 3x}{10x - 15} \cdot \dfrac{8x - 12}{9x + 18} = \dfrac{3x(4x + 1)}{5(2x - 3)} \cdot \dfrac{4(2x - 3)}{9(x + 2)}$

$= \dfrac{3x(4x + 1) \cdot 2 \cdot 2\overset{1}{\cancel{(2x - 3)}}}{5\underset{1}{\cancel{(2x - 3)}} \cdot 3 \cdot 3(x + 2)}$

$= \dfrac{4x(4x + 1)}{15(x + 2)}$

You Try It 5

$\dfrac{x^2 + 2x - 15}{9 - x^2} \cdot \dfrac{x^2 - 3x - 18}{x^2 - 7x + 6}$

$= \dfrac{(x - 3)(x + 5)}{(3 - x)(3 + x)} \cdot \dfrac{(x + 3)(x - 6)}{(x - 1)(x - 6)}$

$= \dfrac{\overset{-1}{\cancel{(x - 3)}}(x + 5)\overset{1}{\cancel{(x + 3)}}\overset{1}{\cancel{(x - 6)}}}{\underset{1}{\cancel{(3 - x)}}\underset{1}{\cancel{(3 + x)}}(x - 1)\underset{1}{\cancel{(x - 6)}}} = -\dfrac{x + 5}{x - 1}$

You Try It 6

$\dfrac{a^2}{4bc^2 - 2b^2c} \div \dfrac{a}{6bc - 3b^2} = \dfrac{a^2}{4bc^2 - 2b^2c} \cdot \dfrac{6bc - 3b^2}{a}$

$= \dfrac{a^2 \cdot 3b\overset{1}{\cancel{(2c - b)}}}{2bc\underset{1}{\cancel{(2c - b)}} \cdot a} = \dfrac{3a}{2c}$

You Try It 7

$\dfrac{3x^2 + 26x + 16}{3x^2 - 7x - 6} \div \dfrac{2x^2 + 9x - 5}{x^2 + 2x - 15}$

$= \dfrac{3x^2 + 26x + 16}{3x^2 - 7x - 6} \cdot \dfrac{x^2 + 2x - 15}{2x^2 + 9x - 5}$

$= \dfrac{\overset{1}{\cancel{(3x + 2)}}(x + 8) \cdot \overset{1}{\cancel{(x + 5)}}\overset{1}{\cancel{(x - 3)}}}{\underset{1}{\cancel{(3x + 2)}}\underset{1}{\cancel{(x - 3)}} \cdot (2x - 1)\underset{1}{\cancel{(x + 5)}}} = \dfrac{x + 8}{2x - 1}$

SECTION 8.2

You Try It 1

$8uv^2 = 2 \cdot 2 \cdot 2 \cdot u \cdot v \cdot v$

$12uw = 2 \cdot 2 \cdot 3 \cdot u \cdot w$

$\text{LCM} = 2 \cdot 2 \cdot 2 \cdot 3 \cdot u \cdot v \cdot v \cdot w = 24uv^2w$

You Try It 2 $\begin{aligned} m^2 - 6m + 9 &= (m - 3)(m - 3) \\ m^2 - 2m - 3 &= (m + 1)(m - 3) \\ \text{LCM} &= (m - 3)\,(m - 3)\,(m + 1) \end{aligned}$

You Try It 3
The LCM is $36xy^2z$.

$\dfrac{x - 3}{4xy^2} = \dfrac{x - 3}{4xy^2} \cdot \dfrac{9z}{9z} = \dfrac{9xz - 27z}{36xy^2z}$

$\dfrac{2x + 1}{9y^2z} = \dfrac{2x + 1}{9y^2z} \cdot \dfrac{4x}{4x} = \dfrac{8x^2 + 4x}{36xy^2z}$

You Try It 4
The LCM is $(x + 2)(x - 5)(x + 5)$

$\dfrac{x + 4}{x^2 - 3x - 10} = \dfrac{x + 4}{(x + 2)(x - 5)} \cdot \dfrac{x + 5}{x + 5}$

$= \dfrac{x^2 + 9x + 20}{(x + 2)(x - 5)(x + 5)}$

$\dfrac{2x}{25 - x^2} = \dfrac{2x}{-(x^2 - 25)} = -\dfrac{2x}{(x - 5)(x + 5)} \cdot \dfrac{x + 2}{x + 2}$

$= -\dfrac{2x^2 + 4x}{(x + 2)(x - 5)(x + 5)}$

You Try It 5 $\dfrac{3}{xy} + \dfrac{12}{xy} = \dfrac{3 + 12}{xy} = \dfrac{15}{xy}$

You Try It 6

$\dfrac{2x^2}{x^2 - x - 12} - \dfrac{7x + 4}{x^2 - x - 12}$

$= \dfrac{2x^2 - (7x + 4)}{x^2 - x - 12} = \dfrac{2x^2 - 7x - 4}{x^2 - x - 12}$

$= \dfrac{(2x + 1)\overset{1}{\cancel{(x - 4)}}}{(x + 3)\underset{1}{\cancel{(x - 4)}}} = \dfrac{2x + 1}{x + 3}$

You Try It 7

$\dfrac{x^2 - 1}{x^2 - 8x + 12} - \dfrac{2x + 1}{x^2 - 8x + 12} + \dfrac{x}{x^2 - 8x + 12}$

$= \dfrac{(x^2 - 1) - (2x + 1) + x}{x^2 - 8x + 12} = \dfrac{x^2 - 1 - 2x - 1 + x}{x^2 - 8x + 12}$

$= \dfrac{x^2 - x - 2}{x^2 - 8x + 12} = \dfrac{(x + 1)\overset{1}{\cancel{(x - 2)}}}{\underset{1}{\cancel{(x - 2)}}(x - 6)} = \dfrac{x + 1}{x - 6}$

You Try It 8
The LCM of the denominators is $24y$.

$\dfrac{z}{8y} - \dfrac{4z}{3y} + \dfrac{5z}{4y} = \dfrac{z}{8y} \cdot \dfrac{3}{3} - \dfrac{4z}{3y} \cdot \dfrac{8}{8} + \dfrac{5z}{4y} \cdot \dfrac{6}{6}$

$= \dfrac{3z}{24y} - \dfrac{32z}{24y} + \dfrac{30z}{24y}$

$= \dfrac{3z - 32z + 30z}{24y} = \dfrac{z}{24y}$

You Try It 9

$2 - x = -(x - 2)$

Therefore, $\dfrac{3}{2 - x} = \dfrac{-3}{x - 2}$.

The LCM is $x - 2$.

$$\dfrac{5x}{x - 2} - \dfrac{3}{2 - x} = \dfrac{5x}{x - 2} - \dfrac{-3}{x - 2}$$

$$= \dfrac{5x - (-3)}{x - 2} = \dfrac{5x + 3}{x - 2}$$

You Try It 10

The LCM is $(3x - 1)(x + 4)$.

$$\dfrac{4x}{3x - 1} - \dfrac{9}{x + 4} = \dfrac{4x}{3x - 1} \cdot \dfrac{x + 4}{x + 4} - \dfrac{9}{x + 4} \cdot \dfrac{3x - 1}{3x - 1}$$

$$= \dfrac{4x^2 + 16x}{(3x - 1)(x + 4)} - \dfrac{27x - 9}{(3x - 1)(x + 4)}$$

$$= \dfrac{(4x^2 + 16x) - (27x - 9)}{(3x - 1)(x + 4)}$$

$$= \dfrac{4x^2 + 16x - 27x + 9}{(3x - 1)(x + 4)}$$

$$= \dfrac{4x^2 - 11x + 9}{(3x - 1)(x + 4)}$$

You Try It 11

The LCM is $x - 3$.

$$2 - \dfrac{1}{x - 3} = \dfrac{2}{1} \cdot \dfrac{x - 3}{x - 3} - \dfrac{1}{x - 3}$$

$$= \dfrac{2x - 6}{x - 3} - \dfrac{1}{x - 3}$$

$$= \dfrac{2x - 6 - 1}{x - 3}$$

$$= \dfrac{2x - 7}{x - 3}$$

You Try It 12

The LCM is $a(a - 5)(a + 5)$.

$$\dfrac{a - 3}{a^2 - 5a} + \dfrac{a - 9}{a^2 - 25}$$

$$= \dfrac{a - 3}{a(a - 5)} \cdot \dfrac{a + 5}{a + 5} + \dfrac{a - 9}{(a - 5)(a + 5)} \cdot \dfrac{a}{a}$$

$$= \dfrac{(a - 3)(a + 5) + a(a - 9)}{a(a - 5)(a + 5)}$$

$$= \dfrac{(a^2 + 2a - 15) + (a^2 - 9a)}{a(a - 5)(a + 5)}$$

$$= \dfrac{a^2 + 2a - 15 + a^2 - 9a}{a(a - 5)(a + 5)}$$

$$= \dfrac{2a^2 - 7a - 15}{a(a - 5)(a + 5)} = \dfrac{(2a + 3)(a - 5)}{a(a - 5)(a + 5)}$$

$$= \dfrac{(2a + 3)\overset{1}{(a - 5)}}{a\underset{1}{(a - 5)}(a + 5)} = \dfrac{2a + 3}{a(a + 5)}$$

You Try It 13

The LCM is $(3x + 2)(x - 1)$.

$$\dfrac{2x - 3}{3x^2 - x - 2} + \dfrac{5}{3x + 2} - \dfrac{1}{x - 1}$$

$$= \dfrac{2x - 3}{(3x + 2)(x - 1)} + \dfrac{5}{3x + 2} \cdot \dfrac{x - 1}{x - 1} - \dfrac{1}{x - 1} \cdot \dfrac{3x + 2}{3x + 2}$$

$$= \dfrac{2x - 3}{(3x + 2)(x - 1)} + \dfrac{5x - 5}{(3x - 2)(x - 1)} - \dfrac{3x + 2}{(3x + 2)(x - 1)}$$

$$= \dfrac{(2x - 3) + (5x - 5) - (3x + 2)}{(3x + 2)(x - 1)}$$

$$= \dfrac{2x - 3 + 5x - 5 - 3x - 2}{(3x + 2)(x - 1)}$$

$$= \dfrac{4x - 10}{(3x + 2)(x - 1)} = \dfrac{2(2x - 5)}{(3x + 2)(x - 1)}$$

SECTION 8.3

You Try It 1

The LCM of 3, x, 9, and x^2 is $9x^2$.

$$\dfrac{\dfrac{1}{3} - \dfrac{1}{x}}{\dfrac{1}{9} - \dfrac{1}{x^2}} = \dfrac{\dfrac{1}{3} - \dfrac{1}{x}}{\dfrac{1}{9} - \dfrac{1}{x^2}} \cdot \dfrac{9x^2}{9x^2} = \dfrac{\dfrac{1}{3} \cdot 9x^2 - \dfrac{1}{x} \cdot 9x^2}{\dfrac{1}{9} \cdot 9x^2 - \dfrac{1}{x^2} \cdot 9x^2}$$

$$= \dfrac{3x^2 - 9x}{x^2 - 9} = \dfrac{3x\overset{1}{(x - 3)}}{\underset{1}{(x - 3)}(x + 3)} = \dfrac{3x}{x + 3}$$

You Try It 2

The LCM of x and x^2 is x^2.

$$\dfrac{1 + \dfrac{4}{x} + \dfrac{3}{x^2}}{1 + \dfrac{10}{x} + \dfrac{21}{x^2}} = \dfrac{1 + \dfrac{4}{x} + \dfrac{3}{x^2}}{1 + \dfrac{10}{x} + \dfrac{21}{x^2}} \cdot \dfrac{x^2}{x^2}$$

$$= \dfrac{1 \cdot x^2 + \dfrac{4}{x} \cdot x^2 + \dfrac{3}{x^2} + x^2}{1 \cdot x^2 + \dfrac{10}{x} \cdot x^2 + \dfrac{21}{x^2} \cdot x^2}$$

$$= \dfrac{x^2 + 4x + 3}{x^2 + 10x + 21} = \dfrac{(x + 1)\overset{1}{(x + 3)}}{\underset{1}{(x + 3)}(x + 7)} = \dfrac{x + 1}{x + 7}$$

You Try It 3

The LCM is $x - 5$.

$$\dfrac{x + 3 - \dfrac{20}{x - 5}}{x + 8 + \dfrac{30}{x + 5}} = \dfrac{x + 3 - \dfrac{20}{x - 5}}{x + 8 + \dfrac{30}{x - 5}} \cdot \dfrac{x - 5}{x - 5}$$

$$= \dfrac{x(x - 5) + 3(x - 5) - \dfrac{20}{x - 5} \cdot (x - 5)}{x(x - 5) + 8(x - 5) + \dfrac{30}{x - 5} \cdot (x - 5)}$$

$$= \dfrac{x^2 - 5x + 3x - 15 - 20}{x^2 - 5x + 8x - 40 + 30}$$

$$= \dfrac{x^2 - 2x - 35}{x^2 + 3x - 10}$$

$$= \dfrac{\overset{1}{(x + 5)}(x - 7)}{(x - 2)\underset{1}{(x + 5)}} = \dfrac{x - 7}{x - 2}$$

SECTION 8.4

You Try It 1

$$\frac{x}{x+6} = \frac{3}{x} \quad \text{The LCM is } x(x+6).$$

$$\frac{\overset{1}{x(\cancel{x+6})}}{1} \cdot \frac{x}{\cancel{x+6}} = \frac{\overset{1}{x(x+6)}}{1} \cdot \frac{3}{\cancel{x}}$$

$$x^2 = (x+6)3$$
$$x^2 = 3x + 18$$
$$x^2 - 3x - 18 = 0$$
$$(x+3)(x-6) = 0$$

$$x + 3 = 0 \qquad x - 6 = 0$$
$$x = -3 \qquad x = 6$$

Both -3 and 6 check as solutions.
The solutions are -3 and 6.

You Try It 2

$$\frac{5x}{x+2} = 3 - \frac{10}{x+2} \quad \text{The LCM is } x + 2.$$

$$\frac{(x+2)}{1} \cdot \frac{5x}{x+2} = \frac{(x+2)}{1}\left(3 - \frac{10}{x+2}\right)$$

$$\frac{\cancel{x+2}}{1} \cdot \frac{5x}{\cancel{x+2}} = (x+2)3 - \frac{\cancel{x+2}}{1} \cdot \frac{10}{\cancel{x+2}}$$

$$5x = (x+2)3 - 10$$
$$5x = 3x + 6 - 10$$
$$5x = 3x - 4$$
$$2x = -4$$
$$x = -2$$

-2 does not check as a solution.
The equation has no solution.

You Try It 3

$$\frac{2}{x+3} = \frac{6}{5x+5}$$

$$\frac{(x+3)(5x+5)}{1} \cdot \frac{2}{x+3} = \frac{(x+3)(5x+5)}{1} \cdot \frac{6}{5x+5}$$

$$\frac{\cancel{(x+3)}(5x+5)}{1} \cdot \frac{2}{\cancel{x+3}} = \frac{(x+3)\cancel{(5x+5)}}{1} \cdot \frac{6}{\cancel{5x+5}}$$

$$(5x+5)2 = (x+3)6$$
$$10x + 10 = 6x + 18$$
$$4x + 10 = 18$$
$$4x = 8$$
$$x = 2$$

The solution is 2.

You Try It 4

Strategy   To find the area of triangle *AOB*:
   • Solve a proportion to find the length
     of *AO* (the height of triangle *AOB*).

   • Use the formula for the area of a
     triangle. *AB* is the base and *AO* is
     the height.

Solution
$$\frac{CD}{AB} = \frac{DO}{AO}$$

$$\frac{4}{10} = \frac{3}{AO}$$

$$10 \cdot AO \cdot \frac{4}{10} = 10 \cdot AO \cdot \frac{3}{AO}$$

$$4(AO) = 30$$
$$AO = 7.5$$

$$A = \frac{1}{2}bh$$
$$= \frac{1}{2}(10)(7.5)$$
$$= 37.5$$

The area of triangle *AOB* is 37.5 cm².

You Try It 5

Strategy   To find the total area that 256 ceramic
     tiles will cover, write and solve a
     proportion, using *x* to represent the
     number of square feet that 256 tiles
     will cover.

Solution
$$\frac{9}{16} = \frac{x}{256}$$

$$256\left(\frac{9}{16}\right) = 256\left(\frac{x}{256}\right)$$

$$144 = x$$

A 144-square-foot area can be tiled
using 256 ceramic tiles.

You Try It 6

Strategy   To find the additional amount of
     medication required for a 200-pound
     adult, write and solve a proportion,
     using *x* to represent the additional
     medication. Then $3 + x$ is the
     total amount required for a 200-
     pound adult.

Solution
$$\frac{150}{3} = \frac{200}{3+x}$$

$$\frac{50}{1} = \frac{200}{3+x}$$

$$(3+x) \cdot 50 = (3+x) \cdot \frac{200}{3+x}$$

$$(3+x) \cdot 50 = 200$$
$$150 + 50x = 200$$
$$50x = 50$$
$$x = 1$$

One additional ounce is required for a
200-pound adult.

SECTION 8.5

You Try It 1

$$A = P + Prt$$
$$A - P = P - P + Prt$$
$$A - P = Prt$$
$$\frac{A - P}{Pt} = \frac{Prt}{Pt}$$
$$\frac{A - P}{Pt} = r$$

You Try It 2

$$s = \frac{A + L}{2}$$
$$2 \cdot s = 2\left(\frac{A + L}{2}\right)$$
$$2s = A + L$$
$$2s - A = A - A + L$$
$$2s - A = L$$

You Try It 3

$$s = a + (n - 1)d$$
$$s = a + nd - d$$
$$s - a = a - a + nd - d$$
$$s - a = nd - d$$
$$s - a + d = nd - d + d$$
$$s - a + d = nd$$
$$\frac{s - a + d}{d} = \frac{nd}{d}$$
$$\frac{s - a + d}{d} = n$$

You Try It 4

$$S = C + rC$$
$$S = (1 + r)C$$
$$\frac{S}{1 + r} = \frac{(1 + r)C}{1 + r}$$
$$\frac{S}{1 + r} = C$$

SECTION 8.6

You Try It 1

Strategy • Time for one printer to complete the job: t

	Rate	Time	Part
1st printer	$\frac{1}{t}$	2	$\frac{2}{t}$
2nd printer	$\frac{1}{t}$	5	$\frac{5}{t}$

• The sum of the parts of the task completed must equal 1.

Solution

$$\frac{2}{t} + \frac{5}{t} = 1$$
$$t\left(\frac{2}{t} + \frac{5}{t}\right) = t \cdot 1$$
$$2 + 5 = t$$
$$7 = t$$

Working alone, one printer takes 7 h to print the payroll.

You Try It 2

Strategy • Rate sailing across the lake: r
Rate sailing back: $3r$

	Distance	Rate	Time
Across	6	r	$\frac{6}{r}$
Back	6	$3r$	$\frac{6}{3r}$

• The total time for the trip was 2 h.

Solution

$$\frac{6}{r} + \frac{6}{3r} = 2$$
$$3r\left(\frac{6}{r} + \frac{6}{3r}\right) = 3r(2)$$
$$3r \cdot \frac{6}{r} + 3r \cdot \frac{6}{3r} = 6r$$
$$18 + 6 = 6r$$
$$24 = 6r$$
$$4 = r$$

The rate across the lake was 4 km/h.

SECTION 8.7

You Try It 1

Strategy To find the distance:
• Write the basic direct variation equation, replace the variables by the given values, and solve for k.
• Write the direct variation equation, replacing k by its value. Substitute 5 for t and solve for s.

Solution
$$s = kt^2$$
$$64 = k(2)^2$$
$$64 = k \cdot 4$$
$$16 = k$$

$$s = 16t^2 = 16(5)^2 = 400$$

The object will fall 400 ft in 5 s.

You Try It 2

Strategy   To find the resistance:
- Write the basic inverse variation equation, replace the variables by the given values, and solve for k.
- Write the inverse variation equation, replacing k by its value. Substitute 0.02 for d and solve for R.

Solution

$$R = \frac{k}{d^2}$$

$$0.5 = \frac{k}{(0.01)^2}$$

$$0.5 = \frac{k}{0.0001}$$

$$0.00005 = k$$

$$R = \frac{0.00005}{d^2} = \frac{0.00005}{(0.02)^2} = 0.125$$

The resistance is 0.125 ohm.

You Try It 3

Strategy   To find the strength:
- Write the basic combined variation equation, replace the variables by the given values, and solve for k.
- Write the combined variation equation, replacing k by its value. Substitute 4 for w, 8 for d, and 16 for L, and solve for s.

Solution

$$s = \frac{kwd^2}{L}$$

$$1200 = \frac{k \cdot 2 \cdot (12)^2}{12}$$

$$1200 = \frac{k \cdot 2 \cdot 144}{12}$$

$$1200 = 24k$$

$$50 = k$$

$$s = \frac{50wd^2}{L} = \frac{50 \cdot 4 \cdot (8)^2}{16} = 800$$

The strength is 800 lb.

Solutions to Chapter 9 "You Try It"

SECTION 9.1

You Try It 1
$$16^{-3/4} = (2^4)^{-3/4}$$
$$= 2^{-3}$$
$$= \frac{1}{2^3} = \frac{1}{8}$$

You Try It 2 $(-81)^{3/4}$

The base of the exponential expression is negative, and the denominator of the exponent is a positive even number.

Therefore, $(-81)^{3/4}$ is not a real number.

You Try It 3 $(x^{3/4}y^{1/2}z^{-2/3})^{-4/3} = x^{-1}y^{-2/3}z^{8/9}$
$$= \frac{z^{8/9}}{xy^{2/3}}$$

You Try It 4 $\left(\dfrac{16a^{-2}b^{4/3}}{9a^4b^{-2/3}}\right)^{-1/2} = \left(\dfrac{2^4a^{-6}b^2}{3^2}\right)^{-1/2}$
$$= \frac{2^{-2}a^3b^{-1}}{3^{-1}}$$
$$= \frac{3a^3}{2^2b} = \frac{3a^3}{4b}$$

You Try It 5 $(2x^3)^{3/4} = \sqrt[4]{(2x^3)^3}$
$$= \sqrt[4]{8x^9}$$

You Try It 6 $-5a^{5/6} = -5(a^5)^{1/6}$
$$= -5\sqrt[6]{a^5}$$

You Try It 7 $\sqrt[3]{3ab} = (3ab)^{1/3}$

You Try It 8 $\sqrt[4]{x^4 + y^4} = (x^4 + y^4)^{1/4}$

You Try It 9 $\sqrt{121x^{10}y^4} = \sqrt{11^2x^{10}y^4}$
$$= (11^2x^{10}y^4)^{1/2}$$
$$= 11x^5y^2$$

You Try It 10 $\sqrt[3]{-8x^{12}y^3} = \sqrt[3]{(-2)^3x^{12}y^3}$
$$= [(-2)^3x^{12}y^3]^{1/3}$$
$$= -2x^4y$$

You Try It 11 $-\sqrt[4]{81x^{12}y^8} = -\sqrt[4]{3^4x^{12}y^8}$
$$= -(3^4x^{12}y^8)^{1/4}$$
$$= -3x^3y^2$$

SECTION 9.2

You Try It 1 $\sqrt[5]{x^7} = \sqrt[5]{x^5 \cdot x^2}$
$$= \sqrt[5]{x^5}\,\sqrt[5]{x^2}$$
$$= x\sqrt[5]{x^2}$$

You Try It 2
$$\sqrt[3]{-64x^8y^{18}} = \sqrt[3]{(-4)^3x^8y^{18}}$$
$$= \sqrt[3]{(-4)^3x^6y^{18}(x^2)}$$
$$= \sqrt[3]{(-4)^3x^6y^{18}}\sqrt[3]{x^2}$$
$$= -4x^2y^6\sqrt[3]{x^2}$$

You Try It 3
$$3xy\sqrt[3]{81x^5y} - \sqrt[3]{192x^8y^4}$$
$$= 3xy\sqrt[3]{3^4x^5y} - \sqrt[3]{2^6 \cdot 3x^8y^4}$$
$$= 3xy\sqrt[3]{3^3x^3}\sqrt[3]{3x^2y} - \sqrt[3]{2^6x^6y^3}\sqrt[3]{3x^2y}$$
$$= 3xy \cdot 3x\sqrt[3]{3x^2y} - 2^2x^2y\sqrt[3]{3x^2y}$$
$$= 9x^2y\sqrt[3]{3x^2y} - 4x^2y\sqrt[3]{3x^2y} = 5x^2y\sqrt[3]{3x^2y}$$

You Try It 4
$$\sqrt{5b}(\sqrt{3b} - \sqrt{10})$$
$$= \sqrt{15b^2} - \sqrt{50b}$$
$$= \sqrt{3 \cdot 5b^2} - \sqrt{2 \cdot 5^2b}$$
$$= \sqrt{b^2}\sqrt{3 \cdot 5} - \sqrt{5^2}\sqrt{2b}$$
$$= b\sqrt{15} - 5\sqrt{2b}$$

You Try It 5
$$(2\sqrt[3]{2x} - 3)(\sqrt[3]{2x} - 5)$$
$$= 2\sqrt[3]{4x^2} - 10\sqrt[3]{2x} - 3\sqrt[3]{2x} + 15$$
$$= 2\sqrt[3]{4x^2} - 13\sqrt[3]{2x} + 15$$

You Try It 6
$$(\sqrt{a} - 3\sqrt{y})(\sqrt{a} + 3\sqrt{y})$$
$$= (\sqrt{a})^2 - (3\sqrt{y})^2$$
$$= a - 9y$$

You Try It 7
$$\frac{y}{\sqrt{3y}} = \frac{y}{\sqrt{3y}} \cdot \frac{\sqrt{3y}}{\sqrt{3y}} = \frac{y\sqrt{3y}}{\sqrt{3^2y^2}} = \frac{y\sqrt{3y}}{3y} = \frac{\sqrt{3y}}{3}$$

You Try It 8
$$\frac{3}{\sqrt[3]{3x^2}} = \frac{3}{\sqrt[3]{3x^2}} \cdot \frac{\sqrt[3]{3^2x}}{\sqrt[3]{3^2x}} = \frac{3\sqrt[3]{9x}}{\sqrt[3]{3^3x^3}}$$
$$= \frac{3\sqrt[3]{9x}}{3x} = \frac{\sqrt[3]{9x}}{x}$$

You Try It 9
$$\frac{3 + \sqrt{6}}{2 - \sqrt{6}} = \frac{3 + \sqrt{6}}{2 - \sqrt{6}} \cdot \frac{2 + \sqrt{6}}{2 + \sqrt{6}} = \frac{6 + 3\sqrt{6} + 2\sqrt{6} + (\sqrt{6})^2}{2^2 - (\sqrt{6})^2}$$
$$= \frac{6 + 5\sqrt{6} + 6}{4 - 6} = \frac{12 + 5\sqrt{6}}{-2} = -\frac{12 + 5\sqrt{6}}{2}$$

SECTION 9.3

You Try It 1 $\sqrt{-45} = i\sqrt{45} = i\sqrt{3^2 \cdot 5} = 3i\sqrt{5}$

You Try It 2
$$\sqrt{98} - \sqrt{-60} = \sqrt{98} - i\sqrt{60}$$
$$= \sqrt{2 \cdot 7^2} - i\sqrt{2^2 \cdot 3 \cdot 5}$$
$$= 7\sqrt{2} - 2i\sqrt{15}$$

You Try It 3 $(-4 + 2i) - (6 - 8i) = -10 + 10i$

You Try It 4 $(16 - \sqrt{-45}) - (3 + \sqrt{-20})$
$$= (16 - i\sqrt{45}) - (3 + i\sqrt{20})$$
$$= (16 - i\sqrt{3^2 \cdot 5}) - (3 + i\sqrt{2^2 \cdot 5})$$
$$= (16 - 3i\sqrt{5}) - (3 + 2i\sqrt{5})$$
$$= 13 - 5i\sqrt{5}$$

You Try It 5 $(3 - 2i) + (-3 + 2i) = 0 + 0i = 0$

You Try It 6 $(-3i)(-10i) = 30i^2 = 30(-1) = -30$

You Try It 7
$$-\sqrt{-8} \cdot \sqrt{-5} = -i\sqrt{8} \cdot i\sqrt{5} = -i^2\sqrt{40}$$
$$= -(-1)\sqrt{40} = \sqrt{2^3 \cdot 5} = 2\sqrt{10}$$

You Try It 8
$$-6i(3 + 4i) = -18i - 24i^2$$
$$= -18i - 24(-1) = 24 - 18i$$

You Try It 9
$$\sqrt{-3}(\sqrt{27} - \sqrt{-6}) = i\sqrt{3}(\sqrt{27} - i\sqrt{6})$$
$$= i\sqrt{81} - i^2\sqrt{18}$$
$$= i\sqrt{3^4} - (-1)\sqrt{2 \cdot 3^2}$$
$$= 9i + 3\sqrt{2}$$
$$= 3\sqrt{2} + 9i$$

You Try It 10
$$(4 - 3i)(2 - i) = 8 - 4i - 6i + 3i^2$$
$$= 8 - 10i + 3i^2$$
$$= 8 - 10i + 3(-1)$$
$$= 5 - 10i$$

You Try It 11 $(3 + 6i)(3 - 6i) = 3^2 + 6^2$
$$= 9 + 36$$
$$= 45$$

You Try It 12
$$(3 - i)\left(\frac{3}{10} + \frac{1}{10}i\right) = \frac{9}{10} + \frac{3}{10}i - \frac{3}{10}i - \frac{1}{10}i^2$$
$$= \frac{9}{10} - \frac{1}{10}i^2 = \frac{9}{10} - \frac{1}{10}(-1)$$
$$= \frac{9}{10} + \frac{1}{10} = 1$$

You Try It 13

$$\frac{2 - 3i}{4i} = \frac{2 - 3i}{4i} \cdot \frac{i}{i}$$

$$= \frac{2i - 3i^2}{4i^2}$$

$$= \frac{2i - 3(-1)}{4(-1)}$$

$$= \frac{3 + 2i}{-4} = -\frac{3}{4} - \frac{1}{2}i$$

You Try It 14

$$\frac{2 + 5i}{3 - 2i} = \frac{2 + 5i}{3 - 2i} \cdot \frac{3 + 2i}{3 + 2i} = \frac{6 + 4i + 15i + 10i^2}{3^2 + 2^2}$$

$$= \frac{6 + 19i + 10(-1)}{13} = \frac{-4 + 19i}{13}$$

$$= -\frac{4}{13} + \frac{19}{13}i$$

SECTION 9.4

You Try It 1

$$\sqrt[4]{x - 8} = 3 \qquad \textit{Check:}$$

$$(\sqrt[4]{x - 8})^4 = 3^4 \qquad \sqrt[4]{x - 8} = 3$$

$$x - 8 = 81 \qquad \sqrt[4]{89 - 8} \mid 3$$

$$x = 89 \qquad \sqrt[4]{81} \mid 3$$

$$3 = 3$$

The solution is 89.

You Try It 2

$$\sqrt{x} - \sqrt{x + 5} = 1$$

$$\sqrt{x} = 1 + \sqrt{x + 5}$$

$$(\sqrt{x})^2 = (1 + \sqrt{x + 5})^2$$

$$x = 1 + 2\sqrt{x + 5} + x + 5$$

$$0 = 6 + 2\sqrt{x + 5}$$

$$-6 = 2\sqrt{x + 5}$$

$$-3 = \sqrt{x + 5}$$

$$(-3)^2 = (\sqrt{x + 5})^2$$

$$9 = x + 5$$

$$4 = x$$

4 does not check as a solution. The equation has no solution.

You Try It 3

Strategy To find the diagonal, use the Pythagorean Theorem. One leg is the length of the rectangle. The second leg is the width of the rectangle. The hypotenuse is the diagonal of the rectangle.

Solution
$$c^2 = a^2 + b^2$$
$$c^2 = (6)^2 + (3)^2$$
$$c^2 = 36 + 9$$
$$c^2 = 45$$
$$(c^2)^{1/2} = (45)^{1/2}$$
$$c = \sqrt{45}$$
$$c \approx 6.7$$

The diagonal is 6.7 cm.

You Try It 4

Strategy To find the height, replace d in the equation with the given value and solve for h.

Solution
$$d = \sqrt{1.5h}$$
$$5.5 = \sqrt{1.5h}$$
$$(5.5)^2 = (\sqrt{1.5h})^2$$
$$30.25 = 1.5h$$
$$20.17 \approx h$$

The periscope must be approximately 20.17 ft above the water.

You Try It 5

Strategy To find the distance, replace the variables v and a in the equation by their given values and solve for s.

Solution
$$v = \sqrt{2as}$$
$$88 = \sqrt{2 \cdot 22s}$$
$$88 = \sqrt{44s}$$
$$(88)^2 = (\sqrt{44s})^2$$
$$7744 = 44s$$
$$176 = s$$

The distance required is 176 ft.

Solutions to Chapter 10 "You Try It"

SECTION 10.1

You Try It 1
$$2x^2 = 7x - 3$$
$$2x^2 - 7x + 3 = 0$$
$$(2x - 1)(x - 3) = 0$$

$$2x - 1 = 0 \qquad x - 3 = 0$$
$$2x = 1 \qquad\quad x = 3$$
$$x = \frac{1}{2}$$

The solutions are $\frac{1}{2}$ and 3.

You Try It 2
$$x^2 - 3ax - 4a^2 = 0$$
$$(x + a)(x - 4a) = 0$$

$$x + a = 0 \qquad x - 4a = 0$$
$$x = -a \qquad\quad x = 4a$$

The solutions are $-a$ and $4a$.

You Try It 3
$$(x - r_1)(x - r_2) = 0$$
$$(x - 3)\left[x - \left(-\frac{1}{2}\right)\right] = 0$$
$$(x - 3)\left(x + \frac{1}{2}\right) = 0$$
$$x^2 - \frac{5}{2}x - \frac{3}{2} = 0$$
$$2\left(x^2 - \frac{5}{2}x - \frac{3}{2}\right) = 2 \cdot 0$$
$$2x^2 - 5x - 3 = 0$$

You Try It 4
$$2(x + 1)^2 - 24 = 0$$
$$2(x + 1)^2 = 24$$
$$(x + 1)^2 = 12$$
$$\sqrt{(x + 1)^2} = \sqrt{12}$$
$$x + 1 = \pm 2\sqrt{3}$$

$$x + 1 = 2\sqrt{3} \qquad\qquad x + 1 = -2\sqrt{3}$$
$$x = -1 + 2\sqrt{3} \qquad\quad x = -1 - 2\sqrt{3}$$

The solutions are
$-1 + 2\sqrt{3}$ and $-1 - 2\sqrt{3}$.

SECTION 10.2

You Try It 1
$$4x^2 - 4x - 1 = 0$$
$$4x^2 - 4x = 1$$
$$\frac{1}{4}(4x^2 - 4x) = \frac{1}{4} \cdot 1$$
$$x^2 - x = \frac{1}{4}$$

Complete the square.

$$x^2 - x + \frac{1}{4} = \frac{1}{4} + \frac{1}{4}$$
$$\left(x - \frac{1}{2}\right)^2 = \frac{2}{4}$$
$$\sqrt{\left(x - \frac{1}{2}\right)^2} = \sqrt{\frac{2}{4}}$$
$$x - \frac{1}{2} = \pm\frac{\sqrt{2}}{2}$$

$$x - \frac{1}{2} = \frac{\sqrt{2}}{2} \qquad\quad x - \frac{1}{2} = -\frac{\sqrt{2}}{2}$$
$$x = \frac{1}{2} + \frac{\sqrt{2}}{2} \qquad\quad x = \frac{1}{2} - \frac{\sqrt{2}}{2}$$

The solutions are $\frac{1 + \sqrt{2}}{2}$ and $\frac{1 - \sqrt{2}}{2}$.

You Try It 2
$$2x^2 + x - 5 = 0$$
$$2x^2 + x = 5$$
$$\frac{1}{2}(2x^2 + x) = \frac{1}{2} \cdot 5$$
$$x^2 + \frac{1}{2}x = \frac{5}{2}$$

Complete the square.

$$x^2 + \frac{1}{2}x + \frac{1}{16} = \frac{5}{2} + \frac{1}{16}$$
$$\left(x + \frac{1}{4}\right)^2 = \frac{41}{16}$$
$$\sqrt{\left(x + \frac{1}{4}\right)^2} = \sqrt{\frac{41}{16}}$$
$$x + \frac{1}{4} = \pm\frac{\sqrt{41}}{4}$$

$$x + \frac{1}{4} = \frac{\sqrt{41}}{4} \qquad\quad x + \frac{1}{4} = -\frac{\sqrt{41}}{4}$$
$$x = -\frac{1}{4} + \frac{\sqrt{41}}{4} \qquad\quad x = -\frac{1}{4} - \frac{\sqrt{41}}{4}$$

The solutions are $\frac{-1 + \sqrt{41}}{4}$ and $\frac{-1 - \sqrt{41}}{4}$.

SECTION 10.3

You Try It 1
$$x^2 - 2x + 10 = 0$$
$$a = 1, b = -2, c = 10$$
$$x = \frac{-b \pm \sqrt{b^2 - 4ac}}{2a}$$
$$= \frac{-(-2) \pm \sqrt{(-2)^2 - 4(1)(10)}}{2 \cdot 1}$$
$$= \frac{2 \pm \sqrt{4 - 40}}{2} = \frac{2 \pm \sqrt{-36}}{2}$$
$$= \frac{2 \pm 6i}{2} = 1 \pm 3i$$

The solutions are $1 + 3i$ and $1 - 3i$.

You Try It 2

$$4x^2 = 4x - 1$$
$$4x^2 - 4x + 1 = 0$$
$$a = 4, b = -4, c = 1$$
$$x = \frac{-b \pm \sqrt{b^2 - 4ac}}{2a}$$
$$= \frac{-(-4) \pm \sqrt{(-4)^2 - 4(4)(1)}}{2 \cdot 4}$$
$$= \frac{4 \pm \sqrt{16 - 16}}{8} = \frac{4 \pm \sqrt{0}}{8}$$
$$= \frac{4}{8} = \frac{1}{2}$$

The solution is $\frac{1}{2}$.

You Try It 3

$$3x^2 - x - 1 = 0$$
$$a = 3, b = -1, c = -1$$
$$b^2 - 4ac = (-1)^2 - 4(3)(-1)$$
$$= 1 + 12 = 13$$
$$13 > 0$$

Because the discriminant is greater than zero, the equation has two real number solutions.

SECTION 10.4

You Try It 1

$$x - 5x^{1/2} + 6 = 0$$
$$(x^{1/2})^2 - 5(x^{1/2}) + 6 = 0$$
$$u^2 - 5u + 6 = 0$$
$$(u - 2)(u - 3) = 0$$

$$u - 2 = 0 \qquad u - 3 = 0$$
$$u = 2 \qquad\quad u = 3$$

Replace u by $x^{1/2}$.

$$x^{1/2} = 2 \qquad\quad x^{1/2} = 3$$
$$\sqrt{x} = 2 \qquad\quad \sqrt{x} = 3$$
$$(\sqrt{x})^2 = 2^2 \qquad (\sqrt{x})^2 = 3^2$$
$$x = 4 \qquad\qquad x = 9$$

The solutions are 4 and 9.

You Try It 2

$$\sqrt{2x + 1} + x = 7$$
$$\sqrt{2x + 1} = 7 - x$$
$$(\sqrt{2x + 1})^2 = (7 - x)^2$$
$$2x + 1 = 49 - 14x + x^2$$
$$0 = x^2 - 16x + 48$$
$$0 = (x - 4)(x - 12)$$

$$x - 4 = 0 \qquad x - 12 = 0$$
$$x = 4 \qquad\quad x = 12$$

4 checks as a solution.
12 does not check as a solution.

The solution is 4.

You Try It 3 $\sqrt{2x - 1} + \sqrt{x} = 2$

Solve for one of the radical expressions.

$$\sqrt{2x - 1} = 2 - \sqrt{x}$$
$$(\sqrt{2x - 1})^2 = (2 - \sqrt{x})^2$$
$$2x - 1 = 4 - 4\sqrt{x} + x$$
$$x - 5 = -4\sqrt{x}$$

Square each side of the equation.

$$(x - 5)^2 = (-4\sqrt{x})^2$$
$$x^2 - 10x + 25 = 16x$$
$$x^2 - 26x + 25 = 0$$
$$(x - 1)(x - 25) = 0$$

$$x - 1 = 0 \qquad x - 25 = 0$$
$$x = 1 \qquad\quad x = 25$$

1 checks as a solution.
25 does not check as a solution.

The solution is 1.

You Try It 4

$$3y + \frac{25}{3y - 2} = -8$$
$$(3y - 2)\left(3y + \frac{25}{3y - 2}\right) = (3y - 2)(-8)$$
$$(3y - 2)(3y) + (3y - 2)\left(\frac{25}{3y - 2}\right) = (3y - 2)(-8)$$
$$9y^2 - 6y + 25 = -24y + 16$$
$$9y^2 + 18y + 9 = 0$$
$$9(y^2 + 2y + 1) = 0$$
$$y^2 + 2y + 1 = 0$$
$$(y + 1)(y + 1) = 0$$

$$y + 1 = 0 \qquad y + 1 = 0$$
$$y = -1 \qquad\quad y = -1$$

The solution is -1.

SECTION 10.5

You Try It 1

Strategy
- This is a geometry problem.
- Width of the rectangle: W
  Length of the rectangle: $W + 3$
- Use the equation $A = L \cdot W$.

Solution
$$A = L \cdot W$$
$$54 = (W + 3)(W)$$
$$54 = W^2 + 3W$$
$$0 = W^2 + 3W - 54$$
$$0 = (W + 9)(W - 6)$$

$$W + 9 = 0 \qquad W - 6 = 0$$
$$W = -9 \qquad\quad W = 6$$

The solution -9 is not possible.

$W + 3 = 6 + 3 = 9$

The length is 9 m.

SECTION 10.6

You Try It 1 $2x^2 - x - 10 \leq 0$
$(2x - 5)(x + 2) \leq 0$

```
2x – 5  ---  |  --------  | +++
x + 2   ---  | ++++++++   | +++
        -3 -2 -1  0  1  2  3
```

```
 -5 -4 -3 -2 -1  0  1  2  3  4  5
```

$$\left\{x \mid -2 \leq x \leq \frac{5}{2}\right\}$$

Solutions to Chapter 11 "You Try It"

SECTION 11.1

You Try It 1

$f(x) = \dfrac{3}{5}x - 4$

$b = -4$

y-intercept: $(0, -4)$

$m = \dfrac{3}{5}$

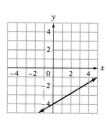

You Try It 2

Strategy
- Select the independent and dependent variables. The function is to predict the Celsius temperature, so that quantity is the dependent variable, y. The Fahrenheit variable is the independent variable, x.
- From the given data, two ordered pairs are (212, 100) and (32, 0). Use these ordered pairs to determine the linear function.

Solution

Let $(x_1, y_1) = (32, 0)$ and $(x_2, y_2) = (212, 100)$.

$m = \dfrac{y_2 - y_1}{x_2 - x_1} = \dfrac{100 - 0}{212 - 32} = \dfrac{100}{180} = \dfrac{5}{9}$

$y - y_1 = m(x - x_1)$

$y - 0 = \dfrac{5}{9}(x - 32)$

$y = \dfrac{5}{9}(x - 32)$, or $C = \dfrac{5}{9}(F - 32)$.

The linear function is $f(F) = \dfrac{5}{9}(F - 32)$.

SECTION 11.2

You Try It 1 x-coordinate of vertex:

$-\dfrac{b}{2a} = -\dfrac{4}{2(4)} = -\dfrac{1}{2}$

y-coordinate of vertex:

$y = 4x^2 + 4x + 1$

$\quad = 4\left(-\dfrac{1}{2}\right)^2 + 4\left(-\dfrac{1}{2}\right) + 1$

$\quad = 1 - 2 + 1$

$\quad = 0$

vertex: $\left(-\dfrac{1}{2}, 0\right)$

axis of symmetry: $x = -\dfrac{1}{2}$

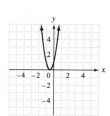

You Try It 2

$y = x^2 + 3x + 4$

$0 = x^2 + 3x + 4$

$x = \dfrac{-b \pm \sqrt{b^2 - 4ac}}{2a}$ • $a = 1, b = 3, c = 4$

$\quad = \dfrac{-3 \pm \sqrt{3^2 - 4(1)(4)}}{2 \cdot 1}$

$\quad = \dfrac{-3 \pm \sqrt{-7}}{2}$

$\quad = \dfrac{-3 \pm i\sqrt{7}}{2} = -\dfrac{3}{2} \pm \dfrac{\sqrt{7}}{2}i$

The equation has no real number solutions. There are no x-intercepts.

You Try It 3

$y = x^2 - x - 6$

$a = 1, b = -1, c = -6$

$b^2 - 4ac$

$(-1)^2 - 4(1)(-6) = 1 + 24 = 25$

Because the discriminant is greater than zero, the parabola has two x-intercepts.

You Try It 4

$f(x) = -3x^2 + 4x - 1$

$x = -\dfrac{b}{2a} = -\dfrac{4}{2(-3)} = \dfrac{2}{3}$

$f(x) = -3x^2 + 4x - 1$

$f\left(\dfrac{2}{3}\right) = -3\left(\dfrac{2}{3}\right)^2 + 4\left(\dfrac{2}{3}\right) - 1$

$\qquad = -\dfrac{4}{3} + \dfrac{8}{3} - 1 = \dfrac{1}{3}$

Because a is negative, the function has a maximum value.

The maximum value of the function is $\dfrac{1}{3}$.

You Try It 5

   Strategy
- To find the time it takes the ball to reach its maximum height, find the t-coordinate of the vertex.
- To find the maximum height, evaluate the function at the t-coordinate of the vertex.

   Solution

$t = -\dfrac{b}{2a} = -\dfrac{64}{2(-16)} = 2$

The ball reaches its maximum height in 2 s.

$s(t) = -16t^2 + 64t$

$s(2) = -16(2)^2 + 64(2) = -64 + 128 = 64$

The maximum height is 64 ft.

SECTION 11.3

You Try It 1   Any vertical line intersects the graph only once. The graph is the graph of a function.

You Try It 2   domain: $\{x \mid x \in \text{real numbers}\}$
              range: $\{y \mid y \in \text{real numbers}\}$

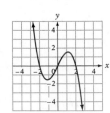

You Try It 3   domain: $\{x \mid x \in \text{real numbers}\}$
              range: $\{y \mid y \geq 0\}$

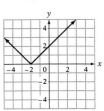

You Try It 4   domain: $\{x \mid x \geq 1\}$
              range: $\{y \mid y \leq 0\}$

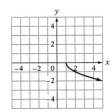

SECTION 11.4

You Try It 1

$(f + g)(-2) = f(-2) + g(-2)$

$\qquad\qquad\quad = [(-2)^2 + 2(-2)] + [5(-2) - 2]$

$\qquad\qquad\quad = (4 - 4) + (-10 - 2)$

$\qquad\qquad\quad = -12$

$(f + g)(-2) = -12$

You Try It 2 $(f \cdot g)(3) = f(3) \cdot g(3)$

$\qquad\qquad\quad = (4 - 3^2) \cdot [3(3) - 4]$

$\qquad\qquad\quad = (4 - 9) \cdot (9 - 4)$

$\qquad\qquad\quad = (-5)(5)$

$\qquad\qquad\quad = -25$

$(f \cdot g)(3) = -25$

You Try It 3 $\left(\dfrac{f}{g}\right)(4) = \dfrac{f(4)}{g(4)}$

$\qquad\qquad\quad = \dfrac{4^2 - 4}{4^2 + 2 \cdot 4 + 1}$

$\qquad\qquad\quad = \dfrac{16 - 4}{16 + 8 + 1}$

$\qquad\qquad\quad = \dfrac{12}{25}$

$\left(\dfrac{f}{g}\right)(4) = \dfrac{12}{25}$

You Try It 4 $g(x) = x^2$

$\qquad\qquad\quad g(-1) = (-1)^2 = 1$

$\qquad\qquad\quad f(x) = 1 - 2x$

$\qquad\qquad\quad f[g(-1)] = f(1) = 1 - 2(1) = -1$

You Try It 5

$f(x) = 3x - 1$

$f(1) = 3(1) - 1 = 2$

$$g(x) = \frac{x}{x^2 - 2}$$

$(g \circ f)(1) = g[f(1)] = g(2) = \dfrac{2}{2^2 - 2} = \dfrac{2}{2} = 1$

You Try It 6

$M(s) = s^3 + 1$

$M[L(s)] = M(s + 1) = (s + 1)^3 + 1$

$\qquad = s^3 + 3s^2 + 3s + 1 + 1$

$\qquad = s^3 + 3s^2 + 3s + 2$

You Try It 7

$V(x) = x^2 + 1$

$V[W(x)] = V(-\sqrt{x - 1}) = (-\sqrt{x - 1})^2 + 1$

$\qquad = x - 1 + 1$

$\qquad = x$

SECTION 11.5

You Try It 1 Because any horizontal line intersects the graph at most once, the graph is the graph of a 1–1 function.

You Try It 2

$f(x) = \dfrac{1}{2}x + 4$

$y = \dfrac{1}{2}x + 4$

$x = \dfrac{1}{2}y + 4$

$x - 4 = \dfrac{1}{2}y$

$2x - 8 = y$

$f^{-1}(x) = 2x - 8$

The inverse of the function is given by $f^{-1}(x) = 2x - 8$.

You Try It 3

$f[g(x)] = 2\left(\dfrac{1}{2}x - 3\right) - 6$

$\qquad = x - 6 - 6 = x - 12$

No, $g(x)$ is not the inverse of $f(x)$.

SECTION 11.6

You Try It 1

$y = x^2 + 2x + 1$

$-\dfrac{b}{2a} = -\dfrac{2}{2(1)} = -1$

axis of symmetry:

$x = -1$

$y = (-1)^2 + 2(-1) + 1$

$\quad = 0$

vertex: $(-1, 0)$

You Try It 2

$x = -y^2 - 2y + 2$

$-\dfrac{b}{2a} = -\dfrac{-2}{2(-1)} = -1$

axis of symmetry:

$y = -1$

$x = -(-1)^2 - 2(-1) + 2$

$\quad = 3$

vertex: $(3, -1)$

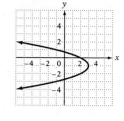

You Try It 3

$y = x^2 - 2x - 1$

$-\dfrac{b}{2a} = -\dfrac{-2}{2(1)} = 1$

axis of symmetry:

$x = 1$

$y = 1^2 - 2(1) - 1$

$\quad = -2$

vertex: $(1, -2)$

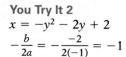

You Try It 4

$(x - h)^2 + (y - k)^2 = r^2$

$(x - 2)^2 + [y - (-3)]^2 = 3^2$

center: $(h, k) = (2, -3)$

radius: $r = 3$

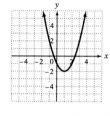

You Try It 5

$(x - h)^2 + (y - k)^2 = r^2$

$(x - 2)^2 + [y - (-3)]^2 = 4^2$

$(x - 2)^2 + (y + 3)^2 = 16$

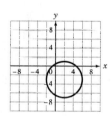

You Try It 6

x-intercepts:

$(2, 0)$ and $(-2, 0)$

y-intercepts:

$(0, 5)$ and $(0, -5)$

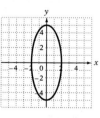

You Try It 7

x-intercepts

$(3\sqrt{2}, 0)$ and $(-3\sqrt{2}, 0)$

y-intercepts:

$(0, 3)$ and $(0, -3)$

$\left(3\sqrt{2} \approx 4\dfrac{1}{4}\right)$

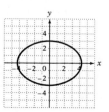

You Try It 8
axis of symmetry:
x-axis

vertices:
$(3, 0)$ and $(-3, 0)$

asymptotes:
$y = \dfrac{5}{3}x$ and $y = -\dfrac{5}{3}x$

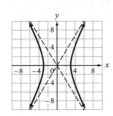

You Try It 9
axis of symmetry:
y-axis

vertices:
$(0, 3)$ and $(0, -3)$

asymptotes:
$y = x$ and $y = -x$

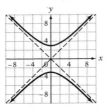

Solutions to Chapter 12 "You Try It"

SECTION 12.1

You Try It 1
$$f(x) = \left(\frac{2}{3}\right)^x$$
$$f(3) = \left(\frac{2}{3}\right)^3 = \frac{8}{27}$$
$$f(-2) = \left(\frac{2}{3}\right)^{-2} = \left(\frac{3}{2}\right)^2 = \frac{9}{4}$$

You Try It 2
$$f(x) = 2^{2x+1}$$
$$f(0) = 2^{2(0)+1} = 2^1 = 2$$
$$f(-2) = 2^{2(-2)+1} = 2^{-3} = \frac{1}{2^3} = \frac{1}{8}$$

You Try It 3
$$f(x) = e^{2x-1}$$
$$f(2) = e^{2 \cdot 2 - 1} = e^3 \approx 20.0855$$
$$f(-2) = e^{2(-2)-1} = e^{-5} \approx 0.0067$$

You Try It 4

x	y
-4	4
-2	2
0	1
2	$\dfrac{1}{2}$
4	$\dfrac{1}{4}$

You Try It 5

x	y
-2	$\dfrac{5}{4}$
-1	$\dfrac{3}{2}$
0	2
1	3
2	5

You Try It 6

x	y
-2	6
-1	4
0	3
1	$\dfrac{5}{2}$
2	$\dfrac{9}{4}$

You Try It 7

x	y
-4	$\dfrac{9}{4}$
-2	$\dfrac{5}{2}$
0	3
2	4
4	6

SECTION 12.2

You Try It 1
$$\log_4 64 = x$$
$$64 = 4^x$$
$$4^3 = 4^x$$
$$3 = x$$
$$\log_4 64 = 3$$

You Try It 2
$$\log_2 x = -4$$
$$2^{-4} = x$$
$$\frac{1}{2^4} = x$$
$$\frac{1}{16} = x$$

The solution is $\dfrac{1}{16}$.

You Try It 3
$$\ln x = 3$$
$$e^3 = x$$
$$20.0855 \approx x$$

You Try It 4
$$\log_8 \sqrt[3]{xy^2} = \log_8(xy^2)^{1/3} = \frac{1}{3}\log_8(xy^2)$$
$$= \frac{1}{3}(\log_8 x + \log_8 y^2)$$
$$= \frac{1}{3}(\log_8 x + 2\log_8 y)$$
$$= \frac{1}{3}\log_8 x + \frac{2}{3}\log_8 y$$

You Try It 5
$$\frac{1}{3}(\log_4 x - 2\log_4 y + \log_4 z)$$
$$= \frac{1}{3}(\log_4 x - \log_4 y^2 + \log_4 z)$$
$$= \frac{1}{3}\left(\log_4 \frac{x}{y^2} + \log_4 z\right) = \frac{1}{3}\left(\log_4 \frac{xz}{y^2}\right)$$
$$= \log_4\left(\frac{xz}{y^2}\right)^{1/3} = \log_4 \sqrt[3]{\frac{xz}{y^2}}$$

You Try It 6   Because $\log_b 1 = 0$, $\log_9 1 = 0$

You Try It 7 $\log_7 6.45 = \dfrac{\log 6.45}{\log 7} \approx 0.95795$

You Try It 8 $\log_3 0.834 = \dfrac{\ln 0.834}{\ln 3} \approx -0.16523$

SECTION 12.3

You Try It 1
$$f(x) = \log_2(x - 1)$$
$$y = \log_2(x - 1)$$
$$2^y = x - 1$$
$$2^y + 1 = x$$

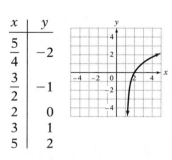

x	y
$\frac{5}{4}$	-2
$\frac{3}{2}$	-1
2	0
3	1
5	2

You Try It 2
$$f(x) = \log_3(2x)$$
$$y = \log_3(2x)$$
$$3^y = 2x$$
$$\frac{3^y}{2} = x$$

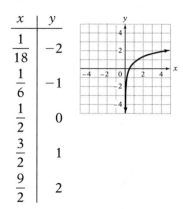

x	y
$\frac{1}{18}$	-2
$\frac{1}{6}$	-1
$\frac{1}{2}$	0
$\frac{3}{2}$	1
$\frac{9}{2}$	2

You Try It 3
$$f(x) = -\log_3(x + 1)$$
$$y = -\log_3(x + 1)$$
$$-y = \log_3(x + 1)$$
$$3^{-y} = x + 1$$
$$3^{-y} - 1 = x$$

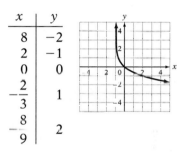

x	y
8	-2
2	-1
0	0
$-\frac{2}{3}$	1
$-\frac{8}{9}$	2

SECTION 12.4

You Try It 1
$$4^{3x} = 25$$
$$\log 4^{3x} = \log 25$$
$$3x \log 4 = \log 25$$
$$3x = \frac{\log 25}{\log 4}$$
$$3x \approx 2.3219$$
$$x \approx 0.7740$$

The solution is 0.7740.

You Try It 2
$$(1.06)^n = 1.5$$
$$\log(1.06)^n = \log 1.5$$
$$n \log 1.06 = \log 1.5$$
$$n = \frac{\log 1.5}{\log 1.06}$$
$$n \approx 6.9585$$

The solution is 6.9585.

You Try It 3 $\log_4(x^2 - 3x) = 1$

Rewrite in exponential form.

$4^1 = x^2 - 3x$
$4 = x^2 - 3x$
$0 = x^2 - 3x - 4$
$0 = (x + 1)(x - 4)$

$x + 1 = 0 \qquad x - 4 = 0$
$\quad x = -1 \qquad\quad x = 4$

The solutions are -1 and 4.

You Try It 4 $\log_3 x + \log_3(x + 3) = \log_3 4$
$\log_3[x(x + 3)] = \log_3 4$

Use the fact that if $\log_b u = \log_b v$, then $u = v$.

$x(x + 3) = 4$
$x^2 + 3x = 4$
$x^2 + 3x - 4 = 0$
$(x + 4)(x - 1) = 0$

$x + 4 = 0 \qquad x - 1 = 0$
$\quad x = -4 \qquad\quad x = 1$

-4 does not check as a solution.
The solution is 1.

You Try It 5 $\log_3 x + \log_3(x + 6) = 3$
$\log_3[x(x + 6)] = 3$

$x(x + 6) = 3^3$
$x^2 + 6x - 27 = 0$
$(x + 9)(x - 3) = 0$

$x + 9 = 0 \qquad x - 3 = 0$
$\quad x = -9 \qquad\quad x = 3$

-9 does not check as a solution.
The solution is 3.

You Try It 2

Strategy To find how many times as strong the San Francisco earthquake was, use the Richter equation to write a system of equations. Solve the system of equations for the ratio $\frac{I_1}{I_2}$.

Solution $7.8 = \log\dfrac{I_1}{I_0}$

$5 = \log\dfrac{I_2}{I_0}$

$7.8 = \log I_1 - \log I_0$
$5 = \log I_2 - \log I_0$
$2.8 = \log I_1 - \log I_2$
$2.8 = \log\dfrac{I_1}{I_2}$

$\dfrac{I_1}{I_2} = 10^{2.8} \approx 630.957$

The San Francisco earthquake was 631 times as strong as one that can cause serious damage.

SECTION 12.5

You Try It 1

Strategy To find the hydrogen ion concentration, replace pH by 2.9 in the equation $\text{pH} = -\log(H^+)$ and solve for H^+.

Solution $\text{pH} = -\log(H^+)$
$2.9 = -\log(H^+)$
$-2.9 = \log(H^+)$
$10^{-2.9} = H^+$
$0.00126 \approx H^+$

The hydrogen ion concentration is approximately 0.00126.

Answers to Chapter 1 Odd-Numbered Exercises

SECTION 1.1

1. $8 > -6$ **3.** $-12 < 1$ **5.** $42 > 19$ **7.** $0 > -31$ **9.** $53 > -46$ **11.** false **13.** true **15.** false **17.** true
19. false **21.** $-23, -18$ **23.** $21, 37$ **25.** -23 **27.** -4 **29.** 9 **31.** 28 **33.** 14 **35.** -77 **37.** 0
39. 74 **41.** -82 **43.** -81 **45.** $|-83| > |58|$ **47.** $|43| < |-52|$ **49.** $|-68| > |-42|$ **51.** $|-45| < |-61|$
53. $19, 0, -28$ **55.** $-45, 0, -17$ **57.** -11 **59.** -5 **61.** -83 **63.** -46 **65.** 0 **67.** -5 **69.** 9 **71.** 1
73. 8 **75.** -7 **77.** -9 **79.** 9 **81.** -3 **83.** 18 **85.** -10 **87.** -18 **89.** -41 **91.** -12 **93.** 0
95. -34 **97.** 0 **99.** -9 **101.** 11 **103.** -18 **105.** 0 **107.** 2 **109.** -138 **111.** -8 **113.** -12
115. -20 **117.** 42 **119.** -28 **121.** 60 **123.** -253 **125.** -238 **127.** -114 **129.** -2 **131.** 8
133. -7 **135.** -12 **137.** -6 **139.** -7 **141.** 11 **143.** -14 **145.** 15 **147.** -16 **149.** 0 **151.** -29
153. undefined **155.** -11 **157.** undefined **159.** -105 **161.** 252 **163.** -240 **165.** 96 **167.** -216
169. -315 **171.** 420 **173.** 2880 **175.** -2772 **177.** 0 **179.** The difference in elevation is 7046 m.
181. The difference between the highest and lowest elevations is greatest in Asia. **183.** The difference is 5°C.
185. The student's score is 93 points. **187.** The difference was $292 million. **189.** The difference is 29°F.

SECTION 1.2

1. 0.125 **3.** $0.\overline{2}$ **5.** $0.1\overline{6}$ **7.** 0.5625 **9.** $0.58\overline{3}$ **11.** 0.24 **13.** 0.225 **15.** $0.\overline{45}$ **17.** $\frac{2}{5}, 0.40$
19. $\frac{22}{25}, 0.88$ **21.** $\frac{8}{5}, 1.6$ **23.** $\frac{87}{100}, 0.87$ **25.** $\frac{9}{2}, 4.50$ **27.** $\frac{3}{70}$ **29.** $\frac{3}{8}$ **31.** $\frac{1}{400}$ **33.** $\frac{1}{16}$ **35.** $\frac{23}{400}$ **37.** 0.091
39. 0.167 **41.** 0.009 **43.** 0.0915 **45.** 0.1823 **47.** 37% **49.** 2% **51.** 12.5% **53.** 136% **55.** 0.4%
57. 83% **59.** $37\frac{1}{2}\%$ **61.** $44\frac{4}{9}\%$ **63.** 45% **65.** 250% **67.** $-\frac{5}{24}$ **69.** $-\frac{19}{24}$ **71.** $\frac{5}{26}$ **73.** $\frac{11}{8}$ **75.** $\frac{1}{12}$
77. $\frac{7}{24}$ **79.** 0 **81.** $\frac{3}{8}$ **83.** $-\frac{7}{60}$ **85.** $-\frac{1}{16}$ **87.** 7.29 **89.** -3.049 **91.** -1.06 **93.** -23.845
95. -10.7893 **97.** -37.19 **99.** -17.5 **101.** 19.61 **103.** $-\frac{3}{8}$ **105.** $\frac{1}{10}$ **107.** $-\frac{4}{9}$ **109.** $-\frac{7}{30}$ **111.** $\frac{15}{64}$
113. $-\frac{10}{9}$ **115.** $-\frac{147}{32}$ **117.** $\frac{25}{8}$ **119.** $\frac{2}{3}$ **121.** 4.164 **123.** 4.347 **125.** -4.028 **127.** -2.22 **129.** -1.104
131. 0.506 **133.** -0.2376 **135.** $-274.\overline{4}$ **137.** -2.59 **139.** -5.11 **141.** -2060.55 **143.** 2401
145. -64 **147.** -8 **149.** -125 **151.** $-\frac{27}{64}$ **153.** 3.375 **155.** -1 **157.** 6.75 **159.** -405 **161.** -8
163. -6750 **165.** -144 **167.** -18 **169.** 4 **171.** 7 **173.** $4\sqrt{2}$ **175.** $2\sqrt{2}$ **177.** $18\sqrt{2}$ **179.** $10\sqrt{10}$
181. $\sqrt{15}$ **183.** $\sqrt{29}$ **185.** $-54\sqrt{2}$ **187.** $3\sqrt{5}$ **189.** 0 **191.** $48\sqrt{2}$ **193.** 15.492 **195.** 16.971 **197.** 16
199. 16.583 **201.** 15.652 **203.** 18.762 **205a.** 47% of *Waterworld*'s total gross was from foreign countries. **b.** *Judge Dredd*'s U.S. box-office gross was 44% of its total gross. **c.** *Judge Dredd* and *Spy Hard* grossed more than half their box-office incomes in foreign countries. **207a.** You would receive 7.1844 million French francs. **b.** $1.66 in U.S. dollars is equivalent to 1 British pound. **209a.** The annual losses for Mattel would be $-$818.496 million. **b.** The average monthly loss was $-$5.614. **211.** 3, 4, 5, 6, 7, 8, 9

SECTION 1.3

1. 0 **3.** -11 **5.** 20 **7.** -10 **9.** 20 **11.** 29 **13.** 11 **15.** 7 **17.** -11 **19.** 6 **21.** 15 **23.** 4
25. 5 **27.** -1 **29.** 4 **31.** 0.51 **33.** 1.7 **35.** $-\frac{1}{16}$ **37.** Answers will vary. For example, $\frac{17}{24}$ and $\frac{33}{48}$.
39. Answers will vary. For example, a. $r = \frac{1}{2}$, b. $r = 1$, c. $r = 2$. **41.** $a = 2, b = 3, c = 6$

SECTION 1.4

1. -9 **3.** 41 **5.** -7 **7.** 13 **9.** -15 **11.** 41 **13.** 1 **15.** 5 **17.** 1 **19.** 57 **21.** 5 **23.** 8

25. -3 **27.** -2 **29.** -4 **31.** 10 **33.** -25 **35.** $25x$ **37.** $9a$ **39.** $2y$ **41.** $-12y - 3$ **43.** $9a$

45. $6ab$ **47.** $-12xy$ **49.** 0 **51.** $-\dfrac{1}{10}y$ **53.** $\dfrac{2}{9}y^2$ **55.** $20x$ **57.** $-4a$ **59.** $-2y^2$ **61.** $-2x + 8y$ **63.** $8x$

65. $19a - 12b$ **67.** $-12x - 2y$ **69.** $-7x^2 - 5x$ **71.** $60x$ **73.** $-10a$ **75.** $30y$ **77.** $72x$ **79.** $-28a$

81. $108b$ **83.** $-56x^2$ **85.** x^2 **87.** x **89.** a **91.** b **93.** x **95.** n **97.** $2x$ **99.** $-2x$ **101.** $-15a^2$

103. $6y$ **105.** $3y$ **107.** $-2x$ **109.** $-9y$ **111.** $-x - 7$ **113.** $10x - 35$ **115.** $-5a - 80$ **117.** $-15y + 35$

119. $20 - 14b$ **121.** $-4x + 2y$ **123.** $18x^2 + 12x$ **125.** $10x - 35$ **127.** $-14x + 49$ **129.** $-30x^2 - 15$

131. $-24y^2 + 96$ **133.** $5x^2 + 5y^2$ **135.** $-\dfrac{1}{2}x + 2y$ **137.** $3x^2 + 6x - 18$ **139.** $-2y^2 + 4y - 8$ **141.** $-2x + 3y - \dfrac{1}{3}$

143. $10x^2 + 15x - 35$ **145.** $6x^2 + 3xy - 9y^2$ **147.** $-3a^2 - 5a + 4$ **149.** $-2x - 16$ **151.** $-12y - 9$ **153.** $7n - 7$

155. $-2x + 41$ **157.** $3y - 3$ **159.** $2a - 4b$ **161.** $-4x + 24$ **163.** $-2x - 16$ **165.** $-3x + 21$ **167.** $-4x + 12$

169. $-x + 50$ **171.** $\dfrac{x}{18}$ **173.** $x + 20$ **175.** $10(x - 50); 10x - 500$ **177.** $\dfrac{5}{8}x + 6$ **179.** $x - (x + 3); -3$

181. $4(x + 19); 4x + 76$ **183.** $\dfrac{15}{x + 12}$ **185.** $\dfrac{2}{3}(x + 7); \dfrac{2}{3}x + \dfrac{14}{3}$ **187.** $40 - \dfrac{x}{20}$ **189.** $x^2 + 2x$

191. $(x + 8) + \dfrac{1}{3}x; \dfrac{4}{3}x + 8$ **193.** $x + (x + 9); 2x + 9$ **195.** $x - (8 - x); 2x - 8$ **197.** $\dfrac{1}{3}x - \dfrac{5}{8}x; -\dfrac{7}{24}x$

199. $(x + 5) + 2; x + 7$ **201.** $2(6x + 7); 12x + 14$ **203.** $B + 40$ **205.** $g, 20 - g$ **207.** $\dfrac{1}{2}L$ **209.** $4d$ **211.** yes

213. $2x$ **215.** $\dfrac{1}{4}x$ **217.** $\dfrac{3}{5}x$

SECTION 1.5

1. $A = \{16, 17, 18, 19, 20, 21\}$ **3.** $A = \{9, 11, 13, 15, 17\}$ **5.** $A = \{b, c\}$ **7.** $A \cup B = \{3, 4, 5, 6\}$

9. $A \cup B = \{-10, -9, -8, 8, 9, 10\}$ **11.** $A \cup B = \{a, b, c, d, e, f\}$ **13.** $A \cup B = \{1, 3, 7, 9, 11, 13\}$ **15.** $A \cap B = \{4, 5\}$

17. $A \cap B = \varnothing$ **19.** $A \cap B = \{c, d, e\}$ **21.** $\{x \mid x > -5, x \in \text{negative integers}\}$ **23.** $\{x \mid x > 30, x \in \text{integers}\}$

25. $\{x \mid x > 5, x \in \text{even integers}\}$ **27.** $\{x \mid x > 8, x \in \text{real numbers}\}$

29.
     −5 −4 −3 −2 −1 0 1 2 3 4 5

31.
     −5 −4 −3 −2 −1 0 1 2 3 4 5

33.
     −5 −4 −3 −2 −1 0 1 2 3 4 5

35.
     −5 −4 −3 −2 −1 0 1 2 3 4 5

37.
     −5 −4 −3 −2 −1 0 1 2 3 4 5

41a. never true   **b.** always true   **c.** always true   **43a.** yes   **b.** yes

CHAPTER REVIEW

1. $-4, 0$ [1.1A]   **2.** 4 [1.1B]   **3.** -5 [1.1B]   **4.** -13 [1.1C]   **5.** 1 [1.1C]   **6.** -42 [1.1D]

7. -20 [1.1D]   **8.** 0.28 [1.2A]   **9.** 0.062 [1.2B]   **10.** 62.5% [1.2B]   **11.** $\dfrac{7}{12}$ [1.2C]   **12.** -1.068 [1.2C]

13. $-\dfrac{72}{85}$ [1.2D]   **14.** -4.6224 [1.2D]   **15.** $\dfrac{16}{81}$ [1.2E]   **16.** 12 [1.2F]   **17.** $-6\sqrt{30}$ [1.2F]

18. 31 [1.3A]   **19.** 29 [1.4A]   **20.** $8a - 4b$ [1.4B]   **21.** $36y$ [1.4C]   **22.** $10x - 35$ [1.4D]

23. $7x + 46$ [1.4D]   **24.** $-90x + 25$ [1.4D]   **25.** $\{1, 3, 5, 7\}$ [1.5A]   **26.** $A \cap B = \{1, 5, 9\}$ [1.5A]

27. [1.5C]   **28.** [1.5C]   **29.** The student's score
was 98. [1.1E]   **30.** The value of the purchase is $10,632.91. [1.2G]   **31.** $2x - \dfrac{1}{2}x; \dfrac{3}{2}x$ [1.4E]   **32.** number of
American League players' cards: A; number of National League players' cards: $5A$ [1.4E]   **33.** number of ten-dollar
bills: T; number of five-dollar bills: $35 - T$ [1.4E]

CHAPTER TEST

1. $-2 > -40$ [1.1A]   **2.** 4 [1.1B]   **3.** -4 [1.1B]   **4.** -14 [1.1C]   **5.** -16 [1.1C]   **6.** 4 [1.1C]

7. 17 [1.1D]   **8.** $0.\overline{7}$ [1.2A]   **9.** $\frac{9}{20}$, 0.45 [1.2B]   **10.** $\frac{1}{15}$ [1.2C]   **11.** -5.3578 [1.2D]   **12.** $-\frac{1}{2}$ [1.2D]

13. 12 [1.2E]   **14.** $-6\sqrt{5}$ [1.2F]   **15.** 17 [1.3A]   **16.** 22 [1.4A]   **17.** $5x$ [1.4B]   **18.** $2x$ [1.4C]

19. $-6x^2 + 21y^2$ [1.4D]   **20.** $-x + 6$ [1.4D]   **21.** $-7x + 33$ [1.4D]   **22.** $\{-2, -1, 0, 1, 2, 3\}$ [1.5A]

23. $\{x \mid x < -3\}$ [1.5B]   **24.** $A \cup B = \{1, 2, 3, 4, 5, 6, 7, 8\}$ [1.5A]

25. ← + + + + + +) + + + + + → [1.5C]   **26.** ← + +] + + + (+ + + + → [1.5C]
         $-5\,-4\,-3\,-2\,-1\;\;0\;\;1\;\;2\;\;3\;\;4\;\;5$ $-5\,-4\,-3\,-2\,-1\;\;0\;\;1\;\;2\;\;3\;\;4\;\;5$

27. $10(x - 3); 10x - 30$ [1.4E]   **28.** The speed of the catcher's return throw is s. The speed of the fastball is $2s$. [1.4E]

29a. The annual losses would be $-\$12,560,000$. **b.** The average monthly loss was $-\$5,070,000$. [1.1E]

30. The price of the Nike stock at the end of the trading day was $\$62\frac{5}{8}$. [1.2G]

Answers to Chapter 2 Odd-Numbered Exercises

SECTION 2.1

1. yes   **3.** no   **5.** no   **7.** yes   **9.** yes   **11.** yes   **13.** no   **15.** yes   **17.** yes   **19.** yes   **21.** no

23. 6   **25.** 16   **27.** 7   **29.** -2 **31.** 1   **33.** 0   **35.** 3   **37.** -10 **39.** -3 **41.** -14 **43.** 2

45. 11   **47.** -9 **49.** -1 **51.** -14 **53.** -5 **55.** -1 **57.** 1   **59.** $-\frac{1}{2}$ **61.** $-\frac{3}{4}$ **63.** $\frac{1}{12}$ **65.** $-\frac{7}{12}$

67. 0.6529   **69.** -0.283 **71.** 9.257   **73.** -3 **75.** 0   **77.** -2 **79.** 9   **81.** 80   **83.** -4 **85.** 0   **87.** 8

89. -7 **91.** 12   **93.** -18 **95.** 15   **97.** -20 **99.** 0   **101.** 15   **103.** 75   **105.** $\frac{8}{3}$ **107.** $\frac{1}{3}$ **109.** $-\frac{1}{2}$

111. $-\frac{3}{2}$ **113.** $\frac{15}{7}$ **115.** 4   **117.** 3   **119.** 4.745   **121.** 2.06   **123.** -2.13 **125.** 28   **127.** 0.72

129. 64   **131.** 24%   **133.** 7.2   **135.** 400   **137.** 9   **139.** 25%   **141.** 5   **143.** 200%   **145.** 400   **147.** 7.7

149. 200   **151.** 400   **153.** 20   **155.** 80.34%   **157.** 19% of the students are in the fine arts college.   **159.** 65% of the amount spent by companies was spent on sports.   **161.** The total electricity used for home lighting is 96.1 billion kWh.

163. There were about 2,482 million shares.   **165a.** More money was spent on new cars in 1986. **b.** $41 billion more was spent on new cars in 1986.   **167a.** Answers will vary. **b.** Answers will vary.   **171.** It is two times its original value.

SECTION 2.2

1. 3   **3.** 6   **5.** -1 **7.** -3 **9.** 2   **11.** 2   **13.** 5   **15.** -3 **17.** 6   **19.** 3   **21.** 1   **23.** 6   **25.** -7

27. 0   **29.** $\frac{3}{4}$ **31.** $\frac{4}{9}$ **33.** $\frac{1}{3}$ **35.** $-\frac{1}{2}$ **37.** $-\frac{3}{4}$ **39.** $\frac{1}{3}$ **41.** $-\frac{1}{6}$ **43.** 1   **45.** 1   **47.** 0   **49.** $\frac{13}{10}$

51. $\frac{2}{5}$ **53.** $-\frac{4}{3}$ **55.** $-\frac{3}{2}$ **57.** 18   **59.** 8   **61.** -16 **63.** 25   **65.** 21   **67.** 15   **69.** -16 **71.** -21

73. $\frac{15}{2}$ **75.** $-\frac{18}{5}$ **77.** 2   **79.** 3   **81.** 1   **83.** -2 **85.** 2   **87.** 3   **89.** -1 **91.** 2   **93.** -2 **95.** -3

97. 0   **99.** -1 **101.** -3 **103.** -1 **105.** 4   **107.** $\frac{2}{3}$ **109.** $\frac{5}{6}$ **111.** $\frac{3}{4}$ **113.** 1   **115.** 4   **117.** -1

119. -1 **121.** $-\frac{2}{3}$ **123.** $\frac{4}{3}$ **125.** $\frac{1}{2}$ **127.** $-\frac{1}{3}$ **129.** $\frac{10}{3}$ **131.** $-\frac{1}{4}$ **133.** $x + 12 = 20; 8$

135. $\frac{3}{5}x = -30; -50$ **137.** $3x + 4 = 13; 3$ **139.** $9x - 6 = 12; 2$ **141.** $x + 2x = 9; 3$ **143.** $5x - 17 = 2; \frac{19}{5}$

145. $6x + 7 = 3x - 8; -5$ **147.** $30 = 7x - 9; \frac{39}{7}$ **149.** $2x = (21 - x) + 3; 8, 13$ **151.** $23 - x = 2x + 5; 6, 17$

153. 19   **155.** -14 **157.** 41,493   **161.** no solution   **163.** -21

SECTION 2.3

1. 20 oz of herbs should be used.   **3.** The cost of the mixture is $1.84 per pound.   **5.** 3 lb of caramel is needed.
7. 2 c of olive oil and 8 c of vinegar are used.   **9.** The cost is $3.00 per ounce.   **11.** 16 oz of the $400 alloy should be used.
13. 37 lb of almonds and 63 lb of walnuts were used.   **15.** 228 adult tickets were sold.   **17.** The cost is $.70 per pound.
19. The resulting gold alloy is 24% gold.   **21.** 20 gal of the 15% acid solution are used.   **23.** 30 lb of the yarn that is
25% wool is used.   **25.** 6.25 gal of the plant food that is 9% nitrogen is used.   **27.** The resulting mixture is 19% sugar.
29. 20 lb of the coffee that is 40% java beans are used.   **31.** 100 ml of the 7% solution and 200 ml of the 4% solution are
used.   **33.** 150 oz of pure chocolate must be added.   **35.** The resulting alloy is 50% silver.   **37.** There must be an additional $5000 added.   **39.** There was $9000 invested at 7% and $6000 at 6.5%.   **41.** There was $2500 deposited in the
mutual fund.   **43.** The university deposited $200,000 at 10% and $100,000 at 8.5%.   **45.** The mechanic must invest
$3000 in additional bonds.   **47.** $40,500 was invested at 8%. $13,500 was invested at 12%.   **49.** The total amount in-
vested was $650,000.   **51.** The total amount invested was $500,000.   **53.** The rate of the first plane is 105 mph. The
rate of the second plane is 130 mph.   **55.** They will be 3000 km apart at 11 A.M.   **57.** The cabin cruiser will be alongside
the motorboat 2 h after the cabin cruiser leaves.   **59.** The distance from the airport to the corporate offices is 120 mi.
61. The rate of the car is 68 mph.   **63.** The distance between the two airports is 300 mi.   **65.** The two planes will pass
each other 2.5 h after the plane leaves Seattle.   **67.** They will meet 1.5 h after they begin.   **69.** The bus overtakes the
car 180 mi from the starting point.   **71.** 3.75 gal must be drained from the radiator and replaced by pure antifreeze.
73. The cyclist's average speed for the trip was $13\frac{1}{3}$ mph.

SECTION 2.4

1. $\{x | x < 5\}$ **3.** $\{x | x \leq 2\}$ **5.** $\{x | x < -4\}$ **7.** $\{x | x > 3\}$ **9.** $\{x | x > 4\}$ **11.** $\{x | x \leq 2\}$ **13.** $\{x | x > -2\}$

15. $\{x | x \geq 2\}$ **17.** $\{x | x > -2\}$ **19.** $\{x | x \leq 3\}$ **21.** $\{x | x < 2\}$ **23.** $\{x | x < -3\}$ **25.** $\{x | x \leq 5\}$ **27.** $\left\{x | x \geq -\frac{1}{2}\right\}$

29. $\left\{x | x < \frac{23}{16}\right\}$ **31.** $\left\{x | x < \frac{8}{3}\right\}$ **33.** $\{x | x > 1\}$ **35.** $\left\{x | x > \frac{14}{11}\right\}$ **37.** $\{x | x \leq 1\}$ **39.** $\left\{x | x \leq \frac{3}{8}\right\}$

41. $\left\{x | x \leq \frac{7}{4}\right\}$ **43.** $\left\{x | x \geq -\frac{5}{4}\right\}$ **45.** $\{x | x \leq 2\}$ **47.** $\{x | -2 \leq x \leq 4\}$ **49.** $\{x | x < 3 \text{ or } x > 5\}$

51. $\{x | -4 < x < 2\}$ **53.** $\{x | x > 6 \text{ or } x < -4\}$ **55.** $\{x | x < -3\}$ **57.** $\{x | -3 < x < 2\}$ **59.** $\{x | -2 < x < 1\}$

61. $\{x | x < -2 \text{ or } x > 2\}$ **63.** $\{x | 2 < x < 6\}$ **65.** $\{x | -3 < x < -2\}$ **67.** $\left\{x | x > 5 \text{ or } x < -\frac{5}{3}\right\}$ **69.** $\{x | x < 3\}$

71. The solution set is the empty set.   **73.** The solution set is the set of real numbers.   **75.** $\left\{x \left| \frac{17}{7} \leq x \leq \frac{45}{7}\right.\right\}$

77. $\left\{x | -5 < x < \frac{17}{3}\right\}$ **79.** The solution set is the set of real numbers.   **81.** The solution set is the empty set.
83. The smallest number is -12.   **85.** The maximum width as an integer is 11 cm.   **87.** The TopPage plan is less expensive for more than 460 pages per month.   **89.** The call must be 7 min or less.   **91.** The temperature range for the
week was between 32°F and 86°F.   **93.** The amount of sales must be $44,000 or more.   **95.** The business writes more
than 200 checks monthly.   **97.** The range of scores is $58 \leq N \leq 100$.   **99.** The ski area is more than 38 mi away.
101. $[1, 2]$ **103.** $\varnothing$

SECTION 2.5

1. $7, -7$ **3.** $4, -4$ **5.** $6, -6$ **7.** $7, -7$ **9.** There is no solution.   **11.** There is no solution   **13.** $1, -5$

15. $8, 2$ **17.** 2 **19.** There is no solution.   **21.** $-\frac{3}{2}, 3$ **23.** $\frac{3}{2}$ **25.** There is no solution.   **27.** $7, -3$

29. $2, -\frac{10}{3}$ **31.** $1, 3$ **33.** $\frac{3}{2}$ **35.** There is no solution.   **37.** $\frac{11}{6}, -\frac{1}{6}$ **39.** $-\frac{1}{3}, -1$ **41.** There is no solution.

43. $3, 0$ **45.** There is no solution.   **47.** $1, \frac{13}{3}$ **49.** There is no solution.   **51.** $\frac{7}{3}, \frac{1}{3}$ **53.** $-\frac{1}{2}$ **55.** $-\frac{1}{2}, -\frac{7}{2}$

57. $-\frac{8}{3}, \frac{10}{3}$ **59.** There is no solution.   **61.** $\{x | x > 3 \text{ or } x < -3\}$ **63.** $\{x | x > 1 \text{ or } x < -3\}$ **65.** $\{x | 4 \leq x \leq 6\}$

67. $\{x | x \geq 5 \text{ or } x \leq -1\}$ **69.** $\{x | -3 < x < 2\}$ **71.** $\left\{x \middle| x > 2 \text{ or } x < -\frac{14}{5}\right\}$ **73.** $\varnothing$ **75.** The solution set is the set of real numbers.   **77.** $\left\{x \middle| x \leq -\frac{1}{3} \text{ or } x \geq 3\right\}$ **79.** $\left\{x \middle| -2 \leq x \leq \frac{9}{2}\right\}$ **81.** $\{x | x = 2\}$ **83.** $\left\{x \middle| x < -2 \text{ or } x > \frac{22}{9}\right\}$ **85.** $\left\{x \middle| -\frac{3}{2} < x < \frac{9}{2}\right\}$ **87.** $\left\{x \middle| x < 0 \text{ or } x > \frac{4}{5}\right\}$ **89.** $\{x | x > 5 \text{ or } x < 0\}$ **91.** The lower limit is 1.742 in. The upper limit is 1.758 in.   **93.** The lower limit is 195 volts. The upper limit is 245 volts.   **95.** The lower limit is $9\frac{19}{32}$ in. The upper limit is $9\frac{21}{32}$ in.   **97.** The lower limit is 28,420 ohms. The upper limit is 29,580 ohms.   **99.** The lower limit is 23,750 ohms. The upper limit is 26,250 ohms.   **101.a.** $\{x | x \geq -3\}$ **b.** $\{a | a \leq 4\}$ **103.a.** $\leq$ **b.** $\geq$ **c.** $\geq$ **d.** $=$ **e.** $=$

CHAPTER REVIEW

1. no   [2.1A]   **2.** 21   [2.1B]   **3.** 20   [2.1C]   **4.** -3 [2.2A]   **5.** $-\frac{6}{7}$ [2.2A]   **6.** $\frac{1}{3}$ [2.2B]   **7.** 4   [2.2B]   **8.** -2 [2.2C]   **9.** 10   [2.2C]   **10.** $\left\{x \middle| x > \frac{5}{3}\right\}$ [2.4A]   **11.** $\{x | x > -1\}$ [2.4A]   **12.** $\left\{x \middle| -3 < x < \frac{4}{3}\right\}$ [2.4B]   **13.** The solution set is the real numbers.   [2.4B]   **14.** $-\frac{9}{5}$, 3   [2.5A]   **15.** 9, -1 [2.5A]   **16.** $\{x | 1 < x < 4\}$ [2.5B]   **17.** $\left\{x \middle| x \geq 2 \text{ or } x \leq \frac{1}{2}\right\}$ [2.5B]   **18.** 30 is 250% of 12.   [2.1D]   **19.** $\frac{1}{2}\%$ of 1600 is 8.   [2.1D]   **20.** $5x - 4 = 16; x = 4$ [2.2D]   **21.** $3x = 2(21 - x) - 2; 8, 13$ [2.2D]   **22.** The airline would sell 177 tickets.   [2.1D]   **23.** The rebate is 6.1% of the cost.   [2.1D]   **24.** 7 qt of cranberry juice and 3 qt of apple juice were used.   [2.3A]   **25.** The cost is $3 per ounce.   [2.3A]   **26.** The percent concentration of butterfat is 14%.   [2.3B]   **27.** 375 lb of the alloy containing 30% tin and 125 lb of the alloy containing 70% tin were used.   [2.3B]   **28.** The total amount invested was $450,000.   [2.3C]   **29.** $1400 was deposited at 6.75%. $1000 was deposited at 9.45%.   [2.3C]   **30.** The jet overtakes the propeller-driven plane 600 mi from the starting point.   [2.3D]   **31.** The average speed on the winding road was 32 mph.   [2.3D]   **32.** The range of scores is $82 \leq x \leq 100$.   [2.4C]   **33.** The lower limit is 1.75 cc. The upper limit is 2.25 cc.   [2.5C]

CHAPTER TEST

1. -5 [2.2B]   **2.** -5 [2.1B]   **3.** -3 [2.2A]   **4.** 2   [2.2C]   **5.** no   [2.1A]   **6.** 5   [2.2A]   **7.** 0.04   [2.1D]   **8.** $-\frac{1}{3}$ [2.2C]   **9.** 2   [2.2B]   **10.** -12 [2.1C]   **11.** $\{x | x \leq -3\}$ [2.4A]   **12.** $\{x | x > -1\}$ [2.4A]   **13.** $\{x | x > -2\}$ [2.4B]   **14.** $\varnothing$ [2.4B]   **15.** 3, $-\frac{9}{5}$ [2.5A]   **16.** 7, -2 [2.5A]   **17.** $\left\{x \middle| \frac{1}{3} \leq x \leq 3\right\}$ [2.5B]   **18.** $\left\{x \middle| x > 2 \text{ or } x < -\frac{1}{2}\right\}$ [2.5B]   **19.** 4, 11   [2.2D]   **20.** The cost of the hamburger mixture is $2.20 per pound.   [2.3A]   **21.** 1.25 gallons of 20% salt solution must be used.   [2.3B]   **22.** $5000 is invested at 3% and $15,000 is invested at 7%.   [2.3C]   **23.** The rate of the snowmobile is 6 mph.   [2.3D]   **24.** You can drive the Gambelli Agency car less than 120 mi per day.   [2.4C]   **25.** The lower limit is 2.648 in. The upper limit is 2.652 in.   [2.5C]

CUMULATIVE REVIEW

1. 6   [1.1C]   **2.** -48 [1.1D]   **3.** $-\frac{19}{48}$ [1.2C]   **4.** 54   [1.2E]   **5.** $\frac{49}{40}$ [1.3A]   **6.** 6   [1.4A]   **7.** $-17x$ [1.4B]   **8.** $-5a - 4b$ [1.4B]   **9.** $2x$ [1.4C]   **10.** $36y$ [1.4C]   **11.** $2x^2 + 6x - 4$ [1.4D]   **12.** $-4x + 14$ [1.4D]   **13.** $6x - 34$ [1.4D]   **14.** $A \cap B = \{-4, 0\}$ [1.5B]   **15.** [number line from -5 to 5, open interval shown]   [1.5C]   **16.** yes   [2.1A]   **17.** -25 [2.1C]   **18.** -3 [2.2A]   **19.** 3   [2.2A]   **20.** -3 [2.2B]   **21.** $\frac{1}{2}$ [2.2B]   **22.** 13   [2.2C]   **23.** $\{x | x \leq 1\}$ [2.4A]   **24.** $\{x | -4 \leq x \leq 1\}$ [2.4B]   **25.** -1 and 4   [2.5A]   **26.** $\left\{x \middle| x > 2 \text{ or } x < -\frac{4}{3}\right\}$ [2.5B]   **27.** $\frac{11}{20}$ [1.2B]   **28.** 103%   [1.2B]   **29.** 25% of 120 is 30.   [2.1D]   **30.** $6x + 13 = 3x - 5; x = -6$ [2.2D]   **31.** 20 lb of oat flour must be used.   [2.3A]   **32.** 25 g of pure gold must be added.   [2.3B]   **33.** The length of the track is 120 m.   [2.3D]

Answers to Chapter 3 Odd-Numbered Exercises

SECTION 3.1

1. 40°; acute **3.** 115°; obtuse **5.** 90°; right **7.** The complement is 28°. **9.** The supplement is 18°. **11.** The length of BC is 14 cm. **13.** The length of QS is 28 ft. **15.** The length of EG is 30 m. **17.** The measure of $\angle MON$ is 86°. **19.** 71° **21.** 30° **23.** 36° **25.** 127° **27.** 116° **29.** 20° **31.** 20° **33.** 20° **35.** 141° **37.** 106° **39.** 11° **41.** $\angle a = 38°$, $\angle b = 142°$ **43.** $\angle a = 47°$, $\angle b = 133°$ **45.** 20° **47.** 47° **49.** $\angle x = 155°$, $\angle y = 70°$ **51.** $\angle a = 45°$, $\angle b = 135°$ **53.** $90° - x$ **55.** The measure of the third angle is 60°. **57.** The measure of the third angle is 35°. **59.** The measure of the third angle is 102°. **61.a.** 1° **b.** 179° **65.** 360°

SECTION 3.2

1. hexagon **3.** pentagon **5.** scalene **7.** equilateral **9.** obtuse **11.** acute **13.** 56 in. **15.** 14 ft **17.** 47 mi **19.** 8π cm or approximately 25.13 cm **21.** 11π mi or approximately 34.56 mi **23.** 17π ft or approximately 53.41 ft **25.** The perimeter is 17.4 cm. **27.** The perimeter is 8 cm. **29.** The perimeter is 24 m. **31.** The perimeter is 48.8 cm. **33.** The perimeter is 17.5 in. **35.** The length of a diameter is 8.4 cm. **37.** The circumference is 1.5π in. **39.** The circumference is 226.19 cm. **41.** 60 ft of fencing should be purchased. **43.** The carpet must be nailed down along 44 ft. **45.** The length is 120 ft. **47.** The length of the third side is 10 in. **49.** The length of each side is 12 in. **51.** The length of a diameter is 2.55 cm. **53.** The length is 13.19 ft. **55.** The bicycle travels 50.27 ft. **57.** The circumference is 39,935.93 km. **59.** 60 ft^2 **61.** 20.25 in^2 **63.** 546 ft^2 **65.** 16π cm^2 or approximately 50.27 cm^2 **67.** 30.25π mi^2 or approximately 95.03 mi^2 **69.** 72.25π ft^2 or approximately 226.98 ft^2 **71.** The area is 156.25 cm^2. **73.** The area is 570 in^2. **75.** The area is 192 in^2. **77.** The area is 13.5 ft^2. **79.** The area is 330 cm^2. **81.** The area is 25π in^2. **83.** The area is 9.08 ft^2. **85.** The area is $10,000\pi$ in^2. **87.** The area is 126 ft^2. **89.** 7500 yd^2 must be purchased. **91.** The width is 10 in. **93.** The length of the base is 20 m. **95.** You should buy 2 qt. **97.** It will cost $74. **99.** The increase in area is 113.10 in^2. **101.** The cost will be $638. **103.** The area is 216 m^2. **105.** 4:9 **109.** $A = \dfrac{\pi d^2}{4}$

SECTION 3.3

1. 840 in^3 **3.** 15 ft^3 **5.** 4.5π cm^3 or approximately 14.14 cm^3 **7.** The volume is 34 m^3. **9.** The volume is 42.875 in^3. **11.** The volume is 36π ft^3. **13.** The volume is 8143.01 cm^3. **15.** The volume is 75π in^3. **17.** The volume is 120 in^3. **19.** The width is 2.5 ft. **21.** The radius of the base is 4.00 in. **23.** The length is 5 in. The width is 5 in. **25.** There are 75.40 m^3 in the tank. **27.** 94 m^2 **29.** 56 m^2 **31.** 96π in^2 or approximately 301.59 in^2 **33.** The surface area is 184 ft^2. **35.** The surface area is 69.36 m^2. **37.** The surface area is 225π cm^2. **39.** The surface area is 402.12 in^2. **41.** The surface area is 6π ft^2. **43.** The surface area is 297 in^2. **45.** The width is 3 cm. **47.** 11 cans of paint should be purchased. **49.** 456 in^2 of glass are needed. **51.** The surface area of the pyramid is 22.53 cm^2 larger. **53.a.** always true **b.** never true **c.** sometimes true

CHAPTER REVIEW

1. $\angle x = 22°$, $\angle y = 158°$ [3.1C] **2.** $\angle x = 68°$ [3.1B] **3.** The length of AC is 44 cm. [3.1A] **4.** $x = 19°$ [3.1A] **5.** The volume is 96 cm^3. [3.3A] **6.** $\angle a = 138°$, $\angle b = 42°$ [3.1B] **7.** The surface area is 220 ft^2. [3.3B] **8.** The supplement is 148°. [3.1A] **9.** The area is 78 cm^2. [3.2B] **10.** The area is 63 m^2. [3.2B] **11.** The volume is 39 ft^3. [3.3A] **12.** The measure of the third angle is 95°. [3.1C] **13.** The length of the base is 8 cm. [3.2B] **14.** The volume is 288π mm^3. [3.3A] **15.** The volume is $\dfrac{784\pi}{3}$ cm^3. [3.3A] **16.** Each side measures 21.5 cm. [3.2A] **17.** 4 cans of paint should be purchased. [3.3B] **18.** 208 yd of fencing are needed. [3.2A] **19.** The area is 90.25 m^2. [3.2B] **20.** The area is 276 m^2. [3.2B]

CHAPTER TEST

1. The radius is 0.75 m.   [3.2A]   **2.** The circumference is 31.4 cm.   [3.2A]   **3.** The perimeter is 26 ft.   [3.2A]
4. $BC = 3$ [3.1A]   **5.** The volume is 267.9 ft^3.   [3.3A]   **6.** The area is 63.585 cm^2.   [3.2B]   **7.** $a = 100°, b = 80°$
[3.1B]   **8.** 75°   [3.1A]   **9.** $a = 135°, b = 45°$ [3.1B]   **10.** The area is 55 m^2.   [3.2B]   **11.** The volume is
169.56 m^3.   [3.3A]   **12.** The perimeter is 6.8 m.   [3.2A]   **13.** 58°   [3.1A]   **14.** The surface area is 164.93 ft^2.   [3.3B]
15. There are 113.04 in^2 more in the pizza.   [3.2B]   **16.** The measures of the other two angles are 58° and 90°.   [3.1C]
17. The bicycle travels 73.3 ft.   [3.2A]   **18.** The area of the room is 28 yd^2.   [3.2B]   **19.** The volume of the silo
is 1144.53 ft^3.   [3.3A]   **20.** The area is 11 m^2.   [3.2B]

CUMULATIVE REVIEW

1. $-3, 0,$ and 1 [1.1A]   **2.** 0.089   [1.2B]   **3.** 35%   [1.2B]   **4.** $-\dfrac{2}{3}$ [1.2D]   **5.** -24.51 [1.2D]   **6.** $-5\sqrt{5}$
[1.2F]   **7.** -28 [1.3A]   **8.** -8 [1.4A]   **9.** $-3m + 3n$ [1.4B]   **10.** $21y$ [1.4C]   **11.** $7x + 9$ [1.4D]
12. $\{-2, -1\}$ [1.5A]   **13.** $\{-10, 0, 10, 20, 30\}$ [1.5A]   **14.** 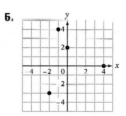   [1.5C]   **15.** 5   [2.2B]
16. $\dfrac{1}{2}$ [2.2C]   **17.** $\{y\,|\,y \le -4\}$ [2.4A]   **18.** $\{x\,|\,x \ge 2\}$ [2.4A]   **19.** $\{x\,|\,x < -3 \text{ or } x > 4\}$ [2.4B]
20. $\{x\,|\,2 \le x \le 6\}$ [2.4B]   **21.** $1, -\dfrac{1}{3}$ [2.5A]   **22.** $\{x\,|\,6 \le x \le 10\}$ [2.5B]   **23.** $\angle x = 131°$ [3.1B]
24. $4x - 10 = 2; x = 3$ [2.2D]   **25.** The third angle measures 122°.   [3.1C]   **26.** $5000 is deposited in
the 9.5% account.   [2.3C]   **27.** The third side measures 4.5 m.   [3.2A]   **28.** 80% of the students went on
to college.   [2.1D]   **29.** The area is 20.25π cm^2.   [3.2B]   **30.** The height of the box is 3 ft.   [3.3A]

Answers to Chapter 4 Odd-Numbered Exercises

SECTION 4.1

1. 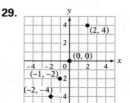   **3.**   **5.**

7. The coordinates of A are $(2, 3)$. The coordinates of B are $(4, 0)$.
The coordinates of C are $(-4, 1)$. The coordinates of D are $(2, -2)$.

9. The coordinates of A are $(-2, 5)$. The coordinates of B are $(3, 4)$.
The coordinates of C are $(0, 0)$. The coordinates of D are $(-3, -2)$.

11. The coordinates of A are $(2, 4)$. The coordinates of B are $(0, 1)$.
The coordinates of C are $(-4, 0)$. The coordinates of D are $(3, -3)$.

13. yes   **15.** no   **17.** no   **19.** no   **21.** $(3, 7)$ **23.** $(6, 3)$ **25.** $(0, 1)$ **27.** $(-5, 0)$

29. 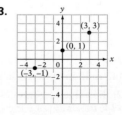   **31.**   **33.**

35. $\{(55, 273), (65, 355), (75, 447), (85, 549)\}$; yes   **37.** $\{(197, 125), (205, 122), (257, 498), (226, 108), (205, 150)\}$; no
39. yes   **41.** no   **43.** yes   **45.** 8   **47.** 9   **49.** 2   **51.** -1 **53.** 22   **55.** $-\dfrac{3}{2}$ **57.** -7

SECTION 4.2

1.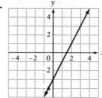

3.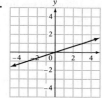

5.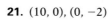

7.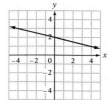

9.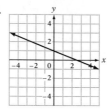

11.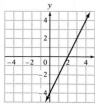

13.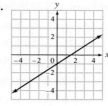

15.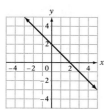

17.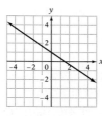

19. $(3, 0), (0, -3)$ **21.** $(10, 0), (0, -2)$ **23.** $(0, 0), (0, 0)$

25.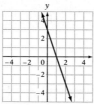

27.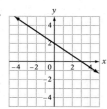

29.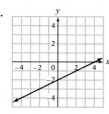

31.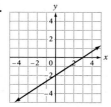

33.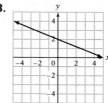

35.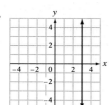

37.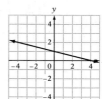

39.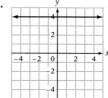

41.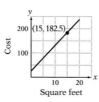

It costs \$182.50 for a custom sign 15 ft^2 in area.

43.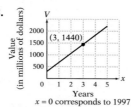

In the year 2000, it is projected that \$1440 million (\$1.44 billion) in stocks will be traded over the Internet.

45. When the value of x changes from 1 to 2, the value of y increases 3 units.
When the value of x changes from 13 to 14, the value of y increases 3 units.

SECTION 4.3

1. -1 **3.** $\frac{1}{3}$ **5.** $-\frac{2}{3}$ **7.** $-\frac{3}{4}$ **9.** The slope is undefined. **11.** $\frac{7}{5}$ **13.** The line has zero slope.

15. $-\frac{1}{2}$ **17.** The slope is undefined. **19.** $m = -0.4$. The percent of the population that can afford a median-priced new home has decreased by 0.4% per year. **21a.** $m = 0.5$. For each additional foot a diver descends below the surface of the water, the pressure on the diver increases by 0.5 pound per square inch. **b.** The y-intercept represents the pressure on a person at sea level. **25.** yes

27. 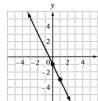 **29.** 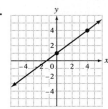 **31.** 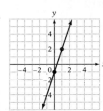 **33.**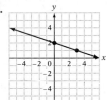

35. 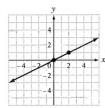 **37.** 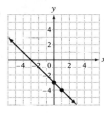 **39.**   **41.** The value of y increases by 2.

43. The value of y increases by 2.

45a. 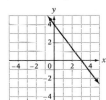 **b.** 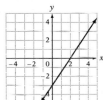 **c.** 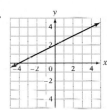 **d.**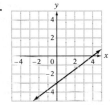

The reciprocals of the coefficients of x and y are the x- and y-intercepts of the graphs of the lines.

47. 10 **49.** -4

SECTION 4.4

1. $y = 2x + 2$ **3.** $y = -3x - 1$ **5.** $y = \frac{1}{3}x$ **7.** $y = \frac{3}{4}x - 5$ **9.** $y = -\frac{3}{5}x$ **11.** $y = \frac{1}{4}x + \frac{5}{2}$ **13.** $y = 2x - 3$

15. $y = -2x - 3$ **17.** $y = \frac{2}{3}x$ **19.** $y = \frac{1}{2}x + 2$ **21.** $y = -\frac{3}{4}x - 2$ **23.** $y = \frac{3}{4}x + \frac{5}{2}$

25. The number of hours of "basic cable" watched per person increases by 12.9 h per year.

27. The number of visitors is decreasing by 2.1 million per year.

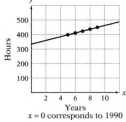

$x = 0$ corresponds to 1990

$x = 0$ corresponds to 1992

29. no **31.** yes **33.** $-\frac{3}{2}$ **35.** $n = -5$ **37.** $y = -\frac{2}{3}x + \frac{5}{3}$

SECTION 4.5

1. The lines are perpendicular.   **3.** No, the lines are not parallel.   **5.** No, the lines are not parallel.   **7.** The lines are perpendicular.   **9.** The lines are parallel.   **11.** The lines are perpendicular.   **13.** No, the lines are not parallel.

15. The lines are perpendicular.   **17.** The lines are parallel.   **19.** $y = \frac{2}{3}x - \frac{8}{3}$ **21.** $y = \frac{1}{3}x - \frac{1}{3}$ **23.** $y = -\frac{5}{3}x - \frac{14}{3}$

27. $\frac{A_1}{B_1} = -\frac{B_2}{A_2}$ **29.** Any equation of the form $y = 2x + b$ where $b \neq -13$ or of the form $y = -\frac{3}{2}x + c$ where $c \neq 8$.

31. The x-intercept is $(9, 0)$. The y-intercept is $(0, 9)$.

SECTION 4.6

1. 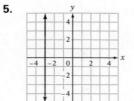   **3.** 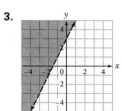   **5.** 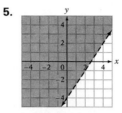   **7.**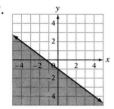

9. 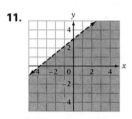   **11.** 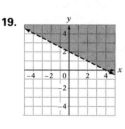   **13.** 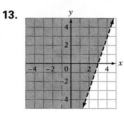   **15.**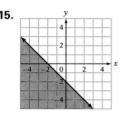

17. 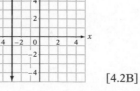   **19.** 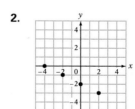   **21.** The inequality is $y \geq 2x + 2$.

CHAPTER REVIEW

1a. 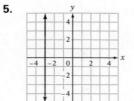   [4.1A]

2. 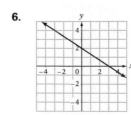   [4.1B]

b. The abscissa of point A is -2.
c. The ordinate of point B is -4.

3. yes   [4.1C]   **4.** -1 [4.1D]

5.   [4.2B]

6.   [4.3B]

7. 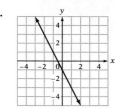 [4.2A]

8. 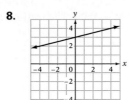 [4.2A]

9. 0 [4.3A]   **10.** $\dfrac{7}{11}$ [4.3A]   **11.** (8, 0) and (0, −12) [4.2B]

12. 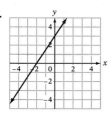 [4.2B]

13. 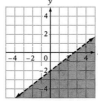 [4.6A]

14. $y = -\dfrac{8}{3}x - \dfrac{1}{3}$ [4.4B]   **15.** $y = -\dfrac{5}{2}x + 16$ [4.4A]   **16.** $y = 2x$ [4.5A]   **17.** $y = 2x + 1$ [4.5A]

18. {(55, 95), (57, 101), (53, 94), (57, 98), (60, 100), (61, 105), (58, 97), (54, 95)} The relation is not a function.   [4.1C]

19.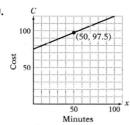

The cost of 50 min of access time for one month is $97.50.   [4.2C]

20.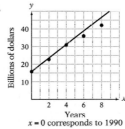

The amount spent on health care increased $3.85 billion per year.   [4.4C]

CHAPTER TEST

1. (3, −3) [4.1B]   **2.** 6 [4.1D]

3. {(3.5, 25), (4.0, 30), (5.2, 45), (5.0, 38), (4.0, 42), (6.3, 12), (5.4, 34)} The relation is not a function.   [4.1C]

4. 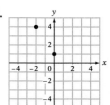 [4.1B]

5. 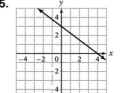 [4.2A]

6. 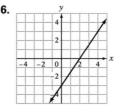 [4.2B]

7. 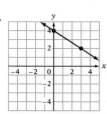 [4.3B]

8. 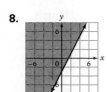 [4.6A]

9. 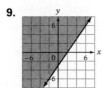 [4.6A]

10.

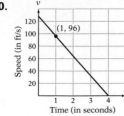

After 1 s, the ball is traveling 96 ft/s. [4.2C]

11. $m = 1500$. The tuition increased by \$1500 per year. [4.4C]

12.

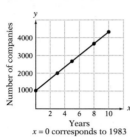

The number of mutual fund companies increased by 330 each year. [4.4C]

13. (2, 0) and (0, −3) [4.2B] **14.** 2 [4.3A] **15.** The slope is undefined. [4.3A] **16.** $-\frac{2}{3}$ [4.2B]

17. $y = \frac{2}{3}x + 3$ [4.4A] **18.** $y = -\frac{2}{7}x - \frac{4}{7}$ [4.4B] **19.** $y = -3x + 7$ [4.5A] **20.** $y = \frac{3}{2}x + 2$ [4.5A]

CUMULATIVE REVIEW

1. −5, −3 [1.1A] **2.** 0.85 [1.2B] **3.** $9\sqrt{5}$ [1.2F] **4.** −12 [1.3A] **5.** $-\frac{5}{8}$ [1.4A]

6. $-4d - 9$ [1.4B] **7.** $-32z$ [1.4C] **8.** $-13x + 7y$ [1.4D] **9.** 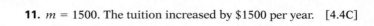 [1.5C]

10. $\frac{3}{2}$ [2.2A] **11.** 1 [2.2C] **12.** $\{x | x > -1\}$ [2.4A] **13.** $\varnothing$ [2.4B] **14.** $\left\{x \middle| 0 < x < \frac{10}{3}\right\}$ [2.5B]

15. $f(2) = 6$ [4.1D] **16.** The slope is 2. [4.3A]

17.

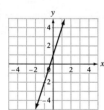

[4.2A]

18.

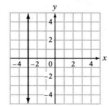

[4.2B]

19.

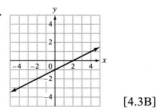

[4.3B]

20.

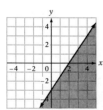

[4.6A]

21. $y = -\frac{1}{3}x - 2$ [4.4B] **22.** $y = -\frac{3}{2}x + 7$ [4.5A]

23. The first plane is traveling at 400 mph. The second plane is traveling at 200 mph. [2.3D]

24. 32 lb of \$8 coffee and 48 lb of \$3 coffee should be used. [2.3A]

25. The slope is $-\frac{10,000}{3}$. The value of the house decreases by \$3333.33 each year. [4.3A]

Answers to Chapter 5 Odd-Numbered Exercises

SECTION 5.1

1. yes   **3.** yes   **5.** no   **7.** no   **9.** no   **11.** yes   **13.** yes   **15.** yes   **17.** no

21.
The solution is $(3, -1)$.

23.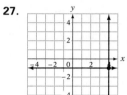
The solution is $(2, 4)$.

25.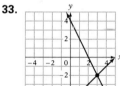
The solution is $(4, 3)$.

27.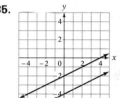
The solution is $(4, -1)$.

29.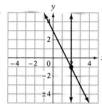
The solution is $(2, -1)$.

31.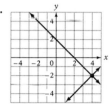
The solution is $(4, -2)$.

33.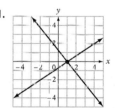
The solution is $(3, -2)$.

35.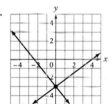
The lines are parallel and therefore do not intersect. The system of equations has no solution.

37.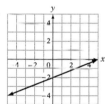
The equations are dependent. The solutions are the ordered pairs $\left(x, \frac{2}{5}x - 2\right)$.

39.
The solution is $(0, -3)$.

41.
The solution is $(1, 0)$.

43. $(1.20, 1.40)$ **45.** $(0.64, -0.10)$ **47.** Answers will vary.

SECTION 5.2

1. $(2, 1)$ **3.** $(4, 1)$ **5.** $(-1, 1)$ **7.** The system of equations is inconsistent and has no solution.   **9.** The system of equations is inconsistent and has no solution.   **11.** $\left(-\frac{3}{4}, -\frac{3}{4}\right)$ **13.** $(1, 1)$ **15.** $(2, 0)$ **17.** $(1, -2)$

19. $(0, 0)$ **21.** The system of equations is dependent. The solutions are the ordered pairs $(x, 2x - 2)$.   **23.** $(-4, -2)$

25. $(10, 31)$ **27.** $(3, -10)$ **29.** $(-22, -5)$ **31.** $k = 2$ **33.** $k = 2$

SECTION 5.3

1. $(6, 1)$ **3.** $(1, 1)$ **5.** $(2, 1)$ **7.** $(-2, 1)$ **9.** The equations are dependent. The solutions are the ordered pairs $(x, 3x - 4)$.   **11.** $\left(-\frac{1}{2}, 2\right)$ **13.** The system is inconsistent and therefore has no solution.   **15.** $(-1, -2)$ **17.** $(-5, 4)$

19. $(2, 5)$ **21.** $\left(\frac{1}{2}, \frac{3}{4}\right)$ **23.** $(0, 0)$ **25.** $(-1, 3)$ **27.** $\left(\frac{2}{3}, -\frac{2}{3}\right)$ **29.** $(-2, 3)$ **31.** $(2, -1)$ **33.** $(10, -5)$

35. $\left(-\frac{1}{2}, \frac{2}{3}\right)$ **37.** $\left(\frac{5}{3}, \frac{1}{3}\right)$ **39.** The system is inconsistent and therefore has no solution.   **41.** $(1, -1)$
43. $(2, 1, 3)$ **45.** $(1, -1, 2)$ **47.** $(1, 2, 4)$ **49.** $(2, -1, -2)$ **51.** $(-2, -1, 3)$ **53.** The system is inconsistent and
therefore has no solution.   **55.** $(1, 4, 1)$ **57.** $(1, 3, 2)$ **59.** $(1, -1, 3)$ **61.** $(0, 2, 0)$ **63.** $(1, 5, 2)$ **65.** $(-2, 1, 1)$
67. $A = 3, B = -3$ **69a.** 14   **b.** $\frac{2}{3}$ **c.** $\frac{1}{2}$ **71.** $A = 1$

SECTION 5.4

1. 11   **3.** 18   **5.** 0   **7.** 15   **9.** -30 **11.** 0   **13.** $(3, -4)$ **15.** $(4, -1)$ **17.** $\left(\frac{11}{14}, \frac{17}{21}\right)$ **19.** $\left(\frac{1}{2}, 1\right)$
21. The system of equations is not independent.   **23.** $(-1, 0)$ **25.** $(1, -1, 2)$ **27.** $(2, -2, 3)$ **29.** The system of
equations is not independent.   **31.** $\left(\frac{68}{25}, \frac{56}{25}, -\frac{8}{25}\right)$ **33.** $\left(\frac{2}{3}, -1, \frac{1}{2}\right)$ **35.** 0   **37a.** 0   **b.** 0

SECTION 5.5

1. The rate of the boat is 15 mph. The rate of the current is 3 mph.   **3.** The rate of the plane is 502.5 mph. The rate of the
wind is 47.5 mph.   **5.** The rate of the team is 8 km/h. The rate of the current is 2 km/h.   **7.** The rate of the plane is 180
mph. The rate of the wind is 20 mph.   **9.** The rate of the plane is 110 mph. The rate of the wind is 10 mph.   **11.** The
rate of the motorboat is 13 mph. The rate of the current is 3 mph.   **13.** The rate of the cabin cruiser is 15 mph. The rate
of the current is 3 mph.   **15.** The cost of the cinnamon tea is \$2.50/lb. The cost of the spice tea is \$3/lb.   **17.** The cost
of the wool carpet is \$26/yd.   **19.** The company plans to manufacture 25 ten-speed bicycles.   **21.** There are 480 g of
the first alloy and 40 g of the second alloy.   **23.** The measure of the smaller angle is 9°. The measure of the larger angle
is 81°.   **25.** There were 155 adult tickets and 90 student tickets sold.   **27.** You have \$1500 in the 6% account and \$3500
in the 8% account.   **29.** The original number is 84.   **31.** There are 30 nickels in the bank.

SECTION 5.6

1. 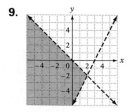   **3.** 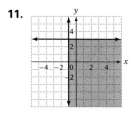   **5.** 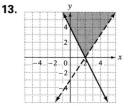   **7.**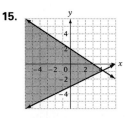

9. 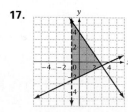   **11.** 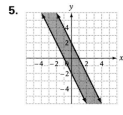   **13.** 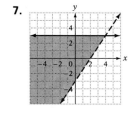   **15.**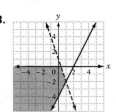

17. 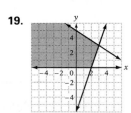   **19.** 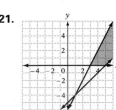   **21.**   **23.**

CHAPTER REVIEW

1.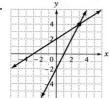

[5.1A]

The solution is (3, 4).

2.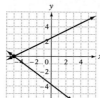

[5.1A]

The solution is (−5, 0).

3.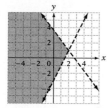

[5.6A]

4.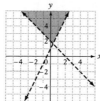

[5.6A]

5. $\left(\frac{3}{4}, \frac{7}{8}\right)$ [5.2A]   **6.** (−3, −4) [5.2A]   **7.** (2, −1) [5.2A]   **8.** (−2, 1) [5.3A]   **9.** The system is inconsistent and therefore has no solution. [5.3A]   **10.** (1, 1) [5.3A]   **11.** The system is inconsistent and therefore has no solution. [5.3B]   **12.** (2, −1, −2) [5.3B]   **13.** 10 [5.4A]   **14.** −32 [5.4A]   **15.** $\left(-\frac{1}{3}, -\frac{10}{3}\right)$ [5.4B]   **16.** $\left(\frac{59}{19}, -\frac{62}{19}\right)$ [5.4B]   **17.** $\left(\frac{1}{5}, -\frac{6}{5}, \frac{3}{5}\right)$ [5.4B]   **18.** (0, −2, 3) [5.4B]   **19.** The rate of the plane is 150 mph. The rate of the wind is 25 mph. [5.5A]   **20.** The cost of the cotton is $9/yd. The cost of the wool is $14/yd. [5.5B]

CHAPTER TEST

1. $\left(6, -\frac{1}{2}\right)$ [5.2A]   **2.** (−4, 7) [5.3A]

3.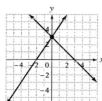

[5.1A]

The solution is (0, 3).

4.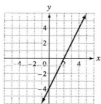

[5.1A]

The equations are dependent. The solutions are the ordered pairs (x, 2x − 4).

5. $\left(x, -\frac{1}{4}x + \frac{3}{2}\right)$ [5.2A]   **6.** $\left(x, \frac{1}{3}x - 2\right)$ [5.3A]   **7.** (3, −1, −2) [5.3B]   **8.** (5, −2, 3) [5.3B]   **9.** 28 [5.4A]   **10.** 0 [5.4A]   **11.** (3, −1) [5.4B]   **12.** $\left(\frac{110}{23}, \frac{25}{23}\right)$ [5.4B]   **13.** (−1, −3, 4) [5.4B]   **14.** (2, 3, −5) [5.4B]

15.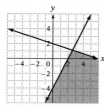

[5.6A]

16.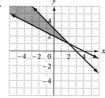

[5.6A]

17. (2, 1) [5.2A]   **18.** The rate of the cabin cruiser in calm water is 16 mph. The rate of the current is 4 mph. [5.5A]   **19.** The rate of the plane in calm air is 175 mph. The rate of the wind is 25 mph. [5.5A]   **20.** On Friday evening, 100 children attended the movie theater. [5.5B]

CUMULATIVE REVIEW

1. $-6\sqrt{10}$ [1.2F]   **2.** 22 [2.2C]   **3.** $3x - 24$ [1.4D]   **4.** -4 [1.4A]   **5.** $\{x \mid x < 6\}$ [2.4B]

6. $\{x \mid -4 < x < 8\}$ [2.5B]   **7.** $\{x \mid x > 4 \text{ or } x < -1\}$ [2.5B]   **8.** $F(2) = 1$ [4.1D]

9. 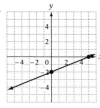 [1.5C]   **10.** $y = -\frac{2}{3}x + \frac{5}{3}$ [4.4A]   **11.** $y = 5x - 11$ [4.4B]   **12.** $y = -\frac{3}{2}x + \frac{1}{2}$ [4.5A]

13. 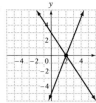 [4.3B]

14. 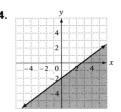 [4.6A]

15. 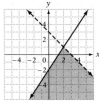 [5.1A]

The solution is $(2, 0)$.

16. $(-5, -11)$ [5.2A]   **17.** $(1, 0, -1)$ [5.3B]   **18.** 3 [5.4A]   **19.** $(2, -3)$ [5.4B]

20. [5.6A]

21. 60 ml of pure water must be used. [2.3B]   **22.** The rate of the wind is 12.5 mph. [5.5A]   **23.** One pound of steak costs \$5. [5.5B]   **24.** The lower limit is 10,200 ohms. The upper limit is 13,800 ohms. [2.5C]   **25.** The slope is 40. The slope represents the monthly income (in dollars) per thousand dollars in sales. [4.3A]

Answers to Chapter 6 Odd-Numbered Exercises

SECTION 6.1

1. a^4b^4 **3.** $-18x^3y^4$ **5.** x^8y^{16} **7.** $81x^8y^{12}$ **9.** $729a^{10}b^6$ **11.** x^5y^{11} **13.** $729x^6$ **15.** $a^{18}b^{18}$ **17.** $4096x^{12}y^{12}$

19. $64a^{24}b^{18}$ **21.** x^{2n+1} **23.** y^{6n-2} **25.** a^{2n^2-6n} **27.** x^{15n+10} **29.** $-6x^5y^5z^4$ **31.** $-12a^2b^9c^2$ **33.** $-6x^4y^4z^5$

35. $-432a^7b^{11}$ **37.** $54a^{13}b^{17}$ **39.** 243   **41.** y^3 **43.** $\frac{a^3b^2}{4}$ **45.** $\frac{x}{y^4}$ **47.** $\frac{1}{2}$ **49.** $-\frac{1}{9}$ **51.** $\frac{1}{y^8}$ **53.** $\frac{1}{x^6y^{10}}$

55. x^5y^5 **57.** $\frac{a^8}{b^9}$ **59.** $\frac{1}{2187a}$ **61.** $\frac{y^6}{x^3}$ **63.** $\frac{y^4}{x^3}$ **65.** $-\frac{1}{2x^2}$ **67.** $-\frac{1}{243a^5b^{10}}$ **69.** $\frac{16x^8}{81y^4z^{12}}$ **71.** $\frac{3a^4}{4b^3}$

73. $-\frac{9a}{8b^6}$ **75.** $\frac{16x^2}{y^6}$ **77.** $\frac{1}{b^{4n}}$ **79.** $-\frac{1}{y^{6n}}$ **81.** y^{n-2} **83.** $\frac{1}{y^{2n}}$ **85.** $\frac{x^{n-5}}{y^6}$ **87.** $\frac{8b^{15}}{3a^{18}}$ **89.** $\frac{8}{5}$

91. 4.67×10^{-6} **93.** 1.7×10^{-10} **95.** 2×10^{11} **97.** 0.000000123   **99.** 8,200,000,000,000,000   **101.** 0.039

103. 150,000   **105.** 20,800,000   **107.** 0.000000015   **109.** 0.0000000000178   **111.** 140,000,000   **113.** 11,000,000

115. 0.000008   **117.** Light travels 2.592×10^{10} km in one day.   **119.** The signals traveled at $1.0\overline{81} \times 10^7$ mi/min.

121. The centrifuge makes one revolution in $6.\overline{6} \times 10^{-7}$ s.   **123.** The sun is 3.38983×10^5 times heavier than Earth.

125. One orchid seed weighs 3.225806×10^{-8} oz.   **127.** The Coma cluster is 1.6423949×10^{21} mi from Earth.

SECTION 6.2

1. $P(3) = 13$ **3.** $R(2) = 10$ **5.** $f(-1) = -11$ **7.a.** -1 **b.** 8 **c.** 2
9. The expression is not a polynomial function.   **11.** The expression is not a polynomial function.
13.a. 3 **b.** π **c.** 5 **15.a.** -5 **b.** 2 **c.** 3 **17.a.** 14 **b.** 14 **c.** 0

19.   **21.**   **23.**   **25.** $6x^2 - 6x + 5$

27. $-x^2 + 1$ **29.** $5y^2 - 15y + 2$ **31.** $7a^2 - a + 2$ **33.** $P(x) + R(x) = 3x^2 - 3xy - 2y^2$
35. $P(x) - R(x) = 8x^2 - 2xy + 5y^2$ **37.** $S(x) = 3x^4 - 8x^2 + 2x; \ S(2) = 20$ **39.a.** $k = 8$ **b.** $k = -4$

SECTION 6.3

1. $x^2 - 2x$ **3.** $-x^2 - 7x$ **5.** $3a^3 - 6a^2$ **7.** $-5x^4 + 5x^3$ **9.** $-3x^5 + 7x^3$ **11.** $12x^3 - 6x^2$ **13.** $6x^2 - 12x$
15. $3x^2 + 4x$ **17.** $-x^3y + xy^3$ **19.** $2x^4 - 3x^2 + 2x$ **21.** $2a^3 + 3a^2 + 2a$ **23.** $3x^6 - 3x^4 - 2x^2$
25. $-6y^4 - 12y^3 + 14y^2$ **27.** $-2a^3 - 6a^2 + 8a$ **29.** $6y^4 - 3y^3 + 6y^2$ **31.** $x^3y - 3x^2y^2 + xy^3$ **33.** $x^3 + 4x^2 + 5x + 2$
35. $a^3 - 6a^2 + 13a - 12$ **37.** $-2b^3 + 7b^2 + 19b - 20$ **39.** $-6x^3 + 31x^2 - 41x + 10$ **41.** $x^3 - 3x^2 + 5x - 15$
43. $x^4 - 4x^3 - 3x^2 + 14x - 8$ **45.** $15y^3 - 16y^2 - 70y + 16$ **47.** $5a^4 - 20a^3 - 5a^2 + 22a - 8$
49. $y^4 + 4y^3 + y^2 - 5y + 2$ **51.** $x^2 + 4x + 3$ **53.** $a^2 + a - 12$ **55.** $y^2 - 5y - 24$ **57.** $y^2 - 10y + 21$
59. $2x^2 + 15x + 7$ **61.** $3x^2 + 11x - 4$ **63.** $4x^2 - 31x + 21$ **65.** $3y^2 - 2y - 16$ **67.** $9x^2 + 54x + 77$
69. $21a^2 - 83a + 80$ **71.** $6a^2 - 25ab + 14b^2$ **73.** $2a^2 - 11ab - 63b^2$ **75.** $100a^2 - 100ab + 21b^2$
77. $15x^2 + 56xy + 48y^2$ **79.** $14x^2 - 97xy - 60y^2$ **81.** $56x^2 - 61xy + 15y^2$ **83.** $y^2 - 25$ **85.** $4x^2 - 9$
87. $x^2 + 2x + 1$ **89.** $9a^2 - 30a + 25$ **91.** $9x^2 - 49$ **93.** $4a^2 + 4ab + b^2$ **95.** $x^2 - 4xy + 4y^2$ **97.** $16 - 9y^2$
99. $25x^2 + 20xy + 4y^2$ **101.** The area is $(10x^2 - 35x)$ ft². .   **103.** The area is $(4x^2 + 4x + 1)$ km².   **105.** The area is
$(18x^2 + 12x + 2)$ in².   **107.** The area is $(4x^2 + 10x)$ m².   **109.** The total area is $(3000 + 60w)$ yd².   **111.** $4ab$
113. $a^3 + 9a^2 + 27a + 27$ **115.a.** $7x^2 - 11x - 8$ **b.** $x^3 - 7x^2 - 7$

SECTION 6.4

1. $x + 8$ **3.** $x^2 + \dfrac{2}{x - 3}$ **5.** $3x + 5 + \dfrac{3}{2x + 1}$ **7.** $5x + 7 + \dfrac{2}{2x - 1}$ **9.** $4x^2 + 6x + 9 + \dfrac{18}{2x - 3}$
11. $3x^2 + 1 + \dfrac{1}{2x^2 - 5}$ **13.** $x^2 - 3x - 10$ **15.** $x^2 - 2x + 1 - \dfrac{1}{x - 3}$ **17.** $2x^3 - 3x^2 + x - 4$ **19.** $2x + \dfrac{x + 2}{x^2 + 2x - 1}$
21. $x^2 + 4x + 6 + \dfrac{10x + 8}{x^2 - 2x - 1}$ **23.** $x^2 - 2x + 4 + \dfrac{-6x - 7}{x^2 + 2x + 3}$ **25.** $2x - 8$ **27.** $3x - 8$ **29.** $3x + 3 - \dfrac{1}{x - 1}$
31. $2x^2 - 3x + 9$ **33.** $4x^2 + 8x + 15 + \dfrac{12}{x - 2}$ **35.** $2x^2 - 3x + 7 - \dfrac{8}{x + 4}$ **37.** $3x^3 + 2x^2 + 12x + 19 + \dfrac{33}{x - 2}$
39. $3x^3 - x + 4 - \dfrac{2}{x + 1}$ **41.** $2x^3 + 6x^2 + 17x + 51 + \dfrac{155}{x - 3}$ **43.** $P(3) = 8$ **45.** $R(4) = 43$ **47.** $P(-2) = -39$
49. $Z(-3) = -60$ **51.** $Q(2) = 31$ **53.** $F(-3) = 178$ **55.** $P(5) = 122$ **57.** $R(-3) = 302$ **59.** $Q(2) = 0$
61. $R(-2) = -65$ **63.a.** $a^2 - ab + b^2$ **b.** $x^4 - x^3y + x^2y^2 - xy^3 + y^4$ **c.** $x^5 - x^4y + x^3y^2 - x^2y^3 + xy^4 - y^5$
65.a. $\dfrac{1}{2}x^2 + \dfrac{3}{4}x - 1$ **b.** $\dfrac{2}{3}x^2 + \dfrac{7}{2}x + \dfrac{10}{3} + \dfrac{64}{6x - 12}$ **c.** $2x^2 - x + 1 + \dfrac{3x - 11}{x^2 - x + 1}$ **d.** $x^2 + 6x + 17 + \dfrac{51x + 56}{x^2 - 2x - 3}$

CHAPTER REVIEW

1. $-6a^3b^6$ [6.1A]   **2.** $9x^4y^6$ [6.1A]   **3.** $\dfrac{c^{10}}{2b^{17}}$ [6.1B]   **4.** 0.00254 [6.1C]

5. -7 [6.2A]   **6.** $4x^2 - 8xy + 5y^2$ [6.2B]   **7.** $\dfrac{18x^5y^4}{z}$ [6.1B]   **8.** $-54a^{13}b^5c^7$ [6.1A]

9.

10.a. 3   **b.** 8   **c.** 5 [6.2A]   **11.** 1 [6.4C]   **12.** $-8x^3 - 14x^2 + 18x$ [6.3A]

[6.2A]

13. $8a^3b^3 - 4a^2b^4 + 6ab^5$ [6.3A]   **14.** $6y^3 + 17y^2 - 2y - 21$ [6.3B]   **15.** $10a^2 + 31a - 63$ [6.3C]

16. 1.27×10^{-7} [6.1C]   **17.** $25y^2 - 70y + 49$ [6.3D]   **18.** $5x + 4 + \dfrac{6}{3x - 2}$ [6.4A]

19. $4x^2 + 3x - 8 + \dfrac{50}{x + 6}$ [6.4B]   **20.** $x^3 + 4x^2 + 16x + 64 + \dfrac{252}{x - 4}$ [6.4B]   **21.** $8{,}100{,}000{,}000$ [6.1C]

22. $-\dfrac{2a^3}{3b^3}$ [6.1B]   **23.** $25a^2 - 4b^2$ [6.3D]   **24.** 68 [6.4C]   **25.** $21y^2 + 4y - 1$ [6.2B]

26. $12b^5 - 4b^4 - 6b^3 - 8b^2 + 5$ [6.3B]   **27.** $a^2 - 49$ [6.3D]   **28.** 7.65×10^{11} [6.1C]   **29.** The area of the Ping-Pong table is $(2w^2 - w)$ ft². [6.3E]   **30.** The Great Galaxy of Andromeda is 1.291224×10^{19} mi from Earth. [6.1D] **31.** There are 6.048×10^5 s in one week. [6.1D]   **32.** The area is $(9x^2 - 12x + 4)$ in². [6.3E]   **33.** The area is $(10x^2 - 29x - 21)$ cm². [6.3E]

CHAPTER TEST

1. $4x^3 - 6x^2$ [6.3A]   **2.** -8 [6.4C]   **3.** $-\dfrac{4}{x^6}$ [6.1B]   **4.** $-6x^3y^6$ [6.1A]   **5.** $x - 1 + \dfrac{2}{x + 1}$ [6.4A/6.4B]

6. $x^3 - 7x^2 + 17x - 15$ [6.3B]   **7.** $-8a^6b^3$ [6.1A]   **8.** $\dfrac{9y^{10}}{x^{10}}$ [6.1B]   **9.** $a^2 + 3ab - 10b^2$ [6.3B]   **10.** -3 [6.2A]

11. $x + 7$ [6.4A/6.4B]   **12.** $6y^4 - 9y^3 + 18y^2$ [6.3A]   **13.** $-4x^4 + 8x^3 - 3x^2 - 14x + 21$ [6.3B]

14. $16y^2 - 9$ [6.3D]   **15.** a^4b^7 [6.1A]   **16.** $8ab^4$ [6.1B]   **17.** $\dfrac{2b^7}{a^{10}}$ [6.1B]   **18.** $-5a^3 + 3a^2 - 4a + 3$ [6.2B]

19. $4x^2 - 20x + 25$ [6.3D]   **20.** $x^2 - 5x + 10 - \dfrac{23}{x + 3}$ [6.4A/6.4B]   **21.** $10x^2 - 43xy + 28y^2$ [6.3C]

22. $3x^3 + 6x^2 - 8x + 3$ [6.2B]   **23.** 3.02×10^{-9} [6.1C]   **24.** The mass of the moon is 8.103×10^{19} tons. [6.1D] **25.** The area of the circle is $(\pi x^2 - 10\pi x + 25\pi)$ m². [6.3E]

CUMULATIVE REVIEW

1. -3 and 3 [1.1A]   **2.** -83 [1.1B]   **3.** 6 [1.3A]   **4.** $-\dfrac{5}{4}$ [1.4A]   **5.** $-50\sqrt{3}$ [1.2F]   **6.** The Inverse Property of Addition [1.4B]   **7.** $-186x + 8$ [1.4D]   **8.** $-\dfrac{1}{6}$ [2.2A]   **9.** $-\dfrac{11}{4}$ [2.2B]   **10.** -1 and $\dfrac{7}{3}$ [2.5A]

11. 18 [4.1D]   **12.** Yes [4.1C]   **13.** $-\dfrac{1}{6}$ [4.3A]   **14.** $y = -\dfrac{3}{2}x + \dfrac{1}{2}$ [4.4A]   **15.** $y = \dfrac{2}{3}x + \dfrac{16}{3}$ [4.5A]

16. $\left(-\dfrac{7}{5}, -\dfrac{8}{5}\right)$ [5.4B]   **17.** $\left(-\dfrac{9}{7}, \dfrac{2}{7}, \dfrac{11}{7}\right)$ [5.3B]   **18.** $5x - 3xy$ [1.4B]   **19.** $4x^3 - 7x + 3$ [6.3B]

20. 5.01×10^{-6} [6.1C]

21.
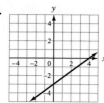
[4.2B]

22.
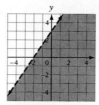
[4.6A]

23.
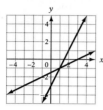
[5.1A]

The solution is $(1, -1)$.

24.
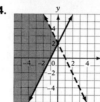
[4.6A]

25. $\dfrac{b^5}{a^8}$ [6.1B]   **26.** $\dfrac{y^2}{25x^6}$ [6.1B]   **27.** The two integers are 9 and 15. [2.2D]   **28.** 40 oz of pure gold must be used. [2.3A]   **29.** The cyclists are traveling at 5 mph and 7.5 mph. [2.3D]   **30.** $4500 must be invested at an annual simple interest rate of 10%. [2.3C]   **31.** The slope is 50. The slope represents the average speed in miles per hour. [4.3A]   **32.** The length is 15 m. The width is 6 m. [3.2A]   **33.** The area is $(4x^2 + 12x + 9)$ m². [6.3E]

Answers to Chapter 7 Odd-Numbered Exercises

SECTION 7.1

1. $5(a + 1)$ **3.** $8(2 - a^2)$ **5.** $4(2x + 3)$ **7.** $6(5a - 1)$ **9.** $x(7x - 3)$ **11.** $a^2(3 + 5a^3)$ **13.** $y(14y + 11)$
15. $2x(x^3 - 2)$ **17.** $2x^7(5x^2 - 6)$ **19.** $4a^5(2a^3 - 1)$ **21.** $xy(xy - 1)$ **23.** $3xy(xy^3 - 2)$ **25.** $xy(x - y^2)$
27. $5y(y^2 - 4y + 2)$ **29.** $3y^2(y^2 - 3y - 2)$ **31.** $3y(y^2 - 3y + 8)$ **33.** $a^2(6a^3 - 3a - 2)$ **35.** $ab(2a - 5ab + 7b)$
37. $2b(2b^4 + 3b^2 - 6)$ **39.** $x^2(8y^2 - 4y + 1)$ **41.** $a^{2n}(2a^{3n} + 1)$ **43.** $y^{2n}(y^{2n} + 1)$ **45.** $b^5(b^n - 1)$
47. $(a + z)(y + 7)$ **49.** $(a - b)(3r + s)$ **51.** $(m - 7)(t - 7)$ **53.** $(4a - b)(2y + 1)$ **55.** $(x + 2)(x + 2y)$
57. $(p - 2)(p - 3r)$ **59.** $(a + 6)(b - 4)$ **61.** $(2z - 1)(z + y)$ **63.** $(4v + 7)(2v - 3y)$ **65.** $(2x - 5)(x - 3y)$
67. $(y - 2)(3y - a)$ **69.** $(3x - y)(y + 1)$ **71.** $(3s + t)(t - 2)$ **73.** 28   **76.** P doubles when $L + W$ doubles.

SECTION 7.2

1. $(x + 1)(x + 2)$ **3.** $(x + 1)(x - 2)$ **5.** $(a + 4)(a - 3)$ **7.** $(a - 1)(a - 2)$ **9.** $(a + 2)(a - 1)$ **11.** $(b - 3)(b - 3)$
13. $(b + 8)(b - 1)$ **15.** $(y + 11)(y - 5)$ **17.** $(y - 2)(y - 3)$ **19.** $(z - 5)(z - 9)$ **21.** $(z + 8)(z - 20)$
23. $(p + 3)(p + 9)$ **25.** $(x + 10)(x + 10)$ **27.** $(b + 4)(b + 5)$ **29.** $(x + 3)(x - 14)$ **31.** $(b + 4)(b - 5)$
33. $(y + 3)(y - 17)$ **35.** $(p + 3)(p - 7)$ **37.** nonfactorable over the integers   **39.** $(x - 5)(x - 15)$ **41.** $(x - 7)(x - 8)$
43. $(x + 8)(x - 7)$ **45.** $(a + 3)(a - 24)$ **47.** $(a - 3)(a - 12)$ **49.** $(z + 8)(z - 17)$ **51.** $(c + 9)(c - 10)$
53. $(z + 4)(z + 11)$ **55.** $(c + 2)(c + 17)$ **57.** $(x + 8)(x - 12)$ **59.** $(x - 8)(x - 14)$ **61.** $(b + 15)(b - 7)$
63. $(a + 3)(a - 12)$ **65.** $(b - 6)(b - 17)$ **67.** $(a + 3)(a + 24)$ **69.** $(x + 12)(x + 13)$ **71.** $(x + 6)(x - 16)$
73. $2(x + 1)(x + 2)$ **75.** $-(x + 2)(x - 9)$ **77.** $a(b + 5)(b - 3)$ **79.** $x(y - 2)(y - 3)$ **81.** $z(z - 3)(z - 4)$
83. $-3y(y - 2)(y - 3)$ **85.** $3(x + 4)(x - 3)$ **87.** $5(z + 4)(z - 7)$ **89.** $2a(a + 8)(a - 4)$ **91.** $(x - 2y)(x - 3y)$
93. $(a - 4b)(a - 5b)$ **95.** $(x + 4y)(x - 7y)$ **97.** nonfactorable over the integers   **99.** $z^2(z - 5)(z - 7)$
101. $b^2(b - 10)(b - 12)$ **103.** $2y^2(y + 3)(y - 16)$ **105.** $-x^2(x + 8)(x - 1)$ **107.** $4y(x + 7)(x - 2)$
109. $c(c + 20)(c - 2)$ **111.** $-4x(x + 3)(x - 2)$ **113.** $(y + x)(y - 8x)$ **115.** $(y + 7z)(y - 3z)$ **117.** $(y - z)(y - 15z)$

119. $4y(x + 1)(x - 18)$ **121.** $4x(x + 8)(x - 5)$ **123.** $5z(z + 2)(z - 12)$ **125.** $5x(x + 2)(x + 4)$ **127.** $4(p + 8)(p - 15)$
129. $p^2(p + 8)(p - 7)$ **131.** $(a - 5b)(a - 5b)$ **133.** $(x + 10y)(x - 6y)$ **135.** $6x(x - 5)(x + 4)$ **137.** $y(x + 6)(x - 9)$
139. $k = -36, 36, -12, 12$ **141.** $k = 22, -22, 10, -10$ **143.** $k = 6, 10, 12$ **145.** $k = 6, 10, 12$ **147.** $k = 4, 6$

SECTION 7.3

1. $(x + 1)(2x + 1)$ **3.** $(y + 3)(2y + 1)$ **5.** $(a - 1)(2a - 1)$ **7.** $(b - 5)(2b - 1)$ **9.** $(x + 1)(2x - 1)$
11. $(x - 3)(2x + 1)$ **13.** $(t + 2)(2t - 5)$ **15.** $(p - 5)(3p - 1)$ **17.** $(3y - 1)(4y - 1)$ **19.** nonfactorable over
the integers   **21.** $(2t - 1)(3t - 4)$ **23.** $(x + 4)(8x + 1)$ **25.** nonfactorable over the integers   **27.** $(3y + 1)(4y + 5)$
29. $(a + 7)(7a - 2)$ **31.** $(b - 4)(3b - 4)$ **33.** $(z - 14)(2z + 1)$ **35.** $(p + 8)(3p - 2)$ **37.** $2(x + 1)(2x + 1)$
39. $5(y - 1)(3y - 7)$ **41.** $x(x - 5)(2x - 1)$ **43.** $b(a - 4)(3a - 4)$ **45.** nonfactorable over the integers
47. $-3x(x - 3)(x + 4)$ **49.** $4(4y - 1)(5y - 1)$ **51.** $z(2z + 3)(4z + 1)$ **53.** $y(2x - 5)(3x + 2)$ **55.** $5(t + 2)(2t - 5)$
57. $p(p - 5)(3p - 1)$ **59.** $2(z + 4)(13z - 3)$ **61.** $2y(y - 4)(5y - 2)$ **63.** $yz(z + 2)(4z - 3)$ **65.** $3a(2a + 3)(7a - 3)$
67. $y(3x - 5y)(3x - 5y)$ **69.** $xy(3x - 4y)(3x - 4y)$ **71.** $(2x - 3)(3x - 4)$ **73.** $(b + 7)(5b - 2)$ **75.** $(3a + 8)(2a - 3)$
77. $(z + 2)(4z + 3)$ **79.** $(2p + 5)(11p - 2)$ **81.** $(y + 1)(8y + 9)$ **83.** $(6t - 5)(3t + 1)$ **85.** $(b + 12)(6b - 1)$
87. $(3x + 2)(3x + 2)$ **89.** $(2b - 3)(3b - 2)$ **91.** $(3b + 5)(11b - 7)$ **93.** $(3y - 4)(6y - 5)$ **95.** $(3a + 7)(5a - 3)$
97. $(2y - 5)(4y - 3)$ **99.** $(2z + 3)(4z - 5)$ **101.** nonfactorable over the integers   **103.** $(2z - 5)(5z - 2)$
105. $(6z + 5)(6z + 7)$ **107.** $(x + y)(3x - 2y)$ **109.** $(a + 2b)(3a - b)$ **111.** $(y - 2z)(4y - 3z)$ **113.** $-(z - 7)(z + 4)$
115. $-(x - 1)(x + 8)$ **117.** $3(x + 5)(3x - 4)$ **119.** $4(2x - 3)(3x - 2)$ **121.** $a^2(5a + 2)(7a - 1)$ **123.** $5(b - 7)(3b - 2)$
125. $(x - 7y)(3x - 5y)$ **127.** $3(8y - 1)(9y + 1)$ **129.** $-(x - 1)(x + 21)$ **131.** $(5a + 7b)(3a - 2b)$
133. $-z(z + 11)(z - 3)$ **135.** $(3a + 2)(a + 3)$ **137.** $k = 7, -7, 5, -5$ **139.** $k = 7, -7, 5, -5$

SECTION 7.4

1. $(x + 4)(x - 4)$ **3.** $(2x + 1)(2x - 1)$ **5.** $(4x + 11)(4x - 11)$ **7.** $(1 + 3a)(1 - 3a)$ **9.** $(xy + 10)(xy - 10)$
11. nonfactorable over the integers   **13.** $(5 + ab)(5 - ab)$ **15.** $(a^n + 1)(a^n - 1)$ **17.** $(x - 6)^2$ **19.** $(b - 1)^2$
21. $(4x - 5)^2$ **23.** nonfactorable over the integers   **25.** nonfactorable over the integers   **27.** $(x + 3y)^2$
29. $(5a - 4b)^2$ **31.** $(x^n + 3)^2$ **33.** $(x - 7)(x - 1)$ **35.** $(x - y + a + b)(x - y - a - b)$ **37.** $(x - 3)(x^2 + 3x + 9)$
39. $(2x - 1)(4x^2 + 2x + 1)$ **41.** $(x - y)(x^2 + xy + y^2)$ **43.** $(m + n)(m^2 - mn + n^2)$ **45.** $(4x + 1)(16x^2 - 4x + 1)$
47. $(3x - 2y)(9x^2 + 6xy + 4y^2)$ **49.** $(xy + 4)(x^2y^2 - 4xy + 16)$ **51.** nonfactorable over the integers
53. nonfactorable over the integers   **55.** $(a - 2b)(a^2 - ab + b^2)$ **57.** $(x^{2n} + y^n)(x^{4n} - x^{2n}y^n + y^{2n})$
59. $(x^n + 2)(x^{2n} - 2x^n + 4)$ **61.** $(xy - 3)(xy - 5)$ **63.** $(xy - 5)(xy - 12)$ **65.** $(x^2 - 3)(x^2 - 6)$
67. $(b^2 + 5)(b^2 - 18)$ **69.** $(x^2y^2 - 2)(x^2y^2 - 6)$ **71.** $(x^n + 1)(x^n + 2)$ **73.** $(3xy - 5)(xy - 3)$ **75.** $(2ab - 3)(3ab - 7)$
77. $(2x^2 - 15)(x^2 + 1)$ **79.** $(2x^n - 1)(x^n - 3)$ **81.** $(2a^n + 5)(3a^n + 2)$ **83.** $3(2x - 3)^2$ **85.** $a(3a - 1)(9a^2 + 3a + 1)$
87. $5(2x + 1)(2x - 1)$ **89.** $y^3(y + 11)(y - 5)$ **91.** $(4x^2 + 9)(2x + 3)(2x - 3)$ **93.** $2a(2 - a)(4 + 2a + a^2)$
95. $b^3(ab - 1)(a^2b^2 + ab + 1)$ **97.** $2x^2(2x - 5)^2$ **99.** $(x^2 + y^2)(x + y)(x - y)$ **101.** $(x^2 + y^2)(x^4 - x^2y^2 + y^4)$
103. nonfactorable over the integers   **105.** $2a(2a - 1)(4a^2 + 2a + 1)$ **107.** $a^2b^2(a + 4b)(a - 12b)$
109. $2b^2(3a + 5b)(4a - 9b)$ **111.** $(x - 2)^2(x + 2)$ **113.** $(x + y)(x - y)(2x + 1)(2x - 1)$
115. $(x - 1)(x^2 + x + 1)(xy + 1)(x^2y^2 - xy + 1)$ **117.** $x(x^n + 1)^2$ **119.** $b^n(3b - 2)(b + 2)$ **121.** $(x - 3)(x - 2)(x - 1)$
123. The dimensions are $(4x + 3)$ m by $(4x + 3)$ m. Yes, x can equal 0. The possible values of x are $x > -\frac{3}{4}$.

SECTION 7.5

3. $3, 5$ **5.** $-8, 9$ **7.** $0, -2$ **9.** $0, -12$ **11.** $0, \frac{7}{4}$ **13.** $0, -\frac{5}{2}$ **15.** $8, -3$ **17.** $11, -11$ **19.** $\frac{1}{4}, -\frac{1}{4}$
21. $\frac{7}{4}, -\frac{7}{4}$ **23.** $3, 5$ **25.** $8, -9$ **27.** $-\frac{2}{3}, -4$ **29.** $\frac{5}{3}, \frac{3}{2}$ **31.** $0, 5$ **33.** $0, 4$ **35.** $-3, 8$ **37.** $-1, 8$
39. $\frac{5}{3}, -2$ **41.** $\frac{6}{5}, 2$ **43.** $12, -1$ **45.** $-3, -5$ **47.** $5, -4$ **49.** $3, 5$ **51.** $15, -1$ **53.** $-6, 3$ **55.** $1, 3$
57. $-12, 5$ **59.** $-\frac{3}{2}, -2$ **61.** The number is -3.   **63.** The numbers are 3 and 5.   **65.** The integers are 8 and 10.
67. The length is 38 cm, and the width is 10 cm.   **69.** 18 consecutive natural numbers beginning with 1 will give a

sum of 171.   **71.** There are 10 teams in the league.   **73.** The object will hit the ground 4 s later.   **75.** The ball will be 64 ft above the ground 2 s later.   **77.** The height of the triangle is 14 m.   **79.** The width of the border is 1.5 ft. **81.** The radius of the original circle is 3.81 in.   **83.** The length is 20 in., and the width is 10 in.   **85.** 1, 18

CHAPTER REVIEW

1. $5x(x^2 + 2x + 7)$ [7.1A]   **2.** $3ab(4a + b)$ [7.1A]   **3.** $7y^3(2y^6 - 7y^3 + 1)$ [7.1A]   **4.** $(x - 3)(4x + 5)$ [7.1B]
5. $(2x + 5)(5x + 2y)$ [7.1B]   **6.** $(3a - 5b)(7x + 2y)$ [7.1B]   **7.** $(b - 3)(b - 10)$ [7.2A]   **8.** $(c + 6)(c + 2)$ [7.2A]
9. $(y - 4)(y + 9)$ [7.2A]   **10.** $3(a + 2)(a - 7)$ [7.2B]   **11.** $4x(x - 6)(x + 1)$ [7.2B]   **12.** $n^2(n + 1)(n - 3)$ [7.2B]
13. $(2x - 7)(3x - 4)$ [7.3A]   **14.** $(6y - 1)(2y + 3)$ [7.3A]   **15.** nonfactorable over the integers [7.3A]
16. $(3x - 2)(x - 5)$ [7.3B]   **17.** $(2a + 5)(a - 12)$ [7.3B]   **18.** $(6a - 5)(3a + 2)$ [7.3B]
19. $(xy + 3)(xy - 3)$ [7.4A]   **20.** $(2x + 3y)^2$ [7.4A]   **21.** $(x^n - 6)^2$ [7.4A]   **22.** $(4a - 3b)(16a^2 + 12ab + 9b^2)$ [7.4B]
23. $(3x^2 + 2)(5x^2 - 3)$ [7.4C]   **24.** $(7x^2y^2 + 3)(3x^2y^2 + 2)$ [7.4C]   **25.** $3a^2(a^2 + 1)(a^2 - 6)$ [7.4D]
26. $\frac{1}{4}$ and -7 [7.5A]   **27.** -3 and 7 [7.5A]   **28.** The length is 100 yd. The width is 60 yd. [7.5B]
29. The width of the frame is $\frac{3}{2}$ in. or 1.5 in. or $1\frac{1}{2}$ in. [7.5B]   **30.** The length of a side is 20 ft. [7.5B]

CHAPTER TEST

1. $(b + 6)(a - 3)$ [7.1B]   **2.** $2y^2(y + 1)(y - 8)$ [7.2B]   **3.** $4(x + 4)(2x - 3)$ [7.3B]   **4.** $(2x + 1)(3x + 8)$ [7.3A]
5. $(a - 3)(a - 16)$ [7.2A]   **6.** $2x(3x^2 - 4x + 5)$ [7.1A]   **7.** $(x + 5)(x - 3)$ [7.2A]   **8.** $\frac{1}{2}, -\frac{1}{2}$ [7.5A]
9. $5(x^2 - 9x - 3)$ [7.1A]   **10.** $(p + 6)^2$ [7.4A]   **11.** 3 and 5 [7.5A]   **12.** $3(x + 2y)^2$ [7.4D]
13. $(3x - 2)(9x^2 + 6x + 4)$ [7.4B]   **14.** $3y^2(2x + 1)(x + 1)$ [7.3B]   **15.** $(2a^2 - 5)(3a^2 + 1)$ [7.4C]
16. $(x - 2)(a + b)$ [7.1B]   **17.** $(p + 1)(x - 1)$ [7.1B]   **18.** $3(a + 5)(a - 5)$ [7.4D]   **19.** nonfactorable over the integers [7.3A]   **20.** $(x + 3)(x - 12)$ [7.2A]   **21.** $(2u - 3b)^2$ [7.4A]   **22.** $(2x + 7y)(2x - 7y)$ [7.4A]
23. $\frac{3}{2}$ and -7 [7.5A]   **24.** The numbers are 3 and 7. [7.5B]   **25.** The length of the rectangle is 15 cm, and the width is 6 cm. [7.5B]

CUMULATIVE REVIEW

1. 7 [1.1C]   **2.** 4 [1.3A]   **3.** -7 [1.4A]   **4.** $15x^2$ [1.4C]   **5.** 12 [1.4D]   **6.** $\frac{2}{3}$ [2.1C]   **7.** $\frac{7}{4}$ [2.2B]
8. 3 [2.2C]   **9.** 45 [2.1D]   **10.** 1 [4.1D]   **11.**   **12.**

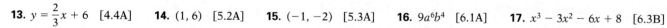

[4.2A]   [4.2B]

13. $y = \frac{2}{3}x + 6$ [4.4A]   **14.** $(1, 6)$ [5.2A]   **15.** $(-1, -2)$ [5.3A]   **16.** $9a^6b^4$ [6.1A]   **17.** $x^3 - 3x^2 - 6x + 8$ [6.3B]
18. $4x + 8 + \frac{21}{2x - 3}$ [6.4A]   **19.** $\frac{y^6}{x^8}$ [6.1B]   **20.** $(a - b)(3 - x)$ [7.1B]   **21.** $5xy^2(3 - 4y^2)$ [7.1A]
22. $(x - 7y)(x + 2y)$ [7.2A]   **23.** $\frac{2}{3}$ and -7 [7.5A]   **24.** $\frac{5}{2}$ and 4 [7.5A]   **25.** The third angle measures 59°. [3.1C]
26. The width is 15 ft. [3.2A]   **27.** The pieces are 4 ft long and 6 ft long. [2.2D]   **28.** $6500 was invested at 11%. [2.3C]   **29.** The distance to the resort is 168 mi. [2.3D]   **30.** The length of the base of the triangle is 12 in. [7.5B]

Answers to Chapter 8 Odd-Numbered Exercises

SECTION 8.1

1. $\dfrac{3}{4x}$ **3.** $\dfrac{1}{x+3}$ **5.** -1 **7.** $\dfrac{2}{3y}$ **9.** $-\dfrac{3}{4x}$ **11.** $\dfrac{a}{b}$ **13.** $-\dfrac{2}{x}$ **15.** $\dfrac{y-2}{y-3}$ **17.** $\dfrac{x+5}{x+4}$ **19.** $\dfrac{x+4}{x-3}$

21. $-\dfrac{x+2}{x+5}$ **23.** $\dfrac{2(x+2)}{x+3}$ **25.** $\dfrac{2x-1}{2x+3}$ **27.** $-\dfrac{x+7}{x+6}$ **29.** $\dfrac{35ab^2}{24x^2y}$ **31.** $\dfrac{4x^3y^3}{3a^2}$ **33.** $\dfrac{3}{4}$ **35.** ab^2

37. $\dfrac{x^2(x-1)}{y(x+3)}$ **39.** $\dfrac{y(x-1)}{x^2(x+10)}$ **41.** $-ab^2$ **43.** $\dfrac{x+5}{x+4}$ **45.** 1 **47.** $-\dfrac{n-10}{n-7}$ **49.** $\dfrac{x(x+2)}{2(x-1)}$ **51.** $-\dfrac{x+2}{x-6}$

53. $\dfrac{x+5}{x-12}$ **55.** $\dfrac{7a^3y^2}{40bx}$ **57.** $\dfrac{4}{3}$ **59.** $\dfrac{3a}{2}$ **61.** $\dfrac{x^2(x+4)}{y^2(x+2)}$ **63.** $\dfrac{x(x-2)}{y(x-6)}$ **65.** $-\dfrac{3by}{ax}$ **67.** $\dfrac{(x-3)(x+6)}{(x+7)(x-6)}$

69. 1 **71.** $-\dfrac{x+8}{x-4}$ **73.** $\dfrac{2n+1}{2n-3}$ **75.** Yes; for example, 3.00000001.   **77.** $5, -5$ **79.** $\dfrac{4x}{3y}$ **81.** $-\dfrac{1}{y^3}$

SECTION 8.2

1. $24x^3y^2$ **3.** $30x^4y^2$ **5.** $8x^2(x+2)$ **7.** $6x^2y(x+4)$ **9.** $36x(x+2)^2$ **11.** $6(x+1)^2$ **13.** $(x-1)(x+2)(x+3)$

15. $(2x+3)^2(x-5)$ **17.** $(x-1)(x-2)$ **19.** $(x-3)(x+2)(x+4)$ **21.** $(x+4)(x+1)(x-7)$

23. $(x-6)(x+6)(x+4)$ **25.** $(x-10)(x-8)(x+3)$ **27.** $(3x-2)(x-3)(x+2)$ **29.** $(x+2)(x-3)$

31. $(x-5)(x+1)$ **33.** $(x-3)(x-2)(x-1)(x-6)$ **35.** $\dfrac{5}{ab^2};\ \dfrac{6b}{ab^2}$ **37.** $\dfrac{15y^2}{18x^2y};\ \dfrac{14x}{18x^2y}$ **39.** $\dfrac{ay+5a}{y^2(y+5)};\ \dfrac{6y}{y^2(y+5)}$

41. $\dfrac{a^2y+7a^2}{y(y+7)^2};\ \dfrac{ay}{y(y+7)^2}$ **43.** $\dfrac{b}{y(y-4)};\ \dfrac{-b^2y}{y(y-4)}$ **45.** $-\dfrac{3y-21}{(y-7)^2};\ \dfrac{2}{(y-7)^2}$ **47.** $\dfrac{2y^2}{y^2(y-3)};\ \dfrac{3}{y^2(y-3)}$

49. $\dfrac{x^3+4x^2}{(2x-1)(x+4)};\ \dfrac{2x^2+x-1}{(2x-1)(x+4)}$ **51.** $\dfrac{3x^2+15x}{(x-5)(x+5)};\ \dfrac{4}{(x-5)(x+5)}$ **53.** $\dfrac{x-3}{(3x-2)(x+2)};\ \dfrac{6x-4}{(3x-2)(x+2)}$

55. $\dfrac{x^2-1}{(x+5)(x-3)(x+1)};\ \dfrac{x^2-3x}{(x+5)(x-3)(x+1)}$ **57.** $\dfrac{11}{y^2}$ **59.** $-\dfrac{7}{x+4}$ **61.** $\dfrac{8x}{2x+3}$ **63.** $\dfrac{5x+7}{x-3}$ **65.** $\dfrac{2x-5}{x+9}$

67. $\dfrac{-3x-4}{2x+7}$ **69.** $\dfrac{1}{x+5}$ **71.** $\dfrac{1}{x-6}$ **73.** $\dfrac{3}{2y-1}$ **75.** $\dfrac{1}{x-5}$ **79.** $\dfrac{7b+5a}{ab}$ **81.** $\dfrac{11}{12a}$ **83.** $\dfrac{11}{12y}$

85. $\dfrac{120+7y}{20y^2}$ **87.** $\dfrac{21b+4a}{12ab}$ **89.** $\dfrac{14x+3}{12x}$ **91.** $\dfrac{8x-3}{6x}$ **93.** $\dfrac{7}{36}$ **95.** $\dfrac{-3x^2-11x-2}{3x^2}$ **97.** $\dfrac{6x^2+5x+10}{6x^2}$

99. $\dfrac{2x^2+1}{x}$ **101.** $\dfrac{4x+2}{x+1}$ **103.** $\dfrac{x^2-x+2}{x^2y}$ **105.** $\dfrac{16xy-12y+6x^2+3x}{12x^2y^2}$ **107.** $\dfrac{3xy-6y-2x^2-14x}{24x^2y}$

109. $\dfrac{9x+2}{(x-2)(x+3)}$ **111.** $\dfrac{2(x+23)}{(x-7)(x+3)}$ **113.** $\dfrac{2x^2-5x+1}{(x+1)(x-3)}$ **115.** $\dfrac{4x^2-34x+5}{(2x-1)(x-6)}$ **117.** $\dfrac{2a-5}{a-7}$

119. $\dfrac{4x+9}{(x+3)(x-3)}$ **121.** $\dfrac{-x+9}{(x+2)(x-3)}$ **123.** $\dfrac{8y}{(y+2)^2}$ **125.** $\dfrac{3x-y}{x-y}$ **127.** $\dfrac{11}{(a-3)(a-4)}$ **129.** $\dfrac{-x-1}{(x+2)(x-5)}$

131. $\dfrac{x+3}{x+5}$ **133.** $\dfrac{x-2}{x+4}$ **135.** $\dfrac{4(2x-1)}{(x+5)(x-2)}$ **137a.** $\dfrac{3}{y}+\dfrac{6}{x}$ **b.** $\dfrac{4}{b^2}+\dfrac{3}{ab}$ **c.** $\dfrac{1}{4mn}+\dfrac{1}{6m^2}$

139. $\dfrac{2}{3},\dfrac{3}{4},\dfrac{4}{5};\ \dfrac{50}{51},\dfrac{100}{101},\dfrac{1000}{1001}$

SECTION 8.3

1. $\dfrac{x}{x-3}$ **3.** $\dfrac{2}{3}$ **5.** $\dfrac{y+3}{y-4}$ **7.** $\dfrac{2(2x+13)}{5x+36}$ **9.** $\dfrac{x+2}{x+3}$ **11.** $\dfrac{x-6}{x+5}$ **13.** $-\dfrac{x-2}{x+1}$ **15.** $x-1$

17. $\dfrac{1}{2x-1}$ **19.** $\dfrac{x-3}{x+5}$ **21.** $\dfrac{x-7}{x-8}$ **23.** $\dfrac{2y-1}{2y+1}$ **25.** $\dfrac{x-2}{2x-5}$ **27.** $-\dfrac{x+1}{4x-3}$ **29.** $\dfrac{x+1}{2(5x-2)}$

31. $\dfrac{5}{3}$ **33.** $-\dfrac{1}{x-1}$ **35.** $\dfrac{y+4}{2(y-2)}$

SECTION 8.4

1. 3   **3.** 1   **5.** 9   **7.** 1   **9.** $\frac{1}{4}$ **11.** 1   **13.** -3 **15.** $\frac{1}{2}$ **17.** 8   **19.** 5   **21.** -1 **23.** 5

25. The equation has no solution.   **27.** 2, 4   **29.** $-\frac{3}{2}$, 4   **31.** 3   **33.** 4   **35.** 9   **37.** 36   **39.** 10   **41.** 113

43. -2 **45.** 15   **47.** 4   **49.** 6.7 cm   **51.** 2.9 m   **53.** 22.5 ft   **55.** 48 m²   **57.** 6.25 cm   **59.** 6 in.

61. 13 cm   **63.** The height of the flagpole is 14.375 ft.   **65.** The width of the ravine is 82.5 ft.   **67.** 20,000 voters voted in favor of the amendment.   **69.** There are 175 mi between the two cities.   **71.** There are 160 ml of water in 280 ml of soft drink.   **73.** It would take 18 min to print a document 45 pages long.   **75.** The window should be 40 ft².

77. No, the shipment will not be accepted.   **79.** Two additional gallons are necessary to cover 1680 ft².

81. The math club receives $75.

SECTION 8.5

1. $h = \dfrac{2A}{b}$ **3.** $t = \dfrac{d}{r}$ **5.** $T = \dfrac{PV}{nR}$ **7.** $L = \dfrac{P - 2W}{2}$ **9.** $b_1 = \dfrac{2A - hb_2}{h}$ **11.** $h = \dfrac{3V}{A}$ **13.** $S = C - Rt$

15. $P = \dfrac{A}{1 + rt}$ **17.** $w = \dfrac{A}{S + 1}$ **19a.** $h = \dfrac{S - 2\pi r^2}{2\pi r}$ **b.** The height is 5 in.   **c.** The height is 4 in.

21a. $S = \dfrac{F + BV}{B}$ **b.** The required selling price is $180.   **c.** The required selling price is $75.

SECTION 8.6

1. It would take 2 h with both sprinklers working.   **3.** It would take both skiploaders 3 h working together.

5. It would take 30 h with both computers working.   **7.** It would take 30 min with both air conditioners working.

9. It would take the second pipeline 90 min to fill the tank.   **11.** It would take the apprentice 15 h to construct the wall.

13. It would take the second technician 3 h to complete the wiring.   **15.** It would have taken one welder 40 h to complete the welds.   **17.** It would take one machine 28 h working alone.   **19.** The rate through the congested traffic is 20 mph.

21. The rate of the jogger is 8 mph, and the rate of the cyclist is 20 mph.   **23.** The rate of the jet is 360 mph.   **25.** The rate of the motorcycle is 48 mph.   **27.** The rate of the car is 48 mph.   **29.** The rate of the wind is 20 mph.   **31.** The rate of the gulf current is 6 mph.   **33.** The rate of the trucker for the first 330 mi was 55 mph.   **35.** The less-experienced helper can complete the job in 30 h.   **37.** The bus usually travels 60 mph.

SECTION 8.7

1. The profit is $80,000.   **3.** The pressure is 6.75 lb/in².   **5.** The object will fall 1600 ft.   **7.** The ball will roll 54 ft in 3 s.

9. The length is 10 ft when the width is 4 ft.   **11.** The gear will make 30 revolutions/min.   **13.** The current will be 7.5 amps.   **15.** The intensity of light will be 48 foot-candles.   **17.** y is doubled.   **19.** inversely   **21.** inversely

CHAPTER REVIEW

1. $\dfrac{b^3 y}{10ax}$ [8.1C]   **2.** $\dfrac{7x + 22}{60x}$ [8.2D]   **3.** $\dfrac{x - 2}{3x - 10}$ [8.3A]   **4.** $-\dfrac{x + 6}{x + 3}$ [8.1A]   **5.** $\dfrac{2x^4}{3y^7}$ [8.1A]

6. 62 [8.4B]   **7.** $\dfrac{(3y - 2)^2}{(y - 1)(y - 2)}$ [8.1C]   **8.** $\dfrac{by^3}{6ax^2}$ [8.1B]   **9.** $\dfrac{x}{x - 7}$ [8.3A]

10. $\dfrac{3x^2 - x}{(2x + 3)(6x - 1)(3x - 1)}$, $\dfrac{24x^3 - 4x^2}{(2x + 3)(6x - 1)(3x - 1)}$ [8.2B]   **11.** $a = \dfrac{T - 2bc}{2b + 2c}$ [8.5A]   **12.** 2 [8.4A]

13. $c = \dfrac{100m}{i}$ [8.5A]   **14.** The equation has no solution. [8.4A]   **15.** $\dfrac{1}{x^2}$ [8.1C]   **16.** $\dfrac{2y - 3}{5y - 7}$ [8.2D]

17. $\dfrac{1}{x + 3}$ [8.2C]   **18.** $(5x - 3)(2x - 1)(4x - 1)$ [8.2A]   **19.** $y = -\dfrac{4}{9}x + 2$ [8.5A]   **20.** $\dfrac{8x + 5}{3x - 4}$ [8.1B]

21. 5 [8.4A] **22.** $\dfrac{3x-1}{x-5}$ [8.2D] **23.** 10 [8.4B] **24.** 12 [8.4B] **25.** The perimeter of triangle *ABC* is 24 in. [8.4C] **26.** It would take 6 h to fill the pool using both hoses. [8.6A] **27.** The rate of the car is 45 mph. [8.6B] **28.** The rate of the wind is 20 mph. [8.6B] **29.** The pitcher's ERA is 1.35. [8.4D] **30.** The current is 2 amps. [8.7A]

CHAPTER TEST

1. $\dfrac{2x^3}{3y^3}$ [8.1A] **2.** $-\dfrac{x+5}{x+5}$ [8.1A] **3.** $\dfrac{x+1}{x^3(x-2)}$ [8.1B] **4.** $\dfrac{(x-5)(2x-1)}{(x+3)(2x+5)}$ [8.1B] **5.** $\dfrac{x+5}{x+4}$ [8.1C]

6. $3(2x-1)(x+1)$ [8.2A] **7.** $\dfrac{3(x+2)}{x(x+2)(x-2)}; \dfrac{x^2}{x(x+2)(x-2)}$ [8.2B] **8.** $\dfrac{2}{x+5}$ [8.2C] **9.** $\dfrac{5}{(2x-1)(3x+1)}$ [8.2D]

10. $\dfrac{x^2-4x+5}{(x-2)(x+3)}$ [8.2D] **11.** $\dfrac{x-3}{x-2}$ [8.3A] **12.** 2 [8.4A] **13.** The equation has no solution. [8.4A]

14. -1 [8.4B] **15.** The area is 64.8 m². [8.4C] **16.** $t=\dfrac{d-s}{r}$ [8.5A] **17.** 14 rolls of wallpaper are needed. [8.4D] **18.** It would take 10 min with both landscapers working. [8.6A] **19.** The rate of the cyclist is 10 mph. [8.6B] **20.** The resistance is 0.4 ohm. [8.7A]

CUMULATIVE REVIEW

1. $\dfrac{31}{30}$ [1.3A] **2.** 21 [1.4A] **3.** $5x-2y$ [1.4B] **4.** $-8x+26$ [1.4D] **5.** $-\dfrac{9}{2}$ [2.2A] **6.** -12 [2.2C]

7. 10 [2.1D] **8.** $\{x|x\le 8\}$ [2.4A] **9.** The volume is 200 ft³. [3.3A] **10.**

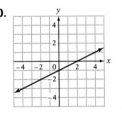

[4.2B]

11. $\dfrac{3}{7}$ [4.1D] **12.** $y=\dfrac{3}{2}x+2$ [4.5A] **13.** -28 [5.4A] **14.** a^3b^7 [6.1A] **15.** $\dfrac{a^5}{b^6}$ [6.1B]

16. 3.5×10^{-8} [6.1C] **17.** $-4a^4+6a^3-2a^2$ [6.3A] **18.** $a^2+ab-12b^2$ [6.3C] **19.** x^2+2x+4 [6.4B]

20. $(y-6)(y-1)$ [7.2A] **21.** $(4x+1)(3x-1)$ [7.3A/7.3B] **22.** $a(2a-3)(a+5)$ [7.3A/7.3B]

23. $4(b+5)(b-5)$ [7.4D] **24.** -3 and $\dfrac{5}{2}$ [7.5A] **25.** $\dfrac{2x^3}{3y^5}$ [8.1A] **26.** $-\dfrac{x-2}{x+5}$ [8.1A] **27.** 1 [8.1C]

28. $\dfrac{3}{(2x-1)(x+1)}$ [8.2D] **29.** $\dfrac{x+3}{x+5}$ [8.3A] **30.** 4 [8.4A] **31.** The alloy contains 70% silver. [2.3B]

32. It would cost \$80. [8.4D] **33.** It would take 6 min to fill the tank. [8.6A]

Answers to Chapter 9 Odd-Numbered Exercises

SECTION 9.1

1. 2 **3.** 27 **5.** $\dfrac{1}{9}$ **7.** 4 **9.** $(-25)^{5/2}$ is not a real number. **11.** $\dfrac{343}{125}$ **13.** x **15.** $y^{1/2}$ **17.** $x^{1/12}$ **19.** $a^{7/12}$

21. $\dfrac{1}{a}$ **23.** $\dfrac{1}{y}$ **25.** $y^{3/2}$ **27.** $\dfrac{1}{x}$ **29.** $\dfrac{1}{x^4}$ **31.** a **33.** $x^{3/10}$ **35.** a^3 **37.** $\dfrac{1}{x^{1/2}}$ **39.** $y^{1/9}$ **41.** $x^4 y$

43. $x^6 y^3 z^9$ **45.** $\dfrac{x}{y^2}$ **47.** $\dfrac{x^{3/2}}{y^{1/4}}$ **49.** $\dfrac{x^2}{y^8}$ **51.** $\dfrac{1}{x^{11/12}}$ **53.** $\dfrac{1}{y^{5/2}}$ **55.** $\dfrac{1}{b^{7/8}}$ **57.** $a^5 b^{13}$ **59.** $\dfrac{m^2}{4n^{3/2}}$ **61.** $\dfrac{y^{17/2}}{x^3}$

63. $\dfrac{16b^2}{a^{1/3}}$ **65.** $y^2 - y$ **67.** $a - a^2$ **69.** x^{4n} **71.** $x^{3n/2}$ **73.** $y^{3n/2}$ **75.** x^{2n^2} **77.** $x^{2n}y^n$ **79.** $x^{4n}y^{2n}$

81. $\sqrt[4]{3}$ **83.** $\sqrt{a^3}$ **85.** $\sqrt{32t^5}$ **87.** $-2\sqrt[3]{x^2}$ **89.** $\sqrt[3]{a^4b^2}$ **91.** $\sqrt[5]{a^6b^{12}}$ **93.** $\sqrt[4]{(4x-3)^3}$ **95.** $\dfrac{1}{\sqrt[3]{x^2}}$

97. $14^{1/2}$ **99.** $x^{1/3}$ **101.** $x^{4/3}$ **103.** $b^{3/5}$ **105.** $(2x^2)^{1/3}$ **107.** $-(3x^5)^{1/2}$ **109.** $3xy^{2/3}$ **111.** $(a^2-2)^{1/2}$ **113.** x^8
115. $-x^4$ **117.** xy^3 **119.** $-x^5y$ **121.** $4a^2b^6$ **123.** $\sqrt{-16x^4y^2}$ is not a real number. **125.** $3x^3$ **127.** $-4x^3y^4$
129. $-x^2y^3$ **131.** x^4y^2 **133.** $3xy^5$ **135.** $2ab^2$ **137a.** false; 2 **b.** true **c.** true **d.** false; $(a^n + b^n)^{1/n}$
e. false; $a + 2a^{1/2}b^{1/2} + b$ **f.** false; $a^{n/m}$

SECTION 9.2

1. $x^2yz^2\sqrt{yz}$ **3.** $2ab^4\sqrt{2a}$ **5.** $3xyz^2\sqrt{5yz}$ **7.** $\sqrt{-9x^3}$ is not a real number. **9.** $a^5b^2\sqrt[3]{ab^2}$ **11.** $-5y\sqrt[3]{x^2y}$
13. $abc^2\sqrt[3]{ab^2}$ **15.** $2x^2y\sqrt[4]{xy}$ **17.** $-6\sqrt{x}$ **19.** $-2\sqrt{2}$ **21.** $3\sqrt{2b} + 5\sqrt{3b}$ **23.** $-2xy\sqrt{2y}$
25. $6ab^2\sqrt{3ab} + 3ab\sqrt{3ab}$ **27.** $-\sqrt[3]{2}$ **29.** $8b\sqrt[3]{2b^2}$ **31.** $3a\sqrt[4]{2a}$ **33.** $17\sqrt{2} - 15\sqrt{5}$ **35.** $5b\sqrt{b}$
37. $-8xy\sqrt{2x} + 2xy\sqrt{xy}$ **39.** $2y\sqrt[3]{2x}$ **41.** $-4ab\sqrt[4]{2b}$ **43.** 16 **45.** $2\sqrt[3]{4}$ **47.** $xy^3\sqrt{x}$ **49.** $8xy\sqrt{x}$
51. $2x^2y\sqrt[3]{2}$ **53.** $2ab\sqrt[4]{3a^2b}$ **55.** 6 **57.** $x - \sqrt{2x}$ **59.** $4x - 8\sqrt{x}$ **61.** $x - 6\sqrt{x} + 9$ **63.** $84 + 16\sqrt{5}$
65. $672x^2y^2$ **67.** $4a^3b^3\sqrt[3]{a}$ **69.** $-8\sqrt{5}$ **71.** $x - y^2$ **73.** $12x - y$ **75.** $y\sqrt{5y}$ **77.** $b\sqrt{13h}$ **79.** $\dfrac{\sqrt{2}}{2}$

81. $\dfrac{2\sqrt{3y}}{3y}$ **83.** $\dfrac{3\sqrt{3a}}{a}$ **85.** $\dfrac{\sqrt{2y}}{2}$ **87.** $\dfrac{5\sqrt[3]{3}}{3}$ **89.** $\dfrac{5\sqrt[3]{9y^2}}{3y}$ **91.** $\dfrac{b\sqrt{2a}}{2a^2}$ **93.** $\dfrac{\sqrt{15x}}{5x}$ **95.** $2 + 2\sqrt{2}$

97. $\dfrac{-12 - 4\sqrt{2}}{7}$ **99.** $-\dfrac{10 + 5\sqrt{7}}{3}$ **101.** $-\dfrac{7\sqrt{x} + 21}{x - 9}$ **103.** $-\sqrt{6} + 3 - 2\sqrt{2} + 2\sqrt{3}$ **105.** $-\dfrac{17 + 5\sqrt{5}}{4}$

107. $\dfrac{8a - 10\sqrt{ab} + 3b}{16a - 9b}$ **109.** $\dfrac{3 - 7\sqrt{y} + 2y}{1 - 4y}$ **111a.** false; $\sqrt[6]{432}$ **b.** true **c.** false; $\sqrt[3]{x} \cdot \sqrt[3]{x} = \sqrt[3]{x^2}$
d. false; $\sqrt{x} + \sqrt{y}$ **e.** false; $\sqrt[2]{2} + \sqrt[3]{3}$ **f.** true **113.** $a + b$

SECTION 9.3

1. $2i$ **3.** $7i\sqrt{2}$ **5.** $3i\sqrt{3}$ **7.** $4 + 2i$ **9.** $2\sqrt{3} - 3i\sqrt{2}$ **11.** $4\sqrt{10} - 7i\sqrt{3}$ **13.** $8 - i$ **15.** $-8 + 4i$
17. $6 - 6i$ **19.** $19 - 7i\sqrt{2}$ **21.** $6\sqrt{2} - 3i\sqrt{2}$ **23.** 63 **25.** -4 **27.** $-3\sqrt{2}$ **29.** $-4 + 12i$ **31.** $-2 + 4i$
33. $17 - i$ **35.** $8 + 27i$ **37.** 1 **39.** 1 **41.** $3i$ **43.** $\dfrac{3}{4} + \dfrac{1}{2}i$ **45.** $\dfrac{10}{13} - \dfrac{2}{13}i$ **47.** $\dfrac{4}{5} + \dfrac{2}{5}i$ **49.** $-i$

51. $-\dfrac{\sqrt{5}}{5} + \dfrac{2\sqrt{5}}{5}i$ **53.** $\dfrac{3}{10} - \dfrac{11}{10}i$ **55.** $\dfrac{6}{5} + \dfrac{7}{5}i$ **57a.** $(y + i)(y - i)$ **b.** $(7x + 4i)(7x - 4i)$ **c.** $(3a + 8i)(3a - 8i)$

59. $-\dfrac{\sqrt{2}}{2} + \dfrac{\sqrt{2}}{2}i$

SECTION 9.4

1. 25 **3.** 27 **5.** 48 **7.** -2 **9.** The equation has no solution. **11.** 9 **13.** -23 **15.** -16 **17.** $\dfrac{9}{4}$

19. 14 **21.** 7 **23.** 7 **25.** -122 **27.** 35 **29.** $-5, -2$ **31.** 45 **33.** 23 **35.** -4 **37.** 10 **39.** 1

41. 3 **43.** 21 **45.** $\dfrac{25}{72}$ **47.** 5 **49.** $-2, 4$ **51.** 6 **53.** 0, 1 **55.** $-2, 2$ **57.** $-2, 1$ **59.** 2, 11

61. The width is 6 ft. **63.** The bottom of the ladder is 10 ft from the wall. **65.** The object has fallen 2500 ft.
67. The periscope must be 8.64 ft above the water. **69.** The length of the pendulum is 4.67 ft. **71.** The distance
is 180 m. **73.** The HDTV screen is 7.15 in. wider. **75a.** 2, -2; integer, rational number, real number
b. $i, -i$; imaginary **c.** 16; integer, rational number, real number **77.** $a = \sqrt{c^2 - b^2}$ or $a = -\sqrt{c^2 - b^2}$ **79.** $x = \sqrt{6}$

CHAPTER REVIEW

1. $20x^2y^2$ [9.1A] **2.** 7 [9.4A] **3.** $39 - 2i$ [9.3C] **4.** $7x^{2/3}y$ [9.1B] **5.** $6\sqrt{3} - 13$ [9.2C] **6.** -2 [9.4A]

7. $\dfrac{1}{x^5}$ [9.1A] **8.** $\dfrac{8\sqrt{3y}}{3y}$ [9.2D] **9.** $-2a^2b^4$ [9.1C] **10.** $2a^2b\sqrt{2b}$ [9.2B] **11.** $\dfrac{x\sqrt{x} - x\sqrt{2} + 2\sqrt{x} - 2\sqrt{2}}{x - 2}$ [9.2D]

12. $\dfrac{2}{3} - \dfrac{5}{3}i$ [9.3D] **13.** $3ab^3\sqrt{2a}$ [9.2A] **14.** $-4\sqrt{2} + 8i\sqrt{2}$ [9.3B] **15.** $5x^3y^3\sqrt[3]{2x^2y}$ [9.2B]

16. $4xy^2\sqrt[3]{x^2}$ [9.2C] **17.** $7 + 3i$ [9.3C] **18.** $3\sqrt[4]{x^3}$ [9.1B] **19.** $-2ab^2\sqrt[5]{2a^3b^2}$ [9.2A]

20. $-2 + 7i$ [9.3D] **21.** $-6\sqrt{2}$ [9.3C] **22.** 30 [9.4A] **23.** $3a^2b^3$ [9.1C] **24.** $5i\sqrt{2}$ [9.3A]

25. $-12 + 10i$ [9.3B] **26.** $31 - 10\sqrt{6}$ [9.2C] **27.** $6x^2\sqrt{3y}$ [9.2B] **28.** The amount of power generated is 120 watts. [9.4B] **29.** The distance required to reach a velocity of 88 ft/s is 242 ft. [9.4B] **30.** The bottom of the ladder is 6.63 ft from the building. [9.4B]

CHAPTER TEST

1. $\dfrac{1}{2}x^{3/4}$ [9.1B] **2.** $-2x^2y\sqrt[3]{2x}$ [9.2B] **3.** $3\sqrt[5]{y^2}$ [9.1B] **4.** $18 + 16i$ [9.3C] **5.** $4x + 4\sqrt{xy} + y$ [9.2C]

6. $r^{1/6}$ [9.1A] **7.** 4 [9.4A] **8.** $2xy^2$ [9.1C] **9.** $-4x\sqrt{3}$ [9.2C] **10.** $-3 + 2i$ [9.3B] **11.** $4x^2y^3\sqrt{2y}$ [9.2A]

12. $14 + 10\sqrt{3}$ [9.2C] **13.** 4 [9.3B] **14.** 2 [9.2D] **15.** $8a\sqrt{2a}$ [9.2B] **16.** $2a - \sqrt{ab} - 15b$ [9.2C]

17. $\dfrac{64x^3}{y^6}$ [9.1A] **18.** $\dfrac{x + \sqrt{xy}}{x - y}$ [9.2D] **19.** $-\dfrac{4}{5} + \dfrac{7}{5}i$ [9.3D] **20.** -3 [9.4A] **21.** $\dfrac{b^3}{8a^6}$ [9.1A]

22. $3abc^2\sqrt[3]{ac}$ [9.2A] **23.** $\dfrac{4x^2}{y}$ [9.2D] **24.** -4 [9.3C] **25.** The object has fallen 576 ft. [9.4B]

CUMULATIVE REVIEW

1. 92 [1.3A] **2.** 56 [1.4A] **3.** $-10x + 1$ [1.4D] **4.** $\dfrac{3}{2}$ [2.2A] **5.** $\dfrac{2}{3}$ [2.2C] **6.** $\{x|x > 1\}$ [2.4A]

7. $\dfrac{1}{3}, \dfrac{7}{3}$ [2.5A] **8.** $\{x|-6 \le x \le 3\}$ [2.5B] **9.** The area is 187.5 cm². [3.2B] **10.** 3 [5.4A]

11. $m = \dfrac{3}{2}$, $b = 3$ 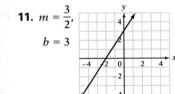   [4.2B]

12. 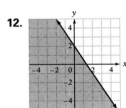   [4.6A]

13. $y = \dfrac{1}{3}x + \dfrac{7}{3}$ [4.4B]

14. $\left(\dfrac{17}{4}, \dfrac{9}{2}\right)$ [5.4B] **15.** $2x^2y^2$ [6.1B] **16.** $(9x + y)(9x - y)$ [7.4A] **17.** $x(x^2 + 3)(x + 1)(x - 1)$ [7.4D]

18. $C = R - nP$ [8.5A] **19.** $\dfrac{y^5}{x^4}$ [9.1A] **20.** $-x\sqrt{10x}$ [9.2B] **21.** $13 - 7\sqrt{3}$ [9.2C] **22.** $\sqrt{6} + \sqrt{2}$ [9.2D]

23. $-\dfrac{1}{5} + \dfrac{3}{5}i$ [9.3D] **24.** -20 [9.4A] **25.** The length of side DE is 27 m. [8.4C] **26.** \$4000 must be invested at 8.4%. [2.3C] **27.** The rate of the plane was 250 mph. [8.6B] **28.** It takes 1.25 s for light to travel to Earth from the moon. [6.1D] **29.** The slope is 0.08. The slope represents the simple interest rate on the investment. The interest rate is 8%. [4.3A] **30.** The periscope must be 32.7 ft above the water. [9.4B]

Answers to Chapter 10 Odd-Numbered Exercises

SECTION 10.1

1. $0, 4$ **3.** $5, -5$ **5.** $3, -2$ **7.** 3 **9.** $0, 2$ **11.** $5, -2$ **13.** $2, 5$ **15.** $6, -\dfrac{3}{2}$ **17.** $2, \dfrac{1}{4}$ **19.** $\dfrac{1}{3}, -4$

21. $\dfrac{9}{2}, -\dfrac{2}{3}$ **23.** $\dfrac{1}{4}, -4$ **25.** $9, -2$ **27.** $-2, -\dfrac{3}{4}$ **29.** $2, -5$ **31.** $-4, -\dfrac{3}{2}$ **33.** $2b, 7b$ **35.** $7c, -c$

37. $-\dfrac{b}{2}, -b$ **39.** $4a, \dfrac{2a}{3}$ **41.** $-\dfrac{a}{3}, 3a$ **43.** $-\dfrac{3y}{2}, -\dfrac{y}{2}$ **45.** $-\dfrac{a}{2}, -\dfrac{4a}{3}$ **47.** $x^2 - 7x + 10 = 0$

49. $x^2 + 6x + 8 = 0$ **51.** $x^2 - 5x - 6 = 0$ **53.** $x^2 - 9 = 0$ **55.** $x^2 - 8x + 16 = 0$ **57.** $x^2 - 5x = 0$

59. $x^2 - 3x = 0$ **61.** $2x^2 - 7x + 3 = 0$ **63.** $4x^2 - 5x - 6 = 0$ **65.** $3x^2 + 11x + 10 = 0$ **67.** $9x^2 - 4 = 0$

69. $6x^2 - 5x + 1 = 0$ **71.** $10x^2 - 7x - 6 = 0$ **73.** $8x^2 + 6x + 1 = 0$ **75.** $50x^2 - 25x - 3 = 0$ **77.** $7, -7$

79. $2i, -2i$ **81.** $2, -2$ **83.** $\dfrac{9}{2}, -\dfrac{9}{2}$ **85.** $7i, -7i$ **87.** $4\sqrt{3}, -4\sqrt{3}$ **89.** $5\sqrt{3}, -5\sqrt{3}$ **91.** $3i\sqrt{2}, -3i\sqrt{2}$

93. $7, -5$ **95.** $0, -6$ **97.** $-7, 3$ **99.** $1, 0$ **101.** $-5 + \sqrt{6}, -5 - \sqrt{6}$ **103.** $3 + 3i\sqrt{5}, 3 - 3i\sqrt{5}$

105. $-\dfrac{2 - 9\sqrt{2}}{3}, -\dfrac{2 + 9\sqrt{2}}{3}$ **107.** $x^2 - 2 = 0$ **109.** $x^2 - 18 = 0$ **111.** $\dfrac{3b}{a}, -\dfrac{3b}{a}$ **113.** $-\dfrac{1}{2}$

SECTION 10.2

3. $5, -1$ **5.** $-9, 1$ **7.** 3 **9.** $-2 + \sqrt{11}, -2 - \sqrt{11}$ **11.** $3 + \sqrt{2}, 3 - \sqrt{2}$ **13.** $1 + i, 1 - i$ **15.** $8, -3$

17. $4, -9$ **19.** $\dfrac{3 + \sqrt{5}}{2}, \dfrac{3 - \sqrt{5}}{2}$ **21.** $\dfrac{1 + \sqrt{5}}{2}, \dfrac{1 - \sqrt{5}}{2}$ **23.** $3 + \sqrt{13}, 3 - \sqrt{13}$ **25.** $5, 3$ **27.** $2 + 3i, 2 - 3i$

29. $-3 + 2i, -3 - 2i$ **31.** $1 + 3\sqrt{2}, 1 - 3\sqrt{2}$ **33.** $\dfrac{1 + \sqrt{17}}{2}, \dfrac{1 - \sqrt{17}}{2}$ **35.** $1 + 2i\sqrt{3}, 1 - 2i\sqrt{3}$

37. $\dfrac{1}{2} + i, \dfrac{1}{2} - i$ **39.** $\dfrac{1}{3} + \dfrac{1}{3}i, \dfrac{1}{3} - \dfrac{1}{3}i$ **41.** $\dfrac{2 + \sqrt{14}}{2}, \dfrac{2 - \sqrt{14}}{2}$ **43.** $1, -\dfrac{3}{2}$ **45.** $1 + \sqrt{5}, 1 - \sqrt{5}$ **47.** $\dfrac{1}{2}, 5$

49. $2 + \sqrt{5}, 2 - \sqrt{5}$ **51.** $1.236, -3.236$ **53.** $1.707, 0.293$ **55.** $x = a, x = -4a$

57. The ball hits the ground in 4.43 s.

SECTION 10.3

1. $5, -2$ **3.** $4, -9$ **5.** $4 + 2\sqrt{22}, 4 - 2\sqrt{22}$ **7.** $3, -8$ **9.** $-3, \dfrac{1}{2}$ **11.** $\dfrac{3}{2}, -\dfrac{1}{4}$ **13.** $2, 12$

15. $\dfrac{1 + \sqrt{3}}{2}, \dfrac{1 - \sqrt{3}}{2}$ **17.** $-1 + i, -1 - i$ **19.** $1 + 2i, 1 - 2i$ **21.** $2 + 3i, 2 - 3i$ **23.** $\dfrac{1}{2} + \dfrac{3}{2}i, \dfrac{1}{2} - \dfrac{3}{2}i$

25. $-\dfrac{3}{2} + \dfrac{1}{2}i, -\dfrac{3}{2} - \dfrac{1}{2}i$ **27.** $\dfrac{3}{4} + \dfrac{3\sqrt{3}}{4}i, \dfrac{3}{4} - \dfrac{3\sqrt{3}}{4}i$ **29.** two complex number solutions **31.** one real number

solution **33.** two real number solutions **35.** $\{p \mid p < 9\}$ **37.** $\{p \mid p > 1\}$

SECTION 10.4

1. $3, -3, 2, -2$ **3.** $\sqrt{2}, -\sqrt{2}, 2, -2$ **5.** $1, 4$ **7.** 16 **9.** $2i, -2i, 1, -1$ **11.** $4i, -4i, 2, -2$ **13.** 16

15. $1, 512$ **17.** $\dfrac{2}{3}, -\dfrac{2}{3}, 1, -1$ **19.** 3 **21.** 9 **23.** $2, -1$ **25.** $0, 2$ **27.** $2, -\dfrac{1}{2}$ **29.** -2 **31.** 1 **33.** 1

35. -3 **37.** $10, -1$ **39.** $-\dfrac{1}{2} + \dfrac{\sqrt{7}}{2}i, -\dfrac{1}{2} - \dfrac{\sqrt{7}}{2}i$ **41.** $1, -3$ **43.** $0, -1$ **45.** $\dfrac{1}{2}, -\dfrac{1}{3}$ **47.** $-\dfrac{2}{3}, 6$ **49.** $\dfrac{4}{3}, 3$

51. $-\dfrac{1}{4}, 3$ **53.** 4

SECTION 10.5

1. The height is 3 cm; the base is 14 cm. **3.** The length is 13 ft; the width is 5 ft. **5.** The dimensions of Colorado are approximately 272 mi by 383 mi. **7.** The cardboard is 90 cm by 90 cm. **9.** The projectile is 64 ft above the ground in 0.54 s or in 7.46 s. **11.** The smaller pipe requires 12 min. The larger pipe requires 6 min. **13.** The rate of the wind is 108 mph. **15.** The rowing rate of the guide is 6 mph. **17.** The Internet revenue will be \$200 billion in the year 2001. The negative value of t corresponds to a year before 1997, which is not between 1997 and 2002.

SECTION 10.6

1. $\{x \mid x < -2 \text{ or } x > 4\}$ **3.** $\{x \mid x \le 1 \text{ or } x \ge 2\}$

5. $\{x \mid -3 < x < 4\}$ **7.** $\{x \mid x < -2 \text{ or } 1 < x < 3\}$

9. $\{x \mid -4 \le x \le 1 \text{ or } x \ge 2\}$ **11.** $\{x \mid x < -2 \text{ or } x > 4\}$

13. $\{x \mid -1 < x \le 3\}$ **15.** $\{x \mid x \le -2 \text{ or } 1 \le x < 3\}$

17. $\{x \mid x > 4 \text{ or } x < -4\}$ **19.** $\{x \mid -3 \le x \le 12\}$ **21.** $\left\{x \mid \frac{1}{2} < x < \frac{3}{2}\right\}$ **23.** $\left\{x \mid x < 1 \text{ or } x > \frac{5}{2}\right\}$

25. $\{x \mid x < -1 \text{ or } 1 < x \le 2\}$ **27.** $\left\{x \mid \frac{1}{2} < x \le 1\right\}$ **29.** $\{x \mid 2 < x \le 3\}$ **31.** $\{x \mid x > 5 \text{ or } -4 < x < -1\}$

33.   **35.**   **37.**

39.

CHAPTER REVIEW

1. $0, \dfrac{3}{2}$ [10.1A]   **2.** $\dfrac{c}{2}, -2c$ [10.1A]   **3.** $4\sqrt{3}, -4\sqrt{3}$ [10.1C]   **4.** $-\dfrac{1}{2} + 2i, -\dfrac{1}{2} - 2i$ [10.1C]

5. $-3, -1$ [10.2A]   **6.** $\dfrac{7 + 2\sqrt{7}}{7}, \dfrac{7 - 2\sqrt{7}}{7}$ [10.2A]   **7.** $\dfrac{3}{4}, \dfrac{4}{3}$ [10.3A]   **8.** $\dfrac{1}{2} + \dfrac{\sqrt{31}}{2}i, \dfrac{1}{2} - \dfrac{\sqrt{31}}{2}i$ [10.3A]

9. $x^2 + 3x = 0$ [10.1B]   **10.** $12x^2 - x - 6 = 0$ [10.1B]   **11.** $1 + i\sqrt{7}, 1 - i\sqrt{7}$ [10.2A]   **12.** $2i, -2i$ [10.2A]

13. $\dfrac{11 + \sqrt{73}}{6}, \dfrac{11 - \sqrt{73}}{6}$ [10.3A]   **14.** two real number solutions [10.3A]   **15.** $\left\{x \mid -3 < x < \dfrac{5}{2}\right\}$ [10.6A]

16. $\left\{x \mid x \le -4 \text{ or } -\dfrac{3}{2} \le x \le 2\right\}$ [10.6A]   **17.** $27, -64$ [10.4A]   **18.** $\dfrac{5}{4}$ [10.4B]   **19.** $-1, 3$ [10.4C]

20. -1 [10.4C]   **21.** [10.6A]   **22.** [10.6A]

$\left\{x \mid x < \dfrac{3}{2} \text{ or } x \ge 2\right\}$ $\left\{x \mid x \le -3 \text{ or } \dfrac{1}{2} \le x < 4\right\}$

23. 4 [10.4B]   **24.** 5 [10.4B]   **25.** $\dfrac{-3 + \sqrt{249}}{10}, \dfrac{-3 - \sqrt{249}}{10}$ [10.4C]   **26.** $\dfrac{-11 + \sqrt{129}}{2}, \dfrac{-11 - \sqrt{129}}{2}$ [10.4C]

27. The length is 12 cm, and the width is 5 cm. [10.5A]   **28.** The three integers are 2, 4, and 6 or -6, -4, and -2. [10.5A]   **29.** Working alone, the new computer takes 12 min to print the payroll. [10.5A]   **30.** The speed of the first car is 40 mph. The speed of the second car is 50 mph. [10.5A]

CHAPTER TEST

1. $\dfrac{2}{3}, -4$ [10.1A]   **2.** $\dfrac{3}{2}, -\dfrac{2}{3}$ [10.1A]   **3.** $x^2 - 9 = 0$ [10.1B]   **4.** $2x^2 + 7x - 4 = 0$ [10.1B]

5. $2 + 2\sqrt{2}, 2 - 2\sqrt{2}$ [10.1C]   **6.** $3 + \sqrt{11}, 3 - \sqrt{11}$ [10.2A]   **7.** $\dfrac{3 + \sqrt{15}}{3}, \dfrac{3 - \sqrt{15}}{3}$ [10.2A]

8. $\dfrac{1 + \sqrt{3}}{2}, \dfrac{1 - \sqrt{3}}{2}$ [10.3A]   **9.** $-2 + 2i\sqrt{2}, -2 - 2i\sqrt{2}$ [10.3A]   **10.** two real number solutions [10.3A]

11. two complex number solutions [10.3A]   **12.** $\dfrac{1}{4}$ [10.4A]   **13.** $1, -1, \sqrt{3}, -\sqrt{3}$ [10.4A]   **14.** 4 [10.4B]

15. The equation has no solution. [10.4B]   **16.** $2, -9$ [10.4C]

17. $\{x \mid x < -4 \text{ or } 2 < x < 4\}$ [10.6A]

18. $\left\{x \mid -4 < x \le \dfrac{3}{2}\right\}$ 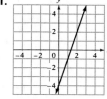 [10.6A]   **19.** The base is 15 ft. The height is 4 ft. [10.5A]

20. The rowing rate of the canoe in calm water is 4 mph. [10.5A]

CUMULATIVE REVIEW

1. 14 [1.4A]   **2.** $\left\{x \mid -2 < x < \dfrac{10}{3}\right\}$ [2.5B]   **3.** The volume is 54π m³. [3.3A]   **4.** $-\dfrac{7}{3}$ [4.1D]   **5.** $-\dfrac{3}{2}$ [4.3A]

6. $\left(\dfrac{5}{2}, 0\right), (0, -3)$ [4.2B]   **7.** $y = x + 1$ [4.5A]   **8.** $(1, -1, 2)$ [5.3B]   **9.**

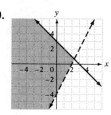

[5.6A]

10. The height of triangle *DEF* is 16 cm. [8.4C]   **11.** $x^2 - 3x - 4 - \dfrac{6}{3x - 4}$ [6.4A]   **12.** $-3xy(x^2 - 2xy + 3y^2)$ [7.1A]

13. $(2x - 5)(3x + 4)$ [7.3A/7.3B]   **14.** $\dfrac{x}{2}$ [8.1B]   **15.** $-\dfrac{3}{2}$ and -1 [8.4A]   **16.** $b = \dfrac{2S - an}{n}$ [8.5A]

17. $1 - a$ [9.1A]   **18.** $-8 - 14i$ [9.3C]   **19.** 0, 1 [9.4A]   **20.** $2, -2, \sqrt{2}, -\sqrt{2}$ [10.4A]   **21.** The lower limit is

$9\dfrac{23}{64}$ in. The upper limit is $9\dfrac{25}{64}$ in. [2.5C]   **22.** The area is $(x^2 + 6x - 16)$ ft². [6.3E]   **23.** The slope is $-\dfrac{25,000}{3}$. The

building decreases $8333.33 in value each year. [4.3A]   **24.** The ladder will reach 15 ft up on the building. [9.4B]

25. There are two complex number solutions. [10.3A]

Answers to Chapter 11 Odd-Numbered Exercises

SECTION 11.1

1. 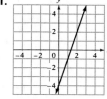   **3.** 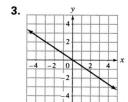   **5.** 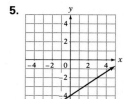   **7.**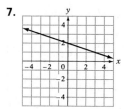

9.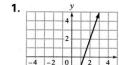

11. If the cost is $150, the markup is $37.50.   **13.** The linear function is $y = -\dfrac{3}{5}x + 545$. If the room rate is $100, 485 rooms will be rented.   **15a.** III   **b.** IV   **c.** II   **d.** I

SECTION 11.2

3.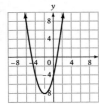

vertex: $(-2, -8)$

axis of symmetry: $x = -2$

5.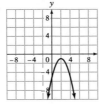

vertex: $(2, -1)$

axis of symmetry: $x = 2$

7.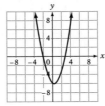

vertex: $\left(\dfrac{1}{2}, -\dfrac{25}{4}\right)$

axis of symmetry: $x = \dfrac{1}{2}$

9.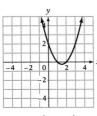

vertex: $\left(\dfrac{3}{2}, -\dfrac{1}{4}\right)$

axis of symmetry: $x = \dfrac{3}{2}$

11.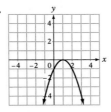

vertex: $(1, 0)$

axis of symmetry: $x = 1$

13.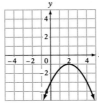

vertex: $(2, -1)$

axis of symmetry: $x = 2$

15. $(2, 0), (-2, 0)$ **17.** $(0, 0), (2, 0)$ **19.** $(2, 0), (-1, 0)$ **21.** $\left(-\dfrac{1}{2}, 0\right), (1, 0)$ **23.** $(-1 + \sqrt{2}, 0), (-1 - \sqrt{2}, 0)$

25. The parabola has no x-intercepts.   **27.** $(1 + \sqrt{3}, 0), (1 - \sqrt{3}, 0)$ **29.** $(2 + \sqrt{5}, 0), (2 - \sqrt{5}, 0)$

31. The parabola has two x-intercepts.   **33.** The parabola has two x-intercepts.   **35.** The parabola has one x-intercept.

37. The parabola has no x-intercepts.   **39.** The parabola has no x-intercepts.   **41.** The parabola has no x-intercepts.

43. minimum: 2   **45.** maximum: -1 **47.** minimum: -2 **49.** maximum: -3 **51.** minimum: $-\dfrac{73}{8}$

53. minimum: $-\dfrac{11}{4}$ **55.** maximum: $-\dfrac{2}{3}$ **57.** minimum: $-\dfrac{1}{12}$ **59.** The maximum height that the diver will be above the water is 13.1 m.   **61.** A price of $250 will give the maximum revenue.   **63.** The pool will have the least amount of algae 5 days after treatment.   **65.** The water will land $31\dfrac{2}{3}$ ft up on the building.   **67.** This shape can enclose a maximum of 39.6 ft².   **69a.** always true   **b.** sometimes true   **c.** sometimes true

SECTION 11.3

1. yes   **3.** no   **5.** yes   **7.**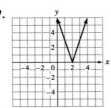

domain: $\{x | x \in \text{real numbers}\}$
range: $\{y | y \geq 0\}$

9.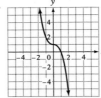

domain: $\{x | x \in \text{real numbers}\}$
range: $\{y | y \in \text{real numbers}\}$

11.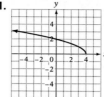

domain: $\{x \mid x \le 4\}$
range: $\{y \mid y \ge 0\}$

13.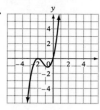

domain: $\{x \mid x \in \text{real numbers}\}$
range: $\{y \mid y \in \text{real numbers}\}$

15.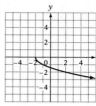

domain: $\{x \mid x \ge -2\}$
range: $\{y \mid y \le 0\}$

17.

domain: $\{x \mid x \in \text{real numbers}\}$
range: $\{y \mid y \ge 0\}$

19. $a = 18$　　**21.** $f(2, 5) + g(2, 5) = 17$　　**23.** $f(14) = 8$　　**25.** $x = -3$

SECTION 11.4

1. 5　　**3.** 1　　**5.** 0　　**7.** $-\dfrac{29}{4}$　　**9.** $\dfrac{2}{3}$　　**11.** 2　　**13.** 39　　**15.** -8　　**17.** $-\dfrac{4}{5}$　　**19.** -2　　**21.** 7　　**23.** -13

25. -29　　**27.** $8x - 13$　　**29.** 4　　**31.** 3　　**33.** $x + 4$　　**35.** 5　　**37.** 11　　**39.** $3x^2 + 3x + 5$　　**41.** -3　　**43.** -27

45. $x^3 - 6x^2 + 12x - 8$　　**47.** $6h + h^2$　　**49.** $2 + h$　　**51.** $h + 2a$　　**53.** -1　　**55.** -6　　**57.** $6x - 13$

SECTION 11.5

1. yes　　**3.** no　　**5.** yes　　**7.** no　　**9.** no　　**11.** no　　**15.** $\{(0, 1), (3, 2), (8, 3), (15, 4)\}$　　**17.** no inverse

19. $\{(-2, 0), (5, -1), (3, 3), (6, -4)\}$　　**21.** no inverse　　**23.** $f^{-1}(x) = \dfrac{1}{4}x + 2$　　**25.** $f^{-1}(x) = \dfrac{1}{2}x - 2$

27. $f^{-1}(x) = 2x + 2$　　**29.** $f^{-1}(x) = -\dfrac{1}{2}x + 1$　　**31.** $f^{-1}(x) = \dfrac{3}{2}x - 6$　　**33.** $f^{-1}(x) = -3x + 3$　　**35.** $f^{-1}(x) = \dfrac{1}{2}x + \dfrac{5}{2}$

37. $f^{-1}(x) = \dfrac{1}{5}x + \dfrac{2}{5}$　　**39.** $f^{-1}(x) = \dfrac{1}{6}x + \dfrac{1}{2}$　　**41.** $f^{-1}(x) = -\dfrac{1}{6}x + \dfrac{1}{3}$　　**43.** $f^{-1}(x) = \dfrac{1}{3}x + \dfrac{4}{3}$　　**45.** $f^{-1}(x) = -\dfrac{3}{2}x + 6$

47. $f^{-1}(x) = \dfrac{1}{3}x + \dfrac{2}{3}$　　**49.** $f^{-1}(x) = -\dfrac{4}{3}x + \dfrac{8}{3}$　　**51.** yes　　**53.** no　　**55.** yes　　**57.** no　　**59.** no　　**61.** yes　　**63.** yes

65.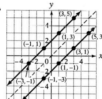

67.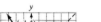

69.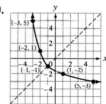

73. $f^{-1}(-1) = 3$　　**75.** $f^{-1}(3) = -3$

77. $f^{-1}(8) = 0$

SECTION 11.6

1.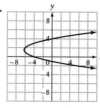

vertex: $\left(-\dfrac{25}{4}, \dfrac{3}{2}\right)$

axis of symmetry: $y = \dfrac{3}{2}$

3.

vertex: $(0, 2)$
axis of symmetry: $x = 0$

5.

vertex: $(-1, 0)$
axis of symmetry: $y = 0$

7.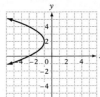

vertex: $(-1, 2)$

axis of symmetry: $y = 2$

9.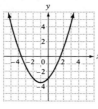

vertex: $\left(-1, -\dfrac{7}{2}\right)$

axis of symmetry: $x = -1$

11.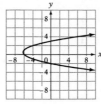

vertex: $\left(-\dfrac{25}{4}, \dfrac{1}{2}\right)$

axis of symmetry: $y = \dfrac{1}{2}$

13.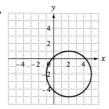

15.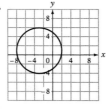

17.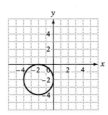

19. $(x - 2)^2 + (y + 1)^2 = 4$

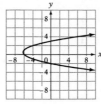

21. $(x + 1)^2 + (y - 1)^2 = 5$

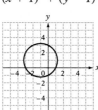

23.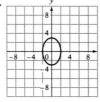

25.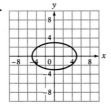

27.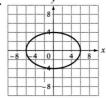

29.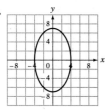

31.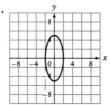

33.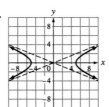

35.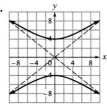

37.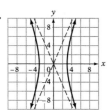

39.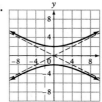

41.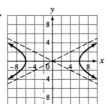

43.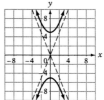

45. $(x - 3)^2 + (y - 3)^2 = 9$

47. $\dfrac{x^2}{25} + \dfrac{y^2}{16} = 1$, ellipse

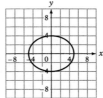

CHAPTER REVIEW

1.
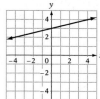
[11.1A]

2.
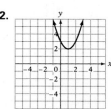
[11.2A]

3. There are no x-intercepts. [11.2B]

4. The maximum value of the function is 9. [11.2C]

5.

domain: $\{x|x \leq 3\}$
range: $\{y|y \leq 0\}$ [11.3A]

6.
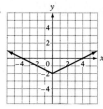
domain: $\{x|x \in \text{real numbers}\}$
range: $\{y|y \geq -2\}$ [11.3A]

7.
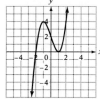
domain: $\{x|x \in \text{real numbers}\}$
range: $\{y|y \in \text{real numbers}\}$ [11.3A]

8. no [11.5A] **9.** -2 [11.4A] **10.** $-\dfrac{13}{2}$ [11.4A] **11.** 5 [11.4B] **12.** $2x^2 - 4x - 5$ [11.4B]

13. $\{(6, 2), (5, 3), (4, 4), (3, 5)\}$ [11.5B] **14.** $f^{-1}(x) = 4x + 16$ [11.5B] **15.**
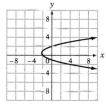
[11.6A]

16.
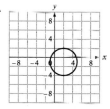
[11.6B]

17.
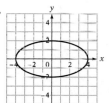
[11.6D]

18.
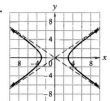
[11.6C]

19. $(x + 3)^2 + (y + 3)^2 = 16$ [11.6B] **20.** The dimensions are 50 cm by 50 cm. The area is 2500 cm². [11.2D]

CHAPTER TEST

1.
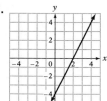
[11.1A]

2.
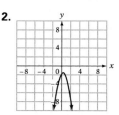
[11.2A]

3. $(0, 0), (-3, 0)$ [11.2B]

4. The maximum value of the function is 3. [11.2C]

5.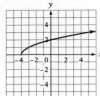

domain: $\{x|x \geq -4\}$
range: $\{y|y \geq 0\}$ [11.3A]

6.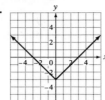

domain: $\{x|x \in \text{real numbers}\}$
range: $\{y|y \geq -3\}$ [11.3A]

7.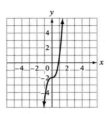

domain: $\{x|x \in \text{real numbers}\}$
range: $\{y|y \in \text{real numbers}\}$ [11.3A]

8. yes   [11.5A]   **9.** 7   [11.4A]   **10.** -9 [11.4A]   **11.** 70   [11.4A]   **12.** $\frac{12}{7}$ [11.4A]

13. $6x^2 + 3x - 16$ [11.4B]   **14.** $f^{-1}(x) = -\frac{1}{6}x + \frac{2}{3}$ [11.5B]   **15.**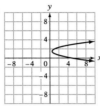

[11.6A]

16.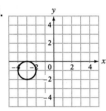

[11.6B]

17.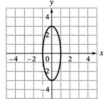

[11.6C]

18.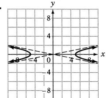

[11.6D]

19. yes   [11.5B]   **20.** The rectangle will have a maximum area when the dimensions are 7 ft by 7 ft.   [11.2A]

CUMULATIVE REVIEW

1.   [1.5C]   **2.** $\frac{38}{53}$ [8.4A]   **3.** -20 [4.1D]   **4.** $y = -\frac{3}{2}x$ [4.4A]   **5.** $y = x - 6$ [4.5A]

6. $\frac{x}{x+y}$ [8.1A]   **7.** $\frac{x-5}{3x-2}$ [8.2D]   **8.** $\frac{5}{2}$ [8.4A]   **9.** $\frac{4a}{3b^{12}}$ [6.1B]   **10.** $2x^{3/4}$ [9.1B]   **11.** $3\sqrt{2} - 5i$ [9.3A]

12. $\frac{-1+\sqrt{7}}{2}, \frac{-1-\sqrt{7}}{2}$ [10.2A/10.3A]   **13.** 6   [10.4B]   **14.** $\{x|-4 < x \leq 3\}$ [10.6A]   **15.** 0   [11.2C]

16. $f^{-1}(x) = \frac{1}{4}x - 2$ [11.5B]   **17.**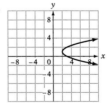

[4.6A]

18.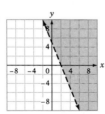

[11.6A]

19.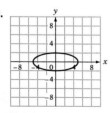

[11.6C]

20.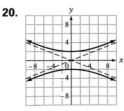

[11.6D]

21. There were 82 adult tickets sold.   [5.5B]

22. The rate of the motorcycle is 60 mph.   [8.6B]   **23.** The rate of the crew in calm water is 4.5 mph.   [5.5A]

24. A gear with 60 teeth will make 18 revolutions per minute.   [8.7A]   **25.** The maximum product is 400.   [11.2D]

Answers to Chapter 12 Odd-Numbered Exercises

SECTION 12.1

1a. $f(2) = 9$ **b.** $f(0) = 1$ **c.** $f(-2) = \dfrac{1}{9}$ **3a.** $g(3) = 16$ **b.** $g(1) = 4$ **c.** $g(-3) = \dfrac{1}{4}$ **5a.** $P(0) = 1$

b. $P\left(\dfrac{3}{2}\right) = \dfrac{1}{8}$ **c.** $P(-2) = 16$ **7a.** $G(4) = 7.3891$ **b.** $G(-2) = 0.3679$ **c.** $G\left(\dfrac{1}{2}\right) = 1.2840$ **9a.** $H(-1) = 54.5982$

b. $H(3) = 1$ **c.** $H(5) = 0.1353$ **11a.** $F(2) = 16$ **b.** $F(-2) = 16$ **c.** $F\left(\dfrac{3}{4}\right) = 1.4768$ **13a.** $f(-2) = 0.1353$

b. $f(2) = 0.1353$ **c.** $f(-3) = 0.0111$ **15.** 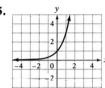   **17.** 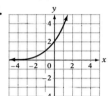   **19.**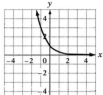

21. 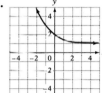   **23.** 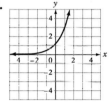   **25.** 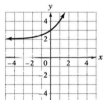   **27.**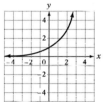

29. 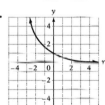   **31.** 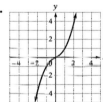   **33.** 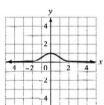   **35.**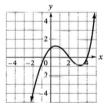

37. 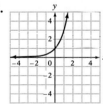   **39a.** 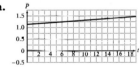   **b.** The point (5, 1.242) means that in the year 1998, the Chinese population was approximately 1.242 billion.

41a. 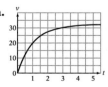   **b.** The point (2, 27.7) means that after 2 s, the object is dropping at a speed of 27.7 ft/s.   **43a.** always true   **b.** always true   **45.** e

SECTION 12.2

1. $\log_5 25 = 2$ **3.** $\log_4 \dfrac{1}{16} = -2$ **5.** $\log_{10} x = y$ **7.** $\log_a w = x$ **9.** $3^2 = 9$ **11.** $10^{-2} = 0.01$ **13.** $e^y = x$

15. $b^v = u$ **17.** $\log_3 81 = 4$ **19.** $\log_2 128 = 7$ **21.** $\log 100 = 2$ **23.** $\ln e^3 = 3$ **25.** $\log_8 1 = 0$ **27.** $\log_5 625 = 4$

29. 9 **31.** 64 **33.** $\dfrac{1}{7}$ **35.** 1 **37.** 316.23 **39.** 0.02 **41.** 7.39 **43.** 0.61 **45.** $\log_3(x^3 y^2)$ **47.** $\ln\left(\dfrac{x^4}{y^2}\right)$

49. $\log_7 x^3$ **51.** $\ln(x^3 y^4)$ **53.** $\log_4(x^2 y^2)$ **55.** $\log_6 \sqrt{\dfrac{x}{y}}$ **57.** $\log_3\left(\dfrac{x^2 z^2}{y}\right)$ **59.** $\ln\left(\dfrac{x}{y^2 z}\right)$ **61.** $\log_4 \dfrac{s^2 r^2}{t^4}$

63. $\ln\left(\dfrac{x}{y^2 z^2}\right)$ **65.** $\log_2\left(\dfrac{t^3 v^2}{r^2}\right)$ **67.** $\log_4 \sqrt{\dfrac{x^3 z}{y^2}}$ **69.** $\ln\sqrt{\dfrac{x}{y^3}}$ **71.** $\log_2\left(\dfrac{\sqrt{xz}}{\sqrt[3]{y^2}}\right)$ **73.** $\log_8 x + \log_8 z$ **75.** $5\log_3 x$

77. $\log_b r - \log_b s$ **79.** $2\log_3 x + 6\log_3 y$ **81.** $3\log_7 u - 4\log_7 v$ **83.** $2\log_2 r + 2\log_2 s$ **85.** $2\ln x + \ln y + \ln z$

87. $\log_5 x + 2\log_5 y - 4\log_5 z$ **89.** $2\log_8 x - \log_8 y - 2\log_8 z$ **91.** $\dfrac{3}{2}\log_4 x + \dfrac{1}{2}\log_4 y$ **93.** $\dfrac{3}{2}\log_7 x - \dfrac{1}{2}\log_7 y$

95. $\ln x + \dfrac{1}{2}\ln y - \dfrac{1}{2}\ln z$ **97.** $\log_3 t - \dfrac{1}{2}\log_3 x$ **99.** $\dfrac{1}{2}\log_7 u + \dfrac{1}{2}\log_7 v - \log_7 x$ **101.** 0.8451 **103.** −0.2218

105. 1.3863 **107.** 1.0415 **109.** 0.8617 **111.** 2.1133 **113.** −0.6309 **115.** 0.2727 **117.** 1.6826

119. 1.9266 **121.** 0.6752 **123.** 2.6125 **125a.** false **b.** true **c.** false **d.** false **e.** false **f.** true

g. false **h.** true

SECTION 12.3

1. 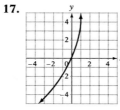 **3.** 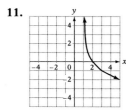 **5.** 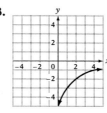 **7.**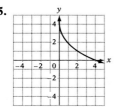

9. **11.** **13.** 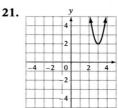 **15.**

17. **19.** **21.**

23a.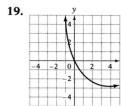

b. The point (25.1, 2) means that a star that is 25.1 parsecs from Earth has a distance modulus of 2.

SECTION 12.4

1. $-\dfrac{1}{3}$ **3.** −3 **5.** 1 **7.** 6 **9.** $\dfrac{4}{7}$ **11.** $\dfrac{9}{8}$ **13.** 1.1133 **15.** 1.0986 **17.** 1.3222 **19.** −2.8074

21. 3.5850 **23.** 1.1309 **25.** $\dfrac{11}{2}$ **27.** −4, 2 **29.** $\dfrac{5}{3}$ **31.** $\dfrac{1}{2}$ **33.** $\dfrac{9}{2}$ **35.** 17.5327 **37.** 3 **39.** 2

41. The equation has no solution. **43.** −0.55 **45.** 1.38 **47.** The equation has no solution. **49.** 0.09

51a.

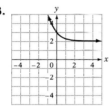

b. It will take the object approximately 2.64 s to fall 100 ft.

SECTION 12.5

1. The value of the investment after 2 years is $5982.   **3.** The company must deposit $16,786 in the account.   **5.** It will take 3.5 h to decay to 20 mg.   **7.** The half-life of the material is 2.5 years.   **9.** It will take 6 weeks of practice to make 80% of the welds correctly.   **11.** The pH of the solution is 1.35.   **13.** The percent of light will be 75% of the light at the surface at a depth of 2.5 m.   **15.** The earthquake in China was 20 times as strong.   **17.** The magnitude is 5.2.   **19.** A normal conversation is 65 decibels.   **21.** The star is 150.7 parsecs from Earth.   **23.** No. Antares is 3.5 times as far.   **25.** 742.9 billion barrels will last 20 years.   **27.** The value of the investment will be $3210.06 in 5 years.   **29.** $r = 243.31(e^{T/14.29} - 1)$ **31.** $r_1 = \sqrt{10 r_2}$

CHAPTER REVIEW

1. 1 [12.1A]   **2.** $5^2 = 25$ [12.2A]   **3.**

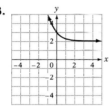

[12.1B]

4.

[12.3A]

5. $\frac{2}{5}\log_3 x + \frac{4}{5}\log_3 y$ [12.2B]   **6.** $\log_3 \frac{x^2}{y^5}$ [12.2B]   **7.** -12 [12.4A]   **8.** $\frac{1}{4}$ [12.4B]   **9.** 1.7251 [12.2C]

10. 32 [12.2A]   **11.** 79 [12.4B]   **12.** 1000 [12.2A]   **13.** $\log_7 \sqrt[3]{xy^4}$ [12.2B]   **14.** $\frac{1}{2}(5\log_8 x - 3\log_8 y)$ [12.2B]

15. $\log_2 32 = 5$ [12.2A]   **16.** 0.4278 [12.2C]   **17.** -0.535 [12.4A]   **18.** $\frac{3}{2}$ [12.1A]   **19.** $\frac{2}{3}$ [12.4B]

20. 2 [12.4B]   **21.**

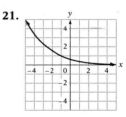

[12.1B]

22.

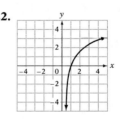

[12.3A]

23. The value of the investment after 2 years is $4692. [12.5A]   **24.** The earthquake is 1000 times as strong. [12.5A]   **25.** The half-life of the material is 27 days. [12.5A]   **26.** Sound emitted from a busy street corner is 107 decibels. [12.5A]

CHAPTER TEST

1. 1 [12.1A]   **2.** $\frac{1}{3}$ [12.1A]   **3.**

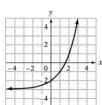

[12.1B]

4.

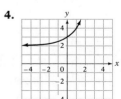

[12.1B]

5. 2 [12.2A]   **6.** $\frac{1}{9}$ [12.2A]   **7.**

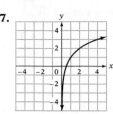

[12.3A]

8.

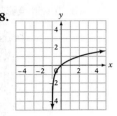

[12.3A]

9. $\frac{1}{2}\log_6 x + \frac{3}{2}\log_6 y$ [12.2B]   **10.** $\log_3\sqrt{\dfrac{x}{y}}$ [12.2B]   **11.** $\ln x - \frac{1}{2}\ln z$ [12.2B]   **12.** $\ln\dfrac{x^3}{y\sqrt{z}}$ [12.2B]

13. -2 [12.4A]   **14.** -3 [12.4A]   **15.** 2.5789 [12.4A]   **16.** 6 [12.4B]   **17.** 3 [12.4B]

18. 1.3652 [12.2C]   **19.** 2.6801 [12.2C]   **20.** The half-life is 33 h. [12.5A]

CUMULATIVE REVIEW

1. $\frac{8}{7}$ [2.2C]   **2.** $y = 2x - 6$ [4.5A]   **3.** $(4x^n + 3)(x^n + 1)$ [7.3A/7.3B]   **4.** $\dfrac{x - 3}{x + 3}$ [8.3A]   **5.** $\dfrac{x\sqrt{y} + y\sqrt{x}}{x - y}$ [9.2D]

6. $2 + \sqrt{10},\, 2 - \sqrt{10}$ [10.2A]   **7.** The length of the side is 26 cm. [9.4B]   **8.**

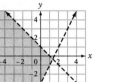

[5.6A]

9. $(0, -1, 2)$ [5.3B]   **10.** $-\dfrac{2x^2 - 17x + 13}{(x - 2)(2x - 3)}$ [8.2D]   **11.** $\{x\,|-5 \le x \le 1\}$ [10.6A]   **12.** $\{x\,|\,1 \le x \le 4\}$ [2.5B]

13.

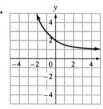

[12.1B]

14.

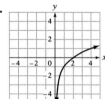

[12.3A]

15. The area is 28 yd². [3.2B]   **16.** 125 [12.2A]

17. $\log_b\dfrac{x^3}{y^5}$ [12.2B]   **18.** 1.7712 [12.2C]   **19.** 2 [12.4A]

20. $\frac{1}{2}$ [12.4B]   **21.** The customer can write fewer than 50 checks. [2.4C]

22. The mixture costs $3.10 per pound. [2.3A]   **23.** The rate of the wind is 25 mph. [5.5A]   **24.** The force will stretch the spring 10.2 in. [8.7A]   **25.** The redwood costs $.40 per foot. The fir costs $.25 per foot. [5.5B]
26. The investment will double in 8 years. [12.5A]

FINAL EXAM

1. -31 [1.3A]   **2.** -1 [1.4A]   **3.** $-10x + 33$ [1.4D]   **4.** 8 [2.2A]   **5.** $4, -\dfrac{2}{3}$ [2.5A]   **6.** The volume is

268.1 ft³. [3.3A]   **7.**

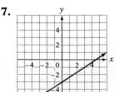

[4.2B]

8. $y = -3x + 7$ [4.4B]   **9.** $y = -\dfrac{2}{3}x - \dfrac{1}{3}$ [4.5A]

10. $6a^3 - 5a^2 + 10a$ [6.3A]   **11.** $(2 - xy)(4 + 2xy + x^2y^2)$ [7.4B]   **12.** $(x - y)(1 + x)(1 - x)$ [7.4D]

geometric solid A figure in space. (Sec. 3.3)

graph of a real number A heavy dot placed directly above the number on the number line. (Sec. 1.1)

graph of a relation The graph of the ordered pairs that belong to the relation. (Sec. 4.1)

graph of an equation in two variables A graph of the ordered-pair solutions of the equation. (Sec. 4.2)

graph of an ordered pair The dot drawn at the coordinates of the point in the plane. (Sec. 4.1)

graphing a point in the plane Placing a dot at the location given by the ordered pair; also called plotting a point in the plane. (Sec. 4.1)

greater than A number that lies to the right of another number on the number line is said to be greater than that number. (Sec. 1.1)

greatest common factor The greatest common factor (GCF) of two or more integers is the greatest integer that is a factor of all the integers. The greatest common factor of two or more monomials is the product of the GCF of the coefficients and the common variable factors. (Sec. 7.1)

half-plane The solution set of a linear inequality in two variables. (Sec. 4.6)

hyperbola A conic section formed by the intersection of a cone and a plane perpendicular to the base of the cone. (Sec. 11.6)

hypotenuse In a right triangle, the side opposite the 90° angle. (Sec. 9.4)

imaginary number A number of the form ai, where a is a real number and $i = \sqrt{-1}$. (Sec. 9.3)

imaginary part of a complex number For the complex number $a + bi$, b is the imaginary part. (Sec. 9.3)

inconsistent system of equations A system of equations that has no solution. (Sec. 5.1)

independent system of equations A system of equations whose graphs intersect at only one point. (Sec. 5.1)

independent variable In a function, the variable that varies independently and whose value determines the value of the dependent variable. (Sec. 4.1)

index In the expression $\sqrt[n]{a}$, n is the index of the radical. (Sec. 9.1)

inequality An expression that contains the symbol $>$, $<$, $\geq$ (is greater than or equal to), or $\leq$ (is less than or equal to). (Sec. 1.5)

integers The numbers $\ldots, -3, -2, -1, 0, 1, 2, 3, \ldots$. (Sec. 1.1)

interior angles The angles within the region enclosed by a triangle. (Sec. 3.1)

intersecting lines Lines that cross at a point in the plane. (Sec. 3.1)

intersection of two sets The set that contains all elements that are common to both of the sets. (Sec. 1.5)

inverse of a function The set of ordered pairs formed by reversing the coordinates of each ordered pair of the function. (Sec. 11.5)

inverse variation A function that can be expressed as the equation $y = k/x$, where k is a constant. (Sec. 8.7)

irrational number The decimal representation of an irrational number never terminates or repeats and can only be approximated. (Sec. 1.2, 9.2)

isosceles triangle A triangle that has two sides of equal length; the angles opposite the equal sides are of equal measure. (Sec. 3.2)

joint variation A variation in which a variable varies directly as the product of two or more variables. A joint variation can be expressed as the equation $z = kxy$, where k is a constant. (Sec. 8.7)

leading coefficient In a polynomial, the coefficient of the variable with the largest exponent. (Sec. 6.2)

least common denominator The smallest number that is a multiple of each denominator in question. (Sec. 1.2)

least common multiple (LCM) The LCM of two or more numbers is the smallest number that is a multiple of each of those numbers. (Sec. 1.2)

least common multiple of two polynomials The simplest polynomial of least degree that contains the factors of each polynomial. (Sec. 8.2)

leg In a right triangle, one of the two sides that are not opposite the 90° angle. (Sec. 9.4)

less than A number that lies to the left of another number on the number line is said to be less than that number. (Sec. 1.1)

like terms Terms of a variable expression that have the same variable part. Having no variable part, constant terms are like terms. (Sec. 1.4)

line A line extends indefinitely in two directions in a plane; it has no width. (Sec. 3.1)

line of best fit A line drawn to approximate data that are graphed as points in a coordinate system. (Sec. 4.4)

linear equation in three variables An equation of the form $Ax + By + Cz = D$, where A, B, C, and D are constants. (Sec. 5.3)

linear equation in two variables An equation of the form $y = mx + b$, where m and b are constants; also called a linear function. (Sec. 4.2)

linear function An equation of the form $y = mx + b$, where m and b are constants; also called a linear equation in two variables. (Sec. 4.2, 6.2, 11.1)

linear inequality in two variables An inequality of the form $y > mx + b$ or $Ax + By > C$. (The symbol $>$ could be replaced by $\geq$, $<$, or $\leq$.) (Sec. 4.6)

linear model A first-degree equation that is used to describe a relationship between quantities. (Sec. 4.4)

line segment Part of a line; it has two endpoints. (Sec. 3.1)

literal equation An equation that contains more than one variable. (Sec. 8.5)

logarithm For b greater than zero and not equal to 1, the statement $y = \log_b x$ (the logarithm of x to the base b) is equivalent to $x = b^y$. (Sec. 12.2)

mantissa The decimal part of a common logarithm. (Sec. 12.2)

matrix A rectangular array of numbers. (Sec. 5.3)

minor of an element The minor of an element in a 3×3 determinant is the 2×2 determinant obtained by eliminating the row and column that contain that element. (Sec. 5.4)

monomial A number, a variable, or a product of a number and variables; a polynomial of one term. (Sec. 6.1, 6.2)

multiplicative inverse The multiplicative inverse of a nonzero real number a is $1/a$; also called the reciprocal. (Sec. 1.4)

natural exponential function The function defined by $f(x) = e^x$, where $e \approx 2.71828$. (Sec. 12.1)

natural logarithm When e (the base of the natural exponential function) is used as the base of a logarithm, the logarithm is referred to as the natural logarithm and is abbreviated $\ln x$. (Sec. 12.2)

natural numbers The numbers 1, 2, 3, . . . ; also called the positive integers. (Sec. 1.1)

negative integers The numbers . . . , $-3, -2, -1$. (Sec. 1.1)

negative slope The slope of a line that slants downward to the right. (Sec. 4.3)

nonfactorable over the integers A polynomial is nonfactorable over the integers if it does not factor using only integers. (Sec. 7.2)

nth root of a A number b such that $b^n = a$. The nth root of a can be written $a^{1/n}$ or $\sqrt[n]{a}$. (Sec. 9.1)

null set The set that contains no elements; also called the empty set. (Sec. 1.5)

numerical coefficient The number part of a variable term. When the numerical coefficient is 1 or -1, the 1 is usually not written. (Sec. 1.4)

obtuse angle An angle whose measure is between 90° and 180°. (Sec. 3.1)

obtuse triangle A triangle that has one obtuse angle. (Sec. 3.2)

odd integer An integer that is not divisible by 2. (Sec. 7.5)

one-to-one function In a one-to-one function, given any y, there is only one x that can be paired with the given y. (Sec. 11.5)

opposites Numbers that are the same distance from zero on the number line but lie on different sides of zero; also called additive inverses. (Sec. 1.1)

order $m \times n$ A matrix of m rows and n columns is of order $m \times n$. (Sec. 5.4)

Order of Operations Agreement A set of rules that tell us in what order to perform the operations that occur in a numerical expression. (Sec. 1.3)

ordered pair Pair of numbers expressed in the form (a, b) and used to locate a point in the plane determined by a rectangular coordinate system. (Sec. 4.1)

ordinate The second number of an ordered pair; it measures a vertical distance and is also called the second coordinate of an ordered pair. (Sec. 4.1)

origin The point of intersection of the two number lines that form a rectangular coordinate system. (Sec. 4.1)

parabola The graph of a quadratic function is called a parabola. (Sec. 11.2)

parallel lines Lines that never meet; the distance between them is always the same. In a rectangular coordinate system, parallel lines have the same slope and thus do not intersect. (Sec. 3.1, 4.5)

parallelogram A quadrilateral that has opposite sides equal and parallel. (Sec. 3.2)

percent Parts of 100. (Sec. 1.2)

perfect cube The product of the same three factors. (Sec. 7.4)

perfect square The product of a term and itself. (Sec. 1.2, 7.4)

perimeter The distance around a plane figure. (Sec. 3.2)

perpendicular lines Intersecting lines that form right angles. The slopes of perpendicular lines are negative reciprocals of each other. (Sec. 3.1, 4.5)

plane A flat surface. (Sec. 3.1)

plane figure A figure that lies totally in a plane. (Sec. 3.1)

plotting a point in the plane Placing a dot at the location given by the ordered pair; also called graphing a point in the plane. (Sec. 3.1)

point-slope formula The equation $y - y_1 = m(x - x_1)$, where m is the slope of a line and (x_1, y_1) is a point on the line. (Sec. 4.4)

polygon A closed figure determined by three or more line segments that lie in a plane. (Sec. 3.2)

polynomial A variable expression in which the terms are monomials. (Sec. 6.2)

positive integers The numbers 1, 2, 3, . . . ; also called the natural numbers. (Sec. 1.1)

positive slope The slope of a line that slants upward to the right. (Sec. 4.3)

prime polynomial A polynomial that is nonfactorable over the integers. (Sec. 7.2)

principal square root The positive square root of a number. (Sec. 1.2, 9.1)

product In multiplication, the result of multiplying two numbers. (Sec. 1.1)

proportion An equation that states the equality of two ratios or rates. (Sec. 8.4)

Pythagorean Theorem The square of the hypotenuse of a right triangle is equal to the sum of the squares of the two legs. (Sec. 9.4)

quadrant One of the four regions into which a rectangular coordinate system divides the plane. (Sec. 4.1)

quadratic equation An equation of the form $ax^2 + bx + c = 0$, where a, b, and c are constants and a is not equal to zero; also called a second-degree equation. (Sec. 7.5, 10.1)

quadratic formula A general formula, derived by applying the method of completing the square to the standard form of a quadratic equation, used to solve quadratic equations. (Sec. 10.3)

quadratic function A function that can be expressed by the equation $f(x) = ax^2 + bx + c$, where a is not equal to zero. (Sec. 6.2, 11.2)

quadratic inequality An inequality that can be written in the form $ax^2 + bx + c < 0$ or $ax^2 + bx + c > 0$, where a is not equal to zero. The symbols $\le$ and $\ge$ can also be used. (Sec. 10.6)

quadratic trinomial A trinomial of the form $ax^2 + bx + c$, where a, b, and c are nonzero constants. (Sec. 7.4)

quadrilateral A four-sided closed figure. (Sec. 3.2)

radical equation An equation that contains a variable expression in a radicand. (Sec. 9.4)

radical sign The symbol $\sqrt{\ }$, which is used to indicate the positive, or principal, square root of a number. (Sec. 1.2, 9.1)

radicand In a radical expression, the expression under the radical sign. (Sec. 1.2, 9.1)

radius of a circle A line segment going from the center to a point on the circle. The fixed distance, from the center of a circle, of all points that make up the circle. (Sec. 3.2, 11.6)

radius of a sphere A line segment going from the center to a point on the sphere. (Sec. 3.3)

range The set of the second coordinates of all the ordered pairs of a relation. (Sec. 4.1)

rate The quotient of two quantities that have different units. (Sec. 8.4)

rate of work That part of a task that is completed in one unit of time. (Sec. 8.6)

ratio The quotient of two quantities that have the same unit. (Sec. 8.4)

rational expression A fraction in which the numerator or denominator is a polynomial. (Sec. 8.1)

rational number A number of the form a/b, where a and b are integers and b is not equal to zero. (Sec. 1.2)

rationalizing the denominator The procedure used to remove a radical from the denominator of a fraction. (Sec. 9.2)

ray A ray starts at a point and extends indefinitely in one direction. (Sec. 3.1)

real numbers The rational numbers and the irrational numbers taken together. (Sec. 1.2)

real part of a complex number For the complex number $a + bi$, a is the real part. (Sec. 9.3)

reciprocal The reciprocal of a nonzero real number a is $1/a$; also called the multiplicative inverse. (Sec. 1.4)

reciprocal of a rational expression The rational expression with the numerator and denominator interchanged. (Sec. 8.1)

rectangle A parallelogram that has four right angles. (Sec. 3.2)

rectangular coordinate system A coordinate system formed by two number lines, one horizontal and one vertical, that intersect at the zero point of each line. (Sec. 4.1)

rectangular solid A solid in which all six faces are rectangles. (Sec. 3.3)

regular polygon A polygon in which each side has the same length and each angle has the same measure. (Sec. 3.2)

relation A set of ordered pairs. (Sec. 4.1)

repeating decimal Decimal formed when dividing the numerator of its fractional counterpart by the denominator results in a decimal part wherein one or more digits repeat infinitely. (Sec. 1.2)

right angle A 90° angle. (Sec. 3.1)

right triangle A triangle that contains one right angle. (Sec. 3.1)

roster method A method of designating a set by enclosing a list of its elements in braces. (Sec. 1.5)

scatter diagram A graph of collected data as points in a coordinate system. (Sec. 4.4)

scientific notation Notation in which a number is expressed as the product of a number between 1 and 10 and a power of 10. (Sec. 6.1)

second-degree equation An equation of the form $ax^2 + bx + c = 0$, where a, b, and c are constants and a is not equal to zero; also called a quadratic equation. (Sec. 10.1)

set A collection of objects. (Sec. 1.5)

set-builder notation A method of designating a set that makes use of a variable and a certain property that only elements of that set possess. (Sec. 1.5)

similar objects Similar objects have the same shape but not necessarily the same size. (Sec. 8.4)

simplest form of a rational expression A rational expression is in simplest form when the numerator and denominator have no common factors. (Sec. 8.1)

slope A measure of the slant, or tilt, of a line. The symbol for slope is m. (Sec. 4.3)

slope-intercept form of a straight line The equation $y = mx + b$, where m is the slope of the line and $(0, b)$ is the y-intercept. (Sec. 4.3)

solution of a system of equations in three variables An ordered triple that is a solution of each equation of the system. (Sec. 5.3)

solution of a system of equations in two variables An ordered pair that is a solution of each equation of the system. (Sec. 5.1)

solution of an equation A number that, when substituted for the variable, results in a true equation. (Sec. 2.1)

solution of an equation in three variables An ordered triple (x, y, z) whose coordinates make the equation a true statement. (Sec. 5.3)

solution of an equation in two variables An ordered pair whose coordinates make the equation a true statement. (Sec. 4.1)

solution set of a system of inequalities The intersection of the solution sets of the individual inequalities. (Sec. 5.6)

solution set of an inequality A set of numbers, each element of which, when substituted for the variable, results in a true inequality (Sec. 2.4)

solving an equation Finding a solution of the equation. (Sec. 2.1)

sphere A solid in which all points are the same distance from point O, which is called the center of the sphere. (Sec. 3.3)

square A rectangle that has four equal sides. (Sec. 3.2)

square root A square root of a positive number x is a number a for which $a^2 = x$. (Sec. 1.2)

square matrix A matrix that has the same number of rows as columns. (Sec. 5.4)

square root of a perfect square One of the two equal factors of the perfect square. (Sec. 7.4)

standard form of a quadratic equation A quadratic equation is in standard form when the polynomial is in descending order and equal to zero. (Sec. 7.5, 10.1)

substitution method An algebraic method of finding an exact solution of a system of linear equations. (Sec. 5.2)

straight angle A 180° angle. (Sec. 3.1)

sum In addition, the total of two or more numbers. (Sec. 1.1)

supplementary angles Two angles whose sum is 180°. (Sec. 3.1)

synthetic division A shorter method of dividing a polynomial by a binomial of the form $x - a$. This method uses only the coefficients of the variable terms. (Sec. 6.4)

system of equations Two or more equations considered together. (Sec. 5.1)

system of inequalities Two or more inequalities considered together. (Sec. 5.6)

terminating decimal Decimal formed when dividing the numerator of its fractional counterpart by the denominator results in a remainder of zero. (Sec. 1.2)

terms of a variable expression The addends of the expression. (Sec. 1.4)

tolerance of a component The acceptable amount by which the component may vary from a given measurement. (Sec. 2.5)

transversal A line intersecting two other lines at two different points. (Sec. 3.1)

triangle A three-sided closed figure. (Sec. 3.1)

trinomial A polynomial of three terms. (Sec. 6.2)

undefined slope The slope of a vertical line is undefined. (Sec. 4.3)

uniform motion The motion of an object whose speed and direction do not change. (Sec. 2.3, 8.6)

union of two sets The set that contains all elements that belong to either of the sets. (Sec. 1.5)

value of a function The value of the dependent variable for a given value of the independent variable. (Sec. 4.1)

value mixture problem A problem that involves combining two ingredients that have different prices into a single blend. (Sec. 2.3)

variable A letter of the alphabet used to stand for a number that is unknown or that can change. (Sec. 1.1)

variable expression An expression that contains one or more variables. (Sec. 1.4)

variable part In a variable term, the variable or variables and their exponents. (Sec. 1.4)

variable term A term composed of a numerical coefficient and a variable part. When the numerical coefficient is 1 or -1, the 1 is not usually written. (Sec. 1.4)

vertex The common endpoint of two rays that form an angle. (Sec. 3.1)

vertex of a parabola The point on the parabola with the smallest y-coordinate or the largest y-coordinate. (Sec. 11.1)

vertical angles Two angles that are on opposite sides of the intersection of two lines. (Sec. 3.1)

volume A measure of the amount of space inside a closed surface. (Sec. 3.3)

x-coordinate The abscissa in an xy-coordinate system. (Sec. 4.1)

x-intercept The point at which a graph crosses the x-axis. (Sec. 4.2)

y-coordinate The ordinate in an xy-coordinate system. (Sec. 4.1)

y-intercept The point at which a graph crosses the y-axis. (Sec. 4.2)

zero slope The slope of a horizontal line. (Sec. 4.3)

Index